R.W. Sutherland

Joseph Chamberlain

J. Chamberlain

Joseph Chamberlain

Entrepreneur in Politics

Peter T. Marsh

Yale University Press
New Haven and London · 1994

Set in Palatino by Best-set Typesetter Ltd., Hong Kong
Printed and bound in Great Britain by Biddles Ltd.,
Guildford and Kings Lynn

Library of Congress Cataloging-in-Publication Data

Marsh, Peter T.
Joseph Chamberlain: entrepreneur in politics / Peter T. Marsh.
p. cm.
Includes bibliographical references and index.
ISBN 0–300–05801–2
1. Chamberlain, Joseph, 1836–1914. 2. Statesmen—Great Britain—
Biography. 3. Industrialists—Great Britain—Biography. 4. Great
Britain—Politics and government—1837–1901. 5. Great Britain—
Politics and government—1901–1910. I. Title.
DA565.C4M35 1994
941.081′092—dc20 [B] 93–47209 CIP

A catalogue record for this book is available from the British Library.

frontispiece: Photograph of Joseph Chamberlain, *c.* 1900.

in memory of
Konstanze
Ein und Alles

Silhouette of Chamberlain, *c.*1890.

Contents

List of Illustrations x

Preface xi

1 The Roots of the Enterprise: *c.*1700–1854 1

2 Screw King: 1854–1869 10
'The city of my adoption and my affection'; Just the
right marriage; Industrial breakthrough; Social impact

3 The Transfer from Business to Politics:
1867–1874 29
Bridging the industrial chasm; The league and the bill;
Repelling an industrial assault; Twisting political combat;
The civic front; 'A working man's representative';
Departure from business

4 Civic Investment: 1869–1880 77
Taking power; Gas and water; The death of faith; Slums
and streets; Ballots and balance sheet

5 Organizational Innovation: 1876–1880 103
Probation; The broader prospect; Departure and debut;
The making of the National Liberal Federation; Despite
the springboard; Upward at last

6 Assertive Apprentice: 1880–1884 132
The spoils of victory; Disjointed cabinet; Between two cities;
Administrative opportunities; Ireland; Africa

7   Rising Expectations: 1884–1885   162
      The genesis of the Radical Programme; Shipping and
      the franchise; Radical imperialism; Hasty prophecy

8   Overextension: 1885   180
      Presenting the programme; Imperial ambivalence; Central
      Board for Ireland; Manoeuvring and electioneering; Meagre
      rewards

9   The Crash: 1885–1886   214
      Cabals at Highbury and Hawarden; The defection of Morley;
      Return to office; Resignation; Tearing asunder; Driving in
      the wedge

10   In Bankruptcy: 1886–1887   255
      Attempted reorientation; Dissolution of partnerships;
      Radical Unionist alternatives; The inadequacy of Unionism;
      No solace

11   New Resources: 1887–1891   281
      Conquests in the New World; Buoyant return to the Old
      World; Setbacks and successes; A power of his own;
      Interweaving fair and foul; Constructing a Radical
      Programme for Unionists

12   Divisional Manager: 1891–1895   332
      Questionable patents, good sales; Marketing costs and
      conflicts; The limits of Radical Unionism; Disheartening
      investments

13   Evading Discredit: 1895–1897   365
      Merger and mandate; Mid-conspiracy; Towards the vortex;
      Subversion; Withholding evidence; Inquest and diversion

14   Imperial Investment: 1895–1898   406
      Cultivating the crown colonies; Commerce with the self-
      governing colonies; The diplomacy of imperialism; Attempting
      to coopt the competition; The home base

15   Test of Investments: 1899   448
      The new proconsul; Hesitation; Other investments; Franchise
      or fight; The deployment of force; The dividends of disaster

16   The Business of War: 1900–1902   482
      The strains of recovery; Reaping the fruits; Joe's mandate;

*The search for postwar security; The profits of war and the
dangers of peace*

17   Dual Directors: 1902–1903   523
     Setbacks; Attempted repairs; Distraction

18   Hastened Culmination: 1903   558
     The new direction; Turbulent current; Exit without escape

19   The All-Consuming Venture: 1903–1906   581
     *The autumn campaign; The political economy of tariff reform;
     Soon beleaguered; Return to impasse; Mutual resistance;
     Transfer of power; Rejection*

20   Paralysis: 1906–1914   632
     *The Valentine compact; Stand-off again; Seizure by
     celebration; Drawing upon diminished force; Unravelling;
     Blessing the fight; Legacy*

     Notes   673
     Manuscript Collections Consulted   712
     Index   716

List of Illustrations

frontispiece: Photograph of Joseph Chamberlain, *c.* 1900, by Lafayette Ltd. Courtesy of Lord Monk Bretton.   ii

Silhouette of Chamberlain, *c.*1890. Courtesy of the University of Birmingham Library.   vi

1. Young Joe, *c.* 1857. Courtesy of J.B. Kenrick.   16

2. George Dawson of the Church of the Saviour. Courtesy of Birmingham Library Services.   40

3. R.W. Dale of Carr's Lane Chapel. Courtesy of Birmingham Library Services.   40

4. Harriet, née Kenrick, 1836–1863. Courtesy of the University of Birmingham Library.   290

5. Florence, née Kenrick, 1848–1875. Courtesy of the University of Birmingham Library.   290

6. Mary, née Endicott, 1864–1957. Courtesy of the University of Birmingham Library.   290

7. Corridor to the greenhouses at Highbury. *Journal of Horticulture and Cottage Gardiner*, 12 March 1896.   442

8. William Strang, etching of Chamberlain, 1903. Courtesy of Diane Maxwell.   582

9. Jesse Collings. Courtesy of Birmingham Library Services.   604

10. William Kenrick. Courtesy of Birmingham Library Services.   604

11. Powell Williams. Courtesy of Birmingham Library Services.   604

12. 'Good ol' Joe' campaigning among his constituents. *The Sphere*, 27 January 1906.   629

13. Bidding farewell. *Daily Sketch*, 8 June 1914.   665

Preface

Drive on—we shall come to the journey's end in time, and perhaps then we shall know where we have been going and whose business we have been doing all the time.

Chamberlain to Jesse Collings, 12 September 1875

Joseph Chamberlain was the first industrialist to enter the highest sphere in British politics. In previous centuries merchants and bankers and in the nineteenth century industrial manufacturers had made their way into Parliament. Some had played a notable part in its proceedings, some had gained office. But few had made the transition from absorption in business to prominence in politics; and none of them set the pace of British politics, before Joseph Chamberlain. His significance was all the greater because his business was located at the centre of 'the workshop of the world', among the metal-manufacturing industries of Birmingham. And though he never became prime minister, by the beginning of the twentieth century he was by all accounts the first minister of the British empire.

His career in business shaped his conduct in politics. It was not just a matter of manners. Chamberlain tackled politics as would an entrepreneur, venture by venture, innovative in organization as well as product or programme, alert to the importance of accounting and, even more, of marketing. His experience of industry had still greater bearing on his achievement in politics. His enduring importance lies in how true he remained to his industrial base and how effectively he brought his roots to bear in the world of high politics where he spent the second half of his life.

There was a remarkable match between the evolution of his career, including its discontinuities, and the maturation and incipient deterioration of Britain as an industrial power. It is hard to avoid a sense of failure in both, and especially in Chamberlain as a politician. A man who took pride in his constructive approach to politics, he proved to be destructive, shattering both the major parties in Britain. Though a great innovator in politics, by the time he died he seemed to have little to show for himself but a succession of lost causes. Yet his name is still one to conjure with; and his life story is one of the most absorbing in modern British history.

It is none the less hard to tell. Everyone who has tried to do so has taken a long time and then abandoned the attempt to tell the whole story. His first official biographer and still the most readable, J.L. Garvin, took fifteen years to carry the story to 1900, and then quit.[1] After the lapse of a decade his work was taken up by Julian Amery, who took a further twenty years to complete the story. Amery tended to lose sight of the man about whom he was writing in order to chronicle his final cause, the crusade for tariff reform.[2] Rather than attempt a biography, Peter Fraser wrote a collection of policy studies.[3] The best single volume on Joseph Chamberlain, by Richard Jay,[4] concentrates on his career in high politics at Westminster to the neglect not only of his personal life but of his business career and also pays little attention to his base and achievement in Birmingham. The present attempt to write a complete Life has taken more than a dozen years.

The difficulty of the enterprise, but also its great reward, arises from Chamberlain's fresh intersection with most of the problems which Britain encountered as a popularly governed industrial power in the half century between the passage of the Second Reform Act and the outbreak of the First World War. Most but not all: Chamberlain had no real interest in one of the motive springs of his age, religion. He lacked the religious conviction that distinguished Gladstone, the romantic interest in religion felt by Disraeli, even the detached intellectual curiosity about the subject which John Morley showed. Chamberlain was brought up in a particularly rationalistic school of Unitarianism; and when confronted by personal tragedy, he angrily abandoned what little faith he had. But anything that kindled the industrial fires or touched the urban interests of Birmingham quickened his imagination. He reflected and throve upon the enterprise of his city.

The discontinuities in Chamberlain's career have often been taken as more significant than any underlying consistency. The Irish Home Rule crisis of 1886 not only broke his political career in half but drove him from the Radical left of the Liberal party into enduring alliance with the Conservatives led from their right by Lord Salisbury. Chamberlain led a campaign in 1884 against the House of Lords; twenty-six years later he urged diehard Unionists to uphold the Lords. Advocate of free trade in the 1880s, Chamberlain died a protectionist. The stock-in-trade of his opponents after 1886 was to quote from his speeches as a Radical to refute his arguments as a Unionist; and other Unionists winced at these reminders.

Yet his basic consistency was apparent to most of those who knew him at close quarters in Birmingham. He was a prophet much honoured in his own country. He was recognized in Birmingham as a man who had contributed in his business career to the industrial ascendancy of the town, the region and indeed the whole country, and who was henceforward determined to extend and ensure the benefits of this collective achievement and keep it strong at home and abroad.

There was something intrinsically Radical about this set of objectives, yet it was hard to place in the conventional spectrum of political opinion. In order to enhance the wellbeing of urban, industrial England, Chamberlain insisted upon widening the accepted social and economic parameters of political action. For more than a decade this insistence placed him on the Radical left of the Liberal party. But during the 1880s, even before his breach with Gladstone, he began to discover historic precursors for his assertion of the powers of the state, precedents predating the detachment of economics from politics by the classical economists to whom Gladstone was devoted. International competition, politically with the powers of Europe and economically with Germany and the United States, pushed Chamberlain in the same direction, towards neo-mercantilist imperialism and the Unionist right.

Throughout his public life there was a further ambivalence in his political stance. He advocated socio-economic reform in order to protect rather than truly to share the ascendancy which the owners of urban wealth acquired alongside the owners of land. Working people were intended to benefit from but not to be partners in his successive public enterprises.

The industrial underpinnings of Chamberlain's politics sometimes distorted his vision. Geographically as well as physically shortsighted, he looked at Britain through the monocle of Birmingham, a lens which was not always correct even for the West Midlands let alone for the rest of industrial and urban Britain or for the countryside. None the less, appreciation of his industrial upbringing helped and can still help those wishing to understand his personal conduct in politics as well as his public policies. His businesslike directness of speech marked a change in the character of public debate, but also offended foreign diplomatic sensibilities, with unfortunate consequences. While members of Britain's traditional elite admired his energy and strength of purpose, they detected a lack of grace; they sensed the cinder and soot of industry clinging to him. He did not share their lifelong associations. His commitment was always to an enterprise rather than to a party; and he was ready to embark upon a new enterprise with fresh partners if his current enterprise went bankrupt or ran short of funds.

But however tenacious his roots, he could not be thought of ab-
stractly as the industrialist in politics. His personality was too strongly
marked for that. Seemingly a man of enormous self-confidence, he was
plagued throughout his life with signs of nervous strain: disabling
headaches, neuralgia, and eventually chronic gout. Seemingly a man of
steely purpose, he acted on instinct and impulse in the most serious
crises of his life. He was an aggressive person who yet craved and
worked best in the harness of close relationships, whether with family
members, wives, partners, collaborators or colleagues. He courted the
votes of the electorate with a frankness which disgusted those who disliked popular government, yet his manner of courtship here as in his
more intimate relationships was imperious. The virtue he most prized
was loyalty, individual and collective. He cultivated patriotism at every
level, personal, civic, national, and imperial. Yet the sort of loyalty he
expected involved subordination if not submissiveness, and hence provoked rebellion. Accordingly the successive phases in his evolution
tended to be accompanied by new sets of friends. Yet he was tortured
by the severance of friendships and commonly attempted sooner or
later to restore them. He was also slow, too slow, to abandon those who
had once been loyal colleagues and still spoke the language of friendship after they had begun to serve him ill, men such as Captain O'Shea
and Arthur Balfour.

A person of such intensity who involved himself in a formative way
with the major concerns of Britain both at home and abroad for half a
century was bound to leave many marks in the archival sands of history. In tracing those marks, in South Africa, Canada and the United
States as well as in the United Kingdom, I have incurred many debts of
gratitude to archivists and others. The manuscript collections which I
consulted are listed at the end of this volume; and to all of those in
charge who assisted me in my enquiry I wish to express my gratitude.
I want to convey special thanks to the late Geoffrey Dyer who introduced me to the rich holdings of the University of Sheffield on Chamberlain's early and late career, to J.M. Fewster for helping me through
the morass of papers of the fourth Earl Grey at the University of
Durham, to Jackie and Hugh McLeod, Linda and Charles Jones,
J.B. Kenrick, and Shiela Southey for their hospitality, to Carole
Hardman of GKN who let me dig into the oldest papers at Nettlefold
and Chamberlain's original Heath Street mill in Smethwick, and to
Maryna Fraser for access to the Barlow Rand archives outside Johannesburg, to Leslie Hannah for telling me how to find my way into the
stockholding records at the Public Record Office, to Frank Bywater for
intriguing conversation about the Crawford divorce, to Simon Restorick
for photographing the Herkimer portrait and the Strang etching, and
very special thanks to Chris Penney in the Heslop Room at the Univer-

sity of Birmingham. John Spiers induced me originally to undertake this enterprise; the John Simon Guggenheim Memorial Foundation kindly launched me on my way with a fellowship; Colin Webb, then at the University of Cape Town, enabled me to spend a remarkable three months in South Africa; John Grenville brought me repeatedly into the company of the history faculty at Birmingham; my own university has given me repeated support; and a succession of honours and graduate history students at Syracuse secured copies for me of all the indexed entries on Chamberlain in *The Times*. Two friends, Andrew Porter from King's College, London, and Michael Dintenfass from the University of Wisconsin, Milwaukee, read and commented on the main draft of this book from beginning to end. Others have done so in part, including members of the European history seminar at Syracuse and the social history seminar at Birmingham, J.B. Conacher from the University of Toronto and Albert Tucker from Glendon College in Toronto, Jack Cell from Duke University, Hugh McLeod at Birmingham, and Alex Rosenberg of the University of California, Riverside. The virtues of the following text owe much to these colleagues; its vices are my own. I wish I could have added the name of Stephen Koss to this list: he died before I commenced the writing of this book; and I miss his friendship often.

I am happy to acknowledge permission as follows to quote from manuscript collections and archives: of Her Majesty Queen Elizabeth II from the papers of Queen Victoria, Edward VII and George V; of the University of Birmingham from the Chamberlain Archive, other archives in the University Library, and University of Birmingham theses; of the Clerk of the Records of the House of Lords from the Ashbourne and Cadogan papers, on behalf of the Beaverbrook Foundation from the Bonar Law and Lloyd George papers, and together with *The Spectator* from the Strachey papers; of the Librarian of the University of Bristol from the Austin papers; of the Huntington Library from a letter of Lady Frances Balfour; of the British Library from the papers of the first Earl Balfour, John Burns, Sir Charles and Lady Dilke, J.E. Ellis, Viscount Gladstone, W.E. Gladstone, and the first Earl Halsbury; of the Harry Ransom Humanities Research Center, the University of Texas at Austin from the W.T. Stead papers; of the Hereford County Record Office from the Lord James of Hereford papers; of Duke University Special Collections Library from the first Earl Midleton papers; of the Librarian and the Archivist of the University of Sheffield Library from the Hewins, Mundella and Wilson papers; of the Centre for Kentish Studies from the Chilston papers; of J.B. Kenrick from the Kenrick papers; of Viscount Esher from the Esher papers; of the Trustees of the Chatsworth Settlement from the Devonshire papers; of the Marquess of Salisbury from the Salisbury papers; of the Bodleian Library from the

Bryce, Selborne, and Sandars papers and a letter to Mrs Farnell; of Lord Monk Bretton from the Monk Bretton papers; of the British Library of Political and Economic Science from the Passfield and Frederic Harrison papers; of the Earl of Rosebery and the Trustees of the National Library of Scotland from the Minto and Rosebery papers; of the Earl of Selborne from the Selborne papers; of the Gloucestershire County Record Office from the St Aldwyn papers; of the Earl of Balfour from the papers of the second Earl; of the Warden and Fellows of New College, Oxford, from the Milner papers; of the Harcourt family from the Harcourt papers; of A.J. Maxse Esq. and the West Sussex Record Office from the Maxse papers; of the Liverpool Record Office from the Melly papers; of Lord Daventry from the Newdegate papers; of Lord Balfour of Burleigh from the Balfour of Burleigh papers; of the Guildford Muniment Room, Surrey Record Office, from the Onslow papers; of Peregrine Churchill from Lord Randolph Churchill's papers; of the Master and Fellows of Churchill College, Cambridge, from the Lyttelton papers; of Barlow Rand Limited from the Barlow Rand archives; of Mrs S.F. Corke from the Farrer papers; of the National Library of Australia from the Alfred Deakin papers; of B. Babington Smith from the Parker Smith papers; of the South African Library from the De Villiers papers; of the Trustees of the Lansdowne MSS. from the Lansdowne papers; of Gillian Ingall from the Bryce papers; of Viscount Ridley from the Ridley papers in the Northumberland Record Office; and of the University of Toronto Press and the Penguin Group to draw in altered form upon chapters which I contributed to B.L. Kinzer, ed., *The Gladstonian Turn of Mind: Essays presented to J.B. Conacher* (University of Toronto Press, 1985) and to J.M.W. Bean, ed., *The Political Culture of Modern Britain: Studies in memory of Stephen Koss* (Hamish Hamilton, 1987). All quotations on the ensuing pages are exactly as in the cited sources, except for those using the Victorian convention of third person verbatim reporting of speeches, which I have turned back into the first person.

There are, finally, three extraordinary tributes which I must pay. One is to the family of Joseph Chamberlain, particularly to his granddaughters and grandsons-in-law, the late Dorothy and Stephen Lloyd, and Diane and the late Terence Maxwell, for the welcome they gave to a foreign intruder into their history and for their continued generous encouragement. Another is to Ben Benedikz, the librarian in charge of the Heslop Room and hence of the unique Chamberlain family archive at the University of Birmingham. He surpasses what any historian or biographer could hope for in an archivist. He led me through the Chamberlain papers, kept me abreast of additions to them including the suitcase of letters between Chamberlain and his third wife Mary which the Maxwells graciously donated, helped me endlessly with copies, read and commented on the manuscript, and always kept my spirits up.

I cannot count the ways to express the love and the loss reflected in the dedication to this book.

1

The Roots of the Enterprise
c.1700–1854

Is it not a curious thing that we always want to know something of the ancestry of a great man although we find that . . . intellect and genius are hardly ever hereditary?

Chamberlain on Milton, 20 April 1864

When still a young businessman, Joseph Chamberlain was observed at a ball in the Birmingham town hall. He was already someone to watch. A precociously successful metal manufacturer, smartly dressed, not tall but lean and alert, he moved easily among the industrial elite of the town. He was affiliated with many of them as a Unitarian and was about to marry into one of the most respected local families. Like the rest of Birmingham's manufacturers, he was proud of what they were doing together to make England the workshop of the world.

But a silk cord ran across the room. The industrial elite were gathered at the lower end of the hall. At the upper, less crowded end stood the landed gentry and the occasional peer from estates outside the smoky town. They were of the class that governed England. Chamberlain stood on the industrial side but along the cord, chatting with an acquaintance in the enclosure of the landed elite.[1] For the moment Chamberlain attempted to ignore the cord; in years to come he would cut it through; but it left an indelible impression on him, stimulating his sense of the need to do battle with the grandees of the British governing establishment. To the end of his life he was inclined to attack 'the same distinguished and superior persons'[2] who time and again resisted his initiatives.

His roots ran deep on the industrial side of England's social economy. Like virtually all English families, the Chamberlains were rural in origin. But as far back as the records run, the men of the family earned their living in businesses of the kind that gave rise to the industrial revolution. The first member of the family for whom records survive,[3] Joseph Chamberlain's great-great-grandfather Daniel, lived out his days in the first half of the eighteenth century in the Wiltshire vil-

lage of Laycock. Daniel Chamberlain was not, however, a farmer but a
maltster, buying local barley to turn it into the malt from which beer
was brewed. He was, in other words, a small businessman in the rural
economy.

He also belonged to one of those kinship networks of Protestant Dissent whose members reinforced each other economically as well as religiously to face the landowners and Church of England clergymen who
governed county and country. Daniel had a brother (or brother-in-law,
the record is not clear) who was a confectioner in the City of London.
Daniel apprenticed his son William, born in 1713, to this brother.
William was a spirited young man. Left on one occasion to sweep out
his uncle's shop, he diverted himself by trying to balance the broom on
the end of his nose. When the broom fell and smashed the dainty goods
set out on the counter, William was packed off to learn a trade in more
durable things.

He became a cordwainer, a worker in new leather and hence a shoe
manufacturer, a trade distinct from that of the cobbler, a worker in old
leather and hence a repairer of shoes. Cordwaining was known to be a
lucrative business, and William prospered. Public responsibilities accompanied his increasing affluence, and he welcomed them. In 1760 he
became warden of St Lawrence Jewry, the church beside London's
Guildhall. Nine years later he was elected Master of the Company of
Cordwainers. On the eve of the American War of Independence, his
business had a capital of £3,800 and made annual profits of close to
£500.[4] War was good for cordwaining: soldiers had to be shod, and then
as now the army paid higher prices than did private customers. The
American war trebled William's capital and quadrupled his annual
profits. The patriotism of the Chamberlain family stood on solid economic foundations.

The decade of peace after the American War of Independence was
hard on the business. It underwent a reorganization in 1783 when
William and his eldest son, also called William, brought the younger
son, Joseph, into full partnership. This Joseph, grandfather of the statesman, was the first of three generations to bear the name. Not long after
the death of the elder William, war broke out again, this time with
revolutionary France, and restored the family fortunes. The capital
worth of the firm steadied at between £9,000 and £10,000, just below the
boom levels of 1781 and 1782; and while profits varied widely from
year to year, they averaged £575.

Before the long war with France was concluded, Joseph emerged as
the dominant partner. He sustained and developed the pattern of loyalties which characterized the family. He was proud of his craft and
guild. He was conscientious in the performance of the public duties that
accompanied his financial position. But those duties were confined to

the local civic sphere. The Chamberlains were strictly urban in their loyalties, uninterested in the acquisition of land, and hence excluded from participation in the higher reaches of government. Joseph was none the less a patriot, martial in his ardour. He was a staunch supporter of the oldest regiment in the kingdom, the Honourable Artillery Company. After all, artillerymen as foot soldiers required an abundance of shoes. He served the regiment as a trustee and on its estate and finance committees, and early in the war against France became captain of the company's northwestern division. This mixture of profit and patriotism formed a legacy which his family did not forget. A century later his grandson would remind his fellow Englishmen of their ancestors who 'with half the population, with one-tenth of the wealth that we possess, stood against a world in arms, and stood successfully. They gave us what we have,' he declared before going on to ask, 'are we going to allow . . . the sceptre of this great dominion to fall from our enfeebled hands?'[5]

The first Joseph Chamberlain clearly did not share the aversion to the war against Revolutionary France which his fellow Unitarian, the famous minister and scientist Joseph Priestley, felt. Joseph I was none the less staunch in his Unitarianism. Both of his wives were descendants of a Puritan minister, Richard Sergeant, ejected from his parish in 1662 by the restored Church of England. The two wives were in fact sisters; and by marrying the sister of his first wife after her death, he defied the proscriptions of the Church of England. His marriages thus deepened the family's sense of the oppression which English Nonconformists had long endured.

At one level, the Unitarianism of the Chamberlains was a religious reflection of their economic position. In the seventeenth century English Presbyterianism, with its respect for ministers but not for bishops, furnished a middle ground between the episcopal Church of England and the congregational Independents and Baptists. Presbyterian chapels attracted middle-class men of enterprise. In the eighteenth century, when the denomination split, the more affluent Presbyterians tended to become Unitarians while poorer members drifted towards the Congregationalists and Baptists.

But the roots of Unitarianism were not crudely economic. What distinguished Unitarians among the ranks of English Nonconformity was their rationalism. Two movements divided English Presbyterians in the eighteenth century. The Methodist revival, appealing to the heart and laying stress on the experience of sin and salvation, drew less educated Presbyterians into the ranks of evangelical denominations like the Congregationalists. But the heyday of the evangelical revival was also the age of reason. One effect of the Enlightenment in England was to transform the better educated Presbyterians into Unitarians; and though nothing is known about the education of the Chamberlains in the eighteenth century, they were among this group.

Well respected in the business community of the City, the Chamberlains still conducted themselves modestly. The second decade of the nineteenth century was bad for their business. It revived in the 1820s, an improvement coinciding with the emergence of Joseph I's sons, Joseph II and Richard, as full partners. The business began to boom and surpassed the prosperity of the 1770s in 1829. When the boom subsided a decade later, it left the business with higher average annual profits than during the French war, never sinking below £500 and rarely below £1,000. When Joseph I died in 1837, his third of the business was valued at £12,000. Yet he lived out his days in rooms over the warehouse in Milk Street.

Joseph II became the dominant partner. He was at least the match of his father in business acumen, and was equally alert to the military market. Sometimes during the ministry of Lord Palmerston, he did nearly half his business and made more than half of his profits with the army. He took a keen interest in politics. Yet he was even more unobtrusive than his father, and also more sensitive. Though he profited from war, corporal punishment horrified him. He never resorted to it himself and would not send his children to schools where it might be used. He also earned a reputation for concern about the well-being of his employees. His sensitivity was, however, kept under severe control: 'nothing could turn him if he had made up his mind', the beadle of the Cordwainers' Company observed; he was 'pleasant and quiet in manner, but not to be moved from what he had said by anybody'.[6] He was at ease only with his wife, Caroline Harben, the mother of Joseph III.

A livelier person than her husband, she brought more adventurous blood to the family. The Harbens had also briefly joined the charmed circle of England's governors. Otherwise for the most part the Harben and Chamberlain families had followed parallel paths. The first Harben of whom anything is known, like the first Chamberlain, was a maltster. His son Thomas, like Daniel Chamberlain's son William, had turned to another craft, in this case clockmaking. At that point, the paths of the two families diverged.

Thomas Harben looked out to sea and became a shipowner, a trader in cargo, and when chance arose a smuggler. When a storm in the winter of 1747 wrecked a Spanish ship against the coast of Sussex near his home, he bought the salvaging rights. The gamble paid off handsomely, for he salvaged £24,000 in quicksilver or mercury from the wreck. With this wealth, he built himself a country house. His son, another Thomas, sought to make his way over the fence that divided the business and governing classes. He diversified his economic base, becoming a banker and ironmonger as well as maltster, and he speculated with ever greater daring. At the same time he managed the parliamentary constituency interests of two Whig dukes, first for the elder Pitt's colleague the Duke of Newcastle and then for the Duke of Richmond, both great land-owners in Sussex. His religious affiliations followed suit. Earnestly Nonconformist to begin with, he moved towards the Established Church. He stretched too far. At the beginning of the war with France which brought prosperity to the Chamberlains, Thomas Harben suf-fered a reverse of fortune. Ten years later he died in the home of his son-in-law, a Church of England parson.

The family underwent a moral split. The eldest son joined the fast circle around the Prince of Wales in Brighton. The second son, Henry, broke off relations with his brother and rejoined the solid business class from which the family had sprung. He established himself as a brewer and provisions merchant in London. It was there that his daughter Caroline met and married the second Joseph Chamberlain.

Both Caroline and her husband brought quiet control to the house-hold which they established. Caroline reinforced her husband's ten-dency to keep to his own social set. But she was anxious to show that her household did not fall below the governing class in grace. She brought her concerns to bear most intently upon her first child, Joseph III. Her mother, his grandmother, taught him fine handwriting. Caroline taught him to speak well, sensitive as she was to 'a good voice and pure pronunciation'.[7] She never raised her own voice in anger, and did not easily forgive outbreaks of childish temper. Her relations with her firstborn were strenuous, for he was an aggressive child. He kept on his bedside table till he died a silver thimble of hers which he had stamped on at the age of three, together with her inscription remind-ing him to control himself. 'You keep telling me that we must forgive seventy times seven,' the little boy complained when sent to bed for disobedience, 'and you won't forgive me even once.'[8] Anxious to rehabilitate himself, he became a conscientious student, coming home with questions which his mother found hard to answer.

Still, the prevailing impression that Caroline and the Harbens gave to the Chamberlain household was one of happiness, even gaiety. Affluent City people and urbane Unitarians, the Harbens drank good wines and were well read. Family gatherings at holiday time were highlighted by plays which they wrote, produced and performed for themselves. Young Joe threw himself into these private theatricals with gusto, even-tually becoming the chief producer and taking the exaggerated charac-ter parts.

To begin with, the Chamberlains lived in a modest but well-built, three-storey Georgian house on Grove Hill Terrace. It stood near the top of a hill in Camberwell on the newly developing southern outskirts of London looking across the river towards the heart of the city. Joseph II bought it just before the arrival of his first child; and it was there that Joseph III was born, on 8 July 1836.

A story survives from his early years of Joseph and his sister Mary playing with toy soldiers and pop guns. Joseph's gun popped Mary's soldiers over while his soldiers withstood her attacks, to her surprise— until she discovered that he had glued his soldiers to the floor! His first teacher, Miss Pace, who taught him at her dame-school down Grove Hill Terrace, remembered an episode with another twist to it. She came upon Joe in the thick of a fight among the schoolboys. It turned out to be over who should be president of a peace society which she and her Quaker aunt had started in the school. Fifty years later when she retold the story, he recalled it differently. He remembered himself as the founder of the society and its largest contributor, having donated to it a fourpenny bit that his uncle had given him. The fight was about what to do with this wealth. 'Eventually,' he recalled with amusement, 'after long consideration, it went to a crossing sweeper near the school, and that was the end of the Peace Society.'[9]

Caroline Chamberlain gave birth to a child every year or two until she had nine. All of them were healthy except the fifth, a son Frank who died at birth in 1845. The shadow of this death precipitated a movement by the family into better quarters north across the Thames at 25 Highbury Place, a private road in Islington. Young Joseph loved the new house. Years later, when he built a mansion for himself in Birmingham, he named it Highbury. Like Grove Hill Terrace, Highbury Place was on a hill. It commanded lovely views both northwest across a meadow and southeast towards the City of London. Each feature of the home etched itself on the growing boy's mind: its enclosed garden, the high bookcases, the china closet. After Grove Hill Terrace, the new house and its garden felt wonderfully spacious, though it seemed small when he came back to look at it thirty years later.

One place held steady in the migrations of Joseph II and his family from Milk Street to Camberwell and then back over the river to Islington. They remained faithful to Carter Lane chapel near their shop in the City. Young Joseph never had a strongly religious sense, though on one occasion, responding to economic opportunity, he tried out what it might be like to be a minister. His father had announced that he would settle £200 a year on any of his sons who would train for the Unitarian ministry. Joseph, aged eight or nine, summoned his eldest sister and a cousin, and, mounting a broad chair-bed, tried his hand at preaching. He never tried again. Nor did any of his younger brothers accept the parental offer.

The Unitarianism of the parents still affected the sons strongly, but it led them in a social and political rather than religious direction. The

Unitarianism of both generations took on an increasingly secular cast. The value which Joseph II prized most explicitly in religion was individual liberty of judgement. He and his family took the rationalist side in a renewed division among Unitarians during the nineteenth century, this time between insistent rationalists who followed a path marked out earlier by Joseph Priestley, and a new school of romantic Unitarians whose best-known spokesman was James Martineau, brother of the still more famous novelist Harriet. James Martineau recognized the emotional impoverishment of strictly rational religion. He sought compensation for the thinness of his theology in romantic mysticism.[10] The disciples of Priestley, including the Chamberlains, stoically rejected this escape.

In doing so, they cut themselves off emotionally from most Victorian believers and indeed from many agnostics. The isolation left a permanent mark on Joseph III. He would never be able to touch the wellsprings of evangelical emotion upon which his fellow countrymen often drew. Yet the rationality of the Unitarians sharpened their capacity for social analysis. Priestley had taught his people to examine the workings of English society with the same rationality which he applied to religious belief. Romantic Unitarians like Martineau lost this capacity for incisive social commentary. Their response to the ills of society degenerated into personal philanthropy. Not so the Priestleyite Unitarians at Carter Lane. They established a mission among the dockers in the East End of London to provide secular, not religious, education; and Joseph III taught there on Sundays in his teens.

In many ways young Joseph Chamberlain was the political heir of Joseph Priestley. Both adhered to the central concept of Radical analysis, the greatest happiness of the greatest number. Though towards this end Joseph Priestley had sought to minimize the powers of the state which Joseph Chamberlain later sought to expand, the Unitarian divine advocated social institutions for the poor which would have been more regulative and authoritarian than anything later introduced by the Radical politician. Young Chamberlain scorned the tendency among men who acquired wealth to lose their early Radicalism. Taunted about being a Unitarian by a Conservative opponent in a Birmingham election, he replied:

> ... in the great struggle for political liberty, which has now been going on for some 100 years, that body, small though it is, has always been on the side of progress, and on the side of the people; and, further, I can say of that body what can be said of few other sects, that its men, when they become rich, do not cease to be liberal.[11]

His rationalism was a tool for practical analysis rather than for philosophical reflection. It nevertheless gave him an appetite for far-reaching social and political ideas. Lord Milner, who worked closely with him later, came to recognize that Chamberlain was 'swayed by big permanent ideas, and they are not external to him, but, wherever he gets them from, *they have their roots inside him*'.[12]

He received his formal education in schools which stressed modern rather than classical subjects: mathematics, some science, and French as well as Latin. When the family moved to Islington, he was sent to an unpretentious but good school under the direction of a Church of England clergyman. When the schoolmaster told Joseph II that his son, by now fourteen, knew as much mathematics as his teacher, Joseph III was enrolled in University College School, a distinguished unsectarian academy in London to which well-to-do Unitarians entrusted their sons. Young Chamberlain's most conspicuous characteristic at school was his appetite for learning, and he did well. He had no interest in team sports. Years later, when called upon to speak at a sports meet, he confessed,

> I do not walk when I can help it; I do not play cricket; I do not play football; I do not play tennis; and I do not even play golf, which I have been assured is an indispensable condition of statesmanship. The fact is I do not take any exercise at all.[13]

The schoolmates of this youth were not amused by the aversion he showed to their games. Once, when the headmaster was called out, the other boys tied Chamberlain to a stanchion in the middle of the room and kept him there until they heard the headmaster's returning footsteps. On prize day, Joe carried away distinctions in mathematics and hydrostatics, Latin and French. His mathematics prize was a book entitled *Eldorado or Adventures in the Path of Empire*.

The public life of London contributed to his education. In common with the business class throughout the country, he was saddened in 1850 by the death of Sir Robert Peel. Two years later the sight of the old Duke of Wellington lying in state in St Paul's Cathedral gripped the teenage lad's imagination. But he scoffed inwardly at the Lord Mayor of London, bedecked in chain and robes of office, who awarded Joe the French prize at University College School with a complacent confession of his own ignorance: 'I hope you will be able to read that book. I cannot "parley vous" myself.' A quarter of a century later, now handing out the prizes himself as mayor of Birmingham, Chamberlain recalled the story and added, 'Nous avons changé tout cela.'[14]

The cultural amenities which he most enjoyed in London were exhibits of new technology. He made use of school vacations to attend lectures on chemistry and electricity as well as literature at the Polytechnic Institution. He loved the scientific exhibits that actually worked, especially a diving bell big enough to take him underwater.

But his school days and school vacations were almost over. His father removed him at the end of two years from University College School, just after his sixteenth birthday, to begin work in the cordwaining business on Milk Street. Young Joe felt no injustice in this. It was part of the order in which he had been raised, and a privileged order at that. University College School expected its students to leave at sixteen. Though he later wished that he could have gone on to university, he valued learning essentially for its utility. The time had come to work. He began at Milk Street, as his forefathers had done, at a bench learning the craft of cordwaining alongside the men who worked for his father.

There were holidays from work, shorter ones than from school, but more interesting because they expanded young Joe's horizons. While most of the Chamberlains were thin-faced and austere, Joe had an uncle of a different sort. Richard Chamberlain was a master cordwainer, but there his affinity with his brother, Joseph II, stopped. Round-faced and ruddy, curly-haired and whiskered, a character straight out of Dickens, Richard loved travel, especially abroad. After young Joe had worked at Milk Street for a year, Richard took him and his sister Mary for three weeks to France and Belgium. The highlight was Paris. Joe and his uncle saw Napoleon III ride by—or, rather, they saw his carriage, for the emperor sat back out of view. They inspected the walls of the Church of St Geneviève which had been battered by cannon and musket balls in 1848. Mary and Joe learned to sample the food and drink. Baedeker in hand, Richard led them up one aisle and down the other of church after church examining everything impartially, or into gallery after gallery where they proceeded methodically from the first painting to the last. Like the Lord Mayor of London, Richard did not know French, so he made use of Joe's knowledge. 'Pardon, Monsier,' Richard would shout at any Frenchman whom he could buttonhole, and then turned him over to Joe to find out what they wanted to know. When things went awry, the exuberant uncle swore like a trooper. Joe's French was good enough to enable him to follow the plays which they attended. He acquired a lifelong zest for foreign travel. He also acquired a motto. When his uncle Richard gave him a ring with a crest for engraving, Joe chose the words, 'Je tiens ferme'—'I hold firm'.

Back at work in London, his apprenticeship at the cordwainer's bench soon came to an end. His father transferred him to the bookkeeping office to learn the craft of accountancy which lay at the heart of the family's enterprise. This apprenticeship too was brief, cut short after little more than a year when he was despatched to travel again, now a shorter distance and on business rather than for pleasure—to Birmingham.

2

Screw King
1854–1869

On the whole I feel certain that to let the Company get fairly into the market would be to abdicate for ever our position as Screw Kings.

Chamberlain to Nettlefold, 10 May 1870

Joseph Chamberlain and Britain's industrial revolution reached prosperous maturity together. His career in business coincided with the Great Victorian Boom. Both stories began with the exhibition of the world's manufactures at the Crystal Palace in 1851. The overseas commercial empire that Chamberlain carved out for his business in the 1860s was one manifestation of the worldwide economic hegemony that Britain asserted in the same decade through a proliferation of free trade treaties. The economic climax for the industrialist and his country came with the Franco-Prussian War, which carried the metal-manufacturing West Midlands to a fever pitch of production. Chamberlain brought his business career to a close in 1874 just before the Great Depression took hold.

His career in business thus coincided with the longest period of sustained economic expansion in modern British history.[1] The boom lasted from the 1850s to the 1870s. Two spurts of inflation, one in the mid-fifties and the other in the early seventies, framed a period of high, relatively stable prices. They were accompanied by a rapid expansion of steam-powered factory-based industry. The steam-powered factory is often considered synonymous with the first stage of the industrial revolution in the late eighteenth and early nineteenth centuries. In fact, the use both of steam power and of production in large factories spread gradually and unevenly. The great expansion in their use did not occur till after 1850. Even then, steam-powered factories were concentrated largely in textiles, coalmining, iron-smelting and heavy engineering. The small, specialized metal-manufacturing industries of the West Midlands were slow to be affected.

The Great Victorian Boom looks golden in retrospect, but it was not really great, nor was it easily achieved. Though the rate of productive growth reached its peak in the third quarter of the nineteenth century, it was not much higher than in the preceding or following decades. Moreover, the boom was not a time of easy profits. The rate of profit was lower than in the first phase of the industrial revolution. Mid-Victorian prosperity was produced by the enterprise of manufacturers like Chamberlain and by the responsive working people whom they employed. The growth in productivity was stimulated as much by compressed profit margins as by widening markets and increasing demand. Opportunities for the acquisition of wealth as a result of technological advances were fewer than in the heroic age of the spinning jenny and flying shuttle, and they were quickly subject to competitive challenge. The mortality rate among businesses ran high. In order to flourish, businesses like the one on which Chamberlain embarked had to have 'some degree of monopoly power ... through patent exploitation, the possession of some unique skill, [or] the differentiation of their products'.[2] The economy that Chamberlain entered in 1854 was 'dynamic, but unstable ... populated by risk-taking entrepreneurs'.[3]

Unlike the landed elite, these entrepreneurs were a mobile lot, moving readily to seize opportunities. Birmingham was particularly full of enterprising immigrants, of whom Chamberlain was to become the most famous. Though ready to move to seek their fortune, the newcomers were rarely rootless. Usually a combination of family connections with economic opportunity induced them to move. Here too, Chamberlain was like the rest. He travelled to Birmingham in 1854, just after his eighteenth birthday, to look after the investment his father was making in a venture by his sister's husband, young Joseph's uncle, John Sutton Nettlefold. Like Joe's father, Nettlefold was a soberly resourceful, modestly affluent manufacturer, in this case of wood screws. Screw manufacturing, like shoemaking, had not yet felt the full force of industrialization. Nettlefold's venture was an attempt to seize an opportunity for such a breakthrough.

At or as a result of the 1851 exhibition in the Crystal Palace, Nettlefold came upon a machine patented by an American, Thomas J. Sloan, which fully mechanized the process of making wood screws. While Britain's industrial accomplishments on the whole dominated the exhibition, acute observers noted the technological superiority which the fledgling American industry had achieved in the manufacture of small metal goods. Like everything else, screws had long been made by hand. The process was laborious and the product therefore costly, yet by modern standards poor in quality. Some of the stages in the manufacture of screws were mechanized in the early decades of the nineteenth century. The process of making small, standard goods from wire was ripe for full automation. It was goaded on in the United States by the high cost of labour. Sloan took out his patent there in 1848, three years before the Crystal Palace exhibition.

The invention opened up the prospect of mass production at much-reduced prices of a much-improved product. The Sloan screw had a sharp gimlet point which enabled the screw to be twisted into wood without first boring a hole. But mass production entailed a daunting rise in the level of initial capital expenditure. The price for exclusive rights to the patent in Britain plus enough machines to exploit its potential was set at £30,000, and upkeep of the machines would be expensive too. Nettlefold was not the largest manufacturer of wood screws even in Birmingham; yet if the patent fell into rival hands, he would be driven out of business.

After taking three years to consider the challenge and how to meet it, Nettlefold responded boldly. He embarked upon the building of a large factory. It was a model of advanced design. Placed alongside the canal which ran from Birmingham westward into the Black Country and close to the London and Northwestern Railway, the building consisted of three long, broad bays with arched cellars below to house shafts driven by steam engines. The shafts were to be connected through band holes in the ceiling to the machines above. 'Thus, with all the services in the cellars, there was exceptional freedom from obstruction, not only over the length of the bays but also between the bays, giving maximum facility for effective lay out of the machinery',[4] and also minimizing the danger of entangling the clothes or limbs of the machine minders in the revolving apparatus. To finance the outlay for plant and machinery, Nettlefold borrowed £10,000 from the elder Joseph Chamberlain.

The elder Chamberlain was able to raise the £10,000 without encroaching upon the capital of his own cordwaining business; and he was happy to do so. The boom in his business had lessened in the 1830s, and its fortunes in the 1850s were indifferent in spite of the Crimean War. Mechanization had barely begun in the shoemaking industry. He was therefore more interested in the opportunities in his brother-in-law's business than in his own. Eventually he had to choose between the two industries because the screw-making venture required further infusions of capital before it could fulfil the hopes of the partners. After meeting these demands, he assumed an equal share with Nettlefold in the business, now called Nettlefold and Chamberlain. In 1863 he sold his cordwaining business and moved to Birmingham. He, rather than his son, was the dominant Chamberlain in the new enterprise during its early years.

Yet for the first decade he was not the man on the spot. That decade was a formative one not only for the business but also for the son who represented him.

'The city of my adoption and my affection'

The young man and the town to which he came breathed each other's spirit. Birmingham was endowed neither with mineral wealth of its own nor with conspicuous geographical or historical advantages. It had built itself up by individual business enterprise. For two centuries, the town had produced or attracted 'generation after generation of energetic men, bent on securing a competence for themselves, accumulating capital and ready profitably to invest it'.[5] No single industry dominated the town and thus narrowed the scope for initiative. Birmingham contained a host of small industries, though most of them involved metal manufacturing of one sort or other; and each industry was further subdivided by stages in the manufacturing process into little shops. The town left the heavy industries of coalmining and iron smelting and also the heavier branches of metal manufacturing to other places, either nearby in the Black Country or farther afield. Birmingham devoted its energies to the making of pens and pins, nails and bolts as well as screws, in fact anything out of wire, anything out of brass, and coins, medals, jewellery and guns. Those who did not make the goods sold them throughout Britain and its empire.

In size of population, Birmingham was fourth among England's cities, behind Liverpool and Manchester as well as London, but it was catching up. From immigration as well as natural increase, its rate of growth peaked in the 1820s, but the slowdown thereafter was slight. Between 1831 and 1871 the population of the town almost doubled, from 144,000 to over a third of a million. Its civic amenities, however, lagged woefully behind. A dense network of streets spread over garden allotments which surrounded the town. The streets, old and new, were badly paved, lit and drained. The air was filled with the smoke of proliferating chimneys. The drink for sale in a host of public houses provided the quickest way to escape from the town. There were no free schools, libraries, art galleries or parks. The town council met in a small room on Moor Street; the mayor worked out of a first-floor parlour on Temple Street. While Birmingham could boast of being the most enterprising town in England, it also put up with one of the least active local governments.

By the 1850s when Chamberlain arrived in Birmingham, its atomized economic and social structure was beginning to prove counterproductive. The problem was not only a matter of civic amenities. It had its economic side in the struggle for survival among small businesses intensified by the development of costly technology. Nettlefold and Chamberlain's venture was designed to meet this challenge in one particular industry. Young Joseph was quick to appreciate the wider bearings of his enterprise.

The religious character of the town also suited him well. In fact he could not have found a religiously more congenial place in England. The popular impression of Birmingham as a citadel of religious Nonconformity was a little misleading.[6] Attendance at the Church of England's places of worship almost equalled that at Nonconformist chapels. The more significant fact was that the proportion of the population attending places of worship of any sort in Birmingham was among the lowest in the country. Birmingham was an unusually secular town.

In keeping with these characteristics, leadership in the town was vested to a considerable extent in its least religiously enthusiastic denomination, the Unitarians, in particular at the Church of the Messiah. Unitarians were proportionately more numerous in Birmingham than in any other urban area of England outside London, a proportion all the greater if the theologically liberal Church of the Saviour under George Dawson was included with them. Upon arriving in Birmingham, Chamberlain as a matter of course joined the Church of the Messiah. It was prominent in the camp of the anti-mystical Unitarians to which his family belonged, and the Nettlefolds were already members of the congregation.

The membership of the Church of the Messiah was small, little over one hundred when Chamberlain joined. The congregation did not seek converts. Composed for the most part of businessmen and their families proud of their austere rationalism, they enjoyed the select character of their gatherings. They were none the less imbued with a sense of social responsibility. They preached and practised a civic gospel. The support they sought among the public was political rather than religious.

They were saved from ineffectual isolation by their classification as Nonconformists. Their bond to other Nonconformists was real: all endured discrimination for their refusal to conform to the Established Church, discrimination the more galling to Unitarians who felt equal in wealth and superior in culture to the privileged gentry. The Unitarians of Birmingham felt particularly close to the nondenominational Unitarian minister, George Dawson, at his own Church of the Saviour, the most original and effective preacher of the civic gospel in which they believed. Still, most worshippers in Birmingham, as in the rest of England, were evangelicals, whether Nonconformist or Anglican by denomination. The civic gospel had not reached them by the 1850s, and it never gained the strength among them that it enjoyed at the Church of the Messiah and the Church of the Saviour. The pace of social concern in the town was set by Dawson and the Unitarians.

Their nearest competitors in influence were the Quakers, another small and affluent sect. But the Unitarians were better attuned than these rivals to another set of emotions in the town. The Quakers were famed for their pacifism, which did not combine easily with the strand of militant patriotism in Birmingham's make-up. The manufacture of small arms formed an important segment in the economy of the town, a segment with which Chamberlain sympathized. While his cord-waining family in London had put shoes on Wellington's soldiers, Birmingham provided them with swords and guns. At the end of the 1850s a wave of enthusiasm in the town for the creation of a volunteer militia prompted one of Chamberlain's earliest initiatives in public life. Working through the Birmingham and Edgbaston Debating Society, he attempted to form a company of volunteer riflemen; and he poured scorn on the lord lieutenant of Warwickshire who declined his offer.

His first few weeks in Birmingham were lonely, when he lived by himself in lodgings. The Nettlefolds were not the most hospitable of families. For two weeks the only local people he came to know were his landlady and a one-legged foreman at the screw factory. Responsible for securing the best return on his father's investment, he began by finding out how the new machinery worked. Then he moved into the bookkeeping office to deploy the skills his father had taught him back at Milk Street. With a view to the Continental market, he hired a French tutor to work with him over breakfast before he walked the half mile north from his lodgings on the fringe of Edgbaston to his office on Broad Street near the centre of the town. At night he read voraciously, often Dickens or good histories, taking note of telling quotations and episodes. But he preferred to be out and about; and within a few months of his arrival, he joined the local debating club.

Aside from its social function, the Birmingham and Edgbaston Debating Society provided the younger business and professional men of the town with a forum to discuss the issues that shaped their world: past history, pieces of legislation like Peel's Bank Act which impinged upon industry, recent novels and current events. Chamberlain had never taken the opportunity in London to observe debate in the House of Commons. He and his fellow debaters in Birmingham did not think of parliamentary careers for themselves; they thought of their town and its business. These confines invested their debates with concrete interest. The club attracted and trained a remarkable generation of men such as George Dixon, William Harris and J.T. Bunce who, a decade later, would transform Birmingham and turn it into a beacon for the country.

Chamberlain did not possess a natural gift for public speaking. Though he spoke often, his early efforts were stilted, obviously the product of painstaking preparation. He rehearsed his speeches in front of a full-length mirror. In front of an audience, if he lost his line of argument, he floundered to everyone's embarrassment. It took a long time before he could think on his feet, and fifteen years before he could speak well.

1. Young Joe, *c.* 1857.

But long before he could speak well, he was outspoken. Soon after the election in 1857 of the famous Radical orator John Bright as Member of Parliament for Birmingham, Bright honoured the Debating Society by speaking at it to defend his general position on the issues of the day. Young Chamberlain led the attack, condemning Bright's pacific inclinations on foreign policy; and he came within one vote of carrying a motion criticizing the great man. Chamberlain rebutted Bright's argument that war was an aristocratic game by insisting that all of England's wars since 1688 had been demanded by the people. He compared the world of nation states to the slums of Birmingham, where it was foolish to go out at night unarmed. No situation restrained Chamberlain from speaking his mind. One of his debating confrères, George Dixon, threw a dinner party in Bright's honour, during which Bright advocated giving Gibraltar back to Spain. While everyone else listened to him respectfully, Chamberlain challenged Bright's suggestion. Fortunately Bright enjoyed the argument. With less august opponents Chamberlain's style of argument had a nasty edge, sarcastic and sneering. A photograph of him from these years shows him looking with imperious suspicion to one side while his arm rests on a tiger skin.

Just the right marriage

Seven years after his arrival in Birmingham, Chamberlain reached the pinnacle of its society through marriage. On his very first Sunday at the Church of the Messiah, he had been 'much impressed when a very tall & handsome family drove up, filed in, took their places in a long pew and immediately after the service, filed out and drove away—very remote. "I mean to get to know those people" he said.'[7] They were the Archibald Kenricks. Heir to a flourishing hollow-ware business established by his father nearby in West Bromwich, Archibald Kenrick was a forbiddingly reserved man. He had relations on both sides of the social divide between town and county. His household was more cultured than most families in the squirarchy. The Kenricks were none the less generously committed to the Unitarian 'religion of works'. Harriet, the youngest child, a few months older than Joseph Chamberlain, taught at an elementary school for children of the working class.

Entry into the Kenrick circle did not come quickly. Five years passed before Harriet took notice of Joseph. She became acquainted with him through her brothers, particularly William, who belonged to the Debating Society. By 1860 the family knew Chamberlain well, and in October they responded happily to his engagement to Harriet. Her father endowed her with a £4,000 mortgage and £800 in Midland Railway stock when they married the following July.

The marriage lived up to all the young businessman's hopes for domestic happiness. The couple spent their honeymoon at a comfortable boarding house in Penzance, scrambling over the seaward promontories when the weather allowed. Orange lichens on the smooth boulders, luxuriant ferns in the clefts between, and 'the fine & fantastic shapes' of the sea rocks delighted them.[8] When it rained, they took turns reading a recently published volume of Buckle's *History of Civilization*, and they read *Pride and Prejudice* aloud to each other, Joe providing a running commentary on the characters: 'he calls most of [them] brutes,' Harriet reported to her sister, 'and Lizzie a very forward and improper young lady'.[9] Joe invented a new name for Harriet every day of their three-week honeymoon.

On their return to Birmingham they moved into a house on Harborne Road. After seven years living in lodgings, Joe luxuriated in the spaciousness. 'We breakfast in the little room,' Harriet reported to Joe's mother, 'dine in the dining room, and pass the evening in the drawing room.'[10] Joe also discovered the delights of gardening, a recreation dear to those who could afford ample grounds. Harriet's father initiated him in the art, which became a consuming hobby for the rest of his life. His cousin, Joseph Nettlefold, with whom he was paired in the family business, shared his passion, and they spent many summer evenings together absorbed in one or other of their gardens. Of these occasions, Harriet commented without unhappiness, 'I walk as the one-eyed among the blind.'[11]

In May of 1862, she gave birth to her first child, Beatrice. Though the prospect of childbirth and motherhood had filled Harriet with apprehension, the delivery went well and she took well to her new responsibility. Beatrice was not a pretty baby and produced a troublesome double row of teeth, but her parents took it all in their stride.

Their happiness was consolidated in the year of Beatrice's birth when Harriet's brother William married Joseph's sister Mary. The fusion of Kenricks and Chamberlains grew ever closer over the years. But this marriage had particular importance for Joe because William became his closest friend, closer even than his own brothers. In appearance William was simply a refined version of Joe, but in temperament and tastes the two men were not at all alike. While Joe rippled with energy, William was withdrawn. 'Kenricks *never* talk at breakfast,' he explained to his bride.[12] He had hoped to become an artist. Yet his greatest gift was common sense, which enabled him to recognize that he did not have enough talent for a career as an artist; and he accepted the necessity of working in his family's firm. His wealth enabled him to support the work of artists such as William Morris and Edward Burne-Jones. The combination in William Kenrick of sensitivity with common sense made him Joseph Chamberlain's most trusted adviser for the rest of their lives.

Testimonials to the respect which Chamberlain had acquired in Birmingham accompanied his marriage. He was elected to the presidency of the Debating Society, put in charge of the financial accounts of the Church of the Messiah, and placed on the council of the Chamber of Commerce. The only cloud in his sky was the treatment his younger brother Arthur received when he joined the firm of Nettlefold and Chamberlain. Their uncle, J.S. Nettlefold, reacted critically to the arrival of another Chamberlain in the firm, and declared that Arthur would never enjoy any authority in '*his* Works'.[13] The problem was not settled until Joseph senior acquired an interest in another business in Birmingham, a firm of brassfounders then renamed Smith and Chamberlain, where Arthur was installed in the summer of 1863.

Harriet delivered her second child, a son Austen, that October. Once again the delivery went well, so quickly in fact that the baby arrived before the doctor; but it was followed by tragic complications. Harriet came down with puerperal fever. As she lapsed into delirium, her mind travelled back to her honeymoon. She saw 'the great blue rolling waves & the deep orange lichens—the great rocks & boulders' which she and Joe had so much admired.[14] She died under leaden skies a few days before the third anniversary of their engagement.

Her death tore Joe from his moorings. 'There is nothing in which I was engaged,' he wrote to her sister, 'none of my actions, hardly any of my thoughts that she did not share & that have not lost with her all present hold & interest.'[15] Afraid that he bore some responsibility for the tragedy because Harriet had died in childbirth, he could not find consolation from his religion. His obvious desolation alarmed his family.

He fled from the house that Harriet and he had so loved. Beatrice and the baby Austen were moved immediately to Berrow Court, the home of Harriet's parents where her older sister could take care of the children. Joe followed. He found, despite his friendship with William, that the Kenrick household was more subdued than he liked; and the Kenricks did not take kindly to the cigars he loved. They gave him his own sitting room in a cottage at the foot of the drive, and he retired there alone after dinner. At his office the staff noted that he no longer cared how he looked. He gave up regular attendance at the Debating Society and resigned from the council of the Chamber of Commerce. With desperate concentration, he threw himself into his business.

Industrial breakthrough

After familiarizing himself with the bookkeeping in his first months at Nettlefold and Chamberlain, he had involved himself with the wholesaling. Gradually day-to-day conduct passed to the original partners' sons, both called Joseph. Joseph Nettlefold, trained as an engineer, took charge of production, Joseph Chamberlain of marketing. But the fathers together with the sons continued to set general policy. As the treatment of Arthur Chamberlain revealed, John Sutton Nettlefold was a force to reckon with until his death in 1866. The elder Joseph Chamberlain moved from London to Birmingham shortly after Harriet's death, deepening his business interests there.

Over the next two years, the four men took a set of decisions which enabled them to realize the potential the Sloan patent offered for domination of their industry. Their exclusive rights to the patent did not extend to the American market where it originated, nor to France, Germany and Russia where the patent had been sold to other buyers. At home, a rival firm in Birmingham, James and Avery, had made independent technological advances, not to the level of the Sloan patent, but enough to give them a goodly share of the industry's expanding production. To achieve the dominance for which they hoped, Nettlefold and Chamberlain pressed up to the next level of industrial advance. To take fuller advantage of Britain's comparatively low raw material costs, the firm extended its production vertically to include ironworks, the drawing of wire from which screws were made, and eventually also production of steel rods. At young Joseph Chamberlain's instigation, in 1864 the partners purchased a wire-making works, called the Imperial Wire Company, situated beside their factory. Now able to reduce the price of their final product, they launched a price-cutting war which induced their two main rivals in Birmingham, James and Avery and the firm of John Hawkins, to sell out to them. One of the few drawbacks to this process of absorption and piecemeal addition to the facilities of the firm was that it lost the physical coherence of operation which the original Heath Street mill had provided.

While the Nettlefold and Chamberlain fathers and sons were taking these decisions, young Joseph Chamberlain threw his still restless energies into a related venture in banking. Lloyds of Birmingham, a private bank, had begun to stagnate in the 1860s in face of competition from a new public company, the Birmingham Joint Stock Bank. Lloyds was thinking of transforming itself into a public joint stock concern when, in 1865, the failure of another private bank in Birmingham, Attwoods, precipitated the change. Though the Lloyds family took more than enough shares in the new institution to retain control, they wanted capital, support and temporarily even leadership from the industrialists who were beginning to dominate the local economy. The Lloyds had Conservative leanings in politics while the manufacturers and merchants whom they sought to recruit were mostly Liberals, but that political difference did not prevent cooperation in business. Timothy Kenrick, younger brother and partner of Harriet's father in the hollow-ware business, became chairman of the provisional committee that transformed Lloyds into a public bank. Joseph Chamberlain took a lead on the committee.[16] Within the new bank's board of directors, Kenrick as chairman and Chamberlain joined three of the Lloyds to form the active core.

Together with the purchase of the Sloan patent, the vertical extension of Nettlefold and Chamberlain in the mid-sixties laid the foundations for its monopoly; and Joseph Chamberlain's banking connections enhanced its access to capital. It soon produced nearly seventy per cent of Birmingham's output of screws. The reduced wholesale prices which its own wire as well as mass production enabled it to offer, a tenth of what prices had been at the beginning of the century, opened up the prospect of almost limitless expansion of its market, already doubled since mid-century. The task of the two sons as they took over from their fathers was to realize this prospect.

They tackled their assignments with unceasing enterprise. Old John Sutton Nettlefold had pioneered the expansion of screw sales by riding across country on horseback, saddle-bag full of samples, from one hardware shop to another. The travels of young Joseph Chamberlain were not initially so picturesque but they were flung far wider. His first voyage for the firm took him to a country whose history would be fatefully entwined with his own, Ireland. Whenever he went on one of the Continental holidays he loved, he took his order book with him. It always came back full.

Foreign travel alerted him to the preferences of foreign buyers. The French were used to screws nicked and wormed but not turned like English ones; so Chamberlain had Nettlefold make some accordingly. The French were also used to blue wrapping paper, which Chamberlain gave them; and they liked the measurements and gauges of the screws to be handwritten on the packages, which was therefore done. But handwritten specifications aroused the suspicions of the Scots, so Chamberlain made sure that they got machine-printed numbering, and also the green wrapping paper they preferred.

As the name and wares of Nettlefold and Chamberlain became well known, Chamberlain spent more time at his office. It was not beside the main mill on the outskirts of the town in Smethwick, but in central Birmingham on Broad Street. There he saw a stream of provincial and foreign agents, independent middlemen, and small aspirants anxious to market the wares of the firm in one quarter or another.[17] In the course of these conversations, Chamberlain established the discounting arrangements and percentage scales that were to dominate the whole screw-making industry for a century. His negotiations with his callers focused on a pair of percentages. The first part of the pair was the percentage off full list price, in other words the wholesale discount, that Chamberlain would give his caller. Direct agents could expect higher discounts than independent middlemen; men who proposed to sell in new markets could bargain confidently for higher figures than those in markets where the name and goods of the firm were known. The second percentage discount, formally for regular cash settlement of invoices, in fact specified the terms of credit that Chamberlain would give to the middleman. This figure, also negotiable, was low, never rising to two digits, whereas the wholesale discounts rarely fell below fifty per cent. The near monopoly which Nettlefold and Chamberlain built up depended as much upon these marketing arrangements as upon the firm's superiority in production.

Responsibility for marketing negotiations went hand in hand with pricing the products of the firm and hence with scrutinizing its costs. Chamberlain was in effect the firm's accountant as well as its commercial manager. Looking towards his later venture into politics, it was fortunate that he worked on the accounting rather than on the engineering side of his business. It was going to be hard to break through the prejudice that excluded industrialists from government. The expertise that Chamberlain acquired in accounting would help him because of its pertinence to the traditional concern of British politicians with finance. But he had little thought of that future yet. His mind was riveted on his business.

No phase of its activity escaped his scrutiny. The economies of scale made possible by automatic machinery and factory production could easily be squandered. To make sure that they were fully utilized, he took systematic note of the type of labour and the sex and age of the workers customarily employed to make each product; the processes involved, for example hot forging or the use of cold wire; the amount and kind of metal used; the 'soife' or steel cuttings from the nicks and threads of the screws, which could be melted down with other steel to improve the quality of the mixture. He worked out percentages for the overhead costs at each mill as well as for packaging, warehousing, taxes, and the expenses of his sales organization. It was a fine craft of calculation that he developed. Yet he never lost sight of the object of the enterprise. As one of his cashiers admiringly observed, 'Money was made very rapidly after Mr. Joseph came.'[18]

His responsibilities extended to every dimension of marketing. Addition of new products went hand in hand with expansion of the market. Apart from a vast array of designs, qualities and sizes of screw, Nettlefold and Chamberlain came to make nuts and bolts, hooks and eyes, nails, rivets, hinges and pins, and revolving centres for chairs and piano stools. They made wire not only for their own products but for sale. They were even prepared to sell the engines of their warfare, the automatic machines for which they held the patent, confident that they could make a profit on the sale and still produce screws more cheaply than the buyer. The range of the firm's wares prompted Chamberlain to initiate an illustrated price list. Good drawings reduced the need for paragraphs of description. Year by year, quarter by quarter, eventually month by month, he revised the printer's copy, adding new items as the firm's list grew, and adjusting the scale of prices to fluctuations in costs and the market.

From commercial management, accounting and advertising, Chamberlain's enterprise extended into still other fields. He negotiated with the Midland Railway, the Great Western Railway and the Shropshire Union Canal Company for special rates for his goods in return for his employment of their facilities.[19] He arranged with the Great Western for a rebate on its charges. He joined the board of directors of the Midland Railway, again in association with Timothy Kenrick, who was its deputy chairman. Yet Chamberlain never attempted to extend his enterprise, in the later fashion of American rubber barons, by taking over the transport and banking concerns with which he and Kenrick were involved.

He was less concerned with extension of the firm at home than with promotion of its sales abroad. Its absorption of competitors in Birmingham disposed for the time being of the threat of serious competition in the domestic market. But Nettlefold and Chamberlain's expanded capacity exceeded British needs. One of the primary objectives of the firm in buying the Imperial Wire Company was to overcome competition abroad with the foreign companies that possessed the Sloan patent. Much of Chamberlain's task as head of marketing was to carve out a commercial empire overseas.

The firm extracted substantial income from the American market in a way which left Chamberlain contemptuous of tariffs. Home of the original patent, the United States raised what was meant to be a prohibitive tariff to keep foreign producers out. In spite of the tariff, Nettlefold and Chamberlain sustained a volume of sales to the United States large enough to make the American manufacturers agree to pay the firm a large annual sum simply to stay away.[20] In some years in the mid-1870s, the turnover of the firm's agency in New York amounted to more than £100,000. A further increase in the American tariff was required to drive Nettlefold and Chamberlain out.

Competition for the lucrative Continental market was stiffer. It came from two French firms. With the lesser of the two, Le Comptoir de Ferches, Chamberlain negotiated in 1869 for a division of the Continent into spheres of influence, Nettlefold and Chamberlain taking the markets washed by the sea, leaving landlocked countries to the Comptoir.[21] But Chamberlain could not make headway against the great Parisian firm of Jappy Frères until providence came to his aid in the form of the Franco-Prussian War. Once the forces of Germany won the battle of Sedan, they surrounded Paris and incidentally cut Jappy Frères off from its customers. Chamberlain seized his opportunity. Nettlefold produced and he marketed furiously throughout the siege of Paris, extending their factory for the purpose. When Paris fell and commerce between the capital and the provinces began again, Jappy regained some of its old customers. Nettlefold reduced his total production only temporarily, and retooled some of his machines from French to English and overseas specifications. When his stockpile of French screws with their metric calibration was exhausted, Chamberlain had English screws packaged in his French wrappers to complete his Continental orders.

Social impact

The expansion of sales overseas was Chamberlain's most spectacular and profitable achievement in business. But the dimensions of the business that stimulated his thinking most profoundly lay at home in Birmingham. Nettlefold and Chamberlain, together with other large metal-manufacturing firms, were making far-reaching changes in the social economy of the town.[22] It had been distinguished, in contrast to the textile towns in the north of England, by its host of small workshops, each specializing in one stage in the manufacture of the small metal goods for which Birmingham was famous. The social composition of the shops was almost as well known as the goods they produced. Organized by small masters who recruited the skilled labour they needed, the shops and hence the town enjoyed more social cohesion than prevailed in the towns to the north, where great textile manufacturers assembled large amounts of unskilled labour in factories. Hence, while the textile towns had been bedevilled by class antagonism, Birmingham provided an example of class cooperation. This cooperation made Birmingham a bastion of Radical democracy in England.

At least that was the popular impression. The economic and social realities were not so clear. Birmingham had never lacked substantial capitalists: bankers like the Lloyds, manufacturers like Matthew Boulton, and the merchants who coordinated the industries of which the small workshops formed part. Far from idyllic, the world of the workshops was grimly competitive. They were at the mercy of the market, unable to ensure security of employment for the worker or independent survival for the small master. Furthermore, the industrial revolution was slowly reaching maturity in the West Midlands. Large factories were springing up around Birmingham. Beginning in the button-making industry, the consolidation of production into factories proceeded apace in the wire-using trades: pins, steel pens, and now screws. Large factory-based firms were not yet common. They were vastly outnumbered by small businesses. But they were beginning to dominate single industries, and they employed a growing proportion of the labour force. As yet beneath the level of public consciousness, this change in industrial organization called for a reformulation of the received political economy of the town.

One of the makers of the change, Chamberlain was the first businessman and one of the first in any occupation in Birmingham to appreciate its social implications. Writing about his particular industry in a survey of the town prepared for the British Association in 1866, he announced that a

> revolution . . . is taking place in the principal hardware trades, and . . . is assimilating the town to the great seats of manufacture in the North, and depriving it of its special characteristic, viz., the number of its small manufacturers, which has hitherto materially influenced its social and commercial prosperity as well as its politics.[23]

This announcement marked an important development in Chamberlain as well as in the social economy of his town. From now on, his insight was as much socio-political as economic.

There were cultural and psychological explanations for his early perception. The rationalist Utilitarian talent for social analysis was at work. It was heightened in Chamberlain after the death of Harriet in 1863. His desperate concentration on business made him unusually knowledgeable about what was happening in the local economy, and also made him anxious to discover some further meaning in what he was doing. As a matter of fact, he exaggerated the socio-economic change which firms such as his were bringing about. It did not amount to a revolution. Small workshops would abound in Birmingham more than in most English towns on into the twentieth century. Moreover, Chamberlain's early perception was shared from the outset by at least one other person, George Dawson at the Church of the Saviour. Chamberlain's special contribution was to recognize the economic forces that underlay Dawson's diagnosis of the civic needs of Birmingham.

The experience of the two men overlapped in a sphere that expanded in significance over the coming decade. The one diversion from business into which Chamberlain threw himself after the death of Harriet was voluntary school teaching, a form of social service in which she had engaged. He spent his Tuesday evenings teaching history to teenage boys in a class organized by the Church of the Messiah. He had taught on Sundays in London and Birmingham since his own teenage years, but a new urgency surrounded his Tuesday evening teaching. It was not just a personal matter of filling up unhappy time. The Church of the Messiah had recently moved into a new building straddling a canal off Broad Street. The decision to move had been contested by some members as a rejection of the poor people crowded in the streets around the old meeting house. The congregation responded to the critics by paying more attention to its schools.

This episode reflected the social tensions created by the growth of big business in the town. Chamberlain's response reflected his own emerging social philosophy. He approved of the move to Broad Street but wanted at the same time to do what he could to prove the critics wrong. As a teacher he did not pretend to be on the same footing as his working-class pupils. He kept his hat and overcoat on while he taught, and carried an umbrella that he used to point at students who were falling asleep after their long working day. Yet he was alert to their social situation. Decades later, when he ran into one of his former students, he could recall the circumstances of the man's family situation. Chamberlain's manner in the classroom was often derisive and sarcastic. Once in a class on the American Revolution, a student dropped his 'h' in speaking about the battle of Bunker's Hill. 'Poor old Bunker!'

Chamberlain jibed, 'What's the matter with him?'[24] Yet even this remark suggested that he wished to eradicate the differences in habits of speech dividing England's social classes.

His account for the British Association of the new organization of industry in Birmingham bore the stamp of liberal capitalism. The dividends Chamberlain identified as coming from large factory production were 'healthier work-places, regularity of hours, economy of labour, increased demand, lower prices, and at the same time higher wages'. The balance among these benefits leaned decidedly towards industrialists rather than labour. Each steam-powered factory embodied an effort by a firm to dominate, rationalize and intensify production in its branch of industry, confronted as all were by stiff competition at home and increasingly abroad. In order to flourish, Nettlefold and Chamberlain felt it necessary not only to buy automatic machinery and reduce raw material costs but also to make the most cost-effective use of labour.

But cost-effective did not simply mean oppressive. Though Nettlefold and Chamberlain did not emulate the high-wage economy of American industry, the practices of the firm were designed to attract a productive workforce. The plant that J.S. Nettlefold built in the mid-1850s reflected the distribution of benefits in the new order of industry. Nettlefold went to the outskirts of the town to locate his mill. He thus weakened its association with the customs of labour in the workshops that clustered near the town centre. In addition to the benefits of physical concentration of labour, he wanted a more disciplined, punctual, regular workforce, less likely to take time off in honour of 'Saint Monday' than were the workers in small workshops. Still Nettlefold's plant was better lit and ventilated, cleaner and safer for its workers than the cramped garrets with which they were familiar elsewhere.

The introduction of the Sloan patented machinery produced a comparable distribution of benefits. One comparatively unskilled woman could tend three or four of the new machines, producing far more and better screws than skilled male artisans had formerly been able to make. Even so, because of the rapid expansion in the business of Nettlefold and Chamberlain, its workforce never shrank in size. On the contrary, by the 1870s its employees numbered more than 2,500, making the firm one of the largest employers in the town. Chamberlain was uneasy about the high proportion of women workers in the mill, though that pattern had always been true of the wood screw industry and was an attraction to people in nearby towns with fewer job opportunities for women. He pointed out that the proportion of male employees in his mill had risen considerably through the need to keep the new machines in repair. Former handcraftsmen were employed at other superior levels in the mass operation without reduction in their wage levels. Wages at Nettlefold and Chamberlain were equal to the best offered for comparable work elsewhere. In contrast to the small workshops where unemployment and underemployment were chronic, employment at Nettlefold and Chamberlain could be relied upon for the full work week. In fact, the high level of demand that Nettlefold and Chamberlain obtained for its products made overtime frequent. Sometimes when big orders came in, employees were expected to work through the night.

On balance the new organization of industry in Birmingham gave workers palpable advantages over what they might expect from the small workshops. The hope of artisans in workshops was to become masters themselves some day. But in the third quarter of the century, that object seemed less attractive than before and also harder to reach. Uncontrolled competition among the workshops kept wages down and made concerted action to raise them virtually impossible. The new factories alleviated both weaknesses from labour's point of view. The consolidation of industry into larger units offered labour a reduced, much reduced, version of the advantages that it gave to the owners. It generated better wages, working conditions and hours as well as profits.

Capital and labour could, furthermore, unite against the common enemy. Small masters in Birmingham continued to obscure the class division that scarred industrial relations to the north, but in a new way. They seemed to pose a common threat to the consolidating industries and to the organization of labour. In truth the danger was less serious to big business than to organized labour. In the very act of establishing themselves, big businesses to a large extent disposed of the challenge from small workshops. The struggle by labour, on the other hand, to overcome its divisions continued beyond the end of the century. Big manufacturers could treat small workshops as the common enemy in order to secure the cooperation of labour in their factories. Even so, the collaboration between big business and organized labour in Birmingham did not amount to just another form of exploitation. In addition to straightforward dividends to labour in wages and hours, the collaboration produced benefits in spheres of common interest, preeminently in education which upgraded worker skills.

Nettlefold and Chamberlain crushed their industrial competitors with such success that in the late 1860s they acquired what amounted to a monopoly. After persuading their main competitors to sell out to them, they did the same with little competitors but in more peremptory fashion. Small masters were presented with reasonable offers of purchase, though these were accompanied by the threat that if they turned the offers down, they would be forced out of business. If the offers were rejected, Nettlefold and Chamberlain made good their threat by lowering prices. Yet once the small masters capitulated, the firm mollified many by employing them as foremen, often at salaries 'larger', so Chamberlain claimed, 'than the average profits of small manufacturers formerly'.

Whatever the benefit to these erstwhile competitors, they were now his employees. Towards the small masters as a breed he remained contemptuous. The collaboration he practised was confined to his employees. Even within these confines he was stern, not given to frequent commendations, and intolerant of stupidity. 'You may take it that we are satisfied if we do not complain,' he told a new employee.[25]

He attempted to demonstrate his goodwill to employees in other ways, but when he moved outside the sphere of economic relations, he discovered the inadequacy of industry as a base for social action. In 1864, improving upon an example set by the Kenricks, he established a club for working men in Smethwick. It was near though not formally associated with the Heath Street mill. He contrived to have the initiative for the club's formation come from working men as well as from the wealthy and influential. Thomas Martineau, a lawyer married to one of Chamberlain's sisters, offered to do the legal work involved in the purchase of land and building a clubhouse. Other business and professional people found well-situated, reasonably priced land for the club, plans for the building from a London architect, and money for furniture and fittings. But working men, canvassed at Chamberlain's instigation by men of their own class, purchased shares from which the money came to buy the land and erect the building. Moving the report of the provisional committee at the meeting called to set up the institution, Chamberlain focused attention on the determination of the men to build their own club.[26] Once in operation, it was run by a committee of workmen under Chamberlain's presidency.

Its fortunes testified more to the liveliness of Chamberlain's commitment than to the viability of his social strategy. The institute organized a glee club, a debating club and for a while a rifle club; it sponsored French classes and ran a library, all at Chamberlain's prompting. He was careful never to stretch the men further than they were happy to go. When an English literature course which he taught attracted only a small clientele, he did not repeat it. He helped to start an independent benefit club to encourage savings for retirement, something for which Nettlefold and Chamberlain, like most companies, made no provision. He attended every variety of the institute's activities. But the club never acquired a vitality of its own. Formed initially as a temperance institution, it tried to make itself more attractive by permitting the sale of beer and spirits, but the change alienated those Chamberlain considered to be 'the better class of artisans'.[27] After he left the firm, the institute degenerated into a drinking club and went bankrupt.

The social upheaval to which in 1866 Chamberlain perceived that his business was contributing could not be dealt with adequately by voluntary agencies for social collaboration like this club. The late 1860s were stirring, searching times in public life as much as in business; and Chamberlain was swept forward by the interaction of the two spheres.

3

The Transfer from Business to Politics
1867–1874

Trades unions and strikes in America quickly come to nothing; they
cannot live in that educated atmosphere.

Alfred Field to the Select Committee on Scientific Instruction,
25 June 1868

From 1867 to 1874 Chamberlain was caught between two movements
which pulled him awkwardly between two careers. During these years
the economy rose to but then passed its crest. At the same time the
political order entered a new phase inaugurated by the enfranchisement
of the urban working class and the rise in power of Gladstone and the
Liberals with a great parliamentary majority. Their momentous legislative achievements, however, precipitated a Conservative reaction coinciding with the onset of economic depression. An industrialist at the
beginning of this confluence of developments in the political economy,
Chamberlain emerged from it totally involved in politics, national as
well as local, but much surer of his footing close to home than in the
still alien national sphere.

Bridging the industrial chasm

Though he began to move into politics at the outset of this period, in
1867, his first steps were closely related to his business and were not
intended to lead to a change of career. His entry into politics was not
something he had always contemplated or for which he had deliberately prepared himself. While he always expressed strong political
opinions and worked against John Bright's reelection in 1859, his political behaviour had generally been that of a very interested bystander.
His frame of reference lay, where to an extent it always remained, in
the social economy of Birmingham.

Still his frantic devotion to work after the death of his wife in 1863
did not give him peace. By 1867 Nettlefold and Chamberlain had made

the extensions in their business that would turn them into the 'Screw Kings'. But Chamberlain was already disappointed with that kingdom. Buying out the firm's chief competitor, James and Avery, had turned out to be a more costly business than he anticipated. 'I am not getting rich very quick or likely to achieve any special distinctions,' he wrote discontentedly to a close friend:

> I work at a lot of things without much serious interest in any. Some-times I manage to forget myself & then I am tolerably contented. You see I fancy it is only the two extremes that are really well off—the very good & the very bad. . . . Now I, who like Mahomet's coffin, hang be-tween earth & heaven, find my position anything but satisfactory, yet feel unable to alter it by my own volition. So I go on working & sin-ning & waiting & remembering—in fact every present participle except hoping—& time is going on & I am 4 years older than I was 4 years ago & sometime or another I shall be dead & perhaps—the other thing—not that this possibility sensibly affects my cheerfulness.[1]

The cure for Chamberlain's despondency lay close at hand in a new venture reinforced by a new love. The new venture had already begun, though he did not yet appreciate its significance for him. At the begin-ning of 1867 George Dixon, newly elected mayor of Birmingham, had invited him along with a number of concerned citizens to his home to discuss the provisions for elementary education in their commu-nity. Dixon accompanied his invitation with a set of statistics on Birmingham outlining its educational destitution.[2] Less than half of the children in Birmingham attended a day school. One third of the boys and seventeen per cent of the girls between the ages of seven and thir-teen worked during the day, earning low wages at a cost to themselves of, among other things, lifelong illiteracy. Another twenty per cent of the boys and a third of the girls went neither to work nor to school. Birmingham was not alone in the proportion of its population who grew up without education. Dixon brought a representative of the Manchester Education Society to the meeting to describe the still worse state of affairs there.

Chamberlain was drawn to the subject as a way to bridge the widen-ing chasm between the middle and working classes in Birmingham as its industrial economy matured. Dixon, senior partner in a firm of mer-chants, shared that concern. Dixon and Chamberlain had toyed with the idea of giving employees in responsible positions a share in the profits of the businesses for which they worked.[3] The two businessmen con-cluded instead that their purpose would be served more comprehen-sively by the provision of free elementary schooling for the working class. They thought of education as a service which middle-class tax-payers could provide for the working class to their mutual benefit.

The benefit to the working class would be substantial though not immediate. Chamberlain did not think, as he explained, that education was 'the specific which would entirely remedy everything they deplored in the condition of the working classes; but he maintained that it was the first step to a remedy, as it would lead to higher wages, a reduction of pauperism and crime, better homes, healthier lives, and temperate recreation'.[4] The cost to the middle-class taxpayer would be immediate and substantial, but it would be more than repaid even in strictly economic terms. It would help to secure industrial peace and prosperity. Basic elementary education (to say nothing of technical) would serve other pressing concerns of business. Like other metal manufacturers in Birmingham, Chamberlain felt the brisk winds of foreign competition. Although Nettlefold and Chamberlain had done well in the American market with some of its products, on other products the tables were turned and not only American but Continental European producers were superseding them.[5] A better-educated workforce, such as the United States and Prussia had acquired, might help to roll back this competition.[6] The process would benefit both workers and owners, earning the former higher wages and secure employment while improving the competitive position and profits of the latter.

For all this social and economic calculation, there was a streak of idealism in Chamberlain's commitment to the cause of education. That idealism, implicit in his 1866 article on the socio-economic revolution which industries like his were causing in Birmingham, was brought out and applied to the civic sphere by George Dawson of the Church of the Saviour in the autumn of the year at the opening of a free reference library in the town centre. The speech which Dawson delivered on that occasion was long remembered by the leaders of the town. Dawson proclaimed a new brand of Radicalism with which, eventually, Chamberlain's name would be synonymous.

The old generation of Radicals, fighting the abuse of power by crown, church and aristocracy, had done their best to reduce the powers of government and discredit its mystique. Dawson taught a new generation of Radicals in Birmingham that they should extend the powers of the state for the wellbeing of the entire community. The tables had turned over the past quarter century. The still oppressive interests of the landed aristocracy and established church used the old Radical philosophy of minimizing the competence of the state in order to minimize their social responsibilities. The Radical fight still needed to be fought, but with a new philosophy and with its own mystique of government. Dawson told the leaders of Birmingham that

A great town exists to discharge towards the people of that town, the duties that a great nation exists to discharge towards the people of that nation—that a town exists here by the grace of God, that a great town is a solemn organisation through which should flow, and in which should be shaped, all the highest, loftiest, and truest ends of man's intellectual and moral nature.[7]

Chamberlain absorbed this extension of his own reflections. Dawson and he were akin in manner as well as outlook; they were both practical and pugnacious, and they took to each other. Dawson was aggressive in argument: 'His opinions . . . provoked fierce prejudice and antagonism; and he took no pains to soothe the prejudice and conciliate the antagonism by his manner of stating his opinions.' As with Chamberlain, 'his policy was a policy of attack'.[8] And however elevated in concept, he always brought his message down to earth. Never leaving his audience with abstractions, he pressed for practical application. In 1867 he focused attention on the subject of elementary schooling.

A potent mixture of idealism, social concern and economic interest thus fuelled the movement in which Dixon sought Chamberlain's cooperation. It was ignited by momentous political events. Gladstone and Disraeli were struggling in the House of Commons to put themselves in power at the head of their respective parties, and in doing so brought the subject of working-class enfranchisement to the fore. In the autumn of 1866, after the defeat of Gladstone's Reform bill, the debate was carried to Birmingham by its MP, John Bright. He came there to launch a national agitation to give labour the vote. A brass band from Nettlefold and Chamberlain's mill took part in a huge procession to the arena where Bright was to speak; and Chamberlain joined the crowd that crushed in to listen. Like all Radicals, Chamberlain echoed the popular demand; and he was glad when it was conceded in the following summer. Yet he shared the uneasiness of many Liberals about giving the vote to the uneducated. Years later while still an arch-Radical he confessed that, '[i]f I had had the making of the Reform Bill of '67, I would have required every voter to write the name of the person for whom he voted and in this way have introduced an ignorance disqualification.'[9]

In the summer of 1867 Chamberlain discovered a new love as well as a new enterprise; and the love confirmed his commitment to the enterprise. Seeking to ease his discontent through travel, he headed north towards Scotland. On the way, he stopped for a few days at the home of his business associate Timothy Kenrick, uncle of his deceased wife Harriet. There, for the first time since her death, Chamberlain's heart began to lift; and he fell in love with Timothy Kenrick's youngest daughter Florence. Less is known about her than about either of the other women Chamberlain married because, at the request of his third wife during their engagement, he burned his correspondence with Florence. But the surviving indirect evidence indicates that Florence was by no means the least important of his wives, and even suggests that she might have kept him true to Liberal Radicalism had she lived longer.

Florence was nineteen when Chamberlain met her, nearly twelve years younger than he. The difference between them in temperament was equally great. She was quiet and diffident while he was brash and impulsive. One of the younger members of a large family, she had been free to follow 'her favourite pursuit of reading without much interruption'. She liked to sit in her father's library or to wander 'through the garden & fields with her younger brother & sister, watching the birds & plants'. There was more, however, to what Joe and Florence now felt for each other than the attraction of opposites. As she had moved into her teenage years, she had become 'a favourite companion of her elder brothers & father for she had read so much & thought so deeply on what she read [that] it was a pleasure for people with minds much more mature to talk with her'.[10] Chamberlain was drawn by the 'world of reflection in her large, thoughtful, brown eyes'.[11]

They were married less than a year later, in June 1868. Joe's second honeymoon was less animated than his first. Both bride and bridegroom were apprehensive. He had not overcome the sense of insecurity with which the death of Harriet had left him. Florence was anxious about the responsibilities she was about to assume as stepmother to two little children, and her health was not strong. Marriage, however, brought out remarkable strengths of character in her. Setting aside their fears and disregarding her fragile health, Joe and she began immediately to produce a family of their own, starting with Neville in 1869, followed each year or two by daughters, Ida, Hilda and Ethel, eventually doubling the family Florence had taken over from Harriet. At the same time Florence fostered Chamberlain's emergence as a Radical politician. In 1869, when his fellow educational enthusiasts urged him to stand for election to the town council, she encouraged him to do so; and she continued to do all she could to help him on.

Each of the major phases in Chamberlain's career was complemented by an accompanying marriage. Harriet had been an ideal wife for the rising businessman. Florence was an equally ideal partner for the coming Radical politician. She clipped out, bound and indexed press reports of his speeches and other pertinent extracts for future use. Though retiring by nature, she enjoyed the society of men in public life and welcomed them to her home. She fully shared, if she did not indeed exceed, her husband's Radicalism. Improving her education through night classes, she was committed to the advancement of women. Few people realized that she edited the blasts of new Radicalism which Chamberlain issued in the *Fortnightly Review*. The two of them discussed each step in his emerging campaign.[12]

The League and the bill

Attempting to form a broad base for action, Dixon had invited a varied group of men to the meeting at his home early in 1867: clergymen of the Established Church to which he himself belonged as well as Nonconformist ministers, Conservatives as well as Liberals. Frederick Temple, the future archbishop of Canterbury, came up from nearby Rugby where he was headmaster. The group agreed that young children should not be employed unless provision was made for their schooling. They undertook to sponsor a fact-finding survey of the provisions for elementary education in Birmingham and in the meantime to raise money to pay the school fees of children from demonstrably poor families. Seeking consensus, they did not directly address the divisive religious dimensions of their concern. But conflicting religious interests lay beneath another issue they wanted to address: the need for increased governmental support for education.

The existing supply of elementary schools in England had been created by charities of one sort or other, almost invariably religious. Since the 1830s, the government at Westminster had made grants to the major philanthropic associations engaged in the work of elementary education. The government grants aggravated denominational dissension. The Church of England's educational agencies, preeminently the National Society for Promoting the Education of the Poor in the Principles of the Established Church, did not welcome the governmental supervision which accompanied the grants. Even so, swallowing its dismay, the National Society accepted the grants, and in doing so consolidated the primacy of the Established Church as England's educator. Alarmed at the prospect, most Nonconformists—with the significant exception of the Unitarians—took issue with the principle of governmental involvement in education. Nevertheless, by the late 1860s it was becoming obvious to all concerned that, even with governmental assistance, the efforts of the religious or, as they were termed, 'voluntary' agencies were unequal to the national need, and that only further governmental assistance could close the great gap. The men who gathered at Dixon's home in 1867, Nonconformists and churchmen alike, agreed that the government must play a larger part in education, and in particular that Parliament should give municipal corporations the power to levy local property taxes or rates for educational purposes.[13] The agreement was deceptive. It ignored the burning questions. Which schools were to receive money from the rates, the existing denominational schools or new civic ones? And for what subjects—religious as well as secular, if indeed the two could be separated?

Dixon wanted to put off these questions until the extent of Birmingham's educational destitution had been fully documented, because his objectives were social rather than denominational. He emphasized his sense of the social urgency by putting another resolution before the meeting, to make the government and hence the courts responsible for enforcing school attendance upon working-class children. Chamberlain seconded the motion. One of the major impediments to comprehensive elementary education stemmed from the refusal of many poor parents to do without the income which they could receive from the labour of their children. Philanthropic payment of school fees for poor children would not solve the problem, nor would the abolition of fees, though Dixon and Chamberlain wanted that too. As long as parents could profit from the labour of their children by sending them to work rather than to school, many children would grow up without education. Compulsory education would be costly for the taxpayer, but that did not deter its advocates. Compulsion could not, of course, be fully implemented until the community had enough schools to accommodate all the children. Dixon and Chamberlain nevertheless sought approval of the principle of compulsion as a pressing goal.

They encountered immediate opposition from supporters of denominational education, later reinforced by men worried about the cost. Compulsory education would involve a great extension of the responsibilities of the state. It was therefore sure to encroach further upon the autonomy of the denominational agencies as well as upon the pocket of the taxpayer. Frederick Temple argued that compulsion had been tried and failed in Massachusetts, a place which Radicals held up as a model of educational advance. Chamberlain questioned Temple's assertion; but since the motion for compulsory schooling did not command anything like unanimous support at the meeting, it was put aside for subsequent consideration. After the meeting, attempting to refute Temple's claim, Chamberlain asked the American consul in Birmingham and the American ambassador in London for information. When their responses supported his reading of the situation in Massachusetts but failed to convince Temple, Chamberlain solicited on-the-spot information from Alfred Field, an agent for Nettlefold and Chamberlain in the United States, but with inconclusive results.[14]

The opponents of compulsion pressed for delay in order to see how much could be accomplished through charitable effort and existing legislation, including the Factory Acts and more recent Industrial Schools Acts which required employers to provide for the education of their child-age employees. The delay only strengthened the case for compulsion. Nothing in the existing legislation applied to the unemployed, nor did the Factory and Industrial Schools Acts apply to small workshops, a fact which galled the larger factory owners and organized labour. Chamberlain secured expressions of working-class support for a compulsory system. The fact-finding inquiry set up after the meeting at Dixon's home revealed that the state of affairs in Birmingham was even worse than had been imagined. There turned out to be enough room in local schools to accommodate only eight per cent of the school-age population. Even so, available places were not always filled and attendance was irregular. The academic results produced by the schools were similarly depressing. Few pupils progressed far enough to acquire a good command of reading, writing and arithmetic. A fund was raised to pay school fees for poor children, but no more than half of the beneficiaries attended at all regularly. The heart of the problem was to ensure general, regular attendance. Impatience mounted; and in October the Birmingham town council passed a resolution in favour of compulsion.

The insistence on compulsion altered the character of the movement Dixon had launched. After he was elected to the House of Commons in the summer of 1867, the leading spirits in Birmingham's education movement abandoned the effort to secure a broad consensus and instead pressed for uncompromising action. Dixon remained more than formally in charge of the movement, but its tone was newly set by Jesse Collings. Fierce and sentimental by turns and prone to nervous collapse, Collings recoiled from compromise as a sign of weakness. He had moved to Birmingham in 1864 when he took charge of a firm of ironmongers. His interest in education, predating his arrival in Birmingham, arose from his exposure as a commercial traveller to educational deprivation in the West of England. A Unitarian by upbringing, he embraced the cause of education as the basic way to improve the lot of the desperately poor. When he came to Birmingham, he fell under the spell of George Dawson and joined the Church of the Saviour. He soon gained election to the town council. Collings was the moving spirit behind its resolution in October in support of compulsion.

Early the next year, in a pamphlet on the schools system in the United States, Collings called for a comparable system in England. '[R]efusing all compromise', he insisted upon 'national secular (or unsectarian) education, compulsory as to rating and attendance', with state aid and inspection, and local management.[15] Using the Anti-Corn Law League as a model, he called for the creation of a society that would publish propaganda, send out lecturers, encourage the formation of local branches, and thus mount a national campaign. Collings scorned half-measures and half-hearted support. In his estimation the clerical moderates who accepted Dixon's initial invitation had done so 'either to retard [the educational movement], or to direct it into some narrow and inefficient channel'.

Here was a man after Chamberlain's heart, even more pugnacious than he was himself, though ultimately less incisive. Chamberlain responded to Collings's appeal by drafting a memorandum to clarify the principles, objects and rationale of what he called a 'National Society for promotion of Universal Compulsory Education'.[16] True to the legacy of Joseph Priestley, Chamberlain cast his memorandum in the language of rationalism. Like Priestley, Chamberlain insisted on an enlarged conception of the natural rights of the individual. But whereas towards this end Priestley, like all old Radicals, had deflated the pretensions of the state, Chamberlain, like George Dawson, insisted on extending the state's sphere of responsibility:

> it is as much the duty of the State to see that children are educated as to see that they are fed ... it is the duty of the State to see that the natural rights of children are asserted & maintained; and failing the action of the proper parties, to interfere for the protection of those who are unable to protect themselves.

He even called to his aid a dictum of that old Tory of Priestley's day, Lord Eldon, '[t]hat the State presumes the responsibility of Parents & their willingness to discharge it but if cases occur when Parents obstinately neglect this duty, it is proper that the State should interfere to enforce its observance'. Compulsory education attracted Chamberlain by temperament as well as in principle. However responsive to those who could not help themselves, the civic order that he envisaged would be imperious. Working-class children needed education; the best of the working class wanted it for them; and the rest must be forced to accept it.

Early in 1869 Dixon convened another meeting at his home, this time restricted to the stalwarts, to launch the national organization and campaign for which Collings had called. The meeting agreed to the creation of a National Education League with an unmistakably Radical agenda. It pressed Parliament for legislation requiring local authorities to ensure that there were enough elementary schools to accommodate every child within their districts, funded by local rates and governmental grants, managed by local authorities, subject to governmental inspection, unsectarian in religious complexion, free of charge to the pupils, and demanding attendance unless the children were receiving education elsewhere. The charter of the National Education League was ambiguous on the fate of the denominational schools but left no doubt that if they received financial support from the rates, they would be subject to management by local government.

The group at Dixon's house undertook to pay for and manage the League; and in doing so they established the model for all subsequent political initiatives from Birmingham. Reaching into their pockets, the men at the meeting donated the money to finance the League. None were more generous than the Chamberlains and their relations. Both

Joseph Chamberlains, father and son, along with J.H. Nettlefold and Archibald Kenrick were among eleven who pledged £1,000, and three other Kenricks offered £500 apiece. At the same time arrangements were made to ensure that control accompanied financial support. Though launching a national campaign, the men brought together by Dixon made sure that it would be directed from Birmingham. Almost all of the officers came from Birmingham. Dixon became president of the national council, Collings its secretary. Chamberlain was to chair the executive committee in charge of day-to-day management, particularly when Dixon was in London for the meetings of the House of Commons.

The leaders of the League chose to defer its inaugural public meeting until the autumn. But they began their countrywide propaganda immediately,[17] mailing out tens of thousands of copies of their platform and of Collings's pamphlet on the American schools system. They sent out speakers to address meetings across the country, collect financial support and organize branches. These efforts elicited an impressive response, encouraging a conviction that the time was ripe for action. Within a month, pledges for £60,000 were received. Within three months, in response to a circular to men prominent in public life, some five thousand joined the League, including forty MPs and between three and four hundred ministers of religion. A hundred branches were established, mainly in the north, the Midlands and Wales but also across the south, including thirteen in London.

The inaugural public meeting of the League in October drew all this support together. To the pleasure of the leaders, there was representation from organized labour. Some trade societies, precursors of trade unions, joined the League and subscribed to its funds. The London Trades' Council sent a message of support, promising 'to use our best endeavours in aid of so laudable a movement'.[18] The secretary of the Amalgamated Society of Carpenters and Joiners, Robert Applegarth, attended the meeting, but he offered only guarded support. He resented the presumption of an essentially middle-class League to speak for the working class. He insisted that the principles of the League did not 'reach exactly and altogether the wants of the working classes, but', he went on, '. . . it goes a step in the right direction'.[19] Recognizing the division of sentiment among the working classes between skilled artisans who prized education and the mass beneath who feared the loss of income from their children, Applegarth sided emphatically with the former. While he blamed the middle class for the degradation of unskilled labour, he lashed out at

> the sot, the careless and indifferent man, who has been so long neglected, and degraded that he does not understand the value of

education . . . him the other class, the better class of working men, have to carry upon their backs . . . those men who do not understand the value of education must be made to understand it.

These words were welcome to the leaders of the League.

They drew their big battalions from religious more than from social sources, from Protestant Nonconformity far more than from organized labour. Yet Chamberlain was less interested in the religious than in the social dimensions of the education controversy. The leaders of the League were divided on the religious dimensions of their crusade, not as between denominations, but between those who favoured unsectarian religious education and those who wanted state schools to confine themselves to secular instruction. The decision for the moment favoured the unsectarians. That meant in effect Protestant trinitarian religious instruction, which did not appeal to Chamberlain. But the prospect did not much immediately trouble him. He seemed to envisage the continuation of denominational schools, at least for a while, though without financial assistance from the state.

His criticism of denominational schooling was essentially social. The tendency of denominational schools to pay greater attention to religious than to secular instruction violated his priorities. He was also repelled by the atmosphere of charity-based paternalism which pervaded Church of England schools. That taint would be minimized in a national network of civic schools. Since the working class had the franchise and also contributed at least indirectly to the rates through rent, they could fairly claim that what the government did for them was a form of self-help; and how better could they help themselves than through education?

Yet inevitably, despite the priorities of its leaders, the campaign of the National Education League took on a deeper religious colour; and Chamberlain followed suit. The chief opposition to the League came from the Church of England, which drove Chamberlain to conclude, 'Our choice is between the education of the people, and the interests of the Church.' He was also naturally responsive to the League's largest and best-organized source of support: Nonconformity. Still, the alliance between the League and Nonconformity was not entirely natural; nor was it ever without strain. Only four of the eight executive officers of the League were Nonconformists; the rest were civic-minded members of the Church of England; and most of the League's Nonconformist leaders were theologically liberal or heterodox, like Chamberlain and Collings. The rank and file members of the League, on the other hand, were for the most part trinitarian Nonconformists whose strongest motive for supporting the League was antagonism towards the Established Church. The traditions of Nonconformity compounded the diffi-

Preachers of the civic gospel:
2. (right) George Dawson of
the Church of the Saviour.
3. (below) R.W. Dale of
Carr's Lane Chapel.

culty of the Education League, for 'the whole inspiration for Nonconformist political effort was the belief that with unrighteous policies
there could be no compromise'.[20]

Whatever its drawbacks, Nonconformist support was indispensable
to the League. It would not have been secured without the cooperation
of another recruit to the ranks of Birmingham's new Radicals: R.W.
Dale, minister at the Carr's Lane Congregational chapel. Dale had come
to Birmingham in 1854, the same year as Chamberlain. The new minister's deepest love was evangelical theology, a pietistic more often than
a socially active creed. Yet Dale combined that creed with his own version of Dawson's civic gospel. A bushy black-bearded embodiment of
the Church Militant, as aggressive in temperament as Chamberlain,
Dale was equally eager to widen the bounds of governmental activity at
home and overseas. Like Chamberlain, Dale's interest in political activity lay latent till roused by Dawson's speech at the opening of the civic
library, Dixon's initiative on education, and the passage of the second
Reform Act. Dale kept his distance initially from the League because he
was nervous about the religious consequences of its demand for an
entirely free network of schools. Once he put that reservation aside in
the interests of the larger cause, he joined in with enthusiasm. His cooperation ensured that, at least in Birmingham, the division between
evangelical and heterodox Nonconformity would be firmly bridged and
that both would march forward under the new Radical banners. Dale
and Chamberlain eventually formed a dual consulship at the head of
the education movement, Chamberlain taking charge of the League,
Dale of the allied Central Nonconformist Committee, both organizations
extending cooperative branches across the country.

The League made rapid headway in its first year, rapid enough to
rouse its critics but not to overcome them. A rival organization, the
National Education Union, was established at Manchester to protect denominational education. The League at Birmingham argued that it had
already compromised in that direction by calling for unsectarian rather
than strictly secular education; and tacitly it was willing to incorporate
denominational schools within the proposed national network, though
without further financial support from the state. But the most ardent
supporters of the League were unhappy with these compromises; and
the antagonism voiced in this faction towards denominational education deepened the anxiety of its defenders. Both sides mobilized their
popular support in order to influence the shape of the bill which the
Liberal government was expected to introduce in the next year or two.

Gladstone had won a commanding majority in the general election at
the end of 1868 with a promise to disestablish the Church of Ireland.
The stand he took on this issue earned him wholehearted support from
Nonconformity. Over fifty Nonconformists were elected to the House of

Commons, more than ever before. Nonconformists were confident that a new era in the progress towards religious equality had opened, all the more so because shortly before the election Gladstone was instrumental in abolishing compulsory church rates. By spending its first year disestablishing and disendowing the Irish Church, the new ministry encouraged Nonconformist hopes for an education bill framed in the same spirit.

Still preoccupied with the discontent in Ireland, Gladstone wanted to devote his second year as prime minister to reform of the Irish land law. Education took a lower place in his priorities. As a high church-man anxious to protect the catholicity of the Church of England and its schools, he had little sympathy for unsectarian religious instruction and was inclined to prefer a purely secular curriculum wherever denomina-tional instruction was not practicable. But he left the designing of the government's bill to the Vice-President of the Committee of Council, W.E. Forster.

That decision bore mixed fruit. Forster lay the legislative foundations on which English elementary education would stand for the rest of the century, but his achievement came at high political cost. Though a sea-soned Member of Parliament, he proved as deficient in political finesse as the neophyte Chamberlain; and they became bitter enemies. Each thought he knew best what the country needed, and neither liked to compromise after he had taken a stand. As a result they hardened each other's intransigence. Forster was an irascible mixture, a rough-hewn former Quaker who enjoyed playing whist with the mistress of the leading Whig lord, a Radical by instinct but torn between the old school and the new. He approached his ministerial assignment with an as-sumption of superiority all too characteristic of the Liberal elite. Deeply concerned about education and imbued with progressive ideas on the subject before the League was born, he had no wish to wait until the League gathered enough strength to force his hand.

Unaware of Forster's intentions but anxious to maximize the strength of the League before the government settled on its proposals, Chamber-lain hoped for delay before the government introduced its bill. While he did not suspect the government of hostility, he feared that it might take a piecemeal approach and propose a measure for the large towns, where the agitation was strongest, to the neglect of the quieter country-side. Forster meant to do much more than that but also, from the League's point of view, much worse. He decided to reject the League's proposals because of the threat they posed to the existing denomina-tional schools and the consequent cost to the taxpayer. He opted instead for a measure 'to supplement the present voluntary system . . . with the least loss of voluntary cooperation'.[21]

The bill which Forster introduced into the House of Commons in the new year did exactly that. It not only incorporated the denominational schools within the national network of elementary schools which it proposed to create. The League might have tolerated that; but the bill went on to promise the denominational agencies another year, with further financial support from the government, to build more schools. Only then, if those facilities fell short of the needs of the school-age population, could local boards be elected to build and manage civic schools. In the meantime children could be obliged to attend denominational schools. Furthermore, once civic schools were established, they could provide whatever religious instruction the majority favoured. These religious provisions of Forster's bill appalled Nonconformists, and hence concentrated the controversy on religious issues. His scheme was nevertheless comprehensive, and his initial presentation of it commanded the respect of the House. Dixon did not immediately recognize its offensive features, and he responded temperately.

But in Birmingham, Chamberlain reacted to the reports of Forster's words with anger. He arranged for protests by the town, by the Nonconformists, and by a large deputation to Gladstone. 'The fight', he told Dixon, 'will be on the Religious question.'[22] He urged Dixon to try not just to amend the bill but to obstruct its passage so that a totally new bill could be introduced the next year. Further reflection on Forster's 'distinct betrayal & contradiction of the principles involved in the Irish Church Bill' whipped Chamberlain to fury, and he censured Dixon's initial moderation.

> If you see Mr Forster you may safely tell him that he has succeeded in raising the whole of the Dissenters against him and if he thinks little of our power we will teach him his mistake.
>
> Letters go out tonight to every dissenting Minister (Independent, Baptist, Unitarian, & Wesleyan) in the country, and you may rest assured that 'all the fat is in the fire'.[23]

Chamberlain's assessment of Nonconformist strength in opposition to the bill was not just wishful thinking. A Central Nonconformist Committee was being formed, with headquarters in Birmingham, to protest against the bill. It sent out a form of protest to 7,300 ministers, and within four days over 5,000 signed and returned it. A majority even of the Wesleyan ministers, customarily averse to political action, subscribed.

When Dixon left for London at the beginning of the parliamentary session, he was recognized as the leader of the League. Chamberlain, still uncertain of himself as a speaker, had not been the most visible even of the League's secondary figures. But the strength of the League lay in the provinces rather than in Parliament, and Dixon initially mistook the response of the League's provincial supporters to Forster's bill.

Chamberlain was the man in command at the headquarters in Birmingham. He took charge of arrangements for the deputation to Gladstone.

When the deputation assembled at 10 Downing Street in front of the prime minister with Forster at his side, Dixon introduced Chamberlain as its main spokesman. Suddenly he stood at the centre of England's political arena. Gladstone sensed the ability of the new man and fastened his attention on him, to the dismay of more moderate souls. Chamberlain returned the compliment by appealing to the prime minister in effect to overrule Forster. Gladstone defended the bill firmly and displayed his sympathy for denominational schooling; yet he did not disguise his preference, if thoroughly denominational religious instruction was not practicable, for secular rather than unsectarian instruction. His response deflected the criticism of the League away from himself but not from Forster and Forster's bill. The League decided to press for its rejection at the second reading. This reaction received so much Nonconformist support that the government undertook to introduce amendments.

Repelling an industrial assault

Amid and partly because of the ensuing political debate, the industrial monopoly of Nettlefold and Chamberlain was confronted by the most serious challenge it had yet faced. The challenge brought Chamberlain's attention back to business, roused his instinct for retaliatory aggression, confirmed his disdain for compromise, and ultimately increased his wealth, enough to sustain him handsomely for the rest of his life.

Word came in May 1870 of the formation of a new firm called the Birmingham Screw Company, with plans to build its mill right across the canal from Nettlefold and Chamberlain's Heath Street works. The new firm wanted at least a slice of the high profits that Nettlefold and Chamberlain were known to be earning. The promoters of the company believed that, even if Nettlefold and Chamberlain lowered its prices, there was plenty of money to be made in the business. Chamberlain had expected the emergence of a rival for some time from any of half a dozen quarters. He was relieved now that he could see the face of his fear. Some men wondered whether he might welcome an opportunity to sell out in order to concentrate on public life in which he had become so conspicuous in recent months. Politics and industry were considered incongruous spheres of enterprise. But whereas his political distraction tempted would-be industrial competitors, their challenge reinvigorated his commitment to his business.

The Birmingham Screw Company brought together a number of

the ingredients of Nettlefold and Chamberlain's success. Alfred Field, a wholesaler who sold Nettlefold and Chamberlain's products in the American market, had bought rights to an American patent for what was claimed to be a better automatic machine than the one used by Nettlefold and Chamberlain. Field sought capital to exploit the invention from Arthur Keen of the Patent Nut and Bolt Company, whose business overlapped marginally with Nettlefold and Chamberlain's. Unsure about the patent for the new machine and quite certain that Nettlefold and Chamberlain were the stronger men, Keen turned Field's offer down. Field turned, this time with success, to John Cornforth, a local manufacturer of wire which could be used in the business, and to Josiah Mason, who had amassed a great fortune manufacturing steel pens. In spite of the wealth now at their command, Field and his associates proposed to sell shares in the new company to the public. In order to begin business before they could fit out a plant for production, Field ordered a supply of screws from Chamberlain's French rival, Jappy Frères, not yet cut off by war. One of Nettlefold's foremen undertook to supervise the building and equipping of the new firm's mill.

When Chamberlain got wind of the venture, he reacted with a mixture of contempt, fatalism, and desire to make hay while the sun still shone. He dismissed Josiah Mason as an ass yet assumed that the new company had come to stay. Believing that it would need five years to reach full production, he advocated a steep rise in the prices his firm would charge during that time to net an extra £20,000 to £30,000. Chamberlain's reactions, while unstable, contained the germ of the strategy which his firm adopted with eventually complete success. His emotions steadied and turned his fatalism into defiance. Joseph Nettlefold's brothers, who were lesser partners in the firm, took fright at Chamberlain's suggestions: surely to raise prices now would encourage competition, while to slash prices in two or three years would reduce profits alarmingly. They wanted the firm to stick to its existing course. Chamberlain had no difficulty proving to Joseph Nettlefold that this alternative would prove less profitable than his strategy, and would also allow their competitors to establish themselves in the industry. He refined his proposal for five years of high profits into a longer-range plan. It began, like the old one, with high prices and profit-taking for however long the new company took to get into production. This profit would then be used to tide Nettlefold and Chamberlain over while they slashed their prices. Forced to match the reduced prices, the new company would be unable to turn a profit and so would exhaust the patience of its shareholders. If the plan did not work out quite as Chamberlain calculated, Nettlefold and he would always be free to offer the promoters of the new company a compromise arrangement; and they would be 'much more likely to treat & be moderate in their views if we have made them feel our strength & power to protect our own'.

Though the confrontation with the Birmingham Screw Company reaffirmed Chamberlain's commitment to his business rather than to politics, he placed greater importance, in summarizing his strategy for Nettlefold, on considerations of power than of wealth. That order of priorities would draw him back into politics once the industrial competition had been met. 'On the whole,' he wrote to his partner,

> I feel certain that to let the [new] Company get fairly in the market would be to abdicate for ever our position as Screw Kings. I do not mean to say that we might not do very well as regards money . . . but for a certainty, our sole supremacy would never be reestablished. . . .
>
> Of course in such a matter as this our decision is partly a Speculation. But I give my vote for the bold game & I believe it will pay in the long run the better of the two.[24]

Once Chamberlain had worked out his plan, he pursued it intently yet with flexible resource. He sought advice among his friends and associates in Birmingham. He worked out his line of thought in tables of statistics. He gathered information by every device he could think up, until he knew as much about the new company as its own promoters. Each day he communicated his findings to his partner, who was in London, in a way intended to stiffen Nettlefold's spine. 'We have got to smash the new Company' was the repeated refrain.

Still restless, he thought up diabolical refinements to his plan. The validity in England of the Ayers patent the new company had bought for automatic machinery was questionable. On the hypothesis that the patent was not valid, Chamberlain proposed that his firm make Ayers patent screws too and market them at a low price as inferior products. He thought of adding steel pens to Nettlefold and Chamberlain's array of wares in order to threaten Josiah Mason's business. He suggested that Nettlefold and Chamberlain offer to fit out its plant at Kings Norton for sale to the new company. He could make a profit on the sale, use the opportunity to consolidate his firm's operation at its main plant in Smethwick, and oblige the new company to begin production at full capacity rather than work its way gradually into the market. The inducement for the new company to accept this proposal would be the hope that Nettlefold and Chamberlain would in effect be offering it a share in the market; but Chamberlain intended explicitly to preserve his freedom to sell Kings Norton and still fight the purchasers. When they eventually gave in, he could buy the plant back at a fraction of the selling price. The promoters of the new company were not foolish enough to fall for this scheme.

During these early skirmishes, Chamberlain took care to communicate with Nettlefold's skilled workmen. He singled out two about whom he was particularly concerned. Through them he warned the rest that Nettlefold and he would never rehire any men who left to work for the new company which, he added, he did not expect to last long. The two men told him that the skilled workers at Smethwick had reached the same conclusion about the prospects of the new firm and would stay in their places, though some of the unskilled men might leave. 'I must say,' Chamberlain commented contentedly to his partner, 'I think all our people believe in us.'[25]

Before Nettlefold returned to Birmingham, Chamberlain was able to report an initial success. Josiah Mason had been on the verge of purchasing a plant in Birmingham owned by a Sheffield firm, the Patent File Company, in order to meet the needs of the new business. Just before Mason concluded the sale, Chamberlain snatched it from him by offering a higher price and buying the plant himself. Driving in the knife, he publicized his purchase in a way calculated to maximize the damage to the new company just as it was offering its shares for sale to the public. He placed a report in the *Birmingham Daily Post* that Nettlefold and Chamberlain had bought the plant in order to meet the increased foreign demand for their goods which they expected 'whenever the competition in the home trade necessitates a reduction in the price'.[26] How better could he have conveyed his threat to deny any dividend to investors in the rival enterprise than by driving his prices down the moment it began production?

The worst way to deal with Chamberlain was to fight him head on. Those who knew him better found subtler approaches more successful. Arthur Keen expected that Nettlefold and Chamberlain would ward off any direct assault. At the end of May, however, Keen enquired whether Chamberlain might welcome a friendly takeover.[27] Keen envisaged an amalgamation of his nut and bolt company with Nettlefold and Chamberlain, taking both of its partners with him; and he did not blanch at the high terms of purchase which Chamberlain suggested in response. But Chamberlain and Keen had different objectives in mind. Keen wanted to harness Chamberlain's talents for the formation of an engineering conglomerate, exactly what Keen achieved some thirty years later with the formation of Guest, Keen and Nettlefold. By now fairly confident of beating off the industrial competition, Chamberlain replied that he would sell out only to free himself for politics; and Keen allowed his offer to lapse.

From Chamberlain's standpoint, the withdrawal of the offer was financially fortunate. The price Keen would have given him fell far short of the value the firm acquired over the next two years. The Birmingham Screw Company managed to get off the ground but it never really flew. Within weeks of its initial formation and Keen's offer, the Franco-Prussian War broke out, vastly expanding Chamberlain's foreign sales and cutting the new company off from its French supplier. In 1871 and 1872, adhering to Chamberlain's strategy, Nettlefold and Chamberlain pushed up their prices by as much as fifty per cent. They rolled in much greater profits than Chamberlain had predicted, for, even apart from the Franco-Prussian War—and this war was 'a marvellous thing for the Midlands'[28]—the early 1870s saw a worldwide economic boom.

Twisting political combat

By temperament, business experience and denominational background, Chamberlain was inclined to view the fight on the Education bill, to which he returned in June, as clear-cut as his fight with the Birmingham Screw Company. But the social and industrial concerns which led him to raise the torch of education were already subordinated to the denominational concerns of Nonconformity. Disconcerted by the religious passions which were aroused, the government focused on denominational issues during the amendment stage of debate on its Education bill, and thus added to their political importance.

The government defeated its opponents by exploiting their division over religious instruction in the new civic or board schools. Given the many conflicting religious groups in England, including Roman Catholics and Jews as well as Dissenters and churchmen, the most logical solution was to restrict the curriculum to secular subjects and leave religious instruction to the churches. That was the alternative which appealed to most of the leaders of the League; and they sensed that Gladstone too preferred it as a way to protect the doctrinal integrity of religious instruction in Church of England schools. But secular education was a repellent option for most Protestant Englishmen, Nonconformists as well as churchmen. The government therefore imposed another solution to the dilemma. So far as denominational schools were concerned, the government satisfied many though not all Nonconformists by introducing a timetable conscience clause which confined religious instruction to the beginning and end of the school day. This stipulation made it easier for dissenting families to withdraw their children from religious teaching in church schools.

But denominational schools were not at the heart of the problem. The question of religious teaching in the new civic or board schools was harder to answer. The government found a way to appeal to Protestant sentiment without severely violating denominational religious instruction. They accepted an amendment proposed by the leader of the National Education Union, Cowper-Temple, which prohibited the use in board schools of catechisms or formularies 'distinctive of any particular denomination'. The Cowper-Temple amendment was enough to calm the fears of moderate Nonconformists, though it prohibited only the forms and not the substance of distinctive denominational teaching. The more resolute spirits stripped away the disguise by supporting a motion by John Bright's brother, Jacob, to prohibit not merely formularies but distinctively denominational doctrine in rate-supported schools. Bright's motion split the Liberals in the Commons into three sections. The smallest third, including twenty-five members of the government, voted against the motion. The remaining two-thirds split equally between supporters of the motion and abstainers. The government escaped defeat only by accepting support from the Conservative opposition.

Repeatedly the government proved willing to defeat its supporters with the aid of its opponents. When Edward Miall, the doughty champion of militant Nonconformity, finally voiced a deep sense of betrayal, Gladstone defied him to withdraw his support. Shocked by the defiance, the friends of the National Education League in the House of Commons sank into sullen inactivity.

Chamberlain opposed the course of the government more vigorously. Speaking in the accents of Nonconformity to the Birmingham town council, he spurned the proffered conscience clause: such an offer proceeded, he said, 'from the spirit of toleration, of which I am heartily sick. Toleration is that spirit of assumption, bigotry, and persecution which for the last few hundred years we have been working to destroy.'[29] As for the rest of the government's concessions on the bill, they did not improve it much. On the contrary, they consolidated denominational education in England and retarded the creation of a truly national system indefinitely. Chamberlain's disgust extended to the dwindling opposition in the House of Commons. He turned his eyes away from Parliament towards the constituencies, and undertook 'to test the feeling of the country ... at every borough election that takes place'.[30] Spurning further attempts to secure amendments, he wrote hotly to Dixon:

> It is not National Education at all—it is a trick to strengthen the Church of England ... we must strengthen ourselves in the House of Commons at all risks. I would rather see a Tory ministry in power than a Liberal government truckling to Tory prejudices.[31]

In its final form, the Education Act of 1870 provided for a dual system of elementary education within which denominational schools would predominate for many years. The demands of the League for compulsory, free and thoroughly unsectarian if not secular education were relegated to the status of options available at the discretion of the new civic school boards; and no locality was required to set up such a board unless the schools provided by denominational agencies proved inadequate.

No one was better placed to lead the provincial assault than Chamberlain, ensconced at League headquarters in Birmingham. Dixon was distracted by his responsibilities in Parliament. No tribune of the people was established in the provinces to overshadow Chamberlain. The heroes of the last great age of Radicalism were gone or going. Cobden was dead, John Bright was ailing and had retired in 1870 from Gladstone's cabinet. Chamberlain moved on to a largely empty stage.

Before the Education bill left the Commons, the executive committee of the League decided to raise £10,000 to extend its agitation. In September, after the bill became law, the executive elaborated a three-pronged campaign. In the first place, they would extend their propaganda. They undertook, secondly, to make what use they could of the Act by encouraging the election of school boards and then urging those boards to exploit their optional powers to provide elementary education which was compulsory, free and unsectarian. Thirdly, to bring pressure to bear upon the government, the executive agreed to ask Liberal candidates at parliamentary by-elections to commit themselves to the principles of the League. Chamberlain spearheaded the campaign for the creation of school boards. Birmingham's town council set the pace by petitioning for a school board even before the bill reached the statute books.

These efforts by the League were soon set back by a pair of blows. Embarrassingly, the League's slate of candidates lost the election for the new school board in Birmingham. The Education Act gave each elector as many votes as there were seats to be filled, fifteen in the case of Birmingham's school board, and allowed the elector to cast all of his votes for one candidate. These provisions were intended to protect minorities. They did so with a vengeance this first time in Birmingham. A Roman Catholic priest headed the poll with 35,000 votes cast by 3,000 voters. Eight Conservative churchmen stood for election, just enough to give them control if all eight won; and they did so, collecting two votes from each of their supporters. The League Liberals, on the other hand, rashly put up a full slate of fifteen candidates; and though they attracted far more voters than their opponents, only six of the fifteen received enough votes to win places on the school board. Chamberlain came close to the bottom of the list of successful candidates.

The Conservative majority on the new school board were quick to make use of their victory. Wickedly they adopted the dearest League demand, for compulsory education. Since as yet there were only denominational schools available, the children of Birmingham would have to attend them. In order, furthermore, to deal with this influx of students, the denominational schools would need financial support from the town council; and the Conservative majority on the school board discovered that the twenty-fifth clause in the 1870 Act entitled them to demand that support. This twenty-fifth clause was the second shock to the League. Amid the pressure and complexity of the amending process in Parliament, the clause had slipped through unnoticed. It violated the declared intention of the government at the amending stage to keep rate financing and denominational education separate. But now that the twenty-fifth clause was law, Forster insisted that school boards enforce the clause.

Like the original disaster in Parliament, these setbacks had some happy consequences for Chamberlain and his colleagues. Though the Liberals elected to the Birmingham school board were too few to implement their policy, they were quite enough to develop the argument for their cause. Their talent for debate was extraordinary, for they included not only Dixon and Chamberlain but also the two most eloquent ministers in the town, Dawson and Dale. The fortnightly debates of the Birmingham school board attracted standing-room audiences, verbatim coverage in the local press, and national attention when reprinted in pamphlet form. It was on the school board and then the town council that Chamberlain shook off his stilted, over-rehearsed uneasiness of speech and turned into an effective orator, by turns persuasive and denunciatory. The twenty-fifth clause was a similar godsend. It infuriated Nonconformists of every stripe. By enforcing the clause, Forster made himself the arch-villain in the rhetoric of the League's leaders, above all of Chamberlain, who had a terrible gift for *ad hominem* sarcasm.

Outside the school board, Chamberlain developed two separate appeals for support of the Education League. In the accents of Cromwell and Priestley he appealed to Nonconformists who had been 'washed in . . . waters of bitterness . . . for the past twenty years'.[32] In the same vein, he placed the Established Church at the heart of all that was wrong in England, and turned the Education Act into the latest chapter in a centuries-old story of injustice. Yet Nonconformity was never his deepest commitment. In other speeches he developed the social case for the League. He described the education movement as 'the first earnest attempt . . . to bridge over the difference between the rich and the poor, and to abolish the gulf . . . that exists between material progress on the one hand, and ignorance and misery on the other'.[33] He demanded a level of secular instruction high enough to enable students to read fluently, write competently, and make out a simple bill or invoice. He pointed out that, for every child taught to do so in England, Prussia taught twenty. Little wonder that Germany was giving England a hard time in foreign markets.

Though he tried sometimes to combine these religious and socio-economic appeals, the groups to which they were directed did not pull readily together. Cooperation with labour made middle-class Nonconformists uneasy. The uneasiness of spokesmen for labour at the middle-class leadership of the League was still outspoken. It erupted over the selection of the Liberal slate of candidates for the Birmingham school board.[34] Though working-class voters formed the bulk of the electorate and so were expected to produce most of the Liberal vote, only one of the fifteen candidates selected by Birmingham's Liberal Association to stand at the first school board election was recognizably working class. When the local branch of the Labour Representation League objected, Chamberlain and Collings undertook to mediate between the Labour League and the Liberal Association. The course of their discussions was cloudy. Though in theory Chamberlain upheld the right of labour to choose its own representatives, in practice he treated labour as an adjective to a predominantly middle-class noun. Even so, labour was more willing to accept what he offered than the Liberal Association was willing to concede it. When the discussions broke down, the Labour League fielded an independent candidate who, however, attracted so few votes as to discredit labour's boasts. The link between labour and Nonconformity in the education movement remained tenuous.

At the same time the bond between the Education League and Nonconformity became strained. For a year after the discovery of the infamous twenty-fifth clause, the League enjoyed fairly solid Nonconformist support. But that support was susceptible to erosion over the question of religious instruction in board schools. Every policy the League devised to deal with that question alienated some group or other. For a while the League clung to an unsectarian policy defined as Bible reading without comment by the teacher. But the policy satisfied no one. Dale shared Gladstone's dislike of unsectarian religious teaching as doctrinally insipid and incapable of commanding conviction. Mere Bible reading was too insubstantial to kindle Nonconformist fervour and yet raised the suspicions of Roman Catholics and secularists.

Though a secularist at heart, Chamberlain for a while defended the unsectarian policy as the least offensive option available. But at the beginning of 1872, he persuaded the executive of the League to accept the more logical policy of confining state-supported instruction to secular subjects, leaving religious instruction strictly up to the religious denominations. The League agreed to insist on this policy for all schools accepting financial aid from the state, whether they were civic or denominational. Led by Dale, a large conference of Nonconformists convened in Manchester and endorsed the new policy.

Working closely with Dale, Chamberlain set out to sell the policy to the Nonconformist rank and file. Presenting himself as 'a Nonconformist to the backbone',[35] he sought to make Nonconformists proud of their historic concern for the rights of others. 'Ours, then,' he told the conference at Manchester, 'is no mere fight between Dissenters on the one hand and a rival Church upon the other; ours is the cause of the nation against sectarianism, the cause of the people against the priests.'[36] But it was an uphill fight. Dale and he could appeal to the Nonconformist mind, but they failed to touch the heart. The need for strictly secular state-supported education was social, not theological, and it looked godless. Even Unitarians responded without enthusiasm. Ministers in the orthodox Nonconformist denominations were repelled, and four hundred of them issued a protest. Still offended by a government which supported denominational education but alienated now from the League, Nonconformity lost its sense of political direction.

Chamberlain's secular policy was intended to reduce not only religious controversy but also the religious identification of the League with Nonconformity. He wanted to broaden the base of support for the education movement and thus to reassert the social purpose which had led him to join the movement in the first place. Towards this end, in the middle of February 1872 he amplified the League's objectives into a trinity of demands: for 'Free land, free schools, and free church'.[37] 'Free schools' was there to epitomize the educational agenda of the League. 'Free church', meaning disestablishment and disendowment of the Church of England, was added to offset the unpopularity in Nonconformist circles of the League's commitment to secular education, and also to provide a way of paying for free education without burdening the taxpayer.

The more remarkable development in Chamberlain's policy was the inclusion of 'Free land'. He did not know, when he adopted this demand, that an erstwhile farmworker called Joseph Arch had just launched a movement which would lead to the formation of the Agricultural Labourers' Union. It was Jesse Collings, not Arch, who interested Chamberlain in the rural potentialities of the education movement. Agricultural labourers, as the poorest of workers, simply could not afford elementary education for their children unless it was free. Furthermore, the National Education League was an essentially urban movement; and until it overcame that limitation it would not command the respect of Parliament. As soon as Chamberlain learned of Arch's Union, he welcomed it as an ally for the Education League.

A plan of political action accompanied Chamberlain's widened agenda. Even before the 1870 Act reached the statute books, he had spoken of League intervention in by-elections. He was encouraged soon afterwards by the defeat in a by-election at Shrewsbury of a ministerial

candidate who would not cooperate with the League. Chamberlain
alerted the salaried agents of the League, as they travelled round the
country, to gather information on electoral circumstances wherever they
went. A member of the League's executive committee stood unsuccess-
fully in a by-election at Truro in 1871. These electoral efforts moved
into higher gear in 1872. Chamberlain and Dale presented the case for
an aggressive electoral strategy to the conference of Nonconformists in
Manchester.[38] Dale argued that Nonconformists should insist upon commitment from each Liberal candidate to their demands in proportion to
their numerical strength in the constituency; and he urged Nonconformists to create their own local electoral associations rather than rely
upon Liberal ones. Chamberlain pointed out that most of the Liberal
MPs who sat for borough constituencies had won by narrow majorities
and hence were vulnerable to Nonconformist threats to withdraw support. In pursuit of these electoral plans, Chamberlain accumulated more
urban constituency information than anyone but the Liberal and Conservative party whips possessed. Deploying his experience in sales and
marketing, he worked with J.T. Bunce of the *Birmingham Daily Post* on
the text and layout of pamphlets and circulars for the Education
League.

Nonconformists responded ambivalently to the policy Dale and
Chamberlain advocated. Some ministers called for even stiffer electoral
tactics. Denominational assemblies of Baptists and Congregationalists,
overcoming their natural aversion, adopted the secular policy which
accompanied the new electoral strategy of the League. But more Nonconformists were repelled than were attracted by both secular education and an electoral strategy which might let the Tories in. Dale and
Chamberlain did not always succeed in convincing the local conferences of Nonconformists they attended; and the passive kind of Nonconformist laymen unlikely to attend such conferences were even less
likely to prove to agree with the impatient leaders of the Education
League.

Meanwhile at the parliamentary level, support for the League crumbled. One of the more advanced Liberals in the Commons, H.S.P.
Winterbotham, the Member for Stroud, began to argue that the 1870
Act should be accepted as an interim settlement of the education question. Chamberlain marched straight into Stroud to condemn such half-
hearted counsel. While admitting that his electoral strategy might lead
to a Tory government, Chamberlain asked his cheering audience: 'What
is that to us? What matters it to education, what matters it to the welfare and prosperity of the nation, whether a Tory Government sits on
the Cabinet benches or a Liberal Government passing Tory measures?'[39]

The League executive decided to test the disposition of the government at the beginning of 1873. Dixon undertook to introduce a bill

requiring universal school boards and compulsory attendance and re-
pealing the 1870 Act's notorious twenty-fifth clause. Hopes rose when
Gladstone announced that the government would itself bring in a bill to
amend the 1870 Act; and Dixon agreed to wait and see. But the bill
Forster brought in turned out to be a slap in the face. Though it made
 the attendance of pauper children at school compulsory, it did not press
for the establishment of school boards in all localities. As for the infamous twenty-fifth clause, Forster proposed in effect to entrench it by
transferring responsibility for its enforcement from school boards to the
Poor Law Guardians.

Infuriated by Forster, the executive of the Education League decided
to take up his challenge in the forthcoming by-election at Bath. Bath
was not a good place for the League because the local Nonconformists
did not want to divide the Liberal vote and thus risk returning a Tory.
The Liberal candidate, a Captain Hayter, refused to have anything to do
with the agent for the Education League who asked him to support
Dixon's rather than Forster's bill. Thereupon the League decided to put
up a candidate of its own, a member of the executive committee, J.C.
Cox. This tactic proved successful. Though Liberals reacted angrily to
the candidacy of Cox, Hayter backed down and agreed to the principles
of Dixon's bill. Cox withdrew, and the Education League gave Hayter a
back-handed endorsement. It was not enough to win him the election,
but he did better than the Liberal candidate at the last election. The
whole episode provoked national debate, and confirmed Chamberlain
and his confederates in their militancy.

As soon as Hayter accepted the League's demand, even before the
electors of Bath went to the polls, Chamberlain proposed to repeat the
Bath tactics in every succeeding by-election. In this way he hoped not
just to enforce the demands of the Education League but to reconstitute
the Liberal party on a Radical basis. He discussed the plan with close
companions in Birmingham and sought the cooperation of the Central
Nonconformist Committee. The plan depended on the recruitment of
fearless candidates for the League. Chamberlain approached thorough-
going Radicals he had come to know around the country. 'Is it not
possible', he asked,

> to form a band of 'irreconcilables' determined to smash up this gigantic
> sham, called a Liberal Party, & to secure reorganisation on a new basis.
> Half a score determined men might yet bring the Govt. to their
> senses.[40]

He argued that, '[t]he only way to bring the Liberal Party to its senses
is to send an extreme man to fight every election, without regard to his
prospect of success, until the important parts of our programme are
incorporated into the platform of the whole Party.'[41]

During these enquiries, Chamberlain came upon the man who was to be his closest Radical companion outside Birmingham for the next dozen years, John Morley. Two years younger than Chamberlain, Morley had followed him at University College School in London. Otherwise they had pursued divergent paths; and they were very different people. Morley lived in the world of ideas and literature.[42] Disowned by his father when the young man recoiled from a career in holy orders, Morley earned his living as a writer in London, where he became a disciple of John Stuart Mill. Morley now edited the *Fortnightly Review*, which he turned into the voice of advanced though still middle-class Radicalism. He was looking for a cause behind which the rising generation of Radicals could unite; and in the first half of 1873 he thought he found what he was looking for in the National Education League.

He was also looking for a leader who could combine action with ideas. John Stuart Mill had just died, and in any case Mill had not been a man of action. Chamberlain was an unlikely candidate for this ideal role because what attracted him to ideas was their utility. Even so, Morley embraced him eagerly; and Chamberlain returned the feeling. Chamberlain admired the intellectual power that Morley possessed, and he craved the familiarity Morley enjoyed with other Radical intellectuals in London. Morley hailed Chamberlain to his associates in London as 'decidedly a leader for an *English* progressive party'.[43]

Once sure of Morley's confidence, Chamberlain admitted to him that the effort to assemble a band of irreconcilables was not going well. 'I am sometimes almost disheartened,' he wrote; 'There is no lack of men who approve . . . but I cannot get a positive pledge to fight, if necessary in person, from the majority of those to whom I have spoken.'[44] The health of Cox, the League's candidate at Bath, was temporarily broken by his fight. Neither Chamberlain nor Morley wanted to contest obviously hopeless constituencies themselves. Liberal dissidents of one sort or other, temperance men or supporters of the Education League, stood against ministerial Liberals in the next four by-elections after Bath. In each case the dissident did better than the ministerialist. But the Conservative candidate invariably won. Chamberlain was particularly shaken by the result in East Staffordshire, admittedly a county constituency but near Birmingham, where the treasurer of the League was badly defeated by a Conservative in a straight fight. The defeat made Chamberlain 'doubt if there are four boroughs in the kingdom where I could find a seat'.[45]

For all its show of militancy, the campaign of Chamberlain and his confederates in the Education League was virtually bankrupt. Radical MPs publicly censured the tactics of the League; and it was almost out of money. Chamberlain's scheme for a band of irreconcilables was designed partly to overcome this financial weakness. He explained candidly to one prospective recruit that the League treasury was 'nearly dry & will not be refilled till next year. I can only suggest a common fund to which each of the "Intransigentes" should bring £200 or £250 & from which the cost of the different fights should be taken.'[46]

An avenue of escape from these straits opened up when John Bright accepted an invitation from Gladstone to rejoin the government. Bright had retired from the cabinet though not from Parliament because of nervous illness shortly before Forster introduced his Education bill. Periodically since then he had tried to mediate between his Birmingham constituents and the prime minister. He warned Gladstone that Forster's extension of denominational education was bearing evil fruit, and warned Dale on the other side that a narrowly Nonconformist agitation would not win working-class support.[47] Shortly after the Bath by-election, Bright condemned the 1870 measure as 'the worst Act passed by a Liberal government since 1832'. Thereupon Gladstone, worried by the Liberal disarray and encouraged by Bright's return to activity, pleaded with him to rejoin the cabinet in the undemanding office of Chancellor of the Duchy of Lancaster. Bright agreed, and then consulted his leading constituents since the law required him to stand for reelection upon his appointment.

The men of Birmingham including Chamberlain who travelled up to Manchester to confer with Bright did not know quite what to make of his appointment. Did it signal a change of heart in the government towards the League or was it just window-dressing? The first word back from Manchester was not encouraging: Bright seemed to resent his constituents questioning the significance of his appointment and thought that 'his presence in the ministry ought of itself to be a sufficient satisfaction to us'.[48] Subsequently, however, he assured Chamberlain of his sympathy with the League, found out what changes in the law would satisfy its leaders, indicated that the government intended to move on other fronts in line with their desires, and sought generally to convey the impression that his inclusion in the cabinet was designed to appease them.[49] Yet he could not disguise the fact that the assurances that he had received from Gladstone were vague and insubstantial.

In fact Gladstone had done little more than ask Bright for sympathetic delay while the government decided its future course. Chamberlain came away doubting that Bright's return to the cabinet would have much impact on its legislative proposals. Nevertheless, Chamberlain decided to welcome the reappointment, and he persuaded the League to do so too. His decision had wider implications than he cared to confess to the executive of the League. He was deeply disappointed by its meagre accomplishment after four years of effort. The cause of education had failed to move either the public or the government as the crusade against the Corn Laws had done in the previous generation. Chamberlain drew the conclusion that '[e]ducation for the ignorant cannot have the meaning that belonged to Bread for the starving'.[50] To make matters worse, the campaign of the Education League had assumed a sectarian character which distorted his objectives without any compensating dividend.

Chagrined at the results of his first venture in public life but unwilling to abandon the basic enterprise, he used Bright's appointment as an opportunity to suspend the agitation of the League and turn to other public ventures. He put the best face he could on this decision by trumpeting Bright's elevation as a promise by the government to mend its ways. He persuaded critics that he could present the decision to the public so as to raise expectations which the government could disappoint only to the League's advantage. In practice, however, he meant to keep the League quiet. Bright said enough in his address to his constituents in October to content the League. But when Forster took public issue with Bright's remarks, Chamberlain responded with unfamiliar restraint, merely expressing the hope that Bright's return to the cabinet would induce Forster to leave.

The civic front

Two other ventures tempted Chamberlain to suspend the agitation of the Education League. One was to have him stand for election to Parliament at Sheffield in alliance with labour more than with Nonconformity. The other was at home in Birmingham, where the Radicals wanted to make him chairman of the school board and mayor of the town. The national attention he attracted dwelt on his parliamentary candidacy at Sheffield. Parliamentary politics far outranked municipal. Moreover, heavy local commitments were regarded in parliamentary circles as a limitation rather than an asset, certainly for those aspiring to national leadership.

Chamberlain was to become the outstanding exception to every generalization about local vis-à-vis parliamentary politics. His three years as mayor of Birmingham became the most outstanding mayoralty in English history; and his association thereafter with Birmingham was to be one of the most remarkable features of his parliamentary career. His accomplishment as mayor will be examined on its own in the next chapter. So noteworthy was it that afterwards, when he sat in the House of Commons, people tended to think that he had entered public life initially through municipal politics.

But on the contrary, he had been drawn into municipal politics by the national campaign for education; and he did not become deeply involved in the town council until the national education campaign began to disintegrate. He was first elected to the town council in the autumn of 1869 in a sense by mistake. His associates in the Education League expected that the coming Act of Parliament would give local responsibility for schools to town councils; and with that in mind Chamberlain was nominated to be councillor for St Paul's ward. One of the central and smallest wards of the town, St Paul's had a predominantly working-class population including many employees of Nettlefold and Chamberlain's Heath Street mill. Chamberlain accepted the nomination with some reluctance. He was on holiday with Florence in Cornwall when the nomination arrived. Encouraged by her, he agreed to it but asked for a delay before he took up the duties. 'I wish very much the invitation had come a year later,' he told one of his proposers; 'I have so many imperative claims on my time in connection with my own business . . . that I a little dread this new labour.' He accepted from a sense of obligation, 'holding firmly that a man who will not [go onto the council] has no right to . . . complain of, or scoff at, the efforts of those who do accept their proportion of public duty'.[51]

No sooner was he elected than the main purpose for his election was invalidated. Forster's Education bill placed responsibility for civic schools on new school boards rather than on existing town councils. Now preoccupied with the campaign against Forster's bill, Chamberlain had little time for the town council. He took care to learn how the council conducted its business, but otherwise was content to support the lead offered by reformers more familiar with civic problems. In 1871, when placed on a demanding special committee to report on urban sanitation, he excused himself, pleading his heavy involvement in the Education League.

Even so, civic controversy tended to focus on Chamberlain; and his bid for reelection to the town council in 1872 was fiercely contested. His tongue in the debates on the council as elsewhere was sharp and attracted antagonism. Yet until he actually became mayor, the issues upon which he spoke out were tangential rather than central to the concerns of the council, and were less civic than national. The hottest issue in the contest over his reelection to the council in 1872 was his republicanism.

Like so many of his political commitments, Chamberlain's republicanism was moderate in substance but abrasive in expression, especially when attacked. His republicanism reflected the resentment he felt at the inherited privilege of England's landed hierarchy, and expressed his preference for equality on the American model. He put the credo to his municipal constituents this way:

that all special privileges that interfere with the happiness of the
people shall be swept away, that men shall have equal rights before
the law, equal opportunities of serving their country; and, lastly, that
the principle of fraternity shall prevail, and that every effort shall
be made to promote, as far as possible, friendly feelings among the
various classes of the community.[52]

There was also a working-class strand in English republicanism in the
early 1870s which Chamberlain was happy to appeal to. But though he
expected a republic to replace the monarchy in due course, he saw no
need to press for the change, because Britain's adaptable constitutional
monarchy did not significantly impede the more substantive reforms
he wanted to bring about. He proposed the toast to the Queen at the
dinners he chaired with an easy grace. Still, he was prepared to
speak up for republicanism. In October 1871 he led a minority of the
town council in objecting to the mayor's refusal to allow the notorious
republican Charles Bradlaugh to speak in the town hall. A year later
Chamberlain objected to expenditure by the town council on a reception for Prince Arthur, the Queen's third son.

That was the issue which William Ellis, Chamberlain's opponent,
exploited when they stood against each other a few weeks later in
the election for St Paul's ward. Chamberlain responded in a rollicking
exchange with the crowd at a ward meeting:

> If Mr. Ellis likes, when next the Prince of Wales comes down to War-
> wickshire to shoot cows out of a cart—(laughter, groans, hisses, and
> loud cheers. A Voice, 'How funny you are to-night.' Other Voices, 'Just
> like Joseph;' 'Monarchism for ever;' 'Keep your temper, Joseph')—
> when that interesting event next takes place, I shall have no objection
> to Mr. Ellis illuminating his warehouses as much as he likes . . . but Mr.
> Ellis has no right . . . to take the taxes from the people, who have great
> difficulty in earning their weekly wages, and to expend that money
> upon that tomfoolery.[53]

The edge of Chamberlain's tongue thus attracted lightning in the
local politics of Birmingham on issues of little substantially civic
moment. His main involvement in the public life of the town was on its
school board. Otherwise the local issues of substance which he dealt
with were industrial more than municipal, subjects such as the application of the Workshops Act to Birmingham, the nine-hour day, and arbitration of labour disputes. On these issues he appealed explicitly as an
industrialist to organized labour against their mutual antagonists, the
small masters who paid low wages to the artisans they employed.
Chamberlain was recognized in the political economy of Birmingham as

a friend of organized labour; and the support he acquired from that source was of crucial importance to his reelection in 1872.

He might well have lost that election but for the intervention by the leader of the recently formed brassworkers union, W.J. Davis. Shortly before voting day, a placard was erected bearing hundreds of signatures, including twenty-one of men in Davis's union, in favour of Ellis, who was the foreman of another business. The old alliance of craftsmen with small masters was rearing its head. However, partly with this election in mind, Chamberlain's brothers Arthur and Richard, who owned a large brassworks, had recently given Davis a concession he needed on wages to get his union off to a good start. Arthur now turned to Davis for help. The new alliance between industry and organized labour came into action. Years later Davis well remembered how it worked.

> Our central offices were then, as now, in the heart of St. Paul's Ward. Day by day, and night by night, [Arthur Chamberlain] accompanied me . . . on a concentration of effort in turning the twenty-one brassworkers. We succeeded in getting every brassworker and his influence on our side.[54]

Joseph Chamberlain held on to his council seat by a slim margin of seventy-two votes. He expressed his gratitude to those in the ward who had worked for him by inviting them for a dinner at the Mason Restaurant on Church Street. 'I have never met a man since', Davis recalled, 'who so captivated his guests . . . the way he encouraged every person present, who had brains, to enjoy the conviviality was marvellous, and yet there was no frivolity, and everyone left thinking that he himself had won the election, and was a political giant.'

Cautioned by the narrowness of the victory, Chamberlain and Davis strengthened and at the same time linked their separate forces in preparation for the next round of local elections. The Birmingham Liberal Association decided, on a motion by Chamberlain, to do all it could in local contests rather than save its energies for parliamentary ones. The Birmingham Trades Council, the omnibus organization for the trade unions of the town, started a fund to encourage working-class representation in its own way, and appointed Chamberlain to be one of the fund's trustees. Both organizations thus readied themselves for a two-stage electoral battle in the autumn of 1873 to seize control of the town council and school board under Chamberlain's captaincy. Looking beyond the battle, Chamberlain had private discussions about the civic enterprises he hoped to build in the event of victory. Even so, he was if anything more interested in his simultaneous attempt at the national level to enter Parliament through a contest at Sheffield.

'A working man's representative'

This was the contest he had mainly in mind when he suspended the agitation of the National Education League. By offering himself as a candidate at Sheffield he modified and extended the mission of the by-election assault force which he had tried to recruit in the summer of 1873. That force was intended not just to revive the fortunes of the Education League but also to reconstitute the Liberal party along Radical lines. His venture at Sheffield was designed to pursue this broader objective by bringing about the alliance between militant Nonconformity and organized labour which had so far eluded him. Dissatisfied with the amount and primarily religious character of the support which the Education League had attracted, Chamberlain saw an opportunity at Sheffield to present himself as 'a working man's representative'.[55] His candidacy there reflected the social concerns he had been expressing since the mid-1860s. Even so, he placed himself as an industrialist in a false position at Sheffield; he misinterpreted the Nonconformist middle classes from which he had sprung; and he emerged with if anything less electoral support than reliance on the Education League could have given him.

Organized labour had been strengthened and at the same time attracted to Chamberlain during the industrial boom of the early 1870s. Membership in trade unions rose as men sought to take advantage of industry's need for labour and ability to pay better wages. There was a doubling between 1866 and 1873 in the number of trades councils, which provided a forum for organized labour on a town by town basis. The boom of the early 1870s also encouraged labour organizers, particularly in the engineering trades, to demand a nine-hour day. When Chamberlain's screw-making business met that demand, he won the admiration of labour.

The subject of shorter hours for labour had been on his mind for some time. After the passage of the Ten Hours Act of 1847 it was discovered in textile mills that a shortened working day could increase the productivity of labour. In the 1850s people in the button industry found that, given the better discipline and organization of a large factory, a five-and-a-half-day week made labour more regular and productive than the usual six days. In 1864, Chamberlain began to keep an abstract of how the wages paid at his Heath Street mill affected the cost per unit of its products.[56] Over the next six years, the productivity of this workforce rose. There was a slight deterioration in 1871, when the men and women worked through many a night to fill the orders the Franco-Prussian War brought in. That deterioration was instructive: productivity lessened as the working day lengthened. Chamberlain was therefore ready, along with one or two other Birmingham employers, to respond to the warning conveyed by a successful strike of the Amalgamated Engineers on Tyneside for a nine-hour day. In 1872, Nettlefold and Chamberlain reduced the working day at Heath Street to nine hours, though still for a six-day week, with provision for two hours of overtime at higher rates of pay. The immediate effect of the change was to increase the labour costs of the firm by 16.5 per cent; but in subsequent years this percentage fell, in other words the productivity of the workforce was further improved.

When Chamberlain agreed to the shortened day, he knew that even strictly in terms of wages and profits he would benefit from the reduction far more than would his employees. Labour leaders were none the less impressed by his enlightenment, which they interpreted as sympathy. During the mid-1870s, Chamberlain acquired a reputation outside his own business for neutrality in industrial conflicts between businessmen and labour, with if anything more sympathy for the latter than the former. He became one of the leading practitioners in the West Midlands of a reconciling approach to industrial relations through arbitration.

The preachers of the new Radicalism had not always endeared themselves to labour. George Dawson had fought compositors in 1858 when they baulked at his attempt to ensure the success of his newspaper at their expense. But the boom in metal manufacturing in the early 1870s encouraged both sides to see new potentialities in arbitration. It offered organized labour a less costly way than strikes to secure a larger slice of the new wealth for their members. Once the concurrent expansion of trade unions proved that they had come to stay, big businessmen began to see how organized labour might serve to control industrial strife and labour costs. Neutral arbitration was possible because both sides agreed that the decision should be governed by the selling price of the goods produced, in other words by the necessities of business more than of labour. Like reducing the hours of labour, arbitration of industrial disputes worked ultimately in the interests of business. Nevertheless, as both arbitrator and employer, Chamberlain showed himself better disposed towards labour than were most industrialists, sometimes including his own brothers and partners. His sympathy on industrial matters disposed labour leaders to sympathize with his political initiatives.

Organized labour also shared his disappointment at the performance of Gladstone's government. Judicial decisions had undermined the legality of trade unions, exposed their funds to theft by dishonest officers, and frustrated the operation of laws originally designed to help labour deploy its strength peacefully. The trade unions looked for remedial legislation from the Liberals, but the Gladstone government dashed the hopes of labour as badly as those of the Education League. While the Trade Union Act of 1871 placed unions on a secure legal foundation, the government accompanied it with a Criminal Law Amendment Act which all but eliminated the capacity of the unions to take industrial action. To make matters worse, when decisions by the courts narrowed the benefit of the Trade Union Act to labour, the government refused to take further remedial action. Conditions therefore appeared ripe for cooperation between the two sets of would-be supporters whom Gladstone's ministry had alienated. Exasperation with the Liberal party among leaders of labour and the League reached a peak simultaneously in 1873. Both groups sponsored candidates who stood against official Liberal nominees in by-elections that spring and summer, the Education League most conspicuously at Bath, independent labour at Greenwich and Dundee.

Chamberlain was invited to Sheffield in May 1873 by a Reform Association recently set up by dissident Radicals at the prompting of a local iron smelter, H.J. Wilson. Wilson was looking for someone to fill the vacancy that was expected when the senior of Sheffield's two MPs retired. Sheffield was only one of several constituencies with their eye on Chamberlain; and at the time he was more interested in Newcastle. But he welcomed every opportunity to fan the sparks of discontent with the government. Sheffield seemed well suited for his purposes. The Education Act had produced acute bitterness there after some Nonconformists including Wilson had their property sequestered over their refusal to pay rates which could be used to defray fees of children in denominational schools. On the labour side, trade unionists were strongly represented in the Sheffield Reform Association.

In his first address to the association that May, Chamberlain sought common ground between Nonconformity and labour. He argued for adult suffrage to enforce respect for the wishes of 'the people' within the system of government which hitherto, whatever party was in power, had been devoted to the propertied classes and the Established Church. Chamberlain gave this Radical argument a less familiar industrial twist. 'I am a manufacturer', he said candidly,

> and am proud in some respects of the class to which I belong. I believe [that] upon the union between the employers and the employed and upon the identity of sympathy and interests between the middle and the working classes, depend the future progress and the prosperity of the country—but I am bound to admit that the middle classes, having used the numbers and the influence and the power of the working classes to secure for themselves representation, have not been too eager to obtain for their allies the benefits which they have obtained for themselves.[57]

The labour leaders of Sheffield did not respond to his appeal immediately. Lacking first-hand knowledge of his performance as an employer, they were less sure than their counterparts in Birmingham of his commitment to their interests. Chamberlain attempted to win wider confidence among the ranks of labour nationally through a manifesto which he issued at the end of the summer in the *Fortnightly Review*.[58] It presented a fourfold 'programme', which he summed up as '*Free Church, Free Land, Free Schools, and Free Labour*'. The first three freedoms merely reordered the demands he had issued on behalf of the Education League in 1872. The distinguishing feature of the new manifesto was Chamberlain's addition of the demand for 'free labour'. Dwelling on the failure of the government to remove the fetters the courts had placed on collective bargaining, he insisted that the amendments which labour requested in the law were modest and did not threaten the interests of property. His challenge to 'The Liberal party and its leaders', as his manifesto was entitled, was more fully defined than anything the advocates of independent labour had issued. The manifesto attracted so much attention that the issue of the *Fortnightly* in which it appeared had to be reprinted.

At the end of September Chamberlain was invited back to Sheffield for another speech. He used the occasion to elaborate his defence of trade unions against middle-class criticism. The growing strength of the unions and the increasingly sympathetic hearing the Trades Union Congress was receiving among critics of the government alarmed many employers. In the spring of the year an Employers' Federation had been formed to make their case. Chamberlain responded, still confident in the closing months of the Victorian boom that industry could afford to be generous. He admitted that the trade unions had pushed wage rates up:

> that, of course, is their primary claim upon the support of the working class. But when I consider the enormous strides which have been made by commerce during the last fifty years; when I know that the profits of trade never were so great as they are at the present time; when I know that enormous fortunes never were so easily or so quickly accumulated, I say it is just and right that the poorer class should also share in this general prosperity. But then it is said that the effect of these unions has been to drive trade out of the country. That is said; but it has never been proved. And when I look at the undoubted evidence of our Government statistics, showing how there is a continuing and enormous increase in the exports of this country, I say that such apprehension is altogether uncalled for.[59]

He defended even the restrictive practices of organized labour, pointing out that the middle-class professions indulged in similar behaviour:

any physician who should presume to do the work of an apothecary
by dispensing his own medicines would never again be met in consultation with any member of that learned body. What is that but the rule
which forbids masons to do bricklayers' work, and bricklayers to do
masons' work?

He concluded with a plea for sympathetic justice in place of the currently hostile rulings of the courts: 'Don't let us exert the full force of
the law to pluck out the mote from the eye of the workman, while we
leave untouched the beam in the eye of the employer.' These were stirring words. Back in Birmingham, the trades council passed a resolution
of thanks and had the speech published. At the school board elections
in November, labour threw itself wholeheartedly behind the campaign
of the Birmingham Liberal Association and then celebrated its triumph
with a torchlight procession.

Though success in the local elections made Chamberlain mayor as
well as the chairman of the school board in Birmingham, these added
responsibilities did not prompt him to draw in his horns at Sheffield.
On the contrary, the Birmingham victories encouraged him to raise his
estimate of Radical prospects everywhere. Yet even for a man of boundless energy, there were only twenty-four hours in the day. His new
civic duties left him little time to devote to Sheffield for the rest of the
year; and the policy of secular education which the Birmingham school
board proceeded to introduce at his prompting alienated Nonconformists in Sheffield. His absorption in Birmingham misled him about Sheffield at a more fundamental level. Superficially the two towns had a
good deal in common.[60] Both had metal-manufacturing economies. But
large units of production had emerged somewhat earlier in Sheffield.
For a variety of reasons the manufacturers of Sheffield tended to ally
themselves with the landed elite around the town rather than with the
local working class as in Birmingham. Because of the resulting weakness of cooperation between masters and employees in Sheffield, labour
was more strongly organized and self-reliant there than in Birmingham.

The Sheffield Reform Association derived its strength primarily from
labour, and Chamberlain responded accordingly. But that was not the
pattern which worked so well for him in Birmingham. The Birmingham
Liberal Association was dominated by industrialists like himself together with allies from the middle-class professions and the leading
Nonconformist ministers. Businessmen of this sort were scarce among
the Radicals of Sheffield and also inferior in ability. H.J. Wilson was at
odds with most other men of his class in his locality. The leading local
newspaper proprietor in Birmingham, John Jaffray of the *Birmingham
Daily Post*, was a firm ally of Chamberlain. But in Sheffield the opposition to him was led by Jaffray's counterpart, Robert Leader of the *Shef-*

field Independent. Mistaking Sheffield for Birmingham, Chamberlain found himself on quicksand.

Unable after the school board elections in Birmingham to size up the situation in Sheffield for himself, he despatched William Harris to do so. Harris was the organizing genius behind the Birmingham Liberal Association. But Chamberlain, in his desire for election to Parliament at Sheffield, confined the inquiries by Harris to those whom Wilson advised him to consult. When Harris returned to report, the new mayor was too deep in civic affairs to see him for more than five minutes. 'I must', Chamberlain wrote Wilson, 'be guided almost entirely by you.'[61] Harris, sensing the problem in Sheffield, recruited a staff member from the headquarters of the Education League to deal with it. But Wilson spurned this help, meanwhile breathing optimism: 'I always try to avoid being sanguine about anything,' he told Chamberlain, 'but really it is very difficult in this case, when we have every element of success on our side.'[62] Two days later, however, he had to confess that '[w]e have a little over-estimated the political knowledge & interest of the people'[63]—not a mistake Birmingham organizers would make.

There was another candidate for the expected parliamentary vacancy, Robert Leader's nominee A.J. Allott, a local worthy, alderman and respected Nonconformist. Critical of Gladstone's government, Allott differed on most issues only in his mildness from Chamberlain. Allott favoured unsectarian religious rather than secular education, but on that issue even Wilson had to admit that Allott was closer to prevailing sentiment in Sheffield than was Chamberlain. Allott was also a generous employer and was not disliked by labour, but he was not at all forceful or exciting. The contest between Allott and Chamberlain was as much a choice between local esteem and charismatic talent as between moderate and advanced Radicalism.

The formal invitation for Chamberlain to become a candidate came from the executive of the Sheffield Trades Council. Its vote on the invitation was 10 to 2, a foretaste of the lack of solidarity among the working class that was to trouble his campaign. Within a week of the trades council's invitation, some trade union secretaries repudiated it. Harris wrote to Wilson in alarm: 'now, for the last time, I entreat you to re-examine your ground before Chamberlain is asked to commit himself'.[64] But knowing his master's ambition, Harris did not press harder: 'After you have considered the matter,' he assured Wilson, 'you will command our adherence.'

Harris discovered further cause for concern closer to home. A rumour circulated in Sheffield that the wire-drawers at Nettlefold and Chamberlain's Imperial Mill were paid substandard wages and prohibited from joining a union. Harris raised the matter with Chamberlain as soon as he could see him. Chamberlain was not directly in charge of that mill and had to inquire himself. What he learned was embarrassing though not discreditable. His partner Joseph Nettlefold had indeed insisted that the wire-drawers he employed must resign from their union, and he paid less per hour for the high quality of wire on which his mill concentrated than was customary in mills drawing wire of varying grades at varied rates. Nettlefold none the less attracted a good workforce because his men could count on regular employment with full hours and hence a better weekly wage than could be had elsewhere. Informed of the damaging rumour in Sheffield, these workers readily signed a letter praising Nettlefold and Chamberlain as employers; and Chamberlain made sure immediately that they joined a union. All the same, the suspicion raised by this episode never quite died down.

On insecure ground even among labour, Chamberlain mistook the situation in Sheffield in other ways. The junior Member of Parliament for Sheffield, A.J. Mundella, who intended to stand for reelection, was arguably the most notable champion of labour in the current House of Commons, though not as trenchant as Chamberlain. Mundella had been elected in 1868; and Chamberlain contended that the people who opposed his candidacy now had opposed Mundella then. But in fact Robert Leader, Allott's sponsor, had been the chief sponsor of Mundella in 1868. Leader's ambition essentially was to dominate the politics of his town. He feared that Chamberlain might threaten this dominance, either by overextending Sheffield's willingness to elect advocates of labour, or by rivalling Leader's local power.

Another figure lurked ominously in Leader's calculations. J.A. Roebuck, one of early Victorian England's more ferocious Radicals, had served as Member of Parliament for Sheffield for nearly twenty years. By the 1860s his chauvinism and dislike of Gladstone got the better of his Radicalism, and he became an admirer of Disraeli, though without changing party affiliation. Roebuck was ousted in 1868 in favour of Mundella. But Roebuck still enjoyed a good deal of covert support in Sheffield, from Conservatives and also from the lower, less politicized ranks of labour who liked his truculent nationalism and disliked the recent efforts of the Liberal government to reduce the availability of beer. If he managed to win votes also from Nonconformists alienated by Chamberlain, Roebuck could quite possibly regain his seat.

Like Allott, who was in effect their candidate, the Nonconformist worthies of Sheffield agreed with the familiar Radical planks in Chamberlain's platform and were prepared under the popular pressures of an election to assent formally to most of his social nostrums. But on those issues, preeminently the use of the Bible in schools and Sunday observance, where the claims of religion ran counter to the demand for full and equitable democracy, these men came down fervently on the side of religion. Chamberlain came down with equal insistence on the other side. Though an advocate of local electoral control of the drink traffic, he opposed Sunday closing of public houses because that 'would practically affect the poor only'.[65] He gave firm support to the principle of one day's rest in seven, but on strictly social grounds; and he insisted on the value of opening museums on Sundays so long as the sabbatarian scruples of the attendants were respected.

Wilson and Chamberlain were aware of the price they would pay for these policies among the local Nonconformist elite. They were confident that the loss would be more than repaid by the enthusiasm Chamberlain could arouse particularly among labour. 'We never pretended to be great men', Wilson commented to Chamberlain,

> — we have always regretted the comparative obscurity of most of our associates, & the absence of monied men. But we say we are the Radicals & working men of Sheffield, and that we are essential to any candidate; and that we have got the *votes*, though we have no money; and we say *now* that we have got a candidate whom it is useless to oppose.[66]

Chamberlain's response belied some of the most notorious characteristics of his behaviour in Birmingham:

> I don't think much of smoke room politics—& as to the 'respectables' I neither expect nor want their aid. I am a working man's representative, if I am any thing, & it is to ensure fair consideration for their claims as to all questions, not merely on special labour legislation, that I chiefly care to enter Parliament.[67]

Caustically he commented to a friend in a similar contest in London:

> the leading London Dissenters are a nasty, narrow, bigoted lot, from whom no help can be expected. . . . You must win, in spite of them, & without them, by the force of the working class vote;—as I hope to win in Sheffield.[68]

On New Year's day 1874, after an absence of three months, Chamberlain returned to Sheffield and accepted the trades council's invitation to make himself available for election. To underscore the popular nature of his candidacy, he delivered his speech out of doors in Paradise Square close to the centre of the town. Some ten to twelve thousand people pressed in to listen, curious but uncertain about their visitor from Birmingham.

He warmed his audience up by proclaiming 'the radical programme of the future'.[69] It combined all the ingredients of the appeal he had developed since his first visit to Sheffield. The programme began with a demand for universal adult suffrage and equal electoral districts. 'Then', he proclaimed, 'we can go on to further legislative changes', which he summed up in his four freedoms: free schools, free labour, free land and a free church. He did not give pride of place this time to free labour because he had said so much about it in the autumn; but he extended that demand to include compensation for industrial injuries caused by the neglect or carelessness of employers. The power of his appeal and the response it evoked were unmistakable.

At the close of his speech someone shouted out a question that was to ring down the years: 'What about Home Rule for Ireland?' There were three thousand Irish electors in Sheffield, and Chamberlain wanted their votes. By responding sympathetically to Home Rule sentiment, he could offset the hostility he was bound to incur from the Catholic clergy over his opposition to denominational education. But his response was not simply an electoral calculation. He knew Ireland first-hand from business trips and had given some thought to the question the heckler raised. Chamberlain declared himself in favour of the kind of Home Rule advocated by the current Irish leader, Isaac Butt, but added, 'I am not in favour of any system which would go further than this, and which would separate the imperial relations which at present exist between the two countries.' Chamberlain would always recall this answer with pride. But amid the pressures of the campaign at Sheffield, things went further than he would care to remember. Harris imported an Irishman called Hogan from Birmingham to woo the extreme Home Rulers; and Chamberlain commented in answer to another question that Parliament 'would move on at an accelerated pace without the Irish members'.[70]

The New Year address in Paradise Square made Chamberlain the front runner for the Liberal nomination for Sheffield's second parliamentary seat. But he could not spend time in Sheffield to consolidate his achievement. He was obliged as mayor of Birmingham to go back and preside over a string of public meetings. Then in mid-January, just as he was presenting plans to the town council for municipalization of the local gas companies, the Trades Union Congress convened in Sheffield for its annual meeting. The metropolitan press headed by *The Times* lavished attention on the meeting. The conflict in timing not only deprived Chamberlain of a good opportunity to make his case in Sheffield but also widened the cracks in his support from labour. Some members of the parliamentary committee of the Trades Union Congress were inclined to favour Allott, and they invited him to the annual meeting.

That meeting served to delay a resolution of the contest between the two candidates, though everyone agreed that it should be settled quickly. The longer the decision was delayed, the deeper the division between the two sides, and the greater the danger that Roebuck would intervene. The problem was how to settle the contest. The alternative methods which the two sides proposed reflected their differing notions of what was desirable in the Liberal party. Allott, placing his trust in established elites, wanted arbitration by independent MPs of national repute. Chamberlain and his supporters insisted that the contest be decided according to which candidate had the greater popular support.

The contestants might propose, but Gladstone disposed. Before the dispute was resolved, Gladstone suddenly called a general election. That news made a settlement urgently necessary but eliminated time for the division between the two camps to heal. The dissolution of Parliament 'could hardly have been worse timed'[71] for Chamberlain, for the news reached him at the death-bed of his father in Birmingham. But it was even worse for Allott. He had to accept the arbitrament of an immediate mass meeting in Paradise Square.

Less than a week after the dissolution, the largest crowd Sheffield had ever seen, perhaps twice the size of the New Year's assembly, crushed into Paradise Square to hear and decide between the two men. The windows of the surrounding offices were filled with the faces of the town's elite, for the moment powerless. Allott tackled his assignment with obvious discomfort. Remarks he made in support of Gladstone provoked disorder that interrupted his speech. Chamberlain's short speech on the other hand was punctuated with cheers which followed wave upon wave at its conclusion. The first show of hands was for Allott and so many went up that it seemed to one reporter 'as if the number could not be exceeded; but when the name of Chamberlain was raised, it seemed as if all the Square . . . had uplifted their hands'.[72]

Winning the Liberal nomination marked the high point of Chamberlain's venture as a working men's candidate. His achievement left the local Liberals divided; and he had no time and little inclination to bridge the division. The situation was worst at the personal level. Allott took his defeat in Paradise Square badly. He told the crowd to its face that he found such a forum 'distasteful'. Though he expressed the hope that Sheffield would present an unbroken Liberal front on election day, he could not bring himself to mention Chamberlain by name. Chamberlain repaid him with contempt.

Allott's sentiments were shared by his supporters. This Nonconformist defection would not have been so serious if Chamberlain had enjoyed solid working-class support. But the unhealed contest between Allott and Chamberlain encouraged Roebuck to enter the field. Roebuck campaigned in favour of 'The Briton's Bible and the Briton's Beer: our National Church and our National Beverage', a manifesto that combined religious and working-class appeals much more successfully than

Chamberlain. 'Our National Church' won solid Conservative support. 'Our National Beverage' attracted working men and turned the public houses of Sheffield into recruiting centres for Roebuck. 'The Briton's Bible' exploited the dismay of Nonconformists in Sheffield at the decision of the Birmingham school board to exclude the Bible from its schools. Roebuck's camp also made use of Allott's candidacy. Some of Roebuck's men may have attended the meeting in Paradise Square to vote for Allott and thus make the result look uncertain. Afterwards they nominated Allott anyway in order to draw support from Chamberlain; and though Allott declined to make the requisite deposit, his name stayed on the ballot.

The campaign between nomination and election was brief and nasty. When Chamberlain and the senior Liberal candidate for Sheffield's two seats, Mundella, tried to hold another rally in Paradise Square, supporters of Roebuck created enough uproar to make the speakers inaudible. Mundella was later struck with half a brick, Chamberlain with a red herring. Between meetings, twenty-two for Chamberlain within five days, he and Mundella walked arm in arm through the streets, sometimes as much for physical support as to demonstrate their solidarity. Yet there was tension between them. The extent of Chamberlain's Radicalism made Mundella uneasy. Beginning to sense the strength of party loyalty, Chamberlain toned down his criticism of the Liberal government. Seeking nevertheless to make the most of his particular supporters, he put posters out on the eve of the election asking Liberals to vote only for him.[73]

Countrywide as well as in Sheffield, Gladstone's sudden dissolution of Parliament caught his Radical critics unprepared. Neither the Education League nor organized labour was ready for a general election. Jerked out of the dormancy in which Chamberlain had placed it, the National Education League managed to induce 300 of the 425 Liberal candidates in Britain to pledge themselves to the repeal of the Education Act's twenty-fifth clause. But the League did not oppose those who rejected this minimal demand. Only a small fraction of the Liberal candidates supported the League's full set of policies. Generally the Nonconformist instinct of loyalty to the Liberal party overrode concern about particular grievances. Initially the Trades Union Congress seemed better prepared and more determined to insist on its objectives. At its annual meeting at Sheffield, the Congress urged members to press candidates for election, regardless of their party, to agree to the needed changes in labour law. But like Nonconformist supporters of the Education League, when it came to the general election with the risk of a Conservative victory, spokesmen for organized labour tended to allow their Liberal loyalties to override their own interests.

Except for the placing of Allott's name on the ballot, the campaign at

Sheffield kept Chamberlain in good spirits. He was stunned by his defeat. Roebuck topped the poll with 14,193 votes, over 4,000 more than he had received in 1868. Mundella, with 12,858, held the second place. Chamberlain was well back with 11,053, saved from the bottom of the poll only by the 621 votes for Allott, too few in themselves to account for Chamberlain's failure. Many Liberals had stayed at home: the total vote was markedly smaller than in 1868. Roebuck won back some of the working-class support he lost in 1868. More than 1,500 Liberals either split their votes between Mundella and Roebuck or plumped for Roebuck.

Beer and the Bible had beaten Chamberlain. The secular brand of his Radicalism had alienated local Nonconformity, while Roebuck's alliance with the brewers ate into Chamberlain's working-class support. Allott claimed that he could have won and offered to place his services at the disposal of his fellow townsmen whenever their next parliamentary vacancy opened up. Letters from his supporters documented the defection of Nonconformists from Chamberlain. But the cruellest blow came from the metropolitan labour leader and erstwhile supporter of the Education League, Robert Applegarth, who told a post-election crowd in Sheffield that he hoped they would take Allott at the next opportunity.

Chamberlain lashed back at Allott. 'There is only one thing which will ever bring me to Sheffield again as a candidate', he declared to Wilson, '—& that is Mr. Allott's offering himself. He has behaved like a "cad" all through, without a spark of nobleness or generosity.'[74] Chamberlain found little comfort from the fact that his defeat was part of a countrywide trend. For the first time in a generation the Conservatives won a solid parliamentary majority. This outcome seemed to magnify Chamberlain's folly in resisting the moderate drift in the Liberal party over the past four years. Before the election he had expected and even looked forward to a spell of Conservative government as good medicine for the Liberals. But his personal defeat coupled with the victory of his arch-enemy W.E. Forster in a similar contest at Bradford furnished evidence to discredit his entire enterprise in national politics. Chamberlain winced at the evidence and sought to put his defeat down to local circumstances.

But he did not accept that excuse himself. He was quick to learn from his failure. He saw that he had misinterpreted the balance of strength between Nonconformity and labour and had underestimated the importance of party unity. He advised the Liberals of Sheffield 'to unite at once on some new man, in case of Roebuck's death';[75] and he suggested Alfred Illingworth of Bradford as someone who would appeal to all Nonconformists but would need warming up to working-class demands. To mobilize and unite both sources of support, Chamberlain urged adoption of the organizational techniques perfected at Birmingham. Thereafter he immersed himself in the civic life of Birmingham. But he did not disengage himself from Sheffield abruptly. He still wanted to enter Parliament; and the persistent loyalty of Wilson and the Sheffield Trades Council together with his own anger at Allott kept him from severing that connection for another two years.

One feature of the working-class scene at Sheffield continued to puzzle Chamberlain: the phenomenon of the Roebuck supporter, the local guise of that national phenomenon, the Conservative working man. 'Even now,' he confessed after the election, 'when the evidence of his existence has been forced upon me in a way which cannot be mistaken, I am bound to say that [the Conservative working man] is a monstrous anomaly and abortion.'[76] He tried to use the monstrosity as grist for his mill. A good many working men, particularly in Lancashire and Yorkshire, had voted for Conservative candidates because they responded more readily than Liberals to the demand for reform in the law governing trade unions. Chamberlain pleaded with Liberals to regain the loyalty of the working class by acceding to that demand.

Otherwise he no longer attempted to put himself forward primarily as a working man's representative. He came to rely instead upon party organization on the Birmingham model to unite labour and Nonconformists within the Radical army. This shift in tactics increased Chamberlain's hostility to independent electoral representation of labour. Reversing his stance as a parliamentary candidate in Sheffield, he boasted to his friends there that Liberal Associations like the one in Birmingham were

> the most magnificent machine ever invented for social, philanthropic, educational & political work. . . . With this organisation we have beaten the Tories till they dare not show their heads . . . we have beaten the publicans . . . we have beaten the priests in the Wards in which the Irish Catholics chiefly live; & now we are going to beat the so called 'Working men's candidates'—a little knot of idle vagabonds who raise this cry in the hope of foisting themselves into notice against the wishes of all the intelligent portion of the working class.[77]

Departure from business

By the time he wrote these words, Chamberlain had completed his movement out of business into full-time politics. He took four years to make the transition. He spoke of the possibility first in 1870, when the threat to the monopoly of the Screw Kings reaffirmed his commitment to his business. Drawn always to 'the bold game', he was not greatly interested in the easy harvest which his business reaped from 1870 to

1873. Though he extended his market during those years, his entries in his notebook of transactions with middlemen tailed away. His dominance within his family's side of the partnership was formalized in 1871. But late in 1873, engrossed in his mayoralty and prospective candidacy at Sheffield, he handed the records of his commercial transactions over to Joseph Nettlefold, taking care to explain the accounting techniques which he had developed. For another year he remained active in the business of Lloyds Bank, where he sought to meet the capital needs of the West Midlands by building more branch offices. He used one firm of architects, Martin and Chamberlain (no relation), to design branch offices for Lloyds Bank and also the new schools whose construction he commissioned as chairman of the Birmingham School Board.

Such congeniality between his business and public interests was, however, the exception rather than the rule, as he discovered in the Sheffield election over the rule against trade unions at one of his mills. Chamberlain's defeat in that election underscored the political cost of such embarrassments. Just as, in 1870, the emergence of a competitor had pulled him back into business, so in 1874 his defeat at Sheffield intensified his commitment to politics. That summer he and his family sold their half of the partnership to the Nettlefolds for some £600,000. After he had made provision for his mother and brothers and sisters, Chamberlain's share amounted to something over one sixth of that sum, quite enough, properly invested, to maintain him in affluence for the rest of his life. He retired from the business on 27 June, twenty years to the day since he had joined it.

Two days later he and his brothers expressed their thanks to their former employees by treating them to a special excursion by train to London and the Crystal Palace. Some 2,300 men, women and children came for the occasion. Chamberlain greeted them individually at the entrance to the dining rooms at the Crystal Palace, where they sat down, in two shifts, to a dinner of roast and boiled meats, veal and ham pies, salad and vegetables, sweets and cheese, and pints of beer.

The timing of his departure from business proved critical. In 1876 depression struck the metallurgical trades of the West Midlands. Though their fortunes thereafter rose as well as fell, they lost their leadership in the market even at home, let alone abroad. This depression, in fact, marked 'the watershed between the era of British industrial supremacy and the era of international competition'.[78] The particular business from which Chamberlain had retired, now called simply Nettlefolds, continued to hold its own in Britain. Adhering to the plan laid out by Chamberlain in 1870, the firm slashed its prices and accepted low profits in the mid-1870s in order to eliminate competition particularly from the Birmingham Screw Company, which Nettlefolds absorbed in 1880. But competition stiffened abroad, particularly on the Continent where France was replaced as the country from which Nettlefolds had most to fear by Germany. Before he retired from the firm, Chamberlain had exported its products to Belgium, Switzerland, Spain, Italy, Malta, Poland, Russia, India, Japan, Australia, New Zealand and Canada as well as France, Germany and the United States. It thus happened that the industrial hegemony which he had helped to establish began to wane as soon as he retired from business.

The economic challenge that Britain faced in the final quarter of the nineteenth century was if anything greater than the political, and might have drawn Chamberlain with his combative instincts back into industry. Like Arthur Keen, whose career as a manufacturer had paralleled his own, Chamberlain might have gone on to greater heights in business. He could have built one of the industrial conglomerates that stood up to international competition at the turn of the century. However, it was not simply his combative sense of the bolder game after his defeat in 1874 that led him to leave business for politics.

Above all other arenas, it was on the front benches in Parliament that the traditional elite of Britain distinguished itself and demonstrated its worth. There were other things with which the landed classes were identified and which other industrialists desired to enhance their social standing, particularly the ownership of a house in the country. Chamberlain spurned such lesser distinctions. Defiantly he dug himself into the soil of Birmingham; it was there, on the suburban edge of the town, that he built his mansion. He wanted to beat the old elite at its proudest game, high politics. He sought to prove that an urban industrialist could play this game in every way better, including of course better for the country. Never one to do things by halves, once he left business he gave himself totally to politics. Though devoted to the welfare of his industrial community, he came to disparage 'mere money-making'.[79] But tragically, the higher he ascended above his industrial base, the fainter became his political vision.

4

Civic Investment
1869–1880

Like Napoleon, [Chamberlain] rushed on from one exploit to another with a rapidity that astounded his friends and confused and overwhelmed his foes.

Thomas Anderton, *A Tale of One City*

Perhaps Chamberlain's greatest accomplishment was as mayor of Birmingham among his own people.[1] There he won widespread, amazed respect for his achievement in civic affairs. That achievement endured in many essentials long past his death. It also laid solid foundations for his career in national politics. And it established a new composite of policies for urban government known as municipal or gas-and-water socialism that inspired emulation throughout the industrialized world.

Gas-and-water socialism amalgamated elements in the other ventures of Chamberlain's early career, in business, the National Education League, and at Sheffield. His civic policy was businesslike in its dependence on accounting; it was entrepreneurial in its eagerness to make the most of economic opportunities; it provided the fullest manifestation of the civic gospel which inspired the Education League; and it displayed the concern about labour which distinguished his candidacy at Sheffield.

He accentuated the contrast between the government of the town in earlier years and under his leadership. What he brought about was sometimes described as a revolution. Yet it developed in almost logical progression from the policy of his predecessors. The story was no older than Chamberlain himself, and its essence was financial. Birmingham did not acquire incorporated municipal government until 1838, and the municipality did not acquire responsibility for all the most important spheres of local government until 1852. Everyone then agreed that the prime consideration in the town council should be true economy; but a debate broke out between the Economists, whose all-consuming policy was to keep local taxation to a minimum, and the Extravagant party (as the Economists called them) who wanted to create efficient local services. The Extravagant party could prove from examples that the slashing of expenditure today often proved terribly costly tomorrow. Unimpressed, the Economists, led by an erstwhile Tory radical, Joseph Allday, gained control of the town shortly before Chamberlain's arrival in Birmingham.

Allday and his men, who did much of their talking over ale and a pipe in the Old Woodman Tavern, belonged to the lower middle class. His closest associates were a draper, a cabinetmaker and a vestry clerk. They reflected the wishes of those, including the enfranchised working class, who struggled to make a living. Government, they insisted, should not make that struggle one whit harder. They were not insensitive to social ills surrounding them—one of the stiffest in the group, Alderman Gameson, took an active interest in child welfare—but they insisted that this sort of thing was the province of philanthropy, not of government.

Allday's grip was broken in 1859. He was succeeded as the pace-setter of government in the town by Thomas Avery. Avery came from the manufacturing elite. He and his brother[2] owned a scale-making business which they had turned into one of the largest enterprises of its kind in England, with four hundred employees. Doubts were rising about the ability of a draper, a cabinetmaker and a vestry clerk to manage the town's budget which, even under a parsimonious council, far exceeded the dimensions of a small business. Furthermore Allday's men, though hostile to large expenditure, were careless in their supervision of small accounts. Avery was the commercial manager of his business, and his achievement in that capacity inspired the hope that he could manage the accounts of the town with similar ability. He took the town's books in hand and improved its financial control with an up-to-date system of accounting.

The emergence of Avery marked a change in the climate of concern about other matters. Hitherto local government had focused mainly on police and poor relief. But the squalor of England's expanding cities extended concern to broader social issues, especially to public health but also to cultural amenities. Under Avery's leadership in the mid-1860s, the council improved the town's drainage, widened streets and opened libraries. Avery, who was Conservative in party allegiance and Gladstonian in financial management, did not entirely abandon Allday's precepts. Avery still feared that municipal expenditure was exceeding the growth in the town's wealth and population; the size of the public debt made him anxious; and he spoke of slowing down the pace of municipal improvements. Through much of the 1860s the new breed of town fathers like Avery and George Dixon, who succeeded Avery as mayor, relied as much on philanthropy as on local government to improve the conditions of life.

The commitment to financial soundness remained fundamental. Yet Avery's application of his skills in financial management showed that this commitment could be less constricting than Allday had assumed. While cautious in approach, Avery opened new ground for civic action. The pride of the town was wounded by the discovery that Manchester, Liverpool, Glasgow and Leeds had done more in one or other of the new fields of civic improvement than Birmingham. Seizing on the subject of public libraries to which Birmingham was unusually responsive, George Dawson sowed the seed of the civic gospel on ground that Avery had cleared. Dawson, Dale and the newly arrived minister at the Church of the Messiah, Crosskey, presented the work of draining, lighting and paving the town as nothing less than 'divine service'.[3] At the same time Dixon led his fellow townsmen to the discovery that the best efforts of philanthropy were not equal to the need at least in one field, education, and that government must take over. The rain of prosperity in metal manufacturing at the end of the decade watered the soil that Avery had cleared and reduced anxiety about increased expenditure by local government.

Dawson was the evangelist of the civic gospel but not its chief apostle. That position was reserved for Chamberlain. It was never easy to think of him as a moralist. Dashingly dressed, with a red tie drawn through a gold ring, already remarkable for his monocle and feared for his acid-tipped tongue, he was more entrepreneurial than altruistic in his endeavours. But that was true also of his gospel. Chamberlain grasped what the more respectable but pedestrian Avery could not: that the reform movement was a politico-economic crusade. And where Avery was numbingly verbose, Chamberlain spoke in lean, sinewy sentences that made men feel they were present at the inception of a great movement. 'Something', he said,

> must be done, and that quickly, to make life a little brighter and a little easier for those who now groan under its burden, if our boasted prosperity is to rest upon its only sure foundation—the happiness, the welfare, and the contentment of the whole community.[4]

While this presentation accentuated the economic dividends to be drawn from the civic gospel, Chamberlain also carried its political implications to the point where the town council replaced the churches as the primary agency of moral action. Though he praised the activities of the churches, he treated them as supplements to the central work of the town council. 'All private effort, all individual philanthropy,' he told the council, 'sinks into insignificance compared with the organised power of a great representative assembly like this.'[5]

Like Allday but on a higher social plane, Chamberlain and his lieutenants convened in two places: in the council chamber, and in the smoking-room of Southbourne, the home that Chamberlain built for his growing family after his marriage to Florence half an hour's walk away from the town centre in Edgbaston. There he displayed a talent for 'infecting his friends and his followers with some of his own magical enthusiasm, so that the stimulation they received gave them a new belief in themselves'.[6] Banded together after their animated evenings, they sallied forth to take Birmingham by storm.

Inspiring as was Chamberlain's gospel, it was based as firmly as Allday's policy or Avery's on financial responsibility. Chamberlain's experience in business exercised a pervasive influence on his investment in civic affairs. Writing years later for an American magazine, he likened the English system of municipal government to

> a joint-stock or co-operative enterprise in which every citizen is a shareholder, and of which the dividends are receivable in the improved health and the increase of the comfort and happiness of the community. The members of the Council are the directors of this great business, and their fees consist in the confidence, the consideration, and the gratitude of those amongst whom they live. In no other undertaking, whether philanthropic or commercial, are the returns more speedy, more manifest, or more beneficial.[7]

Like Avery, Chamberlain commanded confidence in Birmingham as a successful businessman and commercial manager. The financial arrangements in which he encased his proposals, however bold in concept and brilliant in detail, made good sense even under cold scrutiny. Moving beyond Avery, he extended the sphere of calculation in assessing the worth of civic improvements to include the costs of the prison, the hospital and the workhouse which would otherwise continue to rise. But he did not rely on such extended calculations to justify his own initial proposals: his first civic investments were financially self-sufficient.

They also offered real though insubstantial dividends to the big businessmen in his inner circle. The civic service which Chamberlain encouraged industrialists to provide helped to insure their wealth against social discontent. Furthermore the civic prestige that they acquired gave them political credentials to challenge the ascendancy of England's landed elite, upon whom Chamberlain poured scorn at every opportunity. In his mouth, 'gentry' was a term of contempt.

Taking power

For several years after his election to the town council in 1869, he was content to leave the leadership of the forces for civic reform to Avery.

Preoccupied with the Education League and the school board, Chamberlain stood out otherwise on the council mainly as a spokesman for the alliance between industrialists and organized labour. His first initiative on the council was an ultimately unsuccessful effort to secure enforcement of the Workshops Act.[8] A permissive measure, this Act enabled towns to apply to small workshops the same restrictions on child labour and requirements for schooling that the Factory Acts imposed upon large businesses. Led by two aldermen, Sadler and Brinsley, who represented small business, the council had repeatedly refused to apply the Act to Birmingham, the largest town in the country to do so. Chamberlain challenged this course, in the first place because it damaged the reputation of the town and its council. He was also sensitive, as his father had been, to encroachments upon the rights and wellbeing of children. He pleaded with his fellow councillors to imagine their own children being subject to the demands to which less privileged children were exposed so long as the Act was not enforced. Speaking candidly on behalf of his fellow industrialists, he also pointed out the unfairness of exempting small workshops from requirements which larger businesses had to meet.

Aside from this initiative, Chamberlain kept himself within the confines of Avery's policy, scrutinizing the detail of expenditure closely and discouraging notions of extending the council's sphere of enterprise. It was Avery who initiated the abandonment of his own policy. It would be more true to say that the needs of the town forced the council's hand, for Allday's heirs also proposed drastic action. The difference between the two groups boiled down to a matter of competence. Birmingham and its neighbouring countryside were being smothered by the town's sewage. It piled up in the centre of the town, spreading disease. Primitive sewage farms on the outskirts of the town fouled the air of nearby villages. The one river through the town, the Tame, was little better than an open sewer. After picking up its noxious load in the town, the Tame ran past Ham Hall, the country house of one of Birmingham's more important landed neighbours, Sir Charles Adderley. Adderley had bent over backwards to cooperate with the town in tackling their common problem. But he ran out of patience. Together with the inhabitants of the village of Gravelly Hill, he instigated legal proceedings which forced the town in 1871 to come up with a comprehensive response.

The responsibility fell within the sphere of the council's public works committee. Though dominated by Allday's heirs, particularly the grocer Brinsley and Councillor Briggs, this committee recognized at last that the problem was immense, and therefore did its best to propose an adequate response. The dimensions of their proposal startled the rest of the council into a close examination. The ability of Brinsley and company to frame a solution to a big problem failed to command respect. The council called for the appointment of a special sewage committee, and filled it with new men, including Collings, Harris and Chamberlain, with Avery in the chair. Pleading his work for the National Education League, Chamberlain resigned from the committee. It was Avery's enterprise, and he tackled it with brisk assiduity.

Towards the end of the year, Avery presented a massive report. It humiliated the town by proving that, despite its well-drained elevation and comparatively low population density, Birmingham suffered from a death rate which compared unfavourably with other industrial towns. After bitter debate which crystallized the division of the council, it approved the report of Avery's committee and made it responsible for implementation. Over the next three years Avery and his associates saw to the removal of 14,000 middens and associated cesspools, adopted a temporarily effective pan system for the collection and disposal of the town's sewage, and curbed its outflow into waterways. These actions were enough by 1875 to persuade the Court of Chancery to dismiss the threatened legal proceedings. By then the town's demands were higher than the court's, and the sewage committee was soon critical of its own best efforts.

It was thus Avery who first fleshed out the civic gospel. The debates about sewage in 1871 educated Chamberlain alongside the other reforming councillors. But in spite of its debt to Avery, the emboldened civic movement preferred the voice and sought the leadership of Chamberlain. He found words to inspire, though also to infuriate; and his Radicalism on education and industrial issues captured the civic imagination. His contested reelection to the town council in 1872 raised the temperature of civic debate, and the narrowness of his reelection put friend and foe in fighting spirit. Allday's successors decided to put Alderman Brinsley up for mayor if they regained control of the council at the autumn elections in 1873. Their challenge persuaded the friends of Chamberlain to install him as mayor if they won. Both sides brought their electoral organization to a pitch of perfection. A trinity of Nonconformist ministers, Dawson, Dale and Crosskey, held forth on behalf of Chamberlain, while one Church of England clergyman assured his congregation that the angels were looking eagerly for Chamberlain's defeat. The odds were against his election as mayor because more of his supporters than of his opponents on the council were up for reelection. But Chamberlain's forces smashed their way to victory in every contest but one. The mayoralty was his, despite the angels.

Hard on the heels of the council elections came those for the school board. Since Chamberlain's side stood for exclusion of religious instruction from board schools and no payments to denominational schools, the appeal of his opponents to religion grew feverish. As he reported with wicked delight to Morley after the results came in,

> One Rev[eren]d gent[lema]n said the question really was 'whether the Lord God should rule in the land,' and enquiries are freely made today as to whether the Almighty has sent in his resignation!
>
> One parson declared at a public meeting that the Holy Ghost was on their side—on which 'Three cheers for the Holy Ghost' were called for, and, I believe, given.[9]

Chamberlain and his fellow candidates for the school board polled 291,000 votes to their opponents' 195,000, and the Liberals won the victory that eluded them in 1870. All the levers of political power in Birmingham lay in the hands of civic gospellers.

Gas and water

Yet there was little more they could do to put their aspirations into effect, given the financial constraints within which the government of Birmingham worked. While Avery had improved the town's system of accounts and widened its sphere of action, he had not done anything to broaden its financial base. His sewage scheme had pushed the town to the limits of its public financial resources. Chamberlain discovered a way to extend those limits. Everything else that he did as mayor followed from that discovery.

The supply of gas for the town and nearby villages was generated by two private firms, the Birmingham Gas Light and Coke Company and the Birmingham and Staffordshire Gas Company. Both were profitable. The town council had never seriously considered taking them over, though Manchester had set an example of municipal construction of gasworks as far back as 1817 and Leeds and Glasgow had taken over their local gas companies more recently. Relations between the companies and the town were nevertheless strained over the right of both companies to tear up streets for new mains whenever they chose, and were further strained by arguments in Parliament whenever the companies sought to extend the supply of gas to meet ever rising demand. Sensing the insecurity felt by the companies because of these strains, Chamberlain opened talks with their directors privately in the autumn of 1873, perhaps even before the council elections. He had the outline of a settlement in mind within days of his elevation to the mayoralty.[10] He sketched it out immediately for the general purposes committee, and in mid-January 1874 presented it to the full council.

He asked the council to authorize negotiations for a municipal take-over of the gas companies. The main object of his proposal was not municipal control of the town's gas supply so much as a large increase in the financial resource base for further civic undertakings. He spoke to his fellow councillors as businessmen. He warned them that his proposal would increase the debt of the town fivefold; but he also reminded them that unless they found a way to widen the civic financial base without increasing local taxes, the expenditure they already planned would exceed their resources and exhaust the tolerance of the ratepayers. At the same time he raised the vision of the council by enunciating a cardinal tenet of his creed:

> all monopolies which are sustained in any way by the State ought to be in the hands of the representatives of the people, by whom they should be administered, and to whom their profits should go.[11]

Other towns had set the precedent for civic management of the gas supply, but none of them had elevated their action to this philosophic plane. In doing so, Chamberlain opened a new chapter of municipal government in which town councils, so long the domain of Bumbledom, would become 'real local parliaments, supreme in their special jurisdiction'. Whether compelled by the results of the recent election or by Chamberlain's argument, the council approved his motion by an overwhelming majority of 54 to 2.

Three weeks later, Chamberlain hastened back from his defeat at Sheffield to lead the general purposes committee of the council in working out an agreement with the gas companies. The undertaking was large and the financial arrangements complex. Chamberlain compiled, ordered and indexed all the salient detail in a tiny notebook which came to be known as his pocket pistol. Quick to discern the main point at issue and conciliatory on subordinate points, he won the assent of the companies by assuring them of a good and secure reward for their enterprise. Through close examination of their books and plant, he assured himself that the companies were not embarrassed by debt or diminished in value by dilapidated facilities. In working out the financial arrangements for the takeover, he exploited the ability of the town council to borrow money at a lower rate of interest than private companies could obtain. The boom in metal manufacturing was beginning to fail, but even that suited Chamberlain's purposes because it freed funds in the capital market for civic investment.

He presented the outcome of the negotiations to the council in mid-March. Some dividends of municipal ownership made obvious sense: elimination of duplicate gas mains, for example, and reduction in office staff, though Chamberlain insisted on the need for generous efforts to retain the gas companies' ablest employees. He knew how valuable

Nettlefold and Chamberlain had found its recruits from the firms it took over. The dexterity of the financial arrangements he worked out with the gas companies impressed the commercial managers on the council—who now included his brothers Arthur and Richard as well as Collings and Avery—and dazzled the lesser businessmen. What swept the council away was his assurance that in the first year of municipal ownership the town would reap a profit of at least £15,000. If the demand for gas continued to increase as it had in the past, the annual profit would rise to £50,000 within fourteen years. Convinced by his figures and delighted at the prospect, the council approved the proposal with only one dissenting voice.

Convincing the ratepayers was not so easy. Chamberlain had two meetings scheduled with them, which he convened in the evening rather than at the customary hour of noon so that working men could attend. The first meeting had to deal with an increase in the borough rate which the council had requested for an assortment of services to which they were already committed or wished to commit themselves, including a fire brigade (because the current private brigade declined to go on), an overrun in expenditure by the sewage committee, and a heavy bill for cleaning and repairing the streets which the old public works committee had neglected. Chamberlain approached the meeting apprehensively. His fears were born out when the old alliance of small businessmen and working men threw the recommendation out.

But the old allies were unsure of themselves at the second meeting, where Chamberlain sought approval for his gas proposal. They still gave him a rough time. The magnitude of the commitment made them suspicious. But it also made an increase in the rates unnecessary. He was able to convince some of the doubters by repeating a manoeuvre to which he had resorted on the town council. He made the offer 'that if they will take this bargain and farm it out to me I will pay them £20,000 a year for it, and at the end of 14 years I shall have a snug little fortune of £150,000 or £200,000'.[12] Still sceptical, a third of the ratepayers voted against the proposal when it was put to a poll, but it was approved by a strong majority.

In light of the difficulty he experienced with the ratepayer meetings, Chamberlain was careful to nurse the new alliance of industrialists and trade unionists on which his administration depended. He wooed the trade unions by mobilizing sympathy for the Agricultural Labourers Union. A strike among its members spread rapidly from small beginnings in Suffolk, where farmers claimed that they could not afford to add a shilling to their labourers' paltry wage of thirteen shillings a week. Knowing of Chamberlain's sympathy, Joseph Arch, the union's founder, came to Birmingham to plead for support. Chamberlain placed his mayoral prestige behind Arch's efforts and pressed the Birmingham

Liberal Association to open a subscription fund and conduct a ward-by-ward canvass in support of Arch's union. He also welcomed invitations to arbitrate labour disputes closer to home, first among the miners of Staffordshire and then in the building trades of Birmingham. Successful in these and later cases, he used his achievement to encourage workers to trust their union leaders and at the same time to encourage business-men to treat trade unions as partners in the resolution of industrial disputes, partners who could be especially helpful when depression made wage reductions necessary.

One crucial step remained before the town could take over the gas companies. Parliament had to give its approval; and the committees of inquiry in the two Houses gave opponents abundant opportunity to argue against the measure. Some ratepayers carried their opposition to Westminster; but the main opposition came from the villages the gas companies served around Birmingham. Chamberlain acted in effect as the town's legal counsel, and confounded the opposing lawyers with his command of the subject. At the same time he worked out settle-ments with most of the villages. He hoped initially to get through the parliamentary stage in 1874, but the necessary Act did not reach the statute books for another year. Making sure that he was then elected to the chair of the council's new gas committee, he took quick control of the two companies so that the town could reap their profits for the final third of the year.

Throughout these proceedings, particularly on the town council, he displayed a capacity for soothing as well as expediting debate which surprised those who had known him as an opponent. Once in com-mand, he was a different man. The wit that he had used to wound now lowered the temperature of debate with a laugh, but he could be ruth-less in the chair. Sometimes he made motions and put questions so rapidly that opponents could not find a moment to present their objec-tions, though this behaviour was more admired than resented because it expedited business. When he acted as chairman of the gas committee, his talent for business came into its own. As at Nettlefold and Cham-berlain, so now in charge of a large utility, he won respect from the supervisory staff for his technical understanding of the business, his confidence in subordinates, and his capacity to get things done with a minimum of friction. Also as at Nettlefold and Chamberlain, the work-men in the utility's employ drew palpable benefits from his manage-ment. The stokers at the Saltley works were provided with a suitable mess-room. The gas committee turned ten acres of land it did not need at Nechells into a recreation ground, set up a sick fund for their em-ployees, and put an end to work on Sundays.

The performance of the municipalized gas enterprise exceeded Cham-berlain's predictions. Its profits in its first full year, at £34,000, more than doubled his estimate, and they were almost as great the following year despite improvement in the quality of gas provided and a reduction in price to consumers. The gas committee encouraged consumption by arranging an exhibit of gas stoves in the town hall and showing nearby how well gas lamps could light the streets. Drawing up its accounts in 1884, the committee demonstrated that over the past six years it had netted £785,000 which it had returned to the town either in price reductions or contributions to borough funds. Not till 1886, when the Home Rule crisis tore the Liberals of Birmingham apart, did anyone utter a word of disappointment.

Chamberlain's accomplishments as mayor outshone everything else in his civic career. Yet his work as chairman of the school board touched him more deeply. Moreover, because the school board was able to raise its own rate and could count as well on the generosity of the town council, his imagination ranged even more freely in the sphere of education than on the council. He liked the intimate units of work under the school board; he had a feeling for each school and for the lives of the parents and children who surrounded it. He encouraged local communities to initiate proposals more far-reaching in their implications than anything he felt able on his own to persuade the school board or town council to endorse. Some years back he had started a system to provide the poorest children in one school with dinners; and he now asked another to examine that system with a view to inducing the school board to extend it throughout the town. Speaking at a crèche in Bishopsgate Street, he recognized that many girls were kept out of school to look after the babies of their working mothers, and he urged his audience to draw up a plan for nursery accommodation in connection with every large school. From the chair of the school board, he quadrupled the rate of school construction. Aided by the architect John Henry Chamberlain, he persuaded his colleagues to erect 'great schools for your children, provided lavishly with every appliance for education, provided with ground for the recreation of the children, so that their physical as well as their mental health is cared for'.[13] Rivalling the local churches in grandeur, the spired schools that went up around Birmingham reminded the children of the town 'that the bonds which keep them together as fellow-citizens are stronger than the difference which divides them as members of Christian or other sects'.[14]

A succession of celebrations marked Chamberlain's progress through his year as mayor. Plans had been laid some years earlier for a Council House to take the government of the town from its scattered hole-in-the-corner accommodations into a building that reflected the town's rising aspirations. Chamberlain was happy to lay the cornerstone. But the next great occasion seemed calculated to embarrass him. The Prince of Wales decided to pay Birmingham a visit. People wondered how the republican mayor would receive his royal guest. Though Chamberlain assured his fellow citizens that 'a man might be a gentleman as well as a Republican',[15] the day was awaited apprehensively. But he comported himself through the royal visit with superlative aplomb. Dressed smartly in a brown overcoat, he led the Princess of Wales into the town hall at midday, followed by the Prince with Florence at his arm. Proposing the toast to the royal couple at the luncheon, Chamberlain observed that 'the popularity already enjoyed by the members of the Royal House [is] based quite as much on their hearty sympathy, and frank appreciation of the wishes of the nation, as on their high position and exalted rank'.[16] *The Times* purred approval:

> we do not know that we ever heard or chronicled speeches made before Royal personages by Mayors, whether they were Tories, or Whigs, or Liberals, or Radicals, which were couched in such a tone at once of courteous homage, manly independence, and gentlemanly feeling, which were so perfectly becoming and so much the right thing in every way as those of Mr. Chamberlain.[17]

A week later he was elected for a second year as mayor. Though a breach of custom, his reelection was a foregone conclusion long before his first year was over; and the annual round of elections in November further strengthened his support on the council, bringing in his in-laws the Kenricks. He was transforming the office of mayor. Its previous holders had treated it as a disabling honour that required them to preside impartially over the deliberations of the council like Speakers of the House of Commons. Chamberlain, however, behaved from the outset as prime minister. Divesting himself of his business interests in midyear, he devoted all his energies to the service of the town. The *Birmingham Daily Post* eulogized him as 'one of the most popular men in Birmingham'.

> Mr. Chamberlain has exhibited the qualities which Englishmen generally, and Birmingham men especially, approve—ability in the conduct of business, facility of resource, resoluteness in policy, strength of conviction, courage and frankness in expression of opinion, fidelity to friends, and fairness to opponents.[18]

He was reelected in the expectation that he would turn his attention from gas to water. The water supply of the town had been on his mind together with the gas business from the outset of his mayoralty. Both of these utilities were in private hands, an offence against Chamberlain's precept that public services should be owned by the public and serve only the public interest. The social need to deal with the water supply was more urgent than with gas. Water was essentially a social issue, gas a business investment. But gas was dealt with first because the profits from that business would help the town council to deal with financial problems involved in the business of water.

Successive town councils of Birmingham had been impressed by the desirability of taking over the local water company since mid-century, but finance had barred the way. The ratepayers in 1854 rejected a proposal to purchase the waterworks. Fifteen years later the council itself rejected a plea from Avery for action, deterred by the greatly increased price which the water company was now able to demand for its business. Both the need and the price continued to rise. The local water company was a well-conducted enterprise. It had given Birmingham a constant supply earlier than most towns enjoyed, and the prices it charged were reasonable. But of course it provided better service where customers paid up and costs were low; in other words, the inner city suffered. The need for repairs there and the costs of collection were high. The denizens of the central slums had to choose between drawing water from open wells scarcely distinguishable from sewers and stealing it from the company's taps. Their choice was between disease and prison, and often they found both. Birmingham suffered an epidemic of scarlet fever in 1874 which heightened the demand for action. The only alternative to buying out the company was to close the wells; but to do so would increase the commercial worth of the company by enforcing its monopoly and giving it 24,000 more houses to serve. With such prospects, the company had less desire than ever to sell its business. Nor could Chamberlain dangle the prospect of large profits from consolidation in front of the town. The dividends of a municipal takeover would be social rather than financial: they would take the form of comprehensive provision of service, elimination of a threat to public health, and if possible lower prices for water to ease the burden on the poor.

The reception of the takeover of the waterworks which he proposed at the beginning of his second term bore witness to the magnitude of the change in public sentiment that he had brought about in one year. Despite the absence of financial reward and the prospect of a stiff fight with the company, the town council endorsed Chamberlain's proposal unanimously. A town meeting convened on the subject was so supportive that no one demanded a poll. Birmingham sent its bill to Parliament with evidence of support from every quarter barring the water company itself. Parliament's reception of the bill was equally remarkable. Though the bill trampled on private interests, it swept through both Houses with greater ease than the gas bill, and the two bills passed into law together. Four months of hard negotiation with the water company followed before the detail of the municipal takeover could be concluded. Once the new waterworks committee had the business in hand, it honoured Chamberlain's commitment by extending service and reducing charges.

The death of faith

Some months earlier, Chamberlain's pace at work had come to an abrupt halt. Shortly after the town council gave approval to his plan to buy out the water company, Florence died, as Harriet had, in childbirth. The tragedy struck suddenly and all the harder because of disregarded forewarnings. Giving birth to a child every year or two during her marriage, Florence had never gained a firm hold on life. Large crowds brought her to the point of collapse. She had to withdraw from the procession of the Prince and Princess of Wales before they left Birmingham, and she retired again from the town hall in January when John Bright came to speak. Though her health had not been particularly threatened by her earlier deliveries, there was reason to doubt her stamina for further annual births.

Her fragility was masked by the great pleasure she derived from Chamberlain's public life. Secretary, editor, hostess and counsellor, she became his closest political partner, closer to him than anyone had been before or would be after. She found a meaning for herself from her association with his political work. In the last two years of her life she became 'specially interested in . . . all undertakings for the advancement of women',[19] and encouraged Joseph to support the principle of women's suffrage. She hoped that Joseph would be elected to Parliament, and she looked forward to the political life of London.

Early in February 1875, John Morley and Alfred Illingworth of Bradford came to Birmingham for a rally in the town hall on the issue of disestablishment. They were to stay at Southbourne as Chamberlain's guests. Florence was expecting the birth of her next child imminently, so did not go to the meeting. Feeling suddenly that 'her confinement was at hand',[20] she sent Joseph a note towards the end of the meeting suggesting that he put the visitors off. When he reached home, he found her 'poorly but still cheerful'. She seemed better next morning, and he headed off to spend the day on public business in London. He returned late at night to find the same pattern: depression in the evening, better by morning. After another day of this, a little before midnight Florence gave birth to twins, a son and a daughter. All seemed well despite the strain of the double birth. Anxious none the less, Joseph kept the doctor at Southbourne. At 4:30 the next afternoon, a Valentine's Sunday, the doctor came down from Florence's room to say that she was doing well. A few minutes later, when nurses changed her position in bed, she fainted and quickly died. She was twenty-seven years old. Hours later the infant son followed, to be buried in the coffin with his mother. The daughter, Ethel, survived to grow up hauntingly like her mother in appearance.

The death of Florence ripped Chamberlain up from the roots. Acting quickly while he could still control himself, he arranged for the burial. It was marked 'by an absence of the usual display. The mourners did not wear scarves or hatbands; the hearse was of the plainest description, plumes and other customary ornaments being dispensed with; and the mourners followed the hearse in three private carriages, with drawn blinds.'[21] Then, without waiting for the religious service, he fled the country. He did not say and probably did not know where he was going. Accompanied by his unquestioning friend Collings, he passed through France and ended in Algiers. Back across the Mediterranean in Marseilles by 1 March, he tendered his resignation as mayor and did not give an address where he could be reached. Three weeks later he passed through Birmingham just long enough to pick up his brother Arthur and William Kenrick and headed north to lose himself fishing in Scotland. Beginning to find words, he wrote to Dale, 'There is not a fibre in my whole being which has not been roughly torn asunder.'[22] Thirty-eight years old, father of six young children, unable to ease his mind by sharing his grief, he told another friend, 'I must bear my burden, as best I may,—alone.'[23]

After a while he sought to save himself, as after the death of Harriet, through frantic work. Even in tendering his resignation as mayor, he indicated his willingness to keep up his work on the council and in committee, abandoning only the ceremonial and social functions that mayors were supposed to perform. He was not dismayed when the town council refused to accept his resignation. They offered to relieve him of his ceremonial duties but insisted that only he possessed the knowledge and ability to shepherd the gas and water bills through Parliament and that in doing so he would need to speak as mayor.

His cup of sorrow was not yet drained. Chamberlain's mother died in August approaching the age of seventy. She had not been ill but was depressed by her inability to console her son after his tragic loss. Her death was unexpected and quick. She had been the parent whom Chamberlain most loved, and he was shocked by her death. He broke down at the graveside and again at her house. He tried but could not read out her will. Getting a grip on himself, he spoke in envy of her escape from life and expressed the hope that when his turn came he too would have a sudden death. Unable to look back without pain or forward with pleasure, he penned the words that were to characterize the rest of his life:

Drive on—we shall come to the journey's end in time & perhaps then we shall know where we have been going and whose business we have been doing all the time.[24]

The death of Florence tore Chamberlain loose from the Unitarian religious convictions which, though meagre by orthodox standards, had secured his footing. His minister Crosskey prayed,

> that you may be able to trust the Unseen Goodness, which has been veiled in so fearful a shadow & that the peace which may be hoped to follow the devotion & self surrender of a noble heart may not be denied you.[25]

Chamberlain could not discern the Unseen Goodness, he did not believe in self-surrender, and peace was denied him. Aside from Collings, John Morley was the friend who drew closest to Chamberlain through the dark months that followed the death of Florence. As a positivist whose rejection of orthodox Christianity had cost him dearly, Morley was able to identify himself with Chamberlain's agony and thus confirmed his loss of faith. But while Morley accepted his own loss philosophically, Chamberlain reacted to his with anger. In December Morley described a visit he had from Leslie Stephen, who had also been desolated recently by the death of his wife. Chamberlain replied:

> I am very sorry for Leslie Stephen:—but it is no use—no one can help him, and whatever the future may have in store, the charm of his life is gone and can never be restored. The only thing for him to do is to work double tides—to work constantly and not to think. . . . [This life] is a hideous business and our conception of its end & meaning is thoroughly unsatisfying. . . . I refuse to try & buy comfort by forcing myself into insincere conviction—but still I thoroughly abhor the result at which I have arrived, and I think it a grievous misfortune to have been born into such a destiny.[26]

Chamberlain's anger was slow to cool, and it left him hard. He no longer responded sympathetically to individual misfortunes: 'it seems to me sometimes that no one has a right to be happy in this brutal world'.[27] He turned against the women's movement. Eventually contemptuous of vulnerability to the opposite sex, he was willing to exploit the weakness of other men for women to his own political advantage. He placed his faith in the force of his own will and, when his spirits were high, in his luck. Otherwise he observed with dismissive fatalism that 'it will be all the same 100 years hence'.[28]

Slums and streets

Whatever the bearing between the two events, Chamberlain's first major initiative after the death of Florence was a city-centre redevelopment scheme that warped the balance of his civic gospel. Though in earlier proposals he had always dealt first with the financial considerations, their leading purpose was social betterment: the profits from gas were meant to give the town an adequate supply of pure water. The improvement scheme that he developed in 1875 was still more ambitious, but it was more entrepreneurial than socially reforming in character. At the same time it strained his practice of civic finance. Though he had often argued that calculation of the cost of civic improvements ought to take into consideration the resulting economies for law enforcement and medical care, he had not relied on these indirect benefits to justify his gas and water schemes. Those schemes increased the debt of the town but not the rates it had to levy, and consumers benefited from lower charges. His new improvement scheme, however, increased the load on the rates as well as the debt. Annual income from this investment would not match its annual cost for some years. The ultimate dividend from the investment would be enormous, but not until most people then living in Birmingham were dead. The strain that the improvement scheme imposed upon the town's finances, coupled with its questionable social benefits, dissolved the civic consensus that had formed behind Chamberlain's gas-and-water socialism.

The new scheme was designed to improve the centre of the town in two reciprocal ways: by cleaning up the slums and by turning Birmingham into the metropolis of the Midlands. The slum clearance would justify civic expenditure on the commercial heart of the town, while the revenue from the commercial improvement would help pay for the renovation of the slums. But from the outset the dictates of the commercial side proved stronger than those of housing the needy.

As in many towns, the worst slums of Birmingham overlapped its business centre. There was widespread agreement in Birmingham about where the need for urban renewal was most acute, but the problem seemed too large to tackle. Chamberlain was documenting the problem when Florence died. The key term in dealing with it was sanitation. The word applied in the 1870s to everything that threatened the public health: sewage, scarce privies, contaminated water, bad ventilation, and crowded, crumbling houses. Chamberlain convened a national conference on sanitation in January 1875; and in February a recently formed sanitary committee for Birmingham presented a report that shocked the town. The accumulated information and a venture in urban redevelopment in Glasgow helped to shape an Artisans' Dwellings bill which the Conservative Home Secretary, R.A. Cross, introduced in the House of Commons. Cross welcomed Chamberlain's advice on the bill. Enacted in July, it was thus shaped to meet Birmingham's needs. Chamberlain immediately persuaded the town council to appoint a special improvement committee to make use of the Act. In doing so, he sketched out the scheme that he hoped the council would adopt.

The Act gave the local authorities of large towns power to buy up property without paying additional compensation for compulsory purchase in order to tear down slums and let the land to builders for construction of sound working-class housing and other improvements. Responsibility to set the process in motion was placed upon the local medical officer of health. He was to investigate unhealthy areas within his jurisdiction and submit a report to the town council, which would then prepare a remedial scheme for approval by the Local Government Board in London.

Birmingham's medical officer promptly drew up his report. It bore all the marks of inspiration by Chamberlain. Focusing on the centre of the town, the medical officer documented the sewage-infested and disease-ridden condition of its back-to-back houses and 'pudding bag' courts. But though the focus of his concern was social, his recommendations had notable commercial implications. A maze of streets in the old centre of the town overlay and to some extent produced the slums. 'The principal thoroughfares of Birmingham, adequate to the requirements of the traffic of a past time, are quite insufficient for present needs,' the medical officer observed. He insisted that 'no scheme for the improvement of dwellings can be considered satisfactory which does not provide for ample accommodation by means of wide, well-arranged thoroughfares, combining full capacity for traffic with the power of admitting free currents of air and a sufficiency of sunlight'.[29] Before automobiles arrived to pollute the town with their exhaust fumes, broad thoroughfares could be advocated as 'lungs for ... better ventilation'.[30]

As soon as the medical officer's report was received, the improvement committee was ready with its—or rather Chamberlain's—scheme for presentation to the full council. The scheme was a pilot project for the Act, and the proceedings in Birmingham attracted national attention. *The Times* wrote admiringly of the breadth and boldness of Chamberlain's proposals. The chairman of the improvement committee, White, was councillor for the ward where much of the redevelopment was to take place. He described conditions in the slums with vivid examples: a sitting-room window opening over a midden; a fireplace unusable because of percolation through the back wall from an adjacent toilet; a ceiling fallen down on a child's bed, with water pouring to the room below; snow-water flowing down stairs; people leaving their beds and crowding in with neighbours for fear of falling chimney pots; alleys scarcely wide enough for two people to pass; the death of whole families of children from preventible disease.

Seconding White's presentation to the town council, Chamberlain dwelt on the civic improvement side of the scheme. It would drive a wide boulevard, to be lined with attractive shops and handsome offices, right through the old maze of streets and slums. But he was already defensive. The council had given quick, unanimous approval to his initial motion for the appointment of an improvement committee to implement the Artisans' Dwellings Act. His takeover of the gas and water companies had converted almost the entire council to the civic gospel, whether by persuasion or electoral purging. But the converted council still included a Conservative contingent led by the irreproachable Avery. Avery welcomed the prospect of slum clearance; but Chamberlain's emphasis on commercial thoroughfares disillusioned him and turned him eventually into the scheme's most telling critic. Avery thought of the Artisans' Dwellings Act as proof of the Conservative party's urban conscience. Chamberlain, however, insisted that the Conservative ministers responsible for the Act had assured him that Birmingham's scheme with its combination of slum clearance and commercial development was just the kind of thing they had in mind; and the Home Secretary Cross implied as much when he addressed the Conservatives of Birmingham directly. Chamberlain stressed the value of broad thoroughfares for healthful ventilation. He also pointed out the financial rationale behind the combination of commercial improvement with slum clearance. Not only would a large scheme prove cheaper than the accumulation of a number of small ones; the new shops and office buildings and the business they attracted would increase the town's rate base and hence help to defray the expense of slum clearance.

Chamberlain's civic vision had lost nothing of its capacity to stir the heart. He dwelt on the scandalous rates of disease and death in the central wards of the town, sometimes quadruple those of nearby Edgbaston. Of course the improvement scheme would cost a lot of money, more than the town had been willing to contemplate before.

> The town must pay for this state of things in meal or in malt. We must pay in our health, or with our money. Which is the better—to keep our money, and lose our health, or to keep our health, without which money and life itself are practically valueless?

He went on to preach his secular religion according to which social conditions were the source of sin and legislation the basis for salvation:

> We bring up a population in the dank, dark, dreary, filthy courts and alleys such as are to be found throughout the area which we have selected; we surround them with noxious influences of every kind, and place them under conditions in which the observance of even ordinary decency is impossible; and what is the result? . . . I think Mr. White said the other day that to some extent the position of the people was their own fault, and I heard a cheer when that statement was made;

but I am sure Mr. White only meant that to be true in a very limited sense. Their fault! Yes, it is legally their fault, and when they steal we send them to gaol, and when they commit murder we hang them. But if the members of this Council had been placed under similar conditions—if from infancy we had grown up in the same way—does any one of us believe that he should have run no risk of the gaol or the hangman? For my part, I have not sufficient confidence in my own inherent goodness to believe that anything can make headway against such frightful conditions as those I have described. The fact is, it is no more the fault of these people that they are vicious and intemperate than it is their fault that they are stunted, deformed, debilitated, and diseased. The one is due to the physical atmosphere—the moral atmosphere as necessarily and surely produces the other. Let us remove the conditions, and we may hope to see disease and crime removed.[31]

The council approved the scheme. Chamberlain wanted to set to work immediately on its implementation. When the improvement committee discovered that several months would pass before it could legally purchase any of the intended property, Chamberlain and eighteen other men contributed nearly £60,000—including £10,000 from Chamberlain and £15,000 from his brothers and brother-in-law—to a temporary Improvement Trust. Any losses it incurred were the liability of the trust, any profits would accrue to the town. It was indeed a reflection of the contributors' civic dedication. Later, when Chamberlain had left the mayoralty for the House of Commons, he was always able, when called back, to rally conclusive support for the scheme in the council.

None the less, whether for rate-paying or religious reasons, his precept and practice did not convert the Conservatives. They could not make headway with the town council; but they did all they could to defeat or curtail the scheme in the inquiry by the inspector from the Local Government Board who had to give his approval. They came close to success when they convinced the inspector that the provision in the Artisans' Dwellings Act releasing the council from the need to pay additional compensation for land subjected to compulsory purchase applied only to slum clearance and did not extend to the commercial improvement. Chamberlain regarded that claim as fatal to the whole scheme. Making use of the regard he had acquired with the Conservative ministers at Westminister, he persuaded the President of the Local Government Board in effect to overrule the inspector.

In working out the financial provisions of the scheme, Chamberlain reached new heights of audacity. When the Local Government Board would allow him a 3.5 per cent loan for only 30 years instead of the 60 he wanted, he circumvented the Board with the aid of the Bank of England as well as local financial institutions.[32] He offered leases for only 75 years rather than the customary 99 without conceding the lower prices that Avery claimed would be inevitable. One property owner, when offered £50,000 for land which he wanted to sell for £75,000, settled for £51,000. 'That', Chamberlain exulted, 'is the right way to split a difference!'[33] He performed with equal brilliance as, in effect, the town's attorney during the inquiry by the Local Government Board. Single-handed, he warded off the criticisms of a battery of opposing lawyers.

The commercial side of the scheme was a slow but eventually complete success. Work started in 1878 on the central thoroughfare, Corporation Street as it was to be called, 'Rue Chamberlain' to the scornful. They noted with satisfaction that the trees planted along its borders died and had to be replaced. Something much more serious, economic depression, was descending on the metal-working industries of Birmingham as the scheme was launched. By Chamberlain's estimate, three-quarters of the blast furnaces in the neighbourhood were idled. Bidding for leases on Corporation Street was slow. To move things along, the improvement committee sold land on the farther reaches of the street to the government for the construction of county and assize courts, to the annoyance of solicitors who had to move to be near the new site. The annual burden of the scheme on the rates came to double the £12,000 Chamberlain originally predicted. Projections for the year when revenue from the scheme would exceed expenditure were repeatedly pushed forward. It did not come till 1892. Yet, before then, even critics had to admit that the Italianate terracotta stores and offices along Corporation Street were fulfilling Joseph's dream of Birmingham as the mercantile metropolis of the Midlands.

Critics could still point out that the improvement committee's specification for multistoreyed structures along Corporation Street deprived back streets of the light and air they had been led to expect. It was the slum clearance side of the improvement scheme that justified indictment. Some housing was rehabilitated through enforcement of public health regulations. But this effort led to increased rents. Nearly half of the housing in the condemned districts was demolished either as beyond repair or to make way for street construction; and little of it was replaced. Only sixty-two new houses for working men were built on the site of the old central slums.

To arrange for much more was impossible without violating the canons of even Radical finance. The Artisans' Dwellings Act discouraged local authorities from direct involvement in the construction of buildings. The improvement committee was empowered to purchase and clear land but not to erect buildings on it without special permission from the Local Government Board; and the committee was reluctant to request such permission. Chamberlain urged the council to construct blocks of working-class flats such as proved attractive in Glasgow and

London. They were decidedly cheaper than separate houses. But the council rejected the idea because it violated the entrenched preference of the Birmingham working class for individual houses. The council left the task of replacing the demolished housing to private contractors. The area within the scope of the scheme was more than doubled from 43 to 93 acres to find place for the uprooted families outside the town centre. Land was let to builders at less than market prices. But beyond that the council would not go; and no one challenged the assumption that the housing must be let out at rents which allowed for at least a small profit. From the outset Chamberlain indicated that rents for the new or improved separate houses would be a little higher than for the old. Even so, he was liable to criticism because the rationale for the whole scheme and for the special financial terms that made it possible focused attention on the deplorable condition of many artisans' dwellings.

Ballots and balance sheet

In the autumn of 1875, as the improvement scheme began to break up the consensus in the town council on gas-and-water socialism, the electoral alliance among Birmingham's Liberals between industrialists and labour was also threatened with rupture.[34] Chamberlain met this challenge with the same forceful ambiguity he used to defeat the other.

Buoyed up by its victory in the council elections of 1874, the Liberal Association of Birmingham sought to extend its support within the Church of England. The Association put up an Anglican schoolmaster, the Reverend E.F.M. McCarthy, for one of two seats that became vacant on the school board in 1875. W.J. Davis, the trade unionist who helped secure Chamberlain's reelection to the town council in 1872, observed that it seemed more rewarding to be the Association's foe than its friend. Despite all the trumpeting of the part working men played in the Association, it had yet to nominate a working man for public office. Exasperated, the various associations of labour in the town came together to nominate a candidate of their own, and they put up Davis.

Davis and his working-class backers came close to victory in the three-way race they precipitated for two vacancies on the school board. Voting took place on a weekday during working hours, 9 a.m. to 4 p.m., so that labour had only the lunch hour to marshall their strength. Even so, they marshalled a lot. Chamberlain, who presided over the voting as mayor, saw how strongly the vote for Davis was running. He also observed that a hundred of Davis's assistants were serving as scrutineers in voting stations. Seeking to restore good relations with his erstwhile supporter, he drew Davis aside and suggested that his assistants leave their posts in time to vote. Davis appreciated the advice, though it came too late to be useful. He still garnered nearly 10,000 votes, just 600 less than the successful Conservative.

Thereupon Chamberlain made Davis an offer: 'if you want to be on the School Board, or on the Town Council, come to me. As far as I can see your principles are the same as mine, and you have a following which must eventually be recognised.'[35] Davis responded delphically: 'A Labour Party must and will exist.' His election committee put itself on a permanent footing by turning itself into the Birmingham Labour Association. But Davis was willing to settle for the inclusion of working men in the Liberal Association's slate of nominations for public office.

Chamberlain contested that right in theory but conceded it in practice. He claimed that far from behaving as 'a tyrannous middle-class clique', the Liberal Association followed a policy dictated 'solely by a desire to make the lives of the poor somewhat happier, somewhat more comfortable, and to make their lives nobler and better'.[36] Though all the men who carried out this policy currently were middle class, he argued that they could present themselves as 'the representatives of labour in the truest and highest sense'. He also claimed that the interests of labour were better served by selecting candidates for public office on the basis of individual capacity rather than social class. He preached his political religion in the same terms:

> political issues are the greatest and the noblest issues which can be presented to a constituency. In presence of them all local prejudice, all personal considerations, all selfish interests sink into insignificance, and the higher the issue presented, the better are likely to be the representatives selected.[37]

As it was, he made sure that Davis was elected to the school board in 1876. From then on, working men could count on one or two places on the Liberal slate for the board. Three years later, Chamberlain and Davis gave substance to a semi-formal alliance which the Liberal Association concluded with the Labour Association. When the Labour Association nominated Davis for the town council in Nechells ward, Chamberlain prompted the Liberal Association to refrain from putting up an opposing candidate, and thus in effect gave Davis dual nomination. Chamberlain's eulogy of Davis on this occasion left the labour leader glowing with pride. He demonstrated the worth of the 'Lib-Lab' alliance as he carried the ward against his Conservative opponent by an unprecedented majority.

Though that alliance hinged on Chamberlain, he was also at the centre of 'the tyrannous middle-class clique' that controlled the Liberal Association. While he appreciated the need to conciliate the advocates of independent labour representation, he preferred the victories the Liberal Association won on its own. After the election for poor-law guardians in the spring of 1876 he reported jubilantly to Collings:

> We have had another Liberal triumph & carried the whole Board of Guardians by majorities of 3 to 2. Think of that! A representative body of 60, every manjack a Liberal, & carried in the teeth of the Tories, Roman Catholics, publicans, & Labour League, who nominated an 'Independent List'. This is Liberal tyranny with a vengeance & completes the thing beautifully.[38]

Judged by its civic fruits, that tyranny was a blessing. Gas, water and the improvement scheme did not exhaust its benefits. It was hard to find any corner or institution in Birmingham untouched by reform while Chamberlain was mayor. The report of the sanitation committee which prepared the way for the improvement scheme had other effects. It set the agenda to complete the sanitary reclamation of Birmingham that Avery's sewage committee initiated at the beginning of the decade. The report led to building codes governing the restoration of old housing in the town centre and the construction of new housing elsewhere. The codes were even more controversial than the improvement scheme because they posed a threat to the supply of housing. Some Liberals like Harris were prepared to join forces with Alldayites like Brinsley on this issue. But Chamberlain moved so fast that the town council approved the codes before the opposition knew quite what was happening. Meanwhile the department of the medical officer of health was given a great increase of staff, who proceeded to condemn contaminated wells, contain the spread of infectious diseases, and enforce basic sanitation in private working-class homes. Steps were taken to handle the drainage of the town on a comprehensive basis by combining representatives from all the local authorities in the drainage basin of which Birmingham formed the centre. Street paving was closely related to drainage. Chamberlain ensured that roads were surfaced and pavements laid and the principal open spaces landscaped. Collectively these measures helped to make Birmingham one of the healthiest industrial cities in England.

While Chamberlain's civic policy was thoroughly utilitarian, he thought of cultural refinements and amenities as abundantly useful. Trees, flowers and the Italianate décor of Corporation Street drew customers to the town. He advocated municipal museums of art as temples of the new alliance between industrialist and artisan. He urged national authorities to give special collections of jewels to Birmingham as the jewellery capital of the country rather than to the British Museum in London. He gave £1,000 of his own to start a fund for the purchase of objects of industrial art to stimulate local craftsmen. The working men of Birmingham turned out in remarkable numbers to see the new exhibits when they could; and they supported Chamberlain in his effort, against ratepaying and religious opposition among the middle class, to keep museums open on Sundays. The way his various civic policies dovetailed was nicely illustrated in 1880 when the gas committee found itself office accommodation by constructing a handsome building to house the art gallery and museum on its upper floors, leaving the main floor for the business.

From first to last, his municipal administration was based on productive investment. Well-managed civic investment could reverse the process of urban degeneration without increasing the burden on the ratepayer. The financial policy that Chamberlain inaugurated when he took over the gas companies reached a triumph in his final weeks as mayor when he reduced the rates for the coming year by $6\frac{1}{2}$ pence in the pound. The miracle was produced by clever management of the civic debt. Chamberlain increased the debt of the town enormously in taking over its utilities, and he envisaged the improvement scheme as a step towards municipalization of the land on which the town was built. But each of these investments was designed as much for the wealth as for the power it would bring to local government. Each was designed to be profitable: immediately in the case of gas, marginally for water, ultimately and most handsomely through the improvement scheme. In order to make sure this happened, he required each municipal enterprise to keep its own books and account for its own debt. He secured the lowest possible interest rates on the loans the town took out to pay for each investment. Eventually he handed the task of debt management over to a new man on the town council, Powell Williams, who became chairman of the finance committee. Powell Williams worked to convert and consolidate the town's debt to minimize the annual charge. He achieved his goal in 1880–1 with assistance from Chamberlain, by then in the cabinet, through parliamentary legislation.

Chamberlain's civic investments—larger, he boasted, than Britain's purchase of controlling shares in the Suez canal—won admiration from men in Birmingham who liked to pride themselves on their enterprise. His bravura performance earned him an almost invincible ascendancy over the town. Few could resist his magic face to face. He was reelected to the mayoralty in the autumn of 1875 for a third term with the votes of 58 of the 64 members of the town council. By the beginning of the new year he possessed 'almost despotic authority'.[39] He conveyed the character of his ascendancy in a report to Collings:

> We have just had a splendid Council meeting—£250,000 voted—one Park given and another bought—a Chief of Police elected—a Gas Re-

port approved, and not a single division all the afternoon. Brinsley was heard to say . . .'The Mayor's been a-doing this, and *he* can carry anything of course'. . . .

Lastly came the Report of the Public Works Committee with 12 resolutions—among them recommendations that *all* unsewered streets should be at once sewered—that *all* footpaths in the Borough should be paved as quickly as possible, the work to cost £150,000 and the time not to exceed 5 years. . . . Avery objected to the Terms of the resolutions which authorised the Committee to spend £30,000 a year on foot paving for the next 5 years—whereupon I urged that it erred only in not going far enough and the Council at once inserted the words *at least* before the amount of £30,000 a year, and the resolution as amended was carried unanimously before Avery had time to recover from his astonishment.[40]

This dazzling performance had its shadows. The cliquishness of Chamberlain's close associates gave persistent offence. They formed a society named the Arts Club for themselves, with membership limited to seventy-five, all necessarily Liberals. The Conservatives and small masters who resented their exclusion from the centre of power almost welcomed the economic depression that began to descend upon the region. They waited for it to discredit Chamberlain's fiscal calculations; and they did not wait in vain. Uncanny in his luck, he left the mayoralty in 1876 before the improvement scheme took effect, and he left the town council in 1880 before depression affected the gas business. His lieutenants on the council during the 1880s imposed a cautious interpretation upon the general policy he laid down in the 1870s.

Yet even cautiously interpreted, his policy established higher standards of service and more resourceful patterns of financial management for Birmingham. Furthermore, his gift of speech and talent for advertising or propaganda made Birmingham the model for national emulation. During his second term as mayor, the practitioners of his gospel in Birmingham laid plans to enshrine it by turning the stretch of land between the town hall and the Council House into Chamberlain Square. A fountain was to stand at the centre of the square to symbolize Chamberlain's takeover of the water company. John Henry Chamberlain designed the fountain in the Venetian Gothic style he used for the board schools, which were as characteristic of Birmingham as Wren churches were of London. Joseph opened Chamberlain Square shortly after his resignation from the town council to take up high national office.

5

Organizational Innovation
1876–1880

> ...it is another step towards the fulfilment of my destiny—another
> chapter of my life, and while I do not greatly care how soon the last
> one comes, I like the story to keep moving.
>
> Chamberlain to Collings, 30 June 1876, on his election to Parliament

Chamberlain had accomplished a great deal as mayor of Birmingham.
The policy that he worked out combined industrialists and their associates from the professions, including the leading Nonconformist ministers together with organized labour, in an alliance which addressed
palpable needs of the town and established guidelines for future civic
action. This accomplishment raised hope of similar possibilities in the
national arena. At that level, however, constructive success was to elude
Chamberlain. As in the agitation of the Education League, so in parliamentary politics, he could not recreate the Radical alliance which
served him so well at the civic level. Nor did he display the same grasp
of the problems which Britain encountered at home and abroad in the
first phase of the 'Great Depression' as he had shown in handling the
problems of his industrial city at the end of the Victorian boom. Es-
chewing nevertheless any suggestion of uncertainty, he plunged into
the national arena with all the daring and some of the originality which
he had exhibited in municipal politics. He floundered forcefully.

In one corner of the political game, he played with success as well as
originality. Applying one of the distinguishing talents of industrial entrepreneurship, Chamberlain resorted to organizational innovation to
compensate for his lack of parliamentary support and acute policy proposals. The network of constituency organizations which he put together contributed less to the electoral recovery of the Liberals than he
liked to claim. It nevertheless mobilized support for the party in the
provincial towns of England, and thus forwarded his own political
ambitions.

In the first few years after he entered Parliament Chamberlain was
more concerned with the mobilization of popular electoral power than

with the use to which that power might be put. He was candidly opportunistic in choosing policies likely to rouse public support. Such
behaviour looks unprincipled; and at a deep level, after the death of
Florence, he was indeed rootless. Yet during his first years in Parliament few people accused him of being entirely self-interested. His personal ambition was always obvious, but it worried critics all the more
because it was harnessed to advanced Radical purposes and restless
social interests.

Chamberlain entered Parliament at a moment of national tranquillity perplexing to a Radical. The Conservative reaction embodied
by Disraeli's victory in the general election at the beginning of 1874
deepened in the ensuing months. Richard Cross, the new home
secretary, reduced discontent among the trade unions by granting
them all they wanted by way of legal protection; and he directed
the zeal of urban reformers into safe channels by pushing several
enabling measures through Parliament, including the Artisans' Dwellings Act that made the Birmingham improvement scheme possible.
The political waters remained utterly calm at the national level.
Chamberlain and Morley complained that '[a]t Bristol, at Bradford,
at Sheffield, at Manchester, at Edinburgh, we are told half-a-
dozen times in the month by Liberal chiefs and Conservative chiefs,
that time is slumbering, the nation contented, the constituencies
lethargic'.[1]

The economic depression that began in 1873 deepened. Chamberlain
did not have a ready prescription for the unfamiliar ills which the
economy developed, nor did he find the political implications of the
depression easy to gauge. 'I never knew the commercial prospect so
bad as it is at this moment,' he confessed in 1878, '& I cannot see from
what quarter or when relief is to come.'[2] The gloomy economic outlook
deepened Conservative nervousness among the middle class. Falling
revenue from national taxation convinced Chamberlain that local reformers could not expect financial backing from Westminster for further
initiatives. Gas-and-water socialists were too hard pressed at the local
level to encourage or think up anything countrywide. The depression in
commerce and industry was intensified for agriculture by bad harvests.
Yet it did not deepen far enough in the 1870s to produce threatening
social discontent in Britain. In Ireland, on the other hand, agrarian unrest grew alarming. The issues over which the British public therefore
became agitated lay outside their own shores, across the Irish Sea and
beyond. The depression at home drew some attention to the markets
abroad which Britain was losing to competition from the rising industrial powers of the United States and Germany. Even so, the overseas
events which roused the British had little directly to do with their depressed economy.

Chamberlain was elected to the House of Commons just before a tempest erupted in Britain over foreign policy. Shaped and still absorbed by domestic issues, he did not readily see his way forward in the foreign debate. He was nevertheless quick to appreciate the usefulness of the agitation, for it roused the energy of discontent and could be linked to the Radical cause. In informal alliance with Gladstone, Chamberlain showed Liberals how to harness this energy and ride to victory. But the object of this venture, the use to which electoral victory would be put, was left undefined. Lacking essential connection with the industrial society he understood so well in Birmingham, the enterprise of national Radicalism upon which Chamberlain embarked after his election to Parliament was largely a matter of party mobilization and tactics. It gained high visibility and a gratifying measure of political success, but its roots were shallow.

Probation

Chamberlain had hoped to combine the positions of mayor of Birmingham and Member of Parliament for Sheffield. When Sheffield denied him the opportunity, he devoted himself to Birmingham until 'the time of reaction' should give way to 'the revolutionary period which I expect to follow'.[3] He could not meanwhile hide his disappointment at exclusion from Parliament. But during his second term as mayor, with the takeover of gas and water in train and the improvement scheme in mind, his estimate of the comparative importance of municipal and imperial government shifted towards the municipal. Birmingham gave him the eager support he always craved; and he was impressed by how much good he could do for the four hundred thousand citizens of his town. Florence had looked forward to the conversation around Westminster; but after she died, it was the Birmingham town council that called him back from his flight.

John Morley beckoned him towards London. Gas-and-water socialism in the grimy West Midlands did not suit Morley. 'Don't wear yourself out over the sewage question,' he had advised the provincial mayor.[4] He valued Chamberlain's reputation in local government mainly because it raised him in national esteem. Morley wanted Chamberlain to enter the House of Commons at the earliest opportunity, while the Liberals were in opposition: 'It would give you a better chance of making your individuality tell than when the party gets back into power again, and the party chiefs will have prestige at their backs against independent men.'[5]

Chamberlain still longed to enter Parliament. The prestige it offered and the vistas it opened were irresistible for any man with political ambition. But he found it increasingly difficult to think of dividing his loyalties between Birmingham and any other parliamentary constituency. In the spring of 1875 he was offered the possibility of standing for election at Norwich, usually a Liberal town. He placed the decision in the hands of his closest Birmingham lieutenants. When Collings insisted on the primacy of his duty as mayor, Chamberlain turned Norwich down—and thus put Birmingham still more deeply in his debt.

Meanwhile he strove to make himself a force in national Liberal politics without a seat in the Commons. Taking advantage of his friendship with Morley, he used the *Fortnightly Review* to set 'the next page of the Liberal programme'[6] when the first session of Disraeli's Parliament came to an end. Demoralized by defeat in the general election, the Liberals were inclined to lie quiet, in harmony with the evident mood of the country. This timidity angered Chamberlain to sharpen his Radical attack on the moral complacency of moderate Liberalism. He insisted that

> more can be done ... by Act of Parliament ... than by all the private charity and individual beneficence of the upper and middle classes ... a complete system of national education would secure infinitely greater moral and religious progress than all the missions in existence ... the abolition of the Game Laws would do more to reduce the number of criminals than the Howard Association can ever hope to accomplish; and ... anything which would tend by natural causes to a more equal distribution of wealth would go farther to secure the greatest happiness of the greatest number, than all the provident and benefit societies which have ever been started by those who have no need to practise thrift for the benefit of those who have no opportunity.[7]

All that he received for his literary pains was a howl of denunciation from Liberal as well as Conservative editors. 'Cultivate a thick skin and a cool temper,' Morley advised his friend, 'for you will have much need of both before you have done.'[8]

Chamberlain's words nevertheless lifted the spirits of discontented Radicals and kept the parliamentary Liberal party at least dimly aware of a body of provincial opinion which it might be costly to neglect. He therefore proved surprisingly effective during a crisis in the highest councils of the Liberal party, though he was known there only by reputation.

At the beginning of 1875 Gladstone resigned the leadership of the Liberal opposition. Uninterested in the quarrels of a parliamentary party without popular wind in its sails, he sought consolation in religious debate and attacked the claim of Pius IX to papal infallibility. Gladstone's preoccupation with denominational controversy filled Chamberlain with contempt. Writing for publication, he declared that 'an ex-Minister of the first rank who devotes his leisure to the critical examination of the querulousness of an aged Priest is hardly in sympathy with the robust common sense of English Liberalism'.[9] Morley thought that Radicals should hold aloof from the contest for the succession to Gladstone with an ostentatious display of indifference. No genuine Radical could hope to win the leadership in the Commons, where the contest was between a Whig, Lord Hartington, heir to the duchy of Devonshire, and that enemy of the National Education League, W.E. Forster. Morley was not even certain whether affiliation with the Liberal party was a source of strength or weakness to the Radicals.

Chamberlain shared that doubt. But he had found the sentiment of attachment to the Liberal party to be useful in local politics. He hoped to use the same sentiment among Whigs at the national level to induce them to treat the Radicals with tolerant compliance. His desire, furthermore, to stop Forster from becoming leader was intense. Forster still refused even the slightest concession to the National Education League. More generally Forster, as an erstwhile Radical who had never quite forsworn that allegiance, posed a greater threat than any Whig for Chamberlain because Forster could claim to reflect the various factions that the party needed to encompass. Chamberlain therefore attacked Forster's candidacy in a paper free from Morley's control, the *Examiner*. The executive of the National Education League endorsed Chamberlain's stand. Though his rivals in the League and outside Birmingham, like Mundella of Sheffield, favoured Forster, Chamberlain out-trumped them by securing the support of John Bright. Bright presided over the meeting of Liberal Members of Parliament convened to decide on the leadership; and Hartington was elected without dissent.

Chamberlain claimed that he had 'helped more than most—perhaps more than any—to secure Lord Hartington's selection as leader by rendering Forster an impossible candidate'.[10] Though exaggerated, there was a kernel of truth to the claim. Chamberlain's opposition had not only damaged Forster. It also underscored the chief attraction of Hartington as the candidate who did not alienate any section of the party. Hartington was the quintessential Whig, conservative by personal inclination but willing under pressure to accommodate factions more advanced than himself. Chamberlain let Hartington know that the Radicals 'did not expect or want him to accept our views or swallow our programme just yet, but we did hope that he would throw no obstacles in our way & say nothing *against* us'. On those conditions Chamberlain assured him that 'he would find us loyal allies for all questions on which we were agreed & not factious in pressing those on which we differ'.[11] And for a while Hartington lived up to these expectations. Towards the end of his first year as leader, Chamberlain tried to explain to one Radical sceptic how 'we may yet get the important support of

the Whig families for the most radical measures . . . in our modern warfare the General takes up his position in the rear of the Army'.[12]

The broader prospect

The effect of Chamberlain's intervention over the leadership in the
Commons even before he was a member encouraged his national ambitions and led him into spheres of policy debate for which he had no
compass.

In the autumn of 1875, after securing a good reception from the town
council for his improvement scheme, Chamberlain went with Morley to
Paris for a week's holiday. The conversation of the editor and the widowed mayor turned from the spare consolations of agnosticism to the
void-filling activity of public service. Combining their talents, they devised a plan to quicken the pace of debate in England. They were
clearer about the means they would employ to stir up the public than
about what they would say. Chamberlain placed a high estimate on the
influence of the press. Morley offered to write the regular commentary
in the *Fortnightly Review* on 'Home and foreign affairs' in concert with
Chamberlain. Chamberlain, who had ready access to the public platform, undertook to issue pronouncements which the *Fortnightly* could
dwell upon. As for the content of this coordinated effort, the two men
agreed to meet and correspond frequently to discuss the flow of events.
Morley would contribute his talent for philosophic commentary, but
their point of reference, at least as Chamberlain saw it, would be the
precepts and practice of 'the Birmingham school of politicians'.[13]

Disestablishment and disendowment of the Church of England was
to be their central demand. But they did not envisage another single-
issue crusade like that of the Education League. Worried generally
about those often religious enthusiasts who insisted on their particular
cause regardless of its bearing on the Radical cause as a whole, Chamberlain and Morley prided themselves on their 'keen sense of the proportion of things'.[14] They did not think many other people saw things
as clearly as they; Chamberlain put the number at no more than four or
five. The movement they hoped to stimulate was not at all democratic
in its inception, but they hoped to see it gather popular force through
their use of the means of popular persuasion.

Upon his return from Paris to Birmingham, Chamberlain shaped his
speaking engagements as the two men had agreed. He had a standing
invitation from H.J. Wilson to speak at Sheffield whenever he was able
to do so on whatever subject he liked. Seizing the opportunity, he outlined the plan to Wilson and arranged to deliver a major address just
after the other monthly periodicals for December had gone to press, so
that Morley could focus on it in the *Fortnightly*.

This first effort proved disappointing. The speech passed largely unnoticed in London. The provincial papers that commented on it did so critically. Even Morley was uneasy about the look of the speech in print. Annoyed by this reception, Chamberlain lashed out at the press and, beyond it, at the inert, unprocessed public opinion which he wanted to shape. Morley alone escaped his denunciation:

> you have resisted what seems to me the fatal influence of so-called public opinion, i.e. the opinion of ill informed & commonplace people translated and transfigured by the unrivalled literary expression given to it by the writers in the London Press. These writers have ceased to form opinion—they sometimes stereotype it, but more often mirror its fleeting shape, giving it a glamour which conceals its original crudeness and vulgarity.[15]

Soon afterwards Chamberlain thought he discerned a ripple on the surface of public opinion. To his surprise, the breeze originated from overseas. In drawing up their plans for the monthly review of home and foreign affairs in the *Fortnightly*, Morley and he had decided to leave the foreign section to a Parisian journalist. No sooner had they done so than English interest in foreign affairs quickened with Disraeli's irregular purchase of controlling shares in the Suez Canal. Chamberlain ruefully admired this stroke as evidence that the Conservative government was bolder than its Liberal predecessor. At Sheffield he had praised the Artisans' Dwellings Act of the Conservatives as giving effect for almost the first time to the principle that 'the claims of great communities [could be] superior to individual rights and the sacred rights of property'.[16] 'Why then attempt to recall [the Liberals] to power?' he asked Morley after Disraeli's Suez coup was announced; 'Up to the present time it would clearly have been a change for the worse.'[17]

Morley was more critical than Chamberlain about the Suez purchase. But the two men switched sides on foreign affairs at the beginning of the new year. 1876 was to be momentous in foreign policy. A few months earlier the Admiralty had issued a circular directing British ships in territorial waters off the east coast of Africa to surrender to the bordering states any fugitive slaves who came aboard seeking British protection. Disraeli, recognizing the affront to anti-slavery sentiment in England, suspended and then cancelled the circular when it came to his attention, but not before it had provoked a reaction in the provinces. This sentimental movement repelled Morley. But Chamberlain welcomed it as

> wholly good & sound . . . prompted by hatred of injustice & cruelty. . . . If we are to stand aloof, contemptuously pitying the popular ignorance, whenever any great passion stirs the public mind, be-

cause the ordinary local politician does not take account of all the minor issues involved, we shall soon get to the cynical frame of mind of the [metropolitan Conservative journals] and join them in expressing our scorn of the charlatans of politics and those nuisances, the reformers.[18]

The surge of popular sentiment quickly subsided. Chamberlain turned back to domestic issues; and he reacted with contempt to Liberal MPs who protested against Disraeli's bill proclaiming Queen Victoria as Empress of India—'as if it mattered a straw to any one'—while these same Liberals were 'perfectly apathetic on all questions of real importance to the welfare of the people'.[19]

In the early months of 1876 he was strained by municipal work and exasperated by George Dixon's vacillation over his seat in Parliament. Dixon's wife was not well, he had talked for some time about resigning as MP for Birmingham, and at the beginning of the year he again suggested doing so. Here was just the seat Chamberlain wanted. But at the moment he was immersed in the implementation of his civic plans. His friends worried that he was overburdening himself, and his doctor ordered him away to recuperate. The inner group at the Arts Club who controlled the political fortunes of Birmingham therefore arranged for Dixon to defer his resignation for two or three months until Chamberlain could set his civic ventures rolling along their intended tracks. This well-intended arrangement only increased the pace of business on the town council in the first third of the year. In the midst of the rush Dixon began to waver about resigning. His chief political commitment was to education; and in February the Conservative government introduced a measure to amend the Act of 1870. This development made Dixon reluctant to retire, at least until the House of Commons had completed action on the bill; and that date kept being pushed on.

In July Chamberlain would turn forty. Though ambivalent about the relative merits of the work done by municipal and imperial legislatures, he knew that he would never be able to learn the ways of the House of Commons in time to make his mark there if he waited any longer for entry. He had other opportunities for election. The Radicals of Sheffield still wanted him, and the Portsmouth Liberal Association asked him to stand. But Birmingham's response to his mayoralty made him unwilling to contemplate representing any other town in Parliament. Other offers simply deepened his irritation at Dixon's dilly-dallying.

Responsive to Chamberlain's impatience, throughout the spring his lieutenants pressed Dixon to retire. At last, early in June, Bunce forced Dixon's hand by announcing his intended retirement in the *Birmingham Daily Post*; and Dixon duly submitted his resignation. To compensate him, it was agreed that Chamberlain would surrender the chairmanship of Birmingham's school board to Dixon at the next local elections in November. Even so, Dixon let it be known that he had been harried to make the change; and his friends resented his treatment. Chamberlain too felt some bitterness. He had to resign as mayor in order to facilitate the issuing of a writ for the by-election. Though he had realized that entry into Parliament would involve some diminution of his municipal work, he hated to give up the office he had learned to love.

He snapped under the accumulating strain. Provoked by Conservative opposition at the Birmingham school board early in June, he denounced Disraeli as 'a man who went down to the House of Commons and flung at the British Parliament the first lie that entered his head'.[20] Though a crude comment, it would have passed unnoticed if Chamberlain had been a figure of only local significance. As it was, the national press, Liberal as well as Conservative, denounced him. Privately Disraeli matched Chamberlain in abuse, describing his attack as what 'you might expect from the cad of an omnibus'.[21] Chamberlain wrote a letter of apology for publication, hoping 'that it may be accepted as an extenuation of an unwilling offence that I have been greatly overworked lately'.[22] His offending outburst at the school board allowed local resentment at the treatment of Dixon to surface. Moving a resolution of thanks to him at the meeting of the Liberal Association that approved Chamberlain for the parliamentary vacancy, R.W. Dale observed that in the heat of conflict Dixon had never uttered 'words which either he or his friends had occasion to regret or apologise for'.[23]

The populace of Birmingham, however, forgave Chamberlain quickly. Indeed, they seemed almost to sympathize with their champion's lapse of temper. They gave him a thunderous welcome in Bingley Hall after the election, which was uncontested; and he rose to the occasion. He concluded his address with an assertion of his claim to speak for working men:

> No man can sit for Birmingham who does not represent the working classes, which form four-fifths of this great constituency. I, therefore, refuse altogether to consider myself as in any sense the representative of middle-class interests . . . the working classes have much to ask, and much to gain from legislation: and although I do not believe that their interests are antagonistic to those of any other section of the community, because the welfare and security of the whole depend upon the contentment and happiness of every part; yet, as I share their hopes and aspirations, I claim, till you withdraw the privilege, to speak on their behalf and in their name and yours to plead their cause.[24]

Next day, he came down with gout. His doctors informed him that the disease was 'always preceded by great nervous disturbance & depression'.[25] That helped to account for his irritability over the past month; and he laughed at himself for acquiring the disease of statesmen the moment he was elected to Parliament.

Departure and debut

The gout was slow to loosen its grip. Forced to delay his entry to Parliament for two weeks, Chamberlain sank back in depression. 'I have broken with my old life,' he wrote to Collings,

> and have as yet no interest in or hope of my future—everything reminds me of what might have been and recalls my present loneliness. I can neither look back nor forward with any satisfaction & I have lost the dogged endurance which has sustained me so long.[26]

Morley took the train to Birmingham to raise his friend's spirits, and returned to London haunted by 'the picture of you sitting alone in your garden'.[27]

Though Chamberlain recognized that his 'miserable view of things [was] partly due to physical causes', it was a fair reflection of the wrenching passage he was going through. He kept thinking of Florence and of what she would have meant as he entered his new life. Bleakly he ordered rooms for himself in the Westminster Palace Hotel and made plans to find Morley somewhere close to the Commons chamber as soon as he had taken his seat. Leaving the mayoralty for membership in the House of Commons tore Chamberlain from his roots. Though a Londoner by birth, Birmingham had become his home by a kind of baptismal immersion. He knew, as only someone who had come in from outside could know, how citizens of Birmingham earned their living, how they competed and collaborated, argued and worshipped, smoked and laughed and cried. He remained on the town council as an alderman and was pleased to be asked to stay on the gas, improvement and health committees: 'I shall not be quite cut off from my old friends or my old work.'[28]

The circles that he was about to enter in the city of his birth, on the other hand, were alien to him. He no longer knew Camberwell or Islington intimately; and in any case it was not to Camberwell or Islington that he was headed, but to Westminster. The House of Commons, which took pride in itself as the school for statesmen, looked with jaundiced eye on the presumptuous provincial mayor. The Commons furthermore, to say nothing of the Lords, was composed overwhelmingly of members of the landed class and their professional associates. Though they had welcomed bankers and brewers to their midst, manufacturers were still uncomfortably rare, particularly on the front benches. Few industrialists had amassed enough wealth fast enough to devote themselves to public service. Chamberlain might look like a gentleman, immaculately attired as he was and sporting a monocle instead of middle-class spectacles. The modulation of his voice, the cultured accent he had acquired from his mother's family and the Kenricks, and his good judgement in adopting a conversational rather than hectoring manner of speech in the Commons helped him 'catch the ear' of the House. All the same, he bore a clear though invisible stigma as a metal manufacturer. The liability was more than cultural. His familiarity with industry in the West Midlands warped his understanding of the more complex social economy of Britain. Chamberlain sensed his ignorance. He came to London without even an outline of a Radical programme for the country.

His career in Parliament began inauspiciously when he violated the custom of the House by wearing his hat before he was sworn in. Otherwise he comported himself with circumspection, observing the ways of the House and acquainting himself with other Radicals. His native aggressiveness was none the less soon detectable. At dinner with Forster, he found '[t]he old baboon . . . immensely civil', but responded by 'trying to get up an attack upon his educational policy'.[29] Before the month was out, he was trying to combine half a dozen Radicals in or closely associated with the House of Commons into a unified assault force, ready to make 'a devil of a row' in the next year's session with 'strings of notices for Bills & resolutions'.[30]

He enjoyed some quick success in his conflict with Forster. The two men embodied antithetical strategies of Liberal persuasion. Forster was primarily concerned with opinion in the House of Commons, which he sought to impress by presenting his own view but then acquiescing if the majority remained unpersuaded. Chamberlain was primarily concerned with Radical opinion in the constituencies, which he wanted the parliamentary party to treat as its unseen audience and jury. The House was in the final stages of debate on the Conservatives' Education bill. Forster criticized it persistently but intended to let its final reading pass without pressing his opposition to a vote. Chamberlain insisted that the constituencies would regard this course of action as inexplicable and even discreditable. He arranged for a deputation from Liberal associations like Birmingham's to urge Hartington as leader to divide the House against the bill when it came up for the last time. Hartington agreed, and Forster felt obliged to fall into line.

This little victory encouraged Chamberlain to deliver his first speech in the Commons. It amounted to another attack on Forster, this time for supporting a motion to make permanent provision for the payment of school fees for poor children in denominational institutions. The House was pleasantly surprised, not by the substance of Chamberlain's re-

marks, but by his agreeable manner of speaking. He was not the rasp-
ing firebrand they expected. As for Chamberlain himself, he 'felt as cool
& comfortable from the first as if I were addressing my own Council'.[31]

Once the session came to an end, Chamberlain and Collings headed
for the northernmost stretches of Sweden on their way to Lapland. On
returning to England, Chamberlain found the pulse of the public quickened by events in another remote corner of Europe, at the way in which
the Ottoman empire suppressed a rebellion among its Christian subjects
in Bulgaria. Reaction to the atrocities was stronger in the English provinces than in London, and it received early expression in Birmingham.
Chamberlain did not entirely share the feeling himself, though he welcomed the agitation because it embarrassed the Conservative government, whose support for the Ottoman empire had encouraged it to
suppress its dissidents. 'What a hole Dizzy has put his Party into!'[32]

The support which Chamberlain gave the agitation earned him a
great, unanticipated dividend. It enabled him to construct an alliance
with Gladstone. Though neither man was among the first to sense the
significance of the agitation, both were looking for a movement of
popular as distinct from parliamentary opinion to restore their political
hopes. Shortly before Chamberlain returned from Sweden, Gladstone
issued a pamphlet, *Bulgarian Horrors and the Question of the East*. Written
in the language of lofty indignation, it could not be reprinted fast
enough to keep up with demand. The pamphlet heightened the agitation; and the public was further stirred by Gladstone's return to the
political fray.

Chamberlain welcomed both sources of excitement. He called immediately for Gladstone's restoration to the leadership of the Liberal party.
Chamberlain calculated that the return of Gladstone, at nearly seventy
years of age, to the leadership could not last more than a few years, and
during that time he would probably do more for the Radicals than they
could expect from Hartington. Radical domestic purposes continued to
dominate Chamberlain's thoughts; as yet he cared little about the issues
of foreign policy raised by the Bulgarian atrocities agitation, and he discussed them without insight. While denouncing Forster, who as usual
sought for a consensual policy on this subject, Chamberlain had little to
say himself about what the government should do. Far from regarding
Disraeli and his colleagues as hopeless sinners, Chamberlain feared that
they might modify their policy to coincide with the popular will.[33] Enthusiasts on both sides depicted the controversy as a stark choice between the interests of England, identified in this case with Turkish
rather than Russian possession of Constantinople as a crucial link between England and India, and the dictates of morality, which seemed to
require support for the Balkan Christians in cooperation with Russia

against the Turk. Chamberlain evaded the choice by arguing that, regardless of who controlled Constantinople, Britain could maintain its links with India by relying either on Malta or upon Egypt, where British power had been strengthened by the recent purchase of the Suez canal shares: surely, he remarked, 'we did not throw away four millions of money merely for a Stock Exchange speculation'.[34]

His lack of finesse in the discussions of foreign policy which surrounded the opening of Parliament in 1877 was offset by his deepening friendship with Sir Charles Dilke. The band of Radicals in the House of Commons whom Chamberlain tried to rally in the summer of 1876 quickly dwindled to this one. Dilke and Chamberlain made a strange pair. A baronet whose grandfather Disraeli had admired, Dilke moved with ease among the governing elite of France as well as England. His Radicalism was none the less native to him, descended as he was from no less than three men who had condemned Charles I to death. Both Dilke and Chamberlain were avid travellers; but while Chamberlain's travels had been confined to Europe, Dilke had circled the globe in pursuit of the English diaspora. While Chamberlain had used his travels to make his fortune in overseas sales of screws, Dilke had described his travels in a work entitled *Greater Britain* that marked him out as a herald of Liberal imperialism. Six years younger than Chamberlain and elected to Parliament eight years before him, Dilke commanded respect in the Commons on matters of foreign policy. The two men had one experience in common: both were recent widowers shaken by their bereavement. Still, politically they came from different worlds, different but possibly complementary. Dilke offered Chamberlain familiarity with the corridors of power. Chamberlain offered Dilke familiarity with England's industrial electorate. Dilke did much to overcome Chamberlain's sense of alienation in London; he offered to share his home in London with Chamberlain while Parliament was in session, an invitation Chamberlain periodically accepted; and he introduced Chamberlain to the highest circles of the governing elite. 'I am keeping very good Company here,' Chamberlain reported back to Birmingham; 'Last week I dined with the Prince of Wales & next week I am to dine with Earl Granville',[35] Liberal leader in the House of Lords.

Dilke gave Chamberlain a taste of parliamentary power at the beginning of 1877. Through the mediation of Sir William Harcourt, Dilke persuaded Lord Hartington to stiffen his line on the Eastern question in order to conciliate Chamberlain. Puffed up with pleasure, Chamberlain reported to Birmingham that 'the Front Opp[ositio]n. Bench have decided to adopt "my policy" . . . viz. go in for [a] concert of Powers to compel Turkey, by war if necessary, to grant proper security to [the Chris]tian provinces'.[36] However exaggerated, this accomplishment ce-

mented the parliamentary partnership between Chamberlain and Dilke.
'He is a rising man, personally popular in the House and with more of
the true spirit and principle of Liberalism in him than anyone else here,'
Chamberlain told Bunce of the *Birmingham Daily Post*; 'I expect we shall
always be found in the same lobby.'[37] Under Dilke's tutelage, Chamberlain gave some mind to considerations on foreign policy beyond the
reflexes of provincial Radicalism. 'I have read the B[lue]. Book [on]
Turkey carefully and *at present* do not see my way to speak,' he reported with new diffidence to Morley; 'it is like dancing on eggs.'[38]

The making of the National Liberal Federation

Russia went to war with Turkey in April 1877 on behalf of the Orthodox Christians in the Ottoman empire's Balkan provinces, and in doing
so threatened Constantinople. These events abroad intersected with
Chamberlain's plans at home to transform the electoral organization of
the Liberal party nationally through a federation combining features
of the Birmingham Liberal Association and the National Education
League. The developments at home and abroad drew Gladstone and
Chamberlain together in an effort to make the Liberal party in Parliament more responsive to the Liberal electorate.

Ever since 1873, when the failure of the Education League to make an
impression on Gladstone's ministry became obvious, Chamberlain had
contemplated turning the League into an organization on a broader
base with wider objectives. The victory of the Conservatives in the general election of 1874 together with his own defeat at Sheffield and immersion in the civic affairs of Birmingham induced him to bide his
time. Since then the Liberal front bench in the Commons apart from
Forster had moved towards the policy of the Education League. Early
in 1877 Chamberlain had no difficulty in persuading the executive of
the League to bring it to an end, explicitly clearing the way for a federation of Liberal associations that would integrate the cause of education
among other Liberal objectives. By mid-April plans for the new organization were sufficiently well in hand for him to invite Gladstone to
speak at the inaugural meeting, to be held in Birmingham at the end of
May.

Chamberlain baited his hook by telling Gladstone that Birmingham
was the first town in the kingdom 'to move last year in the almost
universal protest against the misgovernment of the Turkish provinces;
& the vast majority of its inhabitants have followed with hearty sympathy & admiration your course in reference to this matter'.[39] At the same
time Chamberlain used the widespread concern about the Middle East
to prepare the public for his new organization. Speaking at a presenta-

tion to the secretary of the Birmingham Liberal Association, he dwelt on the need to overcome the paralysing division of the Liberals in Parliament on foreign affairs.[40] That paralysis became painfully evident when Gladstone attempted to present a set of resolutions in the Commons criticizing Turkey and calling upon Britain to ensure that the Christian provinces of the Ottoman empire gained enough autonomy to protect themselves. Hartington, fearful of the impact Gladstone's policy could have on British interests, tried to make him back away. Chamberlain leapt up to Gladstone's support, insisting that his resolutions 'faithfully represent the opinions of the great mass of the English people which hitherto have had no representation in the House, but only in the agitation out-of-doors'.[41] The tide of opinion in the parliamentary Liberal party was against its old chief and his new supporter on the foreign policy issue: but that was not Chamberlain's primary concern. Gladstone rewarded him with exactly what he wanted. For three weeks Gladstone had held the invitation to address the inaugural meeting of the National Liberal Federation at bay. As soon as the parliamentary debate on his resolutions was over, he wrote to accept.

Not yet aware of this response, worried Whigs wrote to warn Gladstone against acceptance. But he adhered to his decision, insisting that 'the Government will only be kept even decently straight by continuous effort and pressure from without'.[42] Questioned further by the Liberal leader in the Lords, Gladstone echoed Chamberlain's stress on 'unity of action', and then expressed the point still more strongly:

> My opinion is & has long been that the vital principle of the Liberal party . . . is *action*, and that nothing but action will ever make it worthy of the name of a party. . . . What I of course regret is that the action of the party as a whole within the House does not come up to its action and feeling in the country at large.[43]

Chamberlain would not have changed a word. His first reaction after the debate on Gladstone's resolutions in the House of Commons had been one of disappointment: he wrote to Collings that Gladstone had 'lost a splendid opportunity which, unfortunately, was ours as well as his'.[44] But the prospect of Gladstone's arrival and blessing in Birmingham quickly restored his spirits.

Gladstone was duly scheduled to reach Birmingham on the afternoon of 31 May to inaugurate the new organization. The morning was given over to the conference of representatives from Liberal constituency associations and smaller sub-groups which Chamberlain and his Birmingham lieutenants called together to discuss the formation of a federation.[45] Nearly a hundred delegations attended. Though the invited organizations were supposed to rest in some sense on a popular base, many of the delegates were self-appointed. But all the organizations represented at the meeting were avowedly Liberal. Chamberlain kept representatives of the supposedly non-partisan Eastern Question Association away. Most delegates came from provincial towns—there were almost none from London—and industrial counties. None belonged to the county and aristocratic families who controlled the selection of Liberal candidates in rural constituencies.

The assembly was presented with a carefully prepared scheme for federation, the work of William Harris, the organizing genius behind the Birmingham association. Like the Birmingham association, the national federation was to be built on the broadest popular base possible. In the former case the object of that organizational principle was to maximize Liberal voting strength, ensure full cooperation from the enlarged electorate and overcome the division between middle and working class. Harris's further objective for the national federation was to unify the forces of popular Liberalism by transcending its division into single-issue organizations. Chamberlain, for his part, wanted to bring the forces thus unified to bear upon the Liberal party in Parliament. He hoped that, through periodic meetings of 'what will be a really Liberal Parliament outside the Imperial Legislature', the federation would prioritize the various items on the popular Liberal agenda, press those priorities upon the parliamentary leaders of the party, and thus 'give greater definitiveness to Liberal policy, [and] establish clearer aims and more decisive action'.[46]

Chamberlain dominated the proceedings without much difficulty. Radical delegates from around the country expressed gratitude for his leadership. He had attempted beforehand to reduce the fears of associations in industrial cities other than Birmingham that the new federation might impinge on their freedom of action. Harris had worked out the proposals for the federation so carefully, the assembly was so large, and the meeting time so short, that most delegations were ready to accept his scheme as it stood, at least for a year's trial. Even the most suspicious group, the delegation from Manchester, who came strictly as observers, expressed themselves in a cooperative spirit. The Federation of Liberal Associations was duly born.

Though momentous, the accomplishment of the morning was less substantial and more complex than it appeared.[47] Only half of the attending delegations agreed to join immediately. Possible affiliates held back out of a variety of concerns, about local autonomy, membership costs, the importation of party conflict into municipal politics, and above all about Birmingham's assumption of primacy. Chamberlain guarded that primacy at every point. He refused to allow Manchester to join in convening the founding conference, restricting this privilege to the more compliant associations of Leeds and Newcastle. Harris and he weighted the conference with a proliferation of delegations from Birmingham and its environs, and stacked the slate of officers for the Federation with Birmingham men. Still, outside of Manchester and Lancashire, Chamberlain paid a surprisingly low price for this arrogation of leadership—at any rate until 1886. The leaders of associations in other provincial towns seemed to feel that affiliation with the National Federation enhanced their local authority. Robert Leader, Chamberlain's erstwhile enemy at Sheffield, was now president of one of the chief associations sponsoring the Federation, and he took a constructive part in the proceedings of the conference. Chamberlain in return came over to Sheffield to applaud its association. Employing the foreign allusions of the hour, he counteracted jealousy of Birmingham's leadership by exploiting the resentment felt in all provincial cities at the condescension with which they were treated by London:

> men of education can exist in London and know less of the manners and customs of their own countrymen in Birmingham, and Sheffield, and Leeds, and Manchester than they know of the manners and customs of the Jowakis of Afghan and the Galikas of the Transkei.[48]

Jealousy at the pretensions of Birmingham proved less damaging to the Federation of Liberal Associations in its opening years than its failure to absorb any single-issue organizations other than the already defunct Education League. The Liberation Society, for example, insisted on preserving its separate existence; and such organizations enjoyed larger treasuries than the Liberal Federation acquired, eight times as large in the case of the leading temperance society, the United Kingdom Alliance. The resilience of these single-issue societies severely limited the ability of the National Federation to set the order of priorities in the popular Liberal agenda.

The delegates at the founding assembly left the conference hall once their work was done to welcome Gladstone to Birmingham. The spectacle of his reception left an enduring impression on all who witnessed it, including the Grand Old Man himself. It was not so much Gladstone as the populace of Birmingham that impressed observers. The wholeheartedness of the welcome they gave to the Liberal champion seemed to flesh out the future that the leaders of popular Liberalism liked to envisage. As always in Birmingham, painstaking organization had preceded the demonstration. Chamberlain had arranged for a general half-holiday to make good his promise to Gladstone of 'an almost Royal welcome'.[49]

Even so, the reception exceeded Chamberlain's expectations. As an observer later recalled, 'the enthusiasm of the people outside the station was such that they broke the barriers, swept aside the police, and surrounded the carriage in which Mr. and Mrs. Gladstone, accompanied by Mr. Chamberlain and his daughter, were sitting. They pressed forward to shake hands with the great leader, and one, more excited than the rest, patted Mr. Gladstone on the back.'[50] Once some sort of order was reestablished, the tumultuous procession headed on its way to Chamberlain's residence in Edgbaston. The only people to be disappointed were Chamberlain's youngest children 'peering from the nursery window' as the crowd approached their home, who decided 'that Mr. Gladstone had too much of the glory and papa too little'.[51]

That evening Gladstone addressed a meeting in the town's largest arena, Bingley Hall. The estimated capacity crowd of twenty thousand was exceeded almost frighteningly by another ten. Beams were brought in to reinforce barricades which contained the crowd in masses of a thousand, and glass had to be taken out of the roof to let in more air. But once Gladstone started to talk, even men who fainted struggled back to their feet to catch his words. They listened spellbound for over two hours, even when the sound of Gladstone's voice failed to reach the arena's farthest corners.

After pronouncing a blessing on the Federation born that day, he devoted himself to the Eastern question. The agitation on this score and the new Federation had much in common. Both were organized expressions of popular Liberal opinion, particularly in the provinces. Both were concerned to bring that opinion to bear upon the Liberal party in Parliament. Gladstone's preoccupation with the Eastern question helped the Federation in its otherwise vexed task of establishing an order of priorities among the various causes dear to Liberal hearts.

The remarkable events of the day had personal as well as broader political implications for the father and the godfather of the new Federation. In coming to Birmingham to bless the Federation and receive the applause of the people, Gladstone was using popular pressure to reinstate himself among the leaders of the Liberal party. The dividends for Chamberlain promised to be still greater. The model of the Birmingham Liberal Association which the other associations were to follow served two ends: it maximized popular, working-class involvement in the Liberal party through organizations in every municipal ward which anyone could join on payment of a nominal subscription; and at the same time it ensured, through complicated provisions for coopting members at the ascending levels of the organization, that it would be directed by those members of the middle class who had the time, talent and inclination for the task. It was a vehicle for democratic centralism, mobilizing the democratic Liberal energies of provincial England and revolving them with centripetal force around Birmingham, which revolved in turn around Chamberlain. The Federation was not simply a magnification of one man; its democratic base was genuine and its other provincial centres would resent protracted dictation from Birmingham. But so long as Chamberlain paid respectful attention to the forces that revolved around him, they would carry him far. Gladstone left Birmingham much impressed with Chamberlain, his hold over the town, and his ability to use his local and parliamentary positions to reinforce each other. 'He is a man worth watching,' Gladstone reported to Lord Granville, 'of strong selfconsciousness under most pleasing manners and I should think of great tenacity of purpose: expecting to play an historical part, and probably destined to it.'[52]

Despite the springboard

The linked hopes of the former prime minister and the provincial upstart were not quickly filled. Their action at the convention in Birmingham placed the parliamentary leadership of the party in confusion and left Chamberlain to wander in the wilderness for a while longer. By implication the two men were challenging Hartington's leadership of the Liberal party, though they hastened to deny it. Hartington responded with a mixture of concession and defiance which unsettled his challengers. In his opening remarks at the conference in Birmingham, Chamberlain had criticized the foot-dragging of the party's parliamentary leaders on the issue of extending the borough franchise of 1867 to the counties. Hartington promptly accepted that proposal, and waited for a more promising issue over which to dig in his Whig heels.

Meanwhile Chamberlain looked for alliances in Parliament, where he was still weak. Reaching into the upper House, he asked a promising young peer, Lord Rosebery, for dinner with him and Sir Charles Dilke 'to see if it be not possible to arrange some joint action & to secure a fuller discussion in both Houses, of the more prominent points in the Liberal programme'.[53] But Rosebery went his own way.

Chamberlain had already begun, ambivalently, to examine another possible alliance, with the Irish contingent in the Commons. Early in the year he had dismissed them as 'a scurvy lot'[54] because they were not reliably committed to any side in British politics. But in April he worked closely with a recent arrival among their ranks, Charles Stewart Parnell, in debate on the annual Mutiny bill, and then supported the Irish claim for independent representation on Commons committees. In concert with Dilke, Chamberlain sounded out the current Irish leader, Isaac Butt, on the prospects for fuller cooperation. But Irish parliamentary politics were in a particularly volatile state. Parnell mounted a challenge to the ascendancy of Butt, who was reluctant to obstruct debate in the Commons in order to draw attention to Irish demands. When Parnell resorted to obstruction in July, Chamberlain recoiled from the 'rascally Irishmen'.[55]

Towards the end of the year he turned back to Hartington, asking him to address the first annual meeting of the National Liberal Federation. He couched his invitation to Hartington in Hartington's own words about the need 'to promote the organization of Liberals & to secure greater unity & definiteness of aims'. Yet Chamberlain did not hesitate to tell the aristocratic leader of his party that 'the Federation represents the sturdy liberalism of the great towns, rather than the milder form which finds favour in the counties'.[56] However Chamberlain described the Federation, it was not to Hartington's liking, and he pushed the request aside.

Two weeks after Hartington terminated this correspondence, Plevna, the Turkish fortress which had held the Russian army at bay since summer, fell to its attackers. Its fall exposed Constantinople to assault, placed Britain's Middle Eastern interests in deeper jeopardy, and hence intensified the debate at home. The Radical contingent in the House of Commons lost what little cohesion it possessed. Moreover, the threat to Constantinople aroused belligerent spirits among a large stratum of British society that Chamberlain had pushed out of his mind. Jingoism was born. Chamberlain had been taken aback by the working-class chauvinism he found at Sheffield in 1874. Now it reared its head in Birmingham.

After the fall of Plevna, Parliament was called into early session, set for mid-January, and all sides readied themselves for debate. Chamberlain worked on two fronts: he attempted to revive the popular agitation which had greeted the early massacres in Bulgaria, and at the same time he studied the diplomatic question, looking for ways to uphold British interests in the Middle East without involvement in the Russo-Turkish war. He thought of bases that Britain might seize to maintain its primacy in the eastern Mediterranean: perhaps Crete, still better Egypt. The seizure of a protectorate over Egypt would follow naturally from Disraeli's purchase of controlling shares in the Suez canal; and Chamberlain thought such a 'dashing policy' would 'recommend itself to British feeling'.[57] Knowing, however, that Gladstone and John Bright would oppose such action, Chamberlain rejected this option; and thereafter he failed to find his way through the Middle Eastern maze. He was none the less disgusted by the timidity with which the Liberal front bench in the Commons handled the subject, and he was disheartened by the complete disintegration of the Radicals.

But what stunned Chamberlain was the chauvinism that surged through the lower, usually inarticulate ranks of the working class. They expressed their appetite for war in music hall songs and rowdy disruption of rallies for peace. The jingo tide numbed the National Liberal Federation. By March there were few towns in England where anti-war rallies could be convened safely. Birmingham, where Chamberlain's lieutenants held all the levers of power, was one of the few towns where a rally could be held undisturbed. But beneath the fabric of Liberal control, Birmingham and the West Midlands revealed themselves to be a hotbed of jingoism. Chamberlain could scarcely credit the popular passion he saw. Perhaps there was 'an underground current of which we know nothing because it exists amongst a class which is not represented on the Liberal Association & which ordinarily takes no part in politics'. He tried to meet the storm stoically, but the folly of the people made him wish for disaster: in the long run it would be 'the best thing for the country,' he told Collings, 'that we should go into war and suffer the penalties which we so richly deserve'.[58]

There was a more direct assault in Birmingham on Chamberlain. Infuriated by dictation from his emissaries on the school board which he was supposed to have left to Dixon upon entering Parliament, Dixon threw up the chairmanship of the board and attacked Chamberlain's tyranny. Dixon was well liked, and a requisition was drawn up asking him to withdraw his resignation. But Chamberlain crushed the initiative, threatening to resign his parliamentary seat if it went forward. 'I am not going to pretend to be a representative of Birmingham,' he fumed, 'if there is the least colour for the statement that an unprovoked & gratuitous attack on me is approved & sustained by my constituents.'[59] Birmingham duly bowed the knee. Chamberlain remained in an ugly humour, frustrated by the popularity Disraeli gained by standing up to Russia in defence of Constantinople: 'I begin to see that the removal of Jewish disabilities was a mistake,' Chamberlain growled, '& to agree with Carlyle in sighing for the days of King John when we might at least have pulled out all their double teeth.'[60]

Upward at last

At the end of the summer the skies began to clear for the Liberals. They deserved little credit for the change in the political climate; it stemmed from the deteriorating economy. Chamberlain in his capacity as an arbitrator for industrial disputes saw how the depression worsened labour relations. As president of the South Staffordshire Mill and Forge Wages Board, he felt obliged by the collapse of profits in metal manufacturing to agree to three successive wage reductions for ironworkers before the end of 1878. Wishing to blame the government, he linked the economic distress to the foreign policy of the Conservatives, whose expenditure on military preparations drove up the income tax.

Despite the country's economic discontent, the politicians by and large continued to be preoccupied with foreign affairs. Here too the tide turned against the Conservatives. The credit which Disraeli gained by bringing home 'peace with honour' from the Congress of Berlin was lost in setbacks farther afield. The British government of India was embroiled in an expensive and eventually bloody attempt to consolidate its sphere of influence in Afghanistan in face of encroachment by Russia. Chamberlain anticipated disaster with scarcely disguised pleasure: 'I think we shall get rid of the Tories at the next general election,' he assured Mundella, 'but at what a cost! . . . we shall be fortunate if we escape a sharp & terrible retribution for the Jingoism, which has been developed by Lord Beaconsfield's policy.'[61]

Chamberlain's fortunes amid the Liberal revival were bound up with the performance of the National Liberal Federation. Disraeli called the Federation a 'caucus' in order to identify it with the notoriously corrupt forms of electoral organization common in the urban United States. Chamberlain accepted abuse from the Conservatives as a compliment. Yet he took care to explain the basic differences between the associations in his federation, particularly the one in Birmingham, and the American counterpart. The most serious charge against the Birmingham Liberal Association was that, as with an American caucus, its seemingly popular constitution disguised the dictatorial control exercised by its leaders. However valid this criticism, Chamberlain could justly point out how well his association had increased popular political involvement within the city. In contrast to the hole-in-corner conclaves of former years, 'now the representatives are elected at crowded meetings'.[62]

There was one criticism of American caucus politics which was certainly not applicable to Birmingham: it could not be accused of driving the best men out of politics. One of the most impressive features of Birmingham politics in recent years had been the willingness of its leading figures in business and the professions to give themselves to public service. Birmingham-style Liberal associations were nevertheless vulnerable to criticism over their attempts to prevent distinguished Liberal MPs who were opposed to Radicalism from retaining their seats in Parliament. The debate focused on Chamberlain's arch-antagonist, W.E. Forster at Bradford. Forster's relations with his Nonconformist constituents in Bradford had been soured for some time by his handling of the education question. His critics took the lead in forming a Liberal association in Bradford, and then refused to endorse Forster for reelection to Parliament unless he promised to act in conformity with the association's wishes. Chamberlain defended the stand taken by the Bradford association: why, he asked, was a former minister 'entitled to put his personal claims above the interests of the party to which he belongs'?[63]

This line of argument did not convince the godfather of the Liberal Federation. Gladstone thought too well of Forster to condone 'the rule of the association at Bradford'.[64] Yet he drew a distinction between the dictatorial behaviour of the Bradford association, which he condemned, and the Birmingham model, which he praised as a local expression of the *vox populi*. Gladstone's continued endorsement was of crucial importance to Chamberlain, for it blessed his efforts to extend the organization despite resistance from the formal leaders of the party, particularly Hartington.

The conduct of the Bradford association confirmed Hartington's suspicions of the National Liberal Federation. When Chamberlain approached him with another invitation to address the Federation, this time at Leeds, most of Hartington's advisers counselled him to accept. The Federation had grown impressively over the past year, doubling the number of its affiliates to one hundred; and there was remarkably little disagreement between the Federation and the leaders of the parliamentary party at the moment on the policy it should pursue. Chamberlain sought to allay Hartington's fears without disguising their underlying differences. 'I quite agree with you,' he wrote at the end of the year,

> that the first object of all liberals at this moment should be to unite the party in order to put a stop to the reckless foreign policy of the Government.
>
> There are many home questions on which it is possible that I may desire to go farther than you, but these must wait their proper time & for the present I am perfectly content that they should remain in the background.[65]

He added a warning.

> Can the Leader of the liberal party afford to ignore altogether so large a section of it? If he does, the organisation will necessarily tend more & more to separate from the official liberalism & to form a party within the party.

But Hartington accepted that risk and persisted in his rejection of the invitation.

Chamberlain took the rejection calmly, hopeful as never before that on foreign affairs the Liberals were becoming a party of unified action. Addressing the meeting of the Federation that Hartington had refused to attend, Chamberlain warned the associations against becoming

> an instrument to promote the purposes of a section of the party only.... The great need of the Liberal party at the present moment is union... our first duty ought to be... to remove [the government]. Everything must give way to that—personal claims, crotchets of all descriptions—even, I venture to think, some deep-seated convictions, and long-cherished hopes of important reform.

Of course, once they had thrown the Tories out, 'we shall be justified in saying to Lord Hartington that concession is a virtue which gains by being reciprocal'.[66] Even so, it ran against Chamberlain's grain to pull his punches in this fashion; and he experienced severe headaches the following week.

The parliamentary session for 1879 began in encouraging circumstances. Sir Bartle Frere, a distinguished servant of the British government in India, had been sent as high commissioner to South Africa where, against instructions, he embroiled the British in war with the Zulus. Chamberlain, alerted perhaps by his Congregationalist friend R.W. Dale who had missionary connections in the region, was already talking of the situation in South Africa as an example of the government's unnecessarily bullying ways, when news arrived that the Zulus had slaughtered twelve hundred British troops at Isandhlwana. In the ensuing parliamentary debate, Chamberlain damned the government by treating the disaster as an inevitable consequence of its 'new Imperialism'.[67] The disaster gave him an opportunity also to cultivate support among the Irish nationalists led by Parnell who identified the cause of Ireland with imperial oppression everywhere. United for the first time in the life of Disraeli's Parliament, fighting under Radical leadership and supported by a sizeable bloc of Irish MPs, almost all the Liberals in the Commons cast their votes against the government.

Beneath the new Liberal harmony, however, the tension between Hartington and Chamberlain remained unresolved. In July it broke to the surface in an episode that weakened the leader and strengthened the insurgent. The issue in July was the use of flogging to enforce military discipline. It was raised by Parnell, who regarded flogging as an exercise of English suppression, and by Radicals like the miners' M.P. Alexander Macdonald who regarded it as oppression of the working class. Chamberlain joined them from conviction as well as calculation. Corporal punishment was anathema in his family. As a young father, he had only once spanked Austen and shuddered at the memory. One of the features of the jingoism of the past year which repelled him was the pleasure it voiced in brutal manifestations of Britain's overseas power. Shortly before the issue of flogging rose in the Commons, Austen, now a schoolboy at Rugby, was threatened with birching for a trivial offence of trespassing on private land near the school. Chamberlain ordered Austen's removal from the school until the punishment was reduced to detention. Believing, as he told Austen's housemaster, that flogging had 'almost disappeared from the army and navy',[68] he was shocked to discover in July that this was not the case.

The parliamentary episode began quietly enough. Parnell was obstructing debate on the Army Discipline bill in an attempt to reduce if not abolish flogging. A friend of Hartington encouraged the Radicals to take part in Parnell's effort, and they enjoyed an initial success: the government moved to limit flogging to grave offences. Thereupon Chamberlain pointed out, to the government's dismay, that the vague definition of grave offences still left wide latitude for flogging; and he moved for another delay in debate to allow for reconsideration.

Irritated with Chamberlain as well as with the practice of obstruction, Hartington took offence. He opposed the motion, and then casually left the chamber. But other prominent Liberals including even Forster endorsed the Radical obstruction. When Hartington returned to the House and heard one of the obstructives refer to him as leader, he repudiated the proffered leadership. He went on to denounce Chamberlain's motion as 'prejudicial to what he conceived to be a much more important matter than even flogging in the Army—namely, the dignity of Parliament'.[69] Chamberlain struck back with icy repudiation of Hartington:

> It is rather inconvenient that we should have so little of the presence of the noble Lord, lately the Leader of the Opposition, but now the Leader of a section only.[70]

His challenge angered the Whigs and provoked jealous Radical rivals, Fawcett and Mundella, to denounce Chamberlain's impudence. For a few hours he was the target of abuse. Yet it was initially Hartington who had mishandled the situation. Senior members of the parliamentary party including Gladstone and the chief whip W.P. Adam counselled Hartington to make peace. Adam shot down plans for a testimonial dinner in honour of Hartington for fear of consolidating the split. Recognizing his misstep, Hartington sought Chamberlain out privately to dispose of any 'feeling remaining after our little quarrel',[71] and then committed the party to the abolition of flogging in the army.

Chamberlain celebrated discreetly. 'Radicalism below the gangway has been so completely triumphant on this occasion,' he told a friend, 'that I think it will probably be good policy to keep quiet for a little time & not to provoke a revulsion.'[72] True to his own advice, he placed a favourable construction on small advances in policy made by Hartington towards the end of the parliamentary session. He welcomed Hartington's suggestion that the remedy for obstruction might lie in entrusting more public business to local authorities, and he heralded Hartington's mild criticism of the land law as 'the beginning of a new era'.[73] Chamberlain dropped disestablishment from the top of his agenda and instead stressed reforms that Hartington seemed more willing to contemplate, including extension of the county franchise. 'The object', Chamberlain explained to the Liberal Association of Glasgow, 'is that we should be moving, and in the right direction; and when that is secured I think the exact rate of speed, and even to some extent the road that we take, may fairly be left to our chosen leaders.'[74]

The relationship between Hartington and Chamberlain remained fragile. When Hartington travelled up to Newcastle to speak on behalf of Joseph Cowen, a Liberal MP who supported Conservative foreign policy on the Eastern question and South Africa, Chamberlain recalled Hartington's refusal to address the National Liberal Federation. 'I can only hope', Chamberlain bitterly observed, 'that if ever it should be my fate to differ as widely from the leaders & the bulk of my party as Mr. Cowen has done, that I may be as gently treated by both.'[75]

Attention in political circles turned at the end of 1879 towards the next general election, due within a year. Gladstone captured the national spotlight by accepting the Liberal nomination for the Scottish county constituency of Midlothian in a phenomenal succession of speeches, in which he condemned the government and all its works. Chamberlain concentrated on Birmingham and its environs. Utilizing Liberal Federation skills in voter registration, and relying on businessmen who made their fortunes in Birmingham but lived in the surrounding countryside, he launched an assault on Tory seats in rural Warwickshire and Worcestershire. But his primary concern was Birmingham itself.

All was not well there. Brinsley, who had opposed Chamberlain for the mayoralty in 1873 and was now a Conservative, wrested the central ward of Market Hall, with a very mixed population of rich and poor, from the Liberals in the town council elections towards the end of 1879. Then the school board abandoned the policy for which Chamberlain had fought of confining tax-supported instruction to secular subjects, leaving religious instruction to volunteer teachers after hours. Volunteer religious instructors had never come forward in adequate numbers; the Church of England had fought the policy; and it made Nonconformists uneasy. The debate on the school board pitted the more religious Liberals led by Dixon against the Chamberlainite secularists, and at last Dixon's men won. Though Chamberlain was intensely annoyed by these setbacks, they convinced him of the need to repair his electoral alliances, particularly with the Labour Association and its leader, W.J. Davis, who as a member of the school board had sympathized with Dixon.

The prospect of a general election within the year did not, however, rivet Chamberlain's eyes on his constituency. The national preoccupation with foreign and imperial affairs since his entry into Parliament had altered his priorities. 'Under ordinary circumstances, and with an ordinary Government,' he explained to his constituents, 'I am almost inclined to say that local affairs touch more nearly on the interests of the people than questions of Imperial policy. But this is no longer so at the present moment.'[76] When Parliament reconvened in the new year, he concentrated on the situation in South Africa. Schooled by Dale, he displayed less concern about the defeat at Isandhlwana than about the failure of the British authorities elsewhere in South Africa to assert themselves in defence of the natives. He asked the Anti-Slavery Society for information on 'all that concerns . . . the treatment of the black races at the present time by the Colonists'.[77]

The general election was called with unexpected abruptness early in March, but both sides in Birmingham were ready. In the previous general election the Conservatives had surrendered Birmingham to the Liberals without a contest. But after Chamberlain's election to Parliament in 1876, they reorganized themselves, learning from their opponents. Though Birmingham elected three members, the Conservatives decided to concentrate their strength by fielding only two candidates. One, Fred Burnaby, a swashbuckling major in the Royal Horse Guards, had defied the Russians and thrilled English jingoes in 1875 by riding across central Asia. Though a political lightweight, he was thus quite attractive— a claim that could not be made for the other Conservative nominee. The Honourable A.C.G. Calthorpe seemed incapable of speech; and though heir to the owner of all Edgbaston, he had done nothing himself to benefit the town.[78] The Liberals renominated the three sitting MPs, Bright, Chamberlain, and P.H. Muntz, a revered member of a locally revered family. Though on the surface the contest looked unequal, the Liberals were nervous; and they were particularly anxious to make a good showing because Birmingham was scheduled to be the first of the great English towns to vote.

The contest revolved around imperial as well as domestic issues. Burnaby prompted a debate on imperial affairs from which Chamberlain emerged as almost a 'Little Englander'. Latching for the first time on to a phrase of Matthew Arnold about 'the weary Titan' which he would never forget, Chamberlain emphasized the weariness of Britain rather than its titanic stature. Four years of Conservative imperialism led him to suspect, as he told a friend, that even India was overtaxing 'the strength of the giant . . . I don't think we can bear a second India in Asia Minor & I fear it would bring down the whole edifice of our power'.[79] While Burnaby called for a reassertion of British arms to offset the defeats in Afghanistan and South Africa, Chamberlain advocated abandoning the exposed positions into which the Conservative government and its emissaries overseas had thrust Britain.

On the domestic side he trimmed his agenda down to one item which few Whigs would oppose: electoral reform including extension of the county franchise and redistribution. His only fresh initiative had to do with Ireland, and was prompted by electoral considerations in Birmingham as well as by the land war in Ireland precipitated by the fall in agricultural prices. Chamberlain proposed to give Irish tenants security of tenure in order, in part, to staunch the flow of immigrant Irishmen into 'large towns like Birmingham, Manchester, and Liverpool, where their competition necessarily depresses the wages of the English working men'.[80] He also talked vaguely of 'giving to the Irish people equal laws and equal institutions'; but, receding from his stance at Sheffield in the last general election, he threw cold water on 'Home Rule, or . . . any altered system of government of that kind'.[81]

Still the hottest issues in the Birmingham contest were local: control of the drink trade, and the cost of the town's great improvement scheme. Chamberlain sought to lessen the wrath of the publicans by stressing his commitment to full compensation for cancelled licences. Tories none the less heaped their abuse upon him more than on the other Liberal candidates. The Tory *Gazette* floated a rumour that his seat was in such jeopardy that he might seek election for East Staffordshire, and predicted in any case that he would do the poorest of the three Liberal candidates. Under the terms of the 1867 Reform Act, while Birmingham would choose three members, each elector had only two votes; and accordingly the Liberal Association issued instructions as to which two candidates the Liberal electors in each ward should vote for. Chamberlain was assigned a disproportionately large number of the wards in which Conservatives had done well in the recent local elections. When the day for the voting finally arrived he was, as he confessed to Morley, 'horribly anxious. . . . Would it were night and all were well!'[82]

The Conservatives of Birmingham went down to defeat; yet they won more votes than ever before and did better than Conservatives in most other industrial towns. The Liberals of Birmingham also improved upon their previous record. But Chamberlain, though reelected, came in behind Muntz and Bright, as the Tory *Gazette* had predicted. That galled him. 'I feel about 5 years older for the election,' he told Collings, '—and devilishly inclined sometimes to throw the whole thing up . . . after going through the mud of Tory abuse for a fortnight & working like a horse.'[83]

His spirits rose as the results from the rest of the country came in. Well-informed Liberals had expected the party to win only a small majority in the new Parliament; but the party duplicated its triumph of 1868. Liberals won over one hundred seats more than the Conservatives, quite aside from the sixty-five Irish Nationalists. Tories were inclined to give much of the credit for the outcome to Chamberlain's Federation of Liberal Associations; and in a letter to *The Times* Chamberlain happily accepted the credit.[84] He exaggerated the contribution of the Federation to the Liberal victory.[85] The regular Liberal organization under the chief whip, W.P. Adam, accomplished a lot in the many parts of the country which the Federation did not yet touch. Gladstone's Midlothian campaigns had an immense though imponderable impact on the electorate. Underlying everything was the economic depression, which was easing in some industries but not in agriculture. In terms of total votes cast, the Liberal victory was much narrower than the composition of the new House of Commons suggested. The Conservatives received more votes in defeat in 1880 than they had received in victory in 1874. All the same, that achievement only accentuated the fact that the increase in the Liberal vote was much greater. Chamberlain contributed substantially to that increase, not through Radical policies but through Radical organization. As he explained to *The Times*, the Federation of Liberal Associations in Britain's industrial towns had

> deepened and extended the interest felt in the contest . . . fastened a sense of personal responsibility on the electors; and . . . secured the active support, for the most part voluntary and unpaid, of thousands and tens of thousands of voters, who have been willing to work hard for the candidates in whose selection they have for the first time had an influential voice.

The consequences of that accomplishment remained to be seen.

6

Assertive Apprentice
1880–1884

...the charmed circle has been broken, & a new departure made
which is an event in English political history....

Chamberlain to Mrs Pattison, 4 May 1880

The general election of 1880 gave rise to one of the century's most tur-
bulent ministries, with Chamberlain frequently at the centre of the
turbulence. In concrete terms the ministry accomplished little. Yet it
raised many expectations, sometimes hopes, more often disappointments or fears. Chamberlain shared many of these reactions. He
sought Radical alternatives to the moderate, consensual lines of policy
which the cabinet was inclined to pursue. He wanted to prove as no
one had done before that a Radical rooted in the industrial provinces
of England could scale the political heights and still remain true to the
society that bred him, giving political effect to its wishes. His experience as a cabinet minister in the early 1880s encouraged but also
frustrated these hopes. He placed his confidence less in the government of which he was part than in his individual judgement and, above
all, in the enlargement of the popular base of British politics. Spurning
the circumspect arts of the Liberal statecraft, he kept on raising the
stakes.

The spoils of victory

He had engaged in two dialogues during the first three months of
1880 with a view to the expected general election. One, conducted in
public, was with his electorate in Birmingham. He spoke to the voters
with unusual caution, for he was anxious to quieten restive local
interests and to foster Liberal unity nationally in order to defeat the
Tories. His other dialogue had to do with the fruits of the victory

he anticipated and was conducted in private with the official leaders of the party through mediators, Sir William Harcourt and Sir Henry James, as well as with his own associates, Morley and Dilke. It was mainly in this private dialogue that Chamberlain staked out his demands.

The fruits of the expected victory would be twofold: it would place the Liberals in office, and it would make them responsible for the formulation of public policy. Chamberlain was concerned about both. But acceptance of office would not do him any good unless it was accompanied by movement towards some of the goals that he had encouraged the voters to endorse. Gladstone's restoration to the office of prime minister would in itself serve this purpose, though Chamberlain feared that the old man 'would be King Stork and that some of us frogs would have a hard time of it under him'.[1] But a ministry led by one of the current official leaders of the party, Hartington or Granville, would have to offer more to win Chamberlain's support. He talked to them through Harcourt and James about policy. He called for extension of household suffrage and elective local government to the counties and Ireland, for removal of Nonconformist grievances, and for reform of the land law. Office would serve Chamberlain's purposes only so long as he was placed in a sufficiently powerful position in the anticipated Liberal government to influence its conduct; and at the beginning of 1880 he could not count on being offered a seat in the cabinet. Whatever Chamberlain's accomplishments in the country at large, he had been in the House of Commons less than four years and only occasionally to the fore in its debates.

But as soon as the electoral tide became apparent in April, his mind turned to office rather than policy. The contribution of the National Liberal Federation to the Liberal victory emboldened him. Among the possible Radical candidates for office Dilke, with a dozen years in the Commons and recognized expertise in foreign policy, had the parliamentary standing that Chamberlain lacked; but Chamberlain had now demonstrably greater influence outside the House. Chamberlain proposed that Dilke and he combine in 'a thorough offensive & defensive alliance'[2] to make sure that both should be appointed to the cabinet or that both should remain resolutely outside the government, in either case to ensure that the cabinet paid attention to the Radical wing of the party. If either man joined the cabinet alone, he would be 'a radical minnow among Whig Tritons'. Still worse, if they settled for minor office, they would be unable to speak in cabinet and at the same time unable to speak freely in public. But Dilke agreed only in principle to the proposal, and then left for a short holiday in France. The days of waiting for the appointment of a new prime minister sobered Chamberlain and reduced his expectations. He decided that he would settle for minor office if Dilke alone among the Radicals was selected for the cabinet.

Gladstone meanwhile played a more assertive game at a much higher level. For five years he had left Hartington and Granville to lead the Liberal opposition in Parliament. The parliamentary party was ready to support a ministry headed by either leader so long as Gladstone would do so too. But Gladstone intimated that he would neither join nor promise to support a ministry which he did not lead; and he thus forced his way back to 10 Downing Street.

As soon as Gladstone undertook to form a ministry, Dilke returned to London and asked Chamberlain in Birmingham to do so too in view of Gladstone's 'stand and deliver'[3] way of offering positions. Gladstone let it be known that he did not intend to offer cabinet office to either of these presuming Radicals. He insisted that no one should be elevated to the cabinet who had not served an apprenticeship in minor office, though he had violated this rule by appointing Bright to the cabinet in 1868. As soon as Chamberlain reached London, he stiffened Dilke to insist on cabinet office for at least one of them. Chamberlain then warned the party leaders that, if left out, he would 'organise a "pure left" party in the House and the country which should support the Govt. if they brought in Radical measures and oppose them everywhere if they did not', if need be by 'running of Radical candidates in all Borough elections'.[4]

Dilke, the less confident of the two Radicals, was the first to be tested. Gladstone offered him the position of under-secretary at the Foreign Office, an attractive offer because it acknowledged Dilke's expertise in foreign affairs and because the new foreign secretary, Granville, would be in the Lords. Loyal none the less to his partner, Dilke asked Gladstone about Chamberlain. Upon learning that Chamberlain would be offered the secretaryship of the Treasury, a comparably suitable and significant post but also outside the cabinet, Dilke declined to accept Gladstone's offer unless either Chamberlain or he himself was appointed to the cabinet.

Though Gladstone interpreted Dilke's conduct as chivalrous, it did not reward him directly. Bright urged Chamberlain's elevation to the cabinet. Hartington suggested that the Board of Trade would suit Chamberlain and keep him out of mischief. So it was Chamberlain rather than Dilke who was offered a seat in the cabinet as President of the Board of Trade, while the offer to Dilke remained unchanged. Flustered as well as flattered by this turn of events, Chamberlain offered to accept Gladstone's original proposal; but Gladstone dismissed the gesture. He assured the Queen, apparently in his ignorance, that Chamberlain had never expressed republican views and that the Radicals included in earlier cabinets had invariably quietened down.

Disjointed cabinet

That pattern was not to be repeated in Chamberlain's case. From his first days in office he responded to the difficulties the government met at home and abroad as opportunities to display the worth of his Radicalism. He was encouraged to do so by the plasticity of Liberal politics. The unity which the Liberal party had found over the past year and a half in opposition to Disraeli's conduct of foreign policy was not even skin deep. Nor did the Liberals win their majority in the House of Commons by spelling out what they would do once they drove the Tories from power. The implications of the election were still more obscure because the Liberals won their large majority in the Commons by a margin in the popular vote narrow enough 'to mean that a whole variety of factors could be considered decisive'.[5] The crusade that Gladstone conducted at Midlothian against Disraeli's conduct of government had been profoundly moving. Yet it lacked the focus of his campaign in the general election of 1868 on Irish disestablishment. Chamberlain's campaign in the West Midlands was similarly short on specifics. Though the economy of the country was acutely depressed, none of the political leaders concentrated attention on it because all assumed from their common faith in a free economy that there was little any government could do to affect it. During the campaign the Liberals rejected Disraeli's attempt to focus attention on unrest in Ireland, the other spectre that was to haunt the new government. In short, the Liberal party and its leaders had no clear idea of what to do with the power they had gained.

Chamberlain's temptation to take the initiative in these circumstances was increased by the unstable construction of the government. Gladstone was perceived as standing to the left of centre in the Liberal party, and his susceptibility to moral enthusiasms worried the Whigs. Whether to allay their fears or from respect for their prior experience, he placed more Whigs in his cabinet than their strength in the Commons and the country warranted. Aside from Bright who was a spent force and Forster who had become a centrist, Chamberlain was the sole representative of the Radical wing of the party to be elevated to the cabinet. He even looked different. Youthful in appearance because clean-shaven in a bearded age, he was shorter than his colleagues of well-fed aristocratic descent, and he was pale and slightly stooped because less athletic than they.

Even so, the cabinet had some components to offset its political lopsidedness. Forster and Sir William Harcourt provided a potentially conciliatory centre, and the Whig contingent included some devotees of Gladstone, particularly Lord Granville. The inclusion of A.J. Mundella, Henry Fawcett and Leonard Courtney as well as Dilke in offices outside the cabinet did something to satisfy the Radicals. Above all stood Gladstone in dextrous ambiguity.

The ministry was to last for five years. For half that time, until the end of 1882, Chamberlain thought of Gladstone as his mainstay in cabinet. The veteran prime minister gave his new colleague a cordial welcome. On the way back from their swearing-in at Windsor, Gladstone flattered Chamberlain on his physical resemblance to the younger Pitt. Thereafter Chamberlain took pleasure in his likeness to the man Gladstone described as 'a great Reform Minister in his earlier life' but 'carried away later by the miserable wars in which he found himself engaged'.[6] Gladstone felt no such foreboding about Chamberlain. He had echoed Gladstone's denunciation of the miserable wars into which Disraeli had recently plunged Britain, and later spoke of Gladstone's Midlothian speeches as containing 'the whole body of Liberal faith and doctrine'.[7] The two men had more in common than their differences in manner and later in policy would suggest. Gladstone was separated by just one generation from a background in commerce and industry and knew something of what it meant to be a parvenu. The most conspicuous achievement of the two men over the past four years had been to stir up and mobilize the mass electorate. Furthermore, though Gladstone was identified with severe economy in governmental expenditure, he was also capable of extending the regulatory powers of the state, as he had done at the Board of Trade, the office to which he now sent Chamberlain.

Whatever the prospects for cooperation with Gladstone, they did not inhibit Chamberlain from contributing to a pattern of cabinet conduct more often associated with ministerial collapse than with stability. Never sure whether the purposes of his Radical cause would be better served within or free from the constraints of cabinet responsibility, not cowed for a moment by his inexperience in office, and quick to move beyond his province at the Board of Trade, Chamberlain made bold proposals on most major issues that came before the cabinet from its first meeting. While he was willing to modify his proposals or set them aside in deference to the wishes of his colleagues, he threatened to resign whenever the cabinet moved towards policies which he deemed intolerable. Some of the Whig ministers, preeminently Hartington, soon followed suit. Threats of resignation became so commonplace as to suggest that the government was composed of 'frankly hostile elements'.[8] Gladstone eventually resorted to the threat himself. But the worst offenders were the faction leaders: Hartington on the one side, and on the other 'the party of two',[9] Chamberlain and Dilke.

Two and a half years were to elapse before Dilke joined Chamberlain in the cabinet. But from the beginning Chamberlain kept Dilke fully abreast of cabinet deliberations. Knowledge that Dilke and Chamberlain would resign together enhanced their ability to threaten their colleagues. Their compact proved resilient. Such an alliance between natural rivals for the leadership of the Radicals and quite possibly of the Liberal party was remarkable by any standards. It was facilitated by their complementary talents and spheres of particular interest, Dilke for parliamentary debate and in foreign relations, Chamberlain for the provincial arena and in domestic affairs. There was genuine friendship between the two widowers though they handled their loss differently, Dilke by moving on to a fast track, Chamberlain by hardening his heart. This divergent reaction bred one of their few differences in policy: Dilke favoured the enfranchisement of women, which Chamberlain opposed after Florence died. Even so, their commitment to joint resignation extended to issues on which only one felt strongly. Dilke put it effusively: he would, he said, 'resign with [Chamberlain] if he were to resign because he thought Forster did not have his hair cut sufficiently often'.[10]

They used the threat of resignation as a way to manage the tension between their claim to represent the forces of Radicalism outside the ministry and their responsibility as members within it. No previous Radical had found out how to resolve this tension. Some, like Cobden, had declined office in order to preserve their popular representative character inviolate. Those who accepted office had either lost their distinctiveness or, like Bright, had lapsed into ineffectuality. Chamberlain and Dilke wanted to do more than avoid that fate. Unlike Radicals of the old school who aimed to prevent the misuse of state power, Chamberlain and Dilke hoped to demonstrate that the powers of the state could be exercised constructively to ease social tensions at home as well as to provide security abroad. Their tactics and enterprise eventually exhausted Gladstone's patience. Yet paradoxically their repeated threats to resign underscored the earnestness of their experiment in holding office.

Chamberlain's connection to the Federation of Liberal Associations bore upon but did not greatly exacerbate the tensions within the cabinet. Though he resigned the presidency of the Federation upon entering the cabinet, he was succeeded by his friend Collings and remained in close contact with the inner circle of Federation officers in Birmingham. He used the Federation to drum up popular support for measures he wished the cabinet to adopt. In doing so he provoked resentment less inside than outside the cabinet, among Liberal MPs of independent mind and Liberal associations from provincial towns that resented Birmingham's assumption of dominance.

Leaks to the press often proved more useful than the National Liberal Federation for Chamberlain's purposes in soliciting support on issues of contention within the cabinet. He was not the only member of the cabinet to act in this fashion. Forster was as leaky as he; and they fought each other for the allegiance of T.H.S. Escott, who wrote for publica-

tions of varied political complexion. Press leaks began during the formation of the cabinet when word of the compact between Chamberlain
and Dilke reached the press almost as soon as it reached Gladstone.
Suspecting that Chamberlain might not know or respect the customs of
the governing elite, Gladstone coupled his offer of the Presidency of the
Board of Trade with a reminder that his letter of invitation was headed
'Secret' and that 'the rule is . . . to observe the strictest secrecy until Her
Majesty's pleasure has been taken'.[11] Undeterred, Chamberlain thereafter violated the secrecy of cabinet deliberations systematically by
keeping Dilke informed, and Dilke in turn alerted the press. Whenever
leaks occurred, insiders suspected Chamberlain. In addition to his
liaison with the *Birmingham Daily Post*, he was almost ostentatious in his
enjoyment of friendly relations with prominent figures in the London
press. One observer later recalled that 'there was no public man of the
front rank so accessible to journalists as "Joe", a diminutive . . . that in
itself spoke volumes for his popularity with pressmen'.[12]

His attempt to combine membership of the cabinet with close ties to
the press complicated his relationships on both sides. It kept Gladstone
from taking Chamberlain into his confidence, and it strained Chamberlain's friendship with John Morley. Hitherto Chamberlain had been
closer to Morley than to Dilke. Now Dilke and Chamberlain drew together in the bonds of office, while Morley drew away in the service of
what he thought of as the 'spiritual power' of the press. Though Morley
had failed to win election to Parliament, his appointment to be editor of
one of London's leading dailies, the *Pall Mall Gazette*, increased his political importance simultaneously with that of Chamberlain and Dilke.
Morley sought frequent briefings from Chamberlain on domestic affairs
and from Dilke on foreign. But this collaboration could not prevent
occasional serious divergences between the Radical ministers, increasingly impressed with the complications of administration, and the Radical editor more concerned about the principles at stake. Chamberlain
was particularly vulnerable when Morley followed an independent line,
because the longstanding friendship between the two men led others to
assume that Morley's editorials reflected Chamberlain's wishes.

Between two cities

Despite the increase of his work in London, Chamberlain was slow to
buy himself a residence there. Dilke helped him feel at ease in what
Chamberlain still described as 'your beastly metropolis'.[13] He continued
for a while to stay with Dilke or in a hotel and then rented a house in
the fashionable West End, on Prince's Gardens, but did not buy a permanent residence until 1883, when he moved across the road.

He continued meanwhile to sink his roots still deeper in Birmingham. 'Here it is beautiful weather *as usual!*,' he observed smugly to Dilke, '& I naturally do not wish to exchange it for your d-d yellow fogs.'[14] In the summer before the general election he began to build himself a new home there, much grander than Southbourne. Lavishing money on it, he invested the house and surrounding grounds with personal significance. He called it Highbury after the district of London where he had spent his youth. In doing so he suggested that his seat should command attention from the perspective of London as well as Birmingham. Placed near the home of his brother at the edge of Birmingham four miles south of the town centre on a crest of land overlooking a still rural valley, Highbury met Chamberlain's needs to perfection. His family were gathered around him. The eighteen acres of grounds offered him recreation and reflected his aspiration to rival the landed gentry. He could offer hospitality to his associates in national politics approaching what they were accustomed to in country houses. Yet he was still in Birmingham, able to assemble his local associates in his library, to impress carping spirits with the grandeur of his dinners, to open his grounds to fêtes for the faithful, and hence to maintain close contact with the West Midlands. Whenever Chamberlain was present, Highbury was a centre of activity rather than an escape from business. During the parliamentary season he took the three-hour train journey every weekend to Birmingham, where he recharged his batteries. For true holidays he needed to get away from Birmingham as well as London; hence his love for travel abroad.

But the greenhouses and gardens of Highbury gave him at least weekly draughts of the recreation he most enjoyed. Highbury was an oppressive as well as impressive house, designed by John Henry Chamberlain in the Italianate Gothic style of Birmingham's board schools and Corporation Street. Externally the soft orange brick and tan-coloured stone gave an impression of warmth. But tinted glass darkened the interior which was heavy with luxury. 'The drawing-room with its elaborately carved marble arches, its satin paper, rich hangings and choice watercolours has a forlornly grand appearance,' Beatrice Potter—later to become Beatrice Webb—observed censoriously; 'No books, no work, no music, not even a harmless antimacassar, to relieve the oppressive richness of the satin-covered furniture.'[15] The house, however, opened directly on to a long line of greenhouses and was surrounded by gardens. Chamberlain's one hobby was horticulture, which he tackled with his usual combination of zeal and system. He would emerge from a morning's work in the library and head straight for the greenhouses. Donning an apron and replacing his cigar with a short pipe—for he always liked to dress the part—he would experiment with the breeding of new strains of orchids, his favourite flower to which he devoted a dozen of his greenhouses. He would move on to discuss the progress of each bed of plants with the gardeners, first inside and then out of doors. His hobby was partly for diversion, partly applied science, and partly for show. He was a new breed himself in the world of high politics, and the orchid he wore in his lapel became his trademark. Daily some of the choicest specimens were sent up from Birmingham for him to wear while in London; if they were small he would wear as many as three at a time. Another dozen greenhouses at Highbury were reserved for separate cultivation of azaleas, begonias, cyclamens, primulas, chrysanthemums and foliage plants. The conservatory immediately outside the drawing room displayed flowers currently in bloom and was edged by tall palms surrounding a trickling fountain. Outside, in addition to banks of roses and rhododendrons and large fruit and vegetable gardens, the grounds were full of 'delightful surprises': 'dells, rocks and bogs, water scenes and rustic bridges'.[16] The staff of gardeners eventually reached twenty-five and were led by one or two notable experts. Chamberlain concerned himself with the economic security of his gardeners as he had with his employees in industry, and set up a provident fund to which he as well as they contributed.

He moved into Highbury in the summer of 1880 soon after he took office. He reinforced his Birmingham base in other ways. He held out a reconciling hand to George Dixon, who responded 'with great pleasure', admitting that their 'estrangement has been one of the most painful episodes of my life'.[17] Chamberlain made sure that some of his most valued associates in Birmingham—Bunce of the *Daily Post*, the architect John Henry Chamberlain, and Powell Williams who chaired the finance committee on the town council and was secretary to the Federation of Liberal Associations—were appointed by the Lord Chancellor to be borough magistrates. Attentive to the depressed economy in Birmingham, Chamberlain used his influence with the War Office to secure orders for the town's gun trade.

In deciding on the internal arrangements for Highbury, Chamberlain did not consult its primary residents, his six children, even about the decoration of the rooms to which he assigned them. A caring but austere father wrapped up in his own personal pain and engrossed in his work, Chamberlain was the great fact in the lives of his children now ranging in age from seven to eighteen, the god they worshipped, loved and sought to please. He was unstinting in his concern for their comfort, conduct and education. Beatrice, the eldest, completed her education under academically excellent tutelage in France. Austen, Harriet's other child, was sent to Rugby where Chamberlain hoped he would be groomed, like the sons of other politicians, for public life. Neville, the eldest of Florence's four, joined Austen at Rugby but was destined by his father for a career in business. The younger trio, all girls—Hilda, Ida and Ethel—were still at home. Two of Chamberlain's sisters served in succession as surrogate mothers. The second, Clara, postponed her marriage until Beatrice was old enough to take over. But Clara ran a strict nursery and failed to appreciate that the older children needed to be given a freer rein than the young ones. They were delighted when Beatrice succeeded Clara in charge of the household.

It was never a gloomy home. The Chamberlain and Kenrick cousins roamed in happy packs through each other's houses, and spent their summer holidays and winter festivals together. Dilke sent his child Wentworth, also motherless, to Highbury while he was engaged in commercial negotiations with France. Wentworth had run into trouble at school for failing to tell the truth, and Dilke hoped that the environment of Highbury would help to correct the boy's failing. The boy enjoyed his time there so much that he advised his father to move to Birmingham.

Even so, the heart of Highbury was austere. Chamberlain's children served as constant reminders of the wives he had lost. Though he told the children after the death of Florence that they were 'all I have to live for now',[18] he distanced himself from them. He could not bear any mention of Florence, and thus deprived her youngest children of any memory of their mother. They longed for the moments at the end of the day when Chamberlain was in Birmingham and would spend time with them, joining in their games or telling them stories. But his presence could be draining as well as enlivening. For two or three days while he was preparing for a major speech, the household was hushed to leave him undisturbed.

The atmosphere in Highbury retarded the emotional growth of the children, and was particularly hard on Austen. In the absence of a mother and in awe of their father, each set of children looked for leadership to its eldest member, Beatrice among Harriet's two and Neville among Florence's four. Austen was sent away to boarding school at the age of six partly to release him from the dominance of Beatrice; but the towering influence of his father never ceased to shadow him. Once, when Austen criticized Dilke for neglecting his son, Chamberlain blurted out, 'You must remember that his mother died when the boy was born';[19] and Austen suddenly knew why it was hard to touch the heart of his own father. He sought to do so by identifying himself fanatically with his father's opinions and by turning himself physically into the mirror image of his father, complete with monocle and severe countenance. Neville, on the other hand, knew that he feared as much as he loved his father, and he kept politics at arm's length for a very long time. Beatrice could not do so once she took charge of social gatherings for her father. In his presence she was drained of opinions of her own; she was lively only when she had her brothers and sisters or friends to herself.

Chamberlain welcomed this subservient loyalty from his family and close friends. It sustained him in the unwelcoming social environment of Westminster. Lord Granville might be pleasantly surprised at his agreeable manners, which also impressed the Queen and the Prince of Wales. Chamberlain's irreverent repartee certainly delighted the fast set. But the more respectable statesmen disapproved, while young Whigs discussed his aspirations with condescension, and backbench gentry questioned whether he knew the unspoken rules by which gentlemen played the game of politics. In every sense of the words, he too obviously meant business.

These sentiments surfaced in ugly fashion during the spring of 1882. After Chamberlain's appointment to the cabinet he nominated two of his brothers to membership of the Reform Club, the semi-official resort of Liberal members of the two Houses of Parliament and their provincial confrères. The nominations hung fire for more than two years, and then were blackballed by more than sixty members of the club, prompted perhaps by friends of Forster. Alarmed by the potential consequences, Granville and Hartington convened a meeting of the membership to do away with blackballing and thus pave the way for the Chamberlain brothers' election by majority vote. The meeting took place in the wake of news that Chamberlain had helped to negotiate a suspicious settlement between the government and the jailed Irish leader Parnell. Feeling at the meeting in the Reform Club ran against the change of rules, one member declaring that 'there was no right more sacred in the eyes of every true-born Englishman than the right to black-ball anyone he pleased at a club election';[20] and the motion was rejected.

Hypersensitive at the best of times, Chamberlain exploded with fury. Refusing all attempts by Bright and Dilke as well as Granville and Hartington to quieten things down, he launched a suit against one of the leading malevolents, and thus exposed the affair to the press. He recognized that the suit was unlikely to succeed, but resolved to drag it out as long as possible to pile up the legal costs and make the lives of the defendants a burden to them: 'if money & labour can do it, we will bring their gray hairs with sorrow to the grave'.[21] He pursued the defendants for a year before the suit was dismissed. His treatment of them did nothing to remove the suspicion that he was not a gentleman.

Administrative opportunities

The Board of Trade provided the former manufacturer and mayor with the chance to make two points: that he could handle the administrative responsibilities of cabinet office as well as any landed gentleman, and that the prescriptions of Birmingham were applicable to national problems. He soon left no doubt of his competence. He took office with the new Parliament already in session and hence had to speak for his department without time to master its business. Yet he responded immediately to questions in the Commons with crisp, businesslike command. Meanwhile he launched private discussions, like those he once had over Birmingham's gas companies, with spokesmen for the conflicting interests in the initiatives he had foremost in mind. The ease with which he handled statistics stood him in good stead. Though the permanent officials in his department were high priests of classical economic orthodoxy, they learned to respect their new chief and after his departure praised him as the ablest they ever had.

But the other opportunity eluded his grasp. There was to be no repetition at the Board of Trade of the landmark legislative successes that marked Chamberlain's mayoralty of Birmingham. There were plenty of excuses for this contrast. Chamberlain was not supreme in Westminster as he had been in the town council, and like the rest of the cabinet he was distracted by imperial concerns. His experience at the Board of Trade even with modest initiatives was frustrating, and suggested that he could not translate the prescriptions of Birmingham Radicalism for national consumption. He had spent his earlier years in Parliament harnessing every popular discontent, particularly with the Tory foreign policy. But aside from the drinks trade and to a lesser extent land reform, he had paid little attention to the depressed domestic situation. His accession to a domestic office therefore found him unprepared for remedial action.

He reached back to one of his concerns in the mid-1870s when Samuel Plimsoll, the MP for Derby known as 'the Sailors' Friend', had raised his voice against the waste of life at sea.[22] Appalling numbers of merchant seamen drowned in overloaded or badly loaded ships without cost to the owners, who could insure themselves against the risk and even reap a profit when their vessels went to the bottom. Plimsoll's campaign had attracted Chamberlain as Radical chieftain of Birmingham in the mid-1870s because it served to consolidate the Liberal alliance there between organized labour and big business, which had no direct interest in the shipping industry. But Parliament reacted differently from the Birmingham town council. Chamberlain found that big businessmen in the Commons were among his most bitter opponents in this controversy. Shipping magnates were well entrenched on both sides in the House of Commons; the majority of the shipowning MPs were in fact Liberals; and they were not inclined to subject their great industry, vital for the wellbeing of England's island economy, to critical supervision by any screw manufacturer.

Chamberlain thought of his proposals as reasonable, even modest. They were designed to preserve the capitalist economy by ensuring that the wealth it generated for the captains of industry also provided at least security of life if not of livelihood to labour. Even towards this end Chamberlain was willing to use the powers of the state only within severe limits. His experience as a businessman had confirmed him in the faith that

> commerce flourished most when left alone, and that the free breath of competition encourages a healthy growth, while anything in the nature of State interference or protection must of necessity produce an enervated and weakly plant.[23]

He loathed officialism and red tape and welcomed opportunities to reduce governmental involvement in the day-to-day conduct of business. He was confident of his ability to persuade his fellow businessmen of the prudence of his proposals. Nevertheless, if he failed in his best efforts, he was willing to call to his aid the power of public opinion, always sure that it could turn the balance.

One of Chamberlain's first acts in office was to write to Plimsoll and also to C.M. Norwood, Liberal MP for the port town of Hull where he was the leading ship owner, asking each to visit him for private exploratory discussion. Plimsoll responded enthusiastically and postponed a visit to his wife, who was ill at Torquay, in order to meet Chamberlain immediately. But Norwood, who had left London for a fortnight in the country, refused to interrupt his vacation until the House of Commons was reconvened, 'when no doubt we shall meet'.[24] He and his fellow owners had organized a Chamber of Shipping to coordinate resistance to Plimsoll's agitation. Norwood emerged as the fiercest critic of Chamberlain's 'false and bastard Liberalism'[25] which he saw as a threat to the health of British industry and commerce; but for the moment he relied upon the permanent officials at the Board of Trade to educate their chief. The permanent officials would indeed have preferred to move at a more cautious pace than Chamberlain set. Nevertheless, the purpose of the Board as they saw it was to curb the very kind of abuses to which Plimsoll had drawn attention, because they threatened to discredit not only the shipping industry but by implication also the laissez-faire economy.

Encouraged by Plimsoll, Chamberlain moved for appointment of a select committee to enquire into the loss of ships since the passage of the Merchant Shipping Act of 1873, which Norwood had sponsored. Chamberlain also introduced a bill immediately to end the practice of paying sailors by advance notes, a practice which worked to the disadvantage of men in need of quick cash and was condemned by virtually all steamship owners apart from Norwood. Acting on the report of the select committee as soon as that bill passed, Chamberlain introduced another measure to regulate the loading of cargoes of grain to prevent dangerous shifting at sea, and he pushed it through to the statute books in the final weeks of the parliamentary session. Though his pace aroused protests from shippers early in the summer, he managed to mollify most of them by the end of the session with full explanations for his proceedings. Even so, resentment at his initiative and fear of where it might lead him smouldered among ship-owning MPs, reinforced by their railway-owning brethren with similar anxieties.

For the next two years Chamberlain held his fire, distracted by the turmoil in Africa and Ireland. He had two legislative measures on hand, one that was in the administrative pipeline to protect the interests of creditors in cases of bankruptcy, the other to cheapen the taking out of patents in order to encourage the inventiveness of artisans. No one took much issue with either proposal. But lawyers in the House could be relied upon to ask time-consuming questions. Organized labour, and in particular Davis of the Birmingham brassworkers, had a lively interest in the patents bill, but they were weakly represented in the House. Chamberlain was not able to push either measure through to the statute books till 1883.

While the Patents Act proved of enduring benefit, the Bankruptcy Act was just one step in a long process of legislative adjustment. Another piece of legislation, the Electric Lighting Act of 1882, the only significant measure Chamberlain secured that year, had a retarding effect on the industry. The pride Chamberlain took in Birmingham's gas and water prejudiced him against electricity, a new industry which was to lay the foundation for the next stage of industrial advance. Looking at the issue from a municipal perspective, Chamberlain wanted to prevent the creation of another monopoly which local governments would eventually have to buy out at inflated prices. He therefore sought to allow private capital the shortest possible time to prove the worth of the new source of energy before local governments could purchase control. He proposed seven years; and although, in response to pressure from the industry and the House of Lords, he extended the term to twenty-one years, he successfully insisted that local authorities could then purchase the works at cost, allowing private interests no more profit than they had made during their years of ownership. His Act slowed the growth of the electrical industry in Britain for at least half a decade.

Chamberlain was not quick to propose a political cure for the ailing economy of the country. His lack of sympathy for the owners of land led him to put down the depression in agriculture to a succession of bad harvests. He understood the depression in industry better. But its social consequences took time to erupt because the depression was in prices more than in production. Production was up though profits were

down. Owners and shareholders felt the pinch. But the working class
suffered less from unemployment than they benefited from the fall in
consumer prices. The statistics on total volume of transactions in wheat,
tea, sugar, tobacco and spirits enabled Chamberlain to emphasize that
'the consumption of every important article of necessity or luxury by
the working classes has shown a remarkable increase'.[26] The standard of
living of the working classes was at last on the rise.

These facts confirmed Chamberlain's faith in the free economy. His
faith included free trade even though Britain's Continental competitors
returned to tariff protection at the end of the 1870s. Chamberlain knew
from experience how Britain's overseas trade had flourished under free
trade. Because his faith was empirical rather than doctrinaire, he did
not hesitate to recommend retaliatory tariffs in the trade negotiations
with France or Spain. But he restricted his recommendations to wine
and spirits, arguing that Britain had kept duties on these products for
revenue-producing and moral purposes rather than for tariff protection.
Otherwise, he adhered to free trade as an inducement to remain competitive. The depression in trade provoked considerable demand in Britain, particularly in Birmingham, for a restoration of tariffs or 'fair
trade'. But Chamberlain disparaged this chorus as the voice of narrow
interests or simple ignorance. In words which would come back to
haunt him, he interpreted 'fair trade' for his constituents to mean that

> every workman in Birmingham and throughout the country should
> pay more for his loaf, and more for his clothes, and more for every
> other necessary of his life, in order that great manufacturers might
> keep up their profits, and in order, above all, that great landlords
> might maintain and raise their rents.[27]

Ireland

In the ranking of cabinet offices, the presidency of the Board of Trade
stood near the bottom. Its work was deemed lowly in comparison with
foreign and .imperial policy. Though Chamberlain's conduct at the
Board of Trade began to undermine these assumptions,[28] he wanted to
prove his ability to deal with the higher reaches of aristocratic statecraft. As a member of the cabinet he was entitled to participate in its
discussions of the most elevated affairs of state; and Dilke as undersecretary at the Foreign Office kept him abreast of what was going on.
In any case, turmoil in Africa and Ireland subordinated all subjects
closer to home in the mind of the cabinet, Parliament and the politically
conscious public for more than two years. Under calmer circumstances,
imperial concerns might have served to unify a cabinet which was potentially more divided on what was needed at home than abroad. But

the trouble in Ireland and at the edges of the empire was too serious to serve as a diversion. Gladstone's disjointed cabinet had to govern a disunited kingdom and an empire which was coming apart at some of its crucial joints.

Chamberlain threw himself into the cabinet's deliberations on these issues, anxious to make a Radical difference. Like everyone else, he came to regard Ireland as 'the most urgent, the most absorbing, and the most difficult of the questions with which the Government has to deal'.[29] No one could overlook the agrarian war which the recently formed Irish Land League intensified in the second half of 1880; and that conflict raised intractable constitutional as well as socio-economic questions because it was bound up with the fundamental relationship between the two British isles.

This combination of issues brought out tensions within Chamberlain's Radicalism as within every English political creed. Chamberlain's sympathies in England for labour and against landowners led him to favour the agrarian agitators in Ireland. The small tenant farmers of Ireland included some of the poorest in Europe, and they had been affected with particular severity by the bad harvests of the late 1870s. Still, their plight had not met with a generally callous response from their landlords. On the whole, the landlords were inclined to reduce rents and did not press hard for their collection until the improved harvest of 1880 encouraged them to do so. Chamberlain was not impressed by this record and welcomed the opportunity to reduce the legal rights of landlords. At the same time he was aware of the link between agrarian hardship and disaffection with British rule in Ireland. That disaffection threatened the cohesion and safety of the United Kingdom and expressed itself in acts of violence which outraged the English. The tension between the desires of the Irish and the reaction of the English drove Chamberlain to reflect that '[t]he problem of ruling a country against its will by Parliamentary institution has never been attempted by any other nation, and its solution is not an easy one'.[30] Parnell heightened the dilemma. Fast becoming the uncrowned king of Ireland, he derived his power from his ability, through coldly passionate and dextrously ambiguous leadership, to harness agrarian discontent, secure the goodwill of the Catholic clergy, and restrain as well as utilize the clandestine terrorist societies, in pursuit of the nationalist objective of political autonomy for Ireland.

Chamberlain hoped to loosen this tightening knot to his advantage. He and Dilke explored the possibilities of strengthening the relationship with Parnell which had served them on occasion well in opposition to Disraeli's government. But their discussions with Parnell revealed that he was committed to a stiffer conception of Home Rule than Chamberlain and to a lesser extent Dilke were willing to contemplate. Accordingly, when Parnell showed signs of fearing that a generous Irish land bill could reduce popular support for the Home Rule he sought, he increased Chamberlain's interest in that possibility.

Irish unrest assumed alarming proportions soon after the Liberals took office. No one in England had an accurate gauge of what was developing in Ireland or of popular response in England. Agrarian support in Ireland for the Land League was unmistakable. But were the leaders of the League truly agrarian reformers or intent primarily on Home Rule? And to what extent were they responsible for the increasing violence? The cabinet could not even obtain generally convincing statistics on the incidence of disorder and crime. Closer to home, there was no doubt a good deal of Liberal sympathy with the demand for land reform in Ireland and dislike of the use of coercion to suppress the agitation. But to what extent were these sentiments offset by the anger that Liberals also felt over the breakdown of law and order in Ireland? Hence what should come first, reinforcement of the law or reform?

Divided among themselves, the cabinet pursued an essentially negative course during their first eight months in office, rejecting most of the proposals that individual ministers put forward. The confusion in their councils was compounded by the uncertain grip of the minister most responsible for Irish policy, W.E. Forster. By nature a consensus seeker, he confined his search for consensus in this case to the English civil service at Dublin Castle and his cabinet colleagues at Westminster. Because the problem provoked conflicting responses from his advisers and colleagues, he swung back and forth—and thus deepened Chamberlain's feeling of contempt for him. The cabinet did not agree to Forster's initial proposal for stiffened enforcement of the law, whereupon he changed tack and proposed a remedial bill to compensate Irish tenants evicted for non-payment of rent. When this measure encountered opposition in the Commons with which Hartington sympathized, Chamberlain had to threaten resignation to maintain the cabinet's commitment to it. The House of Lords succeeded where Hartington had failed and threw out the bill. Then Chamberlain assumed the initiative. He favoured reconvening Parliament for an autumn session to force the bill through the Lords, but the cabinet was not ready for such resolute action. He instigated inquiries on a public works scheme in France with a view to similar measures in Ireland. But Gladstone's mind turned towards libertarian political solutions. Gladstone suggested the creation of Grand Committees for England, Scotland and Ireland to handle purely regional business. Chamberlain and Bright, welcoming any conciliatory initiative, endorsed the proposal. But the Whig majority in the cabinet turned it down.

They agreed in October to prosecute the ringleaders of the unrest including Parnell for conspiracy. Chamberlain went along with this decision. He was provoked by the decision of the Land League to intensify its agitation after the Liberals took office. He was aware of the anger of middle-class Liberals in Birmingham at the breakdown of law and order in Ireland, and wondered how far this reaction extended among the working class. He also wanted the government to hold together at least long enough to put a major reform of Irish land law on the statute books.

But Chamberlain was fiercely opposed to the introduction of fresh coercive legislation, certainly unless it was accompanied by fresh remedial legislation. 'It may be the work of Tories to crush out disaffection,' he told his Birmingham constituents; '[i]t is the better and higher work of Liberals to find out the cause of disaffection and remove it'.[31] Hence in mid-November when Forster demanded the suspension of Habeas Corpus, Chamberlain threatened to resign. As he explained to Gladstone:

> the arrest of 30 subordinate agents, as proposed by Mr. Forster ... would be like firing with a rifle at a swarm of gnats.... The remedy must be one which affects all—not the arrest of individuals when a whole nation has more or less escaped from the ordinary respect of the laws.[32]

Since Gladstone shared Chamberlain's aversion to coercion, the cabinet put off a decision until the new year when Parliament would be reconvened.

At the last moment the cabinet agreed to present Parliament with a combination of coercive and land-reforming legislation. Neither faction in the cabinet liked the package. The Whigs questioned the need for a land reform bill bold enough to meet Chamberlain's demands, while Chamberlain was dismayed by the Crimes and Arms bills upon which Forster and the Whigs insisted. The coercive bills were given priority over the land bill partly because of the need to await the report of a commission of inquiry into Irish land appointed by the government the previous summer. Chamberlain fumed over the delay. Yet he was neither sure enough of the popular feeling in England about repression in Ireland nor clear enough about the principles at stake to resign in protest against the government's coercive proposals as Dilke wished him to do. Chamberlain's acceptance of the cabinet's course of action estranged him from the pure devotees of conciliation.

English Radicalism approached a crossroads. Two bodies of Radical sentiment turned against coercion. One school now championed by Morley, who had learned their Liberalism from John Stuart Mill and the Italian patriot Mazzini, recoiled from the use of force to crush Irish nationalism; yet these men remained loyal to the Liberal party. Another,

newer group identified the suppression of tenants in Ireland with repression of the working class in England. This group had no more faith
in Liberals than in Tories and questioned the genuineness of Chamberlain's commitment to the working class. The Liberal government's introduction of its coercive proposals turned the doubts of this group to
disgust. In March of 1881, led by H.M. Hyndman, they formed a new
party, the Democratic Federation, the morning star of English socialism.
On the other hand there were some older Radicals such as John Bright
who were hardened by the behaviour of the Irish and began to think of
Parnell and his circle as traitors. This conflict of sentiments was at work
among supporters of the Liberal party at all levels, with disgust at the
disorder in Ireland perhaps stronger among the middle class, and hatred of repression perhaps stronger among the working class: but nothing was certain.

Parnell's tactics deepened Chamberlain's confusion. The Irish Nationalists in the Commons met the introduction of the Crimes and Arms
bills with a filibuster. It could be broken only through arbitrary intervention by the Speaker, who enforced his ruling by expelling thirty-six
Nationalist MPs from the House when they kept up their struggle.
Parnell could have used their expulsion as the moment for Ireland's
secession from the parliamentary union. Instead he chose to return and
renew the struggle in the Commons. Chamberlain missed the significance of that decision. The Nationalists' continued obstruction of debate
particularly angered him because he wanted to get on to the Land bill.
He was further disgusted when Parnell, in order to overcome Irish
uneasiness about his tactics, insisted on the ultimate objective of legislative autonomy.

Chamberlain insisted on a bold land bill as the only way to defeat
Parnell. Chamberlain and also Bright would have liked a land purchase
scheme to turn the Irish tenantry into owners of their smallholdings.
But Gladstone rejected their proposals as wildly expensive. Attention
turned back to the law governing the relationship between landlords
and tenants. Chamberlain insisted on a Radical reform summed up in
three Fs—Fair rents, Free sale, and Fixity of tenure—which would not
only lower rents but turn tenants into co-owners. Gladstone baulked at
fixity of tenure which infringed existing property rights. But he gave
way, and hence kept Chamberlain in the cabinet while losing the Whig
Duke of Argyll.

The Irish Land bill delighted Chamberlain. He half hoped that the
House of Lords would throw it out, thus precipitating a general election
which the Radicals could fight with united enthusiasm. If the Lords accepted the bill and it was enacted, he hoped that it would quieten Ireland enough to enable the Liberals 'to devote ourselves absolutely to
Home legislation and reform'.[33] Instead of rejecting the bill, the Lords

attempted to weaken it with amendments. But Gladstone, now enthusiastic about his handiwork and strongly supported by Chamberlain and Bright, prevailed upon a reluctant cabinet to stick to its guns; and the bill was duly enacted.

Gladstone and Chamberlain were determined to see that their hard-won measure was given a chance to prove its worth. But it threatened Parnell's position—as it was intended to do. If Parnell deterred Irish tenants from taking advantage of the Act, he might forfeit their support; but if he cooperated with the Act, they might still lose interest in his campaign, and he would certainly lose the confidence of determined nationalists. Taking refuge as he so often did in ambiguity, Parnell persuaded the Land League to probe the worth of the Act by bringing test cases before the new land courts, meanwhile aggravating the situation by pressing tenants to withhold their rent until the courts indicated how much reduction they might expect. These tactics again confounded Chamberlain. While the implementation of the Act was held up, outrages continued, provoking a cry for further repression. Chamberlain wished that he had never consented to coercion in the first place. 'I should like to stand aside,' he told Dilke, '—& let the Coercionists & Parnell fight it out together, but I fear this is not now possible. Altogether it is a horrible embroglio & for the moment I don't see my way out of the fog.'[34] Gladstone, however, was infuriated rather than paralysed by the behaviour of Parnell and the leaders of the Land League. He threw them into Kilmainham gaol. In doing so, while he bestowed the mantle of martyrdom on Parnell, Gladstone freed Ireland's tenant farmers to resort to the land courts, to which they flocked. In doing so, Gladstone convinced Chamberlain of the justice of this use of coercion.

Chamberlain responded with zeal, preaching Gladstone's gospel even more trenchantly than the old master himself. In doing so Chamberlain enraged Radicals and Tories alike. His defence of the decision to incarcerate the leaders of the Land League deepened the fracture of Radicalism. Morley took issue with the decision in the press. The socialist and working-class left wing interpreted Chamberlain's defence of the decision as proof that his interests and theirs were fundamentally opposed. But Chamberlain did not back off. 'In for a penny, in for a pound,' he wrote to Dilke; '. . . The electors will better stand a crushing blow, than coercion by driblets.'[35]

Tories were shocked by Chamberlain's expressions of understanding and even sympathy for the unrest in Ireland. Speaking in Liverpool to the National Liberal Federation,[36] he promised a generous response to the needs of Ireland so long as the union was preserved. While insisting that ultimately 'the highest duty of a Liberal was to support and to assert the law', he described coercion as 'a blot upon our civilization'. He declared that, if only the leaders of the Land League kept within the law, 'there never was an agitation promoted in the United Kingdom more deserving of a nation's gratitude and more entitled to complete success'. The ring of Chamberlain's words was deliberate. Averse to ambiguity as a sign of deceit or weakness, he sought to answer the Irish question with balanced yet unmistakable commitments:

> Liberal and Radical as I profess myself to be, I say to Ireland what the Liberals and the Republicans of the North said to the Southern States of America—'The Union must be preserved; you cannot and you shall not destroy it.' Within these limits there is nothing which you may not ask and hope to obtain—equal laws, equal justice, equal opportunities, equal prosperity. These shall be freely accorded to you, your wishes shall be our guide, your prejudices shall be by us respected, your interests shall be our interests; but nature and your position have forged indissoluble links, which cannot be sundered without being fraught with consequences of misery and ruin to both our countries, and we will use all the resources of the Empire to keep them intact.

The auguries at the beginning of 1882 were both exasperating and tantalizing. While 70,000 applications had come before the land courts with more coming in every day, this achievement exposed the limitations of the 1881 Land Act: it did nothing for tenants who fell into arrears on their rent, nor did it embrace leaseholders, groups that together totalled nearly three hundred thousand. The kinds of intimidation such as boycotting for which Parnell and the leaders of the Land League could be held responsible diminished sharply in frequency; but the incidence of violent crimes including murder rose, reflecting the free rein that terrorists enjoyed now that Parnell's hand was removed. So long as tenants could afford to pay their rent, they ignored the command of the Land League to withhold it. In short, the agrarian agitation was being curtailed but within sharp limits and without benefit either to the Land League or to the Liberal government.

One of the less extreme Home Rule MPs, E.D. Gray, approached Chamberlain with a proposal for settlement which began with the tenants in arrears. However attractive the prospect, it would be gravely flawed if it looked like a bargain. No settlement could be concluded without Parnell's consent, yet for British ministers to bargain with the man they had incarcerated would discredit both. If Chamberlain chose to negotiate, he would have to do so through Irish intermediaries. But Irish Nationalist MPs were treated as social outcasts by most other members of the Commons. Chamberlain accepted an almost impossible assignment in pursuing Gray's suggestion. With great reserve, he made the case for each side to the other. But he could not do so and still protect himself from suspicion, as Gladstone managed by adopting a position of judicious detachment. Chamberlain's position was further compromised by his relationship with Forster, the minister responsible for Irish affairs. Forster was rapidly losing the confidence of his colleagues. But Chamberlain's intrusion into the domain of the man he so obviously despised deepened the suspicion that personal motives were at work.

Movement towards 'the new departure', as interested parties on both sides described it, broke promisingly into the open when Irish Nationalist MPs introduced a bill to deal with the problem of arrears, and thus indicated their willingness to extend the effectiveness of the Land Act rather than continue to frustrate it. Even so, Parnell's commitment to the initiative was not entirely clear, nor was there any assurance that he would discountenance further use of intimidation. The government could not with propriety approach him directly while he was in gaol, a constraint which still applied when he was let out briefly on parole to visit his dying daughter. Hence the government had to rely upon emissaries who claimed to represent him.

Three came forward in this murky atmosphere, all Nationalist MPs, F.H. O'Donnell, Justin McCarthy and Captain O'Shea. The government greeted the emergence of the three as evidence of Parnell's conciliatory intent. But O'Shea was in fact an intruder who wished to use his relationship with Parnell to further his own fortunes. Everyone in this business had a private interest, but O'Shea's was particularly distorting. His wife was Parnell's mistress, and the dying infant to whom she had recently given birth was Parnell's daughter, relationships of which no member of the British cabinet was yet aware. A shallow man with ingratiating manners, O'Shea did not want vengeance but position and power, motives which English politicians could understand. His facile flow of words bred some uneasiness. But Englishmen liked to think of excessive readiness of speech as an Irish trait. Chamberlain kept some distance by addressing O'Shea as 'Sir' rather than by name, but otherwise accepted his communications in good faith.

The messages that O'Donnell, McCarthy and O'Shea passed from Kilmainham gaol to Chamberlain enabled him to win cabinet approval for the new departure. The understanding reached with Parnell constituted a victory for the government. The settlement rested upon agreement about the financing of an arrears bill. That agreement enabled Parnell to conclude that agrarian intimidation need no longer be condoned, and in turn enabled the government to conclude that Parnell need no longer remain in gaol. The only member of the cabinet to resist this logic was Forster, who wanted Parnell to denounce all forms of intimidation in absolute terms, which Parnell could do without damaging his leadership. Forster's resignation did not upset the rest of the cabinet. Though the government would have a ticklish time disposing of the inevitable taunts that the settlement was discreditable, neither Gladstone nor Chamberlain was embarrassed by their handiwork.

O'Shea, however, left rotten meat in the stew. He had extracted from Parnell and then showed Forster a statement that

> a practical settlement of the Land Question . . . would I feel sure enable us to co-operate cordially for the future with the Liberal Party in forwarding Liberal principles and measures of general reform.[37]

After the government reached its settlement with Parnell and he was released from gaol, Forster obliged him to read this statement to the Commons. It enabled the Tories to denounce the settlement as an infamous bargain, 'the Kilmainham treaty', concluded by the gaoled Irishman and the Liberal party to their political advantage rather than in the national interest.

O'Shea's meddling damaged everyone he had dealt with, particularly Chamberlain. The settlement with the Irish which he had done much to arrange might otherwise have raised his political standing; and it certainly raised his hopes. But now, after consultation with leading Whigs, Gladstone passed him over in filling Forster's office not just once but again when the first replacement, Lord Frederick Cavendish, was assassinated upon his arrival in Dublin. Dilke was offered the position, but without a seat in the cabinet; and he therefore spurned the offer. Chamberlain tried to change his mind in order to place the Irish office in sympathetic hands.

For the murder of Cavendish threatened further to undermine the new departure. The government felt obliged to bring in a stiff coercion bill to reinforce order in Ireland. Parnell appreciated this necessity and sought only to moderate the severe provisions that Harcourt, as minister in charge of the bill, proposed. Chamberlain resumed his shuttle diplomacy with the Irish leader through O'Shea, ironically the only person to emerge unscathed by his own meddling. But when Gladstone encouraged this dialogue without consulting Harcourt, there was a row. Harcourt refused to make any significant concessions in his coercion bill; and he found enough support in the cabinet to overcome the pleas of Gladstone as well as Chamberlain.

Everything Chamberlain had accomplished over the past year seemed to be lost. He was tarnished by his continuing association with the Irish. He wished to resign but could not do so over the details of a coercion bill the principle of which he had accepted. He was angry by turns with Harcourt and Parnell, who reverted to parliamentary obstruction. Chamberlain had accomplished more than he appreciated, yet his fears were not unfounded. The land legislation of 1881 and 1882 reduced agrarian unrest as he had hoped. But the Crimes Act of 1882, far stiffer than the Act of 1881, kept Irish resentment lively. With the land question temporarily settled, Parnell replaced the Land League with a new National League which had Home Rule as its avowed objective.

In response Chamberlain turned from the economic to the political issue, and sought to weaken the demand for Home Rule by reforming local government. In an article in the *Fortnightly Review*,[38] he drew on the recent use of parliamentary Grand Committees for domestic legislation to suggest the creation of 'Committees of Nations' to deal with 'measures affecting the separate nationalities of the United Kingdom'. If such committees proved effective, it might be 'possible, nay, it may even be said to be probable, that the idea of a separate Parliament, having thus lost all its practical importance, would die away in time'. Whig opposition to the extension of local government in Ireland only confirmed Chamberlain's interest in this line of policy. But he was dissuaded from focusing on it for the moment by his organizational lieutenant in Birmingham, Francis Schnadhorst, who argued that the electorate was fed up with the Irish and wanted attention paid to English business that had been piling up for the past two years.

Africa

Chamberlain had pushed himself to the fore over Ireland as a subject clearly pertinent to Radical interests. His grasp of affairs farther overseas was less firm, and his approach to them was naive. When the government ran into difficulties with Russia, he urged his colleagues to follow 'a policy of perfect frankness. . . . We have to convince her of the absolute honesty of our present policy, and to this end the best way would seem to be to assume her Govt. to be as honest as ourselves.'[39] Insofar as he had an imperial and foreign policy, it was to give effect to the ideals Gladstone had expressed in his Midlothian campaigns. Chamberlain had always been uneasy about John Bright's desire for British withdrawal at any sign of trouble overseas. But Gladstone's international concerns were obviously lively. Chamberlain was deaf to the moral cadences of Gladstone's rhetoric on foreign affairs and never shared his altruistic concern for the comity of nations. As Chamberlain boiled down the message of Midlothian, it offered a way to reconcile Britain's aversion to costly wars with the pride and profit-seeking interest that the British took in their empire. Glossing over the tension between these reactions, he insisted that Britain confine itself to pacifying its existing provinces, already more than adequate to Britain's needs, rather than extend its sway at the troubled frontiers.

He had applied this principle in the closing months of Disraeli's ministry to South Africa. In doing so Chamberlain stumbled upon a part of the world which would both forward and distort his purposes for the rest of his life. Britain was at a crossroads in its relations with South Africa, uncertain whether to minimize or strengthen its interests there. Competition with the rising industrial powers of the United States and Germany increased British interest in undeveloped markets overseas, particularly in the colonies from which British exports could not be excluded by hostile tariffs. On the other hand, the defeat which the Zulus inflicted on the British at Isandhlwana made the risks of imperial expansion terribly clear. Repelled initially by those risks, Chamberlain was one of the few MPs to vote from the outset against the Conservative government's annexation of the Transvaal, a republic formed by dissident Boer emigrants from Britain's Cape Colony. The stand which he took paid him a quick political dividend by widening his cooperation with Gladstone. When British claims that a majority of the population in the Transvaal favoured annexation proved to be ill founded, Gladstone moved toward the position Chamberlain had adopted and expressed sympathy at Midlothian for restoration of the republic's independence.

When the Liberal cabinet met for the first time in 1880 and surveyed the international situation, Chamberlain staked out his position, not the least deterred by his inexperience. He urged his colleagues to repudiate the territorial advances which the Conservatives had attempted and to recall the emissaries responsible for those advances. He was particularly anxious to bring Sir Bartle Frere back from Cape Town and to withdraw from the Transvaal. The cabinet shied away from such a departure from the principle of continuity in foreign policy. Though Frere was recalled, the government with Gladstone's concurrence continued to uphold the annexation of the Transvaal. Partly to muzzle Chamberlain, Gladstone asked him to serve as the cabinet's spokesman in the House of Commons on South African issues. Chamberlain dealt with the assignment by offering only a brief defence of the decisions with which he privately disagreed while expanding vigorously on those he supported; and Gladstone was sufficiently pleased to continue the assignment.

The subsequent course of events in South Africa validated Chamberlain's original advice, to the embarrassment of the rest of the cabinet including the prime minister. The root of the trouble was the encouragement Gladstone had given at Midlothian to the hopes of the Transvaal Boers for independence. When his ministry refused to act in line with those hopes, the Boers took up arms under the leadership of Paul Kruger. By the end of 1880 Britain stood on the brink of war with people Gladstone still hoped to conciliate. The notion of a war of conciliation was absurd and provoked the Radicals in the ministry to rebel. Four of them—Chamberlain and Bright plus Dilke and Courtney—

walked out of the Commons rather than vote against a backbench motion deploring the annexation of the Transvaal.

Then disaster struck, one that scarred Anglo-Boer relations for the rest of the century and was all the more tragic because both sides sought to avoid it. Moved by pressure from the Radical ministers, the Colonial Office opened negotiations with Kruger, who responded with cordiality. But neither side called off its military activity. Contingents of their armed forces moved towards a height of land overlooking a vital access route between Natal and the Transvaal: Majuba hill. Communications between and within the two sides were fatefully slowed by the physical distances that divided them. The British force took up position on the hill, and was wiped out by Boer insurgents.

The defeat at Majuba provoked a cry for retaliation to restore British honour and prestige in South Africa before negotiations with the Transvaal Boers were resumed. And indeed Kruger learned a lesson from Majuba that Gladstone never wished to teach. But the Radicals in the ministry led by Chamberlain rejected the demand for retaliation. They argued that the action of Majuba, however regrettable, was an accident, and they insisted that the otherwise promising negotiations with the Boers be pressed to a conclusion. The parallel argument between coercion and conciliation in Ireland figured prominently in their thinking; and since the argument for coercion of the Transvaal was ultimately illogical, the Radicals welcomed the opportunity to dig in their heels against it. They threatened Gladstone with four or five resignations, from Bright, Chamberlain, Dilke, Courtney and perhaps also Shaw-Lefevre, the Commissioner of Works. Rather than bow directly to this ultimatum, Gladstone gave himself a few days' grace. He used the time to persuade the Colonial Secretary, Lord Kimberley, to resume negotiations with Kruger; and the political crisis was averted. Though the ministry had to endure a hail of criticism for its failure to uphold Britain's prestige, the negotiations moved towards a settlement along lines with which the Conservatives did not fundamentally disagree. Meanwhile respect rose in the cabinet for Chamberlain's judgement.

Learning that he was about to address his constituents, Gladstone and Kimberley encouraged him to make the case for the government's South African policy. Chamberlain complied with more candour than they liked. He explained the government's belated decision to abandon the annexation of the Transvaal in terms that Birmingham could understand:

> if we let [the Transvaal] go, this population of 40,000—a population less than that contained in any one of the sixteen wards of this town ... this dismembered Empire of ours will still contain 250,000,000 of subjects to the Queen ... sufficient even for the wildest ambition.[40]

Thus far Gladstone approved. But Chamberlain went on to say that the Liberal government had been wrong not to cancel the annexation in the first place. Gladstone winced: 'I . . . am not prepared, for myself, to concede that we made a mistake in not advising a revocation of the annexation when we came in,'[41] he wrote reprovingly. Yet he could not help admiring the substance of the speech, which his staff interpreted as 'bold, incisive, powerful and . . . evident indication of statesmanship'.[42]

Understandably Chamberlain was reluctant to face the subsequent deterioration of his achievement. In a Convention signed with Kruger in Pretoria, the government restored the autonomy of the Transvaal subject to British suzerainty, which involved control over the foreign relations of the republic. In return Kruger promised to respect Britain's concern for the black population, who sought protection from Boer enserfment. But the message of Majuba encouraged Kruger thereafter to nibble away at these limitations to full independence. Tacitly he encouraged Boer invasions into native territory. The incursions infuriated a Scottish missionary, John Mackenzie, who returned to Britain to awaken its conscience. Mackenzie enjoyed notable success in Birmingham thanks to R.W. Dale, who had welcomed the government's commitment to the native cause in the Pretoria Convention. Hence Chamberlain was confronted with pressure from his home base to uphold the Convention.

He resisted the demand. 'If the strict execution of the Convention is pressed home,' he explained to Dale, 'we must not conceal from ourselves the probability that we shall be again engaged in a Boer war, the most costly, unsatisfactory, and difficult of all the little wars which we can possibly undertake'.[43] Mackenzie, however, proved a formidable agitator; and Chamberlain joined Dilke and Hartington in pressing the cabinet to stand up to Boer disregard of the Pretoria Convention. Gladstone was dismayed at this reaction in the cabinet. He wooed the Radical pair with an invitation to speak for the cabinet in the forthcoming Commons debate. Dilke turned the offer down. But Chamberlain accepted it, and thus reaffirmed his commitment to an increasingly discredited policy.

Events at the opposite end of Africa pulled him for a while towards the Little England camp. Egyptian army officers led by Arabi combined with Egyptian nationalists to challenge the control that Britain and France exercised over their country in the interests of its foreign creditors. Gambetta at the head of the French government demanded that the two powers defy the challenge; and Britain reluctantly went along. Chamberlain disapproved. The nature of the Egyptian challenge was unclear; but if it was genuinely nationalistic, he thought that Britain would be better advised to accommodate than resist it. At this point

Gambetta suddenly died, leaving the government of France as hesitant as the British, while in Egypt the challenge to the European powers turned menacingly military. Gladstone concluded that Arabi was simply a military adventurer, an assessment which the cabinet did not discuss carefully, as Chamberlain later recalled with regret. But at the time he accepted it readily, and he pressed the government to follow it up more vigorously than Gladstone quite liked. When Arabi fortified Alexandria, Chamberlain supported a request from the navy for permission to destroy the fortifications. The cabinet agreed; and without aid from the French, the British bombarded Alexandria.

This action divided the Radicals. Initially Chamberlain's most anti-imperialistic friends like Morley had been more critical of Arabi's movement than he; but the course of events reversed these reactions. The preponderance of Radical opinion came down on Morley's side against the bombardment of Alexandria. John Bright resigned from the cabinet in protest. But he was content to confine his protest to resignation; otherwise he remained loyal to his colleagues and was anxious 'to treat the Egyptian incident rather as a deplorable blunder than as a crime'.[44] When he finally wrote to the Birmingham Liberal Association to censure the government's action, Chamberlain's henchmen contrived to hush the letter up.

Chamberlain did not regard his argument with the Radical critics as fundamental. He was more impressed than they with Britain's economic interests in Egypt, which were much more substantial than those at stake as yet in South Africa. Pointing out that four-fifths of the shipping through the Suez canal was British, Chamberlain contended that British investment in the mercantile economy of Egypt served to benefit 'many thousands—tens of thousands—of English workmen'.[45] Rather than sacrifice 'all these great interests . . . to the ambition of a military adventurer',[46] he had approved the comparatively small amount of force needed to put Arabi in his place. But Chamberlain was not tempted to ride the wave of popular approval that greeted the bombardment of Alexandria. He was preoccupied with the undercurrent of Radical criticism, and it pulled him back to his Radical moorings. Not opposed to Egyptian nationalism as he fondly imagined it to be, he hoped that Arabi's defeat would release the civic and agricultural interests of Egypt from his military thrall. Once Britain was in control of the country, Chamberlain analysed the situation in terms which Radicals could appreciate. He pressed the cabinet to encourage the speedy growth of representative institutions in Egypt, arguing that when these were in place, Britain could abandon its occupation and rely for protection of its interests upon the gratitude of the Egyptians.

This line of thought did not impress the rest of the cabinet. The bombardment of Alexandria left a vacuum in Egypt which Britain felt obliged to fill and from which it could not then escape. Chamberlain took the dilemma as 'a warning & a lesson to look a little more closely into the beginning of things'.[47] To one degree or another most of his colleagues shared his desire for withdrawal from Egypt, but they began to realize that it would take longer than they dreamt when they unleashed the fleet at Alexandria. Pointing out that '[w]e cannot leave Egypt to anarchy', Chamberlain pleaded with the public for patience.[48]

But Britain sank ever deeper into the Egyptian mire. Seeking release at least from Egypt's southerly domain in the Sudan where British troops faced an uprising under an Islamic leader called the Mahdi, the government despatched General Gordon to conduct the evacuation. Once he reached Khartoum, however, Gordon chose to stay and fight. Though Gladstone wanted simply to repudiate Gordon, the cabinet felt that they could not thus consign Gordon to his fate; and they discussed a further expedition to bring him and his men back to safety. Meanwhile the majority for the government in the Commons crumbled as Radicals and the Irish joined the Tories in censuring its performance. Confounded by the predicament, Chamberlain oscillated between the interventionists in the cabinet led by Hartington and the Little Englanders led by Harcourt who wanted to withdraw from Egypt as well as the Sudan at almost any cost. When a friend wrote to warn Chamberlain of the popular sympathy for Gordon, Chamberlain hotly refused to take it seriously. 'The feeling', he replied, 'is got up in the first instance by Jew-money-lenders & is fostered by educated Jingo's; but you may take my word for it the working classes will never forgive the Government or the party who plunge them into a new Abyssinian war for the sake of persons & interests in which they have not the least concern.'[49]

The balance of Chamberlain's concerns began to shift in the summer of 1884. It was not popular opinion in Britain but competition among the powers of Europe incited by Britain's takeover of Egypt that produced the change. Bismarck seized pieces of territory in Africa and the South Pacific which no European power had yet claimed but which Britain had assumed to be within its sphere. Chamberlain saw little intrinsic worth in the lands at issue, but the challenge of competition always stiffened him to resist. 'I don't give a damn about New Guinea,' he told Dilke at the end of the year; 'but I don't like being cheeked by Bismarck or anyone else.'[50] The revival of imperial competition led Chamberlain to think of Egypt in imperial rather than domestic political terms. He presented his change of mind crudely to the editor of the *Birmingham Daily Post*: 'If we can be sure that no other Power will bar the way to India, or attempt to establish itself in Egypt we may regard with great indifference the struggles of the Egyptian people to work out their own political future.'[51]

Even so, the new frame of reference was unfamiliar to Chamberlain. Not sure quite how great power relationships applied to Egypt, once again he oscillated, this time between conciliating and defying Bismarck. Joseph continued unhappy in his Egyptian bondage.

7

Rising Expectations
1884–1885

For two years Chamberlain had focused his best energies on Ireland and Africa. As 1882 drew to a close he could find little reward for his efforts. The Kilmainham treaty left him under a cloud of suspicion, and both ends of the African continent were restive. The political scene at home was worrying. The government did not fare well in by-elections. The legislative business coming out of the pipeline in the Board of Trade and the other domestic ministries was unexciting. Agrarian Tories such as Henry Chaplin, MP for Mid-Lincolnshire, displayed more initiative than the Liberals by proposing to extend some benefits of the Irish Land Act to English tenant farmers. 'What is the good of bothering about Bankruptcy, or Local Government,' Chamberlain asked Dilke, 'when our real business is to outbid Chaplin & Co with the Farmers?'[1] The Liberal government remained ambiguous in character. While Lord Derby slid in easily as Colonial Secretary in 1882, a protracted struggle was required to counterbalance that appointment by elevating Dilke.

Even so, Chamberlain hesitated to challenge the status quo. He was alarmed by Gladstone's talk of retirement. On the major issues of controversy Chamberlain and Gladstone had come down on the same side in the cabinet; and Chamberlain was not strong enough yet to do without that support. But there was too much he wanted to do to put up with his apprenticeship much longer. Challenges at the turn of the year from Morley, Hartington and Salisbury propelled Chamberlain into action. He proceeded to generate the most famous Radical Programme of the century. The concurrent failure of his main attempt at social legislation suggested that his policy objectives exceeded his political grasp; but he did not heed the lesson. His role in widening the popular base of British politics sent his hopes soaring.

The genesis of the Radical Programme

Morley had exchanged ideas with Chamberlain over the years on every field of political concern bar one, the social economy. That was Chamberlain's province. But at the end of 1882, Morley pressed Chamberlain to give more Radical thought to land reform in response to the rapid spread of extreme ideas among the urban working class. In the spring of the year an American, Henry George, author of *Progress and Poverty*, came to London on his way to Ireland to advocate his panacea of a single tax on the unearned increment in the value of land. Chamberlain and John Bright took George to the Reform Club for dinner to explore his ideas, mainly with regard to Ireland. Elsewhere his book attracted more attention. An English writer, A.R. Wallace, called for nationalization of land. Such ideas found a ready response among people on the fringes of Radical activity in London who were bitterly disappointed at the performance of the Liberal government over the past two years. Some formed socialist societies to give labour an independent voice. These groups were small and disunited. The loyalty of labour to Liberalism remained sturdy. None the less, George and Wallace touched a nerve to which labour could prove acutely sensitive.

Industrial competition from Germany and the United States was eliminating Britain's economic superiority. Falling confidence in the ability of British industry to generate ever greater wealth exposed the maldistribution of the existing wealth. Urban working men might still tolerate and even admire businessmen who grew rich on the rewards of their enterprise, because they had worked for what they earned. But landowners were another matter. The concentration of land ownership in a few hands rose to an all-time height in the 1870s, higher in Britain than anywhere else in the old world. Urban families, often uprooted originally from the countryside, could be easily persuaded that rural landowners had robbed them of their heritage and continued to drive labourers off the land into towns where they drove down industrial wages. Furthermore, landowners in the towns bore responsibility for the cramped, squalid quarters in which the existing and newly arriving working classes had to live.

Morley told Chamberlain that workmen were 'full of the ideas of Henry George' and were 'reading his book by thousands of copies'.[2] Though a dutiful subscriber to laissez-faire economics, Morley concluded that it was no longer enough to call for repeal of the laws which inhibited free trade in land. Fear of Henry George pushed Morley towards the less extreme writings on land reform by John Stuart Mill and Wallace. Morley assured Chamberlain that, at least in London, the proposals of Wallace for nationalisation of the land were 'the one subject that would furnish a base for agitation'.

Though quick to respond, Chamberlain recognized more acutely than Morley the economic dilemma at issue. If by nationalization Wallace meant simply increased taxation on land, owners could pass it on in the form of increased rents. But if nationalization meant more, if it meant ownership by the nation, it would preclude the revival of small peasant owner-farming which Chamberlain and his adviser on these matters, Jesse Collings, advocated for both England and Ireland. They wanted to extend, not to end, the pleasures of property ownership. Small peasant proprietorships would also, they believed, increase the productivity of British agriculture at a time when large capital owners were reluctant to invest in it because of the agricultural depression. Chamberlain asked his ablest officials at the Board of Trade, Thomas Farrer and Robert Giffen, to examine Wallace's ideas. Their analysis was devastating.[3] Knowing that their chief had acquired considerable wealth in business, they rebutted Wallace's claim that most of the wealth generated over the past half century had accrued to the great landowners; and they also pointed out the similarity between landowners who lived on rents and those like Chamberlain who lived on the income from investments. Farrer and Giffen drew Chamberlain back to less drastic prescriptions: to the enhancement of tenant rights as in the Irish Land Act, and to the proliferation of small owner-farmers. Morley was readily convinced. 'Let us go gently,' he concluded.[4]

While Chamberlain too accepted the analysis by Farrer and Giffen, he felt that they did not take the ground swell in public sentiment seriously enough. He had recently delivered a couple of addresses in the industrial heartlands of England, in Lancashire and to his own constituents. Though vigorous, these speeches did not cut any new ground; yet they evoked a response that reinforced the impression Morley had of working-class opinion in London. Chamberlain could not make out the precise nature of the ground swell, but he sensed that it arose from recognition that 'the enormous increase in general wealth has not been accompanied by proportionate improvement in conditions of the poor'.[5] 'Socialism', he told one newspaperman, 'is in the air.'[6]

His discovery went along with a hardening in the lines of conflict within the cabinet. Lord Hartington was more restive than Chamberlain about the ambivalence of the ministry, and was prepared to kick over the traces without waiting for Gladstone's retirement. Provoked by Chamberlain's incursion into Lancashire close to his own constituency, Hartington took public issue with the tenor of his colleague's remarks, particularly on Ireland. Chamberlain rose to the challenge, confident that 'the country—(*our* country that is—the great majority of Liberal opinion) is ripe for a new departure in constructive Radicalism & only wants leaders. So if we are driven to a fight, we shall easily recruit an army.'[7]

The challenge from Hartington prompted Chamberlain to reexamine the terms for Radical collaboration within the Liberal party. 'At present,' he explained to a confidante, 'we are in a transition period when Radicals accept thankfully the crumbs which fall from the rich Whig's table; but sooner or later, "Oliver will ask for more", and it is well that we should consider in time what is the most to which we are entitled as well as what is the least that we may be willing to accept.'[8] The outlines of a programme of constructive Radicalism took shape in his mind. He began, as always, with education, which he wanted to provide free of charge. But the most notable feature of the new programme would be 'changes intended to assist the more equal distribution of wealth', changes which he associated wherever possible with the concentration and privileges of land ownership. Working-class housing could be improved by tapping the wealth of urban landowners, while the number of peasant farmers could be increased by carving small allotments out of the broad acres of the aristocracy.

To temper the alarm of the affluent, Chamberlain spoke of peasant proprietorships as 'the antidote to the doctrines of confiscation which are now making converts'.[9] But he underestimated the divisive potential of his proposals. Property owners would not find it easy to distinguish between his programme and the abyss of true socialism from which he meant to protect them. Chamberlain's brand of constructive Radicalism carried its own price-tag. Free education would cost money, as Leonard Courtney was quick to point out. 'I hope C[ourtney] will some day discover', Chamberlain breezily replied, 'that the duty of a good Government is not to save money but to spend it wisely.'[10] Yet the former cost accountant paid surprisingly little attention to the financial side of his proposals.

These potential conflicts were veiled for the moment by the prerequisite for all of Chamberlain's proposals, extension of the franchise. He set his eyes on the day when a much-widened electorate would come into its own. He was induced, however, to give early expression to the direction of his thoughts by Disraeli's successor as Conservative leader in the Lords, Salisbury. A man whose daring matched his own, Salisbury came to Birmingham to raise the Tory flag in the citadel of the enemy. The acknowledged master of gibes and flouts and jeers taunted the rising master of invective. Two days later, referring to the need for land reform, Chamberlain replied to Salisbury as

> the spokesman of a class—of the class to which he himself belongs—
> 'who toil not, neither do they spin'—whose fortunes, as in his case,
> have originated in grants made long ago, for such services as courtiers

render kings—and have since grown and increased while their owners slept, by the levy of an unearned share on all that other men have done by toil and labour to add to the general wealth and prosperity of the country of which they form a part.[11]

The attack delighted Chamberlain's constituents, but also served Salisbury's purposes. To make sure that the property owners of England took fright, Salisbury pointed out the furthest conclusions to which Chamberlain's rhetoric could be carried.

Pleased by the stir his words had made, Chamberlain pressed on but produced a reaction which made him temporarily pull back. In mid-June the national spotlight returned to Birmingham for the twenty-fifth anniversary of Bright's election as MP for the town. Chamberlain used the occasion to outline the next assignment for Britain's Radicals. The substance of what he demanded was not much in advance of the Liberal consensus. It was 'the tone and colour'[12] of his speech, and the popular response it evoked, that shocked the highest reaches of the British hierarchy, above all the Queen. Chamberlain began by comparing the recent coronation of the Russian tsar with Birmingham's celebration for John Bright:

> Pomp and circumstance were wanting; no public money was expended (hear, hear); no military display (hear, hear) accompanied Mr. Bright. (Cheers.) The brilliant uniforms, the crowds of high officials, the representatives of Royalty were absent (loud laughter and cheers), and nobody missed them (renewed laughter and cheering), for yours was essentially a demonstration of the people by the people (cheers) in honour of the man whom the people delighted to honour (cheers).[13]

Such rhetoric from a minister of the crown was bound to raise more than eyebrows. The Queen demanded that Gladstone call Chamberlain to account.

When the prime minister read the speech, he found further cause for dismay. Chamberlain stretched the conventional confines of public comment by cabinet ministers beyond what Gladstone would tolerate. He instructed Chamberlain to use his next scheduled speech, at the Cobden Club, to redeem himself. Chamberlain resented the order; and his annoyance was raised by the resignation of several members of the Cobden Club over its invitation to him. When he spoke to the club, he reminded its members that the man after whom it was named had favoured a widened electorate, equal electoral districts, compulsory redistribution of landed estates at death, free schools and religious equality. Still, by adapting his style of speech to the parliamentary tastes of the club's membership, Chamberlain satisfied the gentlemen who were sent to judge him.

But not Gladstone, who read the speech afterwards. It contained a demand on behalf of the Radicals in or out of the cabinet for freedom of speech. Chamberlain accepted the need to win consent from the bulk of the party before each Radical policy could be translated into legislation. He was willing to give up his 'liberty of action in the present', but only in return for the right to speak out 'as to the future'.[14] Reluctantly Gladstone accepted the conclusion among those who heard the address that Chamberlain had made amends for his language at Birmingham. But he pressed Chamberlain to agree to his reading of the rules for public ministerial discussion.

Chamberlain felt obliged to do so 'without reserve'.[15] For the rest of the year he expressed himself in public with notable circumspection. He declined even to demand extension of the franchise 'until there is evidence of sufficient general agreement on the subject'.[16] The administrative command which he displayed that summer in shepherding his Bankruptcy bill through Parliament helped to restore him to favour in Gladstone's eyes. But Chamberlain did not expect that favour to last. At year's end he explained to another Radical MP that he expected to 'get the sack sooner or later . . . my object is to get the whole machine as far forward as possible before the smash comes'.[17]

His restraint on the platform that autumn was all the more remarkable in view of the bond he had learned how to forge with mass audiences, particularly in his town. Beatrice Potter was almost overcome by this mastery when she heard him address his constituents in the new year:

> As he rose slowly, and stood silently before his people, his whole face and form seemed transformed. The crowd became wild with enthusiasm. . . . Perfectly still stood the people's Tribune, till the people, exhausted and expectant, gradually subsided into fitful and murmuring cries. At the first sound of his voice they became as one man. Into the tones of his voice he threw the warmth of feeling which was lacking in his words; and every thought, every feeling, the slightest intonation of irony or contempt was reflected on the face of the crowd. It might have been a woman listening to the words of her lover! Perfect response, and unquestioning receptivity.[18]

But for the moment he held this power back.

There was a more discreet way to present his case to the public. The major journals of political opinion, with their select readership and practice of anonymous authorship, offered Chamberlain what he needed. T.H.S. Escott had taken over from Morley as editor of the *Fortnightly Review* and was happy to place the journal at Chamberlain's disposal. In issue after issue for seven months from July 1883 to January 1884, the *Fortnightly* unveiled 'the Radical Programme' of the future.[19]

No names were attached to the articles. Rather than try to master each subject himself, Chamberlain commissioned friendly specialists on each particular field—Collings, for example, on the agricultural labourer, and Francis Adams, the former secretary of the National Education League, on the remaining agenda there—and he entrusted the more general articles to Escott. But from first to last he worked closely with the contributors; and they used his public words and actions as their point of reference. These arrangements enabled him to flesh out a programme that bore his stamp without committing himself to it. The fact that the various authors gave different subjects pride of place widened his room for manoeuvre and the programme's range of appeal.

The programme was predicated on an extension of the working-class electorate, which was widely expected to be the government's next order of business. The authors of the Radical Programme believed that, however partial this electoral reform might be, it would open a new chapter of political history in which the need for social legislation would be the primary concern. They did not expect that this social demand would be pressed immediately by the new working-class voters. They were not even sure that the new working-class voters would be entirely happy to risk higher taxes in order to pay for the social reforms they desired. The articles were as much exploratory as declaratory. Many of them were well informed and pragmatic. But all were imbued with the belief that popular resentment was rising at the unfair distribution of wealth in Britain over the past fifty years and that this resentment threatened the social and economic order of the country.

The Radical Programme called upon the property owners of Britain to reduce this resentment and avert the threat by investing in forms of social insurance. Improved working-class housing for example would function as 'insurance paid by the better class against disease [and] . . . by the rich against revolution'.[20] The kinds of insurance proposed in the programme did not constitute a great advance on what Chamberlain had already advocated. The programme focused on urban housing, land ownership and education. It relied primarily on local government. In theory it did little more than amplify for nationwide consumption the principles upon which the government of Birmingham had been transformed a decade earlier.

Nevertheless the programme violated the assumptions within which national British policy had been confined for more than a generation. Men of state had entrusted the social wellbeing of the country to the beneficence of the free economy, tinctured on the Tory side by vestigial paternalism and on the Liberal side by utilitarian regulation to remove scandalous abuses. The authors of the Radical Programme, by contrast, insisted that the government could and should correct the most offensive aspects of the maldistribution of wealth and privilege in Britain.

The Radical Programme also ran against the moral and religious grain, particularly of many Liberals, by pushing single-issue crusades to the sidelines. Instead of gratifying the prohibitionists, the programme treated the taxes on drink as an indispensable source of governmental revenue. Instead of dwelling on the sectarian concerns of Nonconformists, the article on education treated the need to abolish fees as a question of social justice. This article did not even shrink from suggesting that the terms for abolition of fees might benefit the many elementary schools still run by the Church of England. Still, no matter how great its challenge to cherished assumptions, the Radical Programme did not cause a great stir until Chamberlain began to proclaim it from the platform a year later. The anonymous authors lay their groundwork undisturbed.

The subject of urban housing seized national attention in October, but not at Chamberlain's prompting or on his terms. A Congregationalist minister, Andrew Mearns, touched the public with a pamphlet called *The Bitter Cry of Outcast London* which described the degrading conditions in which the working classes of the metropolis lived. The article in the Radical Programme on the housing of the poor was already due for publication in the *Fortnightly Review* at the end of the month. But the aspect of the problem to which Mearns drew attention was overcrowding inside tenements rather than the insanitary environment produced by building houses back to back as well as side to side. The distinction was fine but crucial, as Lord Salisbury appreciated. Salisbury had already goaded Chamberlain by pointing out that, while Birmingham's famous improvement scheme beautified the town centre by tearing down cramped housing to make way for a broad boulevard, it did next to nothing for the dispossessed workers. Exploiting the point, Salisbury too had an article in the works. Published just after *The Bitter Cry* and before the *Fortnightly*'s piece on the subject, Salisbury's article criticized municipal improvements in London as well as Birmingham which demolished slums without rehousing the dispossessed.

Here was a particularly incisive example of the Conservative criticism that Liberals did both too much and too little on social and Irish issues. Chamberlain undertook to reply in yet another issue of the *Fortnightly*, but he did not fully appreciate the force of the attack. Dismissing Salisbury's article as the vacation essay of a great landowner, he refused to move beyond the prescriptions of Birmingham. He used Birmingham's experience to argue that landowners formed the heart of the problem. Chamberlain calculated that Birmingham had to pay local landowners half a million pounds more than the market value of their property in order to carry out the improvement scheme, an overpayment which accounted entirely for the increase in rates to which the scheme had given rise. He proposed changes in the law in order to place the financial burden for future schemes of this sort squarely on the owners of urban land. By treating great landowners as the villains of the piece, he hoped not only to turn the tables on Salisbury—who owned a substantial tract of land in one of the most overcrowded parts of London— but also to allay the fears of small property-owners. Thereafter the two antagonists sought to drive their knives into each other. Chamberlain despatched agents to investigate Salisbury's management of the housing on his estates in Hertfordshire and London, while Salisbury commissioned the Conservative Central Office to see what Nettlefold and Chamberlain had done for their employees. But neither side discovered anything incriminating.

Chamberlain underestimated the national problem of overcrowded housing because he looked at Britain through the lens of Birmingham, and Birmingham was less densely populated than most industrial towns. The overcrowding in London was obvious, but Chamberlain treated the problem there as exceptional, aggravated by the distances that labouring men had to travel each day unless they remained in tenements near their work. Salisbury continued to set the political pace on this issue, moving for a royal commission on urban housing and then placing his mark on its proceedings.

Shipping and the franchise

All this was skirmishing in anticipation of a big battle over extending the franchise, which Chamberlain saw as the gateway to Radical progress in all other areas. At his prompting, in the autumn of 1883 the National Liberal Federation demanded that electoral reform top the government's legislative agenda for the coming session of Parliament. Gladstone agreed, and at the subsequent meeting of the cabinet only one member, Hartington, demurred.

Chamberlain anticipated a succession of dividends from this decision, each one promising if the preceding one failed. To begin with, Hartington might resign, thus paving the way for Chamberlain to succeed Gladstone as leader of the Liberal party. If Hartington swallowed the pill of electoral reform and stayed in the cabinet, the franchise bill might be defeated in the Commons; but that would enable Liberals to throw an invidious light on Conservatives as opponents of the enlarged electorate that was bound soon to receive the vote. If the Commons passed the bill, the Lords under Salisbury's leadership seemed certain to reject it; and Chamberlain could conduct an exhilarating fight on the favourable theme of the people against the peers.

Only one issue worried him: the redistribution of seats. If that hornets' nest was opened in connection with the straightforward matter of franchise extension, the government was sure to be defeated before it could gain much popular credit. Gladstone, however, saw the force of that argument and agreed that the franchise must be dealt with first and by itself. Once sure of Gladstone's agreement, Chamberlain looked to the future with confidence. Even the existing electorate would return a Liberal majority on the issue of franchise extension. The outcome would be still better, vastly better if the existing Parliament first agreed to extend the franchise and then made way for a general election, leaving the business of redistribution to its successor.

Seeking to confirm the cabinet's decision on the franchise and also to goad Hartington, Chamberlain concentrated his next address on electoral reform and assured his audience that the government would take action. Rising to the bait, Hartington took public issue with his colleague and privately threatened to resign. Gladstone's rival lieutenants thus helped the old man reassert his leadership. Suspicious of Chamberlain's ambition but respectful of his gifts, Gladstone restrained Chamberlain skilfully. 'It is, I know, difficult and disagreeable to . . . rein in a strong conviction, a masculine understanding, and a great power of clear expression,' he wrote when Chamberlain was about to deliver a speech, 'but pray be as cruel as you can to your own gifts.'[21] When Chamberlain's speeches again raised trouble at court, Gladstone remonstrated with but also defended him and coached him on disarming the Queen. Gladstone's blandishments gave Chamberlain the illusion of victory and at the same time kept Hartington in the cabinet when it reaffirmed its decision to make household franchise for the counties its main legislative proposal for 1884.

Chamberlain paid dearly for his seeming success. Once the government staked its credit on the Franchise bill, Gladstone proved willing to abandon other legislative proposals if they threatened its passage. Chamberlain's Merchant Shipping bill was the most conspicuous casualty. He had only himself to blame. The way in which he pressed for this bill maximized the opposition to it and also revealed how far the Radical Programme might repel rather than attract support; yet he failed to learn from the setback.

The case for the Merchant Shipping bill was strong. Chamberlain was not pandering to popular sentiment. The sailors who signed up with the merchant fleet were a migratory, unorganized and ill-informed lot, pathetically unable to help themselves; and Plimsoll's campaign on their behalf no longer enjoyed the public interest that Henry George and *The Bitter Cry* had captured over land and housing. That was part of the problem. Chamberlain had both to rouse concern about and respond to the sailors' plight. What impressed him were the figures, eloquent to the accountant, and advice from his most respected civil servants. Over the past twelve years a staggering total of 36,000 merchant sailors had died at sea, one out of every six who signed on. Many factors contributed to this result, including overloading, undermanning and sailing too fast or without waiting for storms to subside. But the permanent officials at the Board of Trade, Farrer and Thomas Gray, insisted that overinsurance lay at the root of the problem, and the wreck commissioners bore out their conclusions. Through overinsurance, owners profited when their ships went down; and the existing law encouraged risky shipping practices. Insurance could be taken out on ships without deduction for depreciation, on freights including those on the homeward voyage whether or not it occurred, and upon expenses, and the same thing could be insured twice under different headings.

Some large shipping firms, particularly in Liverpool, refused to exploit these possibilities, which they agreed with Chamberlain in deploring. But shippers on the east coast, particularly from Hull and Newcastle, fiercely defended their industry. All of them, western as well as eastern, believed in the free international economy from which they derived their wealth. They were well placed in the House of Commons to defend their interests. They enjoyed the support of insurance underwriters. And they summoned to their aid a host of marginal investors in speculative single-ship companies. Chamberlain met an outcry from an unexpected corner, from 'classes who ought to have had nothing whatever to do with such matters—women, Dissenting ministers, working people, especially in Yorkshire and Lancashire'.[22] These reactions reflected basic flaws in the strategy of the Radical Programme. The investors in shipping, whether large or small, were not idle landowners against whom Chamberlain preferred to inveigh. They were his own economic kith and kin. The major shipowners were captains of industry, though in the mercantile rather than the manufacturing sector. As stockholders they lived off the income from investments, in the way Chamberlain now did.

Blind to these implications, Chamberlain proceeded clumsily in pursuit of a Merchant Shipping bill. Relying solely on the advice of his permanent officials, he did not seek private negotiations with the more reasonable shippers before outlining his bill to the industry. Hence he had to deal with an angry array of all the interested parties under a glare of publicity. Rallies heated the confrontation from both sides. The vivid way in which Chamberlain told the public of the casualty figures and insurance abuses seemed to indict the whole industry for callous inhumanity. Even responsible shippers took umbrage. Chamberlain tried to distinguish between the good majority and a bad few. But the reluctance of all to make concessions in face of his indictment disillusioned him. 'It is not the "black sheep" who are the worst,' he told confidants; 'it is the smug self-righteous ship owners' who, 'like the

Slaveowners of the South . . . were blinded to the misery & suffering caused by the practices to which custom & law had so long lent their sanction.'[23] He used his speech on presenting his Merchant Shipping bill in the Commons to substantiate his indictment in cold detail rather than to conciliate.

By then in any case it was too late. The storm he stirred up had induced the cabinet to postpone the second reading of the bill repeatedly for fear that it would deprive them of vital votes on the Franchise bill. The shippers rejected an attempt by Gladstone to arrange for negotiations. Chamberlain offered to resign and keep up the agitation independently, but he did not insist. He knew that the Franchise bill would be endangered. None the less, the weakness of support for his shipping measure within the parliamentary Liberal party and the unwillingness of the cabinet to stand by it disillusioned him with both. He sought support from the public by arranging for the publication and wide distribution of his speech on the bill's second reading. But his efforts continued to raise more fears among the propertied than hopes among the electorate. And few of the migratory sailors were registered to vote.

He had yet to drink the dregs of the shipping cup. When dropping the bill, the government undertook to appoint a royal commission of inquiry into the industry. Both Chamberlain and the industry were determined to secure strong representation, but Conservatives and moderate Liberals shied away from involvement in a bitter fight. Nominee after nominee rejected the invitation to serve. When Chamberlain's intention of appointing himself to the commission became known, the reaction threatened to bring the government to grief. Gladstone intervened to his colleague's annoyance; and a compromise was worked out, leaving Chamberlain on the commission but strengthening the industry's representation. He served actively on the commission until he left office. A few years later Parliament quietly enacted legislation in the direction of his proposals. In the meantime his exposure of the practice of overinsurance led shippers to abandon its worst excesses. In substance his crusade eventually succeeded, but with no benefit to himself.

His discomfiture in 1884 on merchant shipping was offset, however, by the fortunes of the Franchise bill. At Salisbury's behest, the House of Lords refused in July to pass that measure unless accompanied by a Redistribution bill. Salisbury thus fulfilled Chamberlain's desire for 'a serious collision' between the Lords and the Commons. Radicalism had 'everything to hope and nothing to fear'[24] from a struggle that pitted the peers against the people. The government recessed Parliament to give public opinion time to express itself before the Franchise bill went back to the Lords; and Chamberlain emerged as the central figure in a countrywide agitation. Gladstone welcomed his talent for this purpose. The prime minister stipulated that members of the cabinet confine themselves in public to the subject of the franchise and not talk about how to deal with the Lords if they persisted in their defiance. But he did not care how Chamberlain described the Lords so long as he did not discuss 'future prospects'.[25] Taking advantage of the latitude which the prime minister allowed him, Chamberlain obeyed his injunction for three months, longer than Salisbury would have liked. For Salisbury counted on Chamberlain to polarize the country and frighten moderates into the Conservative fold.

The people of Birmingham lapped up Chamberlain's denunciation of the House of Lords as 'irresponsible without independence, obstinate without courage, arbitrary without judgment, and arrogant without knowledge'.[26] Elsewhere Conservatives assembled creditable audiences but could not rival the many thousands Chamberlain drew. Salisbury was unimpressed by the Liberal demonstrations, whose orderliness he treated as evidence of organizational manipulation rather than popular conviction. In October, shortly before Parliament was to reconvene, his commentary turned ugly. Declaring that he saw 'no great and violent public pressure'[27] for reform, Salisbury seemed to suggest that only violence would persuade him to change his mind. If, he taunted, Chamberlain led a march on London, he would probably have his head broken. Responding in kind, Chamberlain replied that 'if my head is broken it will be broken in very good company'.[28] The Queen was horrified by this response. Gladstone also disapproved and induced Chamberlain to make some amends. Though they fell considerably below the prime minister's desire, Chamberlain escaped further censure on this score because he had not initiated the exchange.

He did not escape so lightly from events closer to home. The rapidly rising young star of the Conservative party and prophet of Tory Democracy, Lord Randolph Churchill, intended to contest Birmingham at the next general election. That was too close for Chamberlain's comfort, though the two men recognized each other as kindred spirits. Both were rebels against the upper echelons in their parties. Churchill appealed to Tory prejudice as stoutly as Chamberlain to Radical. At the same time the Tory Democrat came so close to parts of the Radical Programme that R.W. Dale wondered whether Birmingham's Liberals might coopt him. Once, when opposition to him among the Conservative leadership grew particularly sharp, Churchill enquired whether Chamberlain might allow him to stand as an independent. Uneasy about Salisbury's line, Churchill did not play a prominent part in the franchise agitation over the summer. Nevertheless, in order to plant his standard in Birmingham, arrangements were made for a mass rally for Churchill and Sir Stafford Northcote to address there at Aston Park. Nowhere during the franchise agitation had Conservatives managed to hold a successful rally out of doors. To do so in Birmingham would do much to discredit the claims of the Liberal agitators.

From the moment he learned of the plans, Chamberlain encouraged his lieutenants to disrupt them, though he kept a careful distance from the countermanoeuvres. *'The Tories will not be allowed to hold their meetings here in October,'* he declared privately in August, predicting 'a blazing row'.[29] The Conservatives, anxious for a large audience, played into the hands of their opponents by handing out tickets for the rally indiscriminately. Suddenly fearful of a hostile takeover of the meeting, the Conservatives cut off the supply of tickets, but the Liberals forged counterfeits. Meanwhile they planned for a rival rally nearby. Both sides hired 'roughs'. When the day arrived, upwards of ten thousand townsmen of Birmingham converged on Aston Park to choose between two rallies separated by a few hundred yards and a wall. The trouble may have started when Tory roughs assaulted people coming to their rally with Liberal badges. The injured crossed over to stir up the Liberal rally. Liberals thereupon surged out to the wall, broke off the glass topped coping stones, and poured over. Before taking charge of the Conservative rally, they ignited the fireworks the Conservatives had installed, turning the set piece featuring the head of Sir Stafford Northcote ignominiously upside down. Northcote and Churchill were badly hustled as they beat their retreat, though there was little property damage and no one was seriously hurt.

Breathing fire and brimstone over his treatment, Churchill placed the responsibility on Chamberlain, who had been in town that day, denounced the town's corporation as a creature of the Liberal caucus, and threatened to subject subsequent Liberal rallies to similar disruption. Equally truculent, Chamberlain used his next speech to express, not regret over the events at Aston Park, but indignation at Churchill's disparagement of the Birmingham corporation. When Parliament reopened, Churchill proposed a motion to censure Chamberlain but his remarks lacked their usual fire. Chamberlain responded with, by every account, the best speech that he had yet delivered in the House of Commons. Equipped with affidavits from roughs confessing that they had been hired by Conservative agents, he 'roll[ed] Randolph over like a rabbit'.[30] Churchill's motion was defeated. The Liberals failed to muster their full majority, reflecting disapproval of Chamberlain among moderate Liberal MPs as well as carelessness on the part of the Liberal whip. Still, as Lord Granville ruefully observed, Chamberlain's position was 'strengthened every day' by his notoriety.[31]

His escape was nevertheless lucky. Within two weeks of the debate in the Commons, the affidavits Chamberlain had used to such effect proved to have been suborned, and the roughs who had made the confessions were quietly hustled out of town. Responsibility for this scandal, as for the forged tickets and earlier hiring of roughs, probably lay with the Birmingham Liberals' formidable organizer, Schnadhorst, whose relations with Chamberlain now cooled. Having eluded Churchill's motion of censure, Chamberlain contrived to prevent any revival of the debate. He mended his fences with Churchill by sending him a note of good wishes on his departure for a visit to India, to which Churchill responded with 'the greatest pleasure'.[32]

Radical imperialism

The combat between Chamberlain and the Conservative leaders over the franchise coincided with a sharpening in his imperial thought. The government had embraced the cause of franchise extension partly to offset the unpopularity of its African policy. Its efforts in South Africa were proving no more satisfactory than in Egypt. At the beginning of 1884 the government tried to conciliate the still restive Transvaal republic by modifying the Pretoria Convention with another signed in London. The London Convention left Britain in possession of the 'missionaries road', a crucial stretch of territory to the east of the Transvaal, giving the British at the Cape ready access to the north through land held by Tswana (Bechuana) tribes loyal to Britain. In return, Britain gave the Transvaal responsibility over the native tribes whose allegiance it claimed. But the ink on the London Convention was scarcely dry before Boer freebooters laid claim to much of Bechuanaland with tacit approval from the Transvaal.

The inability of the government to devise an imperial policy that was either consistent or effective dismayed Chamberlain. He found welcome guidance in the autumn of 1883 with the publication of *The Expansion of England* by the professor of modern history at Cambridge, J.R. Seeley. The book impressed Chamberlain so much that he soon claimed to have sent his son Austen to Cambridge because its author was there, though in fact Austen had gone up the year before its publication. *The Expansion of England* struck notes in foreign affairs similar to those struck by the Radical Programme in domestic. Both advocated unapologetic exercise of the powers of government. Both sought to identify the facts in Britain's current situation that were pregnant with implications for the future. Both thought that British statesmen should concern themselves with these facts much more than with the goings on in Parliament. Both were alert to the impact of applied science and saw in trade the mainsprings of the empire. Seeley also wanted to pay less attention to Europe than to Britain's empire overseas, an inclination with which Chamberlain sympathized.

The most salient feature of modern English history as Seeley saw it looking onward rather than back was that '[i]n not much more than half a century the Englishmen beyond the sea . . . will be equal in number to the Englishmen at home'.[33] Seeley thus placed less emphasis on India than on the colonies peopled by emigrants from the United Kingdom. Englishmen beyond the sea and at home would together total more than a hundred million, quite enough if united to hold their own against the rising powers of the future, Russia and the United States. Hence 'the greatest English question of the future'[34] was how to consolidate 'Greater Britain'. It could become 'a robust reality',[35] Seeley argued, through some form of imperial federation. After all, Russia and the United States were demonstrating the practicability of political union over vast land masses; and the distances between Britain and its colonies were effectively shrinking thanks to the steamship and telegraph.

But Seeley's understanding of the colonial empire, like the Radical Programme's reading of the socio-economic dynamics of England, was deeply flawed. He insisted that '[t]he English Empire is on the whole free from that weakness which has brought down most empires, the weakness of being a mere mechanical forced union of alien nationalities'.[36] If the people of the British Isles felt that they were 'for all purposes one nation, though in Wales, in Scotland and in Ireland there is Celtic blood and Celtic languages utterly unintelligible to us are still spoken, so in the Empire a good many French and Dutch and a good many Caffres and Maories may be admitted without marring the ethnological unity of the whole'.[37] Chamberlain knew that this gloss on relations between English and Irish at home was facile, and so was its applicability to relations between British and Boers in South Africa. These shortcomings kept Chamberlain from embracing Seeley's teaching without qualification, but not from welcoming his vision.

By the autumn of 1884 the disregard the Transvaal showed for its recent promises to Britain could not be overlooked. The seriousness of the situation was increased by Bismarck's acquisition of Angra Pequena in southern Africa. These two developments ended Chamberlain's patience with non-intervention and with the reluctance of the Colonial Secretary, Lord Derby, to resist German expansion overseas. In the most incisive memorandum he had yet written on an imperial issue,[38] Chamberlain called for an immediate strengthening of British forces in South Africa, to be reinforced by a colonial contingent, in order to suppress the Boer freebooters and reinstate the Bechuanas loyal to Britain. Since his proposal was contingent on colonial cooperation, the cabinet accepted his advice. But the colonial ministry at the Cape proposed instead to negotiate with the freebooters. Though Chamberlain still pressed for an armed expedition, his colleagues resolved to wait and see what terms the colonial negotiators brought back.

The shift in Chamberlain's thinking showed when he defended government policy in the House of Commons. Observers who hoped to maintain the relationship between Britain and South Africa were pleasantly surprised by the strong sympathy he displayed. J.A. Froude, like Seeley a historian interested in imperial federation, was about to visit Cape Town, and he offered to carry word from Chamberlain. Chamberlain gratified him with a remarkable message: 'Tell them in my name that they will find the Radical Party more sternly Imperial than the most bigoted Tory.'[39]

Hasty prophecy

However significant the development of Chamberlain's imperial thought in 1884, the empire was still of secondary importance to him, overshadowed by affairs at home and above all by the campaign to extend the franchise. Sanguine about the outlook so long as Liberals stuck to their guns on this issue, he feared only that the government might compromise with the Conservatives by bringing in a Redistribution bill and thus place the Franchise bill in jeopardy. He welcomed prolonged confrontation with the Lords. 'Victory will probably be delayed,' he cautioned a Liberal rally as Parliament reassembled in November; 'but the delay will only strengthen our position. . . . If a decision is shortly arrived at we shall gain much; if it is long postponed we shall gain more.'[40]

The turn which events took later that month accordingly disappointed him, all the more so because he could not object. The Conservative leadership agreed to pass the Franchise bill immediately if they could reach agreement with the Liberal leadership on the main features of a scheme of redistribution. In that event both sides would do their best to enact a Redistribution bill before Parliament was dissolved, and a general election would be called on the new basis. A handful of the leaders undertook to negotiate the redistribution. They were dominated on the Conservative side by Salisbury and on the Liberal by Gladstone and Dilke who, as President of the Local Government Board, was familiar with the complications of constituency boundary-making. Like everyone outside this charmed circle, Chamberlain was excluded from its discussions. Preempted since January by Gladstone on the issue of the franchise, he found himself preempted by Dilke on redistribution. The agitation against the Lords from which Chamberlain stood to profit came to a halt. The Third Reform Act, the indispensable precursor of the Radical Programme, would not be his handiwork.

Apart from opposing minority voting, he had not given much thought to redistribution. No one knew quite what to expect from the various ways in which the electoral map could be redrawn to reduce inequities in voter distribution. But for someone who hoped for so much from the new electoral order, Chamberlain's hunches on the subject of redistribution were singularly unsound. Salisbury pressed for single-member constituencies almost universally; he specified only that the new electoral boundaries coincide as far as possible with the lines of economic interest, thus accentuating the differences which ownership of property made. Chamberlain had mixed feelings about this approach but consoled himself that it went a long way towards equal electoral districts and greatly increased the representation of urban areas. He calculated that the Liberals, who had long done well in industrial towns, would now do much better, while the Tories, who had usually done well in rural areas, would find their ranks severely depleted. He recognized that the break-up of big cities like Birmingham into single-member constituencies would foster the election of lesser local figures rather than leaders of citywide or national stature like Bright and himself. But he did not expect an increase in working-class representatives for urban constituencies. In short, though he had little hand in redrawing the electoral map, he saw no reason to revise his sense of what the new electorate would be like or the sort of programme it would find appealing.

Swallowing his disappointment at the abrupt ending of the franchise agitation, he accepted the redistribution scheme that the inner circle agreed upon. Dilke mollified him by giving Birmingham an extra seat, raising its total to seven—though Chamberlain promptly asked for eight—and by raising his hopes that the Redistribution bill might still fail to pass the House of Commons. The skill with which Dilke proceeded to steer the bill through the Commons not only belied this hope but also strengthened the possibility that he rather than Chamberlain would emerge as the Radical leader of the party when Gladstone retired.

That Gladstone would go soon, once the Reform bills were secure, Chamberlain did not doubt: 'what a triumph it is for Mr Gladstone at the end of his career,' he remarked contentedly, 'to have achieved such results!'[41] Trying to flatter the old man but instead deceiving himself, Chamberlain told Gladstone that the Third Reform Act would prove to be 'the greatest Revolution this country has undergone'.[42] Chamberlain's expectations of the sequel to this revolution were boundless. 'If I am not mistaken, this year is the true commencement of the Democratic Gospel,' he prophesied, '& changes which will go to the very root of our present social & political organisation are now brought into the region of practical politics.'[43]

8

Overextension
1885

... it is so difficult in present circumstances to satisfy oneself as to the right course to take,—to be true to one's principles—or to find any principles to be true to. ...

Chamberlain to Mrs Pattison, 13 February 1885

Instead of flowing with Liberal milk and Radical honey, the promised land opened up by the passage of the Third Reform Act turned out to be a Conservative desert. The hopes that the new dispensation encouraged the various Liberal leaders to pursue led them, one and all, into the wilderness. The First Reform Act had been followed by a brief but momentous spate of reforming legislation, the Second by the most productive of all Liberal ministries though it had left Chamberlain angrily impatient. The Third was to yield largely Conservative dividends for twenty years.

Even if no one anticipated this result, it was not entirely unnatural. The procedures for registering to vote operated against members of the working class on the lookout for cheaper or more convenient housing, and so helped to keep the British franchise the least democratic in Europe. In addition, with more canniness than he himself appreciated at the time, Lord Salisbury managed to ensure that the new electoral map reflected residential economic interests and hence undermined the alliance between the urban middle and working classes upon which the Liberal party depended. Yet the extension of household suffrage from the boroughs to the counties, which was the main feature of the Franchise Act, similarly undermined the Conservatives' agrarian base.

The new electoral order would not have disappointed the Liberals so deeply if, after passage of the Reform Act, their leaders had not bid so high and at the same time fallen out among themselves. The cardinal responsibility for this folly lay equally on two men: Chamberlain and Gladstone. In bidding too high and against each other, they bankrupted themselves, broke up their party, and in doing so brought about an enduring diversion in the course of British political history.

However serious the issues in the crisis of 1885 to 1887, it was as much a matter of personalities; and it is best understood as a drama moved forward by its leading characters rather than by impersonal forces. The issues over which Gladstone and Chamberlain were divided, first Chamberlain's mild but abrasive brand of 'socialism' and then Gladstone's initiative over Ireland, were indeed serious. Yet the differences between the two men over both issues were not intrinsically irreconcilable. And though in these years Britain reached the depths of a prolonged economic depression which could have exacerbated Chamberlain's impatience, his sensitivity to it was lessened by the comparative prosperity of Birmingham.

The contrast between laissez-faire Gladstonian Liberalism and Chamberlain's constructive variety was more rhetorical than substantive. The socio-economic and still more the religious reflexes of the two men were undoubtedly quite different. But Gladstone's elaborately qualified and often deliberately obscure manner of speech disguised even from himself the extent to which he was prepared under pressure to violate the canons of laissez-faire orthodoxy. The Irish Land Act of 1881 was only the most conspicuous example of this willingness. That Act's transfer of some of the rights of property from landlord to tenant was extended in muted form to England by the Agricultural Holdings Act of 1883; and Gladstone was soon to offer to apply it to help the dispossessed crofters of Scotland. He had also given sturdy support to the repeated but unsuccessful attempts of his ministry to democratize and strengthen local government in London and the counties, undeterred by the venerable vested interests of the City Corporation and the landed magistracy, measures that were essentially consonant with Chamberlain's municipal socialism. As one historian has put it, 'Consciously or otherwise, Gladstone had by 1885 become capable of countenancing a further extension of constructionist principles.'[1] There were still smaller grounds for divergence in principle between the two men over Ireland, as their agreement during the past four years suggested and as close but helpless observers were to note at the very moment of the separation between the two men in 1886.

As for the economic depression, while it struck the Black Country west of Birmingham in full measure, Birmingham escaped the worst of its rigours, saved by the diversity of its industrial base. Though mature male labourers thrown out of work in one industry might lack the elasticity to find employment in another, their sons could do so; and the women in the family often provided unskilled labour in different industries from those in which their skilled menfolk worked. The various opportunities for employment helped also to keep wages up throughout the town. Even in the Black Country the extended Chamberlain family proved lucky, for the only industry there that did well into the mid-1880s was the manufacture of cast-iron hollow-ware from which the Kenricks derived their wealth. The depression as Chamberlain experienced it in Birmingham was not strong enough to push his Radicalism substantially beyond what he had expressed through the *Fortnightly Review* in 1883. It was political calculation stimulated by the Third Reform Act and Gladstone's expected retirement rather than economic pressure that prompted Chamberlain's initiatives in the opening weeks of 1885.

The underlying issue in the political crisis of the mid-1880s was leadership. So far as the Liberals were concerned, the most salient but also the most deceptive fact was Gladstone's age. A few weeks after working out the agreement with the Conservatives that produced the third Reform Act, he turned seventy-five. Most of his colleagues assumed that he would retire once the Redistribution bill reached the statute books, either before or after the general election that would immediately ensue. After all, he had spoken to them with increasing frequency over the past three years of his wish to retire.

But however sincere these expressions, they were also assertions of his indispensability. Only Gladstone seemed able to hold his cabinet and party together. His talk of retirement drew attention to that fact when his colleagues became embroiled with their rival ambitions. Those ambitions had nevertheless intensified during his ministry. Its record did not kindle collective pride. Ireland was still in turmoil. The unassertive conduct of Lord Granville at the Foreign Office and Lord Derby at the Colonial Office deepened dismay among the stronger spirits in both wings of the cabinet. Its legislative accomplishments were meagre, aside from the Franchise bill; and the process through which that bill was enacted had exacerbated the rivalry among Gladstone's colleagues by discomfiting Lord Hartington while raising Chamberlain's expectations.

But that predictable conflict was overshadowed by the emergence of a rivalry which Chamberlain did not anticipate clearly between himself and Gladstone. Though not imbued with reverence towards the Grand Old Man, Chamberlain assumed that the transition between them would occur naturally as the old generation gave way to the new, the passage between them marked by the Third Reform Act. Preoccupied by the coming dispensation, Chamberlain wanted to stake out his Radical claims. He thought less of Gladstone than of his own generation, of Whigs led by Hartington and of opportunistic Tories such as Lord Randolph Churchill. Yet in proclaiming the new Radicalism Chamberlain implicitly challenged his chief.

Chamberlain's challenge to Gladstone was perceived rather than intended. Gladstone was sensitive to forewarnings of a possible threat. During the agitations of 1884 over merchant shipping and the franchise, young spirits throughout the country looked to Chamberlain as the man of the future. People compared the amount of applause that his name and Gladstone's evoked at Liberal rallies, often to Gladstone's disadvantage. So long as Chamberlain confined himself to forwarding the policies on which the cabinet were agreed, Gladstone welcomed his prowess on the platform. But when Chamberlain sketched out lines of future advance for which his Whig colleagues were not ready, the prime minister took umbrage. The precise moment at which his observation hardened into resentment and then to determination to rid himself of Chamberlain cannot be pinned down. The old man obscured his personal sentiments even from himself. But colleagues like Lord Granville whose future prospects depended on Gladstone's continued leadership lost no opportunity to turn him against Chamberlain. Their efforts were reinforced by a host of other people repelled by the pretensions or policies of the Radical from Birmingham.

The duel between Gladstone and Chamberlain was conducted on ground which they shared uneasily and in arenas where both were vulnerable. Both stood to the left in the Liberal party, though Gladstone to his advantage stood nearer the centre. The two men were the most effective platform orators in their party, a talent which Chamberlain was better able to exploit because he was less encumbered by the work of office and the weight of age. Neither man had cultivated close contacts with the rank and file of the parliamentary party, a weakness which hurt Gladstone less because he could rely on his immense prestige and gratitude for past services. Chamberlain had not built up much of a following for himself among the Radical backbenchers in the Commons. He tended to regard them as will-o'-the-wisps to be forced into line through popular pressure from below and assertive leadership from above. He underestimated the function of the intermediate layers in the structure of political power. Yet during the ensuing crisis, he did better than Gladstone in the decisive engagements in the Commons while Gladstone did better than he among the Liberal masses in the country. The bitterest draught in store for Chamberlain came from a source which had hitherto given him comfort. A person whose talent for friendship was exceeded only by his craving for it, he was to be deserted by some of his closest friends. The experience would sear them all.

Presenting the programme

The first act in the drama of 1885–7 lasted from January to June of 1885, when Gladstone's ministry lost the confidence of the House of Commons in which its original majority had been so large. The disintegration of that majority was reflected from the beginning of the year within the cabinet. It was riddled with dissension and intrigue. Despite the Reform Act and the prospect of a general election on the new basis before the end of 1885, the agenda of cabinet discussion was a familiar one, dominated by unresolved problems in imperial policy: Egypt and the Sudan; competition with Germany in Africa and the Pacific, and with Russia on the western approaches to India; and Ireland, over which the government's coercive powers were due to expire. Unable to reach agreement on these issues, the cabinet was held together by procrastination, by each member's fear of resigning alone, and by their general reluctance to let the Tories take over.

The consideration that pushed the cabinet beyond the business at hand at the beginning of 1885 was Gladstone's health. Its precariousness precipitated discussion behind the scenes in January and February about a possible reconstruction of the ministry in which the new generation would take over. There was less disagreement about the composition of the possible new ministry than about its policy, and less disagreement on domestic issues than on imperial. The common assumption was that the reconstructed ministry would be led by Hartington but include Dilke and Chamberlain in prominent positions. The intrigue to create such a ministry was protracted to the point of failure over Egypt. But there was also a lack of will to succeed, especially on the Radical side. Though on the lookout for opportunities to resign from the existing government along with Dilke, Chamberlain would not commit himself in any intrigue with the rest of his colleagues which could be interpreted as directed against Gladstone.

In the midst of these private discussions, Chamberlain undertook to transmit the Radical Programme from the cool pages of the *Fortnightly Review* to the new electorate through the medium of the platform. The three speeches which he delivered in January 1885 were so evocative that, though the Radical Programme had been articulated first in 1883, thenceforth it was known as the Radical Programme of 1885. The *Fortnightly* articles with four later additions were reissued in book form with a brief introduction by Chamberlain in September 1885 to guide Radicals through the election campaign; but the collected articles were again superseded by the speeches he delivered during the ensuing campaign. Whether heard as delivered or read in the newspapers next day, Chamberlain's speeches produced a far greater impact than any articles or book. The three which he delivered in January 1885 resounded not just for months or years but for decades. At one level these speeches were an ineffectual manoeuvre. They did not lead either Chamberlain or England into the promised land he anticipated. Yet they inaugurated a departure in British public policy which continued even after his death.

The initiative behind these speeches was Chamberlain's alone. He gave Morley and Dilke only a sketchy intimation of his intentions. While the first speech attempted to work out a general approach to the imperial issues vexing the cabinet, the succession of addresses had no direct bearing or impact on his ministerial colleagues' formal or backstairs discussions. He sought to reduce the risk of confrontation in cabinet by developing his themes from speech to speech in an avowedly exploratory mode. Beginning always with the implications of the Reform Act, he invited his audiences to think about the concerns which the new electorate was likely to impress upon the next Parliament and about how those concerns should be met. He did not present demands but rather argued for a socially widened approach to the problems of the nation.

His message was nevertheless politically explosive. Always more Radical in analysing problems than in solving them, Chamberlain propounded a social brand of Radicalism which was modest in substance but sounded like socialism. It caused alarm high and low, to the prime minister and cabinet colleagues and among the electorate. In attempting to set the pace of the Liberal party from the platform, Chamberlain exposed himself to counterattack by opponents more deft in manoeuvre than he. He also misjudged the electorate, and repelled more voters than he attracted. His socio-economic message challenged the moral Liberalism to which Gladstone and other evangelical Victorians were drawn. Dazzled by the doubling of the electorate, Chamberlain assumed that the working class would respond to economic prescriptions. Forgetting the hostility provoked by his Merchant Shipping bill, he sought to persuade middle-class voters that his prescriptions were a kind of social and economic insurance. Though he used the language of natural justice to make his case, he could not quite credit that the deepest motive springs of the electorate, working as well as middle class, might be moral, let alone religious. Furthermore, aggressive in his rhetoric, he created more alarm among the propertied than his proposals actually warranted. When audiences responded by welcoming his oratory with enthusiasm, his Whig colleagues feared that he was raising hopes he could not satisfy.

The first of Chamberlain's speeches, in Birmingham on 5 January, set forth the principles he proposed to follow in the two basic spheres of governmental activity, imperial and domestic. He placed the imperial first. Though increasingly alive to the interests at stake in the scramble for Africa, he was still more impressed by the anti-imperialism of the Radical contingent in the Commons; and he believed that the new electorate would reinforce that disposition. He had no sense yet of the popular imperialism which would surface in the 1890s. 'I do not think', he said, 'that the democracy will have any love for a policy of intervention and aggression, nor any ambition for conquest and universal domination.'[2] The task as he saw it was to secure popular support for the maintenance of Britain's overseas interests. He presented his case in terms that won approval from Morley.

It was the domestic portion of the speech that opened new ground. As a man of wealth Chamberlain was concerned and as a politician he was stimulated at the advent of an electorate made up overwhelmingly of working-class voters, rural as well as urban, labourers who had gained much less than businessmen and landowners from the growth of the capitalist economy. He wanted to preserve social cohesion and sustain economic growth by making the state as protective of small property rights as of large, by making it also more sensitive to the weight of taxation on those with low incomes, and more willing to use its powers to ensure basic social wellbeing. The enunciation of these principles by a prominent cabinet minister made the speeches of January 1885 a point of departure in British public policy.

The examples Chamberlain chose to illustrate these principles did not extend beyond subjects that he and his associates had already raised over the past four years. He spoke of the absorption of common lands by private owners, of the game laws which enabled sporting gentlemen literally to override the rights of farmers, of merchant seamen who drowned to the profit of shipowners, of agricultural labourers driven from the soil, and of urban working-class families 'huddled into dwellings unfit for man or beast'. Fleshed out in this way, the speech did not particularly startle his cabinet colleagues.

But one word went too far. After speaking about the erosion of natural or common rights which had occurred to the benefit of the rights of private property, Chamberlain asked, 'what ransom will property pay for the security it enjoys?' 'Ransom' suggested brigandage rather than social justice.

Nine days later, speaking at Ipswich, he gave his programme more moderate expression. While reiterating his central point 'that the interest of the rich will be found to consist . . . in a full and free acknowledgment of the rights of the poor',[3] Chamberlain repudiated any thought of bringing 'everything down to one dead level'. All he insisted was 'that the community as a whole, co-operating for the benefit of all, may do something . . . to make the life of all its citizens, and, above all, the poorest of them, somewhat better, somewhat nobler, somewhat happier'. He did not translate this gentler formulation into 'any absolute platform'. He meant, he said, simply 'to indicate the nature of the discussion which I think may be with advantage pursued'. He also replaced 'ransom' with the word 'insurance' to convey his meaning. But he could not obliterate the uglier word from public memory. Moreover his development at Ipswich of the themes of his speech in

Birmingham made observers aware that he was engaged in a sustained campaign.

He also introduced the sensitive subject of taxation. Aware that the prevailing canons of public finance had been laid down by Gladstone, Chamberlain confined himself to generalities and conveyed his ideas tentatively. Yet what he said on taxation at Ipswich heralded as momentous a departure in public finance as his Birmingham speech had done in social policy. He pointed out the injustice in local taxation, which forced working men to pay rates on their dwellings on the same basis as those with more disposable income. With regard to the national income tax, Chamberlain appealed to the middling classes who lacked a wide enough margin of income over expenditure to invest in land or securities. He suggested a graduated income tax to fall more heavily on those whose wealth far exceeded their immediate needs. This proposal saved his programme from being just another bid to rally the industrious middle and working classes against the idle owners of broad acres; but it also alarmed men of his own class who derived their wealth from business profits and the dividends from investments.

Reaction to Chamberlain's campaign erupted after Ipswich. Some colleagues found his proposals clever rather than shocking. But backbench Whigs denounced Chamberlain for opening the dykes to socialism. Men like Forster's ally, Wemyss Reid, who were jealous of Chamberlain's ascendancy interpreted his speeches as a blatant bid to supplant Gladstone. Amplified by *The Times*, the hostile reaction took Chamberlain aback. He was stricken appropriately with an abscess in his jaw. The rapturous response he received when he returned to Birmingham at the end of January to deliver the last of his three speeches did something to restore his spirits.

The response from Gladstone, however, was ominous. Gladstone predicted that Chamberlain's cabinet colleagues might take issue with his proposals in public and that the debate was likely to spill over into Parliament. In that event Gladstone warned that he might have to take a stand which would embarrass Chamberlain. Before sending the letter off, Gladstone showed it to Chamberlain's presumed rival, Hartington. Chamberlain understood the threat. 'Mr. G. may defend me,' he explained to Dilke, '—& in doing so may, to all intents and purposes, censure me in such a way as to entail my resignation.'[4] Chamberlain drafted his reply to Gladstone in close consultation with Dilke, reassured by Schnadhorst as to the likely popular reaction if the two Radical ministers resigned together. Though he wished to avoid alienating Gladstone and was quite willing to defend the present conduct of the government, Chamberlain still wanted to preserve his freedom to raise issues for public consideration. But Dilke persuaded him not to insist on this freedom. Accordingly Chamberlain replied to Gladstone penitentially. 'If I have erred in this interpretation of my liberties, I much regret the involuntary mistake.'[5] Though he mentioned the option of resigning in order to forward 'the objects I have most at heart & the promotion of Radical opinions', he assured Gladstone that he was 'chiefly guided by my desire to do whatever you may think best for the Government & least likely to add to your cares'.

Gladstone wrote back on the day that news reached England of the fall of Khartoum. Amid mounting anxiety in England, General Gordon had been holding this outpost against the forces of the Mahdi for nearly a year. Though his own fate was not immediately known, the news of Khartoum overshadowed the flurry aroused by Chamberlain's recent speeches. Whether or not Gladstone received the news before writing, he gave Chamberlain a stern lecture on the political history of the past thirty years:

> Every Liberal Government from & since that of Lord Aberdeen has had one or more Radical members in it, who have sat as representative men. But these gentlemen . . . have not found it necessary to sustain their character as Ministers, as a general rule . . . by drawing on the future and opening up questions not in immediate reach with a view to sustaining faith out of doors in the integrity of their principles.[6]

Though he declined to accept Chamberlain's offer of resignation, he did so without a word of warmth.

Stiffened by the old man's sternness, Chamberlain responded with a lecture of his own. It was not, like Gladstone's, on the history of the passing generation to which the prime minister belonged but on the prospects of the generation that was presumably about to take over. Chamberlain insisted that the new Reform Act invalidated the customs of the past as a guide for the present. 'Popular government', he instructed his leader,

> is inconsistent with the reticence which official etiquette formerly imposed on speakers, & which was easily borne as long as the electorate was a comparatively small & privileged class.[7]

He went on to tell the orator of Midlothian that

> The Platform has become one of the most powerful & indispensable instruments of Government, & any Ministry which neglected the opportunities offered by it would speedily lose the confidence of the People. A new public duty & personal labour has thus come into existence, which devolves to a great extent & as a matter of necessity, on those members of a Government who may be considered specially to represent the majority who are to be appealed to.

Chamberlain was determined not to suffer the fate of former Radical ministers who had forfeited their popular influence when they accepted the constraints of office. Still he sought to persuade Gladstone that the Radical Programme enunciated in January did not contain anything 'inconsistent with the principles professed by the least advanced of Liberals'. Chamberlain also stressed that his more controversial proposals such as a graduated income tax were offered merely 'as examples of what might be done to carry out the objects for which all Liberals might be expected to contend'.

By returning lecture for lecture, Chamberlain deepened the resentment in the old man's breast. An acute observer cautioned Chamberlain that

> Mr. Gladstone is more completely master of the country and of his cabinet than he has ever yet been; and he is reaping the benefit of having always recognised the importance of leading the Liberal party from its left centre rather than from its extreme left. Neither Hartington on his right, nor you upon his left, can afford to dispute with him the direction in which he desires to move.[8]

Whether or not Chamberlain grasped this message, he certainly failed to perceive that Gladstone was deeply hostile to his claim that 'the Community as a whole owed to its poorer members something more in the way of social legislation than it had already conceded'.[9] Along with other members of the cabinet, Chamberlain also failed to recognize the intensity of the old man's ambition to remain leader.

Imperial ambivalence

The deteriorating relationship between the two men was disguised over the next five months by the renewed importance of foreign rather than domestic affairs and by concern with Ireland. Though the government was discredited by its failure to rescue the garrison in the Sudan, the fall of Khartoum called Gladstone's talents into play by heightening the discord among his colleagues. Retaliation against the Mahdi would be no easy matter so far south on the Nile; and the interest in retaliation accentuated the unresolved question of whether Britain should remain in Egypt once the matter of Egypt's international debt was resolved.

Chamberlain felt the dilemma acutely. Aware of the price Britain continued to pay for its refusal to avenge the defeat at Majuba hill, and alert after four years in the cabinet to the range of Britain's interests overseas, he agreed with Hartington on the need for a vigorous response to the fall of Khartoum. As he explained to Morley,

> If we were to adopt the magnanimous course . . . of running away from
> the Mahdi, I fear that noble Savage, as well as all the Powers of Europe
> would misunderstand our motives and sooner or later, under the
> weight of repeated humiliations, we should be driven into war that
> might be more serious than anything we have now to face. . . . If we
> turn tail there is danger to our army in its retreat, danger to the
> friendly tribes, danger to Egypt and danger in India.[10]

Yet the likely length and cost of military action up the Nile would soon
wear out its welcome in England and probably bring the government
down. Chamberlain remained concerned about the extent of the hostility in Radical circles to permanent British occupation of Egypt. He
would therefore approve of nothing that allowed for that possibility. He
wanted simply to 'smash & retire'.

That policy satisfied no one in the cabinet but himself. Still Chamberlain thought he saw a way out, a way that would give rise to a 'smash-
ing' government while he rejoined and strengthened his ties to the
Radicals in the Commons and the country. The fall of Khartoum produced a surge of interest in the possibility of a 'patriotic' ministry under
the leadership of Hartington, probably in some combination with the
opposition, from which Gladstone and other ministers including Chamberlain would retire. Chamberlain talked up this possibility. It need
not exacerbate strain between the remaining and the outgoing Liberal
ministers, at least so far as Chamberlain was concerned, for he would
support the government in implementing its *raison d'être* of retak-
ing Khartoum. Meanwhile he could resume advocacy of his Radical
Programme for domestic consumption. But Dilke, who did not share
his friend's desire for a speedy escape from office, took care to delay
the prerequisite rupture between Gladstone and Hartington over the
demand for military action. Then, when news arrived that Gordon
had died at Khartoum, the case for action to rescue him lost much of
its force, while the survival of the entire government was placed in
jeopardy.

The government escaped censure in the House of Commons by
twenty-two votes. The margin was small enough to force the government to think of resignation. The opportunity for escape that Chamberlain was looking for had come, and he advised his colleagues to take
advantage of the opportunity. But Gladstone induced them to reconsider. His stand was enough to swing Chamberlain round. Uncertain of
his standing with the prime minister, he surrendered his best opportunity to escape from office.

After this misstep, Chamberlain floundered in the cabinet's deliberations on foreign affairs, and in doing so dimmed his reputation in his
colleagues' eyes. In the confrontation that occurred between Britain and

Russia over Afghanistan, and in the continuing contest with France over Egypt, he displayed more concern about Radical reactions at home than about British interests abroad. Though Chamberlain bristled at Russia's 'offensive & insulting' conduct over Afghanistan, he insisted that '[t]he time has passed when the Liberal party can go to war on . . . mere suspicion of intentions which are skilfully cloaked by plausible professions'.[11] He was therefore anxious 'to obtain at any cost & even at the price of personal humiliation & probable defeat of the Government, a settlement of the present difficulty'. Similarly he was willing at one point to abandon not only the Sudan but also Egypt with no more reward for Britain's efforts over the past three years than insistence on the freedom of the Suez Canal.

In contrast to the crudeness of Chamberlain's prescriptions, Gladstone deployed all the skills of traditional statecraft. After Russia seized Pendjeh in Afghanistan, the old master carried the House of Commons wholeheartedly with him by requesting financial support for military action if it should prove necessary in Afghanistan or the Sudan. He then used this support to bring about a settlement with Russia, while he quietly abandoned the Sudan. Meanwhile Chamberlain dithered. Anxious to extend the influence of public opinion in the conduct of state yet increasingly aware of the complexity of international relations, at one moment he thought of drastic solutions. If things should reach the point of war, he told a backbench friend,

> our democracy . . . should understand that no war & no diplomacy is possible if every step is to be the subject of popular criticism & popular agitation. In all times of national crisis the Romans found it necessary to appoint a Dictator, & the English Democracy will have to do something of the same kind if it wishes to avoid a great disaster.[12]

A month later, once the Afghan crisis was on its way to settlement, Chamberlain reverted to conventional Radicalism. 'The old ways of diplomacy are unsuitable to the new Electorate,' he told the editor of the the *Liverpool Daily Post*, 'and if we are to hold our own with foreign nations we must carry our constituents with us step by step by a frank exposition of an intelligible policy.'[13]

Chamberlain felt no such ambivalence about asserting the powers of the state in the domestic sphere, upon which he preferred to focus attention. There he saw no conflict between the needs of government and the wishes of the popular electorate. As he told a club of Liberal MPs towards the end of April:

> When Government represented only the authority of the Crown or the views of a particular class, I can understand that it was the first duty of men who valued their freedom to restrict its authority and to limit

its expenditure. But all that is changed. Now Government is the organised expression of the wishes and the wants of the people, and under
these circumstances . . . it is our business to extend its functions, and to
see in what way its operations can be usefully enlarged.[14]

Central Board for Ireland

Quickened in yet another regard by the expansion of the electorate,
Chamberlain had approached the subject of Ireland even before he
launched his Radical Programme for the kingdom as a whole. Ireland
was affected more than any other part of the kingdom by the Third
Reform Act because the Reform Act of 1867 had left that island largely
untouched. The Franchise Act of 1884 gave the vote to Ireland's poor
tenant farmers, who were expected to send at least eighty Nationalists
into the next Parliament. In the closing weeks of 1884, Chamberlain
sketched the main principles of a proposal he was prepared to advocate
for Ireland. He felt obliged to proceed more discreetly on Ireland
than on England. Yet he repeated the negotiating errors he had made
over the Kilmainham treaty of 1882, this time with more serious
consequences.

Though Ireland had been comparatively tranquil for the past two
years, the endlessly abrasive rhetoric of the Irish Nationalists had done
nothing to improve their reception in England. The 'insatiable agitation'[15] hardened Chamberlain's thinking. He no longer looked for a
union in popular sentiment between England and Ireland. He was willing to concede that the large majority of the Irish might be nationalist at
heart. This recognition of Irish desires reduced the range of Chamberlain's democratic instincts. His fundamental loyalty was to the heartland of England. He explained himself at length to an English
correspondent, W.H. Duigan, with good contacts in Ireland:

> I do not consider that wishes and rights are always identical, or that it
> is sufficient to find out what the majority of the Irish people desire in
> order at once to grant their demands. I can never consent to regard
> Ireland as a separate people with the inherent rights of an absolutely
> independent community. I should not do this in the case of Scotland,
> or of Wales, or, to take still more extreme instances, of Sussex or of
> London. In every case the rights of the country or district must be
> subordinated to the rights of the whole community of which it forms
> only a portion. Ireland by its geographical position, and by its history
> is a part of the United Kingdom, and it cannot divest itself of the ob-
> ligations or be denied the advantages which this condition involves.[16]

He was none the less anxious to bring about a major adjustment in the relationship between England and Ireland which would give the Irish room to deploy their political energies and leave the rest of the kingdom free to take up his domestic agenda. Precluded by the climate of opinion in both islands from presenting his proposals for Ireland publicly, he proceeded privately through intermediaries.

The one Irish politician eager to explore the situation with him was Captain O'Shea. Chamberlain had reason for caution in dealing with O'Shea. His indiscretion in the Kilmainham negotiations had embarrassed all those involved, Chamberlain especially; and there were rumours about the relationship between O'Shea's wife and Parnell of which Chamberlain was probably aware. O'Shea's penchant for intrigue and Chamberlain's for candour made a dangerous combination. Yet these characteristics attracted the two men to each other. More to the point, they were drawn together by Parnell, who commissioned the husband of his mistress to explore the possibilities for agreement with Chamberlain.

The Coercion Act of 1882 was due to expire in 1885. Knowing that the government would not relish a fight to renew the Act on the eve of a general election, Parnell wished to sound out Chamberlain, as the most favourably disposed member of the cabinet, about a possible prior agreement. Through O'Shea, Parnell suggested reducing the severity of the renewal bill, limiting its continuation to one year, and accompanying it with 'a considerable measure of county government with important accessories touching the public boards in Dublin'.[17]

Chamberlain responded with pleased surprise to these suggestions. They corresponded closely with an initiative which he thought of making after the next general election. Concerned to maintain the integrity of his own position, Chamberlain used his correspondence with Duigan to present his ideas to other Irish figures. Chamberlain firmly ruled out political separation between the two islands: 'Sooner than yield on this point I would govern Ireland by force to the end of the chapter.' He forswore his former sympathy with Isaac Butt's conception of Home Rule, on the grounds that it 'would infallibly lead to a demand for entire separation'.[18] On the other hand, he knew from his days as mayor of Birmingham how much good could be done through popularly elected local government. He was willing to offer Ireland that and more.

He proposed the creation of an elective central board for Ireland with legislative powers to deal with a range of questions that concerned Ireland as a whole and might best be handled without reference to the Parliament of the United Kingdom. The most important subjects that Chamberlain proposed to assign to the Irish central board were education, over which Parliament always stumbled because of Ireland's large Catholic majority, and land, vexed by the absence of so many owners of Irish land in England. As the sponsor of public works in Birmingham, he suggested that the Irish central board might also improve the provision of local railways and other forms of public communication. Towards all these ends, the central board would be invested with appropriate powers of taxation. Chamberlain trusted that these responsibilities and resources would divert Irish Nationalists from 'bullying English officials & the English House of Commons, while the Imperial Parliament would continue to regulate for the common good the national policy of the three kingdoms'.

Duigan distributed Chamberlain's proposals in Chamberlain's own words. But O'Shea, who served as the channel for communications between Parnell and Chamberlain, distorted the messages they gave him in order to get round their disagreement. While Chamberlain hoped that his central board would concentrate Ireland's attention on its own material concerns for the foreseeable future, Parnell conceived of the board as a short-term improvement. As Parnell left England for a speaking tour of Ireland, he cautioned O'Shea to make Chamberlain 'understand that we do not propose this Local Self Govt. plank as a substitute for the restitution of our Irish Parliament'.[19] O'Shea protested against this clarification of his instructions. But Parnell demanded 'a clear statement' of his views to Chamberlain after learning of his letter to Duigan. Parnell insisted that '[t]he central Local Govt. body which I propose will not have legislative functions, only administrative'.[20] Chamberlain hoped that the central board would dispose of the land question, which Parnell wished to delay until he could obtain Home Rule. While O'Shea did not entirely suppress his instructions from Parnell in speaking to Chamberlain, he watered them down deceptively. He insisted on a more modest definition of the proposed board's responsibilities than Chamberlain desired. But O'Shea disposed of Parnell's intention to continue insisting on Home Rule by presenting it to Chamberlain as a rhetorical necessity for popular consumption.

Chamberlain was sufficiently encouraged by his discussions with O'Shea to convey their substance to Gladstone who, he learned, had received a similar overture from Parnell through Mrs O'Shea. But when O'Shea sent Chamberlain a copy of the racy report which he had despatched to Parnell, Chamberlain recoiled. As he explained to Morley, '[i]f such a representation were published it would be fatal to the work of reconciliation for it would degrade the whole matter into a mere partisan bargaining in which a bribe for Parnell's support was to be offered by the Radical party'. For the record, he drew up his own description of his conversations with O'Shea.[21]

While Chamberlain was doing so, Parnell issued a resounding declaration of the national aspirations of Ireland:

> no man has the right to fix the boundary of the march of a nation. No
> man has a right to say, 'Thus far shalt thou go and no further'; and we
> have never attempted to fix the *ne plus ultra* to the progress of Ireland's
> nationhood and we never shall.

Indirectly Chamberlain responded by bringing the list of powers for his
Irish central board closer to Parnell's stipulations, saying little more on
the subject of land. The response from other Irishmen to Chamberlain's
letter to Duigan proved too mixed to encourage him to press further.
Chamberlain withdrew the letter from circulation, and for the moment
suspended his initiative.

But the subject of Ireland could not be set aside because of the impending expiration of the Coercion Act. In February Gladstone encouraged the Lord Lieutenant of Ireland, Spencer, to discuss the situation
with his cabinet colleagues individually. Spencer spoke to Chamberlain
among others. Spencer was identified with the Coercion Act, but he
recognized the necessity of renewing it in less severe form and of accompanying the renewal with some measures of reform. An accommodation between Spencer and Chamberlain therefore seemed possible.
But when Chamberlain and Spencer spelled out their ideas to each
other, they could not agree. An honorable but unimaginative grandee
scarred by the hatred which his administration of the Coercion Act had
inspired in Ireland, Spencer recoiled at Chamberlain's proposals because they would in effect scuttle the executive system which he pains-
takingly supervised. Like others in the government who lacked
Chamberlain's experience of city government, Spencer questioned the
stability of an arrangement which would give Ireland a central board
with somewhat more power than a city council but less than provincial
autonomy. Describing Chamberlain's recommendations as 'Mr Parnell's
proposals', Spencer was also disturbed by Chamberlain's willingness to
negotiate with the Irish leader.

Spencer's stance only increased Chamberlain's dependence on indirect channels of communication with the Irish Nationalists. Chamberlain welcomed an opportunity that came unsolicited to him in April
through the leading Catholic prelate in England, Cardinal Manning, on
behalf of the Irish bishops. They doubted that Home Rule would improve their position; they were sure that Irish control of education in
Ireland would serve their interests; and they were therefore attracted by
what they knew of Chamberlain's proposals from his letter to W.H.
Duigan. The Irish bishops encouraged Cardinal Manning to learn more
from Chamberlain and, if possible, to draw Chamberlain and Parnell
towards some agreement. Like O'Shea, Manning relished opportunities

to mediate among the powerful. Like O'Shea also, Manning exaggerated what he managed to achieve. Together Manning and O'Shea persuaded Parnell to restrain his opposition to some renewal of the Coercion Act if it were preceded by legislation to set up a central board for Ireland. But Manning did not tell Chamberlain of the caution with which Parnell accepted this modest and vague agreement.

Even so, Chamberlain secured approval from Gladstone before opening discussions with Manning. Chamberlain knew that Gladstone sympathized, perhaps more than any other member of the cabinet, with the central board scheme. Here surely was an issue on which the younger man and the aging statesman could work in harmony. But the suspicions roused in Gladstone by Chamberlain's Radical Programme at the beginning of the year weakened their springtime agreement on Ireland. Gladstone could have thrown his weight behind the central board and brought most if not all of the cabinet to accept it. Hartington kept his head down on this issue. The only possibly serious defector was Spencer, but he would not make a bitter opponent. For the moment, however, Gladstone was more concerned to keep his distance from the contending factions within his cabinet and so to maintain his indispensability as leader than to hammer out an acceptable Irish policy. When the cabinet met to decide its policy, Gladstone indicated his support for a central board, but declined to deploy his talent for argument on the grounds that it would be 'quite useless'.[22] Thereupon the cabinet rejected the scheme, all the peers but Granville opposing it, though the smaller contingent of commoners except for Hartington supported it.

After the meeting, the prime minister commented that the victorious majority would live to rue the day but that Chamberlain's scheme was now 'dead as mutton'. To chastise his divided colleagues, Gladstone put on a display of resigning, to the point of packing his bags. Yet he employed the usual peacemaker, Harcourt, to patch up an agreement within the cabinet, the pivotal provision of which was a promise from Gladstone to remain as prime minister till the end of the parliamentary session.

Chamberlain's conduct throughout this affair was as self-serving as Gladstone's. Like the prime minister, Chamberlain sought to use the Irish issue to make his mark with the government or, failing that, with the electorate. While anxious to identify himself with a policy to which Gladstone agreed, Chamberlain was content to do without his active support. Frustrated for five years by the cabinet's Whig majority, Chamberlain was eager to discredit them. After the cabinet reached its decision, he let the *Liverpool Daily Post* know that '[a] great opportunity . . . has been lost owing to the pedantry & timidity of the Whigs, and for the moment we seem thrown back on the old worn-out policy of coercion'.[23]

Like Gladstone, Chamberlain talked of resignation but was reluctant to carry out the threat. Instead he looked forward to the coming general election, when the cabinet would be in effect dissolved. He envisaged campaigning, in tacit cooperation with Parnell, for the central board scheme. 'Nothing', Chamberlain told the newest member of the cabinet, 'will induce me to join another Government or to meet a new Parliament except as the advocate of some such plan.'[24]

But the situation was becoming too fluid for such confident prediction. Rather than consent to what they deemed inadequate measures of reform, Dilke and Chamberlain wanted to see the government's Irish policy reduced to bare renewal of the Crimes Act. This tactic frustrated every Liberal faction. Lord Randolph Churchill took advantage of the government's embarrassment by intimating that the Conservatives would not support a renewal of coercion. To parry this threat, after brief conversation with Chamberlain, Gladstone announced that the government would introduce a measure of land reform. Abruptly Dilke sent in his resignation, obliging Chamberlain to follow suit. By now everyone in the cabinet was eager for release. When, at the beginning of June, the government was defeated in the Commons by a combination of Conservative and Irish votes and Radical defections[25] on a clause in the budget, the cabinet decided with almost unseemly haste to resign. A minority Conservative government was installed to look after things until the new electorate could be registered and a general election held.

Manoeuvring and electioneering

The resignation of Gladstone's government brought Chamberlain one step closer, so he felt, to the dawn of the Radical era. Without bearing much blame for the turn of events, he was at last free from the collective responsibilities of cabinet office, free to propound the Radical gospel. In doing so, he could attract the popular following of which he was confident; he could mould that following to support the agenda he thought most expedient under current circumstances; and hence he could place his impress on the construction of the government when the Liberals returned to power after the general election.

But this freedom came at a high price. Emancipation from office made almost all Chamberlain's parliamentary relationships more ambiguous. Though virtually every member of the cabinet had threatened to resign at one time or other, Gladstone left office particularly exasperated with 'the party of two' who had issued the threat most frequently always together. And though their most recent threat had emanated from Dilke, Gladstone's strongest aversion was reserved for Chamberlain, whose ambition to become prime minister struck many observers as blatant. Gladstone believed that the great impending issue was Ireland, and he knew that on this subject Chamberlain had been closer than any other member of the cabinet to his way of thinking. Yet the old man, retained by general consent at the head of the party, was determined to hold Chamberlain more than any other member of that cabinet at arm's length. Chamberlain sensed but underestimated that coolness.

The rivalry that preoccupied Chamberlain was with the Whigs. He thought of the past five years as a long demonstration of their ability in cabinet to frustrate not just Radical advance but bold government of any complexion. He swore that he would never submit to that yoke again. Yet his attitude to the Whigs was less settled than he said. He was willing to work with Whig men if they would not obstruct his measures. It was Chamberlain's relationship with Irish nationalists and particularly with Parnell that deteriorated most severely after the change of government. While aware that Parnell would combine with any faction in England to advance his cause, Chamberlain assumed that the only natural alliance for the Irish Nationalists was with English Radicals. He also felt that his negotiations since the turn of the year with Parnell, though indirect and for the moment fruitless, had turned their seeming agreement on a central or national board for Ireland into a commitment which both men were honour-bound to uphold. Chamberlain knew of course that something else was afoot when the Conservatives and the Irish in the Commons cooperated to bring the Liberal government down. All the same, he could not credit that the Conservatives would offer the Irish anything as substantial as his central board scheme, let alone even more.

For over a month following the change of government, Ireland stood at the centre of the programme that Chamberlain intended to offer the public. He simplified the whole programme under the heading of local government reform. By that he meant first of all a central board or national council for Ireland, sweetened for British consumption by the offer of similar councils for Scotland and Wales. He applied much the same scheme to London, for which he suggested a central board to deal with matters that affected the entire metropolis, while councils for the many boroughs of which London was composed would receive powers like those to be given to the popularly elected county councils that Chamberlain hoped to see throughout the United Kingdom. He also argued that local government reform would help to alleviate the economic depression by promoting the creation of small landholdings for intensive agricultural cultivation. Dilke and Chamberlain planned a tour of investigation through Ireland to prepare themselves for an election campaign of speeches all over the kingdom.

But before they could begin, Parnell kicked over the Irish centrepiece of the scheme. He was lured towards the Conservatives by Lord Randolph Churchill and also by the new Lord Lieutenant of Ireland, Carnarvon, who felt some sympathy for Home Rule. Parnell therefore allowed his confederates in Ireland to conclude that the English Radical leaders would not be welcome there. The nationalist press drove the message home with crude insults. Even the Catholic bishops withdrew their offers of hospitality to Dilke and Chamberlain. Chamberlain was reluctant to recognize the source of the rejection, and pressed O'Shea for an explanation from Parnell. O'Shea brought back word that Parnell had 'a higher bid'.[26] Bitterly Chamberlain concluded that 'we must stand aside and wait events'. He threatened 'to give [the Irish] a bit of my mind in public some day';[27] but he bided his time.

While estranged from the Irish Nationalists, Chamberlain grew more respectful of their Conservative allies. The Conservatives certainly seemed more accommodating than the Whigs to pressures for reform. Chamberlain took to saying 'the Tories are in office, but the Radicals are in power'.[28] He had no thought of changing party and could not conceive of 'an umbrella wide enough to shelter Lord Salisbury and himself'.[29] Still, the minority Conservative government seemed preferable to participation in a Liberal government whose pace was set by Whigs.

Amid the unsettlement of Chamberlain's relationships at Westminster, one stood firm: his friendship and alliance with Sir Charles Dilke. Naturally there were differences of opinion between the two men, but the remarkable fact was that their alliance stood firm. The only issue that the two men could identify as dividing them after the change of government was votes for women, which Dilke strongly supported but which, since the death of his second wife, Chamberlain had come strongly to oppose. Contemporaries were on the lookout for a split between them because, when the Radicals gained supreme power as expected, only one of them could become prime minister. Yet the two men held true to their compact, Chamberlain if anything more loyally than Dilke. While Dilke prevented Chamberlain from resigning from the cabinet on the issue of his choice in February, Chamberlain tendered his resignation in May on a point about which he did not feel strongly, to second Dilke. After the change of government, Chamberlain suggested that the Radicals among the ex-ministers plus Morley should meet frequently to concert their policy. Dilke chaired the meetings, and Chamberlain honoured the arrangement. They needed each other's support in the jockeying for position among the Liberal elite. The friendship had rare personal importance for Chamberlain. Though he drew sustenance from friendships, for example with Jesse Collings and John Morley, those relationships were diminished in significance or twisted by Chamberlain's insistence on subordination. But with Dilke there was a genuine acceptance of equality between the two men, a situation unique in Chamberlain's experience.

In mid-July, an attractive woman of twenty-three, Virginia Crawford, called at Chamberlain's house in London. He was acquainted with her as the youngest daughter of a neighbour, Ellen Smith, Mrs Eustace Smith as she was known. Dilke had introduced him to Ellen Smith, and she had brightened Chamberlain's social life during his first years in the cabinet by inviting him to the salon she kept for rising figures in the arts as well as politics. Her daughters had married early in life to older men at the edge of Chamberlain's circle of acquaintances. Most recently Virginia had married a dull but worthy Scottish lawyer-politician more than twice her age, Donald Crawford. Dissatisfied with their marriages, several of Ellen Smith's daughters including Virginia had plunged into a shadowy world of sexual liaisons. It was a world with which Ellen Smith and Sir Charles Dilke were familiar, for they were erstwhile lovers; but to Chamberlain it was foreign.

He said nothing about the call he received from Virginia Crawford that July day in 1885 until years later when Dilke learned of it independently. Chamberlain then dismissed it, saying that Mrs Crawford did not find anyone but the servants at home and left. He himself was not there when she called; but he arrived soon afterwards. A detective employed by Mrs Crawford's suspicious husband observed her arrival at Chamberlain's house but did not see her leave. She might, therefore, have had an opportunity to tell Chamberlain of an affair which she claimed to have had and was about to confess to her husband, with Dilke.

Whether the affair had indeed occurred and whether she spoke to Chamberlain remain in doubt to this day. As soon as Virginia Crawford's charge could be examined in detail, Chamberlain concluded that it was a tissue of lies. But did he receive prior warning that the charge would be made? If so, did jealousy of Dilke keep Chamberlain from doing all he could to silence the young woman and alert Dilke, as Dilke's secretary came to suspect? However intriguing and impossible to disprove, this suspicion is out of keeping with the remarkable relationship between the two men before and after the scandal was divulged to the public.

Mr Crawford responded to his wife's confession by suing for divorce and cited Dilke as co-respondent. Dilke had been soaring high, politically hopeful and personally happy. He had been encouraged by Gladstone as well as Chamberlain to think of becoming the next leader of the Liberal party; and he was secretly engaged to marry a young widow who shared his political convictions. However, he recognized instantly that Mrs Crawford's accusations would damage him irretrievably. He insisted that they were untrue. But in refuting them his other sexual liaisons, particularly the one with Virginia Crawford's mother, were sure to come to light. Crushed by his reversal of fortune, Dilke turned to Chamberlain.

For political reasons as well as from concern for his friend, Chamberlain was anxious to minimize the seriousness of the setback. 'I trust', he wrote, 'the time may come when we may all look back on this experience as a bad dream which has left no serious trace behind.'[30] Though dismayed by the other sexual relationships that Dilke felt obliged to divulge, Chamberlain assured him of his own full confidence in Dilke's denial of Virginia Crawford's allegations. Dilke's initial impulse had been to leave England for the Continent, but Chamberlain persuaded him that to do so would look cowardly. He brought Dilke to Highbury, where his spirits gradually revived. At the beginning of October when Dilke married his fiancée, Chamberlain stood beside him as best man.

But while the scandal left the friendship between the two men intact, it diminished the value of their political alliance. Lady Salisbury observed with malicious glee that 'we liked Sir Charles Dilke, but we are delighted because [the disaster] will smash Chamberlain'.[31] The scandal expelled Dilke from the innermost councils of the Liberal party until he could restore his reputation. Without Dilke to back him up, Chamberlain's ability to command a respectful hearing among his former cabinet colleagues was sharply reduced.

The events of July 1885, including the defection of Parnell and the discrediting of Dilke, increased Chamberlain's impetuosity. He threw himself into the task of adapting and promulgating his Radical programme. The strategy he pursued was riskier than he appreciated. Schnadhorst, the veteran organizer of the National Liberal Federation, gave him with 'very encouraging' accounts about 'the feeling in the country. I am assured', Chamberlain told Dilke, 'that we (the Radicals) never held so strong a position—that the Counties will be swept for the liberals—& that the whole atmosphere of the H[ouse] of C[ommons] will be changed after November.'[32] However, the electoral situation was new and the outcome less predictable than usual. Both sides expected to do well in the future where they had in the past, Conservatives in the countryside, Liberals in urban areas. The great increase in the number of urban seats raised Liberal expectations. Yet both sides prepared to poach on each other's traditional turf. Liberals wooed agricultural labour, enfranchised for the first time, while Conservatives wooed suburban constituencies which would be detached from the former multi-member constituencies of the large cities, including Birmingham.

Still, most people expected a Liberal victory. The question was, what would be done with it? Chamberlain wanted to mould the expected victory into a mandate for Radical action. He wanted to ensure that the next Liberal government was not hamstrung, like the last, by the vagueness of its electoral rhetoric. He therefore focused attention on the policies he wanted the new Parliament to put into effect. But the programme he propagated exposed his policies to scrutiny and alerted the interests he endangered. The prominence of his campaign, which no other politician matched, accentuated his ambition and quickened jealousy. Chamberlain turned forty-nine in July, not young; he was in a hurry. He hurried enough to make Gladstone sharpen his claws. At the pace that Chamberlain set himself, Morley doubted that he would live another ten years.

The final articles on 'The Radical Programme' came out in the *Fortnightly Review* at the end of June, one on local government including Ireland, the other on taxation. Chamberlain had them assembled and published in book form between red covers. He meant the book to serve as a source of ideas and information for the Radical campaign rather than as a definitive statement of Radical commitments. He wrote a preface for the volume which preserved his freedom of action. Meanwhile he readied himself for the coming campaign, familiarizing himself with the interests of places where he intended to speak, planning what he would say.

The general election could not be held till the new electorate was registered, in effect the end of November. This delay made for an election campaign of extraordinary length, but it was not expected to begin in earnest until September. Chamberlain could not wait. Eager to strike at the Liberal shipowner, Norwood, who led the opposition to the Merchant Shipping bill, Chamberlain headed for Norwood's constituency of Hull at the beginning of August. Huge orange posters heralded Chamberlain as 'Your coming Prime Minister'.

From the outset he made the structure of his appeal to the electorate unmistakable. He demanded 'a definite programme' that discarded 'empty platitudes and generalities, and put a clear issue before the electors'.[33] No longer willing to give Ireland and local government pride of place, he drew attention to the domestic concerns that bulked large in his speeches at the beginning of the year. He insisted that 'the great evil with which we have to deal is the excessive inequality in the distribution of riches'. But he chose his words with more circumspection than in January: there was no mention of 'ransom', and he referred to Gladstone deferentially. He focused on the need for land reform and on the unfair burden of taxation on the working class. Having ascertained that Gladstone did not object to graduated taxation in principle, Chamberlain called for it as 'fair and just to all classes of the community' and intimated that Gladstone agreed. He went on to deliver a blistering restatement of the need for legislation to protect merchant seamen from negligent shipowners.

The comments on taxation and merchant shipping provoked a good deal of public protest from threatened interests. But it was the structure as much as the substance of his electoral strategy that set the tongues of former colleagues wagging. Gladstone privately endorsed Spencer's observation that it was 'very dangerous' to offer the electorate any clear plan or programme.[34] Gladstone headed off for a holiday at sea, leaving his colleagues in the dark as to his intentions; but, as Spencer observed, he no longer said a word about retiring. Chamberlain meanwhile sought to oust the Whiggish party whip, Lord Richard Grosvenor, from control at party headquarters.

By the end of August, even before it was fully under way, Chamberlain's campaign excited Radicals throughout the country. Frederic Harrison exclaimed, 'Chamberlain is the man.'[35] The press announced his plan of march: north to Warrington in Lancashire on 8 September, to Scotland the following week, down to London on the 23rd, up to Bradford for the meeting of the National Liberal Federation at the beginning of October. His campaign was unprecedented in its geographical breadth. Young spirits like Lloyd George would long remember how he quickened their ardour that autumn. Chamberlain stretched his physical resources to the limit, too fast to allow for careful stocktaking. Morley asked, 'Have you had no holiday? Are you going to have none? Are you wise?'[36] But Chamberlain felt unable to lighten his load because Dilke was removed from the fray.

Dilke was not the only prominent Liberal to remain largely silent. Of the members of the late cabinet, only Hartington and Harcourt undertook much speaking. By filling the vacuum, Chamberlain created the impression that he was becoming in effect the leader of the Liberal party. His immediate objective was less ambitious. He wanted to ensure that the electorate delivered a Radical verdict which the next House of Commons and Liberal cabinet would reflect. But his efforts proved counterproductive. He exacerbated the divisions within the Liberal party, frightened moderate Liberals into reconsidering their allegiance, and furnished Conservatives with a welcome bogeyman. These reactions threw him on to the defensive and distracted his attention from the socio-economic issues on which he meant to attract popular urban support.

From the beginning of September, Chamberlain's campaign was as much reactive as constructive. Two speeches by other men towards the end of August did much to bring this about. On the 24th Parnell announced 'a platform with one plank only ... national independence'. On the 29th Hartington spoke out in reaction to Chamberlain's remarks at Hull, objecting in particular to his proposal to give local governing authorities power for the compulsory purchase of land. The danger of pitting Liberal against Liberal about which Gladstone had warned

Chamberlain in January was now a reality. Neither Hartington nor Chamberlain quite desired an open quarrel. But Hartington was as unwilling to accept the kind of Liberal government Chamberlain envisaged as Chamberlain was to accept a repetition of the kind of Liberal government he had known for the past five years. Each man also thought the other's prescriptions electorally suicidal. Hartington could see how Chamberlain alienated moderate Liberals. Chamberlain knew that Hartington would alienate the newly enfranchised agricultural labourers. The quarrel between the two men had the further effect, which neither intended, of accentuating the value of Gladstone's continued leadership.

Opening his autumn campaign at Warrington, Chamberlain replied to Parnell as well as Hartington. He handled Parnell with the anger of a rejected suitor, and refused to bid for his support so long as he talked of national independence. Thereafter Chamberlain watered down his central board proposal, limiting the board to administrative business until the Irish demonstrated that they could handle those responsibilities well. As for Hartington, Chamberlain likened him to Rip Van Winkle for failure to keep abreast of the movement of opinion within the party. However lively his choice of words, Chamberlain did not burn his bridges. Hartington thought that Chamberlain's response 'showed a desire not to push differences to extremities'.[37]

Aside from dealing with the Irish and Whig leaders at Warrington, Chamberlain issued a strong social message:

> We have to ... grapple with the mass of misery and destitution in our midst. ... It is a problem which some men would put aside by references to the eternal laws of supply and demand, to the necessity of freedom of contract, and to the sanctity of every private right of property. But, gentlemen, these are the convenient cant of selfish wealth. ... I shall be told to-morrow that this is Socialism. I have learnt not to be afraid of words that are flung in my face instead of argument. Of course it is Socialism. The Poor Law is Socialism; the Education Act is Socialism; the greater part of municipal work is Socialism; and every kindly act of legislation, by which the community has sought to discharge its responsibilities and its obligations to the poor is Socialism; but it is none the worse for that. Our object is the elevation of the poor, of the masses of the people—a levelling up of them by which we shall do something to remove the excessive inequality in social life which is now one of the greatest dangers as well as a great injury to the State.[38]

He was, however, distracted from this ringing appeal by a more powerful antagonist.

While Chamberlain held forth on the platform, Gladstone did battle with him in private. The pace of Chamberlain's campaign, the fears it raised and the dissent it provoked enabled Gladstone to distance himself from Chamberlain in the interests of party unity. Gladstone's life expectancy and experience kept him from calculating much beyond the general election and its probable outcome. Rejecting long-range programmes, he drew up a short list of items on which he hoped the party could agree, enough to talk about during the election and to occupy the new Parliament for its first year or two. Gladstone also recognized and half hoped that these short-term calculations could be overtaken by the one virtually certain result of the general election: a great increase in the Irish Nationalist contingent in the Commons.

He secured approval for the minimal sort of manifesto he had in mind from Hartington. Armed with Hartington's consent, Gladstone wrote to Chamberlain the day after his speech at Warrington. Gladstone wanted Chamberlain's acquiescence but resented his pretensions and was revolted by his 'socialism'. What most alarmed him was Chamberlain's talk of taking private property for public use. Portraying himself as anxious to resign as leader but willing to remain if that would keep the party united, Gladstone told Chamberlain of the address he was framing and indicated that he did not want to proceed without Chamberlain's approval. But he concluded darkly that 'after having read your telling speech at Warrington . . . I think it will be well for me frankly to introduce your name and to explain our relations'.[39]

Chamberlain responded to the menace with concession and a menace of his own. He narrowed the range of his demands to two: local government reform including the power for compulsory purchase of land for smallholdings, and free education at least in principle. He also reduced the force of his most Radical policy, graduated taxation, by claiming that it was compatible with Gladstone's views. But having conceded this much, Chamberlain in concert with Dilke informed Gladstone that 'it would be impossible for us to join any future Administration which would not concede these points'.[40]

Gladstone went ahead and published his manifesto. It advocated the mildest of reforms in four areas—local government, electoral registration, land laws, and parliamentary procedure—and cast doubts on the wisdom of free education. It was a slap in the face to Chamberlain, though the slap was softened by the blandness of the manifesto. Even Hartington thought it a 'weak production'.[41] Chamberlain gave it a cordial reception in public. As he explained to Dilke, the old man could always be pushed by public opinion, and in any case '[h]is reign [could] not be a long one'.[42] Even so, Chamberlain warned Gladstone again that he would not join a government 'which excluded from practical

& immediate consideration every proposal which I have recently advocated'.[43]

Gladstone countered the threat by playing the Irish card. He asked Chamberlain to contemplate the prospect of a massive Nationalist electoral victory in Ireland, one that would enable Parnell 'to bring forward a plan which [might] contain in your opinion adequate securities for the Union of the Empire. . . . do you think no Government should be formed to promote such a plan unless [your main domestic proposals] were glued to it at the same time?'[44] This scenario implied that Gladstone was ready to give Nationalist Irish demands priority over Radical English ones. Chamberlain responded by stiffening his public opposition to a separate or independent parliament for Ireland.

After a triumphal tour through Scotland, he brought his campaign to London. Under the Redistribution Act, London was about to elect almost one tenth of the House of Commons. Chamberlain had been slow to embrace the city of his birth and still did not know its instincts. His National Liberal Federation had yet to take root there. But he was encouraged by the Radicalism of the variety of organizations in London associated with the Liberal party. It was here that he made his ultimatum public, stating that he would not join a ministry which excluded his proposals from its programme. Crowds cheered his name more than Gladstone's. Radicals looked forward to the new dispensation when Chamberlain won his mandate; and many in the emerging socialist societies of London shared this hope. But Chamberlain's ultimatum aroused his Liberal critics. Seeking to distinguish between the modesty of Gladstone's manifesto and the sweeping declarations of Chamberlain, George Goschen dubbed his proposals the 'Unauthorized Programme'. Chamberlain accepted the label happily, and it stuck. Returning tit for tat, Chamberlain likened Goschen to the skeleton that the ancient Egyptians brought to their feasts as protection against excessive enthusiasm.

Staying out of the public fray, Gladstone invited Chamberlain to his home at Hawarden in North Wales. They spent two days there trying to fathom each other's intentions, and then transmitted what they had learned to their respective friends. Hartington always found Gladstone's conversation mystifying; but Chamberlain and Gladstone got along well in private. Gladstone found Chamberlain 'a good man to talk to, not only from his force and clearness, but because he speaks with reflection, does not misapprehend, or (I think) suspect, or make unnecessary difficulties, or endeavour to maintain pedantically the uniformity and consistency of his argument throughout'.[45] Still the younger man did not escape mystification.

Gladstone wanted to discover whether Chamberlain could be kept in harness. Gladstone was averse to both of the domestic reforms which

Chamberlain regarded as pivotal: compulsory land purchase and free education. Since Hartington apparently was willing to tolerate an innocuous experiment with land purchase, Gladstone did not press that point. On free education, however, he did not want to allow Chamberlain, if in the cabinet, the freedom to take his own stand even in principle. Gladstone hoped to subordinate these domestic issues to the currently most pressing imperial concern. Ireland deepened its grip on his mind. He therefore wanted to nourish Chamberlain's sympathies on this subject. While conveying to Chamberlain that he was 'still very sweet on National Councils',[46] Gladstone encouraged him to place a favourable construction on Parnell's statements. Gladstone also expanded on the basic point about which host and guest were agreed, 'that a prolongation of the present relations of the Irish party to the Parliament would be a national disgrace'.[47] Pleased by Gladstone's invitation to Hawarden and by the implication 'that he was seeking to work with us & had no idea of doing without us',[48] Chamberlain did not immediately sense the direction in which the old statesman was heading.

While Chamberlain talked to Gladstone, Harcourt served as intermediary between Chamberlain and Hartington. The results were not encouraging. In private Hartington was prepared to deal with free education and compulsory land purchase more pragmatically than Gladstone, but the edge of Chamberlain's tongue made reconciliation difficult. As Harcourt reported, '"Rip Van Winkle" stuck a good deal in his gizzard and he is exercised on the question of whether your declaration that you would not join if your programme *was excluded* meant that you insisted it *should be included*.'[49] This reaction provoked Chamberlain, who felt that he had already reduced the substance of his demands to little more than symbolic proportions. 'If we were now to give up the very moderate minimum to which we are committed,' he wrote to Harcourt, 'the very stones would cry out and we should simply be elbowed out of the way to make room for more advanced and less reasonable politicians.'[50] Chamberlain believed that reform of local government would head the agenda of the next Liberal government because every Liberal candidate was committed to it in some form or other. He therefore insisted that it would be 'absolutely necessary to come to a decision upon [the attendant question of compulsory land purchase] before any Govt. was formed'.

These negotiations behind the scenes grew more complicated and confused as the election approached. Gladstone continued his mystifying dialogue with Chamberlain by letter; Grosvenor, the chief whip, replaced Harcourt as intermediary between Chamberlain and Hartington; and Henry Labouchere, a Radical arch-intriguer in touch with Irish Nationalists, Churchill and Gladstone's son Herbert, put Chamberlain in touch with inner movements on the Irish question.

The news from Labouchere should have prompted Chamberlain to reexamine his assumptions. Labouchere reported, first on Herbert Gladstone's authority that his father was disposed to grant a full measure of Home Rule to Ireland; secondly from conversation with Churchill that the Conservatives expected to do well in London; and thirdly from his own experience of Parnell 'that he never makes a bargain without intending to get out of it'.[51] But the third of Labouchere's messages counteracted the first. Mistaking Labouchere's intent, Chamberlain gave his own assessment of the situation:

> I agree with you that the 'modus vivendi' [with Ireland] cannot be found. 1st because all Liberals are getting weary of concessions to Parnell . . . & 2ndly because Parnell cannot be depended on to keep any bargain.
>
> I believe therefore that Mr G.'s plans will come to naught.
>
> I hope that R. Churchill is all out in his calculations. I do not give the Tories more than 200.
>
> Of course the future depends on the result of the elections, but my impression is that Hartington will yield, grumbling as usual, but still yielding.
>
> . . . The idiotic opposition of the Whigs & the abuse of the Tories has turned my gentle hint into a great national policy—& now it must be forced on at all hazards. The majority of new County candidates are pledged to it—ditto Scotch members ditto London. . . .
>
> On the whole I am satisfied with the outlook.[52]

He was reassured by a visit from Gladstone's ally Granville to Highbury, and by Gladstone's own consultation with him—'I have *never* been consulted before'.[53] Seeking clarity where Gladstone used mystery, Chamberlain left his leader in little doubt about his views on Ireland. Chamberlain ruled out pursuit of an accommodation with Parnell not just because he was unreliable but also because 'I would rather let Ireland go altogether than accept the responsibility for a nominal union.'[54] Unable to tell who was reliable when it came to Irishmen, Chamberlain drew comfort from Captain O'Shea's news of dissension in the Irish camp. Undeterred by clear information that Parnell was the lover of O'Shea's wife,[55] Chamberlain endorsed O'Shea's attempt to gain election at Liverpool. Chamberlain still convinced himself that Gladstone would seek agreement with the Radicals rather than with the Irish after the general election.

But Gladstone's sentiments were hardening in the reverse direction. He had come to admit privately that he distrusted Chamberlain more than Parnell.[56] The veteran statesman was pleased to note the miscalculations his strenuous lieutenant was making. The business of national politics, even at election time, was more complicated than Chamberlain appreciated. His plan of campaign was falling apart. The disintegration was most evident over free education.

A mixture of conviction and calculation led Chamberlain to emphasize this issue. He believed that education served better than anything else to improve the lot of labour. Willing by now to pay tribute to the great advance in education brought about by the Act of 1870, he wanted to remove the Act's most serious remaining defect. Though elementary education was made compulsory in 1876, parents still had to contribute towards the cost and so were tempted to evade the law. Chamberlain waxed eloquent on the injustice of forcing the poor man to pay 'not in proportion to his means, but in proportion to his wants'.[57] So far as electoral calculations were concerned, he expected the working classes enfranchised by the Third Reform Act to welcome this form of relief. He also welcomed the hostile reaction of moderate Liberals to free education because it might serve to keep dead Whig wood out of the next Liberal cabinet.

But by mid-October these calculations were being overturned. Working-class householders in urban constituencies were afraid that free education would increase their taxes. The demand for free education alienated many of Chamberlain's otherwise natural supporters and reinforced his natural enemies. Nonconformists feared that if the policy were applied to denominational as well as civic schools, it would perpetuate the ascendancy of the Church of England. Chamberlain tried to lessen this fear by suggesting that eventually the cost of free education could be defrayed by disendowing the established churches. He also suggested that eventually schools which accepted aid from the public purse should be supervised by elected representatives of the public. But since he wanted to institute free education before dealing with either of these eventualities, Nonconformists were not reassured. Instead these distant promises helped Conservatives to raise the cry of the 'Church in danger' and also to consolidate their support among English Catholics.

Gladstone and Salisbury divided the fruits of Chamberlain's impetuosity. Salisbury exploited the alarm in the Church of England by declaring himself against Chamberlain's policy, and he accepted Cardinal Manning's request for a royal commission on education. Gladstone, after questioning the wisdom of free education, was rewarded by a plea from one of Chamberlain's former Nonconformist allies, Alfred Illingworth, who urged the party leader not to be hurried on this issue. Many of Chamberlain's closest associates from the days of the National Education League backed away from free education, some of them quickly. Bunce of the *Birmingham Daily Post* did so before the end of September, Schnadhorst early in October, Morley by the middle of the month. The National Liberal Federation voted at Bradford to reverse Chamberlain's educational priorities, putting electoral control of schools ahead of free education. From then on, Chamberlain played the subject down in public, and in private he sought simply to preserve his freedom in the next Liberal government to speak and vote for free education in principle. But the issue had yet to take its full toll.

In the school board elections in Sheffield at the beginning of November, the anti-denominationalists went down to defeat. Dilke, campaigning for reelection at Chelsea in London, warned Chamberlain that '[t]he Tories are working Free Schools with the ratepayer as well as with the Churchmen & Catholics'.[58] Shortly before the polls opened, Dilke abandoned free education as not ripe for implementation in the coming Parliament.

From the beginning of November, Chamberlain concentrated on Birmingham. The outcome there was not a foregone conclusion. Since 1878 the Conservatives had been garnering support, particularly in poor central wards where labour was unorganized and in affluent residential areas resentful of the costs of Chamberlain's municipal socialism. The tales of adventure on the frontiers of the empire which Colonel Burnaby had recounted on behalf of the Conservatives proved popular in the town, and it was saddened by his death in his last such adventure some months before the election. But the most attractive appeal of the Conservatives in Birmingham was economic. The protracted depression in commodity prices and the resort to protective tariffs among Britain's international trading partners undermined confidence within Birmingham's Chamber of Commerce about the competitiveness of the town. 1885 was the worst year so far; and the multiplicity of the opportunities for labour which the town offered was no longer enough to avoid disturbing levels of unemployment. Earlier in the year, the Chamber had urged the Liberal Colonial Secretary to think of some sort of federation and trading union between Britain and its colonies. When the caretaker Conservative government appointed a royal commission on the depression in trade, the Chamber responded by recommending the imposition of a tariff on foreign manufactured goods, the policy then known as 'fair trade'. Birmingham's Conservatives latched on to the cry. Churchill embellished it with talk of ameliorative social measures.

Buoyantly the Conservatives thought that they might win five of the seven seats into which the Redistribution Act divided the hitherto united constituency. Chamberlain was apprehensive about three: Birmingham North where his brother-in-law William Kenrick, current president of the National Liberal Federation, was standing; the Bordesley Division where Henry Broadhurst, the most eminent labour leader in the previous Parliament, had been persuaded to stand; and Central Birmingham where Churchill challenged John Bright. The weakest aspect of the Conservative effort was their selection of candidates. The most prominent local Conservatives declined to stand themselves. The party resorted for the most part to lesser local men or to imported nonentities. They included a self-styled working man from London with the unfortunate name of Dumphries who stood against Chamberlain. But Henry Matthews, an eminent barrister, was brought in to challenge Kenrick. Churchill was the Conservatives' prize champion.

Always vigilant about the political arrangements of his town, Chamberlain influenced the drawing of the new constituency boundaries to ensure that each of the Conservatively-inclined central wards was combined with two strongly Liberal ones. He feared that the break-up of the town's parliamentary representation might allow greater scope for the advocates of independent labour. He therefore took care to preserve a strong Liberal association for the town as a whole. These arrangements enabled him to keep the representation of labour to one candidate, Broadhurst.

Chamberlain selected West Birmingham as his constituency. It did not include any of the inner Conservative wards. It was none the less heavily working class, as befitted a Radical. Sentimental attachments as well as calculation marked the constituency for Chamberlain. It included the principal works of Nettlefold and Chamberlain and the houses of many of its long-time employees. It included the place where Chamberlain had taught night school and the ward which had first elected him to the town council. His election was not in doubt.

Still, the speeches he delivered to his constituents would be read throughout the country. He had to rally support in all seven of the town's constituencies if Birmingham was to set an example for the rest of the kingdom. Night after night he hammered the same message home. It began with the four points in the manifesto of Gladstone, of whom Chamberlain spoke respectfully. To those four Chamberlain added another three. First he embellished upon Gladstone's willingness to distribute the burden of taxation more fairly between rich and poor. Secondly, he restated his demand for free education, and left no doubt in this connection of his support for disestablishment. Ireland he largely ignored, safe in the knowledge that Birmingham had few Irish-born voters.

Above all he focused on land reform. He expanded on the benefits Britain could draw from the proliferation of garden allotments and small landholdings, the policy famous as 'three acres and a cow'. Its attractions to the newly enfranchised agricultural labourers were obvious. But it was Chamberlain's nostrum for urban ills as well. He claimed that the depression in agriculture shrank the market for urban products and expanded the influx of labour from countryside to town, thus raising unemployment and pulling wages down. British industry did not need tariff protection. Calling on his experience as a manufacturer, he delighted his Birmingham audiences by revealing to them how successfully Nettlefold and Chamberlain had overcome the American hundred per cent tariff on screws. All the same, urban British workers needed protection from their fellow working men in the countryside. If rural labourers were provided with small landholdings for intensive cultivation, they would not only stay at home but increase Britain's agricultural production. And surely this was the barest justice in view of the predatory enclosure of common lands by rich landowners over the past three quarters of a century. Chamberlain united his urban working and middle-class constituents in indignation at this spoliation.

Meagre rewards

The contest in Birmingham was hard fought, though saved from bitterness by the liking Chamberlain and Churchill felt for each other. Fearful for Kenrick, Chamberlain devoted his final two days before the balloting to Birmingham North. As it happened, the result there was the first to be announced. Kenrick carried it by just over 600 votes. Bright carried the Central division by less than 800. These victories were narrow enough to allow the Conservatives to claim moral victory. In fact the Liberals won all seven seats in Birmingham. Chamberlain secured a crushing majority for himself in Birmingham West. Still, he felt less than euphoric about the achievement. The popularity of the patriotic and protectionist drums which the Conservatives beat, and their ability to draw support from both ends of the social spectrum, worried him.

His concern was deepened by Conservative successes in the early returns from other borough constituencies where Liberals expected to do well, and most notably in London. Chamberlain's hopes were cruelly disappointed. When the Third Reform Act enlarged the electorate, he thought that the Liberals would improve conspicuously upon their victory of 1880. As late as the end of October he was encouraged by Schnadhorst to expect a solid Liberal victory with over 360 seats. He had assumed that the Liberals would do their best in the urban areas where they were traditionally strong. The electoral returns from those areas not only disappointed him; they prompted other Liberals to place the blame for the outcome on him, particularly on the offence he had given to religious sentiments with his talk of free education and disestablishment.

The results of the election were not, however, complete. By early autumn Chamberlain had begun to wonder whether the Liberals would do their best in traditionally Conservative county constituencies. And indeed Conservative successes in the early borough results were offset by subsequent Liberal successes in the counties. Chamberlain and Jesse

Collings, who had devoted himself to the agricultural sector, were entitled to much of the credit for these successes. They were due perhaps more to the newly enfranchised agricultural labourers' repudiation of the ancient regime of squire and parson. All the same, the prospect of 'three acres and a cow' tantalized farm labourers, particularly in East Anglia and the southwest, as did garden allotments for working men in essentially industrial 'county' constituencies to the north.

But the gratifying returns no more than matched the depressing ones. The Liberals emerged with a bare half of the new House of Commons. Parnell not only annihilated the 'loyalists' in Catholic Ireland but won a narrow majority of the seats in Ulster. Furthermore, on the eve of the election he had advised Irish voters in Britain to vote Conservative. Estimates of the cost to the Liberals ranged between 20 and 65 seats. Chamberlain put it at 25. 86 Nationalists from Ireland were elected to the new Parliament, neutralizing precisely the majority which the Liberals had won over the Conservatives in Britain.

The stalemate left most men in tense uncertainty. Gladstone dwelt upon the massive Nationalist victory in Ireland, which exceeded his anticipation. Chamberlain meditated on the achievement of the Conservatives. He was puzzled by the Conservatism the urban electorate displayed. The urban working classes were apparently less socialistic in their appetites than he had assumed. As for the affluent residential constituencies, it was there, among Chamberlain's own class, that opposition to the Radical Programme erupted most conspicuously, in Tory rather than moderate Liberal guise. He was also impressed by the capacity of Conservative candidates to adapt themselves to the urban environment. They had proved flexible on social issues, more so than some Whigs. As soon as the disappointing borough results were known, he placed the blame on timid Liberals for watering down his programme. Still, the strongest appeal of the Conservatives was to English national sentiment, partly on foreign affairs but even more with regard to foreign economic competition. The one imperial issue on which the Conservatives had equivocated was Ireland, but Chamberlain did not expect that equivocation to last long.

The election conveyed messages hard to reconcile with the Radical Programme in which he had invested so heavily since January. He needed time—leaving the Conservatives in office to reveal their true colours—time to reassess his enterprise and to gather his forces for the next assault. But what made him pause made Gladstone bold.

9

The Crash
1885–1886

I do not care for the leadership of a party which should prove itself so fickle & so careless of National interests as to sacrifice the unity of the Empire to the precipitate impatience of an old man, careless of the future in which he can have no part.

> Chamberlain to Dilke, 3 May 1886

The political drama of the mid-1880s moved towards its crisis without a pause. The scene shifted from mass meetings to enclaves of rival leaders broadening till they embraced the whole House of Commons. Only when the House reached its decision would the electorate again be consulted.

With the popular chorus silenced, relationships among the main characters assumed crucial importance. They used issues of public policy as weapons of personal combat. Only on the great occasions when Gladstone addressed the House of Commons at length did the grandeur of his unfolding vision of Home Rule for Ireland become apparent. The rival vision of the Radical Programme was dimmed by the disappointing electoral returns. Deprived of a popular mandate, deserted by erstwhile investors in his enterprise, doubtful himself about the viability of the programme, and in this weakened condition challenged at last by his most deadly rival, Chamberlain faced political bankruptcy.

Much more was at stake than the careers of politicians. Gladstone's proposal of a large measure of autonomy for Ireland put the cohesion of the United Kingdom and British empire in question. It also diverted attention from Radical socio-economic proposals. But however great these implications, the crisis that dominated the short life of the new Parliament was not worked out in these terms. It was a tale of rival captains and bemused followers fighting in a fog.

Cabals at Highbury and Hawarden

The leaders of the Liberal party broke into factions within days of the final returns from the general election. Chamberlain summoned some Radicals to Highbury. The men who answered his call were a tattered lot: Dilke clouded by scandal, Shaw-Lefevre defeated at Reading, and Morley who had not yet held office. They did not know what to make of the situation, nor were they willing to defer to Chamberlain. The electoral returns did not require the immediate formation of a Liberal government, let alone enable the Radicals to dictate its policy and composition. The question at Highbury was what course the Radicals should pursue vis-à-vis the rest of the Liberal party and the incumbent Conservative government while they searched for a way to reassert themselves.

Chamberlain was torn between a wish to lie low and his more usual instinct for defiance. He wanted to leave the Conservatives in office long enough to expose their inadequacies. The one thing he did not want was to find himself again in a ministry dominated by Whigs. He ascribed what success the Liberals had achieved in the general election to the Radical offer of 'three acres and a cow', which Whigs and moderate Liberals had done their best to minimize. If Chamberlain accepted any responsibility for the disappointing outcome of the election, it was not because of those he alienated but of those he disappointed. He thought of Scottish Radicals whose enthusiasm for disestablishment he had dampened, and of English Nonconformists fearful that free education unaccompanied by civic control of denominational schools would set back the cause of religious equality. Still, the election forced him to recognize that the voters did 'not care much' about free education[1] and were ambivalent about disestablishment. Writing to Hartington during the Highbury cabal, Chamberlain pointed out that 'we are dreadfully in want of an urban "Cow"'.[2] Yet he could not see one himself; and the election returns did not encourage him to turn his thoughts in the direction of more socialism.

Before coming to Highbury Dilke advised him that 'Ireland is the only question worth discussion'.[3] No government could stay in or take office without reaching some accommodation with the Irish Nationalists, unless some agreement could be reached between the two British parties to hold the Irish at bay. During the conclave at Highbury, Labouchere wrote to Chamberlain about the dividends he could reap from cooperating with Gladstone to reach a settlement with the Irish. It would allow Gladstone to retire and would probably alienate the Whigs, placing Radicals in a position to capture the Liberal party and press on with their agenda of domestic reform. Here was the natural route for English Radicals to choose. It could have altered the future course of Britain's history if Chamberlain had followed it.

But he turned down the advice abruptly: 'we must sit on [Gladstone's] Irish proposals,' he replied.[4] He refused to endorse another initiative on Ireland. With his central board scheme he had made the Irish Nationalists a good offer, only to be insulted by those he sought to conciliate. He would not do more. Aside from personal pique, his vision for Ireland did not extend beyond provincial application of essentially municipal powers. To concede more would, he thought, weaken the imperial government and also diminish the hold of the Liberals on the British electorate.

The men who had gathered at Highbury left to go their separate ways. Dilke nevertheless agreed with Chamberlain on the wisdom of leaving the Tories in office long enough to enable Radicals to benefit from the probable reaction. Dilke offered this advice publicly upon his return to London, less circumspect than usual because of his personal problems. His words confirmed suspicion in Gladstone's household that Chamberlain meant to supplant his leader. Gladstone was too old to be expected to form another government after any considerable delay. He reacted angrily: 'I do not mean to be sat upon by D[ilke] or by D & C[hamberlain], if other things call on me to act.'[5] Still, he resolved to bide his time quietly till the new Parliament assembled. His son Herbert, however, reacted precipitately. To mark the Grand Old Man out as the person to whom Britain should turn, Herbert intimated to the press that his father contemplated the creation of a separate legislature and executive in Dublin for Irish domestic affairs. The disclaimer that the old man immediately issued did little to diminish belief that the press leak, dubbed the 'Hawarden kite', was reliable.

The defection of Morley

Among its reverberations, the Hawarden kite precipitated the rupture of one of Chamberlain's closest friendships, the first of many to be torn asunder over the next six months. Chamberlain drew upon all his relationships, whether family, friends or followers, with a consuming intensity. He was drawn to the circles of people with whom he surrounded himself by a yearning for companionship, an appetite for ideas and information, a need for appreciation, admiration and applause, and by a desire for power. They in turn were drawn to him by his 'vivid and resolute energy, fearless tenacity of will',[6] candour in private and fire in public, his generous loves and contemptuous hates. He encompassed his friends in an embrace that burned both ways. As John Morley recalled,

> The friend . . . was an innermost element in his own existence. To keep a friend, to stand by him, to put a good construction on whatever he said or did, came as naturally to him as traits of self-love come to men in general. This was, of course, bound up with expectations to match.[7]

In the final analysis what Chamberlain required of his friends was loyal subordination. Though he valued hard-hitting conversation and could give as well as take, he could not tolerate fundamental disagreement from those he loved. Those who accepted his terms surrendered their autonomy. Those who knew his love but refused to pay the price eventually pushed him away. But they could not do so completely. They kept on looking back, haunted by wistfulness or consumed by anger. Chamberlain responded to defections from his intimate circle with agonized incomprehension. He could not understand the logic of his departing friend or reconcile close friendship with fundamental disagreement; yet he was no more able than the departing friend to sever the bond completely.

The same pattern applied in milder form to the relations between Chamberlain and followers who were not close friends. He did not expect full agreement from them on all important principles. He recognized the existence of divergent interests among the Radicals. But in accommodating those interests, he insisted on his own order of priorities. Glorious in action as captain of the Radical host, he expected its loyalty. He had no premonition of the resentment against him smouldering among Radicals whose dearest local or religious interests he had subordinated over the past dozen years. Feelings of this sort were to turn Radical against Radical over the next half year. Ireland was often incidental to their alienation from each other—Ireland but not Gladstone. Gladstone catalysed the disruption of party relationships, which in turn crippled him.

In some ways the most decisive of the friendships ruptured during the crisis was between Chamberlain and John Morley. Very close till 1880, their relationship had come under strain once their daily paths diverged with Chamberlain's appointment to the cabinet; and the strain only increased when their paths reconverged with Morley's election as MP for Newcastle in 1883. Chamberlain's ambitions for Morley and Morley's ambitions for himself never quite coincided. Chamberlain hoped that Morley would distinguish himself primarily as a thinker and writer, and so enhance the 'spiritual power' behind Chamberlain's throne. He invested in this prospect by lending Morley enough money to release him from lesser distractions for several years to write a history of the French Revolution. Morley never settled down to write the book. Though he paid off the debt with income from other writing, he sensed Chamberlain's disappointment.

Morley wanted to be more than an educated analyst of politics. Fascinated by men of action, he wanted to be one himself without surrendering his 'spiritual power'. Repeatedly he sought election to Parliament. On each occasion he received loyal support from Chamberlain, though Chamberlain indicated that he would have preferred Morley 'to stick to literature'.[8] Morley owed his successful nomination for Newcastle to Chamberlain and Dilke; and it was at Chamberlain's side that Morley at last entered the House of Commons. But now Morley could be his own man. Once in the Commons, his periodic expressions of dissent from the policies of the government to which Chamberlain belonged took on deeper seriousness. Sparks flew between the two men, particularly over Egypt, which Morley wanted simply to abandon. Chamberlain's crusade against negligent shipowners touched interests in Newcastle too close for Morley's comfort, and he adopted a position of judicious neutrality on the subject. Confronted by Gladstone's challenge to the Radical Programme in January 1885, Chamberlain sensed that he could not take Morley's support for granted.

All the same, Morley believed that the possibility of a rupture with Chamberlain was remote. When Chamberlain rejected Parnell's talk of an independent parliament, Morley wrote to confess that, though he could not bring himself 'up to your pitch about Ireland I do not suppose that we differ an atom as to the next step to be taken, whatever it may be.'[9] The issue of disestablishment kept Morley on Chamberlain's side and away from Gladstone. Morley wrote the chapter on disestablishment and disendowment for *The Radical Programme*, proposing a plan which Gladstone denounced as 'outrageously unjust'.[10] After the general election Chamberlain hoped that Morley would welcome his suggestion to put disestablishment at the top of the Radical agenda.

Yet the election left the two men with different collective loyalties. It aggravated Chamberlain's anger at the Whigs to the point where he hoped the Tories would stay in office for a year or two, while it deepened Morley's disgust at the unprincipled 'imposture' of Toryism.[11] This disagreement quickly became personal. Chamberlain challenged Morley's commitment to himself and the Radical cause by questioning Gladstone's worth as leader of the Liberal party. Morley responded by criticizing Chamberlain for adopting a position of 'deliberate isolation on personal grounds from the rest of the party, at a moment when there is no great *practical* issue that I know of, on which Radicals take a line of their own'.[12] Morley referred respectfully to the party's loyalty to Gladstone, and turned to the subject of Ireland, on which he said he intended to take a line of his own. He made himself clearer to the chairman of his constituency association: if, said Morley, Gladstone was willing to tackle the Irish question, 'we northern radicals [should] support him tooth and nail. . . . Much dirty intriguing is going on. I won't be a party to snubbing the Old Man.'[13]

At this point Herbert Gladstone flew the Hawarden kite. Morley may have encouraged the manoeuvre. He certainly responded to it ardently: 'I shall go with the old man,'[14] he announced. It was a declaration of changed loyalties rather than a statement on Irish policy. When Chamberlain tried to pursue the subject of Ireland with him, Morley only increased his distance. He delayed his reply for several days, and then delivered it in public. Speaking at Newcastle, Morley indicated that he would support Gladstone if he proposed a separate parliament for Ireland. The excuse

Morley gave to Chamberlain for speaking out, that 'it was necessary to my mental peace',[15] was more expressive of personal upheaval than political reflection.

Chamberlain realized that the speech at Newcastle marked a breach in their political comradeship. He told Morley so as calmly as he could manage. His anger flashed only towards Gladstone. Chamberlain's assessment of the state of the relationship between the two friends staggered Morley. He argued that he could combine alignment with Gladstone on Ireland and maintenance of his alliance with Chamberlain. His ambivalence was painfully intense. 'I have no sort of ambition to be an admiral of the fleet', he wrote, 'But I'll be hanged if I'll be a powder monkey.' Alluding to the loan Chamberlain had given him to write a history of the French Revolution, he went on: 'When I read in the newspapers, your threatened advertisement that you will "no longer be responsible for my debts," it will be time enough for me to consider.'[16]

'We can't help ourselves,' Chamberlain concluded. He accepted, indeed exaggerated the fact that the time for reasoned political discussion between the two men had passed. Unable, however, to leave it at that, he exclaimed, 'Have I not . . . done everything in my power, directly & indirectly, to contribute to your well-deserved advance to political power and influence?'[17] Morley accepted that claim, describing his debt to Chamberlain in terms which made his own behaviour almost inexcusable:

> Tacitus says something about his 'dignity' being started by one Emperor, increased by a second, and carried still further by a third. It is always a delight to me to think that 'dignitas mea', whatever it may amount to, has been 'inchoata, aucta, et longius pervecta', not by three men but by one, and that one yourself.[18]

He refused to recognize that he was deserting one emperor for a rival, more congenial one. Yet he would not respond even sketchily about Ireland until Chamberlain gave up attempting to discuss the question with him.

Morley could have accounted for his divergence from Chamberlain more easily by focusing on the subject of Ireland, to which they had often reacted differently. Morley was always more hostile to coercion and more sympathetic towards nationalist aspirations. But other Liberals like Mundella of Sheffield, who had been much more hostile to Irish claims than had Chamberlain, turned away from him now, talking like Morley about party loyalty rather than Ireland. Mundella had disapproved of Chamberlain's sympathy for the Irish as far back as 1874. But two weeks after the general election, Mundella wrote to tell Gladstone that 'I am, *in common with nearly every man I meet*, angry, not to say indignant, that any member of our party, except yourself, should presume to prescribe the course to be taken by the Liberals'; and he assured Gladstone 'that whatever policy you propound will receive the general acceptance of the Liberal party'.[19]

Resentment at the pretensions of Birmingham turned Liberals from rival towns towards Gladstone in order to put Chamberlain down. Liberals from Leeds led by Wemyss Reid, who hated Chamberlain more than he loved Home Rule, prompted the flying of the Hawarden kite. Other Liberals moved in the same direction in reaction to Chamberlain's tolerance for the Tories. F.A. Channing, newly elected for Northamptonshire East, had preached the whole Radical Programme, but he was repelled by Chamberlain's preference for a minority Conservative government over a Liberal one dominated by Whigs.

Return to office

While Chamberlain threatened 'to do anything & everything that may be disagreeable to the Whigs',[20] he responded to Gladstone with remarkable circumspection. News of the Hawarden kite reached Chamberlain when he was about to address his constituents in the Birmingham town hall. Though beginning to suspect 'that a large number—perhaps the majority of the Liberals will support *any* scheme of Mr. G's',[21] Chamberlain felt sure that a generous measure of Home Rule would bring electoral death and damnation. With quick presence of mind Chamberlain developed a line of argument in his speech that combined appreciation of Gladstone's primacy, recognition of the desire of the Liberal rank and file to vent their spleen on the Tories, and his own wish to leave Parnell to find out what he could obtain from his current Tory allies before turning back to the Liberals. Chamberlain wanted to suspend the bidding for Irish support until Parnell lowered his price.

Chamberlain's speech struck Gladstone as a pleasant surprise. It reduced his doubts about Chamberlain's loyalty. It also offered support for the policy of temporizing silence that Gladstone wanted to observe until the Conservative government decided what it would do about Ireland. He wrote to thank Chamberlain for his words and secure his cooperation. But though both men wanted to temporize, there was a critical difference in their sense of timing. Gladstone was waiting for the government to act. If it failed, he was ready to try his own hand: 'the hour glass', he told Chamberlain, 'has begun to run for a definitive issue'.[22] Chamberlain wanted a longer delay, until Parnell learned to accept from the Liberals, and they prepared the English electorate to accept, a settlement less generous than the Nationalists but more generous than the electorate were currently willing to tolerate. He expressed himself clearly to his chief: 'If there were a dissolution on this question, & the Liberal party or its leader were thought to be pledged to a separate Parliament in Dublin, it is my belief that we should sustain a tremendous defeat. The English working classes, for various reasons, are distinctly hostile to Home Rule carried to this extent, & I do not think it would be possible to convert them before a General Election.'[23] Gladstone did not reply to this warning, nor was he anything like this candid with Chamberlain. But the old man was evasive with all of his interlocutors. He urged Chamberlain to be *'very credulous* as to any statements about my views & opinions. Rest assured that I have done & said *nothing* which in any way points to negotiation or separate action.'[24]

Over the next month and more, Chamberlain clung to this assurance and occasional others like it. Every way he looked, he foresaw disaster for the Radicals. 'The question', he told Labouchere, 'is whether it is better to be smashed with Mr. G. & the Parnellites or without them.'[25] The only way out that he could discern lay in taking one step at a time, paying as little attention as possible to the ultimate policy alternatives.

Gladstone too said little about Ireland. He wrapped himself in silence or ambiguity and ignored most of his colleagues. He said nothing in public, and refused to answer letters from his colleagues until the end of the year, when he put them off with polite evasions. By keeping his distance, by immersing himself in works of political philosophy rather than discussion or correspondence, Gladstone focused attention on the uniqueness of his leadership and enhanced its mystique. The same means served to maximize his freedom of action and paralyse his self-willed colleagues.

Chamberlain fluttered helplessly in the web the old man wove. Furious when Gladstone declined to respond to his observations, he was pacified briefly by a note which encouraged him to hope that Gladstone had not yet decided on a generous measure of Home Rule. Chamberlain prompted potential dissidents from the former cabinet—Hartington, Harcourt and Dilke—to concert their opposition to what Gladstone had in mind. But how could they do so when Gladstone refused to reveal it? Chamberlain suggested that the dissidents as a group should confront Gladstone '& call on him to stand & deliver his plans'.[26] Gladstone parried the challenge by inviting them individually to come at different hours. Chamberlain went when he was bidden.

On the substance of the Irish question, Chamberlain had more to say at the turn of the year than most others jockeying for position. He sketched out solutions designed to emphasize the impracticability of a generous measure of Home Rule. He was convinced that such a measure would split and discredit the Liberal party. One alternative he suggested was an adaptation of the American constitution, giving England, Scotland, Wales and possibly Ulster as well as southern Ireland separate legislatures, leaving imperial affairs to Westminster, with a supreme court to arbitrate on the respective limits of authority. As he described it, this solution would involve the abolition of the House of Lords soon and of the monarchy thereafter, a prospect he knew would repel Gladstone. Another solution would be to turn Ireland into a protected state, completely autonomous except for defence and foreign affairs which would remain in British hands. Chamberlain's point in outlining this possibility was to demonstrate that the 'difficulties of any plan are almost insurmountable'. Seeking to discredit any intermediate solution between his central board scheme and complete separation, he remarked—in sharp contrast to the position he would adopt a few months later—that 'the worst of all plans would be one which kept the Irishmen at Westminster while they had their own Parliament in Dublin'.[27]

These scenarios were transmitted to Gladstone without effect. Meanwhile the old man made use of Morley's sympathy for the sort of Home Rule that Chamberlain sought to rule out. Morley and Chamberlain struggled at the beginning of the new year to maintain their private friendship. They tried 'snug' meals together, followed by evenings at the theatre.[28] They discussed possible cabinet arrangements to preserve their collaboration in the event of a Liberal return to power. But at the same time, with other friends, they spoke out against each other. Morley offered his services to Gladstone, proposing to write editorials on Ireland along the lines of Gladstone's thinking for the Liberal *Daily News*, if Gladstone would indicate to him where his mind was tending; and the editorials duly began to appear.

Chamberlain tried to divert attention from constitutional issues to land reform, for Ireland as well as England. He spoke forcefully to the Allotments and Small Holdings Association on the day that Gladstone gave individual interviews to his former colleagues. Chamberlain was largely responsible for a resolution that Jesse Collings wished to move in the opening days of the new Parliament calling for implementation of the Radical Programme on allotments and smallholdings.

Soon after Parliament assembled in mid-January, the Conservative government adopted a coercive policy towards Ireland, and thus courted defeat in the House of Commons, in order to pass the poisoned chalice of office to the Liberals. The Liberal leaders in council (from which Hartington absented himself) adopted Collings's resolution as a way to bring about the Conservatives' defeat without committing themselves on Ireland. Chamberlain welcomed the tactic additionally because it would involve Gladstone's commitment to at least one distinctively Radical policy. Chamberlain also entertained the improbable hope that the tactic might help to focus Parnell's attention on the distress of Ireland's tenant farmers rather than on Home Rule. Parnell flatly rejected the suggestion but was willing to vote for Collings's resolution as a way of bringing Gladstone to power. The House of Commons duly passed the resolution, and the Conservative ministry resigned. Yet the vote was more ominous for the victors than for the vanquished. Eighteen Liberals including Hartington and Goschen voted against the motion, as much because of its Radical substance as of the Irish question that lurked behind it. Another seventy-six Liberals including John Bright abstained. Gladstone thus regained office without a clear expression of confidence even from his party.

Chamberlain entertained a faint hope that the incoming ministry would act in keeping with the resolution that had brought it to office. He was encouraged in this hope by Hartington's refusal to join the ministry. Chamberlain accepted the post of President of the Local Government Board in the hope of implementing something of the Radical Programme. He set to work immediately on a comprehensive local government bill, while Collings followed up the success of his motion by preparing a bill on allotments.

This was shadow play. The new ministry was founded on trust in Gladstone; and Gladstone was preoccupied with Ireland. He was gratified by the cooperation of Chamberlain over Collings's resolution, and Chamberlain was one of the first people Gladstone consulted after accepting the Queen's commission to form a government. But the concord between the two men broke down immediately. Alone among those invited to take office, Chamberlain insisted on what amounted to a letter of contract before accepting Gladstone's invitation. Though both men claimed to be satisfied with the eventual wording of their contract, the strain they generated in reaching it undermined the good faith requisite for its success. Gladstone resented Chamberlain's presumption, and revealed his feeling in a succession of galling slights to Chamberlain.

Their contract took the form of a jointly drafted letter.[29] In it Chamberlain 'recognize[d] the justice of [Gladstone's] view that the question of Ireland is paramount to all others & must first engage [his] attention'; and the two men promised to give fair consideration to each other's proposals on Ireland. Yet Chamberlain indicated his belief that anything beyond a central board or national council would prove incompatible with the needs of the kingdom and empire as a whole. Gladstone spoke of 'examin[ing] whether it is practicable to comply with the wishes of the majority of the Irish people' in terms that suggested more involvement by his cabinet colleagues in the process of examination than he intended.

Once they had concluded their agreement, Gladstone offered Chamberlain the post of First Lord of the Admiralty. Chamberlain declined the offer. As Bright approvingly explained, 'No one of your opinions should go into the military or naval departments, where there is freedom to spend, & no chance of economy or reform.'[30] Instead Chamberlain suggested the office of Secretary of State for the Colonies. Annoyed at his persistent presumption, Gladstone replied witheringly, 'Oh, a Secretary of State!' Chamberlain would have been delighted with the Chancellorship of the Exchequer, but Gladstone assigned that office to Harcourt in a bid for his otherwise uncertain support. The final decision was for Chamberlain to take the least prestigious office in the cabinet, the Presidency of the Local Government Board, because of the importance Chamberlain attached to its responsibilities.

The slights continued. Gladstone agreed to Chamberlain's request for Collings as his undersecretary but insisted, on the grounds of economy, that the salary for this position should be reduced. Furious at this treatment of the man to whom, more than any other, the Liberals owed their recent county victories, Chamberlain threatened to reconsider his own position. Gladstone eventually gave way but gracelessly, 'to Chamberlain's will,' as he put it, 'not to his reasons, which are null'.[31]

This treatment dimmed but did not quite destroy Chamberlain's hopes for the future of the ministry. 'Will Mr. G[ladstone]—at 76—frankly lean on the Radicals for the last steps of his journey?' Chamberlain mused. 'His treatment of myself argues for the negative but that may be due to personal feeling. If so it will yield to the gentle pressure of circumstances. If it does not you will shortly see not a triangular but a quadrilateral duel in which Tories, Whigs, Gladstone Liberals and Chamberlain Radicals will endeavour to eliminate one another.'[32]

His anxieties were deepened by the inclusion of Morley in the cabinet as Chief Secretary for Ireland. A master stroke by Gladstone, this appointment strengthened Radical representation in the cabinet while weakening Chamberlain and paving the way for a bold Irish policy. Morley was writing another of his editorials for the *Daily News* when the summons came to discuss his entry into the ministry. He wanted to accept the offer but hesitated to pay the final price in loyalty. To Gladstone's dismay, he asked for a couple of hours to consult Chamberlain. Chamberlain blanched at Morley's news. It pointed to exactly the sort of Irish policy Chamberlain wished to prevent. Though he said that of course Morley must accept the offer, he left Morley in no doubt of the probable consequences for their political fortunes and friendship. Morley went away hesitant. But when he returned to Gladstone to express his doubts, the old man swept them aside, giving Morley the impression that he meant him to be 'a special ally'.[33]

Morley's switch of allegiance was not quite complete. For a few days he clung to the illusion that he could serve as a buffer between Gladstone and Chamberlain. But Morley and Gladstone quickly agreed on the desirability of a statutory legislature for Ireland. Gladstone sharpened the personal edge of their accord by insisting on 'the necessity of absolute secrecy'[34] between them. Chamberlain on the other hand stiffened his opinion, as he told Morley, that the integrity of the empire and the supremacy of Parliament could not be maintained unimpaired 'in connection with a legislative body sitting in Dublin or in connection with your proposal to put

Ireland in the position of Canada'.[35] The day this message reached Morley, he was asked, 'What is Joe playing at?' 'Fast and loose!' was his reply.[36] For the next few weeks Morley and Chamberlain communicated with each other like foreign powers, rarely and with studied correctness, aware of the impending probability of open war.

For a moment in mid-February, relations between Chamberlain and Gladstone took a more hopeful turn. It may have been prompted by a threat of resignation over the budget from Harcourt, who was never much enamoured of Home Rule. Whatever the reason, Gladstone wrote to Chamberlain in a wooing mood, agreeing to keep Collings's salary at the current level and asking Chamberlain to come to Downing Street and expound his ideas on Ireland. Their ensuing discussion encouraged Chamberlain to 'think that a closer inspection of the difficulties in the way has brought Mr Gladstone nearer to me than he was when he first came to London'.[37] Anxious to focus attention on the agrarian side of the Irish question, Chamberlain sketched out a scheme to help tenants purchase the land they farmed. But the harmony soon faded. It came to an angry end, so far as Chamberlain was concerned, at the beginning of March when Gladstone took away the legislative draughtsman who had been assisting Chamberlain with the local government bill to work on Irish measures.

Throughout these ministerial dealings Chamberlain was isolated. Gladstone had left Dilke out of the ministry. Dilke, who felt his exclusion acutely, was concerned to ensure that at least it did not strain his relationship with Chamberlain, who would be privy to business that he could not readily divulge to outsiders. But in fact Chamberlain was almost as much an outsider as Dilke. How different it would have been but for the Crawford divorce scandal! Dilke in the cabinet, probably at the Foreign Office, able once again to support Chamberlain and prevent the cabinet from taking any course that both of them felt intolerable.

Under the present circumstances, it would have been inconceivably foolish for Chamberlain to deepen the discredit into which Dilke had fallen. Yet Chamberlain was suspected of doing so when the Crawford divorce came to trial in the second week of February. Divorce was never simple or straightforward in Victorian England. For a person in public life it was specially threatening; and this case was unusually murky. Chamberlain knew that much depended on how the case was conducted. Though he believed that the essential charge against Dilke of adultery with Virginia Crawford was untrue, Chamberlain knew that Dilke was not in a position to behave with outraged innocence in court. Not only was there his affair with Virginia's mother, there were shades of other women in his past. Dilke had a reputation among the knowing elite for sexual transgression. Chamberlain hoped accordingly that the Crawford divorce hearing would be confined to the matter on which his friend could claim innocence. To secure this end Chamberlain acted with impropriety and without his usual appreciation of how the public could react.

He arranged to see the judge, Sir Charles Butt, before the trial.[38] The two men knew each other. Butt had been a backbench Liberal MP in the early 1880s before his appointment to the Admiralty division of the courts, to which, oddly, divorce cases were assigned. Because of his knowledge of admiralty business, Chamberlain appointed Butt to the royal commission on merchant shipping in 1884. This association made a meeting between the judge and the best friend of the accused only the more improper. What transpired at the meeting was not recorded. It was fortunate for the reputations of both men that their meeting did not come to light for ninety years.

The part Chamberlain played in the trial and then the verdict of the judge proved quite controversial enough. After the initial proceedings when Mrs Crawford's confession was examined, Dilke's attorneys had a meeting with Chamberlain and decided to advise their client against taking the stand in his own defence. The need for Dilke to do so did not seem compelling, and by not taking the stand he could avoid cross-examination. Dilke's lawyers, Sir Henry James and Sir Charles Russell, were the leading Liberal barristers of the day; hence their advice carried great weight. Chamberlain endorsed the recommendation and conveyed it to Dilke, who accepted it. The lawyers gave this advice in the knowledge that the confession of Mrs Crawford, however damning to herself, could not be accepted as legal proof of Dilke's guilt as the alleged co-respondent. That legal principle formed the basis upon which Sir Charles Butt delivered his judgment. He exonerated Dilke, whom he went out of his way to praise, yet proceeded to grant Mr Crawford the divorce he sought from his wife on the grounds of the adultery which she confessed with Dilke. Apparently Mrs Crawford had committed adultery with Dilke but not he with her!

Initially Chamberlain was pleased with the outcome, and he expected Dilke to move back into the political limelight fairly soon. But the verdict was impossible to accept at face value. The judge was soon suspected of being influenced by his political association with Dilke, while Dilke fell under suspicion for failure to take the stand. A week after the trial the *Birmingham Daily Post*, probably at Chamberlain's prompting, carried an article which attempted to allay these suspicions; but they were voiced with venom in the *Pall Mall Gazette* by its editor, W.T. Stead. Stead had admired Chamberlain in the days of the Bulgarian atrocities agitation but had since turned against him for putting ambition ahead of principle. Directing his venom at Chamberlain, Stead accused him of betraying Dilke by advising him not to take the stand.

Though Dilke's lawyers fully shared responsibility for the advice, it was indeed bad. It added to suspicion of Chamberlain on the eve of his fight for political life. More seriously, it contributed to the ruin of his most valuable ally. Chamberlain still hoped that Dilke would recover but knew now that it would take a long time. Furthermore, though innocent of any wish to damage Dilke, Chamberlain began to sense that he was paying dearly for the friendship.

All this wrenching of old friendships amid the political turmoil prompted Chamberlain to renew a recent acquaintance. The Crawford divorce trial coincided with tumultuous demonstrations among the unemployed in some English cities. The most serious occurred in London when an assembly of 20,000 in Trafalgar Square turned into a riot. The demonstrations extended to Birmingham, where Highbury was threatened. Though ephemeral, they prompted Chamberlain to take action at the Local Government Board. Here was a challenge he welcomed. He issued a circular to the boards of guardians throughout the country. Directing their attention to those whom the depression was throwing out of work rather than to the chronically unemployed with whom these boards were normally preoccupied, Chamberlain urged the guardians to promote public works projects. The Chamberlain Circular became a benchmark in public policy because it broadened the conception of the responsibilities of the state. The departure was more evocative than immediately practical. The public works the circular encouraged did not help the stratum of the unemployed for whom they were intended. Chamberlain foresaw that this might happen. His circular was exploratory rather than dogmatic. He wanted to find out what government could do to alleviate the problem.

He explained his line of thought most fully in reopening an association with Beatrice Potter. Between attacks on him over the Crawford divorce trial, the *Pall Mall Gazette* published an article by her on unemployment in the East End of London where she was a social investigator. The twenty-seven-year-old daughter of a railway promoter who lived near Chamberlain in London, Beatrice Potter moved in circles which overlapped with his. They had met three years earlier. Though in his late forties, Chamberlain looked almost twenty years younger; always immaculately dressed, he cut a handsome figure. Beatrice Potter, though unconventional, was beautiful to look at and stimulating to talk to. He soon became interested in her, and she was fascinated by him. She confided the story of their unfolding relationship to her diary. It was a more intense version of what John Morley experienced in refusing to accept subordination to the man who gripped their emotions.

Beatrice Potter had her first sustained conversation with Chamberlain at a dinner in the summer of 1883. She was seated between him and a Whig peer, and recorded her impression: 'Whig peer talked of his own possessions, Chamberlain *passionately* of getting hold of other people's— for the masses. Curious and interesting character, dominated by *intellec-*

tual passions with little self-control but with any amount of *purpose*.' At the time she was serving as private secretary to Herbert Spencer, the advocate of individualism and strict curbs on the powers of the state, and hence a critic of Chamberlain's politics. 'Herbert Spencer on Chamberlain: "A man who may mean well, but who does, and will do, an incalculable amount of mischief." Chamberlain on Herbert Spencer: "Happily, for the majority of the world, his writing is not intelligible, otherwise his life would have been spent in doing harm."' Beatrice dramatized this conflict as between 'the philosopher' and 'the great man'. She went on: 'I understand the working of Herbert Spencer's reason, but I do not understand the reason of Chamberlain's passion. . . . How I should like to study that man!'[39]

Able to observe Chamberlain at close quarters as well as on the public stage, Beatrice Potter articulated questions about him that troubled people throughout his political life. He held his convictions passionately—she used that word often about him. But were those convictions based on 'honest experience and thought or were they originally the tool of ambition, now become inextricably woven into the love of power, and to his mind no longer distinguishable from it?'[40] The question was compounded for Beatrice Potter by the aversion which Spencer instilled in her about pandering to the masses instead of heeding 'the advice of the more intelligent portion of the community'.[41] She was partially reassured by coming to know Chamberlain's daughter, also named Beatrice and only three years younger than herself, a serious, straightforward, transparently trustworthy woman devoted to her father. 'Coming from such honest surroundings he surely *must* be straight in intention.'[42]

Despite ambivalence on her part and apprehension among her family, Beatrice Potter invited Chamberlain and his elder children to visit her family for new year's festivities. Their prospective arrival threw her into turmoil. She interpreted it as conflict between her sensual and intellectual sides, between her desire for love and marriage and her ambition to devote her mental powers to the wellbeing of society. She assured a friend that 'If . . . the Right Honourable gentleman takes "a very conventional view of women", I may be saved all temptation by my unconventionality. I certainly shall not hide it. He would soon see that I was not the woman to "forward" his most ambitious views.'[43]

Chamberlain accepted the new year's invitation in a rollicking vein:

> I do not despise dancing & I have a great respect for King David who continued the exercise to a late period of his life—but what would the Tories say?
>
> Nero fiddling while Rome was burning would be nothing to a Sybarite President of the Board of Trade dancing on the ruins of his country.[44]

Still, he did not look for anything on political matters from women beyond stimulating banter and sympathetic discussion. It was never quite clear that he had marriage with Beatrice Potter in mind, though she assumed that he did. When they talked politics, she also had love in mind.

The visit went badly. 'At dinner, after some shyness, we plunged into essentials and he began to delicately hint his requirements,' she recorded in her diary.

> That evening and the next morning till lunch we are on 'susceptible terms.' A dispute over state education breaks the charm. 'It is a question of authority with women; if you believe in Herbert Spencer you won't believe in me.' This opens the battle. By a silent arrangement we find ourselves in the garden. 'It pains me to hear any of my views controverted', and with this preface he begins with stern exactitude to lay down the articles of his political creed. I remain modestly silent; but noticing my silence he remarks that he requires 'intelligent sympathy' from women. 'Servility, Mr. Chamberlain,' think I, not sympathy, but intelligent servility. . . . I advanced as boldly as I dare my feeble objections to his general proposition. . . . He refutes my objections by re-asserting his convictions passionately, his expression becoming every minute more gloomy and determined. He tells me the history of his political career, how his creed grew up on a basis of experience and sympathy, how his desire to benefit 'the many' had become gradually a passion absorbing within itself his whole nature. . . . Not a suspicion of feeling did he show towards me. He was simply determined to assert his convictions. If I remained silent he watched my expression narrowly, I felt his curious scrutinizing eyes noting each movement as if he were anxious to ascertain whether I yielded to his absolute supremacy. If I objected to or ventured to qualify his theories or his statements, he smashed objection and qualification by an absolute denial, and continued his assertion. He remarked as we came in that he felt as if he had been making a speech. I felt utterly exhausted, we hardly spoke to each other the rest of the day. The next morning . . . I *think* both of us felt that all was over between us, so that we talked more *pleasantly*, but even then he insisted on bringing me back from trivialities to a discussion as to the intellectual subordination of women. 'I have only one domestic trouble: my sister and daughter are bitten with the women's rights mania. I don't allow any action on the subject.' 'You don't allow division of opinion in your household, Mr. Chamberlain?' 'I can't help people *thinking* differently from me.' 'But you don't allow the expression of the difference?' 'No.' And that little word ended our intercourse.[45]

But it did not. Before the month was out, she was in Birmingham at the invitation of Beatrice Chamberlain to hear 'the great man' address his constituents in the town hall. She identified them with herself as she again fell under his spell:

> Into the tones of his voice he threw the warmth of feeling which was lacking in his words, and every thought, every feeling, the slightest

intonation of irony and contempt was reflected on the face of the crowd. It might have been a woman listening to the words of her lover! Perfect response, unquestioning receptivity. Who *reasons* with his mistress?

Chamberlain's voice lured Beatrice Potter to submit. 'The commonplaces of love have always bored me,' she reflected in her diary.

> But Joseph Chamberlain with his gloom and seriousness, with absence of any gallantry or faculty for saying pretty nothings, the simple way in which he assumes, almost asserts, that you stand on a level far beneath him and that all that concerns you is trivial, that you yourself are without importance in the world except in so far as you might be related to him: this sort of courtship (if it is to be called courtship) fascinates, at least, my imagination.[46]

Away from him she could reassert her other self, but his prominence in public life made him impossible to overlook. Still a disciple of Herbert Spencer, she told herself that she could not marry Chamberlain because of his political creed, yet in its current Radical phase it had a good deal in common with the Fabian socialism she would eventually espouse. Her relationship with Chamberlain continued over the next two years in spasms, as she felt them, at lengthening intervals. Preoccupied by his career, Chamberlain's interest in her persisted but mildly. Beatrice Potter was drawn back to Birmingham shortly before the general election by an invitation from Chamberlain's youngest sister, and confessed the feelings she had entertained towards the great man, only to be told that he 'had never thought of me'.[47]

Her prospects, like his, took a bleak turn at the election of 1885. On the way to cast his vote, her father suffered a stroke. For some years she had served in the comparatively emancipating role of chatelaine to her widowed father. Now she had to be his nurse. She had to leave her work as a social investigator to accompany her father into the country and then to the seaside.

In Bournemouth she wrote the article on unemployment that caught Chamberlain's attention. In her article she criticized the use of public works to alleviate unemployment in London, arguing that they would attract labour from the countryside and Continental Europe and hence fail to serve their intended purpose. Chamberlain wrote to her London address, not knowing of her change of location. When his letter reached her, the sight of the great man's handwriting made her 'ominously excited'.[48] She sent him a lengthy, prickly reply, disparaging governmental action before an official inquiry could be undertaken into the amount and character of employment in each district. Chamberlain replied at even greater length, anxious to understand as well as to be understood. He explained that the Local Government Board over which he presided had 'no official cognisance of distress above the Pauper line. Yet this is surely the serious part of the problem . . . the suffering of the industrious non-pauper class is very great & is increasing.'[49] He was looking for some way to provide an income to conscientious working men thrown out of employment by the depression without encouraging dependence on the state or interfering with the normal labour market. All he could think of was spade labour on public works, though he realized that the suggestion was crude. But he did not want to wait till an extensive fact-finding inquiry could be completed, nor did he think, as Beatrice Potter seemed to suggest, that working men needed simply to be informed about the whereabouts of opportunities for employment. He observed that '[w]henever there is work wanted, the workers find it out very quickly for themselves'.

Beatrice Potter was stung by his disagreement and what she saw as the personal subtext. 'As I read your letter,' she wrote back, 'a suspicion flashed across me, that you wished for some further proof of the incapacity of a woman's intellect to deal with such large matters.'[50] She decried his public works ideas on classical economic grounds: 'if the work were sufficiently unskilled *not* to enter into competition with other employment, it *would* be degrading in its nature . . . & by the subsistence it afforded would increase a parasitic class injurious to the community. I fail to grasp the principle "Something must be done" . . . I have no proposal to make: except sternness from the state, & love & self-devotion from individuals. . . . But,' she continued, returning to the personal wound, 'is it not rather unkind of you to ask me to tell you what I think?. . . it *is* a ludicrous idea that an ordinary woman should be called upon to review the suggestion of Her Majesty's ablest minister!'

Chamberlain pulled back. 'I thought we understood each other pretty well,' he wrote; 'I fear I was mistaken.'[51] He tried to defend himself, unconvincingly on the women's issue, better on the social. He insisted that on many questions he would follow the opinion of an intelligent woman blindly. As for independence of mind, he claimed that 'the only men with whom I have cordially worked are men of striking originality of ideas'. But at a time of alienation from so many friends, he recoiled from this line of reflection. 'I hardly know why I defend myself, for it does not much matter what I think or feel on these subjects.' He turned with relief to the subject of unemployment:

> On the main question, your letter is discouraging; but I fear it is true.
>
> I shall go on, however, as if it were not true, for if we once admit the impossibility of remedying the evils of society, we shall all sink below the level of the brutes.

Beatrice Potter responded with a cry. 'Now I see I was right not to deceive you,' she wrote back. 'I could not lie to the man I loved. But why have worded it so cruelly, why give unnecessary pain? Surely we suffer sufficiently—thank God! that when our own happiness is destroyed there are others to live for. Do not think that I do not consider your decision as *final* and destroy this.'[52] He destroyed the letter as she asked, but she preserved a record of it.

Resignation

Whatever emotions the letter of Beatrice Potter roused within him were repressed by the political crisis. Gladstone had allowed three weeks to pass without pursuing his discussion of Ireland with Chamberlain. Instead Gladstone sounded out an inner circle of colleagues on the principal features of his Irish plans: first the reliable earls Granville and Spencer, then Morley as a committed Home Ruler, and finally Harcourt as the cabinet's potentially decisive swing figure. When Chamberlain, suspecting that such consultations were going on, questioned Morley, the evasiveness of Morley's reply confirmed his suspicion.

Thereupon Chamberlain decided to confront the prime minister. Chamberlain was no longer sure that the British public would reject a generous measure of Home Rule for Ireland. Nor was he certain how the National Liberal Federation would react to a division of opinion on this issue between himself and the Grand Old Man. Undeterred, however, by the precariousness of his support, Chamberlain told his brother that '[i]f Mr. G's scheme goes too far, as I expect it will, I shall leave him'.[53] He knew that this decision would isolate him from most Radicals, and he did not expect significant support from his cabinet colleagues. Yet he assumed that his disagreement with Gladstone would be honoured as a matter of conscientious conviction. He also reckoned that, however Gladstone's Irish plans worked out, eventually the way would be clear for Chamberlain to succeed the old man. 'Either Mr G will succeed and get the Irish question out of the way or he will fail. In either case he will retire from politics and I do not suppose the Liberal Party will accept . . . even John Morley as its permanent leader.'

It was only after Chamberlain took this decisive turn that he received the first direct intimation of Gladstone's Irish plans. The prime minister circulated two memoranda on Irish land to the cabinet. The contrast between what Gladstone proposed and what Chamberlain had suggested on the same subject less than a month before was heavy with implication. Chamberlain's scheme had focused on relief for small farmers and would have been administered by a central board in Ireland designed initially to handle little more than this function. The more costly land scheme of Gladstone was designed to buy out and hence ease the apprehensions of the great landowners. Everything about Gladstone's scheme implied that it was to pave the way for a generous measure of Home Rule for Ireland.

Gladstone's scheme also used up financial resources which might otherwise be available for the British domestic reforms Chamberlain favoured.

Chamberlain resolved to unmask the object behind Gladstone's Irish land proposals. The cabinet met on the Saturday after receiving Gladstone's memoranda to discuss them. Gladstone had scarcely opened the subject at the meeting when Chamberlain interrupted him. Brushing aside the land proposals, Chamberlain demanded to see the plan of Irish government that lay beneath. Gladstone protested at this disruption of the order of business and at the unfairness of a demand for his Irish government proposals which were as yet no more than sketchy. But he admitted that he could see no valid alternative to a separate Irish legislature in Dublin. Chamberlain enclosed himself for the rest of the meeting in steely silence.

His action forced the subject of Home Rule into the centre of the stage. At the same time his manner at this meeting turned the discussion into a contest between himself and Gladstone. When Spencer and Granville consulted their chief next day, the question on their minds was whether Chamberlain was open to persuasion or would use anything they might tell him as fuel for his rebellion. Chamberlain spent the day writing a letter of resignation meant for publication. It argued that Gladstone's proposals were 'tantamount to a proposal for separation' between Ireland and the rest of the United Kingdom.[54]

He was jumping the gun at some risk to himself and to Gladstone. Gladstone's proposals were still in their infancy and could be changed. The prime minister asked Chamberlain to remain in office until he (Gladstone) could fashion a plan of Irish government for presentation to the cabinet; and Chamberlain grudgingly agreed.

To salvage what he could of the lost opportunity for quick attack, Chamberlain developed his ideas on paper to guide the *Birmingham Daily Post* in its editorials. He argued that the creation of a Parliament in Dublin would jeopardize the cohesion of the United Kingdom whether or not Ireland continued to send representatives to the imperial Parliament at Westminster:

> any scheme of the kind attributed to Mr. Gladstone will lead in the long run to the absolute national independence of Ireland. . . . [Great Britain] would sink to the rank of a third rate Power, and its Foreign Policy already sufficiently embarrassing and absorbing would be complicated by perpetual references to the state of feeling in Ireland.[55]

With these words, Chamberlain struck a new chord in his political rhetoric. Hitherto he had identified himself largely with domestic issues. His proposal for a central Irish board paralleled his agenda for domestic reform in Britain. The two were literally bound together in *The Radical Programme*. But if Home Rule meant giving Ireland its own Parliament, then it became for Chamberlain a question of the integrity of the United Kingdom and hence a national and imperial more than a domestic question. He began to develop a corresponding rationale for his opposition to Home Rule. He could have emphasized the domestic reasons for his opposition to Home Rule. But they did not bulk as large as national and imperial considerations in the case which he proceeded to develop against Gladstone's Irish policy. In another way, however, Chamberlain's fight against that policy was an anomaly rather than a turning point in his political development. His opposition to Gladstone's scheme had little to do with the industrial economy of Britain. While Chamberlain objected to giving the Dublin legislature the right to place tariffs on imports from Britain, Gladstone's removal of that right did not reduce Chamberlain's objection to the basic scheme.

Whatever Gladstone's intentions may have been towards Chamberlain before the middle of March, the stiffness of Chamberlain's opposition to his Irish proposals stiffened him in turn. Gladstone had resented Chamberlain's pretensions, disliked his domestic philosophy, and treated him with condescension; yet there had been no clear sign of a wish on Gladstone's part to crush his difficult colleague. Gladstone had put up with worse for longer in his previous ministry. That memory, however, galled him; he was determined never to stomach so much again. Time too was running out for him, almost as fast as patience. Spencer wanted Gladstone to take Chamberlain into his confidence. But the old man complained that 'it is not possible to work a Cabinet on the basis of universal discussion without purpose, at any rate at seventy-seven'.[56] A few days after the cabinet meeting at which Chamberlain behaved so offensively, Gladstone decided against revealing any more of his Irish plans until he could 'find out *absolutely* Chamberlain's intentions'.[57]

Gladstone assigned Harcourt the familiar role of intermediary. But this time Harcourt did not look for peace when he interviewed Chamberlain at the prime minister's behest. Whether disillusioned by the Radical performance in the general election, let down by Chamberlain in dealings with Gladstone at the beginning of the year, or ambitious to establish himself as the old man's heir, Harcourt maximized the gulf between Gladstone's plans for Ireland and Chamberlain's response in his report back to the prime minister. Thereupon Gladstone ordered Granville, Spencer and Morley 'to hold no further communication'[58] with Chamberlain before the meeting of the cabinet at which the projected Irish government bill would be presented. Gladstone and his chosen intimates met with Harcourt to discuss filling the vacancies which the expected resignations of Chamberlain and also Sir George Trevelyan, the Secretary for Scotland, would create.

Meanwhile Chamberlain explored possibilities for realigning his parliamentary relationships. Swallowing his election-time sentiments, he turned to Hartington and the Tories. He had supported the notion of a patriotic ministry under Hartington early in 1885: and what could be more patriotic than a ministry formed to preserve the United Kingdom? Accordingly Chamberlain urged Hartington 'to undertake to form a Government in case of Mr. Gladstone's defeat or resignation'.[59]

In the afternoon the Whig leader, in the evening the Tories. Brazenly experimental, Chamberlain approached them under the gaze of Hartington's close associates, whom he deliberately shocked. R.B. Brett, Hartington's private secretary but an admirer of Chamberlain, had invited him to dinner with a pedigreed young Whig, Albert Grey, and Salisbury's nephew Arthur Balfour. Turning to Balfour, Chamberlain spoke of affinities between his brand of Radical and convinced Conservatives. Both had the courage of their convictions, more so than what Balfour described as 'those lukewarm and slippery Whigs whom it is difficult to differ from and impossible to act with'.[60] Radicals and Tories did not fear strong government as Liberals did. Chamberlain added imperial colour to his commentary: 'a democratic Government should be the strongest Government, from a military and Imperial point of view, in the world, for it has the People behind it'. Bitter at the fruit of his repeated attempts to collaborate with Parnell, Chamberlain suggested that coercion could be effective if 'carried out consistently for five years'. Yet through rhetorical audacity he preserved his freedom of manoeuvre. The alliance he suggested was not the one his fellow guests were hoping for against the Irish, but rather against the Whigs.

His bravado masked deepening insecurity. Gladstone produced his plan for the government of Ireland less than two weeks after Chamberlain demanded to see it. During that interval Chamberlain grew less defiant and wished for a plan on which the cabinet could agree. Though he kept up a stiff front to preserve his dignity and bargaining power, his desire for compromise was evident to Rosebery and even Morley when the cabinet convened to consider the prime minister's proposals. Chamberlain did not ask devastating questions. His points and suggestions[61] could have elicited a conciliatory response.

But Gladstone was cold and uncompromising. After some discussion, he pushed a note to one of his colleagues: 'There is no use in indefinitely prolonging talk.'[62] Later he reflected that with most of his colleagues it was 'safe to go to an extreme of concession. But my experience in Chamberlain's case is that such concession is treated mainly as an acknowledgement of his superior greatness and wisdom, and as a fresh point of departure accordingly.'[63] Chamberlain immediately resubmitted his resignation, and Gladstone accepted it.

Chamberlain parted company from Gladstone more impressed than ever with the old man's powers of intellect. They were, however, warped in Chamberlain's estimation by Gladstone's impatience with the conciliatory style of leadership he had displayed over the previous five years, by a renewed sense of divinely inspired mission, and by readiness to wreak havoc if his lead were not followed. Gladstone's scheme for Home Rule was similarly warped and distended. 'A much smaller scheme', Chamberlain explained, 'would have produced greater friendliness & not have endangered so much. It would have built up things by degrees instead of taking a leap in the dark. This scheme will not be carried: & it will produce infinite mischief for it will make the Irish hostile to any smaller scheme.'[64]

Tearing asunder

At the beginning of March Dilke had counselled his friend to resign, if he must, quietly. 'Go out and lie low. If honesty forces you out, well and good, but it does not force you to fight.'[65] That advice may have been in Chamberlain's mind when he referred to Gladstone's Home Rule proposals as a 'leap in the dark'. The phrase recalled Disraeli's Reform bill of 1867. It too had provoked a rebellion, by Lord Salisbury. He had confined his opposition, however, to cutting words, in the Commons at the beginning, in the press at the end. Between times, he did not attempt to organize opposition in the Commons or the country. As a result, the Conservative party had avoided a split; and eventually Salisbury succeeded Disraeli as leader of the Conservative party.

But Chamberlain could not follow Dilke's advice and Salisbury's example. Chamberlain had been driven to rebel more by Gladstone's treatment of him than by the proposals for Home Rule; and Gladstone's handling of the rebel confirmed the rebellion. Far more than the rebel, the old captain proceeded to treat the debate over Home Rule as a personal contest. It would still have been wiser of Chamberlain to bide his time, waiting (as he had suggested to his brother) for Gladstone either to get the Irish question out of the way or to fail and, one way or other, to retire. But Chamberlain could not possess his soul in peace. He was too angry and too ardent to wait.

Attacked by Gladstone with zeal, jealousy and skill, Chamberlain fought back. Initially desperate, he fought to survive, to secure respect, to frustrate his enemies, and to keep Britain from what he was increasingly convinced would be a disastrous course of action. Bereft of familiar friends outside Birmingham, seriously threatened even there, he learned to match the skill of his former chief in political warfare. He fought with deadly success. But in the process, much of the best within him, in character and in vision, was hardened, twisted or killed.

Chamberlain's departure from the cabinet had a disconcerting reception. For all public purposes he was silenced for two weeks, prohibited by parliamentary convention from explaining himself until the government introduced the legislation that had induced him to resign. He could express himself more freely in private among the members of the parliamentary elite who were out of office. But there he met with a cool response from likely allies and a warm response from erstwhile enemies whose embrace made him nervous.

Far from welcoming Chamberlain as a fellow defector from Gladstone's thrall, Lord Hartington greeted him with suspicion bordering on hostility. The argument they conducted through the election campaign did not fully account for Hartington's behaviour. By political predilection and ambition, the two men were natural rivals rather than allies. Hartington recognized Chamberlain as a competitor for the leadership of the 'body of bewildered and unhappy opinion, of all political shades, which Gladstone's Irish proposals had created within the Liberal party'.[66] Accordingly, while Gladstone was putting the final touches on his Government of Ireland bill, his former lieutenants jockeyed for the position of advantage in opposing it. The tension between Chamberlain and Hartington grew critical as the day for the presentation of the Home Rule bill to the House of Commons drew near. Who had the right to follow the prime minister in debate? Hartington claimed precedence as the senior in terms of service to the country and the Liberal party. Chamberlain claimed the privilege as the person who had just resigned from the cabinet and was entitled to the first opportunity to explain his action to Parliament. Aggravated by Hartington's high-handed yet irresolute conduct, the quarrel continued till the eve of the great debate, when it was resolved to Chamberlain's satisfaction through the mediation of Dilke and Churchill.

In contrast to Hartington, Churchill embraced Chamberlain with open arms when he left the cabinet. The Tory and the Radical dined together the night the press carried news of the resignation. Chamberlain was gratified by this close consultation. But he did not want to turn consultation into full cooperation. He was happy to dine with Tories but refused to share a public platform with them or curb his remarks to avoid hurting their feelings. Whether inside or outside the House of Commons, the audience to which he directed his attention was Liberal, indeed Radical. To express himself in any other fashion would be to discredit himself.

What galled him most during his fortnight of enforced silence after resignation was the misrepresentation of his motives by fellow Liberals. The surge of Liberal support for Gladstone underscored the danger that Chamberlain ran in opposing him. Yet Liberals accused Chamberlain of being motivated to oppose Gladstone's proposals for Home Rule by unprincipled ambition. The most damning form this accusation took was that Chamberlain was acting in collusion with the Tories. He therefore sent a passionate though exaggerated denial of this charge to the editor of the *Birmingham Daily Post*, where it was published almost verbatim.

Things were not going well even in Birmingham. Chamberlain had not kept in close touch with his usual supporters there in reaching his decision to oppose Gladstone's Irish legislation. Like Liberals elsewhere, they were confused by the general situation and hence wanted to follow the leader. But the Liberals of Birmingham had two leaders, Chamberlain as well as Gladstone, and were unhappy to discover that the two pointed in opposite directions. The organizing secretary of the Birmingham Liberal Association, Francis Schnadhorst, warned Chamberlain that on the subject of Ireland Birmingham's Liberals seemed more inclined to follow Gladstone's lead than Chamberlain's. Both the message and the messenger worried Chamberlain. While he sensed that it was too soon to say which way Liberal opinion in the town was moving, he knew that it was unsettled. The uncertainty of the town was reflected in the emptiness of his mail bag. At the turn of the year, based on his reading of opinion in Birmingham, he had been confident that Gladstone could not persuade the party, the Commons and the country to give Ireland its own Parliament. In the dark days that followed his resignation, that confidence was shaken.

Doubts about Schnadhorst's loyalty deepened Chamberlain's anxiety. He had forewarned Schnadhorst in the early days of the current government that he and the prime minister might part company. Instead of emphasizing the Irish question in speaking to Schnadhorst, Chamberlain had dwelt on Gladstone's insulting treatment of himself and Jesse Collings[67] and hence of Birmingham's brand of Radicalism. Schnadhorst felt the affront. But he had too much first-hand experience of Chamberlain's domineering ways to be astonished at the prime minister's reaction. In dealing with Schnadhorst, Chamberlain had 'used the simple power of "You shall" and "You'll go to the devil if you don't"'.[68] Schnadhorst felt inadequately appreciated and wanted to demonstrate that he had opinions of his own. Adopting a position disconcertingly close to Gladstone's, he wrote to Chamberlain questioning the electoral appeal of 'three acres and a cow' and declared that on Ireland 'a bold & thorough policy is the wisest & from every point of view the safest'.[69]

Preoccupied with affairs in Westminster when this letter arrived, Chamberlain did not give much more thought to the state of affairs in Birmingham until he resigned. Then he sensed that Schnadhorst was working against him. But though ready to take Gladstone's side, Schnadhorst appreciated Chamberlain's power too much to welcome a rupture between the young chief and the old. In response to inquiries from ministerial supporters in London about the prospect as he saw it, Schnadhorst expressed his doubt that 'even if Mr. G secures a majority on the Second Reading for Home Rule the Bill can get thro' the Commons or secure a majority in the country if C[hamberlain] is actively hostile'. Schnadhorst further advised that 'if [the Irishmen] have any sense they will be willing to accept something less than Mr. G wd. give them, if by doing so Chamberlain & Bright could be secured'.[70]

There was still a chance that, dismayed by the movement of Liberal opinion towards the prime minister, Chamberlain would reduce his opposition to the government's Irish legislation to modest proportions. He could perhaps take credit for whatever improvements from his point of view were made in the proposals after he resigned from the cabinet, and otherwise lie low, leaving the government to sink or swim with its legislative burden. But that possibility, for which Schnadhorst hoped, was eliminated by the unremitting hostility with which Gladstone treated his former colleague.

The fight between the two men began quietly as soon as Chamberlain resigned. In order to explain his conduct to the House of Commons, he needed permission from the Queen to refer to the pertinent transactions within the ministry and cabinet. By custom that permission had to be sought through the prime minister. Gladstone used this power to curb the freedom of explanation that the Queen was willing to give Chamberlain. The point in question was Gladstone's Irish Land bill which he wished to hold back until he had secured a good hearing for his bill to reconstitute the government of Ireland. Chamberlain wished to draw attention to the Land bill because its generous provision for the landlords would disconcert progressive Liberals. Recognizing his vulnerability on this score, Gladstone strove to confine Chamberlain's initial public explanation of his resignation to the Government of Ireland bill.

Though he saw the muzzle that Gladstone sought to place on him, Chamberlain could not devote all of his attention to this threat. He was also concerned with the possibility of compromise. As the day for Gladstone's presentation of his Government of Ireland bill to the Commons approached, the newspapers were full of reports that great changes had been made in the bill since Chamberlain resigned. Swallowing hard, he approached Morley for confirmation or denial of these reports. The reply that Morley brought from Gladstone brimmed with antagonism from the old master and his new messenger:

> Mr. Gladstone . . . allows me to say this much, that of the four points or propositions on which you parted company from us, there is *one* on which we have been able to move in your direction, and no more than one. Practically and substantially, therefore, the main objections which you took, are still good against our scheme—as good now as they were then.[71]

Steeled but also preoccupied with this exchange, Chamberlain did not pay sufficient heed to word from Lord Salisbury that Chamberlain could ask the Queen directly for permission to make a full explanation of his reasons for resigning.

There was an omen in the House of Commons of particular significance for Birmingham when Gladstone at last presented his epoch-making proposals for the government of Ireland. So many men of note wished to hear him that places for visitors were at a premium. Chamberlain could not secure a place for the man whose support he was most anxious to secure, Dr Dale, the Birmingham Congregationalist. But near the Speaker's chair, together with Cardinal Manning and the editor of *The Times*, was Schnadhorst, obviously by desire of the prime minister.

The essence of Gladstone's plan was to place Ireland's domestic affairs in the hands of a statutory parliament, that is to say a legislature created by and hence ultimately dependent upon an Act of the imperial parliament at Westminster. Subject to this constitutional limitation, the proposed Irish parliament was to be endowed with wide powers, wide enough for Parnell to accept the scheme as a potentially permanent solution to the age-old constitutional problem of Anglo-Irish relations. But the scheme possessed features that left even well-disposed Englishmen uneasy. Instead of specifying the responsibilities of the Irish legislature in Dublin, leaving all others to the imperial government at Westminster, Gladstone's bill identified the subjects that were to be reserved exclusively for Westminster—the crown, defence, foreign and colonial policy, international trade—and assigned everything else to Dublin. There was a real risk that preponderant power would pass to the possessor of the residual subjects of responsibility, in other words to the Dublin parliament, and hence undermine its constitutional subordination to the imperial parliament at Westminster. That risk was deepened by the bill's proposed removal of the elected representatives of Ireland from the imperial parliament. The prospect of getting rid of Irish MPs at Westminster was welcome in view of their infuriating obstruction of parliamentary business in recent years. But the absence of elected representation of Ireland at Westminster would implicitly derogate from the prerogatives of the imperial parliament with regard to Ireland.

There was another widely felt but quite different source of uneasiness with the bill. While it prohibited religious discrimination, it made no special provision for the distinctive concerns of the one Irish province to which the English and the Scots felt akin: industrial, Protestant, loyalist Ulster. Gladstone had altered his original scheme in one regard to conciliate the British economic interests which Chamberlain stood ready to champion: the bill denied the Irish legislature the power to raise protective tariffs against the rest of the United Kingdom. Otherwise the bill stood essentially as outlined to the cabinet when Chamberlain resigned, a bold proposal which was acceptable to the Irish Nationalists but put the cohesion of the United Kingdom in question.

The House of Commons gave Gladstone its rapt attention when he introduced his bill. The proceedings next day opened with Chamberlain's speech to explain his resignation. Though unsurpassed as a platform speaker, he was not yet in the first rank of parliamentary debaters. But what started out as an able explanatory statement was transformed into something more significant by Gladstone's intervention. The moment Chamberlain mentioned the Land bill, 'the old lion' leapt up.[72] He insisted that the permission from the Queen for Chamberlain to speak of cabinet and ministerial business did not extend to 'a subject on which a final decision of the Cabinet had not been taken, and which had not been publicly explained to Parliament'.[73] The blow stunned Chamberlain. In a verbal duel the old man kept cutting off the line of argument Chamberlain wanted to pursue. Gladstone denied him permission even to read from his own letters to the prime minister.

But Gladstone's cleverness backfired. This was clearly not a fight between a vainglorious aggressor and a visionary saint. The malice of the old man was too evident: 'quivering with angry excitement' once he had made his point, he 'sat down pale with ill-concealed passion'.[74] As Chamberlain struggled on his feet to decide how or indeed whether to proceed, it was hard to doubt that he had been misled. What he lost in steadiness of argument he won in sympathy—except from the Irish Nationalists, whose continuing interruptions backfired as Gladstone's had. He found his way at last by dealing with the Land bill hypothetically: he would oppose any scheme framed to compensate the landlords for their loss of political power rather than to benefit needy tenants.

Anxious to suggest an alternative to Gladstone's constitutional proposals, Chamberlain raised the possibility of federation, an idea of increasing interest to Englishmen concerned about the empire, a concept Canada had used to bring its diverse provinces under effective central government. Gladstone had appealed to foreign precedents to justify his scheme. Chamberlain turned the appeal around. He referred to the unifications of Italy and Germany and finally, with great effect, to the United States: 'there you have the greatest Democracy the world has ever seen, and a Democracy which has known how to fight in order to maintain its union'.[75]

Though exultant at his escape from the trap that Gladstone had laid for him, Chamberlain emerged from the ordeal with deepened respect for his redoubtable foe. Who else could win wide support among Liberals for a policy which a few months ago most of them would have dismissed as repugnant? Chamberlain did not find much comfort from the old enemies who were now his allies. The Queen let him know that she had not intended to fetter his freedom of explanation in any way; but this word could not be made public. Among the elite who were in touch with the court, Gladstone's perversion of the Queen's intentions brought discredit upon himself and raised Chamberlain in esteem. But that was of limited value to a man who cared far more about public reaction.

Once the initial duel in the Commons with Gladstone was over, Chamberlain focused his attention on Birmingham. Constituency associations of Liberals around the country were meeting to voice their response to Gladstone's Irish proposals. But so far there had been no word from the usually outspoken Liberals of Birmingham. Schnadhorst held them back, fearful that Chamberlain would resolve the unsettlement in his favour. Nothing could stop Chamberlain from convening a meeting of the Liberal association of his own constituency of Birmingham West. But Chamberlain wanted more. He wanted Liberal Birmingham as a whole to speak with one voice, as no other great town had done. It was for just such a reason that he had preserved a Liberal association for the town when the 1885 Redistribution Act divided it into seven constituencies. Using Bunce of the *Birmingham Daily Post* as his agent, he secured an invitation from this town-wide association to address it on the national controversy. The town hall was reserved for 21 April, at the beginning of Parliament's Easter recess.

During the week before the recess, Gladstone and his lieutenants, particularly Morley and Harcourt, manoeuvred vis-à-vis Chamberlain on the issue of Irish representation at Westminster. Gladstone tried to treat it as a secondary problem to which he would accept any solution on which his cabinet colleagues past and present could agree. Morley and Harcourt, however, sharpened their rivalry with Chamberlain by threatening to resign if the government's scheme were amended to include the Irish at Westminster; and Gladstone did not attempt to test their resolution. For he recognized that Chamberlain would not be satisfied by a clause retaining the Irish in the imperial parliament. That change would lead, if Chamberlain had his way, to a transformation of the bill into something quite different from what Gladstone envisaged.

The question of Irish representation at Westminster acquired crucial significance, both tactical and substantial, for Chamberlain. By focusing his attention on this point he could present himself to waverers as reasonable in his demands. Echoing the prerevolutionary American cry of 'no taxation without representation', he struck a chord to which every Liberal was responsive. It reinforced another of his major themes: that Gladstone's proposals would not settle the strife between England and Ireland because the Irish would not put up for long with an arrangement that left powers of taxation, in particular customs and excise, to the imperial parliament in which they were not represented. Insistence that power and representation went hand in hand stood at the core of Chamberlain's message. Without representation from Ireland, the imperial parliament would lack the title to govern Ireland. Whether as political reformer or party organizer, he had always appreciated the inseparability of power and representation. That principle had helped to make him a Liberal. Now it made him a Radical Unionist.

When he met the massed ranks of the Birmingham Liberal Association in the town hall, his sense of urgency was undisguised. Scorning pleasantries, he plunged immediately into the subject at hand. He drew attention to the broad concerns that Gladstone's proposals slighted: the imperial and the social. The proposal to give Ireland its own parliament not only threatened the cohesion of the kingdom and empire but also deferred consideration of 'those great social problems which had excited our interest and our sympathy'[76] during the recent election. This preface allowed Chamberlain to introduce Gladstone with a combination of admiration and regret as 'the one great, illustrious man' who was responsible for the unfortunate change in the national agenda since the general election.

He proceeded to criticize the prime minister's Irish proposals in detail. He did so more vigorously than he had dared in the House of Commons. He could not hope for overwhelming agreement in the Commons. But that was precisely what he needed from his home base. He therefore pulverized the local opposition with comprehensive, tough, at times contemptuous argument. To drive home his point that the Irish would not remain satisfied with the Dublin parliament which Gladstone offered them, Chamberlain described the fetters and aristocratic privileges with which Gladstone encumbered it. Appealing to Birmingham's experience of civic democracy, he asked his audience how they would react to a similar scheme if applied to their town: 'You would not pick it from the gutter.' Despite the trenchancy of his criticisms, he took up a position of only conditional opposition to the Home Rule bill. But the importance which he placed on his conditions left little doubt of their explosive implications for the bill. He ended with a plea for the same kind of sympathetic understanding that Gladstone had received on former occasions when he too had separated himself from governments on grounds of conscience. With only two votes to the contrary, the meeting passed a motion of unabated confidence in Chamberlain.

But the meeting was not over. The Gladstonians led by Schnadhorst tried to postpone until a later date a vote on the next motion, which was to support the position Chamberlain had adopted on Gladstone's proposals. No sooner was the motion for delay made than Chamberlain intervened to crush it. He did so with rough vehemence, for he needed Birmingham's unhesitating support. He had his way. Birmingham gave him more than support. It gave him its trust. Birmingham was ready to think of Chamberlain as he wished to think of himself. The Unitarian minister, Henry Crosskey, wrote to him next day: 'Permit me to add my warm appreciation—& more than appreciation—of your sacrifice of such splendid opportunities of carrying out long cherished purposes as the Cabinet gave, to conscientious convictions. If all statesmen wd. subordinate the love of power to faithfulness to principle, it wd. be a happier day for our country.'[77]

Still, Chamberlain had had to fight hard for his triumph. The people of Birmingham were of two minds on Gladstone's proposals. Few were as favourable to them as was Schnadhorst; and even he pressed his ministerial friends to retain Irish representation at Westminster in order to conciliate Chamberlain. Few were as hostile as Chamberlain. And though he was delighted at the sound that went out from the town hall, he knew that it was unlikely to be echoed in the rest of the country. Birmingham's Liberals yearned for peace in the party. In the rest of the country that desire turned into anger at any who threatened the peace, preeminently Chamberlain. Other men like Lord Hartington might offer a more uncompromising opposition to Home Rule. But because Chamberlain's disagreement with the Grand Old Man was narrower, and also because of the younger man's obvious instinct for aggression, outside Birmingham it was he who attracted the lightning of Liberal anger. Wisely, after speaking his mind at Birmingham, he adopted a lower profile. Rather than mount a campaign in the country, he mobilized his forces behind the scenes at Westminster.

Before these efforts could prove their worth, he was forced to eat the bitter fruits of apostasy. Delegates from the member associations of the National Liberal Federation met in London on 5 May to define the Federation's response to the Irish proposals of the government. The planning of the agenda rested with associates of Chamberlain from Birmingham. They set down a resolution welcoming the principle of Home Rule but calling for Irish representation at Westminster. The president of the Federation for the year, however, James Kitson from Leeds, represented provincial rivals of Birmingham who supported Gladstone. Supported by Schnadhorst, he put forward an alternative resolution giving the government's proposals wholehearted support. Chamberlain, who did not attend the meeting, braced himself for defeat. It was not so much his defeat as the venom with which the majority of delegates turned on him that burned him to the quick. When Alfred Illingworth called Chamberlain a 'traitor', the audience cheered long and loud. The resignation of six officers of the Federation from Birmingham, an action that Chamberlain angrily encouraged, gave him meagre compensation. He could not understand how he produced such a bitter reaction from men like Illingworth of Bradford and H.J. Wilson of Sheffield who had followed him for more than a decade. He could not understand why it was that he provoked anger while Gladstone inspired veneration.

Morley and Chamberlain lunged ever harder at each other. Chamberlain gave Churchill extracts from Morley's past speeches and writing to use against him in debate. Morley led the opposition in cabinet to retention of the Irish at Westminster. He said that 'Chamberlain wants us to go down on our knees'.[78] By way of reply, Chamberlain revealed Morley's private comment that he did not wish to be 'admiral of the fleet' but would not be a 'powder monkey'. Turning the point round with bitter truth, Chamberlain observed that Morley had 'changed his ship and his captain, but he has to recognise that his position in the service is much the same as before'.[79] With equal truth Morley responded, 'J.C. must be taught that a leader is one thing, and a tyrant another'.[80]

The split between Morley and Chamberlain was the bitterest. But the separation that opened up between Chamberlain and Dilke produced the deepest personal distress. The bond between these two had so intensified during the past year that Chamberlain took for granted that they were in essential agreement on Gladstone's proposals. As Dilke's hopes for eminence in public life crumbled, he identified himself more than ever with the prospects for Chamberlain. Though on the issue of the Irish at Westminster Dilke favoured exclusion, he was ready to keep silent and vote with his friend. But Dilke could not sustain his hopes for Chamberlain without affiliation to the Liberal party. Dilke therefore insisted on the need to support the principle of the Home Rule bill by voting for its second reading. After all, both men accepted the necessity of a substantial measure of self-government for Ireland. Dilke foresaw what would happen if Chamberlain succeeded in defeating the bill and Gladstone called a general election:

> the dissolution will wreck the party, but yet leave *a* party,—democratic, because all the moderates will go over to the Tories,—poor, because all the subscribers will go over to the Tories,—more Radical than the party has ever been,—& yet—as things now stand, with you outside of it.[81]

It was not till the beginning of May when Chamberlain received these words that he sensed where Dilke was heading. Stunned, Chamberlain refrained from writing back till late on 3 May, after Dilke would have announced his decision to his constituents but before the morning newspapers could bring Chamberlain word of what Dilke had said. 'My pleasure in politics is gone,' Chamberlain wrote at midnight. 'The friends with whom I have worked so long are many of them separated from me. . . . You must do what your conscience tells you to be right. . . . But. . . . The present crisis is of course life and death to me.'[82] Next morning, after reading the papers, Chamberlain sent Dilke a short note that ended not with his usual 'Yours ever' but with the formality of 'Yours sincerely'.

Unable to bear the pain he had given his friend, Dilke broke through the reserve he normally maintained on paper. The ardour of his friendship managed as nothing else could do to ease the anguish of Chamberlain, who replied with an outpouring of his own. 'I feel bitterly the action of some of these men, like Morley, Illingworth, & many others, who have left my side at this time although many of them owe much to me,' Chamberlain wrote Dilke, but '[w]ith you it is different. We have been so closely connected that I cannot contemplate any severance . . . as between us two, let nothing come.'[83] 'Nothing', Dilke responded, 'could ever come really between us, because it takes two to make a fight, & even if your mind were turned against me it would come back to me when you found as you would find that nothing could ever turn my mind against you.'[84] 'Let us', Chamberlain concluded, 'agree to consider everything which is said or done for the next few weeks as a dream.'[85]

The magnitude and mood of the pro-government majority among the federated Liberal associations at the beginning of May hardened the rift between Chamberlain and Gladstone. The support of the Federation stiffened Gladstone's resistance to concession. The vituperative reaction among erstwhile supporters of Chamberlain to his 'treachery' intensified his rebellion. Until news of the applause which greeted Illingworth's cruel words reached him, Chamberlain had hoped that his rebellion would involve no more than 'temporary unpopularity with the Radical party'.[86] Afterwards he turned on these former supporters with contempt. Why should he make concessions to preserve the unity of a party whose members abused him while they trooped off like the children of Hamelin to follow the foolish piping of an old man? More familiar than the prime minister with what the Liberal associations could actually deliver, Chamberlain discounted the electoral implications of his defeat within the National Liberal Federation. The tide among active constituency workers outside Birmingham was against him; but he sensed, acutely as it turned out, that opinion among the rank and file was more evenly divided. Come election day, many would demonstrate their uneasiness by staying home—'and it is the men who stay away who turn elections'.[87]

The rift over Home Rule had ever-widening repercussions. It led Chamberlain and Gladstone to reverse the inclination of their social politics. Hitherto the one was notorious for holding property up to 'ransom' while the other was known for his determination to keep down governmental expenditure. Now, on May Day, Gladstone appealed for public support by describing the debate over Home Rule as a battle between those who embodied 'the spirit and power of class' and the popular masses marshalled 'by the upright sense of the nation'.[88] Chamberlain on the other hand, remembering the disappointing response to his Radical Programme, disparaged the masses as ' "kittle cattle" to drive'.[89]

The climactic battle in the fight over Home Rule would be fought in the House of Commons. The action of the National Liberal Federation encouraged Gladstone to believe that, if he held off a vote in the Commons on the second reading of his Home Rule bill for at least another month, pressure from constituency associations would push the Liberal half of the House of Commons, aside from Lord Hartington's Whigs and a scattering of maverick Radicals, into line. Together with the eighty-six Irish Nationalist MPs, that would be enough to carry the bill. But Chamberlain was equally convinced that the minority who followed his guidance had 'the issue in its own hands'.[90] By the beginning of May he was able to alarm the government with his tally of Liberal MPs who could be expected to vote against the second reading of the Home Rule bill as things stood. More than half of the defectors were Whigs or moderate Liberals following the leadership of Hartington. But a good third, by no means all radicals, followed Chamberlain's lead, not so much from personal admiration as from conviction that his analysis of the issue was sound. It was this third that held the balance in the Commons. If they abstained or voted for the second reading of the bill, it would pass. If they voted no, it would fail.

The debate in the Commons on the second reading, scheduled to begin on 10 May, was preceded by a weekend of intense negotiations through Labouchere between Gladstone and Chamberlain, twisted on both sides. The subject of negotiations had narrowed since the introduction of the Home Rule bill from the continuance to the amount and frequency of Irish representation at Westminster. Gladstone was willing to allow the Irish back episodically, while Chamberlain wanted sufficient Irish representation to ensure the effective supremacy of the imperial parliament. Though beneath this narrowed difference there was still an important principle at stake, the contest became a matter of negotiating power. Each protagonist sought to heighten what he demanded of the other while displaying himself as the more reasonable or potentially more successful of the two.

Chamberlain opened the weekend with, by his own admission, a 'devilish ugly letter'[91] in *The Times*. It not only spelled out his demands but censured the entire bill as 'a fulcrum for further agitation' that 'brought us within measurable distance of civil war in Ireland'.[92] Gladstone resorted to vague formulas of concession designed to corner rather than conciliate Chamberlain. Informed of the concessions and apprehensive that they might succeed, Chamberlain trumpeted them as a victory. He was saved by the prime minister's ruffled pride and overconfidence. Opening the debate in the Commons on Monday, Gladstone threw his concessions 'into three sentences, short and ungracious'[93] which served rather to illustrate his inflexibility.

Beneath the old man's dexterity of manoeuvre lay an inflexibility of purpose harder than Chamberlain's. Responding to a Liberal peacemaking mission in mid-May, Gladstone gave the impression that he might be thinking of withdrawing his bill and proceeding instead with a parliamentary resolution. Chamberlain was momentarily softened by the prospect of reunion among the great majority of Liberals willing to give Ireland a substantial measure of self-government. He was disheartened by Hartington who refused to endorse the alternative plans for internal self-government that Chamberlain suggested, and by Lord Salisbury who called repellently for twenty years of resolute government. If Gladstone 'would only postpone the measure', Chamberlain mused to his brother, 'and give us time for consultation we might come together again'.[94] But the wistful moment was brief. Gladstone soon indicated that his accept-ance of the peacemakers' procedure depended on Hartington's approval, which was obviously unattainable.

Gladstone mishandled his ambivalent party. Underestimating its desire for internal peace and its aversion to explicit conflict among its leaders, he allowed his inflexibility and feeling about Chamberlain to show at critical moments; and so in the end he maximized the Unionist defection. Gladstone's final display of conciliatory intent, at a meeting in the Foreign Office for all but diehard anti-Home Rule Liberals, came close to achiev-ing its object of depriving Chamberlain of support. The prime minister offered to withdraw the Home Rule bill after it received approval in principle at the second reading, and to resubmit it later in revised form with particular regard to Irish representation at Westminster. The offer forced Chamberlain to think of walking out with his men at the close of debate on the second reading, thus allowing the Home Rule bill to pass. He was rescued by the skill of the Conservatives in exposing Gladstone's determination to have his own way. Taunted by Conservatives about his willingness to submit the Home Rule bill to genuine reconstruction, Gladstone shot back, 'Never, never, never'—and thus dashed the hopes that his overture at the Foreign Office had raised.

At that point the power of decision passed from Gladstone to Chamber-lain. Those who would follow Chamberlain's lead numbered probably no more than three dozen; they formed the smallest of the voting blocks into which the Commons had divided; but they were crucial. As the debate on the second reading of the Home Rule bill drew to a close, attention focused on the committee room where those who responded to a sum-mons from Chamberlain met to decide how to vote. The skills he had refined over the past two months showed, or rather were disguised, to perfection. While he used the language of judicious moderation, the out-come was stiff determination. A dozen of Hartington's men turned up, enough to tilt the balance firmly against the government's bill. Chamber-lain presented the case for voting against the bill and for abstention with careful impartiality, confining himself to an expression of faint preference for abstention. But he read out a letter from John Bright, the old lion of English Radicalism, who indicated that he would vote with the opposition against the bill. Finally, to reassure Liberal opponents of the bill who were nervous about the individual consequences of their action, the meeting received a commitment that, if Parliament were dissolved after the bill's defeat, they would not be opposed for reelection by Conservatives. Thus braced, the meeting decided its course of action: 3 voted to support the bill, 4 to abstain, and 46 to oppose.

This outcome made the bill's defeat probable. At last sure of himself, Chamberlain broke the silence he had maintained for some time in the House of Commons. His speech was remarkable for the respect he paid Gladstone and his plea for a little of the same respect for himself. He alluded to the argument which friends like Dilke made to him that if only he could bring himself to vote for the bill, the leadership of the Liberal party would devolve upon him:

> not a day passes in which I do not receive dozens or scores of letters urging and beseeching me for my own sake to vote for the Bill and to 'dish the Whigs.' . . . the temptation is no doubt a great one; but, after all, I am not base enough to serve my personal ambition by betraying my country; and I am convinced that when the heat of this discussion is passed and over, Liberals will not judge harshly those who have pursued what they honestly believed to be the path of duty, even although it may lead to the disruption of Party ties, and to the loss of influence and power which it is the legitimate ambition of every man to seek among his political friends and associates.[95]

He continued to receive the trust he desired from Birmingham. Some of the finest men there responded to the mud that was being cast at him with the same uncomprehending dismay that he felt himself. 'How is it', asked Dale, 'that Mr. Chamberlain is the object of so much bitterness? Lord Hartington and Mr. Bright are just as responsible as he is for throwing out the Bill. . . . He is loyally carrying out the principles on this question which he advocated [during the general election] last year. . . . He may be mistaken . . . but he stands by the faith which he professed, and has made the heaviest personal sacrifices in doing so.'[96] Powell Williams, one of Chamberlain's fellow MPs for Birmingham, gave him still sweeter support. Unhappy about the disagreement among Liberals in Birmingham as elsewhere, Powell Williams disliked Chamberlain's decision to vote against the second reading of the Home Rule bill. Yet Powell Williams resolved to follow him, '[p]artly because I value your friendship in a very special degree: and partly because, having supported you in the manly course you have taken, I will not be guilty, whatever may be my own opinion upon the particular point at issue, of the meanness of standing aloof from you in the critical moment'.[97] Henry Broadhurst, the trades unionist who sat for another of the Birmingham constituencies, was still a minor member and supporter of the government; but he parted from Chamberlain regretfully, suspecting that the treatment of Chamberlain by the grandees of the party was actuated by class antagonism.

Gladstone's treatment of Chamberlain as the debate on the second reading reached its close stood in marked contrast to Chamberlain's treatment of Gladstone. The night before the Commons was to vote, Gladstone said that he thought 'with great comfort of the fact that in all human probability all connection between Chamberlain and myself is over for ever'.[98] Gladstone devoted part of his address next evening at the end of the debate to an indictment of his former colleague for lack of principle: 'He has trimmed his vessel and he has touched his rudder in such a masterly way that in whichever direction the winds of Heaven may blow they must fill his sails.'[99] Though otherwise a fine speech, by all accounts it did not sway a single waverer. The Home Rule bill was rejected by a margin of thirty votes, greater than expected. Still, there were stabs of pain for Chamberlain to the end. When the MPs trooped back into the House of Commons after casting their votes, the file of Gladstone's supporters was led by Dilke. When the defeat of the bill was announced, the Irish contingent in the Commons cheered Gladstone and turned on Chamberlain with growls of 'Traitor! Judas!' In doing so they marked him out as the man who killed Home Rule.

Driving in the wedge

He had done so in the immediate parliamentary sense. But Chamberlain was not responsible for the decision that deepened the division of the Liberal party beyond reasonable hope of healing. As soon as the defeat of the Home Rule bill in the Commons appeared likely, Gladstone ordered preparation of the writs for a general election so that he could appeal immediately to the country—as he proceeded to do. The dissolution of Parliament cut off time for tempers to cool and for negotiations to see whether an Irish settlement tolerable to Chamberlain and then Parnell could be worked out. Gladstone forced Liberal MPs to fight for their political lives on the basis of the issue that divided them from each other. Chamberlain regretted the further embitterment of the conflict and was not confident of what the electoral outcome would be. Even so, he met the challenge with determination.

On the eve of the MPs' departure for their home constituencies, the conflict between former friends touched new depths of bitterness. In an address attacking the Radicals who had voted against Home Rule, Morley applied Mark Antony's lines on the assassination of Julius Caesar to Gladstone's defeat:

> Look! In this place ran Cassius' dagger through;
> See what a rent the envious Casca made;
> Through this the well-beloved Brutus stabbed.

The phrase 'envious Casca' immediately stuck to Chamberlain. Morley could just as well have identified himself with the 'well-beloved Brutus' as he stabbed his erstwhile Caesar.

In Birmingham, the first move among Liberals to organize themselves for internecine electoral strife came from opponents of Chamberlain. They called a private meeting almost a week before the rejection of the Home Rule bill. Preoccupied with the contest in the Commons, Chamberlain could not immediately turn his attention to his home base. Still, he appreciated its instincts better than his opponents on the spot. By and large the Liberals of Birmingham felt more strongly about the unity of the party than about the Irish question. Persuaded by the analogy Chamberlain drew between their own experience of local government and the needs of Ireland, they were inclined to agree with him on Irish representation; but they recoiled at the thought of Liberal voting against Liberal, whether in the Commons or closer to home. They hoped to avoid this prospect by returning all seven of the incumbent MPs including the two—Henry Broadhurst and W.T. Cook—who had voted for the Home Rule bill, as well as the five—George Dixon, John Bright, William Kenrick, Powell Williams, and Chamberlain—who had voted against. Pained at the division of the party and perplexed by the issue, men such as Dale, Bunce of the *Daily Post* and Harris the veteran organizer favoured anything that would reduce the electoral dimensions of the conflict.

The Gladstonians of Birmingham prepared to put up candidates against all the incumbents who had voted against the government bill except for the revered Bright. Chamberlain, with more subtlety, refused to challenge the two Home Rule incumbents directly. He paid respect to Liberal sensibilities also by forswearing any wish for Conservative support. He left the hatchet work of the internal contest to his brother Arthur. Quietly, however, he encouraged the Conservatives to put someone up against Cook; and when, to Chamberlain's relief, Broadhurst left the Bordesley Division of Birmingham for a less troubled constituency elsewhere, Chamberlain made sure that his loyal henchman Jesse Collings won the Liberal nomination for the vacancy.

All the same, the official Liberal organization for Birmingham rested in hands that were either neutral or hostile towards Chamberlain. Appreciating better than anyone else the value of an organization, he set about creating one for his Radical Unionists. It was depressing to have to tackle this work all over again. Chamberlain had to rely on members of his family to fill offices in his new organization and carry out its day-to-day assignments. So few others were wiling to lend their names to the enterprise that he decided not to publish a list. The inaugural meeting of the National Radical Union was convened in the Midland Institute's small lecture theatre which was only partially filled.[100] The proceedings were punctuated by the echo of cheers from a meeting of Gladstonian Liberals who filled the town hall across the square.

Preoccupied with Birmingham in the early weeks of the general elec-

tion, Chamberlain paid only passing attention to his national associates
except insofar as they could affect his home base. He raised the possibility of a joint address by Hartington, Bright and himself as the three most
prominent Liberal Unionists; but he was not disturbed when they decided
to speak for themselves. He deleted from his own manifesto a reference to
Canada with which Bright disagreed.

Bright's opponent in the last election, Lord Randolph Churchill, had
been returned to Parliament for a London constituency but remained the
leader whom Birmingham's Conservatives most respected. It was in that
capacity that Chamberlain dealt with him in the middle weeks of June. At
critical junctures in the parliamentary battle against the Home Rule bill
Churchill had provided tactical support for Chamberlain. Both at Westminster and in Birmingham Chamberlain denied that he had any wish to
curry Conservative support, and he pursued a strategy distinctly his own.
Even so, in both places, tacit coordination of effort was indispensable if
Gladstone was to be defeated.

Part of Churchill's function was to stiffen Chamberlain's resolve and
raise his spirits. After Gladstone's persuasive address to the parliamentary Liberal party at the Foreign Office, Churchill had counselled Chamberlain against absenting himself from the vote on the Home Rule bill.
Now in Birmingham Chamberlain was taken aback by the influence of the
Grand Old Man. 'The Gladstone fever is hot upon all the people,' he
observed in dismay, '& no Pasteur has yet discovered the remedy for this
form of rabies.'[101] When the behaviour of the Conservatives in Birmingham threatened to aggravate that fever, Chamberlain wrote frantically to
Churchill, 'I fear the G.O.M. is going to win.'[102] Churchill had already
removed the threat of Conservative opposition to William Kenrick in
Birmingham North. Chamberlain was content in return to leave the
Conservatives free to challenge the Gladstonian incumbent Cook in
Birmingham East.

Chamberlain yearned for more time to give the electorate a clearer
understanding of the issues that Gladstone's Irish policy put at stake. He
feared what Gladstone hoped, that for immediate purposes the sentiment
of loyalty to the Liberal party and its doughty leader would prove
stronger than any sentiment about the Irish. Chamberlain therefore issued
a long manifesto laboriously instructing the voters. He could not take his
rapport with Birmingham for granted because the issue on which he was
forced to concentrate was 'foreign to all the objects with which [he] entered public life'.[103] He pitched his appeal to the patriotism and Protestant-
ism of his fellow townsmen strongly to quicken loyalties which had not
yet acquired an aggressive or particularly anti-Irish edge.

During a campaign of little more than three weeks, he discovered the
resonances of democratic imperialism. 'These two islands', he told the
people of Birmingham,

have always played a great part in the history of the world (cheers). Again and again, outnumbered, overmatched, confronted with difficulties and dangers, they have held their own against a world in arms ('And they will again,' and loud cheering), they have stubbornly and proudly resisted all their enemies, and have scattered them like chaff before the wind (loud cheers). And if in the future, if now you are going to yield to the threat of obstruction and agitation (never), if you tremble at the thought of responsibility, if you shrink from the duty which is cast upon you, if you are willing to wash your hands of your obligations, if you will desert those who trust to your loyalty and honour, if British courage and pluck are dead within your hearts, if you are going to quail before the dagger of the assassin and the threats – (never, and protracted cheering, the audience rising in a body) – and the threats of conspirators and rebels, then I say indeed the sceptre of dominion will have passed from our grasp, and this great Empire will perish with the loss of the qualities which have hitherto sustained it. (Loud cheers, during which the right hon. gentleman resumed his seat.)[104]

Though the imperial note predominated, democratic chords always reinforced it. Speaking in Wales once Birmingham was safe, he reminded his audience that their ancestors had fought off domestic as well as foreign enemies: 'They have resisted the tyranny of kings; they have borne without flinching the terrors of a persecuting Church.'[105] Finally in Lancashire, speaking—so far had things changed—on behalf of Hartington, Chamberlain returned to the theme of his first address to his constituents opposing Gladstone's policy for Ireland: 'the highest idea of the democracy is the union of the people'.[106] As the campaign drew to its close Chamberlain was quietly confident: 'my dear Democracy is coming out all right & will teach [Gladstone] a lesson'.[107]

Hartington was not the strangest bedfellow Chamberlain found in this fight. He embraced the Conservatives ever closer as the campaign progressed. He entered into liaison with them not for his own political survival but for victory on the national scale. Any display of friendship with Conservatives in Birmingham would have threatened his Liberal base. His electoral understanding with Churchill there was kept strictly unspoken. But if Gladstone was to be driven from power nationally, it could only be by the electoral equivalent of the parliamentary alliance of Liberal Unionists with Conservatives that had defeated the Home Rule bill in the Commons. Until tolerably sure of the outcome in Birmingham, Chamberlain held his peace on the contest at large. Then in a succession of published letters he evolved rapidly from refusal to support 'separatist' Liberal candidates, through support for Unionist candidates regardless of 'other considerations', to praise of the Tories for refusing to contest the seats of Liberal MPs who had voted against Gladstone's bill. 'They have

put the Union before everything else, and they naturally claim from
Liberal Unionists a corresponding generosity.'[108]

The results of the election poured in as Chamberlain reached his fiftieth
birthday. They gave him grim satisfaction. All seven seats in Birmingham
went to Unionists. In the end the Gladstonians allowed the five incumbent
Unionist Liberals to be reelected without challenge. The one Gladstonian
incumbent, Cook, was beaten in Birmingham East by a Conservative
protégé of Churchill, Henry Matthews. Only in the Bordesley Division did
the rival Liberal factions confront each other directly. Collings defeated
his Gladstonian opponent by a margin of more than four to one, the
Conservative electors apparently abstaining. Nowhere else in the kingdom did the Gladstonians do so badly.

Even so, elsewhere, though they held their own in West Yorkshire, rural
Wales and eastern Scotland, the results of the election were disastrous for
Gladstone and his supporters. The swing against them averaged 5.7 per
cent, enough to constitute a landslide. The era of Liberal predominance
which began with the Reform Act of 1832 had come to an end. The swing
was worse where Gladstonians had put up candidates against incumbent
Liberal Unionists. The electoral division of the Liberal party proved tragic
for all who had placed their trust in it, for Gladstone and Parnell as much
as for Chamberlain and the Radicals. Only the Conservatives profited. The
319 seats they won did not constitute an independent majority but gave
them much the stronger voice in their partnership with the 79 Liberal
Unionists.

The results of the election held mixed implications for Chamberlain. He
had been right to predict that Liberal voters as a whole would be less
tolerant of Home Rule than the party activists in the federated Liberal
associations. It was also gratifying that the agricultural labourers who
responded so enthusiastically in the general election of 1885 to the prospect of 'three acres and a cow' were disappointed by Gladstone's diversion of all Liberal energies to Ireland: Gladstonians were decimated in the
1886 returns from county constituencies. Yet Chamberlain was not a rural
but an urban Radical; and outside Birmingham the urban working-class
support for Gladstonian Liberals held up well. It was among the middle
classes that the Conservatives and their Liberal Unionist allies made most
headway.

The long-range implications of the electoral returns were still conjec-
tural. Only one thing was certain: the defeat for the moment of
Gladstone's Irish policy. 'I think we have given Home Rule its quietus,'
Chamberlain observed soberly, 'but whether Mr. G will accept his defeat
or not, the future must show.'[109]

10

In Bankruptcy
1886–1887

Our business for the moment is to 'stand and wait'.

Chamberlain to Edward Heneage, 24 July 1886

The pace of the drama eased up once it passed its climax. The situation after the general election reminded Chamberlain of the general election of 1874. Then too, after he and Gladstone opposed each other, Gladstone had led his party to heavy defeat. Now, after a dozen years of work in public life, Chamberlain seemed to be back where he started, a much more prominent figure but otherwise with little reward for his effort except angry recriminations. In some ways things were better in 1874, for his defeat then had not deprived him of his sense of direction. Now he was bewildered.

Of only one thing was he sure—and in that he and Gladstone mirrored each other. Each man lay the blame for the political situation primarily on the other. Apprehensive that he might not live long enough to triumph over his crippling opponent, Gladstone enjoined his disciples to recognize that Chamberlain was 'a most dangerous man, restless, ambitious, unscrupulous'.[1] Chamberlain said the same of Gladstone more pungently: 'as long as he is rampaging about there is no hope for the Liberal Party. He has developed a malignity lately which would do credit to an Invincible or a Thug, & is evidently absolutely careless of the future of his Party or his Country providing that he can crush his recent colleagues & supporters.'[2]

More so, however, than Gladstone or any other political leader, Chamberlain distanced himself from the field of battle. He remained at Highbury even when the formation of a coalition government of Conservatives and Liberal Unionists came under discussion in London. So long as Gladstone remained active, Chamberlain could not see his way forward. He could bid for time but had no strategy for advance. The ardour of his adherence to the Radical wing of the Liberal party was dimmed by its evident rejection of his leadership. Still, he could not credit that these associations were over and done with. Nor could he imagine enduring identification with the Unionist alternatives, whether Hartington Whig or Salisbury Tory.

Attempted reorientation

The results of the general election put the prospects of every British party in question. The rupture of the party system was deep. For none of the leading participants was it deeper or more costly than for Chamberlain. He could count on fewer than a dozen members of the new Parliament to follow him through thick and thin. Yet amid the confusion the place of Chamberlain acquired critical importance for every British party.

On the one side, the presence of Chamberlain made close indentification between Liberal Unionists and Conservatives impossible. Though the Conservatives were much the largest party, they could not command a majority without support from Liberal Unionists. To make sure of the necessary support, Salisbury offered to serve under Hartington in a coalition ministry. But the Conservative leader made his offer conditional on exclusion of Chamberlain. To join him in cabinet, Salisbury explained, would require too abrupt a turn for the arch-Tory and the arch-Radical of recent years. Chamberlain entirely agreed. Hartington had to concur. Though most of the Liberal Unionists in the new Parliament owed allegiance to him rather than to Chamberlain, Hartington appreciated the extent of Chamberlain's electoral appeal, which had saved Hartington from defeat in his own constituency.

On the other side, among the Liberals, the crucial question was party reunion. The results of the general election did not dispel the assumption that, were it not for their division over Home Rule, the Liberals would have a natural majority, probably greater than ever because of the increase in the franchise. Reunion of the party would restore it to power. But here again Chamberlain was the stumbling-block. Hartington was no problem. He commanded almost universal respect. Liberal sentiments on him oscillated gently between wanting him back and accepting the Whig defection from the party as natural. Chamberlain attracted quite different responses. Some Liberals were so disappointed by his defection and so alienated by his duel with Gladstone that they recoiled from and denied the need for reunion with the renegade. A quieter but perhaps equally extensive segment of the Liberal spectrum, however, regretted his departure, feared its consequences, and hoped for his return if only tempers and tongues on all sides would soften for a while.

The path that Chamberlain hewed out for himself sharpened the contours of the new political landscape. His route attracted Conservatives,
neutralized Hartington, and made Liberal reunion impossible. Eventually his path led to a highway. But before doing so it ran a tortuous
course to an apparent dead end.

Chamberlain took his first step in indirect negotiation with Hartington. Without reinforcement from Hartington's contingent in the Commons, Chamberlain's rebellion would be inconsequential. But there was
not a Radical bone in Hartington's body. The slow-moving, unruffled
leadership he offered might be particularly reassuring to Whigs; but it
was antithetical to the Radical brand of Unionism Chamberlain hoped
to imprint. Hartington's kind of Unionism was attractive to Conservatives, indeed too attractive: therein lay its fatal weakness, which Chamberlain was quick to exploit. The distinction between Whig and Tory
was already blurred. If Hartington formed a coalition ministry supported primarily by Tories, he would forfeit 'the name of Liberal and
his position in our Party', as Chamberlain warned him.[3] In these circumstances Hartington's ability to bring Liberal recruits to Unionism
would not last long. Salisbury's refusal to participate in a cabinet that
included Chamberlain only underscored the point. Pinned between
two men of such marked character, Hartington was drained of political
colour.

Just what colours Liberal Unionists should adopt Chamberlain did
not yet know. But he took immediate care to raise the spirits of the new
group. He joined the national Liberal Unionist association from which
he had held aloof before the election because of its Whig character and
public cooperation with the Tories. To accentuate the continuing Liberalism and difference from Conservatism of the Liberal Unionist contingent in the new House of Commons, he induced them to sit on the
opposition, Liberal side of the House. One result of this arrangement
was to place Chamberlain and Hartington on the same bench as
Gladstone. They were separated from him only by the anxious figure of
Morley or the more comfortable corpulence of Harcourt: but Chamberlain was stimulated by close conflict.

While taking his own group in hand, he offered advice for the Conservatives. Chamberlain wanted the Tory leaders to proceed with the
Irish question as he had wanted Gladstone to do at the beginning of the
year, in a consultative and deliberative manner giving precedence to
land over constitutional reform. He wanted the government to set up 'a
small practical Commission to enquire into the working of the Land
Acts & especially into the condition & requirements of the small tenants'.[4] Having thus addressed the pressing problem of agrarian unrest,
the government could approach 'the whole question of Irish Government' in more deliberative fashion; and Chamberlain suggested the

appointment of a joint committee from both Houses in the new Parliament. Ireland was not likely to await the outcome of these inquiries quietly. Analysing the prospective lawlessness, he again discriminated between agrarian unrest and the Nationalist challenge to the maintenance of order. While Chamberlain suggested 'temporary provision against unreasonable evictions', he indicated his readiness to vote for 'any reasonable provisions to secure the execution of the law'.

Here were proposals that Conservatives were willing to consider, whatever they thought of their Radical origin, which was kept quiet. The approach was pragmatic and gave primacy to the bread-and-butter question of land rather than to constitutional reform. Chamberlain's tenderness for small tenants rather than for landlords disconcerted Conservatives. But he could comfort them by supporting the maintenance of law and order in Ireland.

He offered little comfort to the majority of the Liberal party, even though he shared the common assumption that his future lay in a renewal of his affiliation with them. The possibility of reunion depended, he said, on Gladstone's retirement from public life. On balance Chamberlain was optimistic. The old man was seventy-six. But the haste with which Gladstone had plunged into a general election and the vehemence with which he backed Liberal opposition to Liberal Unionist candidates suggested that he would fight for his Home Rule policy regardless of the consequences as long as he was able.

The hostility which this performance roused in Chamberlain extended beyond the messianic old man to those who followed his lead. Chamberlain could not forgive those who refused to honour the conscientiousness of his conduct in their haste, simply at Gladstone's behest, to endorse a policy which they had previously dismissed with scorn. Chamberlain insisted that they confess the error of their ways and 'recognise that the policy they have professed to support is dead & buried'.[5] He expected too much.

His demand suggested a change in Chamberlain's party orientation which he had not yet defined. Gladstone had diverted the Liberal party from what Chamberlain thought should be its prime concerns, as in the Radical Programme. Nothing in the general election angered him more than Gladstone's dismissive treatment of Jesse Collings, whose championing of agricultural labour had contributed to the Liberal victories in county constituencies in the general election of 1885. Nothing gratified Chamberlain more than to see those victories reversed when farm workers, disappointed by the Liberals' failure to act on their promises, stayed at home in the election of 1886 or voted Unionist. By placing a questionable constitutional reform ahead of improving the lot of people near the bottom in Britain's economy, the Gladstonians diminished the worth of the Liberal party in Chamberlain's eyes and revived the doubts he felt about it in the mid-1870s.

He was further depressed after the general election by the ruin of the
man who might otherwise have altered the drift of his thought: Sir
Charles Dilke. He was defeated in his bid for reelection at Chelsea. But
it was the renewal of the Crawford divorce case that destroyed him.
Dilke's failure to take the stand during the trial in February, and the
equivocal verdict that ensued, left him under a cloud. To exonerate
himself, he resorted to a peculiar judicial process associated with the
office of the Queen's Proctor. The case in this way came up for rehear-
ing in July. The procedure proved disastrous to Dilke, for it put him on
trial without the right to defend himself. Formally he was not a party to
the case. The Queen's Proctor, with whom Dilke could have nothing to
do, was the plaintiff, Mrs Crawford the defendant. The procedure allowed her to enthrall the court with tales of Dilke's multiple adulteries
while Dilke could do little to refute her. She not only won the case but
left Dilke liable to imprisonment for perjury.

Chamberlain bore no responsibility for his friend's resort to this disastrous form of appeal. Ironically the person who suggested that Dilke
seek action by the Queen's Proctor was W.T. Stead, the journalist who
accused Chamberlain of treacherously advising Dilke not to take the
stand at the first trial. Still, the second trial and Dilke's response to it
drained the vitality from Chamberlain's friendship for him. While he
still believed Dilke innocent of the main charge, Chamberlain was dismayed by the circumstantial detail with which Mrs Crawford corrobo-
rated her story. Chamberlain's esteem for his friend was further
undermined by the lack of judgement Dilke displayed after the second
trial. Dilke's first thought was to take Holy Orders, an idea that Chamberlain could think of only as 'queer'.[6] Then, against the advice of his
lawyers and Chamberlain, Dilke insisted on staying in England rather
than seek the safety of France until the risk of imprisonment for perjury
had passed. Though eventually able to assure Dilke that the government would not prosecute him, Chamberlain no longer listened to him
as a person of weight.

Dilke's ruin accentuated Chamberlain's isolation. And no sooner had
this link to the Liberal party been broken than Chamberlain's relationship with the Conservatives came under strain. The new cabinet ministers with seats in the House of Commons had as usual to seek
reelection. Among them was the protégé of Churchill, Henry Matthews,
the MP for Birmingham East. Knowing the electoral problems that
Matthews's appointment to office would revive in Birmingham, Chamberlain warned Churchill against making it; but Churchill insisted that
the appointment was *'almost vital* to me'.[7] His action put Chamberlain
'in a devil of a hole'.[8] Among the Liberals of Birmingham, the still primary virtues were the unity of the party and its dominance in the town.
Chamberlain had come close to violating those virtues by lending discreet support to Matthews against the incumbent Gladstonian MP,

Cook, in the general election. Once the issue of Home Rule had for all immediate purposes been disposed of by Gladstone's defeat, the Liberals of Birmingham wanted to set aside their demoralizing disagreement and reassert their primacy by ejecting the town's one Conservative MP from his seat. The Gladstonians were likely to exploit this sentiment by putting a candidate up against Matthews. By doing so they would force Chamberlain to make a clear and open choice between a Liberal Gladstonian and a Conservative Unionist.

The strain that the prospective by-election imposed upon the Unionist alliance extended to the national and parliamentary level. Hartington feared that it might end 'the understanding . . . observed during the general election between us & the Conservatives'.[9] Salisbury censured Chamberlain's resistance as 'very sharp practice'.[10] Chamberlain was rescued only when the local Gladstonians led by Schnadhorst overreached themselves. They emphasized the Gladstonian more than the Liberal commitments of the candidate they had in mind, and thus violated the local preference for party unity. Unable to garner adequate support, they felt obliged to withdraw from the contest; and Matthews was reelected without opposition.

Though the narrowly averted contest in Birmingham kept Conservatives uneasy about Chamberlain, he proved remarkably influential in the formation of government policy. The Conservative ministry found his investigative approach to Ireland appealing and his substantive suggestions worth consideration. Their followers were even more impressed by this anomalous ally. The lean logic with which he argued in the House of Commons and the confidence with which he analysed electoral opinion encouraged Conservative backbenchers to believe that the government was on the right track. 'It is curious but true', Churchill told Chamberlain, 'that you have more effect on the Tory party than either Salisbury or myself. Many of them had great doubt about our policy till you spoke.'[11]

No sooner had the government appropriated Chamberlain's investigative approach to Ireland than Parnell exposed the continuing elements of disagreement among the Unionists. Chamberlain wanted the government to accompany its inquiries with stop-gap measures to deal with immediate dangers, in particular the danger of unrest if landlords evicted tenants who could not pay their rent. But the government opposed further interference with the rights of Irish property, and disregarded this portion of his advice. Thereupon Parnell brought in a bill which addressed the danger Chamberlain had identified but in more drastic fashion than Chamberlain suggested.

While Chamberlain could not disagree with the bill's avowed intent, Hartington, who was heir to vast estates in Ireland, felt if anything more hostile than the Conservatives towards Parnell's measure. The simplest course for Liberal Unionists would have been to abstain when the bill came up for a vote; and so Chamberlain advised. The Conservative government could still defeat the bill so long as the Liberal Unionists did not vote with the opposition. Yet Hartington was determined to vote against the measure. Chamberlain warned him that 'every time we vote with [the Government] we give a shock to the ordinary Liberal politician outside'.[12] But Hartington refused to change his course. Irritated at the consequences of Parnell's manoeuvre, Chamberlain lashed out at Irish Nationalism as a 'vile conspiracy which relies on outrage and assassination'.[13]

Hartington was turning out as hopeless a partner as ever. But Chamberlain was at work on a more promising alliance, one that might help him advance towards the Radical Programme though at a modified pace. Churchill, Chancellor of the Exchequer and Leader of the House of Commons, held a position in the new ministry scarcely inferior to that of Lord Salisbury. The burden of Churchill's responsibilities gave him less time for contact with Chamberlain than Chamberlain quite liked. Even so, whenever he offered advice, Churchill was responsive. He met Chamberlain's proposals for an investigative approach to the needs of Ireland by promising him 'an army of Commissions'.[14] Taking advantage of a delay in Chamberlain's departure for his autumn vacation, Churchill discussed a wide range of concerns with him, foreign as well as Irish and domestic. They agreed in general terms on an updated version of the Radical Programme: 'the National Councils scheme, modified into two Councils, or into Provincial Councils, to pacify Ulster . . . and a three acres and a cow policy for England'.[15] Afterwards Churchill publicized the direction of his thinking in a speech at Dartford.

The adhesion of Chamberlain to Unionism was the most important dividend of the Home Rule controversy in Churchill's estimation. He meant to use Chamberlain to impose his own impress on the government. He availed himself of Chamberlain's persistent Radicalism and fertility in policy-making to push the naturally Conservative majority of the Cabinet in a progressive direction and thus to convince the electorate that resistance to Home Rule need not be an illiberal policy. Chamberlain was happy to be used as Churchill intended. Here again was a 'party of two' who reinforced instead of rivalling each other. Delighted with the way Churchill's 'masterpiece' at Dartford 'flabbergasted the Gladstonians',[16] Chamberlain left England for a leisurely holiday voyage to the Middle East.

The situation was still unsettled; and Chamberlain kept his options open. In connection with the local elections in Birmingham, he sent word of his general support for Liberal candidates regardless of their views on the issue of Home Rule, which was extraneous to municipal purposes. The message he wired to a conference of Liberal Unionists in London expressed more interest in reunion than they liked but in terms that the Gladstonians equally disliked. In mid-December, as soon as he returned to England, he arranged to see Churchill in London, invited Captain O'Shea to Highbury, and sent greetings to Morley.

Dissolution of partnerships

Chamberlain was free to look in every direction because he had no binding affiliations. But the obverse of his freedom was isolation. The paths he followed to escape from his isolation led to quicksand.

Just before Christmas Chamberlain's 'guarantee that [the government] would not pursue a reactionary policy'[17] collapsed with the departure of Churchill from office. During Chamberlain's absence Churchill had been arguing with the prime minister and other colleagues on a range of issues: foreign policy, where Churchill wished to be pacific; defence expenditure, which he wished to keep low; and reform of local government in the counties, which he wanted to be broadly democratic. Particularly on reform of county government, he enjoyed strong support from Chamberlain. Churchill relayed Chamberlain's requirements to Salisbury, indicating that they must be met if the Union with Ireland was to be preserved. Salisbury was not, however, prepared to stomach Chamberlain as 'our guide in internal politics'.[18] The prime minister found support from Hartington, particularly over local government, to counteract the demands of Churchill and Chamberlain. Hence when Churchill, singling out the issue of defence expenditure, tried to force the prime minister's hand by tendering his resignation, Salisbury coolly accepted it.

It all seemed so like Gladstone's treatment of Chamberlain nine months earlier. The renegade Radical welcomed the renegade Tory to 'a bitter pilgrimage'. The Radical knew all too well how willing most Liberals were to follow their party leader even when he placed the unity of the country at risk. Chamberlain told Churchill that '[t]he party tie is the strongest sentiment in this country—stronger than patriotism, or even self interest. But,' he added less confidently, 'it will all come right in the end for both of us.'[19]

The news of Churchill's resignation reached Chamberlain a day before he was to address the Liberal Divisional Council of his constituency. The meeting was called to deal with dissatisfaction over his persistent separation from the national majority of the party. The resignation of the one conspicuously progressive member of the Conservative government increased Chamberlain's difficulty. He believed furthermore that Churchill's resignation spelled doom for the government and created a need 'to reform parties on a new basis'.[20] Therefore, after dealing with his constituents' complaints in the first part of the meeting which was kept private, Chamberlain opened its doors to stimulate the process of party reconstruction.

He spoke of Liberal reunion; but he used that rhetoric to reaffirm the policy priorities which he had attempted to instil since the beginning of the year. If Liberals were agreed on nine points out of ten, why concentrate on the tenth? Why not implement the nine, not least the points of agreement on Irish policy, before worrying about the tenth? He did not point out that to do so would reverse the priorities of Gladstone, who insisted above all that Ireland be given its own parliament.

Chamberlain's list of the points of Liberal agreement began with Irish land: 'without solving this land question Home Rule is impossible, and I believe that if you solve it Home Rule will be unnecessary'.[21] He suggested a round table conference to work out the details of a solution to the land problem. Almost any three leaders of the party, he said, could devise a mutually agreeable scheme to transform the tenants of Ireland into owners of the land they cultivated without great risk to the British taxpayer. After that subject was dealt with, Liberals could go on, still in complete agreement, to the reform of 'purely municipal government' in Ireland before they need concern themselves about an Irish parliament.

His initiative was skilful. There were essentially three forms of party reconstruction he could pursue to regain a political footing: reunion of the Liberal party, creation of some new centre party, or reconstruction of the Liberal Unionist alliance with the Conservatives. His speech kept all these options open. He put the case for Liberal reunion on his own terms in an attractive light. Those terms might be acceptable to Churchill and lead to a consolidation of the progressive forces in Parliament without risk to the Union with Ireland. In any case relations continued sweet between Chamberlain and Churchill, who welcomed the Birmingham speech as fair warning to the Conservatives of the price they would pay if they did not bring him back quickly to their councils.

Chamberlain's speech at Birmingham struck a responsive chord. Gladstonian MPs with West Midlands affiliations, men such as Henry Fowler from Wolverhampton and Henry Broadhurst, welcomed the bid for reunion. But what turned Chamberlain's overture into more than a gesture was the response it evoked from Sir William Harcourt. A Home Ruler from ambition to succeed Gladstone as leader rather than from conviction, Harcourt wished to maximize the party's chances for success. He therefore wanted to bring Chamberlain back to the fold. He was one of the few Gladstonian Liberals to treat Chamberlain with respect for the conscientiousness of his stance on Ireland, respect which Chamberlain gratefully acknowledged. Even so, Harcourt had concluded that Chamberlain sought victory rather than reunion with those

Liberals who differed from him—until Chamberlain's suggestion at Birmingham of a round table conference. Harcourt took immediate hold of Chamberlain's extended hand, and urged Gladstone and Morley to do so too.

This response enabled Harcourt to put his own impress on Chamberlain's proposal. Whereas Chamberlain suggested submitting proposals for a land bill to a conference of middle-level, essentially neutral leaders of the party, Harcourt raised the level of participation to the rank just below Gladstone and extended the exploratory range of the conference to include local government and the possibility of a legislature for Ireland. Chamberlain reluctantly accepted Harcourt's enlargement of the agenda. They worked out an agreement on a conference membership of five: themselves plus Morley as a committed Home Ruler, Trevelyan who had resigned with Chamberlain in March as a second Unionist, and the former Lord Chancellor Herschell as a fairly neutral Gladstonian.

Gladstone and Morley accepted the development suspiciously. If they had spurned Chamberlain's olive branch, responsibility for the continuing disunion of the party would have fallen on their shoulders. Gladstone appreciated that Chamberlain was not likely to accept terms for reunion which involved swallowing Home Rule; and on any other terms Chamberlain's return would dash Gladstone's hopes. He also minimized Chamberlain's following in the House of Commons, 'the six or eight (if they be so many) floating in the air'.[22] Hence, while giving the conference a distant benediction, Gladstone took care to deprive it of any binding or immediately practicable mandate.

Morley writhed with emotion. The prospect of the conference frightened him because it would seat him beside Chamberlain and put Home Rule in question. Morley was able to resist Chamberlain's strength of personality only at a distance; and he identified his own integrity with devotion to Home Rule. He bombarded Harcourt with pleas to be less trusting. But once back in Chamberlain's company, he was almost literally swept away, first into a carriage and then to a box at the opera with Chamberlain to see *Faust*, scarcely reassuring entertainment. Recoiling as soon as he was on his own, Morley proceeded with the conference not to achieve reconciliation with Chamberlain but to 'leave him thoroughly worsted'.[23]

Chamberlain's interest in the conference quickened at the beginning of the new year with the replacement of Churchill at the Exchequer by George Goschen. The most determined Liberal critic of Chamberlain during the election campaign of 1885, Goschen had since distinguished himself as the Liberal Unionist most sympathetic to the Conservatives. In joining, with approval from Hartington, an otherwise Conservative cabinet while continuing to call himself a Liberal Unionist, Goschen strengthened the bond between Whig Unionists and Conservatives and accentuated the anti-Radical character of their alliance.

Yet Chamberlain did not think of forswearing Unionism. The round table conference had some euphoric moments; but the objective of the participants who mattered—Chamberlain and Morley with Gladstone in spirit behind him—was to place the blame for the continuing split in the Liberal party on each other. Chamberlain hoped also to enhance the Radical credentials of his brand of Unionism by showing how close he could come to the Liberal majority on everything but the crucial subject of Home Rule. Here again his object was to increase his ability to fight the Home Rulers.

While members of the conference tried to trap each other, outsiders wondered uneasily what they were up to. John Bright insisted that Chamberlain spoke for no one but himself. When Hartington asked Chamberlain what terms he had obtained from the Gladstonian leadership for opening the discussion, Chamberlain refused to show to him the correspondence. A conference so riddled with suspicion was unlikely to produce much but recrimination. Its initial meetings were nevertheless remarkable. Chamberlain unfolded a plan to turn Ireland's tenant farmers into owners at virtually no risk to the British taxpayer, a plan that thereafter shaped the land policy of both Gladstonians and Unionists. Chamberlain also astonished his fellow conferees by the extent of his agreement with Home Rule as he applied the Canadian federal-provincial model to the United Kingdom. Delighted at his seeming concessions, the conference moved towards acceptance of his cardinal demands. The powers of the Irish legislature would be enumerated, leaving all residual power to the imperial parliament; and Ireland would continue to elect representatives to Westminster.

On this latter point there was no more than a tendency to agree, and Morley soon showed signs of backtracking. For all the seeming consensus, the agreement reached by mid-January did not remove either of the chief obstacles that Unionists saw to Home Rule: Irish representation at Westminster, and protection of Ulster. Uncertain as to whether agreement might be reached on the first, Chamberlain stiffened his stand on the second. He turned special treatment of Ulster into one of his 'fundamental' demands.[24]

Blind to the dark lining of the silver clouds, Harcourt was filled with hope by the first days of discussion. He planned a party meeting to ratify the reconciliation. He described Chamberlain as 'singularly little self-seeking or solicitous as to his own position in the affair'.[25] Morley was astonished at Harcourt's naivety and voiced feelings of revulsion towards Chamberlain which shocked Harcourt. Chamberlain, wrote Morley, 'has found out that his egotism, irascibility and perversity have landed him in a vile mess. . . . He has proved himself to have no wisdom and no temper. Never more let me be asked to believe in his statesmanship. *C'est fini.*'[26]

The round table meetings in mid-January marked the high point of Chamberlain's success in keeping his options open. The ambiguity vital to the continuance of the conference could not be sustained. In order to retain the loyalty of supporters and the trust of allies, the participants needed to issue public statements about their intentions, statements that dispelled the ambiguity. This fatal cycle was quickened by deteriorating relations between England and Ireland. Since Chamberlain had the sharpest tongue, his statements drew the most attention; but he was as much provoked as provocative.

The outlook from Chamberlain's standpoint darkened when the government announced its intention to bring in a new Coercion bill to deal with the unrest in Ireland. Chamberlain was ready to give such a bill favourable consideration but knew it went against the Liberal grain. The bill would also fortify the Gladstonian argument that coercion was the only alternative to Home Rule. Chamberlain therefore felt obliged to use an address to his constituents to stiffen their repudiation of the Gladstonian alternative. He emphasized the inconsistency of the Gladstonians between denial that they were 'Separatists' and sympathy with Irish Nationalist aspirations.

The round table conference reconvened on Valentine's Day for the last time. The meeting might have broken up immediately had it not been for Harcourt's humour. He entered the room wearing an enormous Chamberlainesque orchid, remarking that it was the custom of plenipotentiaries 'to wear the favour of the opposing sovereigns'.[27] The meeting ended much more cordially than it began.

The truce was shattered by the opposing sovereigns. First Gladstone in a letter for publication blamed Liberal Unionists for delaying the disestablishment of the church in Wales. In mid-February Liberal Unionists including Bright and Chamberlain had voted with the Conservatives against a Gladstonian motion for disestablishment in order to save the Unionist government from overthrow. Yet Chamberlain was a better friend of Welsh disestablishment than was Gladstone. Gladstone insisted that the Liberals deal with Home Rule before proceeding to other legislative concerns. He used the primacy he ascribed to Home Rule in order to save himself from Radical measures such as Welsh disestablishment, to which he was indeed opposed. Chamberlain was willing to support Welsh disestablishment at some political cost to himself, as his later conduct proved, so long as it did not jeopardize the Union with Ireland which he deemed of overriding importance.

He seized an opportunity to respond to Gladstone in a Nonconformist paper, *The Baptist*. Gladstone had written of 'poor little Wales' having to wait until Ireland received Home Rule. 'Poor little Wales indeed!' Chamberlain replied:

[It] will not wait alone. The crofters of Scotland and the agricultural labourers of England will keep them company. Thirty-two millions of people must go without much-needed legislation because three million are disloyal.[28]

He went on to link Gladstone's Irish Nationalist allies in Parliament with the Irish-American advocates of terrorism who supported them financially.

That was too steamy a brew for even the most peace-loving Gladstonian. The *Baptist* letter brought the round table conference to a halt and enabled Gladstonians to blame Chamberlain for its failure. The rupture of the conference eliminated the option of Liberal reunion for him, at least under current circumstances. Still, the conference and its ending did not leave a great impression. The only person it affected decisively was Trevelyan, who rejoined the Liberal majority. Individually Trevelyan was not a serious loss to the Unionist cause; but his defection formed part of a steady trickle of Liberal Unionists back to the main fold. The *Baptist* letter produced two dividends for Chamberlain. It clarified the contrast in priorities between the Gladstonians, who put Home Rule for Ireland first, and Chamberlain's adherence to the Radical agenda of 1885. The aggressive tone of the *Baptist* letter also reassured Chamberlain's Unionist associates and strengthened their cooperation.

Even so, he found himself without organized troops or a strategy. Though he welcomed the executive committee of the National Radical Union to Birmingham with bravado, uncertainty was apparent in the substance of his remarks. He was unwilling to challenge the town's Liberal Association, which still encompassed Unionists and Gladstonians. He therefore advocated triangular electoral contests to pit Liberal Unionist candidates against Conservatives and Gladstonians until the Liberal Unionists could enforce their views on one side or other. This was an expression of frustration more than a serious proposal, for it could not be implemented without making enemies all round.

Radical Unionist alternatives

Meanwhile he struggled to secure an Irish policy behind which Radical Unionists could rally. Unionist policy for Ireland had of necessity two sides. One was laid down by Salisbury and the Conservatives: stiffened powers to maintain law and order, in other words coercion. Liberal Unionists had little impact on this side of the policy, which they had to swallow with as good a face as they could manage.

The resort to coercion had a consolidating effect on both sides of the political divide. Gladstonians rallied naturally against the bill which the government introduced to strengthen law enforcement in Ireland. The remarkable thing was how Liberal Unionist MPs rallied to the opposite side. Admittedly four defected. Another small group including Jesse Collings who had pledged themselves unequivocally against coercion in the last election felt obliged to abstain from the vote on the bill. The rest, though, accepted the need for it, however unpopular. For the first time they met together with their Conservative confrères, and heard rousing speeches from Salisbury and Goschen. Thereafter the combined force accepted the strict voting discipline needed to make headway against Gladstonian and Parnellite obstruction.

Chamberlain put a democratic gloss on their action. 'I believe', he told the Commons,

> that the masses in this country have no . . . love for disorder. They have shown . . . notably in the United States, that they can repress it with a sternness which autocratic Governments might envy.[29]

Aside from indicating his preference for only minimal additions to the coercive powers of the government, he gave the bill straightforward acceptance. He accompanied his approval, however, with a stipulation, the indispensable other side of Unionist policy for Ireland, namely that coercion be accompanied by legislation to ease the lot of Ireland's tenant farmers. Unaccompanied by land reform, reliance on repression would be egregiously unjust and too unpopular to keep the government alive for long. The Coercion bill would give landlords ample protection while it did nothing for tenants who were charged excessive rents. Chamberlain therefore demanded revision of the law governing rentals.

Deprived since Churchill's resignation of a private channel for communication with the government, he conveyed his demands from the platform. He kept to general terms, displaying more respect for Conservative susceptibilities than he had for Gladstonian. He received his reward from the cabinet's new Irish Secretary, Arthur Balfour, appointed by his uncle, the prime minister, to replace Sir Michael Hicks Beach, who was suffering from trouble with his eyes. Balfour had hitherto behaved like a dilettante, and Chamberlain, who was twelve years his senior and far more experienced, had treated him without mercy. But over the past year Balfour had come to admire the arrogant Radical for his resolve in resigning from Gladstone's cabinet and for his ideas on Irish industry, technical education and transport. Balfour sent a late draft of the government's proposed Land bill to Chamberlain for his observations.

Time was short. The bill was to be presented to the cabinet within twenty-four hours and to the House of Lords in forty-eight. Chamberlain stayed up past midnight to draw up his commentary for Balfour. It

was sharply critical. Chamberlain implicitly threatened Balfour with
withdrawal of Liberal Unionist support for the Coercion bill unless the
accompanying Irish Land bill was revised 'to protect the tenant against
the alleged injustice of bad landlords, & thus to prevent the Coercion
Bill from being a mere instrument for enabling rack rents to be collected'.[30] Balfour tried to find an hour when he and Chamberlain could
meet to go over the bill together; but Chamberlain's time was already
committed. He could only write back, amplifying his central message:
'What we want broadly is that no tenant shall be evicted or deprived of
his property on the ground of inability or unwillingness to pay an unjust Rent, & we want the Court to say in every case whether the Rent
is under the circumstances unjust. . . . Unless you cut the ground from
under the feet of the agitators . . . & accomplish by law the protection of
tenant against injustice which they endeavour to secure by robbery &
outrage you will have the country against you.'[31]

To concede by law what agitators demanded through intimidation,
and to protect tenants who were able but unwilling to pay rents they
considered unjust, would be hard for Tory flesh to bear, particularly the
flesh of Lord Salisbury, who associated himself frankly with the landlords. Chamberlain did not know what direction the government would
take: 'everything is uncertain here,' he reported from London to
Highbury; 'The feeling runs very high.'[32]

In these circumstances, he responded to an intimation at the end of
March that Gladstone might like to meet him in private. They met a
few days later on the outskirts of London where Gladstone was living.
The two men approached each other equally convinced that for the
moment the Coercion bill was of paramount importance and that it
worked to the political benefit of Gladstonians and the detriment of
Liberal Unionists. Gladstone hoped to exploit his advantage in his conversation with Chamberlain. In the pass to which things had come,
Chamberlain felt some regret over the way he had brought the round
table conference to an end. He would have welcomed an accommodating gesture from Gladstone, but Gladstone saw no need. The two men
parted as they had met, irreconcilable opponents.

'This introduction of coercion', Chamberlain observed, 'has brought
us to the turning-point in the history of the struggle for the Union.'[33] He
threw himself into an effort to stem the tide away from Unionism.
There was no point focusing on Parliament. The lines of division there
had hardened and could be modified only by the force of opinion out
of doors. Chamberlain accordingly embarked upon a speaking tour, up
to the Western Isles of Scotland. A corps of reporters from the national
press accompanied him. Chamberlain's following in the House of Commons might be small; but judged by the press he attracted, his influence
in the country was second only to Gladstone's and Salisbury's.

Though the use to which Chamberlain put the tour was shaped by the immediate exigencies, it had been in the making for several months. A convention of crofters from the Highlands and the Western Isles sought his help to attract the attention of the government. Dispossessed by landowners who had cleared the Highlands and the islands for deer-stalking and sheep-grazing, pushed on to infertile coastal districts with too little land to support the population, the Scottish crofters endured a plight as bad as any in Ireland. They also approached Gladstone, but he put them off, insisting that Irish Home Rule must come first.

Here was an opportunity for Chamberlain to refurbish his Radical credentials and underscore what was wrong with Gladstonian priorities. When spokesmen for the crofters asked him to come and see the situation for himself, he welcomed the invitation and devoted his Easter vacation to the tour. His opponents charged him with opportunism. Even his safety was threatened. There were signs of backtracking among his prospective hosts. Though Chamberlain did not know what awaited him, he went ahead. He took an early opportunity to tell the crofters that if they no longer wished to support his efforts, he was ready to leave; but they demurred. Wherever he went, he was greeted by hisses as well as cheers.

There was a teacher behind the agitator in Chamberlain. He was convinced that, given the necessary information and instruction, people could be induced to abandon their prejudices and come to a proper understanding of great public issues. Towards this end he developed a style that was new to English oratory. Like good teachers, he was responsive to those he wished to guide. At Ayr, a Liberal Unionist stronghold, he tackled the popular dislike of coercive powers to uphold the law in Ireland. In some detail he described a recent convention in the United States of supporters of Irish Nationalism including advocates of violence. He instructed his audience about the Plan of Campaign organized by Nationalist MPs in Ireland. Under its terms, tenants who thought their rents too high could pay what they thought the right level of rent into a fund pending eventual settlement. The offence of the Plan as Chamberlain described it was the intimidation of doubtful tenants to cooperate. He then inveighed against intimidation:

> You are told that the Bill which is now before the House of Commons is a Bill for the repression of liberty. Liberty to do what? Liberty to commit theft, liberty to outrage women, liberty to ruin industrious men?[34]

This was too much for the Irishmen in the audience. The way Chamberlain responded to their interjections made his address a drama. One furious Irishman shouted, 'It is not a characteristic of the Irish people to outrage women.' Chamberlain coolly repeated his charge:

> You want instances of insults to women.
> ('Outrage you said; outrage to women.')
> Certainly.
> ('Outrage was the word, Sir.')
> Certainly.
> ('It is a slander on the Irish people.')

At which Chamberlain told several stories including that of the wife of a farmer murdered by terrorists who then kept her from obtaining a coffin for her husband and jeered at her as she accompanied his body to the station. While he was telling these stories, someone cried out, 'Watch yourself.' Chamberlain seized upon the threat as 'an instance of the demoralization of politics' and blamed 'the assassination party', Irish Nationalists and the Gladstonians who consorted with them. The threat proved his point: 'you must have coercion of one kind or another.... You must either strengthen the law or you must surrender all law to those who break it.'

At Edinburgh he tackled another barrier of popular sentiment for Liberal Unionists to overcome, the idolization of Gladstone. Chamberlain detailed how persistently Gladstone had refused to assure Unionist Liberals that their criticisms of his Home Rule scheme would be met. To drive the point home, Chamberlain reminded his Scottish audience of how Gladstone dealt with their division over Scottish disestablishment in the general election of 1885: he had said that the issue should wait until Liberals disposed of the issues on which they agreed. When that reminder was cheered, Chamberlain responded:

> cheer that if you like.... That was a wise and a statesmanlike policy, becoming the leader of a great party.... But how comes it then that now, twelve months later, the self same man, without any preliminary discussion in the country ... without full or fair consultation with his party or his followers, should have flung this apple of discord amongst us?

He moved on to Inverness. He had last been there to advocate the unauthorized programme of the Radicals in 1885. Now as then, he hoped to use the west of Scotland to change opinion throughout Britain. But what a contrast between the two occasions!

> We were then full of high hopes and expectations.... Now all that we had hoped, all that we had expected, has been ... put on the shelf.[35]

Fishermen reminded Chamberlain of the merchant seamen he had fought for in 1884. Crofters exemplified the agricultural labourers enfranchised in 1884 and targeted in the Radical platform. The plight of the crofters renewed Chamberlain's Radicalism. In Stornoway he insisted that land must be 'treated in every case as a trust, and not as the absolute possession of private owners'.[36] When one man in Skye spoke of their patience in the past, Chamberlain observed, 'it is only when you become impatient that you get any attention'.[37]

Wherever he went, he summarized the pleas and information presented to him, leaving the crofters sure that he understood their situation. He refused to endorse everything they sought, for instance government-provided steamship transport for their produce, which he said would trench on the rightful sphere of private enterprise. The one measure he advocated was a land purchase Act comparable to the measures he had in mind for Ireland. After his tour he drew up such a bill, which he showed to Balfour. But the parliamentary timetable was badly congested. Chamberlain abandoned his scheme when the crofters turned out to be more interested in low rents than in freeholds.

He ended his Scottish tour in Glasgow among people of a quite different sort from crofters. At the Royal Exchange he received an enthusiastic welcome from Glasgow's mercantile classes. It was among electors of this sort that Liberal Unionism drew its support in the west of Scotland. Without abandoning the crofters, Chamberlain adapted his tune to the middle-class ear. He spoke of resistance to terrorism. He told of attempts to frighten him into declining the crofters' invitation. He concluded by speaking of the startling new accusation that Parnell had condoned the murder of the permanent under-secretary for Ireland in Phoenix Park in 1882.

In the midst of Chamberlain's Scottish tour, on the day the House of Commons voted on the second reading of the Coercion bill,[38] *The Times* published a facsimile of a handwritten letter signed apparently by Parnell to this effect. Chamberlain needed no more to convince him of the treachery of the man who had betrayed him. Challenging Parnell to take *The Times* to court over its allegations, he declared that

> if Mr. Parnell . . . fears to face the ordeal of cross-examination, every impartial, every intelligent man will feel that he has put himself in a position in which he is no longer a safe and proper ally for English statesmen. (Loud cheers, the audience rising and waving hats and handkerchiefs.)[39]

Those cheers encouraged him to believe that his tour had been a success. He concluded it with an assertion that

> We have passed through the hottest of the fight. (Cheers.) Our party has been tempered by fire and hardened by pressure, and now there is nothing that will make us yield to what we believe to be dangerous to the country. (Cheers.)

He certainly impeded the advance of Gladstonians in the west of Scotland. The crofters responded appreciatively to his reinvigorated Radicalism. Affluent lowlanders applauded his defiance of Irish Nationalists and their British allies. But could he resolve the tension between these two sources of support? Most of his lowland admirers had opposed his Radical programme in 1885 and were as averse to upheaval at home as in Ireland. Most of the forces of social discontent to which he appealed in 1885 had moved into the Gladstonian camp, giving it everything necessary to become a Radical party except Radical leadership.

The inadequacy of Unionism

He headed straight from Scotland to Birmingham. The battle still raged all over the field. Whenever he turned his attention in one direction, the situation deteriorated in another. While he was in Scotland, his home base came under assault. Rivalry between the Gladstonian and Unionist Liberals there sharpened after the executive meeting of the National Radical Union in mid-March. Each side tried to place its supporters in control of the Birmingham Liberal Association, still the town's most important political organization.[40] At the annual general meeting of the association, which took place during Chamberlain's absence, the Gladstonians secured a motion condemning the return to coercion in Ireland. Feeling at the meeting ran so high that when R.W. Dale attempted to make a case for the new Crimes bill, he was denied a hearing.

Chamberlain lobbied hard upon his return from Scotland; and after two weeks he obtained a motion in favour of the government's bill from his own constituency association of Birmingham West. His Radical Union intensified its recruiting efforts among the lower Liberal ranks in the town, with some success. But it was harder for Chamberlain than for his Gladstonian adversaries to extract commitments of support from the town's leading Liberals. He pleaded with Dale to align himself decisively with the Radical Union, to no avail.

Dale's hesitation was one sign of Chamberlain's failure thus far to carve out a clear, commanding position for himself. Unsure of his new supporters while alienated from the old, he was shifting towards the right. In 1885 he had placed himself firmly on the leftward flank of the Liberal party. Now he consigned Gladstonians to the far left while he claimed the centre left.[41] His social instincts grew less generous. In 1886 he had argued with Beatrice Potter for public works to relieve unemployment. Now he told her that 'State employment would give rise to every form of jobbery & extravagance & would interfere with & repress private enterprise'.[42]

A movement towards the right is not uncommon among men past middle age; and Chamberlain was fifty. It was a widespread movement in the last twenty years of the nineteenth century among his fellow industrialists. It was almost universal among those who applauded his stand on coercion. Still, the bitterness with which Chamberlain turned on former friends did not reflect an easy mind. It was all very well for him to speak of the monarchy with new warmth in the spring of 1887 during Queen Victoria's golden jubilee. But was it necessary to sneer when Morley too spoke well of the monarchy? A former supporter of Chamberlain was so incensed by this evidence of his 'persistent & embittered political treachery'[43] that he offered the press personal letters and reminiscences to prove that Chamberlain had once been an ardent republican.

Chamberlain did not like where the events of the past year had placed him. His political position and the relationships that went with it were not of his choosing. His belief that Gladstone's design of Home Rule would jeopardize the cohesion of the kingdom and the strength of the empire was no doubt genuine. But he had been driven out of communion with the bulk of the Liberal party less by his convictions than by Gladstone. Chamberlain could not circumvent the barrier of Gladstone, nor could he convince most Liberals that Gladstone was the barrier.

What Chamberlain could challenge was the assumption that support for Gladstone was synonymous with progressive politics. Cautioned by the doubts of Birmingham's Liberals, Chamberlain spent the summer of 1887 searching for ways to substantiate this challenge. He never questioned his commitment to the Unionist side on Ireland. He sought to construct a framework of policies, including many he had pursued in the past, with sufficient electoral appeal to secure the Union with Ireland and renew his own enterprise in public life. One after another, however, the efforts he made during the summer towards that end only accentuated the bleakness of his situation.

To begin with, speaking on the anniversary of the formation of the National Radical Union, he sought to overcome the uneasiness all Liberals felt at alliance with Conservatives. He introduced the subject on an invidious note by assuring his audience that 'our allies will be English gentlemen, and not the subsidised agents of a foreign conspiracy'.[44] He moved on to firmer ground when he pointed out that the programme of legislation which the Conservative government hoped to enact for England and Ireland was an improvement on what Gladstone offered the electorate in 1885.

But that was a meagre standard easily surpassed. Chamberlain's argument would not carry much conviction so long as the Conservatives were led by their right wing, which was strong on coercion of Ireland and weak on domestic reform. Though Chamberlain was learning new respect for the prime minister, there was no doubt that Salisbury protected the less progressive components of his party; and no one in the government filled the place Churchill had vacated as champion of Tory democracy.

In mid-June Chamberlain aired the idea of forming a national party in the centre of the political spectrum. The party he envisaged would exclude the Tory far right and at the other end the alliance of Gladstonian Radicals with Parnellites. It would include Churchill and the progressive Tories, all Liberal Unionists, and those Liberals who were willing to modify Home Rule to meet Unionist objections. In policy the centre party would combine two commitments: to uphold Britain's national and imperial interests including the Union with Ireland, and to address urgent social needs at home. For the domestic agenda of the new party, Chamberlain suggested a muted version of the Radical Programme.

The idea of such a party had enormous attractions for him, and he explored the prospects for it eagerly over the coming month. Yet he sensed the unreality of the dream. Its realization depended on its opponents, in particular on Gladstone and Salisbury. Their grip on their respective parties had grown too strong over the past year to be terminated by anything but abdication. Their authority had been strengthened by the rebellions of Chamberlain and Churchill: 'the matter', Chamberlain told Churchill, 'is really out of our hands'.[45]

Accordingly Chamberlain used the idea of a centre party mainly for tactical purposes. It helped ward off the demand for Liberal reunion. His talk of a centre party also increased the pressure on Salisbury to accept Liberal Unionist amendments to make the Irish Land bill more generous. If the present configuration of Unionist government rejected these efforts in deference to its right wing, there was an alternative configuration from which the right wing would be eliminated. Talk about a centre party was thus bound up with a struggle within the Unionist alliance over amendments to the legislation on Ireland. But during these proceedings the nucleus for a centre party disintegrated. And after amending the Land bill to meet Liberal Unionist demands, Lord Salisbury's government set the Crimes Act to work in a way that repelled Chamberlain.

The notion of a centre party had originated in April with Churchill. He and Chamberlain then raised the idea for public consideration in concert with each other. But the two men approached the possibility with differing degrees of seriousness. While Chamberlain could accept it as a useful dream, it offered Churchill his only hope for escape from isolation. In resigning from the government Churchill had seemed to place his personal ambition above the security of the Union with Ireland. Salisbury was hence able to exile him from the Conservative fold as firmly as Gladstone exiled Chamberlain from the Liberal. And whereas Chamberlain had established a niche for himself in the Unionist alliance, Churchill could not do so without encountering Salisbury. Churchill therefore envisaged the composition of a centre party government differently from Chamberlain. Both men agreed that Hartington would be prime minister: but whereas Chamberlain thought of Salisbury for the Foreign Office, Churchill wanted to exclude Salisbury and promised the Foreign Office to Lord Rosebery.

This difference between Chamberlain and Churchill worked its way into the debates on the Land bill. Both men insisted that the bill give more consideration to tenant farmers. Chamberlain hammered out his demands in concert with Hartington. But Churchill insisted upon a more truculent line of his own. Chamberlain pleaded for cooperation among the three men who would form the inner core of the centre party. If, Chamberlain exclaimed to Churchill, 'at the first moment, you decline to make any concession to the views of those with whom you propose to work & insist on having entirely your own way . . . what part do you propose to leave to your colleagues except that of passive acquiescence in your decisions?'[46] But Chamberlain and Hartington were not earnest enough in their pursuit of a centrist government to win Churchill's cooperation. Hartington did not want to demoralize the Conservatives, who after all formed the largest component of the Unionist alliance. He urged postponement of any idea of governmental reconstruction. Chamberlain hoped that the government would recognize its weakness and open the door to a centrist reconstruction; yet he passed Hartington's advice on to Churchill as 'very prudent & wise'.[47]

Rather than submit his government to reconstruction, Salisbury accepted the demand on which Unionist critics of the Land bill placed most emphasis. Violating his sense of what was rightly due the landowners, he agreed to submit rents already revised under the Land Act of 1881—the so-called 'judicial rents'—to further revision in light of the continued depression. He may have been persuaded as much by demand within his own party expressed by Churchill as by Liberal Unionist pressure. No matter. The credit went to the Liberal Unionists, particularly to Chamberlain who had been much more insistent on this and kindred demands than Hartington. The other beneficiary of the concession was Salisbury himself. While the conspicuous grimace with which he agreed to concede reassured his right wing, his willingness to make the concession revived confidence in his ability to lead a government that depended for its survival on the combined forces of the Unionists.

The outcome frustrated Churchill. Unable to censure Salisbury for making a concession that he favoured, Churchill turned on Chamberlain in the Commons and spoke witheringly of his 'characteristic sneer'.[48] When Chamberlain sought privately to minimize the significance of the gibe, Churchill insisted that there was a 'strong difference of opinion between us'.[49]

Chamberlain paid still more heavily for the credit he received for the government's concession over 'judicial rents'. Resentful of the price it had to pay for Liberal Unionist support of the Land bill, the government implemented the new Crimes Act with needless harshness by 'proclaiming' the National League, in effect outlawing the organization that was conducting the Plan of Campaign. This action validated the Gladstonians' charge that the Crimes Act was directed against the government's political opponents in Ireland. Chamberlain was concerned about the impact of the proclamation on public opinion in Britain, and denied its necessity to deal with the situation in Ireland. The incidence of actual crime there had fallen. If particular branches or members of the National League behaved in clearly intimidating fashion, there were less ostentatious provisions of the Act to deal with them. Chamberlain pleaded with the government to change its mind; but to no avail.

He then tried to offset the boost to Gladstonian hopes by elaborating an alternative to Home Rule. If the advocates of a centre party came forward with a scheme to reconstitute the relations between Westminster and Ireland on the model of the relationship between Ottawa and the Canadian provinces, it would accentuate the risks in Gladstone's more extensive proposals. It would also demonstrate constructive vision, always a virtue in Chamberlain's eyes, and never more needed than now, to offset the unpopularity of coercion among the public. But when he sought cooperation from Churchill and Hartington on this escape from the encircling gloom, Churchill encouraged Hartington to reject it. Hartington welcomed Churchill's reaction on tactical and substantive grounds. Straightforward opposition to Gladstone's scheme would, he thought, be more effective than propounding an alternative; and in any case Hartington shied away from the alternative Chamberlain suggested.

Neither Churchill nor Hartington attempted to soften their response to Chamberlain. Churchill declined opportunities to meet him. Hartington told Chamberlain that, if they should drift apart, he would accept the result with regretful understanding. Despairing of Hartington, the centre party, Liberal Unionism and all, Chamberlain predicted that 'the Govt. will be out of office before 2 months have passed of the next session & a general election under present conditions will give Mr. G a majority of at least 150'.[50] His discouragement was deepened by another attempt he made, this time through Morley, to probe Gladstone's interest in reconciliation. Aside from expressing pleasure at *'anything* that pointed towards effective accommodation',[51] the old man cast doubt on the timeliness of communication with Chamberlain and also indicated that arrangements to bring him back to the fold without the addition of Hartington would not be worth the cost. Chamberlain knew all too well from his recent experience how improbable was agreement between Hartington and Gladstone's Home Rulers. The soft language Gladstone used towards Chamberlain scarcely disguised his antagonism. In July Gladstone had told Rosebery that 'Chamberlain is the greatest blackguard I have ever come across.'[52]

On the day the government issued its proclamation of the National League, he left Westminster for Birmingham in disgust. Next day, to local supporters who gathered for a garden party at Highbury, he spoke his mind. He made the best he could of the government's legislative record, describing the Land bill as an incomplete yet 'great and generous concession'[53] to the tenantry of Ireland. But he condemned the proclamation of the League as excessive, carried out against the advice of the Liberal Unionist leaders. He declared his intention of voting against the government on this action if it was challenged in the House of Commons. He also indicated that he might 'put before the country an alternative scheme for the settlement of this perplexed Irish question . . . to show how . . . we may conciliate our desire to grant a great extension of local government to all parts of the kingdom with the continued maintenance of a united Empire'. His remarks lessened the uneasiness of his supporters over coercion but did not ease his own foreboding that 'the game is up unless Providence intervenes to save us'.[54]

No solace

Personal relationships deteriorated along with the political. For a while the Home Rule controversy revived Chamberlain's association with Beatrice Potter despite her resolutions to the contrary. Watching from a seat in the Ladies' Gallery, she was enthralled by the clash in the Commons on the introduction of the Home Rule bill between Gladstone and Chamberlain, for her 'the great man'. Recovering afterwards, according to her diary, from exhaustion at the drama, she 'felt how vastly superior that great man was to me'.[55] Months later, before leaving for his autumn holiday, Chamberlain 'half asked'[56] for an invitation to her family home in the country—which he did not receive. But once he left for the Mediterranean, she visited his sister, Clara Ryland, at Highbury. When Beatrice Potter first saw Chamberlain's home, she had observed its furnishing with condescension. Now she found it 'gorgeous, soft and easy to live in'.[57] Thereafter she kept in touch with the great man's sister and eldest daughter, though she chastised herself in her diary for doing so.

In May 1887, in the midst of his struggle to offset the popular impact of coercion in Ireland, Chamberlain encountered Charles Booth, leader of an investigation on which Beatrice Potter was working into unemployment and poverty in London. Prompted in this way, Chamberlain wrote to her analysing the use of public works or private philanthropy to relieve unemployment, on which he had moved closer to her still conservative views. This overture led to an exchange of invitations to each other's houses.

Hence Beatrice Potter found herself a few steps from the platform when Chamberlain addressed the National Radical Union in Birmingham at the beginning of June:

> He was supported by his brother and the few of the faithful still left in the fold. He was white and agitated, for this was a crucial time, whether or not these meetings would be successful. He has lost none of his old charm of voice and manner, less arrogance and a touch of stern sorrow at the defection of friends, the breaking-up of friendships. But his speech showed no hesitation. Resist unto death was his true motto. And after he sat down it was natural our eyes should meet in the old way.
>
> The town hall was still more crowded in the evening. It was not the crowd of 4 years ago, nor the intoxicating enthusiasm of those brilliant days. It was a gathering of sensible folk. . . . And the speech also had a different flavour. Sentimental sympathy for the wrongs of the downtrodden masses was exchanged for a determination to preserve law and order. The statesman had overcome the demagogue.[58]

Gratified by Beatrice Potter's appreciation at a time when he needed reassurance, Chamberlain strutted in her company after the meeting 'as a man who is sure of his conquest'.[59]

His conduct annoyed but also encouraged her to believe that he shared her reviving passion. She mistook the field of conquest that was uppermost in his mind. Her mounting feeling also renewed her internal struggle between love for a perhaps great but certainly tyrannizing man and desire for a career, mind and integrity of her own. This inner conflict brought Beatrice Potter once again to breaking point, unable either to restrain or to follow her love. When Chamberlain visited her in the country at the end of July, her reserve gave way and she told him how strongly she felt for him. At the same time she insisted that they should not meet again.

He drew back from the emotional outburst but did not want to lose the occasional solace she had given him in a difficult year, now darker than ever. Back in London, he wrote to her:

I cannot help feeling depressed and discouraged at times and I value greatly the sympathy which you have shown me.... Why are we never to see each other again? Why can not we be friends—'comrades'—to use your own expression? I like you very much—I respect and esteem you—I enjoy your conversation and society and I have often wished that fate had thrown us more together.... The circumstances of my past life have made me solitary and reserved, but it is hard that I should lose one of the few friends whose just opinions I value and the sense of whose regard and sympathy would be a strength and support to me.

I cannot say more. You must decide, and if it is for your happiness that we should henceforth be strangers I will make no complaint.[60]

Though these were the gentlest words Chamberlain had ever written to her, Beatrice Potter reacted with an angry sense of injury. She noted at the top of Chamberlain's letter: 'This after he had pursued me for 18 months and dragged me back into an acquaintance I had all along avoided. To insist on meeting a woman who had told you she loved you in order to humiliate her further.' Her feelings did not cool as the year drew to its end. At Christmas she wrote bitterly in her diary,

Happily a feeling of contempt for dishonourable and unchivalrous conduct has killed all other feelings except sadness that the same qualities which wounded me have, perhaps irretrievably, injured his career.[61]

Gladstone might have said much the same.

11

New Resources
1887–1891

Do you remember your telling me in Washington when we were first engaged, that you thought there was something to be done for the colonies, & that you should like to try to do it? I have thought so often of that.

Mary to Joseph Chamberlain, 13 October 1900

By Christmas 1887, while Chamberlain's enemies in England wondered whether he was beaten, he was on an official mission in North America. There he discovered fresh hope, confirmation of his Unionism, and a broader sense of its constructive ramifications. He came upon a path lined with resources to sustain him through an increasingly ugly fight against Home Rule. The path connected him to rising forces in Britain's empire, and hence transformed the complexion of his politics.

Lord Salisbury had asked him late in August to lead a diplomatic delegation to Washington to see whether a solution could be found to a controversy between the United States and Canada over fishing rights in the Gulf of the St Lawrence. The invitation was remarkable. Until the past year Salisbury and Chamberlain had pointed to each other as embodying the worst among their respective opponents. Joint adherents since then of the Unionist alliance, they still thought of each other as standing at its opposite, ultimately irreconcilable poles. The two men had rarely met face to face.

Yet as early as 1883 Salisbury had detected something imperial in Chamberlain's reluctance to abandon Egypt to anarchy. Furthermore, during the fight against Home Rule Salisbury discovered that there was something essentially straightforward about Chamberlain. Gladstonians saw nothing but treachery in the renegade; and early in the controversy Salisbury agreed that Chamberlain lacked trustworthy convictions. But during the negotiations in the spring and early summer of 1887 over Irish legislation between the Liberal Unionist leaders and the Conservative cabinet, Salisbury learned to appreciate Chamberlain's style of conduct. In private Chamberlain emphasized to his Conservative allies the issues on which he would not agree with them, but in public he gave them stout support. He provided a refreshing contrast to Churchill, who sometimes savaged his allies in public. When the Queen visited Salisbury at his home at the height of his controversy with the Liberal Unionists over judicial rents, Salisbury included Chamberlain among the few guests. Speaking afterwards with the Queen, Salisbury contrasted the mischievousness of Churchill with Chamberlain who, though 'rather advanced in some of his views', was 'an honest man' and 'would serve [the Queen] well some day'.[1] The conduct of the Conservative prime minister and the Radical Unionist over the next few weeks accentuated their mutual candour. Salisbury publicized his dislike of the concession he made over judicial rents. Chamberlain gave equally public notice of his intention to vote against the government over the proclamation of the National League. Unruffled by the announcement, immediately thereafter Salisbury asked Chamberlain if he would like the Washington mission.

Chamberlain had already thought of extending his usual autumn travels by visiting India or Australia; and he welcomed the offer of escape. Hartington was the only person he consulted before accepting the invitation. Chamberlain wondered whether he might improve the chances for some constructive alternative to Home Rule by staying close to London; but Hartington responded with another dose of cold Whig water. 'I hope', Chamberlain concluded with disappointment, 'that when I do return politics may be a little less mixed & that I may be less completely isolated than I appear to be at present.'[2]

His assessment of the government rose at the end of August with the passage of a bill to encourage the creation of garden allotments. Chamberlain had urged the government to see that the bill was enacted; and its compliance served to substantiate his claim that Conservatives could provide more domestic reform than Gladstone had offered in his second ministry. Still, the Allotments Act of 1887 did not raise Chamberlain's estimate of Unionist prospects. The more he analysed the essentially negative Unionist strategy against Home Rule, the 'more & more hopeless'[3] it looked. He continued to predict electoral disaster.

Fearful or confident that the electoral foundation of the government could be rapidly undermined, Unionists and Gladstonians threw themselves into a contest for popular support throughout the country on a scale exceeded only during general elections. Feelings rose to a new level of intensity in mid-September when a crowd in Ireland stormed a police station at Mitchelstown and were driven off by officers who shot and killed three of the protesters. The shots resounded throughout the United Kingdom. In Birmingham the executive of the Liberal Association voted to condemn the police and the whole policy of coercion. They booked the town hall for a protest meeting on 30 September, the day after Chamberlain was scheduled to address his constituents. Acting fast, he used an earlier meeting of the National Radical Union to

respond to the deteriorating situation. He accused Gladstonians of using a double standard when they condemned the use of guns by the
police but not by Irish terrorists. He threatened to abandon the current
policy for Birmingham of neutrality in local elections and to oppose any
candidates who had been 'specially aggressive against the Unionists'.[4]
On the other hand, in line with his opposition to the proclamation of
the National League, he criticized the government for issuing blanket
injunctions instead of focusing on trouble spots to prevent eruptions
like the one at Mitchelstown.

His scheduled meeting with his constituents was still stormy. In order to ascertain the size of the opposition, a motion of confidence in
Chamberlain was presented at the beginning of the meeting. Two hundred voted against it, but they were overwhelmed by two thousand in
his favour. Throughout Chamberlain's speech, he had to respond to
hostile interjections. This was popular politics as he believed in it, and
he rose to the challenge. Rather than accept the preoccupation with Ireland, he sought to change the popular agenda. Ireland, he insisted, had
had far more than its share of attention. Britain's domestic needs should
become Parliament's first concern in its next session. Among these
needs he gave pride of place to reform of local government, still handled in English counties by appointed justices of the peace. Welcoming
an indication that the government accepted this order of legislative priorities, Chamberlain called for 'a complete and a universal and a popular system of local representative government . . . [to] develop local life
and local patriotism . . . to protect the rights of the people and to promote their wellbeing'.[5] He also renewed his attempt to deal with the
terrible loss of life among merchant seamen. The royal commission appointed in 1884 had just reported, and it bore out the charges he had
made. Here was a scandal infinitely greater than Mitchelstown:

> We ought not to rest until we have done something to prevent this
> waste of life; and no Irish question ought to be allowed to block the
> way.

Chamberlain argued with every resource at his command. Yet after the
meeting he confessed that he did 'not feel absolutely certain of a single
seat though I *think* that I am safe myself'.[6]

Amid the partisan debate at home, Chamberlain read everything
available on the fisheries dispute in North America. The argument lay
between the United States, whose friendship Britain sought to cultivate,
and Canada, Britain's premier colony. Lacking direct economic involvement in the dispute, Britain looked for a way to reconcile these two
parties. Partisan complications in Washington reduced the prospects for
agreement. Republicans controlled the Senate, which would have to
ratify any treaty, while a Democratic president, Grover Cleveland, held
the White House. Drawing on his experience of British politics, Cham-

berlain did what he could to secure the appointment of a Republican to the American negotiating team. The Republican eventually appointed was, however, a university president, not a politician of weight such as Chamberlain had hoped for.

The Irish controversy led him beyond the immediate diplomatic problem to its bearings on the position of Great Britain as an imperial power. From the outset of the debate over Home Rule he had dwelt on the analogy between the fight to uphold the Union at home and the war fought by the northern states to uphold the American Union. 'They triumphantly vindicated the principle which we seek to establish,' he declared during the election campaign of 1886.[7] The fight for the Union at home also deepened his respect for 'the virtues which distinguished the race when it spread itself over vast continents and established an empire such as the world has never seen before'.[8] The Home Rule controversy drew particular attention to the position of Canada. Chamberlain used the relationship between Canada's federal and provincial governments as a good model to apply to Ireland. Gladstone too referred to Canada as a model, but he spoke of the relationship between the colony and the mother country. That analogy only deepened Chamberlain's alarm at Gladstone's conception of Home Rule for Ireland. The constitutional bond between Britain and Canada was tenuous, sustained mainly by sentiment; and the sentiments of the majority in Ireland would work in the opposite direction.

Chamberlain's diplomatic assignment led him to pay closer attention to Anglo-Canadian relations. What he learned in September increased both his hopes and his fears. On the one hand he was impressed by the vast resources of the dominion, half a continent already crossed by twelve thousand miles of railway. The pattern of its trade impressed him further: per capita, Canadians consumed five times as much of Britain's manufacture and merchandise as did the Americans. On the other hand, Canada defied Britain's interests and belief in free trade by imposing a tariff on all imported goods including those from the mother country. To make matters worse, there was a movement afoot in Canada for commercial union with the United States. The movement attracted the opposition Liberal party in Canada, and the Conservative government of the colony had not decided how to react.

Chamberlain strode in where the Canadian Conservatives feared to tread. Before setting sail for New York he declared that the existing relationship between Canada and Britain was too slender to 'remain as it is. Either, as I hope may be the case, it will be in the future strengthened by ties of federation, or it will be loosened altogether.'[9] Commercial union would weaken the relationship to the point of dissolution. 'Commercial union with the United States means free trade between America and the Dominion, and a protective tariff against the mother country. If Canada desires that, Canada can have it; but Canada can only have it knowing perfectly well that [it] means political separation from Great Britain.'

This interpretation of the imperial outlook in North America in turn intensified Chamberlain's involvement in the Irish debate. Gladstone expected that Chamberlain's diplomatic assignment would prompt him to distance himself from the controversy at home. The British debate over Ireland roused the Irish electorate in the United States. The notoriety of Chamberlain's opposition to Home Rule threatened to reduce the chances for success in his diplomatic mission. Yet instead of distancing himself from the Irish controversy before he left for the United States, Chamberlain headed straight for Ireland. He went to see how determined the Protestant north was to resist subordination to an Irish parliament in Dublin. He braced himself for disappointment.

But the will to defy Home Rule which greeted him along the streets of Belfast matched his own spirit of defiance. He reinforced this response by appealing to all the prejudices of Ulster. He did all he could to deepen the division of Ireland between the south—Nationalist, Catholic, agrarian, poor—and the north—loyal, Protestant, industrial, better educated and more prosperous. He flattered Ulstermen for possessing 'almost all the cultivated intelligence of the country [and] the greater part of its enterprise'.[10] 'There are two races in Ireland,' he declared; and 'to put a race which has shown all the qualities of a dominant people . . . under the other, which . . . has always failed in the qualities which compel success . . . is an attempt against nature [which] can only lead to disaster'.[11] 'Do not forget Ulster,' he reported with satisfaction to Hartington at the conclusion of the tour; '—it is a terrible nut for the G.O.M. to crack.'[12]

Preparations for the diplomatic mission to North America served to inform rather than restrain Chamberlain's rhetoric. To illustrate the incapacity of the Irish for self-government, he described the city government of New York under Irish American control in Tammany Hall as 'the most corrupt, the most immoral, the most ineffective, with which a civilised people have ever been afflicted'.[13] Little wonder that a junior officer at the British embassy in Washington commented, '[t]hey might as well send Judas Iscariot as Ambassador to Heaven as Chamberlain to America'.[14]

Conquests in the New World

Once he sailed from the British Isles, at the end of October 1887, Chamberlain forswore public participation in the Irish controversy. Like many European voyagers before and since, he left for the United States in lively anticipation, with strong but malleable preconceptions, seeking confirmation but open to discovery. He hoped to discover in the New World how to make his way again in the Old. And the New World exceeded his hopes.

He arrived in New York to learn that the Canadian commissioner who was to serve under him, Sir Charles Tupper, had been held back in Canada by election business. Using the delay to pave the way for his mission and sound out reaction in 'the pivotal state' of New York, Chamberlain stayed in the city for a few days. His first task was to counteract the hostile impression which the part he took in British politics had created in American circles. Adept at management of the press, he took New York's notoriously aggressive reporters by surprise. They intended, as one told him, 'to give Chamberlain hell'; yet they would treat any reluctance on his part to submit to their interrogation as British snobbery; and they besieged him in droves. He responded with a novelty which they described as 'interview by wholesale', an early form of news conference. Demonstrating his ease by lighting up a cigar and his hospitality by passing his cigars around, he fielded questions with obliging affability, much more communicative than previous British emissaries yet never revealing more than he intended.

The Americans took to Chamberlain. His assessment of them was more critical. Impressed by success in business, Americans spoke appreciatively of his background in industry; and they liked his no-nonsense style of speech. He took delight in their vitality. But the absorption of New Yorkers in making money made him aware of how his goals had changed. After meeting the elite of New York—its senators, the city's mayor, Whitelaw Reid of the *New York Tribune*, the Astors and the Vanderbilts—he noted that New Yorkers 'have learned to create wealth but have not reached a stage where they know how to spend or enjoy it'.[15]

He looked at New York with Brummagem eyes, and he found the city a poor contrast to Birmingham, let alone London. It was, he concluded, 'the ugliest big city I have ever seen'.[16] Darkened by an overhead railway, illuminated by arc lights that flickered and flared and made everything ghastly, it did not possess one public building of great merit. The finest shops on Broadway displayed their wares with less skill than those on Birmingham's Corporation Street. The expensive houses on Fifth Avenue were architecturally no better than his town house in London. The taste of their interior furniture and decoration was worse. The collections in the main museums were embryonic. Central Park was no match for Hyde Park. The other squares were 'mere open spaces with a few trees & some rusty grass—no flowers no good statues no monuments of any kind'.[17] Municipal taxes were quadruple those in Birmingham, while the municipal services were vastly inferior.

His sense of the inferiority of American civic culture was reinforced at a banquet the New York Chamber of Commerce gave in his honour. Silently he noted the breach of European etiquette when two members of President Cleveland's cabinet were shown to seats of honour ahead of the foreign guest; and he kept smiling through two long speeches in fulsome praise of the United States as about to 'outstrip Great Britain in the race for commercial supremacy'.[18] Chamberlain's turn to speak did not come till late in the evening. He turned the occasion to the benefit of his mission; and in so doing his own vision was stretched. Expressing himself with brevity and grace, he lifted the sights of his audience above the competition between his country and theirs to the 'still greater and more far-reaching nationality of the Anglo-Saxon race'.[19] His remarks made a favourable impression not only in New York but in Washington.

Out of the public gaze, at dinner parties in New York given for him by the rich and their political associates, Chamberlain discovered a combination of attitudes which confirmed his own brand of politics and awakened in him a contempt for American government in the country's gilded age. The news Britain had received about American reaction to Gladstone's proposal for Home Rule suggested overwhelming sympathy for the Irish. But Chamberlain discovered that, in private, all of his American hosts were Liberal Unionists. They were repelled by their experience of the Irish in the United States. The Civil War had turned Americans into staunch unionists so far as the United States was concerned. As for the United Kingdom, Chamberlain's hosts favoured only limited concessions to Irish national sentiment, much less than Gladstone advocated though—like Chamberlain—more than Hartington and Salisbury would endorse. Chamberlain reported his discoveries to friend and foe in Britain with glee. Yet his American hosts, cowed by the Irish vote in the United States, lacked the courage to state their private convictions in public; and they admitted as much to their guest. This spinelessness disgusted Chamberlain and confirmed his belief in the need for strong leadership in democracies. They required leaders willing to step forward and shape public opinion rather than feel out and follow its contours in fear and trembling.

The train from New York to Washington took Chamberlain across stretches of wasteland and marsh which did not impress him. But he warmed to the capital city. The magnificent distances that Dickens admired in Washington had since been filled up with substantial, comfortable houses of red brick or stone, which reminded Chamberlain of English county towns. He sympathized with the Americans who had moved to Washington to escape from 'the bustle & perpetual rattle of dollars in the big cities'.[20] The federal government's smooth conduct of the municipal government of the city after a spate of mismanagement by the local Irish also gratified his prejudice.

Yet the political situation in Washington further lowered his estimate of the workings of the American body politic. The partisan division between a Democratic administration and the Senate under Republican control rendered the Secretary of State who was in charge of the American side of the negotiations, T.F. Bayard, clumsily ineffective. He fell foul of the Senate by asking for its assent to the appointment of a negotiating commission and, when the Senate refused, appointing a commission anyway. President Cleveland's bid for reelection in 1888 with a pledge to reduce tariffs complicated Bayard's stance on reciprocity with Canada over fisheries, so much so that Chamberlain was tempted to charge him with having invited the British delegation to Washington on false pretences. Chamberlain was not much more impressed by President Cleveland, 'rather a rough diamond—very stout with a heavy jowl & bull neck—a rather coarse intonation of voice & apparently no cultivation or interests outside his work'.[21] While admiring the courage of Cleveland in challenging the country's system of protective tariffs, Chamberlain was horrified by the inability of the President to resist intrusions from any 'loafer' or 'impudent fellow' who cared to call on him. 'In time,' Chamberlain commented to his daughter, 'I hope they will see that their Chief Officer should be necessarily raised above them for at least the term of his office & that he represents the dignity & the strength of the whole country.'[22]

The covert Liberal Unionism that Chamberlain discovered among the elite in New York proved to be still more intense in some quarters of Washington. On no one did it have a firmer grip than on the Secretary of the Army, William Crowninshield Endicott. At a dinner for Chamberlain upon his arrival in the capital, Endicott gratified the guest of honour by dwelling on 'the trouble caused by the Irish who congregated in great cities & dominated local politics, causing the corruption so prevalent in American Municipal life'.[23] Afterwards at Endicott's home, Chamberlain discovered that his host was 'of the bluest New England blood',[24] a patrician from Salem, Massachusetts. His wife was a Peabody by birth and hence connected to the Morgan firm of international bankers in London. A nervous conservative in outlook, Endicott had belonged to the American Whig party before the Civil War. Afterwards he joined the Democrats rather than the Republicans as the less radical party of the two. Though he did not speak out publicly against the Irish, that was because, except on official business, he rarely spoke out at all. He accepted the Democratic nomination for Governor of Massachusetts in 1884 on condition that he would not campaign for the office. He was defeated. But Grover Cleveland won the presidency that year, and appointed Endicott to his cabinet to reassure independently minded voters who contributed to his margin of victory.

Mary Endicott, the Secretary's daughter, struck Chamberlain at once as 'one of the brightest & most intelligent girls I have yet met'. He met her at a ball thrown by the British embassy. Never did he so enjoy himself as during his first weeks in Washington, where dances, dinners, floral teas and picnics were organized in his honour. A driven man darkened by the death of two wives, Chamberlain over the past decade had impressed those who knew him well as anxious and essentially melancholy. Official position in London had not encouraged whatever taste he had for the more frivolous forms of social life. The American capital released him from the constraints of London, even though he came as chief of an official mission. 'He has taken to dancing [and] is an accomplished flirt,'[25] observed the astonished embassy official who had lately likened him to Judas Iscariot. Soon after Chamberlain reached Washington he told his homely eldest daughter tactlessly that 'the average of American female beauty is higher than ours. You see a very large number of nice looking girls in the streets & the proportion of good figures . . . is very large.'[26]

All the belles of Washington sought invitations to meet the British emissary who seemed so much younger than his fifty-one years. But Chamberlain was immediately taken with Secretary Endicott's twenty-three-year-old daughter, 'the Puritan maiden from Salem' as he liked to think of her. Serious yet lively, a good listener, an anglophile freshened by New England, familiar with politics from her upbringing, Mary Endicott was just what Chamberlain was looking for in a partner. 'I don't like "superior" women though I should not get on with a silly one either,' he later reflected. He had 'lighted on the exact medium' which he thought of as 'perfection'.[27]

'You managed somehow to attract my intellect—or what passes for such,' he told her afterwards, '—before you captivated my senses.'[28] But his senses did not take long. Mary did not seem at all foreign. In Washington she was regarded as 'an English beauty', and everyone remarked upon the Englishness which a slight drawl gave to her manner of speaking. She had 'an air of natural distinction'. Erect in posture, she was almost as tall as Chamberlain, a man of middle height. He saw her as thin but full figured, her brow 'high & square for a woman', her face open, 'the eyes wonderfully trusting & truthful, & the mouth firm with a tender curve in the lips'.[29] He sensed in her 'an immense & hitherto untried capacity of love & devotion. The deeps have hardly been stirred at present, but there lie hidden in them courage, resolution, intensity of purpose & a great power of self-sacrifice.' Like many Victorian men, he found self-sacrifice an alluring characteristic in a woman and believed it to be indispensable in a wife.

He accepted all the invitations that Washington showered on him in order to see as much as possible of Mary—and also to cultivate support

The wives of Joseph Chamberlain:
4. (*above left*) Harriet, née Kenrick, 1836–1863.
5. (*above right*) Florence, née Kenrick, 1848–1875.
6. (*right*) Mary, née Endicott, 1864–1957.

in the Senate for a treaty. 'If I don't have gout or liver complaint or something of the sort,' he laughed, 'it will be because I am proof against perpetual feasting.'[30] He saw Mary nine times in little more than a month before Christmas when he left for Canada. A week after their first ball, he met her at the home of the Secretary of the Navy, William Whitney. Impatient to ask her to dance, an activity he had refused since the death of Florence, he interrupted a conversation she was having with a young admirer. After Joseph and Mary had taken a few turns on the floor, another young man cut in. Unacquainted with this practice, Chamberlain was furious. 'The next time,' however, 'I managed better & if I saw anyone approaching I asked at once for "another turn".'[31] Once, at a supper, 'I stared at you . . . with the deliberate object of depreciating you & the only result was that I knew that you were the only girl for me'.[32] Holding a plate for her to eat from during another supper dance regardless of the raised eyebrows of onlookers, he allowed neither his 'dignity nor anything else to stand in the way of my determined purpose to make the Puritan maiden my wife if that were humanly possible'.[33] He contrived to have her invited to outings where he was to go. He sent her flowers and books, and even composed a poem:

> The witches of Salem, three centuries ago,
> Were burned at the stake or were hanged in a row;
> > But now milder methods obtain:—
> Yet the charms they exert have more force than of yore;
> Although no one is found their free use to deplore
> > And none dare their owners arraign.
>
> All the wizards & warlocks have ceased from their sins,
> With their cats & their toads,—their wax figures & pins,
> > They cause no more ailments or itching;—
> Still the pains that now rack us are quite as severe
> And while pins raise no heartache we yet have to fear
> > From eyes that are always bewitching.[34]

Mary was swept on but not away. Seeking a man she could admire as well as love, she had set her sights high when she entered the society of Boston and Washington. The passing years, enough to make her reexamine her expectations, had made her only more fastidious. She was 'coming to the conclusion that my chances were against rather than for my marrying'[35] when she met 'the great man', the phrase she unknowingly shared with Beatrice Potter. Feeling old for her age, Mary Endicott was not disconcerted by Chamberlain's fifty-one years, which in any case he bore lightly. And she had always hoped to marry someone in public life.

All she could remember from their first encounter was that Chamberlain 'mentioned Birmingham & expressed the hope that some day [he] would see me there & show me the town'.[36] What struck her afterwards was his earnestness, which she took as sincerity. She could see that, despite his seeming candour, he was 'reserved by nature—we are both like that'.[37] She was flattered by the attention she received from the visiting statesman and lion of the season; and though disconcerted by his intensity, she found his conversation riveting. Before his departure for Ottawa, he asked to call on her at a time when there would not be too many other people around; and she agreed. He took the train north in high spirits with a mounting resolve to make Mary his wife. Her involvement however lagged behind his. 'I feel', she told her cousin, 'like a safety match warranted not to go off—till struck on the right box.'[38]

Invigorated by the social round and his burgeoning love, Chamberlain had pushed his diplomatic negotiations a long way by Christmas. The matter at issue had to do with Canada's rejection of American claims to fishing rights off Canada's eastern shores and similarly with Canada's antagonism towards the American tariff which kept Canadian fish out of American markets. After encouraging the British to enter into negotiations by suggesting reciprocity in this market between Canada and the United States, Bayard got the talks off to a bad start by rejecting the idea. Chamberlain, muffling his anger, proposed a twofold alternative. It called in the first place for mutual surrender by Canada and the United States of fishing rights given them under a Convention of 1818 which had served no purpose except to inflame relations between the two countries. His second, more substantial proposal would permit Canada to impose a licence fee on American fishing vessels that wished to work in Canadian waters.

Chamberlain hoped for a counteroffer, which Bayard duly made. Bayard rejected any surrender of rights under the Convention of 1818 as unacceptable in the current state of American feeling. Instead he suggested free importation of Canadian fish into the United States in return for full access by American deep-sea fishermen to Canadian port facilities; and he accepted Chamberlain's notion of Canadian licence fees as an equitable interim measure until the United States removed its tariff on Canadian fish. President Cleveland endorsed Bayard's suggestions. Cleveland and Bayard thought that the Senate would accept a treaty along these lines. Chamberlain's discussions with Republican senators made him less optimistic. But even without Senate approval, such a treaty would set out the lines on which the controversy could be settled eventually, and in the meantime the licence fee would provide a *modus vivendi*. The Canadian government was the only one that responded to the emerging consensus with uneasiness. Anxious to see Canada for himself, Chamberlain accepted an invitation from the Canadian prime minister, Sir John A. Macdonald, to go to Ottawa where Macdonald thought that Chamberlain's 'personal influence would contribute to a general agreement'.[39]

Ottawa in midwinter was a come-down after Washington. With thick ice but little snow yet, even the winter sports were limited; but Chamberlain donned 'a magnificent fur cap' which he assured his daughter 'would produce a sensation in Piccadilly'.[40] Politically also his visit to Ottawa was disappointing. Because of the Christmas holiday, he saw little of the cabinet beyond the prime minister. After departing for Toronto, Chamberlain had to deal with a burst of resistance to the emerging treaty among the cabinet's lower ranks.

Toronto, however, charmed Chamberlain more than any other city in North America. It passed the ultimate test: it was like Birmingham. 'The streets are broad,' he wrote home, 'the shops, banks, warehouses &c large & good, the public buildings fine & well arranged. The living part of the town reminded me of Edgbaston with its roads of good comfortable detached houses, many of them with small gardens.'[41] Only the art gallery and museum fell below, far below, Birmingham standards. Toronto for its part, responding to hints from the Washington press, welcomed Chamberlain with a dinner party adorned by 'many of Toronto's handsomest young ladies'.[42]

It was imperial stimulation that Chamberlain felt at a banquet the next night. Toronto was torn between pro-British loyalties and economic interests attracted by the notion of commercial union with the United States. Chamberlain had to deal with that conflict when he responded to a toast to '[t]he commercial interests of the Empire'. The toast would be on his mind for the rest of his life.

None of his later responses was more gripping than this first one in Toronto. His public commentary on commercial union between Canada and the United States had already helped to kill interest in the idea among Canada's Conservatives and to make Liberals uneasy. He wanted to nail down the lid of that coffin and generally to strengthen the imperial bond between Canada and Britain. He also wanted to cultivate support for his forthcoming treaty and counteract the rival ambitions which kept the Anglo-Saxon democracies of the north Atlantic at odds with each other. Finally, assured by Sir John A. Macdonald that the relationship between the federal and provincial governments in Canada could indeed serve as a model to settle Britain's relations with Ireland, Chamberlain hoped to turn his visit to Canada to his political advantage in the United Kingdom.

These concerns led Chamberlain to expand upon his conception of Anglo-Saxon nationality. He spoke to his Toronto audience of the greatness and importance of the distinction reserved for the Anglo-Saxon race, that proud, persistent, self-asserting and resolute stock which no change of climate or condition can alter, and which is infallibly bound to be the predominant force in the future history and civilisation of the world.[43]

He appealed in this spirit for a drawing together of the colonies and mother country and, more loosely, of the Anglo-Saxon democracies of Britain and the United States on the basis of their common heritage, their mutual economic interests blended by free trade, and their talent for federal government. Still confident from his experience in business that tariffs ultimately harmed rather than helped the economic interests they were designed to protect, he prophesied that the United States would soon discover the folly of its tariff walls and pull them down. He had further reasons for preaching free trade in Canada. Such a policy would render commercial union with the United States pointless, and would also bring down the Canadian tariffs that strained relations between colony and mother country. There was no conflict, Chamberlain argued, between the natural economic interests of Canada and those of Great Britain. Rather than stimulate local industry artificially, Canada should concentrate on its vast agricultural and mineral resources, newly accessible with the construction of the Canadian Pacific Railway. The cultivation of these resources would attract a large population and thus naturally generate industrial development. Chamberlain was quickly congratulated for 'laying the foundation of a Free trade party' in Canada.[44]

The persuasive power of his speech did not lie, however, in its economic policy, from which Canada and the United States continued to depart, but in the vision it conveyed of the imperial potentialities of English democracy. The relationship between empire and popular government was a subject of widespread uncertainty in the old world and the new. Chamberlain insisted that democratic government tended to reinforce empire. 'The interest of true democracy', he declared in Toronto, 'is not towards anarchy or the disintegration of the Empire, but rather the uniting together [of] kindred races with similar objects.' The English in particular, he claimed, had a gift for unifying kindred races: 'the working out of the great problem of federal government . . . seems to have been left in charge of the English people'.

Yet England still wondered whether it was worthwhile to carry the 'burdens of this vast Empire'. Chamberlain told his fellow Englishmen to look for relief from those burdens 'in widening the foundations of the great Confederation, and not in cutting away the outposts'. Turning back to the colony where he was speaking, he delighted his audience by holding up the federation of Canada as a model not only for the United Kingdom but ultimately for federation of the whole empire:

If [imperial federation] is a dream . . . it is a grand idea. It is one to stimulate the patriotism and statesmanship of every man who loves his country; and whether it be destined or not to perfect realisation, at least let us . . . do all in our power to promote it.

He swept his audience away with enthusiasm. Some wept. Others climbed up on tables, waved dinner napkins, and shouted themselves hoarse.

The response Chamberlain evoked in Toronto nourished his own burgeoning imperialism. So did Washington, to which he immediately returned. He was introduced to a circle of eminent Americans of about his own age, idealists in their youth who had grown cynical about the domestic politics of their country yet were excited by its imperial potentialities. They included Henry and Brooks Adams, descendants of two presidents; Edward Phelps, the American ambassador in London who had returned to Washington for the fisheries negotiations; and John Hay, the disciple of Lincoln who would later work together with Chamberlain when they took charge of their respective countries' imperial growth. Chamberlain embraced Hay as 'decidedly the most European & most cultivated American I have met'.[45] These men intensified Chamberlain's reaction to the corruption of democracy in the United States and heightened his sense of England's imperial mission. They told him that the constitution of the United States dissipated the force of the public will, deprived the country of a supreme locus of power comparable with the House of Commons, weakened the appeal of great issues, discouraged potential leaders, and hence reduced politics to a scramble among scoundrels for the spoils of office.

Secretary Bayard drove the lesson home, when diplomatic negotiations were resumed after Chamberlain's return, by abandoning the proposals which he had made before Christmas and had encouraged Chamberlain to press upon Ottawa. Apparently Democratic insiders had warned Bayard that a treaty on these lines would place the reelection of President Cleveland in jeopardy. Chamberlain accused Bayard of shuffling 'out of all his engagements in the most dishonest manner'.[46] The diplomatic setback also showed Chamberlain the strength in the United States of 'the old feeling against England', a sentiment fuelled by 'envy & a sense of inferiority which even the heroic struggle of the Civil War has not obliterated'.[47]

One evening late in January at dinner with Chamberlain, Henry Adams held forth on the woeful condition of the United States. To deter his guest from drawing comparisons to the advantage of Great Britain, Adams gloomily predicted that Europe would follow in the degenerate footsteps of the United States. Not so, Chamberlain retorted. Most European nations were pursuing some great idea which ennobled their public life. Germany and Italy were building their respective nations.

Even Russia was animated by a sense of her duty to its Slavic peoples. England, he declared, is working out the idea of imperial obligation and responsibility to the vast populations subject to her sway.[48]

This concept impressed itself upon him under personally emotional circumstances. Throughout his sojourn in Canada, he had been nerving himself to propose to Mary. He spoke to her as soon as he returned to Washington. Confident of his intense love for her yet aware that he had not yet stirred the depths of her heart, he told Mary that, given the chance, his love would compel and draw out hers. Such preemptive love-making from a foreigner twice her age whom she had known for less than two months was too much for Mary. She recoiled, telling Joseph coolly that she did not care for him enough to be his wife though she would always feel a certain interest in him.

Three days later, when they met at a dinner in Mary's home, they avoided each other. Joseph thought Mary impassive. Yet he refused to give up. When Mary suggested at a ball that they had better end their relationship then and there, he replied, '[i]f a man is going to be hanged, I suppose he would prefer to postpone his execution for a week or two'. Though Mary's self-possession sometimes almost destroyed his hopes, he continued to badger her. He would fix her in the lens of his monocle and observe condescendingly that her present life was utterly frivolous, that she was worthy of better. It was not, however, his strutting but his interludes of depression that touched her. 'The expression in your face sometimes made my heart ache for you,' she later told him, '& I would go home wretched . . . haunted . . . by a voice which I could not silence, which repeated continually. . . . Are you not going to regret it when it is too late?'[49]

She granted him a reprieve. Meeting him at another ball, she suggested that they step into the front room out of the whirl of the dancers. There she confessed that she might have been a bit hasty in rejecting his proposal. They agreed to enter a period of probation. Joseph returned to his hotel in such boisterous spirits that he kept his astonished secretaries up till 4 a.m. 'Next morning I was up at 9—still as bright as a lark & altogether behaved like a madman as I was. It did not last very long for you took care to cool me down again very soon. You were cruel then.'[50] She was controlled, not cruel. From the beginning of their probation she felt 'drawn on by a fate which could have but one end'. During the early days of February, some lines kept running through her head:

> Unless you can think when the song is done
> No other is soft in the rhythm;
> Unless you can feel, when left by One
>   That all men else go with him;

> Unless you can know when unpraised by his breath
> That your beauty itself wants proving;
> Unless you can swear—'for life, for death!'
>   Oh fear to call it loving.

Meanwhile Chamberlain's negotiations with the Americans and particularly with Secretary Bayard stood deadlocked. The creative period of designing a treaty was over. All that was lacking was the will on Bayard's part to endorse his own handiwork. Ways could readily be found to adjust the remaining points at issue. Chamberlain's impatience mounted. The treaty he wanted was there but just out of his grasp. Otherwise he had found what he came to find, and more. He had escaped from his isolation at Westminster into the warmth of Washington where nearly everyone treated him as a friend. He had discovered in the new world a welcome commentary on the superiority of the old. Canada had excited his imperial imagination. And he had found a woman he wanted to marry. Both Mary and Bayard still eluded him. But if only they would summon up the will to make the decision which he believed each secretly wished to reach, he could sail home in triumph.

It was a sign both of his renewal and of political problems at home that he wanted to return to England quickly. Lord Salisbury's government was going to introduce a bill to extend elective local government to the counties. Chamberlain wanted to keep up the pressure for a genuinely popular measure enabling counties to do what the town council had done for Birmingham. 'Anything less than this will disappoint public expectation,' he warned Salisbury, '& most sorely try the loyalty of liberal Unionists.'[51] Chamberlain was also anxious to stop the erosion of Liberal Unionism in the face of Tory as well as Gladstonian efforts. The Tories were acting badly in his own constituency. Gladstonians drove Jesse Collings out of the presidency of the Allotments and Small Holdings Association which he had founded.

Early in February Chamberlain forced Bayard's hand. Working through the British ambassador in Washington, Chamberlain threatened to break off the negotiations and return home unless Bayard allowed them to move back along the lines envisaged before Christmas. The threat worked. Without a word of explanation from Bayard for his change of heart, the two teams of commissioners picked up where they had left off. They proceeded to straighten out the remaining knots, some of them hard enough to keep the final outcome in doubt.

Once these negotiations were back on track, Joseph put pressure on Mary: 'the time has come at last when I think I ought to pray you to end all uncertainty,' he wrote. 'My work here is rapidly drawing to a close & my public duty will constrain me to return to England as soon as it is completed.'[52] Offering her his love, he promised protection of her happiness, support in fulfilling her own highest aspirations, and a share in 'both the trials & the triumphs of a life full of active—& not unworthy interests'. He argued with her that she really cared for him: 'the strength of my love for you has not left you quite unmoved'.

> Now, therefore, decide. If you are not afraid & will trust me with your happiness, believe me, I will know how to guard it against all the world.

For all the assurance of his words, Joseph was apprehensive about the decision Mary would reach. They had arranged to meet at her home the next afternoon; but he left her free to cancel the engagement or, if they met, to say nothing for the moment about his letter.

It 'came up to my room on the tray with my breakfast', Mary recalled. She had already made up her mind to accept him eventually. When she read the letter, the final shreds of resistance vanished. Still she waited until their meeting was drawing to a close before telling him that 'my Conqueror had won the victory'.[53] Chamberlain left her house 'dazed and in a dream ... like a man recovering from a great illness— all the pain & suffering are forgotten & there is only the promise of a new life'. He dined that night at the home of Cabot Lodge, the Republican senator from Massachusetts who later conspired to defeat his treaty. For the moment, 'all the women were beautiful—all the men were witty—and I was in the seventh heaven because I had all the while a vision of "a little bit of old English" looking through a doorway with her lips parted in pleasant expectation'.[54]

His happiness was quickly overcast by the reaction of Mary's family to the engagement. Her brother William, proud of the family pedigree, squirmed at the thought of alliance with someone who made much of his background in metal manufacturing. Secretary Endicott recoiled at the prospect for deeper reasons, rooted in his early loss of the mother after whom he had named his daughter. He covered his personal aversion by dwelling on political risks. Announcement of the engagement between the daughter of the American Secretary of the Army and the British Chief Commissioner when a treaty was being concluded between their countries might jeopardize not only the treaty but perhaps also the reelection of President Cleveland, in view of the likely Irish American reaction. Endicott insisted on delaying the announcement to avoid this risk. But it was the engagement itself that upset him. He wanted Joseph and Mary to see little of each other before Joseph returned to England, and not to write to each other until the presidential election was over. Mary and Joseph successfully resisted these restrictions. They accepted some delay in the publication of their engagement, though they hoped it would be announced before November.

Four days after Mary accepted Joseph's proposal of marriage, Bayard and he concluded their treaty. It provided for full commercial facilities to American fishermen in Canada as soon as Canadian fish were admitted free of tariff to the United States. Republican friends whom Chamberlain had cultivated in the Senate assured him that, to avoid hasty rejection there, they would at least delay a vote till after the presidential election. Meanwhile the treaty was accompanied by an administrative protocol which did not require Senate approval. For two years, long enough to allow for ratification of the treaty after the presidential election, the protocol established a system of licences which compensated the Canadians for the United States tariff and allowed American fishermen to obtain the Canadian port facilities they needed. The protocol thus disposed of the immediate problems which vexed relations between the two countries, while the treaty offered an enduring solution.

Assured of Mary's love regardless of her family's reservations, Chamberlain exploded with pleasure. 'This is really a tremendous triumph,' he crowed, 'for the difficulties in the way were enormous.... A lady Palmist here says that my line of luck is the most extraordinary that she has ever seen & I begin to believe it. Hurrah! Hurrah! Hurrah! Hurrah!'[55] After a final flurry of dinner parties, quiet mornings with Mary, and forthright speeches in defence of the treaty and Anglo-American understanding, he sailed home.

Buoyant return to the Old World

'With "my feet on my native heath",' he reported to Mary once he reached England, 'the old Adam is reviving & the fighting spirit is coming out.'[56] Chamberlain's achievement in the United States earned him an admiring reception at home. Whether or not the Senate ratified the treaty, it was more than malignant observers in England had expected him to accomplish, and there was a touch of brilliance to the protocol. Chamberlain used his success to reward his friends and discomfit his foes. But he brought back more than the means to settle old scores. He returned with restored energy and fresh vision. His fifty-second year of life saw him through a climactic change. When it began, in the summer of 1887, he 'was much harder—striving to steel myself & to play the game of life till ... the cards [fell] from my hands, & caring little how soon that time comes. Now,' he reported to Mary on his next birthday, 'all this artificial insensibility is broken down. My youth has come back to me & I am as eager & as sensitive as ever I was.'[57]

From now on, his imagination in public affairs worked on three levels: the local, the national and the imperial. He had not been home a month before he distinguished himself on all three.

The reception he met in Birmingham was extremely mixed. On the one hand, to honour their most famous fellow citizen now decked with laurels in international diplomacy, the council of the town chose Chamberlain to be its first honorary freeman. On the other hand, just before his return the Gladstonians in the Birmingham Liberal Association captured nearly all of its divisional organizations, including the one for Chamberlain's own constituency. Personalizing the defection, William Harris, the creator of the old organization, joined Schnadhorst in the Gladstonian camp. Chamberlain had to begin again. Bereft of his most experienced organizers, he had to find and train replacements. In doing so, he showed that he had only increased his talent for this work. The men he chose were to serve him for the rest of their lives, and they proved even more successful than their predecessors. Quite a few of the new cadre came from the Chamberlain and Kenrick families, but not its leaders. Powell Williams, the MP for Birmingham South, took the chair of the new Birmingham Liberal Unionist Association's executive committee, and became henceforth Chamberlain's organizational chief of staff. Charles Vince, the chairman of Chamberlain's constituency association under Liberal auspices, was induced to resign and take up the same position under Liberal Unionist auspices, a pattern that was duplicated by C.E. Mathews in the Edgbaston division.

The task of organizing and hence solidifying the division among the Liberals in Birmingham was sometimes disheartening. Some of the great warhorses of the past, preeminently R.W. Dale, lapsed into neutrality. But others deepened their commitment to Chamberlain's cause. Bunce, editor of the *Birmingham Daily Post*, had detached himself to some extent from Chamberlain over Home Rule. Yet he shared Chamberlain's imperial instincts. As these gained in prominence, Bunce pledged to support him 'through thick & thin in all Imperial matters'.[58]

'My new organisation is going like wild fire,' Joseph reported to Mary; 'I will give my opponents a taste of my quality & teach them not to tread on my tail again.'[59] But before he was fully prepared, he was threatened with embarrassment. A vacancy occurred unexpectedly in the town council, and the Conservatives put up a candidate to stand against the Gladstonian nominee. As a result, the first electoral task of the new Liberal Unionist organization was to persuade its adherents to vote for a Tory. Chamberlain thought the risks high, the Conservative candidate bad, and defeat likely. In the event, however, the Unionist alliance won with a substantial majority; and Chamberlain crowed that 'we have knocked the enemy into a cocked hat'.[60]

He reported his doings to Mary in detail. Night after night before going to bed, and often again during the day, in letters running to as many as forty sides, he told of his doings, poured out his love, and taught his future wife about his world and ways of thought. Recalling the corruption of Tammany Hall under its Irish masters, he wondered how Mary, a fastidious Brahmin, would react to his management of the politics of Birmingham. 'You will think me a "Boss", but at least I make no money by it & have no patronage to bestow. Don't despise me too much my darling I could not bear that from you.'[61]

He gave the news of his engagement to his children, brothers and sisters one by one, but beyond that circle he told only Jesse Collings. The news took all of them by surprise, but they welcomed it because of Chamberlain's evident happiness. Mary was apprehensive about the reaction of Joseph's eldest children, for they were slightly older than her, Beatrice by two years, Austen by one; and she would inevitably displace Beatrice as chatelaine of the household. But Austen foresaw the happiness that his father's marriage would bring home; and Beatrice prepared to resign her responsibilities to Mary with some relief.

Mary's love for her distant partner was confirmed by their correspondence. As strong in written as in spoken word, Joseph's assertions of his love left Mary 'in a positive state of excitement over it all, so that my face is burning & my hands frigid'.[62] Their separation was fated to be far longer than they anticipated. They had hoped that, once Joseph left the United States, the impact of their engagement on the American political scene would become insignificant. Chamberlain hoped for a springtime announcement and a midsummer marriage. But Secretary Endicott procrastinated about seeking the judgement of his colleagues on the political risk until it was clear that something deeper bothered him. Mrs Endicott, though herself sympathetic to the marriage, told Mary not to press her father: 'he thinks he has a right to demand time, & even if the President is favourable I don't know that it will make any difference'. This advice left Mary 'absolutely unstrung'.[63] A few nights later she dreamt that she saw Joseph 'drive up to the door, & [I] was so happy in the thought that in another moment I should be in your arms,—when you leaned forward, gave the coachman an order, &— drove away'.

What infuriated Chamberlain was the deception into which Secretary Endicott pushed Mary and him in order to keep their engagement secret. Rumours of the engagement surfaced in the newspapers of both countries. To fend off congratulations offered to him by his political associates and even by the Prince of Wales, Chamberlain had to resort to evasion and, when that did not work, to outright lies. The humiliation he felt at this enforced behaviour manifested itself in the familiar form of headache, 'cold & neuralgia. Their real name', his daughter told Mary, 'is worry. If you could fix a date ... I would undertake that their cure should be rapid.'[64]

In their endless hours of letter-writing, Mary and Joseph learned more about each other and probed each other's convictions. In the process, Joseph confirmed Mary's willingness to subject herself to him, particularly with regard to the business of politics. Mary gave him the obedience Beatrice Potter had denied, while Joseph gave Mary the love Beatrice Potter had desired. Mary needed no prompting to make her submission. Disclaiming any wish to vote, she offered Joseph her belief that 'a woman can use more good influence behind the scenes in her home than in jostling about in the world of men'.[65] Simultaneously from the other side of the ocean Joseph asserted his 'faith in the instinct of a true woman. Details of policy & modes of action are for men to settle, but the principles that underlie our work are sometimes clearer to the pure in heart than to the well worn consciences of politicians & men of the world.'[66] Though he foresaw no need to exercise the right, he insisted that in their forthcoming marriage ceremony Mary promise 'to love honour & *obey* me' as 'a pretty & simple expression of the natural relation of the woman to him who ought to be her guide & counsellor'.[67] The 'true woman' would 'cling to the stronger & coarser nature, & irresistibly appeal in so doing to all that is chivalrous & manly'.[68] Encouraged by Mary's denial of the right of women to vote, Joseph poured out his loathing for 'the odious crew of strong minded women . . . all of them more or less unsexed'. He scarcely needed to tell Mary later that he considered the book by John Stuart Mill on the subjection of women to be 'stupid. . . . Is it such a bad thing, my darling, this subjection—this sense of surrender to me whom you are ready to trust with your happiness?'[69]

More was confirmed during Chamberlain's first weeks back in England than the bond between him and his fiancée. He returned in time to witness the first satisfactory demonstration that Lord Salisbury's government was willing 'to deal with great practical questions of legislation which are earnestly desired by the majority of the people'.[70] Separated from each other by the Atlantic ocean, Chamberlain had not attempted to negotiate the terms of the prospective bill with Salisbury, nor had Salisbury consulted him about it. But Chamberlain left no doubt about the principle that would guide his action: 'May I express my earnest hope', he wrote to Salisbury, 'that the English Local Govt. Bill will practically establish in Counties the same institutions which have worked so well in the Towns?'[71] Salisbury did not ·need the reminder. On the very day that Chamberlain wrote to him, Salisbury warned Conservatives that, as a result of the Unionist alliance, 'the colour of the convictions of the Unionist Liberals' would have to join with 'the colour of the convictions of the Conservative party in determining the hue of the measures that are presented to Parliament'.[72]

The government accepted the principle Chamberlain had enunciated to Salisbury, but interpreted it narrowly. The Local Government bill 'adopted the Borough constitution & mode of election for the County Council'.[73] But it stuck to Chamberlain's principle even where he wished to go beyond it, particularly in loading the new county councils, like the existing borough councils, with aldermen not popularly elected themselves but chosen by the elected councillors. And the bill fell short of Chamberlain's principle in refusing to give county councils the power that borough councils enjoyed over the local police.

Weighing its pluses and minuses, Chamberlain accepted the bill as 'a good measure, thoroughly liberal in its main provisions & based very much on my lines'.[74] He used it to demonstrate the constructive nature of Unionist government and his own distinctive contribution to it. He exchanged promises with the Conservative minister in charge of the bill, C.T. Ritchie, to support its provisions against critics within their respective parties. If concessions had to be made to the parliamentary opposition, Ritchie undertook to make them in response to interventions from Chamberlain rather than to Gladstonian demand. In the House of Commons Chamberlain upheld the central principle of the bill while pointing out where he wished that it could have been extended. On the matter of control over the police he avowed his intention of voting if need be against the government to give county councils this power, confident that his action would not jeopardize either the bill or the government. Whether he deserved it or not, there was a widespread tendency to credit him for the bill's progressive features. In return he felt able to tell his constituents that 'the alliance with the Conservatives is stronger, firmer, and more permanent in its character than it ever has been before'.[75]

Towards the end of May the bill ran into trouble over its liquor licensing clauses. Though designed to reduce the number of outlets for the sale of alcoholic beverages, these clauses offended the temperance lobby by promising financial compensation to the holders of cancelled licences. Reaction mounted among Conservative MPs for suburban constituencies but was stronger among Liberals; and it found its most insistent leader in W.S. Caine, Chamberlain's own parliamentary whip. Chamberlain defended the clauses firmly. They were consonant with proposals he had made since the mid-seventies to reduce the problem of drunkenness. Hating, furthermore, to withdraw anything when opposed in Parliament, he urged the government to stick to its guns. But opposition among the electorate was a different matter. Once Chamberlain recognized that hostile pressure that was mounting in the constituencies, he counselled the Conservative leader in the Commons, W.H. Smith, to drop the licensing clauses[76]—which Smith did.

Meanwhile Chamberlain had to take care that Conservatives did not use their legislative accomplishments to enhance their interests at his expense. The most sensitive subject of potential conflict between them was elementary education. The Conservative commitment to the Church of England and its schools conflicted with Chamberlain's continuing commitment to the principles of the National Education League. He also needed to preserve his credentials as a Nonconformist in order to maintain his credit in Birmingham with the likes of R.W. Dale. Furthermore, Chamberlain and Dale were among the few Liberal Unionists capable of persuading a significant portion of Nonconformity to support Unionism or at least to recoil from Gladstone's alliance with the Catholic Irish. Worried by the appointment of a royal commission on education, Chamberlain publicly explored the possibilities for reconciliation between the concerns of the Conservatives and his own.[77] Anxious as ever to make elementary schooling free, he suggested a plan whereby the government would replace on an equal basis the income that denominational and civic schools derived from fees. The government showed no interest in the suggestion, and it worried Dale. Still, Dale welcomed the rest of the speech enthusiastically, so much so that next month he resigned from the Birmingham Liberal Association. Chamberlain rewarded him by prevailing upon the government at Dale's request to drop a Technical Instruction bill offensive to Nonconformists.

While cautioning as well as encouraging Conservative enterprise in domestic politics, Chamberlain tried out his imperial wings. The first invitation to do so came from a South African source. John Mackenzie, the missionary who wanted to place Bechuanaland under imperial control, came to confer with him. Chamberlain had learned during Gladstone's ministry to appreciate the significance of Bechuanaland as a link between the Cape Colony and the resources to the north in what became Rhodesia. In 1886, while Britain was preoccupied with the Irish question, Britain's economic interest in southern Africa was heightened while its political grip was weakened by the discovery of gold in the autonomous Boer republic of the Transvaal. Mackenzie's visit revived Chamberlain's interest in the region and quickened his desire eventually 'to be Colonial Minister'.[78]

Though he hesitated to commit himself to Mackenzie, Chamberlain devoted his first major address in London to the colonies. He struck many of the chords that distinguished his new imperialism. He rejoiced in 'the ties between the different branches of the Anglo-Saxon race which form the British Empire'. He spoke hopefully about interesting the colonies in 'a concerted system of defence'. Maintaining that 'trade follows the flag', he stressed that 'a great part of our population is dependent . . . upon the interchange of commodities with our colonial fellow-subjects'.[79] Even so, because of the colonies' reliance for revenue and protection on tariffs and the contrary reliance of the mother country on free trade, he saw little prospect for commercial union. A few days later, persuaded by his own rhetoric and the persistence of Mackenzie, he accepted an invitation to speak at Mackenzie's side to the London Chamber of Commerce.

Before doing so, he connected his rising imperialism with his opposition to Home Rule. He told his constituents that the great reward from the fight over Ireland lay in the evidence it produced 'that the great majority of the British nation are proud of ... the glorious and united Empire'.[80] For him personally, opposing Home Rule had been a regrettable necessity. It was necessary to maintain the integrity of the United Kingdom as well as his political respect vis-à-vis Gladstone. But opposing Home Rule was none the less regrettable because it was a negative policy of little intrinsic socio-political value. It pushed him away from his search till 1886 for domestic reform to secure Britain's social economy. Connected, however, to his recent assignment in North America, the task of opposing Home Rule opened Chamberlain's eyes to an alternative route of socio-economic advance: the march of empire.

So much fell into place on this alternative route. His Kenrick brothers-in-law had long been aware of the importance of the colonial market for their hollow-ware business. Competition from the United States and Germany made Britain more reliant on colonial markets interested in the less sophisticated products of British industry and familiar with British sources of supply. The economic potentialities of the empire also offset the waning faith in free trade, in which Chamberlain continued to believe. Some precarious industries in Birmingham had espoused 'fair trade' and as a result been tempted to switch their political allegiance to the Conservatives. Chamberlain reduced that threat by championing the empire. He thus strengthened his relationship with Birmingham, now more important to him than ever. Outside Birmingham, industrialists embraced him more warmly as a Unionist than they had ever done in his days as an undiluted Radical. But they liked him as much for his destructive opposition to Home Rule as for his constructive vision of the potentialities of the empire.

At the beginning of May, Chamberlain set himself 'to work on South African Policy'.[81] In the midst of his reading, he attended a small dinner party of men interested in the region: the historian J.A. Froude, the Chief Justice of the Cape Colony Sir Henry de Villiers, and Lord Derby, Colonial Secretary in Gladstone's second ministry and now a Liberal Unionist. All three opposed the drift of Chamberlain's thought. Froude and de Villiers wanted Britain to handle southern Africa more in accordance with the wishes of the Cape Colony than of London. Derby still advocated what Chamberlain called the 'shirking' policy of reducing Britain's imperial responsibilities to a minimum. Chamberlain found the argument bracing but also recognized the need to tread carefully.

The speech he delivered to the London Chamber of Commerce in mid-May was a worthy sequel to his speech in Toronto at the turn of the year. As with Canada, so now with South Africa, the complexity of the situation brought out Chamberlain's capacity for constructive policy. In extending this talent from the domestic sphere to the imperial, he also demonstrated his ability to do without Dilke. In effect Chamberlain turned 'the party of two', which had tried but failed to set the pace of Liberal politics earlier in the 1880s, into a still more formidable party of one, which would succeed in setting the pace in Unionist politics for the rest of the century.

He sought to impress the London Chamber of Commerce with the need for, dangers to, and dividends from Britain's imperium. The feeling that Britain, in Matthew Arnold's words, was a 'weary Titan [staggering] under the too vast orb of his fate'[82] had led many Englishmen, Chamberlain among them, to favour minimizing Britain's imperial responsibilities in the late 1870s. But the experience of the early 1880s suggested that such a policy only increased the risk of hostile exploitation of Britain's seeming weakness. Chamberlain therefore called for frank acceptance of 'our obligations and responsibilities'. He insisted at the same time that the primary benefits of this undertaking should accrue to the imperial power rather than to its colonial dependencies. Bechuanaland, for example, should be placed under direct imperial control rather than annexed to the Cape Colony.

The renewed energy which Chamberlain found in North America extended to the gnarled subject of Ireland. After his return from Washington, he advocated state-funded public works to relieve the most depressed parts of Ireland. The innovative substance of his proposals was less remarkable than his development as an advocate. As a Liberal in national politics Chamberlain had presented proposals often confrontationally in public before he met with his colleagues in council. Cautious now in his alliance with Conservatives, he mastered the arts of persuasion. He began privately with Arthur Balfour as Chief Secretary for Ireland. Balfour responded sympathetically to the principle of Chamberlain's policy for public works and indicated that he might act on Chamberlain's ideas for Irish land in the coming year. This evidence of 'power without office—much greater than any power that I could exercise in office at present'[83] gratified Chamberlain greatly. Only after these private conversations did Chamberlain go public with his proposals. Even then he presented them indirectly, through the *Birmingham Daily Post*. He worked his ideas out in consultation with Bunce as editor, an approach which had the further advantage of turning Bunce into a cordial champion of Chamberlain's brand of Unionism. Once Bunce had outlined the plan in the *Daily Post*, Chamberlain presented it to the Liberal Unionist Association of Birmingham.

He did not minimize the Radicalism of the public works part of his proposals. Unionist prejudice, however, against anything redolent of Home Rule induced him to make his suggestions on local government for Ireland vague or guarded. He played down the idea of an all-Irish council on which he had once placed his hopes. Yet even here caution did not quite destroy his imagination. Pursuing the notion of provincial powers for Scotland and Wales as well as Ireland, he described this possibility to Bunce as 'a step in the direction of a general Federation of the Empire'.[84]

These initiatives did not turn the tide of public opinion, which had flowed away from the government over the past year, or reverse the tide among Liberals back to Gladstone. Chamberlain foresaw a 'long & rough' journey.[85] Yet his hopes of eventual success were buoyed up by requests he received each week from people of all sorts—pearl fishers in Australia, free churchmen in Scotland, Chambers of Commerce in England—to intercede with the government on their behalf.

His association with the Conservatives acquired a social dimension. Upon his return from Washington he was welcomed into the town and country houses of the Tory as well as Whig aristocracy, as Gladstonians noted mockingly. For the Ascot races that June he was invited, along with the French Radical Clemenceau, to the nearby home of the Irish Earl Dunraven. Chamberlain enjoyed the company. Yet he looked at and behaved in it as an outsider. He was fascinated by the well-born guests, men like Hartington and Churchill who, 'while able to enjoy the light talk and badinage of this gay society are also at bottom serious politicians'.[86] Chamberlain always talked politics. His cavalier companions knew he was not one of them. They could also see the difference. Dunraven was astonished to see Chamberlain play lawn tennis 'in a closely buttoned black frock coat and top hat'.[87]

He was evidently out of spirits during the festivities, depression the other guests put down to a Unionist by-election loss. But it was the postponement of his marriage which wore him down. Mary's father did not discuss the announcement of the engagement with President Cleveland until 2 July. Cleveland then decided that, since the treaty Chamberlain had negotiated was before Congress, and in view of the Irish vote at large, it would be wiser to wait till the elections were over in November before announcing the engagement. 'What cowards they are!' Chamberlain exploded; 'I despise them from the bottom of my soul.'[88] The endless delay added to his hatred of the Irish—'all liars'[89]—whom he blamed for his misfortune.

Setbacks and successes

The Home Rule controversy turned British political conflict into a cold form of civil war; and Chamberlain was the foremost cold warrior. The war was most intense in the party it divided, between Liberal and Liberal, above all between Radical Liberals and the man they had expected to lead them. The bitterness of the Radical attacks on Chamberlain testified to the severity of their loss and the magnitude of the influence that he transferred to the other side.

Every word that Chamberlain uttered sharpened the conflict. It was in 1888 that the seasoned parliamentary correspondent Henry Lucy reported, 'Chamberlain is the best debater in the House, not excepting Mr. Gladstone.' What most impressed observers was Chamberlain's quickness in debate. Gladstone could be led astray by hostile interjections. Chamberlain returned them with 'deft parrying of his rapier, swiftly followed up by telling thrust at the aggressor'.[90] The accomplishment would have been noteworthy in anyone; it was particularly remarkable in a man brought up in accountancy and business. The awkward plodder of the Edgbaston Debating Society was outstripping the best Oxford and Cambridge could produce. Yet there was something alien and alienating about his conduct in the Commons, perhaps more familiar in industrial competition than hitherto in parliamentary debate. Chamberlain used words in debate to destroy the opposition rather than to persuade the doubtful.

The knife with which he divided the world of British politics was not clean. Angry at Parnell's desertion of him in 1885 and at Gladstone's decision in 1886 to conciliate Parnell rather than himself, Chamberlain pursued every opportunity to discredit the Irish leader. Parnell was vulnerable to attack, most obviously for complicity with the violence which had scarred Ireland since 1880. In order to keep the Nationalist effort united, Parnell had needed at least indirect association with the campaign of physical intimidation which paralleled his own political campaign. Not even the closest of his new-found English admirers were entirely sure that he had kept his ambiguous relations with Irish terrorism inside the confines of the law. His enemies searched for clear evidence of transgression; and Chamberlain encouraged these efforts. They were rewarded in the spring of 1887 with the publication in *The Times* of letters apparently in Parnell's hand indicating that he had condoned murder. It was assumed that, if innocent, Parnell would take *The Times* to court over its charges. But he accepted the advice of nervous English allies not to trust himself to a British jury. A year later, however, after an independent judicial action implied that he was guilty of the charges made by *The Times*, he felt obliged to ask for a parliamentary commission to investigate and dispose of the accusation.

Chamberlain rubbed his hands at the prospect. Though never confident that the main charge of condoning murder would prove valid, he was sure Parnell was 'so mixed up with the conspiracy'[91] that an inquiry would discredit him. Hence, when the government contemplated rejecting Parnell's request, Chamberlain urged them to change their mind. Instead of a parliamentary commission as Parnell requested, the government agreed to appoint a judicial commission with a broad mandate of inquiry. Goading Parnell to take what the government offered, Chamberlain spoke in the Commons of his 'apparent reluctance to face a full enquiry'.[92]

Parnell and Chamberlain faced each other across the chamber: two erstwhile allies, neither quite trusted by the Liberal elite, both masterful organizers of outside forces, both cool in debate, now each other's deadliest enemy. Though Parnell agreed to the inquisition which the government imposed upon him, he returned Chamberlain's attack. Just before midnight at the end of July, he riveted the attention of the House of Commons by accusing Chamberlain, when a member of Gladstone's cabinet, of betraying his colleagues in secret dealings with the Irish leaders. Undeflected by the automatic midnight adjournment, Parnell calmly resumed and concluded his attack the next day.

At first Chamberlain thought of ignoring the attack as beneath contempt. Persuaded by Hartington that this would not do, Chamberlain counterattacked. Turning to look straight at Parnell, he told the story, as he remembered it, of the agreement which the two of them had come close to concluding in January 1885 on an elected central board for Ireland. The Irish leader 'flinched & turned pale', or so Chamberlain thought; 'His followers even began to murmur against him & one of them asked "Why did he engage in these communications without consent or knowledge of his party?"'[93] If Parnell had been willing to settle for something short of a national parliament for Ireland, then Gladstone's subsequent offer of Home Rule was excessive. But Parnell took issue with Chamberlain's version of the story. Chamberlain reacted rashly. 'I have the proof,' he cried, '. . . in letters which are wholly in his handwriting.'[94]

The creation of a judicial tribunal to examine the charges against Parnell prompted several political leaders including Gladstone to reexamine the record of their dealings with the Irish. None of the leaders emerged unscathed from the exercise. But it did Chamberlain more harm than anyone else because he proceeded with the same weakness of judgement which had vexed all his dealings with Parnell. Chamberlain continued to rely in his assessment of Parnell on Captain O'Shea, regardless of repeated evidence of O'Shea's indiscretion. Chamberlain wanted to believe what O'Shea told him about Parnell, whether as a prospective partner earlier in the 1880s or now as a criminal conspirator.

After the confrontation with Parnell in the Commons, Chamberlain and O'Shea prepared their next step. O'Shea wrote a letter to *The Times* which reinforced Chamberlain's interpretation of the central board negotiations. O'Shea also insisted that towards the end of 1884 Chamberlain had received a copy of the Coercion Act of 1882 altered by Parnell's 'own hand into the form in which he proposed that it should be passed'.[95] This revelation, Chamberlain exulted, 'ought to complete Parnell's discomfiture'.[96] Parnell called upon Chamberlain to publish the handwritten proofs he claimed to possess, and Chamberlain instantly agreed to do so.

Only then did he scrutinize his pertinent letters and papers. They did not bear out his claim that Parnell had advanced the central board plan as a substitute for an Irish parliament. The only two letters wholly in Parnell's handwriting were to O'Shea rather than to Chamberlain, who had not seen them till long after they were written. They proved that Parnell had told O'Shea that a board would *not* substitute for a parliament. The letters substantiated lesser but still useful points, in particular that Parnell had suggested a central board as at least a short-term response to the constitutional agitation of Ireland. However, the letters also underscored the place of O'Shea, first as intermediary and now as Chamberlain's chief witness against Parnell. When O'Shea examined his own papers, he found that they discredited him. He came upon a copy of a letter he had sent to Parnell early in 1885 reporting on Chamberlain's response to the central board idea. Shown a copy of the report at the time, Chamberlain had repudiated it—but then forgot about it. Now he realized that O'Shea's letter, the original of which Parnell surely possessed, would portray Chamberlain as a self-interested manipulator. At last but too late, Chamberlain questioned O'Shea's reliability: 'if he misrepresented me, may he not have misrepresented Parnell?'[97]

But to repudiate O'Shea would discredit Chamberlain's earlier judgement. Under these circumstances all Chamberlain could do was minimize the confrontation. After a week of delay while the political world waited, Chamberlain wrote to *The Times* to express 'difficulty in ascertaining what [was] now the issue' between Parnell and himself.[98] Referring only obliquely to letters from Parnell, Chamberlain admitted that they 'corroborate[d] Mr. Parnell's statement that he did not put forward [the central board] proposal as a substitute for an Irish Parliament'. Content to have reduced Chamberlain to such meekness, Parnell dropped the controversy.

The episode left Chamberlain remarkably perky. In its wake he accentuated his Liberal Unionism. The articles in the *Birmingham Daily Post* on Irish policy which Bunce and he had issued since May came out in book form in September with a preface by Chamberlain emphasizing the progressive character of the proposals. At the same time he committed himself unreservedly to Unionism. 'I will not raise a finger to destroy this Government,' he declared at Bedford, 'so long as I know that the Government which would take its place is pledged to . . . a policy . . . which . . . would be fatal to the best interests of the country.'[99]

He proceeded to woo the Conservatives of Birmingham with an eye to the local elections in November. Gladstonian and Unionist Liberals would fight each other for the first time all across the town. Though Liberal Unionists thought that they constituted the largest of the three parties in Birmingham, they needed a formal alliance with the Conservatives to guarantee success. Liberal Unionists kept out of the school board elections, where the contest between Conservative church and Nonconformist chapel was always strong. They concentrated on the town council elections, all the more important because Gladstone was to visit Birmingham five days after the municipal voting. Unionist candidates, mainly Liberal Unionists but including a few Conservatives, were put up for each of the sixteen available seats. To foster a cooperative spirit, Chamberlain invited the leading Conservatives of Birmingham to dine with him at Highbury. So distant were relations between Liberal and Conservative in Birmingham that he scarcely knew his guests. 'Well!' he mused, 'the whirligig of time does bring about its revenge.'[100] To dazzle them, he provided a sumptuous meal with all his silver plate carried by servants in livery round a table covered in blue silk crossed like the Union Jack with red and white begonias. Drawing aside Sir James Sawyer, the most prickly of his guests, Chamberlain virtually offered Sawyer's patron, Randolph Churchill, the parliamentary seat of Central Birmingham where a vacancy was expected as soon as old John Bright, now terminally ill, should die. Chamberlain followed the municipal contest closely. He took pains to prevent a stoppage of government orders to the small-arms industry of Birmingham, and he made sure that the credit for his action extended to the Unionist candidates for the town council. In the event, they won all but two seats, a triumph but never enough to satisfy Chamberlain, who disliked anything less than total victory.

As soon as the votes were counted, he sailed away to claim his bride. He wanted the news of his engagement to be published on 5 November to divert attention from Gladstone's address in Birmingham that night. But the Endicotts insisted on holding the news back till the 7th, the day after the presidential election in the United States—when Cleveland was narrowly beaten. The behaviour of American politicians since his engagement to Mary had deepened his disrespect for them. In addition to delaying his marriage, they rejected his treaty on a straight party vote in the Senate. Fortunately the *modus vivendi* of a licensing system remained in force.

Crossing the Atlantic, Chamberlain learned from detectives employed by the Parnellites that the letters in *The Times* purporting to prove Parnell's approval of murder were the work of a forger named Pigott. Chamberlain was neither convinced nor for the moment much interested. Upon reaching New York, he headed straight for Washington where the marriage promptly took place. The service in St John's, the most fashionable Episcopal church in the capital, was short but stately. President Cleveland, justices of the Supreme Court, and members of the cabinet occupied one side of the church. Afterwards the President proposed the toast to the bride.

The official news of Chamberlain's engagement came to Beatrice Potter as a blow. She spent the eve of his marriage in Westminster Abbey 'listening half-dazed to the solemnly intoned prayers'.[101] Sleepless that night, she pondered the impact the marriage would have on the man she still loved. 'He must become a Tory,' Beatrice Potter told her diary. His shift in this direction would be fostered by his bride:

> [B]y her sympathy with his injured feelings against his old party she will intensify the breach; by her attraction to the 'good society' she will draw him closer to the aristocratic party. She is . . . an American aristocrat.

By 5 p.m. next day Beatrice Potter calculated that the wedding must be over. She spent the following week in 'utter nervous collapse'.

The bride and groom spent the week in the Virginia countryside before heading to the Italian Riviera by way of New York and Paris. Giving a false date for the end of their journey, they contrived to arrive quietly in Highbury on Christmas Eve. The people of Birmingham were delighted with the romantic conquest by the man they all referred to possessively as 'Joe'. Early in the new year, the walls of the town hall were covered with oriental curtains and mirrors, the floor with rugs. There, to the strains of 'Hail, Columbia' and 'Yankee Doodle', Birmingham welcomed the groom and his bride. Mary was showered with the jewellery for which the craftsmen of her husband's constituency were famous, gold bracelets, brooch and collar just like those given to the Princess of Wales when Joe was mayor.

A power of his own

Over the past year, Chamberlain had assembled a political force capable of ensuring his survival and placing his impress on Unionism. He had not created a new party of the centre; he abandoned that hope in the autumn of 1887. Thereafter he lined himself up ever more firmly with Unionism. Its big battalions came from Salisbury's Conservatives and Hartington's Whigs. The followers Chamberlain could fully rely upon in the House of Commons did not exceed ten in number. His power rested on a provincial base, an unfamiliar phenomenon in English politics. Otherwise his influence was a contrivance of policies advanced by the ablest debater and publicist of the era.

His policy for Ireland consisted basically of opposition to Home Rule, praise for Balfour's maintenance of law and order, and advocacy of tenant land purchase and public works to remove the economic roots of Irish discontent. Though Chamberlain did not expect much Irish legislation in 1889, he kept his economic agenda before the eye of the government and the public. There were deepening conservative touches to his talk about Ireland. He accused the Nationalists of willingness to confiscate private property. He dismissed Ireland's past as a 'history of the petty squabbles of a number of hostile tribes, who were only pacified by the British settlement', and disputed the Irish 'claim to be called a nation'.[102] He also brought out the connection between his opposition to Home Rule and his burgeoning imperialism.

The appeal to imperial sentiment diluted but did not destroy Chamberlain's earlier preoccupation with domestic reform. Indeed he paid more attention at the beginning of 1889 to domestic than to imperial needs. In doing so, he set the legislative agenda as much for English as he had already for Irish matters. His English agenda consisted of free education and steps to foster the reemergence of a peasant proprietary as was already occurring in Ireland. He added a cautiously balanced set of measures to help the crofters of Scotland. He pressed this agenda on the government in private and used his speeches to build up public support. To allay the fears of his allies, he asserted that '[t]he greatest Conservative forces in the world are education and the possession of property'.[103] Conservatives were afraid of the governmental cost of free education and the threat it posed to church schools dependent on fees. Chamberlain pointed how costly fees were to collect, and he insisted that a scheme for free education could be devised which left the current proportion of denominational to civic schools undisturbed, though what the scheme would be he did not specify.

A new bond between Chamberlain and his constituents was forged in 1889 with the establishment of the Birmingham Jewellers' and Silversmiths' Association. Though this trade had not flourished in Birmingham until the middle of the nineteenth century, it now claimed to be the most important industry of the town. It was certainly so in Chamberlain's constituency. He embraced the association because its members were among 'the very *élite* of the working classes of Birmingham';[104] and the association embraced him with reciprocal warmth. This relationship reflected a shift of the socio-political affiliations in Birmingham. Trade union leaders such as W.J. Davis with whom Chamberlain had been allied defected to the Gladstonian side. That loss of support was offset by the favour Chamberlain found among the class of small masters who had opposed the municipal socialism of his mayoralty, a class well represented now in the Jewellers' and Silversmiths' Association. Still, this shift in affiliation did not constitute a clear break or sharp change. Chamberlain's municipal policies enjoyed continuing support from the jewellers and silversmiths. One of the first proposals of their association, in true Chamberlain fashion, was to promote art education and technical instruction for the benefit of the industry. Skilled craftsmen catering to an affluent market, the jewellers were men of independent mind, sometimes Radical in spirit but always appreciative of material glory and averse to social upheaval. The social solidarity of Unionism in Birmingham was reinforced by a network of institutions such as the local volunteer and territorial armed forces whose activity Chamberlain encouraged. So effective was this network that Conservative alternatives like the Primrose League made little headway in the city and its environs.

The Conservatives of Birmingham had, nevertheless, a substantial and loyal following. Chamberlain needed their support to sustain his local dominance. Yet he wanted the credit of victory locally to accrue entirely to his Liberal Unionists. He could leaven the Tory and Whig lump of Unionism in Parliament and the country only if he could completely control the representation of Birmingham. Otherwise the distinctiveness of his Radical Unionism would be washed out in the electoral amalgam of Unionism nationally, which would then probably bear the impress of the somnolent features of Hartington. Chamberlain's fear coincided fortunately with Lord Salisbury's anxiety about Randolph Churchill and Churchill's still popular brand of Tory Democracy. When Churchill threatened Chamberlain's sovereignty over Birmingham, Salisbury and Chamberlain combined to frustrate him.

Together Churchill and Chamberlain might have turned Unionism in a centrist direction. But after resigning from Salisbury's cabinet, Churchill followed an erratic course, prone to outbursts against ally and enemy alike. Meanwhile Chamberlain's interest in empire brought out differences in policy between the two men, particularly over defence expenditure, which Churchill sought to reduce and Chamberlain to increase. Even so, in the spring of 1888 Chamberlain discussed the prospective parliamentary vacancy for Birmingham Centre with Churchill in an encouraging manner. Churchill was MP for Paddington, a boringly safe metropolitan constituency; he wanted the lift which election for a provincial capital might give him; and he had enjoyed close relations with Central Birmingham since his contest with Bright for the seat in 1885. Curiously indecisive at critical moments, however, he hesitated to accept Chamberlain's virtual offer.

At the time Chamberlain wanted to assure himself of hearty Conservative cooperation in the next set of local elections. Hence the renewal of his offer when he wined and dined the Conservative leaders of the town in October. But the subsequent Unionist triumph in the local elections showed Chamberlain that he could do without reinforcement from a potential rival. Strengthened by Salisbury's anxiety to keep Churchill out, Chamberlain decided to field a Liberal Unionist candidate for the expected parliamentary vacancy, perhaps Albert Bright, son of the dying lion.

Bright's death on 27 March 1889 accelerated Churchill's nervous oscillation. He wanted to be invited to contest Bright's seat by both the Liberal Unionists and the Conservatives of Birmingham as the only person who could save it from the Gladstonians. These were terms Chamberlain could not possibly accept. Taking advantage of an unpopular attack by Churchill on government proposals for naval defence, Chamberlain expressed doubt as to his chances for election in Birmingham; to which Churchill responded that he was not going to leave Paddington. Yet next day he told the Conservatives of Birmingham that he would stand for election there 'if the circumstances were such as to demand it'.[105]

Chamberlain alerted Conservative party headquarters in London, pressing them to 'send for the Birmingham leaders at once'[106] to ensure that Churchill was not invited. The request was unnecessary. The chief organizer of the Conservative party, Captain Middleton, had already been to Birmingham to bring his hounds to heel. Next day came the news that Albert Bright would stand for election as a Liberal Unionist in his father's place. Salisbury wired instructions in support of the Liberal Unionist candidate to Sir James Sawyer, who was to chair the forthcoming meeting of the town's Conservative association. Sawyer, however, suppressed the wire; and the association unanimously asked Churchill to stand. The Birmingham Conservatives were determined to avoid being chained to Chamberlain's chariot. A deputation from the meeting headed immediately for London to present their invitation to Churchill. But to their consternation, he handed the decision as to what he should do over to three men: his one friend among the Conservative leaders, Hicks Beach, plus Hartington and Chamberlain! And when, inevitably, they advised him not to accept the invitation, he turned it down. In doing so, he damaged his reputation among the Conservatives of Birmingham irreparably.

The reaction did not, however, redound to Chamberlain's benefit, because the angry local Conservatives turned on him. They blamed him for swindling them out of the additional parliamentary seat to which their voting strength in the town entitled them. His talk of the under-representation of Liberal Unionism elsewhere in the country cut no ice with them. So strong was their feeling that Captain Middleton advised Chamberlain, who was in London, to stay away from Birmingham until the by-election was over. Powell Williams counselled him not even to write a letter for publication. And Chamberlain did as he was bid.

1889

The results of the by-election rewarded him. Albert Bright won the seat with a majority of more than 3,000 over his Gladstonian opponent, exceeding the Liberal Unionists' fondest hopes. Since the last general election the Liberal Unionists had lost four seats elsewhere in Britain and gained none. Birmingham gave them their first victory; and it was a great one. The results indicated that Tory voters had turned out well for Bright. When coupled with pre-election canvassing surveys, the final voting figures suggested that the Liberal Unionists were the largest of the three parties in the constituency, and hence could win three-cornered contests if necessary.

Gagged during the campaign, Chamberlain exulted once it was over. Vindicating his claims in a letter to the press, he gave his account of the negotiations with Churchill. Justly angered, Churchill counterattacked. Chamberlain responded mildly because he was sure of his ground. He proposed a joint canvass by the local Unionist parties to establish the comparative size of their electoral support and a joint meeting to reestablish the terms of their compact. While Churchill agreed, his disillusioned former supporters would not. But by now they were divided between Chamberlain-haters and Salisbury loyalists willing to defer to the requirements of the Unionist alliance. Strengthened by the latter faction, Chamberlain assured Balfour and Salisbury that he would never 'let Randolph get into Birmingham'.[107]

For some time Chamberlain was stronger nationally than locally, because the Unionists faced probable defeat at the national level, and the best hope of averting it lay with Chamberlain. Apart from a few results, the best of which was in Central Birmingham, the tide of by-elections flowed against the government at an accelerating rate. Blue-blooded leaders like Salisbury and Hartington knew that the fate of the Union rested ultimately with the ordinary British voter, however much they might regret the fact. Was a popular electorate capable of understanding the needs of a strong kingdom and empire? That they did not know. History afforded no proof. Chamberlain, however, was confident; he was more than willing to put his confidence to the test; and he showed promise of succeeding.

Throughout the autumn of 1889, campaigning from the East Midlands to the West country, he presented the Unionist case to large audiences. They were not made up entirely of supporters; and he welcomed the opportunity to argue his case with Gladstonian hecklers. Chamberlain's addresses had two themes. The secondary one was to boast and insist upon the necessity of accomplishments by the government in the sphere of social reform. He contended that the Gladstonian preoccupation with constitutional issues, preeminently Home Rule, was socially stultifying. For Gladstonian Liberals indeed Ireland blocked the way. The government, on the other hand, had built up a legislative record on local government, allotments and, this year, free education for Scotland, which exceeded what Gladstone had accomplished during the equivalent period in his second ministry. Chamberlain used the government's domestic record to reinforce his other, more prominent theme: that the need for Home Rule was being disproven through a combination of firm maintenance of the law and economic amelioration. The Crimes Act subdued disorder in Ireland with surprisingly little severity; there were less than a hundred people in jail under its terms. Meanwhile the Land Act of 1887 made unfair evictions impossible—or so Chamberlain claimed.

The effectiveness of this campaign remained to be proven; but there could be no doubt about the attention it commanded. Apprehensive of the influence Chamberlain was acquiring, Hartington induced him in the spring of 1888 to accept a territorial treaty so far as Liberal Unionist organization was concerned, extending Chamberlain's province to include the three counties around Birmingham—Warwickshire, Worcestershire and Staffordshire—but leaving the rest of the country to the party's Whiggish regulars. Chamberlain acquired a hand in the national organization through the appointment of Powell Williams as its second-in-command. Chamberlain promptly exceeded these limits by encouraging Liberal Unionist constituency associations outside his 'Duchy' to affiliate themselves jointly with Hartington's network and his own. Hartington managed to push him back. The enforced concentration of Chamberlain's organizational energies gave him one important advantage. If the fight for the Union proved more successful within his assigned province than in the country at large, that would demonstrate the worth of his distinctive brand of Unionism.

At this stage the components of his Unionism were indicators of things to come rather than solid accomplishments, words more than deeds. Invariably they encountered resistance from the Whig and Tory mass of Unionists, well reflected by Hartington and Salisbury. This was as true in imperial as in domestic and Irish policy. Though of recent growth, Chamberlain's imperialism was more expansive than Salisbury's and Hartington's by the end of the 1880s. But Salisbury did not lag far behind.

Chamberlain's imperial attention in 1889 focused on Africa, north and south. Proceedings began in London to give a governmental charter to a commercial company which promised to extend British interests northward from the Cape Colony past the western flank of the Transvaal republic. The company was led by Cecil Rhodes. Already the richest man in Africa, owner of almost all its diamonds and much of its gold, Rhodes was also prominent in the political life of the Cape Colony, where he championed the interests of the white colonists, Dutch as well as English. Chamberlain disliked what he knew about Rhodes. Perhaps they were too much alike. Both had built monopoly businesses, though the importance of Rhodes's monopoly and the ruthlessness with which he achieved it exceeded anything Chamberlain did as Screw King. Chamberlain underestimated Rhodes's devotion to British civilization in the same way that critics of Chamberlain saw only crude ambition or materialism. Chamberlain's fear was that Rhodes would warp the empire by aggrandizing colonial interests in southern Africa to the detriment of the mother country. The risk was real. Yet the way in which Rhodes's focus on Cape Town distorted his imperial vision was in some ways comparable with the distortion of Chamberlain's vision created by his devotion to Birmingham.

Initially Chamberlain hoped to frustrate Rhodes's quest for a charter. As head of an influential committee of men in public life concerned about South Africa, Chamberlain pressed the Colonial Secretary, Lord Knutsford, to resist Rhodes's blandishments. What Rhodes offered proved too attractive for the British government to refuse. Yet Rhodes could not get quite what he wanted from the government. In the country north of the Transvaal which came to be known as Rhodesia, Rhodes and the imperial government needed each other, as Chamberlain came to appreciate. Rhodes needed imperial authorization to confirm his title and develop the territory to which he laid claim by virtue of a concession made by a local chief. The imperial government needed effective occupation by Rhodes in order to resist foreign encroachment. Development by Rhodes's South Africa Company would circumvent the block posed by the Transvaal republic to the northward extension of economic enterprise from the Cape, which was of interest to the Cape Dutch as well as to the British. Profits from the South Africa Company could thus perpetuate the rivalry between the Cape Dutch and the Transvaal Boers who, if joined together, could endanger British primacy in the region. Rhodes's company could do all this without cost to the British taxpayer. Chamberlain therefore came to accept the necessity of a charter. He advised an associate on the South Africa committee, Albert Grey, to accept an offer from Rhodes of a place on his company's board of governors, in the hope that Grey would keep an eye on Rhodes. But Rhodes meant the board to be merely decorative.

As for the other end of the African continent, the ambivalence which Chamberlain had earlier felt about Egypt turned into determination that

Britain must stay in firm control. Chamberlain gave himself a long winter holiday in 1889–90, and chose to spend it in Egypt to test this growing conviction. It did not take him long to conclude that Britain must remain there 'for many long years'.[108] British withdrawal from Egypt before it built up a financially sound and militarily self-sufficient government would only draw in the French.

What Chamberlain most admired in the British occupation of Egypt were the restored, extended or newly built public works, particularly the irrigation network which raised the productivity of the Nile basin to the benefit of rich and poor. In the spring of 1886 before Gladstone derailed him over Ireland, Chamberlain had sought to stimulate public works overseas through construction of railways in China; and he preached the same message later to the Sultan of Turkey. Public works, particularly railways, became for Chamberlain what free trade had been for Cobden: a prescription to solve most if not all problems domestic, Irish and foreign. Public works abroad could help Britain at home, if it financed and constructed them, by absorbing unemployed labour, unused industrial capacity and surplus capital.[109] Railway construction was particularly attractive for the metal manufacturers, machine builders and coal exporters of Birmingham and the Black Country. Egypt convinced Chamberlain of the worth of investment in what he later called 'undeveloped estates'.

This stress on public works to cultivate Britain's overseas assets put Chamberlain in advance of most other advocates of empire. Men like Rosebery and Goschen whose imperialism had older roots reacted to Chamberlain's enthusiasm for public works with amusement. His ideas marked too sharp a break with the canons of Gladstonian finance to win speedy acceptance. He in turn had little respect for earlier accomplishments. He dismissed the art of ancient Egypt as 'monotonous & stereotyped' and its architecture as 'an enormous waste of human energy'.[110]

His brassiness was nevertheless acquiring a gentler patina. Coming as she did from the aristocracy of the New World, Mary helped him make his way among the aristocracy of the Old. Mary delighted the Queen and the still more fastidious Salisbury. She counteracted the feeling that Joe was not quite a gentleman. She drew him fully into the glittering social milieu in which Britain's governing elite did their work. At the same time she took on the role of political wife which Beatrice Potter had disdained. An admirer recorded that Mary

> was always with him, but never spoke on her own. She made no speeches, asked no votes; when he worked on his speeches, she sat quietly by. She listened when he talked, and listened well, without unnecessary questions or comments. When she could she joined

the . . . 'ultra-political' ladies who gathered in the Ladies' and Speakers' Galleries in the House of Commons. There, crowded in hard chairs, peering through a grillwork which hid them from the lawmakers' gaze, a few devoted ladies followed the debates. . . . She always sat up late awaiting the weary warrior's return from the House.[111]

An active hostess, a pleasant guest, a ceaseless correspondent, fascinated by politics, Mary thrived in the part she played.

In matters of substance she had some little influence on Joe. Mary, like Austen, was conservative by nature, fond of aristocratic pastimes, old buildings and old institutions. Mary and Austen, who continued to live with his father, infused Joe's home environment with some of their tastes, in Austen's case doing a little farming at Highbury. They thus made it easier for Joe to assimilate conservative ideas to which, by age and reaction to the Gladstonians, he was already inclined. Yet marriage did not diminish Joe's inner anger, nor did the renewed happiness of his home reduce his driving energy. His fury at the treachery of the Irish and disloyalty of the Radicals burned hot. As for his energy, everything fuelled it—hope, despair, depression, delight—and it displayed itself in every active form: energy for the creation of policy, for decision, adaptation and aggression, and energy to speak in a way that stirred men's blood.

The happiness that Mary gave Joe enabled him to come to terms with his past. He was proud of his roots among the guildsmen of London; but the memory of his first two wives, who had died so young and so senselessly, left him unable to look back at anything which had touched him personally in his first forty years. Suddenly in the summer between his engagement and remarriage he revisited the homes and schools of his childhood in Camberwell and Islington. 'All the happiness of my life has been behind me,' he explained: 'Now, my dear, dearest Mary, you have given me hope, & I can confront the past without fear.'[112]

Mary brought the whole family happiness it had not known since 1875. She took charge of the household in a way that won the affection of Joe's eldest daughter Beatrice; the younger children followed Beatrice's lead; and Austen particularly enjoyed the presence of a fellow spirit. Joe still continued dominant. So conditioned was Beatrice to life under her father's roof at Highbury that she never left it until he died. She never married. Neither did any of her sisters except for the youngest, nor did her two brothers until Joe's active career was at its end. Beatrice claimed that nothing was more fascinating than the conversation round the dinner table at Highbury to which the liveliest spirits in Birmingham and the most famous men in England were invited. Every subject was opened to discussion—except for music: Joe was tone deaf,

and did not recognize even the tune of the national anthem. The extent
to which Chamberlain's children were absorbed by their father seems
unhealthy to modern sensibilities; and so in some measure it was. Yet
the pattern applied widely, to the families of Gladstone and Salisbury
among others. Like the mother country towards the colonies, the father
statesmen of Victorian England tended to drain their children of
autonomy and sometimes individuality.

Marriage markedly increased Chamberlain's financial expenditure.
Though Mary's family endowed her with some independent income,
it could not keep pace with her expenditure in the world of fashion.
In the summer of 1888 Joe added a wing to Highbury to provide
room for Mary, for his growing children, and for the inflow of political
visitors. Though he gave little to charity, he lavished jewels on Mary
and lesser presents on his children. He confessed that he liked
spending money, '& it goes very freely through my hands'.[113] Still,
for the moment the income from his investments rose faster than his
expenditure.

At Highbury he was surrounded by his brothers and sisters. They all
lived nearby till the end of the decade when Richard, MP for Islington
West, moved to London. Joe's brothers kept him alert to the interests of
metal manufacturing. Walter and Herbert still worked with Nettlefold;
Richard and Arthur remained with the brassfounding business established in Birmingham by their father. Arthur, who had no patience
for incompetent management or assertive labour, possessed a talent
for rescuing shaky enterprises. His most notable success was with
Kynoch's, manufacturers of ammunition, which he took over and carried to prosperity on the wave of armaments expenditure which accompanied the growth of the empire.

Interweaving fair and foul

Happy and prosperous on his home ground, Chamberlain was well
equipped to devote himself to the Unionist cause. The need for him to
do so, however, and the means he employed were bound up with and
darkened by his vendetta against Parnell. The inquiry which Chamberlain had fostered into the charges against the Irish leader rebounded
against its promoters. At the end of February 1889, through the confession of the forger about whom Chamberlain had been told on the way
to his wedding, Parnell was cleared of the main charge against him,
condoning murder. The proceedings of the commission of inquiry
dragged on for another year, and substantiated the more general
charges of collusion between the Nationalist party and terrorism in
Ireland. But Parnell's personal acquittal turned him into a hero, at least

in the eyes of British Liberals. The tide of by-election defeats for the government rose to alarming proportions.

Some Conservatives blamed Chamberlain for getting them into this mess. Yet paradoxically, the erosion of electoral support for the government made Conservatives more willing to support Chamberlain's economic prescriptions for Ireland. The main piece of legislation which the government introduced in 1890 was an Irish Land Purchase bill which moved cautiously in the direction that Chamberlain had been pointing since 1886. The bill fell short of his prescriptions, however, in several critical ways. While the facilities to enable tenants to purchase their holdings drew upon purely Irish resources, they were backed up by imperial credit for which, in the last resort, the British taxpayer might have to pay. Furthermore, the bill proposed to use Irish resources without requiring the consent of the local Irish authorities which the government was expected to set up soon. British rather than Irish authorities were to collect the rent-purchase money, a provision that would perpetuate the tenants' sense of alienation from the foreign owners of their land. Chamberlain was prepared to support the bill in spite of these liabilities, but they exposed him to searching Gladstonian criticism.

Excited by the crumbling electoral fortunes of the government, the Gladstonians strove to paralyse it by protracting debate in the Commons. The government made matters worse by introducing proposals like those which offended the temperance lobby in 1888 to license public houses. This action led to the final defection of Chamberlain's whip in the Commons, W.S. Caine, who led the temperance lobby as President of the United Kingdom Alliance. Though Chamberlain could scarcely afford the loss of anyone from his tiny band of followers, he pressed the government to stick to its guns rather than retreat under fire. But the situation was falling out of Unionist control.

Embarrassed by the Land Purchase bill's use of British credit, Chamberlain explored the possibilities for a crossbench compromise to make Irish county authorities, which the government proposed to create next year, responsible for the means by which land ownership would pass from landlord to tenant. In looking for some such settlement, Chamberlain spoke out in a rare attack on Balfour, criticizing him for failure to offer Ireland a really adequate Land Purchase bill before the country calmed down. For the moment, however, Chamberlain did not secure either a crossbench compromise or a more courageous government. The government withdrew its legislative proposals, undertaking to submit them again in an extraordinary autumn session of Parliament.

The dismay Chamberlain felt at this reverse was offset by the prospective explosion of a bomb which he had encouraged Captain O'Shea to ignite under Parnell. O'Shea had not taken legal action over his wife's persistent affair with Parnell for fear of losing a large legacy his wife expected from an elderly aunt. But when the old lady finally died in 1889 and O'Shea discovered that he could gain nothing under the terms of her will, he thought of suing for divorce. His suit would not be foolproof; it could collapse if he were proved to have knowingly tolerated his wife's relations with Parnell. Still, the legal action could lead to an out-of-court financial settlement for O'Shea in return for his abandonment of the case. Failing that, if he adhered to his suit, the damage it would do to Parnell's reputation would at least give O'Shea sweet revenge.

In October 1889 O'Shea told Chamberlain that he contemplated filing for divorce. The prospect was sweet enough for Chamberlain to swallow his distaste at the renewal of an embarrassing relationship. After asserting unctuously that he 'never listened to scandalous reports affecting my friends, & in your case . . . have heard nothing & know nothing beyond what you have told me', Chamberlain encouraged his disreputable associate to proceed. When O'Shea took his advice, Chamberlain responded with more unctuous applause:

> You know that I have never presumed to refer to your private affairs, in regard to which every man must judge for himself but now that you have taken the decisive step I may be allowed to say that . . . any further hesitation would have given rise to an accusation of complacency under an injury which no honourable man can patiently endure.[114]

O'Shea's reminder, however, about the possibility of an out-of-court settlement kept Chamberlain from assuming that the suit would succeed in hurting Parnell. After the abortive parliamentary session in the first half of 1890, Chamberlain left for a holiday in New England wondering whether the Gladstonians might regain power.

His world changed for better and for worse as he sailed home. On 17 November the news broke that Parnell would not defend himself from citation as co-respondent in the O'Shea divorce case. The legal proceedings showed Parnell to have been regularly deceitful and occasionally a liar. The reports damaged all, English as well as Irish, who had allied themselves with him politically. Two days after the news of Parnell came out, Salisbury and Hartington issued a decision upholding Chamberlain's claim to most of the parliamentary representation from Birmingham. But that same week there was a crash in the stock market, particularly among Argentine securities, in which Chamberlain had invested heavily.

The dividends he drew from the exposure of Parnell were mixed though on balance favourable. No longer frightened by the Gladstonian-Parnellite alliance, the government lost whatever sense of necessity it might have felt to amend its Irish Land Purchase bill at Chamberlain's bidding. Otherwise his political fortunes improved along with those of Unionism generally. The adverse tide of by-election results receded. Obstruction in the autumn session of Parliament collapsed. Gladstone repudiated Parnell; and the Irish Nationalists split between Parnell's friends and enemies. Chamberlain exaggerated the consequences. 'Home Rule for our time is smashed,' he wrote, 'banished from the realm of practical politics for our generation.'[115] Cooler heads knew that Home Rule 'would take a good deal more killing'.[116]

Similar rashness was evident in Chamberlain's response to his fall in income, suddenly a good deal lower than his level of expenditure. On holiday in New England before the crash, he travelled to Montreal where he met another Irish adventurer, Sir Ambrose Shea, then Governor of the Bahamas. Shea gave Chamberlain 'a romantic account of the resurrection of his colony . . . due to the discovery . . . that a weed peculiar to the place would give the best quality fibre for hemp'.[117] Like Chamberlain, Shea had come from business into the public service. His primary interest in the empire was to develop it economically. He hoped to alleviate the poverty of the Bahamas through cultivation of a neglected local plant, sisal. This was just the sort of venture to attract Chamberlain, and he despatched his two sons, Austen and Neville, for on-site inquiry in the Bahamas while he returned to England. He thought of taking the risk 'only if there is really a large fortune in it'[118]—until the stock market crashed.

In the wake of the crash his first reaction was to draw back, all the more so because Austen reported that the cost of development would be higher and the selling price for the product lower than Shea had indicated. Chamberlain couched his response to his sons, however, in a way that encouraged them, and particularly Neville, to advocate the investment. Neville had been groomed to maintain the family's economic fortunes by going into business. His path into industry was to be paved, as Joe's had been, through investment by his father in the firm he entered. Joe let Neville know that the prospects for such an investment in Birmingham were not encouraging at the moment. The Bahamas were another matter.

Heartened by an improved report from Austen, who estimated the rate of profit on the Bahamas enterprise at seventy per cent, Joe placed responsibility for deciding about the investment on his sons. Both had less experience of business than Joe when he had gone originally to Birmingham, and Joe's father had made the investment decision then himself. In the present case Joe put the question to his sons in such favourable terms that a negative response was next to impossible. At the same time he indicated that, if they recommended the investment, Neville would have to devote himself for some years to on-site supervision. Joe forgot how much he had depended in the early years of the screw business on the guidance and counsel of his uncle and cousin in Birmingham, advantages Neville would not have in the Bahamas. By Joe's calculations, the investment would not be as good as he had originally stipulated. His Chamberlain brothers and Kenrick brothers-in-law counselled against the venture in itself and because of the burden it would place on Neville. Questions arose about the quality of the Bahamas plant and the fibre it would produce. The price of the fibre might also fall steeply if overproduction occurred. Chamberlain pressed Shea to reduce this risk by curbing the sale of land to other buyers. Otherwise, instead of drawing back, Chamberlain responded to the risk by enlarging his purchase and accelerating his plans for production. 'Our object', he wrote Austen, 'will be to get 2000 acres under cultivation at the earliest possible moment. This ought to give a profit of £10,000 a year & allow us to indulge afterwards in reasonable extravagance'.[119]

Neville, who was left in charge of the plantation, ran into trouble within a year of the purchase. The terms of purchase which the family had negotiated with Sir Ambrose Shea were good enough to expose Shea to official controversy. The terms called for payment of 5 shillings an acre on the first 10,000 acres, the option for another 10,000 at a higher price, construction by the colonial government of a wharf on the island of Andros where the Chamberlains' land was situated, and strict limitations on further sales of government land. The estimates of cost made by Neville and Austen during their preliminary tour of inspection proved reliable for the items they took into account. But every effort to supplement the income from sisal fibre, whether by growing cotton where the soil was good or by selling the pulp of the leaves after fibre was extracted, proved fruitless. Neville also discovered that the sisal plants would have to be renewed every seven years instead of fifteen as originally predicted.

In the autumn of 1893, Chamberlain travelled briefly to Andros to see for himself. He was kept indoors there for most of his time by headache and other minor ills, his usual signs of anxiety. 1893 was a bad year for him financially. All of his investments had deteriorated in value. Yet he could not see how to reduce the expenditure which his prominence in public life required, maintaining a home in London as well as Birmingham, all the more costly now that he was remarried. He had invested nearly £13,000 in Andros and had little further ready capital to spare. The selling price for sisal fibre was deteriorating. There were unforeseen costs of transport to processing centres for the tons of leaves from which fibre would be extracted. Still, Chamberlain refused to reconsider the enterprise in which he had already sunk so much. Instead he authorized heavy further investment for the construction of tramways to move the sisal, plus additional buildings and machinery; and he approved the clearing of more land for planting. To raise the necessary capital, he turned the business into a limited company, disregarding words of caution from the English agents through whom he made this arrangement; and debentures were sold to give him £20,000. Most of it was spent in 1894.

Early the next year Neville sent word of an ominous turn in the fortunes of the enterprise. Most of the purchased and cleared area was classified as 'pine barren', coral-based land on which hitherto only pine trees had grown. Sir Ambrose Shea had assured the Chamberlains that sisal would flourish there; but Neville reported that the plants on 'pine barren' were not doing well. Hard on the heels of this report came news that one of Joe's best investments, in the Canadian Pacific Railway, would not pay its regular dividend and was falling steeply in value.

Out of spirits politically at the time,[120] Chamberlain reeled at the double financial blow. But it did not sober his financial judgement. The news from Neville was not yet disastrous. The plants on 'pine barren' might still come on, and then the amount and quality of the fibre they produced could be assessed. Not content just to wait, Joseph authorized the clearing of another 1,000 acres. In January 1896, preoccupied with the fallout from the Jameson raid, he arranged for a second issue of debentures to raise another £10,000. In doing so, he compounded the disaster which followed almost immediately. Neville intimated in February and confirmed in April that the sisal grown on 'pine barren' was incapable of growing to maturity. His father recalled him to England for consultation; and in August they terminated the business.

In addition to Chamberlain's own capital invested in the plantation, the sum required to pay off the debentures with interest brought the total loss to £50,000, an amount that in today's currency would run to ten figures. The Chamberlains' abandonment of their enterprise so alarmed possible purchasers that the sale of the plantation and its assets netted a mere £550. The loss transformed the economic position of the family. Yet the impact on Joe himself was comparatively small. He and Austen were well-paid ministers of state by the time the disaster struck. Aside from some reduction in his charitable donations, Joe did not change his lifestyle. But to keep it up he had to live off capital. He had quite enough, as he remarked, to last his time; and he could leave enough when he died to look after Mary and his daughters. But his sons would have to find their own resources.

Constructing a Radical Programme for Unionists

Chamberlain's judgement had weakened for private business, but not for public. The euphoria he felt at the fate of Parnell did not last long.

The Gladstonian Liberal party was too obviously 'alive & kicking'.[121] All the same, everything suggested that the fall of Parnell transformed the agenda of partisan debate in Britain. The prime question was no longer Home Rule. The fight that broke out between Parnell's friends and enemies among the Irish indicated that none of them would put up with Gladstone's proposals as a permanent solution to the problem of Anglo-Irish relations. Two key ingredients to Gladstone's design, the promise of permanence and the consent of the Irish, were thus lost. But this situation did not make Chamberlain complacent. The eclipse of Home Rule induced Gladstonians to look for other issues to gain support. Nearly all the issues they raised were domestic. Some, like Welsh disestablishment, were essentially regional. More had to do with the desires of the enlarged working-class electorate. The central question was whether the Liberals or the Unionist alliance could deal with these social questions better.

The Liberal response was ambivalent. Most of the Radical politicians who were concerned about social issues and much of the Radical electorate defected to Gladstone over Ireland. They associated the urban working class of Britain with Ireland's agrarian labour. Attracted by that identification, Gladstone came to sympathize with some lines of Radical social thought, but his primary concern was still to win British support for Irish Home Rule. Some other leading Liberals like Harcourt were stern economists. Aversion to growth in the powers of the state was felt even more strongly at the local level among wealthy men of business, often Nonconformists, who held the party's purse strings, controlled its representation, and often sat in Parliament for their constituencies. So long as Gladstone placed Home Rule at the head of the Liberal agenda, the commitment of the party to social action was open to question.

Once Chamberlain joined the Unionists, the question on that side was whether he still had the vision and they the willingness to do anything socially more substantial than their political opponents. Chamberlain saw the need and the opportunity. The immediate need was partisan advantage and his political survival. Socio-economic considerations also warranted an advance in policy. The economy enjoyed some expansionary recovery in the late 1880s, and although it was depressed again in the early 1890s, there was reason to believe that the country could afford to treat its citizens more generously. Germany set an example in 1889 when it instituted old-age pensions funded by contributions from employer and employee. At the same time there were signs of a new assertiveness in British labour. A successful strike by the dockworkers of London encouraged the creation of unions for unskilled labour. On a much smaller but personally more sensitive level, Austen Chamberlain was beaten in his bid for election to the town council of Birmingham by a local trade union leader.

Joseph Chamberlain's ideas for social policy still stemmed from the vision of cooperation between capital and labour which had first drawn him into public life. Essentially a pacifying, preservative vision, it was Radical simply in its willingness to use the resources of the state, preferably at the local level, to foster social harmony in ways beyond the capacity of private enterprise. Heartened by the fall of Parnell, Chamberlain turned to social issues in the opening months of 1891 with renewed enthusiasm. He announced that the time had come 'to take up once again that great social programme of 1885'.[122] Recalling also the municipal gospel of the 1870s, he talked about the 'distribution of wealth, the conditions of the poor, the sanitary condition of our large towns, the relations between employers and employed'.[123] But for the moment he did not go beyond the measures that he had advocated over the past five years: free schools, treatment of the Scottish crofters like Irish tenant farmers, and creation of small landholdings for the farmworkers and shopkeepers of rural England to keep them away from the overcrowded labour market in the cities.

The problem for Chamberlain was not so much what to do as how to persuade his allies to do it. That problem had confronted him in Liberal form in the first half of the eighties, and he had failed to solve it. He did not expect anything better from the Conservatives at first. But with happy irony the unpromising reputation of the Conservatives induced Chamberlain to improve his tactics. He never appreciated in his Liberal days that frontal assaults like the one on the merchant shipping industry roused more resistance than support. He learned from the failure of Churchill's confrontation with the Salisbury government that gentler persuasion would be necessary with the Tories. On their part the Conservatives proved more forthcoming in the second half of the eighties than Gladstone's Liberal ministry had been in the first—as Chamberlain never ceased to tell the public. While Gladstonians placed constitutional measures at the head of their agenda, Conservatives gave priority to a manageable number of socially more useful reforms: at least, that was how Chamberlain interpreted the evidence. Pressing interpretation and reality to conform to each other, he twisted the arm of the government to turn its hints at reform into firm commitments, and he muffled his disappointment when measures like the Land Purchase bill which he trumpeted in anticipation to the public failed to live up to his expectations.

He did not underestimate the difficulty of expanding the Unionist programme. He wanted more than free education, help for crofters, and smallholdings. He wanted to offer an eight-hour day to selected industries; he hoped for courts of industrial arbitration to avert strikes; inspired by the example Bismarck set in Germany, he contemplated no-fault compensation to workmen for industrial accidents, and old-age pensions. But the arguments likely to win popular support for such a programme were, he feared, 'precisely those which are most resented by strong Conservatives & by the adherents of the older school of political economy'.[124]

Feeling his way, he raised these further proposals first with a Conservative journalist, Alfred Austin, supposed to be close to the prime minister. Going public thereafter, Chamberlain adopted an exploratory approach, inviting the public to participate in the inquiry. He also made the most of any Conservative contributions. Early in March, Lord Salisbury enunciated principles on social reform which, though more restrictive than Chamberlain's, made room for compromise. Parliament had a right to interfere with the economy, said Salisbury, in order to safeguard the health of the community and 'the labour of the unprotected, women and children', though not 'the ordinary labour of the adult man'.[125]

The programme Chamberlain put forward as a Unionist in the opening months of 1891 moved beyond the Radical programme of 1885 in two ways, one imperial, the other social. The imperial development marked another step in Chamberlain's thinking about the commerce of the empire. In the autumn of 1890 while he was in New England, the United States raised its protective wall to new heights with the enactment of the McKinley tariff. Still a convinced free trader, Chamberlain argued that this protectionism hurt American industry by raising the price of imported raw materials. Why else was Britain able to dominate the market in Latin America on the doorstep of the United States?[126] He was none the less worried by the encroachment of American and even more of Continental European competitors upon overseas markets previously dominated by Britain in West Africa and China. The Birmingham Chamber of Commerce responded to the McKinley tariff by urging the government 'to maintain the sphere of British influence in Africa'.[127] Chamberlain called for expansion of Britain's West African colonies, whose prospects he described in glowing terms. Sierra Leone and Gambia had lost their hinterland to foreign rivals, a loss officially recognized in 1889. Competition now threatened the hinterland of the Gold Coast and Lagos. Chamberlain insisted that Britain defy that threat. The need to do so as he saw it was essentially economic, to sustain and increase the wellbeing of the densely populated mother country. Providentially Britain's economic need could be met hand in hand with the advance of civilization:

> when we have put down slave-raiding, the superstitious practice of Fetishism, the inter-tribal conflict which for centuries has desolated these regions and has cost the lives of millions and millions of people, and when we have completed the communications we have already

begun, trade with these West African colonies will rise by leaps and bounds.[128]

As for China, all Britain required was fair access to trading opportunities opened up by other foreign powers.

A by-election at Aston on the edge of Birmingham pushed Chamberlain's programme in another social direction. Aston had been won from the Gladstonians by a Conservative in the general election of 1886 but not by a commanding majority. Chamberlain wanted the by-election to demonstrate the value of Unionist adoption and development of his earlier Radical programme. The fact that the Unionist candidate was a Conservative simply made Chamberlain bolder. The predominantly working-class electorate of the constituency was the kind he most wanted to attract. Accordingly, four days before the voting, he raised the issue of old-age pensions for sympathetic consideration. He was the first political leader in Britain to do so. Nothing he had proposed in his Liberal days was potentially more Radical than this. He took the step carefully. Rather than add the plank to his platform, he led his audience into an examination of the need and feasibility of old-age pensions for the majority of the working class who could not save enough towards this end during their years of employment. While Chamberlain shared the Victorian middle-class belief in the need to encourage thrift among the working class, he sought a way for the state to promote individual insurance for old age. Whatever the practicalities of his suggestion, it immediately increased the significance of the by-election. When the Conservative quadrupled his party's previous margin of victory, the credit went to Chamberlain and his programme.

One month later, the government gave him the top item on his agenda by introducing a measure to make elementary education free. In peculiar fashion the grant caught Chamberlain unprepared. He more than anyone was responsible for bringing this issue to the fore. By 1890 free education had become, he said, 'almost . . . the main object of my public and political life'.[129] Yet his maintenance of this demand as a Unionist had become more symbolic than substantial. There was no way to make elementary education in England free without alienating either Conservative churchmen, who demanded state aid for denominational schools, or Nonconformists, who denounced such aid unless accompanied by civic control. Though Chamberlain believed that the social importance of free education ought to override these denominational susceptibilities, he hoped to avoid the dilemma for the time being by treating free education as a promise to be filled only after the next general election.

He was accordingly disconcerted when Lord Salisbury initiated a measure to make most elementary schools in England, whether denominational or civic, free. While Chamberlain pointed to this proposal as proof of the Unionist commitment to social reform, he suggested that as soon as the measure ran into serious opposition in the Commons, the government should appeal to the electorate. Nonconformist reaction to the government's proposal confirmed his fears but also turned him into an advocate of immediate enactment. He found himself pilloried once again as a turncoat, this time for refusing to insist on civic control of denominational schools that received state funding. But in fact he had abandoned this demand in the early 1880s. He was furious at being 'accused of inconsistency & treachery because I am now willing gladly to accept a concession which, five years ago, I could not get Mr. Gladstone to look at'.[130] Chamberlain's only change was to admit rather than to hide his acceptance of denominational schools as a permanent part of the English elementary network; but that was enough to infuriate Nonconformists. He comforted himself by enhancing the reformist character of the measure, for example raising the age to which children were expected to remain in school from fourteen to fifteen.

The achievement of free education in 1891 brought Chamberlain considerable rewards. Though the actual grant was of Salisbury's devising, no one believed that Salisbury originated the policy. The credit for it went to Chamberlain. How popular his brand of Radical Unionism would prove with the electorate was not at all clear. The Gladstonians continued to make gains in by-elections. Still, Chamberlain's influence had been obvious in the few big by-election victories the Unionists enjoyed, particularly in Central Birmingham and Aston. He had recovered a long way since the desolate summer of 1887, a remarkable achievement for a solitary Birmingham screwmaker surrounded by Whigs and Tories.

12

Divisional Manager
1891–1895

... he has pleasure in putting his cruel knife or probe into quivering,
living flesh.

Charlotte Brontë on Thackeray, Chamberlain's favourite author

Chamberlain's power as a Unionist had been exerted informally. He
was not even leader of his own party. That fact reflected the anomaly of
his place among the landowners and shipping magnates who had been
his enemies through the first dozen years of his political career. Whig
and Tory Unionists remained uncertain about their unsought yet indispensable champion. In order to move them in directions to which they
were not much inclined, he developed techniques for popular persuasion which his better-born associates never quite respected. His attain-
ment in 1892 of formal leadership of his party in the Commons did not
dispose of his problem; nor did his remarkable achievement in that
year's general election. He was an exciting performer in parliamentary
debate, but his pugnacity disturbed some supporters and unified his
Liberal opponents. He advanced financially prudent policies of social
reform which kept the Liberals from evolving into the allies of the
working class. Yet his ability to pursuade Unionists to accept enough of
his policy to make his position among them viable remained unclear.

Questionable patents, good sales

The credit which he received for the policy the Salisbury government
pursued at home and in Ireland had less to do with the content of those
policies than with the way in which Chamberlain interpreted them to
the public. The government's Irish policy was primarily Balfour's
handiwork. Its great achievement by 1890 was the reduction of intimidating crime; and that owed more to Balfour's application of the 1887
Crimes Act than to the public works promised by Chamberlain. The

Land Act of 1887 helped to pacify the Irish countryside; and its reduction of rents already lowered under the Act of 1881 was due in part to
pressure from Chamberlain. But Balfour riddled the Land Purchase Act
of 1891 with precautions which made it ineffective in spite of generous
funding.

The public works which Balfour undertook to 'kill Home Rule with
kindness' began in 1890 as famine relief. In 1891 they took the form of
assistance to 'congested' districts in the west and south of Ireland under
the terms of the Land Purchase Act. Light railways, harbour facilities,
bridges and roads, up-to-date agricultural technology, promotion of local industries with subsidies and technical education: these improvements bore the stamp of Chamberlain, who had advocated them in
public and private since 1887. Their economic returns lay in the future.
But they paid immediate political dividends, dividends which Chamberlain and Balfour shared.

Chamberlain proceeded to set his mark on the next step, the extension of elective county government to Ireland. He was willing to give
Ireland a good deal by way of local government so long as it fell short
of its own parliament. That willingness kept independent Liberals like
R.W. Dale on the Unionist side. But it disturbed the majority of Whigs
and Tories who feared any compromise on local governance for Ireland.
Meanwhile Liberals and Irish Nationalists raked Chamberlain's record
to prove that his opposition to Home Rule was Judas-like betrayal of a
policy, a master and a people he had previously offered to serve.

He was quite prepared to admit by 1891 that 'all that has happened
since 1885' had shaken his confidence in the idea of an elected central
board or national council for Ireland.[1] Yet he remained convinced that
elective involvement of the Irish in their local affairs was indispensable
both for effective Unionist government of Ireland and to maintain electoral support for Unionism in Britain. Balfour looked for some indication of Liberal Unionist wishes on this subject while he worked on
a bill. Hartington feared that the local authorities would abuse their
powers, and he insisted on some overriding authority. Chamberlain
agreed only if the overriding voice came from a court of law and not
from the British executive.

He imposed his mark more effectively on the sphere of the government's domestic policy for Britain. Here too his accomplishment was as
much a matter of interpretation as of substance. He gave the Conservative party 'credit for almost all the social legislation of our time'[2] and
denied that the Gladstonian leaders had shown 'any sympathy at all
with social movements'. There was some basis for this claim, from the
Factory Acts of the 1840s to the Factories and Workshops Act of 1891.
Inspired by a Conservative inquiry in the House of Lords into sweated
labour, the Act of 1891 imposed regulations on all workshops against

dangerous machinery, poor ventilation and inadequate fire protection. It also kept children out of the labour force till the age of eleven and prohibited women from factory work for four weeks after childbirth and otherwise for more than eleven hours a day. An Eight-Hours bill of 1891 sharpened the contrast between the Liberal and Conservative parties. A majority of the Liberals and also of Hartington's people opposed the bill, but a majority of the Conservatives supported it.

Still, Chamberlain exaggerated the contrast. In making his argument he referred repeatedly to the recent grant of free education. Yet the basic Education Act of 1870 was a Liberal accomplishment, which Chamberlain praised in other contexts as the greatest piece of legislation of his time. He did not mean to give Conservatives all the credit for social reform. His point was that they had proved more willing than their Liberal predecessors to enact his Radical programme. His claim alarmed Tories averse to social legislation. H.H. Howorth, MP for South Salford, protested to Lord Salisbury that the government conceded too much to Chamberlain. The prime minister replied sagely that Chamberlain's repetition of his claim offered 'some proof that it is not self–evident, & requires a good deal of special pleading'.[3] Even so, Conservative party organizers recognized that Chamberlain appealed more effectively than any other Unionist to the vital working-class vote.

The National Union of Conservative Associations decided to hold its annual conference for 1891 in Birmingham. Hartington's first concern, when asked 'to indicate some sort of programme for the Liberal Unionists', was to make sure that it was 'of a character which the Conservative party could accept'.[4] Chamberlain instead displayed the socially constructive cost accountancy which he meant by 'ransom'. Shortly before the National Union of Conservative Associations arrived in Birmingham, he applied that notorious term to his new interest in old-age pensions. He pointed out that the underlying claim went back to the Poor Law, under which an annual nine million pounds were currently spent to provide for the aged and destitute: 'the only question is whether a part of this vast sum may not be expended more humanely, more economically, in promoting thrift from the outset rather than dealing with the worst, the most fatal, results of improvidence'.[5]

His alliance as a Unionist with former enemies furthered his skill as a public policy-maker. In his Liberal days he tended to restrict his discussions for these purposes to people in essential agreement with him. Now, when he wanted to think about the social evil for example of intemperance, he invited a brewer, assorted ministers of religion and a teetotaller for dinner. He plunged them into discussion of the issue 'while he kept watch for something practicable that might result'.[6] After raising the subject of old-age pensions for public debate, he accepted the chairmanship of a large committee at Westminster of interested public servants and politicians and then of a small working committee. Charles Booth, the social investigator of poverty in London, came for the weekend to Highbury. Chamberlain used his local party organization to test working-class opinion. He welcomed an opportunity to meet spokesmen for the 'friendly' or provident societies whose working-class members paid subscriptions to insure themselves in the event of sickness and death; but these societies reacted to his initiative as an intrusion. The working committee appointed at Westminster met at Highbury to draw up a scheme for cost analysis by an actuary.

Nothing disguised Chamberlain's intention, in devoting himself to social policy, to serve his political advantage. And he always had a divisive impact. Conservatives in Birmingham who had felt his lash found it hard to forget. Though the Unionist alliance raised Conservative representation on the town council from three seats to nineteen in five years, a conspicuous proportion of the Conservative electorate could not bring itself to vote for Liberal Unionist candidates. On the other side, Chamberlain's former Liberal supporters could not forgive his defection. Labouchere compared him unfavourably with Judas, who at least was ashamed of betraying his master and hanged himself. When Chamberlain denounced the Liberal ministry of the early eighties in which he had played a conspicuous part, Morley attacked him directly. Once again the fight became painfully personal. 'I am sick,' Chamberlain cried, 'really sick of it all.'[7] He jeered publicly at Morley as propertyless. At last, speaking in the Birmingham town hall where he met Salisbury to celebrate their alliance, Chamberlain announced that he neither looked for nor desired reunion with the Gladstonians.

Salisbury understood that Chamberlain's commitment to his new friends was not as solid as his rejection of the old. Yet the alliance between these two men rested on something deeper than their opposition to Home Rule. Though they began from different standpoints and envisaged different objectives, both insisted on the need for a strong state. Both men were determined to prevent any erosion in the capacity of the British state to meet British needs. Standing beside Salisbury, Chamberlain boasted that 'our joint efforts have for ever saved this country from a policy of disintegration which is just as contrary to the democratic instinct of our age as it is to all true Conservative sentiment'.[8]

Salisbury's concern for British strength arose from his preoccupation with the rivalry among the world's most powerful states. Chamberlain's interest in governmental strength arose from his sense of the needs at home. Gladstone's adoption of Home Rule for Ireland roused both of these concerns and thus threw Salisbury and Chamberlain together, to their mutual surprise. They were also drawn towards each other less surprisingly from their growing interest in the empire. The scramble for Africa among the powers of Europe confirmed Salisbury as an imperialist. Ireland and North America as well as Africa led Chamberlain to similar conclusions. Gladstone catalysed the amalgamation between these two men in 1891 when he called for early British withdrawal from Egypt. Salisbury knew better than Chamberlain that France would leap in if Britain left; but he was not confident that the popular electorate could appreciate and insist upon Britain's interests abroad. Providing what Salisbury did not dare to ask, Chamberlain taught the public the fundamentals of British foreign policy as practised by Salisbury. 'Your livelihood', Chamberlain explained, 'and that of your families depend upon our world-wide possessions.'[9] To help the public understand the interests of Britain amid the alliance system which was taking shape on the Continent, Chamberlain presented Austria, Germany and Italy in the Triple Alliance as 'ancient allies of Great Britain' with 'no interests in competition to ours'. In the Dual Alliance, on the other hand, Russia wanted to penetrate the eastern approaches to India while France wanted Egypt. 'Never!' his audience exclaimed.

All the same, his efforts to undermine electoral support for the Gladstonians did not look promising as 1891 drew to a close; and a general election was due within a year. Gladstonians captured South Molton in Devonshire from the Liberal Unionists, a 'smash', Chamberlain admitted, 'and it would be ridiculous to underestimate its importance'.[10] The National Liberal Federation, meeting beforehand at Newcastle, had promised every interest group in the party the piece of legislation it most wanted so long as Home Rule remained the first piece of Liberal business. Chamberlain tried to discredit this strategy by offering fewer but sounder social reforms with the Unionists; but South Molton suggested that the Newcastle programme would succeed.

Just before Christmas, Hartington was elevated to the House of Lords as Duke of Devonshire upon the death of his father. Salisbury and the Whigs had been expecting this development for some time with trepidation, because Chamberlain was Hartington's obvious successor as Liberal Unionist leader in the decisive theatre of the Commons. The prospect made Hartington himself uneasy. Aside from the weakening of his power base, he knew that Chamberlain would not slow his political pace to keep in step with the Whiggish majority among Liberal Unionist MPs. Chamberlain indeed took the leadership without moderating his position. He insisted that the Liberal Unionists in the Commons formally elect him as leader. When they gathered for this purpose before the opening of Parliament in 1892, he laid down his terms by insisting upon his freedom to advocate disestablishment, subject always to the overriding priority of maintaining the Union with Ireland. Though one sturdy Whig insisted on a comparable right to oppose disestablishment, the assembly elected Chamberlain leader unanimously and unconditionally.

The symbolic importance of disestablishment had been underscored at the beginning of the year by opposition among the Conservatives of East Worcestershire to the selection of Austen Chamberlain as Unionist nominee for a vacancy in its parliamentary representation. East Worcestershire was a particularly sensitive constituency because Highbury lay inside its northern boundary. That fact heightened resentment at the Chamberlains' intrusion in a still mainly rural and Conservative constituency. Some of the local Conservatives demanded that Austen forswear support for disestablishment. Their demand threatened to embarrass the national alliance just when his father was joining its leaders. Balfour quelled the mutiny by stressing the loyalty and vital support which the Chamberlains brought to the alliance. Chamberlain was not entirely content with this argument. He argued that his advocacy of disestablishment was positively good for the alliance because it retained the support of some Radicals who might otherwise rejoin the Liberal party. Without Radical assistance, Hartington's people were badly beaten in the by-election for Rossendale, vacated by his elevation to the Lords. That defeat enabled Chamberlain to warn Balfour, 'you cannot . . . keep Radicals in sound faith of Unionism by tickling them with Whiggery. I would undertake to lose Birmingham in 12 months by modelling myself on . . . the speeches of Lord Hartington.'[11]

It was Balfour and Salisbury whom Chamberlain had to worry about, not 'the Duke' as Hartington was hereafter known. Ensconced in the cabinet, the Conservative leaders decided on the government's main legislative proposals for Parliament. They knew as well as Chamberlain that a general election had to be called before the year was out. While that prospect made him eager to bid for still undecided bodies of electoral support, it made Conservative leaders apprehensive of offending the loyalists upon whom the party's electoral exertions would depend. In any case defeat appeared likely. Chamberlain focused on the prospect in the Commons, dismissing the House of Lords as 'a picturesque and a stately, if not a supremely important, part of the British Constitution'.[12] But Salisbury foresaw that, in the event of electoral defeat, he could use the majority he retained in the Lords to protect the interests he cared about.

Accordingly Salisbury and Balfour imposed a cautious character on the government's legislative proposals in 1892, mainly a Small Holdings bill for England and a Local Government bill for Ireland, while Chamberlain took a bolder stand on issues not yet ripe for legislation. He paid as much attention to the sources of electoral support he hoped to attract with each initiative as to the substance of his proposals. Moving away from his earlier electoral alliance between business and organized labour, he displayed increasing interest in the vast majority of the working class that did not belong to trade unions. His emphasis on social issues was designed with this shapeless but electorally decisive mass in mind. Liberals took their policy on a number of domestic issues from the trade unions. Chamberlain sensed that the fluctuating depression of the past two decades had eroded confidence even among organized labour in the existing trade unions. He focused his policy-making imagination in directions which they neglected.

There was little enthusiasm in trade union circles for old-age pensions, a deficiency which only quickened Chamberlain's enthusiasm. Trade union officers could tell from their records that sadly few of their members reached sixty-five, the age Chamberlain proposed for the commencement of a pension; and hence they questioned the worth of a social investment at this point. But professional experts working on national statistics showed Chamberlain that half of the population which reached adulthood lived till sixty-five, and that nearly forty per cent of that half would be obliged in old age to seek assistance under the demeaning provisions of the Poor Law.

In January 1892, Chamberlain drew up an article on which he had been working for some time to present the case for old-age pensions.[13] The article presented a powerful statement of the human need. It derided the classical economic view that the old and indigent had only their own thriftlessness or debauchery to blame for their plight. It enlarged upon the obligation and facilities of the state to address the need, and outlined the scheme on which Chamberlain and his associates in the subcommittee appointed the previous spring by interested Members of Parliament were working. Their scheme was a contributory one, designed to encourage thrift among working people by offering a state supplement to an initial contribution which the worker would make early in his career and to his subsequent annual subscriptions. The scheme made allowance for times when the worker could not keep up his annual subscription, whether through unemployment or illness. It allowed for some payment to the family or designated heir of the subscriber if he died before the age of sixty-five. Chamberlain was very flexible about the details of the scheme, anxious primarily 'to renew his contact with the working-class voter'.[14] He approached the subject as an inquiry calling for careful gathering and sifting of information and reaction. His presentation still drew a withering response from *The Times*. It argued perceptively that any scheme generous enough to attract the working class would be terribly expensive. Yet the reaction of *The Times* served to accentuate the guarded welcome which Chamberlain's initiative received from the Conservative President of the Board of Trade and Lord Salisbury.

The other proposal Chamberlain made to exploit a limitation in the vision of the trade unions stemmed from a suggestion made by a minor Conservative minister, Sir John Gorst, on his return from a conference in Germany. British employers were required to compensate their workers for industrial accidents only if the employer was to blame. The trade unions wanted to extend the liability of the employer to cover the injury or death of an employee as a result of the action of other employees. The trade union plan assumed a conflictual relationship between capital and labour. Chamberlain, envisaging a basically cooperative relationship, proposed even more comprehensive compensation for the employee to cover any accident for which he was not himself directly responsible. With that exception, there was to be no question as to who or what caused the accident. Without accepting responsibility for the accident, the employer would have to provide compensation. In order to do so, he was expected to insure himself and pass this fractional addition in his costs on to the consumer. A suspicious response from the trade unions to Chamberlain's proposal simply confirmed his commitment to it.

He also spoke out strongly, more so than any other leading Unionist or Liberal, in favour of a bill entitling miners working at the coalface to an eight-hour day. He pointed out to Conservative associates that no new principle was at stake here since Parliament had been interfering with the hours of labour for half a century. His concern was primarily electoral, his approach pragmatic. Most mining constituencies demanded support for the measure, but some emphatically did not. Chamberlain wanted the bill to apply only to those districts desiring it. It might reduce production and hence lead to lower wages; but in that case the disillusioned could return to their previous arrangements. He earned immediate political dividends from the stand he took. The Liberal front bench and also the spokesmen for organized labour split on the issue. Chamberlain stood out as a champion of labour while deflecting what might have become a cause for confrontation between labour and capital.

When it came to the government's legislative programme for the coming year, he did not fare so well. Every measure shaped by the government created embarrassments for him, forcing him to resort to his familiar combination of brazenness and dexterity. He was sure that the Unionists were most vulnerable to defeat at the forthcoming election in rural constituencies. He was therefore relieved when the government placed a Small Holdings bill at the head of its legislative agenda for 1892. But he pressed, and he knew that the Gladstonians would press, for the inclusion of a clause permitting compulsory purchase of land for the purposes of the bill where none was otherwise available. To ease Conservative fears, he argued that the clause was purely symbolic. It might prove unnecessary in practice, and it could be hedged with every precaution landowners might desire. Salisbury, however, rejected Chamberlain's plea, contending that he could obtain better

terms for the owners of land from his bastion in the House of Lords
when he was out of office. Chamberlain had thereupon to oppose a
demand in the Commons for the compulsory powers he was known to
favour.

Never in Chamberlain's experience had the electoral tide been so
hard to gauge as in the spring of 1892. It might turn in either direction.
He therefore hoped that the government would defer the dissolution of
Parliament as long as possible and secure what it could of its legislative
proposals to substantiate his claims for Unionism. He made sure of the
Small Holdings bill. He wanted the government to insist on its Irish
Local Government bill even though its elaborate precautions 'filled
[him] with misgivings'.[15] But no one liked this bill, not even Balfour
who had drafted it. By the end of May, the government whips in the
Commons felt that they could no longer rely on the attendance of their
majority, distracted as all were by election fever. Though Salisbury
would have preferred to press on, he agreed to dissolve Parliament for
elections early in July.

If, as Chamberlain claimed, this general election was one of the more
critical of the century, he helped to make it so. The results he achieved
in Birmingham and the surrounding counties reversed a swing nationally towards the Liberals. He thus deprived Gladstone of a popular
mandate for Home Rule. Birmingham in fact gave Chamberlain as a
Unionist markedly greater electoral support than he had ever won as a
Liberal, support which embraced every social layer and approached
communal proportions.

The achievement was hard-earned. Without waiting for the official
announcement of the dissolution, Chamberlain opened his campaign a
month before Birmingham would go to the polls. At Smethwick near
the Heath Street mill which gave him his industrial fortune, he laid out
his political wares. With the exception of Edgbaston, the Gladstonians
put up candidates in every Birmingham constituency including his
own. Two of the six Gladstonian candidates were affiliated to organized
labour. Never before in a general election had the Liberal Unionists of
the town stood in avowed alliance with the Tories.

Chamberlain presented the Unionist case on Ireland in terms the
working men of Birmingham could appreciate. To help them understand how much the government's land legislation had done for Irish
tenant farmers, he described how it would work if applied to the ter-
raced housing his constituents knew so well. Every address he delivered was anchored in defence of the strength and security of the United
Kingdom.

He surrounded that defence with a domestic programme. Subject always to maintenance of the Union, Chamberlain insisted that 'the most
urgent questions of our era are ... social questions dealing with the

material condition of the great masses of population'.[16] The programme he presented as a Unionist in 1892 was clearer and more concrete than the Radical and Unauthorized programmes of 1885. Its most prominent components were old-age pensions for 'the veterans of industry' and workmen's compensation for industrial accidents. To these he often added courts of arbitration for industrial disputes, an eight-hour day for miners where desired, and the extension of electoral control in local government to the district and parish level.

This domestic programme was an inextricable part of Chamberlain's Unionism. Every speech told the same story. Gladstone had diverted the country from the Radical agenda of 1885 by his sudden adoption of Home Rule. Thereafter he used Home Rule to 'block the way' to reforms needed in the larger island. Ireland would indeed block the way, but only for Liberals. No matter how long the list of promises in their Newcastle programme, their first priority was to give Ireland Home Rule, and that would take years. The alternative list of reforms offered by Chamberlain was shorter but more substantial and reliable, as the record of the government served to attest.

Thus far the Conservatives went along with him contentedly. The election manifesto issued by Salisbury did not contradict Chamberlain. But Chamberlain went on to declare that Salisbury's government had enacted 'every item' of the unauthorized programme of 1885. In seeking to reassure Radical Unionists that they had not turned their coats, he seemed to suggest that Conservatives had done so. Salisbury pleaded with Chamberlain to avoid these direct comparisons with 1885. He complied in a variety of ways. He concentrated his fire on Home Rule. He drew attention to Ulster, where a huge convention of delegates left no doubt about the determination to resist subjection to a Parliament at Dublin, if need be by force. He used a manifesto from the Nonconformist ministers of Ireland to undermine the assumption among Nonconformists in England that Home Rule was morally right.

Not content, however, to subordinate his domestic programme for long, he discovered how to present it to woo Conservatives as well as Radical Unionists. Even before Salisbury cautioned him, Chamberlain pointed out what Liberal and Conservative Unionists had learned from each other: 'we Liberals and Radicals have learnt . . . to appreciate more highly the importance of maintaining the great Empire which our forefathers created . . . the Conservative party have learnt from us . . . that it is absolutely necessary that progress should be the order of the day'.[17] Thereafter he repeated his praise of the Conservative record in social legislation. He thanked Conservatives for 'the realization of some of my most earnest hopes formed 20 years ago',[18] for free education, reform of county government, and the construction of a ladder of possibilities for land ownership starting with garden allotments and smallholdings.

He threw everything he had into the campaign, undaunted by symptoms of strain, a twitching eye, headaches and neuralgia. His meetings were disturbed by hecklers, to whom he always responded until they resorted to organized disruption. Since the voting was spread over two weeks and Birmingham voted early, he was free to leave Birmingham and campaign in Manchester on the day Birmingham went to the polls. Otherwise he stuck to his electoral 'Duchy', which included the counties of Staffordshire, Worcestershire and Warwickshire surrounding Birmingham. Most of the Unionist candidates there were Conservatives. Relations with them had improved so much since Austen's trouble in East Worcestershire at the turn of the year that Chamberlain sought a knighthood for the Conservative who had led the rebellion there. Chamberlain was convinced that the fortunes of Birmingham were inseparably tied to the adjacent Black Country. Braced by the results from Birmingham, he campaigned tirelessly through his Duchy, casting a bright light over stolid candidates who were otherwise headed for defeat.

The results exceeded even Chamberlain's expectations. 'You have done gloriously, simply gloriously in the Midlands,' the national chief of the Liberal Unionist organization exclaimed.[19] 30 out of the 39 constituencies in Chamberlain's Duchy returned Unionist candidates. But elsewhere only in Scotland did the Unionists approach this level of success. The new House of Commons gave Gladstone a small majority of 40 and only if Ireland's 80 Nationalists supported him. The Liberal Unionists, defying predictions that they would be wiped out, returned 47 strong to the House of Commons. That halved their strength after the last general election; but it also halved the margin of victory Gladstone anticipated, and ensured that Liberal Unionism would be a force to reckon with for years to come.

The most spectacular results came from the six contested seats in Birmingham and the immediately surrounding four seats of Handsworth, Aston, East Worcestershire and Tamworth. There the Unionist majorities exceeded the normal dimensions of victory. Only one of these constituencies, Tamworth, had returned a Conservative in 1885. The rest had returned Liberals, usually with solid but not overwhelming majorities. Now, as Unionists, the support they received was massive. In no case did it fall below sixty per cent. Chamberlain carried his own constituency with an unheard of majority of 4,387 votes, substantially exceeding his majority of 2,764 as a Radical in 1885. No stratum of the working class could be excluded from such a majority. There is some evidence that in moving from Liberal to Unionist Chamberlain exchanged the support he received from skilled and organized labour in the 1870s for support from the unskilled and the small tradesmen who earlier opposed him. But Chamberlain himself thought his

Unionists did better among skilled workers than among the unskilled. Recent evidence from oral history[20] confirms the impression conveyed by the results of 1892 that he and his men in Birmingham drew their support from every social quarter.

The one working-class element in Birmingham which allied itself with the Gladstonians against Chamberlain in the election of 1892 was the trade union leadership. But they recoiled afterwards and split up politically. Some lingered in the Liberal camp, more opted for independent labour representation, a few joined Chamberlain's Unionists. The election taught all of them new respect for Chamberlain's interest in labour issues.

There were two dimensions to the electoral phenomenon of 1892 in and around Birmingham, one social, the other regional. Chamberlain invested Unionism with a capacity to upstage the Liberals on social issues for working-class consumption, leaving his opponents to make what they could of non-economic constitutional issues, Home Rule, reform of the Lords and the franchise. Simultaneously he accentuated the regional character of British politics. The swing to Unionism in Chamberlain's Duchy, though not as great as in Birmingham, deviated markedly from the national average. Some other regions dashed his hopes. He lost what little he had in the crofter lands of Scotland. The efforts he made, by putting up Nonconformist candidates, to wrest Wales from the Gladstonians proved a total failure. Generally his attempt to woo Nonconformity failed, though his critique of Home Rule and its accompanying priestly peril contributed to the low voter turnout which had bedevilled the Liberals since 1886.

Marketing costs and conflicts

The general election seemed to convince every politician and faction that he or it was on the right tack. Accordingly the new Parliament found itself in an impasse that both sharpened and strained the contending alliances. The election convinced Chamberlain that Unionism needed more of the tonic he manufactured in Birmingham to turn its narrow national defeat into victory. He emerged from the election rippling with ideas and plans. Not content with the performance of his Duchy, he set up a Liberal Unionist Association for the Midlands. He tried to bring about the collapse of the Home Rule alliance by exposing the incompatible aspirations of its component factions. He was struck by how poorly the Unionists had done in London, particularly in working-class constituencies, disappointments underscored by the defeat suffered by the 'Moderate', essentially Conservative and Unionist party in the preceding local election for the London County Council.

Unionism in London needed, said Chamberlain, to offer the quality of municipal service and leadership provided in Birmingham. Applying this message nationally, he wanted the Unionist government, which had not yet resigned, to meet the new Parliament with a statement of the domestic legislation it would introduce if it remained in office.

Lord Salisbury was not afraid of daring tactics. By retaining office rather than resigning as soon as a majority of Gladstonians and Irish Nationalists was elected for the new House of Commons, he attempted to force the Liberals to show their hand and hence to test the loyalty of the Irish to them. His relations with Chamberlain, rarely more than formal until this year, warmed remarkably. Both were devoted to their families, neither entirely liked the world of aristocratic fashion where Devonshire and Balfour were at home; and Mary Chamberlain satisfied Salisbury's expectations of womankind to perfection. The person who provoked Chamberlain was Devonshire. He communicated with Chamberlain as little as possible and never made a forward move until Chamberlain 'threatened to commit suicide in his presence'.[21] Nevertheless, Chamberlain's preoccupation with social issues made Salisbury uneasy. Rather than meet the new Parliament with a bundle of social proposals as Chamberlain urged, Salisbury insisted upon leaving the Gladstonians to make the first move.

The message the general election conveyed to Conservatives was more complicated than the conclusions Chamberlain drew. It made them confident that Home Rule could be beaten. Lacking natural trust in the popular electorate, they had laboured since 1886 under the fear that Gladstone could bring the voters to endorse Home Rule. Chamberlain's efforts in the intervening years to keep the electorate true to its verdict of 1886, and the proof the 1892 election gave of the effectiveness of those efforts, dispelled that fear. Home Rule was not inevitable. Quickened by their new-found freedom from doubt, Conservatives approached the prospect of a period in opposition without dismay.

Nothing filled Unionists with greater enthusiasm for the fight than Chamberlain's sword and fire in debate. When he rose from the Liberal front bench to speak in the new Parliament, the Conservatives opposite roared in anticipation. He exposed the incompatibility of the Liberal pledge to maintain the supremacy of the imperial Parliament with Irish Nationalist insistence on the complete freedom of the Parliament they were to receive. Balfour thought his speech 'most brilliant'.[22] It sent even the Duke of Devonshire into ecstasies as 'one of the best, if not the best speech' he had heard in his many years in the Commons.[23] Emulating Chamberlain's commitment, two dozen young Tory MPs 'formed themselves into a Sacred Band . . . to sit together, vociferously to cheer every Unionist, and to object to the views of every Gladstonian'.[24] But the very confidence that Chamberlain gave Conservatives in the ultimate good sense of the electorate reduced their sense of the need for the further social reforms he advocated. They felt some appreciation for the domestic side of his appeal. But they feared that he would push it too far and infringe upon the interests of the established church and the rights of property.

While confident in his reading of working-class opinion in Birmingham, Chamberlain sensed that it did not provide a fully reliable guide to the thoughts and desires of the working classes of England as a whole. New forms of organization and schools of thought were bidding for their allegiance. Anxious for full information on which to base further development of his domestic programme, he wrote to the newly elected MP for Battersea, John Burns. He did not know Burns personally, but he understood that Burns was in touch with those spheres of labour activity with which he himself was not directly familiar. Formerly a member of the near-Marxist Social Democratic Federation (SDF), and more recently associated with the London dock strike which inspired the formation of trade unions among the unskilled, Burns was a recruit to the band of Labour spokesmen associated with the Liberal party who were known as Lib-Labs. Chamberlain bombarded him with questions about the relative importance, the relationship to the working classes, the leaders, and 'the precise legislative proposals' of the old and the new trade unionists, of collectivists in the Fabian Society, and of full socialists in the SDF.[25]

Taken aback by this probe into divisions which he glossed over even to himself, Burns replied blandly that these groups represented 'different sections of the same movement more or less committed to the same thing . . . "Legislative interference with and for Labour"'.[26] He enclosed a handful of reports and pamphlets, some from the Trades Union Congress. In acknowledging their receipt, Chamberlain summed up his own viewpoint. He still welcomed the prospect of 'the State as representing the whole community undertaking many duties for which it is now considered unsuited'. Yet the Unionist domestic record over the past five years essentially satisfied him. He declared his intention of proceeding along the lines of free education, allotments, land purchase and the Factory Acts, 'to extend . . . the beneficial operations of State control & regulation'.[27]

Burns recoiled from Chamberlain's repeated invitation for discussion over dinner. Chamberlain pressed on independently with his inquiries, and presented their fruits in a substantial article published on 'The labour question'.[28] He drove his coach through the midst of the spokesmen for labour, scattering them to left and right. Defining socialism or collectivism as state ownership of the means of production and state distribution of the fruits of labour in proportion to the work provided, he rejected it with the familiar criticism:

> There would be no reward for originality, no stimulus to exertion or
> initiative. . . . Production would be diminished, and would soon be in-
> sufficient even for the base necessaries of subsistence.

On the other hand he expressed disappointment with the trade unions
and the working-class benefit societies which opposed him over old-age
pensions and workmen's compensation because they wanted their adherents to rely upon their agency rather than on the state in cooperation
with the owners of industry.

In line with this analysis, he added new items to his domestic
agenda, all consonant with the policy he had already developed as a
Unionist. He spoke of legislation to set the maximum number of hours
that shops could be open, to create labour exchanges to put those seeking work in touch with available opportunities, to staunch the flow of
destitute immigrants from eastern Europe, and to give the British working classes the facilities for rent reduction and house purchase that the
Irish now enjoyed. Another recommendation marked the crossroads
between his old municipal Radicalism and his new imperialism. Socialists called for the establishment of municipal businesses to create work
for the unemployed. Chamberlain responded that artificial attempts to
increase production only hurt those already employed in industry. 'The
evil against which we have to struggle', he declared, 'is want of demand.' Referring to the resources of India and Africa, he encouraged
the working classes to urge the government to do all it could to protect,
cultivate and extend Britain's markets overseas.

In advancing these proposals he did not mean to add to the division
between his supporters and Conservatives. For electoral purposes he
insisted that Liberal Unionists preserve their own associations distinct
from Conservative ones to enable Liberals to vote Unionist without
considering themselves Tory. Yet he wanted to foster the solidarity of
the Unionist alliance. He urged Liberal Unionists to seat themselves on
the opposition side in the new House of Commons just down from the
Conservatives. But Irish Nationalists preempted those seats to demonstrate their independence from the Liberal government. Hence Chamberlain found himself still on the Liberal side though below the
gangway. The position proved better for attack than for self-defence. It
enabled Unionists to catch the government in a crossfire, from the Conservatives in front of them and Liberal Unionists to the side. But it also
symbolized the insecurity of Chamberlain's political place.

The Liberals performed more ably than he anticipated. He thought
that their majority would fall apart, perhaps in less than a year. He
expected it to disintegrate either over the Irish demand for greater autonomy for their Parliament or from discontent at the delayed gratifica-
tion of factional Liberal desires. The Liberals frustrated Chamberlain's

hopes with an astute strategy. Their leaders kept quiet until the new House of Commons voted the Unionist government out and enabled them to take over. Then, after half a year's recess to draft legislation, they presented Parliament with an array of proposals. The Home Rule bill, which had first priority, was accompanied by measures to satisfy the government's main British contingents, including a Suspensory bill to prepare the way for Welsh disestablishment, a Local Veto bill to appease the temperance lobby, and an Employers' Liability bill to meet trade union demand. Each measure was presented for preliminary debate and then despatched along the most promising route for enactment, the Employers' Liability bill for example going to grand committee, while the Home Rule bill was debated by the whole House. Recognizing that the Commons could not deal with so many bills if it adhered to its usual customs, the government took full control of the time of the House almost from the outset of the session and prepared to keep it going until it dealt with all the main items in the menu. This strategy disproved Chamberlain's contention that the Newcastle programme was a fraud. Ireland did not block the way to reform for Britain. He had to deal with the substance of the Liberal programme, piece by piece.

The Employers' Liability bill was the Liberals' main bid for working-class support. Framed in close consultation with the trade unions, the bill would oblige employers to pay for accidental injury caused by any employee aside from the victim. Chamberlain trumped this bid with a more comprehensive yet less costly proposal to be funded by the employer ultimately through a slight addition to the consumer price of his products. Whereas the Liberal and trade union scheme accentuated the conflict between worker and employer, Chamberlain's scheme implied cooperation between the two. His scheme drew attention to the difference between trade union leaders, who wanted to encourage reliance on their organizational efforts, and working men preoccupied with their material security. His scheme also reduced opposition from employers fearful of addition to their direct liabilities, and thus reduced uneasiness in Conservative circles.

On Ireland, in the fight against Gladstone's second Home Rule bill, Chamberlain stood forth as the unequivocal voice of British patriotism. Contempt for the Irish and loss of hope for Liberal reunion reduced his support for a central board almost to vanishing point. The conflict over Home Rule in 1893 was more general and at the same time less precisely defined than in 1886. Gladstone, still unable to resolve the dilemmas that would arise from Irish representation in parliaments at Dublin and Westminster, tried first one and then another equally unsatisfactory solution. Chamberlain no longer invested the point with crucial significance, convinced that nothing Gladstone proposed would subordinate the Irish to the imperial legislature effectively. Furthermore, since the fall of Parnell, the Irish refused to treat what Gladstone gave them as more than a temporary arrangement. Gone was the most attractive feature of his initiative in 1886, the promise of an enduring settlement between the two islands.

Though crucial to the rivalry between the two partisan alliances, the debate on the second Home Rule bill threatened to be boring. There was an unmistakable artificiality to the exercise in the Commons. Everyone knew that the Lords would throw the bill out; and no one seriously believed that the government would promptly appeal to the people with another general election. The temptation to languor was strong, and Balfour succumbed. But not Chamberlain. From winter through spring and summer, he led the charge. 'It is he', wrote a veteran reporter, 'who sets the battle in array, sends out skirmishing parties, and is ever ready to lead an attack in person.'[29]

When the monied men of the City of London demonstrated their opposition to the Home Rule bill with a march from the Stock Exchange, Chamberlain was the chosen speaker on their arrival at the Guildhall. Standing a few hundred yards from the shop on Milk Street where his ancestors had their business, he welcomed the marchers to 'your ancient hall, which recalls the patriotism and the resolution of the citizens of London on so many occasions of difficulty and danger'.[30] Again and again that spring, he dwelt on the threat posed by the Home Rule bill to the strength of Great Britain and its empire. With freshness of touch he struck the old notes of patriotism: obligations sanctioned by past history, concern for influence and honour, and the ancient character of Englishmen.[31]

No one could rally the forces of Unionism better than he. Yet no one so helped the government to rally its troops in the Commons. His thrusts at their weak joints pulled them together. No one could parry his quick jabs or relentless logic in argument. But the effect even on wavering opponents was infuriating instead of persuasive. The Irish abused him crudely, the Liberal rank and file fell bitterly silent. Even Dilke, returned to the Commons on the Gladstonian side after an absence of six years, felt that his former partner had 'sold his old true self to the devil'.[32] The Irish knew a fallen angel when they saw one. Describing one of Chamberlain's speeches against the Home Rule bill, T.P. O'Connor wrote that

> in spite of all his efforts at self-control, the hideous and evil passion of
> his heart broke forth, and there was a hoarse and raucous sound of
> hate that almost made one's blood freeze. . . . He stood there—with his
> pale face, his lack-lustre but vicious eye—his voice with cold hatred
> and fell purpose in every accent, and then, as one thought of the hell-

ish passions he was trying to bring into open flame, it became one of the most awful pictures of a lost soul I have ever seen.[33]

The passions roused by Chamberlain eventually shattered the civility of the House of Commons. When months of debate failed to move the House beyond the preamble to the Home Rule bill, the government imposed closure on the committee stage. It was set to end at 10 p.m. on 27 July. As the deadline approached, Chamberlain took the floor. Etching each syllable with a hiss, he spoke with the icy control that marked his moments of most intense feeling. Mindful of the clock, he focused his final words on the willingness of the Commons majority to vote with Gladstone on the Home Rule bill no matter how he changed its crucial provisions.

> The Prime Minister calls 'black,' and they say it is good; the Prime Minister calls 'white,' and they say 'it is better.' It is always the voice of a god. Never since the time of Herod has there been such slavish adulation.[34]

The clock struck ten and the chairman rose to call the vote. But even before Chamberlain finished, at his mention of Herod, the Irish benches led by T.P. O'Connor erupted with cries of 'Judas!' The Conservatives insisted that this breach of verbal decorum be noted by the chairman, and refused to leave their seats for the vote. Some of the Irish surged across to the Conservative benches, and fighting broke out. A Conservative shouted at Gladstone that he was to blame. Chamberlain sat frozen, waiting for the apology due to him. A majestic return by the Speaker to the chamber quelled the storm. He extracted an ambiguous apology from O'Connor, and the embarrassed House adjourned. Its hatreds hardened.

The limits of Radical Unionism

Chamberlain destroyed the Home Rule bill. Its rejection a few weeks later by a ten-to-one majority in the Lords simply confirmed his handiwork. Yet he conceived of himself as a constructive politician. Earlier in July, he had worked productively out of public view in a committee room near the House of Lords. A distinguished royal commission had been appointed, in large part thanks to his efforts, to look into the subject of old-age pensions. Chamberlain was a member of the commission; and he subjected himself to two days of examination by his fellow commissioners[35] to defend the scheme which the informal parliamentary committee on the subject had developed over the past two years.

The examination exposed the limitations of his social vision as a Radical Unionist, limitations that stultified the initiative he had in mind. In retrospect the limits look so severe that it is tempting to dismiss the initiative as a self-serving gesture. Yet the sparks he struck during the examination showed that more was at stake. He challenged some of the most deeply entrenched principles of classical Victorian political economy in his endeavour to ensure the stability and increase the well-being of Britain's industrial society.

He assailed the theory and practice of the provision made for the destitute under the Poor Law of 1834. In order to encourage thrift among the needy and ease the burden on the ratepayer, the Poor Law provided the lowest survivable level of relief to be administered in deterring fashion, symbolized by the workhouse. Chamberlain paid lip service to the Poor Law system on the whole. But he challenged its application to 'the veterans of industry', those who worked diligently through their productive years at wages which did not allow them to save enough to stay out of the workhouse when old age deprived them of their capacity to work. Asked why working men did not do without strong drink in order to provide for their old age, Chamberlain exposed the double standard behind the question: 'in dealing with the poor some economists expect from them a virtue which we certainly do not find in ourselves'.[36] He defended beer for those engaged in physically strenuous work as almost a necessity, and spoke sympathetically of those who resorted to drink at the end of their productive lives when faced with destitution. He proposed old-age pensions for all who made an original deposit and kept up subsequent payments, regardless of anything in their behaviour that might fall short of middle-class expectations.

His fellow commissioners reflected the bodies of opinion he needed to meet if his proposal was to make headway. He violated the devotion to governmental economy that one commissioner, Lord Lingen, had learned as permanent secretary of the Treasury. Albert Pell, who had raised himself from poverty to become a landed gentleman, a Tory MP and authority on the Poor Law, spoke for the contented status quo. Had there not been enough improvement over the past fifty years 'in this England of ours, with all the opportunities that the people have for taking care of themselves', to breed confidence that the improvement would continue without 'disturbing the operation ... by being in a hurry?'[37] C.S. Loch of the Charity Organization Society preached the Poor Law gospel with unflinching rectitude. J.J. Stockall and A.C. Humphreys-Owen spoke for the working-class benefit societies fearful of governmental encroachment on their sphere, little though they had accomplished within it.

Friendly voices countered these hostile ones, but hesitantly. Henry Broadhurst, the Lib-Lab MP who reluctantly parted company with Chamberlain over Home Rule, greeted his old-age pensions scheme sympathetically, though he was also concerned to protect the interests of labour. Sir Herbert Maxwell, Conservative MP for Wigtownshire who served on the parliamentary committee that generated the scheme, reinforced Chamberlain's presentation. But two other sympathizers drew attention to the limitations of his scheme, and in doing so suggested that it might not be worthwhile. Charles Booth, whose researches on poverty in London furnished much of the evidence on which Chamberlain relied, proposed comprehensive non-contributory pensions without any of the limitations to Chamberlain's plan. Chamberlain dismissed Booth's scheme as politically impracticable because it would cost £20,000,000 to £24,000,000 a year, far more than any existing item of domestic expenditure in the British budget. But Booth's questions to Chamberlain suggested that, in searching for the politically practicable, he had come up with the socially useless. The concluding set of questions by C.T. Ritchie left the same impression. Conservative home secretary in the last government, Ritchie had worked so well with Chamberlain that at one time he encouraged the possibility of Ritchie's standing for election in Birmingham. Ritchie was the sort of Conservative from whom Chamberlain needed wholehearted support if his pension scheme was ever to be enacted. But Ritchie concluded that, if the scheme could not be improved upon, then perhaps they should make do with the Poor Law.

Chamberlain's scheme proposed insurance to provide a pension of five shillings a week at the age of sixty-five to anyone who deposited a few pounds by the age of twenty-five and subscribed a few shillings a year for the subsequent forty years. No dividends would be paid for forty years after the scheme was enacted. Chamberlain offered nothing to those already twenty-five, though he expected that Parliament would take this more expensive task in hand once it had agreed to his plan. Nor did his scheme offer anything to 'the submerged tenth', those unable to pay the original deposit or keep up their subscription. He did not even claim that those who took out the insurance would be able eventually to live on five shillings a week. He expected it to be supplemented by support from benevolent employers, family, friends and charity. Chamberlain's scheme was crippled by his refusal to recommend anything requiring a large increase in governmental expenditure. As he calculated the costs of his proposal, it would cost no more than £500,000 and perhaps as little as £50,000 a year. Even so, he advised against introducing his scheme until there was a surplus in the budget to pay for it.

He hoped to launch state-assisted old-age pensions in the same modest but ultimately decisive way that state-assisted elementary education had been launched in 1839 with an exchequer grant of £30,000. That was the example he invariably referred to when the limitations of his scheme were pointed out. Yet he had been willing to spend more in his gas-and-water socialist days as mayor of Birmingham. Unless he assembled more resources for old-age pensions, his initiative would become indeed an empty bid for votes.

He made much more headway with workmen's compensation for industrial accidents. As the Liberal bill reached its final stages in the Commons and headed up to the Lords, another aspect of the controversy became prominent. Hitherto some businesses had 'contracted out' of their responsibilities under the existing legislation by agreeing with their workforce on some form of insurance which gave employees broader coverage than the law required while protecting the employer against litigation. Prompted by the trade unions averse to any diminution of employer responsibility or employee reliance on unions, the Liberal bill prohibited 'contracting out'. The House of Lords under Salisbury's leadership insisted upon it.

Chamberlain wedded Conservative insistence on 'contracting out' with his own policy of comprehensive compensation. In doing so, he secured the dividends that eluded him on old-age pensions. His policy on workmen's compensation was as thorough as Booth's on old-age pensions but without the prohibitive financial cost. In espousing 'contracting out', Chamberlain continued to divide the trade unions from working men who preferred the more rewarding independent schemes. Chamberlain described these men as 'the very flower of the working classes . . . skilled artisans, intelligent, independent men';[38] and he praised the independent schemes for promoting friendly feelings in industry. The fact that some of the employers who used such schemes, like Richard Tangye of Birmingham, were prominent Liberals added to Chamberlain's pleasure. The crowning dividend was consolidation of the Unionist alliance. Salisbury repaid Chamberlain's support for 'contracting out' by accepting the principle of universal compensation. It was, as Chamberlain explained, much preferable to the Liberal alternative of increasing employers' liabilities. Salisbury and Chamberlain kept in step with each other in the manoeuvre of amendment between Lords and Commons. In the end, rather than accept 'contracting out', the government abandoned its bill and hence its most substantial attempt to attract the working classes.

In all these discussions of working-class needs, the mind of the former marketing director harked back to the need for more markets. A delegation of unemployed men waited on Chamberlain to protest against the immigration of paupers from the Continent whom they accused of driving Englishmen out of work. While Chamberlain supported their demand for stricter control of immigration, he belittled what it could do to ease unemployment. Instead he insisted that 'the great cure' lay in 'continuing to do what the English people have always done—namely, to extend their markets and their relations with the waste places of the earth'.[39] He told his Birmingham constituents that 'there was work enough in these undeveloped possessions of England' to provide employment for everyone in the country now and for ages to come.[40]

Here was medicine he could prescribe to the delight of his Unionist allies. They stood in need of some such agreement when the parliamentary session of 1893 dragged on into 1894. The government protracted the session beyond precedent in order to press the major items in its programme for Parliament to a decision. The final measure, a Parish Councils bill, exposed the tensions within the Unionist alliance. Though the bill was poorly drafted and lumbered with extraneous provisions, Chamberlain wanted to see it enacted in its essentials. It was part of his unauthorized programme in 1885 and followed the lines of a bill he drafted at the Local Government Board in 1886 before Gladstone pushed Home Rule to the fore. Furthermore if, after rejecting the Home Rule bill and provoking the withdrawal of the Employers' Liability bill, the House of Lords amended the Parish Councils bill beyond the tolerance of the government, it might call a general election and direct its campaign against the Lords, weakening the case that otherwise Chamberlain was confident could bring the Unionists victory.

He did everything he could to reduce the Lords' amendments to proportions acceptable to the government. But Conservative peers led by Salisbury were determined to defend the rural interests of church and land which the bill threatened. It was a late episode in the old conflict of Whig and Tory. Working privately through Balfour, Chamberlain tried to minimize Salisbury's demands. When that effort failed, Chamberlain spoke out in the Commons, asking Conservatives bluntly whether they were 'going to be so reactionary as to follow the House of Lords'.[41] He enjoyed good relations with the Liberal minister in charge of the bill, H.H. Fowler of Wolverhampton, and approached Fowler confidentially to see what could be done to save the bill from extremists on both sides. Fowler proved more successful on his side than Chamberlain on the other. Salisbury's men insisted on more than Chamberlain thought reasonable. Nevertheless, after throwing the bill back to the Lords twice, the government accepted it for fear of having nothing to show for the long year's work. Luckily for Chamberlain, Salisbury blamed the controversy between Conservative and Liberal Unionists over this bill largely upon the Duke of Devonshire.

In the short interval between the parliamentary session which now ended and the next one for 1894, the change for which Chamberlain had waited so long took place, too late. Eighty-three years of age, with failing eyesight, finding himself alone among his cabinet colleagues in resisting further expenditure on the navy, Gladstone resigned as prime minister and leader of the Liberal party. Chamberlain had paid a high price for Gladstone's longevity. It denied Chamberlain the leadership of the Liberal party and perpetuated the Liberal split beyond hope of healing. The change in Liberal command posed a threat to him when, to some surprise, the person chosen to become prime minister was Lord Rosebery. Home Rule was the rock of offence against which the Unionist alliance was formed; and Chamberlain had endeared himself to the alliance as the man best able to prevent Home Rule. Hence Gladstone's dedication to Home Rule had served the purposes of Unionism and Chamberlain as well as his own. Rosebery, however, was a conspicuously tepid Home Ruler. His appointment threw the current basis of political division in Britain into question. He and Chamberlain eyed each other nervously as contenders for the same ground. Both needed the central, non-Home Ruling Liberal vote that Chamberlain had temporarily captured for Unionism. Both were imperialists ready for social reform. At a dinner with Chamberlain that June, Rosebery recalled the last cabinet meetings which the two of them had attended together in 1886, and observed that, had it not been for Gladstone, 'our differences might have been arranged'.[42] So extensive were their affinities that people wondered periodically whether they would join forces; but the patterns of loyalty entrenched over the past eight years and the inevitable rivalry between the two men kept that possibility illusory.

At the moment of his elevation, the ball lay at Rosebery's feet. He picked it up dexterously by declaring that Home Rule would require the consent of 'the predominant partner', in other words of Britain where the current majority was decidedly Unionist. Then he fumbled. Under pressure from the Irish upon whom he depended for his majority in the Commons, Rosebery backed away from the obvious implication of his words, and renewed the Liberal commitment to Home Rule. Chamberlain headed straight for the hall where Rosebery had announced his retreat, the Corn Exchange in Edinburgh, and dissected his performance. 'Mr. Gladstone was one of whom it was sometimes said that his earnestness ran away with his judgment; but Rosebery'—he had to stop because the audience dissolved in laughter.[43]

It was nevertheless harder, now that Gladstone had gone, to sustain the British electorate's fear of Home Rule. Chamberlain devoted a good half of nearly every speech to exposure of the threat. He enlivened his treatment however familiar the theme. Yet he appreciated better than most that such efforts were not enough. As Home Rule slipped into the shade, domestic British issues moved to the fore. Though the Liberal predilection for constitutional issues continued to assert itself, the government stole some of Chamberlain's socio-economic thunder. Nothing he had proposed matched the significance of the budget which Sir William Harcourt presented in the spring of 1894 inaugurating graduated death duties. Harcourt's budget 'broke decisively with the Gladstonian legacy . . . in the all-important field of finance',[44] as Chamberlain had failed to do in the Radical Programme of 1885 and more recently over old-age pensions. Driving home the accomplishment, Harcourt spoke of funding 'demands not only for the Army and Navy but for every kind of social reform'. Unwilling to challenge the breakthrough and fearful that his fellow Unionists might do so, Chamberlain contented himself with a little carping about details. He voted with his party against the second reading of the Finance bill. But when an exasperated Conservative forced a division against the graduated death duties and carried much of his party with him, Chamberlain spoke and voted for the other side. Thereafter he studiously ignored the subject.

Fortunately from his point of view, the budget of 1894 had little immediately obvious value for the working class. The money Harcourt raised was meant mainly to increase the size of the navy, a bipartisan concern in view of the alliance between France and Russia. His achievement left Chamberlain free to repeat his claim that '[s]ocial reform is . . . the peculiar work of the Unionist party'.[45] His experience over the past year led him to think that Conservatives might be more forthcoming in this regard than Liberal Unionists of Devonshire's stripe. He received encouragement from Conservatives in the royal commission on the aged poor. Devonshire and Sir Henry James were alarmed by the course he pursued over the Employers' Liability bill, but Salisbury rewarded him by accepting the principle of comprehensive compensation.

The success of Chamberlain's collaboration with Conservative peers over employers' liability led him to think more of the upper house which they controlled. He redesigned his social programme, incorporating and accentuating items that appealed to Conservatives. He also recommended new tactics whereby Unionist Lords would present his programme as bills in their House and send them down to challenge the Liberal majority in the Commons. The bills were unlikely to reach the statute books; but no matter. Hitherto all the programmes devised by Chamberlain had been 'unauthorized', launched on his own initiative without endorsement from his party leaders. What distinguished the programme in the autumn of 1894 was his determination to secure explicit commitment and if possible also concrete cooperation from Salisbury and the Conservatives.

The programme was made in Birmingham. Its contents were hammered out in conference between the Birmingham Trades Council and the city's Unionist MPs. Without further consultation, Chamberlain pre-sented the programme to his constituents.[46] He divided his proposals under two headings. The first, 'social reforms', included local control of liquor licensing, facilities to help working men buy their homes, and old-age pensions. The second, 'questions that have special reference to labour', included courts of arbitration for industrial disputes, the eight-hour day on an optional basis for miners, limited hours when shops could be open, reduction of pauper immigration, and workmen's com-pensation for industrial accidents. Some items in the programme, such as encouragement of a home-owning working class and control of alien immigration, had conscious Conservative appeal. The temperance proposal undercut one of the few attractive appeals which the Gladstonians of Birmingham had made at the last general election; and it exploited a bone of contention among Liberals at the national level, where Harcourt favoured local prohibition while Gladstone and others preferred something less restrictive. The offer of an eight-hour day to miners disposed of the demand by the newly formed Independent La-bour party for an eight-hour day throughout the economy. Generally, in place of Liberal and Labour proposals which accentuated lines of social conflict—temperance men against brewers, labour against capital—Chamberlain's programme sought cooperation.

After outlining the programme to his constituents, Chamberlain sug-gested his tactical plan to Salisbury. Approaching Salisbury through his Liberal Unionist son-in-law, Lord Wolmer, Chamberlain asked 'whether it might not be possible for the House of Lords to spoil the game of the Gladstonians by itself dealing with some of the more important social questions by means of Bills?'[47]

Chamberlain did not know it, but Salisbury had recently expressed hostility towards pre-electoral cooperation with him on domestic mat-ters. In the spring of the year a group of Unionist, largely Conservative activists had founded the London Municipal Society to counteract the victories Liberals had won in the London County Council and parlia-mentary elections of 1892. The next elections for the London County Council were due early in 1895. The executive of the London Municipal Society thought of the organization as 'largely Joe's child'[48] and were inspired by Chamberlain's achievement as mayor of Birmingham, so wanted him to kick off their campaign in November of 1894. Chamber-lain welcomed the opportunity, for he sympathized fully with the Soci-ety's moderate reformism. Content with the accomplishments of his famous mayoralty, he was no longer at the forefront of municipal Radi-calism. He also shared the Society's aversion to the centralization of authority in the London County Council. All his experience in local government convinced him that 'the best results of municipal administration can only be obtained in smaller areas'.[49] He was not happy about the current extension of Birmingham's municipal boundaries; and so far as London was concerned, he hoped to enhance the authority of the subordinate borough councils.

Catching wind of the invitation to Chamberlain, Captain Middleton, the Conservatives' chief constituency organizer, sought to head it off. He urged Salisbury to accept a speaking engagement in London before Chamberlain was to address the London Municipal Society. Salisbury accepted by telegram on the very day that Chamberlain announced his programme for Unionism nationally. Embarrassed by Middleton's preemptive strike, the London Municipal Society felt obliged to re-schedule Chamberlain's address for a later date; and he complied. He felt angry at 'the Conservative wirepullers who played me a dirty trick',[50] but he was unwilling to recognize that the wires stretched back to Salisbury.

Salisbury responded to Chamberlain's recommendations for the House of Lords by sympathizing with his 'line of tactics'[51] and indicat-ing that he might himself introduce bills on alien immigration and courts for industrial arbitration. But in regard to workmen's compensa-tion, on which he explicitly agreed with Chamberlain, Salisbury identi-fied the crucial difference between them over electoral strategy for a party in opposition. Salisbury argued that, while employers might 'ac-quiesce in the solution of this question on your lines by a responsible government, which they supported, they might resent the same pro-posal from the same quarter in opposition, as uncalled for, & in a man-ner which might make itself seriously felt at the general election'. Success in elections depended as Salisbury saw it on the efforts of com-mitted supporters, whose zeal might only be dimmed by proposals designed to woo the ever-elusive uncommitted.

His caution was confirmed by other reactions to the social pro-gramme Chamberlain had announced. 'A Liberal Unionist' told *The Times* that, '[m]uch as we all admire Mr. Chamberlain for his patriotic stand against the Home Rule fallacy, he is risking the support of many of his party by his Socialistic proposals and schemes.'[52] Yet Chamber-lain's mail bag told a different story. 'I have an enormous correspon-dence,' he reported to Sir Henry James, '—urging me to go on—*and I will*.'[53] Meanwhile, to reinforce his plan for social legislation by the Lords, Chamberlain defended the upper house against attacks by Rosebery. Chamberlain's well-remembered attacks on the Lords in 1884 for holding up the Third Reform Act did not embarrass him now. Then the Lords were resisting the popular desire for an extension of the fran-chise; now the Lords were identified with the even more popular oppo-sition to Home Rule. He insisted that he was still 'no defender of hereditary legislation, but I am a strong upholder of a second Chamber, and until you can find me a better I am going to stick to the House of Lords'.[54]

Hoping for a more sympathetic response from Salisbury, Chamberlain wrote to him directly, pointing out that he had not mentioned the idea of making use of the upper house 'to anyone but yourself—not even to the Duke of Devonshire whom I have not seen since the close of last session'.[55] He accompanied his letter with a memorandum on many of his proposals including some, such as labour exchanges to provide information on employment opportunities, that had not figured in his speech to his constituents. Salisbury delivered an address at Edinburgh before the letter arrived, and heartened Chamberlain by referring favourably though in very general terms to his domestic initiative. When the National Scottish Conservative Association proceeded to pass resolutions 'supporting *every one* of [Chamberlain's] proposals and urging the Peers to initiate this legislation',[56] his hopes rose. His organizational adjutant, Powell Williams, reported that the programme, and particularly the proposals for home purchase by the working class, had '"caught on" in an extraordinary manner . . . Conservatives seem more enthusiastic than our own people'.[57]

Nevertheless, the direct response from Salisbury to Chamberlain induced him to abandon his plan of action through the House of Lords. Salisbury professed agreement upon policy but reasserted his tactical fear 'that some at least of these measures will provoke the hostility of those of whose support we should otherwise be secure'.[58] In an accompanying memorandum he whittled Chamberlain's proposals for the Lords down to two, artisans' home purchase and industrial arbitration, and even so concluded that 'it would not be prudent' to decide on tactics for the coming session until it was about to begin.

Though Chamberlain replied deferentially, he took issue with Salisbury's tactical teaching. No one had a better title to judge what the House of Lords could handle than Salisbury, but he lacked Chamberlain's familiarity with electoral behaviour, especially among the working class—or so Chamberlain assumed. Through the Conservative network of professional constituency agents whom Captain Middleton supervised, Salisbury knew more about the extent and inclinations of the genuinely Conservative working-class electorate than Chamberlain appreciated. Chamberlain's claim to familiarity with the working class was valid only for Birmingham and the West Midlands, a limitation that enabled Salisbury to discount his advice. In general Chamberlain insisted that 'elections are carried by the shifting votes of a minority who do not strictly belong to either party'. He told Salisbury that the working classes were 'not divided on Party lines as absolutely as the middle & upper classes' and were 'very much influenced by the issues presented to them' at election time.[59] Accordingly, while Chamberlain dropped the idea of embodying his programme in bills from the House of Lords, he urged the Unionist leaders to put it forth in their speeches.

Almost everyone assumed by now that the Unionists would return to power sometime in the coming year. Chamberlain's thoughts turned anxiously to the terms upon which a coalition Unionist government would be formed. 'Is it not desirable', he asked Salisbury, 'that we should, as a Party, make up our minds what we can and will do?' Working through Sir Henry James, Chamberlain sought endorsement from the Duke of Devonshire to some basic formula of agreement on domestic policy. Chamberlain wanted the Unionists 'to leave all questions of Constitutional reform . . . alone for the present and to devote [themselves] to the study and prosecution of social legislation'.[60] He tried to whet Devonshire's appetite by raising the question of the distribution of offices for which Whigs were proverbially always hungry. Chamberlain devoted his next major address, at Heywood near Manchester, to his social programme. But the muted response of the other Unionist leaders crushed his hopes. 'You may read every speech that has been made this autumn by the Duke of Devonshire, by Lord Salisbury, & by Mr. Balfour,' he cried, 'and you will not find a single creative or suggestive idea from beginning to end.'[61]

At last, Balfour responded to a plea from Chamberlain for conversation on his social proposals by inviting him to join Salisbury and himself at Hatfield before Parliament reconvened. The invitation revived Chamberlain's hope for 'some definite & public expression of opinion'.[62] He used the invitation to extract a response from Devonshire, who had not communicated even indirectly with him throughout the autumn. Devonshire duly invited him to Chatsworth shortly before he was to meet Salisbury and Balfour at Hatfield. Chamberlain approached these conferences in an unsettled frame of mind. Reports from the party organization indicated that during the autumn the Unionists gained in popularity, to which his programme undoubtedly contributed. They could look forward to taking office with a commanding majority. Yet Chamberlain was not sure that he agreed enough with the Conservative and Whig leaders to join a government they formed.

The conference at Chatsworth dealt with position more than policy. Devonshire declared that when a Unionist government was formed he would either be prime minister or would not join. He and Chamberlain agreed that the third member of the Liberal Unionist triumvirate, Sir Henry James, should have whatever office he chose, probably either lord chancellor or home secretary. As for himself, Chamberlain made the choice that surprised the country six months later, the Colonial Office.[63] So far as his domestic programme was concerned, all he could report from Chatsworth was the vague comment that there would not 'be any difficulty with the Duke'.[64] No report survives from the subsequent meeting at Hatfield. When it was over, Chamberlain headed to the south of France for a brief holiday.

Once Parliament reconvened, the Home Ruling majority in the Commons held together surprisingly well, if only from fear of a general election. But the Liberals could not postpone the triennial contest which their metropolitan counterparts, the Progressives, had to face at the end of February to retain control of the London County Council. The final month of this campaign began with Chamberlain's delayed speech to the London Metropolitan Society. He rose to the occasion with more insight than the Progressive forces, masterminded by Beatrice Potter's recently acquired husband Sidney Webb, were ready to admit. Even so, the programme Chamberlain offered London showed that his ideas as a municipal reformer had ossified. And in the end Salisbury gave his Conservatives the credit for Chamberlain's efforts.

Chamberlain spoke of the spirit of civic enterprise that had transformed Birmingham twenty years before. He insisted that this spirit was distinctive of small cities like the communes of Renaissance Italy—Siena, Perugia, Bologna and Florence—which he had come to admire. Municipal government on that scale could bring 'the wealth and the influence and the ability of the whole community . . . to bear in order to relieve the pressing wants of its least fortunate members, and . . . raise the general level and standard of the whole population'.[65] Communities of no more than half a million could develop a 'sense of possession' in the civic services, buildings and amenities 'which the poorest share with the richest, the sense that this is their property and not another's'. Chamberlain evoked this spirit in order to attack the tendency of the Progressives to aggrandize the London County Council to the detriment of its component municipal boroughs. These municipal boroughs were a good deal smaller than Birmingham, with populations roughly a third of Birmingham's current 450,000. The London County Council embraced a population of five millions. That was too large, Chamberlain argued, to allow for supervision of municipal works and services by elected councillors.

In some ways he was right, as Beatrice Potter confirmed at the turn of the century when she noted that the generation of businessmen who had led the movement for municipal reform were being replaced by councillors of inferior stamp.[66] The middle-class drift to the suburbs accelerated when cities expanded past the half million mark. Chamberlain also knew that elected municipal councillors protected the public purse more vigilantly than would the salaried officials upon which a vast metropolis had to rely. Yet he used the civic experience of Birmingham to restrain as much as to inspire civic activity in London. He was still Radical enough to focus attention on 'the two greatest of the unsolved problems of local life in London . . . the rehousing of the poor and the question of the unemployed'. But the main solution that he offered was the defective model of the Birmingham improvement scheme. Even within those limits, he stressed the virtue of economy in expenditure, disregarding the initial expensiveness of the Birmingham scheme which was only now breaking even. As with old-age pensions, so in local government, his desire to carry the forces of Unionism with him inhibited his advance.

In the event, the Moderates (as Unionists called themselves for London municipal purposes) wiped out their opponents' large majority on the County Council. Support from appointed aldermen enabled the Progressives to remain in office; but for the next three years it would be office without power. No result could have pleased Salisbury better, because he sympathized with Chamberlain's aversion to the London County Council but not with his proposals for the component municipalities. During the election Salisbury encouraged both the Chamberlainite London Municipal Society and the National Union of Conservative Association's Metropolitan Division under Captain Middleton. The Metropolitan Division campaigned in the accents of undiluted ratepayer Conservatism. The inconsistency in policy between the two organizations did not disturb Salisbury, who welcomed their ability to attract diverse forces. But when the returns for their combined efforts rolled in, he gave all the credit to Middleton's association.

Disheartening investments

The investments Chamberlain had made over the past half decade, political as well as financial, ran into trouble in the spring of 1895. The returns from them turned so poor that he thought of retiring from public life. But instead of drawing back, he deepened his stake without much assurance that the underlying problems had been solved.

The news in February about the poor prospects of his sisal plantation in the Bahamas combined with a collapse in value of his Canadian Pacific Railway shares to threaten his financial security. The setback placed his career in question. Parliamentary life was unremunerative unless in office; and the prospects for him returning to office were not encouraging. 'Why,' he cried to Mary—who, to make matters worse, was away with her parents when the troubles broke—'[w]hy should I ruin myself—incur all this abuse & misrepresentation—only to be a subordinate member of a Cabinet with whose general policy I may not be in hearty sympathy? . . . The simple fact is that the work which has sustained me during the last 8 years has been, for the time at any rate, accomplished. I have largely assisted to make H[ome] Rule impossible,

& now there is nothing but personal ambition to keep me in harness.'[67] Mary replied with reassurance. Yet she continued to spend lavishly on exotic lace for Highbury and dresses for herself. March brought news that a row of small houses was to go up on Kings Heath in Birmingham overlooking Highbury and breaking its view into the Worcestershire countryside. 'I seem', Joe moaned, 'to have no luck at all just now.'[68]

The financial clouds were followed by a political thunderstorm. It arose from Conservative quarters, among party workers who resented the application of the electoral compact with the Liberal Unionists to their constituencies, and among backbench MPs uneasy about Chamberlain's insistent Radicalism. The first storm warning came from the constituency of Hythe in Hampshire. Because the brand of Unionism of the departing MP, Sir Edward Watkin, was unclear, Conservatives disputed the Liberal Unionist claim to replace him. Chamberlain paid little heed to this dispute because it did not fall within his electoral Duchy. But when similar trouble erupted in Warwickshire, he felt touched to the quick. Warwick and Leamington was the constituency of the retiring Speaker of the House of Commons, A.W. Peel. Though understood to be a Liberal Unionist, Peel had kept a low partisan profile because of his parliamentary position. He allowed his constituency organization to be nursed by a local Conservative named Nelson who hoped to become the MP when Peel retired. When Chamberlain heard of Nelson's expectations, he overreacted. 'The Tories seem bent on making my position intolerable,' he told Mary, '& try to grab every seat they can possibly lay claim to.'[69] He induced Balfour to repudiate Nelson's claim and assign the constituency to the Liberal Unionists.

This precipitate decision provoked a reaction on the backbenches in the Commons as well as locally. Sir H.H. Howorth, Conservative MP for Salford South, wrote to The Times decrying the electoral compact in terms that reinforced Chamberlain's suspicions. Why pay such a price for continued opposition to Home Rule, which was by now 'a dead horse', from Radical Unionists who opposed some of the dearest Conservative interests such as the establishment of the Welsh church and denominational education?[70] The Tories of Warwick and Leamington refused to support Chamberlain's nominee, the Speaker's son George. Sinking deeper in depression, Chamberlain was filled 'with increasing disgust at the whole course of politics, & increasing wish to be out of it all'.[71]

A few days later, he defied the likes of Howorth by voting for the second reading of the government's bill to disestablish the Church of England in Wales. He did so to validate his credentials among Nonconformists who might make the difference between defeat and victory for the Unionists. But he meant his action to be no more than symbolic, as he had explained to anxious Conservatives. He explained that he would vote against Welsh disestablishment rather than place a Unionist government in jeopardy; he would insist on more generous treatment for the Welsh church than a Liberal government was likely to allow; and in any case he stood almost alone among Unionists on this issue—only one other Liberal Unionist voted with him for the Welsh disestablishment bill—so why worry? Still, his position was duplicitous. His message to worried Conservatives was quite different from the words he used to woo Nonconformists and the Welsh. Conservatives had reason to wonder whether Chamberlain would steal more than his share of the seats in the new Parliament and use that power to compromise some of the interests they most treasured.

This anxiety surfaced repeatedly during the early weeks of April in the *Standard,* the metropolitan newspaper commonly associated with Lord Salisbury. Though Chamberlain did not suspect that the *Standard* spoke in this particular connection for Salisbury, he feared that it spoke for the sort of Conservatives with whom Salisbury sympathized. Furthermore, the criticisms in the *Standard* were heralded by an attack on Chamberlain in another organ of Conservative opinion, the *New Review,* by an anonymous writer who may have been that most pretentious of aristocrats, George Curzon. The *New Review* writer detected the whiff of 'the back-parlour of the Provincial Mayor' about Chamberlain. Alluding to the strains in the electoral compact, the writer accused Chamberlain of devoting 'his narrow and powerful intelligence' to wirepulling and insisted that 'the right to dictate a policy . . . must ever lie, outside his reach'.[72]

The *New Review* article threatened Chamberlain where he felt least secure. The leaders of the Conservative party backed him up in applying the electoral compact to his Duchy. But Salisbury and also Devonshire had committed themselves to his domestic programme only in the vaguest or most restricted terms. Reversing the concern of Howorth and the *New Review,* Chamberlain feared that the Tory and Whig majority of Unionists would use the electoral rewards which he helped them earn while disregarding his social policy.

Lord Wolmer, who supervised the Liberal Unionist organization nationally, visited Chamberlain early in April to discuss Warwick and Leamington, and found him less concerned about that constituency than about the encompassing wave of Conservative hostility. 'What he wants at the moment is sympathy', Wolmer reported to his father-in-law, Lord Salisbury, particularly sympathy 'from the Conservative party.'[73] But Salisbury also learned from Wolmer that Conservative unrest about Chamberlain and the Unionist alliance had spread to include Sir Michael Hicks Beach, often a good indicator of bedrock Conservative opinion.

Could Chamberlain have seen it, Salisbury's response would not have raised his spirits. His cry for sympathy from the Conservative party struck Salisbury as pitiable emotion to which there was no ready political response. As for the interests at issue between Chamberlain and his Conservative critics, Salisbury extended them to include reform of the land law. If Chamberlain wanted cordial support from Conservatives, Salisbury told Wolmer, 'he has no choice now except to put as far into the shadow as he honestly can his anti-Church & anti-land opinions'.[74]

Nevertheless, Chamberlain received the words of sympathy he craved, from Balfour publicly reading a letter from Salisbury, and privately from Conservatives such as Henry Chaplin who were indignant at the treatment he had received. Chamberlain's spirits picked up but his resolve also hardened. 'If I am to do any good or play any part in the future,' he replied to Chaplin, 'it must be with the hearty—and not the grudging—assent of the Conservative party.'[75] He asked Devonshire to 'take up a firm stand now'.[76] Chamberlain's returning optimism soon exceeded his caution. 'I believe we shall have a great majority,' he reported to Neville in the Bahamas, '& then I suppose there will be a Coalition Government & I shall have to take office once more.'[77] A mutually acceptable compromise was worked out for Warwick and Leamington. The Conservatives rejected Chamberlain's original nominee but accepted an alternative Liberal Unionist. Chamberlain pleased Conservatives in Parliament by cooperating with them over amendments to the Welsh disestablishment bill. But he and Devonshire did nothing more to reach agreement with the Conservative leaders on the terms upon which the anticipated coalition ministry could be formed.

The life left in the Liberal government drained away at the approach of summer. Chamberlain delivered the final blow. Since direct votes of censure only rallied the government's forces, he decided to make use of the votes on budgetary supply. The first opportunity to do so arose on 21 June over the army's store of the new smokeless explosive called cordite. Chamberlain was familiar with it because it was produced by his brother Arthur's firm, Kynoch Ltd. Conservative whipping for the debate was lax, and so was the government's; but the Liberal Unionists were on full alert. The government was narrowly defeated; and after a weekend of uncertainty it decided to resign. Long awaited yet ill prepared for, the moment to form a coalition Unionist government had arrived.

13

Evading Discredit
1895–1897

The Secretary of State for the Colonies: 'Mr. Rhodes ... has shown the capacity, and the energy, and the ability which are required in the development of a new territory. ...'

Sir William Harcourt: 'And the morals?'

Hansard, 8 May 1896

Though Chamberlain had precipitated the fall of the Liberal government, he was not sure quite what would replace it or what place he would find in the new order. In giving a lead to the Unionists in the Commons, he implied that he would join a Unionist government; but he knew he was not in control of the forces he led. He benefited from that knowledge. He had a better sense as a Unionist than ever as a Liberal of what he could and could not do. Moreover, he knew where he wanted to go. Over the past decade he had recovered a sense of political direction and worked out a distinctive agenda. It included domestic and imperial issues, and was flexible as well as focused.

He also knew the particular office of state he wanted: the Colonial Office. His choice surprised almost everyone. His political weight entitled him to a post of higher standing. Rather like the colonies themselves, the Colonial Office ranked among the less important secretaryships of state. But Chamberlain meant to overturn the old priorities. He had talked about domestic affairs and about Ireland far more than about the empire. Yet over the past five years, as concern deepened about unemployment in Britain and the performance of its economy, he had stressed the need to exploit and expand the country's imperial markets.

After some recovery in the late 1880s, the economy had fallen back into depression, triggered by the fall in share values in 1890 from which Chamberlain himself suffered. The Liberals, paralysed by the canons of classical economics, had nothing to offer in response. Some restless Conservatives, with occasional encouragement from Churchill and Salisbury, advocated a return to tariff protection, often with an imperial dimension. Chamberlain directed attention to the colonies. Speaking about the depression in March 1895, he elaborated his imperial theme, undeterred by the poor performance of his own investment in the Bahamas. 'It is not enough to occupy certain great spaces of the world's surface,' he told his constituents,[1] 'unless you are willing to develop them.' He compared Britain's colonies to the undeveloped estates of a landlord, and he insisted that railways were as important to the development of the British empire as roads had been to the Roman. He hoped that cultivation of Britain's imperial estates would stimulate overseas trade, and that the construction of railways in the colonies would ease unemployment among suppliers at home. Thus stimulated, the nation's economy could generate revenue for social reform.

Chamberlain wanted to see how much the Colonial Office could do to cultivate the resources of the empire without violating the British commitment to free trade. Interest in colonial markets was lively among the metal manufacturers of Birmingham who were hurt by every upward twist in the protective tariffs of Germany and the United States. Yet even those who sympathized with demand for a restoration of protective tariffs in Britain hesitated to come out and say so. Chamberlain saw no need to sup with the devils of protectionism before the resources of the imperialism of free trade had been explored.

Domestic considerations fortified his desire for the Colonial Office. Chamberlain's acceptance of a domestic post in a Unionist government, whether the Home Office or the Exchequer, would make many Conservatives uneasy. The springtime outbreak of hostility towards him confirmed that fear. Acceptance of the Colonial Office, on the other hand, would align him with a large body of Conservative sentiment. This choice need not mean abandonment of his domestic proposals. The colonies would, of course, become Chamberlain's first concern. They would replace Home Rule at the head of his agenda if the next election disposed of that threat. Still, as Colonial Secretary, he could shape Unionist domestic policy as effectively as he had while leading the attack on Home Rule during the last Unionist government. Chamberlain did not face up to the ambiguity in that assurance. The extent of his ability to influence the domestic legislation of Salisbury's former ministry was not clear. Responsibility for the Colonial Office was bound to rearrange Chamberlain's priorities and thus dim the prospects for Unionist social reform to which he had drawn so much attention.

That was, however, not the most momentous of the consequences that followed from his choice of the Colonial Office. It placed him on a rising, worldwide wave of international competition for overseas resources, territory and power known as 'imperialism'. The man and the movement would be identified with each other. Chamberlain had encouraged the movement; he possessed a distinctive sense of its potentialities; and the Colonial Office helped him place his impress on it. Yet he could not control the wave he rode. The surge of imperialism carried him to a height of power little short of his highest ambition. But first it nearly destroyed him; and the setback distorted his imperial enterprise.

Merger and mandate

The terms upon which the Unionists formed a coalition gratified Chamberlain. As soon as Salisbury received the Queen's invitation to form a government, he called Devonshire and Chamberlain into conclave with Balfour and himself. His basic question was whether the Liberal Unionists would enter into a coalition with the Conservatives. Yet he did not repeat the offers he made in 1886 to serve under Devonshire as prime minister. Devonshire, suppressing his regret, accepted the primacy of the Conservatives. He asked only about policy, thus adopting Chamberlain's tactics. Referring particularly to Chamberlain's speeches, Salisbury said he foresaw no great difficulty with regard to the general lines of policy apart from the church, which he set aside as an open question. Still, he did not commit himself to anything specific or concrete; and Chamberlain was content to leave the 'details ... open'.[2]

Salisbury thus eluded commitment to Chamberlain on policy. But Chamberlain took Salisbury by surprise over the distribution of offices. The first assignments went as Salisbury intended. Balfour would lead the House of Commons as First Lord of the Treasury. Devonshire as President of the Council would give the armed services the coordination they needed. Salisbury, while serving as prime minister, would also take the Foreign Office, where he had always served with distinction. He offered Chamberlain his choice among all that remained, expecting him to choose the Home Office. When Chamberlain demurred, Balfour assured him that he could have the Exchequer. But Chamberlain asked for the Colonial Office. The only alternative that he suggested, to take charge of the army at the War Office, lacked urgency now that Devonshire had agreed to supervise all the armed forces. Chamberlain explained that he hoped to foster closer union between the colonies and the mother country. Unable to accept his request at face value, Salisbury allowed a day for reconsideration.

Though he had detected Chamberlain's nascent imperial instincts in the early 1880s, Salisbury did not welcome his desire for the Colonial Office. In the hands of a strong and ambitious man, that office could encroach on the sphere of responsibility for Britain's overseas relations which Salisbury most loved and from which he had derived much of his power. When a night for reflection failed to change Chamberlain's choice, Salisbury accepted it with impenetrable grace. He consoled himself with the hope that Chamberlain's interest in the colonies would prove little more than theoretical. Chamberlain soon disposed of that illusion. Yet for a considerable time the linked responsibilities of Salisbury at the Foreign Office and Chamberlain at the Colonial Office strengthened the alliance between the two men. They had much in common as imperialists. Both were determined to use the empire, as Salisbury had put it, 'to make smooth the paths for British commerce . . . for the application of British capital, at a time when . . . other outlets for the commercial energies of our race are being gradually closed'.[3]

In negotiating their agreement to coalesce, the Unionist leaders paid more attention to domestic issues. Before agreeing to take the Exchequer, Sir Michael Hicks Beach asked Chamberlain what he had in mind with regard to old-age pensions. Chamberlain replied modestly: he requested an expert inquiry, but said he did not envisage anything beyond lenient application of the Poor Law, at least until the budget produced a surplus. Hicks Beach in return kept open the possibility of increasing indirect taxation to pay for old-age pensions.

Still, the completed composition of the ministry conveyed the sense among Unionists that imperial issues were more important. Goschen, like Chamberlain, preferred imperial to domestic office, and took the Admiralty rather than the Exchequer before it was offered to Hicks Beach. Of the three minions of Chamberlain to be given subordinate office, only Collings took a domestic position, assisting at the Home Office. Powell Williams was assigned to the War Office under the Liberal Unionist Lord Lansdowne; and Austen Chamberlain went to the Admiralty under Goschen. The prospects for enactment of his father's social programme receded with the transfer of Sir Henry James to the House of Lords as Chancellor of the Duchy of Lancaster. Chamberlain had hoped that James, an able legislator, would draft his social legislation. James would have been better able to do so either as Lord Chancellor, the leading post in the upper house which Salisbury insisted upon giving to the Conservative Halsbury, or as Home Secretary; but his health was not up to the demands of that office.

In an attempt to keep an eye on Chamberlain at the Colonial Office, Salisbury appointed his Liberal Unionist son-in-law Wolmer, now Earl of Selborne, to be undersecretary there. The appointment worked the other way. Chamberlain greeted Selborne with the declaration 'that England had not yet realised what the British Empire really stood for or what a part it might play in the world or of what developments it was capable and that he meant to try and make England understand'.[4] Thereafter Selborne displayed more anxiety to keep his father-in-law up to this vision than to imbue his departmental chief with Salisburian circumspection.

For the moment, attention was riveted on the general election. It did not resolve the uncertain basic policy of the new government. But the huge parliamentary majority won by the government at least confirmed the internal cohesion of the coalition. Chamberlain displayed his desire to work in harness with the Conservatives from the outset by submitting his election address to Balfour for approval. Once the campaign began, there was no time for further consultation of this sort; but Chamberlain still took care to incorporate distinctively Conservative commitments into his appeal.

The first task, however, was to mobilize his electoral machine and also avert local disputes within the alliance such as shocked him in March. Chamberlain had seen to the creation of a Midlands Liberal Unionist Association after the last general election to improve the performance of his party within his electoral 'Duchy'. Funded from Birmingham, and grounded in each polling district, the association created a Liberal Unionist organization in every constituency in Worcestershire, Warwickshire and Staffordshire. It increased party membership ten-, sometimes twentyfold. Inspired by the Liberal Unionist example, the Conservatives of the West Midlands brought their organization up to a level of effectiveness unmatched in the rest of England.

Within Birmingham itself the problem was not organization but cooperation between the allies. The Gladstonian organization, demoralized by its failure at the last general election, collapsed just before the new Salisbury government took office. The Liberals of Birmingham did not even begin to select candidates for the election until July. By putting an Irish doctor up to oppose Chamberlain in West Birmingham, they displayed their despair. But troublesome Birmingham Centre threatened again to disturb the Unionist alliance. John Bright's son neglected the constituency; and when he agreed to retire, the city's Conservatives hoped hungrily to replace him. Chamberlain, in the cooperative spirit of the coalition, responded more sympathetically than would the local Liberal Unionists. His encouragement of Conservatives' hopes for the future eased their surrender on the eve of this election; and the president of the Liberal Unionist association, Ebenezer Parkes, was elected unopposed in Bright's stead. Chamberlain felt so strong at home that he spoke only once in Birmingham during the entire campaign. Otherwise he devoted himself to his surrounding Duchy and the odd marginal constituency elsewhere in the country.

Though Balfour never campaigned better than in this election, it was pervaded, in the judgement of observers, by the personality of Chamberlain. Yet his speeches lacked the fire of 1892 or the social vision of 1894. The object of the Unionist leaders in dissolving Parliament before they could present it with a legislative programme was to direct attention to the sterility of the Liberals' three years in office. Like his colleagues, Chamberlain directed attention backwards more than forwards. He continued to treat Home Rule as 'the great cardinal issue'.[5]

While he could not present the threat as immediate, he dwelt on the way in which this first of all Liberal commitments prevented action on other issues so long as the Liberals were in power. The empire had yet to replace Ireland as the focus of Unionist rhetoric, though the new Colonial Secretary stressed the importance of foreign and colonial trade to deal with 'the lack of employment'.

That, he explained, was 'the greatest of the social problems with which we have to deal'. His social programme ranked lower than Ireland but higher than the empire in his electoral rhetoric. He described the presence of Liberal Unionists in the coalition as 'a pledge that ... the new Government will not be ... backward in its efforts to promote the social amelioration of the condition of our people at home'.[6] At the same time he muted and modified his social agenda to meet Conservative concerns. The manifesto Salisbury issued in calling the election reduced and reordered Chamberlain's programme. Salisbury put relief for agriculture, the most depressed of all sectors in the economy, at the top of his list; he undertook to foster home ownership among the working class; he dealt with old-age pensions simply by mentioning the need to revise the Poor Law; and he said nothing about compensation for industrial accidents. Chamberlain heeded the prime minister under whom he served. Old-age pensions headed Chamberlain's agenda, followed by workmen's compensation and courts to arbitrate industrial disputes. But he gave prominence to measures that appealed to the Conservative instinct for economic protection: curbs on the immigration of destitute aliens and on the import of foreign prison-made goods. He weakened his commitment to an eight-hour day for mining. He also seconded Conservative proposals for agrarian relief, though the way he did so showed that his sympathy was acquired, not natural.

The first results brought Unionist gains crowned by the defeat of Harcourt at Derby. This was too good to be desirable. Harcourt was the Liberal leader with whom Chamberlain preserved the most genuine friendship, in part because there was always some lightness and distance in their relations. Aside from the personal feeling, an electoral tide strong enough to oust Harcourt from a seemingly safe seat might enable the Conservatives to do without the Liberal Unionists. The results on succeeding days placed the Conservatives in a position to do just that. The Unionist tide extended to every corner of the kingdom. Though Chamberlain's midland organization improved on the already good Unionist result of 1892, the performance of his Duchy lost its distinction amid the national tide. Fortunately the tide benefited Liberal Unionists as well as Conservatives. While the larger contingent acquired a small majority of their own, Liberal Unionist representation increased by fifty per cent to give them seventy members in the new House of Commons, making them the most durable splinter party of the century. The size of their parliamentary contingent suggested how much they contributed to the margin of victory in constituencies where the victorious candidates were Conservative. With a majority in the Commons of 152, the victory of the Unionists was greater than any since the Reform Act of 1832, greater even than 1832 in Chamberlain's estimation because on that occasion an enlargement of the electorate accounted for the outcome.

Once the Conservatives came within sight of an independent majority, even before the voting was complete, Chamberlain looked for ways to bypass rocks that threatened the alliance between Conservative and Liberal Unionist. His underlying concern in terms of policy, both domestic and imperial, was finance. He approached the Conservative Chancellor of the Exchequer, Hicks Beach, on ways to give hard-pressed denominational elementary schools more money without violating the current balance between them and the civic board schools dear to Nonconformists. Indirectly through Salisbury, Chamberlain raised the possibility of using the dividends from Britain's shares in the Suez canal to pay for public works in depressed crown colonies.

Beach gave both suggestions an encouraging reception. Salisbury invited 'My dear Chamberlain' to a tête-à-tête with Balfour and himself, asking him to 'drop prefixes'.[7] He meant titles but could as well have meant party labels. Chamberlain did not go so far. Sir Henry James, now Lord James of Hereford, wanted the Liberal Unionists to keep up their separate electoral organization after the election. Devonshire disagreed and referred the question to Chamberlain. Chamberlain would allow weak Liberal Unionist associations to fade away and would not fight others that wished to amalgamate with the Conservatives. But he insisted on the autonomy of Liberal Unionist organizations under his sway, and he encouraged autonomy elsewhere. In doing so he began imperceptibly to take over from the Duke of Devonshire as leader of the Liberal Unionist organization nationwide.

Party organization in the country was nevertheless a minor concern for him after the election. He was tired, sometimes immobilized with headache, exhausted after two years of intense activity without a break. A firm believer in holidays and a lover of travel, he longed to get away. His one political initiative was to press Balfour for a preemptive strike on the opposition in the Commons while its spirits were still low from the election. Chamberlain wanted to tighten the rules against obstruction before the new House adjourned for the autumn, so that the government could take effective charge when Parliament reconvened in January for its first full session. Balfour let the opportunity slip.

Mid-conspiracy

Until he could put the election behind him, Chamberlain was scarcely able to visit the Colonial Office. He managed none the less to convey to its permanent staff the direction in which he hoped to move. Economic cultivation and consolidation of the empire was his goal. It required change in the traditional patterns of government: more directive effort by the Colonial Office than the principles of laissez-faire would encourage, and a stretching of the limitations of strict free trade. Chamberlain approached the changes he envisaged through inquiry. At the beginning of July he let the Colonial Office staff know that he was 'seriously contemplating the possibility and expediency of giving Colonial produce a preference over foreign produce'. At the end of the month he launched an attempt 'to determine the extent to which foreign imports were displacing British goods in the markets of the empire'.[8] He told the new House of Commons about his policy of cultivating the undeveloped estates of the empire. It was to begin with minor estates, crown colonies such as Cyprus.

At the beginning of August, however, as soon as Chamberlain was able to devote his attention to the Colonial Office, he was deflected from his economic agenda and sucked into a conspiracy by Cecil Rhodes to place the destiny of South Africa in British hands. Chamberlain's priorities for South Africa were political more than economic. He wanted to strengthen and extend British imperial authority over the region in face not only of resistance from the Boer republics and competition from other European powers but also of the semi-independent claims advanced by the Cape Colony. Ultimately he hoped to see the various pieces of the British puzzle in the area—the colonies of the Cape and Natal with their white elective legislatures, the black protectorates of Bechuanaland, Swaziland and Zululand, the Boer republics of the Transvaal and the Orange Free State under British paramountcy, and the lands to the north—combined into a federation which would carry the whole empire closer to his dream of imperial federation. The mineral resources of the region fuelled but also troubled his imperial dream, particularly as they were absorbed in the ever widening grasp of Rhodes.

Chamberlain acquiesced in but never fully reconciled himself with the British decision in 1889 to extend imperial interests north of the Transvaal through the private agency of Rhodes's British South Africa Company, commonly known on account of its governmental commission as the Chartered Company. The fiscal limitations that curbed Chamberlain's hopes for old-age pensions also restrained his ambitions for the empire. Until the territory entrusted to the Chartered Company reached economic self-sufficiency, the imperial government could not directly govern and develop it without violating the confines of Victorian governmental finance. Chamberlain's uneasiness about Rhodes intensified in 1890 when he became premier of the Cape Colony, for Rhodes won support from the Cape Dutch by championing the interests of the colony against the pretensions of the imperial government.

Upon becoming Colonial Secretary, Chamberlain accepted the necessity of working with Rhodes and hoped to harness Rhodes's enterprise for imperial purposes. Still, the relationship between the two men was bound to be strenuous. It combined mutual dependency with antagonism. It was further vexed by physical distance, for Rhodes rarely left southern Africa and communicated with Chamberlain through intermediaries. Chamberlain approached these dealings and the business of South Africa with all the wariness at his command; but it was not enough. Rhodes linked him with a flagrantly illegitimate resort to armed force which cast discredit on the entire imperial enterprise in South Africa, placed Chamberlain's career in grave jeopardy, and consumed him for eighteen months in anxious improvisation to control the damage.

The conflict between Chamberlain and Rhodes had flashed into the open in March 1895 before the change of government at Westminster when the appointment of a new governor and high commissioner for the Cape Colony and South Africa was announced. The current high commissioner, Sir Henry Loch, was too devoted to the imperial interest for Rhodes's liking. He prevailed upon Rosebery to bring back Sir Hercules Robinson, who had collaborated closely with Rhodes during his former term as high commissioner and in business. Chamberlain had helped to secure the removal of Robinson and the appointment of Loch in 1889. Since then Robinson had become not merely a shareholder in the Chartered Company but a director of the De Beers diamond monopoly owned by Rhodes. Chamberlain described Robinson's reappointment as high commissioner as little short of scandalous, one 'to which only Americans would stoop'.[9]

Yet Chamberlain had not hesitated in the early 1890s to buy a large number of shares in the South African Gold Trust, a company that raised capital for Rhodes's goldmining interests. Because of the high yields, Chamberlain and his brothers invested in this and at least one other South African goldmining company which was not in Rhodes's network; and the Chamberlains retained their holdings until the turn of the century. In 1882 when a member of Gladstone's cabinet, Chamberlain had invested in the National African Company of George Goldie chartered by the government to extend British interests in west Africa. He retained that investment after becoming Colonial Secretary. But it did not reduce his fundamental dislike of Goldie's enterprise. Chamberlain drew a distinction between income-producing or empire-developing investments, which he thought unexceptionable, and company control, for which he censured Robinson's association with Rhodes.[10] Before accepting reappointment as high commissioner Robinson resigned as director at De Beers; but Chamberlain argued that the association still deprived Robinson of the requisite appearance of impartiality in South Africa, because the 'enormous funds' of De Beers had been 'used again and again for political purposes'.[11]

As a result of this attack, Chamberlain received a hint of the conspiracy that Rhodes was weaving; but it was too obscure to appreciate at the time. Rhodes asked Albert, now fourth Earl Grey, to induce Chamberlain to end his attacks on Robinson's reappointment. Grey was associated with Chamberlain on the South Africa committee of the 1880s, and became a director of the Chartered Company with Chamberlain's encouragement to keep watch on Rhodes in the imperial interest. Then Grey fell under the thrall of Rhodes and used his friendships from the South Africa committee to forward the interests of his new master. Though not fully briefed on the conspiracy of Rhodes, Grey understood why he wanted Robinson as high commissioner at Cape Town. Grey told Chamberlain that '[d]evelopments which are about to take place in the Transvaal will fan up the fire of Race Hatred once more'. Rhodes wanted Robinson as governor because he was 'more likely than anyone else to be able to keep . . . the Dutch party in Cape Colony quiet during the rough times that are coming'.[12]

The developments to which Grey referred were of Rhodes's making. At the end of 1894, Rhodes decided to wrest the power to determine the destiny of South Africa from President Kruger of the Transvaal, as the South African Republic was commonly known. The discovery in 1886 of the world's greatest supply of gold on the Rand, a ridge of land near Johannesburg, brought Kruger's republic from the fringe to the centre of the region's economy. With the opening in 1894 of a railway to Delagoa Bay, the Transvaal no longer depended on the more distant port of Cape Town for access to world markets. Also in 1894, Rhodes's hopes of finding gold fields in the territory of his Chartered Company to counterbalance those of the Transvaal were dashed. Meanwhile there was a conspicuous warming in relations between the Transvaal and Germany, which threatened the paramount standing of Great Britain under the conventions of 1881 and 1884. Complicating the situation, since 1886 a predominantly British immigration had been flowing into the gold fields of the Rand. These outsiders or 'uitlanders' were denied any hope of enfranchisement by the Dutch farmers or 'Boers' whose fathers had trekked in to found the republic. And Kruger, who embodied these origins, had just been reelected to the presidency of their republic, albeit by a narrow margin. This combination of developments destroyed Rhodes's confidence that time was working on the side of British interests in South Africa. His fear was quickened by signs from a weakening heart that, though he was just over forty years of age, time was running out for him too.

He therefore gathered his forces for a putsch to replace Kruger's republic with a regime more fully affiliated with the British. He adapted for his purposes a plan proposed some months earlier by Sir Henry Loch. Impressed by an eruption of anger among the uitlanders of Johannesburg against the Kruger regime, Loch proposed to assemble an armed force in the British protectorate of Bechuanaland across the western border of the Transvaal, ready to invade and protect the uitlanders in the event of an uprising, at which point the high commissioner would present himself to arbitrate between the rebels and the republic in the interests of the paramount power. Rhodes's plan differed in several vital regards from Loch's. Aside from the final intervention of the high commissioner, Rhodes intended to work through his own rather than through imperial agents. He wanted the Bechuanaland protectorate to be assigned to his Chartered Company and to station troops there under Chartered rather than imperial control. He planned to stimulate and supervise the uprising in Johannesburg through his mining company, Consolidated Goldfields, and to supply the rebels with arms and ammunition through De Beers. Furthermore he expected his force on the Bechuanaland border to act parallel with and not simply in support of the rebellion on the Rand. Rhodes meant to orchestrate these events: the rising, the simultaneous invasion, and swift imperial arbitration.

Robinson, though as yet unaware of the plot, was intended to play a vital role in it. Rhodes needed a high commissioner ready to follow his prompting. Robinson possessed the further virtue, as Grey claimed, of being trusted by the Dutch in the Afrikaner Bond, the dominant organization in the politics of the Cape Colony. The Cape Dutch were tied to the Transvaal Boers by what was called racial affinity. Rhodes had reduced the political force of that affinity and won the support of the Bond by appealing to the economic interests of the Cape Dutch, whether against imperial interference or rivalry from the Transvaal. But the alliance between Rhodes and the Bond would be shaken if not shattered by armed attack by Rhodes's men on Kruger's regime. Rhodes hoped that Robinson would retain the confidence of the Cape Dutch and thus help him through the difficult interval when the regime in the Transvaal was being changed.

No change would endure if it permanently estranged those of Dutch descent in South Africa. Their consent was necessary to British control, whether exercised by the Cape, the Chartered Company or London. No knowledge of Rhodes's plot was needed to appreciate the importance of Dutch cooperation at the Cape; and as for the 'rough times' Grey pre-

dicted, the uitlander unrest in Johannesburg was common knowledge.
Grey simply put the two together for Chamberlain. Chamberlain appre-
ciated the point enough to stop his opposition to the reappointment of
Robinson.

When Chamberlain took charge at the Colonial Office four months
later, the first issue to confront him was a request from Rhodes for
Bechuanaland. Anxious to ensure that Rhodes forwarded the interests
of the mother country as well as his own, Chamberlain unwittingly
forced one dimension of Rhodes's conspiracy to the surface.
Bechuanaland came in two parts, a crown colony on the northwestern
border of the Cape Colony, and a protectorate farther north on the
western border of the Transvaal leading to the territories of the Chartered Company. Rhodes wanted both, the crown colony to be assigned
to the Cape, the protectorate to the Chartered Company. Before leaving
office, the Rosebery government had virtually approved the first and
came close to approving the second. Chamberlain attempted to combine
bipartisan continuity with his desire for a greater assertion of imperial
authority by agreeing to the first but delaying the second until he had
time to familiarize himself with the situation. The advocates of imperial
power, Sir Henry now Lord Loch and the missionary Mackenzie,
pleaded with him in the name of the native population of the protectorate to hold on to it. In negotiating the terms for annexation of the crown
colony to the Cape, Chamberlain saw how disinclined the Cape government under Rhodes's premiership was to recognize either native or
imperial claims. The main imperial interest served by the Chartered
Company in the protectorate was construction of the railway beyond
Cape Colony to the north; and Chamberlain was annoyed to discover
how little headway the Chartered Company had made with this project.

But Rhodes wanted the protectorate quickly. Aside from linking his
interests in the Cape with those to the north, it provided the launching
pad he wanted for the invasion to assist a uitlander rising. Emissaries
from Rhodes pressed Chamberlain from the beginning of August: first
Dr Rutherfoord Harris, then Lord Grey, now better informed about
Rhodes's intentions. When Harris and Grey discovered that Chamberlain did not intend to hand over the protectorate for at least a year, they
tried to tell him of the hidden reason for their request, the launching
pad. They tried in effect to ask him to facilitate the invasion of a country whose external relations Britain controlled under the conventions of
the early eighties. The impropriety of such conduct was obvious. Yet if
Chamberlain stood aside and made no provision to protect the largely
British community at Johannesburg, would he not be still more open to
censure? The Colonial Office received many reports emphasizing the
anger of the uitlanders at their oppression by the Boer government.

Nothing suggested that the reported unrest was a product of Rhodes's contrivance.

Even so, Chamberlain saw that he must conduct himself with the utmost circumspection. He tried to draw a line between what he would listen to as Colonial Secretary and what he heard privately from personal associates. When Rutherfoord Harris attempted at the Colonial Office to tell him of the connection between the unrest on the Rand and Rhodes's desire for the Bechuanaland protectorate, Chamberlain silenced him. Afterwards in private, however, he accepted the information from Grey. Chamberlain suggested an immediate compromise while he mulled over a permanent solution. He proposed to grant the Chartered Company just enough land in the protectorate to carry the railway to the north, in exchange for an undertaking from the Company to proceed with the construction immediately. This way he would ensure prompt progress on the railway and Rhodes would acquire the launching pad he wanted: for the railway and hence the land grant would run along the stretch of the Bechuanaland-Transvaal border closest to Johannesburg. Rhodes accepted the offer, which the Colonial Office proceeded to implement, undercutting native resistance in the protectorate. But Chamberlain was not ready yet to approve what Rhodes assumed was the corollary to the land grant: permission to move the armed police force of the Chartered Company down from its territories in the north, ostensibly to protect the railway works along the Transvaal border. Grey gave Chamberlain only a sketchy impression of Rhodes's plan, not enough to show him the necessity for these armed police, quite enough to make him hesitate before agreeing to anything for which there was not obvious justification.

By the beginning of September Chamberlain was so tired that he could do little more than list the problems he had to deal with. He was desperate to be off on holiday far from England to escape the relentless flow of letters and news. To a man who lived for his work, no holiday would be entirely satisfactory if it did not bear in some way on his public responsibilities. He thought of a cruise to South Africa. How differently things might have turned out if he had gone at the beginning instead of the end of his term as Colonial Secretary! But Austen, who was to be in the holiday party, did not want to venture so far. They settled on France and Spain with a visit to Gibraltar.

Before leaving, Chamberlain consulted Salisbury on the major issues of concern between the Colonial and Foreign Office. The two men saw eye to eye across the board: supporting the territorial claims of British Guiana vis-à-vis Venezuela; interested in dividing the spoils of Indochina with France; and determined to uphold imperial interests in South Africa, where Salisbury like Chamberlain wanted 'the Imperial

Government & not Rhodes' to 'exercise the control'.[13] This agreement
enabled Salisbury and Chamberlain to dovetail their efforts nicely when
Kruger severed an alternative trade route between the Transvaal and
the Cape in a dispute over railway freight. First Chamberlain stiffened
the Colonial Office staff to resist Kruger's action. Then, in Chamberlain's absence, Salisbury threatened Kruger with armed force if he
would not back down. Finally Chamberlain made sure that, if the threat
had to be implemented, the government of the Cape Colony would
contribute as much as Britain to the action. Aside from this business,
nothing troubled Chamberlain's holiday.

Towards the vortex

He returned at the beginning of November in excellent health and spirits, and plunged back into work, 'busy as the day is long'.[14] The holiday
had strengthened his vision and for a while lent it balance. Even before
Kruger backed down at the threat of British force and reopened the
trade route to the Cape, Chamberlain urged the Cape government to
moderate its demand for a proportion of the Transvaal trade. A few
days later, he extended his ideas for cultivating the undeveloped estates
of the empire from crown colonies to major ones which elected their
own legislatures and governed themselves internally. For financial as
well as political reasons, the effort in self-governing colonies needed to
be cooperative. They would have to accept complete responsibility for
internal economic improvements, preeminently railways. But Chamberlain offered to cooperate with them in developing the connecting links
of the empire, telegraph cables and steamships. He embodied the economic spirit behind his imperialism in a despatch to all colonial governors, asking for information that could help expand trade with the
mother country. Wishing to move beyond well-meaning generaliza-
tions, the former marketing manager asked for specific information on
factors which might favour foreign as against imperial products, from
prices and freight rates to patterns and packaging. He demanded samples of the colonies' imports, and in return asked for samples of colonial exports which might expand their market in the United Kingdom.

He could not approach the situation in South Africa with the same
freedom of initiative. His return to the Colonial Office coincided with
the delivery of the ultimatum to Kruger on the severed trade route to
the Cape. Meanwhile Rhodes besieged the Colonial Office with telegrams demanding further action on Bechuanaland. The importunity of
Rhodes helped Chamberlain to play the role of arbitrator. Three Tswana
chiefs from the protectorate came to England to plead against being
handed over to the Chartered Company. They won significant support

around the country during Chamberlain's holiday, not least in Birmingham; and their plea to remain under direct imperial rule coincided with Chamberlain's general policy for South Africa. Appealed to by the chiefs and Rhodes, Chamberlain imposed a settlement that gave the Chartered Company the bare minimum of land in the protectorate needed for railway construction, enough to give Rhodes his launching pad; and Chamberlain required Rhodes to surrender a subsidy for £200,000 which the imperial government had promised for the railway. The chiefs accepted the award reluctantly. Rhodes was furious to discover how little land he received for his pains. Loch applauded the settlement.

One part of it bore directly upon the armed force Rhodes wanted to assemble quickly. Since the strip of land assigned to the Chartered Company ran along the Transvaal border, the imperial authorities no longer needed to maintain a substantial border patrol there. Rhodes hoped to take the force over in its entirety, and he expected the imperial high commissioner to press its members to enlist with the Company. But Chamberlain kept his distance from the Company in this matter, and allowed the high commissioner to facilitate but not to urge reenlistment.

The unrest among the uitlanders on the Rand was uppermost in Chamberlain's mind so far as South Africa was concerned. Everything there depended on the validity, extent and objectives of the uprising which was supposed to be brewing. Chamberlain knew little of Rhodes's activities in this regard, though he assumed that the men in Rhodes's company on the Rand played a prominent part in the discontent over which, therefore, Rhodes would have considerable influence. But the reports from the Rand were mixed. The goldmines were booming, distracting their owners and employees from political ills. Chamberlain remained uneasy about the ambiguity in all of Rhodes's enterprises. Were they for Britain's empire or for his own? If uitlander agitators toppled Kruger, to whom would the ensuing regime bear allegiance? Chamberlain recoiled at the thought of an uitlander republic using the power of the mines to strengthen its leadership over the rest of South Africa without reference to distant Britain.

During his holiday Chamberlain had sent Robinson as high commissioner a set of questions about the changes which might take place in the event of an uprising on the Rand. Was an uprising probable in the near future? How should the British authorities respond? Chamberlain's query went by sea and took a month to arrive, Robinson's reply another month. It reached England at the beginning of December. Robinson exaggerated the unrest on the Rand but also quickened doubts about the outcome: 'nine out of every ten Englishmen in the Transvaal would prefer an anglicized & liberalized Republic to a British

Colony in any shape'.[15] He proposed accordingly, when the likely uprising occurred, to facilitate 'a revolution . . . without the loss of a life, and
even without firing a shot', by pursuing a version of Lord Loch's plan.
Robinson would 'issue a Proclamation directing both parties to desist
from hostilities, & to submit to his arbitration'. The mother country
should reinforce him by readying a large force to sail to South Africa. A
constituent assembly should be elected by the white adult males in the
Transvaal, whom he assumed to be for the most part British, to fashion
a new regime. Every non-violent tactic would be used to induce the
convention to transform the old republic into a self-governing British
colony.

How far the influence of Rhodes lay behind this letter, no one quite
knew. Chamberlain assumed that Robinson, as the nominee of Rhodes,
would be fully in his confidence. Rhodes led Robinson to believe that
Chamberlain knew and supported his plans. Just before the letter was
due to reach London, Robinson sent Chamberlain a telegram to report
that the chairman of the Chamber of Mines at Johannesburg was speaking out in despair at the prospects for peaceful reconciliation of the
uitlanders.

The report from Robinson emboldened but also worried Chamberlain. It left him more uneasy about the allegiance of the uitlanders and
still uncertain about the dimensions of the unrest on the Rand. He despatched a telegram to Robinson approving of his proposed course of
action in the event of an uprising but adding: 'I take for granted that no
movement will take place unless success is certain, a fiasco would be
most disastrous.'[16] The pace of developments overseas quickly outran
this caution. During the second week of December, the impression grew
at the Colonial Office that things on the Rand were coming to a head.
There were reliable indications of German sympathy for Kruger's Boers
against the uitlanders. Chamberlain feared that this sympathy might
harden into a firm bond. If that risk was real, it would be better from
the British point of view for the uitlanders to rebel soon, before Kruger
could intimidate them with his German friends.

Chamberlain made the African correspondent of *The Times* in London, Flora Shaw, aware of his line of thought. This was worse than
indiscreet. He could not have intended to publicize his reflections in *The
Times*, for that would alert the Boers and the Germans. He must have
known that the message was likely to reach Rhodes. Shaw had established herself as a channel for information between Rhodes at the Cape
and the Colonial Office. Chamberlain in effect encouraged Rhodes to
trigger the rebellion. Shaw telegraphed Rhodes cryptically, 'Joe sound
in case of interference by European powers but have special reason to
believe wishes you do it imm[ediately]'.[17]

A week later Chamberlain reinforced this advice in response to events on the other side of the globe. On 17 December, President Cleveland astonished Britain with a demand, backed by the threat of force, that its hitherto minor dispute with Venezuela over the border with British Guiana must be submitted to a purely American commission of arbitration. The Cleveland ultimatum replaced South Africa at the head of Chamberlain's agenda and threw him into close consultation with Salisbury. Relations with the United States were Salisbury's responsibility at the Foreign Office, but Chamberlain was responsible for the colony of British Guiana and was the cabinet member most familiar with the United States. His instinctive reaction was to stand up to the Americans; and he discussed what should be done in the event of war among irregular forces on the disputed border.

This distraction prompted Chamberlain's advisers at the Colonial Office to ask whether he would like the upheaval on the Rand to be delayed. He reversed their advice. Anglo-American relations could not turn dangerously ugly for another six months because Cleveland's commission of arbitration would need that long to handle its assignment. Chamberlain told his staff that it would be better for the uitlander rebellion to occur 'at once or be postponed for a year or two at least'.[18] He asked Edward Fairfield, the head of the African department at the Colonial Office, to 'make the situation clear' to Maguire, his current contact with the Chartered Company and hence with Rhodes: 'I again repeat the *worst* time for trouble anywhere would be about 6 months hence. I cannot say that any time would be a *good* one, but can the difficulty be indefinitely postponed?' Chamberlain was not confident that he could set the timing of the rebellion to meet his desires. But he could try. In doing so, he not only showed that he knew more about the conspiracy in South Africa than he could ever admit publicly. He also made himself an accessory to the plot.

The message from Chamberlain was twisted at every stage of its transmission. Fairfield emphasized to Maguire the desirability of delay for at least a year or two. The message was passed to Rhodes with the opposite emphasis, to 'hurry up'.[19] When this message reached Rhodes in Cape Town, he was in some dismay over a difference of opinion among the uitlanders which threatened their agitation with collapse. The bone of contention was the British flag, which the less militant agitators did not want to use. Whatever hesitation Rhodes felt at the foundering agitation was removed by the advice to 'hurry up'.

Despite the impending storm in South Africa, Chamberlain thought more of the United States. Hoping to counteract the anglophobia that Cleveland had unleashed in the United States, Chamberlain suggested to Salisbury on Christmas Eve that they make use of the revulsion which Americans felt in common with the British over atrocities which the Turks were inflicting on Armenians in the Ottoman empire. Chamberlain proposed inviting the United States to join Britain in a naval demonstration at the gates of Constantinople. 'Here is the proper destiny of the two Nations,' he told Salisbury, '—not to cut each other's throats but to bring irresistible force to bear in defence of the weak & oppressed.... The mere fact of their alliance for such a Mission would ... bring the Sultan to his knees.'[20] Chamberlain's failure to heed the limitations on Britain's freedom to take action at Constantinople appalled the prime minister. 'Randolph [Churchill] at his wildest', he told Balfour, 'could not have made a madder suggestion.'[21]

Word from South Africa pulled Chamberlain's attention back there the day after Christmas. He informed Salisbury that 'a rising in Johannesburg is imminent & will probably take place in the course of the next few days'.[22] Apparently Chamberlain had not previously consulted either the prime minister or the cabinet about the trouble brewing to the south. The lack of consultation reflected less, however, on Chamberlain than on Salisbury's management of the cabinet, as his calm reply to Chamberlain's news indicated. The prime minister accorded his colleagues wide freedom of action within their assigned departments. Furthermore, with occasional exceptions of which the worst was the Armenian proposal, Salisbury had been pleasantly surprised at how often Chamberlain at the Colonial Office and he at the Foreign Office found themselves in agreement. Chamberlain had won wide, indeed bipartisan applause for his performance as Colonial Secretary. 'Up to the present,' he reported on 27 December to his American mother-in-law, 'I have been very fortunate in satisfying friends & foes alike.'[23]

But next day things began to crack apart. News reached the Colonial Office that the agitation on the Rand was collapsing. This information was merely disappointing. But it was accompanied by an alarming hint that Rhodes might order Dr Starr Jameson, who was in charge of the force on Bechuanaland's border with the Transvaal, to 'go in' anyway and 'manufacture a revolution'.[24] That prospect horrified Chamberlain. Only a genuine rising on the Rand could justify a protective invasion. Moreover, an invasion was likely to fail if it was not reinforced by armed rebellion on the part of the uitlanders. Chamberlain telegraphed Robinson at the Cape to warn Rhodes that such an incursion would place the charter of his British South Africa Company in grave jeopardy. At the same time Chamberlain alerted Salisbury that the goings-on in the Transvaal were likely to 'fizzle out. Rhodes has miscalculated the feeling of the Johannesburg capitalists,' he explained,[25] thus suggesting how much the entire affair depended on Rhodes.

No sooner had Chamberlain despatched these messages than word reached him that Jameson might act on his own. And so he did, invading the South African Republic, with little more than 500 armed riders to support him, before dawn on 30 December.

The news reached Chamberlain after nightfall at Highbury as he dressed for the servants' annual ball. He clenched his fists. 'If this succeeds it will ruin me,' he said; 'I am going up to London to crush it.' He left as soon as he could without disrupting the party, took a midnight train to London and arrived at his empty London home before dawn. Whatever the military outcome of the Jameson raid, Chamberlain understood that the news was bad politically. No one knew yet how many men rode at Jameson's side, what arms they carried, or what sort of resistance the Boers would be able to mount. The surprise invasion might succeed. But even if it did, it would lack the prior justification of an uprising in Johannesburg. Chamberlain also saw how good an opportunity Jameson's incursion offered Germany to draw Kruger's republic into its sphere. Chamberlain knew that he had to repudiate Jameson's action quickly and vigorously. He attempted in doing so to enhance Britain's paramountcy over the Transvaal and strengthen the political rights of its British residents.

While Jameson rode across the barren pasture land or veldt of the Transvaal towards Johannesburg, Chamberlain did all he could through telegrams to Robinson to turn the invaders back. To deal with international reaction, Chamberlain made sure that the press in South Africa and Britain reported his repudiation of the raid and the steps he took to stop it. He wired his repudiation directly to President Kruger, using the opportunity to urge Kruger to make 'the concessions' required to remove the uitlander agitation. It took some courage to denounce the raid so fast and firmly when the outcome was in doubt. Liberals in Britain and South Africa greeted Chamberlain's stand with profound relief, while Unionist patriots looked at their supposed champion uneasily. Their doubts turned to dismay at New Year when *The Times* published a letter purportedly from the uitlanders of the Rand calling on Jameson to come to the aid of their women and children.

By then one uncertainty troubling Chamberlain was reduced. He believed initially that Jameson invaded at the behest of Rhodes. Rhodes certainly did what he could to allow the raid to succeed if possible. But at last, on New Year's day, word came that Rhodes repudiated Jameson's action. The repudiation was important for imperial purposes. Of course Rhodes was responsible for the basic plot; and his overestimate of the uitlander unrest called his political judgement into serious question. Still, his disavowal helped to lessen suspicion of British involvement. Whatever impact the raid had on Rhodes's usefulness for imperial purposes, Chamberlain was still sure that the empire in South Africa needed the support which the various enterprises of Rhodes could render. Chamberlain therefore incorporated Rhodes's repudiation of the raid in a press release from the Colonial Office on the crisis; and he dismissed the suggestion that Rhodes should resign from office.

Public reaction to Chamberlain's conduct of the situation soared like a roller coaster, up at his prompt denunciation of the raid, down in response to the 'women and children' letter, up higher when Jameson at last surrendered after putting up very little fight, higher still when the German Kaiser telegraphed congratulations to Kruger. Chamberlain stood forth as a national statesman, a sober and strong spokesman when Britain was beleaguered from many sides.

To 'soothe the wounded vanity of the nation', Chamberlain urged Salisbury to display Britain's naval capacity in South African waters, and he agreed. Chamberlain proposed to send troops as well; and though Robinson rejected this suggestion, it served, so Chamberlain believed, to persuade Kruger to release Jameson and the captured soldiers to stand trial in England. The long-range consequences of the raid were not clear, though it soon cost Rhodes his premiership of the Cape Colony. Still, at the end of the first week of January, Chamberlain took the staff of the South Africa department at the Colonial Office out for dinner. 'They well deserve it,' he told Mary, and crowed at his own success: 'I have scored—I do not know what my enemies can invent against me but at present I see no weak point.'[26] Congratulations rained in upon him. The sweetest came from his political opponents, most notably from Harcourt.

Harcourt was the Liberal leader least tainted by the South African involvements of the previous Liberal ministry. He had, for example, been as hostile as Chamberlain to the reappointment of Robinson as high commissioner. Of all the leading Liberals, therefore, Harcourt was freest to probe the suspicious joints in Chamberlain's South African armour. But Harcourt was impressed by Chamberlain's swift denunciation of the raid. Harcourt was also distracted by the quarrel with the United States over Venezuela. War between Britain and the United States was unjustifiable for any reason in Harcourt's estimation, and he was determined to eliminate any excuse for it.

This preoccupation not only protected Chamberlain on his South African flank but strengthened his ties to Salisbury. The prime minister was taken aback to discover that no member of his cabinet shared his desire to stand up to the United States except for the Colonial Secretary. Chamberlain was repelled by Harcourt's wish to assure the Americans that Britain would not seriously resist their demands. One of Salisbury's suggestions was to exclude settled districts from the arbitration on the disputed border between British Guiana and Venezuela. Chamberlain turned the suggestion into a proposal and presented it through an intermediary to the American ambassador in London. When the American

Secretary of State gave the proposal a lukewarm response, Chamberlain and Salisbury refused to accept it as satisfactory.

The demands of the Colonial Office might so well have deflected Chamberlain from his domestic social agenda. Undeterred, he set Lord James of Hereford to work in the new year with the Conservative Home Secretary, Sir Matthew White Ridley, on a bill to compensate workmen for industrial accidents. 'For Heaven's sake stand firm!' Chamberlain urged James; 'A majority of the Unionist members are pledged to the new principle of "compensation for all accidents", and it would be fatal to us if our first social reform were less favourable to the working-classes than [the previous Liberal government's] proposal.'[27]

Chamberlain wanted the Jameson raid to make as little difference as possible to the outlook at home and abroad. The crisis strengthened his nerve. Why should it not strengthen his hand? In one way it had. Jameson's action struck a responsive chord among Canadians and Australians because the events surrounding the raid awakened fears of their own. President Cleveland's ultimatum over the British Guianan border had alarming implications for Canada over its contested Alaskan border with the United States. Kaiser Wilhelm's telegram to Kruger worried Australians who resented the encroachments of Germany in the south Pacific. Before the Jameson raid Chamberlain had rejoiced at the evidence of a 'wider patriotism . . . which encloses the whole of Greater Britain'.[28] After the raid he responded gratefully to the words of solidarity and support sent by Canada and Australia to Britain. The Canadian prime minister spoke proudly of how 'the great mother-Empire stood splendidly isolated'. Chamberlain embraced the sentiment: Britain 'stands secure', he replied, '. . . in the abundant loyalty of her children from one end of the Empire to another'.[29] He observed contentedly that the action of the German Emperor and the American President had 'gone far to tighten the bonds that unite the Empire'.[30]

The imperial patriotism in which Chamberlain took pleasure distorted his vision. To account for the sentiment that bound the countries of the empire together, he spoke of their common origin, language and literature. But those common denominators did not fully apply even within the predominantly white or white-governed colonies. They did not apply to the French of Quebec or to those of Dutch descent in South Africa. The Jameson raid aggravated the division between Afrikaners and English in South Africa and undermined the trust of both in Great Britain. Chamberlain was less concerned about Afrikaner suspicions than about the faith of the South African English shaken by the failure of the raid. The steps he took to reassure the English in South Africa deepened suspicions among the Cape Dutch and their Boer brethren.

He was reluctant to recognize how much the raid had strengthened Kruger's republic. The enemies of the republic stood exposed and defeated while its friends in the Orange Free State and the Cape Colony rallied to its support. When Kruger and Chamberlain began to adjust the relationship between their governments in the wake of the raid, they looked in opposite directions. The Colonial Secretary hoped that the Boer president would enfranchise the uitlanders and remove the other causes of their discontent in order to prevent another upheaval. Chamberlain disregarded how feebly that unrest had displayed itself at Christmas and how much the concessions he required of Kruger would endanger Boer control of the Transvaal. Kruger on the other hand wanted to free his republic of its subordination to Britain and encirclement by British dependencies. He wanted the independence that Chamberlain meant to overcome.

Chamberlain thought he could achieve his goals for the uitlanders fairly quickly. Intermediaries led him to believe that Kruger would come to London to confer with him. 'It will be a great "coup" to get the old man here,' Chamberlain exulted. Believing that 'we have much to gain from him while he has very little to ask from us',[31] Chamberlain botched the preparatory negotiations from start to finish. Kruger had suggested giving Johannesburg municipal government. Chamberlain expanded the suggestion into a proposal for elective local government for the whole of the Rand with more than municipal powers, though under ultimate control by the government of the republic. His scheme of 'Home Rule for the Rand' suffered from many of the defects he had criticized in Gladstone's plan for Ireland. More concerned about parliamentary and British reaction than for Kruger's response, Chamberlain published his proposal in England before Kruger could examine it, and thus further alienated him. When Kruger's aversion to a conference in London became unmistakable, Chamberlain resorted to clumsy threats, and he reacted angrily when the old president finally turned the invitation down.

Subversion

The speed and decisiveness with which Chamberlain dealt with the raid and its consequences in January impressed almost everyone. His lack of tact and the limitations of his vision looked, at least from the British point of view, no worse than venial sins, the excusable accompaniment of his virtues. But one of the decisions he made that month, to uphold Rhodes's Chartered Company as the agency for northward extension of the British empire in South Africa, was bound to be criticized once it became known. Over the ensuing months, as the Rhodes plot was exposed, this decision grew harder to defend, and it deepened suspicions of Chamberlain's complicity in the plot.

Only a minority, though a crucial minority,[32] of the directors of the Company had known about the Rhodes plot. The Company could, therefore, and did claim ignorance. Yet it had always operated as the pliant tool of Rhodes. Jameson was the Company's resident administrator in Bechuanaland. The men who rode with him to Johannesburg were Company troops of one sort and another. Nevertheless, by mid-January Chamberlain decided against revocation of the Charter. The military forces controlled by the Company were placed under imperial command. Otherwise all the powers of the Company were to remain intact, not only for its economic purposes but also for the political administration of its assigned territory to the north.

Chamberlain reached this decision without referring to Rhodes, who had kept his own counsel since the raid. With the enormous exception of the plot and the raid, all the experience Chamberlain had acquired since becoming Colonial Secretary reinforced the wisdom of working through the Chartered Company. Direct imperial rule was impossible. The permanent officials at the Treasury proved the general point by ruling against investing the dividends from Britain's Suez Canal shares in development of the crown colonies. With economizers carping over every sixpence, and with a parliamentary opposition quick to criticize the smallest move, how could the Colonial Office cultivate major portions of the empire? The Chartered Company remained indispensable for northward expansion in South Africa, which Chamberlain desired after the raid as much as ever. And the Chartered Company would be fully effective only under the leadership of Rhodes—though of course from now on, he and his Company would have to operate within the restraints of imperial policy more carefully.

Rhodes did not know of this decision when, having lost his premiership at the Cape, he set sail for London to protect his remaining interests. The opening of Parliament was set for early February. Rhodes came to prevent the parliamentary or judicial inquiry which Chamberlain, recognizing its inevitability, had already promised. The arrival of Rhodes moved the centre of Chamberlain's concern from South Africa to Westminster. There he had to resist the bullying by Rhodes and his solicitor Hawksley, devise an innocuous inquiry, conciliate the Liberal opposition, and through it all if possible strengthen his own position and that of the empire. It was at Westminster that Chamberlain would rise or be crushed. For the next year and a half, amid deepening danger, he pursued a remarkably consistent course to a strong though deeply flawed conclusion.

While Rhodes was still on the high seas, Chamberlain opened discussions with Balfour and the law officers of the crown about the terms for the inquiry. He explained unabashedly that he wanted to grant an inquiry on generously wide terms so that it would lose its way and its power to endanger the interests he meant to protect. He was helped by the insistence of the law officers that the inquiry could not deal with the actual raid until Jameson and his officers stood trial before a British court as agreed with the Transvaal government. Chamberlain also received unintentional help from a group of Radical MPs led by Henry Labouchere who insisted that the inquiry include 'the whole history of the Company'. 'If I were a Director,' Chamberlain observed, 'I think I should prefer this as it will lengthen the enquiry, and so widen the issue, that their guilt—if they be guilty—in connection with the recent raid would be smothered up in comparatively irrelevant detail.' He also welcomed the preference of the House of Commons for a committee of its own rather than for a statutory or judicial commission such as dealt with the charges of *The Times* against Parnell. 'I doubt', he commented, 'whether [a Commons committee] would be the most successful tribunal for arriving at the truth, but they would undoubtedly be most likely to satisfy the feeling in favour of enquiry.'[33]

Rhodes nevertheless adhered to his objective of preventing an inquiry. Once he reached England, he and his inner henchmen warned the Colonial Office that, if an inquiry were held, the ringleaders in the plot would insist that they acted with Chamberlain's encouragement, and would produce telegrams to prove it. Hawksley transmitted the threat to Fairfield at the Colonial Office. After consulting Chamberlain, Fairfield asked Hawksley for copies of the telegrams. Fairfield insisted that Chamberlain 'does not recollect saying anything anent the insurrection which was supposed to be impending which he would greatly care about if it became public'.[34] Hawksley backed off and declined to produce the telegrams, which he did not yet have. But he added menacingly: 'Mr. C. knows what I know and can shape his course with this knowledge.' The telegrams shadowed Chamberlain forever after.

He and Rhodes were due to meet. A mutual associate, R.B. Brett, intervened to prepare the way, fearing that otherwise a confrontation between the two would hurt them both and damage the empire. Brett's task was essentially to convince Rhodes beforehand that confrontational tactics such as Hawksley had used would backfire, that there was, furthermore, no need to blackmail Chamberlain, who already intended to uphold the Chartered Company and keep the inquiry from damaging the interests they shared. Thanks to Brett's intervention, when Rhodes and Chamberlain met they avoided all reference to the past and talked solely about the current outlook in South Africa, particularly for the territory to the north in what was already called Rhodesia. Elated at the turn of their conversation, Rhodes reported jubilantly to the Company's board of directors and immediately headed back for Africa, while Chamberlain turned his attention to the House of Commons.

With great skill he virtually captured the key figures in the Liberal opposition and won widespread approval among the British public; yet in doing so he lost whatever trust his repudiation of the raid had earned him from Kruger, the Boers and the Cape Dutch. Before seeing Rhodes, Chamberlain drew up a 'great despatch'[35] on the situation in South Africa. It provided the fullest account to date of the events surrounding the Jameson raid, and focused attention on the grievances of the uitlanders. The purpose of the despatch was to secure approval for the government's policy from the Liberal opposition. The despatch was shown in draft to Lord Ripon, colonial secretary in the previous ministry, who made a few verbal alterations; to Sidney Buxton, the former colonial undersecretary; and through Buxton to Harcourt as leader of the opposition in the Commons. So preoccupied was Chamberlain with the Liberals that he forgot to clear the despatch with Balfour and Salisbury. Once Chamberlain saw Rhodes, it was published in preparation for the parliamentary debate.

The despatch won Chamberlain praise in the Commons, and served as he hoped to turn attention from the raid to the uitlander grievances. Gratified by his evident concern for their response, the Liberals put up with the need to defer the parliamentary inquiry until Jameson and his officers had been tried by the courts. Harcourt and, still more, Labouchere focused their suspicions on the Chartered Company and Rhodes, including their supposed rigging of the stock market as well as the South African plot. Accordingly the Liberals pressed for a wide-ranging inquiry, to which Chamberlain happily agreed.

Their pleasure at his willingness to inquire into the conduct of the Chartered Company offset their dismay at his continued reliance on the Company. He also persisted in commending Rhodes. There was considerable surprise at Rhodes's abrupt return to Africa when serious questions about him were being asked in England. 'He goes back almost as a private individual,' Chamberlain explained,

> having not the control of a single policeman, having ceased to be Prime Minister, and, for the moment at all events, having seen his work jeopardised, possibly destroyed—the work he set himself of consolidating and bringing together the Dutch and English races. . . . On the other hand, does any one deny that he may be a factor for good? . . . it would be an act of ingratitude if we were, even now, to forget the great services he has rendered . . . his right place is in Africa, and even if he has done wrong in the past he may do a great deal to repair that wrong.[36]

These words delighted Unionists but spread uneasiness among Liberals and suspicion among the Boers and Cape Dutch. The need for Rhodes in Africa received seeming proof in March when the Ndebele erupted in rebellion in Rhodesia and the settlers turned to him for leadership.

The following month closed with revelations which compromised Chamberlain's policy though not yet Chamberlain himself. During the raid, capping the folly of the whole escapade, one of Jameson's officers abandoned not only a set of telegrams which passed between Jameson and the other plotters in Johannesburg and Cape Town, but also a code-book to decipher the messages. The Kruger government published the telegrams at the end of April; and *The Times* of 1 May transmitted the evidence to England. The telegrams revealed how much the supposed upheaval among the uitlanders on the Rand at the end of the year had been of Rhodes's contriving. There was no doubt now of Rhodes's guilt in connection with the raid, though the law officers of the crown said that the evidence was not enough 'to justify the institution of criminal proceedings' against him.[37] The telegrams also raised suspicions of im-perial complicity, though reaching no higher up than Robinson as high commissioner. For the moment the telegrams helped to protect Cham-berlain by revealing that the Jameson raid was modelled on the plan proposed by Lord Loch to the former Liberal ministry.

The revelations reopened the rift between Chamberlain and Rhodes. Knowing that the House of Commons would now expect Rhodes's dis-missal from the Chartered Company's board of directors, Chamberlain urged the board to take this step before the parliamentary debate on the situation, scheduled for 8 May. He hesitated, however, to insist on this advice; and the board also hesitated to accept it because of the war in Matabeleland, which Rhodes used to delay action on his resignation.

Reporting to the Commons, Chamberlain accentuated the pacific fea-tures of his policy. In a prophecy which came back to haunt him, he warned that

> A war in South Africa would be one of the most serious wars that could possibly be waged. It would be in the nature of a civil war. It would be a long war, and . . . it would leave behind it the embers of a strife which I believe generations would hardly be long enough to extinguish.[38]

But his underlying concern was to reduce opposition to continued reli-ance on the Chartered Company. The costs carried by the Company in the Matabele war underscored its indispensability to Britain. As for its leader, 'whatever errors . . . Mr. Rhodes has committed,' said Chamber-lain, 'he had also rendered great services. . . . But for Englishmen like Mr. Rhodes our English history would be much poorer—[*loud Minis-terial cheers*]—and our British dominions would be much smaller. [*Re-newed cheers*]'[39] Liberal reaction to this stalwart defence of Rhodes was muted. But it made some British colonists at the Cape 'doubt [Chamberlain's] innocence in connection with the raid'[40] and fear the Afrikaner reaction.

Withholding evidence

Still, the defence of Rhodes that Chamberlain kept up in the Commons was not enough to satisfy Rhodes's most determined supporters. Hawksley, who served as legal adviser for Jameson and the Chartered Company as well as Rhodes, wanted to use the evidence he possessed of Chamberlain's connections with the previous year's plot to defend Jameson and his officers when they came up for trial, to save Rhodes's position in the Chartered Company, and even to prevent the impending parliamentary inquiry. Rhodes had honoured his tacit agreement with Chamberlain by refusing Hawksley permission to make use of the implicating telegrams. But that did not prevent Hawksley from showing them to the barrister who was to defend Jameson in court or from spreading rumours of Chamberlain's involvement. Exasperated, Chamberlain had the Colonial Office ask Hawksley for copies or the gist of the telegrams about which he had spoken to Fairfield in February. Hawksley took nearly three weeks before complying.

When Chamberlain returned from a weekend in Birmingham early in June, he found waiting for him a set of fifty-one telegrams exchanged between Rhodes's men in London and in South Africa from 2 August to 20 December of the previous year. The telegrams made disturbing reading. Taken at face value, they indicated that Chamberlain gave the Chartered Company its strip of Bechuanaland knowing that it was to be used as a base for invasion of the Transvaal, and that he had precipitated the rising in Johannesburg to meet imperial convenience. But the evidence was embarrassing rather than incriminating. The telegrams were reports by others about him, not directly from himself. The force of the telegrams was weakened by internal contradictions, by stretches of unintelligibility caused in transmission or deciphering, and by the language of stockmarket manipulation in which they were couched.

Together with Selborne and the permanent officials at the Colonial Office, Chamberlain subjected the telegrams to close examination and commentary. Equipped thus to defend himself, he offered his resignation to Lord Salisbury. Though the offer was not an empty gesture, Chamberlain did not expect it to be accepted. He was not admitting guilt, nor did he regard Hawksley's threat as insuperable. But the threat was sufficiently serious for the decision to be placed in the hands of the prime minister. In effect, Chamberlain appealed for endorsement from the prime minister. Salisbury gave it without hesitation. Many years later, when the time came to thank Salisbury for his leadership, the episode Chamberlain remembered with most gratitude was the instant and enduring support Salisbury gave him when faced by Hawksley's aspersions. As Salisbury saw it, Chamberlain had been alert to the need for precautions to uphold imperial interests in the likely event of a rising on the Rand, precautions about which it was impolitic to tell the world. What disgusted Salisbury was the stockjobbery and blackmail apparently habitual among agents of Rhodes.

Sure of Salisbury's support, Chamberlain cut Hawksley's threat down to size. Chamberlain let it be known that execution of the threat would lead to cancellation of the Company's charter. He secured proof that Rhodes was not behind Hawksley's threat. Chamberlain was also comforted by a report that Rhodes had given Lord Rosebery some idea of the plot months before the change of government in England.

Meanwhile the esteem in which Chamberlain was held by the public rose in response to his expressions of imperial vision. Where others saw scattered territories, Chamberlain saw an empire. Where others saw difficulties, Chamberlain saw a way through. Two days after he read the threatening telegrams, he turned attention back to the possibilities for economic consolidation of the empire from which he had been diverted by the imbroglio in South Africa. He addressed the Chambers of Commerce of the Empire, a congress interested in the possibility of a customs union for the British empire on the model of the Zollverein which preceded the unification of imperial Germany. Chamberlain spoke of the 'national unity' reflected by the congress:

> Insensibly the bonds between us are strengthening and multiplying. You have for a long time—you gentlemen who come from the colonies—been in our thoughts; you are now actually in our sight. Your claims, your wishes, the resources of your separate countries, your political conditions—all these are becoming as familiar to us as if we were all provinces in one great kingdom of States in a true Imperial federation.[41]

He embraced the idea of a customs union as a way to preserve tariff protection, upon which the colonies insisted, while extending free trade, to which Britain was devoted, throughout the empire. He promised that 'if a proposal of this kind came to us from the colonies . . . it would not be met with a blank refusal by the people of this country'. The colonies shied away from this proposal because of the loss of tariff revenue and protection vis-à-vis the mother country which it would entail; and Britain recoiled from the abandonment of unlimited international free trade. Still, the spirit which prompted Chamberlain to make the proposal commanded admiration.

On the day that he made this speech, Chamberlain reversed Hawksley's threat by threatening to publish the telegrams himself.

Hawksley replied hastily that he could not consent to publication before Rhodes approved. Hawksley was then warned by Lord Grey, currently administrator of Rhodesia, that he would prefer going to jail himself 'to letting Chamberlain's name come into the matter in such a way as to cause England & Europe to suppose that he had been a party to the "plot"'.[42] Grey was disturbed by the exaggerated impression conveyed by the telegrams of Chamberlain's involvement in the plot. If the telegrams were published, Grey told Hawksley, 'everybody will believe that he was a much more inward conspirator than he really was . . . he has done nothing to be ashamed of. He was led to believe that the inevitable Revolution was abt. to take place & he very properly took precautions to ensure its success when it came about.'

At last Rhodes resigned as managing director of the Chartered Company. He remained—and Chamberlain was glad that he remained—in effective though not in formal charge of the fight against the widespread uprising of the Ndebele in Rhodesia. The resignation of Rhodes and the neutralization of Hawksley put Chamberlain in a good position when it came to arranging for the parliamentary inquiry. So little did Harcourt suspect Chamberlain of complicity in the pre-raid plotting that he pressed Chamberlain to chair the inquiry. That way, the inquiry could have all the resources of the Colonial Office at its disposal and could bind the government to its eventual conclusions. Chamberlain resisted this pressure, confident that he could protect himself as a member of the committee without taking the chair. He promised to place the facilities of the Colonial Office at the committee's command.

The judicial proceedings against Jameson and his officers were completed at the end of July. Once they were convicted and sentenced, Chamberlain moved in the Commons for the appointment of a parliamentary inquiry with 'the widest possible form of reference'[43] as desired by the opposition. The inquiry would have to expire at the end of the parliamentary session, in a matter of days; but it was understood that the committee would be revived when Parliament reconvened in the new year. At its one meeting before the end of the session, the committee decided to begin its inquiry in January with the raid rather than with the general subject of Chartered Company administration. Chamberlain suggested that Rhodes appear as the first witness. The Colonial Office assumed the task of preparing for the new year's investigation.

In the course of these preparations, Chamberlain and Rhodes sought to protect their respective positions. In doing so, they took up antagonistic positions which threatened both men with exposure. Still unaware of the full dimensions of the pre-raid plot, Chamberlain hoped for Rhodes's sake that he had not intended Jameson's force to move without a genuine uprising on the Rand and prior approval from the high commissioner. In other words, Chamberlain hoped that Rhodes was no more guilty than allies of Rhodes insisted Chamberlain to be. But these allies, including Grey as well as Hawksley, feared that Rhodes's guilt was considerably greater than that. The suspension of the parliamentary inquiry till January encouraged them to try to prevent it altogether. Towards this end they wanted Chamberlain to admit at least tacitly that he knew about the plot beforehand. But on this issue he remained elusive.

Once Parliament disbanded for the year, Hawksley gave the Colonial Office a summary statement of his charge. The controverted telegrams, he said, showed that Rhodes and his emissaries had acquainted Chamberlain 'with the paramount reason why ... it was urgently necessary that there should be troops on the Transvaal border without at the same time the suspicions of the authorities of the [South African] Republic being aroused'.[44] Writing the same day to Chamberlain from Rhodesia, Grey sought an excuse to enable Rhodes to refuse to appear before the parliamentary inquiry when it reconvened in January. Grey objected to one of the Liberal nominees on the committee, Labouchere, as intolerable to Rhodes, and also alluded darkly to Hawksley's collection of telegrams.

These tactics backfired. Grey's letter did not arrive till Chamberlain had left England on holiday. But the letter from Hawksley convinced Chamberlain 'that there was a deliberate plot to commit the Colonial Office involuntarily and by partial confidences to a general approval of Rhodes's plans & then to use this afterwards as a screen for the whole conspiracy'.[45] Chamberlain insisted that his staff prepare a further repudiation of Hawksley's charge: 'It is time to have done with him & this blackmailing scheme.'[46]

By mid-autumn so many people had learned 'at any rate in a general way'[47] about Hawksley's telegrams that the parliamentary inquiry was likely to insist upon seeing them. Chamberlain responded by assembling whatever evidence he could find of claims by Rhodes and his emissaries that the Liberal leaders had been told of the plot before the raid. Sir Graham Bower, chief secretary to the high commissioner at the Cape, was induced to testify about Rhodes's claim to have forewarned Rosebery. Rumour had it that even Harcourt was forewarned. Though Chamberlain did not believe the rumour, he sought evidence that it was circulating in order to discredit the charge against himself. As he explained to Selborne, 'If a man says that I murdered his grandmother it may possibly be believed until it is categorically disproved. But if he says that I was assisted in my nefarious work by Lord Salisbury & the Archbishop of Canterbury, he will probably be sent to a lunatic asylum without more ado.'[48]

Chamberlain still hoped to prevent publication of the telegrams. But his confidence was shaken by Grey, upon whom he had relied to refute

Hawksley's charge. The only direct implication of Chamberlain in the South African plot had been through his explicitly private conversation in August 1895 with Grey, who explained the need for a military base in Bechuanaland to reinforce the probable rebellion in Johannesburg. Chamberlain was sure that Grey would never violate the canons of personal confidence—until, upon returning from holiday, he opened Grey's letter referring to the telegrams. Still unaware that Grey was the source of many of the telegrams, Chamberlain wrote back to remind him of their private understanding in 1895. Chamberlain tried to re-assure Grey that, if Rhodes appeared voluntarily as a witness before the parliamentary committee, he would be free to decide 'whether he an-swers questions which may be put to him or not'. Chamberlain also expected the chairman of the inquiry to 'protect witnesses if they refuse to answer questions which may incriminate themselves'. But publica-tion of the telegrams would implicate Rhodes, who received them, and not Chamberlain, whose alleged comments were reported second-hand. Chamberlain threatened, if the telegrams were published, to snap the slender 'thread on which hangs at present the future of the Company and of Mr. Rhodes's connection with its territories'.[49]

Fairfield warned Chamberlain not to expect much from Grey's reply. Assigned to track down the telegrams, Fairfield found that they led back to Grey. Grey might therefore defend the telegrams even though, in doing so, 'he must avow himself a man who on the strength of his private and political friendship with Mr Chamberlain, then betrayed his confidence to a pack of Kimberley speculators'.[50] Grey behaved as Fairfield feared. In concert with Rhodes and referring again to the tele-grams, he renewed the demand that Chamberlain allow the House of Commons inquiry 'to fizzle out'.[51] Instead of reassuring Chamberlain, Grey destroyed his confidence that nothing could prove his complicity in the original plot.

> If [Grey wrote] I am called before the Committee & asked whether I informed you in any way of the impending Revolution at Joh[annesbur]g, I shall be obliged, either to refuse to answer, or to say that I told you privately that the long expected & inevitable rising of the Uitlanders . . . would shortly take place, & that being so it was de-sirable that an armed force shd. be stationed on the Tr[ans]vaal border available for use if required.[52]

Here—not in the telegrams—was the proof of Chamberlain's complic-ity. Grey accompanied it, however, with a promise from Rhodes to suppress the telegrams '*at all costs*'.

The warning and promise reached Chamberlain amid a rising cloud of suspicion generated by Rhodes's associates in London, including the journalist W.T. Stead as well as Hawksley. But the attacks of these men did Chamberlain strangely little harm and even some good in England. Labouchere thought that the innuendoes of Stead and Hawksley were intended to divert blame from Rhodes, and hence felt all the more confident of Chamberlain's innocence.

Inquest and diversion

The impasse between Rhodes and Chamberlain continued right up to the reopening of Parliament in 1897. Rhodes came to London still anxious to prevent the inquiry. He met Chamberlain at the Colonial Office, with Selborne on hand to record their exchange. Afterwards Chamberlain reported that 'the Napoleon of S. Africa' had been 'very cheery— very patriotic & very friendly'.[53] Yet according to Selborne, Rhodes argued strenuously against reappointment of the inquiry. Though he spoke with equal vehemence against publication of the telegrams, the association of the two points continued to suggest a threat. Just as outspoken, Chamberlain attacked Hawksley and forced Rhodes to repudiate the harsh terms in which he too was reported as speaking of Chamberlain. He insisted that the inquiry was unavoidable, all the more so because of rumours Hawksley had generated. Chamberlain no longer attempted to minimize the divergence in outlook between Rhodes and himself. They might both be 'big Englanders'; but that agreement 'applied only to the general objects, not to the means of achieving these objects'.[54] Their interview did nothing to clear the air. So far as the business at hand was concerned, Rhodes might be willing to face the inquiry while suppressing the telegrams. But Hawksley reacted furiously when he learned of Chamberlain's attack, and pressed Rhodes harder than ever to let the telegrams be published.

Three days after meeting Rhodes, Chamberlain moved in the House of Commons for reappointment of the inquiry. He spoke in a matter-of-fact way to minimize excitement. Without referring in particular to Rhodes, he expressed confidence that the Chartered Company would be 'able to make a very good case for itself'. Alluding to the imperial ramifications of the inquiry, he emphasized the need for the inquiry to conduct itself with restraint so as 'to shield great national interests' and 'not to re-open old sores'.[55]

Despite this introduction, the inquiry was bound to rivet attention on the South African fiasco. This was not the kind of interest Chamberlain wanted the work of the Colonial Office to generate. He managed to strengthen his political standing amid the corrosive winds of the South African inquiry by demonstrating his talent as a domestic reformer. His career as a social legislator reached its climax in 1897. He not only substantiated his claim that Unionists could be better social reformers than their Liberal rivals; he effected a breakthrough in British social policy.

He began modestly with the subject of education. In 1896 Balfour had come to grief, and the Unionist majority in the House of Commons failed its first test of legislative capacity, over an Education bill. Meant mainly to help underfunded denominational schools, the bill offered rate aid without ratepayer control to church schools, and it tampered with the clause in the Education Act of 1870 that prohibited denominational religious instruction in civic schools. Chamberlain managed to eliminate the features of the bill most offensive to Nonconformists. But once it entered the Commons, the bill became enmired in amendments, and Balfour had to abandon it.

No longer a Radical on this subject, Chamberlain wanted to protect the existing compromise system from the rival denominational ambitions which threatened to upset it together with the Unionist alliance. Salisbury agreed with this essentially conservative attitude far more than with Balfour's impolitic plans for administrative reform. Chamberlain and Salisbury in concert stripped the 1896 measure down to a simple bill for 1897 to grant hard-pressed denominational schools an additional five shillings per student. Once it passed, Chamberlain pushed through an equally simple measure to assist impoverished civic schools.

This was not a great achievement. Nor could Chamberlain devise a satisfactory plan to achieve what he still spoke of as 'the most valuable social reform that can possibly be propounded':[56] old-age pensions. He endorsed the cabinet's decision to assign the problem to an expert commission of inquiry. But on workmen's compensation for industrial accidents, he knew what he wanted. He had failed to gain a prominent place for this subject on the legislative agenda of the government in its first year. The Conservative home secretary, Sir Matthew White Ridley, dragged his feet. Bypassing Ridley, Chamberlain set to work on a bill with Lord James, who functioned as a Liberal Unionist substitute for Ridley, in preparation for the next year. Chamberlain cultivated parliamentary opinion in cooperation with *The Times*. He put himself in touch with H.W. Massingham of the *Daily Chronicle*, who was unusually knowledgeable about the subject. Anonymous memoranda were despatched to sympathetic business leaders in branches of industry which the bill would affect to sound out opinion. Having shaped his bill in the light of these inquiries, Chamberlain lobbied manufacturers among the government's supporters in the Commons. Before the end of January 1897 he could report that so far, 'without a single exception—I have got them all on my side'.[57]

He almost forgot about Ridley; and when Chamberlain intimated what he had in mind to the cabinet at the beginning of February, Ridley reacted with alarm. Chamberlain offered Ridley a respectful exposition of the proposal. His powers of persuasion and command of the subject turned Ridley into a bemused but loyal adjutant. The cabinet approved Chamberlain's bill somewhat apprehensively in March, and it was introduced in the Commons. Though the measure fell formally within Ridley's sphere, Parliament recognized Chamberlain as the minister in charge.

The bill established the right of an employee to compensation for industrial accidents which were not his own fault. This 'new principle' has been described as 'that of the welfare state'.[58] William Beveridge, who designed the welfare state created after the Second World War, regarded the scheme of workmen's compensation established by Chamberlain as the poineer system of social security. It could not have marked such a breakthrough in social policy unless it avoided offending the canons of Gladstonian political economy that still made old-age pensions impossible. Chamberlain's scheme did not entail any significant increase in governmental expenditure or size. The cost would be passed on by the employer through private insurance to the consumer as a tiny increase in prices. One of Chamberlain's brothers, Herbert, entered the business of providing the requisite insurance. The only responsibilities placed on the Home Office were to appoint medical referees and collect statistics.

Still, the burden on business opened the bill to criticism. The bill tried to reduce the burden in a number of ways. Chamberlain excluded from the scheme those parts of the economy which were likely to oppose and so might defeat it, particularly the shipping industry that had brought him to grief previously, agriculture and domestic service. These exclusions amounted to at least half of the labour force, and thus deprived the scheme of the universality which Chamberlain would have preferred. He defended the arrangement frankly on grounds of expediency rather than of logic, and he assumed that, if his measure proved successful, it would be extended. Having excluded the parts of the opposition likely to be most vociferous, Chamberlain insisted on applying the scheme to coalmining, where he knew it would meet with both resistance and support. He consulted Sir Alfred Hickman, a coalmaster and Conservative MP on the edge of Chamberlain's electoral duchy. With backing from Hickman, he fended off protests from the Mining Association of Great Britain and stood up to Lord Londonderry, a Conservative magnate with coalmining interests in County Durham. Because coalmining was a notoriously dangerous occupation, coalmasters cried that the responsibilities imposed by the bill would ruin them. Chamberlain refuted their cries with careful calculations of cost and the distributive effect of insurance.

Industrialists generally had to be assured that the bill would not markedly increase their costs. That demand was met in the terms of the bill. It placed ceilings on the level of compensation: no more than £300 in case of death, no more weekly than half the preceding weekly wage in case of incapacity. No payment would be made for the first two weeks of disability or for any disability that lasted less than two weeks.

The bill was well designed for passage through Parliament. Since the eruption of the Irish question in the late 1870s, the passage of major bills through the House of Commons had become almost impossible without draconian measures to cut off debate. But Chamberlain showed how it could still be done. He kept his bill lean to reduce the handles for controversy. He left some controversial clauses for introduction in committee. In the Commons his single-minded concern was to expedite debate. Sometimes he played the even-handed statesman pursuing justice between employer and employee. More often he was the brisk man of business, 'arbitrating, conciliating, reconciling warring interests, and stamping the whole proceedings in the House with that spirit of clear and precise bargaining, which', according to the *Daily Chronicle*, 'has always been Mr. Chamberlain's note in politics'.[59]

He had to make more concessions than he liked to neutralize Conservative critics. 'Contracting out', or allowing firms to ignore the national scheme if they had at least as generous a plan of their own, had been a prominent Unionist demand in opposition to the Liberal bill of 1893–4. But the demand had lost much of its point since then, and Chamberlain wanted to ignore it. It was no longer necessary to avoid the unlimited liability that businesses ran under the Liberal bill. But Middleton, the Conservative party organizer, insisted on 'contracting out' because of the pledges given by Conservatives at the general election. Chamberlain had to concede. The concession would not amount to much because the separate business schemes would have to be at least as generous as the national one. Lord Londonderry also threatened the bill. While he failed to exclude coalmining from its terms, he succeeded in making them a little less generous to labour. But otherwise he was unable to upset the government over this measure.

Finally enacted in the last days of the parliamentary session for the year, the Workmen Compensation bill won Chamberlain more admiration than criticism among Conservatives. Uneasy about him until the coalition government was created, they were now inclined to award him the double crown of Disraeli. Like Disraeli he was the champion of empire, and he had renewed the Disraelian tradition in social reform. He succeeded moreover where the current Conservative leaders failed. The contrast between Balfour's performance over the Education bill of 1896 and Chamberlain's on workmen's compensation was unmistakable. Chamberlain stood forth in 1897 as 'the strong man of the Government'.[60]

Yet his achievement in workmen's compensation did not contain the seeds for further social reform. The complaints of Middleton and Londonderry were reinforced by the withdrawal of financial support for the Conservative party from some coalmasters. Salisbury was relieved to note next year that social legislation 'seems to be at a discount'.[61] The discount reflected something more than Conservative resistance. Chamberlain's bag of social reforms no longer had much in it, certainly nothing that could sail as nicely as his scheme for workmen's compensation through the straits of orthodox political economy guarded by the Treasury.

The Workmen Compensation bill could not divert attention for long from the inquest into the Jameson raid. But that probe was blunted by another flare-up in the relations between Britain and the Transvaal republic. Chamberlain persuaded the cabinet to demand repeal of the Aliens Immigration and Expulsion Acts which the Transvaal introduced to curb the size of the uitlander community, and to reinforce that demand by increasing Britain's armed forces in South Africa. These tactics worked: Kruger undertook to repeal the Aliens Immigration Act and to amend the Aliens Expulsion Act to meet British objectives.

Chamberlain's tactics still alarmed Harcourt as the worst sort of truculence; and he blistered Chamberlain in parliamentary debate. But the anxiety which Harcourt voiced in the Commons muted him in the Jameson raid inquiry. He was fearful of adding to Kruger's suspicion of Britain, and therefore refrained from pursuing leads in the testimony which suggested that the British government might bear responsibility for the raid. The Liberals in the committee tried to train their fire on Rhodes and the Chartered Company rather than on Chamberlain. Yet the inquiry was bound to unearth evidence which threw suspicion on him, as the self-appointed defenders of Rhodes such as Hawksley intended. Chamberlain's complicity was also a more prominent question in South Africa than at home. Boers and their sympathizers in the Cape Colony pored over reports of the committee proceedings for any evidence that Chamberlain might share Rhodes's already proven guilt. They were quick to note that, when the inquiry examined Rhodes, Chamberlain acted in his defence rather than as his judge.

At the end of April the prospects turned threatening for Chamberlain. Rutherfoord Harris told the committee of the 'guarded allusion' he made to Chamberlain in August 1895 about the function the Bechuanaland protectorate was intended to serve. Chamberlain intervened to repudiate the implication that he had knowingly paved the way for the raid. Uttering each word with emphasis, he declared:

I never had, any knowledge, or, until, I think it was the day before the actual raid took place, the slightest suspicion of anything in the nature of a hostile or armed invasion of the Transvaal.[62]

Only the touch of ambiguity in the last eight words of this assertion saved it from being an outright lie.

The prospects darkened further when Harris spoke of telegrams the committee had not seen which passed between Rhodes in Cape Town and his agents in London in the months before the raid. The committee asked Hawksley as Rhodes's legal representative to give them these telegrams. But while Hawksley left the committee in no doubt that he possessed the telegrams, he refused to produce them without authorization from Rhodes, who had again left for Rhodesia. The committee had secured copies of most of the telegrams sent after October 1895 from the Eastern Telegraph Company before they were routinely destroyed. But only Hawksley had copies of the earlier telegrams, including reports of Chamberlain's meetings with Rutherfoord Harris and Grey. Hawksley also had copies of later cables sent shortly before the raid, the ones most embarrassing for Chamberlain including the 'hurry up' telegram, of which the Eastern Telegraph Company had mysteriously lost its records. Altogether there were at least eight telegrams in Hawksley's possession which had been examined by Chamberlain, Selborne and the Colonial Office staff in 1896 but were kept from the committee of inquiry in 1897.

In Hawksley's opinion, these telegrams proved Chamberlain's complicity in the Rhodes plot; and Hawksley expected their publication to drive Chamberlain from office. 'I fear', Hawksley wrote to Rhodes,

that Mr. Chamberlain cannot politically survive this disclosure . . . he allowed the troops to be put on the border in connection with the anticipated rising in Johannesburg. . . . At present the real offence is . . . that he has deceived the House of Commons & the country, if not also his colleagues in the Cabinet.[63]

Yet Selborne, whose fate was bound up with Chamberlain's, was sure that they would 'emerge from the ordeal unscathed'[64] if the telegrams were published. They would of course confirm Boer suspicions of Britain's desire to take over their country. But Selborne thought the missing telegrams would have little impact at Westminster. Hawksley, by spreading rumours of Chamberlain's complicity for over a year now to protect Rhodes, had discredited his evidence and inoculated parliamentary observers against suspicion of the Colonial Secretary, particularly where imperial interests were at stake.

Still Chamberlain wished to avoid the ordeal of publication. When the committee learned that he had examined all the telegrams the previous year, he assured the committee that the missing telegrams were 'very similar in character to those that have been produced'.[65] He contrived to remember the passages in the missing telegrams which suggested his innocence. When asked, however, whether he wanted the committee to obtain the missing telegrams, he adopted a stance of uncooperative indifference.

The testimony he and Selborne gave exasperated Hawksley. But Rhodes rejected Hawksley's pleas to release the telegrams for publication. Two members of the committee, Labouchere and Edward Blake, a Canadian Liberal who sat in the imperial Parliament as an Irish Nationalist, tried to insist that Hawksley and Rhodes produce the telegrams. Most of the Liberals on the committee refused to support this demand for fear that it would delay their final report until the next year's session of Parliament and in the meantime allow Rhodes to roam free and unrebuked. Labouchere shared this preoccupation with Rhodes instead of Chamberlain. Even Blake doubted Chamberlain's complicity. The guiding objective of the Liberals on the committee, as Harcourt explained to Chamberlain, was to secure 'a reasoned & uncompromising condemnation of Rhodes'.[66]

Thus the notorious telegrams remained hidden. In the following years every verbatim copy disappeared. The missing telegrams are known now mainly from an analysis of them by Chamberlain which came to light among his papers long after his death.

As the parliamentary inquiry moved towards a close, Harcourt began to suspect Chamberlain of involvement in planning the uitlander uprising of 1895 though not the invasion of the Transvaal. But instead of attempting to establish the degree of Chamberlain's complicity, Harcourt sought to work with him in drawing up the committee's report. In that way, the government and Chamberlain in particular would have to abide by the condemnation of Rhodes which Harcourt was determined to secure. Chamberlain took full advantage of the opportunity Harcourt thus gave him. He pressed Harcourt to warm up the report's expression of sympathy for the uitlanders and to be less severe on the intermediate officials such as the high commissioner's chief secretary and the administrator of the Bechuanaland protectorate who, by their own confession, knew more from Rhodes than they had told their imperial superiors. Chamberlain even pressed Harcourt to play down the significance of the missing telegrams, and also took care that the committee did not attempt to strip Rhodes of his privy councillorship or call for his legal prosecution. So long as the committee and hence Parliament censured Rhodes sternly, Harcourt was willing to concede a great deal. He saw no need for legal prosecution so long as Rhodes was marked by the 'stigma of Parliament . . . of an unsparing character'.[67] As for the missing telegrams, Harcourt promised Chamberlain to deal with that business 'in the form which would be most satisfactory to you'.

One last threat to Chamberlain surfaced at the end of June with the unearthing of telegrams between Rhodes and the South African correspondent of *The Times*, Flora Shaw. They revealed the efforts Rhodes made during Jameson's invasion to prevent the imperial authorities from condemning the raid before its military outcome was clear. The telegrams also suggested that Chamberlain had encouraged a prompt rising in Johannesburg rather than postponement; but Flora Shaw repudiated this implication. Her only effect on Harcourt was to make him more determined than ever 'to damn the rascality'[68] of Rhodes.

Throughout the month of June, the diamond jubilee of Queen Victoria's accession to the throne engulfed London in the sounds and sights of imperial patriotism. Chamberlain loved the festivities, which seemed heaven-sent to reward him. The golden jubilee of 1887 had been a British domestic celebration. The diamond jubilee for the Queen's unprecedented sixty years on the throne celebrated the British empire, the most far-flung and largest the world had ever known. Colourful regiments from every corner of the empire marched through the streets. Premiers from the self-governing colonies, some the size of Europe, gathered to honour their Queen and consult with her Colonial Secretary. According to one report, every member of a delegation from the Malay States turned up for their reception at the Colonial Office sporting a monocle and an orchid. The festivities swept Chamberlain beyond his social depth. He issued too many invitations for a reception at his London home; and when the Prince of Wales drove up, he was infuriated to see his daughter being hustled in the crush.

The absolving waters of the jubilee did not extend to Rhodes in southern Africa. The publication of his exchange of telegrams with Flora Shaw tore away the last thread covering the extent of his guilt. There was little Chamberlain could do now to tone down the censure in the inquiry's report to Parliament. Hawksley despatched one final plea to Rhodes to release the missing telegrams in self-defence. But Rhodes stoically refused. He knew that, whether or not Chamberlain might survive release of the telegrams, their publication would doom the charter of the British South Africa Company.

The heart of the inquiry's report, which Chamberlain signed, was a stern though measured condemnation of Rhodes for the plot before the raid. The committee added an implicit but clear condemnation of his failure to try to stop Jameson once the raid began. The chief imperial authorities, on the other hand, Robinson (now Lord Rosmead) as high commissioner and Chamberlain as Colonial Secretary, were totally exonerated of complicity. Rhodes's refusal to release the missing telegrams was interpreted as tantamount to an admission by him 'that any statements purporting to implicate the Colonial Office contained in them were unfounded'.[69] The committee justified its decision not to bring Rhodes back from Africa to produce the telegrams by stressing the importance of making a report to Parliament without another year's delay. This justification was extended to excuse the committee for not recalling one director of the Chartered Company to London for examination, the one who could have implicated Chamberlain, Lord Grey. Conveniently he was kept far away, serving Chamberlain and Rhodes as imperial administrator of Rhodesia.

Still, the report's condemnation of Rhodes left Chamberlain and his Unionist colleagues uneasy. The problem as they saw it was how to censure Rhodes and yet salvage what remained of his power for imperial purposes. In March Chamberlain had wondered about using Rhodes as a supplier of capital to wean Delagoa Bay from Portugal. In July, while the parliamentary committee was drawing up its verdict, Chamberlain sought to assess and balance the deprivation of official authority which Rhodes was bound to suffer as against the great influence which 'his previous career, his wealth, and his large ideas will always command'.[70]

Chamberlain approached the debate on the report in the House of Commons apprehensively. The missing telegrams and scent of blackmail dogged his footsteps. Rumour later had it that a Liberal MP, D.A. Thomas, sat through the debate in possession of the notorious telegrams, which he was to use if Chamberlain did not speak warmly of Rhodes. The rumour was inherently implausible. Why the choice of a Little England Liberal to protect Rhodes? The tactic would also instantly convict Rhodes of blackmail. And, if Selborne's judgement was right, Chamberlain would emerge unscathed. Even so, all eyes focused on the Colonial Secretary.

The startling thing about his speech, which concluded the debate, was his defence of Rhodes. It was not completely surprising. Every time that the Commons had discussed the raid, Chamberlain delivered exonerating, sometimes eulogistic remarks on Rhodes. Furthermore Hicks Beach, who led off for the government in this debate, coupled condemnation of Rhodes for his plot with appreciation of his otherwise great services to the empire. Chamberlain endorsed the guilty judgment pronounced by the committee. He deserved to be punished and was already punished, said Chamberlain, by the censure of the Commons through its committee and by the loss of his premiership of the Cape Colony and his managing directorship of the Chartered Company. But Chamberlain defended Rhodes against further punishment, particularly from loss of his privy councillorship, in words which eased the censure Harcourt had been so anxious to pronounce.

The exoneration first of Chamberlain by the parliamentary committee and then of Rhodes by Chamberlain bred suspicion abroad. Continental observers saw British hypocrisy at work. Kruger saw proof of British determination to undermine the independence of his republic. The fissure between Boer and Briton widened till it ran across the whole of South Africa, dividing Pretoria from Johannesburg in the Transvaal, and splitting the alliance at the Cape between Dutch and British which Rhodes had put together over the previous decade. Those leaders of the Liberal party in Britain who had *not* served on the inquiry could sense the damage abroad.

But the episode did not damage Chamberlain at home. The indignation of Harcourt and other Liberals on the committee at Chamberlain's amelioration of their verdict on Rhodes was tempered by their recognition that in other ways they too had subordinated their proceedings to the national interest. They continued to believe Chamberlain innocent of the worst charges of complicity. Other observers were impressed by the dexterity with which he contained the damage from the raid and finessed the inquiry. He might not be a paragon of virtue, but one had to admire his virtuosity as a politician. Ironically the British politician most discredited in the wake of the Jameson raid was Harcourt, whose standing as leader of the opposition never recovered. Chamberlain strode forward as exemplar of the new imperialism.

14

Imperial Investment
1895–1898

The eighteen months after the Commons debate on the Jameson raid report were among the most satisfying in Chamberlain's public life. He succeeded during that time in setting the terms of the imperialism by which Britain was captivated. For a short period, perhaps only until the Boer War accentuated the drawbacks, imperialism became, according to its most trenchant critic, 'the most powerful movement in the current politics of the western world'.[1] Britain was the leading imperial power of the time, and Chamberlain the leading practitioner of imperialism. It was a questionable achievement, abhorrent to those it crushed abroad and to Little Englanders at home. As with his domestic Radicalism before the Home Rule split, the accomplishments of his imperialism were more talked about than substantial; and its consequences were bitter. But until 1899 the costs of Chamberlain's imperialism were far less evident than its promise.

The very language of imperialism was his. Concluding his inaugural address as Lord Rector of the University of Glasgow in 1897, he declared his

> ... faith in our race and in our nation. I believe that, with all the force and enthusiasm of which democracy alone is capable, they will complete and maintain that splendid edifice of our greatness, which, commenced under aristocratic auspices, has received in these later times its greatest extension; and that the fixity of purpose and strength of will which are necessary to this end will be supplied by that national patriotism which sustains the most strenuous efforts and makes possible the greatest sacrifices.[2]

Like Elgar's famous march, these were stirring sounds. As with Elgar, the beat of determination was as evident as the soaring confidence, and neither disguised the underlying anxiety.

Chamberlain's central concern as the century neared its close was with the international competition by which Britain found itself assailed. The domestic concern which had led him into politics, for the wellbeing of Britain's industrial society, was overtaken and extended by the deterioration in Britain's international position. During his days in business, Britain towered supreme as the world's first industrial nation reinforced by the world's greatest empire. Since his election to Parliament, the United States had outstripped Britain's industrial achievement, and Germany was matching it. Meanwhile the powers of Europe had divided Africa among themselves and eyed Asia hungrily. Britain, because of its already widespread claims and established interests overseas, did well in this competitive imperial expansion, better than any other power. Imperial success offset but indirectly also accentuated Britain's loss of industrial supremacy. The empire had made only a subordinate contribution to Britain's primacy in the middle of the nineteenth century. Now the empire might be indispensable if Britain wished to maintain its strength abroad and contentment at home.

That supposition lay at the base of Chamberlain's statecraft at the Colonial Office. Ironically for the industrialist turned statesman, the supposition was weaker on the economic side than on the political. Though no one dared call Chamberlain an economic coward, he paid less attention to the technologically demanding and more competitive markets of the industrial world than to the pre-industrial economies of the colonies, whose raw material resources he also overestimated. Concerned furthermore with Britain's shrinking share of the manufacturing sector in the international economy, he did not give much thought to the financial sector, which bulked ever larger in the British economy and where Britain was central internationally.

He sensed the defects of his economic vision only in Birmingham, where he crowned his lifelong concern for industrially applicable education by founding a university. Nationally, he accepted the limitations within which he had to work, though with mounting reluctance. His imperialism amounted to a focused set of concerns more than to answers because the responses he wished to offer were held back by constraints he could not overcome. In order to meet Britain's needs, the empire required cultivation, consolidation and extension, all of which threatened the Victorian canons of economy in governmental expenditure, free trade and a pacific foreign policy. Chamberlain did what he could within these constraints to meet the needs of the empire. To explain his purpose to the public, he punctuated his service at the Colonial Office with speeches at banquets of the influential in London and

on platforms in the provincial cities of England and Scotland. Few
doubted that he carried the public with him. He was, as Winston
Churchill recalled, 'incomparably the most live, sparkling, insurgent,
compulsive figure in British affairs'. Churchill even said that ' "Joe" was
the one who made the weather'.[3] But no man could change the climate.
The popular imperialism of the late 1890s did not run deep enough to
overturn the basic assumptions of the Victorian polity.

Cultivating the crown colonies

As Britain lost ground in competition with the United States and Germany for the markets of Europe and North America, the products and
markets of its tropical dependencies acquired new significance. Chamberlain placed a reassuring interpretation on this shift. 'Our trade', he
explained, '. . . tends more and more in the nature of things to become
an interchange of products between dissimilar countries, between the
temperate countries and the tropical countries, rather than between two
or more temperate countries, where the natural advantages and products are the same.'[4] But the new trade could scarcely begin to replace
the old without substantial investment, especially in the means of transport to open up the tropical dependencies for imperial commerce.

Investment in the undeveloped estates of the empire need not, like
old-age pensions, involve a permanent increase in governmental expenditure. Ultimately the investment was supposed to yield a profit.
Still, at least in the short run, the investment would involve either direct
use of British governmental revenue as capital or indirect but still possibly costly guarantees of loans or stock issues to raise capital in the
open market. Except for cases of emergency, Chamberlain did not intend to resort to direct grants. But he did intend to make greater use of
the powers of the Colonial Office and its officers throughout the empire
to expedite its economic development. He hoped, furthermore, to find
ways to help the crown colonies borrow money without increasing British taxation or compromising Britain's commitment to free trade. An
enterprising policy of development could demonstrate that Britain did
not require protective tariffs in order to make good use of its empire.
Similarly, imperial expansion could serve the precepts of free trade by
preserving markets from the clutches of rival empires which, unlike the
British, surrounded their colonies with protective tariff walls.

Nevertheless, Chamberlain's policy upset conventions that had acquired almost constitutional sanctity. Hitherto the fundamental concern
of the Colonial Office had been 'how best to administer the colonies
. . . with the minimum of expense and involvement';[5] and although the
lassitude in administration which often accompanied this predisposition

found few defenders now, its association with economy in expenditure still commanded admiration. Furthermore any imperial financial commitment, including guarantees for loans, subjected the enterprise to close scrutiny by the Treasury and spasmodic scrutiny in the House of Commons. Chamberlain never managed to gain for his colonial enterprise the freedom it needed.

The arch-mandarin at the Treasury, Sir Edward Hamilton, was impressed at first by Chamberlain as 'a man of ideas', but added, 'it will be interesting to see how he will be able to give effect to them'.[6] He proceeded to undermine Chamberlain's suggestion of using the dividends from the Suez Canal shares as a base for loans to the colonies. The decision rested with Hicks Beach as Chancellor of the Exchequer. He and Chamberlain developed a better relationship than contemporaries could quite credit. Hicks Beach always took his discussions with Chamberlain to matters of financial management and parliamentary debate on which both men felt at home. Still, Hicks Beach's Conservatism was essentially of the cautious kind, and he was ultimately in thrall to the high priests of the Treasury.

After initial discussions with Hicks Beach and Hamilton, Chamberlain drew up an eloquent memorandum.[7] He played on the pride Conservatives took over Disraeli's purchase of shares in the Suez Canal, an imperial coup which proved profitable financially. Citing colonies in the West Indies and Latin America to elaborate his theme, Chamberlain claimed that

> there are untold possibilities of mineral wealth in the shape of gold and other minerals, dye-woods and timber, and all tropical productions, which neither the Colonies themselves nor individual adventurers are in a position to open up . . . because there are no proper means of access. Individual enterprise will till the fields, and cut the timber, and work the mines; but Government, and Government alone, can make the roads and the railways.

He outlined his scheme for low-interest loans to crown colonies for public works such as railways, harbours and irrigation on the security of the Suez Canal shares, the works themselves, and the revenue they produced. But prompted by Hamilton, Hicks Beach whittled down the scheme in the interests of the British taxpayer, raised the rate of interest in the interests of the regular money market, and then declined to give even limited approval. He insisted on the controls by the Treasury and the Commons from which the scheme was designed to liberate the colonies.

The most pressing case of colonial need diverted Chamberlain's attention for a while from his quest for a developmental loan fund. The West Indian colonies were stricken by a sharp fall in the price for their staple sugar crop and could not keep up payment on their existing loans, let alone take out new ones. Britain would have to help them with small grants to meet their basic administrative costs in the emergency. More enduring remedial aid could come in two forms. Britain could make further grants to improve the productivity of the sugar industry in the islands and diversify their economic base. But that was the form of help to which the Treasury was most averse. In any case, the benefits from this investment would not alleviate the immediate distress. Grants-in-aid might not even deal with the root of the problem.

The international price of sugar had been lowered by subsidized production of beet sugar in Continental European states. Britain might correct the situation by threatening to impose countervailing duties to match the foreign subsidies. But to do so would break one of the commandments of free trade, a commandment that ranked even higher in the Treasury's estimation than its aversion to direct grants. Cheap sugar and sugar-based products like jam saved the British taxpayer millions of pounds sterling annually, whereas grants-in-aid were unlikely to exceed tens or a very few hundreds of thousands. There was also some question whether indeed the Continental European subsidies lay at the heart of the West Indies' ills. Sir Charles Dilke noted that sugar production was expanding in places in southeast Asia that did not benefit from bounties.

Chafing at the fetters of doctrinaire free trade, Chamberlain sought to extend his freedom of action. He was still convinced that, in general, free trade was the best policy for Britain. But even Richard Cobden, the Moses of free trade, had departed from strict doctrine in negotiating a reciprocal trade treaty with France. The world's industrial powers with the exception of Britain had abandoned free trade and embraced tariff protection over the past fifteen years. All that Chamberlain asked for was freedom to threaten bounty-paying states with countervailing duties in order to restore free trade.

Still, such a departure from free trade orthodoxy would be inconceivable until Britain was confronted by an unusually clear and acute case of need. Chamberlain therefore despatched a bipartisan royal commission to the West Indies to investigate the situation and report back. Though he left the commissioners free to draw their own conclusions, he pointed out that stimulating alternative industries could not meet the immediate needs of the West Indies, and he implied that countervailing duties were the likely remedy for the ills of the staple sugar industry.

The eventual report of the commission disappointed him. Though the principal commissioners agreed that the European bounties largely accounted for the depression in the West Indian sugar industry, they could not agree on the remedy. They disagreed particularly on countervailing duties. They recommended a package of other measures to diversify and strengthen the local economy. Yet they did not even call for implementation of their recommendations on a bold scale or with generous funding.

The only purpose the report served for Chamberlain was to make clear that the depression in the West Indies was acute and must be eased. Taking that message as his point of departure, he pressed his cabinet colleagues to choose between two alternatives. Both of them went against the Victorian grain. The one he advocated, to threaten the Continental states with countervailing duties in order to get rid of their bounties, would be the more upsetting of the two. He therefore accompanied it with the lowest possible levels of direct grant aid to restore the West Indian colonies to solvency. The alternative, he warned his colleagues, would be far greater direct investment in remedial measures than the 'trifling' scale recommended by the royal commission.[8] The cabinet chose the more expensive alternative, perhaps as Chamberlain intended.

The measures Chamberlain offered the West Indies in 1898 incorporated the best recommendations of the royal commission. A department of agriculture was set up in the West Indies to overcome the technological conservatism of the sugar planters and to encourage the cultivation of new fruit crops. Peasant landownership was encouraged. Steamship service was to be subsidized among the West Indian islands, with neighbouring British Guiana, and on to Canada and Britain. Designed for implementation as a coordinated package, these measures constituted a degree of governmental economic planning that departed from the spirit though not the letter of laissez-faire. A devastating hurricane in the West Indies helped Chamberlain to ensure that the package was well funded. Hamilton continued to oppose special treatment for the West Indies and managed to keep expenditure on the West Indian agricultural department down to the level suggested by the royal commission. Hicks Beach, however, overruled the opposition of his officials at the Treasury to a steamship subsidy, and he remained true to his promise of particular generosity for the West Indies even after the Boer War forced the total expenditure of the government to unprecedented heights.

The direct financial aid for the West Indies incidentally involved the resumption of direct imperial control of the finances of the affected colonies, whether or not the elected members of the various governors' councils agreed. Chamberlain viewed this development without regret. His belief in the Anglo-Saxon gift for government accentuated his assumption of white superiority. He spoke disrespectfully of the 'half breeds' prevalent in West Indian politics and dismissed blacks as 'totally unfit for rep[resentativ]e institutions & the dupes of unscrupulous adventurers'.[9] Yet he respected representative institutions where they worked well; and when the Treasury sought to supersede the longstanding and fairly effective constitution of Barbados, he resisted the attempt.

His experience with the West Indies shaped the developmental policy he pursued with more fortunate colonies. Few were as affluent as Ceylon, whose tea production gave the colonial government a handsome surplus of revenue as well as excellent credit in the open market for loans. But Ceylon had an earlier unhappy experience with coffee; and Chamberlain took warning also from the fate of the West Indies when its staple product fell on hard times. He counselled the governor of Ceylon to use his tax surplus to contribute towards the costs of railway construction rather than 'pile up loans'[10] and to invest in other public works, particularly irrigation for the production of rice, to broaden the colony's economic base.

With its plans for the West Indies on line, the Colonial Office again addressed the general need among crown colonies for developmental loans. The Treasury led by Hamilton resisted the quest of Chamberlain's men for a supply of low-interest loans which they could allocate and the application of which they could supervise without further Treasury control. The two offices eventually came close to agreement on the general terms for borrowing. But Hicks Beach and his advisers backed away as soon as they realized the magnitude of Chamberlain's plans. Hicks Beach contemplated only a few enterprises of direct value to the entire empire. Chamberlain sought a scheme that would enable each colony to construct the form of transport or improvement best suited to its particular needs. Negotiations broke down, but only after some projects had begun in the West Indies and West Africa in anticipation of the funds Chamberlain envisaged. They were rescued by a Colonial Loans bill enacted in 1899 on terms laid down by the Treasury and reserved mainly for these cases.

The following year, the Colonial Office and its allies obtained much of what they wanted through a Colonial Stock Act. It accorded colonial stock issues gilt-edged status and hence lower rates of interest in the open market. Hicks Beach and his advisers were none too happy with this provision of the Act. The Colonial Office overcame their resistance by exploiting a precedent that the self-governing colonies led by Canada managed to set. The Colonial Stock Act of 1900 still did not give Chamberlain the flexibility and freedom from Treasury supervision he desired. Nevertheless, it was under this Act that Britain's imperial dependencies thereafter obtained capital to improve their basic systems of communication, transport and land utilization.

Chamberlain had been Colonial Secretary for five years when the Colonial Stock bill was enacted. The slowness with which he was granted the financial implements he needed to cultivate the resources of the empire irritated but did not exasperate him. He understood the caution of the Treasury because he shared its assumption that the economy was best served by private enterprise. He differed from the Treasury essentially on the extent of supportive activity that the state should provide. The officials at the Treasury shied away not only from direct investment in infrastructure but also from direct contact with businessmen. Chamberlain sought both.

But his efforts to induce business to invest in the tropical empire were unavailing unless they coincided with market forces and private interest. The contribution he won from businessmen did little to augment the meagre assistance he extracted from the Treasury. Businessmen either resisted his blandishments or, when they cooperated, did not succeed in changing the patterns of trade in the imperial interest. Chamberlain pursued Sir Thomas Lipton, the grocery chain millionaire, with generous offers of support to induce him to invest in sugar factories in Barbados, Antigua and St Kitts. But Chamberlain refused to guarantee Lipton completely against risk because the existence of risk was the best guarantee of enterprise. Lipton turned away, deterred by the cloud of depression that hung over the West Indies. On the other hand Sir Alfred Jones of the Elder Dempster Steamship Company accepted the subsidy Chamberlain offered to secure fast transport for fruit, mail and passengers between Jamaica and Britain. But the subsidy did not serve as Chamberlain hoped, to foster trade between Jamaica and Britain and staunch the flow of Jamaican fruit to the United States.

The Gold Coast, already the richest of Britain's possessions in West Africa, furnished the outstanding exception to this pattern of unwilling or ineffective private investment. Crushing machines were needed to extract the gold after which the colony was named, and only rail transport could convey the heavy machinery to mining sites inland. The major mining company in the region, the Ashanti Goldfields Corporation, offered the government annual subsidies of from £20,000 to £30,000 to hasten the extension of the railway which the colony was constructing. Chamberlain accepted the offer eagerly; and it was honoured on both sides even though it eventually doubled the government's construction costs to complete the line as fast as the company required. Yet other British merchants with substantial interests in West Africa 'refused to touch West African colonial railway shares when offered the opportunity for a block subscription at reduced rates'.[11]

Wherever he turned, Chamberlain found himself enmeshed in financial constraints from which he could not escape. Another way to evade the vigilance of the Treasury was by raising revenue in a colony to fund its own development. Chamberlain played fast and loose with conventional practices designed to tide colonial governments over occasional economic reverses. He laid his hands on such moneys to fund the developmental spiral whereby local resources were cultivated to produce greater governmental revenue. He thought that this spiral would reconcile the insistence of the Treasury on colonial self-sufficiency with his desire for economic development. The problem was to get a colony on to the spiral in the first place. Small reserves set aside for a rainy day were not enough.

Another alternative was to tax the native population, a practice which could also serve to press natives into the western cash economy. But action along these lines could prove counterproductive. When the governor of Sierra Leone, Cardew, imposed a hut tax to finance capital development, he triggered an armed revolt which assumed serious dimensions at a time of confrontation between Britain and France in the region. Chamberlain was inclined to scuttle the tax and Cardew along with it. Selborne reasserted the pure Chamberlainite doctrine in face of his faltering chief. Convinced by Cardew that the revolt had deeper roots than the tax, Selborne argued that Sierra Leone needed more and better civil and military officers. 'But this means more money, not less, for administration alone, and then there is the question of development. Are we going to make no roads, no telegraphs, no bridges, to give no industrial or elementary education, to make no effort to survey the territory or explore or utilise its resources?'[12] Touched on his tenderest points, Chamberlain patched up a compromise that retained the offending tax. Still, in the end a tax which had been expected to raise no more than £8,000 cost £55,000 by way of repressing the rebellion to collect. Little wonder that the British merchants with interests in the area censured Chamberlain over the episode.

Among the various imperial utilities in need of development, faster sea transport and the laying of telegraphic cables appealed to Chamberlain as means to control and consolidate the empire. The self-governing colonies, particularly in Australasia, also wanted investment on these improvements. But the Treasury was even more averse to cooperative ventures with self-governing, supposedly self-financing colonies than to investment in dependencies under imperial control. Consolidation of the empire was dismissed by the permanent officials at the Treasury as an immaterial consideration. Only when the projected form of communication possessed military significance was the Treasury content to contribute to it. It took prolonged negotiations to persuade the Treasury to invest in the laying of a Pacific cable between Canada and Australia.

Chamberlain's imperial enterprise proved most effective in a field related to his first love in public life: education. What attracted him was always social application. He took up the cause of research and education in tropical diseases because of the assistance it offered to the imperial cause. Reduction of the toll exacted by disease on the servants of the empire in the tropics would do more for the sinews of imperial control than cables and steamships, more for the imperial armed forces than the addition of regiments, more for the construction of imperial railways or the sinking of colonial mines than additional navvies and diggers. The death-rate among colonial officers in West Africa had persuaded a Commons committee in 1865 to call for withdrawal from Sierra Leone. British insurance companies refused to write life policies for men sent to the region. Throughout the tropical empire, malaria and diseases like blackwater fever slew a horrifying proportion of the men whom the Colonial Office sent out, sapped the energy of the rest, and so shortened the term of service that they rarely quite grasped the nature of their assignment before they returned home.

Early in his tenure at the Colonial Office, Chamberlain requested copies of anything published on tropical disease. The English medical establishment was surprised, for it saw no need to pay special attention to the subject. Chamberlain welcomed the formation in 1896 of a Colonial Nursing Association, founded by a woman who knew from experience in Mauritius about the need of colonial officers for nursing care like that available in England. Mary Chamberlain served the association actively as vice-president.

There was a clear assumption of racial superiority in the activities of the association. Chamberlain explained that its nurses went out to serve those who would otherwise be 'left almost entirely to the tender mercies of dirty and indifferent and ignorant natives'.[13] This prejudice left an unfortunate mark on his entire policy for public health in tropical colonies, segregating, for example, the quarters for white colonial servants to keep them from infection among natives, and reducing opportunities of indigenous doctors for advancement in the colonial medical service.

Yet when abuses of humanitarian principles about which Chamberlain felt strongly in English society were inflicted on natives of the colonies, he reacted sharply. His early revulsion at flogging in the army flared up again, and he did all he could to curb flogging in the colonies. He told his staff that, bad as it was in a European country, flogging was even worse 'where the persons to be flogged are of a different race and colour to the persons who desire to flog them. All experience shows that the European authority is only too ready to inflict a punishment of this kind, which costs nothing, causes him no trouble or compunction, and gratifies his sense of personal power and superiority.'[14]

His most decisive contribution to the fight against tropical disease was to appoint and support Dr Patrick Manson as Colonial Office Medical Adviser. Chamberlain knew from lectures which Manson delivered at St George's Hospital in London on the basis of years of research in Hong Kong that he was the leading investigator in the field.

When the post of Colonial Office Medical Adviser came open for appointment in the summer of 1897, Chamberlain extended the deadline to give Manson time to apply. Manson turned out to possess 'as much talent for efficient administration as for research'.[15] He developed, for example, a standard form for medical reports from the tropical colonies, which Chamberlain enforced along with calls for samples for research.

Within a month of Manson's appointment, his protégé Ronald Ross in India succeeded in tracing malaria to the *Anopheles* mosquito. Manson explained the significance of the discovery to Chamberlain. Ross raced on to develop plans for a comprehensive attack on the breeding grounds of the mosquito. But to his bitter disappointment, Chamberlain would not do more than encourage the colonies to follow Ross's advice. The devotion of Ross to his schemes exceeded their proven worth, and their cost far exceeded the financial resources that the Colonial Office could command.

But Chamberlain wooed and won private resources to fund his greatest achievement in this field, the founding of the London School of Tropical Medicine. Here again the plan came from Manson, its implementation from Chamberlain. In October 1897, Manson issued a public call for the creation of the school. Next year, when plans were announced for expansion of the Greenwich Royal Seaman's Hospital at the Albert Docks, Manson urged Chamberlain to use the opportunity to create the school; and Chamberlain did so. The cost of what Manson originally had in mind, £3,550, was low. Even so, the Treasury offered only half the amount and insisted that the rest be paid by the tropical colonies. They did as the Treasury required, some offering more than requested. Chamberlain lifted the enterprise to a magnitude of which Manson had only dreamed by appealing for private contributions. Using his oratorical talents and personal contacts, he raised £12,000 beyond the various governmental grants in 1899, and another £11,000 in 1905 after he left the Colonial Office.

His efforts helped to extend the crusade against tropical disease to other centres in Britain and beyond. Moved by his example, Sir Alfred Jones of the Elder Dempster Shipping Company raised an even larger sum to found the Liverpool School of Tropical Medicine, which managed to open just before its metropolitan rival. Though a little envious of the achievement in Liverpool, Chamberlain gave the two schools equal privilege to train and certify physicians for service in the tropics. Medical schools in Durham, Edinburgh, Aberdeen and Belfast hurried to offer lectures on the treatment of tropical diseases. Chamberlain also fostered a new kind of investigative agency for tropical diseases. Committees including researchers from the London and Liverpool schools left for the tropics, empowered not just to investigate and recommend but to make and execute policy.

Tropical medicine was not the only field of applied science that Chamberlain fostered at the Colonial Office. He encouraged the Royal Botanical Gardens at Kew, which he knew from his interest in orchids and sisal, to extend its work in tropical botany. In addition to alternative crops for the West Indies, he wanted to find places in the empire to grow cotton to reduce the dependence of Britain on the supply from the United States. Botanical research could also improve the diet in tropical colonies and their raw materials for export.

The foundations laid by Chamberlain for an assault on tropical disease, and the rapid fall in the death-rate among colonial officers, constituted perhaps his most solid achievement at the Colonial Office. He appeared to accomplish a great deal more. He generated a conviction that the hopes for Britain's continued greatness rode on its empire, on the cultivation of its resources and the strengthening of its bonds. That sense invigorated his staff at the Colonial Office. The brightest young graduates of Oxford and Cambridge competed for the privilege of assignment to his department. Yet in administrative terms Chamberlain's accomplishment was strangely mixed and his impact fleeting.

His term at the Colonial Office became almost instantly legendary. In his hands the position of Colonial Secretary assumed an importance second only to that of the prime minister. Yet the Colonial Secretaryship slipped back to its former status as soon as he left. Captivated by his talk of cultivating undeveloped estates, people anticipated that he would do on a grand scale for the empire what he had done for Birmingham, that he would transform the road and rail network of the colonies as he had the streets and utilities of his city. Yet, as things turned out, the scales were reversed. The willingness of Birmingham in the 1870s to endorse civic investments which entailed a huge increase in the municipal debt stood in marked contrast to the inveterate parsimony of the Treasury. The Treasury pared his public works for the empire down to barely symbolic proportions.

So too with his impact on the administrative processes of the Colonial Office. Chamberlain is supposed to have transformed the ambience of the Colonial Office soon after he arrived by replacing its dim gas lighting with bright electric light. But in fact the change took four years and in his time never reached the third floor. Chamberlain managed to increase the size of the Colonial Office staff repeatedly during his tenure. Yet it was never enough to keep pace with the inflow of letters, memoranda and telegrams, which accelerated as he enlarged the department's responsibilities and stimulated the officers overseas.

The increasing frequency of telegraphic communication with the colonies weakened the administrative grasp of the Colonial Office. Communication by cable might have been expected to increase the power of head office to control distant governors. On the contrary, cables enhanced the ability of governors to convey a sense of urgency about situations which only they could gauge and handle with requisite speed. In general the telegraph 'made the [head] office more acutely aware of the need to support rather than curb or direct the actions of the man on the spot'.[16]

The mounting backlog of work at the Colonial Office contributed to a change in Chamberlain's attitude towards the permanent officials. He realized at the outset of his tenure that some of the most important officers, including Meade as permanent undersecretary and Fairfield at the African desk, were old-style Liberals averse to his brand of constructive imperialism. Initially he was inclined to go his own way without seeking their advice. The Treasury's rejection of his Suez Canal shares scheme and the fiasco of the Jameson raid made him more circumspect, though the raid also precipitated Fairfield's retirement by shattering his health. The widening of Chamberlain's concerns as a leader in the cabinet beyond those of his department compounded its own mounting responsibilities. He began to rely on the individual members of the staff within their assigned spheres. He still read and commented on most of the reports and letters that inundated his desk. He never simply rubber-stamped recommendations from his staff, nor did he hesitate to go his own way. He nevertheless gave rise to a strong-minded staff of whose advice he was sometimes insufficiently critical and in whose impartiality the Liberal opposition began to lose confidence.

Steps were taken at Chamberlain's behest to overcome the long-standing alienation between the head office staff in Downing Street and officers serving in the colonies. Several members of the Downing Street staff were appointed to serve under Sir Alfred Milner when he took over from Lord Rosmead in South Africa. Some officers from the colonies were required to serve at the Colonial Office while they were on leave. Chamberlain inaugurated the Corona Club banquets, an annual affair at which the staff from the Colonial Office dined side by side with officers on leave from the colonies. He supplemented these occasions with smaller dinner parties for home staff and colonial officers. Even so, like Napoleon's sleeping corporal, the junior official in from the field who caught the sympathetic ear of the great Colonial Secretary was an inspiring rarity.

The permanent staff at the Colonial Office shared an outlook which Chamberlain modified but which also modified his achievement. Closer instinctively to the Treasury than to Chamberlain, the Colonial Office staff were inclined to believe that their object should be to lead the colonies towards financial self-sufficiency as distinct from maximizing the contribution they could make to the imperial economy. Sensing this bias, Chamberlain turned to the Crown Agents to implement his policy of crown colonial development. Responsible for the construction of public works and other state enterprises in the crown colonies, the crown agents were less subject than the Colonial Office to Treasury supervision. Chamberlain eventually appointed the chief crown agent, Sir Montague Ommanney, to be permanent undersecretary at the Colonial Office. But Ommanney shared only part of Chamberlain's vision. While sympathetic to the crown colonies, Ommanney had little feeling for the self-governing colonies; and they loomed ever larger in Chamberlain's eyes.

Commerce with the self-governing colonies

The self-governing colonies tested the democratic side of Chamberlain's imperialism. Years earlier in Toronto he had asserted that 'The interest of true democracy is . . . towards . . . the uniting together [of] kindred races with similar objects';[17] and he based the imperial mission of the British race on its talent for uniting self-governing peoples. Aristocrats doubted the validity of these claims, doubts which historians have since confirmed. Lord Derby thought that 'Kings and aristocracies may govern empires; but one people cannot govern another.' Professor Hyam delivered that judgement more strongly when he wrote almost a century later about 'the impossibility, in the last resort, of translating the democratic political decisions of one society into the political realities of another'.[18]

The problem focused in the late nineteenth century on the self-governing colonies rather than on India. Britain governed India as a military autocracy, with cooperation from the Indian princes but no elective representation from the vast majority of the population, among whom there was as yet little movement for self-government. British aristocrats took to the task of governing India as a high privilege, much superior to service in the self-governing colonies. Chamberlain was far more interested in the latter than in the former. He did not follow the practice common among the governing elite of a visit to India. India puzzled him without exciting his imagination. After he established himself as one of the leading imperial officers of state, he sought enlightenment on India from Field Marshal Lord Roberts, born there and a veteran of its wars. Roberts left Chamberlain bemused. 'India seems to be between the Devil & the deep sea,' he responded after reading the notes Roberts prepared for him; '—on the one hand most serious danger of attack from outside & internal disturbance unless full preparations are made—& on the other the prospect of most serious financial embarrassment.'[19] With that, he left India to others, and turned back to the colonies that interested him.

For a few years at the turn of the century, Chamberlain was able to set aside the doubts of Victorian Britain about the durability of the bond between the mother country and the self-governing colonies. To the relief of apprehensive aristocrats like Salisbury who could not rival his command over the industrial electorate, Chamberlain quickened popular enthusiasm for the empire. He did so not only among Englishmen and Scots in Birmingham and Glasgow but also in the colonies, as those who heard him in Toronto never forgot. He heightened a sense on both sides in the empire of the strength and grandeur they could acquire from combination with each other.

Questions remained about the effectiveness of this sentiment and its limitation to 'kindred races'. Did it include French Canadians or the Cape Dutch? And how would it respond to the determination of colonial businessmen, not least in Toronto, to protect their infant manufacturing industries against competition from the mother country?

The difficulties in Britain's relations with its self-governing colonies revolved around tariffs, as Chamberlain had sensed during the infancy of his imperialism. In Gladstone's ministry of the early 1880s, when Dilke aired the possibility of a preferential *Zollverein* between Britain and its colonies, Chamberlain gave it a lively welcome. Birmingham sharpened his sensitivity to the colonial market. In light of the prolonged depression at home and the swing towards tariff protection abroad, the business communities of Birmingham and Sheffield were attracted to the notion of a customs union with the colonies, if possible on the basis of free trade within the empire.

Movement among the self-governing colonies paralleled this trend at home. At the first conference of colonial premiers, in connection with the royal jubilee of 1887, J.H. Hofmeyr of the Cape Colony proposed a two per cent, implicitly preferential tariff between Britain and the colonies to provide funds for the navy. Nothing came of the proposal; but the steep McKinley tariff introduced by the United States in 1890 strengthened the case for some concentration on the imperial market. A colonial conference at Ottawa in 1894 expressed itself in favour of a preferential customs union for the empire. But the British government held aloof.

So, still, did Chamberlain. Speaking to the Birmingham jewellers the next spring, he repudiated tariff protection robustly. He pointed out that the foremost practitioners of protection, the United States and France, were suffering as badly from depression as was Britain. In any case, he insisted, 'We depend upon our foreign trade'.[20] The interest of the self-governing colonies in preferential tariffs had nevertheless impressed him; and he raised the subject in his first meetings with the permanent staff when he took over at the Colonial Office.

Canada deepened its impression on him by generating the one ray of light in the dark days that followed the Jameson raid. The Canadians were not so much concerned with the raid as with the preceding ultimatum from President Cleveland over British Guiana, which they saw as reflecting the desire of the United States to dominate all the Americas, north and south. Like the English at Cape Town who were dismayed by Chamberlain's repudiation of Jameson, the Canadians feared at first that Britain would back down in face of the United States threat. They wrote to warn Chamberlain that if so, 'Canadians would lose faith in the empire'.[21] He passed the warning on to Salisbury. The Canadian House of Commons repressed its fears by pledging its loyalty, and unanimously passed a resolution expressing its devotion to Great Britain and the empire. The French Canadian who led the Liberal opposition, Wilfrid Laurier, spoke eloquently in support of the resolution. Meanwhile, all the way from Ontario to the Maritime provinces, officers in the Canadian militia voiced a desire to take their units on overseas service if needed.

The wave of anxious imperialism in Canada began to fall as the risk of war receded. Chamberlain sought to preserve and make enduring use of the fleeting phenomenon. Speaking in March 1896 to the Canada Club in London, he seized upon the words of a Conservative member of the Canadian House of Commons in the recent debate about 'the honour and integrity of our own Empire'.[22] The sense conveyed by this phrase of joint possession of the empire by the colonies and the mother country impressed Chamberlain. As he expressed it, 'the Empire of Great Britain is the common heritage of all her sons, and is not the appanage of the United Kingdom alone'.

But how could the insistence by Britain and each of the internally autonomous colonies on governing themselves be reconciled with the desire for an overarching imperial government? The Imperial Federation League had dissolved itself in 1894 after a decade's fruitless search for a solution. Chamberlain suspended the quest for a constitutional answer, leaving that to 'gradual development'. He proposed 'to approach the question ... on its commercial side'. The unification of Germany had begun that way, with a customs union, the famous *Zollverein*.

But the kind of preferential arrangements to which the colonies were inclined would not do. In a withering analysis which came back to haunt him, Chamberlain rejected a system that would oblige Britain to raise tariffs against foreign imports while the colonies retained tariffs to protect their infant industries against all imports, favouring the mother country merely by imposing a lower tariff on British than on foreign goods. Such a system would raise the British cost of living and production costs, and would further disadvantage Britain because its foreign trade was 'gigantic' in comparison to that of the self-governing colonies. Bargaining like a businessman, he asked them 'to better their offer'.

Still, he was prepared to go a long way to meet them, and in doing so to break seriously with free trade orthodoxy. He was willing to impose tariffs upon foreign imports if the colonies would reduce their tariffs on British goods to a merely revenue-producing level. Protective tariffs against the mother country would have to end. What Chamberlain proposed was an imperial customs union within which free trade would, to all intents and purposes, prevail. He put the proposal forward without endorsement from the government in an attempt 'to provoke discussion—in this country and ... above all, in the colonies'. Speaking in June to the Chambers of Commerce of the Empire,[23] he repeated the proposal. It constituted a fundamental departure from the trading policy Britain had pursued for half a century. Yet the basic plan could be defended from a free-trading point of view as an enlargement of free trade within the empire. The idea had won some sympathy from the previous Liberal Colonial Secretary, Lord Ripon. Chamberlain thought that if the colonies welcomed the proposal, Britain could be induced to follow suit.

Canada was the key. It was the most populous and economically advanced of the self-governing colonies. As a federation, it was easier to deal with than the disunited colonies in southern Africa or Australasia. Canada set the pace to which the other self-governing colonies could be expected sooner or later to conform. Some Canadians were keenly interested in strengthening the economic ties of the empire, most notably Colonel G.T. Denison, the soldier propagandist from Toronto. Banking on his hopes, Chamberlain was confident—so the secretary of the former Imperial Federation League reported—that 'before the end of the year he will have a proposal from the Canadian Government (whichever Government it may be) for a conference to discuss possible Tariff Union'.[24]

A general election approached in Canada. Chamberlain would have liked the Conservatives with whom he had worked well to remain in power, but he was not disconcerted when the Liberals under Laurier won. Shortly after the change of government, however, while Chamberlain was on holiday in Massachusetts, a senior member of the new Canadian cabinet, Sir Richard Cartwright, came to sound him out. Cartwright wanted to know what Chamberlain thought about the possibility of a reciprocal trade treaty between Canada and the United States to give them better terms in each other's market than other countries including Britain would enjoy. Cartwright met a hostile response. Chamberlain said that such a treaty would refute 'the expressions of loyalty and imperial patriotism'[25] Canada had made at the beginning of the year, and lead towards separation between the Dominion and the mother country.

Cartwright's suggestion so daunted Chamberlain that in January 1897 when he invited the colonial premiers to the Queen's forthcoming jubilee, he did not immediately suggest using the occasion for a conference. The Canadian finance minister restored Chamberlain's hopes by reducing the colonial tariff by 12.5 per cent for goods from countries which imposed a particularly low tariff on goods from Canada. In practice the concession was restricted to Britain and New South Wales, though the trade treaties which Britain had concluded on a most-favoured-nation basis with Germany and Belgium confused the situation. The new Canadian tariff fell far short of the imperial free trade union Chamberlain had advocated. The saving grace of the Canadian scheme from his point of view was that it did not require Britain to erect tariffs. Since Britain already had the world's lowest tariffs, nothing more need be done to qualify the mother country for the preferential rate of the colony.

In Canada the defeated Conservatives carped at the so-called imperial preference. In Britain the Board of Trade, the Foreign Office and the law officers of the government criticized its formulation and international bearings. But Chamberlain protected the scheme of the Laurier government from embarrassment on either side of the Atlantic. He even tried, without success, to dampen a crusade which Colonel Denison launched in England to generate enthusiasm for a more assertive imperial policy than Laurier welcomed.

In the midst of the jubilee festivities, just before the colonial conference began, the colonial premiers made a special visit to Birmingham. Welcoming them to his city, Chamberlain seized upon remarks Laurier had made upon his arrival in England at Liverpool. Chamberlain paraphrased Laurier to say that 'either the colonies would draw closer to [Britain] and would take a larger share in the government and administration of the Empire, or else they would insensibly . . . drift apart. That', said Chamberlain, 'is . . . the greatest problem with which the statesmen of the Empire have to-day to deal.'[26]

To encourage spontaneous initiatives, Chamberlain kept the proceedings of his ensuing conference with the colonial premiers private. He opened the conference with a charge, the only speech to be reported in full, in which he suggested how the Canadian suggestions might be pursued. Laurier's remarks at Liverpool emboldened Chamberlain to begin with political federation. He described a hypothetical 'great council of the Empire'[27] composed of distinguished representatives who kept in close touch with their respective colonies. It might begin with minor matters of common interest, but Chamberlain clearly hoped that it would aim higher and acquire executive influence. He added without much subtlety that 'of course, with the privilege of management and of control will also come the obligation ... of contribution towards the expense for objects which we shall have in common'.

Turning to defence, in order to encourage colonial contribution to and integration within the imperial armed forces, he drew attention to the heavy burden shouldered by Britain without help even from the strongest colonies. He referred to the offers in 1896 from the Canadian militia, and suggested a regular interchange between regiments from the mother country and her 'sister' colonies and joint participation 'in the dangers and the glories of the ... expeditions in which the British army may be engaged'.[28] With regard to commercial relations, Chamberlain again improved on the Canadian example. He sought to guarantee the imperial character of the preferential Canadian tariff; he encouraged other colonies to follow the Canadian example; and he indicated that, if they did so, Britain would denounce its most-favoured-nation trade treaties with Germany and Belgium.

Laurier responded to Chamberlain's use of Canadian examples by putting him back on the roller coaster of alarms and excitements to which Sir Richard Cartwright and the new Canadian tariff had introduced him. The ride with Laurier was all the more perplexing because he could make the lows seem so much like highs. Chamberlain and Laurier were masters of words. But whereas Chamberlain's words were noted for their clarity, Laurier used words evocatively. Nowhere was Laurier's talent for mystification more evident than on imperial federation. Most of the colonial premiers indicated that they were not ready for strengthened central government of the empire. They would not tolerate any arrangement, for example representation by population, which subordinated them to the mother country, still less anything which made them responsible for imperial expenditure. George Reid of New South Wales told Chamberlain bluntly that 'we are ready to manage the Empire for you at any time, so long as you pay the piper'.[29] Chamberlain had to confess that Britain was not ready for an arrangement which treated the self-governing colonies as its constitutional equals. But Laurier, while agreeing with the majority of the premiers on the general point, bemused Chamberlain with ambiguity. 'I am quite satisfied with the condition of things as they are,' said the Canadian Liberal, 'but to imagine that will last for ever is a delusion. I venture from my heart', he added vaguely, 'to suggest that there is a good deal in representation.'[30] Outside the conference and afterwards, Laurier reiterated the misleading prophecy he had made at Liverpool.

On imperial defence, Laurier was less ambiguous but also less forthcoming than most of his fellow premiers, though they too disappointed Chamberlain's hopes. The notion of regimental interchange was left for later experimentation. Discussion at the conference focused on the huge and costly British navy, which the premiers saw in majestic review during the jubilee celebrations. Chamberlain sought financial contributions to this guarantee of security in an essentially maritime empire. But Laurier, forgetting the scare over the Cleveland ultimatum, dismissed the notion of Canadian vulnerability and pushed aside the question of what financial contribution Canada might make. The Australian colonies, feeling more vulnerable in their Pacific waters, already made a tiny contribution to the British navy; but no argument about the nature of naval warfare could stop them from insisting that the ships they helped to support should stay close to their port cities. Only Sir Gordon Sprigg of the Cape Colony rose to Chamberlain's call. Nervous about the Transvaal, Sprigg offered Britain the cost of a battleship; but his colony found itself unable fully to honour his commitment.

Only in the commercial sphere did Laurier live up to Chamberlain's hopes. Imperial preference was the perfect way for the French Canadian Liberal to reduce tariffs as the free traders in his party desired without offending Canadian manufacturers of English descent who were attached to the old country. Laurier was happy to assist Chamberlain in emphasizing that the Canadian tariff preference was unconditional and did not involve any restoration of tariffs by Britain. All Britain had to do was cancel the trade treaties with Germany and Belgium which prevented Britain's colonies from giving the mother country the preference they desired. Chamberlain informed the premiers before the end of their conference that Britain denounced the offending treaties. But the Australians responded with Laurier-like ambiguity to the Canadian example of imperial preference. New South Wales adhered to the British policy of free trade. Britain was the exporter the other Australian colonies most feared. These reactions led Chamberlain to conclude that the next step towards imperial federation ought to be regional federation in Australia and South Africa.

Before the conference was over, he concluded that 'Union will not come in a hurry . . . the great thing is—to use a Railway expression—to "get the points right". If we do this we shall go on in parallel lines for the future. If we make any mistake we shall get wider and wider apart till the separation is complete.'[31] Over the next two years, he used his speeches to keep the dream of imperial federation alive. It sustained British confidence at a time of intensified imperial competition among the powers of Europe. Chamberlain assured his audiences that

in a future time . . . the splendid isolation with which our foreign critics sometimes taunt us will be transformed into a close alliance of the British race, and . . . the sons of Britain throughout the world shall stand shoulder to shoulder to defend our mutual interests and common rights.[32]

Otherwise he concentrated on modest devices to draw the self-governing colonies and the mother country together. He continued to look to
Canada for cooperation, impressed by the gradual increase of Canada's
imperial tariff preference from 12 1/2 to 33 1/3 per cent. He worked
with the Canadians to establish an imperial penny postage, 'with a
view', as the Canadian Postmaster General put it, 'to the extension of
the imperial sentiment pari passu with our material development'.[33]
Chamberlain rejected an appeal from Canadian Conservatives who
wished to probe the weaknesses of the Liberal imperial preference. Still
rejecting the restoration of tariffs in Britain, he continued to speak favourably of an imperial free trade *Zollverein*.

The diplomacy of imperialism

Thus Chamberlain could not do a great deal at the Colonial Office to
substantiate the imperial hopes he raised. Yet he conveyed a sense of
accomplishment to his contemporaries. The last thing anyone in the late
1890s would have said of Chamberlain was that he was ineffective.
Ironically it was in foreign affairs that he impressed the nation, ironic
because his vision in international diplomacy never acquired clarity and
his performance was often inept. He was well travelled, had a good
command of French, passable German, early experience in international
marketing and later in North American trade negotiations. Yet he did
not acquire the feeling for great power politics on which the aristocracy
prided itself. He remained a neophyte in matters of high diplomacy
throughout the 1880s, as the British ambassador in Constantinople
noted when they met. The ambassador added however that Chamberlain was obviously 'disposed to learn'.[34]

In the summer of 1891, on the eve of the formation of the Dual Alliance between France and Russia, Chamberlain was approached by the
aspiring French politician Georges Clemençeau in the hope of some
last-minute rapprochement between France and England. With a view
ultimately to regaining the provinces of Alsace and Lorraine seized by
the Germans in the Franco-Prussian war, Clemençeau sought to woo
Britain from its current friendship with Germany by offering an end to
the opposition that France kept up to Britain's occupation of Egypt.
Chamberlain did not leap at the suggestion. France had been the most
assertive of Britain's imperial rivals for more than a decade, and the
actions of the French all over the colonial world exasperated him. He
had also learned enough about great power politics to appreciate that
nothing Britain could do would induce Germany to surrender Alsace-
Lorraine. Still, he wondered about the possibilities for a settlement of
the outstanding colonial disputes between Britain and France, over

Newfoundland, Tunis and Madagascar as well as Egypt. Feeling his way also among the diplomatic entanglements of Continental Europe, he wondered whether Britain might prop up French interests by wooing the swing state of Italy away from its alliance with the Germanic powers.

He relayed his conversation with Clemençeau to Lord Salisbury as Foreign Secretary. Salisbury rejected the suggestions. He belittled the worth of cooperation with France and insisted on 'the friendship of the Central Powers of Europe' as 'almost essential to us'.[35] Salisbury's reaction strengthened Chamberlain's predilections. Shortly before the two men took office together in 1895, Chamberlain criticized the conduct of France in West Africa without any worry about disagreement from Lord Salisbury. 'If [the French] do not take care,' Chamberlain remarked, 'they will some day go too far and find themselves forced to retreat or to go to war.'[36]

His interest in great power politics was derived almost entirely from his colonial concerns. He shared the pride all Unionists took in Salisbury's mastery of international statecraft. Once the two men took office together, Chamberlain discussed international affairs with Salisbury mainly as they related to the colonies and always in deference to Salisbury's judgement.

The conduct of France in West Africa did not return to the fore in Chamberlain's mind for two years. Other colonial matters, especially in South Africa, were more pressing. What interested him in West Africa were its economic potentialities, particularly the lands of the Ashanti in the Gold Coast. He thought they contained 'one of the richest gold fields in the world',[37] a claim similar to one he made for British Guiana—he was dazzled by any prospect of gold. In the autumn of 1895, using Gold Coast administrative revenues to avoid asking the Treasury for support, he sanctioned a military expedition against the Ashanti which opened the wealth of their territory for exploitation. Making similar use of the surplus that each of the main West Africa colonies, Lagos and Sierra Leone as well as the Gold Coast, kept in reserve for emergencies, he launched a programme of railway construction throughout the region.

These interests brought him into conflict with Sir George Goldie, chairman of the Royal Niger Company, and also with the French, whose territory in the region almost completely surrounded the British colonies. The Royal Niger was another of the companies which Britain chartered in the 1880s to assert its title to broad areas of Africa without assuming direct political and financial responsibility. Chamberlain had come to dislike the arrangement in this case even more than in the case of Rhodes's company. Goldie was interested in the Niger river as a trade route rather than as a way to open up the interior for development. Goldie's approach also exposed his province to incursion by the French. He asserted control over the interior through treaties with native chiefs. But the French resorted to a more intensive form of colonizing known as 'effective occupation', introducing small garrisons of troops into the area they hoped to control.

French activity in West Africa was stimulated by every extension of British control up the Nile. This connection opened up a difference of opinion between Chamberlain and Lord Salisbury. In Salisbury's estimation, the issues at stake on the Nile were much more important than those on the Niger. He feared, and the French hoped, that whoever gained control over the upper reaches and headwaters of the Nile in the Sudan and Uganda would be able to control Egypt and the Suez Canal. Anxious to husband his resources for the inevitable confrontation there with the French, Salisbury did not want to aggravate them or disperse his forces elsewhere. West Africa was a subordinate theatre of concern.

Salisbury's estimate of the relative importance of West Africa had prevailed for a long time at Westminster. The British colony of Gambia had been allowed to shrivel to a strip along the banks of the river after which it was named, and British claims to the hinterland of its other colonies in the region had receded. Chamberlain brought this process to a halt. In his estimate, every imperial market was vital. He reminded the Liverpool Chamber of Commerce that

> Our ancestors made great sacrifices to contest the possession with other Powers of the West Indies, of Canada, of India, of the Cape, and it is in consequence of that that we are now the great nation that we boast ourselves to be.... What they did for us we have to do for our successors ... if we are not willing that this country should sink into a fifth-rate Power and the British Empire should be dissolved into its component atoms.[38]

The prosperity of British industry, the livelihood of the working class, and the strength and security of the kingdom, all required Britain to maintain, cultivate and if possible extend every overseas market still open to its traders. Their exclusion from the colonies of rival powers underscored this need. And France was the greatest offender in this regard.

The willingness of Salisbury to conciliate the French in areas other than the Nile sapped Chamberlain's confidence in his handling of British interests. In June 1897 he first challenged Salisbury's response to the French in Tunis, Madagascar and Siam. Though Chamberlain worded his challenge stiffly, he was ready to accept the equally stiff response of Salisbury. He showed by close survey of the agreements in each case that Britain had done well, better in fact than he liked to boast in public for fear of adding to the discomfiture of France. Chamberlain was only sorry that Salisbury did not let the British public appreciate his achievement.

Preoccupied during the parliamentary session of 1897 with the Jameson raid inquiry, workmen's compensation and the colonial conference, Chamberlain did not have much time for the despatches about French encroachment on the territory of the Royal Niger Company. Because the Niger Company fell under the aegis of the Foreign Office, its reports initially went there. But when Chamberlain turned to the despatches while on holiday in September, he was dismayed. The French had pushed in force beyond their colony of Dahomey into territory around the northeastern reaches of the Niger claimed by Goldie's company. The French expansion threatened to cut the coastal colony of Lagos, for which Chamberlain was responsible, off from its hinterland and thus to stunt its growth. The validity of many of the claims to this region—whether by treaty, by military seizure, or as natural hinterland—was uncertain. But there was no doubt that Bussa, a town strategically placed on the navigable upper reaches of the river, had been seized by the French in violation of established British title.

Chamberlain's first suggestion was for Britain to appoint a plenipotentiary, either Salisbury or himself, and convene a congress with the French rather than rely on an ambassadorial conference. He expressed himself as 'perfectly content to accept & support any decision'[39] at which Salisbury might arrive. But Salisbury dismissed Chamberlain's suggestion of a congress as naive, and contended that while the British claim to Bussa was *'really* strong', the rest of their argument was 'shady'.[40] Chamberlain accepted this assessment only long enough to examine the papers more closely. They confirmed him in his determination '—even at the cost of war—to keep an adequate Hinterland for the Gold Coast, Lagos & the Niger Territories'.[41]

His irritation mounted as Britain's representatives in conference at Paris complied with Salisbury's peaceable instructions. Criticizing their conduct with a sharpness which he would not apply directly to Salisbury, Chamberlain complained that 'what they call compromise . . . means in every case giving up something which we believe to be ours and getting nothing in return'.[42] He was willing to make substantial concessions in West Africa if, by doing so, he could bring about a settlement embracing all the areas of colonial or imperial controversy between Britain and France, including the Pacific, Newfoundland, the West Indies and the Nile. Salisbury would have agreed. But the French refused to move in this direction. So long as the French kept their concern about the Nile in the shadows and concentrated on West Africa, Chamberlain would insist on the merits of the situation there; and in his eyes they were wholly British.

Salisbury's control over foreign policy had been protected by his practice as prime minister of deferring on each subject of business to the cabinet minister in charge and by taking the Foreign Office for himself. But the colonies were often central to Britain's disputes with other powers at the end of the nineteenth century, in part because Chamberlain so insisted. Hitherto he and Salisbury had been in essential agreement on the issues where their departmental responsibilities intersected. But West Africa ended that accord.

Unable, because of Chamberlain's departmental responsibility for Lagos, to discount his objections on the Niger negotiations, and disconcerted by the vehemence with which Chamberlain advanced his views, Salisbury began to give way. He instructed the ambassador in Paris, Sir Edward Monson, who led the British delegation at the conference on West Africa, to adopt the assertive tactics for which Chamberlain argued. Monson, Britain's senior ambassador, resented the intrusion of an interloper and followed his instructions with apprehensive scepticism. He was surprised, though not converted, to find that the French responded to his display of stiffness in a 'distinctly apologetic' tone,[43] offering concessions.

This result, far from mollifying Chamberlain, intensified his concern. The French response focused attention on the question of access to the Niger. They asked for a corridor through British territory to connect Dahomey with the Niger and hence by river to the sea. Chamberlain would offer the French nothing more than a guarantee of the free-trading rights that British commercial policy generally allowed. Undismayed at the prospect of a breakdown of the talks over the issue, he made plans to turn the tables on France and send contingents of British troops into the French hinterland. When Salisbury expressed willingness to give France what it wanted, Chamberlain threatened to resign. 'I cannot stand it,' he exclaimed; 'I would rather give up office than allow French methods to triumph in this way.'[44]

In face of this threat, Salisbury felt obliged to give way. Once more he instructed Monson to respond to the French proposals as Chamberlain insisted. Again to Monson's surprise, the reaction of the French commissioners proved to be 'mild and conciliatory'.[45] And again encouraged rather than appeased, the Colonial Secretary continued to harass Monson. Chamberlain remarked about one of Monson's statements that it 'would be an admirable document if it were written by French officials as a brief for a French Minister'.[46]

While the negotiations proceeded in Paris, Chamberlain forced the pace in West Africa by commissioning an armed force under Frederick Lugard to occupy the territory that Britain claimed and to undermine the claims of France. The appointment and deployment of Lugard were master-strokes. Lugard's reputation, which the French knew full well, underscored Britain's determination in the area. He was also a staunch friend of Goldie, whose cooperation was indispensable to Britain's success. The two friends captured each other for Chamberlain's purposes: Goldie felt bound to cooperate with Lugard and in turn persuaded Lugard to follow Chamberlain's instructions. The 'chequerboard' strategy which Chamberlain called on Lugard to follow interposed British units in French territory to neutralize the earlier French incursions in British territory. In some places, units from the two nations took up positions only a few hundred yards from each other. Chamberlain rightly guessed what the British diplomatic commissioners doubted, that the French officers, like the British, would have orders to stop short of fighting. It took calm nerves on both sides in the field to do so. The strategy was risky. Bloodshed on the Niger could have led to gunfire in the Channel; and even Chamberlain might have admitted that the interests at stake in West Africa were not worth a war in Europe.

By March 1898 the French were ready to propose a settlement. After two more months of negotiations, the issue in contention narrowed to Ilo, a town north of Bussa which the French meanwhile had agreed to return to Britain. Salisbury wanted to give way on Ilo. Chamberlain refused. He suspected that the future of the surrounding so-called Empire of Sokoto was at stake; he believed that the stakes were rich; and he doubted that the French cared enough about Ilo to scrap the rest of the agreement. He was ready to give the French another town, Bona, but not Ilo: 'I have gone to the extreme limit,' he informed Salisbury, 'I could not defend any further surrender.'[47]

This time Salisbury would not give in without a struggle. He insisted on referring their disagreement to the cabinet if he could not satisfy himself on the conditions Chamberlain attached to his offer of Bona. Salisbury belittled the supposed wealth of Sokoto. 'There is no loot to get,' he told Chamberlain, 'except in Goldie's dreams.'[48] Chamberlain retorted almost contemptuously, saying that already in the negotiations he had, in deference to the wishes of Salisbury, surrendered everything short of Britain's essential honour and interests. After further consideration Salisbury concluded that Chamberlain's offer of Bona instead of Ilo was satisfactory. So did the French, once again confounding Monson's predictions. In mid-June, the two powers reached agreement, though the French could not bring themselves to ratify it for another year.

It was a stunning achievement for Chamberlain in his first foray into great power politics. Though Britain receded from the height of its claims on the Niger, it retained all that was essential, including control of the river. It acquired control over the inland territories of Sokoto and Bornu, potentially rewarding acquisitions though not fabulous as Chamberlain liked to believe. He carved out generous boundaries for the colony of Lagos and the territory of the Niger Company, eventually

fused as Nigeria. In doing so, he had displayed an acuteness in manoeuvre such as only the aristocratic elite were supposed to possess.
The French succumbed to his tactics on the field in West Africa and at
the conference table in Paris. So had Salisbury.

Chamberlain's achievement on the Niger dimmed the lustre of Salisbury's ensuing triumph on the Nile. As at Bussa on the Niger, so at
Fashoda on the upper Nile, a small contingent of French troops ran up
their flag. By the time they did so, British troops were well advanced to
take possession of the entire Sudan. At Omdurman in September 1898
they annihilated the native forces that fourteen years earlier had swept
over the Sudan. Salisbury was able to announce in November that
France would withdraw its contingent from Fashoda. Yet he declined to
expand publicly on the implications of the French retreat lest France
react by refusing to abandon the rest of the Sudan. He may even have
been willing to allow the French an enclave at Bahr-al-Ghazal so long as
Britain was assured of full control of the Nile.

The victories that Salisbury handled with restraint, Chamberlain
greeted with jubilation. Omdurman emboldened him to embrace the
dream of a Cape-to-Cairo railway and to prophesy that it would be
built within the lifetime of the rising generation. He reacted to the rumour about Bahr-al-Ghazal as he had to the notion of a French corridor
to the Niger. 'Heaven save us from enclaves!' he exclaimed; 'Either they
would be worthless to the French or they would be injurious to us.'
Stressing the unpopularity of Salisbury's inclinations, he added that 'the
country will stand no more graceful concessions'.[49] While Salisbury
played down the triumph of Fashoda, Chamberlain impressed the public with the achievement in West Africa. 'We have now obtained an
undisputed sphere of influence in that great empire of Sokoto,' he announced; and 'as soon as . . . this country is willing to invest some of its
surplus capital in making the necessary communication, Sokoto, or Nigeria, as it has been known, will be one of the great markets of Manchester and Birmingham and for our other commercial centres'.[50]

Attempting to coopt the competition

The success Chamberlain enjoyed during the negotiations with France
on West Africa encouraged him to attempt almost simultaneously to
place the whole foreign policy of Britain on a new footing. In the autumn of 1897, when he was coming to grips with the situation in West
Africa, a greater challenge to Britain's overseas markets arose in China.
Germany seized the Chinese port of Kiaochow, and Russia followed
with the seizure of Port Arthur, initiating a scramble for China. That
scramble differed in one crucial regard from the preceding one for

Africa. Britain did not already have colonies in China—aside from Hong Kong to which, accordingly, Chamberlain's departmental responsibilities were confined. But China bulked large in the informal commercial empire which Britain acquired for itself over the past hundred years without having to pay the costs of direct government, an empire embracing much of Latin America and the Middle East as well as the Orient. It was within this empire that Chamberlain marketed wood screws in the 1860s. The erosion of this empire in face of European and American competition since then increased the importance of the formal empire to Britain. But formal colonies were inferior compensation for the waning of the commercial empire. No part of that empire was more valued than China, though the richness of that market was more prospective than current. Until the 1890s, the British dominated the foreign trade of China and even supervised its tariffs. Britain could therefore only lose from the partition of China. Chamberlain wanted to stop the process.

His mind was on China as 1897 drew to a close. The subject brought out the differences between Salisbury and him, fine differences in objective but yawning differences in approach and crucial differences in underlying priorities. Their immediate objective so far as China was concerned was essentially the same: to keep the market open to all nations. Chamberlain was simply stiffer than Salisbury in his aversion to British acquisition of a Chinese port as a gesture to compensate for the German and Russian seizures. Both men knew that nothing could really compensate the British for even minimal partition of what had been largely their market.

But from the outset they differed fundamentally about how to pursue their common goal. Both knew that they would have to do so in cooperation with one of their competitors. But Salisbury sought a limited, local agreement which would also serve to reduce the attachment of the satisfied power to the antagonists of Britain elsewhere. Thus he hoped to weaken the dual alliance system which split Continental Europe. Initially he sought to cooperate with Russia on China, partly to reduce Russia's concern for its ally France on the Nile.

Chamberlain's alternative was not as clearly defined. From the outset in discussing China he used the loaded term 'alliance'. It was a serious mistake, particularly for someone noted for clarity of expression, yet he continued to make the mistake. The word implied more than he intended, even in the long run. Employing the word for the first time to Salisbury with reference to Japan, Chamberlain excluded anything as formal as a treaty and spoke rather of 'an understanding' to be expressed by elevating Britain's legation in Tokyo to the status of an embassy.[51] There was a good deal of gaucherie as well as imprecision to his search for allies. While Salisbury was crumbling under his weight of

years, Chamberlain, though only six years younger, was at the height of
his powers; and he plunged into talks on great power alliances with the
impetuosity of youth. Still, he appreciated more keenly than Salisbury
that, even with the support of its colonies, Britain could not uphold its
broader commercial empire without cooperation from other countries
interested in those still open markets.

It always came back to markets. Chamberlain reckoned power in essentially economic terms, as access to markets. Salisbury recognized the
importance of markets, but to him they were not the primary consideration in great power diplomacy. Supreme for him in the final analysis
were strategic considerations, at root often matters of naval and military
defence. He was accordingly more selective than Chamberlain in his
designation of Britain's vital interests. Chamberlain tended to think of
all markets as vital, and of China with its teeming millions as particularly so.

Both men laid emphasis, as the century ended, on the spectacle of
rising and decaying empires; and both men were determined to keep
Britain among the former. To Salisbury the spectacle was a curious
phenomenon; Chamberlain was sure that its driving forces were economic. But this difference in interpretation did little to account for
their differences over foreign policy. Where this difference bred misunderstanding was between Chamberlain and the German government
that came to power in 1897 under Prince von Bülow. Chamberlain saw
Germany, and also the United States, as industrial powers like Britain,
admittedly Britain's competitors but motivated by similar economic
considerations. He was impressed that, though Germany protected its
home market with tariffs, it left its colonies open to international trade.
He sensed, by and large rightly, that because of its industrial power,
Germany shared Britain's interest in open access to overseas markets.
Annoyed but not shaken by the seizure of Kiaochow, he failed to grasp
that the key figures in the new German government, including Admiral
Tirpitz and the Kaiser as well as Bülow, placed more importance on
military than on economic considerations, cared more about Europe
than overseas and, when it came to global considerations, were more
jealous of Britain than of any other power. Chamberlain's success over
West Africa with France led him to hope that he fathomed Germany
equally well. His hope was illusory.

When the cabinet took up the subject of China at the beginning of
1898, Chamberlain induced his colleagues to explore the possibility of
alliances along with the alternative, preferred by Salisbury, of a more
modest agreement with Russia. Both options assumed acceptance of the
seizures of Kiaochow and Port Arthur but wanted them to be conducted as 'treaty ports', open to the commerce of all nations. Since
Germany seemed less likely than Russia to impose exclusive control on

its port, attention focused on Port Arthur. Salisbury hoped to induce Russia to keep it open by cooperating with the Russians in making a loan to the needy Chinese government. But Chamberlain suspected the Russians of treating British interests in China with 'special unfriendliness'.[52] He ensured that, while discussing a loan with Russia, Britain would also ask the United States whether they would 'stand with us & Japan in *insisting*' that any concession extracted from China by one power must be shared by all.[53] Soon impatient with Russian procrastination and the passivity of Lord Salisbury, he expanded and stiffened his proposals. He recommended seeking support from Germany as well as the United States for a policy of insistence on open ports, with a view to forcing Russia to open Port Arthur.

Neither of the overtures approved by the cabinet, to Russia and to the United States, elicited the desired response. The cabinet then agreed to British occupation of the Chinese port of Wei-hai-wei in ostensible compensation for the closure of Port Arthur. Chamberlain alone registered his disapproval of this empty gesture. It was not his policy but Salisbury's that suffered discredit from Russia's retention of Port Arthur in defiance of the British, 'a humiliating defeat' even by kind estimation.[54] Salisbury was further weakened by illness. Laid up with bronchitis in February, he was not strong enough even to leave England for convalescence in France until the end of March, when he placed Balfour in temporary charge of the Foreign Office.

No sooner had Salisbury left for France than Chamberlain was presented with an opportunity to explore the alternative foreign policy that was taking shape in his mind. The German ambassador, Count Hatzfeldt, came to see him in search of agreement on the comparatively few points of colonial conflict between their two countries, in West Africa and China. Hatzfeldt took the initiative on his own, hoping that an agreement on these secondary points would convince his masters in Berlin of the wisdom of a broader, ultimately general accord with Britain. But he was taken aback by the enthusiasm with which Chamberlain greeted his initiative. The Colonial Secretary dismissed the points of colonial conflict as 'absolutely trivial in comparison with the great issues involving our relations with other Nations', on which, as Hatzfeldt politely agreed, 'the interests of Germany were really identical with our own'.[55] Revealing his opinion that Lord Salisbury's policy of isolation might have to be abandoned, Chamberlain swept on to suggest that 'an Alliance might be established by Treaty or Agreement between Germany & Great Britain for a term of years ... of a defensive character based upon a mutual understanding as to policy in China & elsewhere'. Though disconcerted by Chamberlain's rashness, Hatzfeldt exaggerated it in reporting to Berlin because he could not reveal his own initiative to his superiors.

Two days later he returned to Chamberlain with a cool response from Bülow. The German minister used pointers he had learned from Lord Salisbury to question the proposal of the Colonial Secretary, in particular Salisbury's insistence on the inability under his country's popular constitution of one Parliament to make commitments binding upon its successor. But the decisive concern for Bülow was the unequal balance of benefit that the two countries would derive from an alliance focused on China and directed against Russia. Though the German occupation of Kiaochow precipitated the crisis in China, Germany was comparatively new in that market and did not entirely mind when Russia retaliated by taking Port Arthur. Absorption in China might distract Russia from its border with Germany. An Anglo-German alliance on China, on the other hand, might turn the eyes of Russia back to eastern Europe.

While Chamberlain received Bülow's response with disappointment, he was not ready to accept it as final, or at any rate to abandon the search for alliances. He looked again to the United States; and this time he elicited a more encouraging response. The United States was heading into war with Spain over its misgovernment of Cuba. The justification for the belligerence of the United States was not obvious to European governments. The American ambassador in London, John Hay, was therefore pleased when Chamberlain raised the subject of an alliance. Here again Chamberlain used the big word. Yet he did not intend anything disconcertingly big. He appreciated that the United States was 'not ready for what they call "entangling alliances"'.[56] He also recognized that the United States did not want anything from Britain with regard to the impending war beyond benevolent neutrality. He gave them that. When the European ambassadors in Washington moved to counsel the United States against hasty aggression, Chamberlain intervened to dissociate Britain from the protest. Americans responded appreciatively.

Chamberlain's interventions in foreign affairs revived the tension common in previous governments between the prime minister and the foreign minister, both of whom were supposed to be in charge of the country's foreign policy. Salisbury had avoided that pattern by combining the two offices. The intrusion of Chamberlain, who held neither office, was irregular; and he paid a price for it. Lacking formal responsibility, he could not make ready use of the normal channels for intergovernmental communication. Hence he found himself caught in a web of deceit reminiscent of his communications through O'Shea with Parnell. Chamberlain and Salisbury began to communicate to each other with more courtesy than candour. The situation was compounded on the German side where Bülow manipulated the Kaiser with flattery. Ambassadors took sides, misleading their ministerial superiors, while cabinet colleagues made critical remarks about each other to ambassadors for foreign consumption. Talk about alliances in this manner was more likely to foster enmity than friendship.

The charming chargé d'affaires at the German embassy in London, Baron von Eckhardtstein, shared Count Hatzfeldt's desire for better Anglo-German relations without sharing the ambassador's skill or caution. Disappointed by Bülow's response to the overture from Chamberlain, Eckhardtstein left for Germany where he gained access to the Kaiser. He brought back an excited report that the Kaiser favoured an Anglo-German alliance and would like to conclude one quickly on terms that were broader and less clearly defined than Chamberlain had suggested. Chamberlain was not carried away by the report. But Balfour, acting as Foreign Secretary in his uncle's absence, was more impressed by Eckhardtstein's news than by the earlier exchange between Hatzfeldt and Chamberlain, which Balfour derided as an 'amateur' play performed by 'a very motley "cast"!'[57]

Hatzfeldt had to play the part of spectre at the feast. Asked by Eckhardtstein to convey the thinking of the government at Berlin to Chamberlain, Hatzfeldt presented a bleaker report than before, whatever the Kaiser had said to Eckhardtstein. Hatzfeldt stressed the threat Russia posed on Germany's eastern borders. When he raised the possibility of British support in Europe to embrace Italy and Austria with whom Germany was allied, Chamberlain backed away. He spoke darkly to Hatzfeldt about missing the brief opportunity for agreement between their two countries and warned him that Britain might turn instead to the Dual Alliance of Russia and France. Yet he did not do anything afterwards to lend credence to this threat.

Hatzfeldt sent Berlin another exaggerated report of Chamberlain's responsibility for the talk of Anglo-German alliance. Chamberlain, reporting to Salisbury upon his return to work, disguised the extent to which he had indeed promoted the possibility. He would not abandon the idea. 'Recent experience', he told Salisbury, 'seems to me to show that we are powerless to resist the ultimate control of China by Russia, and that we are at a great disadvantage in negotiating with France, as long as we maintain our present isolation and I think the country would support us in a Treaty with Germany providing for reciprocal defence.'[58] Rather than stand up to his headstrong colleague, Salisbury responded evasively. 'I quite agree with you that . . . a closer relation with Germany would be desirable,' he wrote; 'but can we get it?'[59]

Rather than argue with each other face-to-face, the two men chose to speak their minds before a vast audience. Each chose an assembly of his party faithful. Salisbury began with the Primrose League, the popular organization of inarticulate Conservatism founded in honour of Disraeli. He brushed aside doubts about the adequacy of isolation or independence as a diplomatic posture. Yet he seemed to refute himself by accepting Britain's inability to resist encroachment on its market in China: 'we shall not be jealous,' he declared, 'if desolation and sterility are removed by the aggrandizement of a rival in regions to which our arms cannot extend.'[60]

Chamberlain responded at the annual meeting of the Birmingham Liberal Unionist Association. After referring respectfully to the 'eloquent speech' and 'courteous diplomacy' of Lord Salisbury,[61] he challenged the underlying policy. He used simple words to convey his message, as befitted someone who wished, as he said, to throw the mysteries of aristocratic diplomacy open to the people: 'You must tell the people what you mean and where you are going if you want them to follow you.' Yet there was more rhetoric than practicality to the proposals he offered. He played the role he often preferred, of a teacher offering new precepts to guide the course of public action, rather than of a statesman responsible for implementing them.

Though he spoke ominously about the alliances dividing the Continental powers, the European alliance system was of secondary concern to him. What worried him was the 'combined assault by the nations of the world upon the commercial supremacy of this country'. It was most evident at the moment in China: there 'our interests . . . are so great, our proportion of the trade is so enormous, and the potentialities of that trade are so gigantic that I feel that no more vital question has ever been presented for the decision of a Government and . . . a nation'. Yet recent events revealed that Britain by itself could not successfully resist encroachment on the Chinese market by the large adjacent land power, Russia. The behaviour of Russia provoked Chamberlain to repeat the proverb, 'Who sups with the devil must have a long spoon.' That remark violated diplomatic civilities. But it was not as severe as the verdict Chamberlain also pronounced on the attempt of the British government—in other words of Salisbury—to come to an understanding with Russia: 'we failed'.

In place of the thus discredited policy of 'strict isolation', Chamberlain presented 'the idea of an alliance with those powers whose interests most nearly approximate to our own'. The one alliance the British would cordially embrace was 'with our kinsmen across the Atlantic . . . an Anglo-Saxon alliance'. The United States fully sympathized with the British wish to keep the Chinese market open. But for the moment the United States was preoccupied with its war with Spain and its fruits in Cuba and the Philippines. That brought Chamberlain to Germany. But there were no cheers to be won from an English audience by referring to Germany, so he spoke in hypothetical terms. What Britain needed in China was to be 'allied with some great military power', one able to deter the Russians from further encroachment in China and perhaps even to open up what they had already taken. He reinforced his point by warning that '[i]f the policy of isolation . . . is . . . maintained in the future, then the fate of the Chinese Empire . . . probably will be, here-after decided . . . in defiance of our interests'.

The speech brought a host of responses. The commercial empire-builders of Birmingham applauded their champion. So did many Tories, worried by Salisbury's failing health and his all too 'courteous' defence of British interests. Chamberlain was even more gratified by the response he won in the United States. The *New York Times* greeted his address as 'the most memorable speech that an English audience in either hemisphere has listened to in a generation'. Though the thought of a formal alliance made Americans uneasy, they could understand the way in which he used the word. Many American newspapers wel-comed the prospect of an Anglo-Saxon alliance in this sense as both 'natural and desirable'.[62]

In the upper political echelons of Germany as well as Britain, the immediate question was how Salisbury would deal with the challenge from Chamberlain. When asked in the House of Lords what he thought of his colleague's speech, the prime minister claimed weakly not to have read it. The criticisms he made to inquiring foreign ambassadors in private could not restore his credit. He was gratified by the cool re-sponse of official Germany to Chamberlain's overture. The Kaiser dis-paraged Chamberlain's public admission of Britain's need for allies as unwise, and stressed that Germany was more concerned about Russia in eastern Europe than in China. Still, the Kaiser expressed interest in alliance with Britain 'on reasonable terms'.[63]

Encouraged by this hint, Chamberlain encroached on Salisbury's authority and convened a ministerial council of those who shared his concerns to meet the British ambassador to Germany, Sir Frank Lascelles, when he was in London. The council included Goschen as First Lord of the Admiralty, Hamilton as Secretary of State for India, and the President of the Local Government Board Henry Chaplin, as well as Chamberlain's parliamentary undersecretary (and Salisbury's son-in-law), Selborne. They commissioned Lascelles, who shared their concerns, to probe the extent of the Kaiser's sympathy for an alliance.

At almost the same time, Anglo-German relations took a turn that produced a temporary rapprochement between Chamberlain and Salis-bury. From the beginning of his tenure as Colonial Secretary, Chamber-lain had his eye on Delagoa Bay. So did President Kruger. Delagoa Bay was the port closest to Johannesburg and belonged to the Portuguese colony of Mozambique. It offered the Transvaal the possibility of access free from British control to overseas markets and support. But if Cham-berlain could gain control of Delagoa Bay, he could rest assured of the ultimate subservience of the Transvaal. He did all he could to persuade Portugal to give him control or at least to keep Kruger and Germany away. Since Portugal was in serious financial straits, Chamberlain offered the Portuguese government a whole range of options for a loan, the essential security for which always involved Delagoa Bay. Portugal, however, resented the humiliating position in which it found itself; and in 1897 it abandoned these talks. Later that year, the German seizure of Kiaochow—here as elsewhere the harbinger of change—prompted the Portuguese to reopen discussions with Britain. Germany got wind of this development in June 1898. Count Hatzfeldt approached Salisbury in search of compensation to Germany for the advantage which Britain seemed likely to acquire.

Britain had always insisted that Delagoa Bay and the Anglo-Portuguese discussions were no business of Germany. Salisbury wished to continue. But Chamberlain, who had hitherto bristled at any hint of foreign rivalry in southern Africa, pressed Salisbury to respond to Hatzfeldt in accommodating fashion. Chamberlain hoped that Germany and Britain could divide the Portuguese spoils in Africa between them in such a way as to give Britain control of Delagoa Bay and the friendship of Germany as well. Four days after his irregular ministerial council with Lascelles, the cabinet decided against Salisbury on German involvement in the Anglo-Portuguese negotiations. Overruling him for the first time on a subject in his own departmental field, the cabinet adopted Chamberlain's advice instead.

But the German appetite for concessions from the British soon had Chamberlain talking like Salisbury. Discussion about the terms on which Germany and Britain would lend money to Portugal looked faintly ridiculous after the middle of July when the Portuguese withdrew their request for a loan. But the unreality of the exercise did nothing to reduce the significance with which the two major powers invested their discussion. They were seeking to assess the worth of their friendship to each other. Chamberlain was aghast that the Germans, not content with an assignment of Portuguese possessions, asked Britain for British possessions. 'Unless [the Germans] are able to modify the opinion they have formed of the value of their neutrality,' he told Salisbury, 'we must certainly look elsewhere for allies.'[64]

Before this rapprochement between the two British statesmen could bear fruit, Salisbury took ill again and headed for France to convalesce, leaving Balfour in charge of the Foreign Office. It was Balfour who pushed for agreement with the Germans. Chamberlain questioned the wisdom of continuing the negotiations unless they were widened to embrace China. They alienated the Kaiser as much as Chamberlain. Concluding that Britain was trying to purchase the friendship of his country on the cheap, the Kaiser declined to respond to the overture from the midsummer cabal of British cabinet ministers which Lascelles managed finally to transmit towards the end of August. When Balfour worked out an agreement with Germany, Chamberlain accepted it with a cynicism that Salisbury would have enjoyed: 'we pay Blackmail to Germany to induce her not to interfere where she has no right of inter- ference. Well! it is worth while to pay Blackmail sometimes.'[65] The one benefit Britain derived from the agreement was its confirmation that Germany 'resigns all concern in Transvaal matters'.[66]

Afterwards Chamberlain thought less about multipurpose, offensive- defensive treaties on the Continental European model. He talked of temporary agreements in support of particular interests, not much be- yond the scale Salisbury preferred, though Chamberlain still had his eye on a general alliance as the eventual object. He paid less attention to Germany than to the United States, now that it had made its debut as an imperial power in the Spanish-American war. The victory of the United States, its annexation of Hawaii, and the acquisition of Cuba and the Philippines gave some Americans new sympathy for Britain as an imperial power. Chamberlain hoped that the war would produce a 'new understanding between the two great English-speaking nations'. Towards that end, he called upon the United States to join Britain in 'the great work of controlling and civilising the Tropics'.[67] He trusted, as he told one of his wife's New England relations, that 'if you become a colonising Nation you will have increased sympathy with us. You will better understand our work & difficulties, & you will be drawn insensibly into closer alliances by community of interests & of senti- ment'.[68] After spending 1898 in search of some kind of alliance, Cham- berlain had little but this hope to show for his efforts.

The home base

The wider Chamberlain spread his imperial wings, the less substantial his achievement. Conversely, the closer that he focused on Birmingham, the more he accomplished. Parliament did not take up much legislation at the national level. Chamberlain was disappointed by the report of the 'expert' committee set up in 1896 to explore the feasibility of state-aided old-age pensions. He hoped that the committee would come up with a scheme consonant with concern for the taxpayer, the social impact so far as thrift and self-help were concerned, and the desirability of co- operation with the friendly societies. But the committee concluded that every scheme that it examined, including the one Chamberlain had sponsored, would 'ultimately injure rather than serve the best interests of the industrial population'.[69] Chamberlain still encouraged the public to hope that the government would be able, before its term ended, 'to

7. Corridor to the greenhouses at Highbury.

do something . . . to secure the veterans of industry . . . from the worst consequences of failing power'.[70] But he did not himself see any fresh way round the difficulties emphasized in the report.

His imagination on domestic matters remained lively only in Birmingham. He was at his happiest there. He elaborated the grounds of Highbury with a succession of variegated gardens to make his hundred acres seem like a thousand. They accommodated the throngs numbering sometimes over a thousand who gathered for the garden parties he threw each summer. Picking up ideas from his travels on the Continent, he put a Dutch garden in one corner, an Italian in another. The greenhouses, where house guests could stroll on rainy days, increased from fourteen to twenty-five. Trees were planted to hide the houses on King's Heath that threatened his view. He won silver medals from the Royal Horticultural Society in 1897 and 1898 for his orchids. The keeper of the national collection of orchids at Kew moved to take charge at Highbury.

In the glow of these years, Chamberlain reached out to old friends. He ended 1897 with a small dinner for friends close to home including Powell Williams his trusty organizer, Bunce of the *Daily Post*, and William Harris, creator of the Liberal machine in the 1870s who deserted to Gladstone over Home Rule. A year later, when Chamberlain's brother-in-law William Kenrick intimated his desire to leave Parliament, Chamberlain poured out his gratitude for 'the comfort & strength' he had received 'through all the ups & downs of political life, by the knowledge that he ha[d] always behind him a few absolutely staunch & loyal friends who ... were, of his own household, & on whom he [could] confidently depend'.[71] Straining precedent, he obtained a privy councillorship for Kenrick instead of a baronetcy. Proud of being a burgher of Birmingham, Kenrick like Chamberlain recoiled from an honour that would have loaded him with a title associated with the landed gentry.

The crowning achievement of Chamberlain's civic career came now at the turn of the century with the founding of the University of Birmingham. It was in some ways the finest of all his accomplishments. The idea had been in his mind for twenty years and more. It was the natural culmination of the enterprise in education that brought him into public life in the first place. Birmingham was now fully equipped with elementary schools. It had removed the social restrictions on entry to its grammar schools, developed an excellent technical school and schools of music and art, and forwarded their collective purpose through a civic library, art gallery and museum. The Midland Institute was available for further, evening education. This network improved the industrial competitiveness and at the same time the quality of life in the city. It reflected Chamberlain's belief that the wellbeing of the entire country depended in large part 'upon the power of our provincial cities to maintain a separate self-sufficing existence', including 'the opportunities of the highest culture'.[72] These were the words he used in 1877 when he first expressed his hope for the creation of a university in Birmingham.

There was as always a contentious side to his aspiration. Josiah Mason, the manufacturer of steel pens who attempted to take over Nettlefold and Chamberlain in 1870, had subsequently endowed a college of applied science which bore his name. Chamberlain disparaged his benefaction. The concentration of Mason College on the technological needs of local industry was indeed too narrow for the good of Birmingham or of the college itself. The limited curriculum of the college reinforced the impression that the higher reaches of culture did not interest Birmingham, and also jeopardized the eligibility of the college for grants made by the national government to encourage higher education. Mason's attachment of his name to his college, which opened in 1880 shortly before his death, diminished the interest of other businessmen in adding to its endowment.

Interest in the creation of a true university for the West Midlands was quickened in 1887 by pleas from H.W. Crosskey, the minister of the

Unitarian church to which Chamberlain was affiliated, and Sir John Seeley, the Cambridge historian whose lectures on 'The expansion of England' had impressed the future Colonial Secretary. Chamberlain re-iterated their pleas in 1888, and subsequently induced the Salisbury government to increase its grants to provincial colleges. The idea of a university in Birmingham did not attract much further attention until 1897. The trustees of Mason College were preoccupied with its deterio-rating financial position, while national and then imperial matters di-verted Chamberlain's attention from any but the most pressing partisan concerns so far as Birmingham was concerned. But his imperial laurels brought him back to Birmingham.

During festivities surrounding his installation as Lord Rector of the University of Glasgow, Chamberlain was impressed with how the pres-ence of a university in 'the middle of a great industrial and manufactur-ing population' could 'elevate the whole mass to higher aims and higher intellectual ambitions than would otherwise be possible to peo-ple engaged entirely in trading and commercial pursuits'.[73] He returned early in December 1897 to Birmingham, where he stayed till the reopen-ing of Parliament, and devoted himself to the creation of a university in Birmingham as if there were nothing else to occupy his thoughts. It was to be the first civic university in England. Oxford and Cambridge were national institutions operating through expensive residential colleges. The University of London, and the composite Victoria University which served three of the northerly cities in England, were essentially examin-ing institutions. The ancient civic universities of Scotland gave Cham-berlain a model he preferred. They offered poor yet ambitious young men lectures, laboratories and living examples of scholarship and re-search, as well as certifying examinations. Chamberlain was still more impressed by the higher education provided by England's industrial competitors, the United States and above all Germany. One reason for the industrial achievement of Germany was the attention it devoted to education, a consideration behind Chamberlain's campaign for elemen-tary education back in the 1870s and now for higher education. 'We look to Germany', he told the people of Birmingham, 'for an example and model of everything in the way of educational organization and progress. Education is made in Germany.'[74] His audience responded with a rueful laugh, knowing all too well how often the label 'made in Germany' appeared in their shops and markets. With its 46,000,000 people, Germany had twenty-one universities. Scotland, with its 4,000,000, had four. England and Wales, with nearly 30,000,000, had just six.

Chamberlain took hold of and transformed the resources to hand in Birmingham. Mason College, in an attempt to overcome its limitations, was already being turned by statute into Mason University College. The officers asked Chamberlain to become president of its council. 'They could not have taken a more suicidal course,' the Vice-Chancellor of the University of Birmingham later remarked.[75] Chamberlain lifted the eyes of the council above its objective of a university college towards a full university. Doing so required transforming the curriculum. So long as the humanities were neglected or treated as lowly servants to the main business of applied science, Mason College would remain a lowly institution. Chamberlain championed the liberal arts not in themselves but because they provided the credentials required for recognition as a true university. In concert with a cabal of sympathizers, he appropriated proposals which the council had just rejected from E.A. Sonnenschein, the Anglo-German leader of the beleaguered liberal arts faculty. He commissioned Bunce of the *Birmingham Daily Post* to draft an appeal for funds—something 'lyric, pathetic, and emphatic'.[76] One observer exclaimed, 'Chamberlain's power and the boldness of his ideas have triumphed over everything.'[77]

Yet his ideas were exploratory. He led and learned simultaneously. He read the messages conveyed by the amount of support he received. Most of his initial ideas for the university underwent considerable change before he was through. The people associated in this work came to regard Chamberlain as its Zeus. 'Armed and equipped,' said the principal of the eventual university, '. . . we sprang from his brain.' He 'created us, and has nourished and guided us,' said the Vice-Chancellor, 'and we have no history outside his remarkable personality'.[78] If so, Chamberlain was a creator of the evolutionary sort.

He introduced his plan in January 1898 at a public meeting of the Mason University College court of governors. He did not want to abandon but rather to absorb the college with its focus on science for local application. The university he envisaged was to take 'all knowledge' as its province and to encourage 'the most important work of original research'.[79] What stunned his audience was his financial objective. He called for an endowment of £250,000, nearly double the largest amount ever raised in Birmingham for charitable purposes. Many people thought this was just Joe talking big. But he was serious about the target. He knew that universities were expensive, far more than any other charity the community had set up. He appealed to the pride of his fellow citizens not to settle for anything 'pinched and mean'. He assured them that he had nothing grandiose in mind. The money was needed to begin with not for 'colossal buildings'—they could come later—but for competitive professorial salaries. He concluded from the experience of Glasgow that the place to begin was with the endowment of 'a certain number of Chairs'.[80] This approach was consonant with the resources of Birmingham. While the city contained few individuals as wealthy as Mason had been, there were men in business and perhaps also in the

professions who might be persuaded to give between £12,000 and
£20,000 to endow a chair that would bear their name. Chamberlain
aimed for fifteen chairs at this rate: hence his target of £250,000.

By dint of strenuous canvassing on his part among his friends and
relations and the college council, the financial campaign made a good
start. It reached nearly £100,000 at mid-year. But then the flow stopped.
It remained dry for months, long enough to put the viability of the
enterprise in question. The disappointing response from the economic
community outside his immediate circle prompted Chamberlain to reconsider the project. Instead of reducing his financial target, he made
the ultimate objective more appealing. Addressing another public meeting of the court of governors in November, he restored Josiah Mason's
focus on applied science in the interests of local industry. Chamberlain
was now convinced that a 'provincial University . . . ought to be redolent of the soil, and inspired by the associations in which it exists'.[81]

Prompted further by the business community, he added something
new to academia. Two days before he addressed the court of governors,
the Chamber of Commerce in Birmingham discussed the idea of a faculty of commerce and sent Chamberlain a memorandum on the subject.
He embraced the suggestion instantly. 'There is one branch of education', he told the court, 'which seems to me hitherto to have been curiously neglected in the Universities that at present exist in this country.
There is . . . nothing like an organised commercial education.' He not
only adopted the idea of 'a faculty for commercial education'. Calling
upon his experience in marketing, he outlined a curriculum including
modern languages, 'commercial geography, commercial law, commercial economy, and other kindred subjects'.

While tailoring the enterprise to enhance its economic appeal, Chamberlain sharpened his fund-raising tactics. He had intended from the
outset to seek contributions from industries as well as individuals. But
so far industry had contributed next to nothing. It was difficult to solicit
funds from industries that were not owned and managed by one person
or family. The phenomenon of non-owning managers acting on behalf
of shareholders raised a so far unanswered question. Were these managers entitled to make charitable donations on behalf of their companies? Chamberlain argued that managers should at least submit
proposals to their shareholders for a corporate contribution proportionate to the size and nature of the business.

He still had little to show for the university he envisaged in Birmingham, as for the main lines of his imperial enterprise in the Colonial
Office, at the end of 1898 when the Unionist ministry reached the mid-
point of its statutory life. The parliamentary majority won in 1895,
though eroded at by-elections, was large enough to assure the govern-

ment another three years of life. That might be enough to assess the effectiveness of Chamberlain's various initiatives, local, national, and imperial, before the familiar pendulum restored the Liberals to office. No one including Chamberlain foresaw at the beginning of 1899 that he was about to subject his handiwork to the most searching of all tests: war.

15

Test of Investments
1899

'Joe has a way of keeping his word.'

Sir Michael Foster to Oliver Lodge, 19 April 1900

Chamberlain risked everything by engaging in war over South Africa. Yet there was a terrible irony for him in the war. For one thing, there was always something disturbingly inadvertent in his enterprise in South Africa. Though the subcontinent bulked large in his imperial thought, only accident and the machinations of others pushed it ahead, for example, of Canada which he thought of as the flagship of the empire. South Africa also gave his interests an unpleasant twist. Concern about relations between capital and labour had led him into politics. No question more concerned the Randlords of Johannesburg. But in South Africa the issue had a twist of colour that dulled Chamberlain's sensitivities. Unable to equate blacks with the workers of Birmingham, he had no sense that the exploitation of black labour on the Rand was more drastic, culturally traumatic and brutal than the treatment of English labour ever was. The concern for popular support which he instilled into big business in Birmingham took on a narrowing imperial twist in the Transvaal, where Chamberlain encouraged the Randlords to cultivate uitlander support against President Kruger. Similarly with regard to education, Chamberlain was less concerned in South Africa with the value of education for labour and more concerned with its bearing on British interests.

He had always championed the virtues of manufacturing industry. Here again South Africa brought about an unfortunate twist. The main product of Transvaal industry was gold, the commodity at the base of the industrial world's monetary system. Inevitably the goldmining of Johannesburg was enveloped in financial speculation, all the more so because mining the low grade ore at the deep levels where the mineral wealth of the Transvaal lay required enormous capital investment. The

resulting stockmarketeering made the Randlords with whom Chamberlain had to associate politically unsavoury.

Chamberlain's interests in South Africa extended of course beyond
his early concerns as a Radical industrialist to his more recent commitments as a Unionist and imperialist. The connections here were more
straightforward. He tended to think of the Boers as he did of the Irish.
Irish nationalists welcomed the association and intensified their criticism of the empire to which they were forced to belong. Irish Nationalists in the House of Commons bombarded Chamberlain with questions
about the misdeeds of the empire around the world. Unionists dismissed the questions as contemptible, but to a later eye they look remarkably well informed and farseeing. The first mention in Parliament
of Sun Yat Sen was in an Irish Nationalist question to Chamberlain
about Sun Yat Sen's expulsion from Hong Kong.

There was one curious application of Chamberlain's Unionism to
South Africa. He seized upon the idea of 'Home Rule for the Rand' as
a way to meet the needs of the uitlander enclave in the Transvaal.
South African response was weak. Kruger entertained the idea merely
as one of the least threatening concessions demanded of him.
Uitlanders thought similarly that the concession would accomplish lit-
tle. Yet Chamberlain kept reverting to it, encouraged by the experience
of Birmingham. He welcomed Home Rule because it could also free the
Rand from its current governors—which was why he opposed Home
Rule for Ireland.

The possibilities for railway construction which figured everywhere
in Chamberlain's plans for imperial development sparkled fantastically
in southern Africa. Rhodes dreamed of pushing his railway from Cape
Town through Rhodesia over the Zambesi river towards Cairo. He
spoke glowingly of the riches to be gathered along the route: gold to
begin with, then 'excellent cattle country, densely populated by natives'[1] so much needed for the mines of the Rand, and farther on rubber
and copper. Chamberlain responded happily. But it was little more than
a dream, as both men should have suspected after the disappointing
results of the mining survey of Rhodesia in 1894.

South Africa figured among the concerns that led Chamberlain into
great power diplomacy. The one benefit from the Anglo-German treaty
of 1898 was its tacit confirmation that Germany no longer thought of
intervention in the region. But that agreement fostered another illusion.
It encouraged Chamberlain to believe that, bereft of solid support from
Europe, the Boers of the Transvaal might threaten but would not actually resort to arms.

Another source of irony in the South African war from Chamberlain's
standpoint lay in war itself. He did not shrink from force. But he did
not contemplate anything more serious than the 'little wars' which

characterized British imperial expansion throughout the century. For Chamberlain, willingness to use force was a sign of determination. He never contemplated war on a scale that would test Britain's imperial institutions. In his confrontation with France he did not think of war beyond the confines of West Africa.

If he could contemplate war with France over West Africa, there could be no question of his willingness to fight for South Africa. The Cape of Good Hope was vital to maritime communications with India. The gold of the Transvaal was crucial to the international economy centred on Britain. Rand gold had further importance for Britain as the only great power which did not withhold a supply of gold from the open market as a reserve in case of major war. These interests intersected. Gold turned the Transvaal into the centre of political gravity for the whole of South Africa, and so affected the security of the Cape. Even so, Chamberlain's ability to use force to defend this nexus of interests was fettered by two restraints. The close governmental scrutiny of expenditure which curbed his investment in the economic development of the empire also curbed his ability to build up the armed force surrounding the Boer republics. Furthermore, he had to carry the self-governing colonies of the Cape and Natal with him despite their economic and, in the case of the Cape Dutch, ethnic gravitation towards the Transvaal. The Jameson raid made this second task more difficult. Chamberlain hoped that time would heal this wound and also allow the flow of English immigration into the Rand to assume commanding proportions.

He never understood the fundamental challenge which subject nationalities posed to the empire. South Africa was tense with ethnic, national and racial conflict, between black and white, Indian and white, and most pressingly among whites. Afrikaners were divided between Boer and Cape Dutch. There were German, Jewish, French and American as well as British uitlanders on the Rand. The tension between British and Afrikaners was pervasive. In these circumstances the democratic imperialism envisaged by Chamberlain was impossible. Violence was endemic, war virtually inevitable. But Chamberlain neither expected the war nor recognized it as the crucial test of the empire he sought to strengthen.

After the parliamentary debate on the Jameson raid report, things were fairly calm in South Africa. It remained the least stable of all the regions under the surveillance of the Colonial Office; but the clouds were not particularly dark at the beginning of 1899, and Chamberlain had little thought of war. He had his mind on the university he was attempting to found in Birmingham, on the government's domestic legislative record which he wanted to improve, on the conflict between the

United States and Canada over Alaska, and on the developmental needs of the crown colonies.

The new proconsul

The signals of stress in South Africa emanated mainly from the man who succeeded Lord Rosmead as high commissioner, Sir Alfred Milner. Part of the rising generation in the public life of Britain, Milner agreed in principle on most matters with Chamberlain but approached their common interests from a different perspective. Though from a poorer stratum of the middle class than Chamberlain, Milner entered the governing elite in traditional fashion by distinguishing himself as a scholarship student at Oxford. The social and political concerns that led Chamberlain from business into politics and from Radicalism to imperialism, Milner grasped faster as concepts. Because his parents had been unable for financial reasons to remain in England, he was German as well as English by upbringing. He responded eagerly to the insistence by the German school of *Katheder-Sozialisten* on the inseparability of economics from society and politics. Milner distanced himself from the British orthodoxy of free trade. As assistant editor of the *Pall Mall Gazette* in the early 1880s, he preached 'the new doctrine of Liberal Imperialism abroad, based on a conviction of the mission of the British Commonwealth, and rational Socialism at home'.[2] He got on famously with those who had known him at Oxford. Yet his dependence on his powers of intellect gave him an austerely independent cast of mind. He wanted to participate in the making of public policy. Yet he despised the collective processes of parliamentary and popular politics. There was nothing like Birmingham in his experience to make him value popular involvement in affairs of state.

He moved from journalism into the public service in the mid-1880s under the aegis of Goschen, and helped organize the Liberal Unionist rebellion in 1886. Impressing all who worked with him, Milner was put in charge of financial accounts for the British administration in Egypt, and then brought back to Britain to take charge of the Board of Inland Revenue. Few positions in the civil service ranked higher. Yet before long he was writing wistfully to his successor in Egypt that 'the sober joys of a well-rendered estimate are tame compared with Empire-Making'.[3]

Word of this wistfulness reached Chamberlain at the end of 1896 when he had to fill a number of key offices including the permanent undersecretaryship at the Colonial Office and the high commissionership in South Africa. Lord Rosmead was afflicted by dropsy and could not remain beyond the spring of 1897. Chamberlain first offered Milner the permanent undersecretaryship. When Milner turned it down, Chamberlain offered and he accepted the high commissionership with its usual accompaniment, governorship of the Cape Colony.

Milner was expected to bring a cool head to a South Africa reeling from the Jameson raid and still in the throes of the parliamentary inquiry. By the time the inquiry reached its conclusion, Chamberlain too had cooled down. He reduced his demands upon the Transvaal government to two: municipal powers for Johannesburg, and instruction in English for the children of English-speakers. He wanted to prevent an accord between Kruger and the Liberal leadership in Britain. Towards that end he refrained from talk of armed intervention in South Africa and relied instead on civil agitation to bring about reform. What he wanted above all was a period of tranquillity to allow the antagonisms roused by the Jameson raid to subside. 'My hope', he told a Liberal member of the inquiry, 'is that everyone will forget the existence of the place for the next year or two, except those who like myself are responsible more or less for its future—& even we shall have to be very dumb & rather deaf.'[4]

One problem remained for Chamberlain to dispose of before Parliament would ignore South Africa. Whatever else the Jameson raid might have shown, it exposed the unreliability of the Chartered Company as custodian of British interests in the region. The parliamentary inquiry had been commissioned to examine the administration of the Chartered Company as well as the genesis of the raid, but chose to concentrate on the raid. During the debate on the committee's report, Chamberlain assured the Commons that he would change the British South Africa Company's charter, if possible before Parliament reconvened in the new year, to ensure 'more direct, efficient control on the part of the Imperial Government'.[5]

He approached the task with the same ambivalence that bedevilled all his dealings with Rhodes. The Matabele rebellion in Rhodesia and the trend of events generally in South Africa in the wake of the Jameson raid impressed Chamberlain again with the inevitability as well as the risks of reliance on Rhodes. Though Rhodes was driven from office at the Cape, nothing reduced the power he held in Rhodesia. Chamberlain 'quite underst[oo]d that as a private individual [Rhodes's] previous career, his wealth, and his large ideas, w[ould] always command great influence'. But Chamberlain did not see how Rhodes could continue to be accorded '*official* influence' in the Chartered Company, let alone in a governmental capacity.[6] So Chamberlain wavered. On the one hand, he assumed that the administrative reorganization would have to be, or at least have to look, extensive. On the other hand, he thought that the old system allowed for plenty of imperial control so long as the Colonial

Secretary and the high commissioner kept the Chartered Company under close surveillance and the imperial government assumed direct charge of the armed forces. Imperial control of the armed forces was secured right after the raid. Surveillance of the Chartered Company was secured with the replacement of Rosmead by Milner. The need for further reform, in Chamberlain's estimation, was a matter of public relations.

For a while he managed the appearance of things well. He made Rhodes wait for the decision on reorganization an unpleasant length of time. No one connected with the Chartered Company could gain access to the Colonial Secretary till mid-autumn. Then he communicated through Milner. But Milner disconcerted Chamberlain by becoming an advocate for Rhodes. Milner felt confident of his ability to subordinate the activities of Rhodes to imperial interests. After disposing of proposals from Chamberlain for fairly extensive reform, Milner in consultation with Rhodes agreed on a minimal scheme. Chamberlain accepted it without demur, persuaded that otherwise the imperial government would find itself saddled with responsibility for Rhodesia. In conversation with questioning Liberals, Chamberlain voiced another fear: that Rhodes, if spurned by Britain, might reunite with the Cape Dutch in opposition to London.

The rehabilitation of Rhodes in the administrative rearrangements for Rhodesia was impossible to disguise, and it embarrassed Chamberlain. Military and police forces remained formally under imperial control. But for all other purposes, executive power remained with officers of the Chartered Company. They would be merely supervised by an 'imperial resident' reporting to the high commissioner in South Africa. The most embarrassing provision of the agreement allowed shareholders of the Chartered Company to elect whomever they wished to its board of directors; and they promptly exercised this privilege to reelect Rhodes. He was back in the saddle less than a year after Parliament found him to blame for the Jameson raid. The one penalty Chamberlain imposed was to deprive Rhodes and the Chartered Company of the Bechuanaland Protectorate which had served as the base for Jameson's incursion. But that penalty was not finally imposed until the summer of 1898, too late to reduce Liberal criticism of the meagre administrative reforms in the House of Commons.

Still, Rhodes did not regain the resources he formerly enjoyed. The diminution of his power became apparent in connection with his plan to extend the Cape-to-Rhodesia railway over the River Zambesi. His financial means no longer matched his dreaming, and he had lost command of the governmental resources of the Cape Colony. He needed financial cooperation from the British government, and sought to engage Chamberlain's sympathies towards this end. But Milner, anxious to focus Chamberlain's energies on a confrontation with Kruger, advised Rhodes against pushing the Colonial Secretary. 'He is very bold & loves the forward game,' Milner explained to Rhodes:

> But it would be a mistake from *your*, I might say from *our*, point of view to get Chamberlain to take up anything wh[ich]. he could not carry with his colleagues, or wh[ich]., if he coerced them into adopting it, would subsequently get them into trouble. It would be a real disaster to weaken or discredit Chamberlain, for it will be a long time before we get another Colonial Minister, who is so likely to back up big schemes of expansion.[7]

Milner would have done well to heed his own words. Rhodes did not do so. He went ahead and asked the British Treasury to place its guarantee behind a large sale of shares to finance the railway extension. Chamberlain supported his request, but in terms which Rhodes could not or would not meet. In order to convince the cabinet of the worth of the enterprise, Chamberlain demanded proof of the mineral riches which were supposed to lie along the route of the extension. When proof was not forthcoming, Chamberlain made financial assistance from the government conditional on eventual government ownership of the railway. This was more than Hicks Beach at the Treasury was happy to offer or Rhodes to accept. Rhodes halted the negotiations. His dream faded, though he never abandoned it. With the fading of his dream, he too faded from Chamberlain's calculations.

Milner took the place of Rhodes as the person locally and hence ultimately in control of British fortunes in South Africa. Whether in Rhodes's time or in Milner's, Chamberlain found South Africa too distant and complex for him to gauge and grasp for himself. He had to depend on regional proconsuls. The problem with the performance of Rhodes in this role, aside from his buccaneering, was that he put his own interests and those of the Cape Colony above imperial ones. The problem with Milner was different. He was as devoted as Chamberlain to the imperial interest. But Milner had none of the experience, which Rhodes and Chamberlain shared, of working with partners in business. Nor was Milner familiar with the arts which helped Chamberlain as an industrialist to secure cooperation from labour. To make matters worse, proud of being a 'race patriot', he was insensitive to ethnic opposition. The ears upon which Chamberlain relied in South Africa were deaf to Afrikaner voices. Only those who invariably sided with Britain against the Boers qualified as race patriots in Milner's esteem.

That was not quite how he saw the situation when he first reached Cape Town in May 1897. There was tension in the air because of Chamberlain's demand that the Transvaal repeal its Aliens Expulsion Act.

Kruger acceded to the demand only after a demonstration of British naval power. Milner regretted the way Britain presented its demand, for he hoped to be blessed as a peacemaker. Yet he reported to Chamberlain after Kruger backed down: 'Feeling all round [here is] much better than when I came, but improvement began with and depends on conviction (of) determination (of) Great Britain not to be ousted, and in matters of Imperial defence not to yield to local pressure. This [is] quite compatible with conciliatory policy, in fact essential to its success.'[8]

Peace in South Africa as Milner saw it had to be based on clear recognition, by Boer and Briton alike, of British supremacy. Just as clearly, Kruger wanted to reduce British influence to vanishing point. The Cape Dutch wanted to fudge the issue. In terms of economic interest and regional power, the Transvaal Boers rivalled, indeed outrivalled the Cape Dutch, who therefore appreciated reinforcement from the British. But the Cape Dutch were no more willing to subordinate their interests to Britain than to the Boers of the Transvaal. There was too much ambiguity in this stance for Milner's liking. He reacted by interpreting the relationship between Cape Dutch and Boer as an Afrikaner plot.

For a while he conducted himself with studious impartiality, hoping that opposition to President Kruger would develop among the more progressive Boers of the Transvaal. But towards the end of 1897, Kruger and his Boer legislature, the Volksraad, turned down the recommendations of a commission formed in cooperation with the mining industry to improve its relations with the Transvaal government. Early in 1898, Kruger was reelected president of the Transvaal by a greatly increased majority. He consolidated his victory by dismissing the Chief Justice of the republic who had challenged the constitutionality of many acts of his government. Milner reacted violently. 'There is no way out of the political troubles of S. Africa,' he wrote to Chamberlain, 'except reform in the Transvaal or war. And at present the chances of reform in the Transvaal are worse than ever.'[9] Abandoning the pursuit of peace, Milner proposed 'to work up to a crisis . . . by steadily and inflexibly pressing for the redress of substantial wrongs and injustices'.

He pursued his own advice with one of the skills associated with Chamberlain. While his letter to Chamberlain was on the high seas, Milner used a visit to Graaff Reinet in Cape Dutch country to rally support, not so much from the audience who heard him, but from the British in the colony and the mother country who would read his words in their newspapers. He drew a sharp distinction between active opponents of Kruger's regime in the Transvaal and those who admired or even just accepted it without voicing criticism. With this speech, he turned himself into a sectional supremacist. A South African League had been organized among the ardently British of the Cape Colony to improve morale after the debacle of the Jameson raid. In 1897 the League established the Progressive party as its arm for Cape elections. Rhodes reemerged in Cape politics as potential leader of the new party; but his leadership was fitful. Milner in effect superseded Rhodes as the leader of the British against the supposed alliance of Dutch and Boer.

Hesitation

The Graaff Reinet speech did not have the impact Milner wanted in Britain because his friends in the British press muffed their instructions. But Chamberlain could not mistake the meaning of the letter he received. He rejected Milner's advice firmly, but in essence only because it was inopportune. He sent Milner a reassertion of the pacific approach upon which they had agreed before he left for South Africa. But Milner always knew that Chamberlain was of two minds about this approach.

The two men agreed that their object in South Africa was to bring it under imperial sway. The subordination of the Transvaal and its resources to Britain was therefore an imperial necessity, whether or not it was justified under the Conventions of 1881 and 1884. The questions that remained were matters of degree and method rather than of objective. How much subordination was necessary for imperial purposes? How far did Kruger wish and how far was he able to press his resistance? How would the public in South Africa and at home respond to the effort to subordinate the Transvaal? And hence how should it be done? Chamberlain wavered between two general responses to these questions. One, which he adopted in his more apprehensive moments, was to meet the minimum needs of the uitlander mining community at Johannesburg without infringing on the power that any self-respecting government of the republic would require. The aggressive alternative, now pushed by Milner, was to seize pretexts to justify a showdown with Kruger, who might then back down as in some previous confrontations.

When the international skies were overcast, Chamberlain wanted to keep South Africa quiet. That was the situation in the spring of 1898 when Milner proposed working up to a crisis: there was trouble with France along the Niger and the Nile, with Russia on the northern approaches to India and China, and possibly with Germany on the margins of South Africa itself. But by November, Germany had abandoned its interest in cooperating with Kruger, and the sharpest conflicts between Britain and France were resolved.

No sooner had France abandoned its pretensions on the Nile than Chamberlain goaded the goldmining interests to stand up to Kruger. Milner, who was back in England for an interval and in consultation

with his chief, undoubtedly encouraged his action; but the central discussion was between Chamberlain and Lord Harris of Consolidated
Gold Fields. Division among the goldmining magnates of the Rand had
contributed to the debacle of the Jameson raid; but they reunited after
the Transvaal government rejected proposals to reconcile the needs of
their industry with those of the republic. The cohesion of the industry
and its alienation from the Kruger regime were vital to the imperial
quest for regional supremacy. When Lord Harris asked Chamberlain
about the propriety of a loan from Consolidated Gold Fields to the
Transvaal government in return for a tightening of governmental regulations on native labour, Chamberlain criticized the proposal as 'selling
the position for a slight pecuniary advantage'.[10] He urged Harris to insist on 'full municipal rights to Johannesburg, including control of education, sanitation & the police'.[11] He mentioned but did not pursue the
greater issue of enfranchising the uitlanders as citizens of the republic.

The year ended with an episode capable of generating a clash between the Boers and the British. It would not have occurred or come to
anything if the uitlanders of Johannesburg had controlled the municipal
police as Chamberlain advocated. A Boer policeman shot and killed a
drunken uitlander called Thomas Edgar when he resisted arrest. Conveying the news to Milner, Chamberlain noted that it might give them
'the right of remonstrance & action—outside the Convention—which
we have not hitherto had'.[12] But until what actually happened could be
ascertained, he kept his attention on the mining magnates.

Lord Harris decided against a loan to the Kruger government. In return Chamberlain let the Randlords know that, so long as they spoke
out fearlessly, he would endorse the industrial reforms they demanded
of the Kruger government. Thereafter collaboration between spokesmen
for the industry and the imperial authorities was fairly close. Public
protests from the president of the Chamber of Mines were reinforced by
despatches from Chamberlain to the Transvaal authorities.

Kruger eventually obtained his loan from the Netherlands. But a loan
was not what his government, or at any rate the livelier spirits within
it, most wanted from the mining industry. J.C. Smuts, the young state
attorney, and F.W. Reitz, the state secretary, entered into competition
with the British government for the favour of the industry. They hoped
to induce at least some mine-owners to reinforce the republic. These
hopes were shared by some of the concessionaires who provided the
industry with goods and services, particularly dynamite and freight, on
a monopoly basis in collusion with the Transvaal government. The Boer
advocates of an accommodation with industry put together a bid which
came to be known as the 'Great Deal'. It even broached the subject of
the franchise by proposing that uitlanders could begin to receive the
vote after five years.

The Boer bid impressed but did not surprise Chamberlain. He concluded that the Transvaal government was worried by the things that heartened and emboldened him, particularly the improvement in Britain's international position and the support the pro-British South African League was attracting in the republic. When emissaries of the industry came to the Colonial Office for advice on how to respond to the Boer proposals, Chamberlain repeated the advice he had given Lord Harris in November: that they should insist on administrative and not just economic reforms, and that the most obvious necessity was 'a bona fide municipality for Johannesburg'.[13] But 'Home Rule for the Rand' held little appeal for the mining magnates and their uitlander employees. They reverted to the issue of the franchise. Smuts and Reitz put it five years off. Kruger spoke of enfranchisement after nine years and even then reserved the right to vote for president and commander-in-chief to 'the old burghers of the country'.[14] Little wonder that Chamberlain, speaking in the Commons, could not see 'the slightest advantage'[15] in such a proposal.

He did not improve matters by adding that 'up to the present time, not one of [Kruger's] promises [to the uitlanders] has been fulfilled, and . . . those grievances have been rather increased than diminished'. In manner though not yet as conscious policy, Chamberlain was absorbing Milner's confrontational attitude. So were spokesmen for the mining industry. Percy Fitzpatrick, the activist in the greatest of the goldmining firms, Werner-Beit, feared that the cohesion of the magnates might dissolve once they entered into talks with representatives from the republican government in Pretoria. As soon as the republican side put its proposals for the franchise in writing, Fitzpatrick revealed them to the press. The negotiations broke down in a welter of claims and denials which widened the rift between the republic and the industry and confirmed the commitment of the industry to the empire.

Other investments

From Chamberlain's point of view, the developments in South Africa were more reassuring than disturbing up to the spring of 1899. Till then he paid more attention to the domestic arena and developments elsewhere overseas. He continued to direct Salisbury's attention to the desirability of cooperation with the United States to keep China open for foreign commerce without fear or favour. But Chamberlain's belief in the natural harmony of the two English-speaking powers was jarred by a collision in their imperial interests. He had hoped that American ex-

pansion in the Caribbean and the Pacific would foster American understanding of Britain's responsibilities. But when it came to defining the
border between the United States and Canada through the supposedly
mineral-rich lands of the Alaskan panhandle, the American expansion-
ists who annexed Cuba and the Philippines stomped all over Canadian
claims. This challenge produced a switch in emphasis between Chamberlain and Salisbury. Now Salisbury was the one more anxious for
good relations with the United States, while Chamberlain encouraged
Canada to stand up to the American ruffians.

On the whole, after the excitements of the previous year, diplomatic
activity quietened down in the first half of 1899. Chamberlain turned to
the domestic scene, neglected since the passage of the Workmen's Compensation Act. In the closing years of the century Parliament displayed
much greater interest in imperial and foreign than in domestic affairs.
But Balfour and Chamberlain sensed that the government was more
vulnerable on domestic issues. Their vulnerability was compounded by
the weakness of the ministers officially responsible for domestic legislation: Ridley at the Home Office and Henry Chaplin at the Local Government Board. At Balfour's request, Chamberlain took Chaplin's place
in charge of a Small Dwellings bill to provide loans for workmen who
wanted to buy their houses.

The lines of division in the cabinet on domestic issues did not always
coincide with party affiliation between Conservatives and Liberal Unionists. Chamberlain and Salisbury sometimes cooperated in opposition
to Balfour, as they did over a bill in 1899 on the government of London.
Salisbury and Chamberlain wanted to strengthen local borough authorities rather than the central London Council. When Balfour, substituting
for Ridley in charge of the bill, gave it a centralized complexion, Chamberlain remarked insinuatingly to the prime minister: 'How greatly the
Gov't of London Bill has grown in Arthur's hands! It may be all right
but I do not think it is what you intended.'[16] The eventual Act bore
more of Chamberlain's mark. A contemporary comment 'that it would
create not one London but twenty-nine Birminghams'[17] may have been
intended as a criticism but would have been taken by Chamberlain as
high praise.

On Liberal prompting, the subject of old-age pensions came up early
in the parliamentary session. It arose while Chamberlain was away, sick
with gout followed by flu. He dealt with the Liberal initiative as an
exercise in political management rather than as an opportunity for creative policy-making. He hoped to avoid the issue when Parliament convened. When that proved impossible, he tried to assign it to a large
parliamentary committee with a divided charge, including housing as
well as pensions. He denounced with a new harshness the suggestion

of pensions for 'everybody—good and bad, thrifty and unthrifty—the waster, drunkard, and idler as well as the industrious'.[18] Still, the Liberal critics of his shortcomings could not agree on anything better. A Liberal friend wrote to compare Chamberlain with 'Asquith & Co'. 'You have Faith and no Works: they have neither Faith nor Works'; and therefore, 'while some of us treat the matter as a mere party or personal dodge of yourself, I . . . cannot help giving you credit'.[19]

The enterprise closest to Chamberlain's heart at the beginning of 1899 was the prospective University of Birmingham. Having renewed its emphasis on applied science and added a faculty of commerce, he invited some thirty West Midlands business leaders to a 'parlour meeting' in his home. He appealed to them to contribute and ask their shareholders to contribute to the redesigned institution from which their companies would so greatly benefit. He pursued individually those who declined his invitation. When Alderman Lloyd questioned the wisdom of trying to match the quality of Oxford or Cambridge, Chamberlain sharpened his analysis of the constituency the local university was intended to serve. Top scholarship winners would probably always head for the older institutions; but 'what we are chiefly deficient in is the higher education of the men who take what I may call second-class positions, as for instance, those of managers, advisers, & experts in manufacturing & other commercial undertakings'.[20]

The endowment stood at £118,936 on the eve of his meeting with local business leaders. They agreed to raise another £50,000. A month later the endowment had reached £135,000. That was still £115,000 short of Chamberlain's £250,000 target for the university. Refusing to concede that Birmingham could not come up with that much, he devised what later became known as challenge grants to stimulate and augment Birmingham's response. He approached two men who had emigrated from Scotland to construct great metal-using enterprises in the New World and had recently come back to Britain. One was Donald Smith, now Lord Strathcona, builder of the Canadian Pacific Railway, the other Andrew Carnegie, the steelmaker of Pittsburgh. Beginning with Strathcona, Chamberlain persuaded him to offer the final £25,000 of the targeted quarter million pounds, but only after the other £225,000 had been raised.

With £90,000 still to find, Chamberlain wrote to Carnegie. Carnegie liked to think of Birmingham as 'the Pittsburgh of the old land'.[21] The interaction between these two men not only accelerated the fund-raising but extended its target and altered the character of the eventual institution. Following Strathcona's example, Carnegie began by offering £25,000 on similar conditions. He then had a conversation with Chamberlain which opened Carnegie's pocket wider and set him thinking about the sort of university Birmingham needed. Carnegie doubled his offer to £50,000 and earmarked it for a purpose outlined in a letter which Chamberlain helped him write. It cited the remark by one British steelmaker that what he most envied about his American competitors was 'the class of scientific young experts you have to manage every department of your works'. Carnegie added, 'this class you must sooner or later secure if Britain is to remain one of the principal manufacturing nations'. Accordingly he specified that his £50,000 should be used 'to establish a scientific department' on the model of the one at Cornell University.[22]

Manoeuvred by Chamberlain, the two donors stimulated each other. Strathcona raised his offer to £37,500, which he earmarked for the faculty of commerce. These challenge grants were more than enough to carry Birmingham to Chamberlain's target. Within a week, £20,000 was raised locally, enough to pass the quarter million pound objective with £4,000 to spare. Swept on by their achievement, Strathcona in concert with Chamberlain declared that £250,000 was not enough for the intended enterprise. He offered an additional £12,500, which would make his donation equal to Carnegie's, if further donations were made to bring the grand total to £300,000 by the end of June. That gave Birmingham six weeks to raise another £33,500.

Everyone till now had danced to Chamberlain's tune. Suddenly Carnegie turned the act around. Chamberlain approached him about the appointment of trustees to ensure that his donation would endow professorships in sciences. But Carnegie's thinking about a science division had moved on since his conversation with Chamberlain. Disdainful of the scientific education he found in Britain, Carnegie wanted his gift to be spent on the building and equipment of a school of science. Chamberlain reacted with dismay. 'We have already the buildings required in connection with Mason University College,' he explained; '. . . what we want to begin with is brains & not architecture.'[23]

Carnegie withstood Chamberlain's arguments. 'Brains of course are necessary,' he replied, 'but the first thing that scientific brains would demand . . . would be that the necessary tools be provided.'[24] Carnegie offered to pay for a tour by one or two Birmingham faculty members to inspect the provisions for science teaching and research at the leading American institutions. Chamberlain could not credit that additions to the facilities of Mason College would be required until enrolment expanded. Anxious nevertheless to mollify the benefactor, Chamberlain offered to buy any scientific equipment Carnegie recommended with whatever funds were left over after salaries for the science faculty had been endowed; and he accepted Carnegie's offer for an inspection tour of American university science facilities. Carnegie reversed Chamberlain's proposal, endowing salaries with whatever was left after proper equipment was installed. Much though Chamberlain disliked this re-

joinder, he felt obliged to acquiesce amid the struggle to reach the new
target of £300,000.

Franchise or fight

By that time he was preoccupied by Britain's deteriorating relations
with Kruger's South African Republic. That subject was on everyone's
mind, including Carnegie's. As an expatriate anti-imperialist, he expressed the hope that Chamberlain would compromise on South Africa
as well as on the university. The people in Birmingham at work for the
new university were amazed that Chamberlain could still give his mind
to it. As Colonial Secretary he held full responsibility for British policy
in South Africa, subject only to approval of the cabinet. He was not
prime minister; but whether people liked it or not, that summer and on
that subject Chamberlain spoke for England. The press watched his
every movement for signs of the direction in which the winds were
blowing.

No matter how important the mines of the Rand were economically,
there was little desire in Britain to fight for them. The mining magnates,
notorious for their stock-market manipulations, had few admirers
among the old aristocracy or the middle- and working-class electorate.
The Randlords themselves recoiled at the prospect of war, which was
bound to be more disruptive.

The termination of the Great Deal negotiations between Kruger's
ministers and the mine-owners nevertheless coincided with an intensi-
fication in the uitlander agitation. The change was triggered earlier with
Edgar's killing by a Boer policeman, who was subsequently acquitted of
wrongdoing and commended by a Boer judge. The events of the case
were open to widely differing interpretations. Still, it pointed up the
danger to Johannesburg, 'where a strong force of police armed with
revolvers have to deal with a large alien unarmed population, whose
language in many cases they do not understand'.[25] At the end of March,
20,000 uitlanders signed a petition to the imperial authorities chroni-
cling their woes. The petition greeted Milner upon his return from Britain, and was quickly transmitted to Chamberlain. It provided proof of
widespread anger among the uitlanders and of their reliance on Britain,
in stirring contrast to their ambivalence in 1895 which discredited the
Jameson raid.

Chamberlain's reaction mixed caution with determination. He drafted
a response that brought the interests of the mines and the uitlander
community under the protective umbrella of the 1884 London Convention without issuing an immediate ultimatum to President Kruger. His
draft failed to please either the cabinet or Milner. Balfour and Hicks

Beach feared that Chamberlain was going too far, Milner that he was not going far enough. And indeed Chamberlain's reluctance to confront the South African Republic with a clear demand left room for misunderstanding of his purpose.

Before the despatch could be issued, intermediaries in South Africa prompted President Steyn of the Orange Free State to invite Kruger and Milner to confer in his capital of Bloemfontein. The invitation upset Chamberlain's plans. Though his despatch was meant to prepare the way for such a conference, he could not now control its agenda. He bowed to the necessity of an independent conference, if only to convince the uncommitted that the imperial authorities had done their best to resolve the tension between Britain and the Transvaal. But Milner's prime concern was to assure the British in South Africa including the uitlanders of the Transvaal that the imperial government would stand by them firmly. Discounting Chamberlain's advice, Milner handled the Bloemfontein conference so as to serve his purposes rather than Chamberlain's.

Chamberlain advised Milner to accept a request from the Cape premier, Schreiner, who was allied with the Afrikaner Bond, to accompany him to Bloemfontein. Milner insisted on proceeding to Bloemfontein alone. The one piece of advice he accepted from Chamberlain was to 'lay all the stress on question of franchise'.[26] Though President Kruger tried to raise other issues, he too accepted the centrality of the franchise question. Going notably further than he had earlier in the year, Kruger offered to reduce the qualifying period of residence before enfranchisement to seven years. The offer was not, however, retrospective; no uitlanders could be enfranchised under it for another seven years. Both Chamberlain and Milner were determined to secure some immediate enfranchisement. Hoping to obtain a better offer from Kruger and in any case to keep up appearances, Chamberlain sent Milner a telegram urging him not to terminate the conference precipitately. But the telegram did not arrive fast enough to catch Milner, who had hastened back to Cape Town.

The news of Milner's abrupt ending of the Bloemfontein conference was accompanied by publication of Chamberlain's response to the uitlander petition and of an earlier inflammatory assessment by Milner of the situation in the Transvaal. These displays of assertive imperialism reduced the likelihood of bipartisan approval in Britain for the government's course in South Africa. Chamberlain needed broad support to impress President Kruger with Britain's determination and convince him that some immediate enfranchisement of the uitlanders was inescapable. Towards that end, Chamberlain sought agreement from the new Liberal leader in the Commons, Sir Henry Campbell-Bannerman, for a reinforcement of 10,000 troops in South Africa. But Campbell-

Bannerman would not approve even of mules for transport to make the existing military force in South Africa more effective.

The suspicions of the Liberals in Britain focused on Chamberlain. They tended to overlook the stridency of Milner because of his impeccable distinction in the public service and his friendship with the rising generation of Liberals such as Asquith. Chamberlain was indeed responsible for the hardening line Britain adopted in South Africa by midsummer. Yet he moved in this direction gradually, by careful stages, anxious to carry British opinion with him.

He defined the British position for the public near the end of June at a meeting of the Birmingham Liberal Unionist Association. For the first time in the two years, he concentrated his remarks on South Africa. He began with the story of oppression told by the uitlanders in their petition. Developing his case from that point, he argued that Kruger's regime was 'not only oppressive and unjust' but constituted 'a menace to British interests and a serious danger to our position as the paramount Power in South Africa'.[27] By identifying the crucial issue as British paramountcy, he heightened what was at stake in the controversy. Even so, to Milner's dismay, he was not yet ready to confront Kruger with an ultimatum. Chamberlain hoped that an ultimatum would prove unnecessary for South African purposes, and he knew that it was premature for British. He ended his speech with an appeal to 'our loyal Dutch subjects in Cape Colony', and in particular to Hofmeyr of the Afrikaner Bond and Schreiner, to help persuade President Kruger 'to make the necessary concessions'.

The note of determination in the speech impressed the Cape Dutch more than its concluding appeal. Schreiner wondered whether Chamberlain wanted war, and questioned his assumption that Kruger would give way under pressure. Beneath such questions lay the uncertainty which the Cape Dutch feared to face about whether the aims of Kruger and Chamberlain were reconcilable. The two men gave different meanings to the same words. Chamberlain insisted that he was willing to uphold the 'independence' of the Transvaal; but he meant independence under British paramountcy, the very thing Kruger had spent his life trying to escape. Reflections of this sort suggested that sooner or later war was inevitable.

For the moment, Chamberlain's words propelled men like Hofmeyr whose hopes straddled the two camps into frantic efforts to patch up an agreement. Chamberlain did not contact them directly for fear of circumventing Milner. But he urged Milner to give efforts like Hofmeyr's time: 'If they afford any basis for settlement so much the better: if not I shall send another despatch pressing urgently for franchise as proposed by you or for full Municipal rights for mining districts and indicating plainly that if satisfactory reply is not given an ultimatum will follow.'[28] When Kruger showed signs of responding to the advice of intermediaries, Chamberlain tried to make Milner responsive. 'If [Kruger's new proposals] appear to be substantial it is our policy' he instructed Milner, 'to accept them as such and not to minimize them. Then if Kruger subsequently plays false we shall have all opinion on our side and shall be able to deal with the breach of faith.'[29] Chamberlain warned Milner that 'opinion here is strongly opposed to war although the necessity of resorting to force in the last resort is gradually making its way among all classes. If we were driven to this extremity I think the Government could rely upon the vast majority of its own supporters & a minority of the Opposition, but the bulk of the Opposition would probably take the opportunity to denounce us.'[30]

Meanwhile Kruger took another obscure step forward on the franchise. When Chamberlain asked to examine it, Kruger improved the offer rather than submit it to imperial investigation. A range of Afrikaners in and outside the Transvaal encouraged this forward movement. Milner interpreted their efforts as proof of the existence of a malevolent 'Afrikaner coalition'.[31] The home government was less suspicious. Still, it added a small reinforcement to the British forces in South Africa. Whatever the motivation, in mid-July Kruger offered a seven-year retrospective residence qualification for the franchise, and he no longer surrounded it with disabling regulations. The only significant omission from his proposals was a guarantee about the distribution of seats in the Volksraad. Two days after the introduction of this measure, the sitting Volksraad passed it.

Before the Volksraad took this preemptive action, and informed by the press that the measure gave the uitlanders five seats, Chamberlain welcomed Kruger's latest proposal as 'a triumph of moral pressure—accompanied by special service officers & 3 Battalions of Artillery'.[32] He authorized a statement to *The Times* that 'assuming the most recent telegrams from Pretoria to be true ... the crisis in the relations between Great Britain and the Transvaal may be regarded as ended'. Congratulating Milner on 'a great victory',[33] he proposed, once the new concession was confirmed, that the high commissioner and the Boer president should meet again to settle the details of the franchise reform and proceed in conciliatory fashion to resolve the remaining points at issue between their countries. When the Volksraad took action, Chamberlain was 'happy to recognize' their measure as providing 'a basis of settlement',[34] although he sought to ensure that the number of predominantly uitlander constituencies would be enough to give them an influential voice in the government of the republic.

His response produced a mixed reaction among his colleagues. The despatch to Milner which he drafted for consideration by the cabinet summarized the argument over the franchise. Balfour and C.T. Ritchie at the Board of Trade questioned the wisdom of including contentious material in a despatch meant to be conciliatory. Salisbury's concerns ran in the opposite direction. He warned Chamberlain 'above all . . . to guard against backsliding'[35] on the part of the Boers, and discussed how to keep up military pressure on the Transvaal. Milner was shocked at Chamberlain's seeming willingness to accept Boer offers at face value. His suspicions were substantiated when the Transvaal State Attorney, Smuts, accompanied the Act of the Volksraad with a long explanatory memorandum. The Uitlander Council reinforced Milner with a telegram telling Chamberlain that it was 'keenly disappointed' by the statement *The Times* had been authorized to publish.[36]

These reactions did not alter the balance of Chamberlain's course. The statement he made in the Commons at the end of the session was so moderate that Liberals thought he must have suffered a setback in the cabinet. Insisting that the uitlanders receive 'some substantial and immediate representation',[37] he welcomed Kruger's latest step as 'a real advance'. Hoping 'to find in it a basis for a satisfactory settlement', he pressed for a joint Boer-British inquiry to see whether the Act of the Volksraad met this standard. At the same time he induced Campbell-Bannerman to admit that there were circumstances under which Britain would have to take up arms. Salisbury reiterated the government's resolve more stiffly in the House of Lords.

The Colonial Secretary was pleased with the way things stood at the end of July. He estimated that, had the Radical opposition dared call for a division, less than twenty MPs would have voted against his policy. Those in Parliament and in South Africa who were most anxious for a peaceful agreement urged Kruger to accept the joint inquiry.

It was a measure of the chasm between the two sides that Chamberlain's offer, which seemed fair to his usual critics, was rejected by Kruger as intolerable. He told Steyn of the Orange Free State that acceptance of a joint inquiry 'would be equivalent to a destruction of our independence'.[38] Unaware of this reaction, Chamberlain maintained his course. The British government decided to send out another military detachment, this time to Natal; and Chamberlain used this action to induce the government of Natal to call out its volunteers. At the same time, he restrained Milner from broadening the diplomatic attack on the Transvaal.

When word that Kruger rejected a joint inquiry reached Milner, he urged Chamberlain to issue an immediate ultimatum. Discouraged but not yet driven off his course, Chamberlain instead asked Milner to appoint a commission of inquiry unilaterally, to consist of three members including if possible 'one independent Africander [sic]'.[39] Because the commission was for fact-finding about the new Transvaal franchise law rather than for policy-making, Chamberlain saw no risk and much advantage in appointing someone sympathetic to the Boers. He questioned and in the event deplored Milner's insistence that no such person could be found who was willing to serve.

The outlook in August oscillated between bleak and bright. Chamberlain was disconcerted to learn that the War Office could not place a whole army corps in Natal within less than three months. The recent pattern of events suggested that Kruger would make concessions to the smallest extent necessary to dissuade the British from resorting to arms. If so, war was unlikely, but so was a truly satisfactory settlement. Prolonged negotiations would diminish the sense of urgency and thus reduce Britain's ability to insist on substantial reform. Accordingly Chamberlain resolved, if the effort at a prompt solution failed, to despatch what he sardonically called 'the Grand Army'.[40] He would then extend his demands to make sure of a satisfactory settlement on all the outstanding issues. He hoped in that case also to make the Transvaal responsible for Britain's military expenses. To reduce the risk of military embarrassment before the Grand Army reached South Africa, he wanted a smaller force to move in from India as soon as Britain issued its broadened ultimatum.

This contingency planning was interrupted by another overture from Pretoria, more substantial than its predecessors but no less wrapped in uncertainty. Anxious to avoid a joint inquiry yet apprehensive of rejecting Chamberlain's demand, Smuts, the Transvaal State Attorney, came to the imperial agent in Pretoria, Conyngham Greene, with an offer that went beyond what Milner had asked for at Bloemfontein. Smuts proposed a five-year retrospective residential qualification for the franchise, ten uitlander seats in the Volksraad of thirty-six with a guarantee that the uitlanders would never have a lower proportion, and entitlement to vote for the president as well as the Volksraad. While unwilling to subject the plan to joint inspection, Smuts offered to go over it in detail with Greene and his legal adviser. In return, Smuts asked Britain to refrain from interference in the domestic affairs of the republic beyond what the Conventions allowed, to say no more about its claim to be the constitutional suzerain of the republic, and to submit disputes about the requirements of the Conventions to a tribunal of arbitration from which, in deference to British insistence, all foreigners except for burghers of the Orange Free State would be excluded. In conversation with Greene, Smuts raised further possibilities including permission to use English in the debates of the Volksraad.

Milner saw nothing in this offer but refusal to accept a joint inquiry and recognize Britain's paramountcy. Chamberlain dismissed this reaction as 'unnecessarily suspicious'.[41] He no longer felt able to give new concessions a warm welcome; they were too obviously eked out under constraint. He wanted to see the offer on paper. Yet he foresaw no difficulty in complying with Smuts's conditions. Fair treatment of the uitlanders by the Boers would render further British intervention in the internal affairs of the republic unnecessary. So long as Britain's de facto paramountcy was respected, Chamberlain had no desire to pursue the constitutional nicety of suzerainty. So long as foreigners were excluded, he was happy to discuss the formation of an arbitration tribunal. 'We must clearly exhaust this new phase of the situation,' he instructed Milner, 'and unless we can prove conclusively that it is dishonestly intended or altogether inadequate . . . you must avoid any language which would lead [the South African Republic] to think we are determined to pick a quarrel.'[42] To allow time for formal presentation and assessment of Smuts's offer, Chamberlain suspended military preparations.

Smuts's proposals were presented formally on 19 August and at first glance looked promising. But two days later, the Boer government stiffened the accompanying requirements. Britain was asked to agree to arbitration of outstanding disputes after the franchise was settled, to refrain from interfering in the internal affairs of the republic, and to refrain expressly from insisting on suzerainty. Chamberlain had no difficulty with the first demand, and might have accepted the second if formulated differently. But there was eventually bipartisan agreement in Britain that the third could not be accepted. The difference between dropping the subject of suzerainty tacitly, as Smuts requested, and explicitly, as now required, was loaded with prestige of vital moment to the empire.

The stiffened Boer conditions blighted Smuts's initiative. Chamberlain issued a chilly response to the franchise proposals at the centre of Smuts's offer, and embarrassed him by treating all the possibilities he had raised in conversation with Greene as promises. The coldness of Chamberlain convinced Smuts that nothing would ever satisfy him. Accordingly, Smuts denied Greene's recollection of their conversation and endorsed the formal proposal with its stiffened conditions. From then on, each step in the negotiations brought the two governments closer to war. By demanding an immediate response to his latest despatch, Chamberlain made it close to an ultimatum. He let Kruger know that failure to reply quickly would lead to a widening of Britain's demands.

In these circumstances Chamberlain again addressed himself to the public. Using the occasion of a garden party at Highbury, he spoke offensively if truly of President Kruger:

He dribbles out reforms like water from a squeezed sponge, and he either accompanies his offers with conditions which he knows to be impossible, or he refuses to allow us to make a satisfactory investigation of the nature and the character of these reforms.[43]

He referred to the Transvaal as 'a subordinate State', thus discrediting the promise he also gave to uphold the Transvaal's 'independence'. He publicized his warning that if Kruger procrastinated much longer, Britain would widen its demands in order to secure 'conditions which once for all shall establish which is the paramount Power in South Africa'. The speech fluttered the dovecotes in Britain. Yet it left Chamberlain on middle ground. The correspondence with which he was deluged afterwards was 'about equally divided between letters from people who abuse me for blood-thirstiness & others who are just as violent on account of my culpable delay'.[44]

He now thought war probable. Still, he insisted that Milner set up an inquiry into the Smuts franchise proposals. Chamberlain needed to establish how substantial those proposals were and how insistent the Boers were on 'the objectionable conditions as to Suzerainty'[45] before he could assess the timeliness of an ultimatum and the degree of public support in Britain that he was likely to enjoy. He recognized that even the 'ordinary patriotic Englishman sees that if there is a war it will be a very big affair—the biggest since the Crimea—with no [?] honour to be gained, if we are successful, and with many most unpleasant contingent possibilities'.[46]

Chamberlain was none the less sure that 'the majority of the people' were now persuaded 'that there is a greater issue than the franchise or the grievances of the Uitlanders at stake'. He had helped to convince most of the British public that not only their 'supremacy in S[outh]. Africa' but their 'existence as a great Power in the world are involved in the result of our present controversy'. He still sensed that 'a large minority' resisted the dominant trend. But that minority shrank when the Transvaal government withdrew Smuts's proposals and reverted to the franchise law passed by the Volksraad. Thereafter Chamberlain possessed the general support at home which he would need in the event of war or—and he had not quite lost hope—to induce Kruger to back down.

The deployment of force

The theatre of debate narrowed in September, so far as Britain was concerned, to the confines of the cabinet. It had to decide how to prepare for the coming contest. This responsibility brought out a fine difference within the cabinet and touched on a crucial flaw in

Chamberlain's policy. He had approached the confrontation with the South African Republic as a battle for the support of the public, most importantly at home but also in the British colonies in South Africa and elsewhere round the world. For years he had pressed his cabinet colleagues, usually in vain, to strengthen the British military presence in South Africa; but he thought of armed force as an intimidating tool in negotiation rather than for deployment in warfare.

Some of his cabinet colleagues, particularly Salisbury, Balfour and the minister in charge of the army, Lord Lansdowne, took the requirements of actual war more seriously; and they insisted that Chamberlain do so too when the prospect of war loomed close. Yet their judgement was no better than his when they contemplated the resort to force. Whatever the arms on their ancestral halls, their craft of leadership was essentially civilian, in contrast to the martial aristocracies of Continental Europe. They remembered that even so half-hearted a struggle as the Crimean war had strained the institutions of the country. The old elite were also more apprehensive than Chamberlain about popular backing in the event of war. And every member of the cabinet felt inhibited by the Treasury. Accordingly, the cabinet handled the preparations for war with nervous fingers.

The needs of the hour, the inhibitions of the cabinet, and ineptitude at army headquarters created an opportunity for Chamberlain to step forward as the war minister, the minister who, whatever his formal office, took charge of the emergency on the eve and in the event of war. One of the leading advocates of military reform, Spencer Wilkinson, thought of Chamberlain for this role earlier when war with France looked likely. At the end of August, Goschen as First Lord of the Admiralty hoped that Chamberlain would take the lead in challenging the slow-moving assumptions of the War Office. No one else seemed willing to do so. Salisbury was distracted by the illness of his wife, who lay dying. Lord Lansdowne would not stand up to the generals. The Duke of Devonshire, who was given responsibility for military coordination and reform at the beginning of the ministry, had done little to meet his assignment; and Balfour had not yet taken it over.

But Chamberlain did not see, let alone seize, the opportunity. He never foresaw that the fundamental struggle with the South African Republic would be a matter of blood and guns rather than of propaganda and public reaction. On occasion he appreciated that war with the Boers, if it came, would be serious. But he never foresaw that the war itself would become the central fact of South African history so far as the empire was concerned and a searing test of his entire imperial enterprise.

Though the Transvaal's withdrawal of the Smuts proposal convinced Chamberlain that 'the time has fully come to bring matters to a head',[47] he continued to deal with the situation in terms of what 'public opinion in this country would stand'.[48] The response of the cabinet to the action of the Transvaal was so modest—despatching 5,700 troops from India and several further battalions of troops and batteries of artillery from England—that the friends of the republic in Britain and South Africa urged Kruger to offer a conciliatory reply. When he refused and seemed bent upon a resort to arms, the British cabinet divided over how to frame its response. The unpreparedness of the army, in particular the time it would take to place a full army corps in South Africa, made Balfour among others anxious to restrain Britain's verbal response until the country could back up its words with military deeds.

Chamberlain minimized the military risk. He thought that anxiety about the black population could inhibit the Boers from attacking the British. His overriding concerns were still political. He was 'aghast at the idea of leaving this country, & above all S[outh]. Africa, in the slightest doubt as to the intentions'[49] of Britain during the time it would take for an army corps to reach the field. Salisbury came down firmly on Balfour's side and disparaged Chamberlain's preoccupation with public opinion. 'Public opinion here is not very irritable,' Salisbury observed. 'Public opinion in South Africa is no doubt rabid: but as they must come to us—because they have no one else to go to—their wrath does not matter very much.'[50] Accordingly, at the end of the third week of September the cabinet ordered unobtrusive mobilization of an army corps and restrained its public language to a warning that they were 'compelled . . . to formulate their own proposals for a final settlement'.[51]

Chamberlain's acceptance of the restraints imposed by the cabinet brought its reward. Though many of his colleagues were pacifically inclined, they all came to accept the need for and justice of the war. Hicks Beach, the minister most critical of Chamberlain's confrontational conduct during the summer, told a confidante at the end of September that 'none of us (except possibly JC though I am by no means sure about him) likes the business. But we all feel that it has got to be done—and though I feel grave doubts as to the effects of a war . . . the Dutch in South Africa can hardly like us less than they do now, and I hope at the end will have learned to respect us.'[52] There was no corresponding closing of ranks in the Cape Colony. At the approach of war, the Cape parliament split along ethnic lines. Afrikaners urged the British government to bend over backwards to reach agreement with the Transvaal. British colonists urged the mother country to stand its ground.

For two weeks at the end of September and beginning of October, Britain hovered with deliberate ambiguity between peace and war. The suspense made Chamberlain intensely anxious but did not improve his judgement. His concerns remained narrowly political. 'What I fear', he told Milner, 'is some suggestion of compromise from [the Boers] which will be totally inadequate to provide a permanent settlement but will nevertheless strengthen the hands of the Opposition at home and make many foolish people inclined to give more time and to patch up some sort of hollow arrangement.'[53] He insisted on the necessity of issuing the British ultimatum before Parliament convened for an emergency session on 17 October. He dismissed the risk of a preemptive strike by the Boers. Milner was belatedly stricken with this anxiety, and called for temporizing negotiations with President Steyn of the Orange Free State. But as the days passed and reinforcements from India neared Natal while the Boers stayed inside their republic, Chamberlain grew contemptuous of such fears. During the earlier negotiations he made much of the munitions which the Transvaal had amassed since the mid-1890s. Now, on the eve of war, he minimized the figures for Boer troop strength, maximized the effectiveness of the British military force in South Africa even at current levels, and assessed 'the risk of a success-ful [Boer] attack on a fortified position chosen by us' as 'very small'.[54] His one glimmer of military perception was to regret 'that our troops, unlike the Boers, cannot mobilise with a piece of biltong & a belt of ammunition, but require such enormous quantities of transport & impedimenta'.[55]

His assessment of the probable impact of the war, if it broke out, was equally shallow. To a Nonconformist minister who pleaded for concili-atory treatment of the Boers, Chamberlain replied:

> supposing war to come, & England to be successful, there is really no fear of permanent discontent either in the Transvaal or any other part of South Africa.[56]

He ignored the evidence offered by Canada that antagonism between peoples of European descent was rarely removed by military conquest.

While resistant to unwelcome lessons elsewhere in the empire, Cham-berlain wanted to make all he could of its far-flung military potential in the current emergency. In the spring of the year when war became a lively possibility, imperial propagandists and military planners in Lon-don suggested the recruitment of troops from the colonies. The sugges-tion was welcomed in the colonies by individual imperialists and by British officers in command of colonial militias. Chamberlain embraced the idea during his summertime negotiations. The prospect of soldiers from all over the empire flocking to support the claims of the uitlanders might impress Kruger with the necessity of concession. For that pur-pose, this military support would best be offered by the colonies rather than requested by the mother country. Accordingly, Chamberlain prompted the governors of the major colonies to find out whether they would 'spontaneously'[57] offer contingents of their local armed forces. By the end of July he was able to tell Parliament of offers from Victoria, New South Wales, Queensland, Canada, West Africa and the Malay States. The announcement provoked the Irish MP John Dillon to inter-ject, 'The British Empire against 30,000 farmers'.[58] That was precisely what Chamberlain wanted Kruger to reflect on.

The roundabout probe of Chamberlain won its best response in Aus-tralasia, especially from New Zealand. Some of the colonies on the sub-continent of Australia responded more slowly, but by the end of the first week in October all had offered troops. The response of Canada, however, was acutely ambiguous. The Governor-General of Canada, Lord Minto, forwarded Chamberlain's inquiry to Sir Wilfrid Laurier in a way designed to appeal both to his desire for peace and to his supposed imperial patriotism. But in stressing how an offer of troops from Canada 'would be a proof to the world that the component parts of that Empire . . . stand shoulder to shoulder to support Imperial interests',[59] Minto only heightened Laurier's anxiety. Laurier recoiled from the suggested commitment as incompatible with the auto-nomous dignity of Canada which, with the support of his fellow French Canadians, he wished to enhance. He vetoed a Canadian contribution to the prospective war in South Africa, and let the public know of his opposition.

Chamberlain continued to seek proof from the South African crisis that 'our colonies . . . will stand side by side and shoulder to shoulder with us in maintaining the honour and interests of the Empire'.[60] He knew of the desire in Canadian imperialist circles to ensure that volun-teers from Canada could enlist for the imperial cause. But Chamberlain did not want to settle for volunteers. He wanted an official commitment from Canada. He also wished to avoid the appearance of an imperial request for aid from the colonies, and was therefore reluctant to offer financial encouragement. But Laurier's recalcitrance induced Chamber-lain to propose imperial payment of colonial troops offered for imperial service. He appeared to accept volunteers, but mainly in order to em-barrass the Canadian government.

His behaviour infuriated the Laurier ministry. Yet they felt obliged to compromise. Minto increased the pressure by stressing how much they 'must depend upon [Britain's] good offices *re* Alaska, and no doubt in many other future questions'.[61] The Canadian government agreed to defray the expenses for equipping and transporting a thousand-man force of volunteers, large enough to maintain its Canadian identity rather than be absorbed in the British corps. The British military au-thorities did not want to accept a contingent of this size, but Chamber-lain prevailed upon them to do so. The Canadian force reached Cape Town on 30 October, a day before the deadline set by Chamberlain. Gracious in success, he asked Minto to assure Laurier 'that I fully appreciate his difficulties and am delighted that he was at last able to overcome them'.[62]

Meanwhile he pushed the tense interval between peace and war towards a close. On 9 October he gave the cabinet the final draft of the British ultimatum. It incorporated most of the recommendations of his colleagues. They kept the focus on the franchise, demanding 'repeal of all legislation since 1881 injuriously affecting the rights and privileges of aliens . . . accompanied by a measure of redistribution in some reasonable proportion to population'.[63] The Transvaal government was sure to reject these terms, which went well beyond the Smuts proposals. The ultimatum was nevertheless restrained. Its franchise demands were modified by an expression of willingness 'to prevent the old burghers from being immediately swamped by the new population'. If Pretoria accepted the demands of the ultimatum, the British government undertook 'to give a complete guarantee against any attack upon the independence of the South African Republic'. Even so, the ultimatum was sure to provoke a confrontation in Parliament with much if not all of the Liberal opposition. Chamberlain was confident that the public would sympathize with the government, but he regretted the prospective loss of bipartisan parliamentary support.

The afternoon that Chamberlain distributed this ultimatum to the cabinet, the Transvaal government gave him all the domestic and imperial support he could desire by issuing its own ultimatum. The Boer ultimatum was marked by military demands for the withdrawal of British troops on the borders of the republic, of the reinforcements that had reached South Africa since 1 June, and of those currently en route. Lord Lansdowne congratulated Chamberlain: 'I don't think Kruger could have played your cards better than he has.'[64] The British responded almost unanimously to the Boer ultimatum as intolerable. It undermined French Canadian opposition to participation in the war. There was no need now for the British ultimatum, and it was suppressed. Britain was free to formulate more stringent terms for the eventual peace. Chamberlain was euphoric. He assured the Queen that the delay in the arrival of the army corps from Britain 'will not be to our disadvantage as the peculiar organisation of the Boer army makes it difficult for them to endure a long campaign and it is even possible that many of them may go home to their farms without waiting for an attack'.[65]

He looked forward to the opening of Parliament, eager to crush his enemies. Trains converged upon Westminster 'full of politicians, some with an air of easy confidence' and soldiers 'who feared there would be no fighting, or that the War, if there was one, would soon be over'.[66] The brief session of Parliament revolved entirely around the Colonial Secretary. In addition to voting supplies for the impending war, there were questions about the imperial cable to connect Britain and Canada with Australia and about federation of the Australian colonies.

There was scarcely any question about voting supplies. Still, the Little England wing of the Liberal party questioned the original necessity for the war. Their spokesmen concentrated on Chamberlain's conduct of the negotiations. They censured his failure to make the extent of his acceptance of the Smuts offer clearer. They also criticized his rhetoric about the Kruger government, the offensive language of his so-called 'new diplomacy'. Chamberlain replied that, whatever might have been true in the days of monarchical or aristocratic government, '[w]e speak now as representatives of people on all sides, and peoples have the right to demand from us that our views, whether right or wrong, shall be made clearly apparent to them so that there shall be no reasonable ground for misunderstanding'.[67] Looking back over the months and years of negotiation with the Transvaal, he concluded that the conflict between the two states was fundamental and war inevitable. What struck him in retrospect was the persistent endeavour of the Transvaal since 1881 to widen its freedom to the point of complete independence and escape from any shadow of British paramountcy. If so, and if Britain was right to maintain its paramountcy as most Liberals agreed, then the details of the prewar diplomacy were unimportant.

His argument won national support. The Liberal imperialist Sir Edward Grey praised Chamberlain's speech as 'the fairest and most telling exposition of the relations between Great Britain and the Transvaal I have yet seen'.[68] The Liberal opposition split three ways on the Little Englander motion of criticism, some voting for it, some voting with the government, and some led by Campbell-Bannerman abstaining.

The dividends of disaster

The coming of the war marked an inevitable watershed for Chamberlain. If the war had produced the quick victory he anticipated, it would have confirmed his imperial policy and allowed him to address the social needs with which he sensed the British public were more concerned. But from the outset the war did not go well. The difficulties which enmired Britain, and the stunning fighting power of the Boers, blighted the imperial cause to which Chamberlain then committed himself more intensely.

The complex impact of the war was apparent from the first bad news, the British surrender at Nicholson's Nek in Natal near the Transvaal border at the end of October. The setback unleashed 'violent imperial passions'[69] in Australia and virtually eliminated opposition there to the war effort. A weaker version of the same reaction occurred in Canada. But in Britain Liberals draw satisfaction from the military embarrassment. Though Campbell-Bannerman had refused to approve of any build-up before the war, he now blamed the government for failure to prepare militarily for the consequences of its South African policy. Liberals of every shade found pleasure in the discomfiture particularly of Chamberlain.

He was sensitive to all these reactions. He relished the martial ardour of the colonies. He enjoyed praise at home from supporters like the writer to *The Times* who lauded his 'striking ability' and 'subordination of personal advantage to patriotic duty'.[70] But Chamberlain was shocked to discover once again the 'terrible amount of hatred' he had accumulated 'during the home rule fight'.[71] He was 'sickened by the special malignity with which my political opponents . . . attempt to single me out from all my colleagues and to impugn my private character & personal honour'.[72]

The government was slow to reorder its agenda. Until 'Black Week' in December when the British lost three battles in a row, the cabinet devoted much of its attention to its purportedly main proposal for the new year's session of Parliament, an old-age pensions scheme. But after Black Week Chamberlain predicted bleakly that 'we shall do no business next session but simply wrangle over the war'.[73] The British defeats set back his plans for civil reconstruction in South Africa as well as for social reform at home. Once the war broke out, he left its conduct to the generals. He meant to devote his attention to the postwar constitution to be imposed upon the allied Boer republics, the Orange Free State as well as the Transvaal. Belying the accusations of his critic J.A. Hobson, Chamberlain did not shape his South African policy hand-in-glove with the mining interests. They were disconcerted by the distance he kept from them, and learned to expect more sympathy from Milner. Nor was Chamberlain as anxious to annex the republics as Little Englanders assumed. Annexation meant full imperial control, which he thought impolitic for more than a limited period of transition.

All this was clear from the report which Percy Fitzpatrick from the mining firm of Wernher, Beit and Eckstein sent to South Africa. To Fitzpatrick's annoyance, Chamberlain sought his opinion at first in typewritten form and agreed to meet him only when Fitzpatrick refused written communication as 'very unfair to Wernher-Beit'.[74] When the two men met, as Fitzpatrick reported to his partners, Chamberlain explained that some members of the government wanted

> to leave the Republics as 'protected' states—i.e. castrate them but let them preserve the name & forms of Republics. I opposed this most strongly. . . . We discussed alternative schemes, Responsible Govt. or Crown Colony. I know you would prefer the latter—so would I, for some time. But he says the Govt. dare not propose that, but he admitted they could decide in principle & promise Responsible Government

but delay the grant until the country is completely settled and reorganized & he agreed that 2 years might be so covered.

Chamberlain also indicated that he was 'dead against pushing any federation' of Britain's colonies and dependencies in South Africa until British loyalists acquired firm control of the Cape Colony. That indeed was his concern for every state in the region. He expected the Transvaal to have a large British majority 'in the course of a year or so'.[75] Though willing to gratify the desire of Natal for some Boer territory, he was anxious to avoid placing the British majority in that colony in any jeopardy. He was perplexed about the Orange Free State, which was sure to remain predominantly Boer for the foreseeable future. All this planning was speculative, dependent on the outcome of the war. But for two months Chamberlain retained 'an optimistic feeling that if we can only get some great victory', the Boer attack would 'suddenly collapse'.[76] That optimism was shattered by Black Week.

Chamberlain's dismay was deepened by the response from Germany to a renewed overture he made for closer understanding. Through most of 1899, relations among the three industrial powers which Chamberlain hoped to bring into concert—Germany, Britain and the United States—revolved around the Samoan Islands in the South Pacific which they jointly occupied. The value of the islands was primarily naval: they lay astride the sea lanes from Australasia to North America. With the acquisition of Hawaii and the Philippines, the United States was extending its influence over the entire Pacific. Britain's Australasian colonies, particularly New Zealand, had a lively interest in the Samoan Islands. Their attraction to Germany was sentimental as well as naval. Imperialists like the Kaiser treasured the islands as the first of Germany's overseas colonies. The advocates of a German navy, led by Admiral Tirpitz, dilated on their strategic worth.

The anti-British strategy of Tirpitz and his school was not yet clear even in Germany. Chamberlain did not discern its menace. His interest in agreement with Germany survived the disappointing negotiations over the Portuguese possessions in Africa. Nothing diminished his uneasiness at the vulnerability of Britain resulting from its diplomatic isolation. The Anglo-German treaty on Portugal did not entirely dispose even of the possibility of German intervention on the Boer side in the event of war between Britain and the Transvaal. Accordingly, in the spring of 1899, Chamberlain was quick to respond to German interest in a *modus vivendi* among the three occupying powers in Samoa.

In September, Germany sought to take advantage of the impending war between Britain and the Transvaal by extending its hold on Samoa at the expense of the New Zealanders. Chamberlain did not take kindly to German exploitation of the situation. 'The policy of the German

Emperor since Bismarck', he observed to Salisbury, 'has always been one of undisguised blackmail.'[77] Yet Chamberlain did not hesitate to subordinate imperial and colonial interest in the South Pacific to the need for a free hand in South Africa. He tried to divert German attention from Samoa by offering generous compensation in West Africa. He indicated that if Germany insisted on Samoa, it would have to compensate Britain generously elsewhere. But on such terms he was ready if need be, as he told Salisbury, to surrender Samoa 'to pay . . . for the German Emperor's support—or neutrality' in South Africa.

And so it turned out. Overcoming the distaste Salisbury felt at the German conduct, Chamberlain secured an agreement with Germany a month after the Boer war broke out. Britain surrendered its share of Samoa to Germany but received compensation in three forms: territory elsewhere in Africa and the South Pacific, freedom of trade for Britain in all areas touched by the treaty, and an official demonstration of German goodwill towards Britain. The German emperor had backed up his demand for Samoa by threatening to cancel a visit he planned to his grandmother, Queen Victoria. That visit now took place. Its occurrence in November was particularly sweet for Britain because a torrent of criticism had descended on it from Continental Europe for pitting all the resources of the British empire against a few thousand Dutch-speaking farmers. Chamberlain was as sensitive to popular criticism from the Continent as at home. 'The Continental Press is disgusting,' he told an old friend; 'It will some day irritate opinion here to such an extent that war will be accepted joyfully.'[78]

The promise of the Anglo-German agreement on Samoa as Chamberlain saw it was expressed by Baron Eckhardtstein, who worked with him to bring it about. In the midst of their negotiations, Eckhardtstein reflected that 'If we come to an agreement on the basis you have suggested, there is nothing left except commercial competition, which could not possibly interfere with the relations of the two countries.'[79] On the eve of the signature of the agreement, Eckhardtstein gave Chamberlain the thanks of the German government for his 'great help in bringing about an arrangement between England and Germany which does not only settle the Samoa question, but abolishes every colonial antagonism between the two countries'.[80]

Bülow as German foreign minister accompanied the Kaiser on his visit to Windsor. Chamberlain welcomed the opportunity to meet the two German leaders. The opportunity was all the greater because Salisbury, with whom the visitors would otherwise have had their most substantial conversations, was kept away by the death of his wife. The permanent officials of the Foreign Office feared the intervention of Chamberlain and cringed at his lack of finesse. 'We can only hope that Birmingham has not given himself away,' Salisbury's assistant undersecretary wrote to the private secretary of the Queen as soon as the discussions at Windsor ended; '. . . He is of a very sanguine temperament. He knows what he wants, but he does not appreciate the difficulties of realizing his fond hopes.'[81]

These fears were all too well founded. Prompted by Bülow, the Kaiser punctured Chamberlain's inflated talk of alliance. Bülow parried Chamberlain's enthusiasm with restrained words of appreciation for his friendship towards Germany. Mistaking the signal, Chamberlain asked eagerly, 'What else can be done?'[82] Loath to propose anything concrete, Bülow suggested that Chamberlain might use his public opportunities to envelop Germany in the climate of goodwill which seemed to exist between Britain and the United States.

Chamberlain left Windsor for Leicester, where he was due to deliver two speeches. Magnifying the meagre encouragement he received from the German leaders, he spoke in Leicester of 'a new Triple Alliance between the Teutonic race and two great branches of the Anglo-Saxon race'.[83] He began with the relationship between Britain and the United States, pointing out the similarity between the current Anglo-Boer war and the recent Spanish-American war. Turning to Germany, he asserted that the immediate conflicts dividing it from Britain had been removed. Friendship between these two Continental powers was, he claimed, almost as natural as between the two English-speaking Atlantic powers:

> the same sentiments which bring us into close sympathy with the United States of America may also be evoked to bring us into closer sympathy and alliance with the Empire of Germany. What do we find? We find our system of justice, we find our literature, we find the very base and foundation on which our language is established the same in the two countries.

He kept on using the heavy word 'alliance'. It was no use adding, as he did, that the term 'understanding' would do as well if not indeed better because 'understanding' implied something broader and more flexible than a treaty. He did not hide his desire for solid agreements as well as for broad sympathy from Germany and the United States to alleviate Britain's isolation.

In the United States, his talk of alliance roused opponents and found no defenders. Even so, the McKinley administration appreciated Britain's benevolent neutrality during the Spanish-American war, and maintained a similar stance towards Britain in its colonial war. German reaction to Chamberlain's speech was more hostile. The popular press in Germany sneered at his appeal. Bülow confined his public response to 'le plus stricte necessaire'.[84] The Leicester speech was particularly inopportune from his point of view because he was about to seek support from the Reichstag for a large increase in the navy to enable

Germany to stand up to Britain on the seas. Chamberlain's disappointment was not alleviated by private assurance from Bülow 'that His
Majesty and he are absolutely at one in their desire to bring about a
permanent and perfect understanding between the two countries'.[85]

On the Friday before Bülow delivered his public reply, the cabinet
deliberated for the last time that year on old-age pensions. Chamberlain
hurried away from the meeting to catch the train for Birmingham and
speak at the distribution of prizes for the municipal School of Art.
Heading straight from New Street station to the town hall, he spoke
under the eye of William Kenrick, his friend who loved art for art's
sake more than for its utility. Chamberlain did not quite agree. Leaving
art to the genius, Chamberlain encouraged the school 'to educate first-
rate craftsmen . . . it is', he said, 'a much nobler task to strive successfully to add grace and beauty to the accessories of our ordinary human
life than to fail ignominiously in producing masterpieces'.[86] Demonstrating nevertheless that he had learned something via Kenrick from
the Pre-Raphaelites, Chamberlain contrasted the wide distribution of
wealth in English society since the reign of Queen Anne with the deterioration in the aesthetic quality of household goods over the same
period. Items once made by skilled craftsmen for the affluent were now
produced in debased form by machine for the mass market. Chamberlain urged his listeners to do what they could to elevate the artistic
quality of mass-produced goods.

At that point, his gift for words deserted him. Shaken by his unhappy
use of the term 'alliance', he groped for the right word to make a point.
He began his sentence several times only to break it off. He turned to
his wife for help, and was rescued by a sympathetic cheer from his
audience. At that, abandoning his search for the elusive word, he
summed up his theme: 'If you can even in the slightest degree introduce into [the ordinary] man's life the element of art, there comes with
it all the freshness of originality, the pleasure of imagination, and the
individual interest which will add so much life to the humblest work.'

After resting for the weekend in Highbury, he turned to the emerging
University of Birmingham. His objectives there were akin to those for
the School of Art. He did not want the university 'to neglect in any way
the older learning,' he explained. 'But beyond this we desire to sys-
tematise & develop the special training . . . required by . . . those
who . . . conduct the great industrial undertakings in the midst of which
our work will be done.'[87] Fund-raising for the university failed to reach
the target of £300,000 so long as Parliament held Chamberlain in London. When he returned to Birmingham at the end of August, he learned
that a special canvass for the final £25,000 had produced a mere £1,500.
He turned once again to the members of his family and the businessmen of the city who were most committed to the new university. Con-

vening them 'in a scene of excitement never to be forgotten',[88] he dug into his own pocket and they into theirs. They exceeded the target substantially before the war broke out.

The one solid achievement of which Chamberlain could be sure at the end of 1899 was the creation of the University of Birmingham. Its successful birth owed something to the Boer War. Writing to Chamberlain shortly after its outbreak, Lord Strathcona observed: 'notwithstanding the interest I take in Higher Education, I should hardly have been led to move in the matter in the case of a Town or City less attached to the cause of Union and the Unity of the Empire, than Birmingham has happily been under your guidance'.[89]

The news of Black Week descended on Chamberlain at Highbury. He was already dismayed by earlier setbacks. In November he asked, 'Is it possible that 26,000 British on the defence are not a match for 28,000 Boers on the aggressive? . . . Is our artillery (of which we were so secure) worse than theirs?'[90] Early in December he foresaw that 'As long as [the Boers] can shoot down our men & run away to fight again another day, they may continue the war indefinitely'.[91] After Black Week, Chamberlain confessed that he was 'broken in spirit'.[92]

His spirit soon revived. Overcoming his diffidence on military matters, he pounded the Secretary for War with suggestions, to cut the Transvaal's telegraph and railway links to Delagoa Bay, and for 'a sort of Sherman's "March through Georgia"' in the Orange Free State.[93] Still, the days of euphoria were over. Chamberlain's mood settled into sober determination, as he reported in a Christmas letter to his American mother-in-law:

> . . . we have a hard job before us—more difficult than we thought . . . we are fighting some 60000 horsemen, of one of the dourest races in the world, in their own country, each man equal to two or three owing to their mobility, all good shots & able to live with very little transport in a climate which from the excessive heat & drought is most trying to British soldiers. . . .
>
> So it happens that although we have sent out the largest army that ever left these shores & must have at least 60000 men with 50000 more on the way, we are in a minority whenever we come to blows owing to the numbers left on the road as guards—or if not actually a minority we are at least too weak to attack successfully strongly entrenched positions.
>
> The next few weeks must be a very anxious time. They will show whether we can relieve the beleaguered garrisons & to what extent the rebellion will spread in Cape Colony, but whether we are successful or whether we have to face further sacrifices I do not doubt the result in the end.[94]

16

The Business of War
1900–1902

I have the lowest opinion of Army administration. Whenever I can test it—Contracts for instance—it is most ludicrously inefficient.

Chamberlain to Dilke, 24 January 1884

No one had expected the new century to begin with a war that demanded more of Britain than its last great fight in the Crimea. Chamberlain found comfort in reading of the troubles the Duke of Wellington encountered in the Peninsular war against the lieutenants of Napoleon. No essentially imperial war had been so serious since the loss of the American colonies.

The war in South Africa was inextricably tied to Chamberlain and his purposes. Whether for blame or praise, he was the focus of attention. Milner might be more responsible for the outbreak of the war, but that possibility was discounted in South Africa and scarcely discerned in Britain. Salisbury disclaimed responsibility by referring to the conflict privately as 'Joe's war'. All of the factions into which the Liberal opposition was divided linked Chamberlain with what they identified as the discreditable features of the conflict. Little Englanders raised questions again about his complicity in the Jameson raid which, they said, led to the war by exacerbating Boer suspicions of the British. Liberal Imperialists criticized his ham-fisted conduct of diplomatic negotiations. On the other hand, those who shared the national and imperial sense of purpose in the Boer War looked to Chamberlain as their leader. The chief civil servant at the Colonial Office observed that Chamberlain was 'consulted, encouraged, abused & applauded from every quarter of the Globe. There is a very prevalent notion that *he* is the Government, so that he gets a mass of letters which should be addressed to other Departments.'[1]

The gravity of the war damaged his imperialism. In a cost-conscious political economy like Britain's, the worth of any policy that entailed serious warfare was doubtful. Yet the war offered some impressive dividends. It evoked a response in the self-governing colonies outside South Africa that disconcerted Liberal critics. Within Britain there was quite enough popular support for the war in the face of repeated military setbacks to remove doubts about the compatibility between assertive imperialism and popular government.

The war elicited popular support, however, on both sides of the fighting, among the Afrikaners as well as the British. And thus the war accentuated the dilemma at the heart of democratic imperialism. British imperialism might appeal to the British as amplified patriotism. It had an ambivalent appeal to citizens of British descent in the self-governing colonies. While they felt proud of their part in 'Greater Britain', the preeminence of Britain in that association threatened the aspirations of the colonies towards independent greatness. For those of different national descent, for example among French Canadians, imperial patriotism was weak. Among the Cape Dutch, it was commonly replaced by the rival sentiment of Afrikaner nationalism, which the Boer War intensified.

Afrikaners took pride in the early Boer victories. They also removed doubts on the other side about the justice of the British cause, for it looked as though the well-prepared Boers 'had all along meant to attack Britain'.[2] These sentiments might have subsided once the struggle reached a natural military conclusion. It was the eruption afterwards of a long guerrilla war that hardened Afrikaner hearts and disheartened the British. But before that, early in 1900, the ethnic tension which the war exacerbated in the Cape Colony menaced the civil order of the empire and upset the accord between Chamberlain and Milner.

The ugliest consequence of Black Week from Chamberlain's point of view was the encouragement it gave the Cape Dutch to support the Boer invaders. Cape Dutch recruits increased the troop strength of the republics—and the Transvaal had stockpiled arms for this eventuality. But the threat that the Cape Dutch defection posed to the British empire was less serious militarily than politically. The burghers of the Boer republics, who continued to constitute the main military threat, were straightforward enemies. Their Cape Dutch supporters were rebels. Their rebellion cast an unbecoming light on the supposed blessings of self-governing British colonial rule. Far from powerless politically, the Cape Dutch commanded the support of more than half the colonial legislature. No executive could long survive without their acquiescence. The balance of sentiment among them on the war was impossible to ascertain exactly. Only a minority actually fought for the Boers. But fewer fought for the British. Kinship and culture made the middling majority sympathetic towards the Boers or at least neutralized the pull of imperial patriotism. Milner wrote off ninety per cent as rebels.

The Cape Dutch defection drove a spear into the joints of Chamberlain's democratic imperialism. Though he remained forever a democrat at home, Ireland had taught him to question the applicability of democracy to the empire. Before becoming Colonial Secretary, he warned Liberal Unionists that

> the great principle that the majority must rule ... will carry you a long way. Of course it will carry you to absolute separation, if the Irish ask for it, and ... there is not the slightest doubt that they will ask for it as soon as they have the leverage which Home Rule will give them. It will carry you in foreign politics to the surrender of Gibraltar, to the withdrawal from Egypt, and to the abandonment of India. In all these cases, if you will consult the people themselves, I do not doubt that they would vote by a considerable majority to get rid of us.[3]

Yet he remained convinced that popular parliamentary support for the empire within the self-governing colonies was not only desirable in principle but indispensable in practice. If the empire had to rely on local agencies like the Chartered Company of Rhodes to cultivate the outer reaches of the empire, how much more did it have to rely on local electoral cooperation in the white settler colonies. Furthermore, the respect which parliamentary government commanded among Unionists as well as Liberals in Britain made any violation of those institutions in the self-governing colonies extremely perilous at Westminster. Chamberlain was quite willing to give the self-governing colonies a strong, even high-handed lead, as his solicitation of 'spontaneous' offers of troops for the war showed. But he drew the line when Milner sought to disfranchise enough of the Cape Dutch to put British loyalists in control of the Cape Colony.

While the war did not worsen Chamberlain's judgement in imperial matters, it numbed his interest in social legislation without stimulating his imagination on military affairs. He was impressed by the ability of the War Office, unrivalled in this regard by its Continental counterparts, to despatch more than a hundred thousand men to South Africa within four months in what still stands as 'an almost flawless mobilisation'.[4] He was not inclined to blame the generals for their setbacks in battle, though their incompetence reached a climax in January under the hapless General Buller at Spion Kop. What puzzled Chamberlain was the consistent ability of Boers to beat larger numbers of British soldiers. Lord Wolseley, the commander-in-chief in London before the war, asserted that professional British troops with maxim guns could overcome untrained Boers twice their number. It was painfully apparent to Chamberlain by the new year that, fighting on his native turf, 'one Boer [was] worth three or four English'.[5] He appreciated the mobility of the Boers without baggage trains or heavy personal equipment.

But it took him, like the professionals at army headquarters, longer to recognize that the sweeping advances and machine guns which mowed down the Sudanese along the Nile would not do against sharp-shooting Boers camouflaged in broken terrain which they knew well. The need for civilian leadership to shake up the soldiers at headquarters and at the front never impressed itself on Chamberlain. This gap in his imagination proved politically costly. It allowed the opportunity to pass to Balfour.

The strains of recovery

Chamberlain did 'not look forward' to the opening of Parliament in 1900 'with much pleasure'.[6] The Liberals had plenty of scope to criticize the government for precipitating a war it was not prepared to fight. Balfour, who happened to be the only member of the cabinet with major speaking engagements between Black Week and the opening of Parliament, deepened the disrepute of the government by failing candidly to accept some responsibility for the military shortcomings. There was reason to wonder whether the government would lose the confidence of the House of Commons and fall.

Chamberlain rose to the parliamentary challenge with a performance even Little Englanders found impressive. The Liberals had submerged their internal divisions with a motion censuring the government for its want of judgement in connection with the war. Chamberlain turned their agreement against them, contrasting it with the consensus in the country that the war was a patriotic duty:

> whatever we may feel—humiliation if you please—at the defects which have been disclosed, that humiliation must be accompanied by the deepest pride. . . . Reverses try the temper of a nation, and our people have borne the test.[7]

He extended the claim to the empire at large: 'every reverse has only been the signal for new offers from our fellow-subjects across the seas'. He used this phenomenon to vindicate his general policy of assertive imperialism, refuting the Liberal claim that the colonies preferred to be left to go their own way.

> What has brought these younger nations of Greater Britain . . . to spring to arms even before you called upon them?
> Sir John Brunner: Liberal policy
> Chamberlain: It is that imperial instinct which you deride and scorn. Our colonies, repelled in the past by indifference and apathy, have responded to the sympathy which has recently been shown to them.

Drawing still more from the response of the self-governing colonies, he declared,

> I will never believe that these free communities would have given their support and approval to any cause which was not just and righteous and which was not based on the principles on which their own institutions have been founded.

His reading of the public mind in England was borne out in a by-election at York, usually a marginal constituency, which the Conservatives carried by a large majority. But Chamberlain's assessment of public opinion was not reliable when it came to Afrikaners. He came to admire the martial daring of the Boers; but his admiration persuaded him that the scars from such honourable conflict would not long outlive its termination. 'When matters have settled down,' he assured the Commons, 'when equal rights are assured to both the white races, I believe that both will enjoy the land together and settle in peace and prosperity.' It was a fond hope, and would be eroded by protracted fighting.

There was a double edge to Chamberlain's imperial rhetoric. He appealed for support in patriotic terms intended, as he said, to transcend partisan divisions. Yet he was only too happy to use the support he thus won for partisan purposes. The imperial emergency turned his impatience with opposition into intolerance. He looked not just for understanding from his opponents but for praise; and when they failed to meet his expectations, he turned on them as dishonourable. Inevitably they compounded the bitterness by treating him as he treated them.

Their venom was fuelled by the publication in Belgium of some of the 'missing telegrams' from the Jameson raid. Purloined from the office of Rhodes's lawyer Hawksley, the telegrams in the *Indépendence Belge* added nothing material to the information available to the parliamentary investigation which Harcourt had in effect led in 1897. Yet they served to sever the friendship Harcourt and Chamberlain had preserved since their separation over Home Rule. The deepened retrospective seriousness which the Boer War lent to the Jameson raid induced Harcourt to support the demand for a new inquiry. Chamberlain branded Harcourt's involvement in 'this conspiracy against the reputation of a single man' as 'dirty work'.[8]

These embittered divisions reached around the country. Word that Chamberlain was to be guest of honour at a dinner given by Methodist leaders in Wesley's Chapel prompted even Liberal imperialists to protest. Those who invited Chamberlain thought they were simply rising to the national occasion. They were taken aback by the cry that Chamberlain's policy in South Africa was 'directly opposed to the teachings of Jesus'.[9] The hosts for the dinner hoped that Chamberlain would save them from embarrassment by stating that pressure of work would prevent him from attending. Contemptuous of such weak patriotism, he deepened their embarrassment by insisting on a public exchange of letters in which they made their request and he complied. He was confident that 'the great majority of Methodists' in England and virtually all of them in Cape Colony and Natal believed in the justice of the war;[10] and he secured outspoken demonstrations of Wesleyan support. But the affair left a nasty taste all round.

When he spoke at the opening of Parliament, he had nothing to raise the spirits of his supporters but his words. 'We do not get on very quickly in S. Africa,' he admitted privately; '. . . I sh[ould]. like to sleep for a month & then see what has been done.'[11] Within a week the fortunes of war changed. The new commander in South Africa, Lord Roberts, struck northward into the Orange Free State. His strategy was rewarded with a string of successes, including the relief of the besieged towns of Kimberley and Ladysmith and the first significant British capture of Boer troops.

From the bleak days of winter through the brightening spring, Chamberlain wrestled with the problems of wartime government in the Cape Colony and plans for the postwar settlement elsewhere in South Africa. The wintertime setbacks stiffened his terms for the postwar order. Britain had gone to war asserting that its paramountcy over the Boer republics could be secured without destroying their independence. That assumption was shaken by exposure to the arsenal the Transvaal had built up for itself and by the price Britain had to pay in blood and treasure to overcome it. Chamberlain remained uneasy about outright annexation of the republics until Black Week. Afterwards he told his colleagues that to restore even the appearance of independence would encourage the republics 'constantly . . . to endeavour to secure the substance' of 'the Africander [sic] ambitions which have produced the present state of things'.[12] He insisted that the republics be placed under the rule of a civil or military governor until Britain could safely grant them the self-governing powers enjoyed by other white settler colonies in the empire.

His recommendations did not differ conspicuously from the views of Milner. More detached than Milner from settler opinion in South Africa, Chamberlain committed himself more firmly to enfranchisement of natives in the Boer republics on the same basis as in the Cape Colony. Concerned like Milner to ensure British supremacy throughout the region, Chamberlain discouraged any idea of regional federation 'until there is a clear British majority with a British Government in four at least of the five States of British South Africa'. Towards that end and also to deal with Milner's troubles at the Cape, Chamberlain toyed with the idea of adding predominantly Dutch areas in the Cape Colony to the Orange Free State, leaving the Cape and the Transvaal in predominantly British hands.

Still, Chamberlain often found Milner harder to deal with than the Afrikaners. The Boer invasion of the Cape Colony and the support they received among the Cape Dutch exhausted what little patience Milner had with the mixed Dutch-British ministry at the Cape led by W.P. Schreiner. By the end of 1899 Milner wanted to get rid of it. He bombarded Chamberlain with pleas, if not to suspend the Cape constitution, at least to disfranchise the districts which had been overrun by invaders and to call a general election in the colony on that basis. 'It is', cried Milner, surely 'out of the question that . . . the people of districts wh[ich]. have revolted almost *en masse* . . . should be allowed, as soon as they have done shooting at the Imperial forces, to turn quietly round and resume the game of disloyalty by the old constitutional means.' Chamberlain persistently rejected these recommendations. A seasoned analyst of electoral returns, he suspected that regional disfranchisement might not produce 'a British and loyal majority'.[13] He knew that suspension of the Cape constitution would lose him the support of some Liberals in the House of Commons who were otherwise 'at one with the Government in the prosecution of the war to a satisfactory settlement'.[14] He was fearful of the kind of ministry Milner wanted at the Cape 'representing the exclusively British section', and thought on the contrary that 'the selection of a Ministry of Moderates would present considerable advantages'. Recognizing that Milner's worries had as much to do with the postwar settlement for the region as with the immediate situation in the Cape, Chamberlain suggested dividing the Transvaal into two provinces, one British, the other Boer.

In mid-May, Chamberlain announced the government's terms for peace. With the army under Lord Roberts at last in the Transvaal on its way to Johannesburg, Chamberlain and his colleagues demanded incorporation of the Boer republics within the empire under crown colonial government until 'it is safe . . . to introduce these States into the great circle of self-governing colonies'.[15]

The mining interests of the Rand had been pressing Chamberlain from the outset of the war to agree to annexation. Now that he had done so, he confronted the Randlords with his bill. He asked for a substantial sum, no less than £25,000,000, mainly to provide compensation in South Africa for injuries caused by the war but also to defray some of Britain's wartime expenses. When Percy Fitzpatrick baulked, Chamberlain responded stiffly, 'I am not going to take less from you than Kruger did', though Chamberlain also promised to provide 'the benefits of good administration'.[16] He was no more forthcoming when Fitzpatrick asked for imperial help for the Transvaal and its mines in raising loans after the war to pay for improved transportation and other public works. The Colonial Secretary knew all too well how averse the Treasury was to developmental loans, to say nothing of its horror at the costs of the war.

Two days before Chamberlain met Fitzpatrick, Lord Roberts marched into Pretoria. His progress precipitated a change of ministry at the Cape. The prospective ending of the war lent urgency to the question of amnesty for the Cape Dutch rebels and strengthened the loyalist British sentiment in favour of punishment as against the Afrikaner wish for leniency. The upshot, which Chamberlain connived to facilitate, was the replacement of Schreiner as prime minister by Sir Gordon Sprigg, whom Chamberlain knew from the Colonial Conference of 1897.

In the self-governing colonies outside South Africa, the war raised Chamberlain's hopes only to perplex him. Participation in the war fostered the imperial patriotism he so wished to cultivate. But the sentiment worked two ways in the colonies. It made them proud of themselves as well as of the empire, and thus frustrated as much as it encouraged plans for imperial consolidation. The war also accentuated ethnic divisions, particularly between French and English in Canada, which made consolidation still more difficult.

No matter how heavy-handedly Chamberlain had contrived to elicit offers of military help from the self-governing colonies before the war, once it began there could be little doubt of the spontaneity with which they doubled and redoubled their contingents for service in South Africa. By the beginning of 1900, the number of colonial troops on service there exceeded the number of British at the battle of Waterloo; and more were to come. Their accomplishment on the battlefield generated pride back home. When Lord Roberts congratulated the Canadians on their contribution to the first capture of Boer troops at the battle of Paardeberg, Laurier asked the Canadian House of Commons, 'is there a man whose bosom does not swell with pride . . . that . . . the fact has been revealed to the world that a new power has arisen in the west?'[17]

These swelling sentiments raised Chamberlain's hopes for some consolidation of the empire, though he did not entirely overlook the deflating ethnic crosscurrents. The former British commander of the Canadian militia, General Hutton, passed through London en route to South Africa, and interested Chamberlain in 'a Militia system of Co-operative Defence applicable to the whole empire'.[18] Though Chamberlain inquired anxiously about 'the racial differences of opinion' between French and English Canadians, he welcomed the proposal.

He referred its military substance to Balfour. Addressing himself to the imperial opportunity, Chamberlain wrote to the governor-general in Canada, Lord Minto, suggesting two constitutional innovations. One was to include advisers from Canada and Australia on an imperial commission which Chamberlain proposed to set up on the terms for peace and postwar settlement in South Africa. He made it quite clear, however, that 'we could not undertake to be guided by the views of Canadian or Australian representatives if these should differ from those of the loyal colonists at the Cape & Natal and of the majority in this country'.[19] His other proposal was more tentative but also more substantial. Chamberlain asked 'whether the time has not now come for the creation of something in the nature of an Imperial Council sitting permanently in London and acting as permanent advisers to the Secretary of State for the Colonies'. He suggested directing the attention of this council in the first instance to Hutton's scheme for a cooperative imperial militia and to 'all schemes for the naval defence of the Empire'. Aware that Laurier might not welcome his proposal, Chamberlain encouraged Minto to discuss it with leaders of the Conservative opposition and influential independents in Canada as well as with the prime minister. Still, what Chamberlain sought was official as well as popular encouragement from Canada to place the proposal before a conference of premiers of the self-governing colonies. Over the next few days he elaborated his suggestion and sent it to the Australian governors for canvassing in their colonies.

Before these ideas could reach Laurier, the Canadian prime minister used words in his House of Commons which boosted Chamberlain's hopes. Yet the object of the Canadian leader diverged widely from that of the British Colonial Secretary. Seeking to allay French Canadian alarm at the precedent set by the Boer War for Canadian involvement in Britain's imperial wars, Laurier argued that Canada would first have the right to tell Britain, 'If you want us to help you, call us to your councils.'[20] At these words, Chamberlain rejoiced: 'the war—with all its losses & sacrifices—has yet brought us in a few months further on our way to a true conception of Empire than a whole generation of peace'.[21] He was not carried away completely. When disciples of Rosebery in the British House of Commons introduced a motion envisaging direct colonial representation in the imperial Parliament, Chamberlain curbed their zeal, afraid that it would frighten the likes of Laurier away from more modest advances.

But he was pushing too fast himself. He was soon pulled back. Minto reported that Chamberlain had misunderstood Laurier. The Canadian premier was first and foremost a Canadian nationalist, Minto explained, and was not animated by 'the British feeling for a united Empire'.[22] Laurier had to accommodate the imperial sentiments of English Canadians, but in so doing he meant to draw Canada, not the British empire, together. Minto tried to end on an encouraging note. He reported that Laurier thought 'the arrangement of tariff questions' was 'far more likely to bring about imperial unity than any joint system of imperial defence'. Otherwise the governor-general had nothing heartening to report. Even Chamberlain's old friend, the Canadian Conservative Sir Charles Tupper, attempted to discredit Laurier among French Canadians by accusing him of favouring tighter links with Britain.

The warmest support for an imperial council came from Australasia, where the flow of volunteers for the war was also greatest. Yet in federating with each other, these colonies threatened one of the few existing institutions that bound the empire together. Chamberlain was the latest in a line of Colonial Secretaries who encouraged regional federation among settler colonies to lift them beyond parochial disputes towards consolidation of the empire. But these intermediate federations generated intermediate loyalties, colonial nationalisms, which strained the bonds of empire. Sentiment in the colonies of Australia was sufficiently unsettled in their hour of federation to allow Chamberlain to maintain imperial features in the federal constitution. But he found it uphill work.

In the spring of 1900, after years of controversy and haggling in convention, the nation builders of Australia came up with a constitutional settlement which they wanted the British Parliament to accept as a package. Chamberlain wanted to accommodate the fledgling nation, and he swallowed his disappointment at being unable to put the finishing touches to its constitution. But he drew the line at the clause in the constitutional bill which restricted the right of appeal to the Judicial Committee of the Privy Council, the body that functioned as supreme appeals court for the empire. The Australians wanted their constitution to be interpreted by their own high court, familiar with the local situation, and not by a British court half a world away. Chamberlain had to restrain such centrifugal forces if the empire was to have a solid centre. He hoped to solve the problem in this case by combining the appellate authorities of the Privy Council and the House of Lords and by securing permanent representation from the self-governing colonies on the combined court. But in the meantime he did not want to do anything to diminish the jurisdiction of the imperial court as currently constituted.

The delegates of the federating colonies of Australia came with their bill to London insisting that they could not accept any amendments. Chamberlain did not deny that they enjoyed strong support in Australia for the clause he wished to contest. But he used whatever shades of resistance he could discover in Australia to fortify his stance on behalf of the empire. He appealed to the colonial premiers in Australia against the *non possumus* of the delegates in London. He voiced the concerns of trading and financial interests in Australia and Britain. He exploited opposition from New Zealand and Western Australia to restrictions on appeals to the Privy Council, even though New Zealand would not and Western Australia might not join the federation. He wooed one of the state delegates in London over to his side. Then he could claim that three of the seven Australasian states agreed with him. When he made his opposition to the offending clause public knowledge, the first reactions from Australia were calm—which Chamberlain interpreted as acquiescence.

He may have been right. The strongest opposition in Australia to imperial claims came from recent immigrants, particularly those from Germany and above all Ireland, rather than from those born in the sub-continent. The delegates in London eventually agreed to a compromise which limited the restriction on the right of appeal to the Privy Council to cases between member states or between a state and the federal government about the interpretation of the constitution; and in special circumstances even these cases could be the subject of appeal to the Privy Council. The agreement was a genuine compromise. Both Chamberlain and the Australian delegates conceded more than they wished. The balance of advantage in the settlement was to Chamberlain, but it did not bode well for his hopes of further imperial consolidation.

Reaping the fruits

He was nevertheless in a sunny frame of mind by midsummer 1900. The war seemed set for a victorious conclusion. It was being won more slowly and at greater cost than anyone in official position had estimated at the outset. Yet the dividends for the empire also were greater than anticipated. And at home the public had demonstrated its willingness to sustain a costly war.

All that remained was to ensure that this national support remained in effect at the end to secure the objectives for which the war was fought. As soon as the government announced its intention to annex the Boer republics, Liberals challenged the decision. Chamberlain returned the challenge by suggesting a general election. Happy to identify the Unionist party with the war effort, he wanted to prevent the Liberals from squandering the fruits of the expected victory and to discourage the Boers from fighting on in the hope of better terms with a change of government in Britain. He was confident that the Unionists could repeat their great victory of 1895. His confidence was fortified by the divided opposition. Voting on the Colonial Office estimates, the Liberals in the Commons split three ways, some for the government, some against, some under Campbell-Bannerman abstaining.

Periodic reverses in the war disturbed Chamberlain's assurance. 'As long as whole detachments of the British Army continue to allow themselves to be mopped up by bands of Boers in different parts of the country,' he complained to Milner in July, 'it is impossible to say that we are really out of the wood.'[23] Otherwise the two men devoted themselves to postwar planning. They hammered out the terms of annexation, drew up schemes for emigration from Britain to guarantee the Transvaal a British majority, and arranged for the despatch of commissions of inquiry from Britain on native affairs and land settlement.

Little clouded their cooperation until September when Milner's nightmare of rebellious Cape Dutchmen in control of the colony prompted him again to urge suspension of the Cape constitution. On this point Chamberlain refused to budge. The two men always differed in their assessment of the Cape Dutch. In capturing Bloemfontein, the British came upon letters written before the war to the Boer leaders by some of their prominent Cape Dutch neighbours and by Little England Liberals in Britain. In Chamberlain's eyes, the letters did not entirely confirm Milner's bad impression of the Cape Dutch. The captured documents showed representatives of the Afrikaner Bond at the Cape urging Kruger to make concessions to the British. Chamberlain was particularly impressed with the 'patriotism & loyalty'[24] evident in the letters from the Cape Dutch chief justice, de Villiers. As a result, whereas Milner urged Chamberlain to impress de Villiers with Britain's unyielding stance on the terms for peace, Chamberlain promised the chief justice to consider favourably 'any suggestions from you as to the policy most likely to secure that reconciliation of the two races which we both earnestly desire to promote'.[25]

The captured letters from the British Little Englanders struck Chamberlain quite differently. The advice they gave the Boer leaders was intrinsically no more serious than that tendered by the Bondsmen of the Cape. But in Chamberlain's eyes, the closer to home, the more reprehensible was such trafficking with Britain's enemies; and there was no cover of ethnic affinity to excuse the British offenders. In order to discredit them, he made preparations to publish the correspondence. The cache of letters did not reach him till late in the parliamentary session. The timing allowed him to smear the Radicals before the evidence could be subjected to parliamentary examination. He wrote to the various correspondents, seeking permission to publish their letters but intimating that he would do so whether or not they agreed. Meanwhile he publicized the existence of the correspondence and suggested broadly that it would be found damning. His opponents fumed at the breach of etiquette in publishing what were meant to be private letters; but otherwise most of them felt powerless to repel his insinuations.

Not so Lloyd George. This as yet minor Welsh Radical was in so many ways akin to Chamberlain. He acted this time on Chamberlain's precept that attack is the best defence. In the closing moments of the parliamentary session Lloyd George deflected Chamberlain's exploitation of the captured letters by accusing his family of exploiting the war to their financial advantage. 'Whatever party in the country suffers by the war,' jibed Lloyd George, 'one party in the country is doing well out of it.'[26] He drew attention to a report just issued by a committee on War Office contracts. The report indicated that the War Office cultivated certain munitions firms, in particular Kynochs under the chairmanship of Chamberlain's brother Arthur, by soliciting bids from them and coaching them on the right levels at which to bid. Kynochs, charged Lloyd George, 'had been practically made by the War Office', thanks to 'certain gentlemen in Birmingham, who had influence with a member of the Government'. When Chamberlain, who had not yet seen the report, accused Lloyd George of proceeding by innuendo, Lloyd George drove the point back at Chamberlain who had 'insinuated treason' over the captured letters. Contemptuous of the upstart, Chamberlain replied indignantly. He denied that he had any connection with Kynochs or ever interfered on its behalf at the War Office. The debates of the Parliament elected in 1895 ended with Chamberlain declaring that 'it is a gross abuse to attack a public man through his relatives, for whom he is not responsible'.[27]

These words did not close the question. Lloyd George, though himself *déclassé*, had exposed a social suspicion which divided the landed or Oxbridge-educated elite still predominant in the government of England from those who made their fortunes from business. So long as Lloyd George was the sole accuser, his charge did not trouble Chamberlain greatly. But he was hurt to find it echoed in the *Spectator*, a leading Unionist weekly edited by St Loe Strachey, another of the men like Milner who had been schooled for national leadership at Balliol College, Oxford. 'I cannot understand', Chamberlain wrote to Strachey, 'how an educated gentleman can encourage the attacks of the baser sort of radicals on the honour of public men.'[28] Chamberlain thought that the old antagonism between industrialists like himself and landowners like Salisbury had been overcome with the formation of the Unionist alliance. They had joined together as men with 'a stake in the country', statesmen of 'character, position & responsibility', dedicated to the well-being of the country, with no thought for their private pecuniary interests. They therefore merited different treatment from mere 'professional politicians' like Lloyd George, an impecunious barrister. While Chamberlain was concerned about how his fellow 'gentlemen' would react to slurs on his honour, he was also unsure how the ordinary people who made up the electorate would react to insinuations that he used public office for private profit.

Strachey knew no better than Chamberlain how to reconcile industrial and public interests. Strachey laid down the maxim that 'the brother of a man with high Cabinet rank should not take while he was in power an active part in obtaining Government contracts'.[29] Yet he saw no comparable conflict with regard to the kinds of private interest common among families in the traditional elite of government: advancement for relations in the armed services or the Established Church, or manipulations of land law. 'If', asked Chamberlain, '... no man must accept office unless he can show that neither he nor any of his relatives have any pecuniary interest in any matter with which the Govt. of the Country have to deal, where are you going to find your Ministers?'

Though hurtful, this argument did not yet appreciably darken the skies for Chamberlain. He was more apprehensive in the summer of 1900 about a violent eruption of nationalist opposition to the intruding Western powers in China, the 'Boxer' rebellion. When news of the siege of the foreign legations in Beijing reached London at the end of June, Chamberlain's mind was on the coming general election. At first he reacted to the news as an unwelcome diversion 'from what is really the main & simple issue of the South African war & the settlement which is to follow it'.[30] But he began to hope for more from the Chinese imbroglio at the end of August when the despatch of an international rescue mission under German command suggested the possibility of broader Anglo-German accord.

The Boer War made Chamberlain and others more uneasy than ever about the isolation of the country. The powers of Europe gloated over Britain's early military humiliations. The eventual turn in the fortunes of the war did not immediately ease the international situation. Britain could not rest secure so long as its military resources were concentrated far from home. Even the unrivalled financial resources of the country showed signs of strain. The borrowing needed to meet the costs of the war threatened to exceed the capacity of the British capital market unless the bank rate was sharply raised. The financial need was almost welcome to Chamberlain because it gave him an opportunity to seek American cooperation. His connections through his wife's Peabody relations with the American banker Pierpont Morgan gave him an opening. Chamberlain used it to secure the first major loan floated by Britain in the American market. The loan allowed him to assure his fellow countrymen that 'the great majority of Americans ... recognize that our aims in this war are as high and our motives as unselfish as those which animated themselves in their recent Spanish-American struggle'.[31]

He was less skilful though more interested in seeking the cooperation of Germany. Disregarding repeated German expressions of concern about their common border with Russia, he sought to convince his cabinet colleagues that 'both in China and elsewhere it is our interest that Germany should throw herself across the path of Russia'.[32] He hoped for an agreement with Germany to prevent Russia from turning Chinese Manchuria into a Russian sphere of influence excluding the trade of other powers. Lord Salisbury recognized the folly of trying to combine with Germany against Russia. Yet Salisbury did not see either the need or the way for Britain to build reliable relationships in a world of rival powers. Because Chamberlain saw the need, the cabinet agreed to follow his way. Britain concluded an agreement with Germany in October which committed the Germans to maintain the so-called 'Open Door' in China 'so far as they can exercise influence'. It was soon clear that the Germans did not intend to use the agreement against Russia. Germany made the agreement in order to keep the lucrative British sphere along the Yangtse river, not the Russian sphere in Manchuria, open to German trade. The agreement thus turned out to be 'a horrible practical joke on England'.[33]

Joe's mandate

England overlooked the joke because the country was absorbed in other business, a general election at home and the eruption of guerrilla warfare in South Africa. The general election in October 1900 inaugurated a paradoxical phase in Chamberlain's career. The election swirled around him individually to an extent without precedent in British history. By duplicating the victory of 1895, he stopped the pendulum that had characterized British elections for a generation. Yet the dividends of victory did not accrue to him personally. The government received the endorsement it sought for its terms of peace in South Africa. But the climate of opinion in which 'the khaki election' was fought and the resurgence of warfare in South Africa kept Chamberlain from gaining clear national approval for his general policy of imperialism. The election was also accompanied by imputations on his personal honour.

The annexation of the Transvaal by Lord Roberts on the first of September brought the conventional war in South Africa to an end. Chamberlain wanted to capitalize on the pleasure of the British electorate at this outcome. He did not minimize early signs that the Boers might resort to guerrilla warfare rather than accept defeat. He used those signs as further grist for his electoral mill, evidence of a Boer desire to keep fighting in the hope of a Liberal return to power and thus to keep at the negotiating table what they lost on the battlefield.

With foreboding Chamberlain also sensed the capacity of the Boer guerrillas to frustrate their presumed conquerors. That prospect made him at last militarily imaginative. In an end-of-summer report to Milner, he outlined much of the strategy against the guerrillas that Britain eventually followed. The objectives of his plan were political as well as military. He wanted to restore peacetime administration and profitable economic activity in the heart of the annexed republics quickly while paralysing the guerrillas on their periphery. It ought to be possible, he argued,

> to establish, if not now, at all events at an early date, a military police, something like the Royal Irish Constabulary, and to echelon these along the lines of communication with instructions to make each post an impregnable position by earth works etc, in which anything from 200 to 500 men might hold their own against all comers for a sufficient time to make certain of reinforcements if necessary.... In addition, of course, the principal towns would also be fortified against attack. This would only leave the open country inhabited almost entirely by the Dutch Boers. What they did there would not matter much, & necessity would force them, I think, to settle down speedily.[34]

His desire for things to settle down was keen. He was dismayed to see that the prospects for a financial contribution from the Transvaal and its mines towards the costs of the war were 'receding into the distance with every week the war lasts'. He was also 'anxious to see the return of a considerable part of the regular army' to Britain in view of 'the troubled state of international politics'.

The brightest prospect in the scene Chamberlain surveyed lay in a prompt general election at home. The triumph of Lord Roberts had transformed the electoral outlook, turning what at the beginning of the year had been the probability of defeat for the Unionists into the certainty of victory. Chamberlain's cabinet colleagues shied away from the blatant opportunism of a 'khaki' election, particularly the peers who did not have to stand for election, and above all Lord Salisbury. But the eruption of guerrilla war in August undermined their resistance. While they might not like pandering to the chauvinistic British electorate, they had to demonstrate to the Boer guerrillas that there was no point in protracting the war.

Chamberlain approached the general election with high expectations. He did not want simply to win. He sought a victory so great that it would commit Britain irrevocably to the imperial cause. The Unionist alliance had evolved by natural stages into a good vehicle for this purpose. The fight against Home Rule enabled Unionists to call themselves 'the national party'. The actions and rhetoric of the coalition Unionist ministry in the past five years had extended the appeal of Unionism in every imperial direction. Chamberlain was further encouraged to identify Unionism with imperialism by the divisive effect imperialism had on the Liberals. They disintegrated by the summer of 1900 into three quarrelling factions, Liberal Imperialists, Little Englanders, and a centre under the party leader, Campbell-Bannerman, tilting indecisively towards the Little Englanders. Chamberlain was emboldened to demand from the electorate 'not merely an ordinary' but 'an overwhelming majority'.[35]

To secure such a national commitment, he fought a paradoxically partisan campaign with weapons that made it still more narrowly personal. To some degree he owed his centrality in the general election to abdication by his cabinet colleagues. Chamberlain orchestrated the preelection speeches by peers in the cabinet. Like other ministers in the Commons, he concentrated his campaign on his locality. He left it only once, to speak at Oldham on behalf of young Winston Churchill. But Chamberlain's 'duchy', embracing the entire West Midlands, was much larger than anyone else's. His speeches around it every other day commanded nationwide attention. Salisbury did not speak at all, contenting himself with a dispirited manifesto. Balfour spoke little and weakly. However unfair it was to speak of 'Joe's war', this was certainly his general election.

That was how the Liberals treated it. Their only point of agreement was on Chamberlain. He evoked every hostile sentiment among Liberals from distrust through disgust to loathing. Only one Liberal, Sir Edward Grey, objected to the abuse hurled at Chamberlain during the election. Chamberlain handled it in public with unctuous indignation. He began to speak of himself in the third person as 'the Colonial Secretary', the abused embodiment of the imperialism all Unionists held dear. Still, he felt each lash of the Liberal tongue. 'Every lie & slander is brought out,' he reported to his wife, '& for one line of argument there are two of abuse of the Colonial Secretary. It is a dirty business.'[36]

It was his own fault. Opening the campaign, he blamed Campbell-Bannerman and the Liberal writers of the Bloemfontein letters for the outbreak and prolongation of the war. Declaring that 'we have come practically to the end of the war', he told his constituents that 'there is nothing going on now but a guerrilla business, which is encouraged by these men ("Shame"); I was going to say those traitors (cheers), but I will say instead these misguided individuals'.[37] He argued that war could have been avoided 'if we had not been undermined by those who were in communication with the Boers, and, still more, by . . . Sir Henry Campbell-Bannerman . . . who made speeches which . . . tended to persuade President Kruger that he could rely upon a large section of the Opposition . . . to oppose any military preparations'.

The Liberals gave as good as they got. Campbell-Bannerman declared that only a man 'not very scrupulous as to personal honour' would have sanctioned publication of the private correspondence captured at Bloemfontein.[38] But the reaction that hurt Chamberlain most deeply came from Lloyd George, back on the track of the war-profiteering by the Chamberlain family. This time Lloyd George struck closer to home and with a stronger case. In the Commons in August he had referred to

Kynochs, the cordite manufacturing firm of Chamberlain's brother Arthur. In his Welsh constituency at the end of September, Lloyd George spoke of Hoskins & Co., the firm in which Chamberlain had set up his son, Neville, after the sisal-growing fiasco in the West Indies. Austen held some shares in the firm, few in number but politically damaging. Hoskins did some supply work for the navy, and Austen held office in the government as Civil Lord of the Admiralty. Respectable Liberals rejected Lloyd George's innuendo as scurrilous; but the substance of his charge was disseminated in party pamphlets and the less reputable Liberal press. In public Chamberlain dismissed the attack briefly as unworthy of a substantial response. But he felt the attack more deeply than he cared to let on.

Otherwise the publication of the Bloemfontein letters served his purposes effectively. The strategy Chamberlain pursued in the election was to exclude Little Englanders from the patriotic pale as 'pro-Boers', and then to maximize the association with them of all other Liberals, including the Liberal Imperialists. The arguments presented by the pro-Boers lent some justification to Chamberlain's crude use of the mayor of Mafeking's saying, 'Every seat lost to the Government was a seat gained by the Boers.' But it was the Liberal Imperialists who most worried Chamberlain, for they laid claim to the mantle of imperialism he wished to reserve for Unionists. 'My great anxiety', he told his wife, 'is to smash the Liberal Imperialist sham.'[39]

That was not, however, the threat on his doorstep in East Birmingham, the only constituency in Birmingham which the Liberals chose to contest. They tried to steer clear of the patriotic tide by drawing the attention to the disappointing record of the government in social reform. They nominated a 'Lib-Lab' candidate, J.V. Stevens, who was secretary of the Amalgamated Tinplate Workers as well as Liberal city councillor for St Thomas's ward. Stevens's candidacy looked promising because the current MP for East Birmingham, Sir Benjamin Stone, was an inactive Conservative backbencher known mainly for his photographs. Stevens adopted the rhetoric of patriotism and added a set of social proposals topped by universal old-age pensions.

Chamberlain met the challenge head on. He attacked Stevens's record on social reform and defended his own. In doing so, Chamberlain demonstrated that his brand of social imperialism had lost little of its electoral potency, however limited in practice. For all his talk, Chamberlain had not found a way for the state to augment the old-age pension funds to which provident working men might contribute without exceeding the constraints of orthodox Treasury finance. Stevens ignored these constraints. Assuming that the working-class electorate of East Birmingham would favour a scheme paid for by the rich, he demanded non-contributory pensions. Chamberlain appealed over Stevens's head to skilled working men who earned enough to worry about taxation. Chamberlain understood how loath these voters would be to pay for a scheme that benefited the ne'er-do-well, who also rarely qualified to vote. Turning to the attack, he pointed out that opposition from the self-styled spokesmen for labour including trade union officials had denied him the support he needed to bring his scheme to pass. He discredited Stevens by recalling that in testimony before the royal commission in 1895 Stevens had opposed not only Chamberlain's but all old-age pensions schemes on the grounds that they would weaken reliance on self-help. Chamberlain concluded his argument by drawing attention to its imperial dimension. The basic form of social security came from 'full employment at fair wages'; and that required 'new markets and the maintenance of the old ones'.[40]

If Unionists elsewhere had added this social line to their imperial rhetoric in the general election, the results might have turned out even more favourably than they did. Chamberlain enabled Sir Benjamin Stone to overwhelm Stevens by more than two thousand votes. In Derby, by contrast, a Lib-Lab team ousted the Conservative incumbents.

In the nation at large, the Unionist alliance did not do as well as Chamberlain desired, though better than the party organizers on both sides expected. He hoped to gain seats. From the first results it was evident that the Unionists would barely maintain their parliamentary majority as at the dissolution, which because of by-election losses was a little smaller than they won in the general election of 1895. Still, such a result was outstanding. No government had been reelected with a large majority since the Reform Act of 1832. The achievement was not significantly diminished by the 243 seats which were left uncontested, for two-thirds of these were abandoned by the demoralized Liberals. All the great towns returned Unionist majorities, though the government did less well in the counties. Chamberlain was disappointed by the lack of increase in the admittedly already large majority of Unionists elected from the West Midlands.

His pleasure mounted at the response of observers in Britain and abroad. He reported to his wife that 'all our people are jubilant'. Foreigners were even more impressed: 'the "Wiener Zeitung" in an article on "Josephus Africanus" goes so far as to say that I am the most successful statesman of the age!'[41] These responses tempted him to invest the election results with more significance than he quite believed. Looking back at the conduct of the election, he wondered whether 'the way in which many of the Liberals tried . . . to compete with us in their newborn fervour of Imperialism' justified him in assuming 'that the vast majority in the country recognise Imperial interests & obligations'.[42] He told one of the London guilds that the war, the election and the beginning of the new century opened a new chapter in the history of the country, to be entitled 'The Unity of the Empire'.[43] Yet his declaration was as much prayer as boast. 'What should we be without our Empire?' he asked his audience:

Two small islands with an overcrowded population in the northern sea. What should [our colonies] be without us? Fractions at present— nations, indeed, but without the fulness of national life, without the cohesion which enables them to look all the world in the face.

The dividends Chamberlain drew individually from his electoral achievement proved meagre. The government was reconstructed with little reference to him. Partly as a result, the electoral success which he gave the government did not renew its credentials effectively. When Lord Salisbury showed no disposition to share the work of ministerial reconstruction, Chamberlain hid his disappointment. Once the electoral returns were in, he headed for the Colonial Office to catch up on his work before going on holiday until the opening of the new Parliament. Yet he hesitated to rush away and dithered over his travel arrangements. Salisbury let him know the ministerial rearrangements he had in mind. They were few, and did not involve Chamberlain directly because he intended to remain at the Colonial Office. He was anxious to keep up the proportion of Liberal Unionists to Conservatives among the appointments. He supported the Liberal Unionists of Ulster who were at odds with their landowning Conservative allies. He gave advice on who might best fill the War Office and the Admiralty. Otherwise he said nothing to affect the character of the new ministry. His one policy recommendation was for the immediate appointment of 'a strong Commission'[44] of inquiry into the conduct of the war, to head off the demand for a parliamentary inquiry like the one which followed the Jameson raid. The appointment which most gratified him was the promotion of Austen to be financial secretary to the Treasury. That appointment paralleled the promotion of Salisbury's eldest son to be undersecretary at the Foreign Office, which Salisbury was leaving to concentrate his dwindling energies on the premiership. Joe was delighted thus to join the ruling families of England.

At the end of his holiday in the Mediterranean he was greeted with sobering news from South Africa. The Boer guerrillas disregarded the British election and expanded their activities, frequently with success. This development threatened the British fruits of victory from the conventional war and spoiled the British appetite for imperialism. Milner's shock at 'the vitality & ubiquity of the enemy'[45] deepened Chamberlain's anxiety. At first the renewed military challenge drew the two men together. They reinforced each other in pressing for a speedy resumption of civilian government and industry in the annexed republics. They were also at one in deploring the army's indiscriminate burning of farms in retaliation for guerrilla attacks.

But the extension of the guerrilla war into the Cape Colony at the end of the year reopened the division between Milner and Chamberlain over the colonial constitution. Milner inveighed against 'the superstition that you can govern a country, in wh[ich]. the majority of citizens are your enemies, by a system of autonomy'.[46] His disagreement with Chamberlain widened to include the terms for peace. Chamberlain favoured a speedy grant of municipal powers to the major towns in the annexed republics in order to demonstrate at home and in South Africa 'that we are not excessive in our demands and that the prolongation of the war is not due to the unreasonableness of our conditions'.[47] Milner feared that gestures of this sort would convey an impression of British willingness to compromise on vital issues.

These were not, however, the issues that interested the new British Parliament when it convened in December. Licking their electoral wounds, the Liberals encouraged Lloyd George to launch another attack on the munitions manufacturing interests of the Chamberlain clan. Ultimately Lloyd George weakened his case by exaggerating it. But in the meantime he unearthed disconcerting evidence of the way in which 'Birmingham had become an arsenal of empire'.[48] Birmingham had long been famous for the manufacture of small arms. That activity naturally involved production for the state. Both involvements were intensified by the industrialization of warfare. One of the ingredients of Britain's imperial power was the capacity to mass-produce metal goods like boilers and ships' berths for naval vessels and technologically improved munitions like cordite. This capacity deepened a political problem. The government was virtually the sole consumer for many kinds of munitions, and hence found itself in the position of a public monopolist dependent on private producers. There was no received body of wisdom to guide public officials and private industrialists in this situation; but it was easier when the two groups were divided socially, as by and large they had been until Chamberlain rose to the front rank among British statesmen.

In the mid-1890s, before and after the change of government at Westminster, his brother Arthur turned the lacklustre firm of Kynochs into one of the three 'giants' of the cordite industry.[49] Other industries in which Arthur and his younger brothers were involved, including Tubes Ltd and Elliott's Metal, produced supplies increasingly for the navy. Herbert Chamberlain was deputy chairman of the Birmingham Small Arms Company. Joe mobilized family capital to establish Neville in Hoskins, avoiding Kynochs because of its conspicuous army connection. Still, Hoskins did a small amount of its business supplying berths for the navy. So it was that when Lloyd George commissioned a couple of men to dig into the business records open to the public at Somerset

House, they came up with evidence of a family federation of companies manufacturing metal supplies and munitions for the armed services to fight a war brought on by the senior member of the family, the Colonial Secretary.

During debate in the Commons in August, Joe disclaimed even indirect involvement in firms manufacturing war materials. So far as he knew, the disclaimer was true. But it turned out that a blind trust in which he had invested some of his capital, the Birmingham Trust Company of which Arthur was chairman, had invested in Elliott's Metal and in Tubes. Moreover, most of the shareholders in Hoskins lived under Joe's roof. He was most vulnerable on the further matter of his brother Arthur's relationship with the War Office as one of its main suppliers of cordite. Joe shared the view common in Birmingham that the success of Kynochs was a tribute to the business acumen of Arthur. Still, Arthur did not scruple in his work at Kynochs to draw attention to his relationship with the Colonial Secretary. Joe had not refrained from using his political position to voice Arthur's concerns, without mentioning his name, most notably over the alleged inadequacy of the army's supply of cordite which precipitated the fall of the Rosebery government in 1895. At the beginning of 1900, Joe gave Balfour information from Kynochs conveying an impression of 'gross want of foresight & arrangement'[50] at the War Office, failings that could be remedied by increasing the orders to Kynochs.

Lloyd George extended his accusations to include every investment and position by members of the Chamberlain family in firms handling government contracts, however indirect or small. Describing Kynochs as 'the worst company of the lot',[51] he cast aspersions on Arthur Chamberlain's conduct of business. Lloyd George did not accuse Joe or Austen Chamberlain, the two family members in the government, of actual corruption. But he treated the entire family as profiteers from a war fomented by the head of the clan. There was considerable sympathy in principle on both sides of the Commons for wider separation between ministers of the crown and directors of businesses supplying the government. But Lloyd George loaded his attack with so much personal malice that the House divided along lines which were more personal than partisan, let alone matters of principle.

Joe was stung as much by the attack on his brother's honour in business as on his own honour in the public service. Unable to hide his outrage at charges that would not be levelled at the traditional elite of government, he turned on the landed gentlemen and lawyers of the party opposite:

> My relations are all men of business. They are all men who have to make their own fortunes or obtain their own subsistence. I come of a family which boasts nothing of distinguished birth, or of inherited

wealth; but who have a record—an unbroken record of nearly two
centuries—of unstained commercial integrity and honour. It may be
weakness, but I admit that an attack upon that affects me more than
any other attack that could be made.[52]

Moved beyond endurance, he left the House after Austen had spoken
and did not return until the Leader of the Opposition rose to conclude
the debate. When the House divided, he reacted to each vote for Lloyd
George's motion as to a grain of salt in a wound. Harcourt 'voted with
Lloyd George', he noted in an outpouring of anger,

> ...I shall not forget that...Grey did not vote, and so with John
> Morley he has always the feelings of a gentleman. But Asquith did...I
> am supposed to feel nothing....It is just my point of honour, of mid-
> dle class commercial honour. Generations of us have had this as our
> point of honour, absolute pecuniary integrity and to be trusted. I have
> not cared to make money. I left it when I went into politics....But
> there is my brother. He does care to make money. And he has such a
> reputation for capacity and they have such confidence in him that he
> cannot touch anything in the part of the country where he is known
> without the shares going up. And to have this charged against me!
> I don't pretend it did not hurt.[53]

Such were the rewards for his assault on the patriotism of his
opponents.

The search for postwar security

The revival of the war protracted the awkward interval in Chamberlain's career between the initial declaration of hostilities and the conclusion of peace. He was responsible for the conduct of affairs in South
Africa. But the commander who replaced Lord Roberts at the end of the
conventional war, Lord Kitchener, was in charge of the fields of combat.
Chamberlain hesitated to do more than make suggestions on the conduct of the war. He overruled Kitchener only when peace terms were
at issue. Into the summer of 1901, the Colonial Secretary paced anxiously up and down the sidelines, trying to accelerate the establishment
of the postwar order with resources which lessened every day the war
went on.

Gradually, however, he came close to being in effect the prime minister for the war. Maddening successes by the Boer guerrillas, deteriorating relations between the British military and civilian authorities in
South Africa, the army's maladministration of the camps it set up for
the wives and children of the Boer commandos, and the prospect of a

crisis in imperial finance, all required resources of leadership which Salisbury no longer possessed and involved subjects with which Chamberlain was centrally concerned. Authority and power devolved upon him naturally, without any need to grasp. Brodrick, the secretary for war, was new to his job, insecure and overworked, and he responded appreciatively to Chamberlain's sympathetic advice. Balfour appeared to be 'fagged out' as leader in the Commons under 'the unchanging burden of anxiety caused by the war . . . Chamberlain on the other hand seem[ed] to grow fresher and more youthful every day'.[54] In private discussion among ministers on matters of controversy requiring resolution, he gathered responses and sought to minimize conflict in prime ministerial fashion. In public his rhetoric, particularly but not solely on imperial themes, assumed the rotund rhythms of classical English oratory.

There were none the less rough edges and severe limits to his political ascent. Often his abrasiveness, sometimes his impetuosity, and occasionally his old Radicalism renewed uneasiness among his Conservative and Whig allies. When a wartime tax on exports of coal evoked protests from the coalowners, Chamberlain criticized them with a tactlessness reminiscent of his attack at the height of his Radicalism on merchant shippers.

In the first half of 1900, he was engaged as usual in a range of enterprises, and no single one of them galvanized his metal. He made a fresh attempt to crack the nut of old-age pensions, which was all the harder when the state was preoccupied with the demands of war. Convinced at last by Carnegie of the need for new buildings for the University of Birmingham, Chamberlain inspired the university governors with his 'vision of a stately pile . . . surrounded by its associated buildings, all specialized for the particular branch of knowledge or training to which they are to be devoted, forming, as a whole, a complete and perfect home of scientific training and scientific research'. For South Africa too he encouraged the formation of colleges, in this case to 'promote the study of English and the spread of English culture, and . . . form a counterpoise to those Dutch colleges at the Cape, some of which [Milner informed him] are nurseries of sedition'.[55]

Meanwhile the problems of postwar pacification were aggravated by the prolongation of the fighting and the severe methods which seemed to be required to crush the guerrillas. Damage to farms in the annexed republics worsened the outlook for postwar recovery. Chamberlain suggested creating a land bank to give economically promising farmers, Boer as well as loyalist, loans rather than outright grants to revive their farms. His insistence on the limitations of this proposal contributed to the collapse in March of the first exploration of the possibilities for peace. Kitchener opened communications with the Boer commandant-general, Louis Botha. Chamberlain welcomed the opening, and ensured that Milner would not wreck it as he had the prewar Bloemfontein conference. But whereas at Bloemfontein Milner had been too stiff, Kitchener proposed greater concessions than Chamberlain thought financially or imperially tolerable.

In an attempt to overcome Boer insistence on some independence for the former republics, Kitchener suggested generous treatment on subordinate matters, including a million-pound British contribution to the Transvaal debt, extension of the terms of amnesty to include rebels in the Cape Colony and Natal, and grants to restore ruined farms. Chamberlain accepted the debt suggestion. But he resisted the others, anxious for financial as well as imperial reasons 'not . . . to allow the Boers to think that they could escape all loss in consequence of the War'.[56] He offered rehabilitative loans but not grants, and stipulated further that the loans would go only to those who swore allegiance to the British crown. He refused amnesty to rebels in the self-governing British colonies. Giving his stiffness a humanitarian shine, he refused 'to purchase a shameful peace by leaving the coloured population [of the annexed republics] in the position in which they stood before the war with not even the ordinary civil rights which the Government of the Cape Colony has long conceded to them'.[57]

After the collapse of the negotiations the Boer leaders indicated that all along they had been set on independence. The outcome left Chamberlain averse to further negotiations or offers of generosity until 'after an unconditional surrender' when they could be given as 'acts of grace'. Liberal criticism of his stiffness in this case was offset by 'a good deal of private dissatisfaction' among Unionists who thought that he had 'gone too far'. Continental observers were impressed by the generosity of the terms the government had offered. Some European commentators even detected a hint of weakness in the generosity and hence 'of doubt on the part of the [British] Government as to their ultimate success'. Content with the balance of this response, Chamberlain stuck to his course.

The powers of Europe did little to exploit the opportunities elsewhere created by the concentration of British armed force in South Africa. But Chamberlain remained fearful of the international insecurity. He blamed the continuing erosion of the Chinese market on Britain's lack of allies. In January 1901, when Russia moved to legitimize its control over Manchuria, he made his final overture to Germany. With some prearrangement he met the German chargé, Eckhardtstein, under the roof of the Duke of Devonshire at Chatsworth. Precisely what Chamberlain said on this occasion remains unknown because the only surviving report of the conversation originated with Eckhardtstein, who never hesitated to distort what he heard in his anxiety to bring about an

Anglo-German alliance. Chamberlain, warned by the failure of his former bids to Germany, appears to have suggested at Chatsworth a gradual approach, beginning with a reconciliation of German and British interests in Morocco across from Gibraltar. He accompanied his suggestion with a warning that if Germany did not respond constructively, he would turn to the dual alliance of Russia and France even though they were Britain's imperial rivals.

The German response was hastened by the final illness of Queen Victoria the week after the Chatsworth meeting. Moved by veneration for his grandmother, the Kaiser defied anti-British feeling in Germany and sped to her bedside. When she died, he took an impressively dutiful part in the funeral ceremonies. His presence in England enabled Eckhardtstein to give him an enthusiastic account of the conversation with Chamberlain, to which the Kaiser responded with delight. Apprehensive lest he commit Germany, Bülow who was now Chancellor urged the Kaiser to keep to a middle course between Britain and Russia. With some reluctance the Kaiser obeyed the advice. He made no attempt to pursue matters with Chamberlain. That may have only mildly disappointed Chamberlain under the circumstances. But he was deeply disappointed to learn before the Kaiser returned to Berlin that Germany had no intention of resisting Russian encroachments in China.

Thereupon Chamberlain's hopes for an Anglo-German alliance died. When, with the arrival of spring, Eckhardtstein made another unofficial bid for such an alliance, Chamberlain met it coldly. He was already thinking of France. At the beginning of March the French ambassador, Cambon, suggested exchanging French fishing rights on the coast of Newfoundland for British territory in Gambia. Chamberlain sought to amplify the proposal. But progress was slow. First the new British foreign secretary, Lansdowne, and then Cambon hesitated to advance at the pace Chamberlain desired. In encouraging Lansdowne forward, Chamberlain aligned himself with the tide of Unionist opinion away from Germany in reaction to its naval build-up. Still, Chamberlain did not place himself on the flowing edge of this tide. With his change of diplomatic heart, he lost some of his enthusiasm for great-power diplomacy. The prospect of association with Russia as the ally of France repelled him. Though responsive when asked for advice, he no longer thrust himself into the centre of the diplomatic arena.

It was the Boer War that raised Chamberlain towards the summit of power. The resilience of the guerrillas in South Africa and impatience at home among Unionists pushed him to assert himself in military matters. The failure of the negotiations for peace sent Kitchener back to war with a fierceness intensified by exasperation with his political masters as well as with his foes in the war zone. At the end of May, he warned that stiffer tactics might have to be employed. Less than two weeks later, he recommended that Botha and the other Boer commanders be threatened with banishment 'if hostilities do not cease within a month, . . . that all prisoners of war will not be allowed to return, that their wives and families will be sent to them, [and] that no more volunteer surrenders will be accepted'.[58] Though Chamberlain agreed on banishment of the leaders, the rest of Kitchener's proposals struck him as the worst kind of bluff, violating the conventions of war with little likelihood that the threats would be enforced.

While Kitchener threatened Botha with banishment, Chamberlain pressed for the creation of a lightly armed corps, 'able to move without guns, waggons, or baggage . . . as fast and as long as the Boers themselves . . . to bring back Botha, alive or dead'.[59] Preferring to move in strength, Kitchener responded by talking of five such corps. That was too many, in Chamberlain's estimation, to ensure that only the finest manpower was employed; and he was filled with scorn when he learned that Kitchener's supposedly mobile corps carried pianos and harmoniums with them. Chamberlain continued to prod the military with suggestions. He proposed to protect train transport by placing empty cars in the van, keeping the engine at the rear to push, and by including Boer prisoners as hostages in all trains through dangerous districts, following examples set in the American Civil and Franco-Prussian Wars.

Sometimes the news made his efforts seem pointless. On a single day in September, Louis Botha inflicted heavy losses on a large British force in Natal, while J.C. Smuts, the former state attorney turned soldier, cut up the 17th Lancers inside the Cape Colony. Chamberlain was sickened 'to find that with inferior numbers [the Boers] could hold defensive positions against masses of our troops and yet that we are not infrequently surprised and defeated in similar positions'.[60] The dismal showing of the troops endangered the mandate of the government. If the prospects for a victorious end to the war faded much further, Parliament would expect to be called into emergency session. It would convene in a mood of deepened doubt about the war, and might proceed to examine the crisis in governmental finance which the war had exacerbated.

Hicks Beach as Chancellor suggested a December session of Parliament on this score alone. A war so far from England's shores was bound to be expensive. The Chancellor strained the conventions of Victorian finance to produce the necessary funds. He raised the income tax, borrowed heavily, and even imposed low, strictly revenue-producing tariffs on sugar and coal. These emergency measures brought the underlying, basic problem in governmental finance to a head. Governmental expenditure had risen forty per centy since 1895 quite apart from the war. Four spheres of expenditure stood out. Hicks Beach noted without disapproval that expenditure on elementary education had risen as a result of increases in attendance and higher required standards of scholastic achievement. He was not unsympathetic to the rise in expenditure on overseas possessions. In fact he hoped to use the autumn vacation with Chamberlain to take a look at the government's investment in the West Indies. What mainly disturbed the Chancellor was the steep rise, quite apart from the Boer War, in expenditure on the army and navy. Their estimates had leapt up year by year before the war at the insistence of military experts alarmed at the mounting might of the Continental powers. The wartime expenditure on South Africa increased but also disguised and seemed to excuse the rise in mainline military expenditure. The prospective end to the South Africa war would strip away that disguise, and prompted Hicks Beach to call for an end at least to increases in basic expenditure on the armed services.

He sounded out the leaders of the government before deciding whether to approach the full cabinet. He wrote first to Chamberlain, then to Salisbury and Balfour. Formally the most important letter was to Salisbury: it was accompanied by a threat of resignation if his budgetary warning went unheeded. Salisbury responded with full agreement but without hope. 'I think it is the duty of all of us', he wrote, '. . . not to do anything which may bring about that catastrophe [a break-up of the government over the armed service estimates] *while the war lasts.*'[61] Balfour did not respond at all, at any rate by letter. Substantively the most important exchange was with Chamberlain. And it was Chamberlain who assumed the prime ministerial task of assembling responses from other members of the cabinet to head off a collision.

In his exchange with Hicks Beach, Chamberlain sharpened the focus of the Chancellor's concern to exclude expenditure on the war in South Africa and to reduce its application to the Colonial Office. Meanwhile Chamberlain alerted the two armed service ministers, Brodrick at the War Office and Selborne at the Admiralty, to the Chancellor's alarm at their ever escalating estimates. Both men were new to their posts, having been appointed in the reconstruction of the government after the general election. Chamberlain coached them to scrutinize the Chancellor's forecasts in detail, and at the same time readied them to make concessions. Chamberlain pressed Brodrick to do so 'either by reducing the expenses in Africa or by postponing expenditure in this country'.[62] With Selborne, his former undersecretary, Chamberlain played the elder statesman: 'after the war is over,' he wrote, 'the people will [not] long stand a continuance of war taxation. Our forefathers did not'—and he reminded Selborne that 'everything was cut down immediately' after the Napoleonic Wars.[63]

Concessions by the service ministers could not dispose of the basic points at issue between Chamberlain and Hicks Beach. Chamberlain contended to the Chancellor that expenditure would have to remain high for a year or two after the war to offset the drain it caused and the deficiencies it exacerbated in the defensive arrangements of Britain and the empire. Even so, Britain would barely be keeping up with 'what other Nations are doing'.[64] Hicks Beach replied with a restatement of the fiscal philosophy under which Britain had prospered in the mid-nineteenth century:

> one of the main causes of the increase of the wealth and comfort of our population in the last 50 years, far greater than in any other European nation, has been the lightness of our taxation: and if our peace taxation is to grow largely, as it must if our present rate of expenditure continues, wealth & comfort will be so diminished as to cause grave danger to our social system.[65]

The fundamental difference that opened up between the two men was evident to both. The gruff but essentially pacific Conservatism of the Chancellor, in this regard a true Victorian, stood in contrast to the apprehensive militancy with which the Colonial Secretary wanted Britain to move into the twentieth century. The threatened rupture of the government was put off, however, by the persisting guerrilla war. Chamberlain was not sorry to report to Hicks Beach, '[a]nother reverse in S. Africa. It looks badly for economy.'[66] The vicissitudes of the war enabled the Colonial Secretary to extend his command in the government—but only so long as the war dragged on.

Towards the end of 1901 Chamberlain's rivals accentuated the boundaries to his authority and the precariousness of his political base. Their achievement occurred significantly in the domestic arena, the sphere where Chamberlain had been obliged to tread with most circumspection since allying himself with the Whigs and Tories. Poignantly, the particular subject on which he was set back was education, the subject which first drew him into public life and usually integrated his industrial and political interests.

Preoccupied with the war, he no longer had an overarching domestic agenda except to put out the occasional brush fire. When he returned to Birmingham for the autumn parliamentary recess, he found that another old concern of his, restriction of the drinks trade, was exciting local passions. The magistrates of Birmingham, led by his brother Arthur, used their regulatory powers to compel brewers to surrender many of their public house licences. This action upset the powerful drinks trade without entirely satisfying the temperance lobby, which sought local prohibition and cancellation of current licences without payment of compensation. Joe first familiarized himself with the local situation, with which he confessed he had 'a little lost touch'.[67] He then produced a tolerable compromise which allowed the magistrates to extend their activity within limits. In doing so, however, he revealed the extent to which his philosophy had changed. Speaking at the reopening of a local temperance hall in the accents of the purest Conservatism, he defied anyone 'to point to any Act of Parliament passed during the last seventy years which has had any effect whatever in reducing drunkenness'.[68]

However lively an issue in Birmingham, temperance did not head the domestic agenda of the government for the coming legislative year. Elementary education reemerged as a pressing concern with the exhaustion of the funds provided in 1897 to ease the plight of denominational schools, still providing half of the schooling in the country. The costs of meeting the higher standards of performance imposed by the Education Office precipitated the loss of some sixty denominational schools a year. Devotees of the Church of England, who bulked large in the ranks of Unionism, were in no mood to tolerate the deterioration of their educational arm. Some of them took action in the courts to challenge the right of rate-financed civic schools to move into secondary education. The denial of that right in the Cockerton judgment, delivered in the spring of 1901, exacerbated the general situation. The rivalry between the civic and denominational networks in elementary education crippled the effort to provide national schooling at the secondary level. The government felt obliged to tide the threatened secondary schools over for a year and use the interval to prepare an enduring legislative solution.

Balfour and the Duke of Devonshire assumed responsibility for this task, with Chamberlain's tacit assent. Throughout the ministry he had accepted supervisory responsibility for social legislation but left elementary education to Balfour, intervening only when Balfour foundered on the rocks of sectarian prejudice. Those rocks had turned Chamberlain, like Salisbury, into an apprehensive minimalist in pre-university education. Yet here was a domestic problem that could be addressed with little further strain on the nation's finances. The needs of the denominational schools could be met locally by allowing them to be funded like the civic board schools from the local rates or property taxes. At the same time the inequities between civic school board districts could be ironed out by lifting responsibility for education from the municipal to the county level. All that stood in the way of this administratively compelling solution was Nonconformist prejudice against rate funding for Church of England schools, a sentiment of diminishing popular force which paled in the face of the national need.

Devonshire and Balfour prided themselves on their freedom from the distorting passions of the masses, Devonshire as the patrician embodiment of common sense, Balfour by his coolly philosophic intellect. Jealousy confirmed the dispassionate conclusions the two men reached on education. Devonshire resented his loss of primacy within the Unionist alliance. Balfour envied the attention everyone focused on the able but brash man who sat beside him in the House of Commons. With the best financial and administrative arguments on their side in the educational debate, Balfour and Devonshire had no wish to give way once again to Chamberlain.

The Liberal Unionism of Birmingham, where Nonconformity retained its grip, found itself isolated. Some Liberal Unionists elsewhere like Lord Selborne who were close to Chamberlain on all other issues differed from him on education because they were ardent churchmen. Chamberlain warned Selborne that 'a Bill giving Rate aid to denominational Schools . . . would lose Birmingham & the Birmingham influence';[69] but to little avail. Most members of the cabinet would have been content to follow the lead of Chamberlain and Salisbury on the prospective bill, minimizing its scope and stepping around bones of contention to avoid denominational controversy. But national need, administrative requirements and the pressure of churchmen on the backbenches enabled Balfour and Devonshire to convince their colleagues of the necessity for a potentially enduring measure.

All but one of the provisions for which Chamberlain pressed were rejected. He would have been happy to increase the grant to denominational schools from national taxation, which did not strain the tolerance of Nonconformists; but his war in South Africa had exhausted all the available funds. He hoped to restrict the bill to secondary education, where the industrial need was greatest. He tried to make municipal rather than county councils the governing authority for education, and to enable ratepayers to assign their rates to the school of their choice. All to no avail. The only alleviating clause in the impending bill from Chamberlain's standpoint, the provision making rate aid for religious schools optional rather than mandatory, would diminish the effectiveness of the ultimate Act and perpetuate local controversy. There was handwriting on the wall of the cabinet chamber as the Education bill for 1902 was finalized. The message was particularly ominous for the person usually considered the strongest man in the room.

The profits of war and the dangers of peace

The war, however, preserved his centrality to the government and raised him to a pinnacle of acclaim. The resurgence of guerrilla warfare that postponed a confrontation with Hicks Beach also subjected the government to a crossfire of criticism. Unionists like Winston Churchill on one side called for more effective military action. Liberals on the other side inveighed against the 'methods of barbarism' to which the British forces resorted in South Africa, and called for more attractive terms for peace. Churchill showed no subservience to the man who helped him enter Parliament but had kept his father in the political wilderness. Observing the old courtesies of political combat, the young man informed Chamberlain of his intention to challenge the government's reluctance to interfere with the army's conduct of the war. 'If Kitchener cannot settle the question,' Churchill insisted, 'you will have to interfere.'[70] Writing in a style of command, he ordered the government to 'make some sort of plan: and make sure that we end the matter with the next bitter weather', in other words by the middle of 1902, 'whatever happens'.

Privately Chamberlain attempted to make the British performance in South Africa both more humane and more effective—with greater success as usual on the civilian than on the military side. Publicly he upheld the doctrine of separation between civilian and military responsibilities: 'I hope', he declared, 'that no Government will ever be found in this country that will ever take the details of military operations out of the hands of the military authorities.'[71] Censured by Unionists demanding tougher treatment of the Boers and by Liberals horrified at current British practices, he held to middle ground. While agreeing that 'measures of greater severity' might become necessary, he revealed that he had discouraged wholesale confiscation and executions as ineffective for military purposes and harmful for purposes of peaceful settlement after the war. He transmitted some of Churchill's remarks for Kitchener's consumption and amplified his own proposals to release more areas for economic revival and to form 'flying columns' to capture the Boer leaders.

Milner, wearily aware that Kitchener would treat all such advice with resentful disregard, responded to his chief with a disjointed letter, first acquiescing in the obstinacy of Kitchener and then suggesting his removal. Milner's letter merely strengthened Kitchener's position. Chamberlain was inclined to agree to his removal. But Milner's ambivalence in making the proposal enabled Salisbury to reject it. Thereafter Milner was locked into a dual structure of authority in South Africa which he could not supersede until the war was won, and Chamberlain was locked out of military influence.

In the administrative sphere over which he could seize control, however, Chamberlain proved conspicuously effective, enough to overcome humanitarian and Liberal protests at the most notorious of the 'methods of barbarism': the concentration camps. The army set up camps in the wake of Lord Roberts's farm-burning policy to accommodate the dispossessed Boer women and children and prevent them from supplying their menfolk in the guerrilla war. None too worried about the wellbeing of the inmates, the military administrators of the camps paid little attention to public health dangers and allowed the camps to grow too large. The death-toll soared into the thousands, casualty figures proportionately far higher than those on the fields of battle. The scandal was disclosed to the British by an intrepid humanitarian, Emily Hobhouse.

Until she raised the cry, Chamberlain did not appreciate the dimensions of the scandal. He looked upon the camps as one of the draconian practices adopted by the army the wisdom of which he questioned but the continuance of which he tolerated in deference to the military command. Although responsibility for administration of the camps was formally shared by the civilian and military authorities, in practice the latter were in control. When questioned about the camps in Parliament, Chamberlain put up what defence he could and neither voiced reservations nor took remedial action. But in the autumn of 1901, as the scandal escalated, strengthening Little Englanders' case against the war, he looked into the situation more closely. What he saw shocked him as one who had done much to improve public health in Birmingham and more recently in the tropical empire.

He still refused to criticize the army administration in public. He insisted that the army had pursued the principles he now laid down for civilian administration of the camps. But even critics recognized that a new and effective rule was begun. Chamberlain came up with directives on this subject as readily as Churchill on the military. 'Are you satisfied', he asked Milner without a question mark, 'that the medical and nursing staff is sufficient, and that adequate steps are taken to have infectious cases immediately detected, isolated, and specially treated ... we cannot tolerate the present situation if forethought and science can suggest any expedients for preventing or curing it. If necessary, the Camps must be moved and broken into units ... as soon as a Camp becomes unhealthy, and the water supply affected it must be evacuated.'[72] He did not hesitate to override the army. 'If you feel that you are really hampered in the efficient administration of the Camps by military exigencies,' he told Milner, 'I must be informed.' By the end of the year the death-rate in the camps had halved. By the end of the war it was below the normal death-rate in the South African countryside.

When Parliament reconvened in January, Chamberlain felt the government to be 'stronger than ever'.[73] Kitchener was allowing the mines to reopen more rapidly. The report which Chamberlain published about the concentration camps, as he told Milner, 'cut the ground from under the feet of most of our critics'. These developments served to reduce the pressure from the Liberals for softened peace terms. Chamberlain assured Milner that there was not 'any influential opinion in favour of approaching the Boers or indeed on any thing but unconditional surrender, although many men dislike the particular words used to describe an inevitable result'.

Chamberlain did not, however, forget the fundamental budgetary problem Hicks Beach had raised of how the costs of imperial development and defence were straining the customary limits of British governmental finance. Before expanding those limits at home, Chamberlain wanted to make full use of the contribution the empire abroad could make. His mind kept turning to the mineral resources of South Africa. In probing them, Chamberlain spelled out his priorities as chief minister of the empire. So far as he was concerned, Britain was not engaged in a capitalists' war. Though cooperation between industry and the state would serve the best interests of each, in the final analysis industry was to serve the state rather than the other way round. The enterprise to which Chamberlain had committed himself was the enterprise of England.

He pressed Milner to settle before the war ended the amount and means by which the Transvaal would contribute towards its cost. '[W]e cannot safely leave it to the future,' Chamberlain explained: 'If we do, all the local interests, both British and Dutch, may combine against us, and try to repudiate liability.'[74] He had in mind a contribution of £100,000,000 which the Transvaal would assume in the form of a debt to be paid over twenty years, largely by the mining industry. He envisaged a special fifteen per cent tax of mining profits over and above the current ten per cent tax, and in addition 'a considerable share of the profits of the sale of new [mining] undertakings'.[75] He argued that a surcharge on profits would not impede mining development, for good mines were paying their original shareholders high rates of interest mounting in some cases to one hundred per cent.

It was Balliol-bred Milner rather than the Birmingham Screw King who voiced the protest of the mining industry. Milner's protest lacked the convincing specificity which a businessman familiar with the industry would have deployed. Milner sought to instruct Chamberlain that 'the chief benefit the State derives from the mines will always be what they contribute indirectly. Every working mine, whether it pays its shareholders or not, pours money into the coffers of the Government through indirect taxation. It is in our interest by every means in our power to encourage development.... Mining is at best a risky enterprise ... expenses are owing to present conditions exceptionally heavy and this will continue for some time.'[76] These clichés did not impress Chamberlain. While conceding that it might be impossible 'immediately to fix any definite sum for war indemnity', he could not see 'any objection to ear-marking certain sources of revenue' for the purpose, and he insisted on a large estimate in order to 'get our fair proportion'.[77]

His effort was sidetracked by another military setback. In the first week of March, the Boers captured the British general Lord Methuen, scattered or destroyed his column, and briefly broke Kitchener's nerve. Chamberlain could only counsel 'patience and a stiff upper lip'.[78] But the empire gave him more. New Zealand offered another thousand men for the war, and New Zealanders fell over one another in their enthusiasm to enlist. South Australia showed itself ready to offer a further thousand. Chamberlain used these examples to elicit yet another thousand from Canada. 'It is all very satisfactory,' he commented, '& must make the pro-Boers gnash their teeth.'[79]

The esteem in which Chamberlain was held by his fellow countrymen reached its height in the spring of 1902. What delighted the British could infuriate foreigners. Speaking at Edinburgh in October about the treatment of the Boers, Chamberlain had defended the conduct of the British army against international aspersions by citing Continental European examples. Whenever the time came for 'measures of greater severity', he remarked, the British could 'find precedents for anything that we may do in the action of those nations who now criticize our "barbarity" and "cruelty," but whose example in Poland, in the Caucasus, in Algeria, in Tongking, in Bosnia, in the Franco-German war . . . we have never even approached'.[80] This affront to the martial honour of Germany and France was not necessary to his argument; and while it drew cheers from his Scottish audience, it raised 'a perfect storm of indignant protest',[81] especially in the German press. Chamberlain did not expect this reaction. He recalled a conversation with General Sherman, who led a devastating march through Georgia during the American Civil War. Sherman told Chamberlain that

> 'in our civil war there had to be a deal of killing done.' And when I asked him to explain, he said that dealing with men of the character, courage & resolution of the Southerners, no lasting peace would have been possible unless they had first been convinced by the most bitter suffering that they were hopelessly overmatched.[82]

Chamberlain applied those observations to South Africa. He compared the Boers to the American Southerners as 'men of grit and resolution'. Accordingly, to treat them generously 'while they refuse to own themselves utterly defeated, would be to provoke a new African struggle at a future time'. He regretted the offence Germans took at his remark in Edinburgh. But the abuse they hurled at him deterred him from apologizing. They only confirmed his loss of hope for an alliance. He opened the new year with a declaration that

it is the duty of the British people to count upon themselves alone, as
their ancestors did. I say alone, yes, in a splendid isolation, surrounded
and supported by our kinsfolk.[83]

Two days later, speaking in the Reichstag, Bülow deepened the estrangement between the two countries with an attack on Chamberlain.
Bülow galled Chamberlain by implying that he had apologized for his
aspersions on the conduct of the German army. Then the German
Chancellor recalled the response of Frederick the Great to similar criticism: 'Let the man alone, and don't get excited; he is biting granite.'
Chamberlain's tactlessness in the autumn had damaged him among the
British aristocracy as evidence that he lacked the finesse their upbringing instilled. 'Clever as he is,' remarked Lord Esher, 'he has never learnt
the self-restraint which everyone learns at a great public school or at a
university.'[84] The attack from Bülow more than restored Chamberlain's
credit at home. He met the attack with words the English relished.
'Gentlemen,' he declared at the annual dinner of the Birmingham
jewellers:

> what I have said I have said. I withdraw nothing. I qualify nothing. I
> defend nothing. . . . I do not want to give lessons to a foreign Minister
> and I will not accept any at his hands. I am responsible only to my
> own Sovereign and to my own countrymen.[85]

His audience punctuated every phrase with cheers and erupted after
the last sentence in 'a scene of wild enthusiasm'.[86]

Outside Birmingham, the response was even greater. The City of
London organized a special presentation in the Guildhall to honour
Chamberlain. *The Times* heralded it by pointing out the match between
the wishes of the nation and the talents of the man. 'By a sound instinct
the nation desires to be led by some one who has a mind, who knows
how to handle facts, and who can go to the root of the matter while
others are fumbling with words or losing themselves among non-essen-
tials. We do not want to disparage any of the servants of the Crown,
but it is mere plain fact that at home and abroad Mr. Chamberlain is
recognized as the one among them who pre-eminently stands for efficiency of national effort.'[87]

A month later, 'the respectable middle classes' of London crowded
along the route of the procession. They greeted Chamberlain with a
continuous 'storm of cheers' as he rode, with Mary at his side, in an
open carriage to the Guildhall to receive its address of tribute enclosed
in a golden casket.[88] At the luncheon given by the Lord Mayor afterwards in the Mansion House, the assembled members of the cabinet led
by Balfour accorded Chamberlain 'a position on the roll of statesmen of

this country second to none'. The Lord Mayor and Balfour lay special emphasis on the loyalty to the empire that Chamberlain had evoked 'from our distant fellow-countrymen unparalleled in depth and intensity throughout our long and glorious history'. '... in those outlying and most important portions of our Empire,' said Balfour, 'it is to my right hon. friend that they look as the man who, above all others, has made the British Empire a reality.' Next day *The Times* greeted Chamberlain as 'the most popular and trusted man in England'.

This acclaim inevitably suggested that Chamberlain was the man to succeed old Lord Salisbury when he retired, rather than Balfour who, as Conservative leader in the Commons, was the otherwise natural successor. Voices to this effect were raised in the Unionist press. Individual Unionists including Conservatives approached Chamberlain privately to urge him on. The possibility made Balfour anxious. But Chamberlain did not promote it. He appeared to be fully gratified by serving in effect as the first minister of the empire. Thanks particularly to the response of the self-governing dominions, the Boer War took the empire one more step towards consolidation. Chamberlain described this consolidation glowingly at the Guildhall as

> the aspiration of our ancestors ... striven for by patriotic statesmen of all parties, and now ... within measure of practical accomplishment. It is fraught with consequences of incalculable importance in the coming years. We watch these new nations rising like stars above the horizon, and we hope and believe that they will run their orbit in harmony with our own.[89]

With such a departmental sphere of responsibility, why attempt to seize the prime ministership, which would more naturally devolve upon the leader of the largest division in the governing alliance at home?

Ten days after the triumphal celebration in the City, Chamberlain went out of his way to reassure Balfour. He drew Balfour's private secretary into his room at the House of Commons, and told him 'with great earnestness & almost passionate emphasis' that he was '*not a candidate*' for prime minister:

> I have my own work to do and it is not done yet & I am quite content to stay where I am. ... I shall be quite willing to serve under Balfour—but—mark—I wd. not serve under anyone.[90]

He said the same thing afterwards to would-be backers: 'please remember', he told Leo Maxse who advocated his candidacy in the *National Review*, 'that, in the true and not the ironical sense of the words, *nolo episcopari*. I am very well where I am and have still work to do there which attracts me.'[91] He discouraged any further demonstrations that 'might be regarded as a bid for an office which I have no ambition to hold'.[92]

But while his imperial position seemed unassailable, its domestic underpinnings were cracking. The movement for old-age pensions passed him by. The benevolent societies, after a decade of jealous opposition to his modest pension proposal, leapt beyond it to favour a universal scheme, as did the Trades Union Congress. As for the Education bill, Chamberlain kept up a rearguard action against it well into the new year. But in mid-March the cabinet finally decided on a measure along the lines recommended by Devonshire and Balfour. When the mutiny that Chamberlain expected among Nonconformist Unionists duly erupted, he accepted his share of collective cabinet responsibility for the bill and made what defence of it he could. To companions from the days of the National Education League, he stressed how the bill would implement one of the League's 'main objects'[93] by establishing a local educational authority in every district. To nervous associates in Birmingham, he argued wishfully that 'the mass of people' would turn out to be 'educationalists rather than sectarians'.[94] To the general public he presented the bill as a reorganizational effort to maximize the effectiveness of the network of educational institutions, primary and secondary, denominational and civic. To Nonconformist Unionists who remained unconvinced, he pleaded for them not to place domestic concerns above imperial.

His main imperial concern was how to secure a reliable settlement in South Africa. He wanted unconditional surrender by the Boers. Rather than compromise to expedite peace, he hoped that the British forces would reduce the scope of the war so that it could be sustained without great expense and without exhausting the patience of the British public while waiting for the final Boer surrender. But instead of narrowing the theatre of war and sending some troops home, Kitchener demanded ever more. Even among Unionists, ardour for the war flagged. Those who worried about its cost, preeminently Hicks Beach at the Exchequer, wondered whether Chamberlain would be sufficiently responsive to Boer overtures for peace.

He was indeed none too happy when Boers approached Kitchener at the beginning of April. Their initial proposals were easy to reject because they still called for recognition of the old republics' independence. The Boer spokesmen nevertheless asked what terms Britain would be prepared to offer while rejecting independence. Chamberlain felt obliged to respond. He did so by coupling insistence on the basic features of the offer of 1901 with willingness 'to go further to secure peace' so long as that could be done without 'concessions which may encourage future rebellion, or . . . justify the loyal section in saying that they have been betrayed'.[95]

The negotiations were vexed on the British side by divided counsels in Pretoria. Chamberlain took pains to keep the cabinet abreast of everything from South Africa, including private as well as official communications from Milner, and he sought to incorporate the suggestions of his colleagues in drafting responses to South Africa. Most of the cabinet were more willing than Chamberlain to accommodate the Boers. But Salisbury backed him up consistently; and Chamberlain retained control of the negotiations so far as Westminster was concerned. In Pretoria, however, Milner and Kitchener, who shared responsibility in the face-to-face talks, were divided by a gulf of suspicion. Milner would have preferred to wait more insistently than Chamberlain till the Boers simply surrendered. But with Kitchener beside him anxious for peace, Milner needed steady reinforcement from Chamberlain, and hence could not elude Chamberlain's control. Chamberlain intimated that the government was prepared to respond more generously than in the previous year on two issues: amnesty for Cape rebels and financial aid for Boer farms.

For a month from mid-April to mid-May, while the Boer commandos in the field mulled over the British rejection of their demand for independence, the prospects for the negotiations remained unclear. Chamberlain addressed the Liberal Unionists of Birmingham just as the Boer spokesmen were returning to the negotiating table; and he did nothing to raise hopes for a speedy settlement. He sought instead to lift attention beyond the immediate war to a promising imperial possibility which the war had raised. To help meet the costs of the war, Hicks Beach had recently imposed a low registration duty on imported wheat or corn. At three pennies per hundredweight, the duty had little effect on the price of bread. Even so, British Liberals treated the duty as a violation of free trade, the more shocking because of its inevitable association with the notorious Corn Laws imposed after the Napoleonic wars. Yet the Liberal prime minister of Canada, Sir Wilfrid Laurier, saw the registration duty as giving Britain an opportunity to respond to the imperial tariff preference he had instituted in 1898: Britain could exempt Canadian wheat from the new tax.

Chamberlain welcomed the prospect. Dining a few weeks earlier as the guest of some young rebels in the Unionist party, he offered his hosts 'a precious secret. Tariffs! There are the politics of the future, and of the near future. Study them closely, and make yourselves masters of them, and you will not regret your hospitality to me.'[96] Now he divulged the secret to the public. He began by describing the international challenge:

> The position of this country is not one without anxiety to statesmen and careful observers. The political jealousy . . . the commercial rivalry

more serious than anything we have yet had, the pressure of hostile tariffs, the pressure of bounties, the pressure of subsidies, it is all becoming more weighty and more apparent. What is the object of this system adopted by countries which, at all events, are very prosperous themselves—countries like Germany and other large Continental States? . . . the intention is to shut out this country as far as possible from all profitable trade with those foreign States and at the same time to enable those foreign States to undersell us in British markets.[97]

Then he suggested the basis for a response:

It is impossible that these new methods of competition can be met by adherence to old and antiquated methods. . . . At the present moment the Empire is being attacked on all sides and in our isolation we must look to ourselves. We must draw closer our internal relations, the ties of sentiment, the times of sympathy, yes, and the ties of interest . . . if we do not take every chance in our power to keep British trade in British hands . . . we shall deserve the disasters which will infallibly come upon us.

Attention was diverted from this potentially momentous pronouncement by the return of the Boer negotiators to Pretoria. They came willing to recognize the republics' loss of independence, but they pressed insistently for a comprehensive amnesty and payment of the republics' war debt. There was no trouble on the first score. Milner was aghast, however, at the audacity of the demand that Britain 'virtually pay . . . for conduct of the war against us'.[98] He was not much more sympathetic to the Boers' other financial demand, for aid in restoring their war-torn farms. Milner argued that ultimately all of these costs would fall on British loyalists, many of whom also needed help. In the meantime this expenditure would deprive him of funds the wanted to cultivate 'the finest "undeveloped estate" in the Empire'.[99] But Chamberlain wired back that 'a mere question of money should [not] prevent termination of war which costs more than a million per week'.[100] Reluctantly, Milner cooperated in developing a formula for financial aid which obscured but still covered the payment of Boer War debts.

He was more successful in gutting another provision that Chamberlain wanted: application of the Cape Coloured franchise to the annexed republics. Defence of the rights of the native population and also of British Indians in South Africa had figured prominently in the official British rationale for the war. Milner knew, however, that these claims were intensely unpopular among the white population of the region, British as well as Boer. He bid for their cooperation in the postwar reconstruction by ensuring that under the terms of peace nothing would be done about the enfranchisement of 'Kaffirs' until the new colonies with their purely white electorates had regained the institutions of self-government.

The final accord was signed silently on the last day of May with only an hour to spare before the deadline set by Britain expired. After two and a half years of costly effort, the peace treaty, which Chamberlain preferred to call 'terms of surrender', was an anticlimax. Though he presented it as a vindication of the war effort, he did not greet it with jubilation. 'I wish', he grumbled, that 'K[itchener]. had not allowed them [to retain] their rifles.'[101]

The war was decisive, though not as Chamberlain desired, and not so much for South Africa as for Chamberlain himself and for the cause he had at heart. Milner was already afraid that the war he had precipitated might prove counterproductive. The victors had so little time and money to build the promised land. In Britain too the war had drained the resources available for the imperial cause and cooled the sentiments in its support. Cooled yet not chilled: the willingness of the British public to support the imperial cause was not in immediate doubt. Though bloodier than any war in which Britain had engaged since the defeat of Napoleon, the Boer War was not a terribly sanguinary affair: less than 6,000 British were killed in action, and perhaps as many Boers. The worst losses to the British forces were from disease—some 16,000—and a similar number on the other side, plus some 20,000 from the unsanitary concentration camps. More disturbing from the British standpoint was the fact that almost half a million men had been required to defeat an enemy a tenth that number.

The war proved less costly in blood than in treasure, as Hicks Beach had been warning for some time. The limits of Victorian governmental finance were stretched close to breaking point by the war's ultimate price of nearly a quarter million pounds. Chamberlain did not belittle that cost. But he had begun to discern a way to meet it, a way which accorded with his whole philosophy of governmental expenditure. Just as he tried to keep social reforms along self-financing lines, so now he envisaged an empire financing and thus strengthening itself, through tariffs.

17

Dual Directors
1902–1903

Thanking Lord Salisbury for his congratulations on the Boer surrender, Chamberlain commented, 'Now a new chapter begins'. He knew it would 'not [be] a very easy one to write'.[1] The Boer War had dammed the flow of British politics. It arrested the ebbing of Unionist support evident in prewar by-elections. It gave the government a renewed raison d'être and made Chamberlain its central figure. The war aggravated the divisions among the Liberal opposition. With the end of the war, the floodgate lifted. The waters flowed out with such force that they generated whirlpools as well as forward momentum, threatening to drag those on the surface down as well as thrusting them on.

The most immediately obvious impact was upon the Liberals, who derived nothing but benefit from the onrush. It submerged their wartime differences. Nothing distracted them from drawing together to fight against the corn tax and the Education bill under two historic banners of Liberalism: free trade and fairness to Nonconformists.

The impact upon the Unionists was less straightforward and more dangerous. Military victory exposed problems which the long-fought war had magnified, problems of taxation, neglected social needs, military inadequacy, and international competition both economic and political. The Unionists were tired by their long stretch in office and discredited to some extent by the exhausting war. Still, they had learned from their experience. They were arguably better aware of the country's needs than was the Liberal opposition, committed as it was to old shibboleths.

Among themselves, the Unionists revolved in a variety of circles at different rates and sometimes in different directions. Among the older generation there were squires who longed for a return of the Corn

Laws, not to be confused with another circle, the provincial business interests that had advocated 'Fair Trade' for the past twenty years. There were two interrelated but distinct circles among the younger generation: neomercantilists like W.A.S. Hewins and William Ashley, and geopolitical imperialists led by J.L. Garvin, Leo Maxse and Leo Amery. Most of these men had been Liberals and even supporters of Home Rule or Fabians in their early youth. Moved by a mixture of social and imperial concerns, the neomercantilists grew dissatisfied with the classical Liberal picture of a society composed of rational, purely economically motivated individuals. Taking economic history seriously, they were impressed by the old mercantilist system in which the state encouraged or restrained private economic interests 'to promote national strength and independence'.[2] The leading geopolitical imperialists, on the other hand, were journalists rather than academics; and they were less concerned about Britain's economy than with its deteriorating diplomatic and military position. The geographical orientation of both younger groups lay beyond London. Garvin was Irish, while Hewins and Ashley gravitated like Chamberlain towards the Midlands. Both younger groups paid a lot of attention to Germany. The neomercantilists were impressed by Germany as an intellectual and industrial example; the geo-imperialists were preoccupied with the political threat it posed.

The ministerial elite constituted another circle, remote from the rest, proud of its accumulated wisdom but regarded by ardent spirits with despair. Kipling described the highest tier as '[a]rid, aloof, incurious, unthinking, unthanking, gelt'.[3] The reconstruction of 1900 increased the aristocratic, familial composition of the ministry—the Hotel Cecil, it was dubbed—and failed to bring in new blood. The resurgence afterwards of guerrilla warfare accentuated the impression of ministerial incapacity. Chamberlain alone escaped criticism for lassitude. With the end of the war, criticism quickened among the outer Unionist circles, exasperated with the ministry's unhurried pace.

Chamberlain's understanding of these postwar crosscurrents, though better than most people's, was only partial. He could not face the fact that the Boer War damaged more than it strengthened the imperial cause. That setback was tied up with a personal one. The arrival of peace precipitated a change of command in the government. Physically Lord Salisbury could not carry on. His impending departure accentuated the anomaly of Chamberlain's position. Strong man of the government but leader of its smallest and most idiosyncratic faction, the still Radical Unionists of Birmingham, Chamberlain was likely to be superseded by Balfour. Twelve years junior to Chamberlain and without any of his skills for popular government, Balfour seemed nevertheless to be a reliable ally; he was certainly a courageous administrator; and he was above all leader of the Conservative multitude. While Chamberlain gave up his ambition to be prime minister, he sought to be recognized as first minister of the empire. That, however, was a position without precedent or security.

Furthermore, Chamberlain did not emerge from the war with a clear agenda for his imperial ministry. He was unsure of his course on imperial trade, and it was not yet established as his highest imperial priority. In the early 1890s when he first toyed with the notion of tariffs, his interest had been as much in raising revenue for social reform as in consolidating the empire. After his appointment to the Colonial Office, he thought of tariffs primarily for imperial purposes. But aware that the subject was loaded with controversy, he handled it in gingerly fashion, equally ready to suggest departures in policy and to pull back. Canada's introduction of imperial preference generated a momentum of its own. German academics, concerned about the impact of imperial preference if adopted by Britain, invited the director of the London School of Economics, W.A.S. Hewins, to write an article on 'Imperialism and its probable effect on the Commercial Policy of the United Kingdom'.[4] The invitation led Hewins to contact Chamberlain as the likely leader of a movement for economic consolidation of the empire. But when Hewins's letter arrived, Chamberlain was preoccupied with the Boer War and the impending general election. He chilled Hewins by questioning the likelihood of 'any considerable change in the commercial policy of the United Kingdom'.[5] The guerrilla war kept Chamberlain cautious. For a while he had 'no belief in the possibility of any great or far-reaching change' in imperial relations. 'Until we can persuade the self-governing Colonies to make suggestions to us (even if they have been first "suggested" to them),' he explained to the new secretary for war with regard to imperial defence, 'we shall not succeed.'[6]

Beneath the surface of these remarks, however, Chamberlain's imperial thought moved forward. Only two states, the United States and Germany, could rest assured that their future lay among the greatest powers. In the closing weeks of the war and the first weeks of peace, Chamberlain was haunted by fear that Britain would be demoted from this circle. While Britain fought in South Africa, Germany moved past it in industrial production and prepared to challenge Britain's naval supremacy. The United States raced far ahead and began to supersede Britain in spheres where Britain thought itself supreme, as a supplier of international capital and in merchant shipping.

The war opened up a few resources to help Britain offset these alarming trends. 30,000 troops from Australia, New Zealand and Canada ral-

lied to the imperial colours in South Africa. Hicks Beach revived registration duties on imports, particularly the corn tax, which he envisaged
as a permanent increase in the financial resources at the disposal of
the government. He still opposed any form of tariff protection,
including imperial preference; but having come so far, perhaps he could
be pushed farther. There was hope as well as caution in Chamberlain's
remark to the First Lord of the Admiralty about Hicks Beach in the final
days of the war: 'at present we must take what we can get & proceed
slowly'.[7] In truly mercantilist fashion, Chamberlain also thought of
reviving the old Navigations Acts.

His preoccupation with the political economy of the empire affected
his industrial concerns. He felt little respect for devotees of international trade who did not heed its impact on growth at home. He
reacted sharply when coalmining magnates cried out against the small
excise Hicks Beach imposed on exported coal to help pay for the
war. Chamberlain criticized them not just for unwillingness to share
the imperial financial burden but also because their vast exports of
coal 'help our competitors to carry on their competition with our
trades and manufactures'.[8] His knowledge of manufacturing helped
him understand that, if British industry was to regain the technological and marketing edge it was losing to the Americans and Germans,
Britain needed higher education in applied science and business
management. On the other hand, his responsibility for undeveloped
colonies and his association with Tory squires like Henry Chaplin
made him sympathize with some of the least advanced segments of
the British and imperial economy. The export on which he first took
issue with the Germans was beet root sugar. It was Germany's most
rewarding export in the early 1890s but was then surpassed by manufactured goods. Despite the German trend towards technologically sophisticated exports, Chamberlain paid more attention as Colonial
Secretary to agricultural goods. The fight to defend the inefficient West
Indian cane sugar made Chamberlain an advocate of countervailing
duties.

Despite all the talk of trade, ultimately Chamberlain's concept of
empire was more political than economic. He attracted the rising generation of geopolitical imperialists with his recognition of Britain's need
for reinforcement amid the rivalry of the international powers at the
turn of the century. Garvin and Leo Maxse welcomed the exchange of
insults with Bülow as evidence of Chamberlain's alienation from Germany, the power they most feared. Maxse introduced him in the spring
of 1902 to George Saunders, the Berlin correspondent of *The Times*, who
warned Chamberlain of the German world mission being preached,
among others, by the Germanized Houston Stewart Chamberlain, no
relation of Britain's Colonial Secretary.

Setbacks

For two months after the Boer surrender, Chamberlain found little to say in Parliament. Meanwhile his position was undermined by his cabinet colleagues, imperial associates, and his own illusions. The first blow, bordering on treachery, was dealt by Milner. The way Chamberlain handled it broadened respect for him at home. Still, the blow drew attention to the unending precariousness of everything he did with regard to South Africa.

From the beginning of the year, hidden by distance, Milner had been fomenting a demand among the British of the Cape Colony for the very thing Chamberlain had ruled out: suspension of the colonial constitution. The end of the war would have to be accompanied by the ending of martial law in the Cape and the restoration to power of Sir Gordon Sprigg's government, which depended on the tolerance of the Afrikaner Bond as well as of British Progressives. Milner recoiled at the prospect. A minority of the Dutch, particularly in the western and northern Cape, had fought for the Boers, and most of the other Cape Dutch felt some sympathy with them. The genuine rebels were sure to lose their franchise with the return of civilian government; but the other Cape Dutch would remain politically decisive until fresh elections were held on an electoral map redrawn to reflect the shift in population to urban, predominantly British areas. Meanwhile, as Milner put it, the loyalists 'would not count for more, man for man, in the hour of victory than the people who in the struggle have been against us'.[9] Milner was also anxious 'to get on as fast as possible with all recuperative work',[10] including the resumption of mining, enlargement of the British population, and federation of the British affiliated states in southern Africa. An uncooperative government at the Cape could delay action on these measures during the precious few years that would elapse before Britain restored self-government to the former republics.

Disregarding Chamberlain's injunctions, Milner prompted Rhodes to persuade the Progressive party in the Cape legislature to demand temporary suspension of the colonial constitution. When Rhodes died at the end of March before completing his task, Milner took it over himself, ostensibly in his private rather than official capacity. The Boer overtures for peace quickened his pace. He hurried south from Johannesburg to Cape Town—for a holiday, he told Chamberlain—in fact to raise support for suspension and secure the cooperation of the newly appointed Governor of Cape Colony, Hely-Hutchinson. In mid-May, Milner issued a statement supporting suspension, for publication in the *Cape Times*. He kept news of his statement from being telegraphed to Britain. On the last day of May, while waiting for the final Boer decision on the terms of surrender, he sent Chamberlain a long despatch on the topic of suspension without mentioning the course he had taken, and he sent the despatch by sea mail. What Milner pressed Chamberlain for by telegram in the first days of peace was generous funding for economic rehabilitation. 'My sole reliance', he wired unctuously to the Colonial Secretary, 'is on you personally.'[11] By mid-June, Chamberlain was aware of the mounting clamour in the Cape Colony, and he assured Parliament at Westminster that the Cape constitution would not be suspended without its approval. Not suspecting the identity of the leader of the agitation, Chamberlain ordered Hely-Hutchinson to preserve official neutrality towards the local movement.

Milner's despatch of 31 May on the subject of suspension reached Chamberlain on the day that *The Times* in London published news of the stand Milner had taken in Cape Town. Chamberlain reacted with a sense of personal betrayal. 'I am sure', he wired to Milner,

> you will admit that I have supported you with absolute loyalty & that I have done my best to shield you from criticism. . . . Under these circumstances I am deeply hurt to find that in a matter of cardinal importance in which I desired the utmost caution you should have fully expressed your views to private individuals without giving me the opportunity of considering them beforehand.[12]

Chamberlain could not disguise from the cabinet the extent to which Milner had misled him, nor did he attempt to minimize the dilemma in which the government found itself. Liberal imperialists went out of their way to assure Chamberlain of their support in resisting the demand for suspension. But Chamberlain found no comfort in assistance from his opponents, and he knew that Milner's advocacy of suspension would find some sympathy among the government's supporters. A few members of the cabinet, preeminently Selborne, hesitated to stand up to Milner. Chamberlain did not. He continued to insist that '[n]othing but the safety of the state or the clearly expressed desire of a great majority of the white population' of the colony, Dutch as well as British, would justify suspending its constitution.[13]

Though disconcerted by the intensity of Chamberlain's reaction, Milner deepened his commitment to the underlying policy, 'to fight the Bond, or its analogues, when it spreads to the new Colonies, . . . tooth & nail'.[14] Rather than compromise, he proposed to resign his office after a discreet interval of months and in the meantime to abstain 'from any dealing whatever with political questions at the Cape'.[15] He recognized, as Chamberlain never did, that the trust needed for effective working between them had gone. Chamberlain tried to minimize their difference, though he continued to damn the demand for suspension as 'likely rather to produce discontent and agitation than to pacify race hatred'.[16] On the difference in basic policy, Chamberlain could go no farther in Milner's direction than to wish that both organizations of ethnic militancy, the (British) South African League as well as the Afrikaner Bond, would dissolve themselves.

The break in his accord with Milner was followed by a quick succession of blows at home. The first was physical. Chamberlain was hurrying between engagements in a horse-drawn cab over a slippery stretch of Whitehall on 7 July when the horse plunged down, loosening a pane of window glass. It fell, gashing Chamberlain's forehead to the bone. Pouring blood though never losing consciousness, he was taken nearby to Charing Cross Hospital. He refused anaesthetic as the broad wound was stitched. After two days he was allowed home with orders from his doctors to stay in bed and avoid all work for two weeks. The long-term consequences of the accident remain imponderable; but it was bound to shake the system and draw attention to the age of a man who had just turned sixty-six. Occasionally during the past two years, he had confessed to close associates that he 'felt very tired, & could wish (but for patriotic considerations) that the [Liberals] could come in for a short time & give [him] a holiday'.[17] The accident could only deepen his fundamental fatigue—and when he was tired, he tended to act rashly.

Politically, the most significant thing about the accident was what it did *not* prevent from happening. Two days after it occurred, Balfour allowed a free vote on the clause in the Education bill that made rate aid for denominational schools optional rather than mandatory. The optional clause was all that mitigated the offence of this use of rate aid in the eyes of many Nonconformists. Austen Chamberlain, in place of his father, spoke to uphold the option. But Balfour not only indicated his own sympathy for making the aid mandatory; he also stipulated that the increased governmental grant which he had recently announced for county councils to help them meet their educational responsibilities would apply only to those that took over the school boards. Voting in the interests of their pocket and the Established Church, the Unionist majority decided in favour of mandatory rate aid.

Next day, on 10 July, without forewarning the cabinet, Lord Salisbury tendered his resignation as prime minister to the king. His haste in resigning had nothing to do with Chamberlain's temporary absence from the scene, but rather with the rescheduling of the coronation. Edward VII was to be crowned on 26 June but was taken ill shortly beforehand, and the coronation was postponed till August. The old prime minister, in crumbling health, could not hold on till then. Anxious about the governing alliance, he declined the customary responsibility for advising the king on whom to appoint in his stead. There was no need to do so. Salisbury recognized that the bulk of the party was inclined towards Balfour; and the king had intimated that he shared that inclination. Furthermore, at the height of the talk earlier in the year about Chamberlain for prime minister, Chamberlain had informed Salisbury 'that if at any time you contemplated retirement my supposed ambition would not prevent me from giving to Arthur any support that it might be in my power to render'.[18] The only way in which the prime ministership might come to Chamberlain would have been for Balfour to decline it in his favour.

The four men involved in the change of command—the king, the old prime minister, the new, and the one who would not be—handled the affair gracefully. Immediately upon receiving the royal commission, before anyone else knew of it, Balfour hastened to Chamberlain's bedside to make sure of his approval, which was cordially given. Yet this transaction between the two was based upon illusion on both sides. Chamberlain thought that he could hold coordinate, in some ways even superior, authority in the reconstituted government as first minister of the empire. If Balfour detected this illusion, he did nothing to upset it, for he suffered from another: that his mastery in his own government would not require rough assertion.

Chamberlain acted according to his illusion in the reallocation of offices that followed the change in prime minister. He could have had any department he wished. Some of those who looked to him for leadership hoped that he would either move to the Exchequer or take overall responsibility for reform of the armed services. The Exchequer was vacated by Hicks Beach, who retired along with Salisbury in reaction to evidence of Balfour's willingness, particularly on education and the army, to exceed the limits of peacetime expenditure on which Hicks Beach wanted to insist. If Chamberlain took over the Exchequer, he would be in a position to supervise expenditure in all fields and shape the financial policy of the government, for instance in response to the Canadian suggestion that Britain give the corn tax an imperially preferential character. But Chamberlain did not stop to consider these possibilities. The moment Balfour's appointment as prime minister was announced, Chamberlain let it be known that he would remain where he was. 'Mr. Chamberlain has no thought of leaving the Colonial Office,' *The Times* was authorized to announce, 'his view being that the work he has undertaken for the welding together of the Empire is as yet by no means accomplished.'[19]

He was in the midst of that work when his cab accident took place. It occurred during the second week of a conference he had convened with the premiers of the self-governing colonies—Canada, Australia,

New Zealand, the Cape, Natal and Newfoundland—in connection with the coronation. Chamberlain hoped to make much of this opportunity to weld the empire together; and his determination was only deepened by the disappointing first sessions of the conference. Disregarding doctor's orders, he returned to chair the conference ten days after his mishap.

British expectations of the conference were raised by Chamberlain's presidency over its deliberations. Imperialists believed and Little Englanders feared that his dealings at the Colonial Office with the self-governing colonies had gained him 'a popularity greater [beyond the seas] than any other Imperial statesman has ever commanded'.[20] His own hopes were quickened by the contribution of the self-governing colonies to the recent war. In his first speech after the Boer surrender, he gloried in the fact that the colonies had

> leapt to arms, in order to show the world a united Empire, in order to prove that the outlying parts, although separated from us by the expanse of ocean, although they are in themselves free and independent countries as far as their local affairs are concerned, yet constitute one people, under one flag, under one Sovereign, pursuing together a common destiny.[21]

The discussions he had over the next few weeks sustained but also sobered his hopes. In debating the new corn tax, the House of Commons concerned itself mainly with its possible reduction in favour of Canada; and Hicks Beach refused to rule out that possibility for the future. In the context of this debate, Chamberlain transmitted to the Canadian prime minister a suggestion that in return for exemption from the corn duty Canada might exempt certain British textiles from its tariffs. Laurier leapt at the suggestion, hoping that Hicks Beach would act on it while the Finance bill was still before Parliament. Hicks Beach was not willing to act that quickly if at all, and the proposal collapsed. But it impressed Chamberlain with the possibility of driving a bargain with the Canadians.

He was also impressed with the need to improve the bargain from the British perspective. The free-trading instincts prevalent among the British civil service were reflected in a memorandum from the President of the Board of Trade, Arthur Balfour's brother Gerald. It emphasized the difficulty of devising a preferential system that reconciled the interests of the various colonies with those of the mother country. Instead the Board of Trade suggested shipping subsidies to reduce freight rates on trade within the empire.

The colonial conference opened at the end of June in a climate of excited anticipation, from which it sought to protect itself by reporting only briefly to the public. The participants were further distracted by the postponement of the coronation, which upset their plans for summer travel and return home. Unsettled himself, Chamberlain stumbled in his opening address between pursuing a vision and driving a bargain. His agenda was clear enough: 'our paramount object', he told the half dozen colonial premiers, 'is to strengthen the bonds which unite us'. He identified and ranked the three main avenues towards this end: first development of unifying political institutions, secondly commercial union, and in third place imperial defence. Despite the smallness of his audience, he presented the paramount object with eloquence. He began with the line from Matthew Arnold which struck him even before he became an imperialist: 'The weary Titan staggers under the too vast orb of its fate.' Chamberlain continued: 'We have borne the burden for many years. We think it is time that our children should assist us to support it.'[22] Later, referring to defence and thinking of Canada where the standard of living was already higher than in Britain, he returned to his initial theme:

> now that the Colonies are rich and powerful, that every day they are growing by leaps and bounds, their material prosperity promises to rival that of the United Kingdom itself, and I think it is inconsistent with their position—inconsistent with their dignity as nations—that they should leave the mother country to bear the whole, or almost the whole, of the expense.[23]

It was easier to express his objective than to secure it. Try though he might, he could not convince the assembled premiers that he appreciated the autonomous desires of the colonies they led. Adhering to the pattern he set in securing colonial troops for the South African war, Chamberlain made suggestions to the premiers in the hope of winning a 'spontaneous' response from them. While he spoke encouragingly of an imperial council to which executive and legislative powers could be added he insisted that the demand for such a council 'must come from the Colonies. If it comes,' he promised, 'it will be enthusiastically received in this country.' Yet he roused anxieties he needed to allay. He argued that what distinguished the member states of the empire from each other was qualitatively no greater than the differences the United States or Canada had overcome in unifying themselves. But he understood these distinctions within narrowly ethnic British confines. Heedless of Laurier's Francophone susceptibilities, Chamberlain spoke about the desirability of filling up 'the spare places in your lands with . . . above all, a British population'.[24] Fearing that at heart he was a Big Englander, the colonial premiers simply ignored his proposals for constitutional consolidation of the empire.

The way in which Chamberlain opened the subject of imperial trade was more tactless. He did not yet fully understand his own priorities on the commercial issue. The primary objective in uniting the empire through commerce was the political one of imperial strength rather than the economic one of prosperity. The two were of course bound up together, but to say that was to miss the point. If prosperity were the overriding concern, why discount the enormous worldwide market in favour of the much smaller imperial one? That was the question which Sir Robert Giffen, the renowned statistician formerly with the Board of Trade, asked Chamberlain privately during the conference. Chamberlain boasted that the empire could become economically self-sustaining, and he deplored the fact that Britain conducted most of its trade with foreign countries. But that pattern had grown up in response to economic opportunity undeflected by the concerns of state. Chamberlain argued that concentrated development of the imperial economy would be ultimately in the economic interests of its member countries: but, at least for Britain, that was to prefer a long-term gamble to the lucrative game on hand. In the final analysis, commercial consolidation of the empire was a mercantilist policy designed to build up such an economy as would strengthen the state.

Chamberlain began to grasp that point during the colonial conference. But at its outset he missed it. Prompted by the Board of Trade, he discussed imperial preference as a matter of economic advantage, and played down its political significance. The colonial premiers listened to his presentation 'with astonishment and disappointment'.[25] The issue revolved around the tariff preference Canada gave Britain in 1898 and raised in 1900 without prospect of reward from Britain—until the introduction of the corn duty kindled Canadian hopes. Chamberlain trod roughly on those hopes. The Board of Trade convinced him, and he tried to convince the conference, that the preference of 1898–1900 had done nothing more than offset the decline that British exports to Canada had undergone with the imposition of the Canadian protective tariff in 1888. He wanted more from the Canadians before exempting Canadian wheat from the British corn duty. He wanted Canada to exempt some British manufactured goods from its tariff, so that he could demonstrate to the British that imperial preference was a substantial benefit. Economically he was right. After a battle of figures with the Board of Trade, the Canadians had to confess that their basic table of tariffs had indeed been designed to protect nascent Canadian manufactures against British competition. But the confession was a dubious gain from Chamberlain's standpoint. Instead of utilizing the generous sentiments behind the Canadian preference, he exposed the division in economic interest between the colony and the mother country without generating hope for improvement unless the basic fiscal policy of one or the other were radically altered.

With regard to the third item on the agenda of the conference, imperial defence, Chamberlain left the initiative from the British side to the British service ministers, Selborne for the navy and Brodrick for the army. Like Chamberlain, they pushed too hard and ended up with empty hands. They even lost the one substantial proposal on offer from the colonial premiers. Seddon of New Zealand, the only imperial enthusiast among them, called for the creation in each colony of an imperial reserve force. It would initially be composed of seasoned troops returning from the Boer War, and would be available for service outside the colony at the joint expense of and within limits agreed upon by the colonial and imperial governments.

Selborne and Brodrick were eager for contributions from the colonies to ease the burden of imperial defence. But the British service ministers were reluctant to accept restrictions from the colonies along with their contributions. Chamberlain did not help matters by contrasting the 'backward' failure of Canadians and Australians to understand the need to pay for their defence with the 'wiser opinion' of New Zealand.[26] Instead of simply accepting New Zealand's offer for an imperial reserve force, Brodrick insisted that the contingent from New Zealand be free to serve anywhere including India and Europe, whereas Seddon wanted to limit its liability for service to China, South Africa and Canada. When protracted discussions between the British service ministers and the colonial premiers produced little result, Chamberlain tried to patch together some agreement. He proposed giving New Zealand more control over its contingent than Brodrick liked. Chilled by all the wrangling, Seddon withdrew his offer. At the close of the conference, the Canadians explained that their objection to participation in an imperial reserve force stemmed 'not so much from the expense involved, as from a belief that [it] would entail an important departure from the principle of Colonial self-government'.[27] Thereafter Chamberlain abandoned this route to imperial unification.

But he was not willing to give up the commercial route. Nor was Laurier. He sought a meeting with Chamberlain as soon as possible after his cab accident. Upon returning to the chair of the colonial conference, Chamberlain put its deliberations about trade on to a better footing. He now saw clearly and stated that the primary issue was not economic advantage but 'the unity of the Empire'.[28] No longer willing to be held back by the Board of Trade or the Treasury, he alluded to his own 'private and personal conviction on the subject'. He showed himself willing to consider and, if opportune, to advocate a remarkable variety of means to increase imperial trade: fixed rates of preference, tariff exemptions, shipping subsidies, navigation laws, bounties on imports. But he was still not ready for a fundamental British departure from international free trade unless he could bring about free trade within the empire.

Laurier arranged to meet Chamberlain again; and they agreed to intensified negotiations between the individual colonies and the Board of Trade. The ensuing discussions with the Canadian delegation revealed that they did not mean to alter their basic trading policy or cease protecting their manufacturing industry from British competition. Rather than reduce their tariffs against British manufactures, the Canadians proposed to heighten their tariff against foreign countries. That alternative had no attractions for Chamberlain. Far from leading to imperial free trade, the Canadian proposal might not even increase Canadian consumption of British goods. Yet the Canadians began to threaten that unless their four-year-old preference received some reward, they might withdraw it.

They did not want, however, to end up with recriminations. Working back and forth with the other participants in the conference, the Canadians devised a set of resolutions. All the participants agreed that preferential trade would strengthen the empire; and they recommended that every colony should 'give substantial preferential treatment to the products and manufactures of the United Kingdom'.[29] In a further resolution to which Chamberlain could not commit himself officially, the colonial premiers urged the British government to grant preference to colonial produce and manufactures 'either by exemption from or reduction of duties now or hereafter imposed'. The Canadians let it be known that they expected early compliance by Britain, without which they reserved the right to reconsider their original grant of preference.

Though disappointed by the outcome and disillusioned with each other, Chamberlain and Laurier refused to be discouraged. Ignoring the fact that the Anglophone province of Ontario was the heartland of protectionist manufacturing, Chamberlain trusted the British population of Canada to keep the French premier of the country up to the imperial mark. Laurier still wanted preferential access to the British market, particularly for the wheat from the Canadian prairies. He assured Chamberlain that the discussions at the conference put him in 'high hope' that the trade between their two countries would be 'very much improved in the near future'.[30]

Attempted repairs

Wherever Chamberlain looked that August, his affairs lay in disarray. He had to scramble to salvage anything from the colonial conference.

His achievement in South Africa was assailed by Milner's advocacy of constitutional suspension. At home Chamberlain was taken aback by his inability to shape policy as he thought best. On occasion in the late summer and autumn of 1902 he conveyed his frustration to questioners by saying, 'If I were dictator . . .', only to point out that the policy he preferred was unattainable and that they must reconcile themselves to constraints which he could not elude.

For more than a month after his accident, he could not put in the long days at his desk or at meetings and the nights in conversation that he needed to keep abreast of events. Once he acquired some sense of his bearings, he wrote to the new prime minister. 'My dear Arthur,' he began, '. . . From what I hear & read I fear that things are not going well, and I confess that I am exceedingly anxious as to the future.'[31] His immediate concerns were the Education bill and the reconstruction of the government.

Encouraged by Balfour's request for his approval before accepting the prime ministership, Chamberlain had approached the reconstruction as a task which the two men might share as party leaders in the governing alliance. But Balfour acted entirely according to his own lights. The argument between the two men revolved around the lacklustre Conservative Secretary of State for India, Lord George Hamilton. His removal from the India Office, on top of the resignation of Hicks Beach from the Exchequer, would make room for a substantial reconstruction, enough to give the government some new life, which Chamberlain felt it needed. But instead of Hamilton, Balfour dropped Lord James of Hereford, whose post at the Duchy of Lancaster had no intrinsic administrative significance. The misuse of opportunity was all the worse in Chamberlain's eyes because Lord James was one of the senior Liberal Unionists in the cabinet and had done yeoman service for Chamberlain in drafting domestic legislation. Jesse Collings, Chamberlain's ailing henchman, wrote to condole with James on Balfour's galling devotion to 'his own exclusive circle'[32]—only to receive word that Balfour was dropping him too! Austen Chamberlain was promoted to cabinet office but in the position of Postmaster General where, as his father noted regretfully, he would have little time to bring his weight to bear on political issues of general importance.

Before the reconstruction was complete, the electoral consequences of Balfour's Education bill became painfully apparent. They enhanced Chamberlain's ability to criticize the bill and enabled him to neutralize its impact on Nonconformist Unionism, but only in Birmingham. In the end, the bill accentuated the narrowness of his base and left him feeling estranged within the cabinet. Preoccupied by South Africa and the colonial conference, he had been unprepared for, and because of his accident he may even have been unaware of, the mid-July amendment to the Education bill that made rate aid for denominational schools mandatory. But the Unionists' loss of a previously safe seat at Leeds woke him up. Though the chief agent of the Conservative party argued that the corn tax and not the Education bill was responsible for the party's misfortune, the seriousness of the Nonconformist defection was clear. The victorious Liberal candidate had concentrated his campaign on the iniquities of the bill from a Nonconformist standpoint and was aided by well-organized Nonconformist forces both local and national. 'After Leeds,' Chamberlain told Balfour, 'I do not think that any seat where there is a strong Nonconformist electorate, can be considered as absolutely safe.'[33]

Under different pressures from their respective parties, Chamberlain and Balfour groped their way towards a solution of the education question acceptable to all but the most rabid religionists on either side. Chamberlain quelled a mutiny among the Liberal Unionists of Birmingham by promising that the secular as distinct from the religious instruction provided by denominational schools in receipt of rate aid would be subject to popular control. Meanwhile Balfour discovered that Conservative backbenchers, though anxious to uphold Church of England schools, did not want to place them under the control of the Church of England clergy. Interested himself in educational efficiency more than denominational controversy, he accepted an amendment to the bill ensuring that control of religious instruction in denominational schools would rest in lay rather than clerical hands. That change helped to mute reaction in Birmingham when Chamberlain's promise proved barren. He was saved from discredit afterwards by the effective use which the Liberal Unionist educators of Birmingham made of the administrative improvements in the new Education Act.

Chamberlain could understand that Balfour as a Conservative had to accommodate Conservative supporters of the Established Church. But there was no such excuse for the Duke of Devonshire. He seemed, as co-sponsor of the Education Act, to betray the Whig tradition of protecting Nonconformists from oppression. Chamberlain could only account for Devonshire's stance on rate aid for denominational schools as spinelessness, the Whig vice he had always suspected in Devonshire. Frustrated beyond endurance in September when the reaction to the Education bill in Birmingham looked most threatening, he exploded to Devonshire over the whole range of issues confronting them, foreign as well as domestic:

> I never can get any real support from you or any one else in the Cabinet, in support of my own convinced opinion that we ought not to give

way to the bluffing of any Foreign Power & that if the worst come to the worst we could hold out, as our ancestors did, against the lot of them. . . .

The political future seems to me—an optimist by profession—most gloomy.

I told you that your Education Bill would destroy your own Party.

It has done so. Our best friends are leaving us by scores & hundreds & they will not come back. . . .

We are so deep in the mire that I do not see how we can get out.[34]

Though the subsequent *modus vivendi* with Balfour on the Education bill calmed Chamberlain down, he continued to feel that he was walking on quicksand.

While Balfour kept control of the composition and domestic policy of the government, he encouraged Chamberlain to treat the empire as his own. It was a heady assignment, and Chamberlain accepted it with euphoria. Hopeful about the postwar outlook in South Africa, he tried to convince Milner that they were 'in entire agreement' on all fundamental issues. Discounting the bitterness of the Afrikaners, he assured Milner that 'as long as the physical force is under our control British rule will be firmly established and nothing can touch our more important interests'.[35] Milner, however, was as gloomy as the Boers. He defied Chamberlain's injunctions over suspension of the Cape constitution by urging British loyalists to stand up to the Afrikaners, whether at the Cape or in the annexed republics. 'A few years ago,' he told one of the stalwarts, 'we had two great weights resting upon us—the Bond supremacy of the Cape Colony, and the hostile Transvaal. . . . I had hoped that the tremendous struggle which we have just gone through, would rid us of both; as a matter of fact it has only rid us of one.'[36] Unable to persuade Chamberlain to declare political war on the Bond, Milner persisted in his resolve to resign the high commissionership within a few months. In the meantime he slowed down his replies to inquiries from the Colonial Office. By the end of October Chamberlain recognized that his differences with Milner involved basic policy, and he arranged for Milner's eventual replacement by the Conservative Secretary for Scotland, Lord Balfour of Burleigh.

Chamberlain was somewhat sobered also by his first encounter with the defeated Boers. Three of the Boer generals, Botha, De Wet and De La Rey, sailed for England to see if they could ease the terms of the surrender and raise financial support for reconstruction from Continental sympathizers. Chamberlain hoped to woo his erstwhile adversaries with a mixed display of British might and sympathy. But they saw more mastery than sympathy. No sooner had the travellers landed at Southampton than they were swept out to meet the Colonial Secretary on the deck of a British man-of-war. He invited them to watch the British fleet sail past in honour of the coronation, 'your ships,' he remarked with heavy grandeur, 'as you have sworn to be loyal British subjects'.[37] He was annoyed when they declined that invitation and a subsequent one to dine with him after their first day in conference. Alerted by their sour response, he requested a list before the conference of the items they wished to discuss. He was indignant when they asked for an entire revision of the agreement that ended the war. In Birmingham at the time, he refused to go to London to confer with the generals until they undertook not to ask for anything inconsistent with the terms of surrender signed in Pretoria.

The generals quickly recognized their misstep in asking more from Chamberlain than they realistically expected him to grant; and their conference with him began without further delay. Eager once again for the Boer spokesmen to bear out his hopes, Chamberlain responded cordially to their requests for improvement in the detailed application of the Pretoria agreement. He purred afterwards that the generals were now 'mild as new milk'.[38] He asked Botha and De La Rey to serve on the governor's council in the crown colonial government of the Transvaal, and they were inclined to agree.

But Chamberlain's delight did not last. After leaving for the Continent, the generals launched their campaign for financial help with an appeal couched in the language of endless suffering. It infuriated Chamberlain. Contempt was added to his anger when the generals raised little more than a hundred thousand pounds from their Continental sympathizers, in contrast to the three millions pledged by Kitchener and Milner at Pretoria. His reaction was further embittered by the secrecy with which the generals covered the treasury Kruger had carried with him when he fled from his republic to Holland. The generals refused even to commit those funds publicly to help the widows and orphans over whose plight they wrung European hearts. At a final meeting back in London, the generals quarrelled with Chamberlain over the interpretation of the original terms of surrender, and Chamberlain suspended his invitation for Botha and De La Rey to serve on the governor's council.

The only promising development in the imperial sphere for Chamberlain that autumn came from Canada. Dazzled, however, by a grander opportunity which opened in South Africa, he did not give the Canadian seed the patient cultivation it needed. At the end of August, the Canadian finance minister Fielding visited Chamberlain at Highbury. Fielding still wanted a reciprocal agreement on the British corn tax. He encouraged Chamberlain to press his cabinet colleagues for preferential exemption of Canada with a view to reducing the Canadian tariff on British manufactured goods. Such an agreement would not come easily; it would encounter strong resistance in both governments. Nor would the opportunity to work out an agreement last long. The cabinets in both countries needed to settle the main features of their budgets before their parliaments opened for the new year.

Chamberlain agreed to recommend preferential modification of the corn tax to the British cabinet and promised also to keep Fielding informed so that he could work out the Canadian response. Early in October, on his way back to Ottawa, Fielding reminded Chamberlain of their accord. Before the month was out, Chamberlain did as he had promised and asked the cabinet to allow colonial corn into the United Kingdom free of duty. Balfour responded cautiously, aware that the proposal 'raises very big questions indeed—colonial and fiscal—and [that] the Government which embarks upon it provokes a big fight'.[39] The cabinet undertook to mull over Chamberlain's proposal for consideration when they next met.

But he was already thinking of other things. With encouragement from Balfour, before Chamberlain raised the subject of the corn tax with his cabinet colleagues, he informed them that he intended to embark the next month on a tour of imperial reconciliation to the war-torn colonies in South Africa. He envisaged the trip as the first in a succession he might take to the major colonies as first minister of the empire. Balfour heralded the South African tour as a reflection of Chamberlain's 'special relation with the Colonies'.

Though duly impressed by the grand gesture, Fielding reacted to the news with dismay. The Canadian finance minister sensed better than the British Colonial Secretary that the tour might take him away from England before he won the decision they both desired from the British cabinet. Chamberlain came close to securing the decision before he left for Africa. The opposition in the cabinet was led by Hicks Beach's replacement as Chancellor of the Exchequer, C.T. Ritchie. An earnest but unoriginal politician from the mercantile upper-middle class, Ritchie had distinguished himself at the Home Office by sponsoring the domestic reforms commonly associated with Chamberlain. As Chancellor he came under the tutelage of the mandarins of the Treasury led by Sir Edward Hamilton. Through Ritchie, they presented the well-polished case against deviation from free trade. Ritchie embellished the case by relaying the concern of Captain Middleton, the chief organizer of the Conservative party, at the unpopularity of the corn tax in the constituencies.

But Ritchie found himself in a rearguard position when the cabinet met to discuss the tax a week before Chamberlain's departure. Balfour knew of Middleton's further judgement that constituency opinion would turn round if the corn tax led to 'a general scheme of fiscal reform in the direction of protection'.[40] The only member of the cabinet to reinforce Ritchie in support of the Treasury's position was Lord Londonderry, a Tory grandee notorious for his incoherence in debate and, as the leading coal magnate in County Durham, hostile to Chamberlain since the passage of the Workmen's Compensation Act. Lord Balfour of Burleigh disliked any departure from free trade but held his peace, perhaps in view of his likely appointment to succeed Milner. Ritchie could not stop the cabinet agreeing in principle to amend the corn tax preferentially 'in favour of the British Empire'.[41]

On the other hand, Chamberlain could not turn the agreement in principle into a commitment for communication to the Canadians. Ritchie asked for time to see whether evidence would accumulate to suggest dropping the corn tax altogether. He was given until the end of February or beginning of March, when Chamberlain was due back from South Africa and the budget would have to be settled. Unable to carry his agreement with Fielding into effect, Chamberlain tried to leave things up to him. Scrupulously respecting the cabinet's decision not to communicate their agreement in principle to the Canadians lest it be taken as a commitment, Chamberlain suggested to Fielding that he draft two alternative budgets. In one of them he could spell out the tariff concessions Canada would offer Britain in return for exclusion from the British corn tax. By doing so Fielding could strengthen Chamberlain's hand when he returned to England for the final decision on the corn tax. But the suggestion had no appeal for Fielding. Disappointed, he sat back to follow the international press coverage of the British Colonial Secretary's voyage to see his empire.

Distraction

Chamberlain was content to leave without nailing down an agreement. It would have nailed him down as well, to a policy with an uncertain reward, since the Canadians were more likely to raise tariffs against foreign imports than lower them in favour of the British. He had not yet committed himself to the economic principle of protection. Speaking on his way down the east coast of Africa to British merchants in Zanzibar, he chided them for looking to government for help: 'They tell me you want bounties,' he said; 'That's not English.'[42]

He approached his visit to South Africa as a kind of escape. An imperial mission away from England would release him from the ascendancy of Balfour. When Balfour became prime minister, one of Chamberlain's first responses was to say that he was thinking of 'a visit to all the self-governing Colonies'.[43] Hicks Beach, when he heard of the plan, immediately recognized that it would place Chamberlain 'in the eyes of foreigners and colonials, in something of a Royal position as compared with his colleagues, as representing this country by himself'.[44] The mission to South Africa would also distance him from the unfortunate Education Act.

His cab accident left him longing for a real holiday, the first after seven years of extraordinary work. Mary was worried by his fatigue. Her concern turned his thoughts of a South African trip into a firm plan. She too looked tired: he thought often of her that autumn, of the former voyage of escape and recovery he had taken to Washington in 1887, and of what he had found there. What most impressed the farewell audience in Birmingham when he left for South Africa was the tribute he paid to Mary. Further concerns for family and friends were on his mind. His youngest child, Ethel, the only one so far to be married, had been worryingly ill for some months. Jesse Collings was depressed and failing. When John Morley, who had been commissioned to write the official life of Gladstone, wrote to Chamberlain for information on his years of service under the Grand Old Man, Chamberlain seized the opportunity to repair the broken friendship. All in all, for personal and political reasons, he wanted opportunity for recovery.

Still, from every angle, the trip proved to be a mistake. It exhausted rather than restored him. Any analogy with his mission to Washington was misleading. In 1887 Chamberlain needed to jump political tracks; and his trip to the New World helped him find his way again in the Old. There was no such option for him in 1902. He was not adrift but fettered by responsibility and shared power. The task now was to find a way forward within fetters which empowered as much as they restrained him.

Chamberlain explained his desires at length when he asked Milner whether he thought the trip desirable. After giving priority to his need for a holiday, Chamberlain stated that 'the time has come, when, if a further marked advance is to be made in the relations between the mother-country and the Colonies, I must take some new step of a rather sensational kind'.[45] He suggested that the points on which he and Milner were at odds might be better settled in conversation than correspondence. He wished to confine his public speaking to one address of summation as he left South Africa. Otherwise he wanted simply to meet people and listen.

Milner replied promptly that the plan was 'the best thing that could happen for all of us'.[46] But his words barely masked his chagrin at a proposal which implicitly rebuked him. Moreover, Milner could sense beneath it the fundamental difference in their practice of imperialism. He ran his province as an autocrat in alliance with ethnic partisans.

Chamberlain, though by temperament also imperious, was by conviction and experience a democrat. Beginning with his business, he attempted to secure the cooperation of groups whose antagonism he feared, a practice at which he was particularly adept when he could meet them face to face. His practice did not work well at a distance. So long as Chamberlain attempted to govern the far-flung British empire from its centre, Milner's practice prevailed within his assigned province; and Milner's order might possibly be restored after Chamberlain departed. In that case the tour would prove useless. But so long as Chamberlain was in South Africa, he would place Milner's work in jeopardy. Therefore, like Fielding in Canada, Milner stood back. He planned to join the tour episodically and only during its middle stretch. He did not act with his usual vigour to prevent Chamberlain's itinerary from being swamped by public engagements, on which after all Chamberlain normally thrived.

For a month after Milner sent his approval, the vicissitudes of the Education bill kept Chamberlain from seeking authorization for the tour from the cabinet and the king. It was nevertheless in Chamberlain's mind when the pioneer of Zionism, Theodor Herzl, came to see him on behalf of the Jews who were fleeing persecution in eastern Europe. Their plight reminded Chamberlain of the upheaval in the Balkans when he first entered Parliament, an upheaval which he still thought Disraeli had handled insensitively. Now heir to Disraeli as upholder of the empire, Chamberlain wondered whether Jewish needs and British interests might be combined. Jewish immigration into the sweated trades of east London spelled trouble for British labour. Could a place be found for the immigrants in the Middle East through which he might soon pass?

Between meetings with Herzl, Chamberlain had another conference, more obviously pertinent to his prospective tour, with prominent goldmining financiers in London. They were dismayed by the plans he announced during the summer for taxation of their industry in the Transvaal. A ten per cent tax had been immediately imposed on the profits of the mines. He intended to exact a further 'fair return'[47] from the sale of all new tracts for mining development. The gold magnates questioned his estimate of the revenue-producing capacity of their industry. They argued that any surplus left in the colonial treasury after meeting the regular costs of administration should be spent on internal economic development, which would serve his interests as well as theirs. Far from convinced, Chamberlain reserved the subject for decision when he reached South Africa.

When his prospective trip was announced at the end of October, it captured the imagination of the public and the politicians, of friend and foe, and of the foreign as well as national press. Hitherto all mother countries had held their responsible statesmen at home. Now the most famous minister in the world's greatest empire, the embodiment of the new imperialism, was heading out to bind up the wounds of a remote but fabled province. The only place to greet the announcement with some anxiety was South Africa itself, where people of all persuasions feared tightened control from London. King Edward VII commissioned one of the newest and biggest naval cruisers, paid for partly by contributions from the Cape Colony, to carry Chamberlain to his destination. The route and timing of the tour added to its drama. In order to postpone his introduction to the vexed politics of Cape Town till the end of the tour, Chamberlain chose to sail through the Mediterranean and the Suez Canal down the east coast of Africa to land at Durban in Natal close to Christmas.

As always, the place most excited by his venture was his home town. With bipartisan cooperation, Birmingham planned to give Chamberlain a farewell to dwarf all previous celebrations in his honour. It began with a banquet in the town hall. The privileged hundreds who dined with him or watched from the galleries heard him identify the characteristics which distinguished their town among the cities of the empire, characteristics which he liked to think he shared: public spirit, local patriotism, vigour, independence of mind, and (less convincingly) toleration. The Lord Mayor read telegrams of welcome from men of Birmingham now resident in the South African cities he would soon visit.

But the remarkable feature of this celebration was the spectacle when Chamberlain left the town hall that night to ride home. He was met by a 'sea of fire-lit faces'.[48] Four thousand men, who had competed for the honour, from the local artillery, naval reserve, yeomanry and university student body, lined the square and the streets towards his home carrying torches. Coloured fires, Chinese lanterns and fairy lights in the windows of the houses along the route heightened the effect. As Chamberlain's carriage moved along, 'the cheering broke into a deep-tongued roar'. He stood up frequently in his carriage, hat in hand, to bow in acknowledgement. The crowds responded with boisterous familiarity. 'There's Joey!'—'Look at 'im now!'—'Wish you a pleasant journey, Joe!' As the carriage rolled past, the torch-bearers swung in behind, eight abreast, creating a river of flame. The fireworks at the end of the evening were an anticlimax.

The cruise south was the one part of the tour that fulfilled Chamberlain's hopes. Mainly it gave him a holiday. The weather was rough in the Bay of Biscay and the Mediterranean. But Chamberlain enjoyed displaying how good a sailor he was by smoking his biggest, blackest cigars during the storm while seasickness felled the crew. The engine bearings of the cruiser overheated in the stormy weather, forcing it to stop at Malta for repair. The delay postponed the scheduled arrival in Durban from just before to just after Christmas; but that did not disconcert the travellers. Once the weather improved, Chamberlain became 'quite frolicsome'.[49]

He broke his journey for three visits. The first, to Cairo, enabled him to discuss Herzl's dream of a Jewish return to the Middle East with the British proconsul in Egypt, Lord Cromer, who received the suggestion without enthusiasm. His reaction led Chamberlain to think of an alternative possibility when he stopped for the second time, at Mombasa, to travel on the recently built Uganda railway into the Kenyan highlands. The main purpose of this excursion was for Chamberlain to examine the local supply of native labour. The mining interests of the Transvaal thought of tapping this supply to reduce the shortage on the Rand where the work force had been disrupted by the war. But the Foreign Office, which was in charge of the Uganda protectorate including Kenya, wanted to keep the local labour in place for further railway construction and agricultural development. The roads along which Chamberlain travelled were lined with Masai warriors for his inspection.

He was more impressed by what he saw of the few white families farming in the Kenyan highlands. Chamberlain reported that the highlands were 'a White man's country where English children live & thrive & every kind of European fruit & vegetable can be grown...but the population is at present so sparse that no early progress can be expected unless a considerable immigration can be arranged'.[50] He concluded that the protectorate needed all the labour it could find, and therefore could do little to meet the needs of the Transvaal 'for a long time'.[51] The desirability of white immigration brought Herzl's Zionists to mind; but Chamberlain supposed that the country was 'too far removed from Palestine'[52] to attract them. During his third excursion, to Zanzibar, Chamberlain observed how German merchants were outdoing the British in a British protectorate.

The welcome he received when he reached Natal, the most British of the South African colonies, was enthusiastic. He reached agreements with the elected government of the colony without difficulty. The colony agreed to pay a large portion of the costs it incurred in the recent war, and it assumed primary responsibility for postwar defence. What took Chamberlain aback was the amount of administrative decision-making that was thrust upon him the moment he arrived. He came with a small staff of three, designed for a policymaker rather than for administration. But Milner let the role of high commissioner in effect devolve upon Chamberlain as long as he was in South Africa. Chamberlain knew the notes he wished to strike in his mission, but he had not foreseen that he would have to orchestrate their implementation. He refused to recognize that Milner was intent on playing a different theme.

The note of reconciliation between Dutch and British ran throughout Chamberlain's remarks in South Africa, always accompanied by a note of firmness in upholding the gains Britain had fought to achieve. In his first significant speech of the tour,[53] he announced that his object in South Africa was to see if 'out of these two great and kindred races we cannot make a fusion—a nation stronger in its unity than either of its parts would be alone'. Using the French and English in Canada and the Scotch and English in Britain as prior examples (but ignoring Ireland), he treated the recent war as a natural struggle between the governing races of the region for supremacy. Now that this issue had been resolved, he pleaded for cooperation as equally necessary and natural.

But before he could concentrate on this objective, he was faced with a welter of compensation claims arising from wartime pledges of protection and commandeering of supplies by the British army. From an unending stream of complainants he learned that the army, to which the task of examining and paying these claims had been entrusted, handled it very slowly and also inconsistently, because the officers in charge were frequently changed. As he travelled north into the Transvaal, interrupted repeatedly by petitioners, he worked out a plan for the immediate transfer of this responsibility, together with £3,000,000 which the army had been given for the purpose, to expeditious civilian commissions. He estimated that another £1 million would be needed to meet the claims. The additional sum would also allow Britain to deal more generously with the claims of the Boers who had either surrendered before the end of the war, the 'Hands-Uppers', or actually fought for the British, the 'National Scouts'. As soon as he reached Pretoria, he sent his plan by telegraph to the cabinet in London, 'beg[ging] most earnestly for immediate reply as feeling runs very high here and I desire to make a statement before I leave Transvaal'.[54]

On the journey north, Chamberlain was able to tour some of the recent battlefields. Otherwise he found himself cut off from the land he had come to see. He worked 'under the greatest pressure, every moment of my time being taken up with interviews or with public functions which I have found it impossible to refuse without giving offence'.[55]

The consensual practice of government Chamberlain wished to forward within the empire was limited to white races. He saw no evidence in other races of capacity for self-government. Even so, he did not completely forget how useful for imperial purposes he had found appeals to London from native peoples against local white oppression. So far as indigenous black Africans were concerned, his overriding concern in the wake of the war was to meet the need of the mines for labour. But the community of immigrants from India, numerous in Natal and expanding into the Transvaal, had greater imperial significance. Not only had the imperial government used Indian grievances, like those of indigenous Africans, as sticks with which to beat the Boer republics; the Indians, as citizens of the greatest of all British imperial possessions, had powerful imperial spokesmen, a viceroy in Delhi and a secretary of state in London, to protect their dignity. Still, their presence in South Africa repelled the white population, the British of Natal as much as the Boers of the Transvaal. They resented commercial competition from Indians who worked harder at lower cost than their British counterparts and possessed good trading contacts. In the name of public health and sanitation, the white governments imposed humiliating restrictions on freedom of movement and mercantile activity in Indian communities. The Indians in the Transvaal hoped for better after the British annexation. Milner recognized, however, that nothing would unite the white population of the colony against imperial authority faster than a lenient response to Indian or indigenous African demands. He proposed a set of regulations for the Indian community in Johannesburg and Pretoria more oppressive than Chamberlain, under pressure from the India Office, could accept. The problem was left for resolution when Chamberlain reached South Africa.

Once the Indians of Natal and the Transvaal learned of his intended visit, they recalled their ablest spokesman, Mohandas K. Gandhi, from India to present their case. Drawing upon what he learned in England while reading for the bar, Gandhi had seized upon imperial citizenship as a useful concept to assert the rights of Indians in Natal, where he had lived for almost a decade. Shortly before Chamberlain's visit was announced, he had returned to India. He arrived back in Durban a few days before the Colonial Secretary, and stayed eventually for another decade, during which he developed the practice of passive disobedience. He led one of the last deputations to Chamberlain in Durban before his departure for the Transvaal. Unaware of the momentousness of the occasion, Chamberlain thus presided over a confrontation between Milnerite imperialism and its evolving Gandhian antithesis.

The Colonial Secretary dealt with the Indian deputation, as with all the others, by listening and reserving judgement. He intended to hammer out imperial policy on this issue, as on most others, in consultation with Milner. The only significant thing about the meeting between Chamberlain and Gandhi was that it was not repeated. The foremost concern of Gandhi and the Indians who called him back was not Natal but the Transvaal, because it was the economic centre of the region and had not yet settled its regulations for Indians. Gandhi and his associates envisaged their deputation to Chamberlain in Durban as a precursor to the more important one which would wait on him in Pretoria. But W.E. Davidson, the chief executive assistant to the lieutenant governor for the Transvaal, was unhappy about Indians petitioning Chamberlain in Pretoria and took a particular dislike to Gandhi. Davidson excluded Gandhi from the deputation in Pretoria on the grounds that he had not established residence in the Transvaal. Though a deputation of Transvaal Indians was eventually allowed to see Chamberlain, Davidson insisted that they turn up in full Indian dress even if they did not possess it—simply a turban would not do—rather than in European garb. Deprived of its desired spokesman, the deputation came and went without making much impression on Chamberlain. Ultimately, after his resignation from the Colonial Office, their position in the Transvaal was regulated along lines tolerable to the local white community.

The difference between Chamberlain and Milner over the Indians was, in any event, quite negotiable, more so than their difference over the Afrikaners. When Chamberlain met the Boers in the Transvaal, he found in them something akin to his Calvinist forebears. They were almost more to his liking than the British on the Rand, who struck him as 'a cosmopolitan population devoted to money making & their own interests & apparently indifferent to the higher claims of the Empire . . . clamorous for further benefits, impatient of the slightest restraint & discontented if all their demands are not immediately complied with'.[56] Milner, on the other hand, blamed the discontent in the colony largely on 'the return of the more undesirable section of the Boer population', especially 'those Parsons of the Dutch Reformed Church who were rightly deported during the war because they were incurably, and in most cases treacherously, hostile'.[57]

Paradoxically, these contrary reactions made Chamberlain anxious to keep Milner at his post. Chamberlain sought to treat their differences as complementary. He thought himself able, from his background in Nonconformity and the National Education League, to help Milner accept the need to conciliate the Dutch Reformed clergy over instruction in the schools of the colony. Chamberlain also recognized the confidence that Milner inspired in the British community of the Transvaal; and in Chamberlain's estimation, they held the 'key of the South African situation'.[58] He concluded that Milner's early departure 'would be a calamity'.

Milner met Chamberlain as he entered the Transvaal and escorted him as far as the colonial capital, Pretoria. Chamberlain remained there for a few days while Milner went on to the British environs of Johannesburg where he preferred to reside. Still the two men spent much of their time working together in one or other of the neighbouring cities. Chamberlain's objectives were fourfold: to reconcile the Boers to their defeat, to quicken imperial patriotism in the British community, to bring Milner round to alleviate discontent in both groups, and to settle the lines for the postwar reconstruction.

Chamberlain began on 8 January with a pair of speeches, in the morning to Boer delegates in the legislative council house of the old republic in Pretoria, and in the afternoon to the British community in the largest sports ground in Johannesburg. The Boers, sensing the criticism of Milner implicit in Chamberlain's tour, attempted to get him to take a fresh look at their situation. They presented him with a petition renewing the call of the Boer generals in September for a general amnesty and return of all prisoners of war. Chamberlain rejected the call but did so calmly with a candour which produced more respect than resentment.

Aside from this encounter, Chamberlain saw little of the Boers over the next two weeks. He paid more attention to the British, on the assumption that they possessed the determining voice in the Transvaal. With the mining and mercantile British his technique was to praise them for virtues he was none too sure they possessed, in order to induce them to live up to his praise. He reinforced this approach with threats, for example to withdraw the British garrison from the Transvaal. The technique worked long enough for him to put together a generally acceptable financial settlement on the war debt and on developmental funds, though the debt settlement did not survive the year.

In these two weeks he worked at a pace that exceeded his usually heavy pace in England—'Six hours sleep & 18 hours work—& such work!'[59]—deputations, briefing sessions, talks with business leaders, tours of inspection, receptions and speeches. Still, he seemed to thrive. Mary pulled him away when she could for tea out of doors. Though gout, his familiar signal of stress, threatened to rise in Durban and again in Johannesburg, he managed to keep it down.

He managed also to keep an eye on developments at home. There was nothing to throw him off track. The Conservatives' loss of a seat to the Liberals in the Newmarket division of Cambridgeshire, where Nonconformity was strong, confirmed his belief that the government would pay dearly for the Education Act. At the same time, he was pleased to find Ritchie acting more resolutely against Continental European sugar bounties than Hicks Beach had done. Were the protectionist instincts that Ritchie had displayed back in the 1880s reasserting themselves?

During a lull in the financial discussions in Johannesburg, and prompted by a working man in one of the deputations who mentioned the 'bread tax' recently imposed in London, Chamberlain mused aloud about the scheme taking shape in his mind. There were only two men with him at the time, Milner and the mining spokesman, Percy Fitzpatrick. They listened intently to the monologue, which Fitzpatrick recalled twenty years later, perhaps amplifying the original sketch. The plan began modestly with the current one shilling corn tax, but then mushroomed into

> a policy of Imperial Preference and Empire development, by means of which . . . the essentials for life, industry, and trade within the Empire should be available for the Empire, assured as to quantity and regularity of supply, and gradually reduced in cost . . . under a defensive tariff against the outer world and a preferential abatement in favour of all parts of the Empire. He spoke of the enormous possibilities of Canada, Australia and New Zealand in the matter of food supplies, etc., of the illimitable quantity and variety of products from different parts of Africa and the world wide possessions of the British Empire. . . . He spoke . . . of how obvious it was that the superabundance in one portion should make good the shortage in another; of how it would absorb the surplus population; of how a sane, business-like, practical policy, free of all fanaticism and prejudices, made the proper course seem so obvious and simple. . . .

Then he spoke of himself,

> as though a period or stage in his career had been reached. . . . Position, safety, administration, do not attract, he seemed to say; there was something great to be done for the Empire, and he was willing to risk a fall. . . . Perhaps it might not be adopted at the first attempt—the first General Election—but at the next it would triumph.[60]

However prophetic, it was all still visionary, not a commitment. Though the rush of political waters released by the ending of the Boer War had carried him far, he was not yet swept away.

When Chamberlain left the room for a rest, Milner responded to the scheme he had just heard. His commentary was incisive and realistic, sympathetic but deflating, the Oxford antidote to enthusiasm. It would take not one but several general elections before Britain could be convinced to abandon free trade, longer than a man approaching seventy years of age could expect to enjoy. Milner added 'very gently that he did not think Mr. Chamberlain . . . thoroughly understood the magnitude and financial intricacies of this question . . . that he was not ready with the constructive measures; that it did not appear that he had anyone to work this out for him. . . . It was not an undertaking for one man; it called for the most thorough preparation and an organisation of well-informed workers.'

On the business at hand in South Africa, tariffs with a view to imperial preference were among the first subjects on which Milner and Chamberlain reached some agreement. Milner was less concerned about economic consolidation of the empire than about the need to reduce the tariffs that kept the cost of living in the Transvaal high and retarded the inflow of British immigration. He undertook to raise the possibility of a twenty-five per cent imperial preference at the conference he was to convene in March among representatives of all the South African colonies. On the subject of education, Chamberlain negotiated separately with a spokesman for the Dutch Reformed clergy and Milner, and produced a compromise. It gave the clergy 'a qualified kind of veto on teachers whom [they] may consider disqualified either on moral or religious grounds, or who are not efficient as teachers of Dutch'.[61] Drawing further on his Birmingham background, Chamberlain prevailed upon Milner to speed up the establishment of elective municipal governments in Pretoria and Johannesburg. They agreed on the composition of the Legislative Council for the crown colony, just under half to be composed of non-official appointees representative of the mines, other socio-economic interests in the British community, and both factions of Boers, 'Bitter-Enders' as well as 'Hands-Uppers'. Finally they agreed that, after a holiday later in the year, Milner would return to South Africa for another year, with the possibility though not the likelihood of a further extension. Milner consented, so he told Chamberlain, 'in the teeth of every personal consideration and inclination'.[62]

These subjects of negotiation were overshadowed by three issues important to the mining economy of the Rand and hence to the political outlook for the Transvaal and all South Africa: the supply of labour, a contribution to the British war debt, and a loan for infrastructural development. Chamberlain discussed these questions with the resident mining directors as well as Milner. Before leaving Johannesburg Chamberlain recommended an approach to the problem of labour supply and announced a pair of loan arrangements. But the problems remained intractable. His labour policy did not command local support, and the local promise to help defray the war debt proved insubstantial.

The only durable agreement Chamberlain concluded was on a developmental loan. It was for £35,000,000, guaranteed by the imperial government and secured upon the resources of the annexed republics. Like most of Chamberlain's other developmental loans, this one focused to a large extent on railways. There was also something about it reminiscent of gas-and-water socialism: it placed the existing railway network under public control while providing for its extension. In order to secure a colonial contribution to the war debt, Chamberlain settled for a lower sum than he originally desired, thirty instead of fifty million pounds. Even so, and even though the mining magnates offered to take up the

first ten millions of the loan floated for this purpose, the whole arrangement was allowed to die in 1904.

But the problem which contained the most dangerous potentialities
was the labour supply. Though Chamberlain saw the dividends that
could accrue from a good solution and the dangers that would surely
follow a bad one, his contribution proved ineffective. The potential
margin of profit from goldmining at the deep levels on which the Rand
increasingly relied was narrow, all the more so because of a sharp fall
in the world price for gold. The margin would be turned to deficit by
any substantial rise in labour costs. To make the problem more acute,
throughout the region native labour seemed in short supply, unsettled
by the war and alienated by the folly of the mine managers who had
taken advantage of the war to slash wages. Unable to see a solution
locally, the industry looked beyond, to Uganda, India and the British
sphere of influence in China.

Chamberlain discouraged this search. He was willing to include
Rhodesia within the labour catchment sphere of the Rand. He was
willing also to tighten the economic screws on the African population
to oblige them to work. But after his glimpse of the Kenyan highlands
he did not want to extend the Rand's sphere north of the Zambesi.
The way in which the whites of the Transvaal treated Indians precluded permission from British authorities in India for the emigration of
any more. Chamberlain sensed, better than the local administrators, that
the entry from China of another colour into the racial mixture of the
Transvaal would arouse a mixed reaction among whites in the colony;
and he foresaw the reaction in Britain. He therefore turned back to the
labour supply in the Transvaal and its environs. In addition to tougher
policing of the African population, he pleaded for various efforts to
increase the employment of white and particularly of British labour in
mining, an increase which would also ensure the ascendancy of the
British.

As so often when the social economy was at issue, he thought of
education. In the South African context, given the assumption that education among other things distinguished whites from blacks, better
education would enhance white ascendancy as well as productivity.
Chamberlain urged Johannesburg, like Birmingham, to build itself a
university. That was his only educational recommendation which interested the city. Otherwise, as he was obliged to recognize, the mine-
owners had no intention of paying the higher wage rates needed to
attract even uneducated white labour; nor would white workers work
beside black.

Chamberlain made his recommendations and announced agreements
in a parting address. The cordial response he received from the British

community in Johannesburg did not delude him into believing that all of his prescriptions would be followed. Yet Chamberlain was fascinated rather than discouraged by what he had found. 'I like the fight,' he reported, 'with all the strong conflicting elements in this new community, which has the making of a great people & with all its faults is essentially British, loyal & patriotic.'[63]

After leaving Johannesburg, Chamberlain moved back and forth between Afrikaner and British communities. His immediate destination was the country town of Potchefstroom, as thoroughly Boer as Johannesburg was British. From there he headed out beyond the railway line, pulled by mule in a Cape cart or covered wagon over the scorching veldt to the remote villages of Ventersdorp and Lichtenburg, rarely visited by the British except in war. The British were impressed by the daring of this summertime trek, urged on him by the Boer leaders. In later months his evident fatigue was put down to this exertion. Yet far from flagging during their trek, he and Mary flourished. They were well looked after. The tents in which they occasionally slept were carpeted and comfortably furnished, 'veritable palaces of Aladdin in the middle of the rural simplicity of the Dutch township'.[64] Five hundred pounds of ice were sent ahead to each halting-place. The travellers were surprised by the warm welcome they received from the Boers, sometimes former collaborators but more often former foes. Chamberlain was moved by 'the mystery and beauty of the solitude of the illimitable veld';[65] and he was haunted by the ravages of the war, worse than he anticipated.

They left the Transvaal to enter the northernmost tip of the Cape Colony at Mafeking, and then moved south to Kimberley. These were British towns which withstood Boer sieges in the first phase of the war and were now fiercely loyalist. Over the border from Kimberley into the Orange River Colony on the way to Bloemfontein, the Chamberlains again changed ethnic environment. Here they received a quieter, less fervent but still genuine greeting on the thinly populated land from clusters of Boer men and women who rode out to meet them.

But in Bloemfontein, where Milner briefly rejoined the party, the Boers broke into three camps. The mildest were the 'Hands-Uppers', those who supported the Boer republic until Britain seemed certain to win the war, whereupon they surrendered and adopted a position of neutrality. Now they simply wanted to be left alone to earn a livelihood. The other two camps were led by men embittered by brotherly hate, Piet de Wet at the head of the National Scouts who had fought for the British, and Christian de Wet who had held out against them to the bitter end. The two brothers had fought each other most recently for the right to represent their district in a general deputation to Chamberlain.

While Christian commanded majority support among the inhabitants, Piet was elected by the contrivance of British magistrates.

The brothers presented their contrary grievances to Chamberlain. Christian presented a prickly version of the demands Chamberlain already knew from the Boer generals in London and the Boer assembly in Pretoria; and he replied with corresponding stiffness. Piet was angry because his National Scouts seemed to receive less generous compensation for their wartime losses than the Bitter-Enders. 'British magnanimity in this country perhaps may not always work well,' he told Chamberlain in a remark with which Milner fully sympathized, 'as it may be taken for weakness.'[66] Chamberlain advised him to wait until the business of compensation had been disposed of, and in the meantime assured him that 'those who laugh last laugh longest'.

Otherwise Chamberlain continued to preach the civic virtue of reconciliation between British and Boer, subject always to the further civic virtue of loyalty to the constituted colonial and imperial authorities. He preached his message more insistently as he approached the Cape Colony, where the civil war had shattered both virtues. The Cape Dutch who had sympathized with the Boer republics accused the minority who went along with the British of disloyalty. The same accusation was applied by the British in the colony to all the Cape Dutch who had not joined the fight against their Boer kinsfolk. Nothing roused Chamberlain more than a debate about loyalty. He used the pride which so many Cape Dutch took in their loyalty to the 'volk' to insist on respect for the loyalty which a minority of their brethren gave during the war to the colonial government; and he called upon the leaders of the Cape Dutch to repudiate the persecution of the minority in their ranks. At the same time he urged the militantly British Progressives to moderate their demands for demonstrative loyalty from the Dutch, and to shake whatever hands might be stretched out towards them.

Throughout his tour Chamberlain ran into the charge that loyalty did not pay. The charge exasperated him with its implication that loyalty and, *a fortiori*, the empire depended on calculations of profit and loss. That was not how he wanted to think of the empire, man of business though he was. He stressed that unless the empire was inspired by a vision transcending profit and loss, it would be doomed like all preceding empires. He made the point to the Chamber of Commerce in Cape Town, bearing in mind the 'Recessional' poem of Rudyard Kipling, who was in the city at the time and in touch with Chamberlain:

The object of a man in business is to get the largest possible return upon his capital, his skill, and his labour. Under a principle of that sort

he cannot be expected to turn aside at every moment to consider sentimental, or even philanthropic, considerations. But the Empire cannot
be run on those principles. . . . If we were to open . . . in an office in
Downing Street, a ledger account with every one of our colonies, if we
were to write them off as a bad debt, whenever we cannot prove there
is an immediate profit upon our mutual transactions . . . we shall have
a very miserable conception of the true Imperial spirit. No, gentlemen,
the British Empire . . . does not mean mere pettifogging considerations
of profit and loss. It means a spirit infused into the whole race which
raises and elevates us above the petty and sordid considerations of
ordinary life. The British Empire is based upon a community of sacrifice. Whenever that is lost sight of, then, indeed, I think we may expect
to sink into oblivion like the empires of the past, which . . . after having
exhibited to the world evidences of their power and strength, died
away regretted by none, and leaving behind them a record of selfish-
ness only.[67]

Even so, Chamberlain accepted the necessity of proving at least that
'disloyalty does not pay'.[68] Until he entered the Cape, he dealt with this
suspicion mainly with regard to compensation for wartime losses; and
he secured £2,000,000 from the British government to be awarded
through special tribunals to those who had cooperated during the war.
Suspicion reared up in uglier form in the Cape Colony. The weak colonial government of Sir Gordon Sprigg conciliated its supporters in the
Afrikaner Bond by leaving magisterial power in Dutch districts in dis-
affected hands. Some of these magistrates handled demobilization in
their districts by taking rifles away from wartime supporters of the
British while returning the rifles of those who had supported the Boers.
Chamberlain secured a reversal of this policy.

He wanted more substantial results than these from his mission of
reconciliation. From every colony he sought a financial contribution to
Britain's imperial expenses. From the Cape Chamberlain looked for a
large contribution—perhaps as much as £10,000,000, certainly more
than the annual £50,000 the colony currently contributed—to the British
navy. After all, the colony relied on it for defence of the sea lanes and
harbours vital to its livelihood. He expected a warmer response from
the British than from the Dutch in the colony. Sprigg was agreeable. But
the British at Grahamstown and Port Elizabeth in the eastern Cape
which Chamberlain visited after leaving Bloemfontein disappointed
him. Their patriotism expended itself in hostility to the Dutch rather
than in willingness to pay for imperial defence.

To his surprise and passing delight, the leaders of the Afrikaner Bond
proved more forthcoming. His party was joined at Graaf Reinet in the
Cape Dutch heartland by N.F. De Waal, secretary of the Bond. On the

train to the next stop at Middelburg, Chamberlain sounded De Waal on two possibilities. One was a coalition between moderate leaders from the two existing parties, the Bond and the Progressives, to overcome the political division of the Cape along ethnic lines. The other was a financial contribution from the colony to the imperial navy, a contribution which would go far, if sponsored by the Bond, to meet the colonial British demand for proof of Dutch loyalty. De Waal met the first suggestion evasively. But he responded encouragingly to the second. He raised Chamberlain's hopes further by stepping forward at the meeting in Middelburg, which was De Waal's town, to accept Chamberlain's demand for an expression of loyalty from the Dutch. De Waal not only accepted the annexation of the Boer republics as irrevocable; he praised the liberty which the Cape Dutch enjoyed under the British flag, and proposed 'to prove our loyalty by our acts'.[69]

Chamberlain pursued his suggestions to De Waal with the leader of the Bond, Jan Hofmeyr. Overcoming obstruction from the colony's British bureaucracy, Chamberlain made sure that he met Hofmeyr in Cape Town. In private conference with Chamberlain, Hofmeyr dismissed the notion of a moderate coalition. But instead of dismissing the idea of a defence contribution, Hofmeyr coupled it with a suggestion of general amnesty for wartime offences. Three days later, at the head of a deputation to Chamberlain from the Bond, Hofmeyr echoed De Waal's declaration of loyalty in words Chamberlain could not have improved upon. Hofmeyr undertook to follow up his declaration with a detailed appeal to his people, a promise he proceeded to honour.

By embracing Hofmeyr's declaration immediately as 'a most hopeful and most happy augury for the future',[70] Chamberlain forced the British party to accept the pledge at least formally. But Hofmeyr's private suggestion of making a defence contribution conditional on a general amnesty placed Chamberlain in an awkward position. Even in the best of situations, such an agreement would look like a crude bargain. Amnesty for the Cape was particularly vexed not only because the war there had been a rebellion but also because of the political consequences. The minimum punishment of the rebels was disfranchisement, and that penalty cut deeply into the voting strength of the Bond. It was oddly easier to release the most serious rebels from prison than to reenfranchise the rank and file. Hofmeyr was anxious to secure, and Chamberlain helped to bring about, the more limited amnesty for prisoners. But the general amnesty which Hofmeyr also wanted could restore the Bond's former sway and keep the Progressives in a minority. Chamberlain set the matter aside for further consideration after his return to Britain.

He left Cape Town uncertain about the success of his mission and anxious about the prospect at home. In his farewell address he remarked that 'my time for active service to the Empire is necessarily coming to a close'.[71] That was not the comment of a man sure of his political direction. Word reached him from Austen that Ritchie had hardened 'dead against the remission of the corn duty to the Colonies' and might resign 'if we insist', in which case he might join forces with Hicks Beach on the backbenches.[72] The buoyancy with which Joe met the demands of his tour gave way once he set sail for home. He came down with a heavy cold, and was crippled by gout for half of the return voyage. Milner, who remained behind, also took to his bed. He expressed disgust at Chamberlain's rapprochement with Hofmeyr as 'too theatrical', and advised a confidant at the Cape to 'keep your powder dry'.[73] Word reached Chamberlain at Madeira that Ritchie had issued his threat to resign.

18

Hastened Culmination
1903

Chamberlain doesn't deserve all the bad things that are said of him, but he is essentially a dangerous man, because being very masterful, impulsive and sanguine he always believes he can get through a tight place by pushing. He is like an engine driver, who running at speed finds that parts of his engine get hot, & who instead of slowing down to let them cool & oiling them, crams on more speed in the hope of reaching the end of the journey before anything gives way.

Sir Edward Grey to Lord Northbrook, 28 July 1900

'All Hail. The Universe is ringing with your praises,' wrote Lord James in a letter that reached Chamberlain at Madeira; 'Your work represents the greatest act of known Statesmanship.'[1] Though similar greetings awaited him in England, they were transparently inflated. He returned to his desk at the Colonial Office thin, tired and dispirited. From almost every angle, the political outlook was disturbed; and he was deprived of the tools he wanted to deal with the situation.

Birmingham stood out as sound. A deputation from the city sent to meet him at Southampton boarded the medical tugboat that inspected the ship before it reached port. Chamberlain was delighted by this characteristic enterprise. He was also relieved to learn that the Education Act had been neutralized in Birmingham through the replacement of the recently church-dominated school board with a council authority led by Nonconformist Unionists. But in this as in so many ways, Birmingham was the exception, not the rule.

There was one sphere in which the country as a whole was performing almost too well for Chamberlain's current purposes: the economy. Although in international competition Britain was pressed hard by Germany and surpassed by the United States, the domestic economy had pulled out of depression after the Unionists took office in 1895. It was now doing well—too well to prompt radical reconsideration of the country's fiscal policy. 'The Home trade', which Chamberlain thought of as 'always the main stand by' of the economy, was 'still very good—as it has been for the last eight years', he noted, 'and there is no sign at present of any set back'.[2]

In every other sphere, the prospect was disheartening. A Labour candidate won the east London constituency of Woolwich three days before Chamberlain reached Southampton: his social policy no longer appeased the urban working class. Balfour had failed to pull his government together, as he could not disguise when he drew Chamberlain aside for conversation at Victoria Station when he reached London. There was open revolt on the Unionist backbenches against a scheme of army reform prepared by Brodrick. Within the cabinet Chamberlain felt isolated and was quick to quarrel. His failure to secure a substantial contribution from the Cape towards the costs of imperial defence weakened his hand in the cabinet's discussion of army reform and the budget. Canadians questioned the worth of the imperial connection because Britain refused to challenge President Roosevelt's highhanded conduct over the boundary with Alaska. Their quickness to criticize irritated Chamberlain in view of Canada's unwillingness to share the financial burden of imperial defence. He was also vexed by the interest of Lord Lansdowne at the Foreign Office in collaborative ventures with Germany. In concert with the Unionist press Chamberlain shot down a plan which Lansdowne made with encouragement from Balfour for British participation in a primarily German project for railway construction in the Ottoman empire. Generally frustrated, Chamberlain retired 'rather sadly'[3] to Birmingham during the Easter vacation to reexamine his bearings.

The concerns he brought back from South Africa and the messages he received from Canada suggested somewhat differing strategies for imperial consolidation. He was not yet sure which was the less troubled or more promising. Upon his return to the Colonial Office he encountered a chorus of disappointment from Canada over the delayed British decision on preferential amendment of the corn duty. Fielding warned that the Canadian government might rescind its imperial tariff preference. It faced opposition from Canadian manufacturers allied to the Conservative party; and France and the United States might offer 'material concessions' in return for its cancellation.[4] Colonel Denison, the leading Canadian advocate of imperial preference, confirmed Fielding's report and echoed his discouragement. Denison was alarmed by a movement in the United States for reciprocity with Canada; and he pleaded with Chamberlain 'to get something done this Session that will give us a preference, no matter how small'.[5]

Chamberlain had to tell Fielding that the British corn tax was likely to be repealed rather than amended preferentially. The only hope Chamberlain could offer was that the next depression in trade might induce Britain to embrace tariff protection and preference. He pleaded, as in South Africa, for an imperialism which transcended calculations of profit and loss: 'If we are to have an Empire at all in which our Colonies are to share we must all be prepared . . . to make sacrifices to maintain it.'[6]

He had nothing better to report to South Africa. Milner persuaded the conference of South African colonies which he convened after Chamberlain's departure to approve of a preferential tariff on the Canadian model. When Britain did not immediately respond, Milner despatched a telegram designed almost too obviously to strengthen Chamberlain's hand. Milner pointed out that the colonies 'expected some decided mark of appreciation', and that it would be 'quite sufficient' for the moment 'if something, however slight, was done for Canada'.[7] Chamberlain had to send back a limp response. He reported that in Britain, 'we are all suffering from slight reaction. We are feeling our taxation & the general opinion is that Colonies have not done & are not doing their share. Therefore we cannot gush although I rejoice personally at every step however small towards closer Union.'[8] The message did not surprise Milner, who had little faith in the preferential cause. In his return letter, he was happy to discredit Hofmeyr by reporting that the 'slight reaction' was not confined to Britain: 'You would have laughed to see [Hofmeyr at the colonial conference] trying to wriggle out of "preferential trade"'.[9]

So far as South Africa was concerned, Chamberlain's mind turned less towards trade and tariffs than towards defence. While on tour he began to work out a scheme to station 30,000 men from Britain's 'Home' army permanently in South Africa. The permanent presence of such a large force in the region would discourage any thought of rebellion among Afrikaners, and would eventually expand the British population if recruits decided to settle in South Africa on their retirement. The terrain was good for training. Keeping the force formally as part of the 'Home' army would release it from the expensive system of 'linked' battalions which applied to India, and would also protect it from the economizing knife of the Liberals when they returned to power. The crucial issue was financial. Chamberlain argued that his scheme would cost less than maintenance of a force of the same size in England.

His proposal ran into stiff resistance from Brodrick, who was annoyed by Chamberlain's lack of sympathy with his grander plans for enlargement and reform of the army. Brodrick agreed that the crucial issue was financial, but argued that Chamberlain's scheme would increase rather than diminish Britain's military expenses. The argument between the two men grew so acrimonious that Balfour intervened to submit Chamberlain's scheme for cost analysis. Chamberlain secured an auditor of his choice, his party organizer Powell Williams, who had served in a junior capacity at the War Office. But when Powell Williams ascertained that Chamberlain's scheme would indeed cost more, Chamberlain had to abandon it.

He was drawn in the course of this argument to the school of geopolitical activists led by Leo Amery. Barely thirty years old, one of the bright lights from Balliol and All Souls, Amery had been converted from Fabianism to imperialism by Milner. Commissioned to write the official history of the Boer War, Amery became severely critical of Brodrick's reform proposals. Chamberlain contacted the young man to strengthen his own argument with Brodrick. Flattered by this approach from the first minister of the empire, Amery sharpened Chamberlain's appreciation of the military dimensions of imperial security—until the statesman abruptly shifted the focus of discussion to tariffs.

The new direction

Chamberlain had found it hard to concentrate on the news at Madeira that Ritchie would resign if the cabinet adhered to its decision to amend the corn tax preferentially. The target of Ritchie's protest was important enough to make Chamberlain also think of resigning. Yet it was not of such obvious importance that the public would readily understand his reason for resigning, right after a spectacular mission. Preferential amendment of the corn tax was not the flag for a crusade. It appealed to Chamberlain as a disarming way to begin consolidating the empire through tariffs. He had learned, against his natural inclination, that great departures in British politics are best made from modest beginnings. Ritchie spoiled this modest option. His resignation would emphasize the departure in principle implicit in preferential amendment of the corn duty, and thus turn an unpretentious tool for empire-building into flag of offence to free traders.

When the cabinet came to discuss Ritchie's budget, his proposal for outright repeal of the corn tax was coldly received. There was considerably more support for Chamberlain's proposal to amend the tax preferentially in favour of the Canadians; but four or five members of the cabinet stood out against it. With intense lobbying, Chamberlain might have reduced the number of those who would resign rather than accept his amendment to one or two, including Lord Balfour of Burleigh as well as Ritchie. But they were enough to frustrate his purposes. Failing preferential amendment, he insisted almost petulantly on repeal as less offensive to the Canadians than the maintenance of the duty without amendment. The cabinet acquiesced unhappily, aware that the decision would please no one.

Though he had insisted on it, the decision to repeal the corn tax constituted a defeat for Chamberlain. He brooded over the setback and considered ways to move past it. He thought of raising the general issue of imperial preference with his constituents, whom he was scheduled to address in May. Still, as the day for Ritchie's presentation of the budget drew near, Chamberlain prayed that the cup might be taken from him, that some accident might throw the government out. When the day came, Ritchie embittered the potion by elevating repeal of the corn tax into a matter of principle, ridding the food of the people from a regrettable wartime imposition. Balfour tried to reduce the offence to Chamberlain by insisting that the repeal did not prejudge the general question of imperial preference.

Two weeks later, Chamberlain had an opportunity to speak for himself in presenting another budget, this one for the annexed Boer republics. He concluded by drawing attention to the preferential customs rate of twenty-five per cent which the recent intercolonial conference under Milner's presidency had recommended to the member colonial legislatures. Chamberlain took this recommendation 'as an evidence of true loyalty, as a recognition of obligation which we most gratefully acknowledge'.[10]

Meanwhile Ritchie's treatment of the corn tax angered the growing number of protectionists in the Unionist parliamentary party; and they arranged for a deputation to Balfour. In preparation for that encounter, scheduled for 15 May, and for the meeting Chamberlain was to have the same day with his constituents, the cabinet convened to work on a common response. They agreed that Balfour should respond 'in such terms as would indicate the possibility of reviving the [corn] tax, if it were associated with some great change in our fiscal system'.[11] Balfour followed this guidance in calming fashion. He dampened hopes of immediate change without killing them for the future.

Chamberlain adhered to the letter of the cabinet advice, but he expressed it with a spirit all his own. He left the cabinet meeting feeling free to advocate the great change in fiscal policy which Balfour treated as a distant possibility. Instead of deflecting him, the contretemps with Ritchie deepened Chamberlain's commitment to preferential tariffs as the best way to consolidate the empire. A month before the cabinet met to discuss how to handle the protectionist deputation, Chamberlain asked the leader of his constituency organization, Charles Vince, to gauge local response to the policy he had in mind, and Vince had responded encouragingly. Two days before the cabinet meeting, Chamberlain encouraged William Ashley, the economist he recruited to create a commerce faculty for the University of Birmingham, to prepare a book on tariff reform. When Chamberlain addressed his constituents, he was careful not to commit the government to an immediate change in policy. Still, the way in which he presented imperial preference left no doubt about his personal commitment to it and his desire to make it the centre of debate for the next general election.

The juncture was as critical in domestic as in imperial terms. The Liberal opposition, united after a decade of dissension, eagerly anticipated the government's demise. While Chamberlain was on his southern tour, the Liberal chief whip concluded a pact with the newly formed Labour Representation Committee to cooperate against Unionists at the next general election. Nonconformists flocked back to the Liberal fold in reaction to the Education Act. Trade unionists were angered by the government's refusal to protect their rights from the erosion by the courts. Liberal imperialists scented blood in the fight against Brodrick's army reforms.

Chamberlain upset all predictions by changing the political agenda. He began his speech by expanding on Canada's tariff preference. He described the increasing trade Britain had done with Canada since its grant of preference, 'chiefly in textile goods—cotton, woollen, and goods of that kind—and in the manufactures of hardware and iron and steel'.[12] He pleaded for 'a treaty of preference and reciprocity with our own children'. He warned that Canada might repeal its preference if Britain persisted in its refusal to respond. He pressed Canada to increase its preference by lowering the tariff against Britain rather than by raising its tariff against foreign exporters. He extended his policy to foreign competition by calling for retaliatory tariffs 'whenever our own interests or our relations between our Colonies and ourselves are threatened by other people', particularly Germany. He invested his appeal with the sense of urgency Balfour avoided. 'You have an opportunity,' Chamberlain told his audience; 'you will never have it again.' He concluded by turning his objective into a question,

> whether the people of this country really have it in their hearts to do all that is necessary, even if it occasionally goes against their own prejudices, to consolidate an Empire which can only be maintained by relations of interest as well as by relations of sentiment.

Turbulent current

These words plunged Chamberlain into the rush of waters released at the end of the South African war. The force of his entry and the force of the current produced changes in everyone's course, including his own. The policy he had chosen generated a momentum of its own. Some circles attached themselves to his cause with an eagerness which modified his movement. A strong swimmer himself, he churned up waters which deepened the turbulence. The direction in which he and his supporters attempted to swim cut across the prevailing flow of Britain's political economy. The Liberals united to ride that flow, though they were not entirely certain that they made the most farsighted choice.

Chamberlain plunged on as if he knew where he was going. In fact he was unsure and ill-prepared. He had taken an imperial initiative, and he looked for an imperial response. His first instructions after delivering the momentous speech were to find out 'how it is received in Canada & the Colonies generally'.[13] The response was gratifying. Both parties in Canada welcomed his overture warmly, as did New Zealand. From Cape Colony, Hofmeyr's welcome was cooler but clear. The Australian response was mixed but not discouraging. Outside the empire, Britain's great protectionist rivals, the United States and Germany, reacted with some sympathy to Chamberlain's suggestion that Britain follow their example.

But the response among the working class in Birmingham made him uneasy. A few days after his speech, he issued a statement asserting that increased trade with the colonies was sure to be accompanied by an increase in wages, which would outweigh any rise which tariffs might bring about in the cost of living. After another few days, he suggested that old-age pensions could be funded with the revenue from tariffs. Thus belatedly and tentatively, his imperial initiative acquired a social dimension.

The crusade of the Colonial Secretary also acquired an industrial dimension, more enduring and complicating than the social. Remarkably, the former Screw King had not given careful thought to the industrial purposes tariffs might serve. Anxious to limit the offence his initiative caused to the faith in free trade, he specifically repudiated the use of tariffs for protection when he spoke to his constituents. But the support his speech evoked from industry induced him to change his mind. The response of the working class in general to his initiative might be uncertain; but the metal-manufacturing interests of the West Midlands, masters and men alike, and in particular the metal wire industries depressed by German and American competition, offered him support too enthusiastic to refuse. His imperial initiative thus mushroomed into a full-blown challenge to the politico-economic creed to which Britain had subscribed for half a century.

He responded happily to the challengers of that orthodoxy who had held back for lack of leadership. Ashley placed his talents at the service of tariff reform. In accepting Ashley's offer, Chamberlain laid out the lines on which a study of the tariff problem needed to proceed for his purposes.[14] His grasp of the problem, after a quarter century in public life, was shaped by the needs of political debate more than of the industrial economy, and he had little familiarity with the academic study of economics. He knew where his case was politically most vulnerable, and he pressed Ashley to focus his economic inquiry on that point: the impact a tariff on imported foodstuffs including wheat would have on the working-class standard of living. Chamberlain wanted Ashley to marshal evidence on how little effect the recent corn tax had on the price of bread, how little correlation there was between the price of bread and the standard of living of the working class, and how much they stood to gain from high wages like those in the tariff-protected United States. Ashley threw himself into the study immediately. He published a book, *The Tariff Problem*, in time to accompany the campaign of speeches which Chamberlain projected for the autumn. By all accounts the most persuasive book-length rationale for tariff reform, Ashley's work commanded the respect even of John Morley. Ashley insisted that he developed his argument with little guidance from Chamberlain, but the case and conclusions of the two men were very similar.

The rapid social and industrial expansion of Chamberlain's initiative threw his relations with his cabinet colleagues into turmoil. Most members of the cabinet suppressed their reaction to Chamberlain's speech to his constituents, though the octogenarian Lord Chancellor, Halsbury, wrote to him in ecstasy. But the connection which Chamberlain drew between tariffs and old-age pensions alarmed those who recoiled from additions to the responsibilities of the state. Balfour's concern was for the cohesion of his government. His anxiety turned to alarm after Liberals in the Commons precipitated a debate on the fiscal policy of the government. He responded by endorsing Chamberlain's request for an inquiry on imperial trade while treating his policy suggestions with benevolent agnosticism. But no sooner had Balfour spoken than Chamberlain carried his proposals further than ever, violating an undertaking he had given not to worsen the cabinet's dissension. Provocatively, without awaiting the fruits of Ashley's researches, Chamberlain accepted the necessity of 'a tax on food'.[15] Recognizing that such a tax would fall mainly on the working class, he offered to use the revenue, including the portion paid by the middle and upper classes, to pay for old-age pensions. Here was the Radical doctrine of 'ransom' in imperial guise. Bidding at the same time for industrial support, Chamberlain dwelt on the dangers raised by the growth of large trusts in Germany and the United States, particularly in iron and steel, that dumped their excess production on to the British market at prices British producers could not match. The style of Chamberlain's statement in the Commons assailed Balfour as much as its substance. As the Liberal *Daily News* observed, Chamberlain spoke 'more like a Monarch than a Minister'.[16]

The 'gratuitous challenge'[17] from Chamberlain angered Balfour. Yet Chamberlain's divisiveness underscored Balfour's importance to the Unionist party. He was its bond of peace. So long as Unionists on both sides of the debate appealed to him and claimed his approval, he would hold the balance of power in his government. Furthermore, Chamberlain was preoccupied with the future, the issue for debate at the next general election and the mandate for the next Parliament. Balfour was concerned with the existing Parliament and the current ministry. Accordingly Balfour did not rebuke Chamberlain after the Commons debate. But the prime minister was quite ready to reassure colleagues who doubted the wisdom of Chamberlain's proposals and were not prepared 'to be committed by silence to a policy which has not been adopted by the Cabinet'.[18]

After the Commons debate, Chamberlain sparred with his other co-leader, Devonshire, still titular chief of the national Liberal Unionist organization. Chamberlain had installed Powell Williams as secretary in charge at the national headquarters in London; and at Chamberlain's behest, Powell Williams began to distribute copies of his address to his constituents through the Liberal Unionist network. Devonshire objected. Chamberlain was surprised, but ordered Powell Williams immediately to desist. Having kept to himself since the South African tour, Chamberlain thought that the cabinet remained as sympathetic to imperial preference as they had been back in November. When Devonshire shattered this illusion, Chamberlain threatened to give a national mandate for propaganda to the regional office of the Liberal Unionists in Birmingham.

Of all the members of the cabinet, only Ritchie had much wish to stand up to Chamberlain. The aversion between Devonshire and Chamberlain was old but, like Devonshire, not lively. The other eventual dissidents, Balfour of Burleigh and Lord George Hamilton, diverged from Chamberlain reluctantly. Balfour of Burleigh was simply the soul of orthodoxy, on free trade as on everything else. Hamilton had been part of the Chamberlain cabal on foreign policy in Salisbury's day, and had given West Indian cane sugar preferential admission to India as secretary of state. But he could not see how to accommodate Indian interests in a preferential system of tariffs designed in the interests of the self-governing colonies.

Chamberlain had no satisfactory answer. He was not ready to meet subordinate criticisms of his grand design or provide substantial answers to specific questions. In cabinet government, even points of conflict involving matters of principle can often be resolved through examination of the practicalities. But as Milner foresaw, Chamberlain opened the great debate on imperial preference before doing his homework. What he offered was an objective, not a well-worked plan, still less the grubby commercial bargain Churchill thought he saw. Chamberlain modified his proposals repeatedly over the summer. Yet the terms in which he articulated his vision sounded like concrete conclusions.

Equipped with expressions of concern from five members of the cabinet, Balfour summoned it together. Chamberlain was disconcerted to discover how guarded his colleagues were about the cause he had taken to heart. Most were preoccupied with departmental responsibilities or held older priorities higher, like the Union with Ireland and party unity. Chamberlain thought of resigning. But none of his colleagues, apart from Ritchie, wanted or were ready for that yet, least of all Balfour. He persuaded the cabinet to launch an inquiry, which was after all what Chamberlain had called for in his original speech. Balfour kept the inquiry within the cabinet and stipulated that, while it was going on, members of the cabinet must not conduct their debate in public. The arrangement did not work easily. In announcing it to the House of Commons, Ritchie made no secret of his stand on the issue. In presenting the agreement to the Lords, Devonshire drew a distinction between skilled workers, whose security of employment and wage rates might be improved through tariff protection, and the unskilled poor who could not afford any increase in the cost of food.

Chamberlain's campaign entered a quieter phase, expected to last until the autumn speech-making season. The decision of the cabinet only confirmed him in his independence and deepened his reliance on alternative agencies for policymaking and publicity. Tariff reform seemed to rejuvenate Chamberlain. Though approaching his sixty-seventh birthday, he refused to feel old. When his younger brother Herbert died at the end of May, Joe declared himself confident that he would 'live to win this last battle for a United Empire',[19] even though it would probably take two more general elections. He thought of the cause he embraced as young. He was ready to admit that Britain was 'an old country. . . . But the Empire . . . is in its infancy. Now is the time when we can mould that Empire, and . . . decide its future destinies.'[20]

The rejuvenated leader devised new means to develop his case and organize support. The statistics provided by the Board of Trade on Britain's overseas trade were woefully inadequate. The controversy over imperial preference exposed this inadequacy, which left the controversialists on quicksand. To find his footing, Chamberlain turned to independent analysts like the Conservative backbencher Sir Vincent Caillard, an expert on tariffs from his years as British representative on the Ottoman Debt Council. Similarly for examination of policy, he turned away from cabinet colleagues to unofficial shapers of the public mind, young men mostly in their thirties. There were economists in this cadre including Hewins at the London School of Economics as well as Ashley. But its most conspicuous members were journalists, J.L. Garvin from the *Daily Telegraph*, Leo Amery at *The Times*, and Leo Maxse editing the *National Review*. In an interactive process, they pressed their vision of the world and their impression of their readers upon the statesman they revered. One after another that spring and summer, these men offered themselves for Chamberlain's service, Maxse with enthusiasm, Amery more slowly because of his prior concern for army reform, Ashley always at a distance. Hewins was commissioned to write a series of articles on the cause for *The Times*. They fed Chamberlain with information he could not get from the civil service, and with ideas with a radical edge. This core of advisers was circled by encouraging grandees from the newspaper world including Moberly Bell, manager of *The Times*, and Arthur Pearson, owner of the *Daily Express* and a host of provincial papers.

Chamberlain also mobilized his parliamentary support in an unfamiliar way, worrisome to those who held party cohesion in high esteem. Prohibited by the cabinet from leading the campaign from the front, he encouraged Unionist backbenchers to mount one from behind. 130 of them convened for this purpose before the end of June. The resolution which they passed in favour of imperial preference had to be worded vaguely to secure this much support. It was still pointed enough to provoke the formation of a contrary camp of 53 Unionist backbenchers committed to free trade. Chamberlain expected party loyalty to shrink the free trade minority to small proportions. In the meantime, before the contest hardened along party lines, he did what he could to win support from Liberal imperialists. The effort bore little fruit. Liberals as far apart as Sir Edward Grey and Lloyd George thought privately that Chamberlain's adoption of imperial preference might turn out to be wise; but free trade was too deeply rooted in the Liberal mind for any significant deviation in public. The party rallied as solidly against Chamberlain's proposals as it had against Balfour's Education Act. None of the dozen self-styled Liberals who signed a letter in support of Chamberlain to *The Times* in late July had been eminent as Liberals, and they all now became Unionists.

Even so, led by the one duke among them, Sutherland, they played an essential part in another organizational innovation in Chamberlain's campaign, the formation of a non-partisan Tariff Reform League. While agreeing to personal silence about the fiscal controversy, Chamberlain secured permission from his cabinet colleagues for impersonal discussion in pamphlet form. They had no notion how he would exploit this opening, particularly through the Tariff Reform League. Presided over by Sutherland, chaired by Pearson, energized by dedicated Unionist MPs, and well funded from industry, the Tariff Reform League produced a flood of printed works, large and small, to counteract the propaganda of the Cobden Club over the past generation.

The Tariff Reform League was based in London. An avowedly partisan organization was created at the same time in Birmingham: the Tariff Reform Committee, affiliated to the city's Liberal Unionist Association. With Chamberlain's constituency organizer, Charles Vince, in the chair, and with Neville Chamberlain, a Kenrick, a Nettlefold and Powell Williams on the executive, the committee was tightly under Joe's control. It became his command centre in the battle for support.

Using its party credentials, the committee sent its propaganda to Union-ist associations around the country. Using the industrial credentials of Birmingham, the committee solicited economic information as well as support from chambers of commerce in other cities.

By the end of the summer, the printed propaganda for Chamberlain's cause exceeded anything since the heyday of the Anti-Corn Law League. Within Birmingham the achievement was nevertheless marred by two defections, neither serious but one especially bitter. The *Birming-ham Post*, hitherto identified with Chamberlain, turned against his latest initiative. Arthur Pearson's *Midland Express* offset this defection. But nothing could remove the other sting. Arthur Chamberlain came out in favour of free trade, and he lambasted his elder brother for preparing 'a raging, tearing propaganda'.[21] Though the two men had stood solidly together to repel the attacks of Lloyd George on their business dealings, that episode had left Joe uneasy about Arthur's management of Kynochs. Arthur was exasperated by Joe's success in limiting the power of the Birmingham magistrates to reduce the number of licensed public houses. The two brothers were at each other's throats when Joe re-turned from South Africa. Though hitherto Arthur had upheld his brother's political cause through all its twists and turns, their quarrel stretched back to their conduct in industry. Joe advocated alliance in one form or other between capital and labour to defuse their conflict, an objective still with tariff reform. Arthur was a devotee of laissez-faire, and opposed trade unions in his firms as resolutely as he now opposed governmental interference with the freedom of trade. The quarrel be-tween the two men was too personal, however, to be conducted calmly in terms of principle.

Arthur's defection did not reflect a breach in Joe's relations with the Birmingham business community. Any such risk was removed by Joe's move towards protectionism. Like the Tories who longed for a return to Corn Laws, the metal manufacturers of the West Midlands welcomed a change in fiscal policy to protect their threatened interests. But both groups felt little love for reforms which did not directly serve their needs. The link Chamberlain suggested between tariffs and old-age pensions roused uneasiness in these quarters without greatly enhancing his appeal to labour. Quick again to adjust his message, he played down pensions and played up the industrial appeal of protection to labour as well as to capital. Gathering that the working class cared less about old age than about their immediate standard of living, he com-posed a letter to a trade unionist for publication in *The Times* in which he stressed that workers in the tariff-protected economies of Germany and the United States enjoyed higher wage rates than those prevalent in Britain.[22] He reiterated his related concern at the increasing proportion of raw materials and semifinished goods rather than of high-level manufactures among British exports, in contrast to the performance of Britain's rivals.

The adjustments in his message strengthened his cause. Towards the end of June, a group of MPs and industrialists connected with iron and steel, engineering and electrical manufacturing gathered to raise money for the speech-making campaign Chamberlain was to launch in the autumn. Among them was Arthur Keen, once Chamberlain's business rival, now his successor through the merger of Guest, Keen & Co. with Nettlefolds. With names such as Hickman, Lawrence and Wrightson, and from firms such as Westinghouse, GKN and Bessemer, this group gave Chamberlain his hard core of parliamentary and industrial support.

The day after this meeting, fulfilling an engagement made before and hence exempted from the cabinet's self-imposed gag, Chamberlain addressed the Constitutional Club, a citadel of the government's Conservative majority. There he painted a gloomy picture of the economy, emphasizing the threat to the staple exports, the iron and steel products and textiles, upon which Britain's industrial primacy was built. He also refined the social side of his proposals to meet Conservative susceptibilities. From every standpoint, working-class as well as Conservative and Whig, it seemed more important to hold down the cost of living than to pay for old-age pensions. Bowing to the consensus, Chamberlain offered to reduce the existing revenue tariff on tea and sugar or tobacco to offset the tax on corn which he wished to reinstate with preferential modification in favour of Canada. Gerald Balfour at the Board of Trade welcomed the shift in Chamberlain's policy as 'a long step back towards . . . the safer and better direction'.[23]

Thereafter, for the rest of the summer, the crucial forum for the fiscal inquiry was the cabinet. But Chamberlain paid little attention to it, as did his opposing colleagues. Preoccupied elsewhere, he stepped on the toes of ministers in the middle who were not sure which way to turn. He worked at breakneck pace, his independent discussions and organizations adding to the continual demands of the Colonial Office.

The outcome of the cabinet deliberations depended to a great extent on the Duke of Devonshire. If he could be brought around, the remaining opponents of fiscal reform in the cabinet could be readily dispensed with. Chamberlain therefore focused his attention on the duke. Their ensuing correspondence was remarkable. It exposed the imperial limitations of Chamberlain's initiative, accentuated its industrial strength, helped him work out the basic terms for his proposed fiscal reform, and in the process threw more light on the gulf that divided him from the duke.

India did not figure in Chamberlain's imperial thought. He neither visited India nor appreciated the place of the country which the older generation, and some of the new, thought of as the heart of the empire. The Colonial Office, which had no responsibility for India, increased his preoccupation elsewhere. He included the figures for India whenever he wanted to emphasize the population of the empire. But he paid no attention to its special economic circumstances, including its low tariffs designed to give the textiles of Lancashire free access to the Indian market as well as to keep down the cost of living among India's always famine-threatened masses. Chamberlain also belittled the military contribution of India to the empire, though the Indian army helped Britain meet a whole succession of imperial crises, particularly in Africa. Chamberlain's ignorance of India undermined any inclination Devonshire had to listen to his fiscal proposals with respect.

But when Devonshire questioned the worth of the proposals from a domestic perspective, Chamberlain worked out a strong industrial rationale for his cause, though too radical for Devonshire. It challenged the supremacy which finance enjoyed in the classical school of political economy. Devonshire could not understand Chamberlain's preoccupation with solid imports and exports. One of the greatest capitalists in the country but not a manufacturing industrialist, the duke saw no special merit in paying for imports with visible exports. He argued that 'if, to take the extreme case, our Imports were balanced by our shipping receipts and by the interest on our foreign investments, the country would be just as much better off than it is now, as a man who lives on invested capital is better off than the man who has to work with his hands'[24]—as he knew from experience.

The argument of the duke drove Chamberlain back to his industrial roots and original social vision. Wishing for reinforcement from academic economics, Chamberlain asked Hewins for help; but Chamberlain accompanied his request with questions which pointed to the answer he sought. What, he asked Hewins, 'is the effect of payment for imports by interest on securities? Is it not the effect that such payment does not promote employment of labour, and that, therefore, although the *wealth* of the country so paid may not be less in aggregate, the *national health* will be worse in the sense that it will tend to cease being a manufacturing and producing nation and will become instead a nation of consumers, chiefly rich men and their dependents?'[25] The old antagonism between the landed aristocrat and the metal manufacturer resurfaced.

Leaving little time for help from Hewins, Chamberlain prepared a short memorandum for the duke. In the memorandum Chamberlain contended that it was 'better to keep the employment in this country even though the workmen (and everyone else) had to pay a little more for the articles manufactured at home than for those coming from abroad, where wages may be lower and the conditions of employment more favourable to the manufacturer'.[26] The last clause contradicted Chamberlain's earlier contention that protectionist econo- mies paid higher wages; yet the priority which he gave to labour was unmistakable.

It was through discussion with politicians such as Devonshire and businessmen such as Arthur Keen rather than through economic or sta- tistical analysis that Chamberlain evolved his ideas. 'All economic argu- ments are speculative,' he wrote in summarizing fashion to the duke.[27] 'I prefer a little common sense & business experience. Both tell me that there is ample room for the investment of untold millions in this coun- try', and that there 'will also be a sufficiency of labour although its cost per man will increase. Not necessarily its cost on the goods made,' he added with technological alertness, 'as new inventions constantly take the place of manual labour.' Thus spoke a man who thought of wealth in terms of manufacturing capacity and equated welfare with the em- ployment of labour, seeking to convince a man who thought of wealth in terms of investments and equated happiness with leisure. There was no meeting of minds.

The subject always came back to exports. Chamberlain pointed to the stagnancy of British exports over the past decade as evidence of the country's economic debility. He maintained that this stagnancy would have amounted to 'an immense decline but for the increase of Colonial trade &', he added disapprovingly, 'the larger export of coal'.[28] He pre- dicted that worse was to come with the dumping of excess goods from tariff-protected German and American industry on British markets at home and abroad.

At the end of the summer, Chamberlain gave the duke an outline of his fiscal proposals, revised and developed in light of what he had learned since mid-May. Gone was the link with old-age pensions, in view of mounting evidence that the working class was not interested in this offer. Instead, any increase in the cost of living from a tariff on corn and also now on meat would be offset by reduced taxation of other basic items of consumption: indeed more than offset. Chamberlain planned a net reduction in the taxes on consumption large enough to create a budget deficit, which he proposed to meet through a tariff on imports of manufactured goods. The taxes on consumption, with pref- erential amendment in favour of the colonies, were designed for pur- poses of imperial consolidation. The tax on manufactured goods was designed to give some tariff protection to domestic industry.

That promise enabled Chamberlain to exploit the most popular aspect of customs duties, namely the capacity to retaliate against countries that kept Britain out of their markets by surrounding them with high tariffs. Retaliation was popular because it was directed against an obviously unfair practice and also because it could serve to restore free trade. But

Chamberlain did not desire the elimination of tariffs. He wanted a modest level of tariff to become a permanent feature of the fiscal order in Britain. That was justified, he argued, to protect the country against 'unfair competition'[29] from other countries where, quite apart from tariffs, the burden of taxation and the standard of living might be lower and where industry was less regulated for the protection of workers. The revenue which accrued from tariffs would also enable the government to improve the armed defences of the country and its social services.

The outline Chamberlain drew up did not yet amount to, nor did he present it as, a fully worked system of tariffs. He offered it as a fair indication of his fiscal intentions. He hoped to implement his scheme in three steps: first to win 'a general mandate' from the electorate, then to open discussions with the colonies on preference and with foreign countries on the excesses of their protective systems, and only then, in light of those discussions, to draw up a concrete tariff scheme for Parliament to enact. His opponents naturally sought to jump to the third stage and examine the detailed application of Chamberlain's scheme immediately. They also seized on early evidence of colonial and foreign response to his proposals in order to predict and dissect his ultimate plan.

Chamberlain was disappointed that response in the colonies was not more enthusiastic. The government of Germany indicated privately that it would be willing to do business with him in revising the tariff relations between the two countries. Protectionists in the United States smiled approvingly at his efforts to persuade the old country to follow their young example. But colonial reaction was more mixed. Australia was conspicuously divided on the issue. But by all accounts the crucial colony was Canada. Chamberlain's speech of mid-May was widely applauded there. Free-trading sentiments were strong only in the Canadian west. Imperial sentiments masked the aversion of English-Canadian manufacturers in Ontario to British imports. Chamberlain received private assurance of support from the Canadian government. But to his disappointment, and to the relief of his British enemies, the usually eloquent prime minister of Canada, Laurier, offered no response to him in public. In private too, speaking to the governor-general Lord Minto, Laurier deepened Chamberlain's anxiety by saying that he did not sense any particular urgency in the relations between Britain and Canada.

It was Lord Minto who felt this urgency, and he impressed it upon Chamberlain: 'if we miss our present chance,' Minto wrote, 'that is to say if the old country appears to throw cold water on what were the deliberately expressed suggestions of the Colonial representatives at the recent Conference, we shall never get another. From what I have seen of Canadian life I am convinced that we have arrived at the parting of the ways—either we are going to unite our Empire or to lose it.'[30] Disregarding Laurier's assessment, Chamberlain took Minto's counsel to heart. Chamberlain's sense of fleeting opportunity was heightened personally as he turned sixty-seven. And however disappointed by Laurier, he was heartened by the Canadian finance minister. Fielding led him to believe that Canada would not only welcome a preferential trade agreement with Britain but might go on to ease the burden of imperial defence on Britain.

Still, the doubtful response to imperial preference in the colonies, like Devonshire's at home, induced Chamberlain to clarify his proposals. In correspondence with sympathizers in Canada and Australia, he outlined a plan to reconcile the colonial desire for protection of their infant industries with the desire of British manufacturers for freer access to the colonial market. But while his plan allowed for the preservation of existing industrial interests in the colonies, it would keep them from rising higher. The colonies could retain tariffs to protect whatever they already did in 'the great primary industries such as Iron Making and Cotton Spinning'.[31] In return, however, for preferential access of their agricultural produce to the British market, the colonies would have to open their markets freely or almost freely to specialized British goods not yet manufactured in the colonies: merely raising the colonial tariff against foreign producers would not suffice. In this way something approaching free trade in agriculture and the advanced levels of industry could be attained within the empire. That, for the British, would be tariff reform in its most popular shape. Not so for the colonies. Yet there were compensating rewards. Under imperial preference, the colonies could count on enormous growth in their primary production for export to Britain, growth that would expand their domestic market for local manufacturing. The political rewards would be still greater. In place of 'the parochial life and small ambitions of little States . . . insignificant, powerless and uninteresting', the colonies would possess a historic destiny as vital contributors to and participants in the world's greatest empire.

The plans which Chamberlain thus evolved over the summer contained unresolved tensions, imperial and domestic. Furthermore, the logic of his scheme and the support it attracted drove him ever further from free trade towards protection, and thus maximized his challenge to the fiscal practice under which Britain had flourished for half a century. The pace at which he moved towards protection increased uneasiness among his colleagues. He was obviously improvising under the pressure of the controversy he had precipitated, improvising with an enthusiasm which excited some but frightened more. The manner in which he propounded his ideas was as disconcerting as his message, not least to those who treasured the time-honoured crafts of parliamentary gradualism and consensual government in cabinet.

Exit without escape

Chamberlain was tired of those constraints. He was impatient too with the governmental lassitude which prevailed before his arrival at the Colonial Office, allowing colonies to go their own way and encouraging business at home to pursue its own interests without regard to Britain's national needs and international performance. Though his command of many of the traditional skills of government was unrivalled, he longed for release after eight years of ceaseless work in office, and he doubted the necessity of his continuing in office for the purposes he now had in mind.

To put the matter differently, he was dissatisfied with the dual leadership he had formed with Balfour when Lord Salisbury retired. Thirteen months after his retirement, Salisbury died; and the dual leadership did not long outlive him. During the final weeks of his life, in parting interviews with former colleagues, Salisbury denounced the dual leadership as an unstable arrangement and censured Balfour for allowing it to develop. Over the past three months Chamberlain had strained the arrangement to its limits, not so much by embracing imperial preference—after all, his assigned sphere in the dual leadership was the imperial—as by developing it, heedless of Balfour, into a full-blown scheme of tariff reform involving domestic fiscal, social and economic policy. Balfour's patience, though tried, never snapped. But when the members of the cabinet gathered for the memorial service to Salisbury in Westminster Abbey at the beginning of September, Balfour was on the lookout for some way to make himself master in his own house. Beginning that day, he and Chamberlain worked out a new arrangement between themselves. It was ill-considered on Chamberlain's part, deceptive on Balfour's, and for both proved worse than the dual leadership.

In calling for imperial preference and increasingly for tariff protection, Chamberlain attracted quite enough support among Unionists to transform the agenda and shake the composition of the party. Though the tariff reformers had their eye on the next general election rather than on the immediate business of government, the character and composition of the cabinet could not but be affected by the upheaval in the party. By August it was obvious that some resignations were imminent: the question was no longer whether but who. When the cabinet met in mid-August to debate the fiscal issue, it saw no prospect of compromise between the stiff free traders, including Hamilton and Balfour of

Burleigh as well as Ritchie, and the enthusiastic tariff reformers, including Selborne and Halsbury as well as Chamberlain. The debate was adjourned for a month.

Until 8 September, a week after the memorial service for Salisbury, Balfour gave his colleagues the impression that he was in basic sympathy with Chamberlain's proposals for imperial preference, including tariffs on foreign foodstuffs, as well as retaliation against protectionist foreign countries that exploited the open British market. He differed from Chamberlain only in emphasis, displaying greater aversion to tariff protection and greater anxiety to keep down the working-class cost of living. The thinking of the two men evolved after the mid-August meeting of the cabinet, still along parallel lines. Both men were disconcerted by the popular aversion to food taxes but were encouraged by the popularity of retaliation.

They were also impressed by the desirability of conciliating the Duke of Devonshire. Though Chamberlain had done his best to bring him around, the duke sympathized far more with the ministerial trio of free-trading Conservatives than with the Liberal Unionists who were ardent for tariff reform, including his former lieutenant Selborne. Balfour feared that if the government fell apart over the fiscal controversy, Devonshire might supplant him as prime minister. Balfour and Chamberlain also wondered if the duke could be used to release them from each other. Chamberlain thought he saw a way of keeping Devonshire in office while escaping himself with increased ability to shape the thinking of the country and the government. Balfour hoped to use Devonshire to reduce Chamberlain's ability to set the government's pace.

Balfour may not have quite credited Chamberlain's suggestion when he first made it at the Salisbury memorial service. Chamberlain repeated it in writing on 9 September for Balfour to consider before the cabinet reconvened on 14 September. Point after point in Chamberlain's letter manifested his desire to escape from office.[32] His inability under the cabinet's summertime truce to speak out in defence of his proposals had, he feared, allowed 'the superstition about the "dear loaf"' to gain strength. It was desirable to keep the duke in the cabinet; and if Chamberlain remained there too after the cabinet truce came to an end, he would still feel unable to make a strong case for his proposals for fear that Devonshire would take umbrage. Chamberlain suggested that Balfour try to keep the duke and let Chamberlain himself go by excluding imperial preference with its unpopular corollary of food taxes from the government's fiscal policy for the moment while adopting the popular policy of retaliation. Chamberlain said that he would feel honourbound to resign in this case, because otherwise 'the Colonies would think I had betrayed them'. He would use his freedom to do what he could to convert the public at home to his views, and thus enable the

Unionist leadership to embrace them. His list of the advantages to be drawn from this strategy began with the freedom it would give him 'to put my own case in my own way', and ended with relief at the prospect of 'a little more rest after the strain of so many years'.

His offer of resignation was not meant as a protest. On the contrary, he thought it was consistent 'with an absolutely loyal support of the Government afterwards'. In order to demonstrate the friendliness of his departure, he offered to persuade his son Austen to remain in the cabinet. In effect Joe expected the dual leadership to continue after his resignation, but at a distance, Balfour remaining in charge at Westminster while Joe took to the platform in the provinces. He counted on receiving a lot of cooperation from the government. Placing his trust in Balfour's expressions of agreement in principle with imperial preference and a tariff on foodstuffs, Chamberlain expected the ministry to wish his campaign well. He expected Balfour and the cabinet meanwhile to commit themselves to retaliation by asking for 'powers to negotiate with foreign countries'. Such a course of action would, Chamberlain thought, lead to imperial preference perhaps quickly, despite its exclusion at the outset.

These were the expectations of a frustrated crusader, not the calculations of a seasoned minister. In his eagerness to throw off the yoke of collective responsibility, Chamberlain did not subject his proposal to examination by anyone before offering it to Balfour. Nor did he discuss it with anyone while Balfour had it under consideration. Austen was on holiday and did not see his father until the meeting of the cabinet. Mary was with Joe in Birmingham, but he said nothing to her. Like Lord Randolph Churchill when he tendered his resignation to Salisbury in 1886, Chamberlain plunged on alone.

Like his uncle on that occasion, Balfour took his time responding to Chamberlain, who remained in Birmingham. They did not discuss the letter, which Chamberlain wrote on a Wednesday, until an hour before the cabinet met the following Monday. In the interim Balfour had to be reticent about Chamberlain's suggestion for fear that the free-trading ministerial minority would treat his departure as their triumph. But Balfour discussed the proposal with his brother and also showed Chamberlain's letter to Selborne. As the husband of a Cecil, former protégé of Devonshire, and now an ardent tariff reformer, Selborne would be of pivotal importance in reconstructing the cabinet.

Balfour welcomed the prospect of Chamberlain's departure, though only if the uncompromising free traders in the cabinet resigned at the same time. Otherwise Balfour would alienate the broad body of support within the Unionist party for some regulation of trade through tariffs. He wanted to keep Devonshire if he could; but he was not confident of success on this point, and was willing to lose him as well as Chamberlain. Losing the duke would not be as unpleasant as continuing in harness with Chamberlain. Balfour could not say quite this to Selborne. But after giving Selborne his impression that the duke had 'finally resolved to go',[33] Balfour sought to persuade Selborne that the simultaneous departure of Chamberlain would alleviate the danger of the cabinet's disruption.

While Balfour conferred with colleagues of his choice, the dissident free-trade ministers met to prepare themselves for the cabinet council set for 14 September. Chamberlain kept to himself. Balfour half expected him the day before. But he did not leave Birmingham until the morning of the meeting, scheduled for 3 p.m. He arrived in time for an hour's conversation beforehand with the Balfour brothers, Gerald as well as Arthur. They settled the lines on which they would proceed in the full meeting. The prime minister would insist on the '[n]ecessity for change in recognised fiscal policy . . . [to give the government] liberty of negotiation & to promote fiscal union of empire',[34] but he was also to rule out imperial preference as impracticable in the current state of British opinion. On that issue, 'everyone would be free to express his own opinion . . . but the official programme would be confined to the point upon which the Party could most probably be united'.[35] When Balfour enunciated that limitation, Chamberlain would explain that, in view of his exceptional situation vis-à-vis the colonies, he felt obliged to resign though he would continue to support 'those who remained to carry out the policy' outlined by the prime minister. The agreement which the three men reached was to be confirmed by the promotion of Austen Chamberlain in the cabinet, probably to replace Ritchie as Chancellor of the Exchequer.

The ensuing meeting of the cabinet proceeded as Balfour and Chamberlain arranged. The only person who threatened to upset the plan was Austen, who returned to London just in time for the cabinet council without being forewarned. Visibly agitated during the meeting by his father's suggestion of resignation, he was held back from following his example only by a note which Gerald Balfour pushed to him across the table. On the other hand, the prime minister virtually demanded the resignations of the free-trading trio. Joe left the meeting satisfied. He prepared his formal letter of resignation, which bore the date of the letter in which he had initially developed his scheme for Balfour.

Their accord came under immediate strain. Chamberlain had gained the release he sought. He wanted a prompt and becoming presentation of the news to the effect that, while the free-trading trio had been dismissed, he left the ministry with the prime minister's blessing to carry the cause of tariff reform to the country. But Balfour did not place quite that gloss on their joint action; and while he welcomed Chamberlain's departure, he was anxious to make private use of that news in order to keep Devonshire in the cabinet. Chamberlain regarded this effort with neutrality, aware that the retention of Devonshire would shore up the weakened government but would also obscure the government's commitment to fiscal reform. Chamberlain kept silent while Balfour baited his hook for Devonshire with hints at and then long passages from Chamberlain's letter of resignation. The procedure wounded Chamberlain by indicating that only his resignation would keep Devonshire in the cabinet. Never a dogmatist, the duke found the impassioned debate between free traders and tariff reformers perplexing; but his deepest political instinct was aversion to activism; and he knew that Chamberlain was bound to invest the fiscal policy of any government to which he belonged with that dreaded quality. The debate over fiscal policy had become terribly personal.

After two days of uncertainty, Balfour landed his fish. Once Devonshire agreed to remain in the ministry, the news of the ministerial resignations could be released. The free-trading resignations were announced without adornment. The announcement with regard to Chamberlain was accompanied with publication of an exchange of letters with Balfour in which the prime minister praised his departing colleague for doing 'more than any man, living or dead, to bring home to the citizens of the Empire the consciousness of Imperial obligation, and the interdependence between the various fragments into which the Empire is geographically divided'.[36] Yet he expressed no more than passive regret at Chamberlain's decision to resign from the government. And he placed a negative gloss on Austen's remaining within it: Austen's action was treated as 'conclusive evidence that in your judgment, as in mine, the exclusion of taxation on food from the party programme is, in existing circumstances, the course best fitted practically to further the cause of fiscal reform'.

Balfour used Austen as a rope to tie his father down. The cabinet was Balfour's sphere of authority, all the more so after Joe departed. There Austen could be flattered, overawed or overruled into submission. Joe did not foresee this danger, and he was taken aback when it was first pointed out to him. The public concordat between Joe and the prime minister also protected Balfour from the risk of 'frontal attack by the most savage political fighter of their day'.[37] The agreement in effect left the Commons as well as the cabinet to Balfour while Joe devoted his attention to the country. Balfour was content. He neither felt nor fared well on the platform.

Yet his insidious adaptation of the arrangement which Chamberlain had proposed only heightened its essential danger. The dual leadership, which had been kept together over the past year within the constraints of the cabinet, was now loosened by the adoption of a dual forum. The two men surrendered different but none the less vital spheres of power and authority to each other; and the release cost them both dearly. What Chamberlain lost in the cabinet and the Commons he gained in the national party and the country; and Chamberlain's gain was Balfour's loss. Chamberlain fortified his side of the dual forum by creating his own civil service to compensate for the inadequacies of the Board of Trade and the hostility of the Treasury. On this unorthodox basis, he launched the most serious challenge to the prevailing political economy which Britain had experienced in half a century. The only thing which could be predicted with certainty about this climactic venture of his was that it would be explosive.

19

The All-Consuming Venture
1903–1906

I suggested that why Chamberlain would make headway, in spite of
his bad arguments, was because he had a vision, desired to bring about
a new state of affairs and was working day and night for a cause, that
no one else wished anything but a quiet life and the *status quo*.

Beatrice Webb in her diary, 3 November 1903

Once Chamberlain resigned from the cabinet, the crusade for tariff reform carried him back to Birmingham. Until he became Colonial Secretary, he had kept in close touch with his provincial base. But since then
the demands of office had held him for long stretches in London; and
for a while he had lost the ability to head off problems in Birmingham
before they arose. His return after resignation took him back to his
roots, as did the whole policy of tariff reform. The way he sought to
propagate his policy also reflected his basic instincts in public life: he
was engaged in another 'work of enquiry & education'.[1]

In one way tariff reform marked a deviation in Chamberlain's career,
and that deviation had upsetting consequences. Tariff reform sup-
planted opposition to Home Rule as the pivot around which his politics
revolved. His commitment to the new cause was absolute, as his Unionism had not been, for he had always appreciated the need to supplement opposition to Home Rule with a more constructive policy for
Ireland and by raising other issues in England and abroad. His new
policy disrupted his party by altering the basis on which the Unionist
alliance was formed.

The single-mindedness of Chamberlain's commitment to tariff reform
was not a sign of health, personally or politically. He knew that this
venture would be his last. He accompanied expressions of confidence in
the triumph of tariff reform with the proviso, 'if I have life & strength
for a few years more';[2] and he did not hide this anxiety from the general public. Everyone was impressed by his seeming youthfulness and
boundless energy, until the summer of 1903 when he turned sixty-
seven. Thereafter observers detected signs of failing force. No longer
diverted by the varied responsibilities of cabinet government, he threw

8. Etching of
Chamberlain,
1903.

all he had into the effort to convert Britain to tariff reform before the
opportunity faded. His daughters noticed sadly that his range of subjects for dinnertime conversation narrowed to tariff reform, which became 'almost an obsession'.[3] His obsession furthermore debilitated his
party. He turned Unionists into internecine fanatics, each faction more
interested in suppressing its opponents within the party than in defeating the Liberals, while Balfour turned party unity into an absolute, arid
dogma.

Chamberlain's vision was narrowed in yet another way by his return
to Birmingham. While his local lieutenants and daily experience quickened his appreciation of the needs of the metal-manufacturing West
Midlands, his appreciation of the economic interests of other regions of
the country was correspondingly reduced. He was also under less pressure in Birmingham than at the Colonial Office to pay attention to the
ambitions of the colonies.

The autumn campaign

Between his resignation and his first scheduled speaking engagement, he had barely three weeks to prepare a campaign meant to change the direction of Britain's political economy. Chamberlain immured himself in Highbury to read, organize his thoughts and prepare his words. He had to give attention to changes in the ministry, respond to would-be advisers, and settle arrangements for his first meeting and the preceding conference of the National Union of Conservative Associations in Sheffield at which Balfour would announce the stance of the reconstructed government on the fiscal controversy. The way things worked out during these three weeks surprised everyone and disconcerted the friends of Chamberlain. But he was not dismayed or deflected from his course, confident that his concordat with Balfour was being honoured.

His one anxiety in his first days after resignation was lest middle-rank Conservative worthies, particularly in Glasgow where his first meeting was to be held, would distance themselves from his policy in deference to Balfour's supposed desires. Having surrendered office in order to convert the country to imperial preference, he interpreted any opposition from Conservatives as rank ingratitude. 'I have made *my* sacrifice,' he wrote to his Glasgow lieutenant, 'and the least they can do is to show some appreciation of it.'[4] It was, however, soon evident that Balfour had more to fear from the constituency leaders of the Conservative party than did Chamberlain.

Speaking in Sheffield at the beginning of October, Balfour enunciated a policy in strict but unenthusiastic accord with his agreement with Chamberlain. The prime minister called for eventual electoral though not immediate parliamentary approval of retaliatory tariffs to induce foreign states to lower their protectionist walls. At the same time, citing the popular aversion to taxes on foodstuffs, he declared himself against imperial preference. The audience greeted this declaration 'in stony silence'.[5] When Balfour rhetorically offered to resign if the party did not endorse his stand, the meeting was disrupted with a call, 'What about Joe?' The seeming spinelessness of the lead that Balfour offered did not impress even neutral observers. 'It is rather new in politics,' a British diplomat remarked, 'that we should have a Prime Minister who openly says he has no convictions until he has found out whether it pays or not. Of the two I prefer Chamberlain.'[6] Chamberlain's supporters at Sheffield reacted to the official leader of the party with acute disappointment.

But Chamberlain urged them to be patient. He insisted that Balfour could not possibly have spoken differently: 'his first duty', Chamberlain argued, was 'to try and prevent a serious split'.[7] 'We are making for the same port but in different boats.'[8] He had been gratified by Balfour's consultation with him in filling the ministerial vacancies and by the prominence of Liberal Unionist tariff reformers in the reconstruction: Arnold-Forster to the War Office as well as Austen to the Exchequer. He was also gratified that the Duke of Devonshire, after days of dithering, resigned when Balfour committed himself to retaliatory tariffs at Sheffield. It had been galling to know that Devonshire remained in the cabinet only on the assurance that Chamberlain left. Chamberlain was looking for an opportunity to 'have it out with the Duke'[9] when the news of his resignation arrived. The resignation increased Balfour's dependence on Chamberlain. Moreover, the way in which Devonshire's earlier conduct was now explained and statements from the sacked free-trading ministers created the impression that Balfour had intrigued in mid-September to hang on to the duke. For once, it was Balfour rather than Chamberlain who looked unprincipled.

The obvious Conservative sympathy for Chamberlain at Sheffield was not enough to make him euphoric during his opening trip to Scotland. He headed into parts of the country where the decision hung in the balance, to Glasgow and then Newcastle, where shipbuilding interests profited at least as much from international as from colonial trade, and on to Liverpool, which owed its wealth to freely admitted raw materials including cotton. On the eve of his opening expedition to Glasgow, Chamberlain felt that he would either triumph or utterly fail. A week later, he felt 'somewhat in the position of Athanasius contra mundum'.[10]

He remained fettered by his anxiety to keep relations with Balfour and the cabinet sweet. Mary Chamberlain kept in touch with Balfour's sister Betty. Chamberlain prefaced his campaign in Glasgow with a remarkable statement of loyalty to Balfour: 'Understand', he told his audience, 'that in no conceivable circumstances will I allow myself to be put in any sort of competition, direct or indirect, with my friend and leader, whom I mean to follow.'[11] He sought to endorse the official programme of the party as well as to move it forward, no more disloyal than 'scouts, or pioneers, or investigators, or discoverers'.

It was as 'a missionary of Empire' that he presented his case. Though he called his policy 'tariff reform' to encompass retaliation and some tariff protection as well as imperial preference, he stressed the imperial side. The imperial emergency was sharper than the domestic. The recession that set in after the war was not deep. Things at home would have to get much worse—as Chamberlain anticipated they would—before the popular devotion to cheap food could be shaken. But he believed that relations between the colonies and the mother country were already at a turning point, brought there by Britain's refusal to respond to Canada's tariff preference by amending the wartime corn tax in Canada's favour. If steps were not taken to coordinate the economic growth of the empire, the self-governing colonies would develop towards independence. 'We must either draw closer together,' Chamberlain warned, 'or we shall drift apart.'

But as he analysed the danger, he emphasized domestic considerations. The concern he pressed upon his Glasgow audience was for 'the national strength and the prosperity of the United Kingdom'. He spoke of 'cracks and crevices in the walls' of British trade which had been opened up by protectionist competition from the United States and Germany. In his speech next day at Greenock, those cracks and crevices yawned wide: 'Agriculture...has been practically destroyed. Sugar has gone; silk has gone; iron is threatened; wool is threatened; cotton will go!'[12]

The more he dwelt on the domestic danger, the more economic his message became. His imperial gospel grew very mundane to harness the material interests of his countrymen. It all came down to tariffs, from which the colonies were to be preferentially exempt: two shillings a quarter on corn excluding maize, and a corresponding duty on flour; five per cent on meat and dairy produce excluding bacon; and, with an eye to South African production, an indeterminate amount on wines and perhaps fruits. To offset the increased cost of living which these food taxes would entail, Chamberlain proposed to reduce the existing revenue duties on tea, sugar, cocoa and coffee. Those reductions would produce a net budgetary deficit, which he proposed to make good by instituting 'a moderate duty on all manufactured goods, not exceeding 10 per cent. on the average, but varying according to the amount of labour' involved in their manufacture. The variable tariff on imported manufactures was designed to appeal to the complex of industrial interests in Britain. Chamberlain recognized, however, that the value of the tariff on manufactures would not be obvious to the working class, particularly now that he had dropped all mention of old-age pensions. He therefore wound up his tour of Scotland by translating industrial tariffs to mean protection of working-class employment.

The ultimate verdict on his programme would be delivered by the electorate. Accordingly Chamberlain couched his appeal in the terms he thought the popular electorate would understand. Because his case was dependent in part on economic comparisons, he had to use statistics. But he knew that statistics would quickly bore and would never convince a popular audience. He had not been driven to tariff reform himself by poring over statistical returns. Though by training he was an accountant, his vigilance in this sphere had dulled with disuse. He claimed to approach public problems as a man of business, yet he was more creative than careful in his approach to economic data. He reacted with impatience when critics of his programme seized on its statistical weak points. In Scotland he had selected 1872 as a benchmark year for

British exports, ignoring the upward distortion in that year when—as he could have remembered—British manufacturers reaped extraordinary dividends from the disruption of their Continental competitors in the wake of the Franco-Prussian war.

He insisted that his argument was not affected by these statistical fine points. But he was forced to recognize that they had a considerable effect on the educated middle class. The best way to reach them was through the quality press. While he continued to concentrate his own efforts on the platform, he entrusted the more refined kinds of economic argument to his scholarly and journalistic assistants, including the sociologist Benjamin Kidd as well as Hewins and Garvin. Chamberlain insisted that the scholars keep the publicity of their efforts in mind. 'Anonymous letters in small type are of little value,' he instructed Hewins, 'but an article or letter from a recognised authority which the Editor will place in the front and comment upon is of the utmost advantage.'[13]

Back in Birmingham, uncertain about the impact of his efforts in Scotland, Chamberlain came down with gout. A week later when he had to leave for Newcastle, he could not walk without assistance and had a migraine headache. He nearly blacked out during his address at Newcastle, and he wondered how much longer he had to live. Conceptually, none the less, his speeches in and around Newcastle marked some development in his argument. He dwelt on the qualitative deterioration in British exports over the past thirty years, from a preponderance of manufactured goods to less finished products and even raw materials. Britain exported less and imported more of the sort of production that involved a high input of labour. So here again the issue was employment. His analysis on the colonial side was less compelling than on the British. He exaggerated the degree to which Britain's exports to the colonies offset the deterioration in its exports to foreign markets.

With similarly uneven justification, he rewrote the history of the British economy in the past century to discredit the myth of a mid-Victorian boom fuelled by free trade. Chamberlain argued that the prosperity of the 1850s owed more to railway construction at home and the discovery of gold abroad than to the country's adoption of free trade in the late 1840s. He stood on weaker ground when he gave credit for the mid-century prosperity to the preceding system of protective tariffs. Whatever the merits of his case, with each step in its development he widened his estrangement from laissez-faire. He translated it to mean 'let[ting] matters alone. My judgment is that this country of ours has let things alone too long. We have been too ready to drift.'[14]

The crucial development at Newcastle was not in his argument, however, but in the party organization. The host group there, the Durham and North Riding Liberal Unionist Association, greeted Chamberlain with a resolution endorsing tariff reform. The resolution was all the more significant because the Duke of Devonshire as president of the national organization had written to prevent the local association from taking such a stand. Angry at the disregard of his warning, the duke threatened to withdraw financial support from branches of the national association which committed themselves to tariff reform. The threat played into Chamberlain's hands. It was Devonshire, not Chamberlain, who had first divided Liberal Unionists on an issue other than Home Rule, by sponsoring the recent Education Act. It was the Free Food League of which the duke was now president which threw the first electoral stone at fellow Unionists over the fiscal issue by working against Alfred Lyttelton in the by-election necessitated by his appointment as Colonial Secretary. Chamberlain felt confident that Liberal Unionist opinion in the country was swinging towards tariff reform. He therefore advocated freedom for local associations to deal with the issue as they saw fit. Devonshire beat a temporary retreat.

This quarrel gave a foretaste of the disruption Chamberlain's campaign was likely to cause in every Unionist organization, Liberal or Conservative. Balfour recoiled at the prospect. Not having heard from him since Glasgow, Chamberlain sensed that Balfour was distancing himself from the campaign. The former Colonial Secretary wrote to the prime minister in a collegial vein, but received no response. Balfour prevented members of the cabinet including Austen Chamberlain from giving public support to anything beyond the official policy of tariff retaliation.

One result of this prohibition was to concentrate the campaign for tariff reform upon Joe alone. He complained of being 'deprived of the active cooperation of the members of the Cabinet, who ... would have carried the war over a much wider country'.[15] Still, he seemed to take the country by storm. He put in perhaps his best performance at Liverpool. He went there under the auspices of the Liverpool Working Men's Conservative Association. The Trades Union Congress had recently declared against tariff reform. Never did Chamberlain appeal beyond the trade unions to the working class more astutely than on this occasion at Liverpool.

He reminded his audience that the original campaign for free trade by the Anti-Corn Law League had been decidedly middle class rather than working class in inspiration. He pointed out the incompatibility of laissez-faire with the collective philosophy of trade unionism and also with the legislation enacted over the past generation 'to benefit the condition of the working men and to raise the standard of living'.[16] 'What is the good', he asked, '... of prohibiting sweating in this country, if you allow sweated goods to come in from foreign countries?' The cordial response of his audience encouraged him to emphasize his exasperation with laissez-faire, 'this feeble and futile policy of official in-capacity or official apathy, which makes it either below the dignity or below the duty of a British Government to take care of British trade'.

He did not deal so well with the issues raised by Liverpool's ship-ping industry, whose interests were greater in foreign than in imperial trade. None the less, after a month's campaigning, he had pulled the central ideas of tariff reform together. Its middle-class supporters re-sponded like the apostles. 'We had had [these ideas] all of us vague in the back of our minds,' one wrote with more excitement than coher-ence, '& they wd. never have been fertilized with being if it had not been for you, & that you felt the moment to call them out.—Now that you have done it, we can all see it is right.'[17] Chamberlain knew that he was not himself the source of the ideas he pulled together. But that realization gave him a sense of being moved by forces greater than him-self at the forward edge of the history of his country and its empire.

Tariff reform was a logical working-out of a set of essentially mercan-tile impressions that struck Chamberlain and those who thought with him as unmistakable. Accordingly when Sir Robert Giffen, his former official and the embodiment of statistical objectivity at the Board of Trade, wrote to *The Times* to question his figures, Chamberlain replied to him serenely:

> I imagine that no one doubts that certain general tendencies have de-veloped themselves in the trade of this country during the last thirty years—that is to say that, we are on the whole doing less with the protected countries; that what we are doing with them has somewhat changed its character and consists more of raw materials in proportion to finished manufacture than it used to do; and that the trade with British Possessions has in the meantime greatly increased and has not been subject to this deterioration of quality. But whether the figures that have been given to me, or that I have found for myself, and used as illustrations of these changes are the best that could be chosen I do not know.[18]

He was disconcerted to receive a denial from Giffen that the statistics on trade bore out these assumptions.

Still, Giffen's use of these statistics, which were in any case unreli-able, served to demonstrate their limited use in economic argument. It all came down to interpretation. It came down in particular to the meaning of the statistics of trade with South Africa, which had unques-tionably increased, and with Canada, which had revived from a slump. Provokingly, Giffen insisted that the trade with South Africa should be treated as foreign up to the war because the Transvaal had been an essentially independent country. Since then, of course, the figures had been inflated by war. As for the trade with Canada, while Giffen stressed that it had only returned to the level of former years, Chamberlain emphasized the role of Canada's imperial preference in bringing about that return. Ultimately Giffen was as doctrinaire in his handling of the evidence as was Chamberlain. Chamberlain was driven to point out that the argument transcended not only statistics but economics. He reaffirmed what he had known at the outset, that tariff reform was ultimately a matter of imperial faith. Even if tariff reform involved 'a loss of material wealth', that 'would be amply compensated for by the union of the Empire'.[19] The debate on tariff reform made him contemptuous of statistics. 'The more I deal with the subject,' he commented wearily to Ashley, 'the more I distrust all figures—those which tell for us as well as those which tell against us.'[20]

Nevertheless, Chamberlain's thought on the economic situation of Britain was pushed further by this argument. Giffen emphasized the 'enormous business and gain' Britain derived from its international commerce, particularly through the so-called invisible items in the balance of payments including shipping, insurance, and to an increasing extent the return on exports of capital. Chamberlain placed greater importance on exports and imports of manufactured goods than on financial services, no matter how lucrative. It was not just a question of preferring one sector of the economy to another: the difference between visible and invisible trade brought him back to the issue of employment. Far more than financial services, manufacturing meant jobs: 'while our investments abroad may provide a sufficient return to the capitalists . . . they tend directly to a transfer of employment from this country to our rivals & competitors'.[21]

His economic credo found its most convincing demonstrations of validity in Birmingham, where he spoke midway through his autumn campaign. The jewellers of the town, many of them his constituents, responded appreciatively when he pointed out how their trade was being lost to foreign producers whose domestic markets were tariff-protected. In another of the trades for which Birmingham was famous, small brass manufacture, imports from foreign countries had increased threefold. Yet another, the pearl button trade, famous since the eighteenth century, was being overtaken by American producers sheltering behind the McKinley tariff.

Cumulatively these examples converted Chamberlain to protectionism. Though he still spoke of free trade within the empire as his ideal, he was ever more impressed with the prosperity, economic muscle and invasive power built up by Britain's industrial rivals behind their tariff walls. For Britain to follow their example would involve a radical departure from the fiscal policy which served the country well in the past: but Chamberlain asked his constituents, 'are we really so conservative a nation that, while such a change has taken place . . . we are still to say,

"We stick to our well-tried policy"?'[22] At the end he came back to the imperial faith that had led him to launch his crusade. 'For my part,' he told his audience,

> I care very little whether the result will be to make this country, already rich a little richer. . . . What I care for is that this people shall rise to the height of its great mission . . . and, in co-operation with our kinsmen across the seas . . . combine to make an Empire . . . greater, more united, more fruitful for good, than any Empire in human history.

From Glasgow to Newcastle, across to Liverpool, home at Birmingham, then over to Cardiff, back up to Leeds; a solo performance concentrating on one theme: there had never been anything quite like this in the political history of the old country. The campaign of the Anti-Corn Law League in the 1840s had been a team effort. Gladstone's campaigns were personal demonstrations without clear policies and revolved around his parliamentary constituency. The only true precedent came from the New World, in William Jennings Bryan's campaign against the gold standard. Bryan came to Cardiff to observe his English counterpart. It was there that Chamberlain declared: 'What Washington did for the United States of America, when he made . . . a self-contained and self-sufficient empire of some 80 millions of souls, what Bismarck did for Germany when he united between 50 and 60 millions of people . . . it is our business and our duty to do for the British Empire.'[23]

But Washington and Bismarck did not unite their empires by themselves. Chamberlain was angrily aware of his need for help. He no longer had help from the civil service to cope with his correspondence. Letters poured in on him and his private secretary at the rate of two hundred a day. What disturbed him more was the minimal cooperation he received from the cabinet. By the time he reached the end of his tour at Leeds, some twenty leading Liberals headed by Asquith and Unionist free traders led by old Devonshire and young Churchill had spoken out against tariff reform with all the oratorical fire at their command. The best help Chamberlain received from the leading tier of the Unionist party came from Henry Chaplin, who was prominent in the National Union of Conservative Associations but had been dropped for incapacity from the cabinet when it was reconstructed in 1900. Chaplin was abler than the caricature squire he seemed to be. Yet on his feet he was inarticulate. The only members of the cabinet to speak that autumn in full support of tariff reform were Selborne and Austen Chamberlain. Balfour discouraged pronouncements which went beyond the official policy of retaliation, but did not discountenance explanations of why it was wrong to go further.

Chamberlain was dismayed to discover how many of his former colleagues wanted to stay in the official halfway house. He had no time for the half-hearted. When Brodrick in an address to his constituents questioned the desirability of agricultural tariffs, Chamberlain wrote to him stiffly: 'The time is very close when we must all take sides ... I had hoped that you would be wholly with me. ... I want to know on whom I can depend.'[24] When Brodrick pleaded for tolerance, Chamberlain refused to give it: 'in my judgment, confirmed by the best electioneers I know,' he replied, 'there will be in the end only two policies—one of absolute free trade of the most orthodox type, and the other my policy of a moderate tariff with a preference to the Colonies'.[25]

He was similarly impatient with the reluctance of the Canadian government to declare itself in favour of tariff reform for Britain. At last the Finance Minister Fielding wrote to Chamberlain reaffirming Canada's commitment to the resolutions of the Colonial Conference of 1902. The letter arrived in time for public reading at Chamberlain's last provincial engagement of the year in Leeds. But he was not satisfied with anything less than the ardent imperialism displayed by New Zealand. Lord Minto, the British governor-general of Canada, convinced Chamberlain that he could find imperialism of that sort there below the ministerial level. He encouraged Chamberlain to take the resolutions of chambers of commerce from Ontario in favour of his proposals at face value, without questioning their willingness to reduce tariff protection vis-à-vis the mother country. Minto said that, while Laurier was committed to a further measure of imperial preference, he lacked the smallest spark of 'Imperial enthusiasm'[26] and dreamed instead of Canadian independence.

The coolness of the Canadian and British governments increased Chamberlain's already dangerous self-reliance. He offered to serve as imperial ambassador with full powers to work out preferential trade treaties which the colonies and the mother country would find mutually beneficial. He ended 1903 exhausted and anxious yet exhilarated. 'What a year it has been!' he exclaimed: 'I do not think I could stand many more like it. ... Why is there so much work in the world to do and so few men to do it?'[27]

He was buoyed up by achievements as the year ended. On 15 December, tariff-reforming candidates in by-elections for two south London constituencies halted the postwar electoral swing against the government. The victories were all the sweeter because Conservative party headquarters put pressure on the Unionist candidates to stay within the confines of Balfour's policy, only to be overwhelmed by local and national tariff reformers. Observers at home and abroad wondered whether the great campaigner would once again sweep all before him.

The day after the metropolitan by-elections, Chamberlain announced his establishment of a Tariff Reform Commission. It was another of his institutional innovations in politics and reflected the originating force of tariff reform. Remarkably, Chamberlain had to be reeducated by an academic about what was congenial to industry before he agreed to set up this body, a commission of business interests designed to supersede the agencies of the state on the subject of tariffs. Chamberlain approached the task of designing tariffs with a parliamentary concern: the House of Commons floundered when confronted with detailed legislation, and a tariff bill might have to deal with a thousand articles of trade. He thought therefore of devising 'something perfectly simple, such as a 10 or 20 per cent. duty on everything, and force it through ruthlessly'.[28]

Whatever the parliamentary merits of this high-handed approach, 'it was not business', as the economist Hewins noted: 'English manufacturers would not stand that sort of thing.' Hewins derived his understanding of the process of tariff-making from the German experience, which involved 'close intercourse and elaborate discussion . . . between businessman and bureaucrat'.[29] The needs of the various sectors of British industry were too complex and controversial—they were not yet even fully ascertained—to tolerate the uniform tariff Chamberlain thought to impose. Yet if he left the task of designing a system of tariffs until the moment was ripe for political action, the opportunity might be lost during the preparatory industrial inquiry which would have to take place. Without appreciating the political audacity of his advice, Hewins wanted Chamberlain to set up the needed inquiry himself. Unable to argue the case with the great man face to face, he left Chamberlain to be brought round through his closer associates and through articles which Hewins wrote for *The Times*.

By mid-October, Chamberlain appreciated the wisdom of working out the desired tariff in consultation with domestic business interests and with the colonies. He was led forward by Arthur Pearson, the newspaper magnate who chaired the Tariff Reform League. The two men reached agreement on an industrial commission late at night after Chamberlain's speech in Birmingham. Pearson headed straightaway for London to secure the assistance of Hewins as administrative secretary for the commission. Chamberlain did not envisage the secretaryship as a full-time job, nor did he like to ask Hewins to resign his position as director of the London School of Economics for a temporary assignment. But the enthusiasm of Hewins overcame Chamberlain's hesitation. With Hewins in daily charge and Pearson as intermediary, planning for the commission and the recruitment of participants went ahead rapidly.

Acting like a prime minister nominating a royal commission, Chamberlain announced the terms for his Tariff Reform Commission in mid-December and issued an initial list of men who agreed to serve on it.

He gave the commission a national rather than imperial assignment: it was to devise a general tariff for the United Kingdom, leaving imperial preference to be worked out with the colonies afterwards. Yet the imperial dimension of the task was evident at the start. The chair of the commission went to Sir Robert Herbert, the former permanent undersecretary at the Colonial Office. Chamberlain asked the agents general of the various colonies who were resident in London to accept watching briefs at the commission for their home governments.

The membership of the commission also reflected Chamberlain's sense of the proportional importance of the component parts of Britain's economy. Eight members were associated primarily with engineering enterprises and five with iron and steel, eight with textiles and five with other types of manufacturing, nine with the production of food and drink (a pair of industries expanding rapidly in Birmingham), six with wholesale and retail marketing and shipping, and only two with banking.[30]

Whatever the limits of economic coverage in the composition of the commission, there was no denying the distinction of those who agreed to serve or their willingness to invest time and money in the enterprise. When the commissioners were first convened, a hat went round to defray the anticipated expenses, and it was promptly filled with £27,000. Some of the greatest businessmen in Britain agreed to serve on the commission: Sir Alfred Hickman in iron and steel, the Liverpool shipping magnate Sir Alfred Jones, Sir Andrew Noble from the munitions makers Armstrong and Whitworth, and Arthur Keen of GKN. Other interests attached to tariff reform were embodied on the commission by Henry Chaplin for agriculture, Sir Vincent Caillard for mercantile protectionism, Sir Charles Tennant, Asquith's father-in-law, as a Liberal convert to the cause, and Charles Booth, the esteemed social investigator, who threw himself into the enterprise because he believed that 'the well-being of the poorer classes . . . depends very much more on . . . employment, than on changes in the level of prices'.[31]

The political economy of tariff reform

Although Chamberlain had arrived at his policy of tariff reform impulsively, it posed an acute challenge to the general philosophy of political economy which had guided Britain for more than half a century. Two principles were central to that philosophy: free trade, and laissez-faire or minimal governmental management of the economy. Those principles, which were avowed as well as observed, were accompanied by an equally important but unspoken, semiconscious set of assumptions: assumptions of the superior importance of the export to the domestic market, and of the superior importance also of banking, particularly in the City of London, to manufacturing industry, largely in the provinces.

The central pair of principles, though believed to be of timeless validity, had been established and confirmed within living memory in Britain by the domestic boom and international ascendancy it enjoyed during the third quarter of the nineteenth century. The memory of that high noon was all the more glorious because it was preceded by forty years of turbulence and hunger associated with the Corn Laws enacted after the Napoleonic wars and repealed in 1846 during the darkness that preceded the dawn. The set of assumptions which accompanied free trade and laissez-faire, particularly the superiority of City finance over provincial manufacturing, had received their confirmation more recently, in the final quarter of the century, when the 'invisible' services of shipping, insurance, banking and overseas capital exports flourished more than ever, offsetting the deterioration the British balance of trade suffered in the face of competition from the United States and Germany. No longer the workshop of the world, Britain served increasingly as its financial centre. British free traders might not be oblivious of the compensatory character of this achievement; they might thus be aware of some vulnerability in the national economy at the turn of the century. Still, they belittled the costs to Britain of a deteriorating balance of trade. In any case they could not see how to improve it through the imposition of tariffs without doing more harm than good to the British economy.

Nothing eased Chamberlain's anxiety about the deteriorating performance of British trade and industry in comparison with its foreign rivals. Whatever uneasiness free traders felt about industrial competition abroad was quietened by the increase in prosperity at home: Englishmen at all but the bottom levels of society were demonstrably better off in 1903 than they had been thirty years earlier. Though tariff reformers belittled the increase in prosperity at home, they could not do away with that evident fact. But the economies of Germany and the United States were growing faster than Britain's. Their achievements eroded Britain's standing abroad and encroached upon the market at home.

Chamberlain's alarm at the threat posed by Germany made him an envious admirer of the example set by Germany, where banking functioned as the partner rather than the master of industry and where governmental protection of industry was national policy. Because the standard of living was lower in Germany than at home, British free traders scorned the comparison. But Chamberlain pointed out how much faster industrial exports and also rates of employment and wages were rising in Germany than in Britain. Still, he was no more willing than the free traders to stand up to the competition from German industry directly. While free traders relied on financial and commercial services to sustain the British economy, Chamberlain urged Britain to make the most of the colonial market where competition was less severe than in the markets of the rival industrial powers. He had lost the confidence he had in his days as Screw King that Britain could sell its wares anywhere in the world.

He assessed the deterioration in Britain's economic performance perceptively. But he could not demonstrate the validity of his assessment conclusively. The available statistics on economic performance were still embryonic, limited in the British case to visible exports and imports, and ambiguous even within those limitations. There were no reliable measurements for aggregate income or industrial production nationally or internationally. While Chamberlain's sense of Britain's comparative deterioration has in large part been validated later by economic historians, it was denied at the time. Lacking statistical proof of his reason for alarm, he had to hope that the British economy would become sufficiently depressed to make his fellow countrymen question their commitment to free trade.[32] But the fates turned against him. He was encouraged at the beginning of his campaign by signs of a recession in exports, only to see them rebound in 1904 and remain buoyant for the remainder of his career. While statistics were available to document the export recovery, there were none at hand to document the continuing comparative deterioration in Britain's industrial capacity.

Chamberlain's understanding was based, as so often, upon the experience of Birmingham and its metal-manufacturing environs. The economy there had undergone important changes in the thirty years since he left business for politics. Birmingham was no longer so preoccupied with metal manufacturing. Food production and brewing had become major local industries, taking advantage of Birmingham's central location in the English domestic market. Metal manufacturing still remained the primary industry of the West Midlands, but its character had changed, shifting from the manufacture of hardware to more sophisticated engineering associated with the electrical and cycle trades. Yet the engineering trades were particularly vulnerable to competition from Germany. Both new and old metal-manufacturing industries in the West Midlands experienced 'a fall in the relative importance of the export trade; while the Colonies were taking a larger proportion of the total foreign sales than they had a quarter of a century before'.[33] The correspondence between the needs of the metal-manufacturing West Midlands and the prescriptions of tariff reform was complete. The affinity between the two extended to their world view. Like Chamberlain, West Midlands metal manufacturers felt some kinship with industrial Germany. They admired German industrial practice because they feared German competition. The protective side of tariff reform was a prescription tried and tested in Germany to counter a threat to Britain from Germany.

Though no one understood the metal-manufacturing West Midlands better than Chamberlain, his application of their regional requirements to the whole country and the empire remains controversial. His programme has been criticized for offering to protect backward sectors of British industry instead of concentrating on newer, technologically more sophisticated industries which needed 'sheltering ... from competition in the early stages of their growth'.[34] Yet the persistence of foreign competition under free trade did not force the old industries to modernize themselves. New and old in the West Midlands spoke with one voice in calling for protection from Germany. No one questioned the appreciation of the technological needs of industry which Chamberlain demonstrated in founding the University of Birmingham. He simply contended, against his periodic Liberal collaborators in higher education such as Richard Haldane, that improved technological training was not enough by itself. After all, Germany insisted on tariffs as well as technological education.

Chamberlain was more vulnerable to criticism for discounting sectors of the economy which did not bulk large from the vantage point of Birmingham. He never had much regard for agriculture, a thin sector in the British economy. He was gratified that tariff reform with its demand for a duty on foreign foodstuffs won enthusiastic support from Henry Chaplin. Chamberlain trusted that the squires would follow Chaplin's lead even though they wanted protection against colonial as well as foreign produce: 'I may not be giving them much,' Chamberlain commented, 'but I am giving them something'.[35] Still, his electoral sense was sharp enough to make him doubt whether the agricultural labourers would follow the farmers' and squires' electoral lead.

While Chamberlain attempted to disguise his limited rapport with agriculture, he left no doubt about the limits to his appreciation of a far more important sector of the economy, City banking. Interestingly he showed no awareness that here too, in the relationship between banking and industry, Germany provided an enviable alternative to the British model. Chamberlain knew from experience that British manufacturers met their capital needs from internal family resources or from local joint-stock banks like Lloyds in Birmingham. Manufacturing industry in Britain derived little benefit from the great central banking firms in the City of London. They served the world, financing governments and overseas enterprises, into which they funnelled British investment capital. The rewards which Britain earned in that way 'handsomely covered its massive trade gap in "visible" goods'.[36] But this achievement only confirmed the 'historic disjunction' in Britain 'between finance and industry, [and also between] metropolitan and provincial England', which 'now proved a severe handicap'.[37] The City failed to evolve a form of finance capitalism such as developed in Germany and the United States, interlocking banking and industrial corporations to build up the national economy. Chamberlain had been accustomed at the Colonial Office to dealing with City bankers on overseas enterprises or on industries such as shipping which were crucial to overseas trade. But when it came to devising a tariff, he did not ask City bankers to play much part in his Tariff Reform Commission.

In his view, manufacturing industry was the horse that pulled the national economic cart. Even the wealth the country received from its financial sector depended ultimately, he insisted, upon 'the productive energy and capacity which is behind it'. Britain owed its centrality in international finance to the primacy it had acquired as an industrial power. Driving the point home in the Guildhall at the heart of the City of London, he challenged the City's order of economic priorities: 'banking', he declared, 'is not the cause of our wealth, but it is the consequence of our wealth'.[38]

While he spoke of wealth, the wealth of the nation was not in fact his main objective. With a shudder, he contemplated the possibility of Britain becoming very rich simply as a financial centre and trading entrepôt, 'with no productive industry whatever' and no working men, 'a home for millionaires and for their dependents'. His objection to this prospect was more political than economic: he warned his constituents that Britain might become 'richer, but not greater'.[39] The erosion of Britain's comparative power in recent decades worried him, and he was not comforted by its simultaneous prosperity.

His conception of the prime manufacturing interest was rather narrowly domestic. A substantial number of British industries including some metal manufacturing made profitable use of component materials 'dumped' at low prices on the British market by foreign producers. Cheap sheet steel from Germany, for example, kept costs down for British shipbuilders. Chamberlain recoiled from this practice as shortsighted, allowing crucial segments of the British productive base to shrivel in the face of foreign competition, thus weakening the country as a whole. His desire for domestic and imperial self-sufficiency alarmed industries such as cotton textiles which depended on foreign sources of supply for their raw materials. And indeed what interested him was domestic industry at all stages of the productive process, the more domestic the better. He paid a heavy political price for his economic biases. They undermined his title to speak for British manufacturing industry as a whole, let alone for the non-manufacturing segments of the national economy. As a result, he could not assemble a group of economic forces strong enough to force their will on the political community.

His domestic concern also fettered his imperial imagination. Though he spoke glowingly about the economic consolidation of the empire, he pictured the growth in its manufacturing capacity as taking place primarily in the mother country. While he denied that he had any wish to reduce the manufacturing capacity of the colonies, he certainly did not wish to see it expanded, particularly to new fields, at Britain's expense. The tariff preferences he envisaged for the colonies were confined to agricultural production. That limitation reduced the appeal of his policy to all the colonies, and to some even more than to others. His proposals for imperial preference were shaped with Canada and to a lesser extent Australia and New Zealand in mind. Regardless of his long preoccupation with South Africa, tariff reform had so little to offer the mineral-rich but agriculturally rather poor colonies in that region that he had to deny that he intended to exclude them from his proposals. In spite of his denials, the culmination of Chamberlain's career in tariff reform suggested how far the events in South Africa had distracted him from his essential politico-economic interest in the empire. 'Of course until South Africa exports something besides Wool and Feathers,' he wrote to a questioning disciple, 'there is not much opportunity for her to take advantage of the preference, but she can have Wine [from the Cape Colony] at once and Corn and Meat will be added to her as soon as she is able to produce a surplus beyond her own needs.'[40]

There was nevertheless some validity to Lord Minto's contention, which so impressed Chamberlain, that the empire had 'arrived at the parting of the ways' and that the moment had come when Britain had to decide whether 'to unite our Empire or to lose it'.[41] Appreciation of the economic utility of the empire had been growing in recent years both in the colonies and in the mother country, as evidenced by Canada's introduction of imperial preference and the gratitude in some industrial circles in Britain for the colonial market in the face of stiffening foreign competition elsewhere. Those sentiments were heated by the Boer War; and though the temperature was cooled by the prolongation of the war and fell with its close, it was still high enough to encourage hopes of strengthening imperial relationships—but only if Britain grasped the hand which the colonies extended over preferential tariffs. There was unlikely to be another such opportunity. Unless manufacturing interests in the colonies were soon shaped by the harness of imperial tariffs, they were sure to assume dimensions uncongenial to British industry. The motivating concern in this set of calculations was, nevertheless, British rather than colonial.

While Chamberlain's industrial interests narrowed his imperial vision, other domestic forces reduced his social vision. The sources of support which his proposals drew served to minimize its potentialities. After the summer of 1903, he said little about using revenue from tariffs to pay for social insurance, particularly old-age pensions. Some Conservatives regretted his abandonment of this appeal which would have drawn attention to the lack of social reforming imagination among free-trading Liberals. On balance, however, the impact of Conservative support on Chamberlain's formulation of tariff reform was to emphasize its protection of beleaguered economic interests. 'Radical' became a term of abuse in Chamberlain's rhetoric, obscuring the fact that, even in its protective vein, tariff reform constituted the most radical challenge in half a century to the established canons of British political economy.

Economically, the balance of advantage on tariff reform remains doubtful. But to leave it at that is to miss its point. Tariff reform was an act of political will, a refusal to remain politically passive while the industrial economy of Britian was surpassed by international competitors. Though an industrialist to begin with, Chamberlain had long since transferred his primary sphere of enterprise from private to the political economy. As he told one sympathizer, 'It is by legislative & fiscal action and not by private effort that we can secure the object which we all desire.'[42] The refusal to give even the thinnest film of tariff protection to vital domestic industrial interests was an act of national abnegation on Britain's part which none of its rivals was tempted to emulate. The justification for the purity of British devotion to free trade was doctrinaire rather than empirical. The political will of Britain was paralysed, so far as the economic performance of the country was concerned, by past glories. Like all declining empires, Britain clung to beliefs which it identified with its era of supremacy long after the supporting circumstances had changed.

Chamberlain sought to rouse Great Britain to adapt its policy to the changed circumstances. He urged the British to shake off the politically enervating effects of laissez-faire and free trade. Whatever his particular proposals—and the tariffs he suggested were modest by American and German standards—his challenge to prevailing British policy was likely to give the economy at least 'a once-for-all shot in the arm'.[43] At the same time there was an opportunity, genuine so far as Canada was concerned, to test the feasibility of mercantile consolidation of the maritime British empire.

Soon beleaguered

The genuineness of that opportunity from the British side was thrown into doubt at the beginning of 1904 before Chamberlain reached the Guildhall for the final engagement in his three months of platform addresses. Displaying some reluctance to go to London, Chamberlain kept his foray brief. In the first days of the year no one knew quite how to

measure the success of his campaign. Free-trading Unionists and leaders of the Liberal party reached out to each other in anxiety. The former
offered indirectly to support Liberal candidates in by-elections against
tariff-reforming Unionists, while Liberals weighed the merits of an alliance—until they saw the campaign for tariff reform falter.

The possibility that Chamberlain would sweep all before him receded
markedly in the week before he spoke at the Guildhall. First Balfour
spoke to his constituents in Manchester, dwelling on the impediments
to imperial preference from the British and Canadian perspectives, and
urging tender treatment of Unionists who had difficulty stomaching
any departure from free trade. Then a tariff-reforming Conservative
was defeated at a by-election in the hitherto fairly safe Conservative
constituency of Norwich. At the same time the Board of Trade released
figures on exports and imports showing that the British economy had
recovered from the postwar recession.

A chorus of top-hatted members of the stock exchange marched in
front of Chamberlain's carriage towards the Guildhall, singing 'He's
coming!' to the tune of 'Old Black Joe'. 'Good Old Joe' spoke defen-
sively that day to a City crowd which was obviously in two minds
about his message. He tried to turn the statistics released by the Board
of Trade to his advantage. The increase in imports was large, he
pointed out, but not in exports. Exports of manufactured goods to
tariff-protected foreign markets had decreased. Foreign imports had
grown faster than British into Britain's own colonies. Generally, in fact,
the rate of growth in German exports was double that for British.
Chamberlain also exposed the spectre, veiled by the Board of Trade's
figures, of an increase in national wealth accompanied by a loss in imperial power. He cited the case of Holland, richer now than at the
height of its maritime empire but no longer a power to reckon with. 'Is
it wished that we should follow in the same lines?'

He did not exaggerate the effectiveness of the campaign of speeches
which ended at the Guildhall. He liked to think of his efforts for tariff
reform as a crusade transcending party politics. Yet he understood that
the need for electoral purposes was to reinvigorate the forces of Unionism which had lost their sense of purpose at the end of the Boer War.
He held Balfour to blame for the persisting Unionist discontent, for alienating Nonconformist supporters with his Education Act and for failing to satisfy the public desire for radical reform of the army. These
were the issues which Chamberlain referred to privately when the response to his campaign for tariff reform proved disappointing. He had
not expected speedy success during the autumn. Only in the wake of
the December by-elections did he think that victory might be within his
grasp. In January he cautioned supporters not to anticipate victory at
the next general election: he would, he said, 'be satisfied if we were

beaten by a small majority: the election after that will be the crucial one'.[44]

To prepare his followers for the long haul, he fostered the formation of an inexpensive dining club of young tariff reformers in London to exchange ideas for use on active service as speakers. He gathered the faithful around him in the House of Commons. They assembled on the third and fourth benches below the gangway on the government side, leaving the first two benches to the Unionist free traders who could thus reveal their inclination to lean towards the Liberals.

No matter how complicated the fight in Parliament, in the sphere of party organization Chamberlain moved from strength to strength. The dynamics of party organization worked differently from those of Parliament, to the embarrassment of the official leaders, Balfour of the Conservatives and Devonshire of the Liberal Unionists. A small quarter of the Unionists in the House of Commons, including more than a quarter of the Liberal Unionists, were committed free traders. There were enough of them to keep the survival of the government in question and hence to check the more numerous tariff reformers. But in party organizations it was the big battalions that mattered. Devonshire's grip on the Liberal Unionist organization proved so feeble that at the beginning of 1904 he virtually abdicated in Chamberlain's favour. An era of patrician party management came to an end with the departure of the duke, superseded by Chamberlain's upper-middle-class manipulation.

The duke floundered badly in his last contest with the Screw King. Sensing the weakness of his support among party activists outside Parliament, Devonshire concluded that the only way to avoid a tariff-reforming capture of the national Liberal Unionist organization was to scuttle it. But in proposing to do so, he appeared to violate the cause for which the organization had been originally created, the defeat of Home Rule. He compounded his offence by attempting to seize the funds of the national organization before he lost control of it. When Chamberlain convened a meeting of the governing grand committee, the Central Liberal Unionist Association, at the beginning of February, most of its hundred members accepted his summons; and only two declined to vote as he wished. Sweeping beyond the question of preserving the association, he secured a mandate for the organization to reconstitute and extend itself on a popular, elective basis to augment the constituency machinery available for the purposes of tariff reform. This task was assigned to Chamberlain's organizational chief of staff, Powell Williams. Repudiated by the association he had founded, the old duke advised free-trading Unionists to vote for Liberals in preference to any tariff reformer—and then joined the ranks of the ineffectual.

Chamberlain paid a terrible price for all these battles, whether won or lost. Tariff reform consumed him. He could still entertain other ambitions, for example to make the University of Birmingham 'the greatest institution for the teaching of the highest applied Sciences in the World'.[45] But he did not allow anything to detract from his pursuit of tariff reform. Instead of pushing his university ever upward, for a while he discouraged the University Court of Governors from adding to their building plans and to the financial demands on the government. His devotion to tariff reform overtaxed his energies. He pushed himself in his solitary campaign too hard. When his old enemy, gout, drove him to his doctors late in January, they discovered evidence of strain to his heart and warned him to take a complete holiday as soon as possible, preferably for four months. Aware himself that he was worn out, Chamberlain was ready to comply, though only for half the recommended time.

In the few days of parliamentary activity for which he went back to London before leaving for holiday, his spirit was tested and then shaken. Balfour too was ill, and was unable to take his accustomed place at the opening of Parliament for the year. Austen Chamberlain as Chancellor of the Exchequer led off for the government in the opening debate. Unsure of himself in his awkward role as surrogate for Balfour but son of Joe, Austen floundered badly. Embarrassed Unionist back-benchers watched in silence. Afterwards in private, while implicitly admitting Austen's failure, Joe subjected his supporters to a tongue-lashing. They should back each other up, he insisted, all the more so when things went badly: 'If it is a good speech cheer it & if a bad speech cheer it louder.'[46] When his own time came to speak in the Commons, he rose as usual to the occasion. Yet some observers thought that his recent grandstanding on provincial platforms dulled his skill in the parliamentary debate. And one Unionist backbencher noted that 'his colour, a luminous sallow hue, does not connote good health, while a certain hesitation in the selection of words, and an occasional lack of grammatical construction, showed that preoccupation or excitement were disconnecting the structure of his remarks'.[47]

Able to rely totally on only a small band, anxious to make the most of the historic but fleeting opportunity, Chamberlain drove his lieutenants too hard. Suddenly Powell Williams broke. Chamberlain had relied heavily on Powell Williams, for he was a seasoned organizer and gave Chamberlain the devoted loyalty he craved. Taking all that Williams offered, Chamberlain loaded him with responsibility for organization in the Commons, in Birmingham, and nationally in both the Tariff Reform League and the Liberal Unionist Association, including the delicate parleys with Devonshire. Williams shouldered it without flagging until suddenly in the Commons he suffered an apoplectic seizure. He recovered consciousness for little more than a day, and then died. Chamberlain, who stayed at his bedside, was shattered not only by the loss of his lieutenant and friend but by his own guilt. 'It is my fault,' he told Williams's wife, 'I have worked him to death.'[48]

So shaken was Chamberlain by the death of Powell Williams that it threatened his own health. He felt unable to return to the Commons for debate on a Liberal motion designed to probe the government's fiscal divisions. Chamberlain's doctors prevented him from attending Williams's funeral in Birmingham and hurried his departure for the Continent. Chamberlain made no attempt to hide the severity of his loss. The press was informed that no letters would be forwarded to him during his absence. People wondered whether they would ever see him well again. It was not a sign of returning health but of persisting political anxiety that brought him back sooner than his doctors prescribed.

Return to impasse

On doctor's orders anxiously enforced by Mary, Chamberlain relaxed as they sailed to their holiday destination, Egypt. Once there, he did a little languid touring of the temples and tombs. He was less impressed by the ancient glories than by the modern accomplishments of industrial technology, particularly the dams and irrigation works constructed at Britain's behest along the Nile. After barely a month away, he turned slowly towards home. The holiday had not fulfilled its purpose. He caught a chill in Cairo, and suffered from neuralgia and biliousness as he crossed the Mediterranean for Italy.

The political situation in England was deteriorating rapidly. Chamberlain had left the House of Commons in the grip of debate, provoked by the Liberals but conducted mainly among Unionists, about fiscal policy. In the absence of both Balfour and Chamberlain, members of the cabinet argued with each other on the floor of the House. Closing for the government, the Home Secretary and chief Conservative organizer Akers Douglas virtually turned his back on the Liberal opposition in order to persuade the Unionists to agree on Balfour's policy of retaliation while retaining their freedom to move under pressure from their local associations towards Chamberlain's policy of imperial preference. The twenty-six Unionists who voted with the Liberals at the conclusion of the debate were not enough to overthrow the government. But the further twenty-six Unionist free traders who either abstained on this division or voted with the government held its survival in their hands.

Concentrating on Parliament, Balfour followed the advice of his private secretary, J.S. Sandars, to 'avoid either frightening or irritating'[49] this crucial free-trading contingent. Since they would take fright at any hint that the prime minister saw hope for imperial preference, including food taxes, Balfour emphasized his commitment to nothing beyond

Lifelong loyalists:
9. (*above left*) Jesse Collings.
10. (*above right*) William Kenrick.
11. (*right*) Powell Williams.

retaliation. But when he tried to impose that restraint upon the Unionist parliamentary party as a whole, the tariff reformers forced him to desist. He resorted thereafter to a stance of unfriendly neutrality towards anything beyond retaliation. While the Unionist parliamentary party was locked in debate, the country displayed its leanings through by-elections. The Liberals enjoyed a string of successes, interrupted only in 'dear Birmingham',[50] where their attempt to win Powell Williams's former seat was crushed.

On leaving Cairo, Chamberlain surveyed the situation at home in letters to his sons. He started with Austen, his originally intended political heir. Now that he was Chancellor housed at 11 Downing Street beside Balfour, Austen was no longer simply an extension of his father. Joe began to understand that his elder son served two masters. Uncertain how to deal with the situation himself, Joe explained that Balfour's policy of strict neutrality towards anything beyond retaliatory tariffs would render Unionist victory at the next general election a setback for imperial preference. Joe nevertheless assured Austen that 'as long as you are doing good constructive work, like the Army Reform, you have a reason for existence & a right to hold on'.[51] The words scarcely rang with conviction. Yet Joe went on to declare that '[i]n no case am I going to fight against Balfour's Government. I would rather go out of politics & if things remain as they are I do not see any alternative.'

After another two weeks of rumination, still on the way home, Joe wrote at greater length and with greater candour to Neville. The letter in effect installed Neville as Powell Williams's replacement as tariff reform organizer, though only for Birmingham and the West Midlands. Joe began by ascribing the by-election reverses to the long overdue swing of the electoral pendulum. The Unionists were sure to lose the next election; but the pendulum would swing back, propelled by disillusionment at the spectacle of Liberal government in action. The ailing warrior wanted to position his forces to take advantage of the pendulum when it swung their way. 'The battle will be a hard one & probably a long one,' he predicted, a grim prophecy for an old man. 'Qui m'aime, me suivra—& one of the most important things to be done now is to see who are the stalwarts.'[52] The first wobbler Joe dismissed in his confidential letter to his younger son was the prime minister. Balfour's refusal to go 'one inch' beyond retaliation was 'worse than nothing' in Joe's estimation, because such a policy would 'postpone Preference to the Greek Kalends'. He therefore felt obliged, 'without publicly separating myself from Balfour, to hope that he will fail' at the next election. The sooner the defeat came, the better. In the meantime, 'the delicate point & difficulty of the situation' was to commit the Unionist party to tariff reform before the electoral pendulum reversed itself. 'Are we to work for the success of the Unionist Party & then find the Balfourites in command of the ship feebly steering her on the rocks of a partial & half-hearted retaliation? And how are we to prevent this without quarrelling politically with Balfour? It needs careful management.'

Remembering his unauthorized campaigns as a Liberal, the old master-organizer gave his son-apprentice detailed guidance on how to put another ambitious enterprise together. The plan included elimination of the Unionist free-trading contingent in the House of Commons, the '*common* enemies' who voted against the government in Parliament and opposed tariff reformers in by-elections. But that assignment was initially parliamentary. Neville's assignment was organizational. Joe wanted to appeal beyond the Balfourite 'Wirepullers' who controlled party headquarters to 'the people', by which he meant party activists in the constituencies, the stratum where tariff reform ran strongest. Back in 1886, the National Liberal Federation had sided with Gladstone; but Chamberlain was confident that the same sort of contest in Unionist garb would go his way. Just as the former victory was vital to Gladstone, so this latter one was vital to Chamberlain. If all went according to plan, Balfour would have to defer to the demand of the local party troops upon whom electoral victory depended.

Neville was to start with the Birmingham Liberal Unionist Grand Committee. It would be asked to endorse a motion supporting Balfour's government while approving of imperial preference, thus binding the two together. Joe did 'not mind if there is a little opposition, providing we are sure of an overwhelming majority, & if there are any unsound men in the Association . . . I should be glad to be rid of them'. Once assured of cooperation from the Liberal Unionists of Birmingham, Neville was to see that their example was followed by Liberal Unionists throughout the West Midlands, while Joe would contact Francis Lowe, the leader of Birmingham's Conservatives, to see that they did the same. 'If the movement starts well in our district, I should then see how far our friends in the House of Commons could work it in other parts of the Kingdom. . . . Wherever the local Conserv. or Lib U Association refused to pronounce in our favour by resolution, we must have a local Association of our own.' In this way as well as through test questions, Joe and his lieutenants would try to gain pledges to tariff reform from a majority of the prospective Unionist candidates before the general election.

No matter how effective, such action could not be relied upon to precipitate a general election. That power lay with the prime minister, who could be forced to call an early election only by defeat in the House of Commons. Chamberlain proposed to assume responsibility for the parliamentary side of the campaign himself, marshalling the tariff reformers in the Commons and negotiating with Balfour. 'I must have a serious talk with B. soon after my return,' Joe told Neville.

Accordingly, in Naples about to leave for home, Joe wrote asking Balfour to see him as he passed through London on his way to Birmingham. With pointed geniality, Chamberlain commiserated with the prime minister on the poor by-election returns, commented that the public would soon tire of the Liberals once observed in office, and offered congratulations on the accomplishments of the government in army reform and the diplomatic understanding with France. 'You have not lived in vain if you carry through these two great affairs.'[53] A week later the two men met privately and parried each other's probes.

Chamberlain spent the Easter vacation at Highbury in council with his sons, local lieutenants, and a small gathering of experts on commerce led by Ashley. Then, disregarding the anxieties of his wife and doctors, he threw himself into the whirl at Westminster. His object there was to bind the Unionist leaders to the cause of tariff reform by joining forces with them in a variety of ways, excluding those whose commitment to free trade overrode their devotion to the Union. For a moment even the Duke of Devonshire seemed tempted to avoid exclusion. But when he insisted on his right to oppose tariff-reforming candidates in by-elections, Chamberlain refused to let him escape: he denounced Devonshire's electoral policy as *'war to the knife* with all who hold my opinions'.[54] Chamberlain took over the national organization of the Liberal Unionist party, reconstituted it on an elective basis, and turned it into an army of tariff reformers.

Meanwhile he took care to attach all the Liberal Unionist members of the government, including those who were neutral on the fiscal issue, to the reconstituted organization. He assumed its presidency himself, and divided the vice-presidency between Selborne, a dedicated tariff reformer, and Lansdowne, a fiscal Balfourite. At the inaugural rally of the reconstituted organization, Chamberlain tried to associate Lansdowne with a resolution in favour of imperial preference. When Lansdowne baulked, the two men settled on a resolution which made the most of Balfour's declaration at Sheffield of willingness to consider imperial preference once the political situation ripened.

Balfour still eluded capture. When Chamberlain had assured himself of bipartisan support in Canada for imperial preference, he contemplated a colonial conference at which the colonies could counteract the domestic considerations in Britain which kept Balfour away from preferential tariffs. Chamberlain also argued that the best way to counteract criticism of the government on other issues like education, licensing of public houses, and recruitment of Chinese labour for South Africa, was 'to take the offensive, and ... carry out a flank attack with Fiscal Reform'.[55] But his arguments and manoeuvres left Balfour cold.

Chamberlain encountered some timidity about full-blooded tariff reform even on his own Tariff Commission. After the businessmen on the commission examined the information it gathered on the iron and steel industry, they hesitated to specify what level of tariff the industry needed. Chamberlain wanted the commission to issue a specific recommendation 'as an example of the sort of thing which we think it would be wise for the Country to adopt'.[56] For general purposes he proposed a three-tier tariff: zero for the colonies that offered substantial imperial preference in return, a high rate to force protectionist foreign countries to lower their tariffs against imports from Britain, and a comparatively low rate for countries that agreed to lower their tariffs. But most of the Tariff Commissioners hesitated to endorse anything precise. Aside from Hewins, who helped Chamberlain shape his proposal, only Booth gave it an immediate welcome. Even so, after a little delay, the commission came round to what Chamberlain wanted.

After two months of lobbying and committee work at Westminster, he was tired and subject to 'bad fits of depression'.[57] Beatrice Potter, who never entirely recovered from her infatuation with him despite her marriage to Sidney Webb, sat beside Chamberlain at a luncheon. She found him obsessed with tariff reform: 'He looks desperately unhealthy . . . a restless look in the eyes, bad colour, and general aspect of "falling in". But,' she added, 'I should imagine that there is plenty of force in the man yet, an almost mechanically savage persistence in steaming ahead.'[58]

Concentrating relentlessly on his chosen course, he returned to the platform in the summer for a succession of speeches, mainly in London. They emphasized the imperial dimension of his cause, and reached a climax at the beginning of August when he called for a conference with the colonies to see how far they would go to achieve imperial preference. His emphasis on the imperial theme served a variety of purposes. It kept his achievements as Colonial Secretary in the public mind; it offset those tariff reformers who were interested only in the protective aspect of the cause; it appealed in principle to all Unionists; and it placed a positive gloss on his increasingly evident difference from 'my right hon. friend the Prime Minister'[59] who did not want to go beyond retaliatory tariffs. Two of the occasions on which Chamberlain spoke demonstrated the progress he was making within the active ranks of the Unionist alliance. Two hundred Unionist MPs, a clear majority of the parliamentary party, indicated their wish to attend a dinner in his honour at the beginning of July. As they arrived, they pinned orchids to their lapels. 'I am a fiscal reformer mainly because I am an imperialist,' Chamberlain told them, and he gave the economic side of the question only 'secondary' significance.[60] A week later, his inaugural address as president of the national Liberal Unionist association left no doubt that he had captured it.

The headway he made in the parliamentary and organizational ranks of the party was not, however, reflected among the electorate. Chamberlain discounted the significance of the by-election setbacks the government suffered through the spring and early summer of 1904, because the Unionist candidates kept to the Balfourite line on fiscal reform. He hoped for better from two by-elections scheduled for the end of July and beginning of August where the Unionist candidates were 'whole-hoggers', as supporters of imperial preference and food taxes came to be known. The first of these contests looked particularly promising, for it was in the hitherto safe Conservative constituency of West Shropshire on the edge of Chamberlain's duchy. But the Liberals pulled off a resounding victory. The message was driven home two weeks later in Northeast Lanarkshire, where the Liberals won again.

Grimly Chamberlain readied himself to ride out the electoral gale. Nothing abroad diminished the setback at home. He kept on trying to secure an unmistakable endorsement of his stand from the Canadian government. But all that Laurier would give him was a marked passage from Fielding's springtime budget address, a mode of reply reminiscent of Parnell. Chamberlain was forced to recognize that instead of drawing support from the colonies for his purposes in Britain, he would have to carry his campaign overseas 'when the battle is finished here'. Disappointed by the Australians as well as Canadians, he damned them as 'very provincial and very selfish'.[61] The colonial reaction lengthened the time that Chamberlain would have to spend in the wilderness before he could reach his goal. Four general elections might be necessary, one each to replace the governments of Australia and Canada with 'strongly Imperial' alternatives, and two in Britain to install and then remove a Liberal government. 'If . . . we can keep the matter open for *a year or two longer*,' he wrote to Minto, minimizing the likely interval, 'I hope we may look forward to a general [Colonial] Conference held under the most favourable auspices.'[62]

His immediate proposal for a colonial conference was not, therefore, entirely serious. It was a manoeuvre designed to drive Balfour to make a statement in favour of a conference, and hence to accept the possibility of agreeing to imperial preference, before the next general election in Britain. The ploy backfired. Exploiting the unpopularity of the tariffs on foodstuffs which imperial preference would require, Balfour amended Chamberlain's proposal for a colonial conference to require not just one general election in Britain, but two. If the Unionists retained power through the next general election, Balfour would summon a colonial conference; and if the conference agreed on a scheme for imperial preference, he would refer it to the judgement of a second general election. The point of difference might seem immaterial since both men expected the Unionists to lose the coming general election. But the vehemence with which Austen Chamberlain protested against Balfour's suggestion revealed how electorally vulnerable the Chamberlains felt on food taxes.

Joe had only himself to blame for this turn in the argument. With singularly poor timing, a sign of deteriorating judgement, he followed his call for a colonial conference with several addresses to communities involved in agriculture, an industry he neglected in his original campaign. In this context he could not avoid dwelling on the tariffs he proposed on imported foodstuffs, for this was the feature of tariff reform which most attracted the agricultural interest, however unpopular with the electorate at large. Chamberlain's appeal to agriculture also drew attention to the aristocratic alliances he had formed. Whenever he addressed rural audiences, he was accompanied by a bevy of dukes.

While Chamberlain retired between speeches to Highbury, Austen pleaded his case with Balfour. Ignoring his father's anxiety to escape from office in the autumn of 1903, Austen accused Balfour of betrayal.

> You encouraged my Father to go out as a 'pioneer'; you gave your blessing to his efforts for closer union with the colonies; you assured us who remained that we too thus served the interests of imperial union & we were thus induced to leave him for the time almost single-handed at his herculean task. He undertook this work believing ... that, when he had proved that the obstacles were not insuperable, you & your Government would be prepared to make some advance; & had he not been led to believe this ... I believe he wd. never have set out.[63]

Balfour's reply was almost contemptuously dilatory.

He was fortified by the agreement he received for his double election idea from Lord Selborne. Selborne had been one of the few cabinet ministers to speak out in favour of imperial preference, and he continued to do so. But as First Lord of the Admiralty, he was grateful for the support Balfour gave him to modernize the navy. That need in Selborne's scales outweighed the hypothetical point at issue between the Chamberlains and Balfour about a colonial conference and the general election after next. Assured of Selborne's support, Balfour in his next speech at Edinburgh surrounded the call for a colonial conference with general elections in the colonies as well as with two in Britain. Furious but unable publicly to do much, Joe had to 'make the best of it ... and ... attempt to minimise the difference'.[64] He emphasized Balfour's agreement to a colonial conference but disagreed with the requirement for subsequent elections: 'how long is it going to take?' he cried; 'How long?'[65]

He secured a sympathetic response from Balfour's party. The National Union of Conservative Associations convened for its annual conference at the end of October while Chamberlain was on another convalescent holiday in Italy. In concert with Chamberlain, Henry Chaplin presented the conference with a resolution which maximized Balfour's sympathy with tariff reform. The conference passed it by an overwhelming majority, all the sweeter because an attempt by free traders to amend the motion in accordance with Balfour's speech at Edinburgh received only thirteen votes. The achievement was overshadowed, however, by news of a Russian attack on British fishing ships in the North Sea. The news enabled Balfour, in his address at the conference, to ignore its resolution on tariff reform and dwell entirely on the international storm. Chamberlain's priorities had been so turned around that he responded to the international crisis as a chance to advance tariff reform. He wondered, before the news proved to be false, if the prospective war would have to be paid for by revenue raised through tariffs, and how far it might strengthen the commitment of the colonies to the empire.

Mutual resistance

The situation which Chamberlain faced at the turn of the year strained his temper but also cleared his vision. Fretful even on holiday, he wrote home to berate his daughters and the servants at Highbury for their neglect of the garden. When Edward Goulding, the Unionist MP for East Wiltshire, briefed him on efforts that some of his most aggressive followers, known as 'Confederates', were making to deprive free-trading Unionist MPs of their seats, Chamberlain criticized the effort as insufficiently stiff.

His aggressiveness was increased by estrangement from his former colleagues in government. No member of the cabinet seemed ready to place his office or the life of the government at risk for tariff reform, not even Austen; or so Joe suspected. Finding the old man at Highbury before Christmas 'in a hurt frame of mind', Lord Selborne urged Balfour 'to *see* him oftener . . . he is emotional, he is overworked & he gets down in his luck'.[66] Lord Esher brought Balfour and Chamberlain together to improve the parliamentary prospects of army reform; but the prime minister would not invite his erstwhile colleague for another of their tête-à-têtes of former years. The colonies did nothing to alleviate Chamberlain's gloom. He learned that the United States was testing Canada's adherence to imperial preference with talk of North American reciprocity. The report he received on Australia was no more encouraging. Everywhere, in the colonies and at home, he found politicians prevented by local concerns 'from taking a broad view of Imperial matters'.[67]

Driven on rather than discouraged by this prospect, he undertook another campaign of speeches between the end of his autumn holiday and the reopening of Parliament. Once again he called Ashley into conference at Highbury for preparatory economic analysis, and turned to Hewins at the Tariff Commission in London for statistics to substantiate his arguments. He took his winter campaign to potentially decisive areas, Lancashire, London and Lincolnshire; and he dealt with weak points in the case for tariff reform, particularly its social dimension and its applicability to Britain's premier export industry, cotton textiles.

Beginning at Limehouse in East London, Chamberlain appealed to labour, emphasizing the protective character of tariff reform rather than its potential as a source of revenue for social reform. He argued that tariff reform would protect British labour from foreign competition, particularly from countries where labour was cheapened by the absence of protective social legislation like his Workmen's Compensation Act. Exploiting the widespread revulsion in East London at sweatshops using immigrant labour, he argued for limitations on imports of sweated goods from abroad as well as for curbs on immigration. Though thus chauvinistic as well as protective, Chamberlain's case for tariff reform was more radical than the Liberal alternative of continued free trade. Derisively he argued that 'the most retrograde Tory in the most retrograde of times never committed himself to such an insane policy of stagnation as has now been accepted by the party which calls itself Radical'.[68]

Three weeks later at Preston in Lancashire, he tackled the problems raised for tariff reform by cotton textiles. The falling off that Chamberlain observed in other industries faced with tariff-protected foreign competition was not clear in cotton textile manufacturing, and it relied on cheap imports of raw material. To apply his nostrum to this industry, he resorted to a more complicated, less straightforward analysis than he needed in other cases. His perception of the eroding export market for British cotton goods was farsighted but not immediately persuasive. The closing remarks of the chairman of the meeting were noncommittal, to Chamberlain's obvious annoyance.

Three days after this disappointing reception, his youngest child Ethel died. Hauntingly like her mother Florence in appearance, Ethel had been the only one of Chamberlain's children to leave him for marriage and a home of her own. But she shared her mother's delicate constitution as well as her independence of spirit. After giving birth to a daughter in 1902, Ethel was found to have tuberculosis. She was sent alone, without husband or child, to a Swiss sanatorium in the autumn of 1904. Her sister Hilda headed there after Christmas to keep her company. They had barely a day together before Ethel's condition deteriorated sharply and she died. Chamberlain reeled in his grief, unable either to flee abroad or to drown himself in work. He felt obliged to keep the final speaking engagement of his winter campaign, at Gainsborough; but beyond that, as he told his Scottish lieutenant, 'I am not fit for politics or anything else just now & all the brightness has gone out of my life.'[69] This speech proved almost more than he could handle. Minutes before he was due to leave for Gainsborough, Mary found him slumped in despair. She rallied him; but later, in the midst of his address, he fell silent. Mary had to prompt him past the momentary blackout.

Yet the Gainsborough address was perhaps the best statement of the imperial case for tariff reform that Chamberlain ever delivered. He was as emphatic about the limitations of Britain's empire as he was visionary about its potentialities. Britain and its overseas possessions did not constitute an empire 'in the sense in which other empires have existed on this globe'. It was not like the German empire or the American union.

> It is a great potentiality, the greatest that was ever given to man. But for the moment it is a loose bundle of sticks, bound together, indeed, by a thin tie of sentiment and sympathy, but a tie, after all, so slender that a rough blow might shatter it and dissolve it into its constituent elements.

Belying the aristocratic sneers of the Cecils and Churchill at the materialism of his cause, he insisted that the British empire

> was won by sacrifice. It can only be maintained by sacrifice. Partly it is the result of conquest and of war, and of all the sufferings that war brings; partly the result of discovery, the work of pioneers . . . which involved them, at any rate, in the greatest of hardships.

Encouraging his audience to recognize that Britain and its colonial empire stood at a crossroads, he opened up a transforming vision:

> the position you have held hitherto cannot be permanently held unless you take your children into your counsels, and make the Empire theirs as well as yours. If that be done, then although it may be that the separate work of this kingdom may have ceased to be the guiding principle of the world, or of the civilisation in which we have taken part, yet our destiny may be continued and fulfilled in the British Empire.

Finally, urging his audience not to mistake the 'musty dogma' of free trade for 'the principle of your progress', he summed up his sense of the historical moment:

> In the past this country was ... the workshop of the world. ... That is
> no longer the case. ... Our competitors are gaining upon us in that
> which makes national greatness ... it is only the beginning. ... Those
> are the wise nations that look a little ahead and see a difficulty before
> it overwhelms them ... amongst those nations may we not hope our
> own will be counted?[70]

After Gainsborough, Chamberlain stayed away from the public platform until Easter. But he could not escape from other demands. He had
to make changes in the small circle of men on whom he relied. He lost
one of his few friends in the cabinet when Selborne replaced Milner as
high commissioner in South Africa. Chamberlain gained parliamentary
assistance from Lord Minto during the interlude between his governor-
generalship of Canada and his viceroyalty of India. One departure from
the inner circle left Chamberlain with increased responsibility. Arthur
Pearson, the newspaper publisher who chaired the Tariff Commission,
had done more than anyone to capture the Unionist press and much of
the provincial Liberal press for tariff reform. But Pearson was more
concerned about the popularity of tariff reform as reflected in the circulation of his newspapers than about the intrinsic strength of the creed.
Hewins as secretary of the Tariff Commission reported in alarm to
Chamberlain that Pearson was about to present a watered down version of tariff reform, minimizing the offence of food taxes, in the
columns of the *Standard*. While Chamberlain could not do anything
about the *Standard*, he would not allow the chairman of the Tariff Commission to 'alter one jot the lines on which I have been going'.[71] Pearson
was promptly replaced as chairman by Lord Ridley, son of the former
Conservative Home Secretary and a capable though undistinguished
organizer. Anxious to ensure that the commission was under complete
control, Chamberlain arranged for weekly meetings of its executive
committee during the parliamentary session, and he undertook to attend the meetings himself 'whenever I can possibly do so'.[72] In effect it
was Hewins, not Ridley, who replaced Pearson as the leader of the
Tariff Commission in Chamberlain's estimation. Chamberlain drew
upon Hewins's resources to identify advocates of tariff reform in the
business community who might be willing to stand as candidates at the
general election.

The demands upon Chamberlain grew inside as well as outside Parliament. In a bid to improve their reputation in ministerial circles, tariff-
reforming MPs undertook to dine together on Mondays and Thursdays
to assure the government of a majority in the Commons. Chamberlain
added these dinners to his obligations in order to encourage cooperation between what he liked to think of as 'the Pioneer & the main
army'.[73]

The prospects for this cooperation hinged on the relationship between Chamberlain as commander of the irregular pioneers and Balfour as the Unionist commander-in-chief. At Chamberlain's request, the two men met at the opening of Parliament for dinner in Chamberlain's London home 'alone & *absolutely free from interruption*'.[74] But one dinner was not enough to dispose of their differences. They discussed two subjects: Balfour's insistence on surrounding a colonial conference with two general elections, and the parliamentary candidacy of Lord Hugh Cecil. Beneath those subjects lay differences about the depth of the electoral aversion to food taxes and more generally on the psychology of popular government. Balfour insisted that the opposition to food taxes was 'deep-rooted . . . affecting the large mass of voters, especially the poorest class, which it will be a matter of extreme difficulty to overcome'.[75] Chamberlain recognized the strength of the prejudice but refused to respect it. He believed that he could overcome it with other forces: his imperial vision, a dedicated party, remorseless organization, and 'house to house education'[76] on the realities of Britain's economic situation. This frontal assault on the problem repelled Balfour as a threat to his primacy, and it struck the likes of the current Lord Salisbury as distastefully vehement. But it thrilled Unionists of more ardent spirit, old and young, because it transformed the dreams of the Young England movement of the 1840s into an industrial and imperial programme to confront the geopolitical demands of the new century.

The least attractive aspect of Chamberlain's campaign was the attempt to drive advocates of free trade, no matter how eminent, out of the Unionist parliamentary party. The most outspoken and gifted of them was the youngest son of the late Lord Salisbury, Lord Hugh Cecil, MP since 1895 for the safely Conservative metropolitan constituency of Greenwich. The Greenwich Conservative Association, infuriated by his opposition to tariff reform, deselected him as candidate for the coming general election and chose a whole-hogger named Benn to replace him. Though often exasperated by Lord Hugh, Balfour drew comfort from his insistent loyalty to the Conservative party and from the proof he provided that only Balfour could hold the party together. Before dining with Chamberlain, Balfour ordered Conservative party headquarters to ask the Greenwich association to reconsider its decision; and over dinner he asked Chamberlain to treat Lord Hugh with forbearance.

Forbearance was a virtue Chamberlain did not possess or respect. The support Lord Hugh received from Conservative party headquarters provoked Chamberlain. He told Lord Ridley to do 'everything in our power to help Benn'.[77] Chamberlain gave Benn his best advice and abundant financial support for an aggressive campaign. He was not deterred by the offence he thus gave to the gentlemanly mores of Unionism. He admitted that '[o]ur Greenwich policy is unpopular', but added, 'I have gone through all this before',[78] remembering how he had used the original Liberal caucus to expel enemies.

The inability of Chamberlain and Balfour to bridge their differences exposed them both within a matter of weeks to acute embarrassment. It seemed that if they failed to support each other, they would bring each other down, a possibility the old pioneer sensed more clearly than the regular commander. The springtime humiliation was all the bitterer for Chamberlain because Austen let him down. At issue was the lifespan of the government, which was sure to end with the general election. That prospect held no terrors for Joe. He wanted to see the Liberals in and then out of office as soon as possible. But Balfour wanted to hang on. Though he admitted that the government no longer enjoyed the confidence of the electorate, with patrician assurance he flattered himself that the Unionist government was 'best for the country',[79] particularly in strengthening Britain's armed defences and diplomatic relationships.

Austen was pulled both ways. In temperament and outlook, he was one of nature's conservatives. Were it not for his parentage, he would have found service under Balfour congenial. He performed as Chancellor of the Exchequer to the complete satisfaction of the mandarins at the Treasury, balancing direct and indirect taxation in the best Gladstonian tradition. He was gratified, after twenty years under his father's tutelage, to stand at this height on his own two feet. But that was not how others saw him, nor sometimes how he saw himself. Physically the mirror image of his father complete with monocle, Austen was unable to detach himself from home until he was forty. He had been Chancellor for three months before he took up his official residence as Chancellor on Downing Street, next door to Balfour. The night after he moved in, he poured out his overmastering devotion to his father:

> I cannot close my first evening away from your roof ... without writing a line to you. It is so great a change in my life & all about me is so strange that as yet I hardly realise it. But what I do realise is how much I owe to you & how very dear to me is the close friendship which you have encouraged between us ... my prayer tonight is that the perfect confidence which I have enjoyed for so long may continue unimpaired by our separation and that I may do something to help you in the great work which you have undertaken.[80]

Beneath this unbounded filial piety, the gentlemanly conservative in Austen struggled to be true to itself. But this was an uphill struggle because his father did not encourage autonomy among those close to him.

Hoping to bring down the government, the Liberals in the Commons promoted a succession of resolutions on fiscal policy worded to divide free-trading Unionists and Balfourites from the tariff-reforming wing of the party. The first motion was against imperial preference. Finding that they could not defeat it, the government preserved its majority by moving 'the previous question'. But the government whips discovered that this tactic might not work against all the ensuing motions, especially those directed at Chamberlain's proposals for a general industrial tariff and a tariff on foodstuffs. Conservative loyalty to Balfour would probably serve to defeat the motion directed against his policy of retaliation. The whips therefore suggested a free vote on the anti-Chamberlainite motions, which would thus go down to defeat, putting the life of the government on the line only for the motion on retaliation.

Horrified at the prospect, Chamberlain pressed the government to stick to its stratagem of moving the previous question. The risk was that the government would be defeated, precipitating a general election; but that risk he only welcomed. Nor was he disconcerted by the prospect of the government falling on a motion which drew attention to its divisions on fiscal policy. Such an outcome would focus attention on the issue he had raised, and would increase the pressure on Unionist candidates from their local associations to fall in line with the tariff-reforming majority in the party.

Balfour, however, threatened to resign rather than stake the life of the government on fiscal policies which he was not ready to sponsor. He had quite enough support in Parliament to enforce his stand. Chamberlain had already been warned by some Conservative tariff reformers that, out of loyalty to Balfour, they would 'not do anything to bring about the fall of the Government'.[81] Many Unionist MPs were deterred from hastening the fall of the government by the prospect of losing their seats at the next election. All but the most fanatical tariff reformers blanched at the thought of a fiscal fight among Unionists in the midst of a general election. Even so, Balfour felt unable to defy Chamberlain by condoning differential treatment of the various fiscal resolutions. Balfour therefore asked the cabinet to deal impartially with the remaining Liberal motions by walking out of the Commons chamber when they came up for a vote—in effect by running away.

Austen saw no way to refute Balfour's argument, yet he writhed at the offence he knew his father would take. After a sleepless night, Austen joined his cabinet colleagues in accepting Balfour's advice, and then tried to explain it to his father as in the best interests of tariff reform. Still, the son knew that he was refusing to stand by his father and would, if need be, vote to uphold the prime minister.

Joe felt the lack of support from Austen all the more because he could not fight for himself. He was in bed with influenza when the crisis opened, and as it worsened, so did his illness. Mary also fell ill; and when the crisis entered its most serious phase, they had to leave London for recovery in Highbury. Joe cringed at the impression he might convey of fleeing the scene of battle.

The spectacle of a mass Unionist exodus in the face of the Liberal attack discredited the government. Even so, for Chamberlain the outcome could have been worse. He expected that, out of loyalty to the prime minister, the Unionists would vote down the anti-retaliation motion, concentrating the humiliation of the Unionist flight on the tariff reformers. Fearing his wrath, Balfour made sure that the Unionists adhered to his pusillanimous tactics for the whole debate; and he endured the same humiliation he caused Chamberlain to suffer.

The tariff reformers were nevertheless disheartened. Over the next three months, while Chamberlain sought to regroup his forces, Balfour manoeuvred around him to hold the Unionist army together under his command. For all their dexterity, Balfour's tactics were self-defeating. He prevented Chamberlain from concentrating on persuasion of the electorate, as Balfour originally hoped he might do. Balfour's tactics also provoked Chamberlain to attack him for obstructing the commitment of the Unionist party to tariff reform. Refusing help from Chamberlain to hold up the temple, Balfour maddened him to shake it down.

The issue over which the two men jockeyed for position was still the connection between a colonial conference and general elections. To Chamberlain's surprise, Balfour welcomed one possibility that seemed to offer both men what they wanted: a prolongation of the government for Balfour, imperial preference for Chamberlain, and even a chance to win the next election. But Balfour raised Chamberlain's hopes only to dash them. After the humiliations of March, Balfour asked for conversation with Chamberlain and Sir Herbert Maxwell, a tariff-reforming MP who admired both leaders. Chamberlain expected a chilly encounter. To the astonishment of both tariff reformers, Balfour met them sympathetically. Encouraged by this reception, Maxwell remembered that the next colonial conference was scheduled tentatively for the summer of 1906, before the maximum constitutional lifetime of the current Parliament would expire. He asked whether Balfour might be willing to use the scheme of imperial preferences to which the colonial conference might agree as the basis for the government's appeal at the ensuing general election. That way, Balfour's double election pledge could be obviated, he could stay in office for another year, and the Unionists could go to the people with a proposal for imperial preference strengthened by endorsement from the colonies. After checking with his secretary, Balfour reported that nothing he had said on the subject would prevent him from following this course.

The meeting was not all smiles. Chamberlain embraced the prospective agreement with a warmth that put Balfour on guard. He could not miss the purr of triumph beneath Chamberlain's promise 'to give up all claim to colonial preference as being his own plan ... provided the Cabinet would adopt it and carry it through'.[82] Chamberlain underlined the threat to Balfour's ascendancy by asking him to 'consider the expediency of readmitting [Chamberlain] to the Cabinet'. The suggestion was 'not accepted'.

Chamberlain left the meeting in uncertainty. The cordiality of the prime minister did not last long. His willingness to remain in office long enough to preside over the colonial conference threatened to deprive him of Unionist free-trading support in the Commons. Given full support from the tariff reformers as well as his own loyalists, his government might still have survived. But rather than take the gamble, Balfour forswore his intention of remaining in office past the spring of 1906.

Having placated the Unionist free traders, he had to guard himself against desertion from the tariff reformers. He gave Chamberlain two pieces of compensation. Balfour told Parliament that his double election pledge with regard to the colonial conference would not remain binding if he lost the coming election. He also promised to treat tariff reform including colonial preference as the foremost issue in the Unionist campaign at that election. But when he made this promise in public, he embedded it in a speech in such a way as to hide its significance.

The way that Balfour jerked Chamberlain back and forth, often from a distance through intermediaries, was bound to infuriate him. Chamberlain's impatience turned to anger. He almost broke under the strain. While drafting a public reply to Balfour's evasions, the old fighter found himself momentarily unable to write or speak. Though he quickly recovered, his doctors ordered him to cancel his speaking engagement. Chamberlain refused, knowing that 'If I don't do it, I shall never speak again.'[83] Heading immediately for Lancashire to deliver his reply, Chamberlain criticized Balfour's obscurity and imposed his own interpretation on the prime minister's remarks.

> What did Mr. Balfour say? He said ... tariff reform will be the most important part of Unionist policy. He said, Colonial preference is the most important part of tariff reform. He said, Colonial preference will therefore be the first item in the future Unionist programme. ... Here is the official programme to which I most heartily subscribe.[84]

Unionist free traders reacted with horror to this translation. Balfour insisted that his meaning should be sought in his own speeches rather than in those of Chamberlain. But Balfour's words did not speak for themselves.

During this infighting, reports from North America heightened Chamberlain's sense of the imperial urgency of tariff reform. Balfour was preoccupied with foreign affairs, currently a threat from Germany to the Anglo-French entente, naval war between Japan and Russia, and a strengthened British treaty with Japan. But Chamberlain was convinced that economic consolidation of the empire was the way to strengthen Britain's competitive position. His greatest geopolitical anxiety in the spring of 1905 was the rapid rise of American interest, endorsed by President Roosevelt, in a reciprocal trade agreement with Canada. The leader of the Conservatives in Canada warned that reciprocity would lead ultimately to amalgamation between the two countries. Chamberlain warned his fellow countrymen that things would move in that direction if they continued to refuse the trading preference Canada sought. When the Tariff Commission completed its survey of the major British industries, Chamberlain charged the commission to find out what lines and terms of imperial preference British industry would like to secure.

But his main concern in the early summer of 1905, aside from jockeying for position with Balfour, was the appeal of tariff reform to the working-class electorate. Speaking to the branch of the Tariff Reform League set up specifically for organized labour, Chamberlain dwelt on the affinity between trade unionism and tariff reform: 'you cannot be Free Traders in goods and not be Free Traders in labour'.[85] He insisted again and again that the heart of the matter was 'the question of employment'. Tariffs to guard British manufactured goods would keep up British wages, preserve British social legislation, and protect British jobs. 'Give me the power to give you more employment,' the erstwhile manufacturer declared to the working men of Lancashire, 'and everything will follow. It will be easy enough then for your employers to give you higher wages; it will be easy enough then to promise all the legislation which is intended to raise the standard of your life; but, believe me . . . it is the comparative decrease in the employment of this country that is answerable for the greater part of the ills of which you complain.'[86]

Transfer of power

The duel between Chamberlain and Balfour entered its decisive phase towards the end of July. Crumbling morale on the Unionist benches in the Commons allowed the government to be defeated on 20 July on a motion involving Ireland, the original raison d'être of the Unionist alliance. Balfour secured a reversal of the vote; but it still implied that he had exhausted his title to govern.

The day after the defeat though by earlier arrangement, Chamberlain met an emissary of the Canadian government; and together they coordinated the proceedings of Chamberlain's Tariff Commission with a commission the Canadian cabinet set up to revise its tariff. In effect Chamberlain took the right to formulate British imperial policy on this subject out of Balfour's hesitant hands. Thereafter Chamberlain encroached upon one after another of Balfour's official powers, including control over his party organization, the timing of the general election, and setting the Unionist agenda.

Yet Chamberlain's achievements remained equivocal. Regardless of his ever more obvious contest with Balfour, each man knew that he needed the other. The Unitarian metal manufacturer had no hold on the loyalties of traditional Conservatives. The aristocratic Scottish philosopher knew that the hearts of the ardent men in his party were against him. Neither man would therefore risk a showdown with the other. But they were equally unwilling to reinforce each other. Accordingly the dual leadership under which the Unionist party had laboured since Lord Salisbury's retirement remained in force, or rather in diminishing force, each consul going his own way, ignoring the injunctions and appeals of the other. By doing so, they dug themselves an electoral grave deep enough to bury them both. Instead of offsetting, they compounded each other's electoral liabilities. They thus contributed to a massive transfer of power from the Unionist alliance to the Liberals. That transfer confirmed Britain's commitment to free trade.

Skirmishes within the Unionist leadership continued throughout the summer. The by-election victory of a tariff reformer in Chamberlain's electoral duchy at the beginning of July heartened him with its evidence 'of what could be done with well organised and well directed effort'.[87] While Balfour devoted himself to high diplomacy and military reform, his government lurched from crisis to crisis in Parliament, accident-prone like any dying regime. On education, temperance and Ireland, its measures alienated friends without conciliating foes. The association of tariff reform with a government sinking ever deeper in public esteem did neither any good. Yet Chamberlain shrank from severing the connection. He wanted the tariff-reforming wing of the party to win over rather than break with the Balfourite centre. If not to win over, then to conquer: during the summer he and his adjutants discussed a 'scheme of capturing the party organisation'[88] of the Conservatives. Whole-hoggers were prevalent in the National Union of Conservative Associations but had not overcome the Balfourites in control at party headquarters. Chamberlain's zeal for this fight intensified when the central office cancelled its financial support for parliamentary candidates who moved beyond Balfourite fiscal policy towards tariff reform.

These crosscurrents absorbed the attention of political observers. But in the privacy of Chamberlain's West End home, a negotiation of greater moment took place. One of the more imperially minded mem-

bers of the Canadian Liberal cabinet, Sir William Mulock, came on behalf of his colleagues to find out how the impending revision of their
tariff could serve to 'help forward Mr. Chamberlain's movement'.[89] The
directive Chamberlain had given his Tariff Commission to study imperial preference from the British standpoint dovetailed nicely with a
commission the Canadian government had set up to examine their tariff
with a view to its revision the following spring. At Mulock's suggestion, the two men undertook to harmonize the two inquiries by having
Hewins as secretary of Chamberlain's commission cross the Atlantic for
confidential discussion with the Canadian commissioners before they
submitted their report.

The agreement was irregular because Chamberlain lacked official
government position. The irregularity of the undertaking made smooth
progress unlikely; and so it proved. On his return to Ottawa, Mulock
reported, sooner than he had led Chamberlain to expect, that the Canadian commission would be happy to meet Hewins in the early part of
October. Mulock underlined the need for discretion by advising Hewins
to travel via New York rather than Montreal. The letter was slow in
reaching Chamberlain, who had gone in the meantime for a cure at
Aix-en-Provence. As soon as the message arrived, he sent Hewins to
Canada. The unlucky emissary arrived to find that Mulock had just
been elevated from the cabinet to the Chief Justice of the Exchequer
division of the Canadian Supreme Court. Not only was he therefore
politically inaccessible, Hewins also discovered that Mulock had presented Chamberlain with a more glowing overture than Laurier and his
finance minister, Fielding, had intended.

Hewins found himself treated by Laurier and Fielding as Chamberlain was by Balfour. Hewins was beyond his political depth, and tackled his mission like an exercise in economics. He came accompanied by
a statistician, an array of diagrams, and a portable cabinet made to contain 12,000 summary cards on 'practically every article & every subject
which can arise in the discussions'.[90] Laurier and also Fielding who was
in charge of the tariff revision inquiry treated Hewins with evasion and
delays interspersed with sudden meetings to which the poor man hurried with his chest of note cards.

Despite their cavalier conduct, the Canadian ministers made it clear
that they were seriously interested in preferential tariffs which would
allow British manufacturers greater access to the Canadian market than
they had hitherto enjoyed. Hewins was also encouraged by independent talks he had with Canadian manufacturers. They led him to believe that the two economies could be drawn together on a broader
front than he had anticipated before coming to Canada. His hopes were
however matched by rising fears. He could sense from the atmosphere
in the board rooms of Canadian business that the economic pull towards a common market with the United States was strong. He also

saw that Laurier and, less clearly, Fielding were free traders at heart. They embraced imperial preference as a way to lower the tariff wall which the dominion had built round itself. Their objective in revising the tariff was to lower it further, towards Germany and the United States as well though not as much as towards Britain. Hewins believed none the less that the situation in Canada gave Britain a crucial opportunity for imperial economic consolidation—if only Chamberlain could seize it.

That 'if' governed Chamberlain's response to these negotiations. They had value for him insofar as they bore upon the coming general election in Britain and thereafter upon the situation with which the new, presumably Liberal government would have to deal. The prospective Unionist loss of power lent an air of unreality to the Hewins mission. It nevertheless opened up the possibility for a startling change in Chamberlain's campaign, to drop the unpopular corn tax. From his opening conversation with Mulock, through all the letters of instruction to Hewins, Chamberlain pressed the Canadian ministers to consider whether they could do without a preferential British tariff in favour of Canadian wheat. Though that tariff was the point over which the controversy over fiscal reform had erupted, a corn tax was not in principle essential to imperial preference and it threatened to make preference impossible for Britain.

The Canadian response was tantalizing but ultimately negative. The Canadian ministers confessed that, in strictly economic terms, their economy could fare even better if Britain gave tariff preference to other Canadian exports instead of wheat. Yet Laurier insisted on preferential treatment for wheat: 'it is what I have been fighting for,' he told Hewins, '& what I want'.[91] With as keen an understanding of the electorate in Canada as Chamberlain had in Britain, Laurier knew that no symbol in the Canadian debate was more persuasive than the tax which would reserve the British market for the boundless supply of wheat growing in the Canadian prairies.

Moreover, Laurier had no wish to further Chamberlain's imperial purposes. Whether through imperial preference or trade agreements with the United States or Germany, Laurier wished to make the most of the rich resources of his northern dominion. He was a nationalist, economically and politically. In his discussions with Hewins, he stressed his hostility to any tightening of the bonds of empire, whether through military arrangements or unifying political institutions in London. He insisted on an imperial preference for wheat for purely Canadian reasons. How Britain responded to it was, he remarked with a shrug, entirely up to the British. His insistence on a preferential corn tax forced Chamberlain to adhere to it and trust in his ability to sway the electorate by the sheer strength of his commitment.

Refreshed by his cure at Aix, Chamberlain returned to England in

October determined to capture the forces of Unionism for the cause of tariff reform. The battle turned into another duel with Balfour, whose priorities changed after his last major accomplishment in foreign affairs, the signing in September of a strengthened treaty with Japan. Previously he had tried to keep his party together in order to preserve his government and hence his ability to strengthen Britain's diplomatic and military position. Thenceforth he tried to preserve his government in order to reinforce his ability to hold his party together, including as many as possible of the free traders. Though the purposes of Balfour and Chamberlain were thus incompatible, each man recognized that an explicit, decisive break with the other would be self-defeating. They therefore lunged at and parried each other from a distance, from platforms in different corners of the kingdom and through third-party attempts at conciliation.

Conciliation was never to Chamberlain's liking, least of all during the autumn parliamentary recess when he could hold forth from the platform and fight on the favourable terrain of the annual party conferences. He refused the olive branches extended to him behind the scenes by apprehensive Balfourites on behalf of the Unionist free traders. Austen welcomed these efforts to reconcile the prime minister he esteemed with the father he worshipped. But Joe insisted that his objectives and those, for example, of Hugh Cecil were so different that 'no compromise could possibly bridge over the divergence of opinion.... The Prime Minister has to choose.'[92]

The quarrel was heated at the beginning of November by Balfour's least intelligent supporter in the cabinet, Lord Londonderry. An inveterate opponent of Chamberlain, Londonderry declared that his fiscal proposals had been discredited in the past two years of debate, and that therefore the Unionist party should reject them in order to recover its peace. Chamberlain used Londonderry's attack to indict Balfour's leadership without mentioning the prime minister by name. Declaring that he 'would infinitely rather be part of a powerful minority than a member of an impotent majority', Chamberlain called for an end to 'the apathy which has been born of timorous counsels and of half-hearted convictions'.[93] Balfour measured support by its extent, Chamberlain by its intensity.

The National Union of Conservative Associations convened for its annual meeting, this year on Londonderry's doorstep in Newcastle. Together with Henry Chaplin, Chamberlain drew up plans for an endorsement of tariff reform. Balfour had arranged to stay with Londonderry during the conference, and spoke in complimentary fashion about his host before it opened. Balfour might be leader of the Conservative party and Chamberlain merely allied to it; but Chamberlain's lieutenants took command of the conference. It voted overwhelmingly in favour of his fiscal proposals against those of the prime minister. It also resolved to replace Balfour's lieutenants at party headquarters with an elected committee representing the tariff-reforming majority among constituency activists. Balfour affected to ignore the triumph of the tariff reformers in his speech as leader at the conclusion of the conference, and dwelt instead on the need to accommodate all wings of the party. But the fact remained that the soldiers of his army had marched off without him, under the banner of the alternative commander.

Chamberlain and Balfour found themselves together a few days later in a railway compartment on their way to Windsor to meet the king of Greece. Chamberlain pressed Balfour to dissolve Parliament immediately: 'you will wreck the Party if you go on'.[94] To drive the message home, Chamberlain delivered another public criticism of Balfour's style of government, this time at the Liberal Unionist party conference in Bristol. After securing the now customary commitment to tariff reform from the conference, Chamberlain disparaged attempts to conciliate the free traders. 'No army', he declared, 'was ever led successfully to battle on the principle that the lamest man should govern the march of the army.'[95] He may have had Hugh Cecil in mind as 'the lamest man', but the words were applied to Balfour.

The prime minister still procrastinated; but he had run out of options. Two weeks after Chamberlain spoke at Bristol, Balfour tendered his resignation to the king. By resigning rather than advising the dissolution of Parliament, Balfour probed the joints of the Liberal leadership between Little Englanders and Liberal Imperialists in the hope that they might fail to agree on the composition of a government; but to no avail. The Liberals put together a team of ministers conspicuously stronger than the Unionists had provided since Chamberlain's resignation. The way was cleared for a general election at the beginning of the new year.

Rejection

Chamberlain was the ablest electioneer of his generation. The only general election which did not produce results in line with his expectations was in 1885. His mastery in popular politics was also evident between times, especially after the general election of 1886 when his recurrent platform campaigns confirmed the unpopularity of Home Rule and made the most of the Unionist bent for social reform. But would his campaign for tariff reform prove similarly effective? The crucial test for all interim campaigns came with the ensuing general election: in popular politics, that was the bottom line.

He never lost sight of that fact. Though the enlargement of the electorate by the third Reform Act disappointed his expectations in 1885, he never forgot the electoral preponderance of the working class. Recognizing thereafter that Home Rule neutralized but did not overturn the popular inclination to vote Liberal, he favoured general elections at mid-year when registration procedures and seasonal considerations reduced the number of voters. He hoped that the cause of empire would give Unionism the positive appeal which opposition to Home Rule did not provide; and the election of 1900 seemed to bear out his hopes. Still, throughout his campaign for tariff reform, he appreciated the need to convince working-class voters about the worth of his policy from their socio-economic point of view.

But he had no sense that the working-class electorate which he failed to rouse at infancy in 1885 was waking up from its twenty-year sleep. He approached the general election set for January 1906 in a sober mood. He expected a national defeat for the Unionists as heavy as either British party had suffered in his lifetime. He thought the Liberals might win a majority over the Conservatives in the Commons of as much as 140. Still, he assumed that the majority would include the contingent of 85 Nationalists which Ireland had returned with little variation for the past twenty years. His calculations for the future depended on the instability which the Irish component would create in the governing majority. That instability was all the more promising from the Unionist point of view because Sir Henry Campbell-Bannerman had watered down the Liberal commitment on Ireland to Home Rule only by instalments. Chamberlain also reckoned on the longstanding interest of Irish Nationalists in tariff protection for their island economy. He counted on the instability of the Irish-Liberal alliance to reduce the lifetime of the new government to a year or two, within his own probable lifespan and before the colonies were likely to move off in autonomous directions.

He approached the general election with singleness of purpose. He sought a slimmed down army of Unionist MPs, divested of free traders, dominated by tariff reformers whose strength of conviction would press the weaker Balfourite brethren into line. He shuddered at the thought of a narrow Unionist victory which left the Balfour government dependent on free traders for survival. Even so, Chamberlain wished to focus his attack on the Liberals rather than on other Unionists. He sought to divert attention from the sins of the Balfour ministry by emphasizing the promise of tariff reform. In effect he ignored Balfour, being 'absolutely determined not to make a breach with him'.[96] Balfour too shied away from an overt break, but he laid public stress on his ability to retain the loyalty of Unionist free traders.

In the business of electoral mobilization, Chamberlain all but superseded Balfour. Conservative party headquarters remained under Balfourite control but was replaced as the effective organizing force in most areas by the Tariff Reform League. Chamberlain filled its war chest with financial resources that rich supporters had placed at his disposal. He did his best to ensure that tariff reformers expelled Unionist free traders from the Commons. His only serious setback in this effort came in the safely Conservative constituency of Marylebone where mismanagement by the local Conservative association enabled Balfour to instal Hugh Cecil's brother Robert as the Conservative nominee.

Chamberlain's campaign retained the regional character of former general elections. He concentrated his personal efforts on the West Midlands, declining for example to head north to aid his Scottish lieutenant, Parker Smith. Chamberlain made only one foray outside his electoral duchy, to Derby where the Unionists faced a strong challenge from a Labour party candidate allied to the Liberals. The only countrywide activity he undertook was to publish letters of endorsement to beleaguered tariff-reforming candidates. He used every occasion to stress the appeal of tariff reform to the working class. He traversed the West Midlands from corner to corner, delivering a substantial address every other night. The Liberal Unionist organization worked at full throttle. The city organization, led by businessmen in touch with each subdivision and with the auxiliary tariff-reforming associations, saturated the urban and suburban constituencies with every form of propaganda. Conservative organization in the region was much less formidable.

Chamberlain's family staffed the command centre for this effort—all but Austen, whose health broke down upon his return to his father's roof. Neville was the local custodian of the family's political interests. Mary became Joe's principal political secretary. She prompted him when he was lost for a word while speaking, an increasingly frequent occurrence; and she commented confidently on the political outlook to his main lieutenants round the country. Beatrice organized support for Austen in his East Worcestershire constituency, though she refrained from the public activity of which her father disapproved in women. Giving him all this support, the family pleaded with Joe to reduce his pace for fear of a stroke. But the old warrior, now almost seventy, refused. 'I cannot go half speed,' he said unrelentingly; 'I must either do my utmost or stop altogether and though I know the risks I prefer to take them.'[97]

His health and hopes were buoyed up by the contest. Mary was surprised at the resilience he displayed in the thick of the fight. More attention focused on him than on anyone else in the country, including the past and present prime ministers. The rally in London where the Liberals kicked off their campaign revised the old negro spiritual to sing, 'No more Joe'. Some Unionists were sufficiently encouraged by the response their efforts seemed to be winning to predict a narrow victory. Chamberlain revised his prediction of the Liberal majority in the next House of Commons downward from 140 to 80.

The results from the balloting, which extended over the second half of January, opened with personal defeat for Balfour and every other Unionist in the six constituencies of Manchester. At a stroke, all of Chamberlain's calculations were confounded. The unanticipated possibility of his replacing Balfour as leader of the Unionist alliance was overshadowed by the probability that Unionists would find themselves out of power far longer than Chamberlain ever imagined. The Liberals were likely to secure a majority independent of the Irish. The window of imperial opportunity might close and Chamberlain's life energies might be exhausted before the Liberals could be expelled from office.

In response to a letter of commiseration from Chamberlain, Balfour made clear that he had no intention of resigning the leadership: 'nothing', he wrote, 'would induce me at such a time to abandon my share of the work'.[98] As the tide of Unionist defeats rolled on, attention turned to Birmingham and its environs. While Joe's defeat in Birmingham West was inconceivable, Balfour wrote solicitously about Austen in East Worcestershire, half hoping that it might go the way of Manchester. The polling date for the seven Birmingham constituencies had been set, to Joe's annoyance, for the end of the voting in the urban areas of England, too late to set the nation an example.

He remained confident that his Unionists were safe in six of the city's seats. But once again the seventh, Birmingham East, was vulnerable. The Conservative incumbent, Sir Benjamin Stone, was undistinguished, the Conservative organization frail, and Stone was confronted by an able Labour candidate, James Holmes of the Amalgamated Society of Railway Servants. Holmes had cultivated the constituency for two years, enjoyed local support from his union, and exploited the lack of attention Stone had paid to social issues. Chamberlain intervened to spike Holmes's social guns, and in the final few days called in his best Liberal Unionist organizers. All that was left for Sir Benjamin was to remind his constituents that 'a vote given for Stone is a vote given for Chamberlain'.[99] Polling day began with a call in the city press from Chamberlain to 'the men of Birmingham when other cities have fallen away once more to shew their generous loyalty to old friends and to the old cause'.[100]

Apart from the national dimensions of the Liberal victory, the most remarkable returns in the general election of 1906 were from Birmingham. The crowds which cheered Chamberlain off to South Africa in 1903 massed anxiously on the night of 17 January in front of the Council House for the outcome of the voting in their city. The first result to come in, from West Birmingham, told them that their Joe had crushed his opponent by a margin even greater than in the Unionist landslide of 1895. His triumph was repeated on a reduced scale in one constituency after another in the city. But the crowd remained anxious until the final

12. 'Good ol' Joe' campaigning among his constituents.

result was announced, from East Birmingham. Stone carried it with a majority slim by Birmingham but not by national standards. At a distance from the erupting cheers, Chamberlain telephoned his thanks to the crowd in words which were emblazoned in lights: 'Well done, Birmingham! My own people have justified my confidence, and I am deeply grateful to all who have assisted in winning this great victory. We are seven.' The results from Birmingham ran diametrically against the national trend. The contrast between his city and the rest of the country enabled Chamberlain to argue that the 'uncertainty about Fiscal Reform, due largely to the temperament of Arthur Balfour, prevented anything like a definite issue except in Birmingham'.[101]

The returns from Birmingham did not change the national tide. The Liberals and Labour won seats in the adjacent Black Country, though by margins below the national average. Elsewhere tariff reformers fared well only in Sheffield, economically akin to Birmingham in its dependence on metal manufacturing, and in Liverpool, where aversion to Irish Catholics did more than love of tariffs to impel working-class electors to vote Unionist. The rural returns, which rolled in after Birmingham had voted, were almost as bad as the urban ones. They began with the defeat in Lincolnshire of Henry Chaplin. In despair, Chamberlain cried, 'Campbell-Bannerman and his motley crew will be able to do what they like.'[102] The returns from Scotland were still worse.

But Chamberlain rallied quickly. Like Balfour, he pointed beyond the Liberal to the Labour victories. But whereas Balfour observed the phenomenon with passive curiosity, Chamberlain aimed to build past it.

Before the voting began, he had dismissed the new Labour party as a mere appendage of the Liberals. He paid little attention to the anger of organized labour at the Taff Vale decision which crippled its legal rights. He was used to appealing over the heads of trade union leaders to the working men beyond. But the first week of returns in 1906 woke him up. The achievement of Labour in Manchester, at Derby where the Labour candidate headed the poll, the substantial vote for Holmes in East Birmingham, and more successful incursions by Labour elsewhere in the West Midlands induced Chamberlain to revise his assessment. The support he won from the working men of Birmingham still encouraged him to believe that the electorate had not decided against tariff reform. He emphasized instead how much the issue of Chinese labour in South Africa benefited the Labour party because of the rooted working-class 'prejudice against the employment of cheap labour anywhere'.[103] But otherwise he took the challenge from Labour seriously. In response, he sharpened the socio-economic debate.

He presented the country with a choice between the only two policies which came seriously to grips with its socio-economic needs: tariff reform as proposed by his Unionists, and the socialism of the Labour party. Chamberlain continued to insist that the Liberals, regardless of their electoral achievement, had nothing to offer. That was certainly the case in Birmingham, where independent Labour activists were as contemptuous as he was of the emptiness of the Liberal social cupboard. Everywhere Liberalism seemed paralysed by its commitment to laissez-faire and free trade. Chamberlain scoffed at John Burns, the former dockers' leader now president of the Local Government Board in the Liberal government, for offering the unemployed and destitute nothing but sermons on thrift and self-help. Liberals preferred moral to social issues. Labour candidates, on the other hand, preferred to talk about the legal repression of trade unions, unemployment, old-age pensions and housing.[104]

At the end of the voting Chamberlain initiated a threefold approach towards Labour. He sought to weaken the alliance between Labour and the Liberals by emphasizing their different social priorities. He sought to reduce the hostility of Labour to tariff reform by emphasizing their common concerns, preeminently domestic employment: 'Sooner or later they would find that they could not protect labour without protecting also the products of labour.'[105] Finally he argued that tariff reform would secure those agreed ends more effectively than socialism, which would only reduce the aggregate wealth of the country by redistributing it.

But this was the argument for the next election. It did not affect the results of the one just past. In the worst defeat any party had suffered since 1832, the Unionist contingent in the Commons was reduced by more than half to 157. They were faced by 377 successful Liberals allied to a Lib-Lab and straight Labour contingent of 54, to say nothing of the 83 Irish Nationalists. The popular vote was just as extraordinary. After twenty years of voter turn-outs reduced by the unpopularity of Home Rule, the electorate created by the third Reform Act went to the polls in unprecedented numbers. While there was a substantial improvement in the Unionist vote over the 1900 result, it was overwhelmed by a doubling of the Liberal vote. The era of popular politics which Chamberlain vainly anticipated in 1885 had begun at last—and it began by deserting his banner.

20

Paralysis
1906–1914

... the final rocket at a display of fireworks ... makes more noise, goes higher & is more brilliant than all the rest. People wait in expectation of another—but no—the show is over.

Mary Endicott to Joseph Chamberlain, 20 July 1888

'The disaster has been complete,' Chamberlain admitted to an admirer.[1] At the end of January, a week after the election returns were complete, he still could 'not fully understand [the outcome] nor can I foresee all that it portends'.[2] Outside Birmingham, tariff reformers had experienced the same fate as Balfourites and Unionist free traders. Chamberlain's lieutenants, Parker Smith in Scotland as well as Chaplin in East Anglia, were among the fallen.

Yet the rout and the contrasting outcome in Birmingham propelled Chamberlain into faster activity than the narrower national defeat he anticipated would have done. He had planned to recover after the election with a fortnight's holiday on the Riviera. But the returns left him more excited than exhausted. The absence of Balfour from the Commons at the opening of the new Parliament raised questions about the leadership and policy of the shattered opposition, questions which were too urgent, at least in Chamberlain's estimation, to be put off.

His eagerness to plunge into the fray at Westminster was increased by the composition of the Unionist force in the new House of Commons. Though all factions in the party suffered in the general election, those who followed Balfour's ambiguous lead in the fiscal debate fared worse than those with firmer convictions, whether tariff reformers or Unionist free traders. The composition of each faction was not entirely clear; but something like twenty per cent of the Balfourites in the old House had survived, as compared with almost forty per cent of the other two factions. Equal in number to the tariff reformers in the old House, the followers of Balfour were outnumbered in the new by more than two to one, according to *The Times*. Tariff-reforming candidates kept five of the most notorious Unionist free traders including Hugh

Cecil from returning to the Commons. Even so, that faction fared comparatively well, though only in proportion to its previous numbers: it would have a hard core of sixteen in the new House, too few, even with support from the surviving Balfourites, to withstand the tariff-reforming majority in the parliamentary party. Thus though the Unionist contingent in the Commons was far smaller than Chamberlain had anticipated, it lived up to his hope for a parliamentary force largely committed to his cause.

But that way of achieving fiscal agreement was undercut by conflicting leadership loyalties, older partisan commitments, and the still more basic conflict which tariff reform aroused between those who wished to resist and those who wished to meet the demand, accentuated by the emergence of the Labour party, for far-reaching change. These forces served on balance to strengthen Balfour. They enabled him to remain leader of the party but not to neutralize its fiscal policy. He and Chamberlain still could not do without each other. 'Both had the power to destroy the effectiveness of the party; only together could they successfully preserve it'[3]—a fact which Chamberlain was always quicker to recognize. Under these circumstances, the Unionist party in the new House of Commons was able to impose its will upon its leaders. For some time the parliamentary party got what it wanted: the policy of Chamberlain under the leadership of Balfour. But the balance was never stable. The two men continued to pursue conflicting objectives.

The Valentine compact

Just before Birmingham went to the polls, Chamberlain publicly reaffirmed his allegiance to Balfour as leader of the party regardless of his defeat at Manchester. Some of the most ardent tariff reformers, men such as Ridley, Leo Maxse and Parker Smith, pressed Chamberlain to take the leadership: that was the only way, they argued, to commit the party to their cause and end the divisions and evasions which had deepened the electoral disaster. But Chamberlain insisted in private as in public on the necessity of Balfour as leader. Some admirers and later commentators accounted for Chamberlain's restraint by saying that he was mistakenly confident of Balfour's friendship. Yet there is no evidence that Chamberlain still made this mistake, nor was it necessary to explain his refusal to seek the leadership. He offered compelling reasons for his action: as a Liberal Unionist he belonged to much the smaller of the two parties in the Unionist alliance; he was known to be out of sympathy with most Conservatives on a subject dear to their hearts, the Church of England; and on this and other grounds, many old-fashioned Conservatives still regarded him as an interloper. Chamberlain knew what some admirers could not understand: that the leadership was not his to seize.

Yet he also appreciated that the results of the election strengthened his ability to gain official Unionist commitment to his policy. The final electoral grist for his mill came with late returns from the environs of Birmingham. The Handsworth division of Staffordshire and Austen's constituency of East Worcestershire reelected their Unionist representatives with increased majorities. Fortified by these results, Joe wrote to Balfour, seeking to confer about the temporary leadership of the party in the Commons pending Balfour's return at a by-election. There were important corollaries of the leadership, such as the appointment of whips, which Chamberlain raised. But he indicated that his primary concern was with policy rather than personal leadership.

Balfour, at home in Scotland, refused to be hurried into conference. He sought to detach questions of policy from the matter of the temporary leadership by assuming that it would devolve naturally upon Chamberlain. This reply reached Chamberlain along with news that one of the MPs for the City of London was vacating his seat to make way for Balfour. The need for a temporary leader was therefore likely to be short. But that development did not deflect Chamberlain from his course. He replied to Balfour that he would not even sit on the front bench if the party would not accept the main features of his policy. Insisting that Balfour meet him shortly in London, Chamberlain outlined two proposals he wanted to discuss. One was for a meeting of the parliamentary party to indicate its wishes on fiscal policy. His second proposal was for reform of the Conservative party organization, partly through amalgamation—except in Birmingham—with the Liberal Unionist organization and the Tariff Reform League, and partly through democratization along Liberal Unionist lines. He wanted to introduce 'our system of voluntary workers chosen from the working classes and [get] rid of the existing system of privilege for subscribers and so called men of influence'.[4]

Meanwhile Chamberlain kept in touch with close supporters through John Boraston at Liberal Unionist headquarters. Balfour, he insisted, 'is the only leader with whom we can hope to win, but we cannot win with him unless he is willing to move to meet us. . . . It would be an absolute waste of my life to go on for another five or six years'—the probable lifetime of the new Parliament—'to find myself at the end in the same sort of position in which we have struggled during the last two years.'[5] Balfour felt much the same, though from the opposite side. When Lord Balcarres, one of the party whips, told Balfour that the majority of the party preferred him to Chamberlain as leader but would also prefer 'to go for Joe's fiscal scheme rather than for mine', Balfour confessed 'to feeling some reluctance in remaining leader'.[6]

Word of the impending confrontation between the two men reached Unionist peers and MPs, including many of the defeated as they gathered in London for the opening of the new Parliament. They divided into three schools, turning the Carlton Club into 'a hotbed of intrigue'.[7] At one end were pure Conservatives such as the current Lord Salisbury and traditional Whigs such as Lord Lansdowne, who urged Balfour to stand firm. Salisbury recoiled from tariff reform as 'an effort to drive the Conservative elements of our society into a policy of far-reaching change'.[8] Lansdowne had learned from the previous Lord Salisbury that the business of a party in opposition was simply to oppose the incumbent government. As Lansdowne put it to Balfour, '[w]ith a majority of over 200 against us, we are—for the moment, at all events—relieved of the necessity of bringing forward a constructive policy of our own'.[9] At the other end of the spectrum, men such as Ridley and Leo Maxse did what they could to elevate Chamberlain to the leadership. But most of the parliamentary party fell somewhere between these two stools. Even Henry Chaplin shrank from a rupture with Balfour.

The conference between the two leaders was set for the evening of 2 February. Chamberlain expected Balfour to 'advance in his direction'.[10] He was taken aback to find Balfour heading the opposite way. Balfour disagreed with the common assumption that support for tariff reform among Unionists in the new House of Commons was more extensive than in the old. He was more averse than ever to food taxes and a general tariff. Echoing Lord Lansdowne, Balfour argued that tariff reform would not be practical politics in the lifetime of this Parliament and perhaps even the next.

The rebuff steeled Chamberlain. He insisted on a meeting of the parliamentary party to ascertain its thinking. If the outcome went contrary to his views, he planned to organize the tariff reformers as a distinct parliamentary group among the Unionists, with its own whips. But the assurance with which Balfour held his ground led Chamberlain to raise his estimate of the strength of party loyalty as against fiscal conviction. This lesson was reinforced by Unionist reaction to the reported failure of the conference. It provoked sharp *ad hominem* argument, from which Balfour emerged better than his challenger.

To clear the air, Chamberlain issued a manifesto. It began by reasserting that 'in no circumstances would [he] be a candidate for the leadership of the Unionist party'.[11] Having thus sought to dispose of the personal issue, he made the question of policy equally clear. He identified the disagreement between Balfour's fiscal policy and that of tariff reformers as essentially twofold: over 'a moderate duty on corn' for imperial preference, and over a general tariff for retaliatory use against foreign duties on British goods. If Balfour would accept these requirements, Chamberlain assured him of 'hearty support' from tariff reformers. But Chamberlain warned that, if the party decided to put fiscal reform aside, committed tariff reformers would organize themselves for independent action. He also connected tariff reform with 'the necessary revenue' for social reform.

Before this manifesto was published, Balfour conceded Chamberlain's demand for a party meeting in principle but stressed the problems that would arise in practice. Hitherto the parliamentary party had met only to ratify recommendations from the leaders, not to thrash things out itself. Chamberlain responded that surely some form of words could be found to give the meeting a choice between the policies of the two leaders without mentioning their names. But try though he might, there was no way to separate policy from leadership. As Balfour pointed out, the parliamentary party could not reject either policy without expressing lack of confidence in the leader associated with it. Staunch tariff reformers fortified Balfour's argument by telling Chamberlain that 'if we pass our resolution at the Party Meeting',[12] they would want him to take over as leader of the Unionist party. But they also warned him that they did not want to operate in the new Parliament as a separate camp. Disconcerted by these reactions, Chamberlain prepared to lie low in Parliament and concentrate his energies elsewhere, particularly on party organization, where Balfour promised to be more cooperative.

With help from Austen, Joe tried to draft a resolution on fiscal policy which Balfour and he might recommend jointly to the party meeting. The Chamberlains sought 'to prevent any wider severance between Balfourites & T[ariff]. Reformers while putting in a wedge between Balfourites & Free Fooders who insist on committing themselves against a general tariff and against any tax on corn.'[13] Presented to Balfour as 'the charter of our cooperation',[14] the resolution was drawn 'almost verbatim' from Balfour's speeches. It committed the Unionist party to fiscal reform 'to secure more equal terms of competition for British trade and closer commercial union with the Colonies'. While the resolution did not endorse a general tariff and a duty on foreign corn, it treated them as reasonable means towards the desired ends.

Despite the careful crafting of the resolution, Chamberlain was not surprised when Balfour put off responding to it until he had addressed his prospective constituents in the City of London. In that address Balfour put his own stamp on the case for tariff reform, keeping his distance from a corn tax or a general tariff. But as always, his speech lacked fire, and it irritated those with strong convictions, free fooders as well as tariff reformers. He arranged to meet afterwards in conference with the two Chamberlains. He reinforced himself by including his brother Gerald, Lord Lansdowne, and the loyal chiefs at Conservative party headquarters, Akers Douglas and Acland Hood.

Balfour and his allies argued stiffly against the resolution which the two Chamberlains wanted to present to the party meeting. The conferees did not make headway at their first meeting on 13 February or when they reconvened next day, until Austen suggested turning the resolution into an exchange of letters between his father and Balfour. Joe agreed to the proposal and to a brief recess for the purpose, but with little hope. The format of an exchange of letters, however, removed Balfour's most serious objections, which were less to the substance of the resolution than to the procedure of asking the party meeting to make a choice. Akers Douglas and Acland Hood made a few modifications to the fiscal commitment. As amended, it steered clear of 'artificial protection against legitimate competition', and it placed the burden of proving the necessity for a general tariff and a corn tax on their advocates.[15] With those changes, Balfour agreed to the exchange of letters. They carried the day's date: Valentine's Day. Joe accepted the agreement with pleasure.

To everyone but Balfour, the Valentine compact looked like a victory for Chamberlain. The circle of tariff reformers who met with him that night were overjoyed by the turn of events. Chaplin called it 'the greatest political triumph since . . . Disraeli captured the Conservative Party'[16]—but of course Chaplin was glad to escape the necessity of choosing between Chamberlain and the regular party leader. On the other side, those in the Cecil clan were horrified at the 'surrender by Arthur', and were not persuaded by his own claim that it was 'a surrender by Joe'.[17] The Unionist peers, MPs and defeated candidates who convened next day for the party meeting read the exchange of letters in the morning papers; and they greeted Chamberlain with enthusiasm. The meeting passed a motion of continued confidence in Balfour as leader apathetically but unanimously; and that was the only resolution made at the meeting. Opposition to the substance of Balfour's fiscal commitments in the Valentine's accord was minimal. The protests of Devonshire and Hugh Cecil were received with conspicuous annoyance.

Yet Hicks Beach later observed that Balfour had written nothing which a free trader could not bring himself to accept. Before the year was over, the Valentine letters would be used by the old guard who were still in control at party headquarters to freeze rather than facilitate discussion of a corn tax and general tariff.

Chamberlain did not foresee this possibility. He hoped that the Valentine compact 'finally closed the chapter of ambiguities and explanations' and cleared the way 'to secure a definite issue on the fiscal question at the next election'.[18] The committee Balfour promised to appoint on combined Conservative and Liberal Unionist party reorganization led Chamberlain to think of reducing the Tariff Reform League to 'an office for statistics & information'.[19] Yet his confidence in the new accord was not robust. The three weeks and all the unpleasantness it had taken to bring Balfour round deprived the entente of true cordiality.

Stand-off again

Two months after the two men signed their 'charter', one of their junior colleagues, Arnold-Forster, compared the two. He felt that Chamberlain was 'in touch with the real public of this country. His whole view of public life seems to me far wider & far truer than A.J.B's.' But Arnold-Forster was worried that 'J.C. is getting old, & is naturally enough a little disappointed by the terrible set-back of the elections. His courage is wonderful and admirable; but I can't help feel he is tired of organizing, tired of the detail . . . & for these reasons not likely to break up this lamentable dualism which is playing the mischief with our Party.'[20]

Chamberlain was indeed feeling his age. He saw little prospect of breaking down the governing majority in the Commons in less than three years, a long time for a man approaching his seventieth birthday. The prospects were further darkened by the 'exceptional prosperity' which Britain by his own admission was experiencing.[21] Sometimes he admitted feeling 'near to the end of a very active and strenuous career'.[22]

As soon as the post-electoral negotiations subsided, he came down with influenza. Balfour too was stricken with illness; and the enforced absence of the Unionist leaders from the House of Commons did nothing to restore harmony in the party. The Duke of Devonshire warned the House of Lords that Chamberlain's proposals were as socialistic as anything proposed by Labour: tariff reform would enable the state to 'tell us where we are to buy, where we are to sell, what commodities we are to manufacture at home, and what we may . . . import'.[23] Chamberlain made so much trouble over the terms of the fiscal amendment to be moved from the Unionist benches in the Commons that one of the whips felt sure the party would split. George Wyndham, a Balfour loyalist in the former ministry who switched allegiance to Chamberlain after the election, presented an amendment to give tariff reformers a chance to make their case. The government delayed debate on Wyndham's motion until the Unionist leaders were well enough to attend, then diverted debate by raising a free-trade motion from the Liberal side of the House, and finally forced Wyndham's motion to a vote without discussion. Acland Hood did not want to serve in his official capacity as chief whip for the vote on Wyndham's motion. Austen Chamberlain had to rouse Balfour from his room outside the Commons chamber to push Acland Hood into line. A few of the free-trading Unionists including Lord Robert Cecil voted with the government against Wyndham's motion, and others abstained, while waverers followed the reluctant chief whip in supporting the motion. The split allowed Acland Hood to claim that the free-trading contingent in the Commons was larger than Chamberlain allowed. Balfour parried Chamberlain's rebuttal by claiming that there had really not been a vote on Wyndham's motion at all.

Though enervated by this continued infighting at home, Chamberlain remained the imperial statesman best known in the colonies. That reputation gave him opportunities which neither Balfour nor the Liberal ministers officially in charge at the Colonial Office enjoyed. The colonial conference due to meet in 1906 was put off for a year. Chamberlain still trusted that it would demonstrate the colonial desire for imperial preference in trade. He was irritated by the persistent refusal of the Liberal government in Canada to reaffirm its agreement. But the feeble imperialism of the Canadians made the overture he received from the prime minister of Australia, Alfred Deakin, all the more welcome. An outspoken advocate of imperial preference, Deakin sought Chamberlain's advice on how to express 'our convictions' at the coming year's conference.[24] Chamberlain responded proudly as 'the undoubted leader of the movement for Tariff Reform and Preference in this country'.[25] He advised Deakin to arrange for a detailed study of the reciprocal benefits the colonies and the mother country would gain from imperial preference. Chamberlain made preparations for a corresponding statement from the British side by the Tariff Commission.

He did not make such effective use of his opportunities in the House of Commons. Nowhere was his loosening grip more apparent. Once the sharpest in the House, his edge had been dulled by disuse since 1903 when he left that sphere to Balfour. MPs complained that Chamberlain addressed the Commons as if it were another of his public meetings. He was slow to understand the temper of the new House, with its horde of inexperienced Liberal backbenchers. Balfour fared worse with his philosophical word games; but that was little consolation to Chamberlain. He was put off by the disrespect and sometimes derision with which the Liberal majority treated him. He no longer argued tightly, he could not always find the right word, and his voice was sometimes hard to make out.

Gradually, however, on the subject of education which first brought him into politics, Chamberlain began to impress the new House with his old acumen. The subject threatened again to accentuate the foreignness of a Unitarian leading a party of Established Churchmen. But Chamberlain devised a strategy that improved his cooperation with Balfour, impressed all but the most ecclesiastical Unionists on the

backbenches, and made the government pause. The government
brought in a bill to remove the offence its Nonconformist supporters
felt under the Education Act of 1902 which authorized local tax support
for denominational schools. Yet the government failed to escape from
the religious dilemma that bedevilled English education. The Education
bill of 1906 reversed the offence of 1902 by requiring local taxpayers to
support nondenominational religious education acceptable to most
Nonconformists but not to dogmatic Anglicans. Inconsistent in applying
even that principle, the bill sought to pacify the Irish by authorizing
local tax support for denominational schools where four-fifths of the
local citizenry subscribed to one denomination, a preponderance rare
outside Catholic Ireland. Chamberlain cut through the conundrum by
returning to his original principles on the subject. He proposed to confine tax support to secular education, making religious education voluntary though encouraged by the state. His proposal was unlikely to
satisfy church-loving Unionists as a permanent solution; but it served
their purposes for the moment by exposing the injustice of the Liberal
bill. That bill dominated debate in the Commons through June. Hence
education was the subject of Chamberlain's last speech there, as it had
been of his first.

It was not the only old issue to which he was pulled back in these
months. The electoral potential of Labour stirred thought in both major
parties but did not carry either of them far. The government resorted to
two measures in its first year, one of them flattering to Chamberlain.
They extended the terms of his Workmen's Compensation Act. They
also undertook to protect trade union funds from their liability under
the Taff Vale decision to pay compensation for losses to industry from
strike action. No longer a pacesetter in this sphere, Chamberlain
thought that both measures went too far. He feared that the first, by
reducing the period of time before compensation became due from two
weeks to one, would prove hard on industry and discourage thrift and
self-reliance among labour. The second would place trade unions in a
legal position of irresponsible privilege. He took care, nevertheless,
to allow Labour to have its way on these issues, leaving the Liberal
government to bear any blame for excess generosity.

His stand on these measures was not constructive; and his thinking
on the increasingly pressing subject of old-age pensions did not advance. Sticking to his self-financing schemes of former years, he denounced 'anything in the nature of a universal old-age pension' as
'impracticable from the point of view of expense . . . and undesirable
from the point of view of its influence upon thrift and industry'.[26] None
the less, moved by the electoral needs of his campaign for tariffs, he
began to think of yet 'another "unauthorized programme" which will
show how that in the matters of social reform our party is ahead'[27] of

the Liberals. He turned for suggestions to the political leaders of New Zealand and Australia who combined imperial commitment to preferential tariffs with domestic commitment to social insurance and arbitration of industrial disputes.

He did not find anything concrete to recommend for Britain. But at the end of June he indicated the lines on which he wanted his party to move forward. Speaking to Unionist MPs from the old Parliament and the new, he admitted that his social policy over the past two years had been inadequate. He urged them to think of socialism as admirable in objective, however misguided in method, and discussed the financing of welfare legislation. Extensions in social insurance would require 'extension of the basis of our taxation'.[28] That necessity brought him to fiscal reform. There were good ways and bad to extend the national tax base. Tariffs were the best because they involved 'the least interference' with the trade from which the country derived its wealth. The next 'unauthorized programme' would be protective of industry as well as responsive to labour and all the while imperial.

In order to propel Unionists forward along these lines, Chamberlain had to make good on the Valentine compact. The most pressing task was to nourish the popular roots of the party's organizational machinery. But Balfour's prolonged illness, which he nursed through the spring, left this matter 'hanging fire', to Chamberlain's annoyance. The business of reorganization was frustrated by Acland Hood, who selected Chamberlain's old adversary Lord Londonderry to represent the Conservative leadership on the reorganization committee. In the brief private conferences which Chamberlain was able to secure with Balfour, he found that Balfour was 'opposed to our views, or at all events not eager to adopt them at the expense of a difference with Hood'.[29] When Lord Ridley suggested in despair that they scuttle the attempt to join up with the Conservative organization and channel their efforts once again through the Tariff Reform League, Chamberlain was inclined to agree. He extended his independence of action to the parliamentary arena, and appealed over the heads of the regular whips to younger members of the party in both Houses. By midsummer Acland Hood and his lieutenants regarded Chamberlain's doings with pre-Valentine hostility. Four months after it was signed, the compact served little purpose except to preserve decorum within the dual leadership.

Seizure by celebration

Like the oligarchs of the Renaissance Tuscan cities to which Chamberlain likened Birmingham, the businessmen-politicians who grouped themselves around him used civic celebrations to forward their purposes. For twenty-five years these celebrations revolved around Chamberlain personally as the city's leading citizen. They began in 1880 with the opening of Chamberlain Square between the old town hall and the new Council House. They continued in the spring of 1888 upon Chamberlain's election as the first honorary freeman of the recently elevated City of Birmingham, and again the next January with the reception for Mary and Joseph after their wedding. The celebrations assumed the proportions of a national spectacle upon the occasion of Chamberlain's departure on his mission to South Africa.

Before Easter in 1906, word reached the national press of planning in Birmingham to celebrate two anniversaries of Chamberlain together at the beginning of July, the thirtieth anniversary of his election to the House of Commons, actually on 7 June, and his seventieth birthday on 9 July. The first suggestion came from non-partisan civic sources and envisaged a celebration by the whole city. But Chamberlain's Liberal Unionist lieutenants were quick to demand a celebration designed to 'give encouragement to tariff reform'.[30] Chamberlain threw his personal weight on this side. He wanted Birmingham once again to be a show-case, this time of the difference that tariff reform could make to the Unionist party; he wanted the public to remember how Birmingham reversed the national tide in the general election. He did not recoil from the focus which the celebration would place on him personally. The collapsing Valentine accord showed that there was no escape from the issue of Unionist leadership. Birmingham displayed the difference the leadership of Chamberlain could make.

His insistence on a partisan rally induced the celebration's organizers in Birmingham to work 'upon a much more ambitious scale than was originally anticipated'.[31] A planning committee of twenty was set up. It included eight each from the Liberal Unionist and Conservative associations for the city plus the editors of the three local newspapers. It was presided over by Henry Payton, the goldsmith and jeweller who had been Chamberlain's friend for nearly fifty years and looked after his constituency interests in West Birmingham. Eventually fifteen sub-committees were appointed, one to select a commemorative medal, one for the motorcade, one for the festivities in each city party, and so forth, most of them chaired by a member of the City Council. The plans for July spread over a long weekend: Saturday for the civic celebration, Sunday a day of rest though it was Chamberlain's actual birthday, and Monday for the political rally. The Tariff Reform League planned simultaneous demonstrations elsewhere in England.

Ever more elaborate in their plans for Birmingham, the organizers crammed the weekend with spectacles and speeches, prizes and parades. Chamberlain's recurrent ill-health might have prompted him to restrain the enthusiasts. But the signs that time was running out for him only quickened his pace. Down with flu in the first half of March, he was stricken again in April with gout while holidaying on the Riviera. A visitor who had not seen Chamberlain for four years was struck by the change in his appearance when he welcomed his constituents to a party in the grounds of Highbury at the beginning of June: 'His face wore a parchment look, and his handshake was feeble.'[32] A week later he had a brief attack of gout, and at the beginning of July a cold. Yet he threw himself into his engagements with gusto. Sitting beside Chamberlain at a dinner for the Unionist parliamentarians he was about to address, Sir Herbert Maxwell 'could not but wonder at the freedom with which he ate, drank and smoked large cigars. "My friend," thought I to myself, "it is hardly possible that you can escape paying smartly for this." '[33] Instead of arranging to take things easy after the Birmingham festivities, Chamberlain accepted a string of engagements for the following days to work up support at home and abroad, with the Tariff Commission, the Liberal Unionist Council, the executive of the Tariff Reform League, a delegation from the Canadian chambers of commerce, and an agricultural audience in Kent.

The festivities in Birmingham started a day early, on Friday 7 July, at the educational institutions which Chamberlain had built up. Commemorative medals were distributed to all the elementary schoolchildren, who cheered the former chair of the school board. Faculty and students at a University of Birmingham degree-day congregation sent congratulations to the founder. Saturday morning the flower-sellers did a brisk business in artificial orchids. The railway companies ran special cheap trains to Birmingham from all parts of the Midlands. By noon the factories as well as the shops of the city closed so that their employees could enjoy the events of the afternoon and evening. The city centre was dense with crowds by the time Chamberlain arrived, modern as ever in a motor car, at the steps of the Council House for the select civic luncheon with which the celebrations formally began.

There was something truly moving about the civic celebration that Saturday. As Chamberlain entered the Council House, he was greeted by his lieutenants from past battles. Liberals who had left him over Home Rule stood alongside those who had followed him through every stage in his evolution. At the end of the luncheon, Chamberlain rose to speak but for a moment could not. 'However strenuously,' he started . . . and could not go on. Whether from a surge of feeling or excess of strain, he stood with tears in his eyes while his comrades reassured him with cheers. When he regained his voice, the level of feeling remained high as he expressed his 'pride and thankfulness that, with the greater part of my life behind me—an open book which all of you may read and criticise—I yet have been able to retain the distinction which I have most coveted and which I most prize—the affectionate regard of those amongst whom I live.'[34] He spoke of their remarkable civic accomplishment in the 'struggle with disease, the provision . . . for health, for recreation, and for everything which contributes to raise the standard of life and increase the happiness of the masses of the population'. He concluded by describing the relationship that united him to the city:

> I feel that if I have been permitted to serve this community no man has ever had more generous masters. They have been my teachers also. What I am, for good or for ill, they have made me—this city of my adoption and of my affection. It has been the home of strong convictions, of great ideals, of frank expression, of earnest endeavour to carry out its ideals, and I have tried to interpret what I believe to be the spirit of the town; and I have found in the affection of my own people an overwhelming reward for a strenuous life of work and contest.

His account of the relationship was borne out during the day. After leaving the Council House, Chamberlain was driven at the head of a motorcade through seventeen miles of cheering crowds to one after another of seven parks in the city. Each park put on a display of local talent—marching drill by schoolboys and maypole dancing by schoolgirls, athletic and aquatic displays, choirs, jugglers and puppet shows—to entertain the people till Chamberlain arrived. The streets along which he drove were decked with bunting, windows with flowers and flags. Householders linked their homes with streamers and garlands. The poorer districts were particularly dense with colour. As he drove into sight, the crowds called out familiarly, 'Good ol' Joe'. The residents of Sladefield Lane ran a banner across their street: 'From lies, hypocrisy, and deceit, Joey, deliver us.' The townspeople and their champion basked in mutual appreciation. 'We know what Joey wants!' cried someone in Calthorpe Park, at which Chamberlain, 'in a half-confidential, half-ironical tone, replied, "Yes, and I generally manage to get it."' At nightfall the festivities came to an end in all seven parks with fireworks, the display in each park ending with a dazzling orchid which turned into a portrait of Chamberlain.

The Saturday celebrations were unmistakably popular, and the mood was mellow. The spirit on Monday was militant. The plans were tighter and more calculating. The events of Monday, as a regular working day, had to be compressed into the evening. Still, it was to be a long one; and the pubs were encouraged to stay open past their usual closing time to refresh the marching torch-bearers before they headed home. The focal event of the evening was a rally which Chamberlain would address in Bingley Hall, the enormous arena where Gladstone inaugurated the National Liberal Federation in 1877. Every detail of the programme was carefully considered. The chairman of the city's

Conservative association, Sir Francis Lowe, was selected instead of a Liberal Unionist to preside at the rally in order to impress the stamp of Chamberlain and tariff reform on the larger partner in the Unionist alliance nationally. Balfour sensed the intent, and sent only a grudging letter of support for Lowe to issue to the press.

Five thousand men who would later serve as torch-bearers, some of them students from the university, assembled at the beginning of the evening in the drill-hall and some of the city schools. Then they marched off, six abreast, to take up their assigned positions on the route along which Chamberlain would ride at the conclusion of the rally. In place of the usual marching command, they kept in step to the call of 'Joe, Joe, Joe'. The crowds waiting outside Bingley Hall for Chamberlain to arrive worked themselves up with a rhythmic chant, familiar in Birmingham, of 'Where's Joe?' which turned into 'Here's Joe!' at the first glimpse of him. Inside, the audience of nine or ten thousand had no time for anyone but Joe. They greeted him with an explosion of cheers, and then sang, to the familiar tune,

> We'll follow Joe
> Through Weal and Woe
> For the sake of Auld Lang Syne.
>
> His blows are like the stroke of steel
> His words like burning wine;
> For England's fame he plays the game
> Like the kings of Auld Lang Syne.

Deputations from 115 organizations proceeded up to the platform where they handed Chamberlain addresses of congratulation from all over the kingdom and many points in the empire. Once this procession had passed and 'Rule Britannia' had been sung, he spoke.

In contrast to his civic address on Saturday, this speech was forward-looking and full of fight. He heralded his final 'unauthorized programme'. Pursuing the lines he laid out the previous month, he enunciated the two distinguishing principles of what he called 'the Birmingham school'. Each principle he sharpened by identifying its enemies. The first principle was readiness to use the powers of the state to promote the welfare of the country. It was an essentially Radical principle, the same one that underlay his Radical Programme of 1884–5. As then, so now, he meant to put the principle into practice only modestly. He liked tariffs because they involved the least governmental interference with trade. Yet as in 1885, so now, he presented the principle provocatively. He rejoiced in the 'bitter opposition' which his unauthorized programmes invariably met from 'the descendants and representatives of the old Whig party' led by the Duke of Devonshire. Though Chamberlain invidiously singled out Whigs as the 'superior persons' who always opposed him, his words could be applied to the Cecils and Lord Londonderry. Free traders all, they were 'against the Factory Acts ... against trades unions—they were in favour of unlimited competition—they would buy everything in the cheapest market, and especially labour'.[35]

The rationale for this rhetoric was to appeal to labour. But Chamberlain had a point to make and a bone to pick in that direction also. The working class had to be wooed away from its self-appointed spokesmen in the Labour party. The second principle Chamberlain enunciated for the Birmingham school was readiness to strengthen the empire. Labour MPs disparaged the empire. But Chamberlain knew that the working men of Birmingham were militantly patriotic: 'never in our history has Birmingham sympathised with the Little Englander'. The results of the general election indicated that the rest of England did not always feel the same. Still, he insisted that the anti-imperialism of the Labour party was not representative of the working class: 'never yet in our history, or in the history of the British race, has the great democracy been unpatriotic'.

He bound the two principles of the Birmingham school together by praising the capacity of the imperial state to rise above the selfish interests of the individual to meet the needs of the country. He spoke first of international power: 'England without an empire ... would be a fifth-rate nation, existing on the sufferance of its more powerful neighbours.' But in the final analysis, his heart stayed at home. His primary objective was 'national prosperity'. By that he did not mean merely 'a greater aggregation of national wealth which ... may never be properly distributed'. The prosperity of the nation would be insecure without co-operation between industrialists and labour. That had always been his message. The object of tariff reform, as he presented it for the last time, was to 'secure for the masses of the industrial population in this country constant employment at fair wages'.

His voice flagged towards the end of his speech; and he concluded it with a string of premonitions that he might not be able to implement the unauthorized programme he foreshadowed. He wondered aloud whether these words might be the last that he uttered in public, and whether he would 'live to congratulate you upon our common triumph'. He ended with a couplet:

> Others I doubt not, if not we,
> The issue of our toil shall see.

He was carried home that night on the same river of fire that sent him on his way to South Africa. The torch-bearers who lined his route swung in behind his carriage as it passed. They followed it in waves separated by marching bands. At the entrance to Cannon Hill Park, the marchers threw their torches on to a mounting bonfire and headed in for the final display of fireworks, while Chamberlain and Mary drove on to Highbury along streets lit by Chinese lanterns. The celebration ended with an aeronaut in a balloon a thousand feet over the city igniting a nine hundred square foot 'Fire Portrait' of the incomparable leader.

He took the afternoon train to London next day for a midweek meeting with the Tariff Commission, the first of his engagements to sustain the momentum from the celebrations in Birmingham. After receiving further congratulations from the commission, he opened discussion of its report on agriculture. Then he hurried off for another meeting before returning home, tired and unusually flushed, for tea with Mary. After a warm bath, he was dressing for dinner when he suffered a stroke. It paralysed his right side. He fell to the ground but remained all too aware of what was happening. When Mary, who wondered what was keeping him, came to the door behind which he had been dressing, he dragged himself over to open it. But his active life had closed.

Drawing upon diminished force

Later that year, while impressions of Chamberlain remained vivid, a journalist noted that 'the spell he lays on men . . . is singularly impersonal. People think of him rather as a force than as a man.'[36] While the man sat encased in 'a palsied frame, watching undimmed from afar the conflict which [he] had hitherto inspired and controlled',[37] his family and supporters sought to make what they could of his inimitable force.

As soon as Mary realized what had happened, she sent word to their hosts for the evening, saying that she—not Joe—had been taken ill. After examining Chamberlain, his doctor confirmed Mary's fear. Chamberlain had indeed suffered a stroke. He had lost the use of his right side. His foot and leg dragged. He could not hold a pen in his hand or the famous monocle in his eye. His voice had so thickened that it was hard to make out. The doctor held out hope of recovery, given immediate rest and eventual exercise. But at best Chamberlain would be out of commission for many months.

The family kept the diagnosis from the public. They issued a statement that he had suffered an unusually severe attack of gout. The family's deception arose from their knowledge that Chamberlain's personal resources were crucial to his cause. He was also of consuming importance to his family. Apart from Ethel who had gone and Neville whose time had not yet come, all of them felt unable to flourish unless warmed by his flame. Now that it could only flicker, they denied that it had lost any of its brightness, which they bent all their efforts to restore.

As custodians of the flame, they also modified its light, which was in any case changed by immobility. The words which used to flow from Chamberlain came out in often unintelligible grunts. The stroke rigidified his politics along with his body. 'If you don't give in,' he observed during his years of paralysis, 'something always happens.'[38] The only way he felt able to make things happen now was by not giving in. That tendency was confirmed by his main custodians, Mary and Austen. Both were by nature conservative, Mary the Brahmin Episcopalian from Boston, and Austen a retiring gentleman at heart. Though they did their best to transmit Joe's missives to the outside world, the message rarely came through with Radical edge. Mary even turned Joe into a patron of Church of England charities.

Austen found his trusteeship for Joe difficult. The tension between the aggressive tactics his father pushed him to adopt and his own pacific inclinations left Austen prone to illness. He surrendered what little independence he had previously acquired vis-à-vis his father, and received no reward for his pains. He merely alienated his natural friends, the centrists in the party, without gaining much respect from the 'whole-hoggers' who never found the father's light in the son's eyes. In the spring of 1906, at the age of forty-two, after a whirlwind courtship, Austen announced his engagement to the daughter of a retired army officer. He was thus about to move under a roof of his own, when his father was struck down. Joe's absence from the marriage, which went ahead on 21 July, gave the public its first intimation that his illness was serious. When Austen returned from his honeymoon in September, he attempted to assume the leadership of the tariff reform movement, including the Tariff Reform League, which he had not previously joined. He felt obliged to identify himself entirely with his father and serve as his surrogate.

By the beginning of August, Joe was able to communicate through his private secretary with Hewins, who took charge of the Tariff Commission. He was taken for carriage rides through Battersea Park away from the eyes of his neighbours in Kensington, most of whom in any case were on holiday by this time. In mid-September he made the trip from Princes Gardens to Highbury. He escaped notice until the train reached Snow Hill station in Birmingham.

There the familiar face was glimpsed in a wheelchair, quickening suspicions of the extent of Chamberlain's illness. The family issued a statement ascribing the wheelchair to a sprained ankle. Within less than a week, however, they had to announce his withdrawal from all of his engagements for the autumn. Austen still claimed that there was 'nothing that need cause his [father's] friends any disquietude'[39]. But enough had been seen at Snow Hill to make the rumours about Joe's condition fairly accurate. In mid-October he asked Mary to advise Ridley at the Tariff Reform League not to 'delay any action in order to consult him'.[40]

Ardent tariff reformers lost patience. The flow of funds to the Tariff Commission had dried up as soon as Joe was stricken. Garvin cast about for someone more rousing than Austen to take over the leadership of their cause. Milner spoke out on behalf of the social imperialism proclaimed by Joe in his last speech; but Austen defeated an attempt to replace Ridley with Milner in the chair of the Tariff Reform League. Another leader of the movement, Sir Joseph Lawrence, alluded publicly to the suspicion of a conspiracy at Highbury 'to mislead the people as to the real state of Mr. Chamberlain's health'.[41]

When Austen left Highbury for the new year's session of Parliament, Joe encouraged him to act as leader of the committed tariff reformers, 'with or *without* Mr. Balfour',[42] and to extend their aggressive tactics to subjects including education on which Balfour favoured peace. Joe then went in Mary's custody to the south of France in search of sun. She took pains to avoid public notice on their way through London to the coast. But her precautions only deepened suspicion. Before their departure, Balfour secured from a cardiologist an assessment of Chamberlain's condition based on a photograph. It was enough to indicate that his right side was paralysed with little hope of recovery now that half a year had elapsed since the stroke. The warmth of France did not save Joe from recurrent gout, invariably accompanied by depression.

At home, however, the prospects for tariff reform improved. The long-discussed and delayed Colonial Conference, now called Imperial, was convened. Its pace was set by the colonies led by Deakin of Australia. Overcoming considerable reluctance from Laurier, they called for imperial tariff preference, to which the British ministers responded with blank hostility. Chamberlain pressed Halsbury in the Lords as well as Austen in the Commons to censure the government. But to his delight, Balfour took this step without prompting.

After the conference Deakin reported to the man he still regarded as the imperial leader. Unimpressed by Balfour and sure from Australian experience that the social dimension of tariff reform was as vital as the imperial, Deakin said that Chamberlain's return to active leadership was indispensable. In a long response dictated to his daughter Ida, Chamberlain interpreted the recent developments differently. To begin with, he explained that he would never be able to throw himself into public life as completely as in the past. He reconciled himself to this prospect because the Imperial Conference and its reception among Unionists led him to conclude somewhat ruefully that his cause did better in his absence, when attention was not diverted by 'the personal feeling & abuse' which he aroused.[43]

These conclusions were confirmed when he returned to England in June. His incapacity was apparent to observers at the Channel; and Mary no longer tried to hide him. When he reached Birmingham, a crowd of his fellow townsmen were waiting for him; and they were moved by the obvious difficulty he had in raising his hat to acknowledge their cheers. Willing to be open about his disability and longing to be in touch with the political world, he returned after a few days to London, and saw visitors including Balfour for the first time since his stroke. That autumn the National Union of Conservative Associations met for its annual conference in Birmingham. Balfour used the occasion to turn Chamberlain's unauthorized programme into official party policy, known thereafter as 'the Birmingham programme'. In principle Balfour endorsed the social as well as imperial dimensions of tariff reform, and he moved towards protectionism. After speaking to the conference, he visited Chamberlain at Highbury and reinforced his public speech with private words of commitment to tariff reform. Chamberlain subsequently pressed 'whole-hog' tariff reformers who were still rebellious to curb their hostility to Balfour for the common good.

The promising political outlook turned even better over the winter. The recession to which Chamberlain had candidly looked forward for the past four years set in. Unemployment approached ten per cent in 1908 for the first time in a generation. The prospects for tariff reform rose even faster than the economy declined. By the summer Acland Hood was refusing assistance from party headquarters to candidates who declined to accept preference and a general tariff.

But meanwhile Chamberlain's health deteriorated; and his inability to ride the political wave accentuated his personal depression. Even on days when he could speak clearly, his voice sounded like 'some clumsy mechanical contrivance'.[44] Friends had mixed reactions about visiting him, saddened 'to see that sort of power nearing its end'.[45] Chamberlain admitted to his old friend Collings that 'recovery is very slow, and I have been rather discouraged of late'.[46] To shield himself from the feeling of uselessness, he declined to pay attention to the news Mary relayed to him from the outside world. She had difficulty securing political advice for Austen when he sought it. Joe's secretary could not bring correspondence to his attention. Trying to write with his left hand, Joe scrawled a note to Mary and then looked at it with embarrassment: 'This letter is worse than a child's,' he added; 'I am ashamed of it.'[47]

Only a fight could draw him out of his private world. His one political action in the early weeks of 1909, before Mary took him to Cannes, was to support an effort to expel all Unionist free-trading MPs and in particular Lord Robert Cecil from the next Parliament. When papers arrived with news of the budget presented by Lloyd George as Chancellor of the Exchequer, Chamberlain refused to have the speech read out to him verbatim and contented himself with a summary. But as soon as he grasped the implications of the budget, he and Mary left Cannes for London. Lloyd George had come up with an alternative to tariff reform. In order to meet the demands on the Treasury for social services and the armed forces without resorting to tariffs, he jacked up the income and inheritance taxes on the wealthy and introduced new taxes to fall on major owners of land.

Looking stronger after his stay in Cannes, Chamberlain did what he could to precipitate a fight. On Empire Day, 24 May, he issued a letter, his longest public statement since his stroke, to make the most of an offer from New Zealand, belittled by the British government, to contribute £2 per head from its small population towards the cost of a dreadnought for the imperial navy. The same day he had Garvin, the leading journalist of tariff reform, over for lunch. He sought the service of Garvin's pen to rouse the House of Lords to reject Lloyd George's budget. It was an audacious proposition. The man who scourged the House of Lords in 1884 for exercising its undoubted right to delay passage of the third Reform bill now wanted the Lords to resurrect a defunct right to reject a finance bill. When Garvin pointed out the dangers, Chamberlain dismissed them and exhilarated him with 'his cool and resolute will'. Despite his 'smothered' speech, Chamberlain expressed himself with humour that made his luncheon guests 'shout with laughter'.[48] He felt sure that the inevitable Liberal appeal of 'the peers versus the people' could be countered as Salisbury did in 1884, by pointing out that the peers were merely forcing the government to consult the people through a general election.

The physical strength Chamberlain gained at Cannes did not last long, and his political judgement had lost some of its edge. He did not look well when he returned to Birmingham after his lunch with Garvin. He also failed to keep his distance from the property defence associations which sprang up during the summer, shifting the emphasis in the campaign against the budget away from tariff reform towards self-defence by the owners of wealth.

His influence nevertheless revived through the efforts of others. Little had been done to mark his birthday since the tragic festivities of 1906. But in 1909, accepting the fact that Chamberlain could not return to active leadership personally, the officers of the Tariff Reform League organized celebrations to keep his torch burning in the public eye. The idea occurred first to Lord Grey, Minto's successor as governor-general of Canada. Right after the seventieth birthday demonstrations but before learning of their unhappy consequence, Grey expressed the hope that 'every successive anniversary [of Chamberlain's birth would] be regarded & kept by British Imperialists all the world over as a day of rejoicing & of hope'.[49] A year later Kipling, on a visit to Canada, did what he could to foster a cult of Chamberlain, prophesying that

> Our children will tell their sons of the statesman who in the evening of his days, crowned with years and honour, beheld what our Empire might be made, who stepped aside from the sheep tracks of little politicians, who put from him ease, and comfort, and friendship, and lost even health itself, that he might inspire and lead the young generation to follow him along the new path.[50]

Acting in that spirit, the Tariff Reform League marked Chamberlain's birthday in 1909 with a banquet in the Albert Hall for nearly three thousand people. The hero of the occasion spent the day quietly at home in Birmingham, where he received a thousand letters and telegrams from all over the kingdom and empire (though least of all from Canada).

That autumn Chamberlain's course against the Liberal budget prevailed in all sections of the Unionist party. He continued to employ aggressive tactics. He was the last Unionist leader to endorse a compromise arrangement with Lord Robert Cecil in Marylebone, and he did not approve of extending the arrangement to other free-trading Unionist MPs. When Balfour came to Birmingham for a rally, he embraced tariff reform as the alternative to Lloyd George's budget but refrained from giving the Lords advice on what to do with it. Not so Chamberlain. In a letter read out at the rally, he urged the upper House 'to force a general election'.[51] When Balfour toyed with thoughts of compromise, Chamberlain deterred him. He moved to London to keep the Lords up to the mark. They duly threw the budget out, giving him the general election he asked for.

But by the time they did so, his confidence of victory was ebbing. Balfour contrived to use tariff reform as the best 'defence of the propertied classes against higher direct taxation'[52] rather than as a constructive alternative to the Liberal budget. Without quite identifying the distortion, Chamberlain sensed something wrong. The beginnings of economic recovery towards the end of the year did nothing to restore his confidence. In the midst of the election in January 1910, Amery found him 'rather pessimistic'.[53]

Yet he did all he could to win. If he could not speak in public, he could dictate messages. Within days of the Lords' rejection of the budget, he despatched a manifesto to the press on 'The National Crisis'.[54] Though he tried to turn the question from 'the peers versus the people' to 'tariff or budget', he felt obliged to give the constitutional question first place. But when Balfour devoted his electoral address almost entirely to the constitutional position of the Lords, Chamberlain saw the mistake and thereafter avoided it. His own electoral address summarized the case for tariff reform. It focused on the opportunity for 'closer union of the Empire'[55] and on domestic employment, though he offered nothing concrete by way of social reform.

Until the voting came to an end, the newspapers carried column after column of letters from Chamberlain to individual Unionist candidates in which he presented the points in the case for tariff reform which were pertinent to the particular candidate and constituency. Sometimes he spoke of the imperial need. More often he dwelt on the promise to restore industrial production and employment. He invested both themes with a sense of urgency. Liberals feared the effect of his letters enough to spread the rumour that they could not possibly be the work of the stricken old man in Highbury.

In print, none the less, his words failed to come across with the force he used to give them from the platform. Nor did they come to his mind with the former fluency. When Maxse and Garvin asked him for a final statement to publish on the eve of the voting, the best thing he could give them was excerpts from his former speeches. They still made stirring reading—'England without an Empire! England in that case would not be the England we love'[56]—yet they lacked the power of spoken oratory. Deprived of his voice, Chamberlain was no match for the titans of the Liberal party, particularly for Lloyd George who was rising to the heights of oratorical power. The Unionists lacked other great guns to back Chamberlain up. Balfour never moved the public, and the rising generation of Unionist orators such as F.E. Smith did not yet command national attention. The Liberals' David slung his stones against a Goliath already fallen.

Unravelling

Birmingham voted on the first day, not late in the election as in 1906. Chamberlain, unopposed in Birmingham West, was the first candidate to be elected to the new Parliament. Elsewhere in the city the Unionists won by their greatest margins ever. They went on in the rest of his electoral duchy to regain the dominance they lost in 1906. A Liberal in Yorkshire remarked sourly that if Chamberlain had proposed 'an expedition on aeroplanes to annex and colonize the planet Mars, the people of Birmingham would vote for him'.[57]

But Britain was not Birmingham. The election results in the country as a whole divided along regional lines. Nowhere else did Unionists prove as strong as in the West Midlands. They recovered from 1906 in the Southeast. But they failed to dent the Liberal strength in East Lancashire and West Yorkshire where textile manufacturing was prospering. The regional pattern was interwoven with a social one. Outside

Birmingham, where a record voter turnout expanded the Unionist victory, the working-class electorate reacted to tariff reform sceptically, particularly where it was identified with the propertied classes. Thus Unionists fared far better in predominantly middle-class constituencies than in the working-class districts of East London and the industrial North; and the Liberals profited generally from their continuing cooperation with the Labour party. The 'class feeling' which tariff reform, like all of Chamberlain's political prescriptions, was designed to neutralize proved stronger than the intended antidote. In total, almost as many Unionists as Liberals were elected to the new Parliament; but the Liberal alliance with Irish Nationalists as well as Labour kept the government in power.

The results of this election were more disappointing to Chamberlain than the worse ones of 1906. While he still persuaded himself that Unionist candidates who dwelt constructively on tariff reform fared better than those with a different emphasis, he saw no hope for improvement wherever the cotton and woollen trades were secure. After the election he told Hewins that 'we shall have to wait our time and to move slower than we expected'[58]—a hopeless prospect for a man of seventy-three in a wheelchair.

He left Birmingham at the beginning of February en route to Cannes, stopping in London just long enough to take the oath as a Member of the new Parliament. Margot Asquith, the sociable wife of the prime minister, called on him. In an attempt to show him some fellow feeling, she recalled an illness which made her feel '*so* ill that I thought I was *done*'. 'Better to *think* it, Mrs. Asquith,' Chamberlain replied, 'than to *know* it as I do.'[59] Afterwards, taking advantage of a quiet interval, Chamberlain was led into the Commons from behind the Speaker's chair. His voice was audible as he took his oath, but Austen had to sign for him. He asked to sit for a few minutes on the Treasury bench. Then he was led out, and left for Cannes.

He regretted the promptness of his departure from London, for soon afterwards the pace of politics quickened. Difficulties with the Irish placed the Liberals in danger of defeat in the Commons and thus raised the possibility of a Unionist minority government. Austen was inclined to agree with Balfour, who backed away from the opportunity, remembering the embarrassments Lord Salisbury endured when he formed his caretaker ministry in 1885. But Joe hoped to save the Unionists from a second election fought more explicitly than the last to uphold the House of Lords. He therefore wanted the Unionists to seize power if they could, to secure emergency funding particularly for old-age pensions in place of the budget which had not yet been enacted, and to dissolve Parliament swiftly for a second election fighting for tariff reform. If they could win even the slimmest of majorities, he hoped to push a tariff-reforming budget through: 'such a splendid policy', he told Balfour, '...is worth any effort'.[60]

Balfour came to Cannes to convalesce from the elections, which always made him sick. His first luncheon there with Chamberlain was not a success. Chamberlain's voice was muffled, and Balfour found him incomprehensible. Rescued by the arrival of a companion for golf, Balfour excused himself, to Mary's exasperation, by saying 'he understood that golf in Cannes had to be over before 5 so that they could get back in time for Baccarat at the Casino'.[61] To avoid such frivolity, Mary arranged the next meeting 'for 5 o'clock, when he will have finished his golf'.[62] When Balfour returned to London, Chamberlain sent him a quotation from Mirabeau, 'De l'audace, et toujours de l'audace'. But it came too late and in any case was not welcome.

From this point on, the cause to which Chamberlain had devoted himself unravelled. Asquith's government emerged solidly entrenched and intent on eliminating the veto power of the House of Lords. Chamberlain dreaded an election on this issue, and for once was not sure how to handle it. The constitutional issue eroded Unionist commitment to tariff reform. In the fight against Lloyd George's budget, most Unionist free traders including Hugh Cecil came to accept tariff reform as the lesser of two evils. But the general election in January turned things round. By confirming the Liberals in office, enabling them to enact their budget, encouraging them to move against the Lords, yet making their security in office dependent on the Irish, the results of the election made the original objective of Unionism, prevention of Home Rule, a more urgent concern than tariff reform.

Away from the corridors of power, Chamberlain withdrew into his private world. He proposed to retire from the House of Commons at the next general election, which was expected as soon as the government joined battle with the House of Lords over its reform. Mary despatched a plea to Austen for help, fearful that Joe would become 'a hopeless invalid with all incentive gone'.[63] Her anxiety was compounded by word from Neville that his father's finances had deteriorated seriously since his illness. Mary persuaded Neville to hide the situation from Joe as far as possible. What drained their pocket, she told Neville, was the effort to keep Joe in touch with the inner circles of politics—the house and entertaining in London as well as Birmingham—and the restorative villa in Cannes. Joe was all too ready to relapse by his hearth in Highbury; and his family could not reconcile themselves to that yet.

He was stirred by the accession in May of a new monarch, George V. With encouragement from Chamberlain when Colonial Secretary, George as Prince of Wales had visited all the major self-governing colonies, Australia, New Zealand, South Africa and Canada. Chamberlain wrote to him on the death of his father, encouraging him to cultivate those associations and thus make his monarchy 'the symbol of the Empire as a whole'.[64] Within days of Chamberlain's return to London, the new king came to Princes Gardens to see 'Joe', as he called him in his diary;[65] and they talked for more than an hour.

The talk between Chamberlain and the new king 'ranged over many things'.[66] They may have spoken about a proposed conference between the leaders of the two major parties to avert the impending clash over the House of Lords. Garvin had already discussed the possibility with Chamberlain, and thought he overcame Chamberlain's initial opposition. Some people thought his conversation with the king served the same end. The conference was agreed to, with Austen Chamberlain and Bonar Law participating along with Balfour from the Unionist side. Mary reported that Joe was 'much exercised in his mind over the situation' and reluctant to accept the need for a conference; but he came to regard it more favourably. Remembering his experience with the Round Table conference of 1887, he told Austen, '[i]f it succeeds all will be well—if not—there may be a bad time to go through, but . . . you need [not] fear utter annihilation.'[67] The old man hoped that somehow the conference might save the Unionists from fighting an election on the issue of 'the peers versus the people'. Inside the paralysed body in the wheelchair, the Radical Unionist of the 1880s began to stir, still interested in a federal solution to the Irish question. Mary warned Austen that his father was 'inclined to be Liberal in some of his views, & would yield certain points which would hardly meet with general approbation among Conservatives'.[68] Joe moved from Birmingham to London to keep abreast of developments with Austen who, however, was left on the margins of the conference.

The liveliest of the Liberal negotiators, Lloyd George, had been a secret admirer of Joe from the days of the Radical Programme. But the propensity to aggression in debate which Lloyd George shared with Chamberlain deepened the differences between them into a chasm, particularly after he accused the Chamberlains of war profiteering. Their fights blinded Chamberlain to their affinities in policy, and he dismissed Lloyd George with contempt. Lloyd George resented this treatment; yet he was among the minority of Liberals who recognized that simple reaffirmation of free trade was an inadequate response to tariff reform. What drew him to Chamberlain in the first place and continued to impress him was Chamberlain's willingness to extend the powers of the state to address social needs.

That was the burden of remarks which Lloyd George made about Chamberlain in an address to the Liberal Christian League as the interparty conference approached its climax. Lloyd George paid tribute to the 'outstanding service' Chamberlain had rendered 'to the cause of the masses' by drawing attention to 'real crying evils' in the industrial society of Britain and by 'seeking a remedy, not in voluntary effort, but in bold and comprehensive action on the part of the State'. Lloyd George damned tariff reformers for attempting to enrich the colonies at Britain's expense and for threatening to ruin those sectors of the national economy which did well under free trade. None the less, he gave credit to Chamberlain as the man who converted the Unionist party to tariff reform for opening 'a prospect which is full of hope for those who wish well to the wretched and those who walk in despair'.[69] This was quite enough praise to impress *The Times* and alarm those who feared the purpose which might lurk behind the honeyed words.

Lloyd George had meanwhile propounded a remarkable offer in the privately conducted inter-party discussions. He suggested that the Liberals grant imperial preference and a strengthened army and navy to the Unionists in return for a federal resolution of the Irish question, disestablishment of the Church of England in Wales, and some changes in Balfour's Education Act. The proposal seemed tailor-made for Chamberlain. But it was offered to begin with only to Balfour, who did not find it attractive. Balfour did not immediately show the proposal to Austen. Nor did Lloyd George make sure that the Chamberlains learned of it independently. But when at last Balfour informed Austen, Lloyd George showed him the similarity between the part of the proposal on Ireland and suggestions made by his father in the 1880s. Austen responded with cautious interest, and transmitted the proposal to his father.

For whatever reason, no response of any sort came from Highbury. Thereafter the whole negotiation was brought to a halt from the Unionist side. In allowing Lloyd George's offer to slip through his fingers, Joe lost the best chance he ever had to bring tariff reform into effect. He failed to remember the proverb he had repeated to Austen that very spring: 'He that will not when he may, may not when he will.'

As soon as the conference collapsed, the government introduced its bill to curtail the veto power of the House of Lords and, without waiting for it to be rejected, dissolved Parliament for another general election, to take place before Christmas. Faced with the situation he had hoped to avoid, Chamberlain tried to combine defence of the second chamber with a renewed call for tariff reform. But most Unionists reacted differently, defending the Lords as a bulwark against Home Rule. Few dared challenge tariff reform in its entirety. But almost everyone admitted that the duties on foodstuffs which imperial preference entailed were not popular with the electorate. A chorus of Unionists called for postponement of food duties or for a pledge to submit them after the election for further electoral consideration through a referendum. The chorus was conducted by Chamberlain's hitherto foremost champion in the press, J.L. Garvin.

Chamberlain moved in mid-November to London, where Leo Amery found him 'full of the zest of battle, convinced of the folly of surrender'.[70] To all appeals for compromise on the food duties, he replied simply, 'I cannot consent.'[71] To his relief, Balfour refused to bow to the pressure for yet another change in his fiscal posture, and he upheld tariff reform fully. But at last, four days before the polling was to begin, he made the demanded concession. Chamberlain retired to Highbury. In a published letter, he reformulated his order of priorities. He still refused to focus on the House of Lords, but for the moment gave pride of place to prevention of Home Rule, ahead of tariff reform. Thereafter he said nothing.

The results of Balfour's capitulation were unimpressive. What the Unionists gained in free-trading Lancashire, Cheshire, Yorkshire and Scotland, they lost in the counties and the South of England, particularly London. In total, the results of the December election duplicated those of January almost exactly. Chamberlain used the results to reaffirm the wisdom of opposing 'anything in the nature of a compromise'.[72] But he closed the year 'very depressed physically & mentally'.[73]

The tide which turned away from tariff reform after the first general election of 1910 ebbed rapidly after the second. Chamberlain's health and spirits followed the fortunes of his cause. The Liberal government of Canada concluded a reciprocal trade agreement with the United States. But in the ensuing general election the Canadian Conservatives defeated Laurier's Liberals, and promptly repudiated the trade agreement with the United States. Within a week of the Canadian election, Hilda Chamberlain reported that 'Papa . . . got back his speech' and that it was 'quite distinct,—even if not very fluent'.[74]

He oscillated between withdrawal into private life and defiance in public. He left Highbury for London in the summer of 1911 to stiffen the Unionist Lords against the Liberal bill to curb the powers of their House. Though he had sought to avoid electoral battle on this issue, he welcomed the parliamentary fight. 'You can't do wrong,' he told Austen, 'if you fight to the end.'[75] In a message read out at a banquet which diehard opponents of the government bill gave in honour of their senior spokesman, Lord Halsbury, Joe praised Halsbury because 'he has refused to surrender his principles'.[76]

The wording was explosive. It implied that Unionists who followed a different course of action were surrendering their principles; and the Unionists who did so were led by Balfour. Chamberlain's message intensified the division among Unionists between Balfour's 'hedgers' and Halsbury's last 'ditchers'. The division ran along new lines, uniting the

Cecils with the Chamberlains while Chaplin joined the hedgers. But the unaccustomed lineup did little to reduce the sharpness of the division.

It precipitated Balfour's resignation as leader of the party. He concluded that if, under his leadership, Unionists could not find the party unity he had been anxious to secure, they should find themselves another leader. Though Chamberlain did not promote this conclusion, he had been convinced since December by Balfour's concession of a referendum on food duties that he was no longer the best leader for the party. When news of mounting dissatisfaction with Balfour's leadership reached Chamberlain at the beginning of October, he welcomed it. This news as much as the results of the election in Canada roused him out of his late summer slump. He saw an opportunity for Austen, who was on holiday in Lugano. Neville forwarded the news to Austen by telegram, and reinforced its message: 'now is the time for you to come forward and given them a lead'.[77] The whole family hoped for Austen's advancement, all, that is, but Austen himself.

Austen came home reluctantly. He wanted Balfour to stay on, partly out of devotion to him, but also because he did not want the position. He buried his emotional ambivalence towards his father and Balfour with effusions of devotion. He had recently expressed his debt to his father with a sense of foreboding: 'He has been more ambitious for me than ever I have been for myself—infinitely more ambitious for me than he was for *himself*—and that is the only point on which I have ever had to resist his counsels.'[78] When Balfour finally resigned at the beginning of November, Austen conveyed the news to his father with an effusion about Balfour. 'The blow has fallen and I am as sick as a man can be,' wrote Austen, '. . . for I love the man . . . though as you know he has once or twice nearly broken my heart politically.'[79] Joe tried to put steel into his son. Austen agreed that he was the most eligible and best person for the vacated leadership in the Commons, better than the other candidate, Walter Long, a petulant man of little administrative weight. But Austen was unwilling to fight for the post. Long was favoured by traditional Conservatives, less for his own merits than because of the bond between Austen and his father. Though pacific by nature, for five years Austen had fought stiffly as Joe's surrogate. He was an honourable sheep in the old wolf's clothing.

As soon as it became clear that neither he nor Long could win the leadership without a fight, Austen abandoned the contest. Pointing to the damage which another fight would inflict on the party, Austen persuaded Long to join him in retiring in favour of a third candidate, Bonar Law. Law was less experienced than the other two but broadly acceptable as a tariff reformer who endorsed the referendum in December and compromise over the Lords in July; and he was duly chosen by acclamation. Austen greeted the outcome with 'unmixed relief' except for the 'immense disappointment to his father'.[80] Joe tried but failed to hide his disappointment. He criticized Austen by commending Bonar Law. 'The strength which he has shown in resolving to fight for the leadership', Joe commented, 'perhaps is an indication that ... he has developed strength of which we did not suspect him.'[81]

For some time after Austen's withdrawal from the leadership contest, the cause of tariff reform held up well, better than his father. In Cannes, where Mary took Joe as usual from February to May, he could not speak intelligibly. Back in Birmingham over the summer, he suffered a severe attack of gout which left him legally blind. Yet politically, for a while longer, the old man held his own. He secured good terms for the Liberal Unionists in their organizational fusion with the Conservatives to form one Unionist party. For most of 1912 the Unionist commitment to tariff reform seemed to strengthen in Bonar Law's custody. His reputation as a tariff reformer had not been greatly damaged by the encouragement he gave Balfour to issue his referendum pledge. The pledge was withdrawn as official party policy in November by Lansdowne as party leader in the Lords.

But that action produced such panic within the party that by the end of the year Bonar Law was ready to abandon the Unionist commitment to food taxes almost entirely. All along it was the protective rather than the imperial side of tariff reform which attracted Bonar Law; and the main object of tariffs on foreign foodstuffs was imperial. He cared still more for the Union with Ireland than for the protectionist dividends of tariff reform. After curbing the powers of the House of Lords through passage of the Parliament Act, the government had introduced its Home Rule bill. Bonar Law wanted to mobilize all possible support for Unionism to prevent the enactment of that bill.

Even so, he feared that any backtracking on his part over tariff reform would compromise and weaken his leadership. Eyes kept turning to the old man in the wheelchair. Only Joe Chamberlain could make a concession on food taxes which tariff reformers generally would accept. In March the Cecil brothers, Hugh and Robert, appealed to him as one who had done more than any other living man to prevent Home Rule to do so again by authorizing the desired concession. He refused. So too, when Bonar Law came to tell him 'of the immense number of letters he had received urging him to drop the food taxes', Chamberlain replied that it was impossible to do so 'if we were to do anything for the Colonies'.[82]

For a man approaching eighty who could not speak clearly or hold a pen, Chamberlain continued to command astonishing influence. In the summer of 1912, in an effort to restore the finances of the Tariff Reform League, Lord Ridley announced the formation of a birthday fund in Chamberlain's honour and opened it for the shillings of working men as well as for the guineas of the rich. The response was stunning symbolically, though in straight financial terms the League raised much more privately from its wealthiest backers. Shillings poured in daily by the thousands, forcing the organizers to recruit help with the mail. Contributions came from Hong Kong, from members of the Melbourne stock exchange, from Sir Starr Jameson of the ill-fated raid who led the English party in the new Union of South Africa. 'Would that people at home could recognize as clearly as people in the Dominions almost universally do,' wrote Jameson, 'that in this policy for which Mr Chamberlain stands is wrapt up our whole national existence!'[83]

Chamberlain presented the assault on food taxes to Bonar Law as a question of leadership rather than of policy. Sensing at the end of the year that Bonar Law was crumbling, Chamberlain sent him word that 'the present crisis is in the nature of a try-on to see how far you are "squeezable." If the Free Fooders [and] the rest of them can pretend to their followers that every assault will be followed by a weakening on your part, the party would be in pieces in a month.' Firm resistance would 'kill the movement just as soon' and go far to establish Bonar Law as a 'great' political leader.[84]

'If I had been your father,' Bonar Law later told Austen, 'I might have carried it through successfully.'[85] As it was, Bonar Law could not find enough support within the parliamentary party to act on Joe's advice. Early in January it became apparent that the still committed 'whole-hoggers' in the Commons numbered no more than forty and perhaps as few as seventeen. Bonar Law concluded that the party should give up the proposed food taxes; but loath to turn his coat as leader, he offered to resign. The effect of his offer was to pass responsibility for the abandonment of food taxes to the tariff reformers. A letter was drafted, revised by some of them, and then circulated among the Unionist backbenchers, accepting Bonar Law's guidance on food taxes and asking him not to resign. Here again Austen did the gentlemanly thing. Though he would not sign the letter himself, he encouraged at least one of the hard-line tariff reformers to do so. All but six backbenchers duly signed; and Bonar Law stayed on. Thereupon, though he did not repudiate food taxes completely, he passed the onus of asking for them on to the self-governing colonies; and even if they did so, he undertook to submit their request to the judgement of another general election in Britain.

Though thus muffled, his statement rang the death-knell of tariff reform as a way to consolidate the empire. Food taxes and with them imperial preference were removed from the short- and middle-term agenda of the Unionist party, pushed off far enough to exceed the fleeting imperial opportunity which Chamberlain had hoped to seize. The self-governing colonies were sure to have gone their separate ways before Unionists in Britain surmounted all the hurdles Bonar Law placed on the path to imperial preference. After that, it would be nothing but an insubstantial courtesy.

Blessing the fight

The old man met this ultimate disappointment with resilience. Doggedly he insisted 'that even now a great deal can, & will be done, if there is any grit left in the party'.[86] He did what he could to hearten 'the small group of men who now represent the whole Imperial policy'.[87] In addition to Austen they included Amery, Hewins, Chaplin, Selborne, Wyndham, Page Croft, Ridley, Maxse and a repentant Garvin. One by one they visited their frail leader in Princes Gardens or at Highbury to reconfirm their apostolic commission.

Yet the blow from Bonar Law led Chamberlain to accept that his own political life had effectively ended. He left Birmingham within a week, pausing only briefly in London before heading on to Cannes. There, early in February, he told Mary that he would retire from Parliament at the next general election. Though she said nothing to prompt it, she realized the necessity for this decision. For nearly seven years she had encouraged his involvement in high politics as the best way to keep his spirits vital. Even now she feared that he would 'not altogether recover' from the decision 'in the sense that it sets a seal, & renders it more difficult to keep in touch with things'.[88] But she could see that his capacity to express himself was deteriorating. Recurrent attacks of gout made it ever more difficult for him to dictate messages. What went out over his name was no longer quite his: when he could not find words, Mary or Austen drew up something for his approval.

Joe was anxious to keep his decision to retire quiet for a while, partly from reluctance to make the break but also for political reasons. The Liberals in Birmingham had declined to contest his reelection in the two general elections of 1910, but they were restive now and would field a candidate the moment his retirement was announced. Unionist organization in Birmingham had slackened during his illness, a situation worsened by the illness and inactivity of Jesse Collings. Chamberlain intended privately to use his decision to retire to encourage Collings to follow his example. Chamberlain also wanted to strengthen Austen and through him the cause of tariff reform by having Austen succeed him as Member for West Birmingham, a constituency which, with its large working-class population, carried more political clout than East Worcestershire.

These political calculations were not, however, the daily concerns of Chamberlain's shrinking world. Sardonic in the happiest of times, his

wit turned bitter. Irritable with the company surrounding him, he remarked at the announcement of cold veal pie for lunch that '[c]old veal
is as insipid as sisters kissing!'[89] He was painfully dependent on
Beatrice, Hilda and Ida, the daughters who devoted their passing years
to the care of their father. He was even more dependent on Mary,
harshly though he had reacted to dependence on women after the death
of Florence. Neville sensed the irony:

> He who had been so self reliant was now dependent on a woman for
> every act of life . . . and allowed himself to be dragged out to walk his
> daily round panting and sweating with the exertion, to be thrust into
> his coat and piled with rugs on the hottest day, to have his gloves
> pulled on and off, to have his cigars cut down and to be sent to bed
> early.[90]

In the days of his strength Chamberlain had more than once expressed his wish eventually for a swift death. After his stroke he told
Mary repeatedly that he wished to die. 'I thought the work might kill
me,' he said to Neville, 'but I never expected this.' His need for Mary
was only accentuated during the spring of 1913 at Cannes when her
appendix broke, peritonitis set in, and she lay dangerously ill for some
days before she recovered. Back in Birmingham during the autumn,
death narrowed the circle of Chamberlain's oldest associates. In October
Arthur, his fiercely estranged yet deeply fond brother, passed away
after spending some years like Joe in a wheelchair. Charles Vince, the
doughty constituency chairman for West Birmingham, followed in
November.

On New Year's day 1914, Chamberlain resolved to announce without
further delay that he would not stand at the next general election—
which might be precipitated by the crisis over Home Rule. The announcement appeared five days later in the *Birmingham Daily Post* in the
form of a letter from Chamberlain to the new constituency chairman for
West Birmingham, George Titterton, whom Chamberlain always remembered as the best student in the night school classes he taught fifty
years before at the Church of the Messiah. The letter read sadly: 'I cannot hope again to do my work in Parliament.' The announcement
proved more wrenching for Chamberlain than he anticipated. Alone
with Mary, he talked 'a great deal of the active life we have led together
with its keen interests & its clash of swords in the stormy times & its
development, & fulfilment in quieter days'.[91] They left England almost
immediately for the Riviera.

The final stretch of Chamberlain's life was shadowed by the spectre
of Home Rule. The issue had always complicated his political career. It
ruptured his relations with the Liberals and placed him in unnatural
alliance with the opponents of Radicalism. It pushed him towards im-

perialism only to keep him, with the spectre's recent revival, from the realization of his imperial hopes through tariff reform. He had done more than anyone else to defeat Home Rule, yet his opposition to it had not been straightforward because he advocated a federal solution to the Irish problem.

In the winter of 1913–14, Home Rule seemed likely to become law within a matter of months under the terms of the Parliament Act. While the prospect turned many Unionists into violent fanatics, some of those close to Chamberlain including his elder son pointed to his federal proposals in the 1880s as a way to resolve the crisis. But the old man was slow to reach that conclusion himself. He did not want to find a way out of the deadlock; he hoped for a fight. In the previous spring, describing the government's procedure with its Home Rule bill as 'a constitutional outrage',[92] he had encouraged Unionists to press their fight against Home Rule to unconstitutional extremes. That autumn, when the leader of the Irish Unionist extremists, Edward Carson, came to visit, Chamberlain backed him up with advice to 'fight it out to the finish'.[93] When Bonar Law accompanied Carson to rally the faithful in Birmingham, Chamberlain sent five words for their meeting: 'Hold fast and fight hard.'[94] He was contemptuous when Austen used the meeting to accept the conditions Bonar Law laid down before preferential food taxes could become law. Joe saw no need to moderate his fight for tariff reform in order to fight against Home Rule.

After he announced his intention to retire from Parliament at the next election, Chamberlain withdrew increasingly into himself; and his messages to Austen grew 'rather telegraphic'.[95] Still his reactions on Ireland remained rigid. Bonar Law and Carson toyed with the notion of excluding Ulster from the imposition of Home Rule as a better way out of the crisis than federal schemes. But the exclusion of Ulster struck Joe as worse because the concession of Home Rule to any part of Ireland would place the cohesion of the kingdom in jeopardy. He wanted Unionists to leave the proposing of alternative solutions up to the government, and 'then to tear them to pieces'.[96] He did not, however, like the idea of tampering with the annual Mutiny bill in order to force the government to soften its stance on Home Rule. Eventually he gave more favourable thought to a federal solution for Ireland, not so much to get out of the current crisis but as a step towards federation of the empire. But once Asquith proposed an Amending bill as a means out of the parliamentary impasse, Chamberlain reverted to his preferred stance of dogged defiance.

He returned to England in the middle of May, and to Birmingham at the end of the month, for a garden party in the grounds of Highbury to bid farewell to his constituents. This would be Joe's first appearance in public since his stroke—apart from glimpses of him as he was lifted in

13. Bidding farewell.

or out of trains—and it was also to be his last. Garden parties at Highbury had always been massive affairs, and this was no exception: four thousand people came. They did not know whether they would catch a last glimpse of the man who had been hidden for nearly eight years. The reporter from *The Times* captured the moment:

> When it was reported that Mr. Chamberlain was on the terrace people hurried from all directions to pay their respects to him. He was seated in a bath chair. Every one was enabled to see Mr. Chamberlain as he was drawn backwards and forwards along the terrace in front of the house and round the footpaths intersecting the lawn. . . . Now and again there were little bursts of cheering which Mr. Chamberlain acknowledged by raising his hat, and as he passed along men who had been in many a political fight with him bared their heads and shouted, 'Long life to you,' and 'I wish we had you with us now.' Mr. Chamberlain smiled and shook his head and occasionally put out his hand, as he was wheeled about, to grasp that of some old political friend whom he recognized.

Before the speeches which Austen and others were to give, the old man 'turned to his guests, raised his hat . . . wished them good-night',[97] and was wheeled back indoors. Less than two weeks later, he left Birmingham, for the final time, and travelled back to London, the city of his birth.

His frame was frail but his spirit remained aggressive. He anticipated civil war over Ireland and did not draw back at the prospect. Leo Amery came to Princes Gardens to discuss the situation with him at the end of June. 'As I was leaving the room,' Amery later recalled, 'he called me back to say "Amery, if I were the House of Lords I would fight" . . . . "Fight", indeed, was the last word I heard him utter.'[98]

Later that day, when Chamberlain came downstairs to go out for a drive, he had a heart attack. Mary was at hand. She was to have gone out for a dinner to meet the King and Queen of Portugal, but the dinner was cancelled because of the assassination of the Archduke Ferdinand at Sarajevo. In pain for the first time since his initial paralysis, Chamberlain was taken to bed. The pain continued through the next day. He was obviously failing, but was still able to talk to Austen about the situation in Ireland. Anxious to stiffen Austen's resolve to uphold the loyalists of Ireland, he discussed the latest overture from Asquith. 'Somebody has got to give way,' was the final sentence of the dying fighter to his gentle son, 'but I don't see why it should be always us.'[99] 'The great "Joe"', as Amery liked to call him, spent a restless night, had the newspaper read to him next morning, but grew steadily weaker through the day. He died at 10.15 that night, in the arms of Mary and surrounded by his children.

The striking feature of his funeral four days later was its austere simplicity, upon which he had insisted. He was offered burial in Westminster Abbey, but the family declined. The coffin was conveyed without procession or ceremony through London in an open hearse and by train to Birmingham. The funeral service was conducted without sermon or oration in the Unitarian Church of the Messiah, an unimpressive building to the eyes of *The Times* reporter from London. The family and those connected with Birmingham were invited to attend, including the mayor and city councillors, the Members of Parliament for the city, and the officers of the university. The great figures of the kingdom and empire were gathered elsewhere, for a memorial service in St Margaret's, Westminster.

The casket was of plain oak. Its only conspicuous ornament was a cross of white roses, placed there by Mary. The casket was carried without pomp through the streets of Birmingham to a bleak civic cemetery in the heart of Chamberlain's West Birmingham constituency not far from the factory where he had worked. The streets were lined densely by the people of Birmingham, bareheaded and silent. Only eleven were allowed to follow the minister into the Key Hill Cemetery: Chamberlain's wife and sons and daughters, his one surviving brother Walter and his brother-in-law William Kenrick, his long-serving private secretary, and the Members of Parliament to represent the city. He was buried in a small ground vault with the two women to whom he had been married so many years before. The inscription added to the stone covering reads simply

Also of

Joseph Chamberlain

Born July 8th 1836

Died July 2nd 1914

Close round the stone lay the graves of the industrialists and civic leaders among whom he had been chief: Kenricks and Martineaus, the Nonconformist ministers Dawson, Dale and Vince, and the long-faithful Powell Williams.

Legacy

The valuation of the estate which Joseph Chamberlain left was placed just over £125,000. Though not the estate of a wealthy man, it was respectable for an industrialist. Despite the losses he incurred from his sisal-growing venture in the 1890s, he left somewhat more at his death than he had taken from his metal-manufacturing partnership upon retiring from business in 1874. If he had not gained, neither had he lost much from his movement into politics. The estates which his brothers Arthur and Herbert left after devoting their lives to business ranged in valuation from roughly £25,000 more than Joe's to £25,000 less.

Still, his will made sombre reading for his eldest son. Mary, who had a private income from her family and other American legacies, fared well under her husband's will, receiving £40,000 to guarantee her an annual income of at least £2,000. Joe's three surviving daughters received £20,000 apiece, and £10,000 went to Ethel's daughter Hilda Mary. After the specified bequests were met and death duties paid, the residue of the estate amounted to just over £12,000, of which Austen was to receive three-quarters and Neville one. Neville, as the businessman of the family, would fare comfortably though he was never as affluent as his father. But on an inheritance of £9,000 and no official income apart from the small salary which Parliament had recently instituted for Members of Parliament, Austen was left in precarious financial circumstances.

His situation, and Mary's departure for London, necessitated the sale of Highbury. Though 'so much a part of Joe that it seemed almost a sacrilege to be pulling it to pieces', Highbury had not endeared itself to Mary. She found it 'a relief to get away'. London she loved, not Birmingham. She settled herself into Princes Gardens by Christmas after his death. Joe's daughters, released from nursing the father they adored, also set up house for themselves, Beatrice in London, Hilda and Ida together in Hampshire where they settled in with all the excitement that goes with 'a new toy', as Mary observed. But Austen spent the autumn, with help from Mary, breaking up Highbury, both of them weighed with 'a sense of tragedy ... well nigh unbearable'.[100]

The rapid dismantling of Highbury could be looked upon as a metaphor for Chamberlain's political achievement. When war broke out on the Continent instead of Ireland in August and the self-governing colonies including South Africa joined in on Britain's side, Beatrice Chamberlain exulted, 'The Empire has stood together! My father is vindicated.'[101] However, a former Unionist whip in the Commons, Lord Crawford, observed at Chamberlain's death that it occurred 'at a moment when the Tariff Reform movement is weaker than at any time since its inception—and he lived long enough to see Home Rule become an impending reality. The two great ideals of his life are thus shattered before his deathbed.'[102] Home Rule was placed on the statute books at the outbreak of the war, though suspended for its duration.

To the eyes of Conservatives such as Crawford, Chamberlain's career which once looked so substantial had little to show for itself by the time he died. But Crawford's understanding of the ideals which animated Chamberlain did not stretch back beyond the rupture of the Liberal party in 1886 over Home Rule. Nor did landowners like Crawford grasp the full measure of Chamberlain's impact close to his industrial home. It was mainly there that his achievement proved solid and durable.

Joseph Chamberlain was the first industrialist to enter the highest circles of the state. He was born and bred, educated and apprenticed for manufacturing industry; and he was outstandingly successful at it, good enough to get out before the age of forty with a fortune and the trappings of affluence for the rest of his life. Though his movement then from business into politics was complete and wholehearted, his genius as a politician lay in keeping in touch with his urban industrial roots.

He failed to find answers to the great questions familiar to the traditional elite of British government into which his experience of urban industry gave him no special insight: the denominational dilemma in elementary education, more importantly the Irish question, and how to consolidate a maritime empire composed of self-governing states. Though the traditional elite also failed to solve these problems, they produced masters of the ancient craft of international diplomacy at which Chamberlain proved particularly inept.

Yet his experience in industry enabled him to present fresh responses to many of the questions, old and new, with which the political leaders of Britain were confronted between the passage of the Second Reform Act and the outbreak of the First World War. He widened the range of the questions, as much on overseas matters as on domestic. He escalated debate on how the powers of the state should be used to meet the needs of an industrial economy and urban society. The urban programmes which he implemented and the responses which he worked out to national and imperial questions found enduring favour in the industrial city where he made his home. The monuments of the traditional elite are at Westminster. The memorials of Joseph Chamberlain are all over Birmingham.

Education was the issue which first drew Chamberlain into politics, and it persisted as a concern until tariff reform consumed him. He was goaded into action by the superiority of education in the United States and Germany and by the economic edge as well as the social strength which those countries derived from that superiority. Arguably his most enduring achievement came in higher education, founding the University of Birmingham with its emphasis on applied science and its pioneering faculty of commerce. Nothing in his career was more impressive than his work towards this end amid the demands of the Boer War. Once he was convinced that the university needed more space and equipment for the sciences, he secured a generous donation of land in Edgbaston and commissioned one of the leading architects in the country to design a coordinated set of buildings. He raised money for the university from the city and neighbouring county governments. In return for contributions from local industry, he encouraged the creation within the university of schools for 'railway engineering, electric lighting, railway management, and every large trade in the town'.[103] Though the first year of campaigning for tariff reform turned him away from the university, he gave his attention to it again in 1905. He joined forces with R.B. Haldane of the Liberals to increase support at the national level, and commissioned the construction of a high tower to draw attention for miles around to the institution which was rising in Edgbaston. The university felt the loss of Chamberlain's driving force as soon as he was stricken. The stream of financial donations diminished to a trickle. He no longer had vision to spare for the university, and did not encourage the proposals which were made to raise endowments for the university in his honour, preferring to leave the magic of his name to tariff reform. The university continued nevertheless to distinguish itself long after the cause of tariff reform faded away.

The culminating passion of his life was the empire; and here his accomplishment was most equivocal. His ideal of a maritime federation of states drawn together by trade and, when possible, by military and naval cooperation and imperial institutions to fortify their collective international position was attractive but probably chimerical. He certainly never solved 'the great problem of federal government' which he claimed at the nativity of his imperialism in Toronto 'to have been left in charge of the English people'.[104] He backed away from the various federal solutions he propounded in the mid-1880s to deal with the Irish question. Though he eventually acquired some sympathy for the Afrikaner loyalties of Jan Hofmeyr at the Cape, he never learned how to accommodate the French Canadian nationalism of Sir Wilfrid Laurier. South Africa diverted and drained his imperial energies away from constructive ends. His most substantial contributions to the empire were threefold: the expansion of Nigeria, improvement of tropical medicine, and, in a nice combination of traditional agrarian imagery with industrial enterprise, cultivating the empire's undeveloped estates.

Conservative contemporaries and disciples ranked his imperial achievement much higher. Balfour maintained that as an imperial statesman, Chamberlain had 'done the greatest . . . work which perhaps has ever fallen to a single statesman in this country'[105] by refusing to stand by as the self-governing colonies went their separate ways and instead by doing all he could to cultivate a common imperial patriotism. This sentiment grew indeed in many parts of the empire from the end of the 1880s through the First World War; and Chamberlain made a greater contribution than any other person to that growth. The question remains: what difference did the sentiment make? The claim that Beatrice Chamberlain made for her father at the outbreak of the First World War was based on the growth of empire-wide patriotism; and a similar claim can be made for the Second. But the vindication of Joseph Chamberlain is more often found in his son Neville's introduction of tariff reform as Chancellor of the Exchequer in 1931 and in the agreements reached with the dominions at Ottawa a year later. The imperial content of those measures was slim. They did more to protect the interests of the individual states of the Commonwealth than to promote trade among them.

The characteristic of Joseph Chamberlain which made the greatest impression on Liberals was his concern for the wellbeing of the working man. Liberals rarely questioned the genuineness of his concern, at least after his stroke reduced his threat to their power. Asquith paid tribute in the House of Commons at his death to his responsiveness to human suffering, as had Lloyd George during the inter-party conference of 1910. The tribute from Chamberlain's inveterate enemy in the press, W.T. Stead, was still more remarkable. Stead wrote that '[f]rom his boyhood up, Joseph Chamberlain has been consumed with a passionate longing to benefit the lot of the common people. Not [John] Burns, nor Keir Hardie [of the Labour party] is more constantly preoccupied by the necessity for doing something to make the cottage of the labouring man less of a hovel and more of a home.'[106] The leaders of the Liberal party knew to their cost how politically rewarding this concern of Chamberlain's could be. They elaborated their social vision to counteract his.

Yet his social vision became blurred and his constructive capacity for these purposes lessened after he moved from the Birmingham town council to the House of Commons. His domestic initiatives in Gladstone's ministry accomplished little. The Radical Programme was ill-judged and an electoral failure, at least in urban constituencies, the part of Britain about which he truly cared. In a curious way the Unionist alliance sharpened the cost-accounting tools Chamberlain used so well as mayor of Birmingham, and helped him work out self-financing schemes of social insurance for the whole country. Even so, his social accountancy reached its limits with the enactment of workmen's compensation for industrial accidents. His social prescriptions as a tariff reformer were timorous and vague. Unionists by and large were not game for more.

The concerns which carried Chamberlain into public life arose from his discovery of the needs and impact of his business. His business also generated the methods of marketing and accounting which he applied to politics. But above all, his business provided work and wages, fairly good wages, for its employees and profits, excellent profits, for its owners. He entered public life to ensure those benefits. Thereafter he upheld them in the face of intensifying international competition. His essential purpose as a statesman was to meet the needs of Britain's industrial economy. His most significant achievement was the extent to which he induced both political parties in Britain to endorse that objective and exercise the powers of the state in one way or other towards that end.

He began by constructing efficient models for civic control of utilities to raise the quality of life in the cities where industry concentrated. He failed to adapt this model to national purposes as a Liberal. But as a Unionist in the late 1880s when Britain's economy remained in the grip of depression and lost its pride of place to foreign competitors, he focused his attention on markets in the colonies and employment at home as crucial to the wellbeing of the country. The passivity with which Gladstonian Liberals were prepared to watch the colonies go their separate ways and foreign competitors outstrip Britain as an industrial power repelled Chamberlain. He moved as Colonial Secretary to energize British government on both fronts. Loss of standing in international economic competition was not just unfortunate in his estimation but dangerous, even more so for those who depended on British industry for their employment than for those who derived their wealth from investments.

Many Unionists supported his extensions or attempted extensions of state action because they promised to strengthen Britain's standing as a great power and centre of an empire. His self-financing social reforms and his reliance on tariffs to fund further reform also attracted Unionists as less threatening to the ownership of property than the workmen's compensation plan of Asquith and the budget of Lloyd George. From one perspective, tariff reform was a scheme for general self-financing of social reform, to be paid largely by the working-class consumer for his own benefit. As such, tariff reform was suspect to progressive Liberals and Labour. Yet Chamberlain's financial policy was as Radical as theirs in assuming that social insurance was a responsibility of the state. His insistence that redistributive taxation would kill the industrial goose that lay the golden social egg fuelled a debate on the economics of social reform which continues today.

Still, his most substantial achievements were in the city of his adoption, in Birmingham, to which he repaired as often as he could for refreshment from the strains of life in London. The grandly designed civic schools of the 1870s, the improvements surrounding Corporation Street, the street lighting, paving and parks, Chamberlain Square, the clock towers erected in his honour upon his return from South Africa and still higher at the university, all these and more bore testament to the man everyone in town spoke of as 'Joe'. He was the one major figure in British history who 'from beginning to end, contrived to be both a great national and a great local force'. As with the empire, so with his city, he fostered an unfamiliar level of patriotism. The best testimony to this achievement came oddly from a metropolitan source, *The Times*. In one of several obituary articles, *The Times* praised Chamberlain for creating 'a feeling of local and civic patriotism in the people of Birmingham' which had been 'peculiarly and signally deficient in it'.

> He preached and . . . practised, a pride in Birmingham such as the Greeks in classical times and the Italians in the Middle Ages felt in their cities. He held up the ideal of a self-sufficing community with stately and beneficent public institutions and a dignified public life— not dependent on London for picture galleries, museums, and libraries, or on Oxford or Cambridge for the best educational facilities, but in all things complete in itself.[107]

He made an enduring mark upon the heart and public life of his city. The distinctive polity which he and the men who lay around him in Key Hill Cemetery had established in Birmingham showed disturbing cracks before his death. Liberals and independent Labour made gains in the municipal elections of 1911, gains particularly for Labour which undermined the Unionist hegemony.[108] But it was not shattered. It survived the First World War and persisted, though much eroded, till 1945. Even now the footmarks of Joseph Chamberlain can be traced in the life of his city.

Notes

Abbreviations

AC   Austen Chamberlain papers
JC   Joseph Chamberlain papers
NC   Neville Chamberlain papers
Garvin, *Life of Chamberlain*   J.L. Garvin, *The Life of Joseph Chamberlain*, vols i–iii
                                (London, 1933–5)
Amery, *Life of Chamberlain*   Julian Amery, *The Life of Joseph Chamberlain*, vols iv–vi
                                (London, 1951–69)

Preface

1. Garvin, *Life of Chamberlain*, vols 1 and 3 (London, 1933–5).
2. Amery, *Life of Chamberlain*, vols iv–vi (London, 1951–69).
3. Peter Fraser, *Joseph Chamberlain: Radicalism and empire, 1868–1914* (London, 1966).
4. Richard Jay, *Joseph Chamberlain: A political study* (Oxford, 1981).

1. The Roots of the Enterprise: c. 1700–1854

1. F.J. Ryland, *Specks on the Dusty Road* (Birmingham, 1937), 41.
2. Chamberlain's last speech, at the Bingley Hall celebration of his seventieth birthday, in C.W. Boyd, ed., *Mr Chamberlain's Speeches*, introd. Austen Chamberlain (London, 1914; reprinted in one vol., New York, 1970), ii, 366.
3. See Austen Chamberlain, *Notes on the Families of Chamberlain and Harben* (privately printed, 1915).
4. Abstract of returns of the Milk Street business, 1775–1863, AC1/2/4/1.
5. Chamberlain in Birmingham, 27 June 1905, in C.W. Boyd, *Mr Chamberlain's Speeches*, ii, 334–5.
6. Quoted in N. Murrell Marris, *The Right Honourable Joseph Chamberlain* (London, 1900), 8.
7. Garvin, *Life of Chamberlain*, i, 31.
8. Quoted by J.M. Hughes in *Emotion and High Politics* (Berkeley, 1983), 193. Professor Hughes provides very interesting reflections on Chamberlain's psychological

make-up.

9. Quoted in N. Murrell Marris, *The Right Honourable Joseph Chamberlain*, 13.

10. I am specially indebted here to largely unpublished work of Professor R.K. Webb on the British Unitarians.

11. At an election rally on behalf of George Dixon in All Saints' Ward, 19 Sept. 1868, JC4/1/3.

12. Milner to Lady Edward Cecil, 16 May 1903, in Cecil Headlam, ed., *The Milner Papers* (London, 1931), i, 123.

13. Chamberlain to the Birchfield Harriers, reported in *The Times*, 3 Oct. 1892.

14. Speech at the Birmingham and Edgbaston Proprietary School, 23 Dec. 1875, JC4/5/11–12.

2. Screw King: 1854–1869

1. This chapter draws upon G.C. Allen, *The Industrial Development of Birmingham and the Black Country, 1860–1927* (New York, 1966, corrected reprint of the London, 1929 ed.); Edgar Jones, *A History of GKN*, vol. i, *Innovation and enterprise, 1759–1918* (London, 1987); Conrad Gill, *History of Birmingham*, vol. 1 (London, 1952); P.L. Payne, *British Entrepreneurship in the Nineteenth Century* (London, 1974); R.A. Church, *The Great Victorian Boom, 1850–1873* (London, 1975); R.A. Church, ed., *The Dynamics of Victorian Business* (London, 1980); A.F. Hooper, 'Mid-Victorian radicalism: Community and class in Birmingham, 1850–1880', University of London Ph.D. dissertation, 1978; and W.J. Ashley, 'Birmingham industry and commerce', in G.A. Auden, *A Handbook for Birmingham and the Neighbourhood*, prepared for the 83rd annual meeting of the British Association for the Advancement of Science

(Birmingham, 1913), 353–64.

2. P.L. Payne, *British Entrepreneurship in the Nineteenth Century*, 187. In *The Book of Business* (privately printed, 1899), 27, Joseph's brother Arthur Chamberlain classified the firm of Nettlefold and Chamberlain among the 'Businesses for the supply of common articles, but which are more or less protected, by reason of some peculiarity in the manufacture or goodwill which has been created'.

3. J.R.T. Hughes quoted in R.A. Church, *The Great Victorian Boom, 1850–1873*, 55.

4. Description provided by Stephen Lloyd, dated June 1982.

5. W.J. Ashley, 'Birmingham industry and Commerce', 534.

6. See Hugh McLeod, 'Class, community and region: The religious geography of nineteenth-century England', in Michael Hill, ed., *A Sociological Yearbook of Religion in Britain: 6* (London, 1973).

7. Cecily Debenham's recollections, copy, William Kenrick papers.

8. Chamberlain to Caroline Kenrick, 13 Aug. 1861, AC1/1/5/41.

9. Harriet to Caroline Kenrick, 12 Aug. 1861, AC1/1/5/40.

10. AC1/1/5/4.

11. Harriet to Mrs Chamberlain, 1 July 1862, AC1/1/5/12.

12. Cecily Debenham's recollections, copy, William Kenrick papers.

13. Harriet to Mrs Chamberlain, 25 February 1863, AC1/1/5/15.

14. Chamberlain to Emma Hutton on 5 Nov. 1863, which would have been Harriet's twenty-eighth birthday, AC1/1/5/31.

15. Ibid.

16. Lloyds Bank Co. Ltd, Board of Directors Minute Books; Lloyds Bank Register of Shareholders; Samuel Lloyd, *The Lloyds of Birmingham* (Birmingham, 1907), 74ff.; R.S. Sayers, *Lloyds Bank in the History of English Banking* (Oxford, 1957), 31.

17. With the marketing in London

Chamberlain had little to do. That was reserved by the terms of the partnership for the Nettlefolds' original and continuing sales establishment on High Holborn.

18. Quoted in 'The history of the screw', section III, 28, typescript, GKN archives (Smethwick).

19. Transcript of Chamberlain's notebook, entries for 21 Feb. 1867, 10 June 1869 and 21 July 1870, JC1/18/2.

20. *Iron Trade Circular* (Ryland's), 14 July 1877; *New York Times*, 27 April 1888.

21. Transcript of Joseph Chamberlain's notebook kept at Nettlefold and Chamberlain, Broad Street, Birmingham, 1866–74, JC1/18/2, pp. 23–4.

22. The following discussion benefits greatly from A.F. Hooper's closely informed and acute work, 'Mid-Victorian radicalism: Community and class in Birmingham, 1850–1880', University of London Ph.D. dissertation, 1978.

23. Joseph Chamberlain, 'Manufacture of iron wood screws', in Samuel Timmins, ed., *The Resources, Products, and Industrial History of Birmingham and the Midland Hardware District* (London, 1866), 604–9.

24. The Rev. C.A.J. Fellows, 'The Right Hon. Joseph Chamberlain as a Sunday school teacher', JC1/17/1.

25. Quoted in the *Birmingham Daily Post*, 7 July 1906, p. 8, col. 1.

26. *Birmingham Daily Post*, 11 Feb. 1864.

27. Chamberlain to the House of Lords select committee on intemperance, 16 Mar. 1877.

3. The Transfer from Business to Politics: 1867–1874

1. Chamberlain to H. Peyton, 15 Aug. [1867], JC5/58/3.

2. JC6/3/2/22.

3. A.F. Hooper, 'Mid-Victorian radicalism: Community and class in Birmingham, 1850–1880', University of London Ph.D. thesis, 1978, 52.

4. Chamberlain lecturing on education in connection with the Mutual Improvement Society at the Church of the Messiah, 28 April 1870, JC4/1/11–12.

5. Alfred Field's testimony to the Select Committee on Scientific Instruction, Parliamentary Papers, 1867–8, xv, 336–40.

6. Chamberlain's speeches at Scarborough, 27 January 1871, and Newcastle, 26 February 1872, JC4/1/16–17 and 34.

7. Quoted in Wright Wilson, *The Life of George Dawson* (Birmingham, 1905), 151.

8. R.W. Dale, 'George Dawson: politician, lecturer, and preacher', *The Nineteenth Century* (August 1877), 44.

9. Chamberlain to Mr Cox, 22 Jan. 1884, copy, JC6/4f/3.

10. Louise Chamberlain to the children of Florence, n.d., NC1/6/4/16.

11. Emily Martineau to Chamberlain, 6 Apr. 1875, NC1/6/4/15.

12. Letter from Chamberlain 'For Florence's children', 5 Apr. 1875, Beatrice, Ida and Hilda Chamberlain papers.

13. The best account of these and the subsequent proceedings in Birmingham is in J.A. Langford, *Modern Birmingham and its Institutions* (Birmingham, 1873–7), ii, 394ff.

14. Chamberlain to Charles Francis Adams, 15 Feb. 1867; Adams to Chamberlain, 18 Feb.; Temple to Chamberlain, 19 and 20 Feb.; Chamberlain to Field, 2 Mar.; Field to Chamberlain, 29 Mar.; William Emerson to Chamberlain, 23 May; Temple to Chamberlain, 18 June 1867, JC6/3/2/2, 4, 5, 6, 12, 15, 19 and 20.

15. Quoted in E.P. Hennock, *Fit and Proper Persons: Ideal and reality in nineteenth-century urban govern-*

ment (Montreal, 1973), 86. This book provides the best account of the educational movement in Birmingham.

16. JC6/3/2/24.

17. For the best contemporary account of the activities of the League, with a helpful introduction, see Francis Adams, *History of the Elementary School Contest in England*, ed. Asa Briggs (Brighton, 1972).

18. J.A. Langford, *Modern Birmingham and its Institutions*, 419.

19. National Education League, *Report of the 1st general meeting* (Birmingham, 1869), proceedings on 12 Oct. 1869.

20. D.W. Bebbington, *The Nonconformist Conscience: Chapel and politics, 1870–1914* (London, 1982), 157.

21. Quoted in Asa Briggs, introduction to Francis Adams, *History of the Elementary School Contest in England*, xxii.

22. Chamberlain to Dixon, 26 Feb. 1870, copy, JC5/27/12.

23. Chamberlain to Dixon, 3 Mar. 1870, copy, JC5/27/13.

24. Chamberlain to Joseph Nettlefold, 10 May 1870, NC1/6/3/3.

25. Chamberlain to Joseph Nettlefold, 23 May 1870, NC1/6/3/13.

26. *Birmingham Daily Post*, 23 May 1870.

27. Transcript of Chamberlain's notebook, pp. 26–7, JC1/18/2.

28. F. Brett Young, *Portrait of Clare* (London, 1938), 240.

29. 8 March 1870, JC4/1/9.

30. Chamberlain to Harcourt, 2 July 1870, MS Harcourt Dep. 59.

31. Chamberlain to Dixon, 16 July [1870], JC5/27/14.

32. Chamberlain at the Birmingham Town Hall, 23 Nov. 1870, JC4/1/15–16.

33. 27 Jan. 1871, JC4/1/16–17.

34. For accounts of this episode, see A.F. Hooper, 'Mid-Victorian radicalism', 422, and J.S. Hurt, *Elementary Schooling and the Working Classes, 1860–1918* (London, 1979), 87.

35. Chamberlain at Sedgeley, 2 Dec. 1872, JC4/1/59.

36. Chamberlain in the Manchester Free Trade Hall, 22 Jan. 1872, JC4/1/36.

37. Speech at the Temperance Hall on 19 Feb. 1872, JC4/1/32–3.

38. For accounts of this campaign, see D.A. Hamer, *The Politics of Electoral Pressure: A study in the history of Victorian reform agitations* (Atlantic Highlands, New Jersey, 1977), 122ff.; and Patricia Auspos, 'Radicalism, pressure groups, and party politics: From the National Education League to the National Liberal Federation', *Journal of British Studies*, 20 (fall 1980), 181–204.

39. Chamberlain at Stroud, 26 Mar. 1872, JC4/1/40.

40. Chamberlain to Admiral Maxse, 26 June 1873, Maxse papers, 205, p. 18.

41. Chamberlain to W.H. Duigan, 28 June 1873, copy, JC8/3/1/1.

42. See the excellent biography by D.A. Hamer, *John Morley* (Oxford, 1968).

43. 17 July 1873, quoted in F.W. Hirst, *Early Life and Letters of John Morley* (London, 1927), i, 276.

44. Chamberlain to Morley, 19 July 1873, copy, JC5/54/3.

45. Chamberlain to Morley, ?10 Aug. 1873, copy, JC5/54/7.

46. Chamberlain to Admiral Maxse, 26 June 1873, Maxse papers.

47. Keith Robbins, *John Bright* (London, 1979), 212.

48. Chamberlain's report to J.T. Bunce, 10 Aug. 1873, copy, JC5/8/8a.

49. Chamberlain to H.J. Wilson, 12 Aug. 1873, Wilson papers (University of Sheffield); to Morley, 14 Aug. 1873, copy, JC5/54/10; and to Maxse, 28 Aug. 1873, Maxse papers, 205, pp. 19–20.

50. Chamberlain to Morley, 19 Aug. 1873, copy, JC5/54/13.

51. Chamberlain to Villiers Blake-

52. Chamberlain at a post-election dinner in St Paul's ward, 6 Dec. 1872, JC4/1/62.
53. JC4/2/7.
54. W.J. Davis, 'Early recollections of a great statesman', *Searchlight of Greater Birmingham*, 13 Nov. 1913.
55. Chamberlain to H.J. Wilson, 25 Dec. 1873, Wilson papers (University of Sheffield).
56. Abstract of Cost (Wages) of Screws at Smethwick commencing in January 1864, GKN archives (Smethwick).
57. Speech to the Sheffield Reform Association, 14 May 1873, JC4/1/74.
58. xiv n.s. (1 Sept. 1873).
59. 23 Sept. 1873, in C.W. Boyd, *Mr Chamberlain's Speeches* (London, 1914), i, 28ff.
60. See Dennis Smith, *Conflict and Compromise: Class formation in English society, 1830–1914: A comparative study of Birmingham and Sheffield* (London, 1982).
61. Chamberlain to Wilson, 13 Dec. 1873, Wilson papers.
62. Wilson to Chamberlain, 14 Dec. 1873, JC6/5/2/7.
63. Wilson to Chamberlain, 16 Dec. 1873, JC6/5/2/10.
64. Harris to Wilson, 17 Dec. 1873, Wilson papers.
65. Chamberlain to Wilson, 23 Dec. 1873, Wilson papers.
66. Wilson to Chamberlain, 24 Dec. 1873, JC6/5/2/22.
67. Chamberlain to Wilson, 25 Dec. 1873, Wilson papers.
68. Chamberlain to Admiral Maxse, ?Dec. 1873, Maxse papers 205, p. 14.
69. Speech at Sheffield, 1 Jan. 1874, JC4/3/23–31.
70. Wilson to Chamberlain, 27 Dec. 1873, and T. Paynter Allen to Chamberlain, 6 Jan. 1874, JC6/5/2/25 and 33; Mundella to Wilson, 9 Jan. 1874, Chamberlain to Wilson, 12 Jan. 1874, and Harris to Wilson, 21 Jan. 1874, Wilson papers; the *Sheffield Independent*, 30

Jan. 1874; and *Hansard*, 3rd ser., cccvi, 680–1 (1 June 1886).
71. Chamberlain to Wilson, 24 Jan. 1874, Wilson papers.
72. *Sheffield Post*, 31 Jan. 1874.
73. W.H.G. Armytage, *A.J. Mundella, 1825–1897* (London, 1951), 366 n. 46.
74. Chamberlain to Wilson, 9 Feb. 1874, Wilson papers.
75. Ibid.
76. *Sheffield Post*, 19 Mar. 1874.
77. Chamberlain to Wilson, ?15 Oct. 1875, Wilson papers (Sheffield City Library collection).
78. G.C. Allen, *The Industrial Development of Birmingham and the Black Country, 1860–1927* (New York, 1966, corrected reprint of the London, 1929 ed.), 211.
79. Chamberlain quoted by Lady Stanley, 5 Feb. 1887, in Garvin, *Life of Chamberlain*, iii, 299.

4. *Civic Investment: 1869–1880*

1. There are a number of excellent studies of the Chamberlain era in the government of Birmingham though not of the place of this era in his career. See J.T. Bunce, *History of the Corporation of Birmingham*, ii (Birmingham, 1885); Asa Briggs, *History of Birmingham*, ii: Borough and city, 1865–1938 (London, 1952) and *Victorian Cities* (London, 1963); E.P. Hennock, *Fit and Proper Persons: Ideal and reality in nineteenth-century urban government* (Montreal, 1973); Derek Fraser, *Urban Politics in Victorian England: The structure of politics in Victorian cities* (Leicester, 1976) and *Power and Authority in the Victorain City* (Oxford, 1979); and L.J. Jones, 'Public pursuit or private profit? Liberal businessmen and municipal politics in Birmingham, 1865–1900', *Business History*, xxv, 3 (Nov. 1983), 240–59.
2. His brother, as partner in James and Avery, had been for a while

in competition with Nettlefold and Chamberlain.

3. E.P. Hennock, *Fit and Proper Persons*, 96.
4. Chamberlain speaking on the sanitary condition of large towns, in Birmingham, 13 Jan. 1875, in C.W. Boyd, ed., *Mr Chamberlain's Speeches* (London, 1914), i, 65.
5. Quoted in E.P. Hennock, *Fit and Proper Persons*, 143.
6. M.H. Tiltman, *Quality Chase* (London, 1939), 262.
7. Chamberlain, 'Municipal institutions in America and England', *Forum* (Nov. 1892), 281.
8. Chamberlain to the town council, *Birmingham Daily Post*, 3 Aug. 1870, and JC4/1/12. There is an excellent discussion of this issue in A.F. Hooper, 'Mid-Victorian radicalism: Community and class in Birmingham, 1850–1880', University of London Ph.D. thesis, 1978, 235–41.
9. Chamberlain to Morley, 19 Nov. 1873, copy, JC5/54/28.
10. Chamberlain to H.J. Wilson, 8 Dec. 1873, Wilson papers.
11. Quoted in J.T. Bunce, *History of the Corporation of Birmingham*, ii, 347.
12. Chamberlain to the ratepayers meeting in the town hall, 13 Apr. 1874, JC4/1/117.
13. C.W. Boyd, ed., *Mr Chamberlain's Speeches*, i., 53.
14. Chamberlain to the school board, 18 June 1875, JC4/5/27.
15. 17 Oct. 1874, C.W. Boyd, ed., *Mr Chamberlain's Speeches*, i, 47. But he was reported to have commented to a friend before the festivities, 'I shall be ashamed of myself and the whole business.' Arthur Mee, *Joseph Chamberlain* (London, 1901), 59.
16. *Birmingham Daily Post*, 4 Nov. 1874.
17. 4 Nov. 1874.
18. 9 Nov. 1874.
19. Louise Chamberlain to Florence's children, n.d., NC1/6/4/16.
20. Chamberlain to the children of Florence, 5 Apr. 1875, Beatrice, Ida and Hilda Chamberlain papers.
21. NC1/6/4/23.
22. Chamberlain to Dale, 25 Mar. 1875, JC5/20/29.
23. Chamberlain to Samuel Timmins, 4 Apr. 1875, JC/L.Add./152.
24. Chamberlain to Collings, 12 Sept. 1875, copy, JC5/16/47.
25. Crosskey to Chamberlain, 18 Feb. 1875, NC1/6/4/6.
26. Chamberlain to Morley, 7 Dec. 1875, copy, JC5/54/61.
27. Chamberlain to Collings, May 1876, quoted in Garvin, *Life of Chamberlain*, i, 210.
28. Chamberlain to Mrs Pattison, 13 Feb. 1885, copy, JC5/24/409.
29. Quoted in J.T. Bunce, *History of the Corporation of Birmingham*, ii, 458.
30. Chamberlain to the town council, 12 Oct. 1875, ibid., 464.
31. 12 Oct. 1875, ibid., 464–5.
32. Jennifer Tann, *Joseph's Dream: Joseph Chamberlain and Birmingham's improvement* (Birmingham, 1978), 8.
33. Chamberlain to Collings, 12 Mar. 1876, JC5/16.
34. The best accounts of this episode are by W.J. Davis in *The Searchlight of Greater Birmingham*, 13 Nov. 1913, by A.F. Hooper, 'Mid-Victorian radicalism', 440ff., and by J.S. Hurt, *Elementary Schooling and the Working Classes, 1860–1918* (London, 1979), 88–9.
35. Quoted in Davis's recollections in *The Searchlight of Greater Birmingham*, 13 Nov. 1913.
36. Chamberlain in Bordesley ward, 1876, JC4/5/16–18.
37. Speech on 2 May 1876, JC4/5/39.
38. Chamberlain to Collings, 10 Apr. 1876, copy, JC5/16/51.
39. Chamberlain to Dilke, 29 Jan. 1876, Dilke papers.
40. Chamberlain to Collings, 6 June 1876, copy, JC5/16/54.

5. *Organizational Innovation: 1876–1880*

1. *Fortnightly Review* (Jan. 1876), 150.

2. Chamberlain to Mundella, 16 Oct. 1878, Mundella papers.

3. Chamberlain to Admiral Maxse, 5 July 1874, Maxse papers, 205, p. 22.

4. Morley to Chamberlain, 22 Nov. 1873, JC5/54/29.

5. Morley to Chamberlain, 28 May 1875, JC5/54/44.

6. *Fortnightly Review* (Oct. 1874), 405–29.

7. Ibid., 416.

8. Morley to Chamberlain, 16 Nov. 1874, JC5/54/40.

9. Chamberlain to the *Examiner*, 21 Jan. 1875.

10. Chamberlain to H.J. Wilson, 18 Dec. 1875, Wilson papers (Sheffield City Library).

11. Chamberlain to H.J. Wilson, 10 Jan. 1876, Wilson papers (Sheffield City Library).

12. Chamberlain to Cox, 31 Dec. 1875, copy, JC6/4f/2.

13. Chamberlain to H.J. Wilson, 6 Nov. 1875, Wilson papers (Sheffield City Library).

14. Chamberlain to Morley, 7 Dec. 1875, copy, JC5/54/61.

15. Ibid.

16. Chamberlain at Sheffield, 25 Nov. 1875, JC4/5/7–11.

17. Chamberlain to Morley, 27 Nov. 1875, copy, JC5/54/57.

18. Chamberlain to Morley, 30 Jan. 1876, copy, JC5/54/78.

19. Chamberlain to H.J. Wilson, 10 Apr. 1876, Wilson papers (Sheffield City Library).

20. Quoted in Garvin, *Life of Chamberlain*, i, 227.

21. Disraeli to Lady Chesterfield, 22 June 1876, written but not sent, quoted in G.E. Buckle, *The Life of Benjamin Disraeli, Earl of Beaconsfield* (N.Y., 1920), v, 480.

22. In *The Times* and the *Birmingham Daily Post*, 19 June 1876.

23. *Birmingham Daily Post*, 16 June 1876.

24. Chamberlain in Bingley Hall, 28 June 1876, JC4/5/45–8.

25. Chamberlain to Collings, 30 June 1876, JC5/16/55.

26. Chamberlain to Collings, 9 July 1876, copy, JC5/16/56.

27. Morley to Chamberlain, 10 July 1876, JC5/54/111.

28. Chamberlain to Collings, 30 June 1876, copy, JC5/16/55.

29. Chamberlain to Bunce, 26 July 1876, copy, JC5/8/18.

30. Chamberlain to Collings, 27 July 1876, copy, JC5/16/58. The half dozen included Sir Charles Dilke, MP for Chelsea, Joseph Cowen, MP for Newcastle, Thomas Burt, MP for Morpeth, L.L. Dillwyn, MP for Swansea, E.D. Gray, soon to be elected at Tipperary, and John Morley.

31. Chamberlain to Morley, 5 Aug. 1876, copy, JC5/54/114.

32. Quoted in R.T. Shannon, *Gladstone and the Bulgarian Agitation, 1876* (London, 1963), 120.

33. See what amounted to his article in the *Fortnightly Review*, Nov. 1876, pp. 686–690. This attribution is borne out by the exchange of letters between Morley and Chamberlain between 14 October and 3 November 1876, JC5/54/123, 125 and 126.

34. Chamberlain in Deritend Ward, 23 Oct. 1876, JC4/5/53–5.

35. Chamberlain to Henry Peyton, 23 Feb. 1877, JC/L.Add/93.

36. Chamberlain to Collings, 8 Feb. 1877, copy, JC5/16/59.

37. Chamberlain to Bunce, 16 Feb. 1877, copy, JC5/8/25.

38. Chamberlain to Morley, 20 Feb. 1877, copy, JC5/54/159.

39. Chamberlain to Gladstone, 16 Apr. 1877, Gladstone papers, Add.MS 44125.

40. Chamberlain in the Birmingham town hall, 9 Apr. 1877, JC4/5/85–7.

41. *Hansard*, 3rd ser., ccxxxiv, 455–6 (7 May 1877).

42. Gladstone to Granville, 17 May 1877, in Agatha Ramm, ed., *The Political Correspondence of Mr Gladstone and Lord Granville, 1868–1886* (London, 1952), i, 38–9.

43. Gladstone to Granville, 19 May 1877, ibid., 40; cf. Chamberlain to Gladstone, 16 Apr. 1877; and Gladstone to Granville, 23 May 1877, ibid., 42.

44. Chamberlain to Collings, 10 May 1877, copy, JC5/16/67.

45. *Proceedings attending the formation of the National Federation of Liberal Associations; with report of conference held in Birmingham, on Thursday, May 31st, 1877* (Birmingham, 1877).

46. Ibid., 16.

47. There is a wealth of good literature on the National Liberal Federation, including F.H. Herrick, 'The origins of the National Liberal Federation', *Journal of Modern History*, xvii, 2 (June 1945), 116–29; H.J. Hanham, *Elections and Party Management: Politics in the time of Disraeli and Gladstone* (London, 1959); Barry McGill, 'Francis Schnadhorst and Liberal party organization', *Journal of Modern History*, xxxiv, 1 (March 1962), 19–39; D.A. Hamer, *Liberal Politics in the Age of Gladstone and Rosebery* (Oxford, 1972); and Patricia Auspos, 'Radicalism, pressure groups, and party politics: From the National Education League to the National Liberal Federation', *Journal of British Studies*, 20 (fall 1980), 181–204.

48. Chamberlain at Sheffield, 5 Dec. 1877, JC4/5/114–18.

49. Chamberlain to Gladstone, 24 May 1877, Gladstone papers, BL Add.MS 44125.

50. N. Murrell Marris, *The Right Honourable Joseph Chamberlain* (London, 1900), 156.

51. David Dilks, *Neville Chamberlain* (Cambridge, 1984), i, 18.

52. 1 June 1877, in Agatha Ramm, ed., *The Political Correspondence of Mr Gladstone and Lord Granville, 1868–1886*, i, 43.

53. Chamberlain to Rosebery, 28 June 1877, Rosebery papers.

54. Chamberlain to Bunce, 16 Feb. 1877, copy, JC5/8/25.

55. Chamberlain to Morley, 3 Oct. 1877, copy, JC5/54/182.

56. Chamberlain to Hartington, 17 Nov. 1877, Devonshire papers.

57. Chamberlain to W.T. Stead, 21 Dec. 1877, Stead papers.

58. Chamberlain to Collings, 2 Apr. 1878, copy, JC5/16/81.

59. Chamberlain to Collings, 7 May 1878, copy, JC5/16/85.

60. Chamberlain to Admiral Maxse, 1 May 1878, Maxse papers, 205, p. 28.

61. Chamberlain to Mundella, 16 Oct. 1878, Mundella papers. Disraeli had been ennobled as Earl of Beaconsfield in 1876.

62. 'The caucus', *Fortnightly Review* (November 1878), 735. See also Chamberlain's earlier letter to *The Times*, 31 July 1878.

63. 'The caucus', 737.

64. Gladstone to Granville, 25 Aug. 1878, in Agatha Ramm, ed., *The Political Correspondence of Mr Gladstone and Lord Granville, 1868–1886*, i, 74–5.

65. Chamberlain to Hartington, 22 Dec. 1878, Devonshire papers.

66. Chamberlain to the National Liberal Federation Council, 22 Jan. 1879, JC4/5/155.

67. *Hansard*, 3rd ser., ccxliv, 1911 (27 Mar. 1879).

68. Chamberlain to H. Lee Warner, 8 Apr. 1879, copy, JC1/9/2.

69. *Hansard*, 3rd ser., ccxlvii, 1804–5 (7 July 1879).

70. Ibid., 1807.

71. Chamberlain to Morley, 22 July 1879, copy, JC5/54/265.

72. Chamberlain to Admiral Maxse, 17 July 1879, Maxse papers, 205, p. 31.

73. *Fortnightly Review* (August 1879), 195. On responsibility for this article, see Morley to Chamberlain, 23 Aug. 1879, JC5/54/270.

74. 14 Oct. 1879, JC4/5/170–4.

75. Chamberlain to W.T. Stead, 30 Sept. 1879, Stead papers.

76. Chamberlain to St Mary's Ward

Liberal Association, 8 Jan. 1880, JC4/5/185–8.

77. Chamberlain to F.W. Chesson, 7 Feb. 1880, Anti-Slavery Collection, Rhodes House, Oxford.

78. See David Cannadine, *Lords and Landlords: The aristocracy and the towns, 1774–1967* (Leicester, 1980), 191–4.

79. Chamberlain to Henry Peyton, 23 Oct. 1879, JC5/58/14.

80. Newsclipping dated 20 Mar. 1880, JC4/3/99–100.

81. Newsclipping dated 16 Mar. 1880, JC4/3/87.

82. Chamberlain to Morley, 31 Mar. 1880, copy, JC5/54/301.

83. Chamberlain to Collings, 9 Apr. 1880, copy, JC5/16/93.

84. In *The Times* for 13 Apr. 1880.

85. See H.J. Hanham, *Elections and Party Management* (London, 1959), particularly p. 144, n. 2; and Trevor Lloyd, *The General Election of 1880* (Oxford, 1968), chap. 6.

6. Assertive Apprentice: 1880–1884

1. Chamberlain to Morley, 25 Jan. 1880, copy, JC5/54/283.

2. Chamberlain to Dilke, [4 Apr. 1880], Dilke papers.

3. Dilke to Chamberlain, 24 Apr. 1880, JC5/24/15.

4. Chamberlain to Collings, 27 Apr. 1880, copy, JC5/16/94.

5. Trevor Lloyd, *The General Election of 1880* (Oxford, 1968), 158.

6. Chamberlain to his sister Clara, 4 May 1880, AC1/4/4/3.

7. Chamberlain at Birmingham, 30 Mar. 1883, in H.W. Lucy, ed., *Speeches of the Right Hon. Joseph Chamberlain, M.P.* (London, 1885), 38.

8. A.G. Gardiner, *The Life of Sir William Harcourt* (London, 1923), i, 368.

9. T.H.S. Escott, *Personal Forces of the Period* (London, 1898), 69ff.

10. Dilke to Granville, April 1882, in Stephen Gwynn and G.M. Tuckwell, *The Life of the Rt. Hon. Sir Charles W. Dilke, Bart., M.P.* (London, 1917), i, 424.

11. Gladstone to Chamberlain, 27 Apr. 1880, JC5/34/1.

12. Quoted in Stephen Koss, *The Rise and Fall of the Political Press in Britain* (Chapel Hill, 1981), i, 219.

13. Chamberlain to Dilke, 20 Sept. 1880, Dilke papers.

14. Chamberlain to Dilke, 19 Jan. 1882, Dilke papers.

15. Entry for 16 Mar. 1884 in Norman and Jeanne MacKenzie, ed., *The Diary of Beatrice Webb* (Cambridge, Mass., 1982), i, 105–6.

16. Darby Stafford, 'The Colonial Secretary's Country Home', *English Illustrated Magazine*, xxv (1901), 229–39, and the *Journal of Horticulture and Cottage Gardiner*, 12 Mar. 1896. I am indebted to Phillada Ballard for showing me her paper, '"Rus in Urbe": Joseph Chamberlain's gardens at Highbury, Moor Green, Birmingham, 1879–1916'.

17. Dixon to Chamberlain, 30 Apr. 1880, JC5/27/4.

18. Austen Chamberlain to Mr Sayle, 27 Oct. [no year], AC.L.Add.68.

19. Quoted in C.A. Petrie, *The Life and Letters of the Right Hon. Sir Austen Chamberlain* (London, 1939), i, 3.

20. Quoted in T. Wemyss Reid, *Life of the Rt Hon. W.E. Forster* (reprinted, New York, 1920), 330.

21. Chamberlain to Dilke, Christmas eve 1882, Dilke papers.

22. For a thorough exploration of all of his initiatives on merchant shipping see Geoffrey Alderman, 'Joseph Chamberlain's attempted reform of the British mercantile marine', *Journal of Transport History*, n.s.i (1972), 169–84.

23. Chamberlain at a livery dinner of the Carpenters' Company, *The Times*, 25 Nov. 1884.

24. Norwood to Chamberlain, 5 May 1880, JC2/14/13.

25. *Hansard*, 3rd ser., cclii, 964 (1 June 1880).

26. *Hansard*, 3rd ser., cclxiv, 1790 (12 Aug. 1881).
27. 30 Mar. 1883, in H.W. Lucy, ed., *Speeches of the Right Hon. Joseph Chamberlain*, 43.
28. For an analysis of this broad change, see José Harris, 'The transition to high politics in English social policy, 1880–1914', in Michael Bentley and John Stevenson, eds, *High and Low Politics in Modern Britain* (Oxford, 1983), 58–79.
29. Chamberlain in Birmingham reported in *The Times*, 17 Nov. 1880.
30. Chamberlain to Lord Spencer, 21 Nov. 1882, copy, JC8/9/3/14.
31. Chamberlain in Birmingham reported in *The Times*, 17 Nov. 1880.
32. Memorandum by Chamberlain, 18 Nov. 1880, Gladstone papers.
33. Chamberlain to Bunce, 6 May 1881, JC5/8/56.
34. Chamberlain to Dilke, 4 Oct. 1881, Dilke papers.
35. Chamberlain to Dilke, 12 Oct. 1881, Dilke papers; cf. Chamberlain to Granville, 18 Oct. 1881, Granville papers PRO30/29/117.
36. 25 Oct. 1881, in Joseph Chamberlain, *Home Rule and the Irish Question: A collection of speeches delivered between 1881 and 1887* (London, 1887).
37. Parnell to O'Shea, 28 Apr. 1881, quoted in J.L. Hammond, *Gladstone and the Irish Nation* (London, 1938), 277.
38. *Fortnightly Review* (January 1883), 149. On Chamberlain's responsibility for this article, see W.E. Houghton, ed., *The Wellesley Index to Victorian Periodicals, 1824–1900* (Toronto, 1972), ii, 235, item 1992.
39. Note by Chamberlain, [Aug. 1880], Devonshire papers.
40. Chamberlain in Birmingham, 7 June 1881, in H.W. Lucy, ed., *Speeches of the Right Hon. Joseph Chamberlain*, 18.
41. Gladstone to Chamberlain, 8 June 1881, JC5/34/5.

42. D.W.R. Bahlman, *The Diary of Sir Edward Walter Hamilton, 1880–1885* (Oxford, 1972), i, 145.
43. Chamberlain to Dale, 14 Sept. 1882, JC5/20/41.
44. Bright to Chamberlain, 4 Jan. 1883, JC5/7/20.
45. Chamberlain at Birmingham reported in *The Times*, 20 Dec. 1882.
46. *Hansard*, 3rd ser., cclxxii, 1796 (25 July 1882).
47. Chamberlain to Labouchere, 18 Dec. 1883, copy, JC5/50/18.
48. Chamberlain at Newcastle, 15 Jan. 1884, in H.W. Lucy, ed., *Speeches of the Right Hon. Joseph Chamberlain*, 70.
49. Chamberlain to Admiral Maxse, 30 Apr. 1884, Maxse papers, 205, p. 65.
50. Chamberlain to Dilke, 29 Dec. 1884, quoted in Ronald Robinson and John Gallagher with Alice Denny, *Africa and the Victorians* (London, 1961), 179.
51. Chamberlain to Bunce, 19 June 1884, copy, JC5/8/74.

7. *Rising Expectations: 1884–1885*

1. Chamberlain to Dilke, 9 Sept. 1881, Dilke papers.
2. Morley to Chamberlain, 24 Dec. 1882, JC5/54/66.
3. Memorandum on 'Nationalization of Land', undated, JC6/5/10/1.
4. Morley to Chamberlain, 24 Jan. 1883, JC5/54/481.
5. Chamberlain to Dilke, 31 Dec. 1882, Dilke papers.
6. Chamberlain to E.R. Russell, 22 Jan. 1883, copy, JC5/62/4.
7. Chamberlain to Dilke, 20 Jan. 1883, Dilke papers.
8. Chamberlain to E.R. Russell, 22 Jan. 1883, copy, JC5/62/4.
9. Chamberlain to Lady Dorothy Nevill, 4 Jan. 1883, JC/L.Add. 138.
10. Chamberlain to Mundella, 20 Jan. 1883, Mundella papers.
11. Chamberlain in Birmingham, 30

Mar. 1883, in H.W. Lucy, ed., *Speeches of the Right Hon. Joseph Chamberlain, M.P.* (London, 1885), 41.

12. Gladstone to Sir Henry Ponsonby, 30 June 1883, in Philip Guedalla, *The Queen and Mr Gladstone* (NY, 1934), 573.

13. Reported in *The Times*, 14 June 1883.

14. Chamberlain to the Cobden Club, 30 June 1883, reported in *The Times*, 2 July 1883.

15. Chamberlain to Gladstone, 2 July 1883, Gladstone papers, BL Add.MS 44125.

16. Chamberlain to the Battersea Radical Association, in *The Times*, 7 Sept. 1883.

17. Chamberlain to Henry Labouchere, 22 Dec. 1883, copy, JC5/50/20.

18. Diary entry for February 1884 in Beatrice Webb, *My Apprenticeship* (Penguin Books, 1971), 143.

19. Belying its title, the *Fortnightly* was published monthly. Extended, compiled and revised for publication in book form in July 1885, *The Radical Programme* has been published more recently in a well-edited edition by D.A. Hamer (Brighton, 1971).

20. D.A. Hamer, ed., *The Radical Programme*, 79.

21. Gladstone to Chamberlain, 3 Dec. 1883, JC5/34/20.

22. Chamberlain to the House of Commons, *Hansard*, 3rd ser., cclxxxviii, 731 (19 May 1884).

23. Chamberlain to Admiral Maxse, 19 Mar. 1884, Maxse papers, 205, p. 63, and to Frederic Harrison, 9 June ?1884, Harrison papers.

24. 'The Radical Programme. II.—Measures', *Fortnightly Review* (Sept. 1883), 439.

25. Gladstone to Chamberlain, 26 July 1884, JC5/34/28 and Gladstone to Ponsonby, 7 Aug. 1884, in Philip Guedalla, *The Queen and Mr Gladstone*, 620.

26. Chamberlain in Birmingham reported in *The Times*, 5 Aug. 1884.

27. See the printed extract in the Chamberlain papers, JC6/1/J/19.

28. Chamberlain at Newtown reported in *The Times*, 20 Oct. 1884.

29. Chamberlain to Morley, 16 Aug. 1884, copy, JC5/54/569.

30. Harcourt to Spencer, 31 Oct. 1884, in Peter Gordon, ed., *The Red Earl: The Papers of the Fifth Earl Spencer* (Northants Record Society, 1981–1986), i, 279.

31. Granville to Spencer, 8 Nov. 1884, ibid., 281.

32. Churchill to Chamberlain, 27 Nov. 1884, JC5/14/4.

33. J.R. Seeley, *The Expansion of England*, ed. John Gross (Chicago, 1971), 15.

34. Ibid., 17.

35. Ibid., 63.

36. Ibid., 41.

37. Ibid., 43.

38. Memorandum dated 1 Oct. 1884, JC9/1/1/6.

39. Froude to Chamberlain, 1 Dec. 1884, JC5/32/3.

40. Reported in *The Times*, 5 Nov. 1884.

41. Chamberlain to George Melly, 27 Nov. 1884, Melly papers.

42. Chamberlain to Gladstone, 28 Dec. 1884, Gladstone papers, BL Add.MS 44126.

43. Chamberlain to C.P. Ilbert, 19 Dec. 1884, copy, JC9/1/ 2/1.

8. Overextension: 1885

1. Michael Barker, *Gladstone and Radicalism: The reconstruction of Liberal policy in Britain, 1885–94* (New York, 1975), 15.

2. C.W. Boyd, ed., *Mr Chamberlain's Speeches* (New York, 1970), i, 134.

3. Ibid., 142.

4. Chamberlain to Dilke, [2 Feb. 1885], Dilke papers.

5. Chamberlain to Gladstone, 3 Feb. 1885, Gladstone papers, BL Add.MS 44126.

6. Gladstone to Chamberlain, 5 Feb. 1885, JC5/34/34.

7. Chamberlain to Gladstone, 7 Feb. 1885, Gladstone papers, BL Add.MS 44126.

8. R.B. Brett to Chamberlain, 9 Feb. 1885, JC5/6/5.

9. Ibid.

10. Chamberlain to Morley, 15 Feb. 1885, copy, JC5/54/612.

11. Memoranda by Chamberlain, 17 Mar. and 23 Apr. 1885, JC7/1/2/1 and Devonshire papers 340.1749.

12. Chamberlain to Henry Broadhurst, 6 Apr. 1885, Broadhurst papers.

13. Chamberlain to Edward Russell, 17 May 1885, copy, JC5/62/18.

14. Chamberlain to the Eighty Club, 28 Apr. 1885, in C.W. Boyd, ed., *Mr Chamberlain's Speeches*, i, 161.

15. Chamberlain to Morley, 21 Jan. 1885, copy, JC5/54/598.

16. Chamberlain to Duigan, 17 Dec. 1884, JC8/3/1/24.

17. C.H.D. Howard, 'Joseph Chamberlain, Parnell and the Irish "central board" scheme, 1884–5', *Irish Historical Studies*, viii, 32 (Sept. 1953), 328.

18. Chamberlain to Duigan, 17 Dec. 1884, JC8/3/1/24.

19. Parnell to O'Shea, 5 Jan. 1885, copy, JC8/7/3/4.

20. Parnell to O'Shea, 13 Jan. 1885, copy, JC8/7/3/5.

21. Chamberlain to Morley, 21 Jan. 1885, copy, JC5/54/598.

22. Quoted in A.B. Cooke and J.R. Vincent, *The Governing Passion: Cabinet government and party politics in Britain, 1885–86* (Brighton, 1974), 231.

23. Chamberlain to Edward Russell, 17 May 1885, copy, JC5/62/18.

24. Chamberlain to Lord Rosebery, 17 May 1885, Rosebery papers.

25. Chamberlain may have borne some responsibility for this. See J.L. Hammond, *Gladstone and the Irish Nation* (London, 1938), 373, n. 1.

26. Chamberlain to Spencer, 26 July 1885, copy, JC8/9/3/27.

27. Chamberlain to O'Shea, 3 Aug. 1885, copy, JC8/8/1/51.

28. Chamberlain speaking at Hackney, reported in *The Times*, 25 July 1885.

29. W. Wooding (Chamberlain's private secretary) to J. Wright, in *The Times*, 1 Aug. 1885.

30. Chamberlain to Mrs Pattison, 29 July 1885, copy, JC5/25/17.

31. Quoted in Roy Jenkins, *Sir Charles Dilke: A Victorian tragedy* (London, 1958), 354.

32. Chamberlain to Dilke, 30 June 1885, Dilke papers.

33. Chamberlain at Hull, 5 Aug. 1885, in C.W. Boyd, ed., *Mr Chamberlain's Speeches*, i, 166ff.

34. Spencer to Granville, 8 Aug. 1885, in Peter Gordon, ed., *The Red Earl: The Papers of the Fifth Earl Spencer* (Northants Record Society, 1981–1986), ii, 68.

35. F.W. Hirst, *Early Life & Letters of John Morley* (London, 1927), ii, 247.

36. Morley to Chamberlain, 29 Aug. 1885, JC5/54/619.

37. A.D. Elliot, *The Life of George Joachim Goschen, First Viscount Goschen, 1831–1907* (London, 1911), i, 309.

38. Chamberlain at Warrington, 8 Sept. 1885, in H.W. Lucy, ed., *Speeches of the Right Hon. Joseph Chamberlain, M.P.* (London, 1885), 188–9.

39. Gladstone to Chamberlain, 9 Sept. 1885, JC5/34/38.

40. Chamberlain to Gladstone, 10 Sept. 1885, Gladstone papers, BL Add.MS 44126.

41. Quoted in Michael Barker, *Gladstone and Radicalism: The reconstruction of Liberal policy in Britain, 1885–94* (New York, 1975), 20.

42. Chamberlain to Dilke, 20 Sept. 1885, Dilke papers.

43. Chamberlain to Gladstone, 20 Sept. 1885, copy, JC5/34/79.

44. Gladstone to Chamberlain, 26 Sept. 1885, JC5/34/42.

45. Gladstone to Granville, 8 Oct. 1885, in Agatha Ramm, ed., *The Political Correspondence of Mr*

Gladstone and Lord Granville, 1868–1886 (London, 1952), ii, 403ff.

46. Chamberlain to Dilke, 7 Oct. 1885, Dilke papers.

47. Gladstone to Granville, 8 Oct. 1885, in Agatha Ramm, ii, 403ff.

48. Chamberlain to Dilke, 9 Oct. 1885, Dilke papers.

49. Harcourt to Chamberlain, 7 Oct. 1885, JC5/38/37.

50. Chamberlain to Harcourt, 9 Oct. 1885, copy, JC5/38/151.

51. Labouchere to Chamberlain, 18 Oct. 1885, JC5/50/28.

52. Chamberlain to Labouchere, 20 Oct. 1885, copy, JC5/50/29.

53. Chamberlain to Morley, 8 Nov. 1885, copy, JC5/54/657.

54. Chamberlain to Gladstone, 26 Oct. 1885, Gladstone papers, BL Add.MS 44126.

55. Labouchere to Chamberlain, 10 Nov. 1885, JC5/50/32.

56. Robert Rhodes James, *Rosebery* (New York, 1963), 173.

57. Chamberlain in Birmingham, reported in *The Times*, 16 Jan. 1883.

58. Dilke to Chamberlain, 21 Nov. 1885, JC5/24/156.

9. The Crash: 1885–1886

1. Chamberlain to Labouchere, 4 Dec. 1885, copy, JC5/50/41.

2. Chamberlain to Hartington, 6 Dec. 1885, copy, JC5/38/152.

3. Dilke to Chamberlain, 30 Nov. 1885, JC5/24/157.

4. Chamberlain to Labouchere, 7 Dec. 1885, copy, JC5/50/43.

5. Gladstone to Rosebery, quoted in Robert Rhodes James, *Rosebery* (New York, 1963), 175.

6. John Morley, *Recollections* (New York, 1917), i, 147.

7. Ibid., 209.

8. Chamberlain to Admiral Maxse, 25 Apr. 1885, Maxse papers, 205, p. 79.

9. Morley to Chamberlain, 19 Sept. 1885, JC5/54/627.

10. Gladstone to Chamberlain, 6 Nov. 1885, JC5/34/44.

11. Morley to Chamberlain, 13 Dec. 1885, JC5/54/663.

12. Morley to Chamberlain, 16 Dec. 1885, JC5/54/666.

13. Morley to Spence Watson, 15 Dec. 1885, in F.W. Hirst, *Early Life & Letters of John Morley* (London, 1927), ii, 272.

14. Edward R. Russell, *That Reminds Me* (London, 1899), 55. Cf. R.B. O'Brien, *The Life of Charles Stewart Parnell, 1846–1891* (1898; reprinted, New York, 1968), ii, 116.

15. Morley to Chamberlain, 24 Dec. 1885, JC5/54/670.

16. Morley to Chamberlain, 28 Dec. 1885, JC5/54/674.

17. Chamberlain to Morley, 29 Dec. 1885, copy, JC5/54/676.

18. Morley to Chamberlain, 1 Jan. 1886, JC5/54/677.

19. Quoted in D.A. Hamer, *Liberal Politics in the Age of Gladstone and Rosebery* (Oxford, 1972), 106.

20. Chamberlain to R.B. Brett, 19 Dec. 1885, Esher papers.

21. Chamberlain to Dilke, 19 Dec. 1885, Dilke papers.

22. Gladstone to Chamberlain, 18 Dec. 1885, JC5/34/46.

23. Chamberlain to Gladstone, 19 Dec. 1885, Gladstone papers, BL Add.MS 44126.

24. Gladstone to Chamberlain, 18 Dec. 1885, JC5/34/46.

25. Chamberlain to Labouchere, 3 Jan. 1886, copy, JC5/50/60.

26. Chamberlain to Harcourt, 27 Dec. 1885, Harcourt papers.

27. Chamberlain to Labouchere, 3 Jan. 1886, copy, JC5/50/60.

28. A.B. Cooke and J.R. Vincent, *The Governing Passion: Cabinet government and party politics in Britain, 1885–86* (Brighton, 1974), 321.

29. Chamberlain to Gladstone, 30 Jan. 1886, Gladstone papers, BL Add.MS 44126.

30. Bright to Chamberlain, 4 Feb. 1886, JC5/7/26.

31. Gladstone to Harcourt, 8 Feb.

1886, in A.G. Gardiner, *The Life of Sir William Harcourt* (London, 1923), i, 568.

32. Chamberlain to R.B. Brett, 8 Feb. 1886, Esher papers.

33. A.B. Cooke and J.R. Vincent, *The Governing Passion*, 351.

34. Morley to Gladstone, 2 Feb. 1886, and Gladstone to Morley, 2 Feb. 1886, copy, Gladstone papers, BL Add.MS 44255, ff.54–5.

35. Chamberlain to Morley, 4 Feb. 1886, copy, JC5/54/685.

36. R.B. Brett's journal, entry for 5 Feb. 1886, in M.V. Brett and Lord Esher, *Journals and Letters of Reginald Viscount Esher* (London, 1934–8), i, 123.

37. Chamberlain to Labouchere, 15 Feb. 1886, copy, JC5/50/68.

38. Chamberlain to Sir Charles Butt, 5 Feb. 1886, Dilke-Crawford-Roskill papers.

39. Norman and Jeanne MacKenzie, eds, *The Diary of Beatrice Webb*, vol. i: 1873–1892 (Cambridge, Mass., 1982)—hereafter cited as *Diary of Beatrice Webb*—entry for 15 July 1883, 90.

40. Ibid., 26 Sept. 1883, 94–5.

41. Ibid., 95.

42. Quoted in Jeanne MacKenzie, *A Victorian Courtship: The story of Beatrice Potter and Sidney Webb* (London, 1979), 21.

43. Beatrice Potter to Mary Playne, Oct. 1883, quoted in *Diary of Beatrice Webb*, i, 99.

44. Chamberlain to Beatrice Potter, 16 Dec. 1883, Passfield papers.

45. *Diary of Beatrice Webb*, 12 Jan. 1884, 102–3.

46. Ibid., 16 Mar. 1884, 108 and 111.

47. Quoted in Jeanne MacKenzie, *A Victorian Courtship*, 33.

48. *Diary of Beatrice Webb*, 6 Mar. 1886, 156.

49. Chamberlain to Beatrice Potter, 28 Feb. 1886, Passfield papers.

50. Beatrice Potter to Chamberlain, Feb. 1886, JC5/59/1.

51. Chamberlain to Beatrice Potter, 5 Mar. 1885, Passfield papers.

52. *Diary of Beatrice Webb*, 6 Mar. 1887, 156.

53. Joseph to Arthur Chamberlain, 8 Mar. 1886, copy, JC5/11/5.

54. Chamberlain to Gladstone, 15 Mar. 1886, Gladstone papers, BL Add.MS 44126.

55. Enclosure with W. Wooding to J.T. Bunce, 17 Mar. 1886, copy, JC5/8/83.

56. Gladstone to Harcourt, 20 Mar. 1887, in A.G. Gardiner, *The Life of Sir William Harcourt* (London, 1923), i, 576.

57. Notes dated 18 Mar. 1886, Gladstone papers, BL Add.MS 44647, ff.44 and 45.

58. Note by Gladstone, 22 Mar. 1886, Gladstone papers, BL Add.MS 44647, f.50.

59. Lord Askwith, *Lord James of Hereford* (London, 1930), 172.

60. Balfour wrote a full report of the conversation to Salisbury, 22 Mar. 1886, copy, Austen Chamberlain papers, AC1/4/4/6.

61. Recorded in Gladstone's notes on the cabinet council of 26 March 1886, Gladstone papers, BL Add.MS 44647, ff.56–7.

62. Gladstone papers, BL Add.MS 44647, f.54.

63. Quoted in J.L. Hammond, *Gladstone and the Irish Nation* (London, 1938), 495.

64. Memorandum by Sir Thomas Farrer, 1 Apr. 1886, Farrer papers.

65. Quoted in Roy Jenkins, *Sir Charles Dilke* (London, 1958), 254.

66. A.B. Cooke and J.R. Vincent, *The Governing Passion*, 107.

67. Collings had been elected as MP for Ipswich but was unseated on charges of electoral corruption just after the resignation of Chamberlain, whose sense of isolation in the crisis was thus aggravated.

68. *Diary of Beatrice Webb*, March 1884, 90.

69. Schnadhorst to Chamberlain, 13 Feb. 1886, JC5/63/9.

70. Schnadhorst to Labouchere, 4 Apr. 1886, Viscount Gladstone papers,

BL Add.MS 46016, ff.23–4.

71. Morley to Chamberlain, 7 Apr. 1886, JC5/54/687.

72. In spite of still being in love with Chamberlain, Beatrice Potter sat among the observers, and she left a vivid description of the occasion in her diary: *Diary of Beatrice Webb*, 12 Apr. 1886, 160–3.

73. *Hansard*, 3rd ser., ccciv, 1186 (9 Apr. 1886).

74. *Diary of Beatrice Webb*, 12 Apr. 1886, 160–3.

75. *Hansard*, 3rd ser., ccciv, 1205 (9 Apr. 1886).

76. Reported in *The Times*, 22 Apr. 1886.

77. Crosskey to Chamberlain, 22 Apr. 1886, JC8/5/3/14.

78. Quoted in Chamberlain, *A Political Memoir, 1880–92*, ed. C.H.D. Howard (London, 1953), 213.

79. Chamberlain to Labouchere, 2 May 1886, copy, JC5/50/88.

80. Morley to Spence Watson, 11 May 1886, quoted in A.B. Cooke and J.R. Vincent, *The Governing Passion*, 417, note.

81. Dilke to Chamberlain, May Day 1886, JC5/24/177.

82. Chamberlain to Dilke, 3 May 1886, Dilke papers.

83. Chamberlain to Dilke, 6 May 1886, Dilke papers.

84. Dilke to Chamberlain, 6 May 1886, JC5/24/179.

85. Chamberlain to Dilke, 21 May 1886, Dilke papers.

86. Chamberlain to Labouchere, 24 Apr. 1886, copy, JC5/50/82.

87. Chamberlain to Labouchere, 30 Apr. 1886, copy, JC5/50/24.

88. A.B. Cooke and J.R. Vincent, *The Governing Passion*, 410–11.

89. Chamberlain to Harcourt, 5 May 1886, copy, JC5/38/160.

90. Chamberlain to Labouchere, 2 May 1886, copy, JC5/50/88.

91. Joseph to Arthur Chamberlain, 7 May 1886, copy, JC5/11/6.

92. Chamberlain to T.H. Bolton, 7 May 1886, in *The Times*, 8 May 1886.

93. So they were described by the Gladstonian apologist, J.L. Hammond, in *Gladstone and the Irish Nation* (London, 1938), 527.

94. Joseph to Arthur Chamberlain, 17 May 1886, copy, JC5/11/9.

95. *Hansard*, 3rd ser., cccv, 698–700 (1 June 1886).

96. Dale to J.P. Perkins, 10 June 1886, in A.W.W. Dale, *The Life of R.W. Dale of Birmingham* (London, 1898), 464.

97. Powell Williams to Chamberlain, 3 June 1886, JC5/72/6.

98. Quoted in A.B. Cooke and J.R. Vincent, *The Governing Passion*, 431.

99. *Hansard*, 3rd ser., ccccvi, 1233 (7 June 1886).

100. This is the meeting that Lloyd George is alleged to have missed because he travelled to Birmingham on the wrong day. The mistake saved him from a premature declaration of support for Chamberlain's Unionist brand of Radicalism, which Lloyd George's home province of Wales firmly rejected in the ensuing general election. John Grigg, *The Young Lloyd George* (London, 1973), 51.

101. Chamberlain to St John Brodrick, 15 June 1886, Midleton papers.

102. Chamberlain to Churchill, 17 June 1886, Lord Randolph Churchill papers.

103. Chamberlain's first public address of the campaign, in Birmingham on 19 June 1886, in Joseph Chamberlain, *Home Rule and the Irish Question: A collection of speeches delivered between 1881 and 1887* (London, 1887), 149.

104. Speech of 2 July 1886, ibid., 198–9.

105. Speech in Cardiff, 6 July 1886, ibid., 211.

106. Speech in Rawtenstall, 8 July 1886, ibid., 216.

107. Gladstone to Sir Thomas Farrer, 4 July 1886, Farrer papers.

108. Chamberlain's reply to T.K. Tapling in *The Times*, 29 June 1886, 7, to Thomas Guest in *The Times*, 3

July 1886, 11, and to a Liberal elector in *The Times*, 3 July 1886, 14.

109. Chamberlain to Lady Dorothy Nevill, 11 July 1886, JC5/56/42.

10. *In Bankruptcy: 1886–1887*

1. Recollection of James Bryce quoted in A.B. Cooke and J.R. Vincent, *The Governing Passion* (Brighton, 1974), 439.
2. Chamberlain to Sir Henry James, 14 July 1886, James of Hereford papers. The Invincibles and the Thugs were notorious terrorists, the one group in Ireland, the other in India.
3. He warned him through their intermediary, Sir Henry James. Chamberlain to James, 16 July 1886, James of Hereford papers.
4. Chamberlain to Sir Henry James, 23 July 1886, James of Hereford papers.
5. Chamberlain to the Rev. H.E. Dowson, 17 July 1886, copy, in the Bryce papers, U.B.4.
6. Chamberlain to Sir Henry James, 14 July 1886, James of Hereford papers.
7. Churchill to Chamberlain, 7 Aug. 1886, JC5/14/20.
8. Chamberlain to Churchill, 8 Aug. 1886, Churchill papers.
9. Hartington to Chamberlain, 6 Aug. 1886, JC5/22/15.
10. Salisbury to the Queen, 6 Aug. 1886, in G.E. Buckle, ed., *The Letters of Queen Victoria* (London, 1930), 3rd ser., i, 172.
11. Churchill to Chamberlain, 27 Aug. 1886, JC5/14/23.
12. Chamberlain to Hartington, 9 Sept. 1886, JC5/22/124.
13. Letter from Chamberlain, 2 Oct. 1886, in *The Times*, 5 Oct. 1886.
14. Churchill to Chamberlain, 12 Aug. 1886, quoted in R.F. Foster, *Lord Randolph Churchill* (Oxford, 1981), 279.
15. Chamberlain's report to Dilke, quoted ibid., 293.
16. Chamberlain to Churchill, 5 Oct. 1886, Churchill papers.
17. Chamberlain to the Liberal Divisional Council of West Birmingham, 23 Dec. 1886, in *The Times*, 24 Dec. 1886.
18. Salisbury to Sir James Stephen, 30 Dec. 1886, quoted in J.P.D. Dunbabin, 'The politics of the establishment of County Councils', *Historical Journal*, vi, 2 (1963), 248.
19. Chamberlain to Churchill, 26 Dec. 1886, Churchill papers.
20. Chamberlain to Churchill, 23 Dec. 1886, Churchill papers.
21. Chamberlain to the Liberal Divisional Council of West Birmingham, 23 Dec. 1886, *The Times*, 24 Dec. 1886.
22. Gladstone to Harcourt, 7 Jan. 1887, quoted in A.G. Gardiner, *The Life of Sir William Harcourt* (London, 1923), ii, 26.
23. Morley to Harcourt, 6 Jan. 1887, quoted in D.A. Hamer, *John Morley* (Oxford, 1968), 221.
24. Chamberlain's notes on the conference of 14 Jan. 1887, JC8/9/2/3.
25. Harcourt to Morley, 17 Jan. 1887, in A.G. Gardiner, *The Life of Sir William Harcourt*, ii, 603.
26. Morley to Harcourt, 18 Jan. 1887, ibid., 29.
27. Quoted ibid., 32.
28. *The Baptist*, 25 Feb. 1887.
29. *Hansard*, 3rd ser., cccxii, 1418 (24 Mar. 1887).
30. Chamberlain to Balfour, 30 Mar. 1887, Balfour papers (British Library).
31. Chamberlain to Balfour, 31 Mar. 1887, Balfour papers (British Library).
32. Joseph to Beatrice Chamberlain, 30 Mar. 1887, Beatrice Chamberlain papers.
33. Chamberlain at Glasgow, in *The Times*, 4 May 1887.
34. Reported in *The Times*, 14 Apr. 1887.
35. Reported ibid., 18 Apr. 1887.
36. Reported ibid., 25 Apr. 1887.
37. Reported ibid., 29 Apr. 1887.

38. Chamberlain, and also Jesse Collings who accompanied him on this tour, thus missed this critical vote. Both were absent unpaired. Chamberlain declared afterwards that he would have voted for the second reading and had tried but found himself unable to pair on the question: note in *The Times* of 11 May 1887.

39. Reported in *The Times*, 4 May 1887.

40. The best account of this subject is by R.A. Wright, 'Liberal party organisation and politics in Birmingham, Coventry and Wolverhampton 1886–1914, with particular reference to the development of Independent Labour representation', University of Birmingham Ph.D. dissertation, 1977.

41. Chamberlain to R.B. Brett, 5 June 1887, Esher papers.

42. Chamberlain to Beatrice Potter, 19 May 1887, Passfield papers.

43. The Rev. J. Charles Cox to the editor of the *Sheffield Independent*, 21 May 1887, H.J. Wilson papers.

44. National Radical Union, *Report of the Proceedings of the Annual Meeting & Conference, held in Birmingham, on Wednesday, June 1st, 1887* (Birmingham, 1887), 13.

45. Chamberlain to Churchill, 13 July 1887, Churchill papers.

46. Chamberlain to Churchill, 12 July 1887, Churchill papers.

47. Chamberlain to Churchill, 13 July 1887, Churchill papers.

48. *Hansard*, 3rd ser., cccxviii, 828 (1 Aug. 1887).

49. Churchill to Chamberlain, 2 Aug. 1887, JC5/14/33.

50. Chamberlain to Churchill, 19 Aug. 1887, Churchill papers.

51. Morley to Chamberlain, 14 Aug. 1887, JC5/54/702.

52. Quoted in Robert Rhodes James, *Rosebery* (New York, 1963), 196.

53. Speech on Saturday, 20 Aug. 1887, reported in *The Times* of 22 Aug. 1887.

54. Chamberlain to Churchill, 19 Aug. 1887, Churchill papers.

55. Norman and Jeanne MacKenzie, eds, *The Diary of Beatrice Webb* (Cambridge, Mass., 1982), i, 163.

56. Ibid., 177.

57. Ibid., 179.

58. Ibid., 209–10.

59. Ibid., 212.

60. Chamberlain to Beatrice Potter, 7 Aug. 1887, in *Diary of Beatrice Webb*, i, 210–11.

61. Ibid., 226.

11. New Resources: 1887–1891

1. Queen Victoria's journal, 17 July 1887, Royal Archives.

2. Chamberlain to Churchill, 6 Sept. 1887, Churchill papers.

3. Chamberlain to Collings, 18 Sept. 1887, copy, JC5/16/124.

4. Report of Chamberlain's remarks to the executive of the National Radical Union, in *The Times*, 24 Sept. 1887.

5. Report in *The Times*, 30 Sept. 1887.

6. Chamberlain to Churchill, 2 Oct. 1887, Churchill papers.

7. Chamberlain at Barrow, 24 June 1886, in *Home Rule and the Irish Question* (London, 1887), 181.

8. Ibid.

9. Chamberlain at Belfast, 12 Oct. 1887, in C.W. Boyd, ed., *Mr Chamberlain's Speeches* (London, 1914), i, 296.

10. Speech at Belfast, 11 Oct. 1887, ibid., 282.

11. Speech at Belfast, 12 Oct. 1887, ibid., 287.

12. Chamberlain to Hartington, 27 Oct. 1887, copy, JC5/22/128.

13. Speech at Belfast, 12 Oct. 1887, *Mr Chamberlain's Speeches*, 289.

14. Cecil Spring Rice to a friend, 28 Oct. 1887, in Stephen Gwynn, *The Letters and Friendships of Sir Cecil Spring Rice* (London, 1930), i, 77.

15. Joseph to Beatrice Chamberlain, 14 Nov. 1887, AC1/4/5/37.

16. Joseph to Beatrice Chamberlain, 12 Nov. 1887, AC1/4/5/37.

17. Joseph to Beatrice Chamberlain, 14 Nov. 1887, AC1/4/5/37.
18. Remark by Mr Lamar, Secretary of the Interior, in the report by *The Times*, 17 Nov. 1887.
19. Chamberlain to the New York Chamber of Commerce, 16 Nov. 1887, AC1/4/6/10.
20. Joseph to Beatrice Chamberlain, 25 Nov. 1887, AC1/4/5/37.
21. Joseph to Beatrice Chamberlain, 18 Jan. 1888, AC1/4/5/47.
22. Joseph to Beatrice Chamberlain, 15 Dec. 1887, AC1/4/5/42.
23. Joseph to Beatrice Chamberlain, 25 Nov. 1887, AC1/4/5/37.
24. Joseph to Beatrice Chamberlain, 9 Dec. 1887, AC1/4/5/41.
25. Cecil Spring Rice to a friend, 20 Dec. 1887, in Stephen Gwynn, *The Letters and Friendships of Sir Cecil Spring Rice*, i, 79.
26. Joseph to Beatrice Chamberlain, 2 Dec. 1887, AC1/4/5/40.
27. Chamberlain to Mary Endicott, 11 July 1888, JC23/A1/37.
28. Chamberlain to Mary Endicott, 8 June 1888, JC28/A1/28.
29. Chamberlain to Mary Endicott, 30 June 1888, JC28/A1/34.
30. Chamberlain to Dilke, 11 Dec. 1887, Dilke papers.
31. Chamberlain to Mary Endicott, 18 July 1888, JC28/A1/39.
32. Chamberlain to Mary Endicott, 28 Apr. 1888, JC28/A1/16.
33. Chamberlain to Mary Endicott, 21 June 1888, JC28/A1/31.
34. Chamberlain to Mary Endicott, 13 Dec. 1887, JC28/A2/1/1.
35. Mary Endicott to Chamberlain, 18 July 1888, JC28/B1/36.
36. Mary Endicott to Chamberlain, 15 Oct. 1888, JC28/B1/61.
37. Mary Endicott to Chamberlain, 1 May 1888, JC28/B1/14.
38. Mary Endicott to Fanny Mason, 27 Dec. 1887, in Diana W. Laing, *Mistress of Herself* (Barre, Mass., 1965), 41.
39. Chamberlain to Salisbury, 11 Dec. 1887, Salisbury papers.
40. Joseph to Beatrice Chamberlain, 28 Dec. 1887, AC1/4/5/44.
41. Joseph to Beatrice Chamberlain, 3 Jan. 1888, AC1/4/5/45.
42. Report in the *Toronto World* of 30 Dec. 1887 quoted in Willoughby Maycock, *With Mr Chamberlain in the United States and Canada, 1887–88* (London, 1914), 98.
43. The best report of this speech, delivered on 30 December 1887, is in Willoughby Maycock, ibid., 100ff.
44. Lord Lansdowne to Chamberlain, 3 Jan. 1888, JC3/1/115.
45. Joseph to Beatrice Chamberlain, 18 Jan. 1888, AC1/4/5/47.
46. Ibid.
47. Ibid.
48. Entry for 26 Jan. 1888 in Chamberlain's Diary in America, JC3/14.
49. Mary Endicott to Chamberlain, 13 and 27 Apr. 1888, JC28/B1/10 and 13.
50. Chamberlain to Mary Endicott, 21 June 1888, JC28/A1/31.
51. Chamberlain to Salisbury, 13 Jan. 1888, Salisbury papers.
52. Chamberlain to Mary Endicott, 'Friday night', 11 Feb. 1888, JC28/A2/1/5.
53. Mary Endicott to Chamberlain, 28 Sept. 1888, JC28/B1/57.
54. Chamberlain to Mary Endicott, 'Saturday night 2 a.m.', 12 Feb. 1888, JC28/A2/1/6.
55. Joseph to Beatrice Chamberlain, 17 Feb. 1888, AC1/4/5/51.
56. Chamberlain to Mary Endicott, 10 Mar. 1888, JC28/A1/5.
57. Chamberlain to Mary Endicott, 8 July 1888, JC28/A1/36.
58. Chamberlain to Mary Endicott, 7 Apr. 1888, JC28/A1/10.
59. Chamberlain to Mary Endicott, 21 Apr. 1888, JC28/A1/14.
60. Chamberlain to Mary Endicott, 12 May 1888, JC28/A1/20.
61. Ibid.
62. Mary Endicott to Chamberlain, 23 Mar. 1888, JC28/B1/5.
63. Mary Endicott to Chamberlain, 10 Apr. 1888, JC28/B1/9.
64. Beatrice Chamberlain to Mary Endicott, 11 May 1888, Endicott

papers.

65. Mary Endicott to Chamberlain, 6 Apr. 1888, JC28/B1/8a.

66. Chamberlain to Mary Endicott, 7 Apr. 1888, JC28/A1/10.

67. Chamberlain to Mary Endicott, 10 Apr. 1888, JC28/A1/11.

68. Chamberlain to Mary Endicott, 19 Apr. 1888, JC28/A1/13a.

69. Chamberlain to Mary Endicott, 20 May 1888, JC28/A1/22.

70. Chamberlain speaking on the second reading of the Local Government bill, *Hansard*, 3rd ser., cccxxiv, 1362 (16 Apr. 1888).

71. Chamberlain to Salisbury, 13 Jan. 1888, Salisbury papers.

72. Salisbury at Liverpool, 13 Jan. 1888, quoted in Peter Marsh, *The Discipline of Popular Government* (Hassocks, 1978), 127.

73. Salisbury to Chamberlain, 1 Feb. 1888, JC3/1/88.

74. Chamberlain to Mary Endicott, 18 Mar. 1888, JC28/A1/7.

75. Chamberlain in Birmingham, 18 Apr. 1888, in *Speeches on the Irish Question* (London, 1890), 89.

76. Chamberlain to Mary Endicott, 7 June 1888, JC28/A1/27, refuting his later claim in *A Political Memoir, 1880–92*, ed. C.H.D. Howard (London, 1953), 280.

77. Reported in *The Times*, 26 May 1888.

78. Chamberlain to Mary Endicott, 19 Mar. 1888, JC28/A1/7.

79. Chamberlain to the Devonshire Club, 9 Apr. 1888, in C.W. Boyd, ed., *Mr Chamberlain's Speeches*, i, 322–4.

80. 18 Apr. 1888, in Joseph Chamberlain, *Speeches on the Irish Question: A collection of speeches delivered between 1887 and 1890* (London, 1890), 93.

81. Chamberlain to Mary Endicott, 1 May 1888, JC28/A1/17.

82. Quoted once again by Chamberlain at the close of this speech, reported in *The Times*, 15 May 1888.

83. Chamberlain to Mary Endicott, 4 May 1888, JC28/A1/18.

84. Chamberlain to Bunce, 28 June 1888, copy, JC5/8/103.

85. Chamberlain to Mary Endicott, 26 June 1888, JC28/A1/32.

86. Chamberlain to Mary Endicott, 14 June 1888, JC28/A1/30.

87. Lord Dunraven, *Past Times and Pastimes* (London, 1922), i, 259.

88. Chamberlain to Mary Endicott, 3 July 1888, JC28/A1/34a.

89. Chamberlain to Mary Endicott, 10 July 1888, JC28/A1/36b.

90. H.W. Lucy, *A Diary of the Salisbury Parliament, 1886–1892* (London, 1892), 145 and 147.

91. Chamberlain to Mary Endicott, 7 July 1888, JC28/A1/36.

92. *Hansard*, 3rd ser., cccxxix, 351 (24 July 1888).

93. Chamberlain to Mary Endicott, 31 July 1888, JC28/A1/42a.

94. *Hansard*, 3rd ser., cccxxix, 968 (31 July 1888).

95. O'Shea to *The Times*, 1 Aug. 1888, in Henry Harrison, *Parnell, Joseph Chamberlain and Mr Garvin* (London, 1938), 243.

96. Chamberlain to Mary Endicott, 1 Aug. 1888, JC28/A1/43.

97. Chamberlain to Mary Endicott, 8 Aug. 1888, JC28/A1/45.

98. *The Times*, 13 Aug. 1888.

99. Reported in *The Times*, 21 Sept. 1888.

100. Chamberlain to Mary Endicott, 5 Oct. 1888, JC28/A1/61.

101. Norman and Jeanne MacKenzie, eds, *The Diary of Beatrice Webb* (Cambridge, Mass., 1982), i, 265–7.

102. Speech at Dundee, 14 Feb. 1889, in *Speeches on the Irish Question* (London, 1890), 171–2.

103. Speech in Glasgow reported in *The Times*, 13 Feb. 1888.

104. Chamberlain's address to the first annual dinner, reported in *The Times*, 29 Jan. 1889.

105. Powell Williams to Chamberlain, 28 Mar. 1889, JC6/2/1/3.

106. Chamberlain to Akers-Douglas, 31 Mar. 1889. Chilston papers.

107. Balfour to Salisbury, 2 July 1889, cited by John France in 'Personali-

ties and politics in the formation of the Unionist alliance, 1885–1895', Cambridge Ph.D. thesis 1985, p. 357.

108. Notes by Mary Chamberlain, JC19/3/1.

109. Chamberlain's memorandum on development of the resources of Turkey, JC7/4/1/4.

110. Chamberlain to Mrs Endicott, 22 Jan. 1890, AC4/5/1.

111. Diana Whitehall Laing, *Mistress of Herself* (Barre, Mass., 1965), 78.

112. Chamberlain to Mary Endicott, 21 July 1888, JC28/A1/40.

113. Chamberlain to Mary Endicott, 17 Oct. 1888, JC28/A1/64a.

114. Chamberlain to O'Shea, 10 Jan. 1890, copy, JC8/8/1/131.

115. Chamberlain to Mrs Endicott, 1 Dec. 1890, AC4/5/3.

116. Lord Derby's entry for 6 Dec. 1890 in John Vincent, ed., *The Later Derby Diaries* (Bristol, 1981).

117. Joseph to Mary Chamberlain, 27 Sept. 1890, JC28/A2/3/5.

118. Chamberlain to Collings, 28 Oct. 1890, copy, JC5/16/127.

119. Joseph to Austen Chamberlain, 18 Dec. 1890, AC1/4/3/3.

120. See below, pp, 361–4.

121. Joseph to Austen Chamberlain, 16 Jan. 1891, AC1/4/3/4.

122. Chamberlain speaking in Birmingham, reported in *The Times*, 23 Feb. 1891.

123. Chamberlain in Birmingham, reported in *The Times*, 16 Jan. 1891.

124. Chamberlain to Alfred Austin, 16 Feb. 1891, Austin papers.

125. Salisbury to the Associated Chambers of Commerce, reported in *The Times*, 5 Mar. 1891.

126. Interview with Chamberlain reported in the *Boston Herald*, 7 Nov. 1890.

127. G.H. Wright, *Chronicles of the Birmingham Chamber of Commerce* (Birmingham, 1913), 348–9.

128. Chamberlain in Birmingham at the Jewellers' annual banquet, reported in *The Times*, 31 Jan. 1891.

129. 10 Apr. 1890, in *Speeches on the Irish Question* (London, 1890), 259.

130. Chamberlain to R.W. Dale, 29 Apr. 1891, JC5/20/72.

12.   *Divisional Manager: 1891–1895*

1. Letter in *The Times*, 10 July 1891.

2. Chamberlain in Sunderland, reported in *The Times*, 22 Oct. 1891.

3. Salisbury to Howorth, 12 Dec. 1891, copy, Salisbury papers.

4. Hartington to Salisbury, 14 June 1891, Salisbury papers.

5. Chamberlain speaking in Birmingham, reported in *The Times*, 19 Nov. 1891.

6. Louis Creswicke, *The Life of the Right Honourable Joseph Chamberlain* (London, 1904), i, 8.

7. Chamberlain to Jesse Collings, 3 Nov. 1891, copy, JC5/16/129.

8. Reported in *The Times*, 26 Nov. 1891.

9. Chamberlain speaking at Sunderland, reported in *The Times*, 22 Oct. 1891.

10. Chamberlain to Harcourt, 16 Nov. 1891, copy, JC5/38/206.

11. Chamberlain to Balfour, 29 Jan. 1892, Balfour papers (British Library).

12. Chamberlain at the annual dinner of the Birmingham Jewellers' and Silversmiths' Association, reported in *The Times*, 21 Mar. 1892.

13. 'Old-age pensions', *National Review*, xviii, 108 (Feb. 1892), 721–39, actually published before the end of January.

14. E.P. Hennock, *British Social Reform and German Precedents: The case of social insurance, 1880–1914* (Oxford, 1987), 120.

15. Chamberlain to Balfour, 19 May 1892, Balfour papers (British Library).

16. Chamberlain at Smethwick, reported in *The Times*, 10 June 1892.

17. Chamberlain to his constituents, reported in *The Times*, 18 June 1892.

18. Reported in *The Times*, 1 July 1892.

19. Lord Wolmer to Chamberlain, 10 July 1892, JC5/74/19.
20. Carl Chinn, 'The anatomy of a working class neighbourhood, West Sparkbrook 1871–1914', University of Birmingham Ph.D. thesis, 1986.
21. Balfour, quoting Chamberlain, to Salisbury, 24 July 1892, Salisbury papers.
22. Balfour to the Queen, 11 Aug. 1892, Royal Archives C39/62.
23. Devonshire to Chamberlain, 21 Aug. 1892, JC5/22/68.
24. Sir Henry James to Chamberlain, 26 Sept. 1892, JC5/46/29.
25. Chamberlain to Burns, 19 Sept. 1892, Burns papers.
26. Burns to Chamberlain, 20 Sept. 1892, draft, Burns papers.
27. Chamberlain to Burns, 22 Sept. 1892, Burns papers.
28. *Nineteenth Century*, xxxii, 189 (November 1892), 677–711.
29. H.W. Lucy, *A Diary of the Home Rule Parliament, 1892–1895* (London, 1896), 143.
30. Report in *The Times*, 4 May 1893.
31. See Chamberlain, 'A bill for the weakening of Great Britain', *The Nineteenth Century*, xxxiii, 194 (Apr. 1893), 553.
32. Quoted in Henry Harrison, *Parnell, Joseph Chamberlain and Mr Garvin* (London, 1938), 234.
33. Quoted in *The Times*, 20 Feb. 1893.
34. *Hansard*, 4th ser., xv, 724 (27 July 1893).
35. A verbatim report of the proceedings is provided in the Parliamentary Papers (1895), xv, 657–77 (4 July 1893) and 693–704 (11 July 1893).
36. Ibid., 659.
37. Ibid., 675.
38. *Hansard*, 4th ser., xviii, 1569 (23 Nov. 1893).
39. Reported in *The Times*, 5 Dec. 1893.
40. Speech at the annual meeting of the West Birmingham Relief Fund, reported in *The Times*, 23 Jan. 1894.
41. *Hansard*, 4th ser., xxi, 520 (15 Feb. 1894).
42. Quoted in Garvin, *Life of Chamberlain*, iii, 599.
43. Reported in *The Times*, 23 Mar. 1894.
44. David Brooks, ed., *The Destruction of Lord Rosebery: From the diary of Sir Edward Hamilton, 1894–1895* (London, 1986), 16.
45. Speaking at Leeds, reported in *The Times*, 26 Sept. 1894.
46. Speech reported in *The Times*, 12 Oct. 1894.
47. Chamberlain to Wolmer, 12 Oct. 1894, copy, JC5/74/23.
48. As put by Lord George Hamilton, quoted in Ken Young, *Local Politics and the Rise of Party: The London Municipal Society and the Conservative intervention in local elections, 1894–1963* (Leicester, 1975), 62.
49. Chamberlain to St Loe Strachey, 10 Oct. 1894, Strachey papers.
50. Chamberlain to Sir Henry James, 17 Nov. 1894, Lord James of Hereford papers.
51. Wolmer to Chamberlain, 15 Oct. 1894, JC5/74/24.
52. Letter in *The Times* of 15 Oct. 1894.
53. Chamberlain to James, 18 Oct. 1894, copy, Lord James of Hereford papers.
54. Speaking at Durham, reported in *The Times*, 17 Oct. 1894.
55. Chamberlain to Salisbury, 29 Oct. 1894, copy, JC5/67/21.
56. Chamberlain to Sir Henry James, 7 Nov. 1894, copy, Lord James of Hereford papers.
57. Chamberlain reporting to Parker Smith, 17 Nov. 1894, Parker Smith papers.
58. Salisbury to Chamberlain, 9 Nov. 1894, JC5/67/22.
59. Chamberlain to Salisbury, 15 Nov. 1894, copy, JC5/67/24.
60. Chamberlain to James, 11 Dec. 1894, copy, Lord James of Hereford papers.
61. Chamberlain to St Loe Strachey, 18 Dec. 1894, Strachey papers.
62. Chamberlain to St Loe Strachey, 22 Dec. 1894, Strachey papers.

63. List for the 1895 Cabinet, in Chamberlain's hand, Devonshire papers, 340.2619A.
64. Chamberlain to James, 9 Jan. 1895, copy, Lord James of Hereford papers.
65. Reported in *The Times*, 7 Feb. 1895.
66. E.P. Hall Jr, 'Localism in Joseph Chamberlain's social politics, 1869–1895', University of Massachusetts Ph.D. thesis, 1977, 205–6.
67. Joseph to Mary Chamberlain, 28 Feb. 1895, JC28/A/2/8/27.
68. Joseph to Mary Chamberlain, 6 Mar. 1895, JC28/A/2/8/32.
69. Joseph to Mary Chamberlain, 13 Mar. 1895, JC28/A/2/8/39.
70. Quoted in David Brooks, ed., *The Destruction of Lord Rosebery*, 75.
71. Joseph to Mary Chamberlain, 21 Mar. 1895, JC28/A/2/8/47.
72. 'Z', 'Two demagogues: A parallel and a moral', *New Review*, XII, 71 (Apr. 1895), 363–72.
73. Wolmer to Salisbury, 7 Apr. 1895, Salisbury papers.
74. Salisbury to Wolmer, 13 Apr. 1895, Selborne papers.
75. Chamberlain to Chaplin, 19 Apr. 1895, copy, JC5/13/13.
76. Chamberlain to Devonshire, 19 Apr. 1895, copy, JC5/22/156.
77. Joseph to Neville Chamberlain, 25 Apr. 1895, NC1/6/9/26.

13. *Evading Discredit: 1895–1897*

1. Chamberlain to the Birmingham Jewellers' and Silversmiths' Association, reported in *The Times*, 1 Apr. 1895.
2. Chamberlain's notes on the meetings of 24 and 25 June 1895, JC 6/6/1D/2.
3. Quoted by R.E. Robinson in 'Imperial problems in British politics, 1880–1895', *The Cambridge History of the British Empire* (Cambridge, 1959), iii, 161.
4. So Selborne later recalled: Selborne papers, MS Selb. 191. In fact Chamberlain expressed his desire for 'a strong policy' as much at home as abroad: Chamberlain to Selborne, 3 July 1895, Selborne papers.
5. Speaking in Lambeth, reported in *The Times*, 8 July 1895.
6. Chamberlain's manifesto, in *The Times*, 9 July 1895.
7. Salisbury to Chamberlain, 25 July 1895, JC5/67/27.
8. R.V. Kubicek, *The Administration of Imperialism: Joseph Chamberlain at the Colonial Office* (Durham, North Carolina, 1969), 155.
9. Chamberlain's comment to Edward Hamilton, quoted in David Brooks, ed., *The Destruction of Lord Rosebery: From the diary of Sir Edward Hamilton, 1894–1895* (London, 1986), 233.
10. After the Jameson raid, Chamberlain became more scrupulous; and he required army officers serving in southern Africa to rid themselves of any goldmining shares they might possess, though he did not do so himself until the Boer War was under way.
11. *Hansard*, 4th ser., xxxii, 432 (28 Mar. 1895).
12. Grey to Chamberlain, 1 Apr. 1895, JC10/6/1/1.
13. Selborne to Chamberlain, 7 Sept. 1895, Selborne papers.
14. Report by Mary Chamberlain quoted in D.W. Laing, *Mistress of Herself* (Barre, Mass., 1965), 98.
15. Robinson to Chamberlain, 4 Nov. 1895, JC10/2/4B/3.
16. Quoted in Garvin, *Life of Chamberlain*, iii, 63.
17. Shaw to Rhodes, 12 Dec. 1895, copy, Jameson Raid file, *The Times* archives.
18. Chamberlain writing from Highbury to Sir Robert Meade, 18 Dec. 1895, secret, JC10/1/20.
19. This was the most important of the subsequently notorious 'missing' telegrams, for which no full text has survived.
20. Chamberlain to Salisbury, 24 Dec. 1895, Salisbury papers.

21. Salisbury to Balfour, 27 Dec. 1895, Balfour papers (British Library).
22. Chamberlain to Salisbury, 26 Dec. 1895, Salisbury papers.
23. Chamberlain to Mrs Endicott, 27 Dec. 1895, AC4/5/6.
24. Edward Fairfield to Chamberlain, 28 Dec. 1895, JC10/1/22.
25. Chamberlain to Salisbury, 29 Dec. 1895, Salisbury papers.
26. Joseph to Mary Chamberlain, 8 Jan. 1896, JC28/A/2/9/5.
27. Chamberlain to James, 27 Jan. 1896, copy, Lord James of Hereford papers.
28. At a banquet to celebrate the completion of the railway between the Transvaal and Natal, reported in *The Times*, 7 Nov. 1895.
29. Chamberlain at a banquet in honour of the new governor of Queensland, Australia, reported in *The Times*, 22 Jan. 1896.
30. Chamberlain through H.F. Wilson to Sir Charles Tupper, 10 Mar. 1896, Tupper papers.
31. Chamberlain to Salisbury, 24 Jan. 1896, Salisbury papers.
32. Including Grey, Rutherfoord Harris and Alfred Beit.
33. Memorandum to the law officers on 'The invasion of the Transvaal', copy enclosed with Chamberlain to Balfour, 2 Feb. 1896, Balfour papers (British Library).
34. Fairfield to Hawksley, 4 Feb. 1896, in Jean van der Poel, *The Jameson Raid* (London, 1951), 156–7.
35. It was so called in the Colonial Office. Chamberlain to Meade, 2 Feb. 1896, AC2/1/2/11.
36. *Hansard*, 4th ser., xxxvii, 327–8 (13 Feb. 1896).
37. Opinion of 5 May 1896, JC10/1/41.
38. *Hansard*, 4th ser., xli, 914–15 (8 May 1896).
39. Ibid., 919–20.
40. R. Solomon to James Rose Innes, 13 May 1896, in H.M. Wright, ed., *Sir James Rose Innes, Selected Correspondence (1884–1902)* (Cape Town, 1972), 186.
41. 9 June 1896, in C.W. Boyd, ed., *Mr Chamberlain's Speeches* (London, 1914), 366 and 371.
42. Grey to Hawksley, 12 June 1896, draft, Grey papers.
43. *Hansard*, 4th ser., xliii, 1060 (30 July 1896).
44. Hawksley to Fairfield, 20 Aug. 1896, JC10/1/60.
45. Chamberlain to Fairfield, 22 Aug. 1896, JC10/1/61.
46. Chamberlain to Fairfield, 23 Aug. 1896, JC10/1/62.
47. Sir Robert Meade to Chamberlain, 14 Oct. 1896, JC10/1/7/1.
48. Chamberlain to Selborne, 30 Dec. 1896, Selborne papers.
49. Chamberlain to Grey, 13 Oct. 1896, Grey papers.
50. Minute by Edward Fairfield, 27 Oct. 1896, JC10/1/77.
51. Grey to Chamberlain, 25 Nov. 1896, JC10/6/1/8.
52. Grey to Chamberlain, 10 Dec. 1896, JC10/6/1/9.
53. Chamberlain to Lord James, 26 Jan. 1897, Lord James of Hereford papers.
54. Selborne's notes in Garvin, *Life of Chamberlain*, iii, 118.
55. *Hansard*, 4th ser., xlv, 806–8 (29 Jan. 1897).
56. Speech to the Birmingham Jewellers' and Goldsmiths' Association reported in *The Times*, 1 Feb. 1897.
57. Chamberlain to Lord James, 23 Jan. 1897, James papers.
58. P.S. Bagwell, *Industrial Relations* (Dublin, 1974), 79.
59. Quoted in N.M. Marris, *The Right Honourable Joseph Chamberlain* (London, 1900), 312.
60. A.S.T. Griffith-Boscawen, *Fourteen Years in Parliament* (London, 1907), 126.
61. Quoted by John France in Robert Blake and Hugh Cecil, eds, *Salisbury* (Basingstoke, 1987), 244.
62. Jameson Raid Enquiry, Report and Minutes, Parliamentary Papers, 1897, vol. ix, 30 April 1897, Question 6223.
63. Hawksley to Rhodes, 22 May

1897, Hildersham Hall papers.

64. Selborne to Milner, 24 May 1897, quoted in J.E. Butler, *The Liberal Party and the Jameson Raid* (Oxford, 1968), 173.

65. Jameson Raid Enquiry, Question 9565.

66. Harcourt to Chamberlain, 15 June 1897, JC5/38/115.

67. Ibid.

68. Harcourt to Chamberlain, 18 June 1897, JC5/38/116.

69. Jameson Raid Enquiry, Report, xv.

70. Chamberlain to Milner, 5 July 1897, Milner papers.

14. *Imperial Investment: 1895–1898*

1. J.A. Hobson quoted in Eric Hobsbawm, *The Age of Empire, 1875–1914* (London, 1987), 60.

2. Chamberlain on 'Patriotism', 3 Nov. 1897, reported in *The Times*, 4 Nov. 1897.

3. W.S. Churchill, *Great Contemporaries* (London, 1937), 57.

4. Chamberlain to the Colonial Nursing Association, 26 July 1899, reported in *The Times*, 26 July 1899.

5. J.D. Fage in Prosser Gifford and W.R. Louis, ed., *Britain and Germany in Africa* (New Haven, 1967), 696.

6. Quoted in R.M. Kesner, *Economic Control and Colonial Development: Crown colony financial management in the age of Joseph Chamberlain* (Westport, Conn., 1981), which is the outstanding work on the subject.

7. Memorandum by Mr Chamberlain respecting the Suez Canal Shares, 15 Nov. 1895, printed for the use of the Cabinet, 8 Jan. 1896, with Modifications and a further Memorandum by the Chancellor of the Exchequer, St Aldwyn papers.

8. Chamberlain to Hicks Beach, 26 Nov. 1897, in 'Correspondence on the subject of a countervailing duty against sugar bounties', Cabinet paper dated 7 Dec. 1897,

St Aldwyn papers.

9. Chamberlain to Dilke, 15 Apr. 1896, Dilke papers.

10. Chamberlain to Sir J. West Ridgeway, 27 Apr. 1898, copy, JC9/2/2/9.

11. R.E. Dumett, 'Joseph Chamberlain, imperial finance and railway policy in British West Africa in the late nineteenth century', *English Historical Review*, xc, 355 (1975), 316.

12. Quoted in J.D. Hargreaves, 'The establishment of the Sierra Leone hut tax and the rebellion of 1898', *Cambridge Historical Journal*, xii, 1 (1956), 79.

13. Chamberlain's address to the Colonial Nursing Association, reported in *The Times*, 26 July 1899.

14. Quoted in R.V. Kubicek, *The Administration of Imperialism: Joseph Chamberlain at the Colonial Office* (Durham, N.C., 1969), 34.

15. R.E. Dumett, 'The campaign against malaria and the expansion of scientific medical and sanitary services in British West Africa', *African Historical Studies*, i (1968), 162.

16. R.V. Kubicek, *The Administration of Imperialism*, 32.

17. See above, p. 294.

18. Ronald Hyam, 'The Colonial Office mind 1900–1914', *Journal of Imperial and Commonwealth History*, viii, 1 (Oct. 1979), 30–1.

19. Chamberlain to Lord Roberts, 2 Nov. 1897, Roberts papers, 7101–23–16–8.

20. Reported in *The Times*, 1 Apr. 1895.

21. R.J.D. Page, 'Canada and the empire during Joseph Chamberlain's tenure as Colonial Secretary, 1895–1903', University of Oxford D.Phil. thesis, 1971, 173.

22. Quoted by Chamberlain in his speech, reported by *The Times* on 26 Mar. 1896.

23. See above, p. 392.

24. H.O. Arnold-Forster to his wife, June 1896, in Mary Arnold-Forster, *The Right Honourable Hugh Oakley*

Arnold-Forster (London, 1910), 213.

25. Copy of a memorandum by Chamberlain, JC9/2/1E/1.
26. Reported in *The Times*, 22 June 1897.
27. 'Proceedings of a Conference between the Secretary of State for the Colonies and the Premiers of the Self-governing Colonies at the Colonial Office, London, June and July, 1897', 131.
28. Ibid., 135.
29. Quoted in J.E. Kendle, *The Colonial and Imperial Conferences, 1887–1911* (London, 1967), 27.
30. Quoted in Garvin, *Life of Chamberlain*, iii, 190.
31. Chamberlain to Devonshire, 4 July 1897, Devonshire papers.
32. Chamberlain to the Liverpool Chamber of Commerce, reported in *The Times*, 19 Jan. 1898.
33. William Mulock to Chamberlain, 12 Aug. 1898, JC9/2/1N/1.
34. Sir William White quoted in Stephen Gwynn and G.M. Tuckwell, *The Life of the Rt Hon. Sir Charles W. Dilke, Bart., MP* (London, 1917), ii, 292.
35. Copy of a diary entry by Chamberlain, dated 16 July 1891, JC8/1/5.
36. Chamberlain to Frederick Lugard, 1 June 1895, Lugard papers.
37. Chamberlain to Hicks Beach, 5 Jan. 1898, St Aldwyn papers.
38. Reported in *The Times*, 19 Jan. 1898.
39. Chamberlain to Selborne, 12 Sept. 1897, JC9/4/2D/4.
40. Salisbury to Chamberlain, 17 Sept. 1897, JC5/67/81.
41. Chamberlain to Selborne, 29 Sept. 1897, JC9/4/2D/10.
42. Minute by Chamberlain, 16 Nov. 1897, copy, JC9/4/3/1.
43. Quoted in J.E. Flint, *Sir George Goldie and the Making of Nigeria* (Oxford, 1960), 288.
44. Chamberlain to Selborne, 1 Dec. 1897, Selborne papers.
45. J.E. Flint, *Sir George Goldie and the Making of Nigeria*, 290.
46. Memorandum by Chamberlain of 24 Jan. 1898, Public Record Office CAB37/46.
47. Chamberlain to Salisbury, 2 June 1898, draft, JC5/67/96.
48. Salisbury to Chamberlain, 3 June 1898, JC5/67/97.
49. Chamberlain to Lord Lansdowne, 27 Oct. 1898, Lansdowne papers.
50. Chamberlain in Manchester, reported in *The Times*, 17 Nov. 1898.
51. Chamberlain to Salisbury, 31 Dec. 1897, Salisbury papers.
52. Chamberlain to Salisbury, 4 Jan. 1898, Salisbury papers.
53. Chamberlain to Lord James, 11 Jan. 1898, Lord James of Hereford papers.
54. J.A.S. Grenville, *Lord Salisbury and Foreign Policy* (London, 1970, corrected ed.), 145. This book remains the classic study of its subject.
55. Draft memorandum by Chamberlain, 29 Mar. 1898, JC7/2/2A/3.
56. Chamberlain to H.W. Massingham, 8 Apr. 1898, JC/L.Add.337.
57. Quoted in J.A.S. Grenville, *Lord Salisbury and Foreign Policy*, 157.
58. Chamberlain to Salisbury, Apr. 1898, Salisbury papers.
59. Salisbury to Chamberlain, 2 May 1898, JC6/67/91.
60. Reported in *The Times*, 5 May 1898.
61. Reported in *The Times*, 14 May 1898.
62. Stuart Anderson, *Race and Rapprochement: Anglo-Saxonism and Anglo-American Relations, 1895–1904* (East Brunswick, N.J., 1981), 123.
63. Lascelles to Salisbury, 27 May 1898, copy, JC7/2/2A/9.
64. Chamberlain to Salisbury, 25 July 1898, Salisbury papers.
65. Chamberlain to Balfour, 19 Aug. 1898, Salisbury papers, A/92.
66. Assessment by Balfour, 5 Sept. 1898, quoted in Ronald Robinson and John Gallagher, with Alice Denny, *Africa and the Victorians: The official mind of imperialism* (London, 1961), 448.
67. Chamberlain, 'Recent develop-

ments of policy in the United States and their relation to an Anglo-American alliance', *Scribner's Magazine* (Dec. 1898), 676 and 682.

68. Chamberlain to Morton Prince, 7 July 1898, Morton Prince papers.

69. Quoted in an editorial of *The Statist*, 16 July 1898.

70. Chamberlain to the National Liberal Unionist conference at Manchester, reported in *The Times*, 16 Nov. 1898.

71. Chamberlain to William Kenrick, 24 Nov. 1898, Kenrick papers.

72. Chamberlain to the Birmingham and Midland Institute, 7 Oct. 1877, JC4/5/96.

73. Chamberlain's speech at the first public meeting of the court of governors of Mason University College, reported in *The Times*, 14 Jan. 1898.

74. Reported in *The Times*, 14 Jan. 1898.

75. Alderman Beale at the annual degree congregation, reported in *The Times*, 7 July 1906.

76. Chamberlain to Bunce, 6 Dec. 1897, JC5/8/123.

77. G.H. Kenrick to Sonnenschein, 9 Dec. 1898 in E.W. Vincent and Percival Hinton, *The University of Birmingham: Its history and significance* (Birmingham, 1947), 16.

78. Principal Lodge and Vice-Chancellor Beale, reported in *The Times*, 7 July 1906.

79. Reported in *The Times*, 14 Jan. 1898.

80. Mary to Beatrice Chamberlain, 1 Dec. 1897, Beatrice Chamberlain papers.

81. Reported in *The Times*, 19 Nov. 1898.

15. Test of Investments: 1899

1. Rhodes to Chamberlain, 28 Apr. 1898, copy, Rhodes papers.

2. Cecil Headlam, ed., *The Milner Papers* (London, 1931), i, 13.

3. Quoted ibid., 27.

4. Chamberlain to J.E. Ellis, 14 Oct. 1897, Ellis papers.

5. *Hansard*, 4th ser., li, 1174–5 (26 July 1897).

6. Chamberlain to Milner, 5 July 1897, Milner papers.

7. Milner to Rhodes, 6 March or May 1898, Rhodes papers.

8. Milner telegram to Chamberlain, 9 July 1897, in Cecil Headlam, ed., *The Milner Papers*, i. 61.

9. Milner to Chamberlain, 23 Feb. 1898, ibid., 221.

10. Memorandum by Chamberlain, 29 Nov. 1898, JC10/4/2/36.

11. Chamberlain to Salisbury, 30 Nov. 1898, Salisbury papers.

12. Chamberlain to Milner, 30 Dec. 1898, Milner papers.

13. Minute by Lord Selborne, 9 Mar. 1899, quoted in J.S. Marais, *The Fall of Kruger's Republic* (Oxford, 1961), 250–1.

14. Quoted ibid., 254.

15. *Hansard*, 4th ser., lxviii, 1377 (20 Mar. 1899).

16. Chamberlain to Salisbury, 26 Jan. 1899, Salisbury papers.

17. Quoted in Asa Briggs, *Victorian Cities* (London, 1963), 337.

18. Chamberlain to the Grand United Order of Oddfellows, reported in *The Times*, 25 May 1899.

19. E.R. Russell to Chamberlain, 18 Mar. 1899, JC5/62/29.

20. Chamberlain to Alderman Lloyd, 1 Feb. 1899, JC1/i/3.

21. Carnegie to Chamberlain, 30 Mar. 1899, JC12/1/1/7.

22. Carnegie to Chamberlain, 9 May 1899, University of Birmingham Collection.

23. Chamberlain to Carnegie, 27 May 1899, copy, University of Birmingham Collection.

24. Carnegie to Chamberlain, 3 June 1899, University of Birmingham Collection.

25. Draft despatch from Chamberlain to Milner, 10 May 1899, JC10/3/4/III.

26. Chamberlain telegram to Milner,

24 May 1899, Milner papers.

27. Report in *The Times*, 27 June 1899.

28. Chamberlain telegram to Milner, 3 July 1899. Milner papers.

29. Chamberlain telegram to Milner, 6 July 1899, no. 1, Milner papers.

30. Chamberlain to Milner, 7 July 1899, Milner papers.

31. Quoted in J.S. Marais, *The Fall of Kruger's Republic*, 297.

32. Chamberlain to Salisbury, 18 July 1899, Salisbury papers.

33. Chamberlain telegram to Milner, 18 July 1899 II, Milner papers.

34. Chamberlain draft despatch to Milner, printed for the use of the Colonial Office, 19 July 1899, Public Record Office CAB37/50/8388.

35. Salisbury to Chamberlain, 19 July 1899, JC5/67/114.

36. The Uitlander Council telegram to Chamberlain, 19 July 1899, Milner papers.

37. *Hansard*, 4th ser., lxxv, 706 ff. (28 July 1899).

38. Quoted in Garvin, *Life of Chamberlain*, iii, 431.

39. Chamberlain telegram to Milner, 18 Aug. 1899 IV, Milner papers.

40. Chamberlain to Selborne, 14 Aug. 1899, Selborne papers.

41. Chamberlain to Salisbury, 16 Aug. 1899, Salisbury papers.

42. Chamberlain telegram to Milner, 16 Aug. 1899 IV, Milner papers.

43. Reported in *The Times*, 28 Aug. 1899.

44. Chamberlain to F.A. Newdegate, 31 Aug. 1899, Newdegate papers, CR136/BS267.

45. Chamberlain telegram to Milner, 31 Aug. 1899 I, Milner papers.

46. Chamberlain to Milner, 2 Sept. 1899, Milner papers.

47. Chamberlain to the cabinet, 5 Sept. 1899, PRO CAB37/50/8388.

48. Chamberlain's memorandum for the cabinet, 6 Sept. 1899, JC10/3/4/IV.

49. Chamberlain to Salisbury, 18 Sept. 1899, Salisbury papers.

50. Salisbury to Chamberlain, 19 Sept. 1899, JC5/67/124.

51. Draft despatch by Chamberlain, 21 Sept. 1899, JC10/3/117.

52. Hicks Beach to Lady Londonderry, 30 Sept. 1899, quoted in Ronald Robinson and John Gallagher, with Alice Denny, *Africa and the Victorians* (London, 1961), 455–6.

53. Chamberlain to Milner, 5 Oct. 1899, Milner papers.

54. Chamberlain to Hicks Beach, 7 Oct. 1899, St Aldwyn papers.

55. Chamberlain to Milner, 5 Oct. 1899, Milner papers.

56. Chamberlain to the Rev. H.E. Dowson, 5 Oct. 1899, copy, Bryce papers.

57. Chamberlain to Lord Minto, 3 July 1899, Minto papers.

58. *Hansard*, 4th ser., lxxv, 703 (28 July 1899).

59. Minto to Laurier, 19 July 1899, copy, JC9/2/1K/4.

60. Speech at the Highbury garden party, reported in *The Times*, 28 Aug. 1899.

61. Minto to Chamberlain, 14 Oct. 1899, quoted in John Buchan, *Lord Minto* (London, 1924), 141–2.

62. Chamberlain to Minto, 26 Oct. 1899, Minto papers.

63. Chamberlain's circular to the cabinet, 9 Oct. 1899, PRO CAB37/51/77.

64. Lansdowne to Chamberlain, 10 Oct. 1899, JC5/51/89.

65. Chamberlain to the Queen, 12 Oct. 1899, Royal Archives, P.2/75.

66. Lady Frances Balfour writing from the Speaker's Gallery, 17 Oct. 1899, in Lady Frances Balfour, *Ne Obliviscaris* (London, 1930), ii, 298.

67. *Hansard*, 4th ser., lxxvii, 646 (25 Oct. 1899).

68. Grey to Chamberlain, 20 Oct. 1899, JC10/5/2/4.

69. C.N. Connolly, 'Manufacturing "spontaneity": The Australian offers of troops for the Boer War', *Historical Studies*, xviii, 70 (1978), 117.

70. 'X' to the editor in *The Times*, 7 Dec. 1899.

71. Chamberlain to Alfred Lyttelton, 23 Dec. 1899, Lyttelton papers.
72. Chamberlain to Selborne, 9 Nov. 1899, Selborne papers.
73. Chamberlain to Devonshire, 25 Dec. 1899, Balfour papers.
74. Fitzpatrick to Eckstein, 18 Nov. 1899, Barlow Rand archives.
75. Chamberlain to Milner, 6 Dec. 1899, Milner papers.
76. Ibid.
77. Chamberlain to Salisbury, 18 Sept. 1899, Salisbury papers.
78. Chamberlain to Admiral Maxse, 11 Nov. 1899, Maxse papers, 205, p. 124.
79. Eckhardtstein to Chamberlain, 12 Oct. 1899, JC7/2/2B/9.
80. Eckhardtstein to Chamberlain, 9 Nov. 1899, JC7/2/2B/16.
81. Francis Bertie to Arthur Bigge, 28 Nov. 1899, Royal Archives, RA I 62/71.
82. Chamberlain's memorandum of December 1911 for his son Austen, JC7/2/2A/24.
83. Reported in *The Times*, 1 Dec. 1899.
84. Chamberlain to Ambassador Lascelles, 12 Dec. 1899, copy, JC7/2/2A/36.
85. Eckhardtstein to Chamberlain, 17 Dec. 1899, JC7/2/2B/19.
86. Reported in *The Times*, 9 Dec. 1899.
87. Chamberlain to an unindentified 'President', 11 Dec. 1899, copy, JC12/1/1/25.
88. Vice-Principal R.S. Heath on 'The University' in *The Times*, 7 July 1906.
89. Strathcona to Chamberlain, 30 Oct. 1899, JC12/1/1/24.
90. Chamberlain to the Duke of Devonshire, 5 Nov. 1899, Devonshire papers.
91. Chamberlain to Milner, 6 Dec. 1899, Milner papers.
92. Lady Betty to Gerald Balfour, 'Sunday' [17 Dec. 1899], Gerald Balfour papers.
93. Chamberlain to Lansdowne, 21 Dec. 1899, copy, Earl Roberts papers, 7101–23–16–10.
94. Chamberlain to Mrs Endicott, 24 Dec. 1899, AC4/5/8.

16.   *The Business of War: 1900–1902*

1. Lord Ampthill to J. Parker Smith, 15 Jan. 1900, Parker Smith papers.
2. An impression James Bryce pointed out with regret to J.X. Merriman, 29 Dec. 1899, in Phyllis Lewsen, ed., *Selections from the Correspondence of John X. Merriman, 1890–1905* (Cape Town, 1966), ii, 128.
3. Chamberlain to the Durham and North Riding Liberal Unionist Association, reported in *The Times*, 17 Oct. 1894.
4. Howard Bailes, 'Technology and imperialism: A case study of the Victorian army in Africa', *Victorian Studies*, xxiv, 1 (autumn 1980), 86.
5. Chamberlain to Milner, 1 Jan. 1900, Milner papers.
6. Joseph to Mary Chamberlain, 16 Jan. 1900, JC28/A/2/13/1.
7. *Hansard*, 4th ser., Lxxviii, 621–3 (5 Feb. 1900).
8. *Hansard*, 4th ser., Lxxix, 634 (20 Feb. 1900).
9. Dr H.S. Lunn to the Rev. T.E. Westerdale in *The Times*, 20 Feb. 1900.
10. Chamberlain to the Rev. T.E. Westerdale in *The Times*, 28 Feb. 1900.
11. Joseph to Neville Chamberlain, 10 Feb. 1900, NC1/6/9/32.
12. Chamberlain's Memorandum on the Future Settlement of British South Africa, 12 Jan. 1900, JC14/4/II.
13. Chamberlain telegram to Milner, 23 Feb. 1900, PRO CAB37/52/31.
14. Chamberlain's Memorandum for the cabinet on 'The Political Situation in the Cape Colony', 7 Mar. 1900, PRO CAB37/52/32.
15. Chamberlain to the Birmingham Liberal Unionist Association, reported in *The Times*, 12 May 1900.

16. Paraphrase by Fitzpatrick in his letter to Beit, 8 June 1900, in A.H. Duminy and W.R. Guest, eds, *Fitzpatrick, South African Politician: Selected papers, 1888–1906* (Johannesburg, 1976), 259.

17. Quoted in R.J.D. Page, 'Canada and the empire during Joseph Chamberlain's tenure as Colonial Secretary, 1895–1903', University of Oxford D. Phil. thesis, 1971, 411.

18. Quoted in R.H. Wilde, 'Joseph Chamberlain's proposal of an imperial council in March, 1900', *Canadian Historical Review*, xxxvii, 3 (Sept. 1956), 240.

19. Chamberlain to Minto, 2 Mar. 1900, Minto papers.

20. Quoted in J.E. Kendle, *The Colonial and Imperial Conferences, 1887–1911* (London, 1967), 36.

21. Chamberlain to Lady Frances Balfour, 20 Mar. 1900, Huntington Library.

22. Minto to Chamberlain, 14 Apr. 1900, quoted in John Buchan, *Lord Minto* (London, 1924), 159.

23. Chamberlain to Milner, 23 July 1900, Milner papers.

24. Chamberlain to de Villiers, 9 Aug. 1900, de Villiers papers.

25. Chamberlain to de Villiers, 16 Aug. 1900, de Villiers papers.

26. *Hansard*, 4th ser., lxxxvii, 1012 (8 Aug. 1900).

27. *Hansard*, 4th ser., lxxxvii, 1014 (8 Aug. 1900).

28. Chamberlain to Strachey, 18 Aug. 1900, Strachey papers.

29. Strachey to Chamberlain, 21 Aug. 1900, copy, Strachey papers.

30. Chamberlain to Milner, 23 July 1900, Milner papers.

31. Chamberlain to the Women's Liberal Unionist Association, reported in *The Times*, 20 June 1900.

32. Chamberlain's memorandum for the cabinet on 'The Chinese Problem', 10 Sept. 1900, JC14/4/1/1.

33. The words of the American ambassador to Britain and then Secretary of State, John Hay, quoted in

P.M. Kennedy, *The Rise of Anglo-German Antagonism, 1860–1914* (London, 1980), 243.

34. Chamberlain to Milner, 10 Sept. 1900, Milner papers.

35. Chamberlain to his constituents in West Birmingham, reported in *The Times*, 24 Sept. 1900.

36. Joseph to Mary Chamberlain, 30 Sept. 1900, JC28/A/2/13/39.

37. Reported in *The Times*, 24 Sept. 1900.

38. Quoted in M.E.Y. Enstam, 'The "khaki" election of 1900 in the United Kingdom', Duke University Ph.D. thesis, 1967, 135.

39. Joseph to Mary Chamberlain, 28 Sept. 1900, JC28/A/2/13/37.

40. Chamberlain in East Birmingham, reported in *The Times*, 1 Oct. 1900.

41. Joseph to Mary Chamberlain, 10 Oct. 1900, JC28/A/2/13/49.

42. Chamberlain to Lord Minto, 22 Oct. 1900, Minto papers.

43. Chamberlain to the Fishmongers' Company, reported in *The Times*, 25 Oct. 1900.

44. Chamberlain to Balfour, 21 Oct. 1900, Balfour papers (Whittinghame).

45. Milner to Chamberlain, 28 Oct. 1900, JC13/1/78.

46. Milner to Chamberlain, 14 Nov. 1900, JC13/1/91.

47. Chamberlain to Milner, 22 Dec. 1900, Milner papers.

48. L.H. Gann and Peter Duignan, *The Rulers of British Africa, 1870–1914* (London, 1978), 36.

49. R.C. Trebilcock, 'A "special relationship"—government, re-armament and the cordite firms', *Economic History Review*, xix, 2 (Aug. 1966), 364–79.

50. Chamberlain to Balfour, 2 Jan. 1900, Balfour papers (British Library).

51. *Hansard*, 4th ser., lxxxviii, 413 (10 Dec. 1990).

52. Ibid., 440.

53. Parker Smith's memorandum of conversation with Chamberlain 'as to Lloyd George attacks', 1900,

Parker Smith papers.

54. Entry for 9 Aug. 1901 in J.R. Vincent, ed., *The Crawford Papers: The journals of David Lindsay, twenty-seventh Earl of Crawford and tenth Earl of Balcarres, 1871–1940, during the years 1892 to 1940* (Manchester, 1984), 64.

55. Chamberlain to Milner, 22 Jan. 1901, Milner papers.

56. Chamberlain to Milner, 1 Apr. 1901, Milner papers.

57. Chamberlain draft telegram to Milner, 4 Mar. 1901, JC14/4/ II.

58. Kitchener telegram to Chamberlain, 19 June 1901, Kitchener papers.

59. Chamberlain to Brodrick, 24 Aug. 1901, copy, JC11/8/44.

60. Chamberlain to Brodrick, 19 Sept. 1901, copy, JC11/8/57.

61. Quoted in P.T. Marsh, *The Discipline of Popular Government: Lord Salisbury's domestic statecraft, 1881–1902* (Hassocks, 1978), 310.

62. Chamberlain to Brodrick, 17 Sept. 1901, copy, JC11/8/54.

63. Chamberlain to Selborne, 26 Sept. 1901, Selborne papers.

64. Chamberlain to Hicks Beach, 12 Sept. 1901, St Aldwyn papers.

65. Hicks Beach to Chamberlain, 2 Oct. 1901, draft, St Aldwyn papers.

66. Chamberlain to Hicks Beach, 21 Sept. 1901, St Aldwyn papers.

67. Chamberlain to Earl Grey, 3 Oct. 1901, Grey papers.

68. Reported in the *Birmingham Daily Post*, 15 Oct. 1901.

69. Chamberlain to Selborne, 7 Nov. 1901, Selborne papers.

70. Churchill to Chamberlain, 14 Oct. 1901, JC11/9/5.

71. Chamberlain at a Unionist demonstration in Edinburgh, reported in *The Times*, 26 Oct. 1901.

72. Chamberlain telegram to Milner, 16 Nov. 1901, I, copy, Milner papers.

73. Chamberlain to Milner, 20 Jan. 1902, Milner papers.

74. Chamberlain telegram to Milner,

75. Chamberlain telegram to Milner, 20 Feb. 1902, III, Milner papers.

76. Milner telegram to Chamberlain, 9 Mar. 1902, JC13/1/211.

77. Chamberlain telegram to Milner, 12 Mar. 1902, Milner papers.

78. Chamberlain to Milner, 12 Mar. 1902, Milner papers.

79. Joseph to Mary Chamberlain, 18 Mar. 1902, JC28/A/2/15/3.

80. Chamberlain to the Unionist demonstration in Edinburgh, *The Times*, 26 Oct. 1901.

81. *The Times*, 28 Oct. 1901.

82. Chamberlain to C.F. Adams, 8 Dec. 1901, Adams papers.

83. Chamberlain in West Birmingham, reported in *The Times*, 7 Jan. 1902.

84. M.V. Brett and Lord Esher, *Journals and Letters of Reginald Viscount Esher* (London, 1934–8), i, 318–19.

85. Reported in *The Times*, 13 Jan. 1902.

86. Recalled by Francis Webb in the *Searchlight of Greater Birmingham*, 13 Nov. 1913.

87. *The Times*, 17 Jan. 1902.

88. Reported in *The Times*, 14 Feb. 1902.

89. Reported in *The Times*, 14 Feb. 1902.

90. J.S. Sandars, Memorandum on a conversation with Mr Chamberlain, 25 Feb. 1902, AC42/6/26.

91. Chamberlain to Maxse, 7 Mar. 1902, Maxse papers, 450, p. 503.

92. Chamberlain to Lord James, 18 Apr. 1902, James of Hereford papers.

93. Chamberlain to James Grey Glover, in *The Times*, 24 Apr. 1902.

94. Chamberlain to Charles Vince, 26 Apr. 1902, copy, JC11/39/166.

95. Chamberlain telegram to Milner, 13 Apr. 1902, PRO CAB37/61.

96. Recalled by Winston Churchill in *My Early Life* (London, 1930), 385.

97. Reported in *The Times*, 17 May 1902.

98. Milner telegram to Chamberlain, 21 May 1902, PRO CAB37.

99. Milner to Chamberlain, 21 Apr.

19 Feb. 1902, Milner papers.

1902, JC13/1/235.

100. Chamberlain telegram to Milner, 22 May 1902, Milner papers.
101. Chamberlain to Brodrick, 1 June 1902, copy, JC11/8/100.

17. Dual Directors: 1902–1903

1. Chamberlain to Salisbury, 1 June 1902, copy, JC11/30/229.
2. Hewins quoted in G.M. Koot, *English Historical Economics, 1870–1926: The rise of economic history and neomercantilism* (Cambridge, 1987), 167.
3. 'The Islanders' (1902).
4. W.A.S. Hewins, *The Apologia of an Imperialist* (London, 1929), i, 48.
5. Chamberlain to Hewins, 5 Sept. 1900, Hewins papers.
6. Chamberlain to Brodrick, 26 Dec. 1900, copy, JC16/4/2.
7. Chamberlain to Selborne, 29 May 1902, Selborne papers.
8. Chamberlain to the Birmingham Liberal Unionist Association, reported in *The Times*, 11 May 1901.
9. Milner to Chamberlain, 27 June 1902, JC13/1/266.
10. Milner telegram to Chamberlain, received 10 June 1902, PRO CAB37.
11. Ibid.
12. Chamberlain telegram to Milner, 24 June 1902, Milner papers.
13. Ibid.
14. Milner to Chamberlain, 27 June 1902, JC13/1/266.
15. Milner telegram to Chamberlain, 29 June 1902, JC13/1/267.
16. Chamberlain to Hely-Hutchinson, 2 July 1902, copy, Milner papers.
17. G.E. Buckle to Chamberlain, 22 July 1902, JC11/39/18.
18. Chamberlain to Salisbury, 11 July 1902, Salisbury papers.
19. 15 July 1902.
20. Leader in *The Times* after his accident, 8 July 1902.
21. Chamberlain at the opening of the Colonial Troops Club, reported in *The Times*, 7 June 1902.
22. Report of the proceedings in Maurice Olliver, ed., *The Colonial and Imperial Conferences from 1887 to 1937* (Ottawa, 1954), i, 153.
23. Ibid., 155.
24. Ibid., 156.
25. As Seddon of New Zealand put it, ibid., 160.
26. Ibid., 183.
27. Ibid., 209.
28. Ibid., 173.
29. Ibid., 207.
30. Laurier to Chamberlain, 25 Aug. 1902, quoted in R.J.D. Page, 'Canada and the empire during Joseph Chamberlain's tenure as Colonial Secretary, 1895–1903', University of Oxford D.Phil. thesis, 1971, 113.
31. Chamberlain to Balfour, 4 Aug. 1902, Balfour papers (British Library).
32. Collings to James, 12 Aug. 1902, Lord James of Hereford papers.
33. Chamberlain to Balfour, 4 Aug. 1902, Balfour Papers (British Library).
34. Chamberlain to Devonshire, 22 Sept. 1902, Devonshire papers.
35. Chamberlain to Milner, 24 July 1902, Milner papers.
36. Milner to Charles Southey, 16 July 1902, Southey papers.
37. Quoted in Amery, *Life of Chamberlain*, iv, 82.
38. Joseph to Mary Chamberlain, 5 Sept. 1902, JC28/A/2/15/5.
39. Balfour's report to the king, 21 Oct. 1902, Royal Archives, R23/4.
40. Report quoted in Alan Sykes, *Tariff Reform in British Politics, 1903–1913* (Oxford, 1979), 32.
41. Balfour to the king, 19 Nov. 1902, copy, JC17/1/13.
42. Admiral Fawkes's diary of the voyage, typed excerpts, JC13/2/1/19.
43. Chamberlain to Milner, 4 Sept. 1902, Milner papers.
44. Hicks Beach to Lady Londonderry, 9 Nov. 1902, in Lady Victoria Hicks-Beach, *Life of Sir Michael Hicks Beach (Earl St Aldwyn)* (Lon-

don, 1932), ii, 182.

45. Chamberlain to Milner, 4 Sept. 1902, Milner papers.

46. Milner telegram to Chamberlain, 26 Sept. 1902, Milner papers.

47. *Hansard*, 4th ser., xl, 46 (29 July 1902).

48. *Birmingham Daily Mail*, 18 Nov. 1902.

49. Mary to Ida Chamberlain, 11 Dec. 1902, Ida Chamberlain papers.

50. Chamberlain to Edward VII, 4 Jan. 1903, Royal Archives, W6/22.

51. Chamberlain to Lord Onslow, 16 Dec. 1902, quoted in Alan Jeeves, *Migrant Labour in South Africa's Mining Economy: The struggle for the gold mines' labour supply, 1890–1920* (Kingston, Ont., 1985), 221–2.

52. Chamberlain's diary for 21 Dec. 1902, quoted in Amery, *Life of Chamberlain*, iv, 263.

53. 27 Dec. 1902, in C.W. Boyd, ed., *Mr Chamberlain's Speeches* (London, 1914; reprinted in one vol., New York, 1970), ii, 76–81.

54. Chamberlain's telegraph to the Acting Secretary of State for the Colonies, 7 Jan. 1903, Milner papers.

55. Chamberlain to Edward VII, 4 Jan. 1903, Royal Archives, W6/22.

56. Ibid.

57. Memorandum delivered to Chamberlain upon arrival in South Africa, 26 Dec. 1902, JC13/2/1/14.

58. Chamberlain to Edward VII, 4 Jan. 1903, Royal Archives, W6/22.

59. Joseph to Austen Chamberlain, 9 Jan. 1903, AC8/2/16.

60. Quoted in Amery, *Life of Chamberlain*, iv, 529–32.

61. Memorandum by Chamberlain, 7 Jan. 1903, Milner papers.

62. Milner to Chamberlain, 20 Jan. 1903, copy, JC18/15/51.

63. Chamberlain to Lord Balfour of Burleigh, n.d., but from Johannesburg, Balfour of Burleigh papers.

64. *With Chamberlain in South Africa* (Central News Agency, 1903), 47.

65. Chamberlain speaking in Bloemfontein, 7 Feb. 1903, in W.B.

Worsfold, *The Reconstruction of the New Colonies under Lord Milner* (London, 1913), i, 204.

66. Manuscript report of the proceedings, JC13/2/1/28.

67. Quoted in W.B. Worsfold, *The Reconstruction of the New Colonies under Lord Milner*, i, 226.

68. Chamberlain's memorandum of 18 Feb. 1903, JC13/2/1/26.

69. Quoted in T.R.H. Davenport, *The Afrikaner Bond* (London, 1966), 242.

70. Quotation in Amery, *Life of Chamberlain*, iv, 374.

71. 23 Feb. 1903, in C.W. Boyd, ed., *Mr Chamberlain's Speeches*, ii, 110.

72. Austen to Joseph Chamberlain, 5 Feb. 1903, JC18/15/7.

73. Milner to Charles Southey, 24 Mar. 1903, Southey papers.

18   Hastened Culmination: 1903

1. Lord James of Hereford to Chamberlain, 25 Feb. 1903, JC18/14/7.

2. Chamberlain to Sir John Forrest, 1 Apr. 1903, copy, JC18/2/7.

3. Chamberlain to Lady Dilke, 19 Apr. 1903, Lady Dilke papers.

4. Fielding to Chamberlain, 11 Mar. 1903, copy, Monk Bretton papers.

5. G.T. Denison to Chamberlain, 23 Mar. 1903, in G.T. Denison, *The Struggle for Imperial Unity* (London, 1909), 346.

6. Chamberlain to Fielding, 2 Apr. 1903, JC18/4/6.

7. Quoted in W.B. Worsfold, *The Reconstruction of the New Colonies under Lord Milner* (London, 1913) ii, 314.

8. Chamberlain telegram to Milner, 28 Mar. 1903, JC18/15/72.

9. Milner to Chamberlain, 6 Apr. 1903, copy, JC18/15/55.

10. *Hansard*, 4th ser., cxxi, 1549 (6 May 1903).

11. Balfour to the king, 12 May 1903, in Amery, *Life of Chamberlain*, v, 182.

12. Speech in Birmingham, 15 May

1903, in Chamberlain, *Imperial Union and Tariff Reform: Speeches delivered from May 15 to Nov. 4, 1903* (London, 2nd ed., 1910), 13.

13. Note by Chamberlain on a letter from Lord Strathcona, 17 May 1903, JC18/4/38.

14. Their correspondence is in JC18/18/7–10.

15. *Hansard*, 4th ser., cxxiii, 185 (28 May 1903).

16. Quoted in A.M. Gollin, *Balfour's Burden: Arthur Balfour and imperial preference* (London, 1965), 61.

17. As Balfour later described it to Devonshire, quoted in Denis Judd, *Balfour and the British Empire* (London, 1968), 111.

18. Devonshire to Balfour, 31 May 1903, in Amery, *Life of Chamberlain*, v, 241.

19. Chamberlain to the Rev. Mr. Dowson, 15 May 1903, copy, JC18/19/28.

20. Speech in Birmingham, 15 May 1903, in Chamberlain, *Imperial Union and Tariff Reform*.

21. Reported at a meeting of the Birmingham Chamber of Commerce, in *The Times*, 23 July 1903.

22. Letter dated 3 June in *The Times* of 8 June 1903.

23. G.W. Balfour to Bonar Law, 29 June 1903, Bonar Law papers.

24. Devonshire to Chamberlain, 13 July 1903, draft, Devonshire papers.

25. Chamberlain to Hewins, 14 July 1903, Hewins papers.

26. Memorandum with Chamberlain to Devonshire, 15 July 1903, Devonshire papers.

27. Chamberlain to Devonshire, 20 July 1903, Devonshire papers.

28. Chamberlain to Devonshire, 20 July 1903, Devonshire papers.

29. Chamberlain to Devonshire, 25 Aug. 1903, Devonshire papers.

30. Minto to Chamberlain, 17 July 1903, JC18/4/24.

31. Chamberlain to Minto, 31 July 1903, Minto papers; cf. Chamberlain to Wise, the Attorney-General of Australia, 31 July 1903, copy, Alfred Deakin papers, NLA MS 1540/14/372–3.

32. Chamberlain to Balfour, 9 Sept. 1903, J.S. Sandars papers.

33. Balfour to Selborne, 11 Sept. 1903, in D.G. Boyce, ed., *The Crisis of British Unionism: Lord Selborne's domestic political papers, 1885–1922* (London, 1987), 30–1.

34. The formulation recorded by Lord Balfour of Burleigh in his memorandum on the ensuing meeting, Balfour of Burleigh papers.

35. This was the formulation which Balfour subsequently used, according to Chamberlain's 'Recollections of the Cabinet of 14th Sept., which led to the Ministerial Resignations', typed copy, JC18/16/4.

36. Balfour to Chamberlain, 16 Sept. 1903, in *The Times*, 18 Sept. 1903.

37. A.M. Gollin, *Balfour's Burden*, 127.

19. The All-Consuming Venture: 1903–1906

1. As Balfour put it to Edward VII, 16 Sept. 1903, Royal Archives, W.63/24.

2. Chamberlain to Milner, 25 Sept. 1903, Milner papers.

3. Hilda Chamberlain's memoir of her sister Beatrice, Hilda Chamberlain papers.

4. Chamberlain to Parker Smith, 21 Sept. 1903, copy, Parker Smith papers.

5. Arthur Pearson reporting to Chamberlain, 2 Oct. 1903, JC18/18/104.

6. Spring Rice to a friend, 1 Oct. 1903, in Stephen Gwynn, *The Letters and Friendships of Sir Cecil Spring Rice* (London, 1930), i, 365–6.

7. Chamberlain to Henry Chaplin, 3 Oct. 1903, copy, JC18/18/26.

8. Chamberlain to Leo Maxse, 5 Oct. 1903, Maxse papers, 451, p. 702.

9. Collings to Chamberlain, 1 Oct.

1903, JC19/7/34.

10. Chamberlain to W.A.S. Hewins, 12 Oct. 1903, Hewins papers.

11. Chamberlain at Glasgow, 6 Oct. 1903, in *Imperial Union and Tariff Reform: Speeches delivered from May 15 to Nov. 4, 1903* (London, 2nd ed., 1910), 21.

12. Chamberlain at Greenock, 7 Oct. 1903, ibid., 59.

13. Chamberlain to Hewins, 12 Oct. 1903, Hewins papers.

14. Chamberlain at Tynemouth, 21 Oct. 1903, *Imperial Union and Tariff Reform*, 123.

15. Chamberlain to Lord Onslow, 11 Nov. 1903, Onslow papers.

16. Chamberlain at Liverpool, 27 Oct. 1903, *Imperial Union and Tariff Reform*, 135.

17. Parker Smith to Chamberlain, 29 Oct. 1903, JC18/18/101.

18. Chamberlain to Giffen, 24 Oct. 1903, JC L.Add 48a.

19. Chamberlain to Giffen, 2 Nov. 1903, JC L.Add 51a.

20. Chamberlain to Ashley, 14 June 1905, JC20/4/4.

21. Chamberlain to the editor of the *Sun*, 27 Nov. 1903, JC18/18/125.

22. Chamberlain in Birmingham, 4 Nov. 1903, *Imperial Union and Tariff Reform*, 185.

23. Chamberlain at Cardiff, reported in *The Times*, 21 Nov. 1903.

24. Chamberlain to Brodrick, 8 Dec. 1903, Midleton papers (Duke University).

25. Chamberlain to Brodrick, 24 Dec. 1903, ibid.

26. Minto to Chamberlain, 14 Dec. 1903, JC18/4/30.

27. Chamberlain to Collings, 30 Dec. 1903, copy, JC19/7/31.

28. Chamberlain speaking to W.A.S. Hewins, 1 July 1903, quoted in Hewins, *Apologia of an Imperialist* (London, 1929), i, 69.

29. A.J. Marrison, 'The development of a tariff reform policy during Chamberlain's first campaign, May 1903–February 1904', in W.H. Chaloner and M.B. Ratcliffe, eds,

Trade and Transport (Manchester, 1977), 232.

30. A.J. Marrison assigns different numbers to each category in an able article: 'Businessmen, industries and tariff reform in Great Britain, 1903–1930', *Business History*, xxv (July 1983).

31. Booth to Chamberlain, 15 Dec. 1903, AC1/4/2/29.

32. The best discussion of these statistics and their impact on the debate is in A.L. Friedberg, *The Weary Titan: Britain and the experience of relative decline, 1895–1905* (Princeton, 1988), chap. 2.

33. G.C. Allen, *The Industrial Development of Birmingham and the Black Country, 1860–1927* (New York, 1966, corrected reprint of the London, 1929 ed.), 277.

34. P.J. Cain, 'Political economy in Edwardian England: The tariff-reform controversy' in Alan O'Day, ed., *The Edwardian Age* (London, 1979), 49.

35. Chamberlain to Lord Onslow, 11 Nov. 1903, Onslow papers.

36. P.M. Kennedy, *Strategy and Diplomacy, 1870–1945* (London, 1984), 96.

37. P.J. Cain and A.G. Hopkins, 'The political economy of British expansion overseas, 1750–1914', *Economic History Review*, 2nd ser., xxxiii, 4 (Nov. 1980), 484.

38. Reported in *The Times*, 20 Jan. 1904.

39. Speech at the annual dinner of the Birmingham Jewellers' and Silversmiths' Association, reported in *The Times*, 12 Jan. 1904.

40. Chamberlain to Leo Amery, 19 Oct. 1903, copy, JC21/1/7.

41. Minto to Chamberlain, 17 July 1903, JC18/4/24.

42. Chamberlain to Mrs Farnell, 11 Dec. 1905, Bodleian MS Don. c.150, f.110.

43. Michael Balfour, *Britain and Joseph Chamberlain* (London, 1985), 286.

44. Chamberlain to Leo Maxse, 21 Jan. 1904, Maxse papers, 452, p. 734.

45. Chamberlain to Lord Halsbury, 27 Dec. ?1904, Halsbury papers.
46. Note probably by Parker Smith, dated 5/4/02 in error for 5/2/04, JC19/7/85.
47. Entry for 5 Feb. 1904 in *The Crawford Papers: The journals of David Lindsay, twenty-seventh Earl of Crawford and tenth Earl of Balcarres, 1871–1940, during the years 1892 to 1940*, ed. J.R. Vincent (Manchester, 1984), 70.
48. Quoted in Amery, *Life of Chamberlain*, vi, 555.
49. Quoted in Alan Sykes, *Tariff Reform in British Politics, 1903–1913* (Oxford, 1979), 78–9.
50. Joseph to Austen Chamberlain, 11 Mar. 1904, AC1/4/5/32.
51. Ibid.
52. Joseph to Neville Chamberlain, 25 Mar. 1904, NC1/6/9/36.
53. Chamberlain to Balfour, 8 Apr. 1904, Balfour papers (British Library).
54. Chamberlain to Devonshire, 15 May 1904, Devonshire papers.
55. Chamberlain to Lady Dorothy Nevill, 1904, quotation in the Lloyd George papers, C/9/4/70.
56. Report in the Minutes of Proceedings of the First Meeting of the Tariff Commission to consider a Preliminary Report: The Iron and Steel Trades, 28 June 1904, pp. 2–3, Tariff Commission papers, TC2 1/8.
57. Chamberlain to Jesse Collings, 25 July 1904, typed extract, JC19/7/33.
58. Entry for 17 June 1904 in Norman and Jeanne MacKenzie, eds, *The Diary of Beatrice Webb* (Cambridge, Mass., 1983), ii, 328.
59. *Hansard*, 4th ser., cxxxiv, 347 (1 Aug. 1904).
60. Reported in *The Times*, 9 July 1904.
61. Chamberlain to Jesse Collings, 25 July 1904, typed extract, JC19/7/33.
62. Chamberlain to Minto, 17 Aug. 1904, Minto papers.
63. Austen Chamberlain to Balfour, 24

Aug. 1904, copy, AC17/3/1.
64. Chamberlain to Alfred Lyttelton, 4 Oct. 1904, Lyttelton papers.
65. Chamberlain at Luton, reported in *The Times*, 6 Oct. 1904.
66. Quoted in R.A. Rempel, *Unionists Divided: Arthur Balfour, Joseph Chamberlain and the Unionist Free Traders* (Newton Abbot, 1972), 125.
67. Chamberlain to Sir Frank Swettenham, 24 Jan. 1905, copy, JC20/4/118.
68. Chamberlain at Limehouse, 15 Dec. 1904, in C.W. Boyd, ed., *Mr Chamberlain's Speeches* (two vols, London, 1914; reprinted in one vol., New York, 1970), ii, 258.
69. Chamberlain to Parker Smith, 20 Jan. 1905, Parker Smith papers.
70. Chamberlain at Gainsborough, 1 Feb. 1905, in C.W. Boyd, ed., *Mr Chamberlain's Speeches*, ii, 294–314.
71. Chamberlain to Hewins, 3 Feb. 1905, Hewins papers.
72. Chamberlain to Lord Ridley, 18 Feb. 1905, Ridley papers, ZRI. 25/99.
73. Chamberlain to Lyttelton, 13 Mar. 1905, Lyttelton papers.
74. Chamberlain to Balfour, 12 Feb. 1905, Balfour papers (British Library).
75. Balfour to Chamberlain, 18 Feb. 1905, copy, Balfour papers (British Library).
76. Chamberlain to Balfour, 24 Feb. 1905, copy, JC20/4/10.
77. Chamberlain to Lord Ridley, 13 Mar. 1905, Ridley papers, ZRI. 25/99.
78. Chamberlain to Parker Smith, 29 Mar. 1905, JC20/4/105.
79. Parker Smith's memorandum on 'Debate on Ainsworth motion', 22 Mar. 1905, JC20/4/101.
80. Austen to Joseph Chamberlain, 11 Jan. 1904, AC1/4/5/31.
81. Herbert Maxwell to Chamberlain, 25 Feb. 1905, in Amery, *Life of Chamberlain*, vi, 664.
82. Memoire headed '(*Vespertilia.*)' by Maxwell, JC18/18/93.
83. Quoted in Amery, *Life of Chamber-*

lain, vi, 718.

84. Chamberlain at St Helens, reported in *The Times*, 5 June 1905.

85. 17 May 1905, in C.W. Boyd, ed., *Mr Chamberlain's Speeches*, ii, 318.

86. Chamberlain to Lancashire Conservative Working Men's Federation at St Helens, reported in *The Times*, 5 June 1905.

87. Chamberlain's comment reported in 'Additional matter from the interview between Mr. Chamberlain & Sir W. Mulock on July 21' 1905, JC20/2/36.

88. Parker Smith's report of his conversation with Chamberlain on 5 July 1905, JC20/4/106.

89. Notes of an Interview between Mr Chamberlain and Sir W. Mulock, with Mr Hewins present, on Friday July 21st, 1905, at 40 Princes Gardens, JC20/2/35.

90. Hewins to Chamberlain, 8 Oct. 1905, JC20/2/14.

91. Hewins to Chamberlain, 7 Nov. 1905, JC20/2/25.

92. Chamberlain to Lord Tennyson, 24 Oct. 1905, copy, JC20/4/120.

93. Reported in *The Times*, 4 Nov. 1905.

94. Quoted in Amery, *Life of Chamberlain*, vi, 755.

95. Reported in *The Times*, 22 Nov. 1905.

96. Chamberlain to Leo Maxse, 21 Dec. 1905, Maxse papers, 453, p. 187.

97. Quoted by Neville Chamberlain in Amery, *Life of Chamberlain*, vi, 779.

98. Balfour to Chamberlain, 15 Jan. 1906, copy, JC21/2/1.

99. Quoted in Stephen Roberts, 'Politics and the Birmingham working class: The general elections of 1900 and 1906 in East Birmingham', *West Midlands Studies*, xv (1982), 12.

100. Quoted in *'The Man and the City.' A souvenir of Mr. Chamberlain's connection with the Midland City*, AC1/6/2/21.

101. Chamberlain to Earl Grey, 31 Jan. 1906, Grey papers.

102. Chamberlain to Chaplin, 18 Jan. 1906, copy, JC21/2/22.

103. Chamberlain to Parker Smith, 27 Jan. 1906, copy, Parker Smith papers.

104. Pat Thane, 'The working class and state "welfare" in Britain, 1880–1914', *Historical Journal*, xxvii, 4 (1984), 892.

105. Chamberlain at Halesowen, reported in *The Times*, 23 Jan. 1906.

20. Paralysis: 1906–1914

1. Chamberlain to Lord Roberts, 27 Jan. 1906, Roberts papers, 7101–23–16–26.

2. Chamberlain to Mrs Endicott, 30 Jan. 1906, AC1/8/8/30.

3. Alan Sykes, *Tariff Reform in British Politics, 1903–1913* (Oxford, 1979), 109.

4. Chamberlain to Balfour, 25 Jan. 1906, copy, JC21/2/4.

5. Chamberlain to Boraston, 26 Jan. 1906, AC2/1/3/57.

6. Balfour to Sandars, 26 Jan. 1906, in Max Egremont, *Balfour* (London, 1980), 208.

7. As observed by a newly elected Conservative MP quoted ibid., 205.

8. Quoted in Alan Sykes, ibid., 106.

9. Lansdowne to Balfour, 28 Jan. 1906, in Amery, *Life of Chamberlain*, vi, 809.

10. Report by G.E. Buckle to John Walter, 1 Feb. 1906, quoted in Stephen Koss, *The Rise and Fall of the Political Press in Britain* (London, 1984), ii, 69.

11. The manifesto took the form of a letter to Lord Ridley, published in all the major papers including *The Times* on 8 Feb. 1906.

12. Gilbert Parker to Chamberlain, 8 Feb. 1906, in Amery, *Life of Chamberlain*, vi, 830.

13. Chamberlain to Ridley, 9 Feb. 1906, Ridley papers, ZRI. 25/99.

14. Chamberlain to Balfour, 10 Feb. 1906, and enclosure, Balfour pa-

pers (British Library).

15. Balfour to Chamberlain, 14 Feb. 1906, draft, Balfour papers (British Library).

16. Mary Chamberlain to Mrs Endicott, 17 Feb. 1906, in Amery, *Life of Chamberlain*, vi, 848.

17. Salisbury to Selborne, 25 Feb. 1906, in Alan Sykes, *Tariff Reform in British Politics, 1903–1913*, 111.

18. Chamberlain to Hewins, 16 Feb. 1906, Hewins papers, and to Leo Amery, 27 Mar. 1906, copy, JC21/1/12.

19. Chamberlain to Boscawen, 17 Feb. 1906, Ridley papers, ZRI. 25/99.

20. Arnold-Forster to Bonar Law, 24 Apr. 1906, Bonar Law papers.

21. Chamberlain to the Tariff Commission, 3 May 1906, Tariff Commission papers.

22. Chamberlain to the Australian Merchants' annual banquet, reported in *The Times*, 9 May 1906.

23. 22 Feb. 1906, quoted in Bernard Holland, *The Life of Spencer Compton Eighth Duke of Devonshire* (London, 1911), ii, 398.

24. Deakin to Chamberlain, 14 Mar. 1906, copy, JC2/2/42.

25. Chamberlain to Deakin, 26 Apr. 1906, Deakin papers, NLA MS 1540/1/1384.

26. *Hansard*, 4th ser., clvi, 457 (1 May 1906).

27. Chamberlain to Alfred Deakin, 26 May 1906, copy, JC21/2/44.

28. Chamberlain to the 1900 Club, reported in *The Times*, 26 June 1906.

29. Joseph to Austen Chamberlain, 4 May 1906, AC8/2/18.

30. Reported in *The Times*, 17 Apr. 1906.

31. Reported in *The Times*, 3 May 1906.

32. Recollections of R.S. Kirk in the *Searchlight of Greater Birmingham*, 13 Nov. 1913.

33. Unpublished memoir by Sir Herbert Maxwell, JC18/18/93.

34. Reported in the *Birmingham Daily Post*, 9 July 1906.

35. Reported in the *Birmingham Daily Post*, 10 July 1906.

36. 'Mr. Chamberlain — the Man' in *The Reader*, 27 Oct. 1906.

37. Unpublished memoire by Maxwell, JC18/18/93.

38. Quoted in a letter from Fabian Ware, *The Times*, 1 Nov. 1941.

39. Announcement and report in *The Times*, 26 Sept. 1906.

40. Mary Chamberlain to Ridley, 10 Oct. 1906, Ridley papers, ZRI. 25/99.

41. Note in *The Times*, 6 Dec. 1906.

42. Mary to Austen Chamberlain, 13 Feb. 1907, AC4/2/1.

43. Chamberlain to Deakin, 16 May 1907, Deakin papers, NLA MS 1540/15/1536.

44. The impression of Hewins on 12 Feb. 1908 in his *Apologia of an Imperialist* (London, 1929), i, 221.

45. Spring Rice to Lord Cranley, 24 Mar. 1908, in Stephen Gwynn, *The Letters and Friendships of Sir Cecil Spring Rice* (London, 1930), ii, 114.

46. Chamberlain to Collings, 26 Apr. 1908, copy, JC22/41.

47. Joseph to Mary Chamberlain, 14 Oct. 1908, JC28/A/2/20/2.

48. Garvin's report to Lord Northcliffe, 27 May 1909, in A.M. Gollin, *The Observer and J.L. Garvin, 1908–1914* (London, 1960), 100.

49. Grey to Chamberlain, 18 July 1906, AC1/4/4/22.

50. Kipling to an audience in Toronto, 19 Oct. 1907, reported in *The Times*, 21 Oct. 1907.

51. Reported in *The Times*, 23 Sept. 1909.

52. As put in the ablest study of this subject, Alan Sykes, *Tariff Reform in British Politics, 1903–1913*, 205.

53. L.S. Amery, *My Political Life* (London, 1953), i, 344.

54. Manuscript dated 4 Dec. 1909, JC27/57.

55. In *The Times*, 30 Dec. 1909.

56. From his last speech in Birmingham, reprinted in the Appeal by Mr. Chamberlain, *The Times*, 14 Jan. 1910.

57. Herbert Samuel quoted in *The Times*, 18 Jan. 1910.
58. Chamberlain to Hewins, 28 Jan. 1910, Hewins papers.
59. Quoted in Amery, *Life of Chamberlain*, vi, 947.
60. Quoted in Mary to Austen Chamberlain, 18 Mar. 1910, AC4/2/70.
61. Mary to Austen Chamberlain, 8 Mar. 1910, AC4/2/66.
62. Mary to Austen Chamberlain, 12 Mar. 1910, AC4/2/68.
63. Mary to Austen Chamberlain, 23 Mar. 1910, AC4/2/71.
64. Chamberlain to George V, 22 May 1910, Royal Archives, GV AA55/82.
65. Entry for 4 June 1910, Royal Archives.
66. Mary to Austen Chamberlain, 14 June 1910, AC4/2/82.
67. Mary to Austen Chamberlain, 15 June 1910, AC4/2/83.
68. Mary to Austen Chamberlain, 17 June 1910, AC4/2/84.
69. Reported in *The Times*, 18 Oct. 1910.
70. L.S. Amery, *My Political Life*, i, 378.
71. Mary to Austen Chamberlain, 28 Nov. 1910, AC4/2/91.
72. Chamberlain to Hewins, 13 Dec. 1910, Hewins papers.
73. Mary Chamberlain's diary for 31 Dec. 1910, Miscellaneous Chamberlain papers, C.
74. 2 Oct. 1911, AC1/8/8/28.
75. Reported by Austen Chamberlain to Garvin, 14 July 1911, in Amery, *Life of Chamberlain*, vi, 968.
76. Reported in *The Times*, 27 July 1911.
77. Quoted in D.J. Dutton, *Austen Chamberlain* (Bolton, 1985), 88.
78. Austen to Mary Chamberlain, 7 May 1911, in Austen Chamberlain, *Politics from Inside: An epistolary chronicle, 1906–1914* (London, 1936), 337.
79. Austen to Joseph Chamberlain, 4 Nov. 1911, ibid., 377–8.
80. Austen to Mary Chamberlain, 10 Nov. 1911, AC4/1/724.
81. Mary to Austen Chamberlain, 12 Nov. 1911, AC4/2/124.
82. Mary to Austen Chamberlain, 21 Feb. 1912, AC4/2/130.
83. In *The Times*, 25 July 1912.
84. H.A. Gwynne to Bonar Law, 29 Dec. 1912, Bonar Law papers.
85. Bonar Law to Austen Chamberlain, 8 Jan. 1913, in Austen Chamberlain, *Politics from Inside*, 510.
86. Mary to Austen Chamberlain, 8 Jan. 1913, AC4/2/157.
87. Mary to Austen Chamberlain, 25 Jan. 1913, AC4/2/158.
88. Mary to Neville Chamberlain, 5 Mar. 1913, NC1/20/2/8.
89. D.M. Laing, *Mistress of Herself* (Barre, Mass., 1965), 184.
90. Neville Chamberlain to his children, dated 6 July 1914, typed copy, NC1/6/11.
91. Mary to Austen Chamberlain, 12 Jan. 1914, AC4/2/181.
92. Letter from Chamberlain to J.T. Middlemore, published by *The Times* on 27 May 1913.
93. Reported in a speech by Carson, in *The Times*, 29 Nov. 1913.
94. Reported in *The Times*, 22 Nov. 1913.
95. Mary to Austen Chamberlain, 5 Apr. 1914, AC4/2/196.
96. Mary to Austen Chamberlain, 11 Apr. 1914, AC4/2/197.
97. Reported in *The Times*, 18 June 1914.
98. Transcript of a radio broadcast by Amery, 1 Aug. 1952, JC23/4/13.
99. Austen Chamberlain, *Politics from Inside*, 21.
100. Mary Chamberlain to Fanny Prince, 17 Dec. 1914, Endicott papers, and to Leo Maxse, 21 Nov. 1914, Maxse papers, 431, p. 158.
101. Quoted in her obituary in *The Times*, 22 Nov. 1918.
102. Diary entry for 3 July 1914 in J.R. Vincent, ed., *The Crawford Papers* (Manchester, 1984), 337–8.
103. Chamberlain to the governors of Mason College, in *The Times*, 19 Jan. 1900.
104. See above, p. 294.
105. Reported in *The Times*, 7 July 1914.

106. Quoted in D.H. Elletson, *The Chamberlains* (London, 1966), 291.
107. *The Times* leader, 7 July 1914.
108. R.A. Wright, 'Liberal party organisation and politics in Birmingham, Coventry and Wolverhampton 1886–1914, with particular reference to the development of Independent Labour representation', University of Birmingham Ph.D. thesis, 1977, 365.

Manuscript Collections Consulted

The papers of

Adams, Charles Francis, Jr, Massachusetts Historical Society.
Adams, Henry, Massachusetts Historical Society.
Anti-Slavery Collection, Rhodes House.
Arnold-Forster, H.O., British Library.
Ashbourne, Edw. Gibson, 1st Baron, House of Lords Record Office.
Austin, Alfred, University of Bristol.

Bagshawe Collection, Sheffield City Library.
Balfour, A.J., 1st Earl, British Library and Whittinghame.
Balfour, Gerald, 2nd Earl, Whittinghame.
Balfour of Burleigh, A.H. Bruce, 6th Baron, in possession of the present Lord
  Balfour of Burleigh.
Barlow Rand Archives, Sandton, South Africa.
Barton, Edmund, National Library of Australia.
Bayard, T.F., Library of Congress.
Benson, E.W., Lambeth Palace.
Bessborough MS, West Sussex County Record Office.
Boyd Carpenter, Wm, British Library.
Bower, G.J., South African Library.
Bright, John, British Library.
Broadhurst, Henry, British Library of Political and Economic Science.
Bryce, James, Viscount, Bodleian Library.
Burns, John, British Library.

Cadogan, G.H., 5th Earl, House of Lords Record Office.
Campbell-Bannerman, Henry, British Library.
Cape Archives, Government House series, Cape Town.
Cecil of Chelwood, E.A.R. Gascoyne-Cecil, Viscount, British Library.

Chamberlain, Beatrice, Ida and Hilda, University of Birmingham.
Chamberlain, Joseph, University of Birmingham.
Chamberlain, J. Austen, University of Birmingham.
Chamberlain, A. Neville, University of Birmingham.
Childers, H.C.E., Royal Commonwealth Society, and Letterbook, South African
    Library.
Chilston, A.A., 1st Viscount, Kent Archives Office.
Churchill, Lord Randolph, Churchill College.
Courtney, L.H., 1st Baron, British Library of Political and Economic Science.
Cowan, Joseph, Tyne and Wear County Record Office.
Cranbrook, Gathorne Gathorne-Hardy, 1st Earl, Ipswich and East Suffolk
    Record Office.
Croft, H.P., 1st Baron, Churchill College.
Cromer, Evelyn Baring, 1st Earl, Public Record Office.
Cross, R.A., 1st Viscount, British Library.

Dalrymple, Charles, National Library of Scotland.
Deakin, Alfred, National Library of Australia.
Denison, G.T., Public Archives, Ottawa.
De Villiers, J.H., 1st Baron, South African Library.
Devonshire, S.C. Cavendish, 8th Duke, Chatsworth.
Dilke, C.W. and Lady, British Library.
Dilke-Crawford-Roskill Collection, Churchill College.
Dixon, George, University of Birmingham.
Duke University MSS, Durham, North Carolina.

Eckstein & Co., H., Barlow Rand, Sandton, South Africa.
Elliot, Arthur, National Library of Scotland.
Ellis, J.E., British Library.
Endicott, W.C., Massachusetts Historical Society.
Escott, T.H.S., British Library.
Esher, R.B. Brett, 2nd Viscount, Churchill College.

Farrer, T.H., 1st Baron, Surrey Record Office.
Fiedler-Harding Letters, University of Birmingham.

Garvin, J.L., University of Texas, Austin.
Gell, P.L., Transvaal and Central Archives.
Gladstone, H.J., Viscount, British Library.
Gladstone, W.E., British Library.
Goschen, G.J., 1st Viscount, Bodleian Library.
Granville, G.G., Leveson-Gower, 2nd Earl, Public Record Office.
Green, Alice Stopford, National Library of Ireland.
Grey, A.H.G., 4th Earl, University of Durham and National Archives of
    Zimbabwe.
GKN, 22 Kingsway, London, and Heath Street, Smethwick.

Haldane, R.B., Viscount, National Library of Scotland.

Halsbury, H.S. Giffard, 1st Earl, British Library.
Hambleden MSS, W.H. Smith & Son Ltd, Strand House, London.
Harcourt, Lewis, Viscount, and W.G.G.V.V., Bodleian Library.
Harrison, Frederic, British Library of Political and Economic Science.
Hewins, W.A.S., Sheffield University.
Hildersham Hall (Rhodes family) Collection, Rhodes House.
Hofmeyr, J.H., South African Library.
Hutton, E.T.H., British Library.

Innes, James Rose, South African Library.

James of Hereford, Henry, Baron, Hereford County Record Office.

Kenrick, Wm, in possession of Mr J.B. Kenrick.
Kidd, Benjamin, Cambridge University.
Kitchener, H.H., 1st Earl, Public Record Office.

Lansdowne, H.C.K. Petty-Fitzmaurice, 5th Marquess of, Bowood.
Law, Andrew Bonar, House of Lords Record Office.
Lee of Fareham, A.H., Viscount, Courtauld Institute.
Leonard, C.L., Transvaal and Central Archives.
Lloyd George, David, 1st Earl, House of Lords Record Office.
Lloyds Bank, 71 Lombard Street, London, and Colmore Row, Birmingham.
Loch, H.B., 1st Baron, Scottish Record Office.
Lodge, Oliver, University of Birmingham.
Long, W.H., 1st Viscount, Wiltshire Record Office.
Lugard, F.J.D., Baron, Rhodes House.
Lyttelton, Alfred, Churchill College.

Mackenzie, John, University of Witwatersrand.
Maxse, F.A. and L.J., West Sussex Record Office.
Maxse, Cecil, Kent Archives Office.
Meade, Robert, Swansea University College.
Melly, George, Brown, Picton & Hornby Libraries, Liverpool.
Merriman, J.X., South African Library.
Midleton, St John Brodrick, 1st Earl, Public Record Office and Duke University.
Milner, Alfred, Viscount, Bodleian Library.
Minto, G.J.M.K. Elliot, 4th Earl, National Library of Scotland.
Molema-Plantje MSS, University of Witwatersrand.
Monk Bretton, J.G. and J.W. Dodson, 1st and 2nd Barons, Bodleian Library.
Morgan, J.S. (Guildhall Library).
Morton Prince, Massachusetts Historical Society.
Mundella, A.J., Sheffield University.

Newdegate, F.A., Warwickshire Record Office.

Oliver, F.S., National Library of Scotland.
Olney, Richard, Library of Congress.

Onslow, Wm Hillier, 4th Earl, Guildford Muniment Room.
O'Shea, W.H., National Library of Ireland.

Pace: Miss Pace's School account book, Southwark Local Studies Library.
Passfield, Sydney Webb, Baron, and Beatrice Potter, Lady, British Library of Political and Economic Science.
Playfair, Lyon, 1st Baron, Imperial College.

Quickswood, Lord Hugh Cecil, Baron, Hatfield.

Rhodes, C.J., Rhodes House.
Ridley, M.W., 1st Viscount, and 2nd, Northumberland Record Office.
Ripon, G.F.S. Robinson, 1st Marquess, British Library.
Roberts, F.S., 1st Earl, National Army Museum.
Rosebery, A.P. Primrose, 5th Earl, National Library of Scotland.
Rothschild Archive, New Court, London.
Royal Archives, Windsor Castle.
Rutland, J.J.R. Manners, 7th Duke, and Duchess, and 8th Duke, Belvoir Castle.

St Aldwyn, M.E. Hicks Beach, 1st Earl, Gloucestershire Record Office.
Salisbury, R.A.T. Gascoyne-Cecil, 3rd Marquess, and 4th Marquess, Hatfield.
Sandars, J.S., Bodleian Library.
Schnadhorst, Francis, University of Birmingham.
Selborne, Roundell Palmer, 1st Earl, Lambeth Palace.
Selborne, W.W. Palmer, 2nd Earl, Bodleian Library.
Smith, J. Parker, Strathclyde Regional Archives.
Southey, Charles, in possession of Sheila Southey.
Sprigg, J.S., Cory Library, Rhodes University.
Spring-Rice, C.A., Churchill College.
Stead, W.T., Transvaal and Central Archives, and Humanities Research Center archives, University of Texas at Austin.
Strachey, J. St L., House of Lords Record Office.

Tariff Commission Collection, British Library of Political and Economic Science.
Tennyson, 2nd Baron, National Library of Scotland.
The Times Archives, London.
Transvaal and Central Archives, High Commissioner, Governor, and Secretary for Native Affairs series.
Tupper, Charles, Public Archives, Ottawa.

University of Birmingham Collection, University of Birmingham.

Wilkinson, Spenser, Army Museums Ogilby Trust.
Wilson, H.J., University of Sheffield and Sheffield City Library.
Wolseley, G.J., Viscount, Hove Central Library.

Index

Adam, W.P. 127, 130
Adams, Brooks and Henry 295
Afrikaner Bond 375, 463–4, 493, 527, 529, 538, 555–6
Akers Douglas, Aretas 603, 636–7
alien immigration 346, 353, 356, 370, 612
Allday, Joseph 78, 81–2
Allott, A.J. 67–8, 71–3
American Civil War 508, 516
Amery, Leo 524, 560–61, 567, 652, 658, 662, 666
Anglo-German alliance 433 ff., 479–80, 507, 516
Anglo-Saxon race 287, 293–4, 304, 411, 479
Anti-Corn Law League 36, 569, 587, 590
Applegarth, Robert 38–9, 73
arbitration 60, 63, 86, 123, 328, 341, 356, 358, 370, 641
Arch, Joseph 53, 85–6
Arnold-Forster, H.O. 584, 638
Artisans' Dwellings Act 93 ff., 104, 109
Arts Club 102, 110
Ashley, William 524, 562, 564–5, 567, 589, 607, 612
Asquith, H.H. 504, 590, 593, 654–5, 664, 666, 670, 672
Australia
  Nettlefold and Chamberlain in 76
  support from 385, 473, 475, 516, 525, 661
  federation 422, 474, 491–2
  resistance to imperial consolidation 424
  trade policy 425, 550, 564, 573, 598, 609, 611, 639, 641, 649
  imperial interests 477, 655

imperial council 489–90
colonial conference, 1902 530, 534
Avery, Thomas 78 ff., 89, 95, 97, 102

Balcarres, Earl of see Crawford, Earl of
Balfour, Arthur
  relationship with Chamberlain xiv, 517–18, 670
  link for Chamberlain to Salisbury and the Conservatives 235, 272, 316, 337, 344, 353, 359, 362, 364, 367, 369
  Irish Secretary 268–9, 306, 332–3, 340
  parliamentary leadership 348, 371, 399, 505
  South African policy 387, 389, 462, 465, 471
  on education 397, 511–12, 519
  foreign policy 435, 437, 440–41
  domestic policy 459
  military policy 470, 489, 503
  on the platform 485, 498
  fiscal policy 509, 540, 582–4, 600 ff., 632 ff., 645, 649–50, 652 ff.
  dual leadership 524, 529–30, 536–8, 541
  prime minister chapt. 18
Balfour, Gerald 531, 570, 577–8, 636
Balfour of Burleigh, Lord 538, 541, 561, 566, 575–6
banking 593–4, 596–7
bankruptcy legislation 145, 162, 167
Bayard, T.F. 288, 292, 295, 297–9
Beaconsfield, Earl of see Disraeli, Benjamin
Bechuanaland 176, 304, 306, 372, 375–6, 378–9, 382, 391, 395, 400, 402, 453
Birmingham xiii, 13–15, 24–8, 60–61,

77–80, 85, 98
  and Edgbaston Debating Society
    15 ff., 308
  Screw Company 44 ff., 75
  school board 50–52, 66, 72, 75, 81–3,
    87, 98–9, 111, 123, 128
  Liberal Association 52, 61, 66–7, 74,
    85–6, 98–100, 116, 118, 130, 159, 211,
    238, 242–3, 251, 267, 273, 282, 300,
    304
  sanitation 59, 81–2, 93, 100
  Trades Council 61, 66, 355
  gas 70, 83 ff., 145
  water 88 ff.
  improvement scheme 92 ff., 108, 130,
    169, 361
  Liberal Unionist Association 300, 307,
    438, 464, 520, 568, 602, 606, 627
  Jewellers' and Silversmiths'
    Association 313–14, 420, 517, 589
Bismarck, Prince 160–61, 177, 328, 478,
  590
Boer War 469 ff., chapt. 16, 523–5, 532,
  534, 546 ff., 561, 563, 598, 600, 669
Booth, Charles 279, 335, 351, 593, 608
Botha, Louis 506, 508, 538
Brett, R.B. see Esher, Viscount
Bright, Albert 315–16
Bright, John
  challenged by Chamberlain 16, 29
  support from and for Chamberlain
    32, 107, 134, 142, 166
  brother Jacob 49
  Gladstone's first ministry 50, 57–8,
    137
  foreign policy 122
  general election, 1880 129–30
  Gladstone's second ministry 135,
    150–51, 163, 179
  Africa 155ff.
  challenged by Randolph Churchill
    210, 212
  Home Rule crisis 223, 239, 248–9,
    251–2, 265–6
  contest to succeed him 311, 314–15,
    369
Brinsley, Alderman 81–2, 100, 102, 128
British Guiana see Venezuela
Broadhurst, Henry 210–11, 249, 251, 263,
  351
Brodrick, St. John 505, 509, 534, 559–61,
  563, 591
Bulgarian atrocities 114–17
Bülow, Prince von 434, 436–7, 478–80,
  507, 517, 526
Bunce, J.T. 15, 54, 110, 116, 140, 209, 251,
  300, 306–7, 310, 442, 445
Burnaby, Fred 129, 210
Burns, John 345, 630, 670

Butt, Isaac 70, 121

Caillard, Vincent 567, 593
Caine, W.S. 303, 322
Campbell-Bannerman, Henry 463–4, 466,
  475–6, 492, 497–8, 626, 629
Canada
  Nettlefold and Chamberlain in 76
  analogy with Ireland 225, 241, 252,
    265, 277
  fisheries negotiations 281, 283, 292 ff.
  tariffs 284–5, 421 ff., 525, 539–41, 550,
    559–60, 563–4, 573–4, 584, 588–9,
    598–600, 607, 609, 611, 614, 620 ff.,
    639, 643, 651–2, 658–9
  support from 385, 412, 472 ff., 516, 655
  flagship of the empire 448
  Alaska boundary 451, 459
  French Canada 483, 546, 670
  imperial council 489–91
  colonial conference, 1902 530 ff., 591
Canadian Pacific Railway 294, 326, 361,
  460
Cape Colony see South Africa
Carnegie, Andrew 460–62, 505
Cartwright, Richard 422–4
Cecil, Hugh 615, 624–5, 627, 632–5, 637,
  655, 660
Cecil, Robert 627, 639, 650, 652, 660
Central Nonconformist Committee 41, 43
centre party 263, 275–6, 312
Chambers of Commerce 18–19, 210, 287,
  305–6, 392, 422, 428, 554, 591, 643
Chamberlain, Arthur 18–19, 61, 85, 91,
  251, 321, 364, 494, 502–4, 510, 569, 663,
  667
Chamberlain, Austin
  birth and mother's death 18–19, 141
  education 126, 140, 176
  and Mary Chamberlain 301, 320
  investments 324–6, 499, 503–4
  electoral difficulties 327, 337, 342,
    628, 634
  appointments to office 368, 501, 536,
    577–9, 584
  health and temperament 377, 627
  representative of his father 529, 557,
    636–8, 648–50, 654 ff.
  yoked by Balfour 587, 590, 602, 605,
    610–11, 616–17, 624
Chamberlain, Beatrice 18–19,
  140–41, 228–9, 301, 320, 627, 663, 668,
  670
Chamberlain, Caroline née Harben 4, 91
Chamberlain, Ethel 33, 90, 141, 542,
  612–13, 647, 667
Chamberlain, Florence née Kenrick 32–3,
  59, 80, 88, 90 ff., 104–5, 112, 137, 141, 291,
  663

Chamberlain, Harriet née Kenrick 17–19, 33, 90–91, 141
Chamberlain, Harbert 321, 502, 667
Chamberlain, Hilda 33, 140, 613, 658, 663, 668
Chamberlain, Ida 33, 140, 649, 663, 668
Chamberlain, J.H. 75, 87, 102, 139–40
Chamberlain, Joseph I 2–4
Chamberlain, Joseph II 4–7, 12, 38, 71
Chamberlain, Joseph III
   industrialist in politics xi–xiv, 1, 112–13, 494, 668–9, 671
   religion xii, 6–8, 25, 91–2, 95–6, 99, 106
   health xiv, 111–12, 301, 342, 459, 529–31, 536, 542, 557, 567, 581, 602–3, 617, 619, 638, 643, 647 ff.
   as teacher 7, 17, 25–6, 438, 581
   education 8–9, 517
   accountancy 9, 15, 19, 21–2, 80, 83 ff., 93, 101, 585, 671
   gardening 17–18, 139–40
   courtship and marriages 17–19, 32–3, 289 ff., 311–12
   mayoralty 58, 66, 70, 75, chapt. 4, 103, 105, 111–12, 143
   republicanism 59–60, 88, 134, 274
   women's movement 92, 137, 229, 231, 302
   imperialism 126, 176 ff., 185, 233–4, 252–3, 293 ff., 304–6, 317, 335–6, 354, 366–8, 405 ff., 419, 482–4, 496 ff., 526, 542–4, 559, 608, 669–70
   at the Board of Trade chapts 6–8
   at the Local Government Board 223 ff., 353
   Colonial Secretary 223, 304, 359, chapts 13–18
   mission to the United States 281 ff., 542
   'Duchy' 317, 342, 362, 369–70, 398, 498
   sisal investment 324–6, 361, 366, 417, 499, 667
   as war minister 470 ff., 476, 484–5, 496–7, 504, 507–8, 513
   tour of South Africa 540 ff., 566, 642
Chamberlain, Mary née Endicott 32, 289 ff., 311–12, 319–21, 344, 362, 415, 542, 549, 577, 584, 603, 613, 617, 627, 642, 647 ff.
Chamberlain, Neville
   birth and childhood 33, 140–41
   investments 324–6, 499, 655, 667
   lieutenant of his father 568, 605–6, 627, 647, 659, 663, 670
Chamberlain, Richard (brother) 61, 85, 321

Chamberlain, Richard (uncle) 4, 9
Chamberlain, Walter 321, 667
Chamberlain Square 102, 642, 672
Chaplin, Henry 162, 364, 439, 459, 526, 590, 593, 596, 611, 624, 629, 632, 635, 637, 659, 662
China 319, 329–30, 432 ff., 456, 458, 495–6, 506–7, 534
Chinese labour 552, 607, 630
Church of England 2–3, 5, 14, 34, 39, 42, 48–9, 51, 64, 98, 108, 128, 169, 209, 304, 345, 367, 511, 529, 537, 633, 648
Church of the Messiah 14, 17–18, 25, 79, 666
Churchill, Randolph
   Aston Park riot 174–6
   exploratory alliances 182, 197, 199, 207–8, 212, 237, 252–4
   desire for a Birmingham constituency 210–11, 311, 314–16
   Salisbury's second ministry 259 ff.
   resignation 262, 268, 328, 577
   centre party 275–7
   comparison with Chamberlain 282, 307, 382
   tariffs 365
Churchill, Winston
   on Chamberlain 408
   support from Chamberlain 498
   military policy 512–14
   tariffs 566, 590, 613
civic gospel 41, 77, 79–80, 82–3, 92–3, 95, 102
Clemençeau, Georges 307, 426–7
Cleveland, Grover 283, 288, 292, 298, 307, 311–12, 381, 385, 421, 425
Cobden, Richard 50, 137, 319, 410
Cobden Club 166, 568
Collings, Jesse
   on education 36–8
   Birmingham politics 52, 82, 85, 106
   agricultural concerns 53, 164, 168, 212–13, 222–3
   friendship with Chamberlain 91–2, 199, 251, 301, 542
   National Liberal Federation 137
   Gladstonian treatment of 224–5, 238, 258, 297
   election, 1886 254
   on coercion 268
   appointment, removal, and retirement 368, 536, 662
colonial conferences
   1897 423–5, 429, 489
   1902 530 ff., 573, 591
   1907 607 ff., 615, 618–19, 639, 649
concentration camps 513–14
contracts 493–5, 502–4
Conventions of Pretoria and London 158,

176, 374, 456–7
Cook, W.T.   251–2, 254, 260
cordwainers   2–4, 9, 15
Corn Laws
    early nineteenth-century   58, 520, 524, 594
    Chamberlain's proposals   523, 530, 540–41, 550, 557, 559, 561–2, 564–5, 570, 623, 635–7
    Hicks Beach's measure   526, 531, 533, 537, 549
    see also food taxes
corporal punishment   4, 126–7, 415
Corporation Street   97, 100, 139, 286, 672
Courtney, Leonard   135, 156–7, 165
Cox, J.C.   55–6
Crawford, Earl of   634, 668
Crawford, Virginia   200–201, 225–6, 259
Cross, R.A.   93, 95, 104
Crosskey, H.W.   79, 82, 92, 243, 443
Crystal Palace, 10–12, 75

Dale, R.W.   40–41, 51 ff., 79, 82, 91, 111, 126, 128, 158, 174, 240, 249, 251, 273, 300, 304, 333, 344, 667
Davis, W.J.   61, 98–9, 128, 145, 314
Dawson, George   14, 25, 31–2, 36–7, 40–41, 51, 63, 79, 82, 667
Deakin, Alfred   639, 649
Delagoa Bay   374, 404, 439–40, 481
Denison, G.T.   422–3, 559
Derby, Earl of   162, 177, 182, 305, 419
de Villiers, Henry   305, 393
Devonshire, Duke of
    leadership in the Commons   107–8, 113–15, 117, 121, 126 ff.
    National Liberal Federation   122, 125
    Gladstone's second ministry   133–4, 136, 142, 148, 158, 160, 162, 164–5, 170–71, 182, 184, 187, 189–90, 196
    election campaign, 1885   203 ff.
    Home Rule crisis   215, 221–2, 235, 237, 244, 246–8, 252–3
    Salisbury's second ministry   256–7, 260–62, 264–5, 276–8, 282, 285, 287, 307, 309, 313 ff., 323, 303–4
    removed to the Lords   336–7, 344, 353, 355, 358
    coalition   359–60, 363–4, 367, 371
    military coordination   470
    Education bill, 1902   511–12, 519, 537–8
    tariffs   566–7, 570–71, 574, 576 ff., 584, 590, 601–2, 607, 637–8
    Liberal Unionist organization   587, 601–2
    recurrent opponent of Chamberlain   645
de Wet, Christian   538, 553–4

Dilke, Charles
    the party of two   115–16, 121, 133 ff., 141–2, 147, 149, 151, 154, 156–8, 160, 162, 178–9, 184–5, 187, 190, 197–8, 205, 210, 217, 306, 420
    the Crawford divorce   199–201, 225–7, 259
    Home Rule crisis   215–16, 221, 236–7, 245–6, 249–50, 348
    sugar production   410
disestablishment
    Irish   41–3
    Welsh   266, 327, 347, 362–4, 657
Disraeli, Benjamin   xii, 68, 437, 115
    second Reform bill   32, 236
    second Ministry   104, 106, 114, 123–4, 126, 135–6, 147
    Suez Canal purchase   109, 122, 409
    insulted by Chamberlain   111
    Chamberlain acquires his mantle   399, 543, 637
Dissent   see Nonconformity
Dixon, George   15–16, 30, 34 ff., 49 ff., 78–9, 110–11, 123, 128, 140, 251
drink trade   69, 130, 143, 303, 356, 510–11, 569

Eckhardtstein, Baron von   437, 478, 506–7
Edgar, Thomas   457, 462
Edgbaston   80, 120, 129, 293, 340, 669
education, elementary   30 ff., 34 ff.
Education Act
    1870   42–4, 48 ff., 59, 110, 209, 334, 397
    1876 amending Act   110, 113
    1902   510–12, 519, 523, 529, 536–8, 542–3, 549, 558, 563, 568, 587, 600, 640, 657
    1906 bill   640
Edward VII   60, 87–8, 90, 115, 142, 301, 403, 529–30, 544
Egypt   115, 122, 158 ff., 176, 184, 189–91, 218, 281, 319, 336, 426 ff., 451, 484, 545, 603
eight-hour day   328, 334, 339, 341, 356, 370
Ellis, William   60–61
Employers' Liability bill   see workmen's compensation for industrial accidents
employment   353, 358, 365–6, 370, 500, 552, 586, 589, 593, 620, 646, 653, 671
Endicott, W.C.   288, 298, 301
Escott, T.H.S.   137, 167–8
Esher, Viscount   235, 388, 517, 611

Fabian Society   345, 524, 561
Factory Acts   35, 81, 333, 345, 646
'fair trade'   146, 210, 305, 524
Fairfield, Edward   381, 388, 391, 395, 418
Farrer, T.H.   164, 172

Fawcett, Henry 127, 135
Field, Alfred 29, 35, 45
Fielding, W.S. 539–41, 543, 559, 574, 591, 609, 622–3
Fitzpatrick, Percy 458, 476, 488–9, 550
food taxes 565, 572, 576, 583, 585, 603, 609–10, 614–15, 657 ff.
  see also Corn Laws
Forster, W.E. 42–4, 51, 55, 57–9, 73, 107, 113–14, 116, 124, 127, 135, 137, 142, 148–9, 153–4, 187
Fortnightly Review 33, 56, 65, 106, 108–9, 167, 184
Fowler, Henry 263, 353
France 9, 76, 146, 191, 336, 355, 377, 420, 426 ff., 433–4, 437, 456, 507, 516, 620
Franco-Prussian War 10, 23, 48, 62, 426, 508, 516, 586
free education 53, 165, 169, 205, 207, 209 ff., 215, 304, 313, 317, 328, 330–31, 341, 345
free trade
  advocated by Chamberlain xii, 294
  reinforced by business experience and observation 23, 146, 211–12
  Canada's departures from 284, 425
  imperial reinforcement and stretching 305, 372, 407–8, 410, 430, 478
  comparison to public works 391
  U.S. and German tariffs 329, 366
  within the empire 392, 422
  Milner on 451
  departure from 520, 523, 531, 535, 541, 550, 561 ff.
  attacked 586–7, 589, 593 ff., 613, 615, 619–21, 626, 646
  Lloyd George's doubts about 656
Frere, Bartle 126, 156
Froude, J.A. 178, 305

Gambia see West Africa
Gandhi, M.K. 547–8
Garvin, J.L. xii, 524, 526, 567, 586, 649, 651, 653, 656, 658, 662
gas-and-water socialism 77 ff., 104–5, 210, 551
George, Henry 163, 171
George V 655–6
Germany
  competition xiii, 76, 104, 156, 163, 184, 305, 407–8, 521, 524, 558, 563, 565, 572, 595–6, 600
  a model 31, 51–2, 241, 295, 327, 339, 421, 426, 444, 524, 569, 590, 592, 594, 597, 613, 669
  alliance 336, 433 ff., 477 ff., 495–6, 506–7, 559, 620
  tariffs 366, 423, 425, 564, 573, 623
  interest in the Transvaal 374, 380,

383, 385, 456
  estrangement 516–17, 526
  see also William II
Giffen, Robert 164, 533, 588–9
Gladstone, Herbert 207–8, 216, 218
Gladstone, W.E. 68
  religion xii
  economic credo xiii
  first ministry 29, 67
  second Reform bill 32
  Education Act, 1870 41 ff., 48 ff.
  defeat, resignation, and return 71–2, 106–7, 128, 130, 590
  support from and for Chamberlain 105, 114, 116–17, 119 ff., 124–5, 127, 644
  second ministry chaps 6–7, 180–97, 305, 671
  general election, 1885 197–213
  Home Rule crisis chapt. 9, 353, 443, 606
  enmity towards Chamberlain 255 ff.
  efforts at rapprochement 263 ff., 269
  persisting antagonism 270–71, 274 ff., 280, 285, 287, 309, 311, 324, 327, 331, 335–6, 340–41, 344, 347, 349
  comparisons with Chamberlain 308, 321
  retirement 354
  Liberal disagreements 356
  Morley commissioned to write his Life 542
gold 427, 448, 450, 586
Gold Coast see West Africa
Goldie, George 373, 427–9, 431
Gordon, General 160, 188, 190
Goschen, G.J. 206, 223, 264, 268, 319, 368, 439, 451, 470
Granville, Earl 115, 121, 133–5, 142, 175, 182–3, 196, 208, 232–4
'Great Deal' 457–8, 462
'Great Depression' 10, 75, 97, 102–4, 123, 131, 135, 181–2, 198, 210, 365–6, 420, 558, 671
'Great Victorian Boom' 10–11, 586, 594
Greene, Conyngham 467–8
Grey, Edward 475, 498, 504, 568
Grey, Albert, Earl 235, 318, 374 ff., 393–5, 401, 404, 651
Grosvenor, Richard 203, 207
Guest, Keen and Nettlefold (GKN) 47, 570
gun trade see small arms trade

Haldane, Richard 596, 669
Halsbury, Earl of 368, 565, 576, 649, 658
Hamilton, Edward 409, 411–12, 540
Hamilton, George 439, 536, 566, 575
Harcourt, William 203, 207, 356, 370, 384

mediator   115, 133, 135, 196, 257
Ireland   154, 221, 224–5, 232, 234, 242
Little Englander   160
round table conference   263–6
financial policy   327, 355
Jameson raid   389, 393–4, 400, 402ff.,
   486
voted against Chamberlain over
   contracts   504
Harris, Rutherfoord   376–7, 400–401
Harris, William   15, 67, 82, 100, 118, 251,
   300, 355, 442
Hartington, Marquess of   see Devonshire,
   Duke of
Hatzfeldt, Count   435, 437, 440
Hawksley, B.F.   387–8, 391ff., 400ff., 486
Hay, John   295, 436
Heath Street mill   12, 20, 26, 28, 44, 46, 59,
   62–3, 340
Hely-Hutchinson, Walter   527–8
Herzl, Theodor   543, 545
Hewins, W.A.S.   524–5, 567, 571, 586, 592,
   608, 612, 614, 622–3, 648, 654, 662
Hickman, Alfred   570, 593
Hicks Beach, Michael   268, 315, 536
   indicator of bedrock Conservative
      opinion   363
   negotiations as Chancellor of the
      Exchequer with Chamberlain   368,
      371, 409, 411–12, 454, 508–10, 512,
      515, 522, 549
   South Africa   404, 462–3, 471, 519
   tariffs   520, 526, 531, 557, 637
   retirement   530, 536, 540
   on Chamberlain's 'Royal position'
      541–2
Highbury   6, 139–41, 227, 321, 362, 442,
   665, 667–8
Hofmeyr, J.A.   420, 464, 556–7, 560, 564,
   670
Home Rule
   for Ireland
      crucial yet distorting for
         Chamberlain   xii, 148, 152, 581,
         668
      Chamberlain's early views   70, 130,
         147, 155, 193–5
      disruptive for Liberals   87, 256, 351,
         353, 406, 443, 643
      Conservative sympathy for   199
      crisis over   208, 214, 220ff., 258,
         261, 263ff., 270, 274
      prolonged fight against   277, 281–2,
         284–5, 287, 307–8, 313, 317, 324,
         327, 333, 335–6, 340–41, 343–4,
         347–9, 354, 357, 360–62, 366, 369
      connection to imperialism   305, 484,
         497, 524
      Liberal Unionist cohesion   587, 601

unpopular   626, 631
revival   655, 657–8, 660, 663–4
for the Rand   386, 449, 457–8, 464
Hong Kong   415, 433, 449, 661
Hood, Acland   636ff., 650
Hoskins & Co.   499, 502–3
House of Lords   173ff., 337, 357–8, 651–2,
   654ff.

Illingworth, Alfred   73, 90, 209, 244–5
Imperial Council   490, 532
imperial defence   424–5, 534, 555–6,
   559–60, 571
imperial federation   210, 294–5, 307, 372,
   392, 421–2, 425
imperial preference   372, 420ff., 490,
   525–6, 530–31, 533–5, 539–40, 550–51,
   559ff., 583ff., 603, 607ff., 635, 639, 641,
   649–50, 657, 661
income tax, graduated   187, 189, 202, 205,
   355
India   76, 129, 160, 190, 282, 419, 450, 456,
   467, 471–2, 484, 534, 547, 552, 560, 566,
   570–1, 614
Ireland   146–55, 546
   land law   42, 104, 129–30, 150ff., 181,
      222, 225, 232–3, 239, 241, 257–8, 263,
      265, 268–9, 272, 275ff., 317, 322, 333
   coercion of   148ff., 193, 195, 197, 222,
      258, 266ff., 277–9, 282–3
   central board for   192ff., 198, 204, 207,
      215, 222–3, 232–3, 261, 333, 347
   national council for   see central board
      for
   see also Home Rule for Ireland
Isandhlwana   126, 129, 156

James and Avery   19–20, 30
James of Hereford, Henry, Baron
   133, 226, 355, 357, 359, 368, 371, 385, 397,
   536, 558
Jameson, Starr   382ff., 661
Jameson raid   326, 372–87, 421, 457
   the enquiry   387–405, 429, 452, 501
   continuing reverberations   418, 450,
      482, 486
Japan   76, 433, 435, 620, 624
Jappy Frères   23, 45
jingoism   122–4, 126, 160
Jones, Alfred   413, 416, 593
Judas Iscariot   250, 285, 289, 333, 335, 349

Keen, Arthur   45, 47–8, 76, 570, 572, 593
Kenrick, Archibald   17–18, 38
Kenrick, Mary née Chamberlain   6, 9, 18
Kenrick, Timothy   20, 22, 32
Kenrick, William   17–19, 91, 96, 210, 212,
   251–2, 443, 480, 667
Kenya   545, 552

'Kilmainham treaty' 153–5, 162, 192
Kipling, Rudyard 524, 554, 652
Kitchener, Earl 504–6, 513–14, 516,
519–20, 522, 539
Kruger, Paul
uprising, 1880–81 156–8
pattern of defiance and retreat
374–5, 378, 400
reaction to the Jameson raid and
enquiry 383–4, 386, 389, 405
Delagoa Bay 439
prelude to war 448–9, 452, 454 ff.,
462 ff., 493
Chamberlain to tax the mining
industry as heavily as 488
treasure to Holland 539
Kynoch's 321, 364, 494, 499, 502–3, 569

Labouchere, Henry 207–8, 215, 221, 247,
335, 388–9, 394, 396, 402
Labour party 563, 630–31, 633, 638, 640,
646, 654, 670, 672
laissez faire 163, 204, 372, 411, 569, 586–8,
593–4, 599
Lansdowne, Marquess of 368, 470, 474,
507, 559, 607, 635–6, 660
Lascelles, Frank 439–40
Laurier, Wilfrid 421 ff., 473, 489–90, 520,
532, 534–5, 573–4, 591, 609, 622–3, 649,
658, 670
Law, Bonar 656, 659 ff.
Leader, Robert 66, 68, 119
Lloyd George, David 203, 493–4, 498–9,
502–4, 568–9, 650 ff., 670, 672
Lloyds Bank 20, 24, 75
Local Government Board 94, 96–7
see also Joseph Chamberlain at the
Local Government Board
local government reform 283, 297, 302–3,
341, 353
Loch, Henry 373, 375–6, 379–80, 390
London, local government of 181, 198,
343–4, 356–7, 360–61, 459
Londonderry, Marquess of 398–400, 541,
624, 641, 646
loyalty xiv, 216–17, 220, 224, 285, 443,
518, 554–6, 562
Lugard, Frederick 430–31

Mackenzie, John 158, 304, 376
Majuba 157–8, 189
Manning, Cardinal 195–6, 209, 240
Manson, Patrick 415–16
markets 21–3, 305, 329, 346, 352–3, 366,
426, 428, 432–4, 438, 500, 572, 586, 594
Mason, Josiah 45–7, 443, 446
Matthews, Henry 211, 254, 259–60
Maxse, Leo 518, 524, 526, 567, 633, 635,
653, 662

Maxwell, Herbert 351, 618, 643
mercantilism 524, 526, 533, 588
merchant shipping 143–5, 171–3, 182,
185–6, 202–3, 218, 226, 283, 328
Middleton, Captain 315–16, 357–8, 361,
399–400, 540
Midlothian 128, 130, 136, 155–6
Mill, John Stuart 56, 149, 163, 302
Milner, Alfred
appointed high commissioner 418,
452
background 451
early policy in South Africa 452 ff.
seeks armed confrontation 462 ff.
Boer War chapt. 16, 539
estrangement from
Chamberlain 527–9, 536, 538
Chamberlain's trip to South Africa
542–3, 545 ff.
tariffs 560, 562, 566, 614, 649
converted Amery to imperialism 561
Minto, Earl of 473, 489–90, 573–4, 591,
598, 609, 614, 651
Morgan, Pierpont 288, 495
Morley, John 167
religion xii, 92
friendship with Chamberlain 56, 83,
90, 104 ff., 112, 130, 133, 138, 162–4,
185–6, 194, 199
Liberalism 149
disagreements with Chamberlain
151, 159, 189, 202–3, 209
switch in allegiance 215 ff., 222,
224–5, 227, 232, 234–5, 239, 242,
244–5, 250
committed opponent of Chamberlain
257, 262, 264–5, 277, 335
repaired friendship 504, 542
tariffs 565
Mulock, William 622–3
Mundella, A.J. 68, 107, 127, 135, 219
municipal socialism see gas-and-water
socialism
Muntz, P.H. 129–30

Natal see South Africa
National Education League 34 ff., 49 ff.,
62, 64–5, 67, 72, 77, 81–2, 103, 107–8,
116, 168, 209, 304, 519, 548
National Liberal Federation 103
foundation 117 ff., 644
opposition to 124–5, 128
achievement 130–31, 133
use during Gladstone's second
ministry 137, 140, 151, 170
election campaign, 1885 203, 206,
209–10
turns against its founder 232, 244,
246, 254, 336

a model 606
National Liberal Unionist Association
601, 607–8, 625, 643
National Radical Union 251, 267, 273–4,
279, 282
National Union of Conservative
Associations 334, 583, 590, 611, 621,
624, 650
Navigation Acts 526, 534
Nettlefold, John Sutton 11–12, 18 ff., 26
Nettlefold, Joseph Henry 18–21, 23, 38,
45–7, 68, 75
Nettlefold and Chamberlain 12, 18 ff.,
26 ff., 35, 44 ff., 63, 67–8, 85–6, 170,
211–12, 443
New South Wales see Australia
New Zealand 76, 473, 477, 491, 516, 525,
530, 534, 550, 564, 591, 598, 641, 651, 655
Newcastle programme 336, 341, 347
Nigeria see West Africa
nine-hour day 60, 62–3
Nonconformity
Chamberlain's background 2–3
Birmingham 14
education as an issue for 34, 39, 41 ff.,
48 ff., 64, 68, 128, 169, 209, 215, 304,
330–1, 371, 397, 511–12, 519, 523,
529, 536–7, 548–9, 558, 563, 600, 640
alliance with organized labour 62, 69,
71 ff., 103, 327
grievances 133, 343, 362–3
Home Rule 341
Boer War 486–7
Norwood, C.M. 144, 202

old-age pensions
Nettlefold and Chamberlain 28
German example 327
Chamberlain's proposals 330, 334–5,
338, 341, 346, 349 ff., 355–6, 361, 370,
372
failure to implement 368, 397–8, 408,
441–2, 459–60, 476, 480, 499–500,
505
movement beyond Chamberlain 519,
630, 640
tariff financing 564–5, 569–70, 572,
585, 599, 654
Orange Free State see South Africa
orchids 140, 266, 403, 417, 442, 608, 643–4
organized labour see trades unions
O'Shea, W.H. xiv, 153–4, 193 ff., 199, 208,
262, 309–10, 322–3, 436
Ottoman empire see Turkey

Parnell, C.S.
early dealings with Chamberlain 121,
126–7
Kilmainham treaty 142, 147 ff.

central board scheme 193 ff.
throws Chamberlain over 198–9, 201,
203–4
election manœuvres, 1885 207–8, 218
Home Rule crisis 213, 220, 222, 235,
240, 250, 254
vendetta 260–61, 272, 308–10, 312,
321, 323, 326–8, 348
recollections 388, 436, 609
patriotism
prized by Chamberlain at every level
xiv
ancestral 2–3
Home Rule quickens 252, 347–8
imperial 385, 403, 422, 483, 486–7,
489, 499, 504, 549, 553, 670
Milner's racial 454
civic 544, 672
'a community of sacrifice' 555
national 646
Pearson, Arthur 568–9, 592, 614
platform 108, 183–4, 188, 583 ff., 608, 612,
614, 624–5, 563
Plimsoll, Samuel 143–4, 171
Portugal 439–40, 477
Potter, Beatrice see Webb, Beatrice
press 109, 137–8
Priestley, Joseph 7, 37, 51
Prince of Wales see Edward VII
Princes Gardens 138, 648, 668
Prussia see Germany
protectionism 366, 564, 569, 572, 574–6,
585–6, 589, 594–6, 599, 608, 612, 650, 660

Radical programme
first, 1874 69–70
lack of 113
in *Fortnightly Review*, 1883–4 163 ff.,
176, 178–9, 218
from the platform, 1885 184 ff., 192,
196, 202 ff., 213–14, 223, 258, 656, 671
under the Unionists 261, 273, 275,
328–30, 334, 341, 353, 355, 640, 645
railways 559
dealings with in business 22–3
a panacea 319, 586
imperial development 366, 412–13,
415, 417, 427
South Africa 374, 376 ff., 449, 453–4,
551
ransom 186, 202, 246, 334, 565
Reform Act
second (1867) xii, 32, 41, 130, 180,
192, 236, 669
third (1884–5) 170–71, 173–6, 178–9,
180, 182, 184, 188, 192, 206–7, 212,
625, 631, 651
Reform Club 142, 163
Reid, Wemyss 187, 220

Rhodes, Cecil   318, 372ff., 449, 452–4, 484,
    486, 527
Rhodesia   304, 390, 393, 401, 404, 452
Ridley, second Viscount   614–15, 633, 635,
    641, 649, 660, 662
Ridley, M.W.   385, 397–8, 459
Ripon, Earl of   389, 422
Ritchie, C.T.   303, 351, 465, 540–41, 549,
    557, 561–2, 566–7, 576, 578
Roberts, Earl   419, 487–9, 496–7, 504, 513
Robinson, Hercules   373–5, 379–80,
    382–4, 390, 403, 418, 451, 453
Roebuck, J.A.   68, 71–4
Rosebery, Earl of
    early approach to   121
    too close to be friends   235, 276, 319,
        354, 357, 490
    South Africa   373, 376, 392, 394
Rosmead, Lord see Robinson, Hercules
round table conference   263–7, 656
Russia   114–15, 123–4, 155, 177, 184, 191,
    296, 336, 355, 426, 432ff., 456, 495–6,
    506–7, 611, 620

Saint Paul's ward   59–61, 211
Salisbury, third Marquess   635, 654
    partnership with Chamberlain   xii,
        199
    housing   162, 169–70
    use of Chamberlain as enemy   165–6,
        209
    third Reform bill   173–4, 178–80, 651
    Home Rule crisis   236, 239, 247–8
    Unionist ally   256–7, 260–62, 267–9,
        275–6, 281–2, 287, 297, 302, 313ff.,
        323, 328ff., 334ff., 352–3, 355, 357ff.,
        363–4
    liking of Mary Chamberlain   344
    prime minister, 1895–1902   chapts
        13–16, 566
    succession to   523–4, 529–30, 575–7,
        621
Salisbury, fourth Marquess   615, 635
Samoa   477–8
Sawyer, James   311, 315
Schnadhorst, Francis   155, 176, 187, 201,
    209, 212, 238–40, 242–4, 260, 300
Schreiner, W.P.   463–4, 488–9
Seeley, J.R.   176–8, 444
Selborne, Earl of
    liaison with Salisbury and Devonshire
        356, 363–4
    under-secretary at the Colonial Office
        368, 414, 439
    Jameson raid   391, 394, 396, 401–2,
        404
    First Lord of the Admiralty   509, 512,
        528, 534
    tariff reformer   576–8, 590, 607,

        610–11, 614, 662
Shaw, Flora   380, 403
Shaw-Lefevre, G.J.   157, 215
Shea, Ambrose   324–6
Sheffield   58, 61ff., 77, 84, 105, 108–10,
    116, 119, 122, 210, 420, 583, 629
Sierra Leone   see West Africa
Sloan patent   11–12, 19, 23, 26
small arms trade   15, 140, 502
Smith, Parker   627, 632–3
Smuts, J.C.   457, 466ff., 470, 475, 508
Social Democratic Federation   150, 345
socialism   164, 181, 185, 204–6, 213, 215,
    230, 345, 357, 630, 638, 641
    see also gas-and-water socialism
South Africa
    Chamberlain's early interest   126,
        128–9, 155ff.
    maturing concern   176–8
    imperial policy for   304–6, 318, 427,
        655, 668
    Jameson raid   372ff.
    Anglo-German negotiations   439–41
    coming of the Boer War   448–58,
        462ff.
    Boer War   chapt. 16
    post-war concerns   525ff., 534, 536,
        538–9
    mission to   540ff., 628, 646, 670, 672
    tariffs   559–60, 562, 564, 585, 588, 598,
        614, 661
    Chinese labour   607, 630
South African League   455–6, 458, 529
Southbourne   80, 90, 139
Spanish-American war   436, 438, 441, 479,
    495
Spencer, Earl of   195–6, 203, 232–4
Spencer, Herbert   228–30
Sprigg, Gordon   425, 489, 527, 555
statistics   567, 585–6, 588–9, 595, 600
Stead, W.T.   226, 259, 395, 670
Stone, Benjamin   499–500, 628–9
Strathcona, Lord   460–61, 481
Sudan   161, 184, 189, 191, 428, 432
Suez Canal   428, 544
    Chamberlain's response to purchase
        101, 109, 115, 122, 159, 191
    plan for revenue from   371, 387, 409,
        418
suspension of the Cape constitution   488,
    493, 502, 527–9, 536, 538

Taff Vale decision   630, 640
tariff reform   520–22, 525, 541, 550, chapts
    18–20
Tariff Reform Commission   591–3, 597,
    607–8, 612, 614, 620–22, 639, 643, 647–9
Tariff Reform Committee   568–9
Tariff Reform League   568, 592, 602, 620,

626, 634, 637–8, 641–3, 648–9, 651–2, 660–61
Temple, Frederick   34–5
'three acres and a cow'   211, 213, 215, 238, 254, 261
trades councils   62, 67, 74
    see also Birmingham Trades Council
Trade Union Act, 1871   63–4
Trades Union Congress   65, 70, 72, 345, 519, 587
trades unions
    National Education League   38
    Chamberlain's alliance with   53, 61 ff., 75, 81, 85–6, 103, 143, 342–3, 569
    Conservative conciliation   104
    new assertiveness   327
    Chamberlain appeals beyond   337ff., 345–7, 352, 499–500, 587, 646
    opposition from   563, 628, 630, 640
    tariffs   620
Transvaal   see South Africa
Trevelyan, George   234, 264, 267
tropical medicine   414ff., 670
Tupper, Charles   286, 491
Turkey   114ff., 319, 382, 559

Ulster   240, 265, 285, 341, 501, 664
Unauthorized programme   206, 640–41, 650
    see also Radical programme
'undeveloped estates'   319, 366, 372, 378, 408ff., 521, 670
Unitarianism   3, 6–7, 14
United States
    competition   xiii, 104, 156, 163, 177, 407–8, 413, 444, 525, 558, 594
    a model   31, 241, 526, 532, 590, 597, 613, 669
    Nettlefold and Chamberlain in   76
    mission to   281, 283–4, 286ff., 305
    tariffs   329, 366, 420, 564–5, 569, 572–3, 599
    diplomatic conflicts   381–2, 384, 451, 458–9, 559
    Canadian trade   422, 611, 620, 622–3,

658
    alliance   434–6, 438–9, 479
    imperial sympathy   441, 477, 495
University of Birmingham   443ff., 450, 460–62, 480–81, 505, 552, 562, 596, 602, 643, 669, 672

Venezuela   377, 381, 384–5, 421
Victoria, Queen
    Chamberlain's early attitude towards   110, 134
    early reaction to Chamberlain   142, 166, 171, 174
    permission at resignation   239–41
    jubilees   274, 403, 423
    later reactions   282, 319, 474
    Kaiser's visits   478–9, 507
Vince, Charles   300, 562, 568, 663

Wallace, A.R.   163–4
'weary Titan'   129, 306, 532
Webb, Beatrice   139, 167, 227ff., 273, 278–80, 291, 302, 312, 319, 360, 608
West Africa   329–30, 413–14, 427ff., 434–5, 450, 473, 478, 670
West Indies   409ff., 429, 509, 526, 566
William II   384–5, 434, 436–7, 439–40, 477–9, 507
Williams, Powell
    financial manager   101, 140
    Home Rule crisis   249, 251
    trusty organizer   300, 316–17, 358, 442, 566, 568, 601, 605, 667
    War Office   368, 560
    death   602
Wilson, H.J.   64, 66–7, 108, 244
Wolmer, Lord   see Selborne, Earl of
workmen's compensation for industrial accidents   70, 328, 339, 341, 346–7, 351–3, 355–7, 370, 385, 397ff., 429, 459, 541, 612, 640, 671–2
Workshops Act   60, 81
Wyndham, George   638–9, 662

Zollverein   392, 420